VOICES OF THE MARTYRS

A.D.34–A.D.203

KINGSTONE

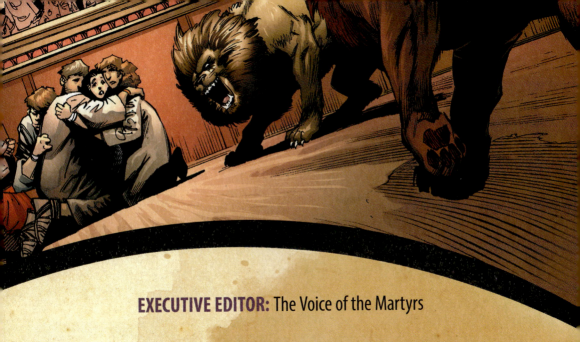

EXECUTIVE EDITOR: The Voice of the Martyrs

EDITOR:	Kelly Ayris		
WRITERS:	Ben Avery	Art Ayris	
PENCILS:	Edgar Bercasio	Rich Bonk	Danny Bulanadi
	Caio Cacau	Sergio Cariello	Karl Comendador
	Frank Fosco	Eduardo Garcia	Kyle Hotz
	Geof Isherwood	Daniel Kopalek	Ariel Medel
	Agapito De Los Santos	Jeff Slemons	Claude St. Aubin
INKS:	Charles Barnett	Edgar Bercasio	Danny Bulanadi
	Sergio Cariello	Karl Comendador	DYM
	Randy Emberlin	Frank Fosco	Geof Isherwood
	Chris Ivy	Daniel Kopalek	Al Milgrom
	Jason Moore	Roland Paris	Agapito De Los Santos
	Jeff Slemons		
COLORISTS:	Joel Chua	Andrew Crossley	Fabricio Guerra
	Emily Kanalz	Mark McNabb	Ben Prenevost
	Josh Ray	Tom Smith	Chris Sotomayer
LETTERS:	Zach Matheny	Lisa McMahon	
DESIGN:	Lisa McMahon	Duncan Weachock	

The Voice of the Martyrs

KINGSTONE

VOICES OF THE MARTYRS

A.D. 34 – A.D. 203

Published by Kingstone Comics
1330 Citizens Boulevard
Suite 701 – Second Floor
Leesburg, FL 34748 U.S.A.

Kingstone Comics
An imprint of
Kingstone Media Group, Inc.

Unless otherwise indicated, Scripture quotations are from The
Holy Bible, New Living Translation, copyright © 1996, 2004, 2015 by
Tyndale House Foundation. Used by permission of Tyndale House
Publishers, Inc., Carol Stream, Illinois 60188. All rights reserved.

ISBN 978-0-88264-114-0

First Edition 2017
Second Edition 2020

Printed in India

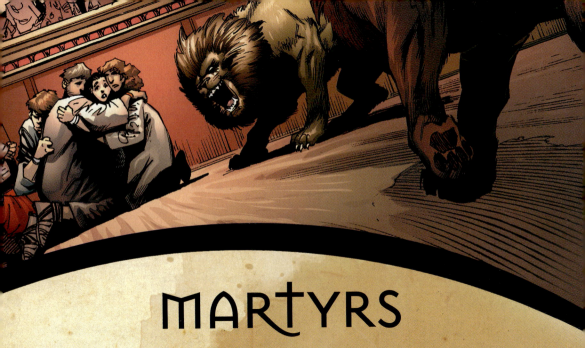

MARTYRS

Before ascending to Heaven, Jesus told his followers, "You will be my witnesses (μάρτυρες, martures), telling people about me everywhere – in Jerusalem, throughout Judea, in Samaria, and to the ends of the earth" (Acts 1:8). Later Peter wrote, "I, too, am an elder and a witness (μάρτυς, martus) to the sufferings of Christ" (1 Peter 5:1). In both verses, and in dozens more throughout the New Testament, the Greek word (μάρτυς, martus) is consistently translated "witness."

Μάρτυς (martus) is also where we get the English word "martyr." The consequences of being a faithful "witness" for Jesus Christ were so severe that the commonly accepted definition of the word changed over time. Paul confessed, "And I was in complete agreement when your witness Stephen was killed. I stood by and kept the coats they took off when they stoned him" (Acts 22:20). Three decades later, Paul also gave his life for being a faithful witness for Christ. Eleven of the men Jesus selected as his apostles suffered the same fate, as did many early Christians. But it didn't end in the first or second century. Today Christians around the world continue to give their lives rather than compromise their witness for Jesus Christ.

While it might not be death, being a μάρτυς (martus) for Jesus Christ always has, and always will, come with a price. However, for over 2,000 years many of those who have claimed the name "Christian" have come to the same conclusion — it is worth it, whatever the cost.

Hebrews 12:1 says, "Therefore, since we are surrounded by such a huge crowd of witnesses (μαρτύρων, marturon), to the life of faith, let us strip off every weight that slows us down, especially the sin that so easily trips us up. And let us run with endurance the race God has set before us." The examples of Christianity's first witnesses are crucial to our faith. It is our prayer that the faithful witness of these early followers of Christ will encourage and inspire each of us to "run with endurance."

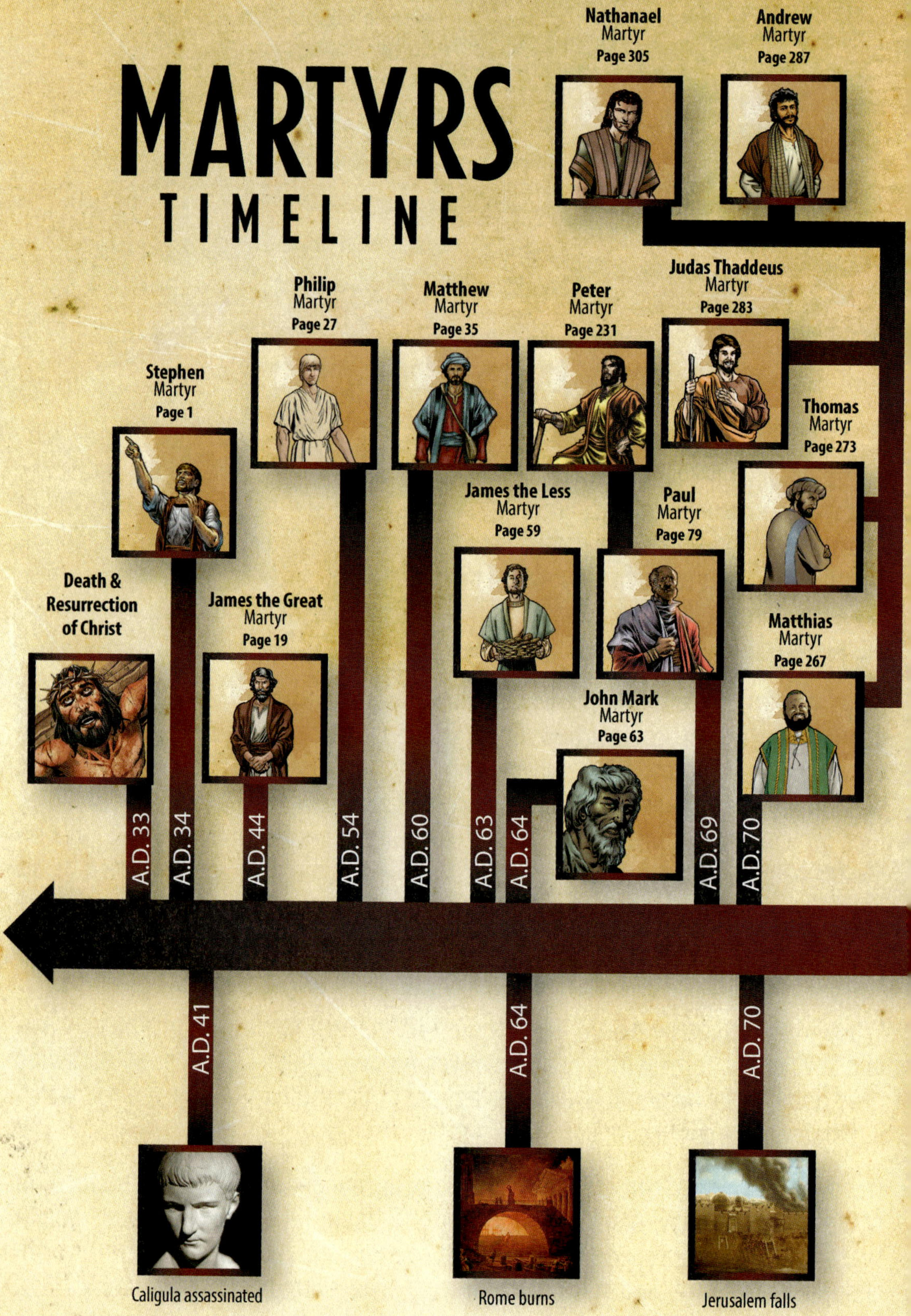
MARTYRS
TIMELINE
Nathanael
Martyr
Page 305
Andrew
Martyr
Page 287
Philip
Martyr
Page 27
Matthew
Martyr
Page 35
Peter
Martyr
Page 231
Judas Thaddeus
Martyr
Page 283
Stephen
Martyr
Page 1
Thomas
Martyr
Page 273
James the Less
Martyr
Page 59
Paul
Martyr
Page 79
Death & Resurrection of Christ
James the Great
Martyr
Page 19
Matthias
Martyr
Page 267
John Mark
Martyr
Page 63
A.D. 33
A.D. 34
A.D. 44
A.D. 54
A.D. 60
A.D. 63
A.D. 64
A.D. 69
A.D. 70
A.D. 41
A.D. 64
A.D. 70
Caligula assassinated
Rome burns
Jerusalem falls

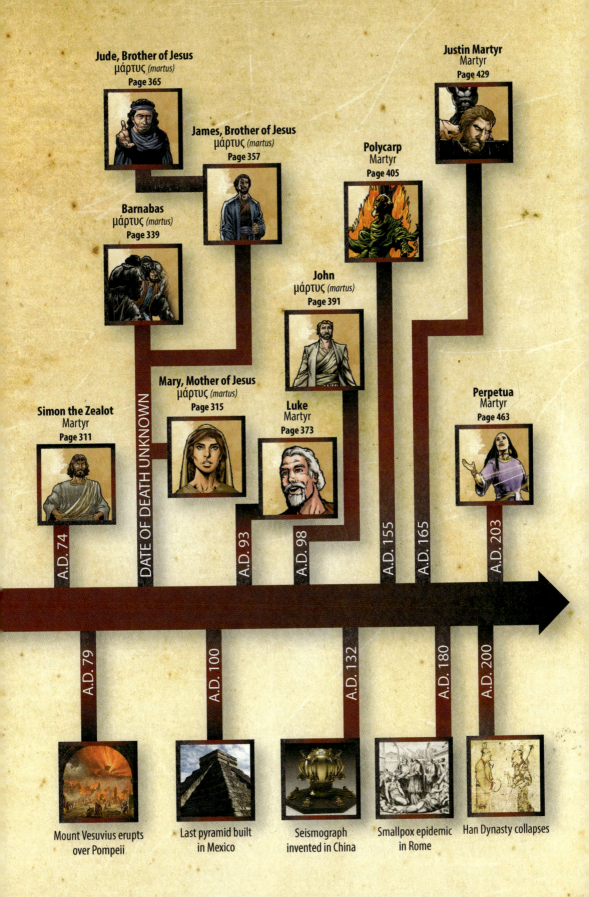

Jude, Brother of Jesus
μάρτυς (martus)
Page 365

James, Brother of Jesus
μάρτυς (martus)
Page 357

Justin Martyr
Martyr
Page 429

Polycarp
Martyr
Page 405

Barnabas
μάρτυς (martus)
Page 339

John
μάρτυς (martus)
Page 391

Mary, Mother of Jesus
μάρτυς (martus)
Page 315

Simon the Zealot
Martyr
Page 311

Luke
Martyr
Page 373

Perpetua
Martyr
Page 463

A.D. 74

DATE OF DEATH UNKNOWN

A.D. 93

A.D. 98

A.D. 155

A.D. 165

A.D. 203

A.D. 79

A.D. 100

A.D. 132

A.D. 180

A.D. 200

Mount Vesuvius erupts
over Pompeii

Last pyramid built
in Mexico

Seismograph
invented in China

Smallpox epidemic
in Rome

Han Dynasty collapses

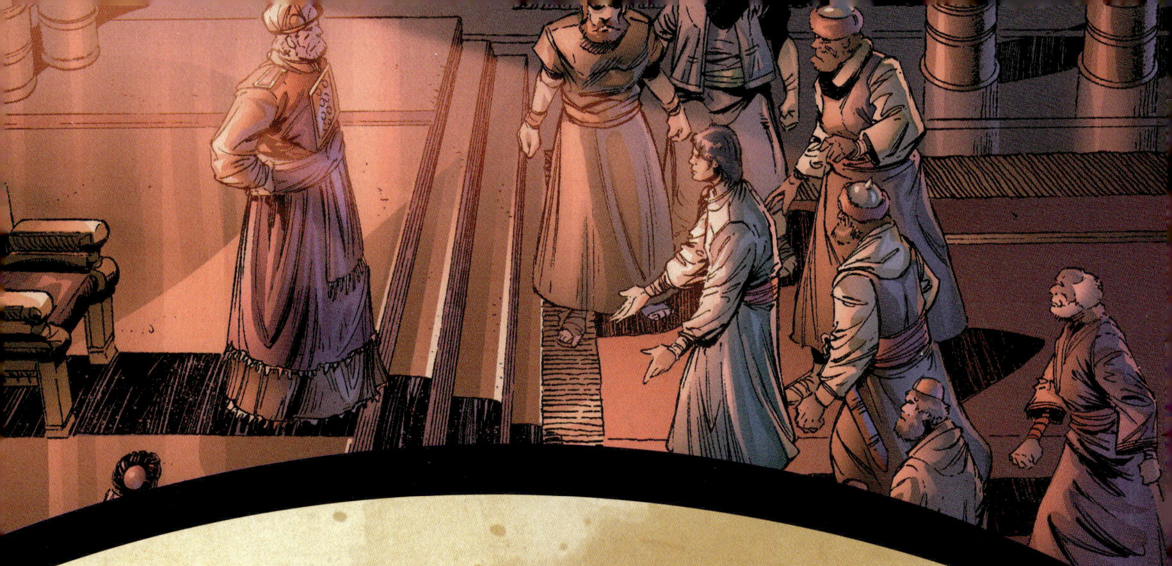

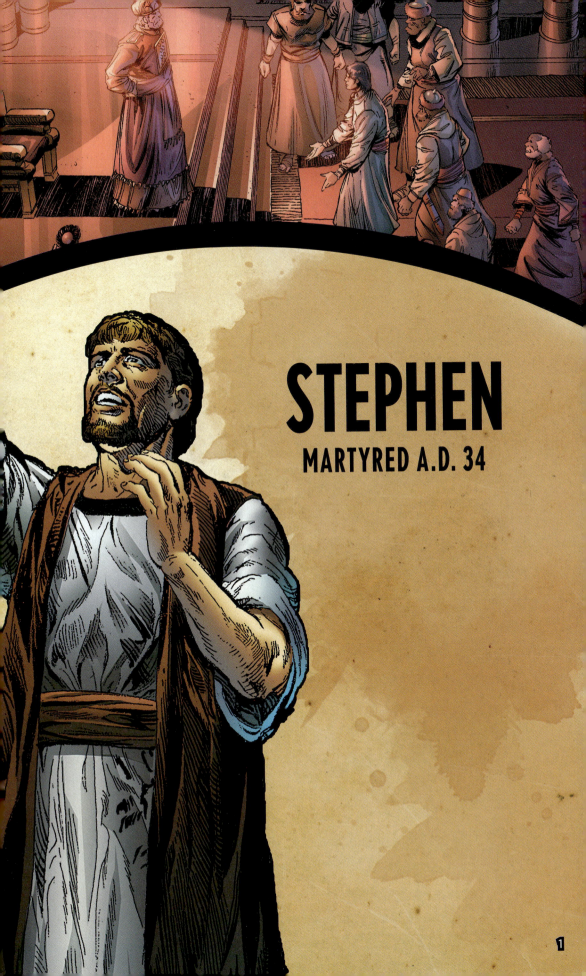

STEPHEN

MARTYRED A.D. 34

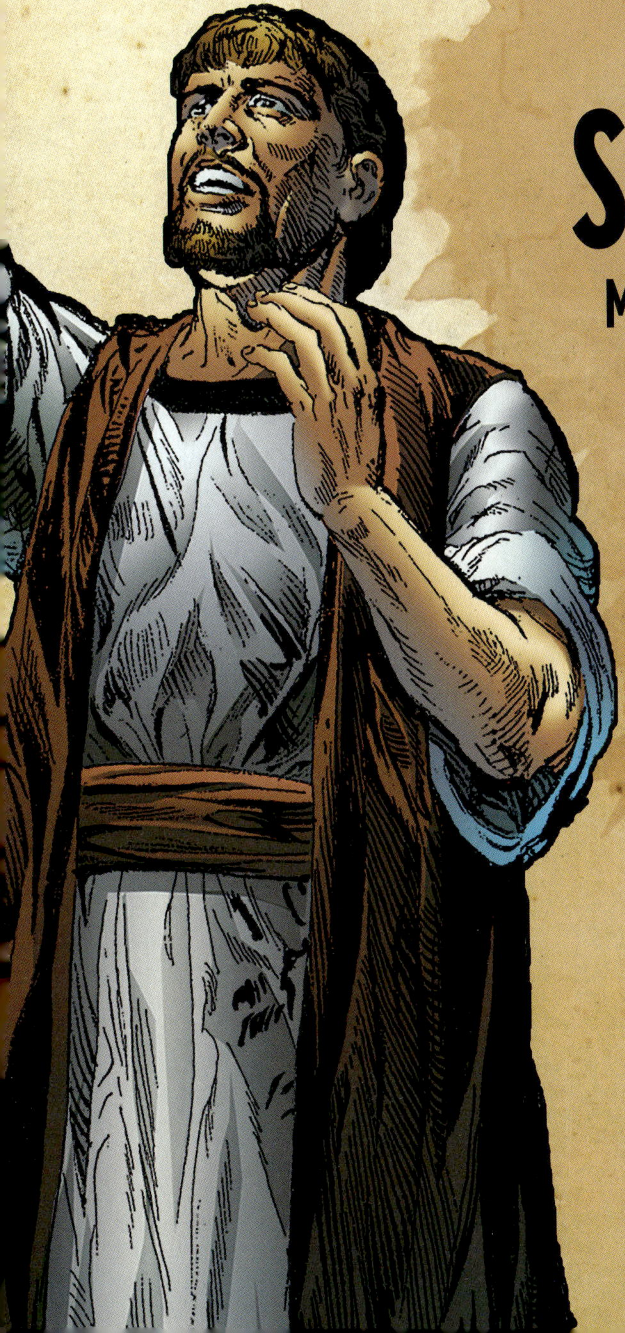

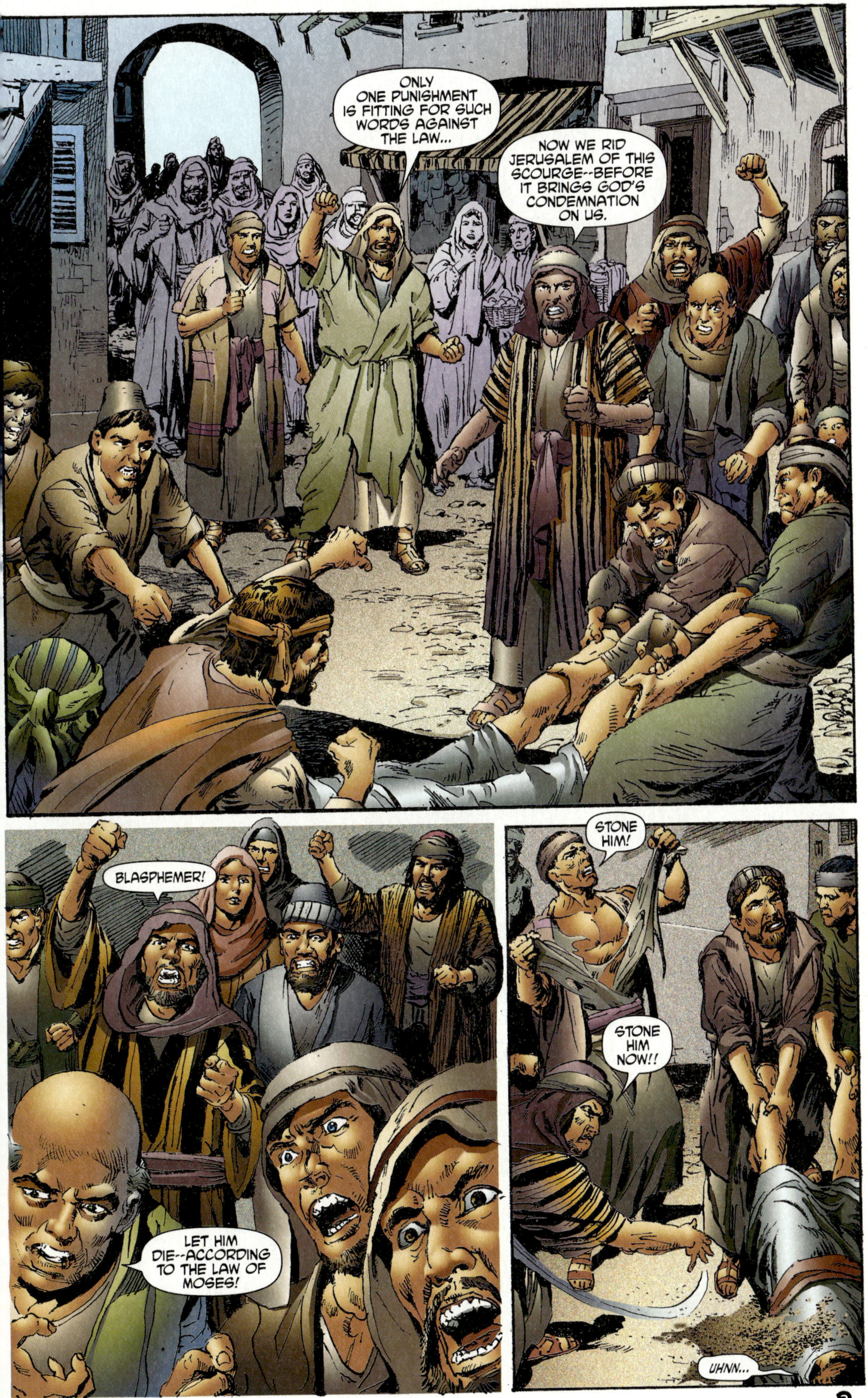
ONLY ONE PUNISHMENT IS FITTING FOR SUCH WORDS AGAINST THE LAW...
NOW WE RID JERUSALEM OF THIS SCOURGE--BEFORE IT BRINGS GOD'S CONDEMNATION ON US.
BLASPHEMER!
LET HIM DIE--ACCORDING TO THE LAW OF MOSES!
STONE HIM!
STONE HIM NOW!!
UHNN...

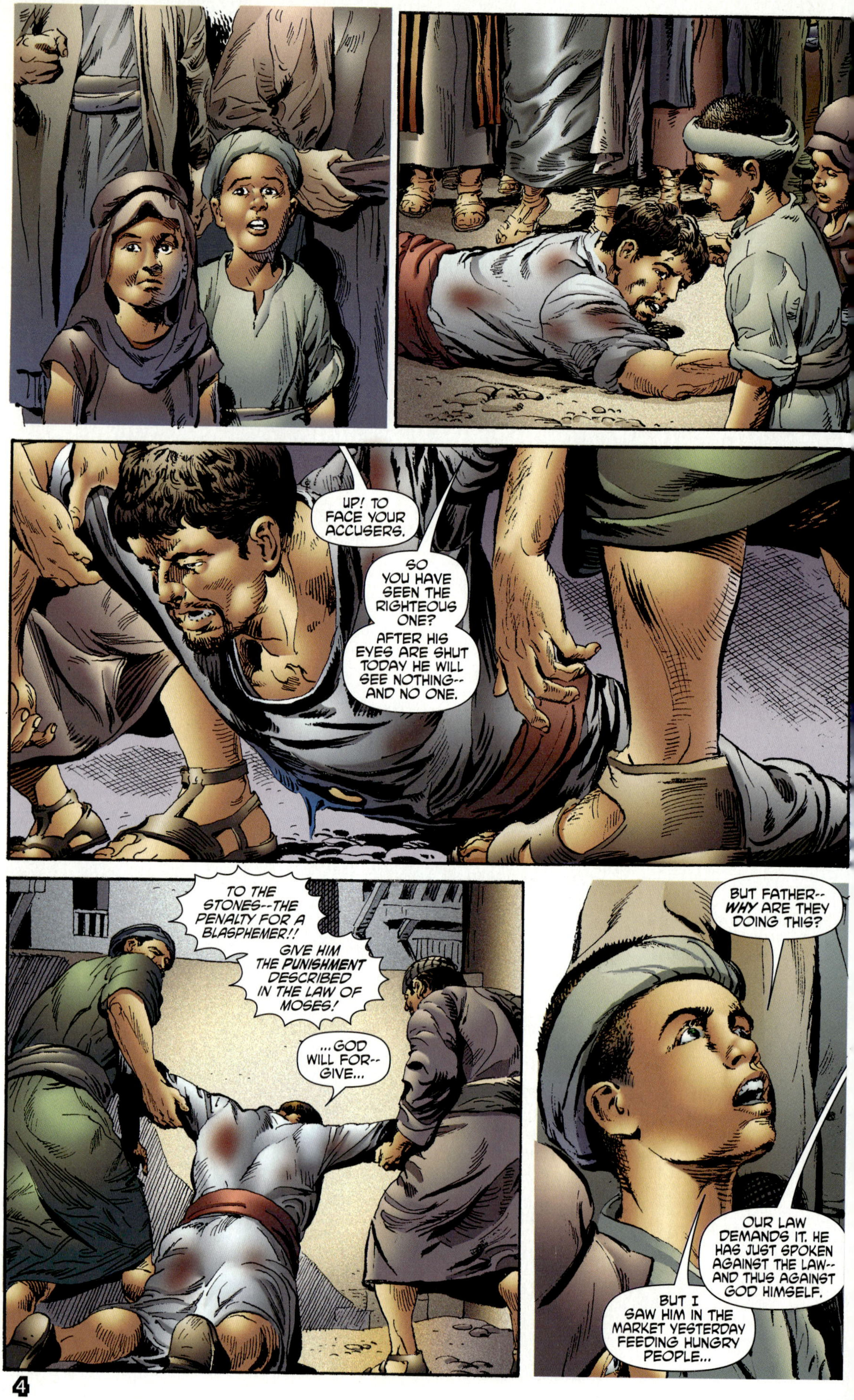

UP! TO FACE YOUR ACCUSERS.
SO YOU HAVE SEEN THE RIGHTEOUS ONE?
AFTER HIS EYES ARE SHUT TODAY HE WILL SEE NOTHING-- AND NO ONE.
TO THE STONES--THE PENALTY FOR A BLASPHEMER!!
GIVE HIM THE PUNISHMENT DESCRIBED IN THE LAW OF MOSES!
...GOD WILL FOR-- GIVE...
BUT FATHER-- WHY ARE THEY DOING THIS?
OUR LAW DEMANDS IT. HE HAS JUST SPOKEN AGAINST THE LAW-- AND THUS AGAINST GOD HIMSELF.
BUT I SAW HIM IN THE MARKET YESTERDAY FEEDING HUNGRY PEOPLE...

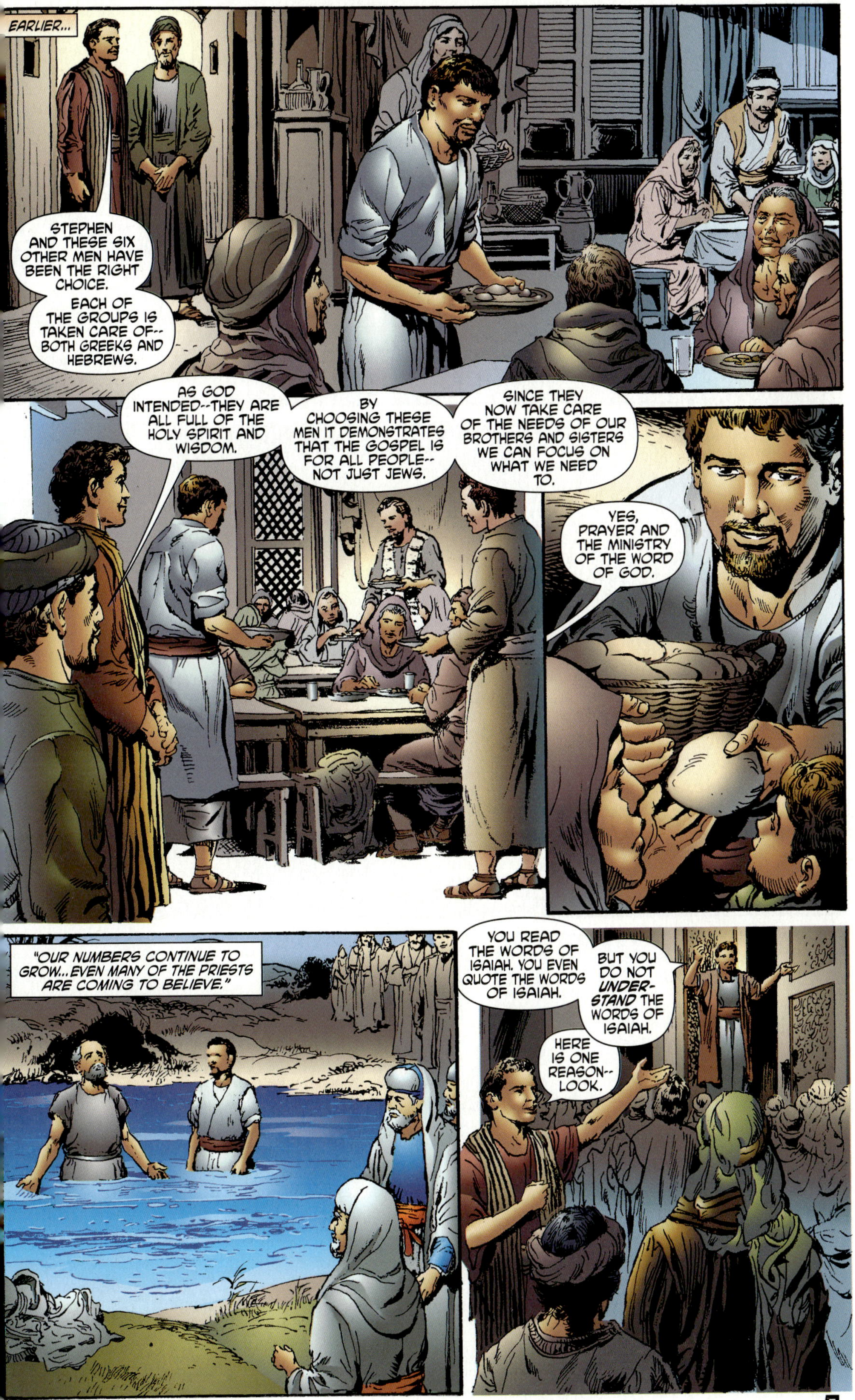
EARLIER...
STEPHEN AND THESE SIX OTHER MEN HAVE BEEN THE RIGHT CHOICE.
EACH OF THE GROUPS IS TAKEN CARE OF-- BOTH GREEKS AND HEBREWS.
AS GOD INTENDED--THEY ARE ALL FULL OF THE HOLY SPIRIT AND WISDOM.
BY CHOOSING THESE MEN IT DEMONSTRATES THAT THE GOSPEL IS FOR ALL PEOPLE-- NOT JUST JEWS.
SINCE THEY NOW TAKE CARE OF THE NEEDS OF OUR BROTHERS AND SISTERS WE CAN FOCUS ON WHAT WE NEED TO.
YES, PRAYER AND THE MINISTRY OF THE WORD OF GOD.
"OUR NUMBERS CONTINUE TO GROW...EVEN MANY OF THE PRIESTS ARE COMING TO BELIEVE."
YOU READ THE WORDS OF ISAIAH. YOU EVEN QUOTE THE WORDS OF ISAIAH.
BUT YOU DO NOT *UNDER-STAND* THE WORDS OF ISAIAH.
HERE IS ONE REASON-- LOOK.

AS ISAIAH PROPHESIED--HE WAS LED LIKE A LAMB TO THE SLAUGHTER. JUST AS A SHEEP BEFORE ITS SHEARERS IS SILENT, SO HE--JESUS--DID NOT OPEN HIS MOUTH.

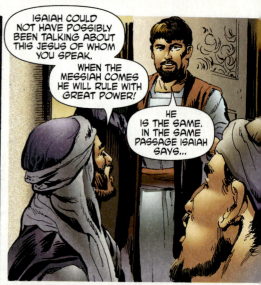

ISAIAH COULD NOT HAVE POSSIBLY BEEN TALKING ABOUT THIS JESUS OF WHOM YOU SPEAK.

WHEN THE MESSIAH COMES HE WILL RULE WITH GREAT POWER!

HE IS THE SAME. IN THE SAME PASSAGE ISAIAH SAYS...

...HE WAS ASSIGNED A GRAVE WITH THE WICKED, AND WITH THE RICH IN HIS DEATH.

A MAN OF WEALTH GAVE HIS BURIAL PLACE TO JESUS-- THOUGH DEATH COULD NOT CONTAIN HIM!

WHAT ARE YOU DOING?!

THIS MAN IS TO APPEAR BEFORE THE SANHEDRIN.

WHAT RIGHT DO YOU HAVE TO TAKE HIM FROM US?

FOR PREACHING REBELLION.

BEN NATHEN-- COME WITH ME!

WHAT'S THE RUSH?

ANOTHER CHRIST FOLLOWER IS BEING BROUGHT TO TRIAL.

FOR WHAT?

BLASPHEMY, OF COURSE.

6

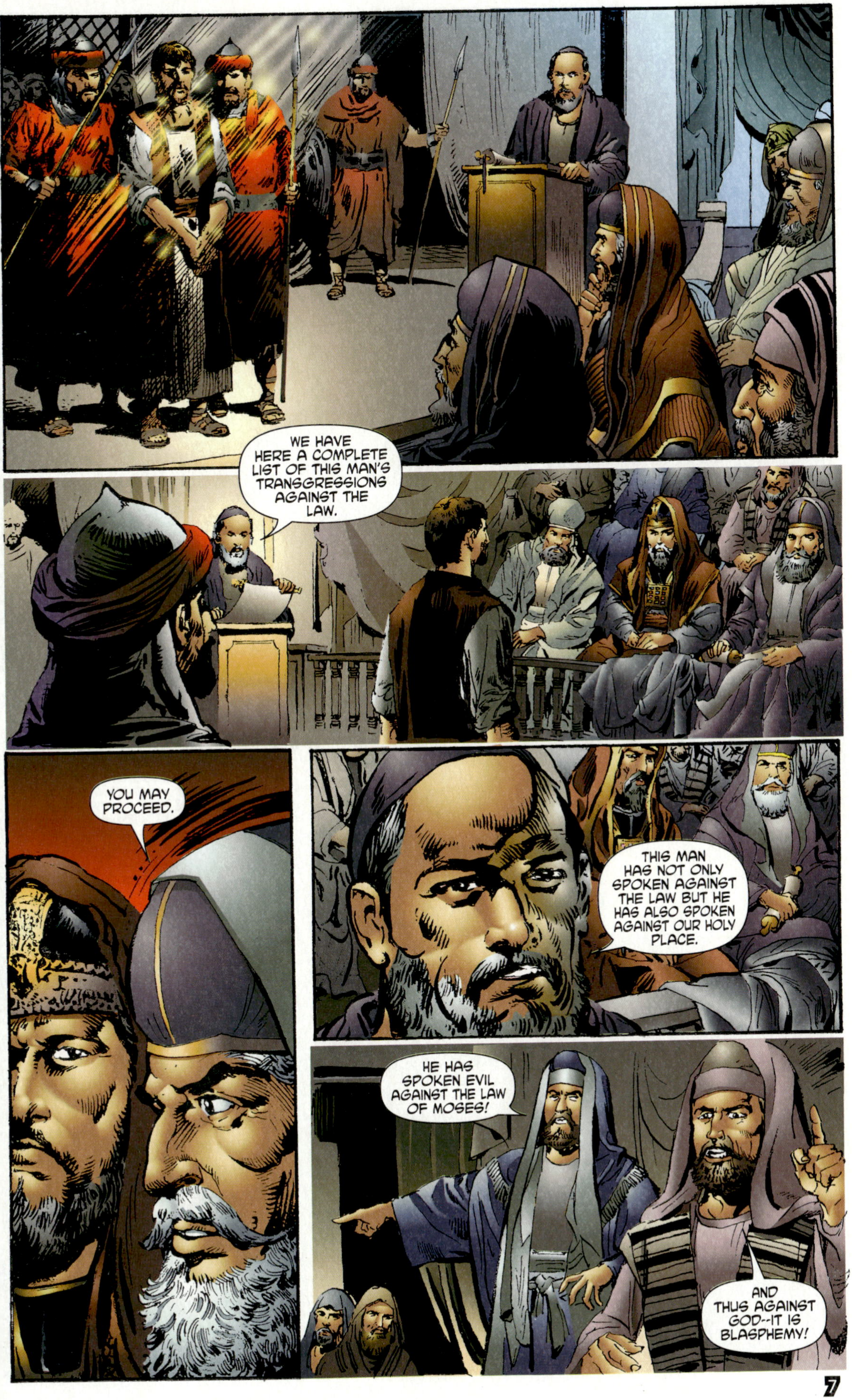
WE HAVE HERE A COMPLETE LIST OF THIS MAN'S TRANSGRESSIONS AGAINST THE LAW.
YOU MAY PROCEED.
THIS MAN HAS NOT ONLY SPOKEN AGAINST THE LAW BUT HE HAS ALSO SPOKEN AGAINST OUR HOLY PLACE.
HE HAS SPOKEN EVIL AGAINST THE LAW OF MOSES!
AND THUS AGAINST GOD--IT IS BLASPHEMY!

ARE THERE ANY WITNESSES?

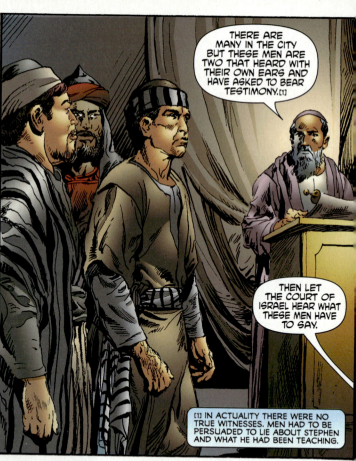

THERE ARE MANY IN THE CITY BUT THESE MEN ARE TWO THAT HEARD WITH THEIR OWN EARS AND HAVE ASKED TO BEAR TESTIMONY.[1]

THEN LET THE COURT OF ISRAEL HEAR WHAT THESE MEN HAVE TO SAY.

[1] IN ACTUALITY THERE WERE NO TRUE WITNESSES. MEN HAD TO BE PERSUADED TO LIE ABOUT STEPHEN AND WHAT HE HAD BEEN TEACHING.

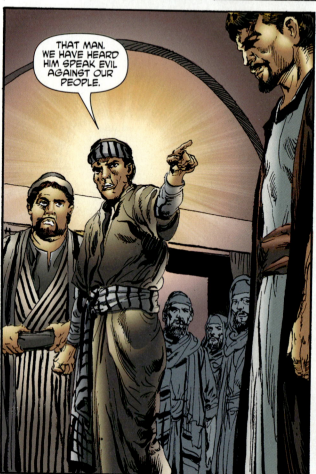

THAT MAN, WE HAVE HEARD HIM SPEAK EVIL AGAINST OUR PEOPLE.

HE SAID THAT THE DEAD MAN JESUS WOULD DESTROY THIS VERY PLACE WHERE WE STAND AND CHANGE ALL OF OUR CUSTOMS GIVEN TO US BY OUR FATHER MOSES.

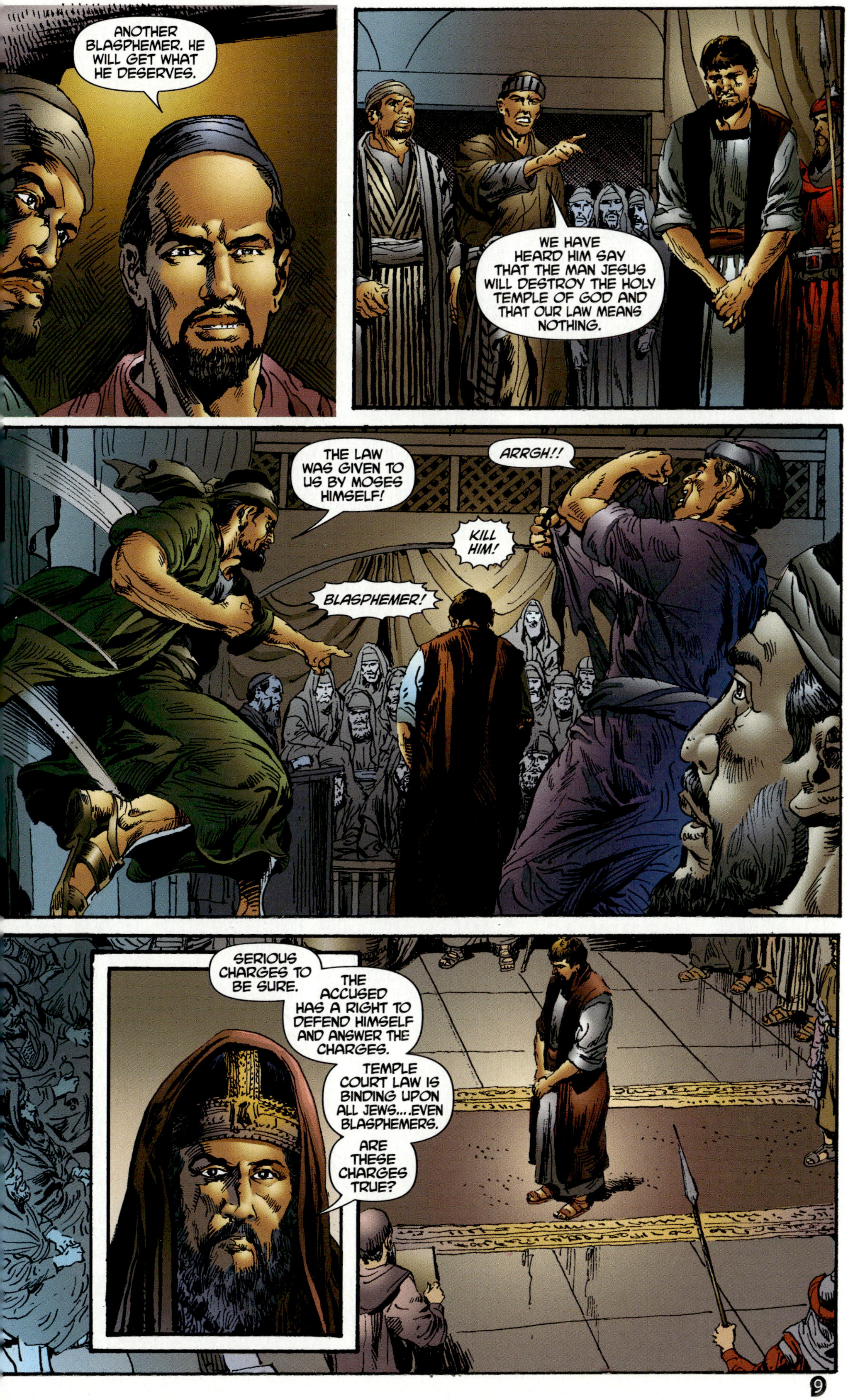
ANOTHER BLASPHEMER. HE WILL GET WHAT HE DESERVES.
WE HAVE HEARD HIM SAY THAT THE MAN JESUS WILL DESTROY THE HOLY TEMPLE OF GOD AND THAT OUR LAW MEANS NOTHING.
THE LAW WAS GIVEN TO US BY MOSES HIMSELF!
ARRGH!!
KILL HIM!
BLASPHEMER!
SERIOUS CHARGES TO BE SURE.
THE ACCUSED HAS A RIGHT TO DEFEND HIMSELF AND ANSWER THE CHARGES.
TEMPLE COURT LAW IS BINDING UPON ALL JEWS....EVEN BLASPHEMERS.
ARE THESE CHARGES TRUE?

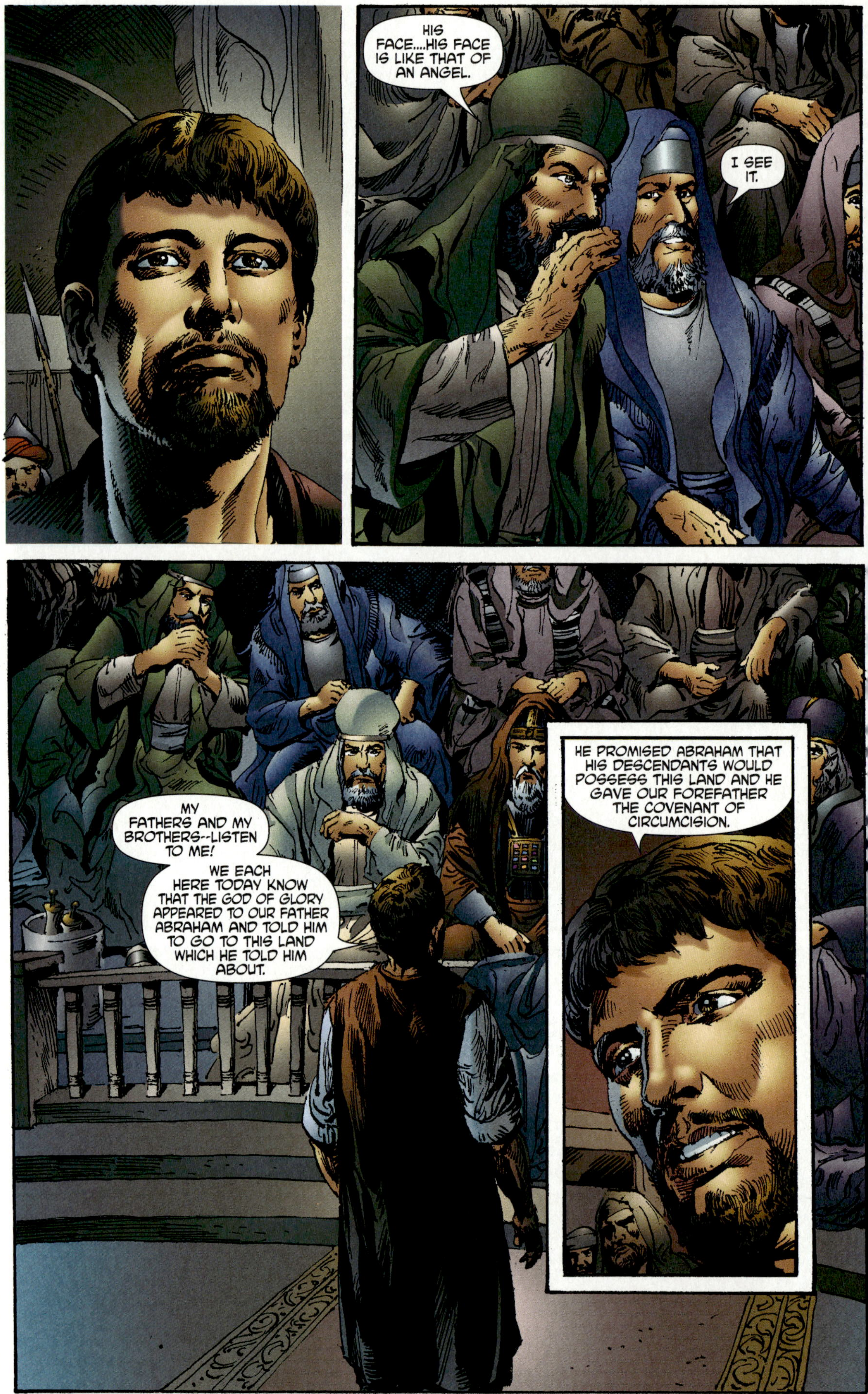
HIS FACE....HIS FACE IS LIKE THAT OF AN ANGEL.
I SEE IT.
MY FATHERS AND MY BROTHERS--LISTEN TO ME!
WE EACH HERE TODAY KNOW THAT THE GOD OF GLORY APPEARED TO OUR FATHER ABRAHAM AND TOLD HIM TO GO TO THIS LAND WHICH HE TOLD HIM ABOUT.
HE PROMISED ABRAHAM THAT HIS DESCENDANTS WOULD POSSESS THIS LAND AND HE GAVE OUR FOREFATHER THE COVENANT OF CIRCUMCISION.

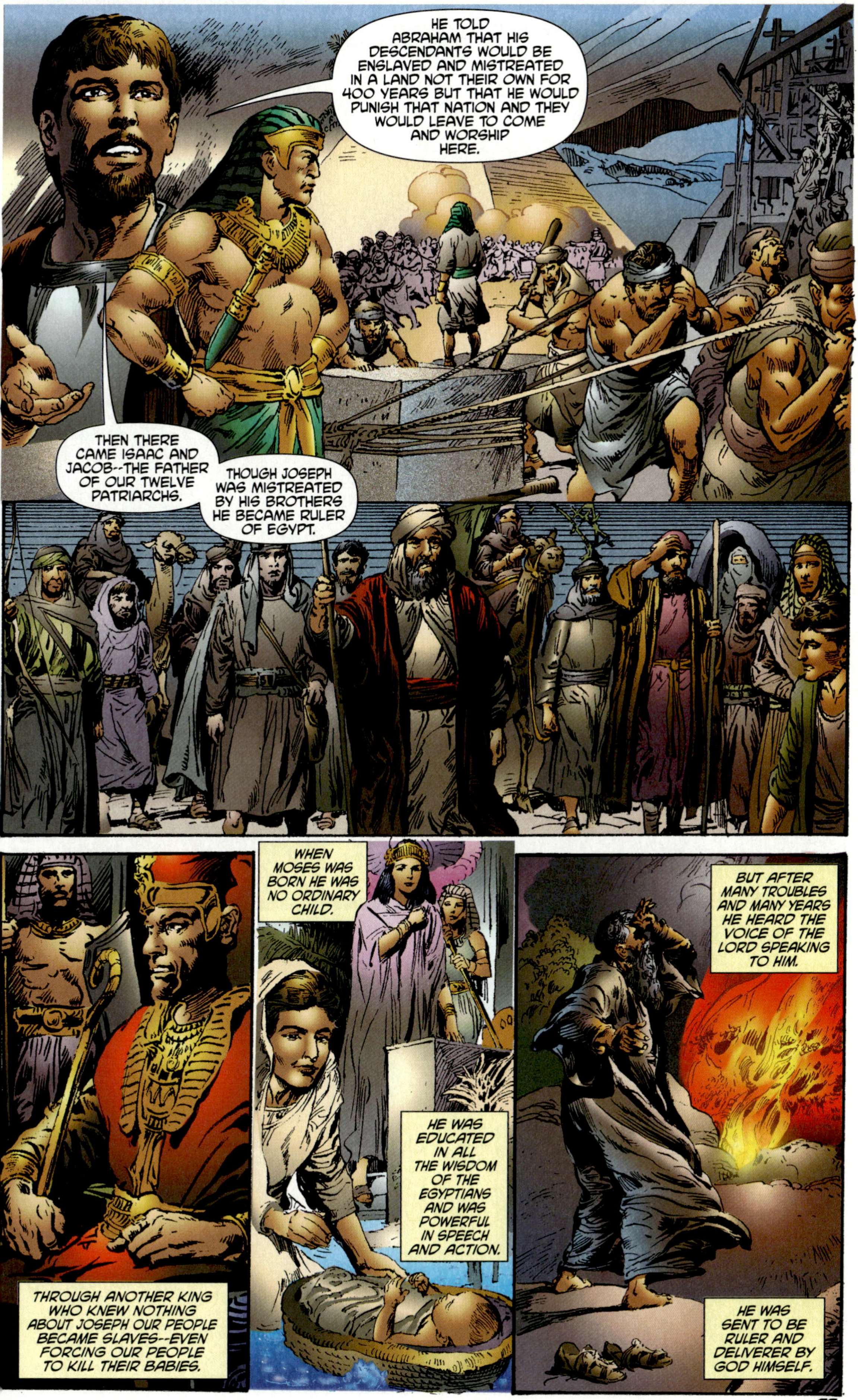

HE TOLD ABRAHAM THAT HIS DESCENDANTS WOULD BE ENSLAVED AND MISTREATED IN A LAND NOT THEIR OWN FOR 400 YEARS BUT THAT HE WOULD PUNISH THAT NATION AND THEY WOULD LEAVE TO COME AND WORSHIP HERE.
THEN THERE CAME ISAAC AND JACOB--THE FATHER OF OUR TWELVE PATRIARCHS.
THOUGH JOSEPH WAS MISTREATED BY HIS BROTHERS HE BECAME RULER OF EGYPT.
THROUGH ANOTHER KING WHO KNEW NOTHING ABOUT JOSEPH OUR PEOPLE BECAME SLAVES--EVEN FORCING OUR PEOPLE TO KILL THEIR BABIES.
WHEN MOSES WAS BORN HE WAS NO ORDINARY CHILD.
HE WAS EDUCATED IN ALL THE WISDOM OF THE EGYPTIANS AND WAS POWERFUL IN SPEECH AND ACTION.
BUT AFTER MANY TROUBLES AND MANY YEARS HE HEARD THE VOICE OF THE LORD SPEAKING TO HIM.
HE WAS SENT TO BE RULER AND DELIVERER BY GOD HIMSELF.

BUT THIS SAME MOSES TOLD OUR PEOPLE THAT GOD WOULD SEND A GREAT PROPHET LIKE HIMSELF FROM AMONG US.

YET OUR FOREFATHERS REFUSED TO OBEY GOD.

THEY WANTED TO GO BACK TO EGYPT AND HAD AARON MAKE FOR THEM A GOLDEN CALF AS AN IDOL TO WORSHIP AND LEAD THEM.

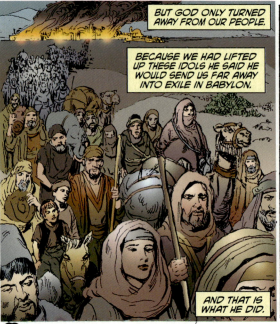

BUT GOD ONLY TURNED AWAY FROM OUR PEOPLE.

BECAUSE WE HAD LIFTED UP THESE IDOLS HE SAID HE WOULD SEND US FAR AWAY INTO EXILE IN BABYLON.

AND THAT IS WHAT HE DID.

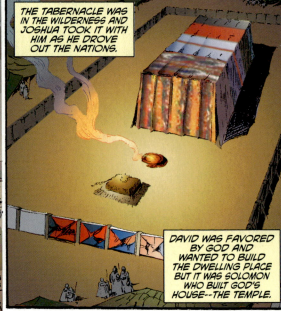

THE TABERNACLE WAS IN THE WILDERNESS AND JOSHUA TOOK IT WITH HIM AS HE DROVE OUT THE NATIONS.

DAVID WAS FAVORED BY GOD AND WANTED TO BUILD THE DWELLING PLACE BUT IT WAS SOLOMON WHO BUILT GOD'S HOUSE--THE TEMPLE.

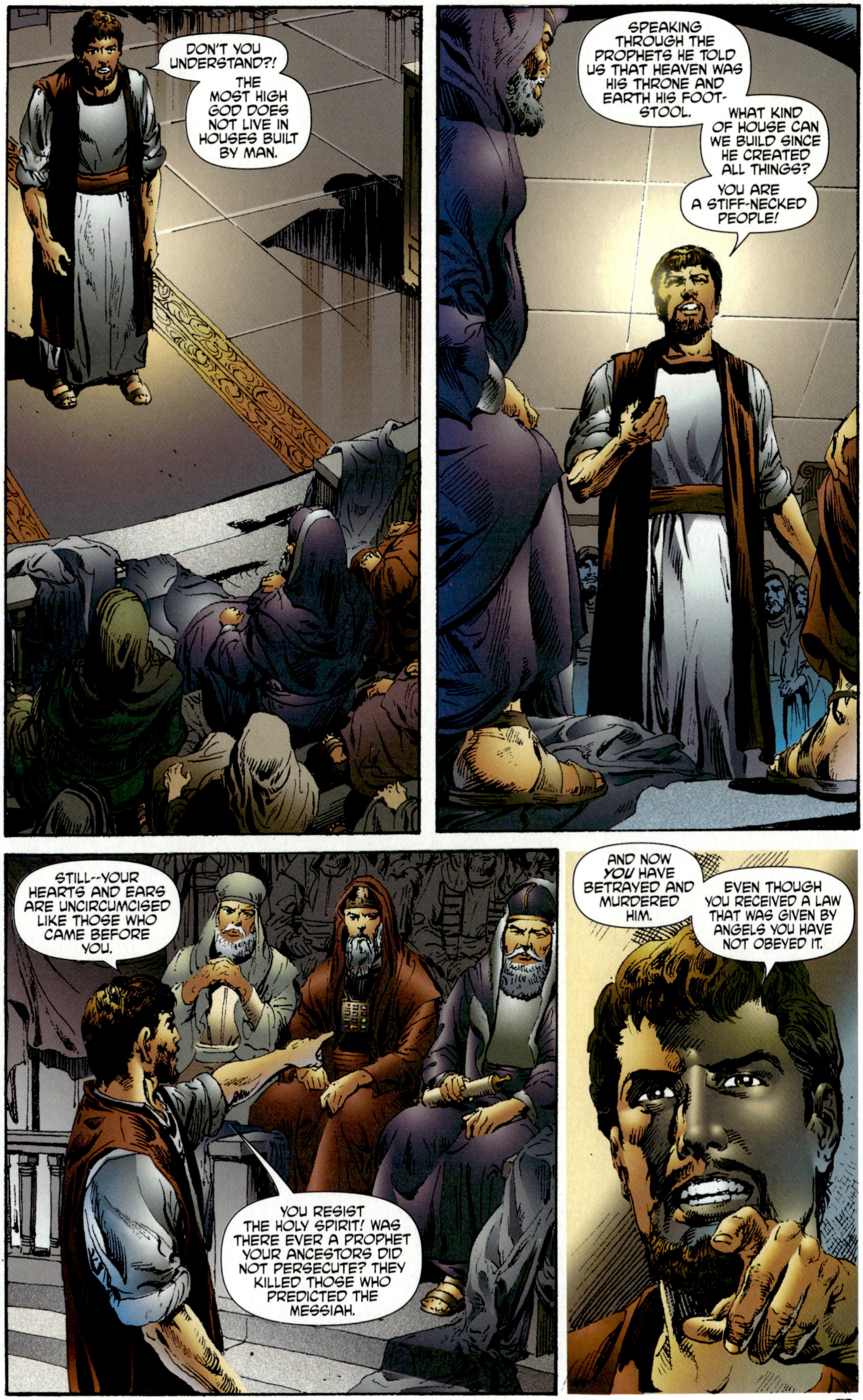
DON'T YOU UNDERSTAND?!
THE MOST HIGH GOD DOES NOT LIVE IN HOUSES BUILT BY MAN.
SPEAKING THROUGH THE PROPHETS HE TOLD US THAT HEAVEN WAS HIS THRONE AND EARTH HIS FOOT-STOOL.
WHAT KIND OF HOUSE CAN WE BUILD SINCE HE CREATED ALL THINGS?
YOU ARE A STIFF-NECKED PEOPLE!
STILL--YOUR HEARTS AND EARS ARE UNCIRCUMCISED LIKE THOSE WHO CAME BEFORE YOU.
YOU RESIST THE HOLY SPIRIT! WAS THERE EVER A PROPHET YOUR ANCESTORS DID NOT PERSECUTE? THEY KILLED THOSE WHO PREDICTED THE MESSIAH.
AND NOW *YOU* HAVE BETRAYED AND MURDERED HIM.
EVEN THOUGH YOU RECEIVED A LAW THAT WAS GIVEN BY ANGELS YOU HAVE NOT OBEYED IT.

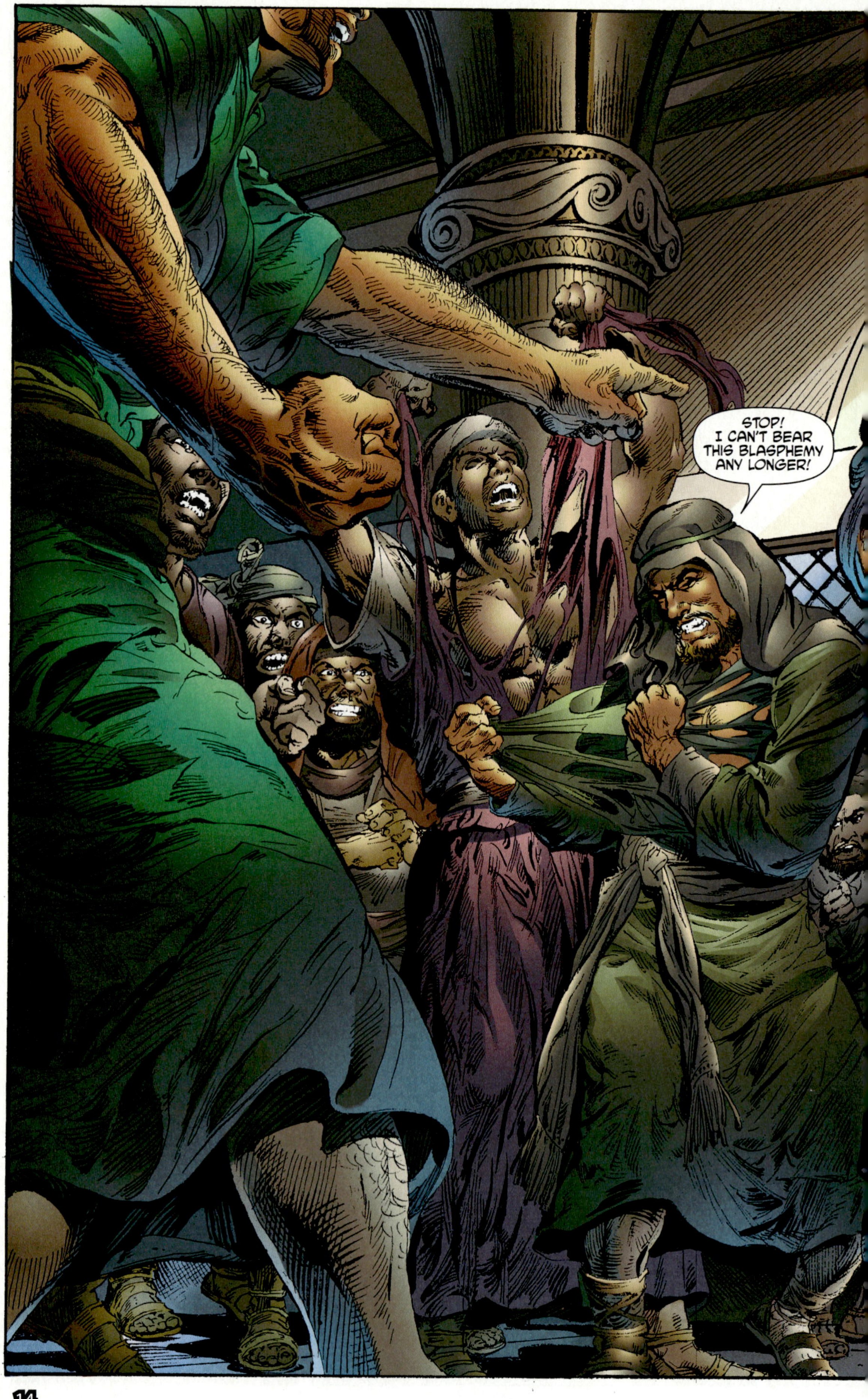
STOP! I CAN'T BEAR THIS BLASPHEMY ANY LONGER!

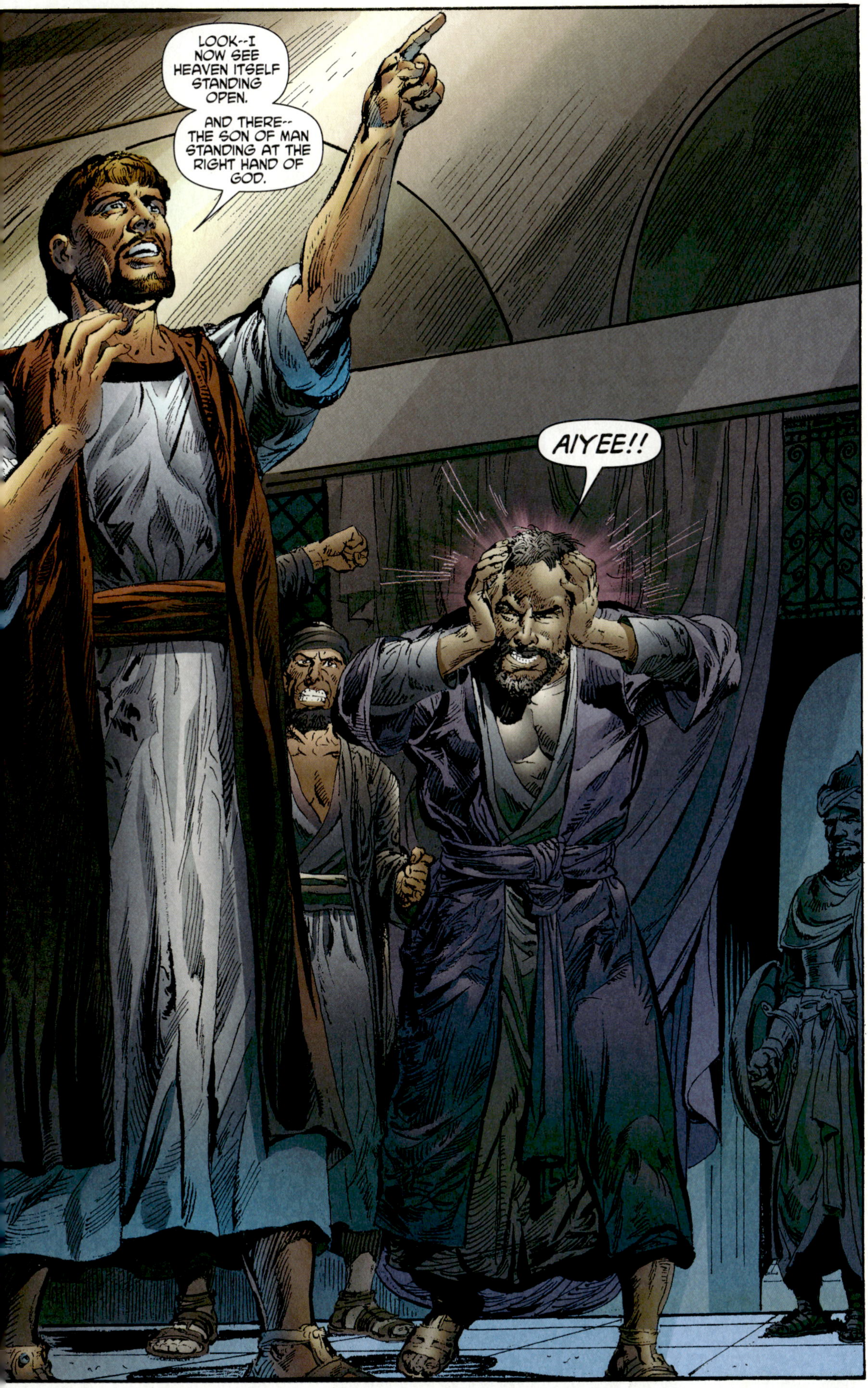
LOOK--I NOW SEE HEAVEN ITSELF STANDING OPEN.
AND THERE-- THE SON OF MAN STANDING AT THE RIGHT HAND OF GOD.
AIYEE!!

STONES OF GOD'S JUDGMENT.

STONES OF GOD'S PLEASURE...

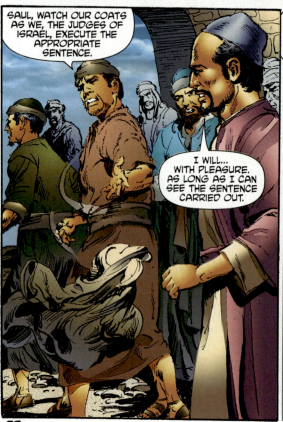

SAUL, WATCH OUR COATS AS WE, THE JUDGES OF ISRAEL, EXECUTE THE APPROPRIATE SENTENCE.

I WILL... WITH PLEASURE. AS LONG AS I CAN SEE THE SENTENCE CARRIED OUT.

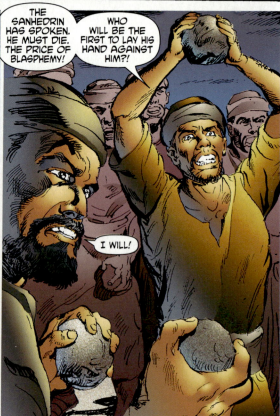

THE SANHEDRIN HAS SPOKEN. HE MUST DIE. THE PRICE OF BLASPHEMY!

WHO WILL BE THE FIRST TO LAY HIS HAND AGAINST HIM?!

I WILL!

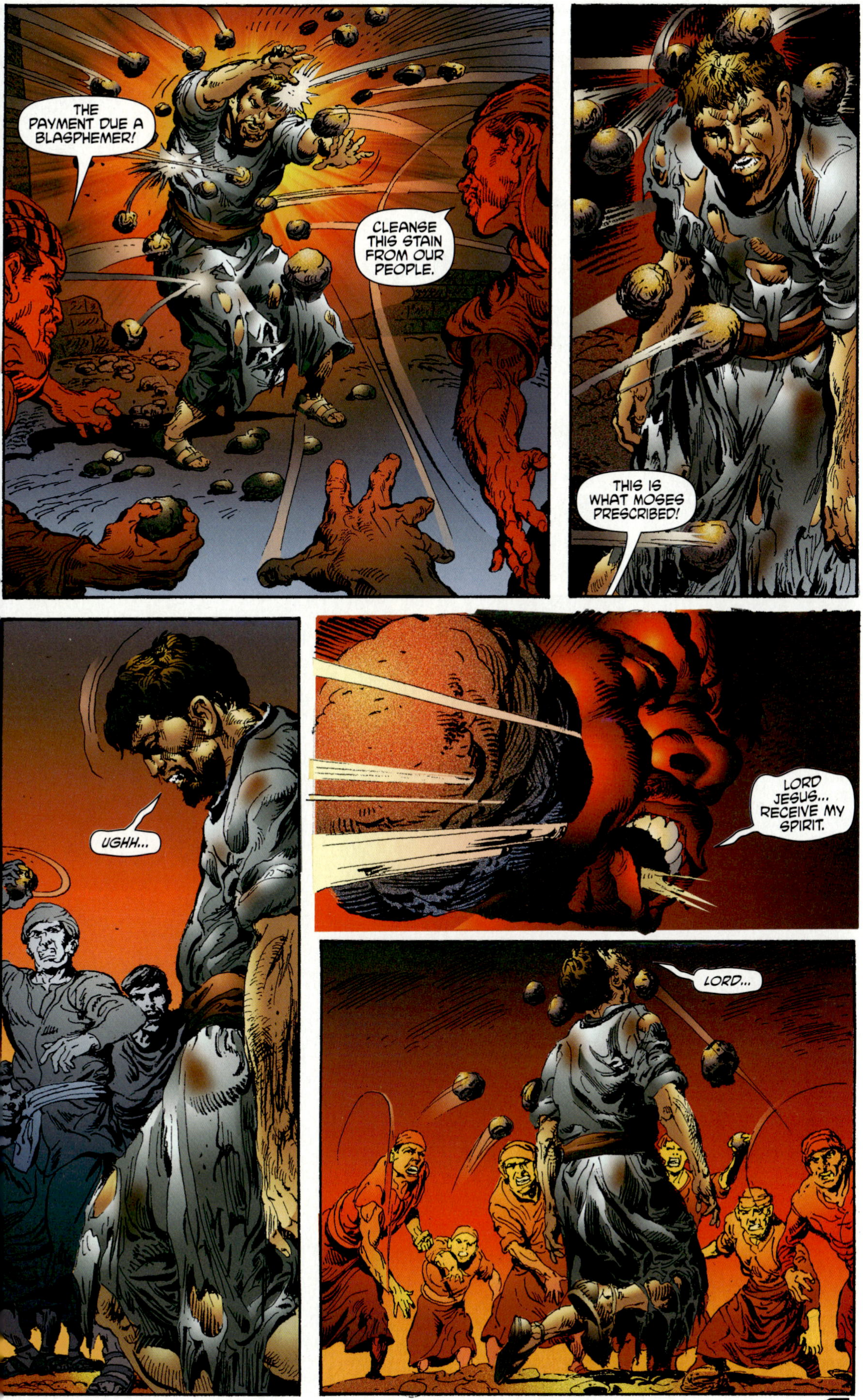
THE PAYMENT DUE A BLASPHEMER!
CLEANSE THIS STAIN FROM OUR PEOPLE.
THIS IS WHAT MOSES PRESCRIBED!
UGHH...
LORD JESUS... RECEIVE MY SPIRIT.
LORD...

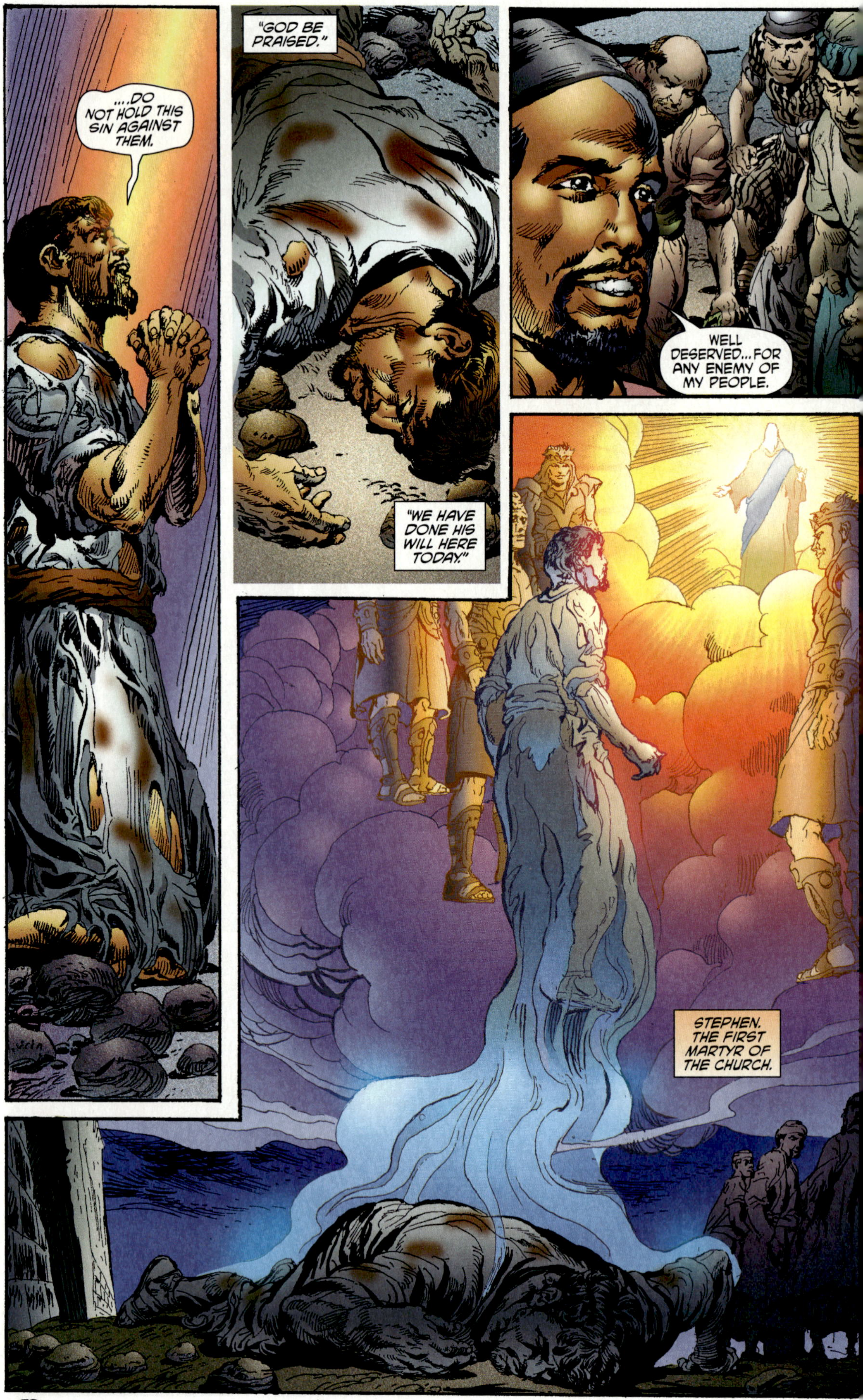
...DO NOT HOLD THIS SIN AGAINST THEM.
"GOD BE PRAISED."
"WE HAVE DONE HIS WILL HERE TODAY."
WELL DESERVED...FOR ANY ENEMY OF MY PEOPLE.
STEPHEN. THE FIRST MARTYR OF THE CHURCH.

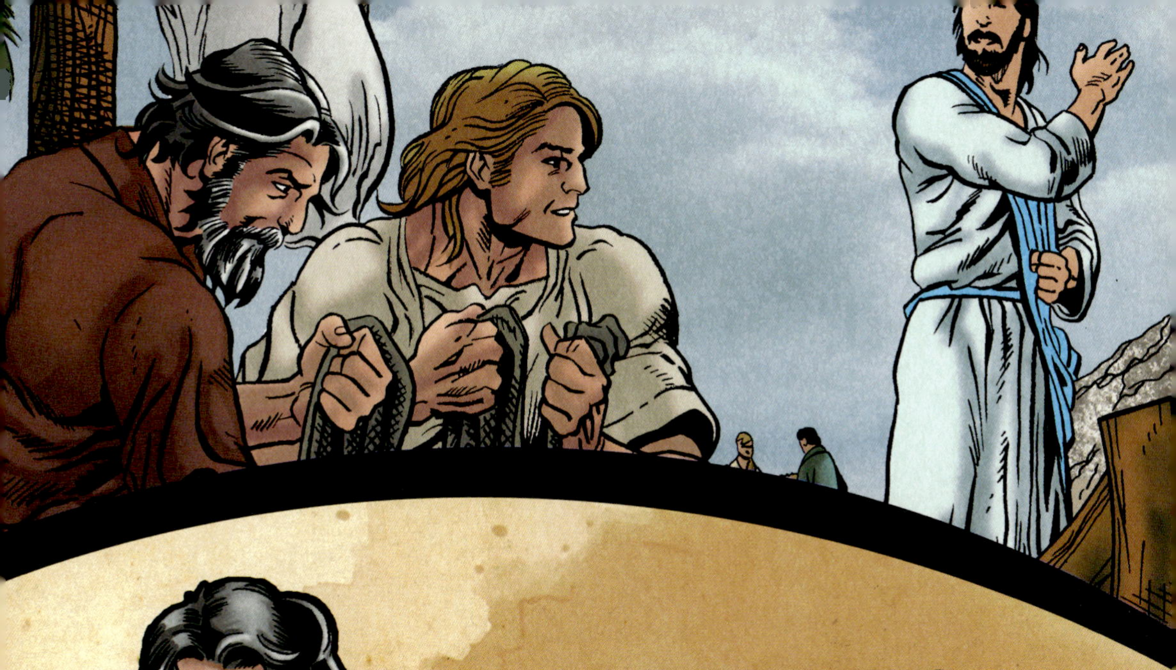

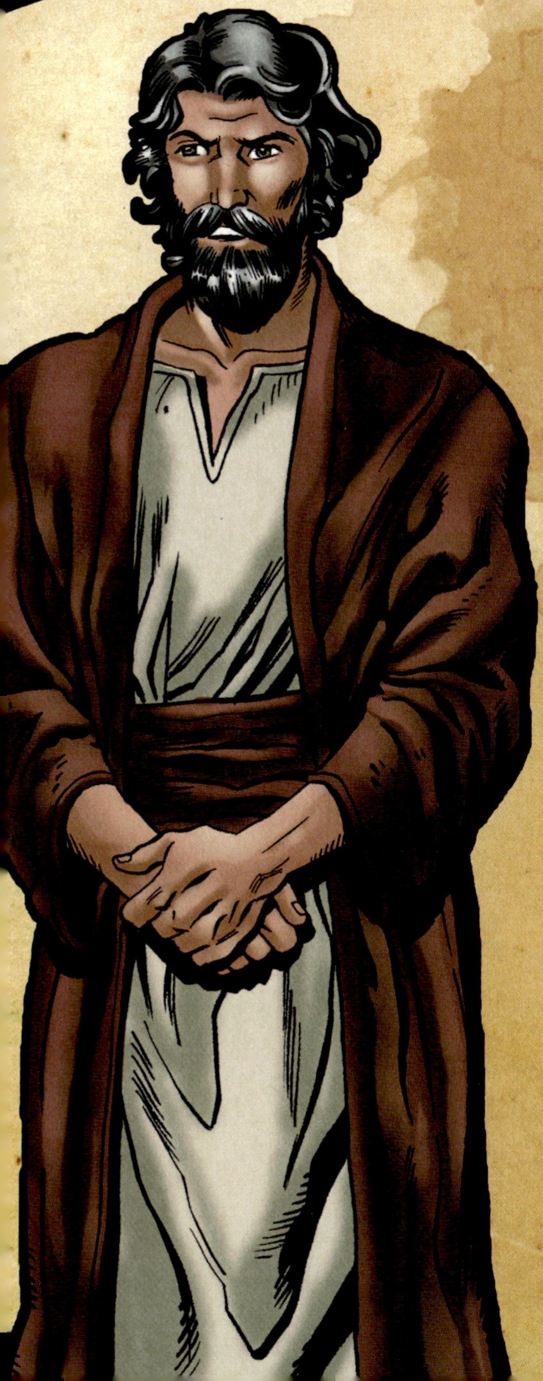

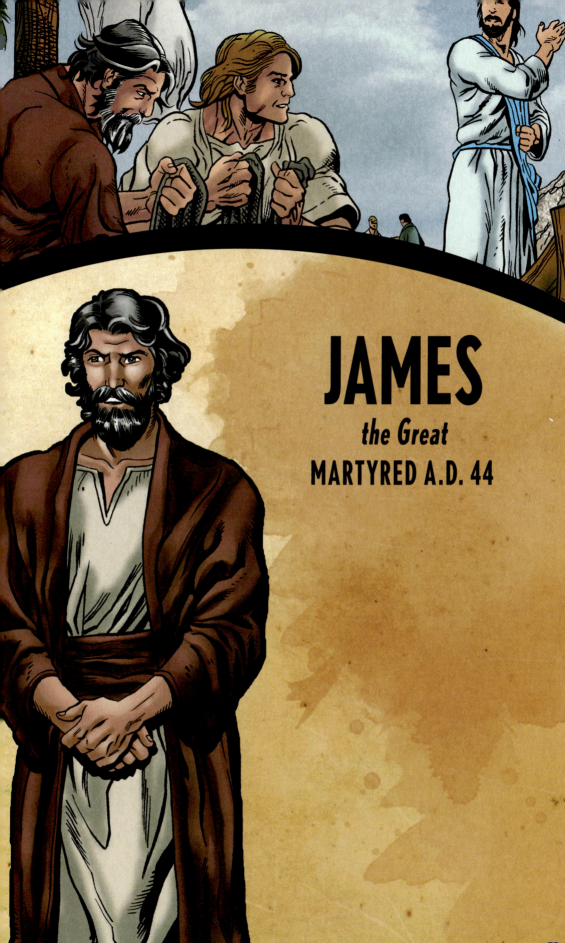

JAMES

the Great

MARTYRED A.D. 44

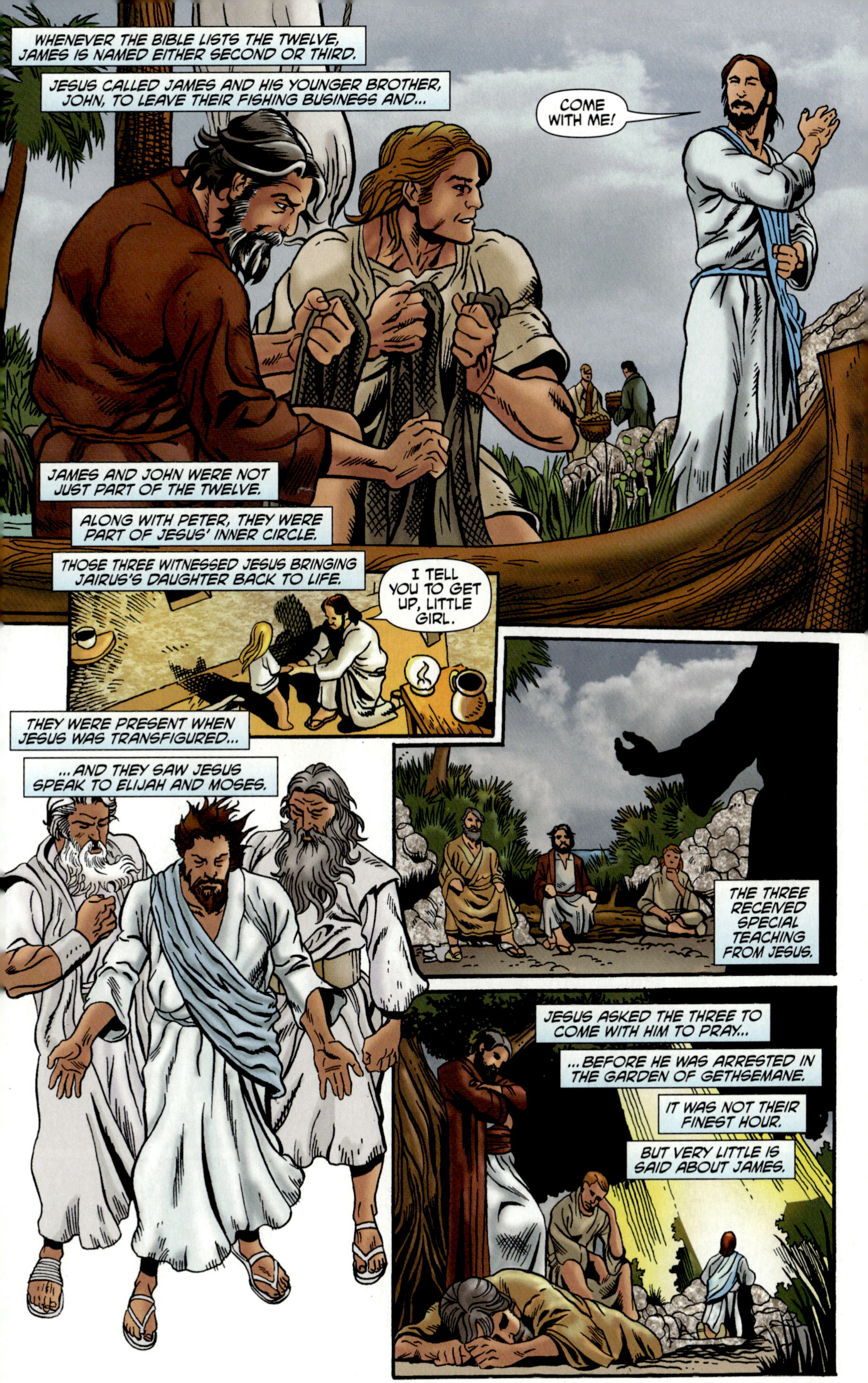
WHENEVER THE BIBLE LISTS THE TWELVE, JAMES IS NAMED EITHER SECOND OR THIRD.
JESUS CALLED JAMES AND HIS YOUNGER BROTHER, JOHN, TO LEAVE THEIR FISHING BUSINESS AND...
COME WITH ME!
JAMES AND JOHN WERE NOT JUST PART OF THE TWELVE.
ALONG WITH PETER, THEY WERE PART OF JESUS' INNER CIRCLE.
THOSE THREE WITNESSED JESUS BRINGING JAIRUS'S DAUGHTER BACK TO LIFE.
I TELL YOU TO GET UP, LITTLE GIRL.
THEY WERE PRESENT WHEN JESUS WAS TRANSFIGURED...
...AND THEY SAW JESUS SPEAK TO ELIJAH AND MOSES.
THE THREE RECEIVED SPECIAL TEACHING FROM JESUS.
JESUS ASKED THE THREE TO COME WITH HIM TO PRAY...
...BEFORE HE WAS ARRESTED IN THE GARDEN OF GETHSEMANE.
IT WAS NOT THEIR FINEST HOUR.
BUT VERY LITTLE IS SAID ABOUT JAMES.

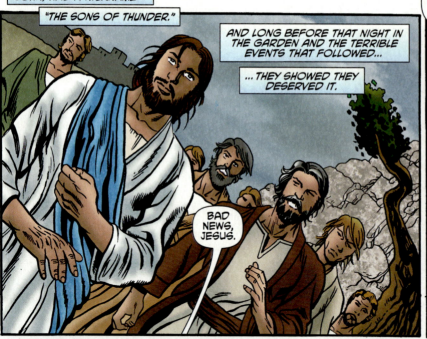

JAMES AND HIS BROTHER, JOHN, HAD A NICKNAME--

"THE SONS OF THUNDER."

AND LONG BEFORE THAT NIGHT IN THE GARDEN AND THE TERRIBLE EVENTS THAT FOLLOWED...

...THEY SHOWED THEY DESERVED IT.

BAD NEWS, JESUS.

THE VILLAGE AHEAD HAD ROOM FOR US...

UNTIL THEY HEARD WE WERE TRAVELING TO JERUSALEM.

I KNEW WE SHOULD HAVE AVOIDED SAMARIA.

THIS IS NOT RIGHT!

JERUSALEM IS WHERE THE TEMPLE IS.

THEY KNOW PASSOVER IS COMING.

SINCE THE TIME OF ELIJAH, THIS REGION HAS BEEN FULL OF HEATHENS...

...IDOLATERS AND PAGANS!

JESUS, DO YOU WANT US TO CALL DOWN FIRE ON THAT VILLAGE...

...AS ELIJAH DID WHEN AHAZIAH'S MEN CONFRONTED HIM?

DO YOU EVEN KNOW WHAT KIND OF SPIRIT YOU SPEAK WITH?

THE SON OF MAN DID NOT COME TO DESTROY MEN'S LIVES.

THE SON OF MAN CAME TO SAVE THEM.

WE WILL GO TO THE NEXT VILLAGE AND INQUIRE THERE.

JAMES AND JOHN KNEW JESUS WAS SPECIAL...

...BUT THEY STILL DID NOT FULLY UNDERSTAND WHY...

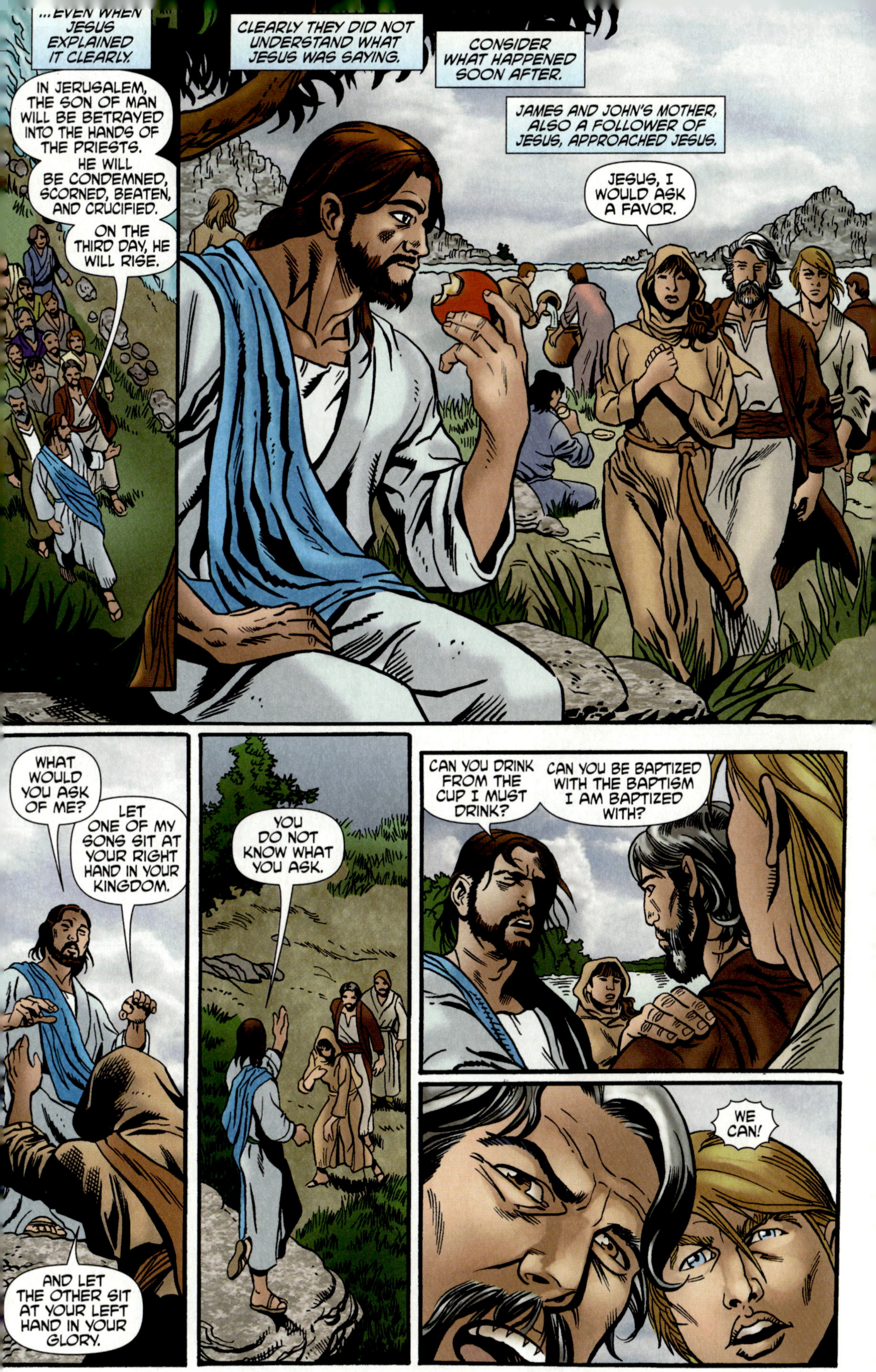
...EVEN WHEN JESUS EXPLAINED IT CLEARLY.
IN JERUSALEM, THE SON OF MAN WILL BE BETRAYED INTO THE HANDS OF THE PRIESTS.
HE WILL BE CONDEMNED, SCORNED, BEATEN, AND CRUCIFIED.
ON THE THIRD DAY, HE WILL RISE.
CLEARLY THEY DID NOT UNDERSTAND WHAT JESUS WAS SAYING.
CONSIDER WHAT HAPPENED SOON AFTER.
JAMES AND JOHN'S MOTHER, ALSO A FOLLOWER OF JESUS, APPROACHED JESUS.
JESUS, I WOULD ASK A FAVOR.
WHAT WOULD YOU ASK OF ME?
LET ONE OF MY SONS SIT AT YOUR RIGHT HAND IN YOUR KINGDOM.
AND LET THE OTHER SIT AT YOUR LEFT HAND IN YOUR GLORY.
YOU DO NOT KNOW WHAT YOU ASK.
CAN YOU DRINK FROM THE CUP I MUST DRINK?
CAN YOU BE BAPTIZED WITH THE BAPTISM I AM BAPTIZED WITH?
WE CAN!

YOU WILL, INDEED.

YOU WILL DRINK FROM MY CUP.

YOU WILL BE BAPTIZED WITH MY BAPTISM.

BUT AS FOR YOUR QUESTION, TO SIT AT MY RIGHT OR LEFT HAND?

THAT IS NOT MINE TO GRANT.

MY FATHER HAS PREPARED THOSE PLACES.

AND THOSE PLACES BELONG TO THE ONES HE PREPARED THEM FOR.

CAN YOU BELIEVE THEM?

TRYING TO BE FIRST IN THE KINGDOM AGAIN...

COME HERE, MY FRIENDS.

ALL OF YOU.

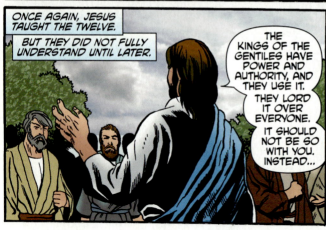

ONCE AGAIN, JESUS TAUGHT THE TWELVE.

BUT THEY DID NOT FULLY UNDERSTAND UNTIL LATER.

THE KINGS OF THE GENTILES HAVE POWER AND AUTHORITY, AND THEY USE IT.

THEY LORD IT OVER EVERYONE.

IT SHOULD NOT BE SO WITH YOU. INSTEAD...

"WHOEVER WANTS TO BE GREAT AMONG YOU...

"...MUST BE A SERVANT.

"WHOEVER WANTS TO BE FIRST...

"...MUST BE THE SLAVE TO ALL.

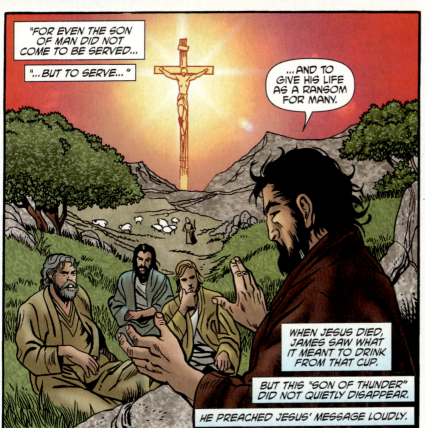

"FOR EVEN THE SON OF MAN DID NOT COME TO BE SERVED..."

"...BUT TO SERVE..."

...AND TO GIVE HIS LIFE AS A RANSOM FOR MANY.

WHEN JESUS DIED, JAMES SAW WHAT IT MEANT TO DRINK FROM THAT CUP.

BUT THIS "SON OF THUNDER" DID NOT QUIETLY DISAPPEAR.

HE PREACHED JESUS' MESSAGE LOUDLY.

HEROD AGRIPPA DID NOT LIKE THIS.

HE PERSECUTED THE FOLLOWERS OF CHRIST.

WE ARREST YOU IN HEROD THE KING'S NAME!

JAMES IS THE ONLY APOSTLE WHOSE DEATH IS RECORDED IN THE BIBLE.

HE WAS ALSO THE FIRST OF THE TWELVE TO DIE A MARTYR.

AS JESUS SAID HE WOULD, JAMES "DRANK FROM THE CUP."

A "SON OF THUNDER," FIRST NOT BECAUSE HE HONORED HIMSELF...

...BUT BECAUSE HE WAS A SERVANT TO ALL.

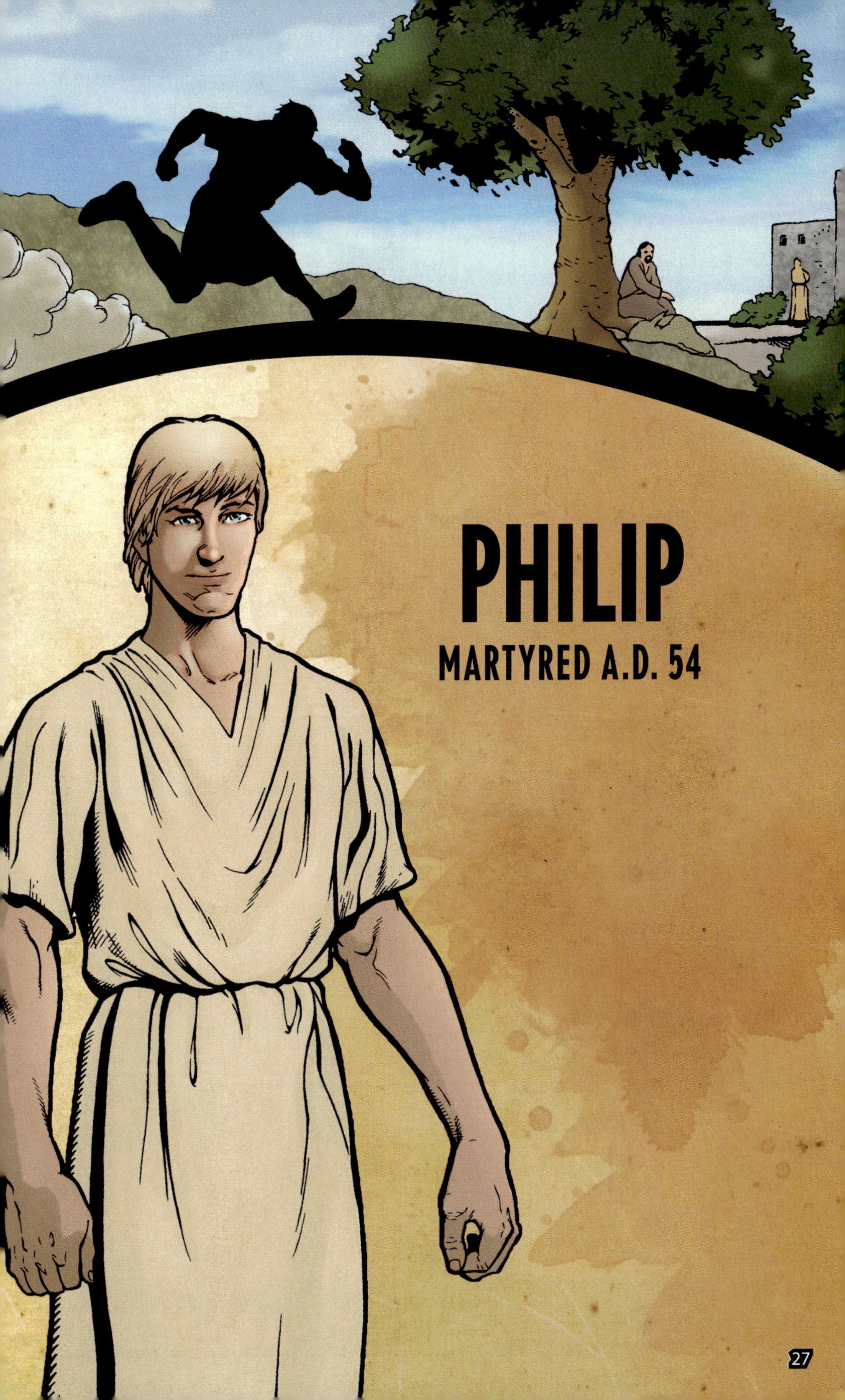

PHILIP

MARTYRED A.D. 54

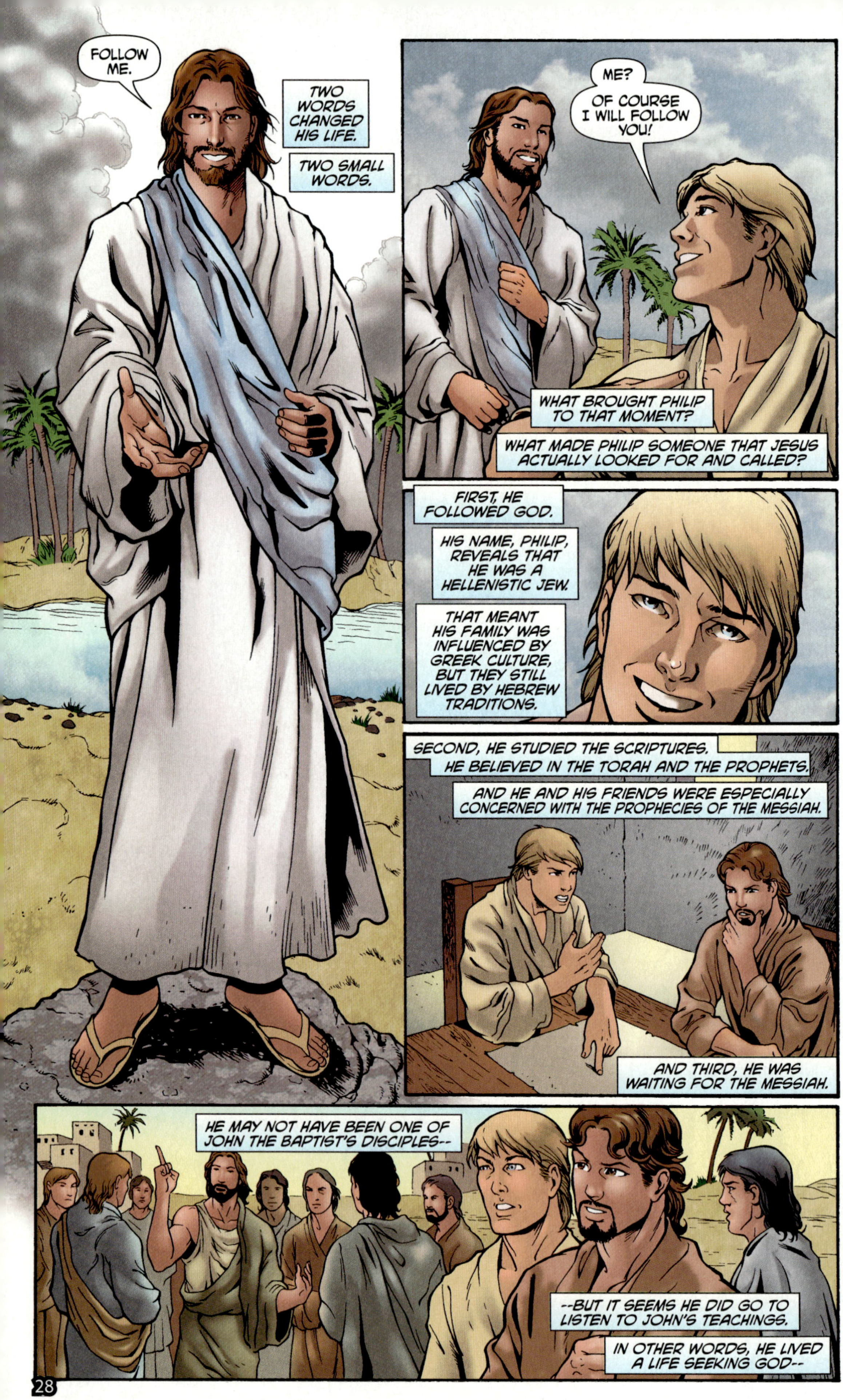
FOLLOW ME.
TWO WORDS CHANGED HIS LIFE.
TWO SMALL WORDS.
ME?
OF COURSE I WILL FOLLOW YOU!
WHAT BROUGHT PHILIP TO THAT MOMENT?
WHAT MADE PHILIP SOMEONE THAT JESUS ACTUALLY LOOKED FOR AND CALLED?
FIRST, HE FOLLOWED GOD.
HIS NAME, PHILIP, REVEALS THAT HE WAS A HELLENISTIC JEW.
THAT MEANT HIS FAMILY WAS INFLUENCED BY GREEK CULTURE, BUT THEY STILL LIVED BY HEBREW TRADITIONS.
SECOND, HE STUDIED THE SCRIPTURES. HE BELIEVED IN THE TORAH AND THE PROPHETS.
AND HE AND HIS FRIENDS WERE ESPECIALLY CONCERNED WITH THE PROPHECIES OF THE MESSIAH.
AND THIRD, HE WAS WAITING FOR THE MESSIAH.
HE MAY NOT HAVE BEEN ONE OF JOHN THE BAPTIST'S DISCIPLES--
--BUT IT SEEMS HE DID GO TO LISTEN TO JOHN'S TEACHINGS.
IN OTHER WORDS, HE LIVED A LIFE SEEKING GOD--

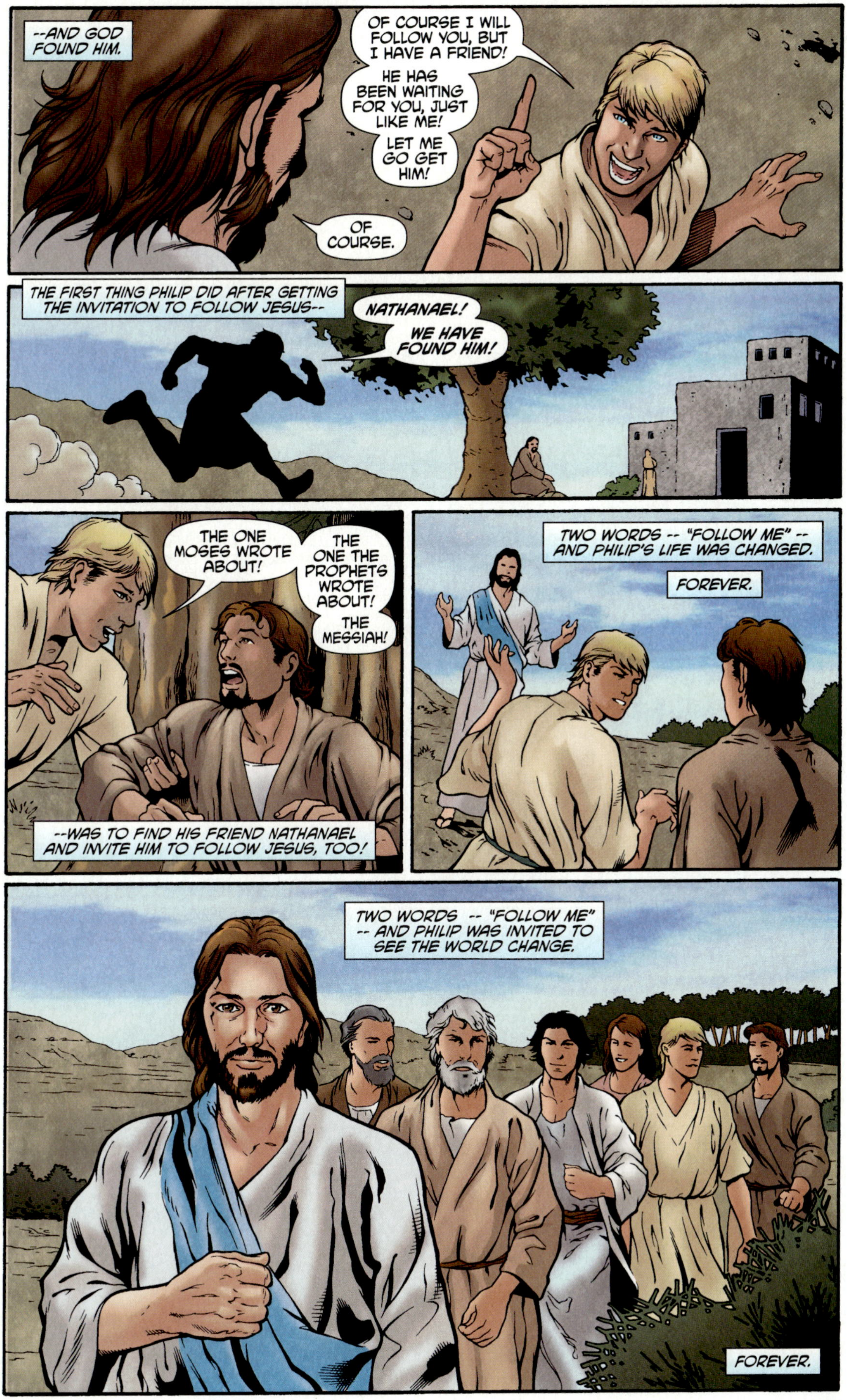
--AND GOD FOUND HIM.
OF COURSE I WILL FOLLOW YOU, BUT I HAVE A FRIEND!
HE HAS BEEN WAITING FOR YOU, JUST LIKE ME!
LET ME GO GET HIM!
OF COURSE.
THE FIRST THING PHILIP DID AFTER GETTING THE INVITATION TO FOLLOW JESUS--
NATHANAEL!
WE HAVE FOUND HIM!
THE ONE MOSES WROTE ABOUT!
THE ONE THE PROPHETS WROTE ABOUT!
THE MESSIAH!
--WAS TO FIND HIS FRIEND NATHANAEL AND INVITE HIM TO FOLLOW JESUS, TOO!
TWO WORDS -- "FOLLOW ME" -- AND PHILIP'S LIFE WAS CHANGED.
FOREVER.
TWO WORDS -- "FOLLOW ME" -- AND PHILIP WAS INVITED TO SEE THE WORLD CHANGE.
FOREVER.

THE WAIT WAS OVER, BUT PHILIP STILL HAD MANY LESSONS TO LEARN ABOUT FOLLOWING CHRIST.
HE WAS THERE WHEN JESUS WAS TEACHING THE 5,000 PEOPLE IN THE WILDERNESS.
5,000 PEOPLE WHO DID NOT EXPECT TO BE THERE SO LONG, AND WHO WERE GETTING HUNGRY.
WE SHOULD SEND THE PEOPLE HOME, JESUS.
THEY ARE HUNGRY.
SO FEED THEM.
GIVE THEM SOMETHING TO EAT.
WHERE CAN YOU BUY THEM SOME BREAD?
"BUY THEM BREAD"?
IT WOULD TAKE EIGHT MONTHS OF WAGES TO BUY ENOUGH BREAD FOR EACH PERSON TO JUST HAVE A BITE!
SO WHAT DO WE HAVE THAT WE CAN GIVE THEM?
THIS BOY HAS FIVE SMALL LOAVES OF BREAD AND TWO SMALL FISH.
THAT WON'T DO MUCH WITH SO MANY.
GIVE IT TO ME AND HAVE EVERY-ONE SIT DOWN.
JESUS THANKED GOD FOR THE BREAD, THEN BROKE THE BREAD--
--GIVING IT TO THE DISCIPLES TO GIVE TO THE PEOPLE.
TWELVE BASKETS OF BREAD WERE LEFT OVER. ONE BASKET FOR EACH OF THE TWELVE DISCIPLES.
PHILIP LEARNED ABOUT GOD'S PROVISION THAT DAY.

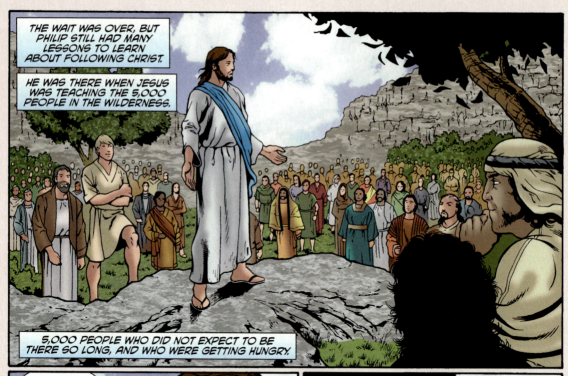

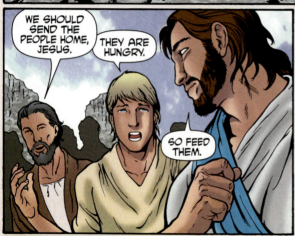

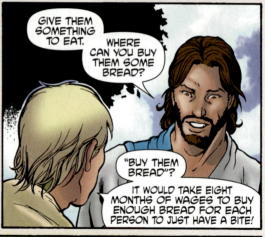

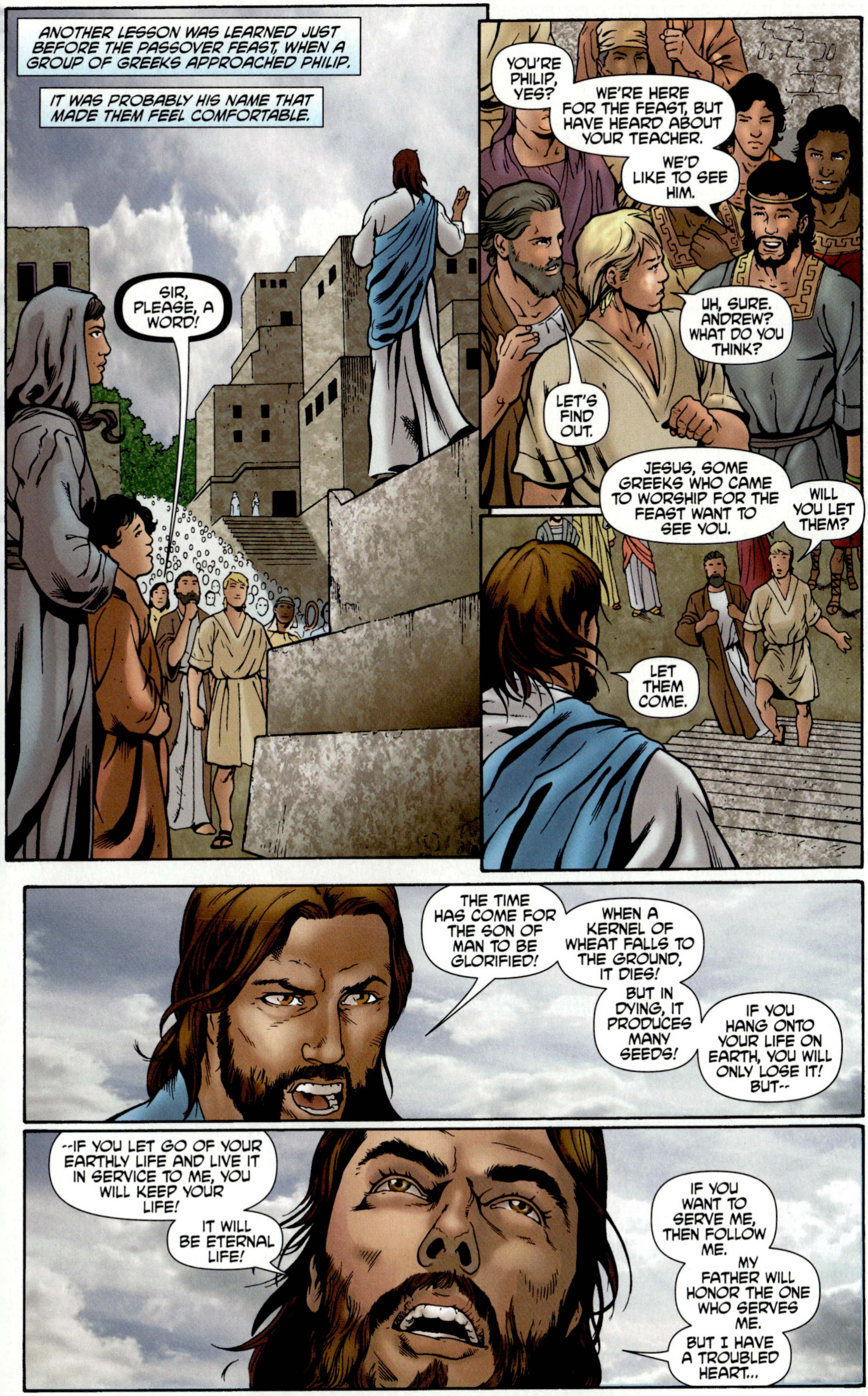

ANOTHER LESSON WAS LEARNED JUST BEFORE THE PASSOVER FEAST, WHEN A GROUP OF GREEKS APPROACHED PHILIP.
IT WAS PROBABLY HIS NAME THAT MADE THEM FEEL COMFORTABLE.
SIR, PLEASE, A WORD!
YOU'RE PHILIP, YES?
WE'RE HERE FOR THE FEAST, BUT HAVE HEARD ABOUT YOUR TEACHER.
WE'D LIKE TO SEE HIM.
UH, SURE. ANDREW? WHAT DO YOU THINK?
LET'S FIND OUT.
JESUS, SOME GREEKS WHO CAME TO WORSHIP FOR THE FEAST WANT TO SEE YOU.
WILL YOU LET THEM?
LET THEM COME.
THE TIME HAS COME FOR THE SON OF MAN TO BE GLORIFIED!
WHEN A KERNEL OF WHEAT FALLS TO THE GROUND, IT DIES!
BUT IN DYING, IT PRODUCES MANY SEEDS!
IF YOU HANG ONTO YOUR LIFE ON EARTH, YOU WILL ONLY LOSE IT! BUT--
--IF YOU LET GO OF YOUR EARTHLY LIFE AND LIVE IT IN SERVICE TO ME, YOU WILL KEEP YOUR LIFE!
IT WILL BE ETERNAL LIFE!
IF YOU WANT TO SERVE ME, THEN FOLLOW ME.
MY FATHER WILL HONOR THE ONE WHO SERVES ME.
BUT I HAVE A TROUBLED HEART...

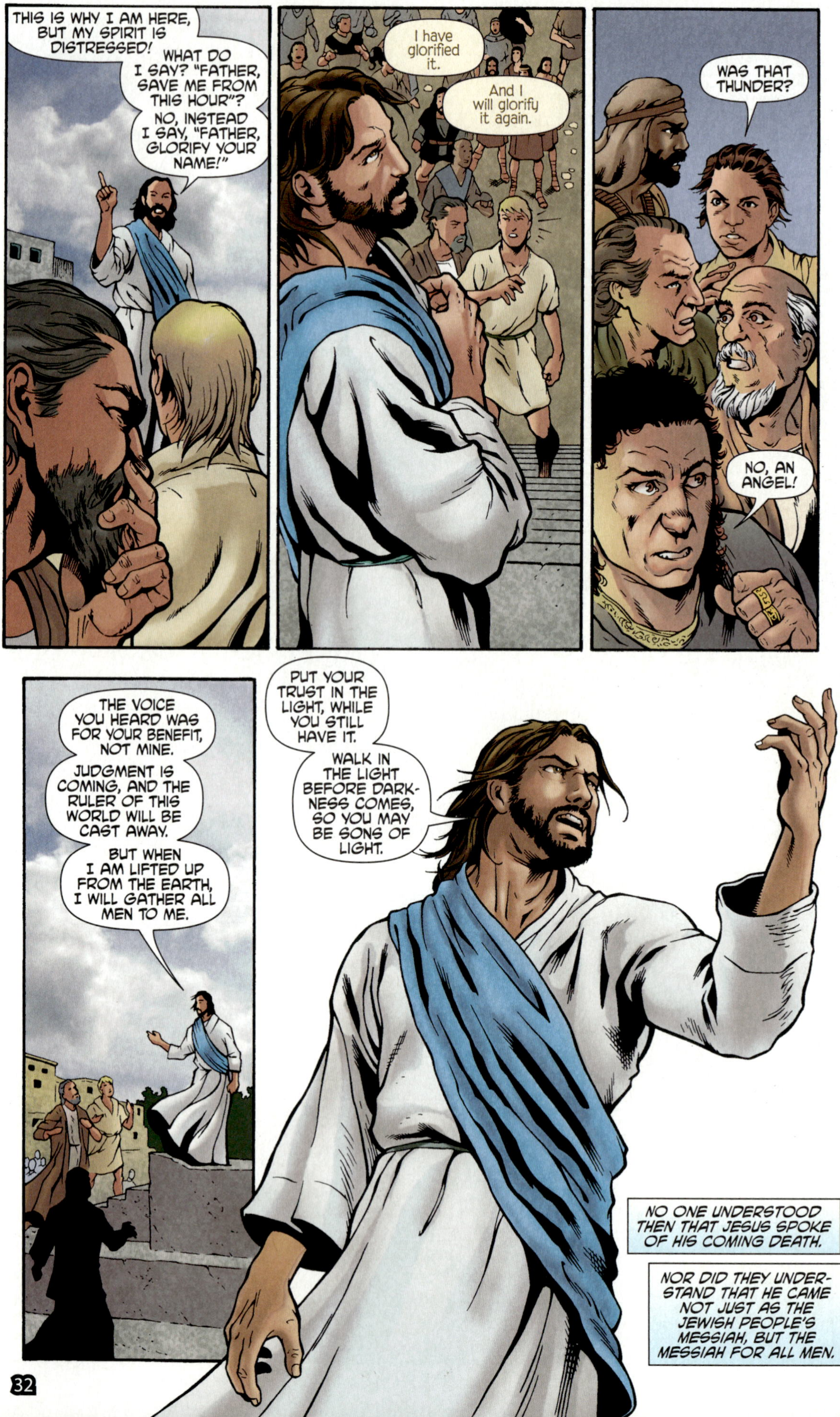
THIS IS WHY I AM HERE, BUT MY SPIRIT IS DISTRESSED!
WHAT DO I SAY? "FATHER, SAVE ME FROM THIS HOUR"?
NO, INSTEAD I SAY, "FATHER, GLORIFY YOUR NAME!"
I have glorified it.
And I will glorify it again.
WAS THAT THUNDER?
NO, AN ANGEL!
THE VOICE YOU HEARD WAS FOR YOUR BENEFIT, NOT MINE.
JUDGMENT IS COMING, AND THE RULER OF THIS WORLD WILL BE CAST AWAY.
BUT WHEN I AM LIFTED UP FROM THE EARTH, I WILL GATHER ALL MEN TO ME.
PUT YOUR TRUST IN THE LIGHT, WHILE YOU STILL HAVE IT.
WALK IN THE LIGHT BEFORE DARKNESS COMES, SO YOU MAY BE SONS OF LIGHT.
NO ONE UNDERSTOOD THEN THAT JESUS SPOKE OF HIS COMING DEATH.
NOR DID THEY UNDERSTAND THAT HE CAME NOT JUST AS THE JEWISH PEOPLE'S MESSIAH, BUT THE MESSIAH FOR ALL MEN.

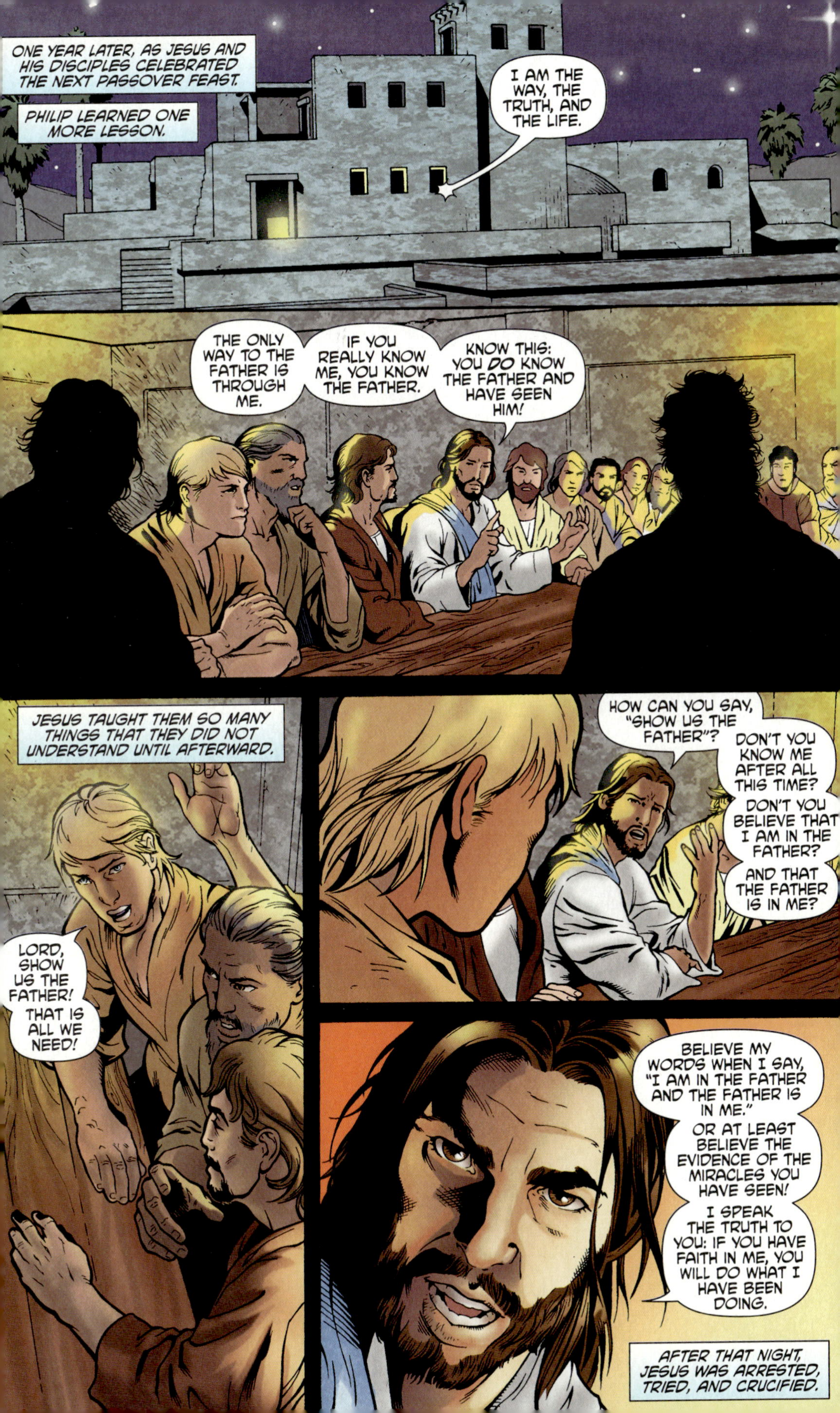
ONE YEAR LATER, AS JESUS AND HIS DISCIPLES CELEBRATED THE NEXT PASSOVER FEAST,
PHILIP LEARNED ONE MORE LESSON.
I AM THE WAY, THE TRUTH, AND THE LIFE.
THE ONLY WAY TO THE FATHER IS THROUGH ME.
IF YOU REALLY KNOW ME, YOU KNOW THE FATHER.
KNOW THIS: YOU DO KNOW THE FATHER AND HAVE SEEN HIM!
JESUS TAUGHT THEM SO MANY THINGS THAT THEY DID NOT UNDERSTAND UNTIL AFTERWARD.
LORD, SHOW US THE FATHER!
THAT IS ALL WE NEED!
HOW CAN YOU SAY, "SHOW US THE FATHER"?
DON'T YOU KNOW ME AFTER ALL THIS TIME?
DON'T YOU BELIEVE THAT I AM IN THE FATHER?
AND THAT THE FATHER IS IN ME?
BELIEVE MY WORDS WHEN I SAY, "I AM IN THE FATHER AND THE FATHER IS IN ME."
OR AT LEAST BELIEVE THE EVIDENCE OF THE MIRACLES YOU HAVE SEEN!
I SPEAK THE TRUTH TO YOU: IF YOU HAVE FAITH IN ME, YOU WILL DO WHAT I HAVE BEEN DOING.
AFTER THAT NIGHT, JESUS WAS ARRESTED, TRIED, AND CRUCIFIED.

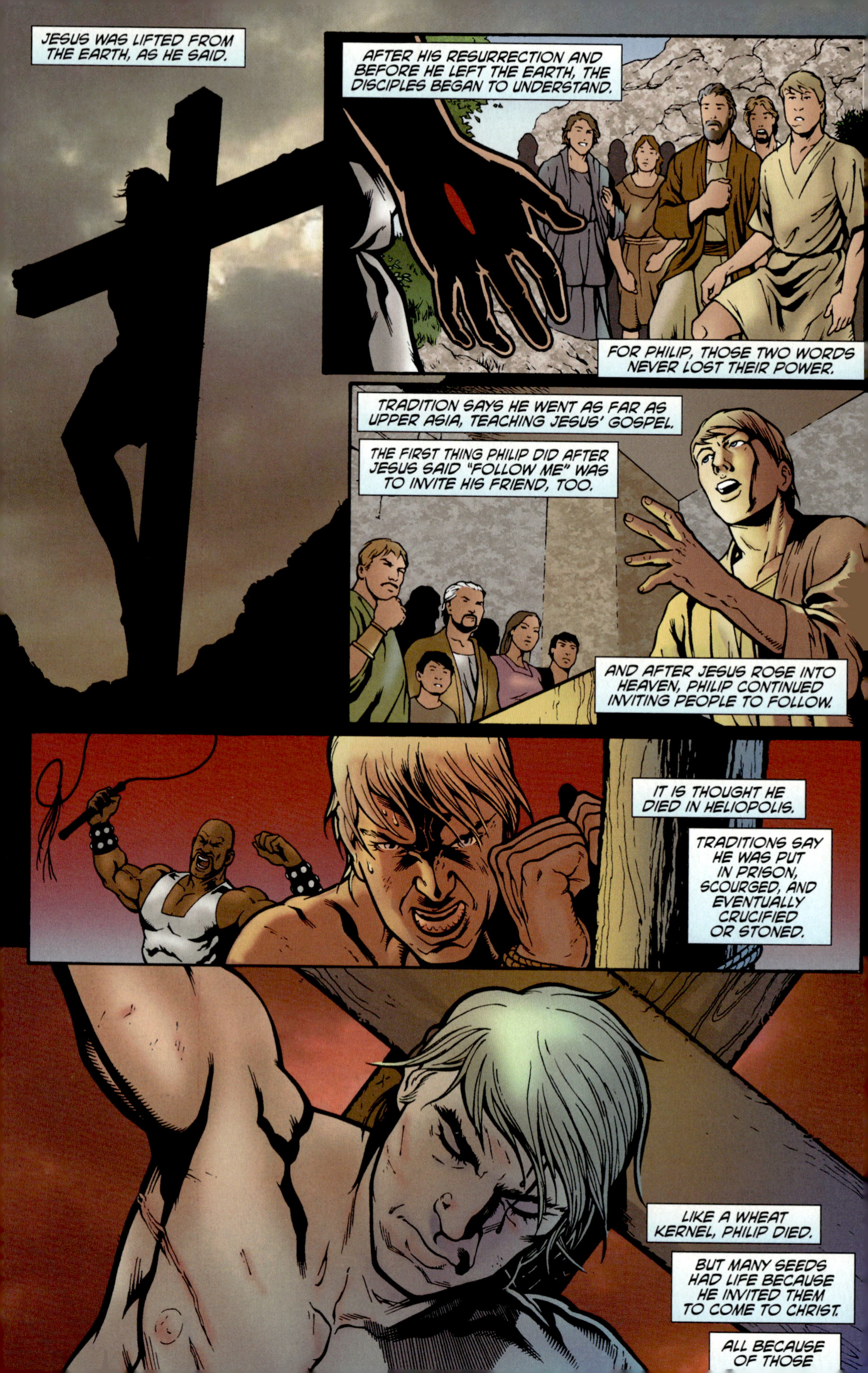
JESUS WAS LIFTED FROM THE EARTH, AS HE SAID.
AFTER HIS RESURRECTION AND BEFORE HE LEFT THE EARTH, THE DISCIPLES BEGAN TO UNDERSTAND.
FOR PHILIP, THOSE TWO WORDS NEVER LOST THEIR POWER.
TRADITION SAYS HE WENT AS FAR AS UPPER ASIA, TEACHING JESUS' GOSPEL.
THE FIRST THING PHILIP DID AFTER JESUS SAID "FOLLOW ME" WAS TO INVITE HIS FRIEND, TOO.
AND AFTER JESUS ROSE INTO HEAVEN, PHILIP CONTINUED INVITING PEOPLE TO FOLLOW.
IT IS THOUGHT HE DIED IN HELIOPOLIS.
TRADITIONS SAY HE WAS PUT IN PRISON, SCOURGED, AND EVENTUALLY CRUCIFIED OR STONED.
LIKE A WHEAT KERNEL, PHILIP DIED.
BUT MANY SEEDS HAD LIFE BECAUSE HE INVITED THEM TO COME TO CHRIST.
ALL BECAUSE OF THOSE

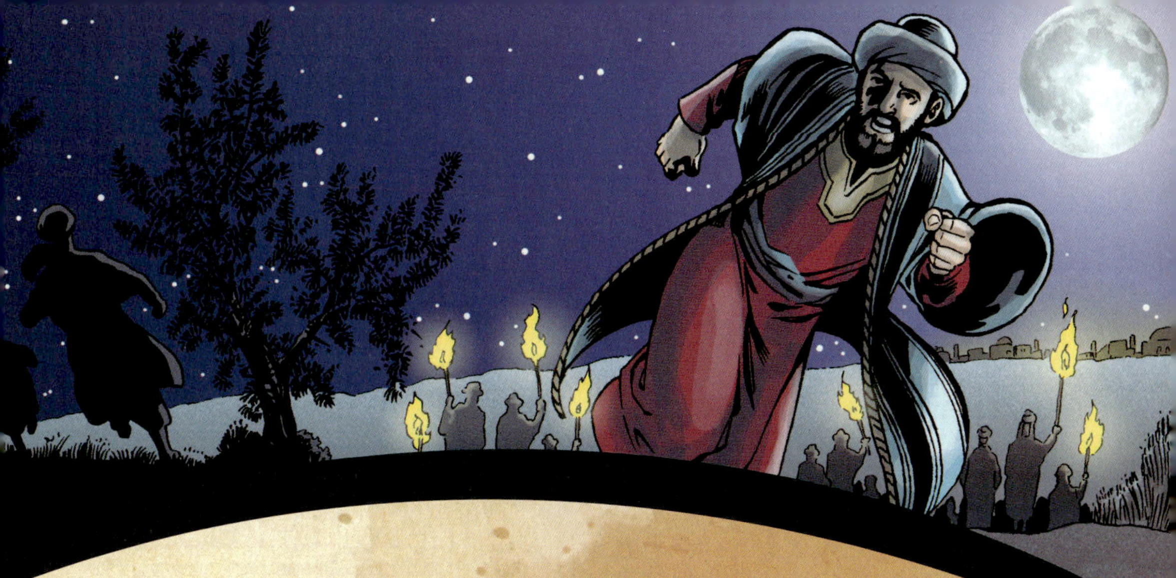

MATTHEW

MARTYRED A.D. 60

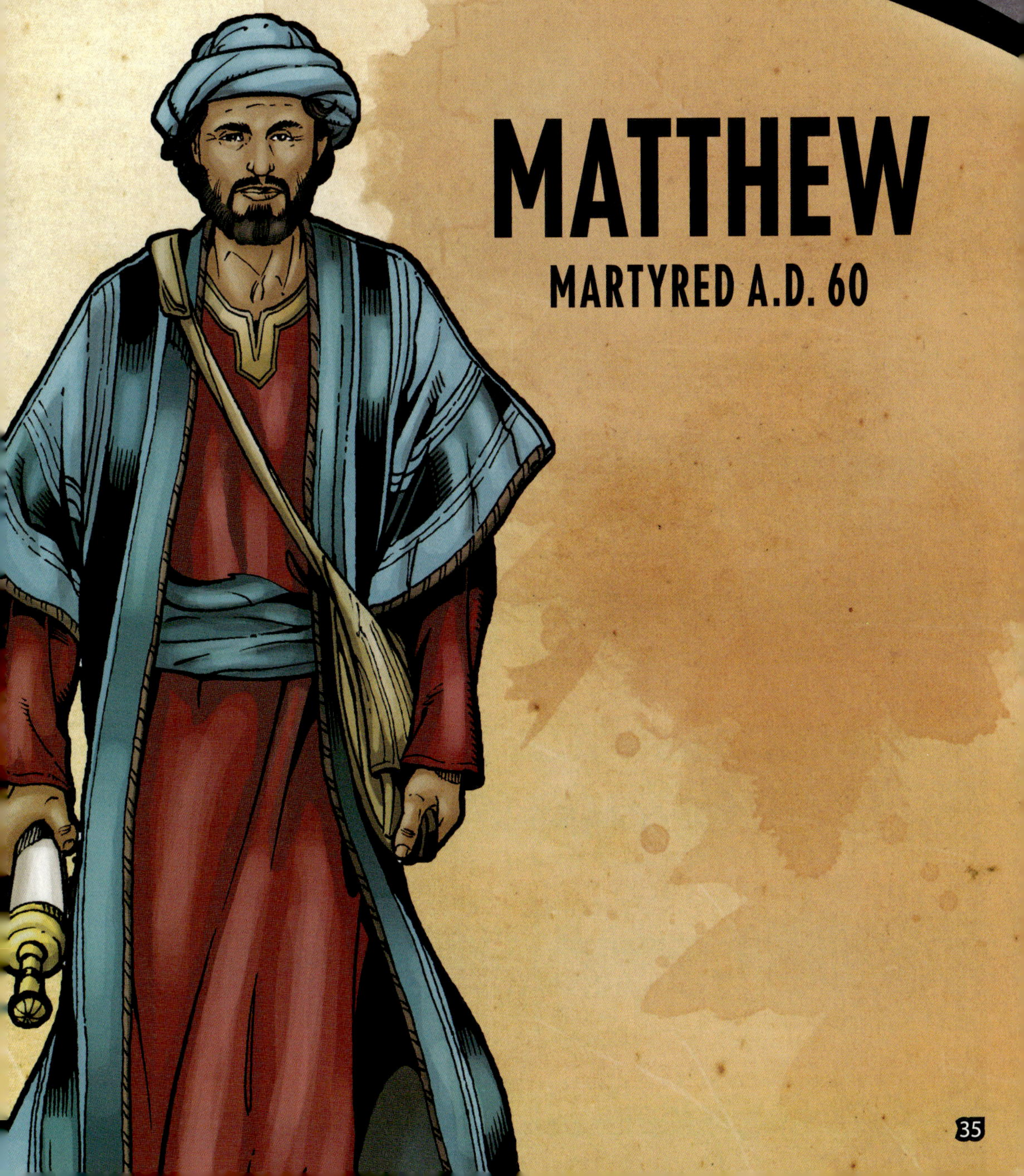

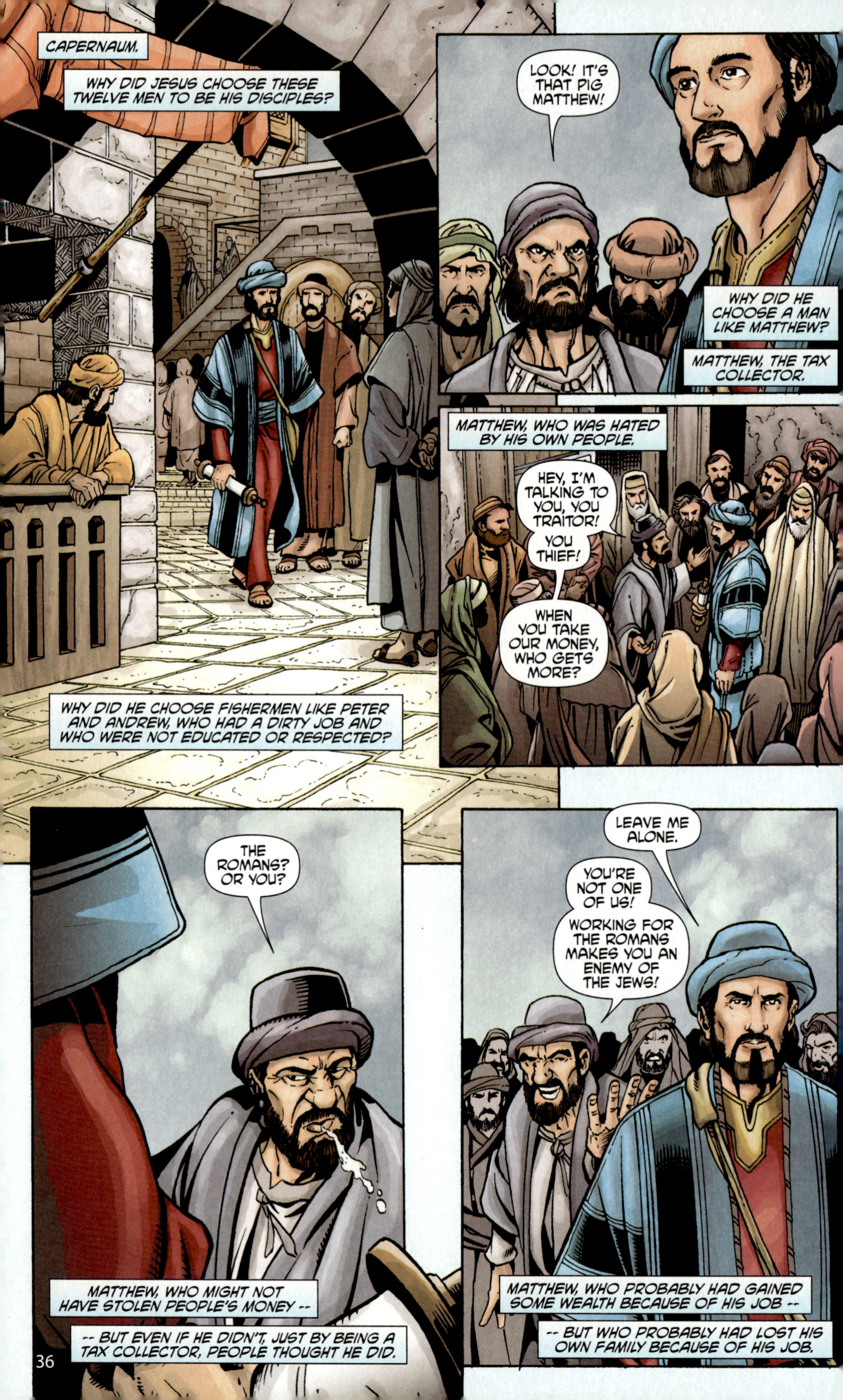

CAPERNAUM.
WHY DID JESUS CHOOSE THESE TWELVE MEN TO BE HIS DISCIPLES?
WHY DID HE CHOOSE FISHERMEN LIKE PETER AND ANDREW, WHO HAD A DIRTY JOB AND WHO WERE NOT EDUCATED OR RESPECTED?
LOOK! IT'S THAT PIG MATTHEW!
WHY DID HE CHOOSE A MAN LIKE MATTHEW?
MATTHEW, THE TAX COLLECTOR.
MATTHEW, WHO WAS HATED BY HIS OWN PEOPLE.
HEY, I'M TALKING TO YOU, YOU TRAITOR!
YOU THIEF!
WHEN YOU TAKE OUR MONEY, WHO GETS MORE?
THE ROMANS? OR YOU?
MATTHEW, WHO MIGHT NOT HAVE STOLEN PEOPLE'S MONEY --
-- BUT EVEN IF HE DIDN'T, JUST BY BEING A TAX COLLECTOR, PEOPLE THOUGHT HE DID.
LEAVE ME ALONE.
YOU'RE NOT ONE OF US!
WORKING FOR THE ROMANS MAKES YOU AN ENEMY OF THE JEWS!
MATTHEW, WHO PROBABLY HAD GAINED SOME WEALTH BECAUSE OF HIS JOB --
-- BUT WHO PROBABLY HAD LOST HIS OWN FAMILY BECAUSE OF HIS JOB.

GREETINGS, MATTHEW.

YES, YES.

MATTHEW, WHO, BECAUSE HE WAS JEWISH, WAS EDUCATED IN THE SCRIPTURES AND WAYS OF THE JEWS.

MATTHEW, WHO COLLECTED TAXES FROM THE JEWISH PEOPLE, BUT COLLECTED THE MONEY FOR THE ROMAN GOVERNMENT.

MATTHEW! YOU DID NOT COME TO ARION'S FEAST LAST WEEK!

I WAS NOT IN THE MOOD FOR FEASTING.

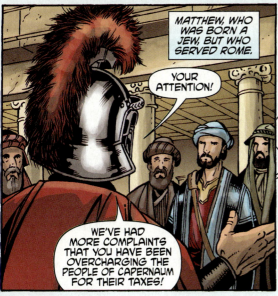

MATTHEW, WHO WAS BORN A JEW, BUT WHO SERVED ROME.

YOUR ATTENTION!

WE'VE HAD MORE COMPLAINTS THAT YOU HAVE BEEN OVERCHARGING THE PEOPLE OF CAPERNAUM FOR THEIR TAXES!

I DO NOT CARE ABOUT THOSE COMPLAINTS.

BUT YOUR COLLECTIONS HAVE BEEN LOW.

PEOPLE HAVE BEEN REFUSING TO PAY ME!

I AM AUTHORIZED TO ALLOW YOU TWENTY EXTRA SOLDIERS TO USE AS YOU SEE FIT.

IF YOU CANNOT COLLECT WHAT IS EXPECTED, BE ASSURED YOU WILL LOSE SOME, OR ALL, OF YOUR PAY FOR THE MONTH!

DO YOU MIND IF I TAKE FIVE OF THOSE SOLDIERS?

I KNOW EXACTLY WHERE I WANT TO GO FIRST.

I DO NOT THINK I WILL NEED ANY OF THEM TODAY.

OTHER THAN THE USUAL GUARDS I NEED FOR PROTECTION.

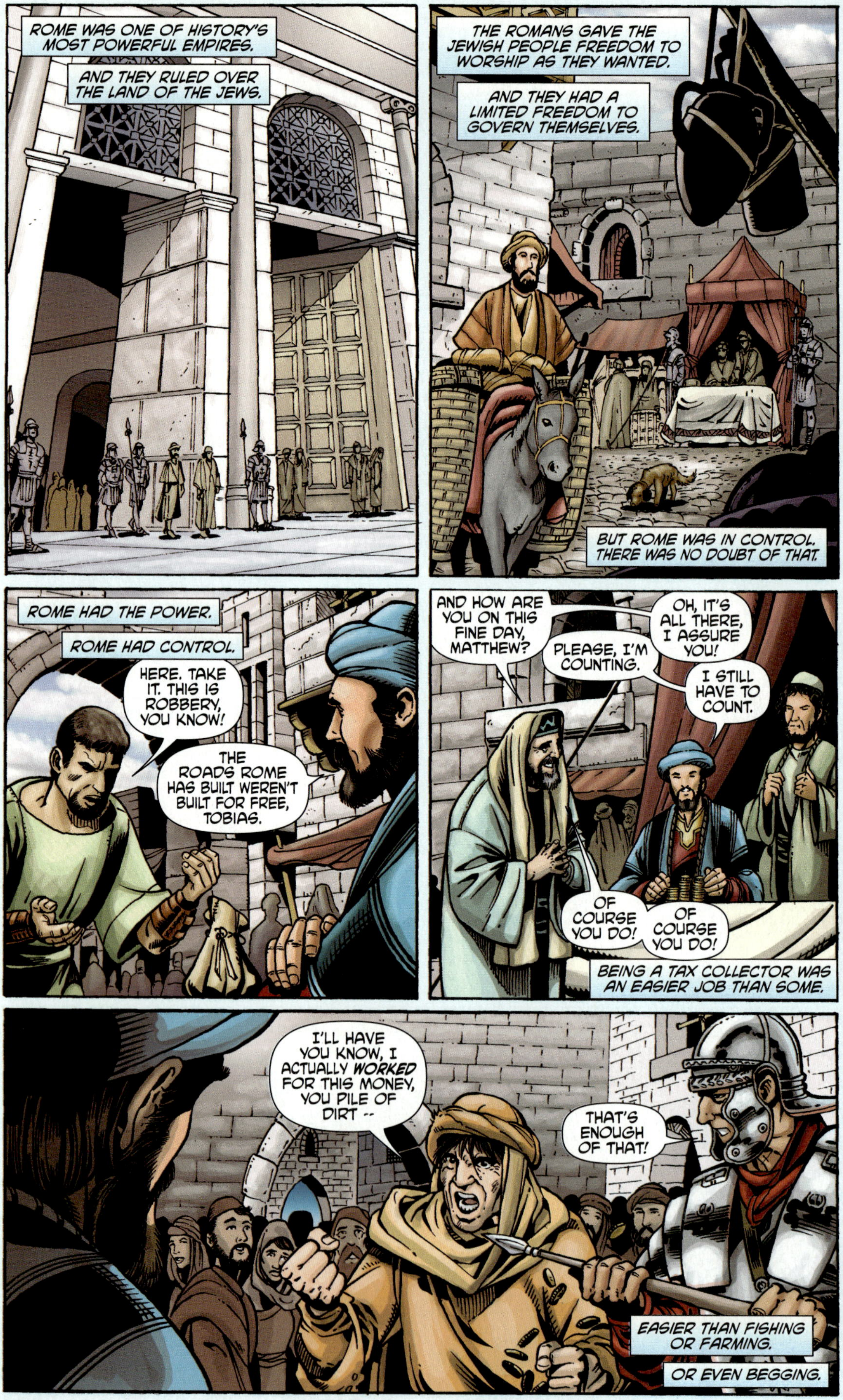
ROME WAS ONE OF HISTORY'S MOST POWERFUL EMPIRES.
AND THEY RULED OVER THE LAND OF THE JEWS.
THE ROMANS GAVE THE JEWISH PEOPLE FREEDOM TO WORSHIP AS THEY WANTED.
AND THEY HAD A LIMITED FREEDOM TO GOVERN THEMSELVES.
BUT ROME WAS IN CONTROL. THERE WAS NO DOUBT OF THAT.
ROME HAD THE POWER.
ROME HAD CONTROL.
HERE. TAKE IT. THIS IS ROBBERY, YOU KNOW!
THE ROADS ROME HAS BUILT WEREN'T BUILT FOR FREE, TOBIAS.
AND HOW ARE YOU ON THIS FINE DAY, MATTHEW?
OH, IT'S ALL THERE, I ASSURE YOU!
PLEASE, I'M COUNTING.
I STILL HAVE TO COUNT.
OF COURSE YOU DO!
OF COURSE YOU DO!
BEING A TAX COLLECTOR WAS AN EASIER JOB THAN SOME.
I'LL HAVE YOU KNOW, I ACTUALLY *WORKED* FOR THIS MONEY, YOU PILE OF DIRT --
THAT'S ENOUGH OF THAT!
EASIER THAN FISHING OR FARMING.
OR EVEN BEGGING.

I WORK TO FEED MY FAMILY, NOT THE FAMILIES OF CORRUPT POLITICIANS AND TAX COLLECTORS LIKE YOU! YOU'RE LUCKY YOU HAVE THOSE BRUTES THERE TO PROTECT YOU NOW!

IF THE ROMANS WERE HATED, THE JEWISH MEN WHO HELPED THE ROMANS WERE EVEN MORE HATED.

SO MATTHEW WAS AN UNUSUAL MAN FOR JESUS TO CHOOSE.

HAD MATTHEW BEEN THINKING ABOUT THIS JOB?

HAD HE BEEN FEELING BAD ABOUT WHAT HE WAS DOING?

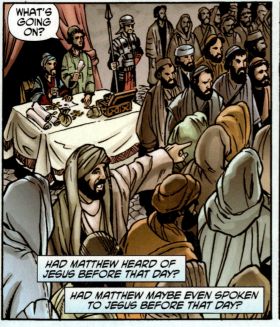

WHAT'S GOING ON?

HAD MATTHEW HEARD OF JESUS BEFORE THAT DAY?

HAD MATTHEW MAYBE EVEN SPOKEN TO JESUS BEFORE THAT DAY?

OR WAS THIS THE FIRST TIME THEY EVER MET?

DID MATTHEW HEAR JESUS TEACH BEFORE THAT DAY?

IT'S QUITE POSSIBLE. THERE IS NO WAY TO KNOW.

ALL WE KNOW IS THAT MATTHEW HEARD JESUS ON THAT DAY.

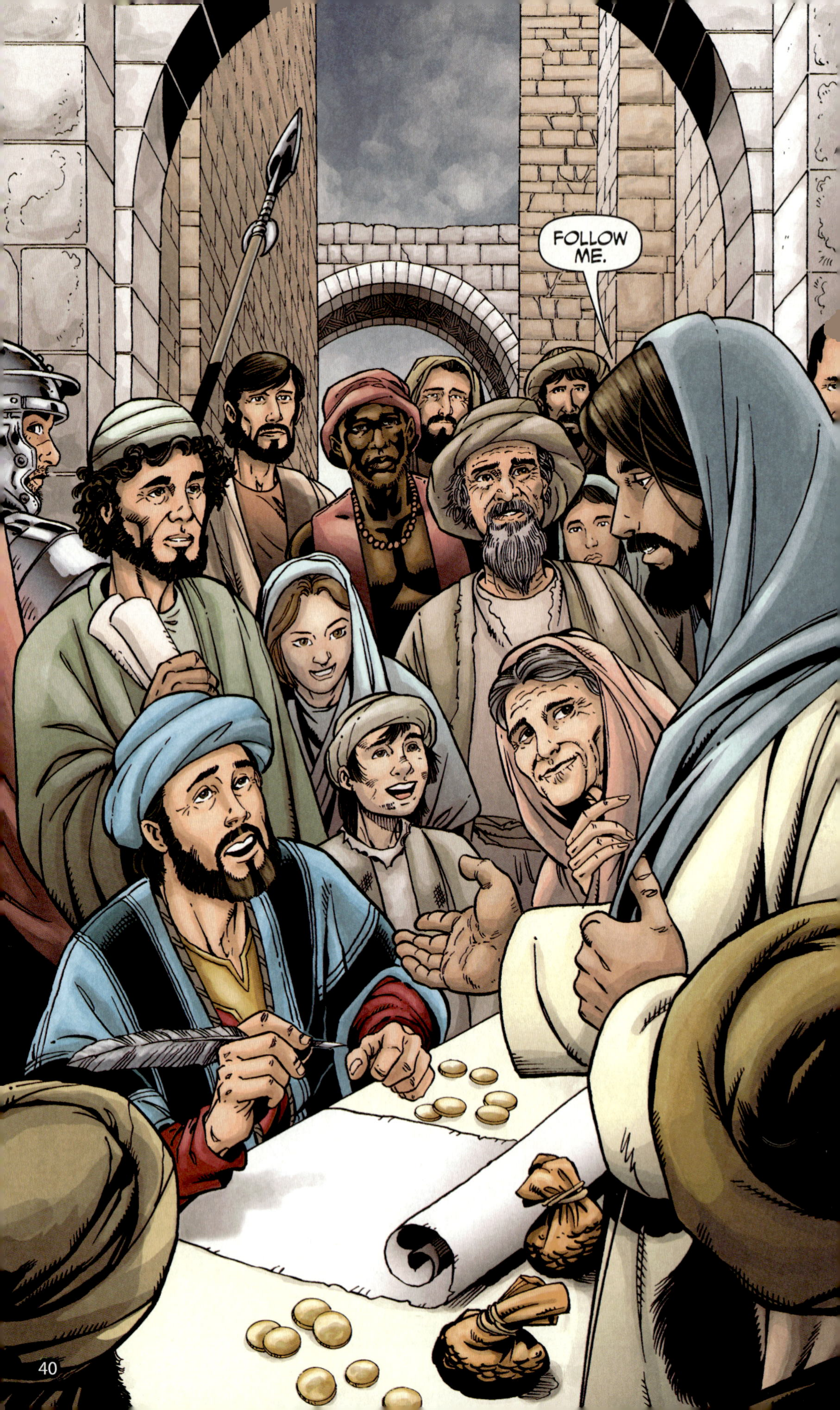
FOLLOW ME.

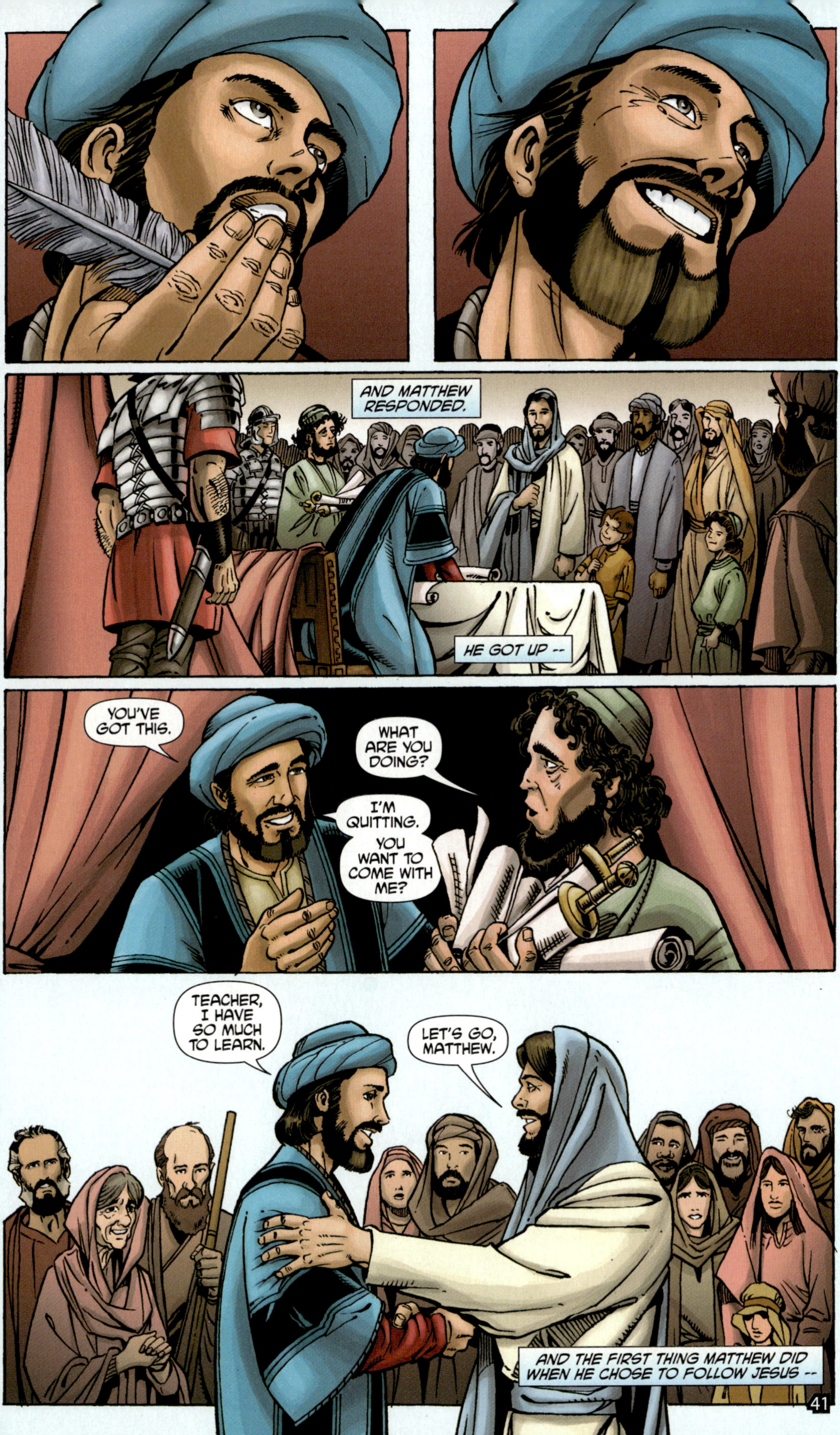
AND MATTHEW RESPONDED.
HE GOT UP --
YOU'VE GOT THIS.
WHAT ARE YOU DOING?
I'M QUITTING.
YOU WANT TO COME WITH ME?
TEACHER, I HAVE SO MUCH TO LEARN.
LET'S GO, MATTHEW.
AND THE FIRST THING MATTHEW DID WHEN HE CHOSE TO FOLLOW JESUS --

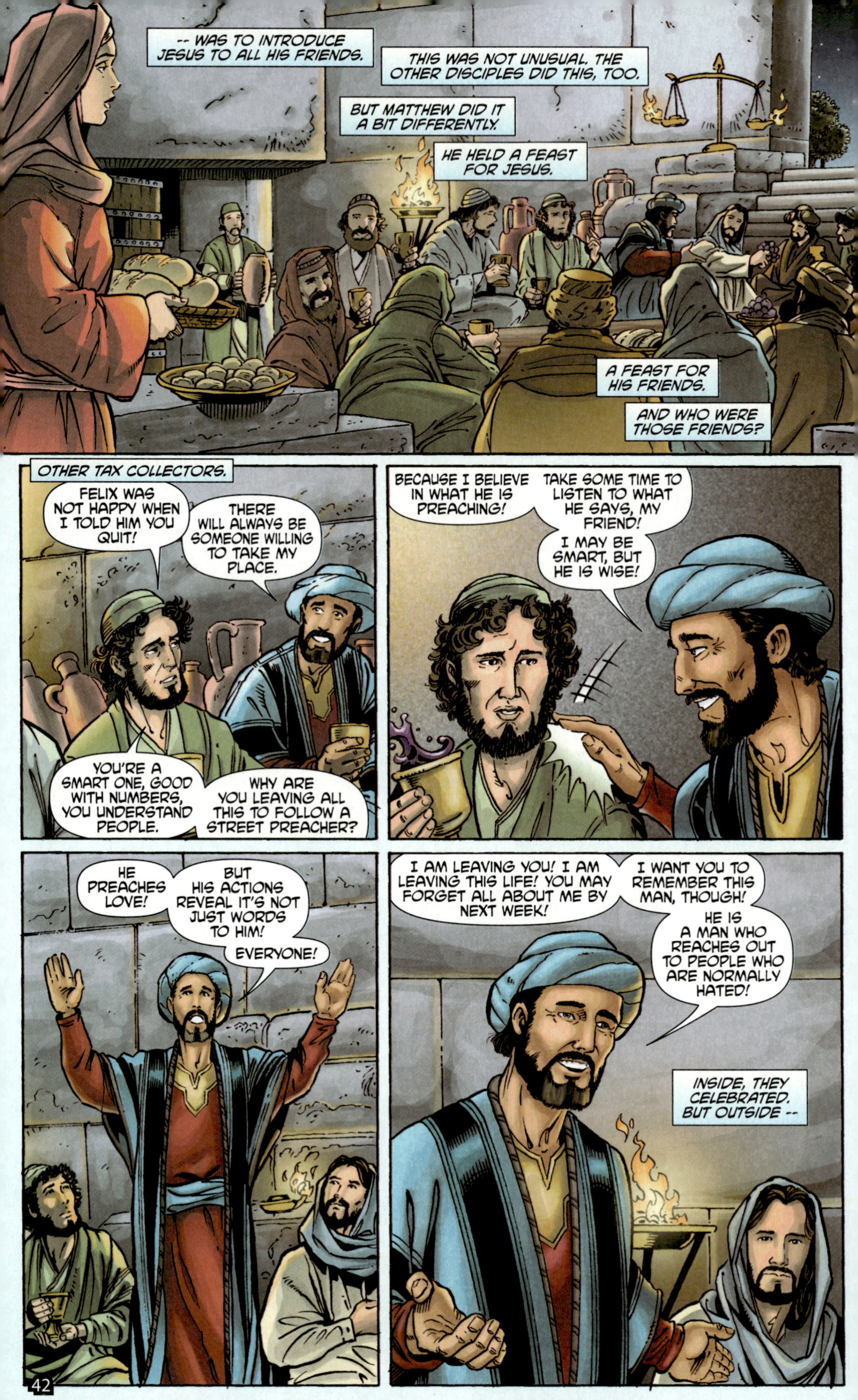

-- WAS TO INTRODUCE JESUS TO ALL HIS FRIENDS.
THIS WAS NOT UNUSUAL. THE OTHER DISCIPLES DID THIS, TOO.
BUT MATTHEW DID IT A BIT DIFFERENTLY.
HE HELD A FEAST FOR JESUS.
A FEAST FOR HIS FRIENDS.
AND WHO WERE THOSE FRIENDS?
OTHER TAX COLLECTORS.
FELIX WAS NOT HAPPY WHEN I TOLD HIM YOU QUIT!
THERE WILL ALWAYS BE SOMEONE WILLING TO TAKE MY PLACE.
YOU'RE A SMART ONE, GOOD WITH NUMBERS, YOU UNDERSTAND PEOPLE.
WHY ARE YOU LEAVING ALL THIS TO FOLLOW A STREET PREACHER?
BECAUSE I BELIEVE IN WHAT HE IS PREACHING!
TAKE SOME TIME TO LISTEN TO WHAT HE SAYS, MY FRIEND!
I MAY BE SMART, BUT HE IS WISE!
HE PREACHES LOVE!
BUT HIS ACTIONS REVEAL IT'S NOT JUST WORDS TO HIM!
EVERYONE!
I AM LEAVING YOU! I AM LEAVING THIS LIFE! YOU MAY FORGET ALL ABOUT ME BY NEXT WEEK!
I WANT YOU TO REMEMBER THIS MAN, THOUGH!
HE IS A MAN WHO REACHES OUT TO PEOPLE WHO ARE NORMALLY HATED!
INSIDE, THEY CELEBRATED. BUT OUTSIDE --

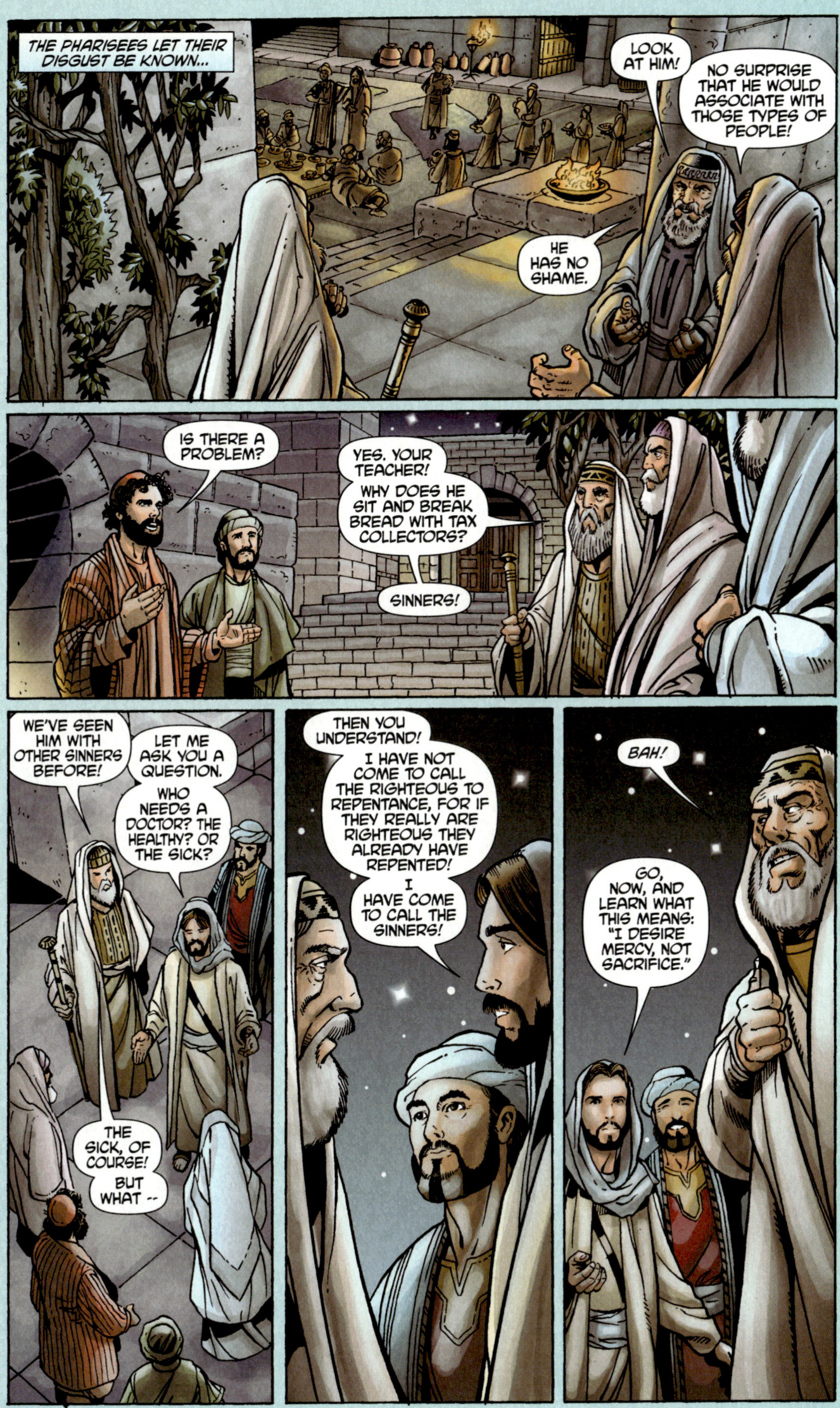
THE PHARISEES LET THEIR DISGUST BE KNOWN...
LOOK AT HIM!
NO SURPRISE THAT HE WOULD ASSOCIATE WITH THOSE TYPES OF PEOPLE!
HE HAS NO SHAME.
IS THERE A PROBLEM?
YES. YOUR TEACHER!
WHY DOES HE SIT AND BREAK BREAD WITH TAX COLLECTORS?
SINNERS!
WE'VE SEEN HIM WITH OTHER SINNERS BEFORE!
LET ME ASK YOU A QUESTION.
WHO NEEDS A DOCTOR? THE HEALTHY? OR THE SICK?
THE SICK, OF COURSE!
BUT WHAT --
THEN YOU UNDERSTAND!
I HAVE NOT COME TO CALL THE RIGHTEOUS TO REPENTANCE, FOR IF THEY REALLY ARE RIGHTEOUS THEY ALREADY HAVE REPENTED!
I HAVE COME TO CALL THE SINNERS!
BAH!
GO, NOW, AND LEARN WHAT THIS MEANS: "I DESIRE MERCY, NOT SACRIFICE."

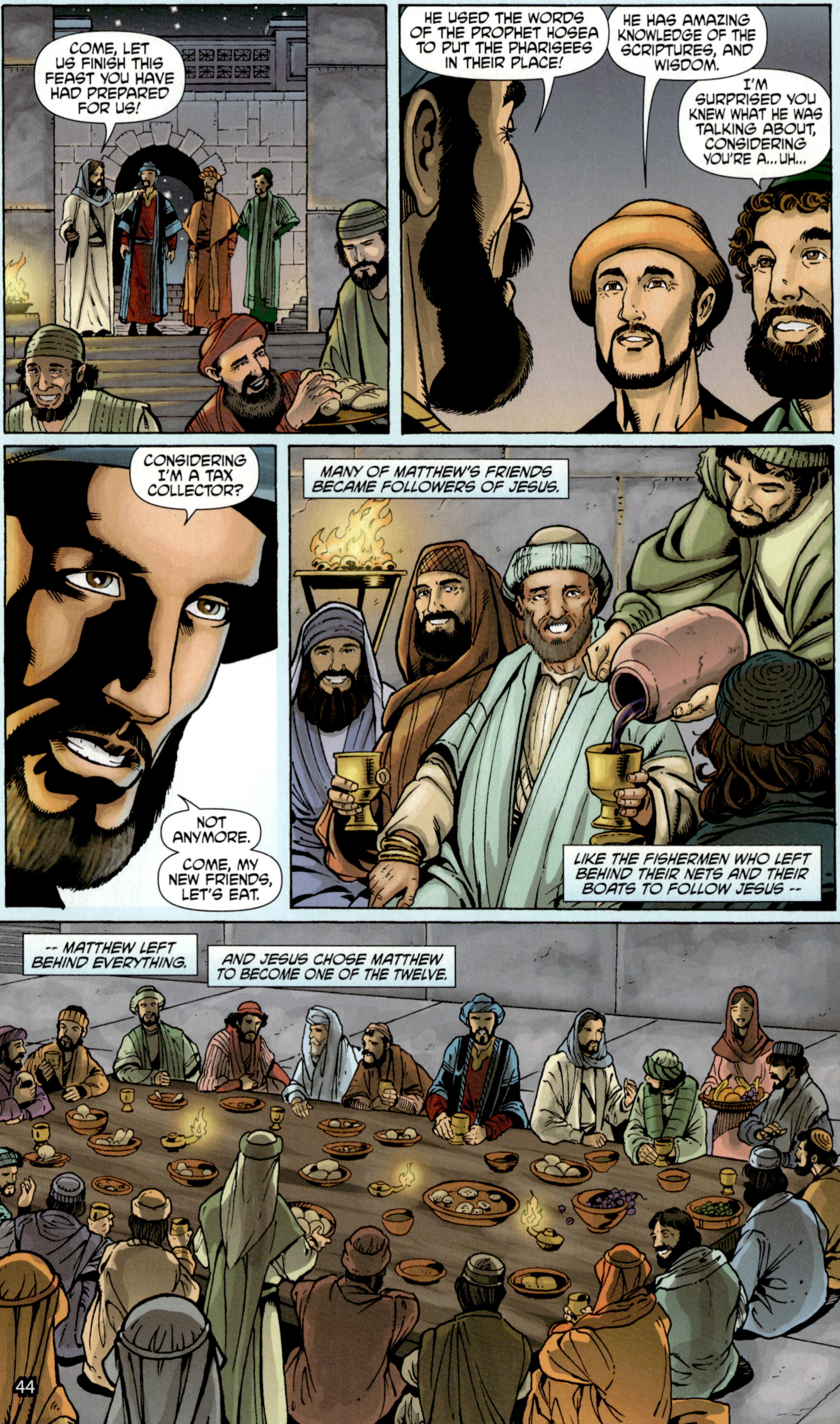
COME, LET US FINISH THIS FEAST YOU HAVE HAD PREPARED FOR US!
HE USED THE WORDS OF THE PROPHET HOSEA TO PUT THE PHARISEES IN THEIR PLACE!
HE HAS AMAZING KNOWLEDGE OF THE SCRIPTURES, AND WISDOM.
I'M SURPRISED YOU KNEW WHAT HE WAS TALKING ABOUT, CONSIDERING YOU'RE A...UH...
CONSIDERING I'M A TAX COLLECTOR?
NOT ANYMORE.
COME, MY NEW FRIENDS, LET'S EAT.
MANY OF MATTHEW'S FRIENDS BECAME FOLLOWERS OF JESUS.
LIKE THE FISHERMEN WHO LEFT BEHIND THEIR NETS AND THEIR BOATS TO FOLLOW JESUS --
-- MATTHEW LEFT BEHIND EVERYTHING.
AND JESUS CHOSE MATTHEW TO BECOME ONE OF THE TWELVE.

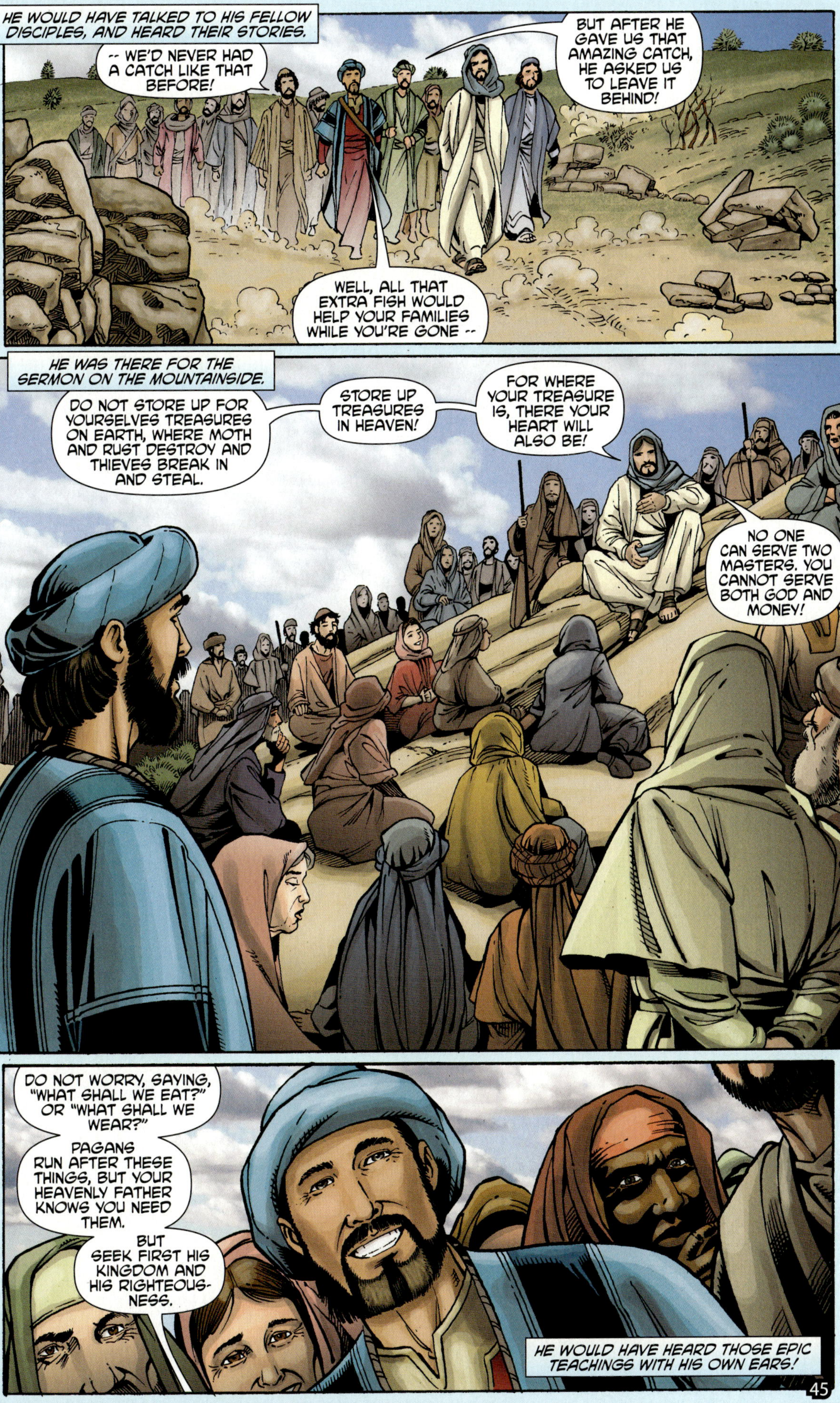
HE WOULD HAVE TALKED TO HIS FELLOW DISCIPLES, AND HEARD THEIR STORIES.
-- WE'D NEVER HAD A CATCH LIKE THAT BEFORE!
BUT AFTER HE GAVE US THAT AMAZING CATCH, HE ASKED US TO LEAVE IT BEHIND!
WELL, ALL THAT EXTRA FISH WOULD HELP YOUR FAMILIES WHILE YOU'RE GONE --
HE WAS THERE FOR THE SERMON ON THE MOUNTAINSIDE.
DO NOT STORE UP FOR YOURSELVES TREASURES ON EARTH, WHERE MOTH AND RUST DESTROY AND THIEVES BREAK IN AND STEAL.
STORE UP TREASURES IN HEAVEN!
FOR WHERE YOUR TREASURE IS, THERE YOUR HEART WILL ALSO BE!
NO ONE CAN SERVE TWO MASTERS. YOU CANNOT SERVE BOTH GOD AND MONEY!
DO NOT WORRY, SAYING, "WHAT SHALL WE EAT?" OR "WHAT SHALL WE WEAR?"
PAGANS RUN AFTER THESE THINGS, BUT YOUR HEAVENLY FATHER KNOWS YOU NEED THEM.
BUT SEEK FIRST HIS KINGDOM AND HIS RIGHTEOUS-NESS.
HE WOULD HAVE HEARD THOSE EPIC TEACHINGS WITH HIS OWN EARS!

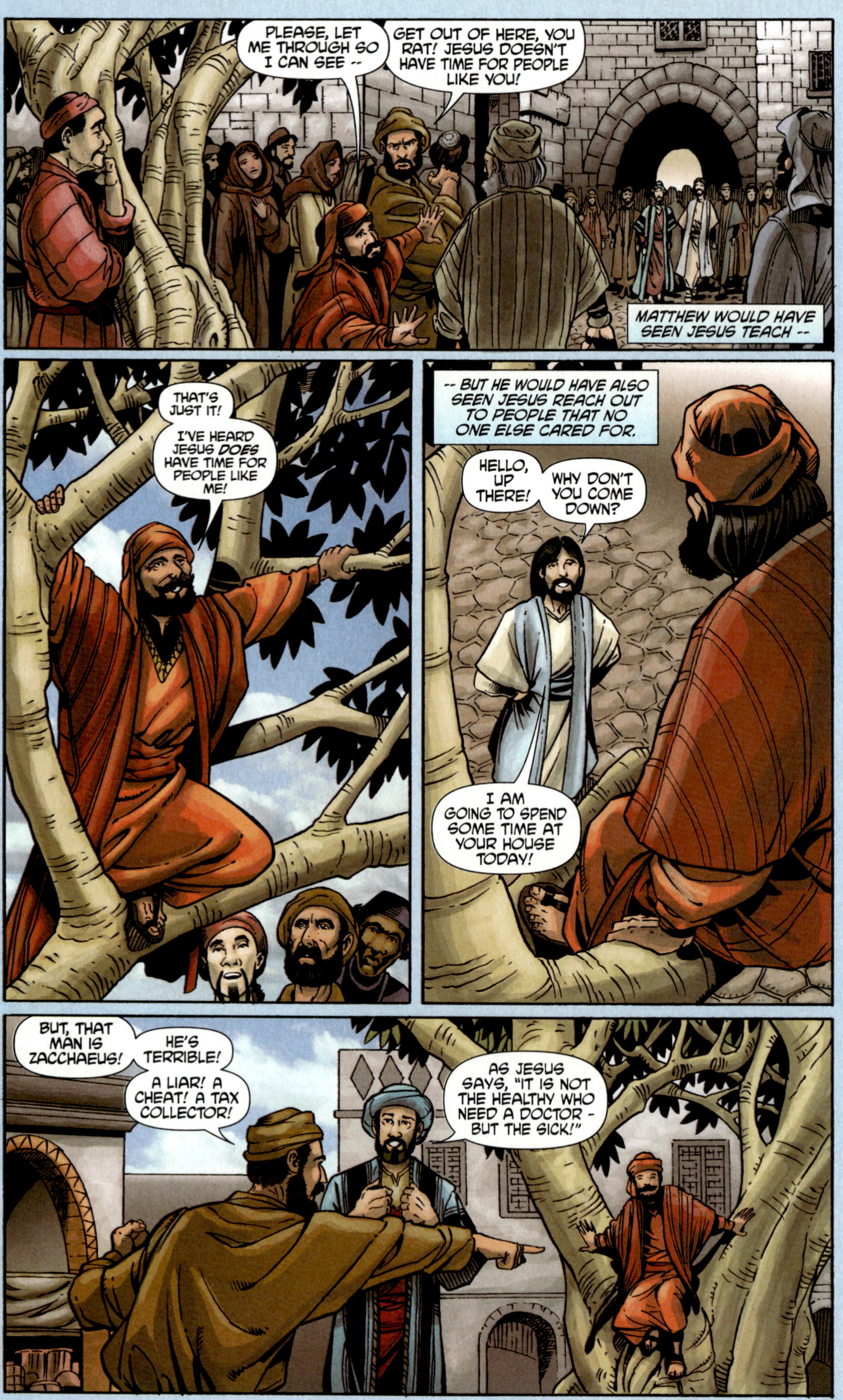
PLEASE, LET ME THROUGH SO I CAN SEE --
GET OUT OF HERE, YOU RAT! JESUS DOESN'T HAVE TIME FOR PEOPLE LIKE YOU!
MATTHEW WOULD HAVE SEEN JESUS TEACH --
THAT'S JUST IT!
I'VE HEARD JESUS DOES HAVE TIME FOR PEOPLE LIKE ME!
-- BUT HE WOULD HAVE ALSO SEEN JESUS REACH OUT TO PEOPLE THAT NO ONE ELSE CARED FOR.
HELLO, UP THERE!
WHY DON'T YOU COME DOWN?
I AM GOING TO SPEND SOME TIME AT YOUR HOUSE TODAY!
BUT, THAT MAN IS ZACCHAEUS!
HE'S TERRIBLE!
A LIAR! A CHEAT! A TAX COLLECTOR!
AS JESUS SAYS, "IT IS NOT THE HEALTHY WHO NEED A DOCTOR - BUT THE SICK!"

HE WOULD HAVE HEARD JESUS TELL THOSE FANTASTIC, MEANING-FILLED STORIES.

THE PARABLES.

LET HE WHO HAS EARS LISTEN!

THE KINGDOM OF HEAVEN IS LIKE A TREASURE, HIDDEN IN A FIELD!

WHEN A MAN FOUND IT, HE HID IT AGAIN!

AND THEN IN HIS JOY, HE WENT AND SOLD EVERYTHING HE HAD.

AND BOUGHT THAT FIELD!

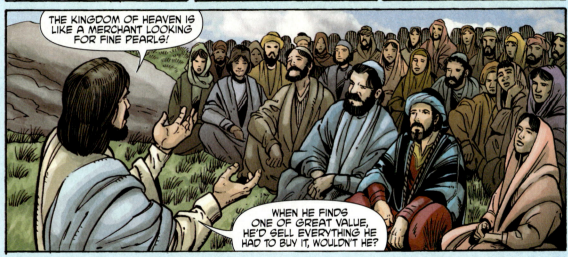

THE KINGDOM OF HEAVEN IS LIKE A MERCHANT LOOKING FOR FINE PEARLS!

WHEN HE FINDS ONE OF GREAT VALUE, HE'D SELL EVERYTHING HE HAD TO BUY IT, WOULDN'T HE?

47

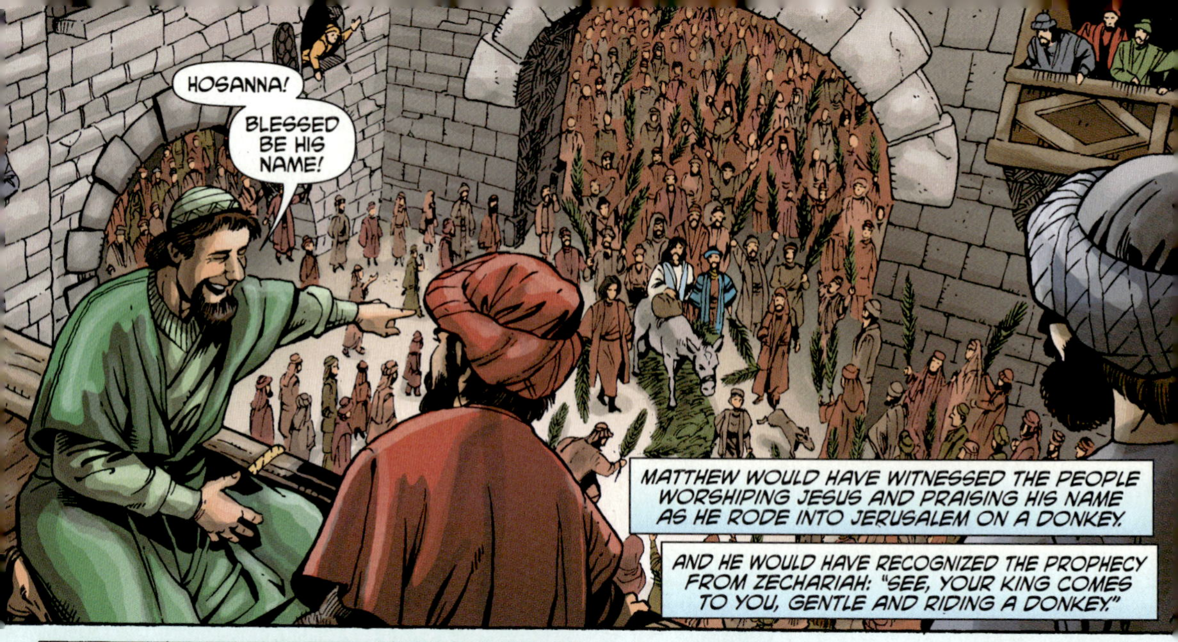
HOSANNA!
BLESSED BE HIS NAME!
MATTHEW WOULD HAVE WITNESSED THE PEOPLE WORSHIPING JESUS AND PRAISING HIS NAME AS HE RODE INTO JERUSALEM ON A DONKEY.
AND HE WOULD HAVE RECOGNIZED THE PROPHECY FROM ZECHARIAH: "SEE, YOUR KING COMES TO YOU, GENTLE AND RIDING A DONKEY."

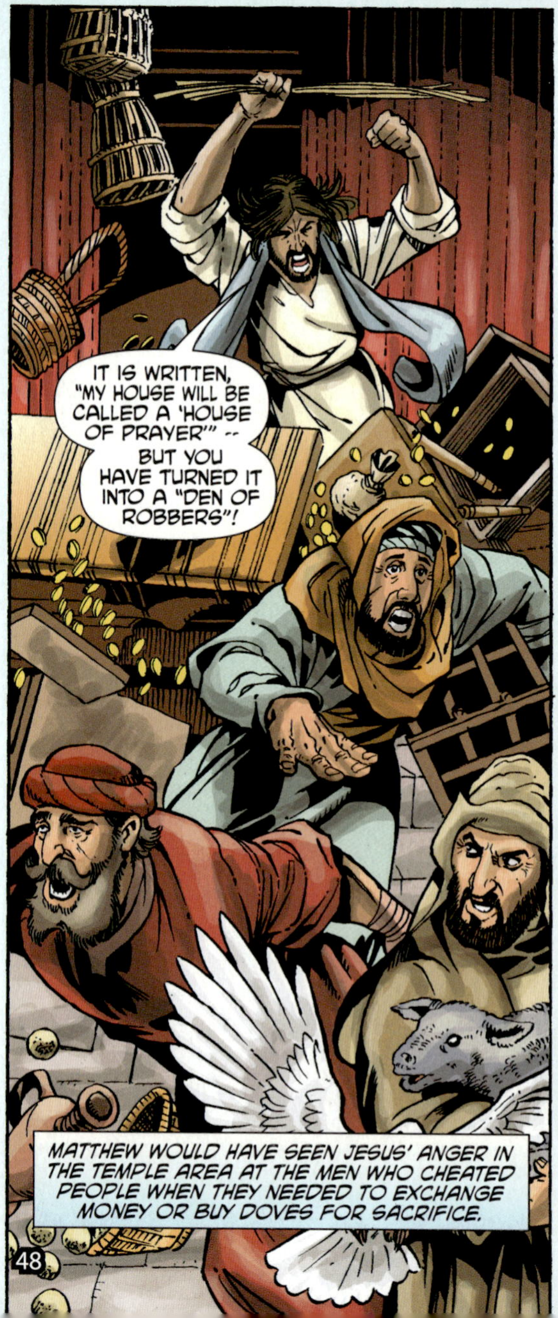
IT IS WRITTEN, "MY HOUSE WILL BE CALLED A 'HOUSE OF PRAYER'" --
BUT YOU HAVE TURNED IT INTO A "DEN OF ROBBERS"!
MATTHEW WOULD HAVE SEEN JESUS' ANGER IN THE TEMPLE AREA AT THE MEN WHO CHEATED PEOPLE WHEN THEY NEEDED TO EXCHANGE MONEY OR BUY DOVES FOR SACRIFICE.

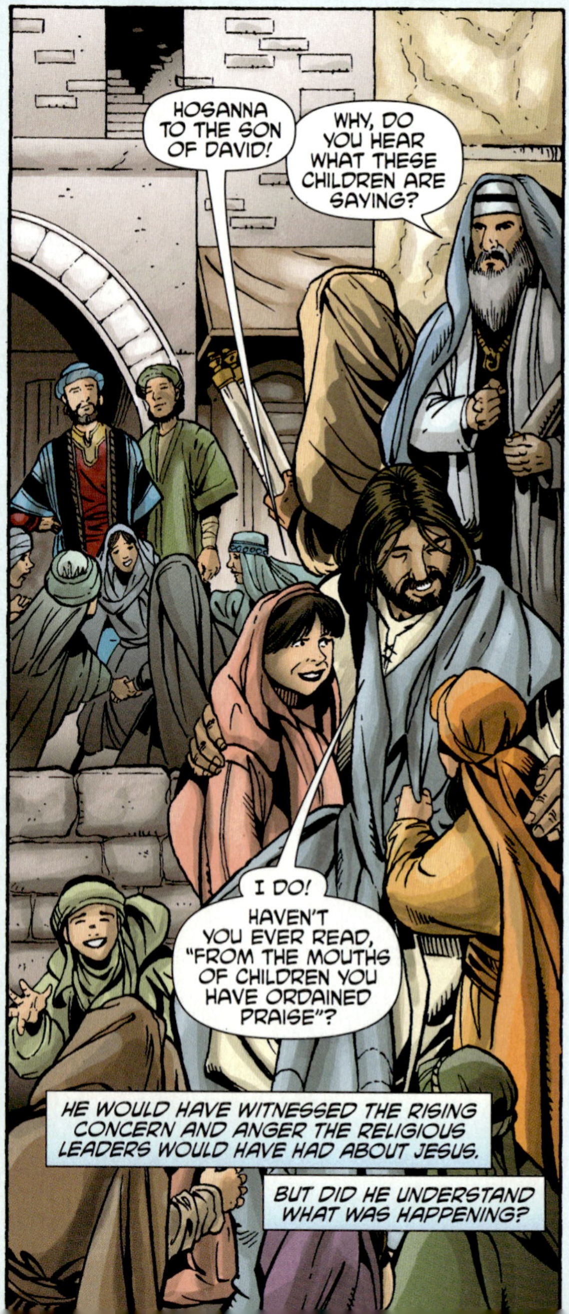
HOSANNA TO THE SON OF DAVID!
WHY, DO YOU HEAR WHAT THESE CHILDREN ARE SAYING?
I DO!
HAVEN'T YOU EVER READ, "FROM THE MOUTHS OF CHILDREN YOU HAVE ORDAINED PRAISE"?
HE WOULD HAVE WITNESSED THE RISING CONCERN AND ANGER THE RELIGIOUS LEADERS WOULD HAVE HAD ABOUT JESUS.
BUT DID HE UNDERSTAND WHAT WAS HAPPENING?

AFTER SEEING ALL OF THESE THINGS, WHEN MATTHEW SAT AND ATE WITH JESUS AND THE OTHERS --

TAKE THIS BREAD AND EAT IT.

FOR THIS BREAD IS MY BODY.

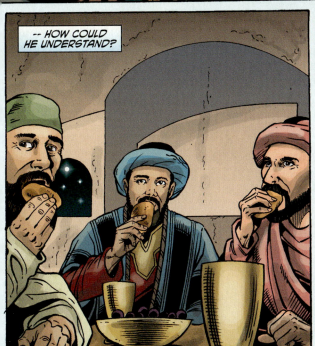

-- HOW COULD HE UNDERSTAND?

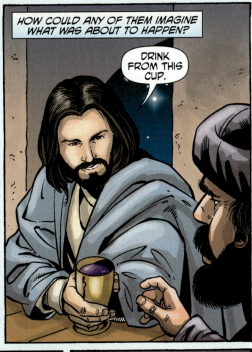

HOW COULD ANY OF THEM IMAGINE WHAT WAS ABOUT TO HAPPEN?

DRINK FROM THIS CUP.

THIS IS MY BLOOD.

IT IS A COVENANT, POURED OUT FOR YOU.

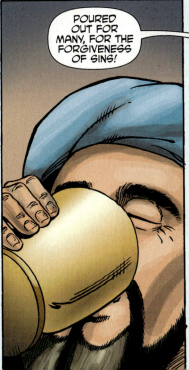

POURED OUT FOR MANY, FOR THE FORGIVENESS OF SINS!

AND NOW I TELL YOU, I WILL NOT DRINK OF THE FRUIT OF THE VINE UNTIL THE DAY WHEN I DRINK IT WITH YOU.

IN MY FATHER'S KINGDOM.

HE COULD NOT KNOW. NONE OF THEM DID.

EVEN THOUGH JESUS HAD ALLUDED TO IT MANY TIMES.

49

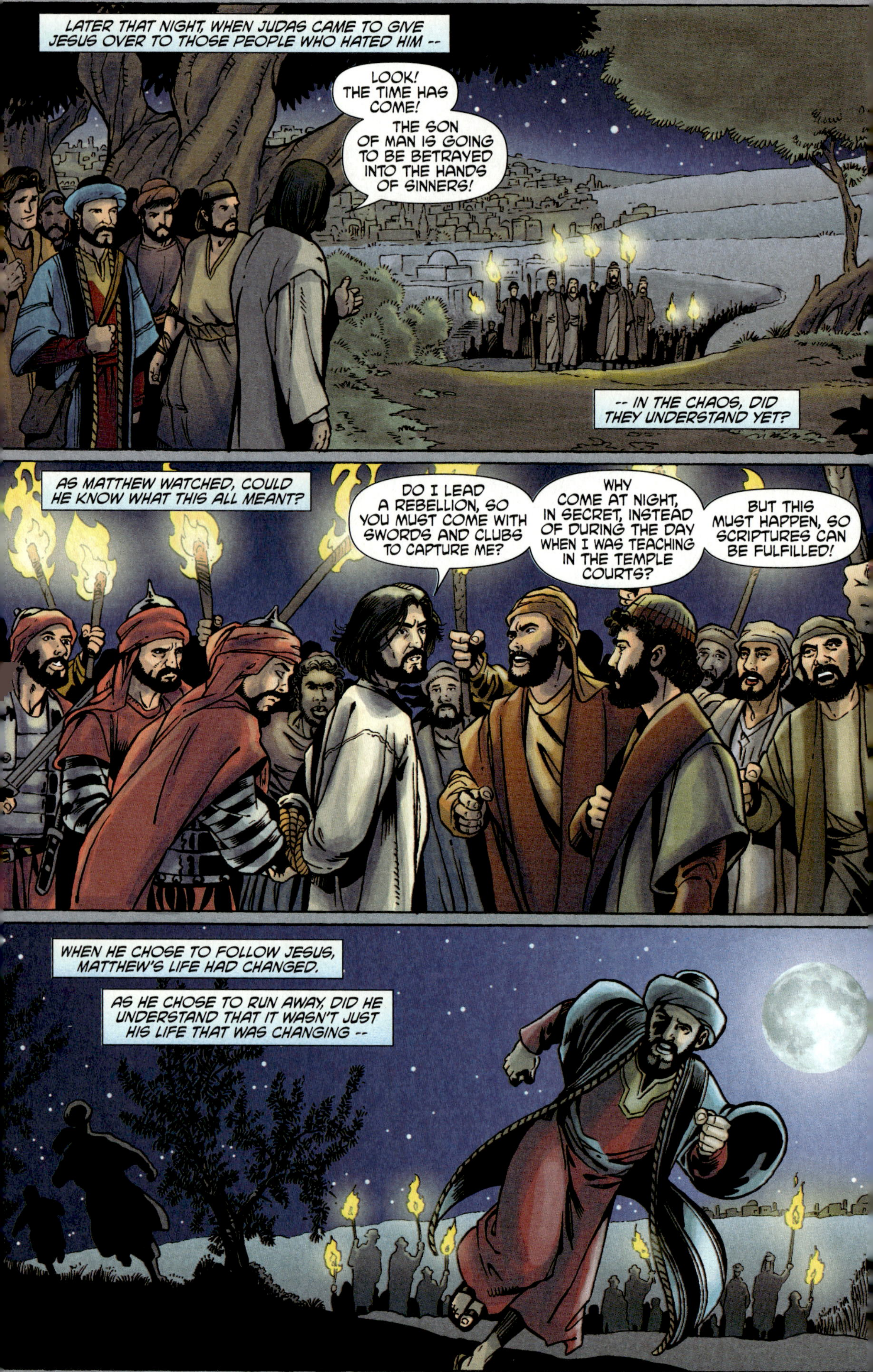
LATER THAT NIGHT, WHEN JUDAS CAME TO GIVE JESUS OVER TO THOSE PEOPLE WHO HATED HIM --
LOOK! THE TIME HAS COME!
THE SON OF MAN IS GOING TO BE BETRAYED INTO THE HANDS OF SINNERS!
-- IN THE CHAOS, DID THEY UNDERSTAND YET?
AS MATTHEW WATCHED, COULD HE KNOW WHAT THIS ALL MEANT?
DO I LEAD A REBELLION, SO YOU MUST COME WITH SWORDS AND CLUBS TO CAPTURE ME?
WHY COME AT NIGHT, IN SECRET, INSTEAD OF DURING THE DAY WHEN I WAS TEACHING IN THE TEMPLE COURTS?
BUT THIS MUST HAPPEN, SO SCRIPTURES CAN BE FULFILLED!
WHEN HE CHOSE TO FOLLOW JESUS, MATTHEW'S LIFE HAD CHANGED.
AS HE CHOSE TO RUN AWAY, DID HE UNDERSTAND THAT IT WASN'T JUST HIS LIFE THAT WAS CHANGING --

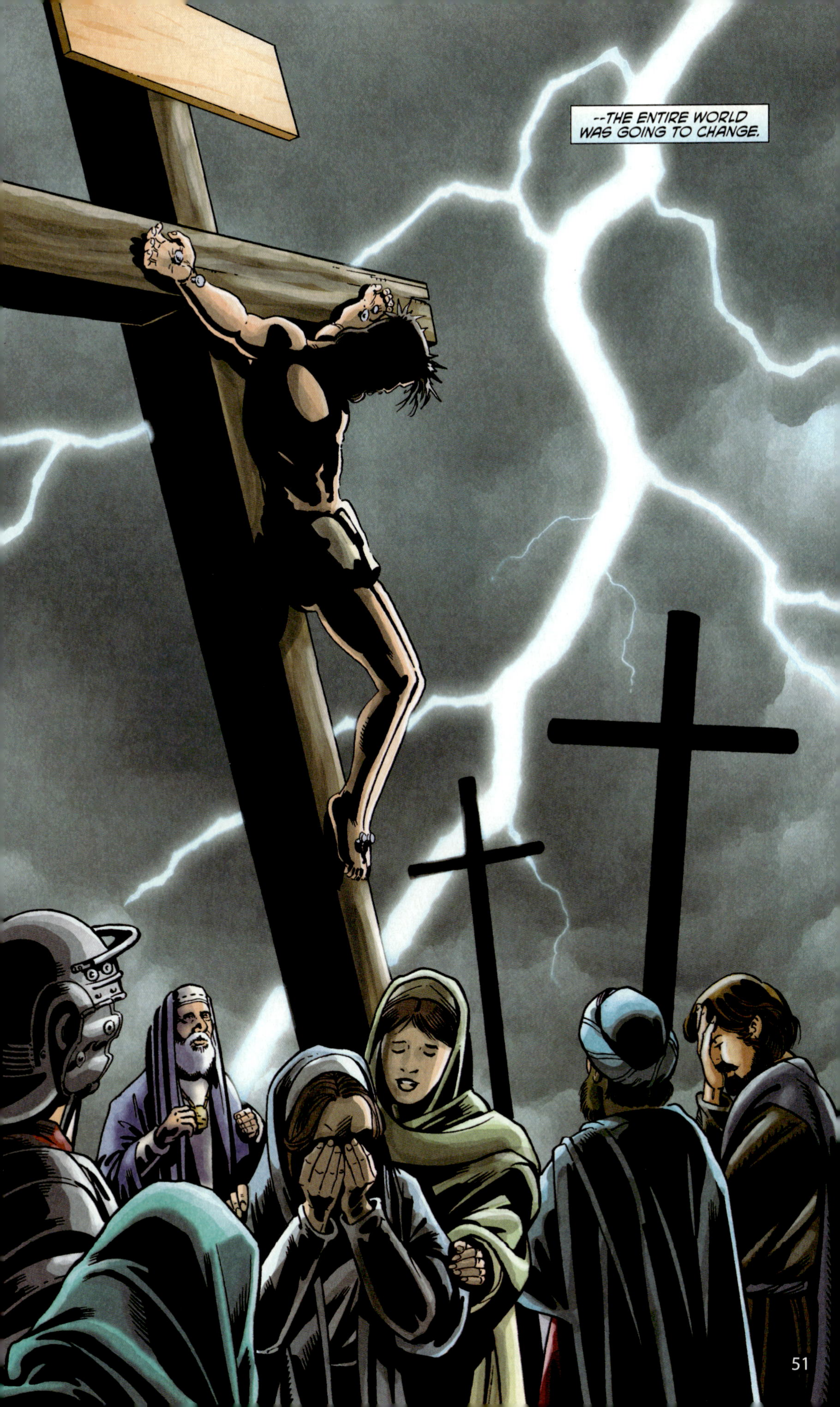
--THE ENTIRE WORLD WAS GOING TO CHANGE.

WHILE JESUS' BODY WAS BURIED IN A TOMB, SEALED BY A STONE, THE DISCIPLES HID, BEHIND LOCKED DOORS.

EVEN WHEN SOME OF THE WOMEN WHO FOLLOWED JESUS REPORTED HIS TOMB WAS EMPTY, THEY HID.

EVEN WHEN PETER SAW THE TOMB, THEY FEARED.

EVEN WHEN AN ANGEL TOLD THE WOMEN JESUS HAD RISEN, THEY DID NOT UNDERSTAND.

BUT THEN THEY HEARD THAT VOICE.

PEACE BE WITH YOU!

AN IMPOSSIBLE VOICE.

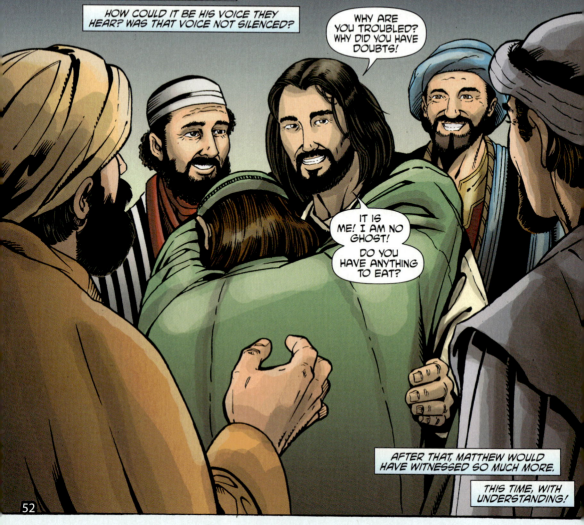

HOW WAS ANYONE HERE? WERE THE DOORS NOT LOCKED?

HOW COULD IT BE HIS VOICE THEY HEAR? WAS THAT VOICE NOT SILENCED?

WHY ARE YOU TROUBLED? WHY DID YOU HAVE DOUBTS!

IT IS ME! I AM NO GHOST!

DO YOU HAVE ANYTHING TO EAT?

AFTER THAT, MATTHEW WOULD HAVE WITNESSED SO MUCH MORE.

THIS TIME, WITH UNDERSTANDING!

52

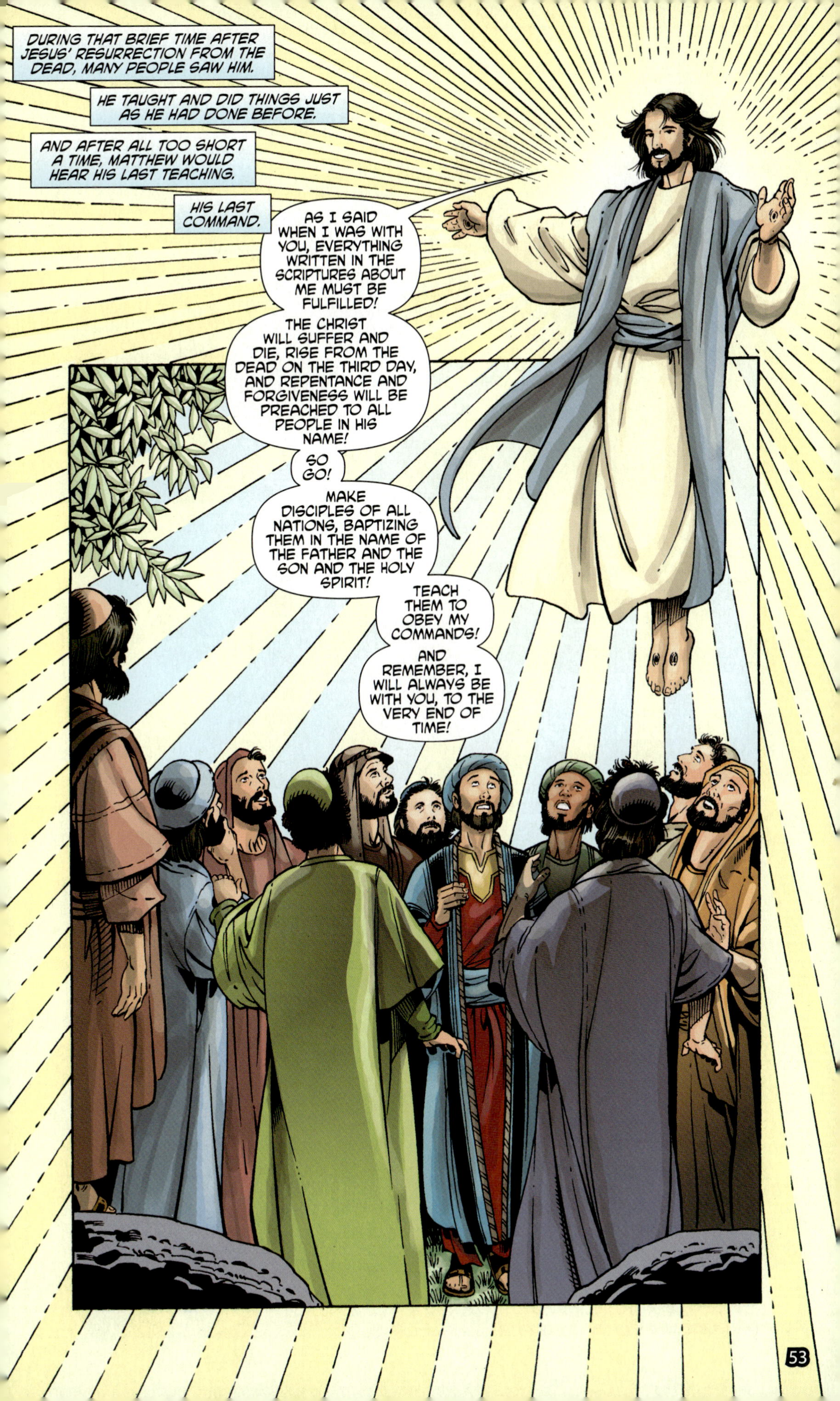
DURING THAT BRIEF TIME AFTER JESUS' RESURRECTION FROM THE DEAD, MANY PEOPLE SAW HIM.
HE TAUGHT AND DID THINGS JUST AS HE HAD DONE BEFORE.
AND AFTER ALL TOO SHORT A TIME, MATTHEW WOULD HEAR HIS LAST TEACHING.
HIS LAST COMMAND.
AS I SAID WHEN I WAS WITH YOU, EVERYTHING WRITTEN IN THE SCRIPTURES ABOUT ME MUST BE FULFILLED!
THE CHRIST WILL SUFFER AND DIE, RISE FROM THE DEAD ON THE THIRD DAY, AND REPENTANCE AND FORGIVENESS WILL BE PREACHED TO ALL PEOPLE IN HIS NAME!
SO GO!
MAKE DISCIPLES OF ALL NATIONS, BAPTIZING THEM IN THE NAME OF THE FATHER AND THE SON AND THE HOLY SPIRIT!
TEACH THEM TO OBEY MY COMMANDS!
AND REMEMBER, I WILL ALWAYS BE WITH YOU, TO THE VERY END OF TIME!

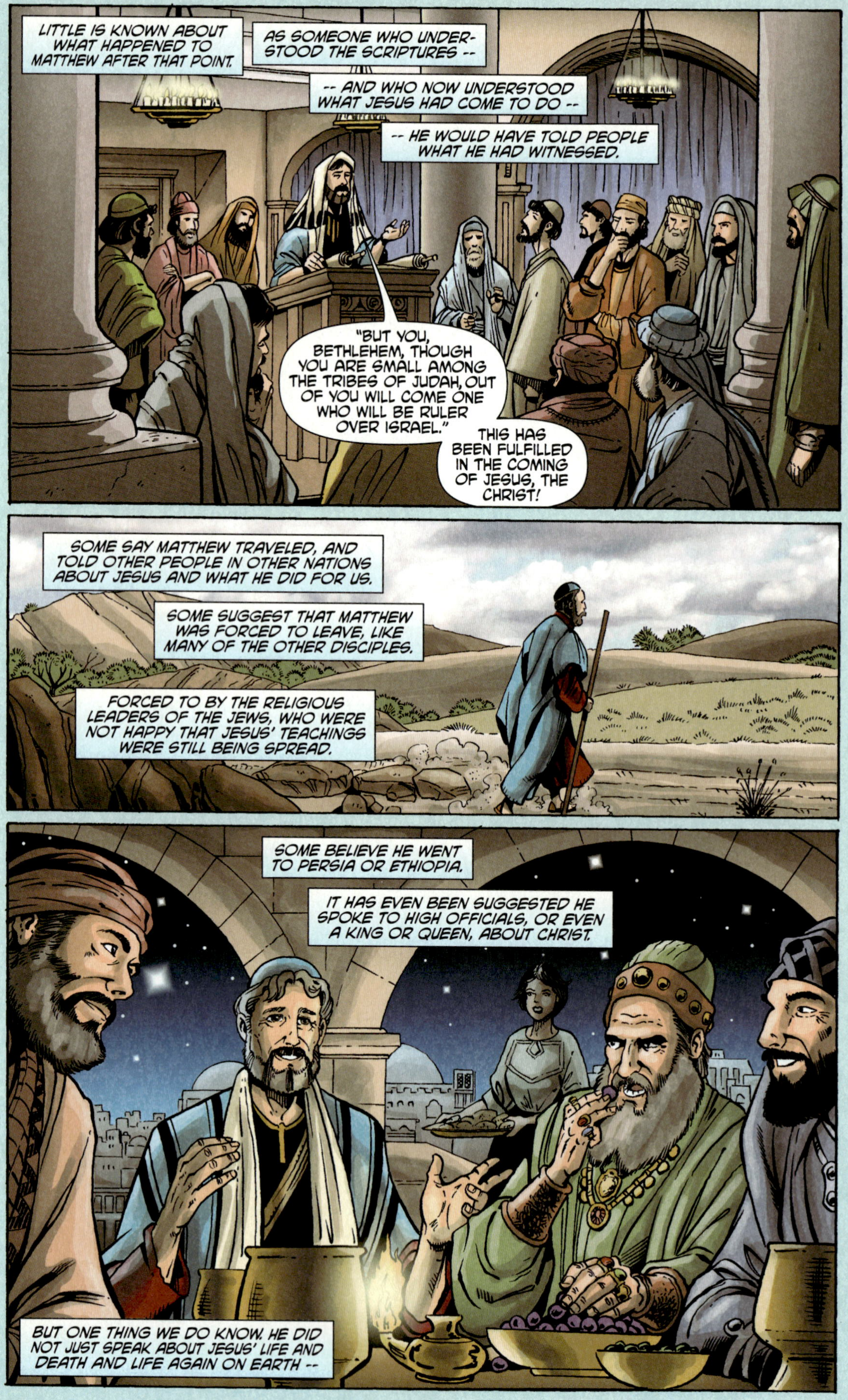
LITTLE IS KNOWN ABOUT WHAT HAPPENED TO MATTHEW AFTER THAT POINT.
AS SOMEONE WHO UNDER-STOOD THE SCRIPTURES --
-- AND WHO NOW UNDERSTOOD WHAT JESUS HAD COME TO DO --
-- HE WOULD HAVE TOLD PEOPLE WHAT HE HAD WITNESSED.
"BUT YOU, BETHLEHEM, THOUGH YOU ARE SMALL AMONG THE TRIBES OF JUDAH, OUT OF YOU WILL COME ONE WHO WILL BE RULER OVER ISRAEL."
THIS HAS BEEN FULFILLED IN THE COMING OF JESUS, THE CHRIST!
SOME SAY MATTHEW TRAVELED, AND TOLD OTHER PEOPLE IN OTHER NATIONS ABOUT JESUS AND WHAT HE DID FOR US.
SOME SUGGEST THAT MATTHEW WAS FORCED TO LEAVE, LIKE MANY OF THE OTHER DISCIPLES.
FORCED TO BY THE RELIGIOUS LEADERS OF THE JEWS, WHO WERE NOT HAPPY THAT JESUS' TEACHINGS WERE STILL BEING SPREAD.
SOME BELIEVE HE WENT TO PERSIA OR ETHIOPIA.
IT HAS EVEN BEEN SUGGESTED HE SPOKE TO HIGH OFFICIALS, OR EVEN A KING OR QUEEN, ABOUT CHRIST.
BUT ONE THING WE DO KNOW. HE DID NOT JUST SPEAK ABOUT JESUS' LIFE AND DEATH AND LIFE AGAIN ON EARTH --

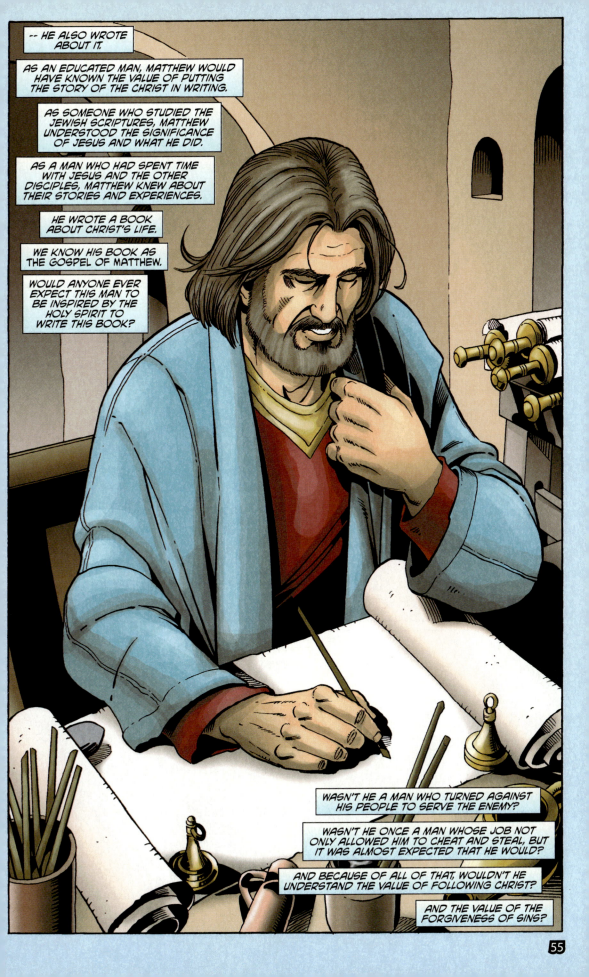

-- HE ALSO WROTE ABOUT IT.

AS AN EDUCATED MAN, MATTHEW WOULD HAVE KNOWN THE VALUE OF PUTTING THE STORY OF THE CHRIST IN WRITING.

AS SOMEONE WHO STUDIED THE JEWISH SCRIPTURES, MATTHEW UNDERSTOOD THE SIGNIFICANCE OF JESUS AND WHAT HE DID.

AS A MAN WHO HAD SPENT TIME WITH JESUS AND THE OTHER DISCIPLES, MATTHEW KNEW ABOUT THEIR STORIES AND EXPERIENCES.

HE WROTE A BOOK ABOUT CHRIST'S LIFE.

WE KNOW HIS BOOK AS THE GOSPEL OF MATTHEW.

WOULD ANYONE EVER EXPECT THIS MAN TO BE INSPIRED BY THE HOLY SPIRIT TO WRITE THIS BOOK?

WASN'T HE A MAN WHO TURNED AGAINST HIS PEOPLE TO SERVE THE ENEMY?

WASN'T HE ONCE A MAN WHOSE JOB NOT ONLY ALLOWED HIM TO CHEAT AND STEAL, BUT IT WAS ALMOST EXPECTED THAT HE WOULD?

AND BECAUSE OF ALL OF THAT, WOULDN'T HE UNDERSTAND THE VALUE OF FOLLOWING CHRIST?

AND THE VALUE OF THE FORGIVENESS OF SINS?

WOULD MATTHEW HAVE EXPECTED THAT THIS WRITING WOULD STILL BE READ TODAY, TWO THOUSAND YEARS LATER?

WOULD HE EVEN BELIEVE THAT GENERATIONS OF PEOPLE HAVE BEEN INSPIRED AND EXCITED AND ENTERTAINED AND EDUCATED BY THIS BOOK?

"SO JOSEPH GOT UP, TOOK THE CHILD AND HIS MOTHER DURING THE NIGHT AND LEFT FOR EGYPT."

"AND SO WAS FULFILLED WHAT THE LORD HAS SAID THROUGH THE PROPHET: 'OUT OF EGYPT I CALLED MY SON.'"

THIS TELLS US THAT HUNDREDS OF YEARS BEFORE JESUS WAS BORN, THE PROPHET HOSEA WROTE ABOUT HIM!

BECAUSE OF THE WAY MATTHEW'S BOOK IS WRITTEN --

-- IT IS THOUGHT THAT HE WROTE HIS BOOK FOR JEWISH PEOPLE.

"ON THE FIRST DAY OF THE FEAST OF UNLEAVENED BREAD, THE DISCIPLES CAME TO JESUS..."

IT EXPLAINS HOW JESUS FULFILLED THEIR PROPHECIES, ESPECIALLY THE PROPHECIES OF THE MESSIAH.

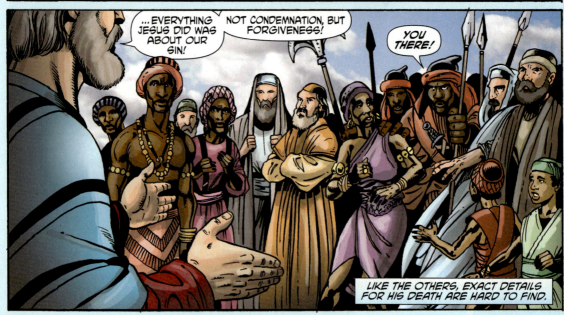

...EVERYTHING JESUS DID WAS ABOUT OUR SIN!

NOT CONDEMNATION, BUT FORGIVENESS!

YOU THERE!

LIKE THE OTHERS, EXACT DETAILS FOR HIS DEATH ARE HARD TO FIND.

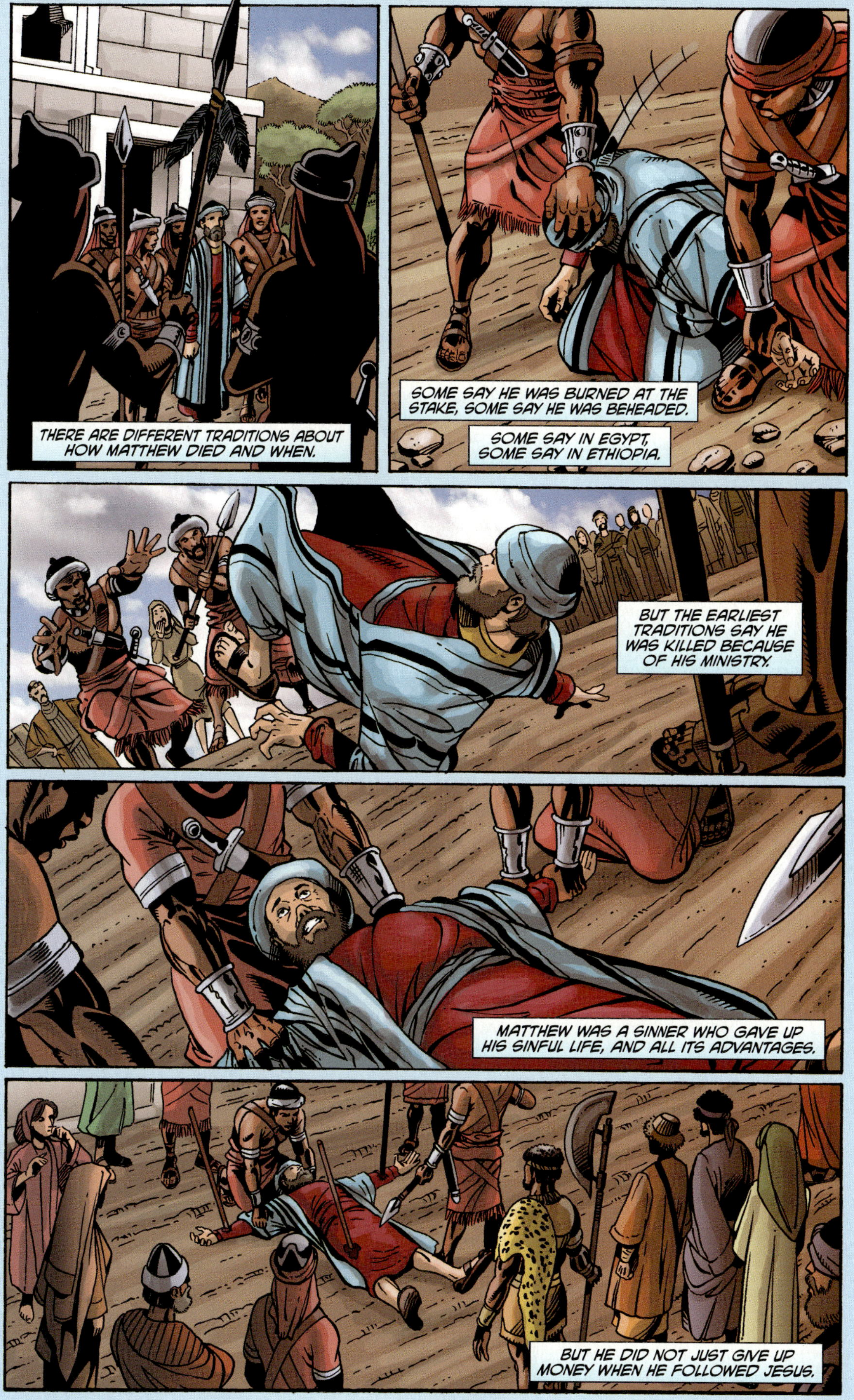
THERE ARE DIFFERENT TRADITIONS ABOUT HOW MATTHEW DIED AND WHEN.
SOME SAY HE WAS BURNED AT THE STAKE, SOME SAY HE WAS BEHEADED.
SOME SAY IN EGYPT, SOME SAY IN ETHIOPIA.
BUT THE EARLIEST TRADITIONS SAY HE WAS KILLED BECAUSE OF HIS MINISTRY.
MATTHEW WAS A SINNER WHO GAVE UP HIS SINFUL LIFE, AND ALL ITS ADVANTAGES.
BUT HE DID NOT JUST GIVE UP MONEY WHEN HE FOLLOWED JESUS.

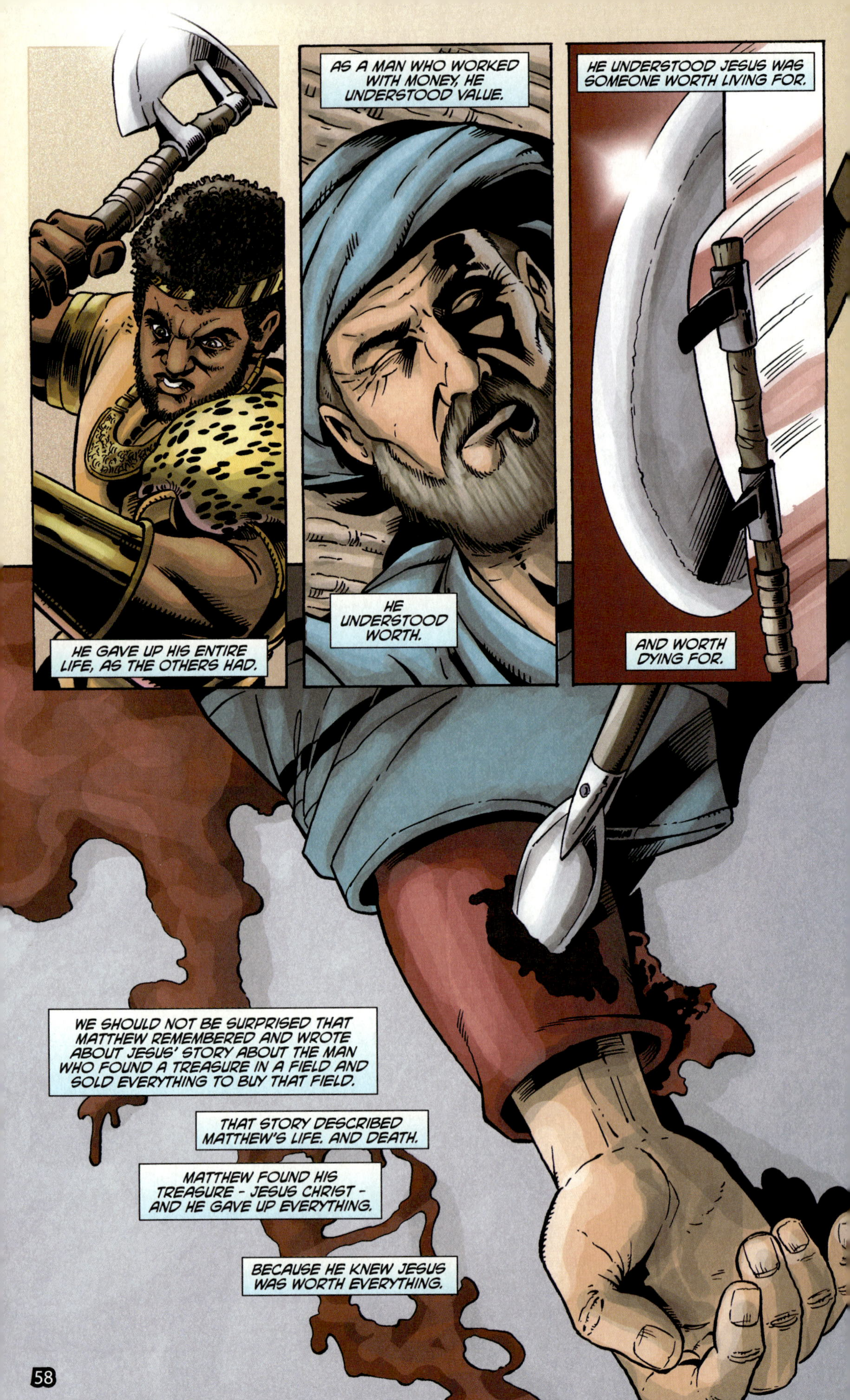
HE GAVE UP HIS ENTIRE LIFE, AS THE OTHERS HAD.
AS A MAN WHO WORKED WITH MONEY, HE UNDERSTOOD VALUE.
HE UNDERSTOOD WORTH.
HE UNDERSTOOD JESUS WAS SOMEONE WORTH LIVING FOR.
AND WORTH DYING FOR.
WE SHOULD NOT BE SURPRISED THAT MATTHEW REMEMBERED AND WROTE ABOUT JESUS' STORY ABOUT THE MAN WHO FOUND A TREASURE IN A FIELD AND SOLD EVERYTHING TO BUY THAT FIELD.
THAT STORY DESCRIBED MATTHEW'S LIFE. AND DEATH.
MATTHEW FOUND HIS TREASURE - JESUS CHRIST - AND HE GAVE UP EVERYTHING.
BECAUSE HE KNEW JESUS WAS WORTH EVERYTHING.

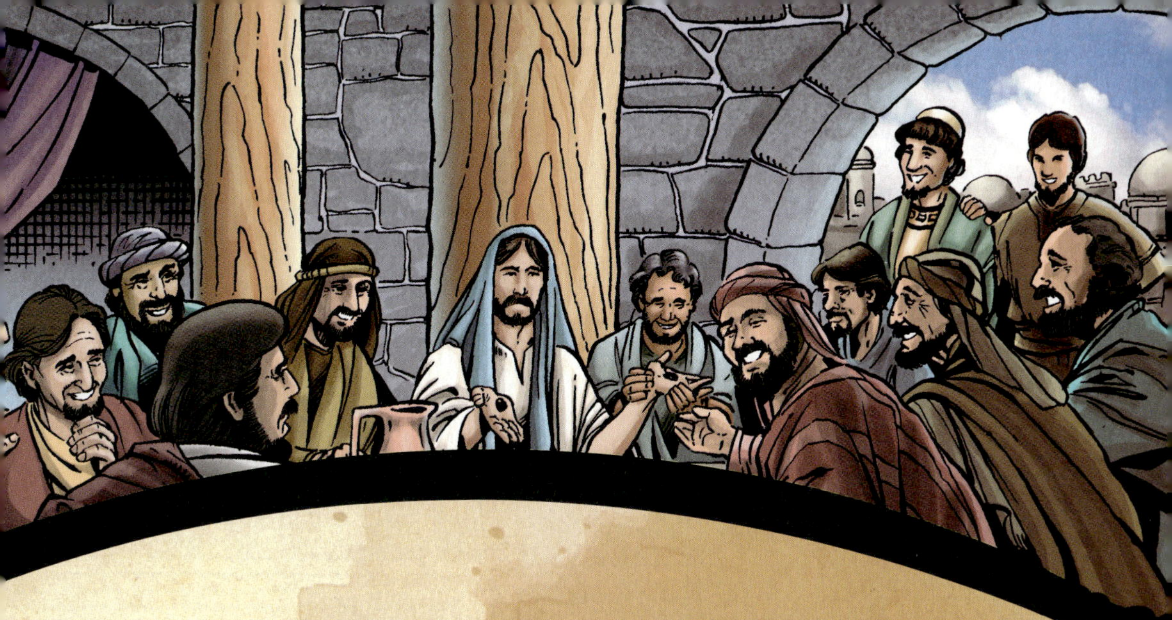

JAMES

the Less

MARTYRED A.D. 63

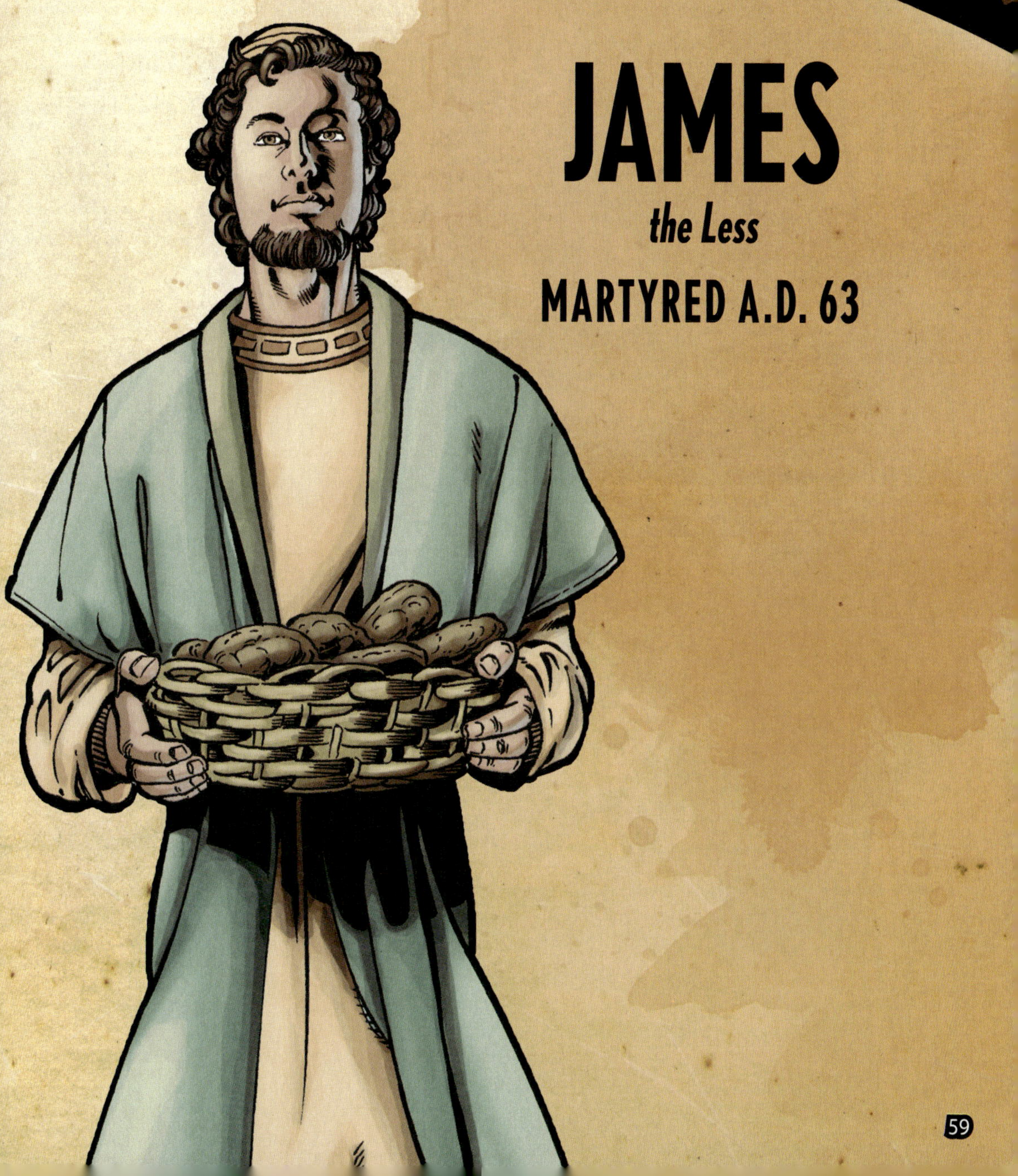

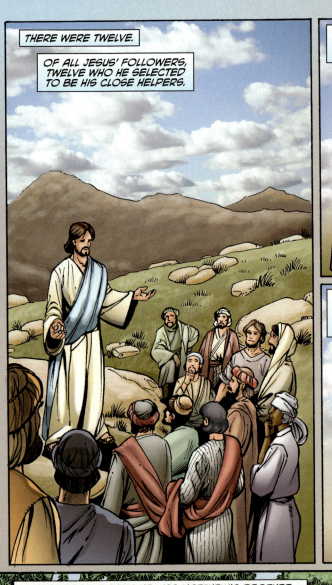

THERE WERE TWELVE.

OF ALL JESUS' FOLLOWERS, TWELVE WHO HE SELECTED TO BE HIS CLOSE HELPERS.

SOME WE KNOW MUCH ABOUT, LIKE PETER. OR ANDREW. OR EVEN JUDAS.

BUT OTHERS?

WE KNOW VERY LITTLE.

AND ONE OF THESE TWELVE, WE HAVE ONLY A NAME.

JAMES, SON OF ALPHAEUS.

SOME PEOPLE THINK HE WAS MATTHEW'S BROTHER, BECAUSE THEY BOTH HAD FATHERS NAMED ALPHAEUS.

IT'S POSSIBLE, BUT UNLIKELY, BECAUSE WE ARE TOLD ABOUT OTHER BROTHERS IN THIS GROUP--

--BUT THEY ARE NEVER MENTIONED AS BROTHERS.

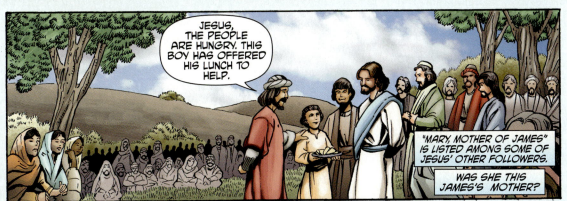

JESUS, THE PEOPLE ARE HUNGRY. THIS BOY HAS OFFERED HIS LUNCH TO HELP.

"MARY, MOTHER OF JAMES" IS LISTED AMONG SOME OF JESUS' OTHER FOLLOWERS.

WAS SHE THIS JAMES'S MOTHER?

WE CANNOT KNOW FOR SURE.

BUT SOME THINGS WE DO KNOW FOR SURE.

JAMES LEFT EVERYTHING TO FOLLOW JESUS. ALL OF THE TWELVE DID.

HE SAW JESUS PERFORM MIRACLES, JUST LIKE THEY ALL DID.

UNBELIEVABLE! FEEDING EVERYONE WITH THAT SMALL LUNCH!

AFTER ALL THAT, THERE'S STILL BREAD LEFT OVER!

TWELVE BASKETS FULL.

ONE FOR EACH OF US!

HE SERVED IN JESUS' MINISTRY--

--AND JESUS SERVED HIM.

YOU CALL ME TEACHER AND LORD, AND THAT IS WHAT I AM.

NOW THAT I, YOUR LORD, HAVE WASHED YOUR FEET, FOLLOW MY EXAMPLE.

THAT SAME NIGHT, JAMES RAN AND HID LIKE THE OTHERS.

WHILE JESUS WAS ARRESTED, TRIED, AND CRUCIFIED THE NEXT DAY.

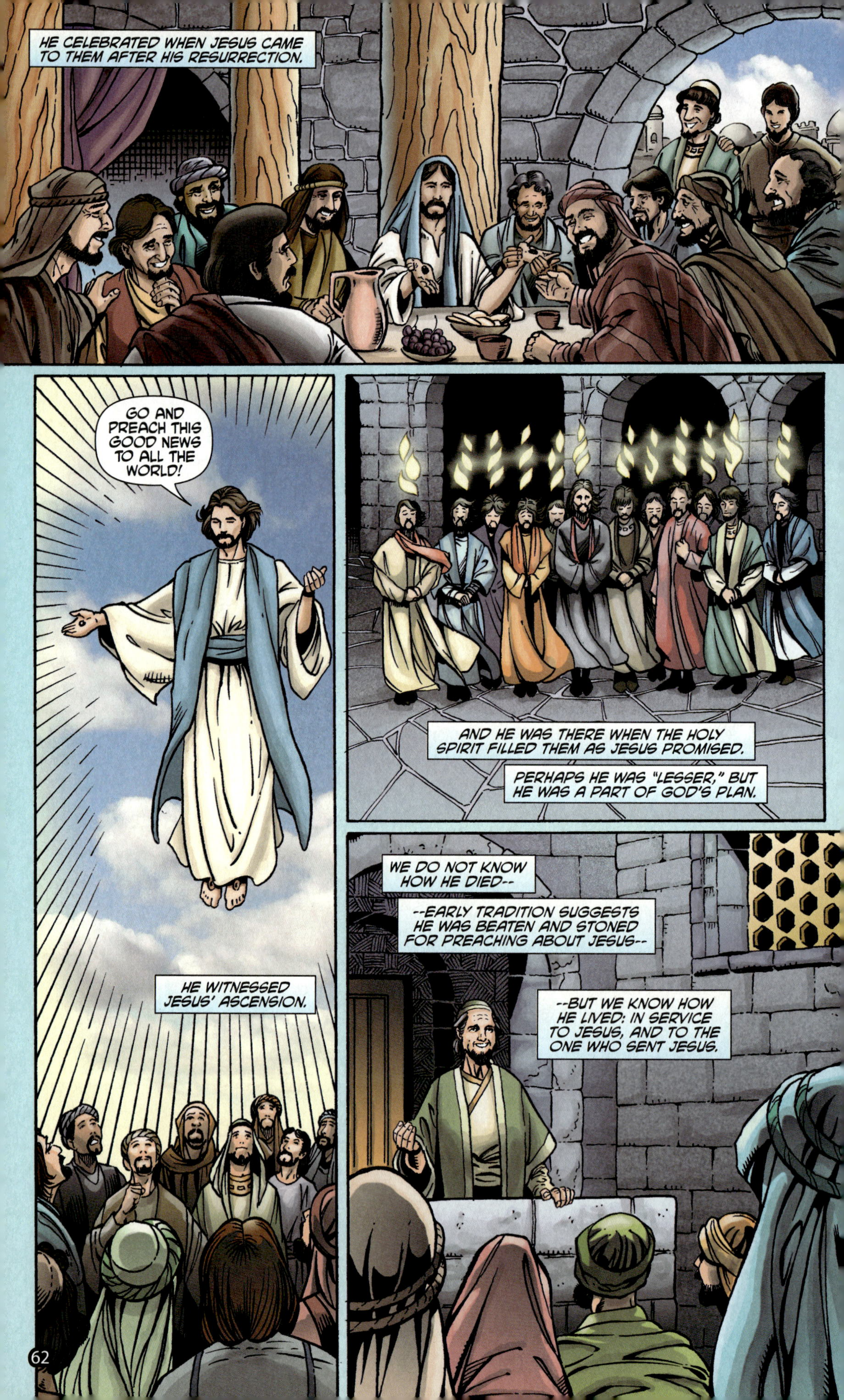
HE CELEBRATED WHEN JESUS CAME TO THEM AFTER HIS RESURRECTION.
GO AND PREACH THIS GOOD NEWS TO ALL THE WORLD!
HE WITNESSED JESUS' ASCENSION.
AND HE WAS THERE WHEN THE HOLY SPIRIT FILLED THEM AS JESUS PROMISED.
PERHAPS HE WAS "LESSER," BUT HE WAS A PART OF GOD'S PLAN.
WE DO NOT KNOW HOW HE DIED--
--EARLY TRADITION SUGGESTS HE WAS BEATEN AND STONED FOR PREACHING ABOUT JESUS--
--BUT WE KNOW HOW HE LIVED: IN SERVICE TO JESUS, AND TO THE ONE WHO SENT JESUS.

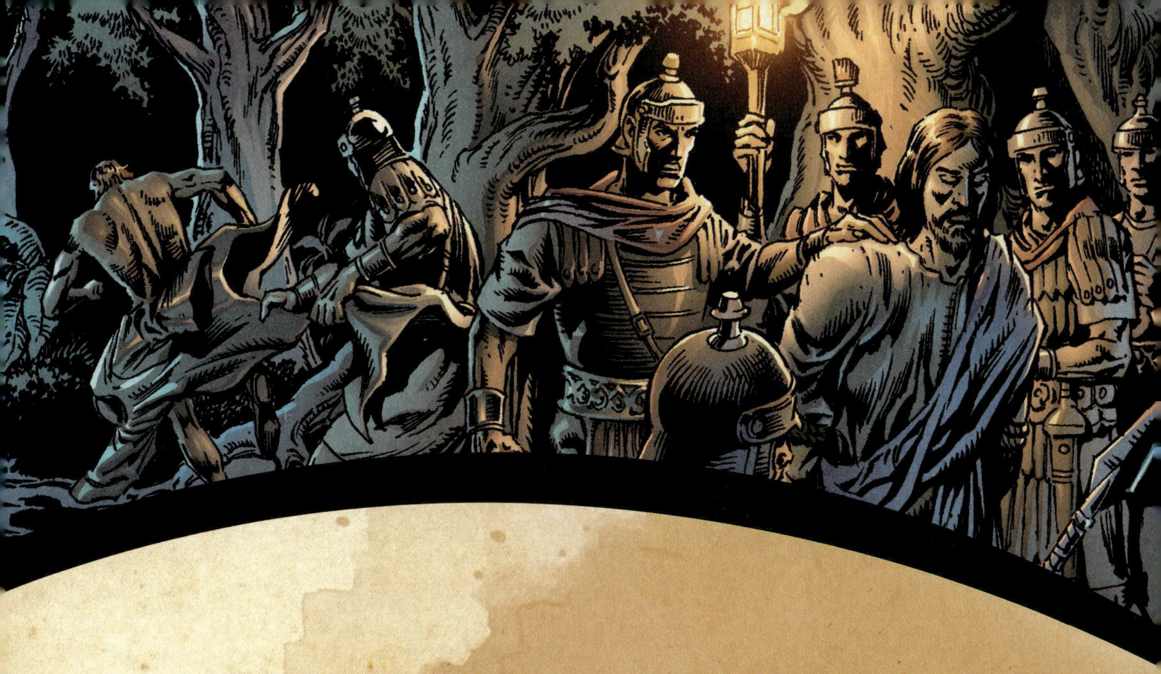

JOHN MARK

MARTYRED A.D. 64

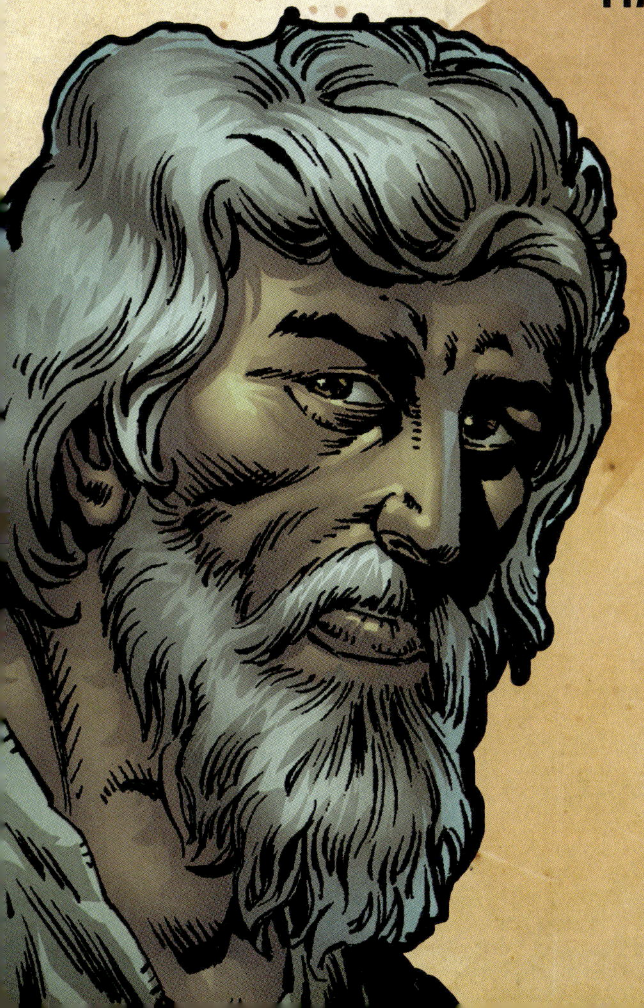

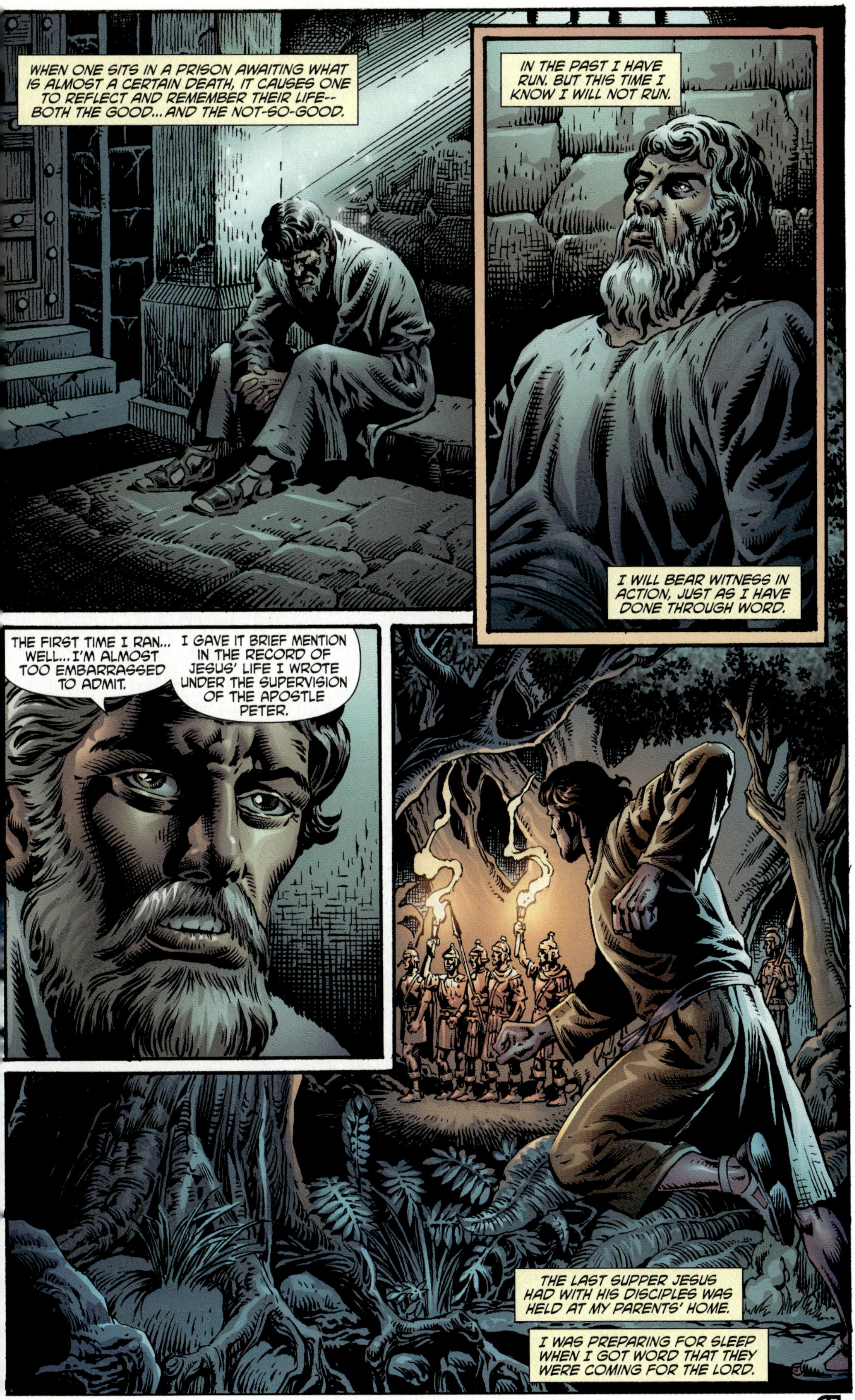
WHEN ONE SITS IN A PRISON AWAITING WHAT IS ALMOST A CERTAIN DEATH, IT CAUSES ONE TO REFLECT AND REMEMBER THEIR LIFE-- BOTH THE GOOD... AND THE NOT-SO-GOOD.
IN THE PAST I HAVE RUN. BUT THIS TIME I KNOW I WILL NOT RUN.
I WILL BEAR WITNESS IN ACTION, JUST AS I HAVE DONE THROUGH WORD.
THE FIRST TIME I RAN... WELL... I'M ALMOST TOO EMBARRASSED TO ADMIT.
I GAVE IT BRIEF MENTION IN THE RECORD OF JESUS' LIFE I WROTE UNDER THE SUPERVISION OF THE APOSTLE PETER.
THE LAST SUPPER JESUS HAD WITH HIS DISCIPLES WAS HELD AT MY PARENTS' HOME.
I WAS PREPARING FOR SLEEP WHEN I GOT WORD THAT THEY WERE COMING FOR THE LORD.

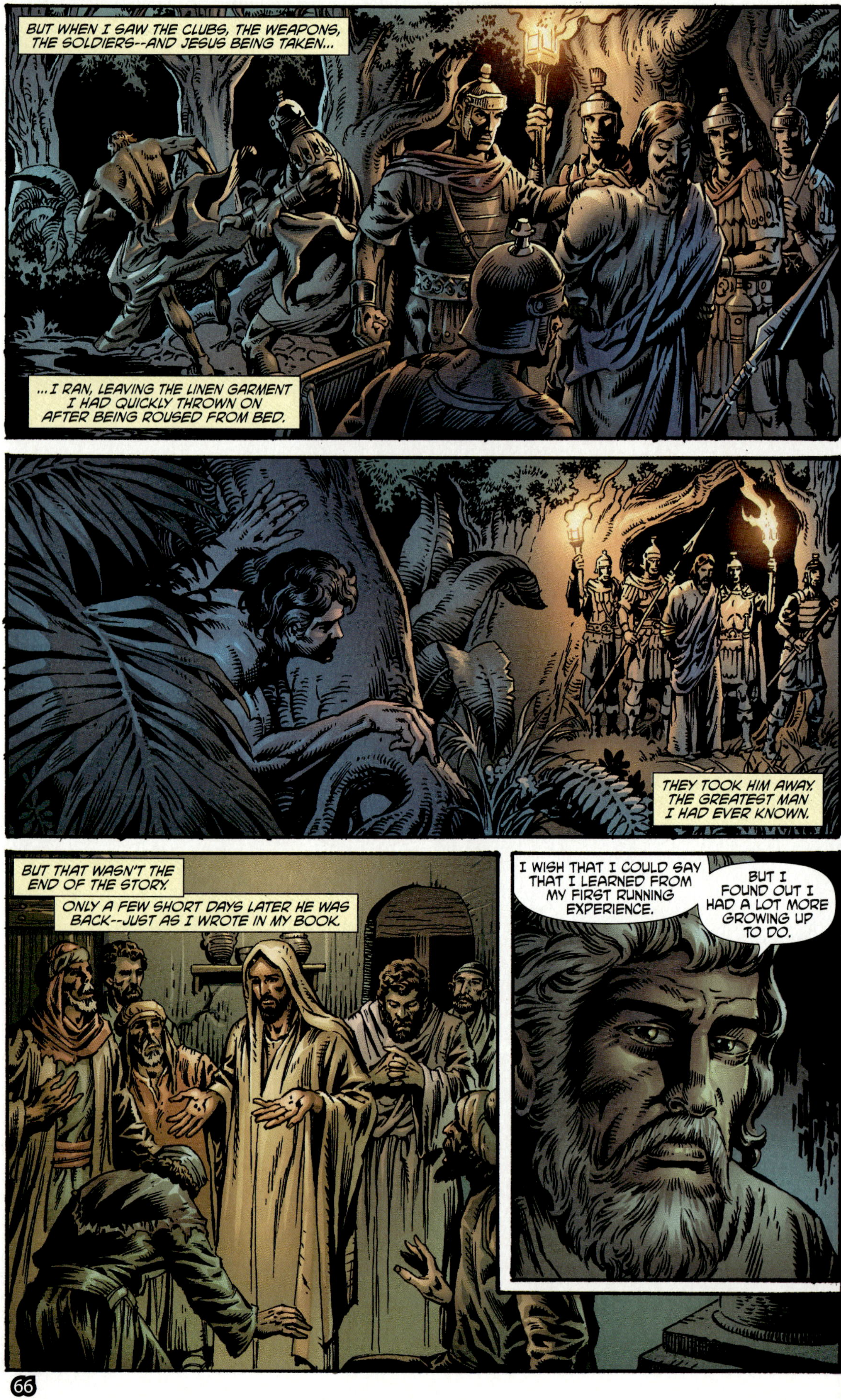
BUT WHEN I SAW THE CLUBS, THE WEAPONS, THE SOLDIERS--AND JESUS BEING TAKEN...
...I RAN, LEAVING THE LINEN GARMENT I HAD QUICKLY THROWN ON AFTER BEING ROUSED FROM BED.
THEY TOOK HIM AWAY. THE GREATEST MAN I HAD EVER KNOWN.
BUT THAT WASN'T THE END OF THE STORY.
ONLY A FEW SHORT DAYS LATER HE WAS BACK--JUST AS I WROTE IN MY BOOK.
I WISH THAT I COULD SAY THAT I LEARNED FROM MY FIRST RUNNING EXPERIENCE.
BUT I FOUND OUT I HAD A LOT MORE GROWING UP TO DO.

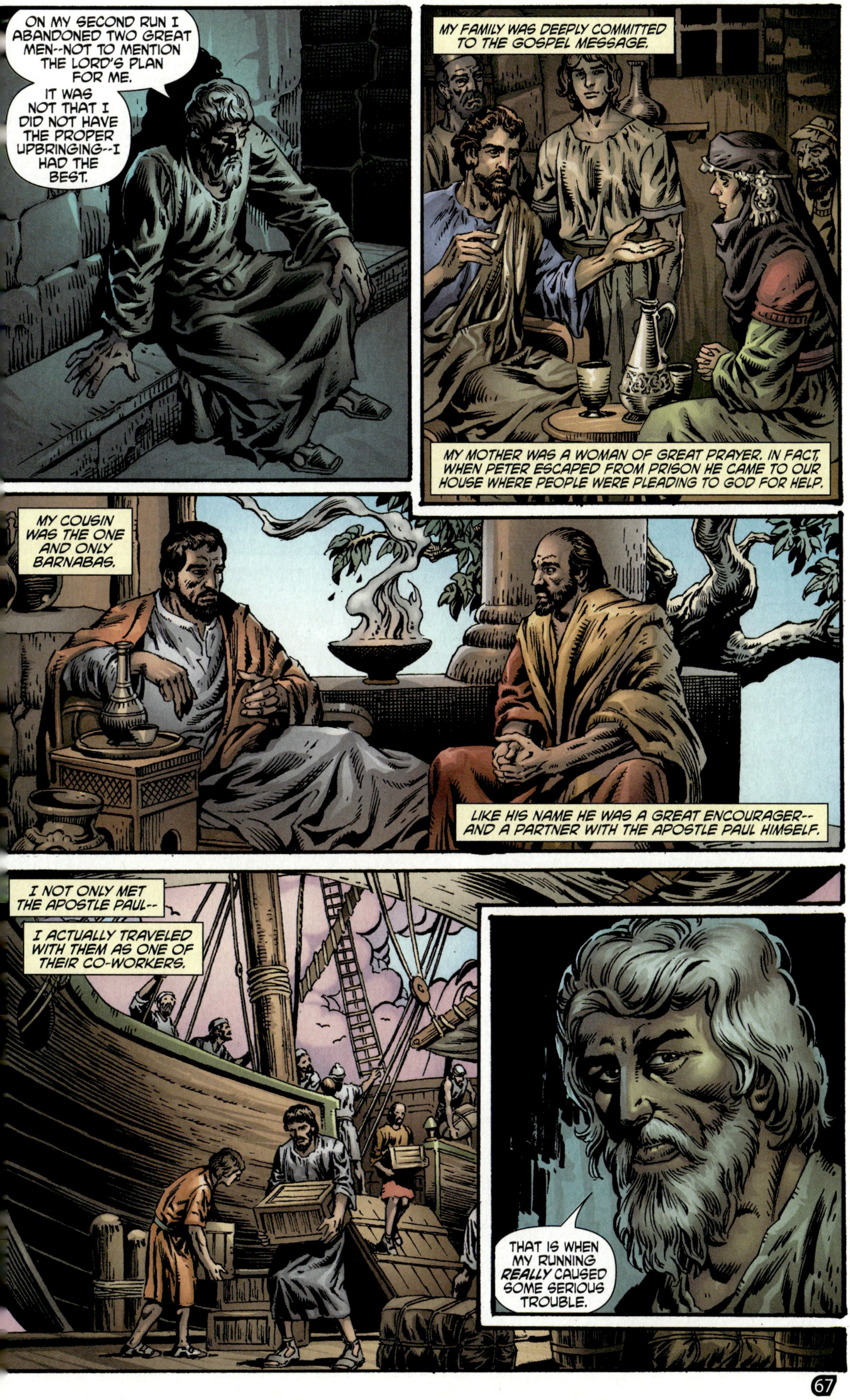
ON MY SECOND RUN I ABANDONED TWO GREAT MEN--NOT TO MENTION THE LORD'S PLAN FOR ME.
IT WAS NOT THAT I DID NOT HAVE THE PROPER UPBRINGING--I HAD THE BEST.
MY FAMILY WAS DEEPLY COMMITTED TO THE GOSPEL MESSAGE.
MY MOTHER WAS A WOMAN OF GREAT PRAYER. IN FACT, WHEN PETER ESCAPED FROM PRISON HE CAME TO OUR HOUSE WHERE PEOPLE WERE PLEADING TO GOD FOR HELP.
MY COUSIN WAS THE ONE AND ONLY BARNABAS.
LIKE HIS NAME HE WAS A GREAT ENCOURAGER--AND A PARTNER WITH THE APOSTLE PAUL HIMSELF.
I NOT ONLY MET THE APOSTLE PAUL--
I ACTUALLY TRAVELED WITH THEM AS ONE OF THEIR CO-WORKERS.
THAT IS WHEN MY RUNNING *REALLY* CAUSED SOME SERIOUS TROUBLE.

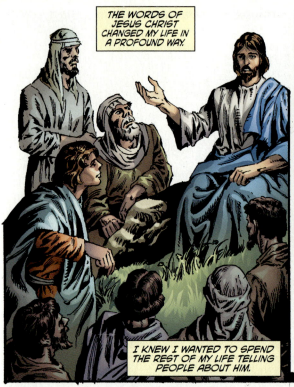

THE WORDS OF JESUS CHRIST CHANGED MY LIFE IN A PROFOUND WAY.

I KNEW I WANTED TO SPEND THE REST OF MY LIFE TELLING PEOPLE ABOUT HIM.

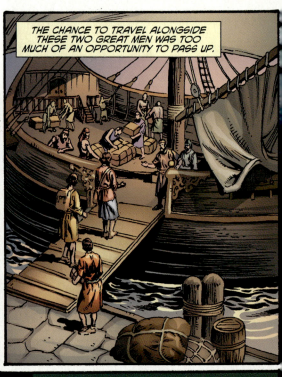

THE CHANCE TO TRAVEL ALONGSIDE THESE TWO GREAT MEN WAS TOO MUCH OF AN OPPORTUNITY TO PASS UP.

BUT MY TIME WITH THESE MEN-- INCLUDING MY COUSIN--CAME TO AN END WHILE IN THE CITY OF PERGA.

EVEN NOW, I AM NOT SURE EXACTLY WHY I QUIT. THERE WERE LIKELY MANY REASONS.

I SAW PAUL AFFLICTED WITH MALARIA AND I SAW HIS EYESIGHT AFFECTED.

WE WERE HARASSED IN EVERY CITY.

I WAS HOMESICK.

BEING A MISSIONARY WAS HARDER THAN I IMAGINED.

AND SO I SIMPLY LEFT THEM--TO THE CONSTERNATION OF MY COUSIN BARNABAS.

AND TO THE GREAT IRRITATION OF PAUL.

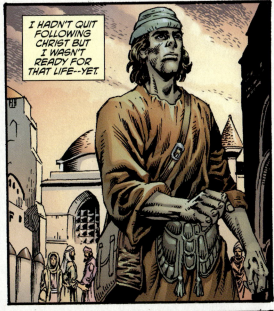

I HADN'T QUIT FOLLOWING CHRIST BUT I WASN'T READY FOR THAT LIFE--YET.

IN ANTIOCH--THE CITY WHERE WE WERE FIRST CALLED CHRISTIANS, I FINALLY FELT I WAS READY TO REJOIN THE MISSIONARY FORCE.

I WAS READY. BUT THE APOSTLE WAS NOT...

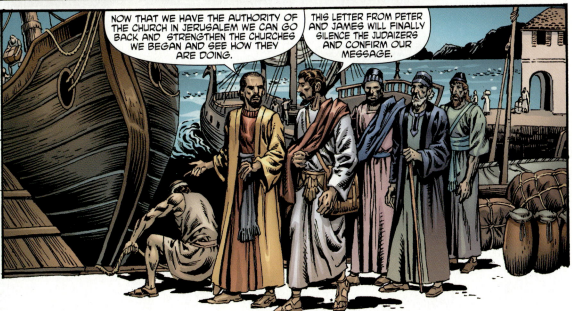

NOW THAT WE HAVE THE AUTHORITY OF THE CHURCH IN JERUSALEM WE CAN GO BACK AND STRENGTHEN THE CHURCHES WE BEGAN AND SEE HOW THEY ARE DOING.

THIS LETTER FROM PETER AND JAMES WILL FINALLY SILENCE THE JUDAIZERS AND CONFIRM OUR MESSAGE.

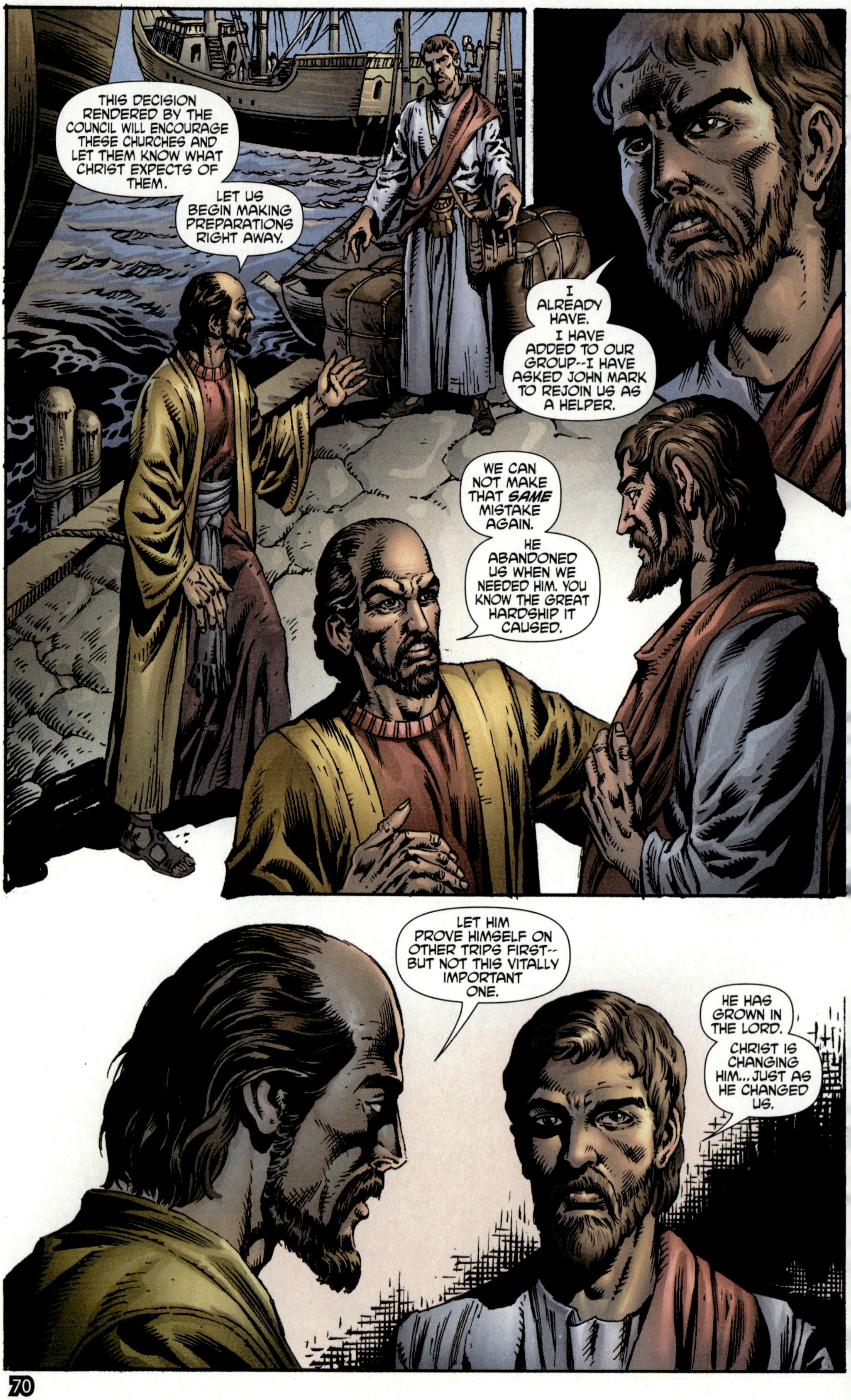
THIS DECISION RENDERED BY THE COUNCIL WILL ENCOURAGE THESE CHURCHES AND LET THEM KNOW WHAT CHRIST EXPECTS OF THEM.
LET US BEGIN MAKING PREPARATIONS RIGHT AWAY.
I ALREADY HAVE.
I HAVE ADDED TO OUR GROUP--I HAVE ASKED JOHN MARK TO REJOIN US AS A HELPER.
WE CAN NOT MAKE THAT *SAME* MISTAKE AGAIN.
HE ABANDONED US WHEN WE NEEDED HIM. YOU KNOW THE GREAT HARDSHIP IT CAUSED.
LET HIM PROVE HIMSELF ON OTHER TRIPS FIRST-- BUT NOT THIS VITALLY IMPORTANT ONE.
HE HAS GROWN IN THE LORD.
CHRIST IS CHANGING HIM... JUST AS HE CHANGED US.

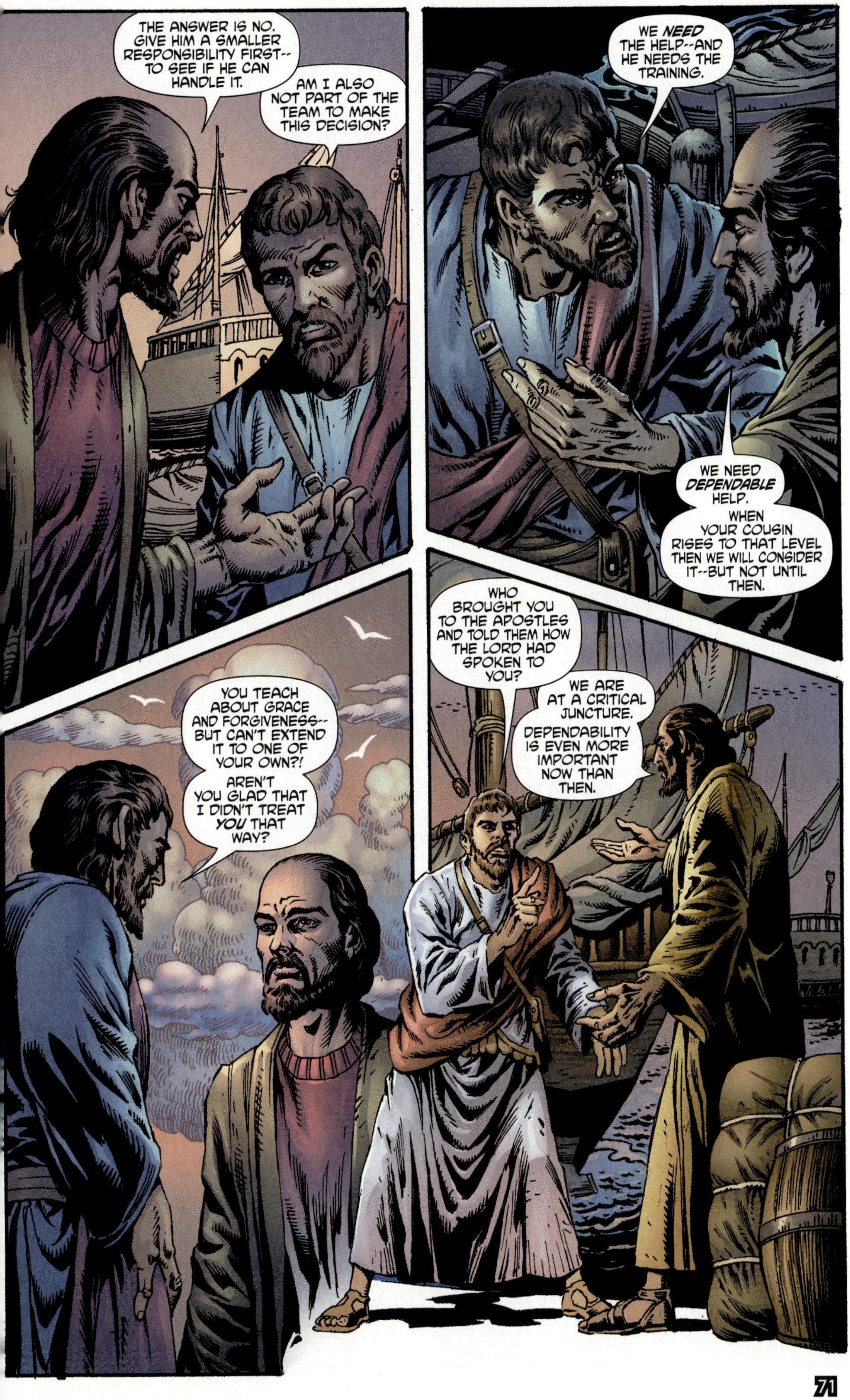

THE ANSWER IS NO. GIVE HIM A SMALLER RESPONSIBILITY FIRST-- TO SEE IF HE CAN HANDLE IT.
AM I ALSO NOT PART OF THE TEAM TO MAKE THIS DECISION?
WE NEED THE HELP--AND HE NEEDS THE TRAINING.
WE NEED DEPENDABLE HELP.
WHEN YOUR COUSIN RISES TO THAT LEVEL THEN WE WILL CONSIDER IT--BUT NOT UNTIL THEN.
YOU TEACH ABOUT GRACE AND FORGIVENESS-- BUT CAN'T EXTEND IT TO ONE OF YOUR OWN?!
AREN'T YOU GLAD THAT I DIDN'T TREAT YOU THAT WAY?
WHO BROUGHT YOU TO THE APOSTLES AND TOLD THEM HOW THE LORD HAD SPOKEN TO YOU?
WE ARE AT A CRITICAL JUNCTURE.
DEPENDABILITY IS EVEN MORE IMPORTANT NOW THAN THEN.

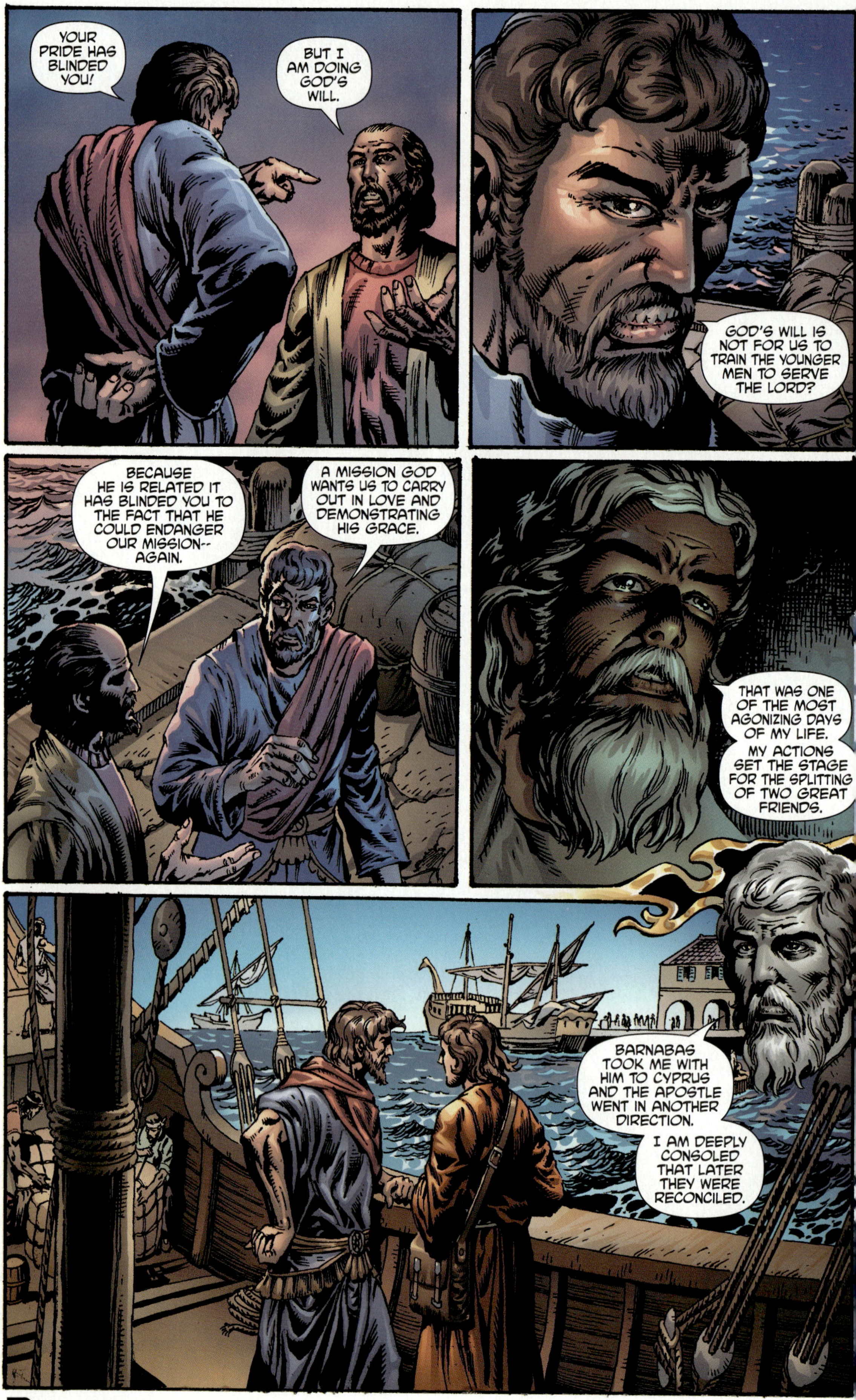
YOUR PRIDE HAS BLINDED YOU!
BUT I AM DOING GOD'S WILL.
GOD'S WILL IS NOT FOR US TO TRAIN THE YOUNGER MEN TO SERVE THE LORD?
BECAUSE HE IS RELATED IT HAS BLINDED YOU TO THE FACT THAT HE COULD ENDANGER OUR MISSION-- AGAIN.
A MISSION GOD WANTS US TO CARRY OUT IN LOVE AND DEMONSTRATING HIS GRACE.
THAT WAS ONE OF THE MOST AGONIZING DAYS OF MY LIFE.
MY ACTIONS SET THE STAGE FOR THE SPLITTING OF TWO GREAT FRIENDS.
BARNABAS TOOK ME WITH HIM TO CYPRUS AND THE APOSTLE WENT IN ANOTHER DIRECTION.
I AM DEEPLY CONSOLED THAT LATER THEY WERE RECONCILED.

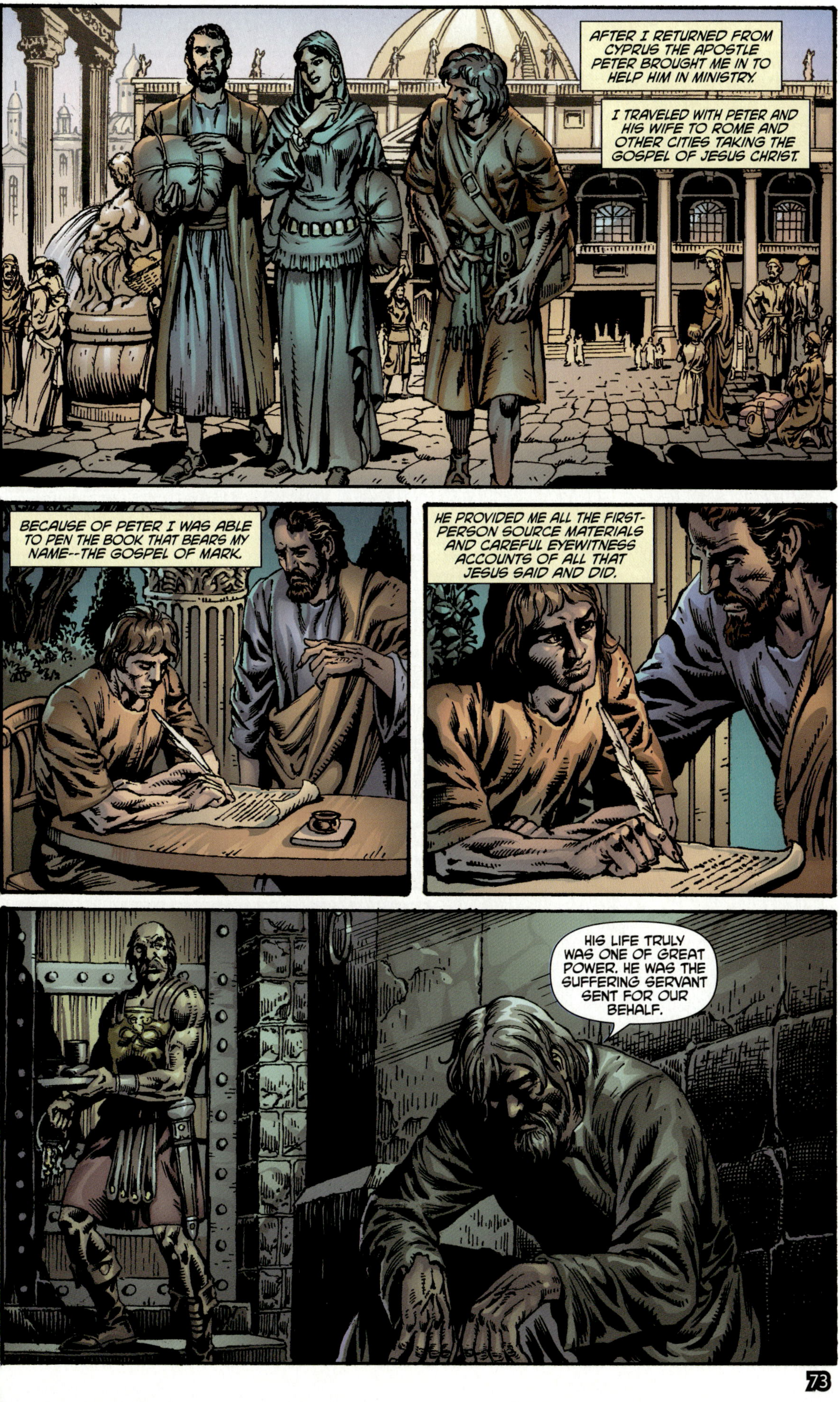
AFTER I RETURNED FROM CYPRUS THE APOSTLE PETER BROUGHT ME IN TO HELP HIM IN MINISTRY.
I TRAVELED WITH PETER AND HIS WIFE TO ROME AND OTHER CITIES TAKING THE GOSPEL OF JESUS CHRIST.
BECAUSE OF PETER I WAS ABLE TO PEN THE BOOK THAT BEARS MY NAME--THE GOSPEL OF MARK.
HE PROVIDED ME ALL THE FIRST-PERSON SOURCE MATERIALS AND CAREFUL EYEWITNESS ACCOUNTS OF ALL THAT JESUS SAID AND DID.
HIS LIFE TRULY WAS ONE OF GREAT POWER. HE WAS THE SUFFERING SERVANT SENT FOR OUR BEHALF.

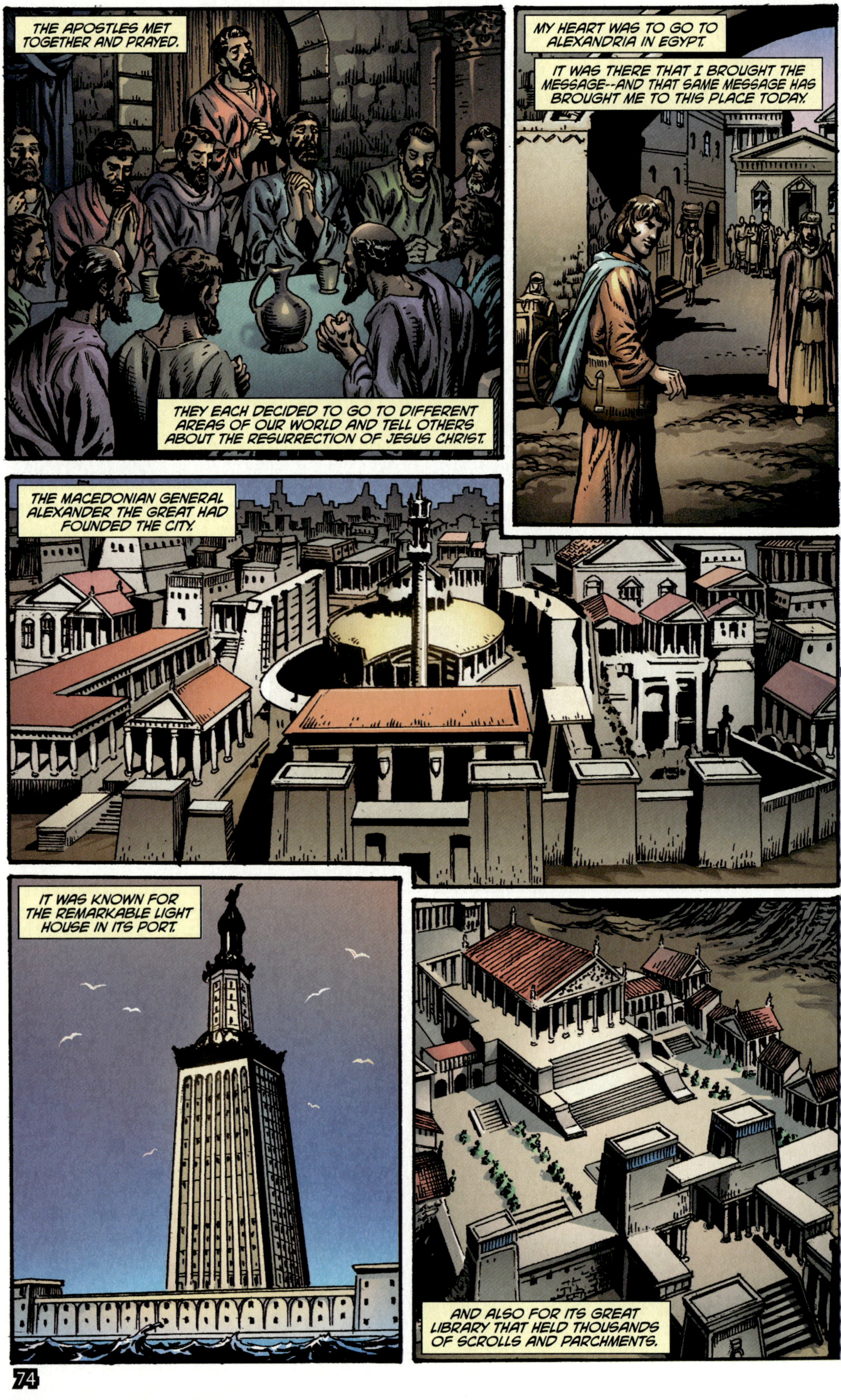
THE APOSTLES MET TOGETHER AND PRAYED.
THEY EACH DECIDED TO GO TO DIFFERENT AREAS OF OUR WORLD AND TELL OTHERS ABOUT THE RESURRECTION OF JESUS CHRIST.
MY HEART WAS TO GO TO ALEXANDRIA IN EGYPT.
IT WAS THERE THAT I BROUGHT THE MESSAGE--AND THAT SAME MESSAGE HAS BROUGHT ME TO THIS PLACE TODAY.
THE MACEDONIAN GENERAL ALEXANDER THE GREAT HAD FOUNDED THE CITY.
IT WAS KNOWN FOR THE REMARKABLE LIGHT HOUSE IN ITS PORT.
AND ALSO FOR ITS GREAT LIBRARY THAT HELD THOUSANDS OF SCROLLS AND PARCHMENTS.

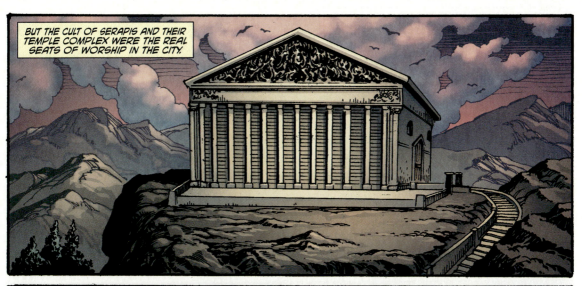

BUT THE CULT OF SERAPIS AND THEIR TEMPLE COMPLEX WERE THE REAL SEATS OF WORSHIP IN THE CITY.

BUT THEY CALLED ME MARK THE EVANGELIST FOR A REASON.

I HAD AN UNDYING PASSION FOR OTHERS TO KNOW ABOUT HIM-- EVEN THESE PAGANS.

THEIR GOD, SERAPIS, WAS IMAGINARY.

BUT BY THE POWER OF THE HOLY SPIRIT I PREACHED A REAL, COME TO EARTH GOD IN FLESH AND BLOOD.

THE MESSAGE BORE GREAT FRUIT AND SOON A BODY OF BELIEVERS SPRANG TO LIFE IN THIS CITY OF DARKNESS--AND EVEN BEGAN TO THRIVE.

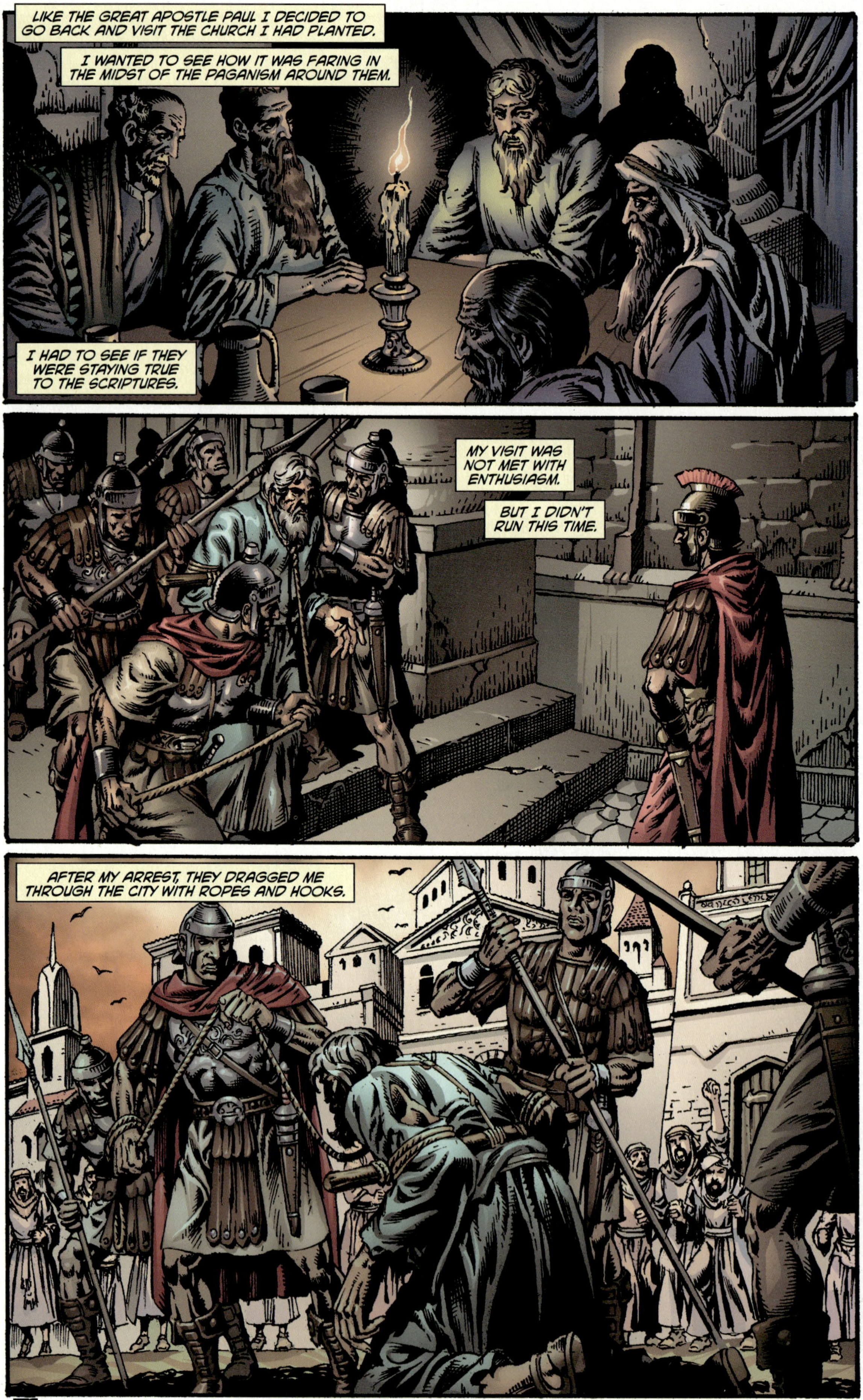
LIKE THE GREAT APOSTLE PAUL I DECIDED TO GO BACK AND VISIT THE CHURCH I HAD PLANTED.
I WANTED TO SEE HOW IT WAS FARING IN THE MIDST OF THE PAGANISM AROUND THEM.
I HAD TO SEE IF THEY WERE STAYING TRUE TO THE SCRIPTURES.
MY VISIT WAS NOT MET WITH ENTHUSIASM.
BUT I DIDN'T RUN THIS TIME.
AFTER MY ARREST, THEY DRAGGED ME THROUGH THE CITY WITH ROPES AND HOOKS.

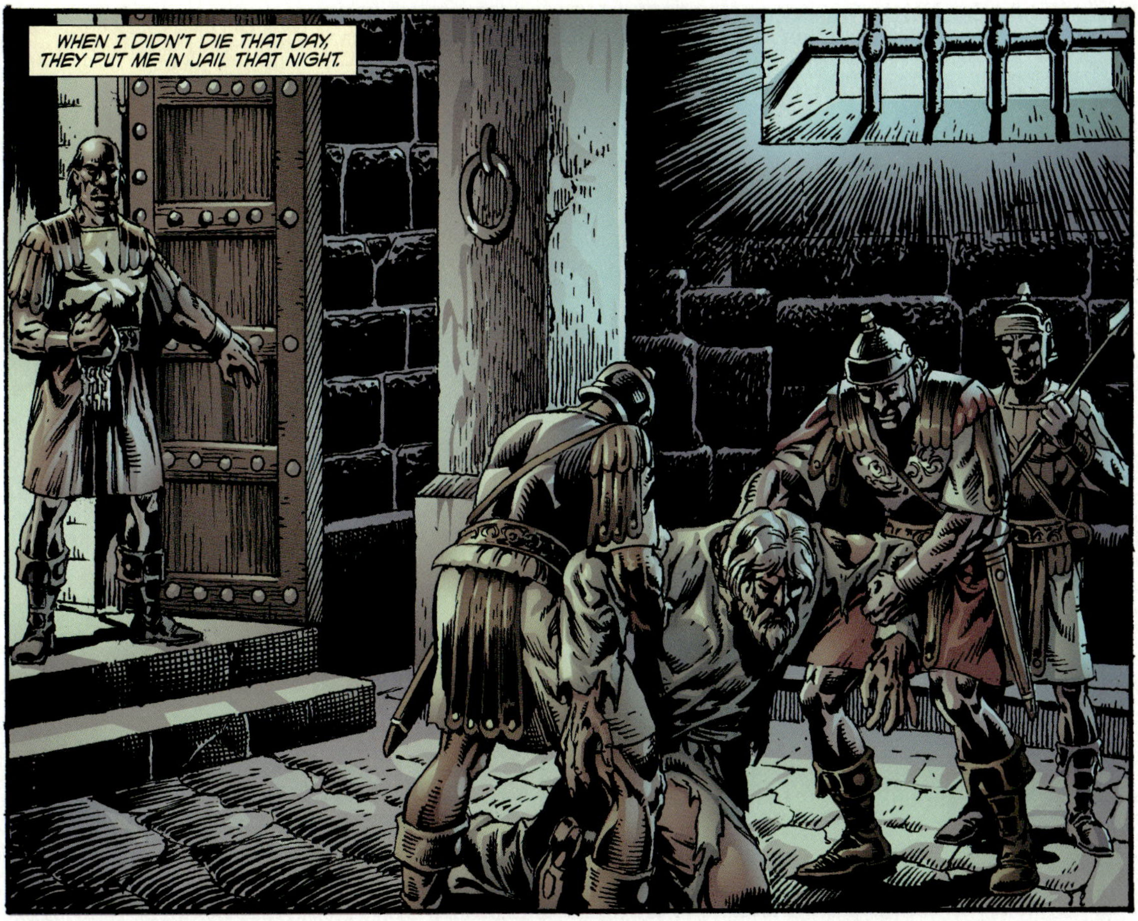
WHEN I DIDN'T DIE THAT DAY, THEY PUT ME IN JAIL THAT NIGHT.

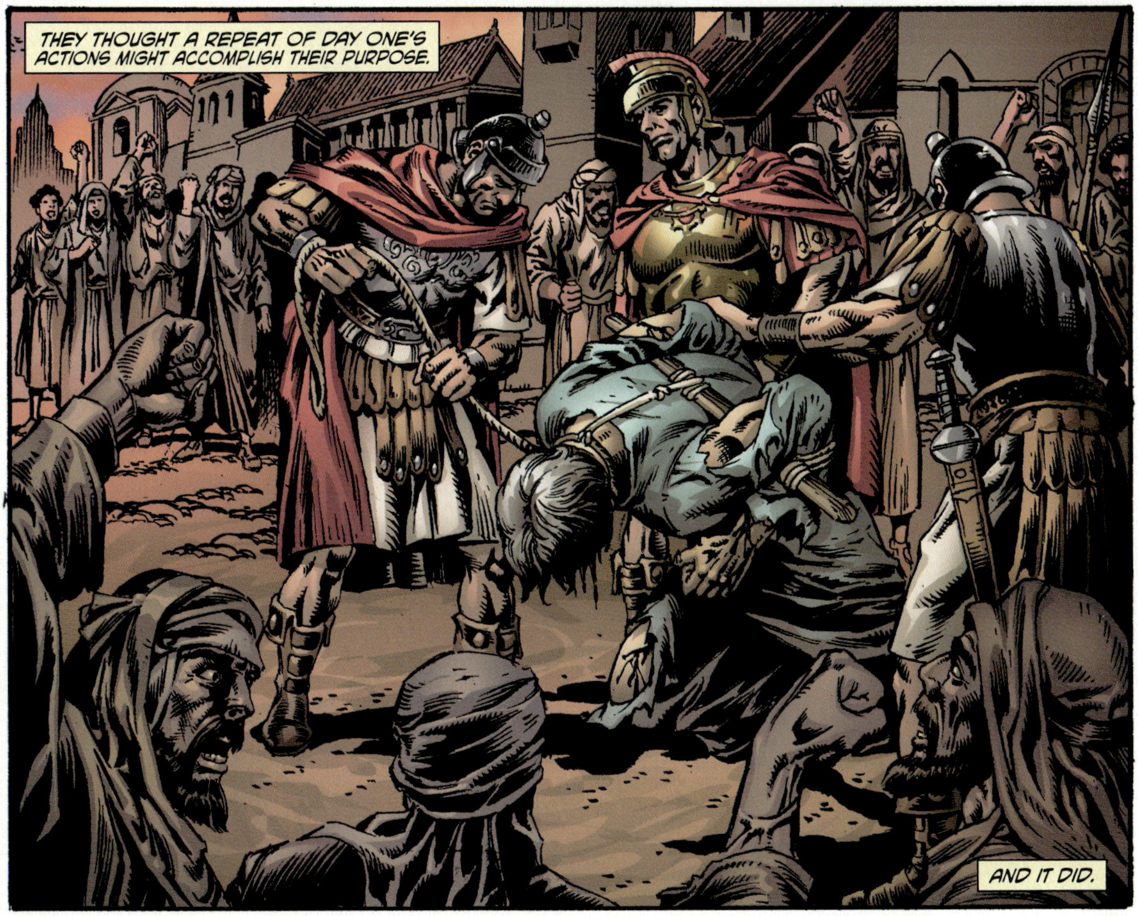
THEY THOUGHT A REPEAT OF DAY ONE'S ACTIONS MIGHT ACCOMPLISH THEIR PURPOSE.
AND IT DID.

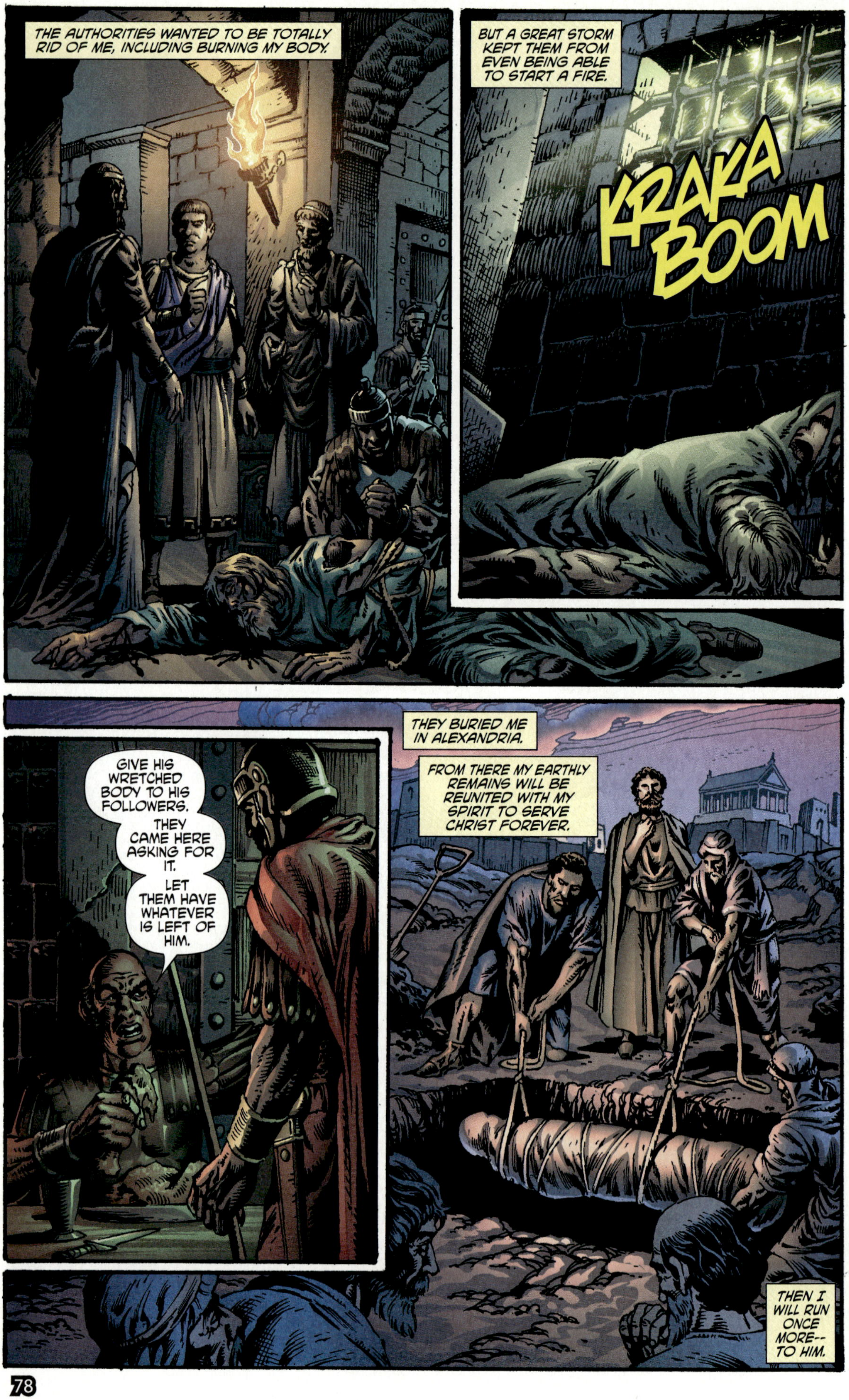
THE AUTHORITIES WANTED TO BE TOTALLY RID OF ME, INCLUDING BURNING MY BODY.
BUT A GREAT STORM KEPT THEM FROM EVEN BEING ABLE TO START A FIRE.
KRAKA BOOM
GIVE HIS WRETCHED BODY TO HIS FOLLOWERS.
THEY CAME HERE ASKING FOR IT.
LET THEM HAVE WHATEVER IS LEFT OF HIM.
THEY BURIED ME IN ALEXANDRIA.
FROM THERE MY EARTHLY REMAINS WILL BE REUNITED WITH MY SPIRIT TO SERVE CHRIST FOREVER.
THEN I WILL RUN ONCE MORE-- TO HIM.

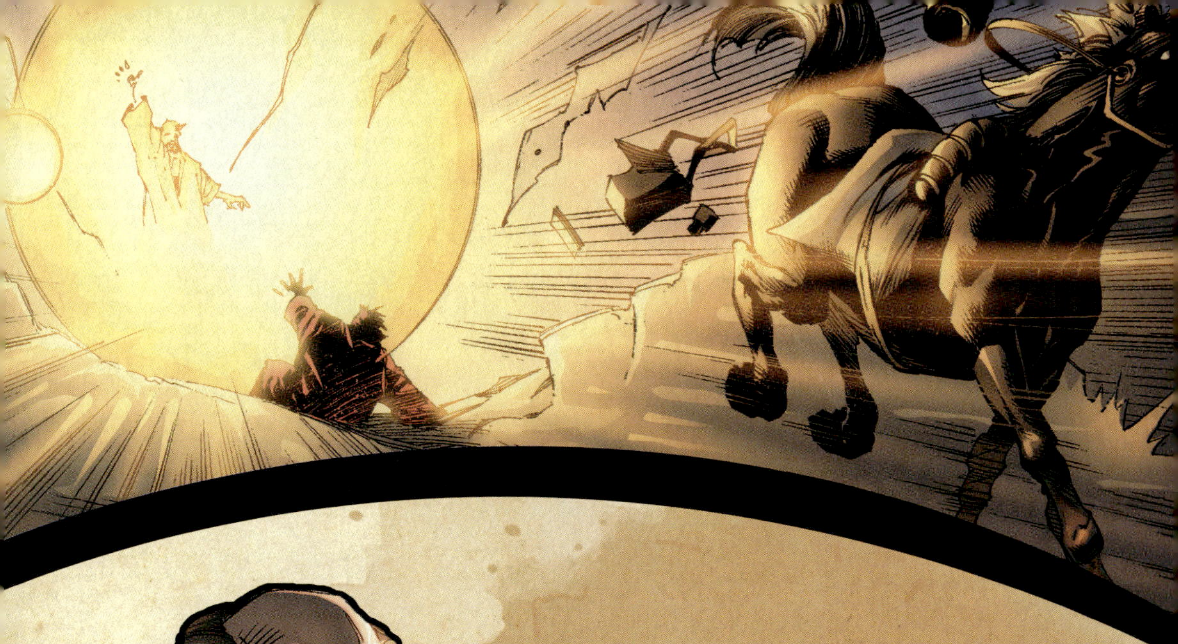

PAUL

MARTYRED A.D. 69

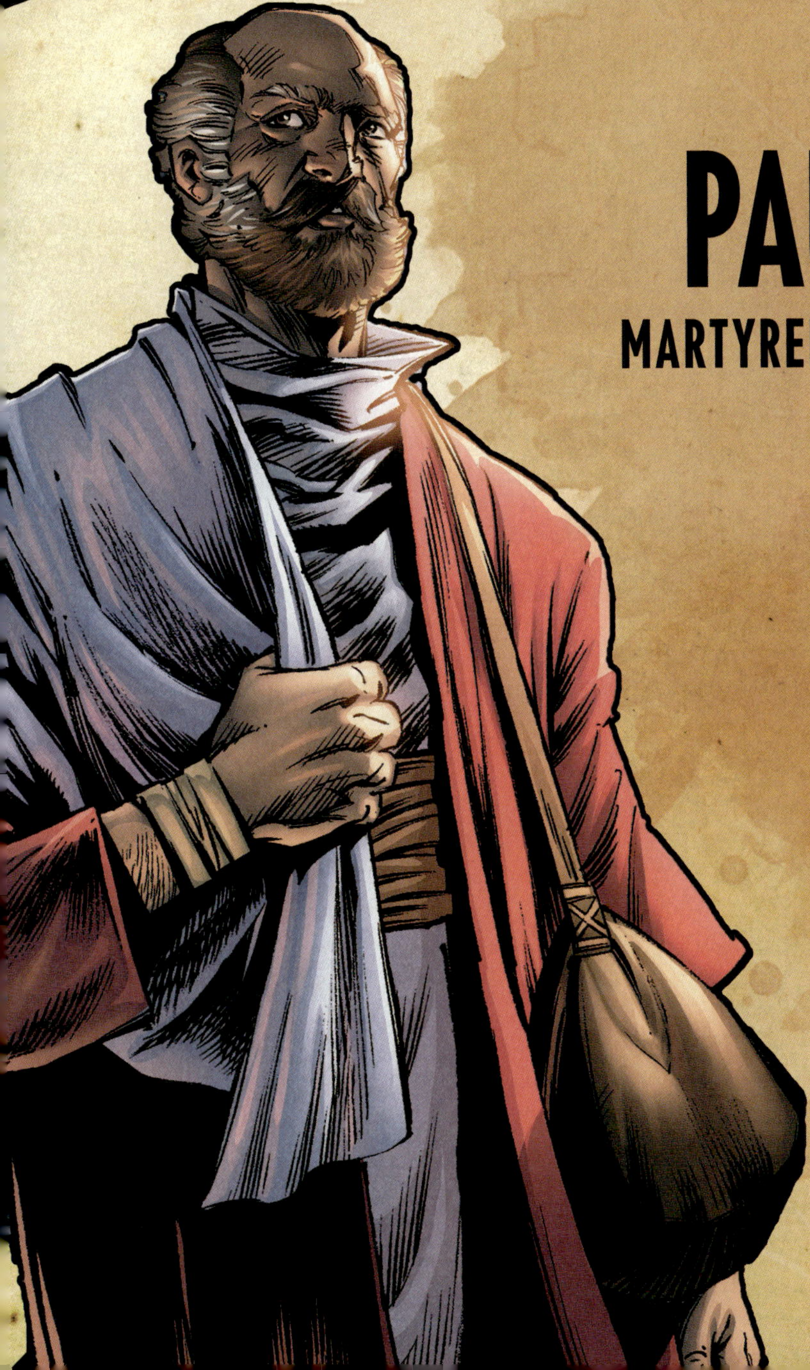

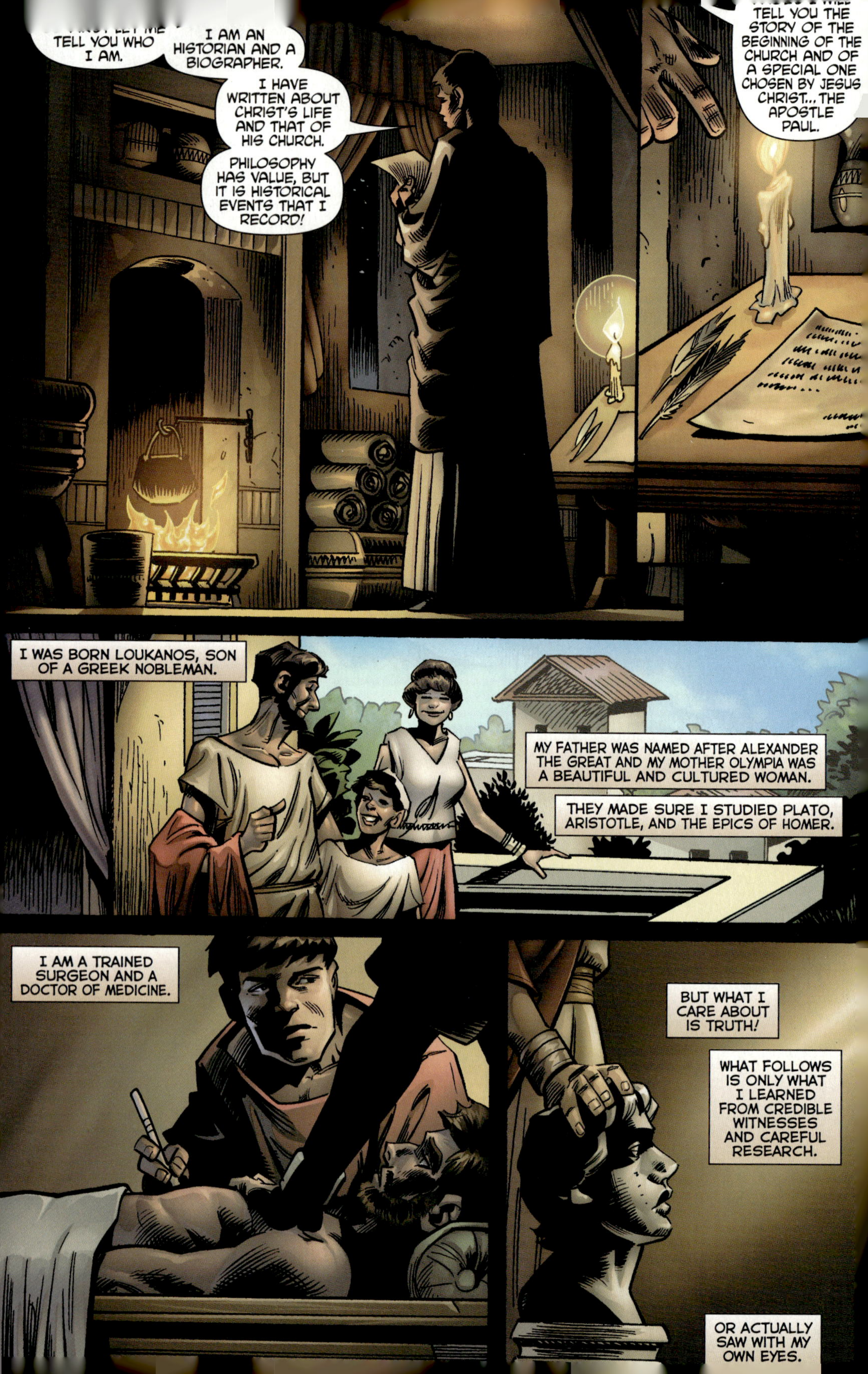
TELL YOU WHO I AM.
I AM AN HISTORIAN AND A BIOGRAPHER.
I HAVE WRITTEN ABOUT CHRIST'S LIFE AND THAT OF HIS CHURCH.
PHILOSOPHY HAS VALUE, BUT IT IS HISTORICAL EVENTS THAT I RECORD!
TELL YOU THE STORY OF THE BEGINNING OF THE CHURCH AND OF A SPECIAL ONE CHOSEN BY JESUS CHRIST... THE APOSTLE PAUL.
I WAS BORN LOUKANOS, SON OF A GREEK NOBLEMAN.
MY FATHER WAS NAMED AFTER ALEXANDER THE GREAT AND MY MOTHER OLYMPIA WAS A BEAUTIFUL AND CULTURED WOMAN.
THEY MADE SURE I STUDIED PLATO, ARISTOTLE, AND THE EPICS OF HOMER.
I AM A TRAINED SURGEON AND A DOCTOR OF MEDICINE.
BUT WHAT I CARE ABOUT IS TRUTH!
WHAT FOLLOWS IS ONLY WHAT I LEARNED FROM CREDIBLE WITNESSES AND CAREFUL RESEARCH.
OR ACTUALLY SAW WITH MY OWN EYES.

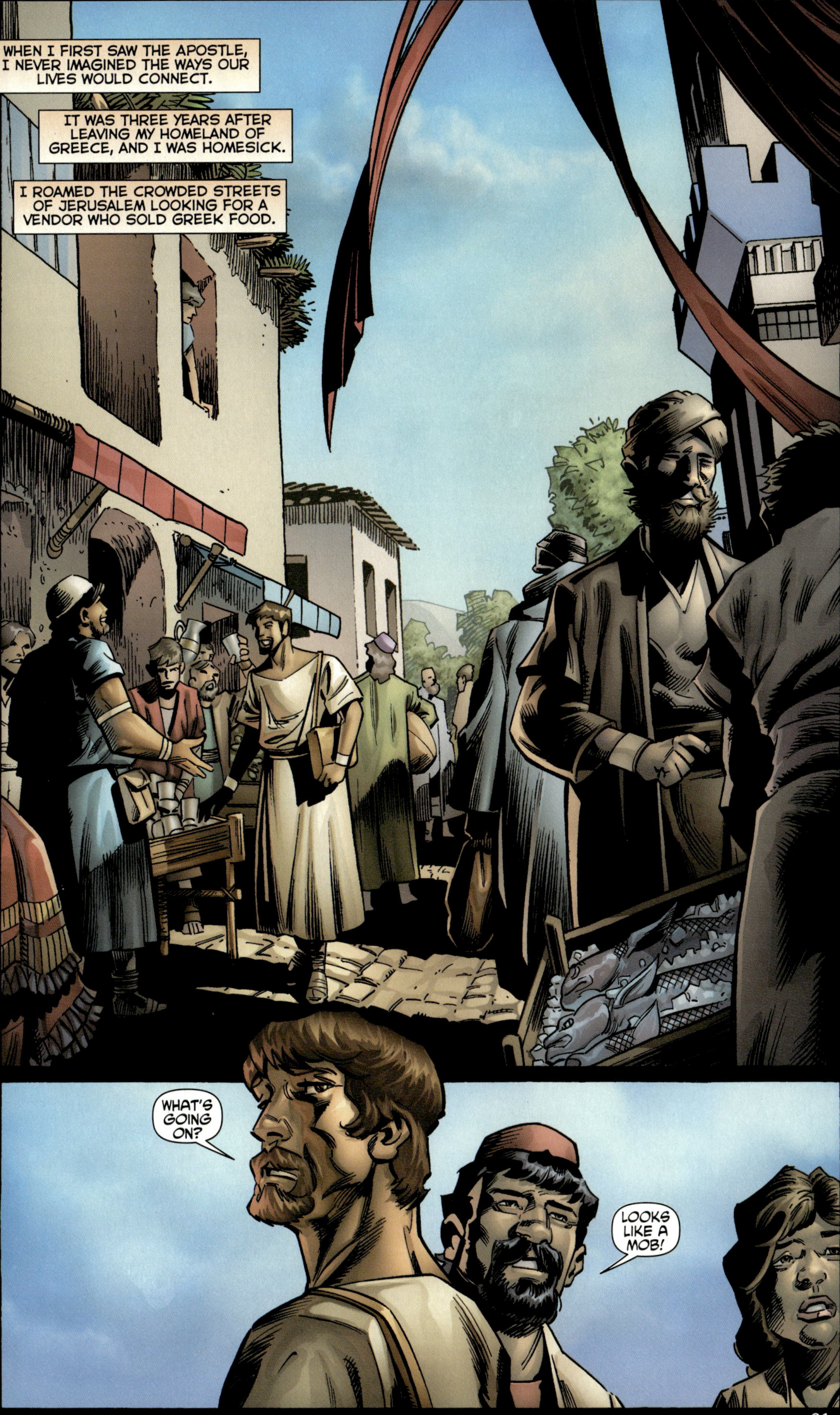
WHEN I FIRST SAW THE APOSTLE, I NEVER IMAGINED THE WAYS OUR LIVES WOULD CONNECT.
IT WAS THREE YEARS AFTER LEAVING MY HOMELAND OF GREECE, AND I WAS HOMESICK.
I ROAMED THE CROWDED STREETS OF JERUSALEM LOOKING FOR A VENDOR WHO SOLD GREEK FOOD.
WHAT'S GOING ON?
LOOKS LIKE A MOB!

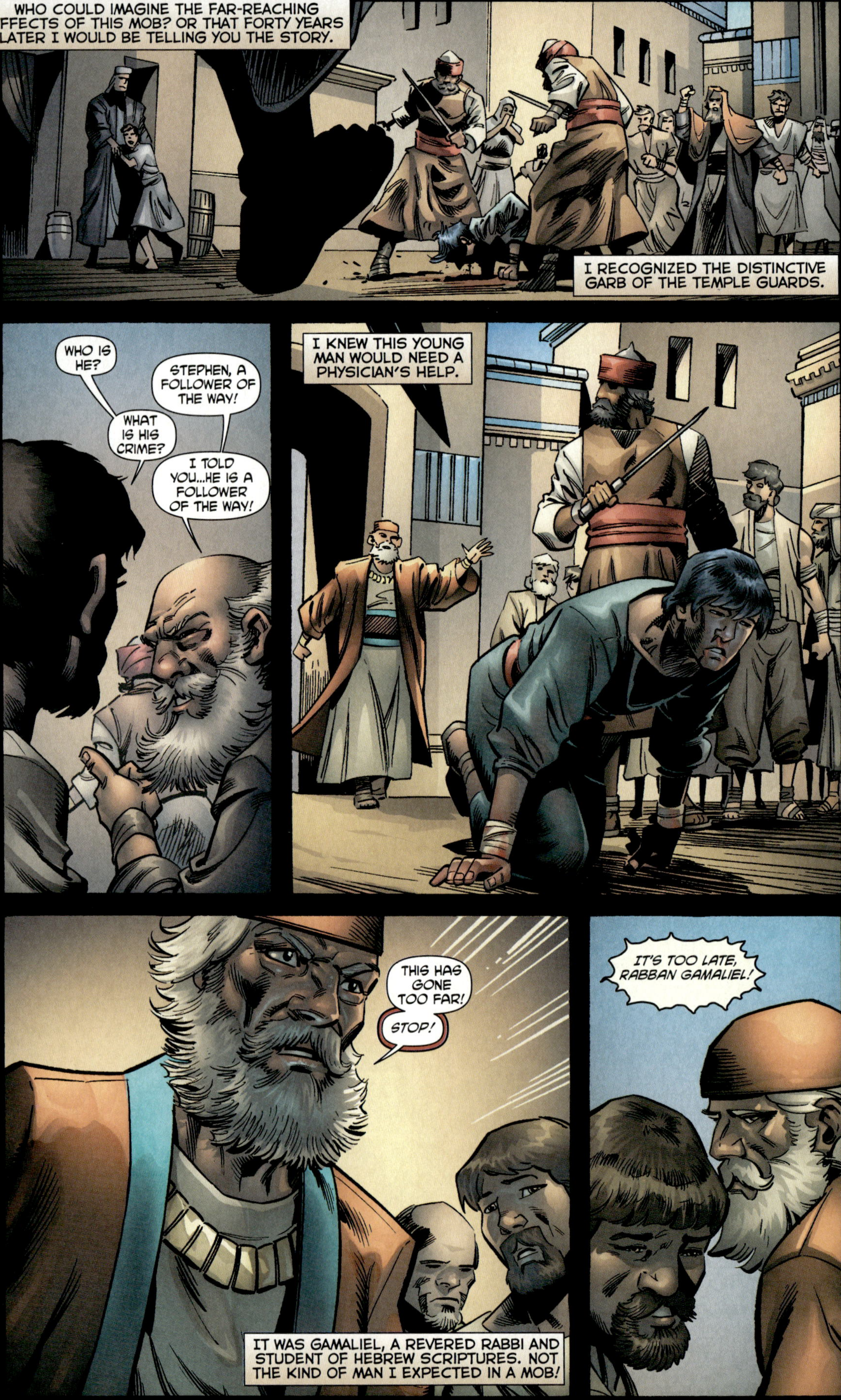

WHO COULD IMAGINE THE FAR-REACHING EFFECTS OF THIS MOB? OR THAT FORTY YEARS LATER I WOULD BE TELLING YOU THE STORY.
I RECOGNIZED THE DISTINCTIVE GARB OF THE TEMPLE GUARDS.
WHO IS HE?
STEPHEN, A FOLLOWER OF THE WAY!
WHAT IS HIS CRIME?
I TOLD YOU...HE IS A FOLLOWER OF THE WAY!
I KNEW THIS YOUNG MAN WOULD NEED A PHYSICIAN'S HELP.
THIS HAS GONE TOO FAR!
STOP!
IT WAS GAMALIEL, A REVERED RABBI AND STUDENT OF HEBREW SCRIPTURES. NOT THE KIND OF MAN I EXPECTED IN A MOB!
IT'S TOO LATE, RABBAN GAMALIEL!

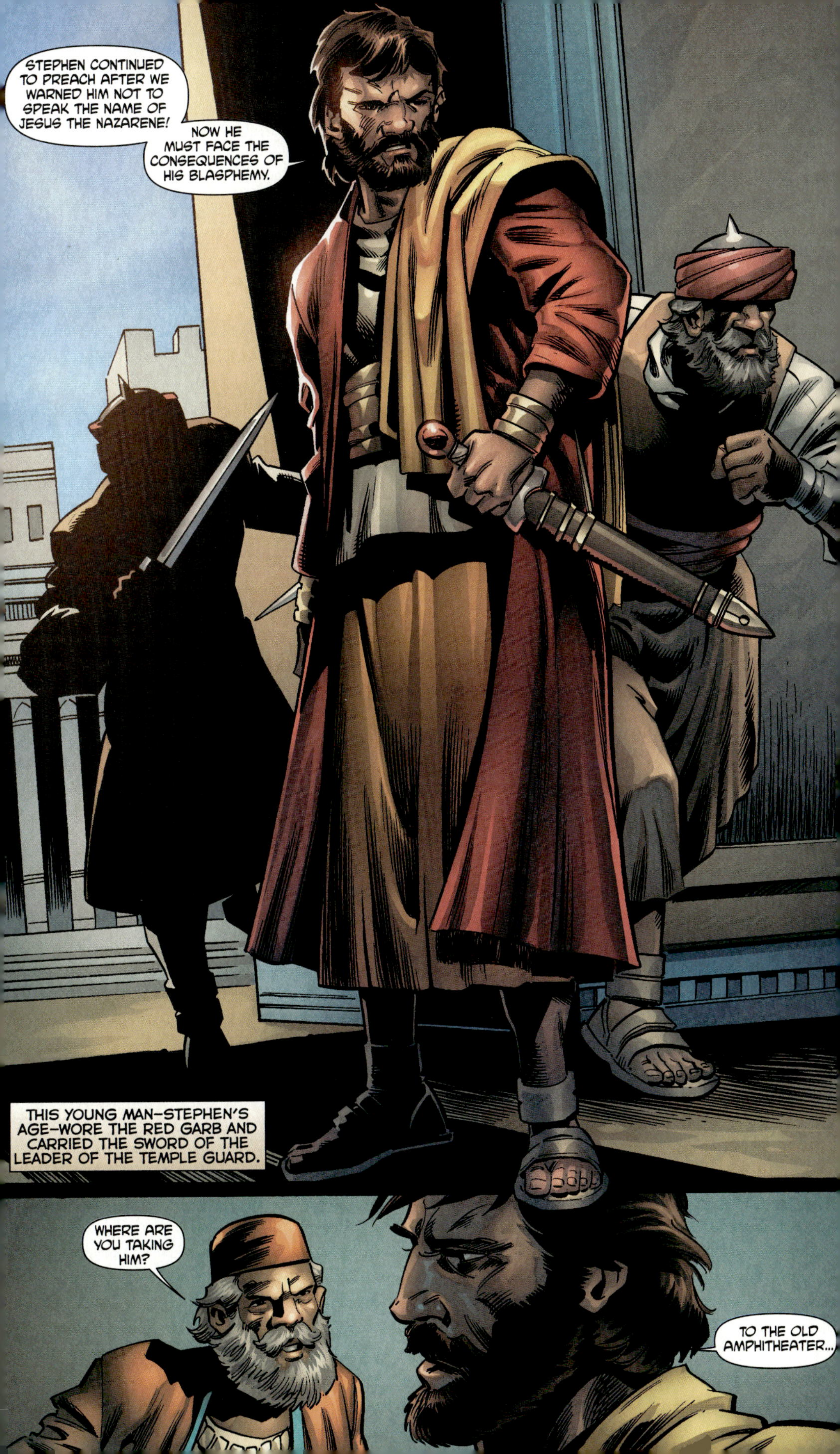
STEPHEN CONTINUED TO PREACH AFTER WE WARNED HIM NOT TO SPEAK THE NAME OF JESUS THE NAZARENE!
NOW HE MUST FACE THE CONSEQUENCES OF HIS BLASPHEMY.
THIS YOUNG MAN—STEPHEN'S AGE—WORE THE RED GARB AND CARRIED THE SWORD OF THE LEADER OF THE TEMPLE GUARD.
WHERE ARE YOU TAKING HIM?
TO THE OLD AMPHITHEATER...

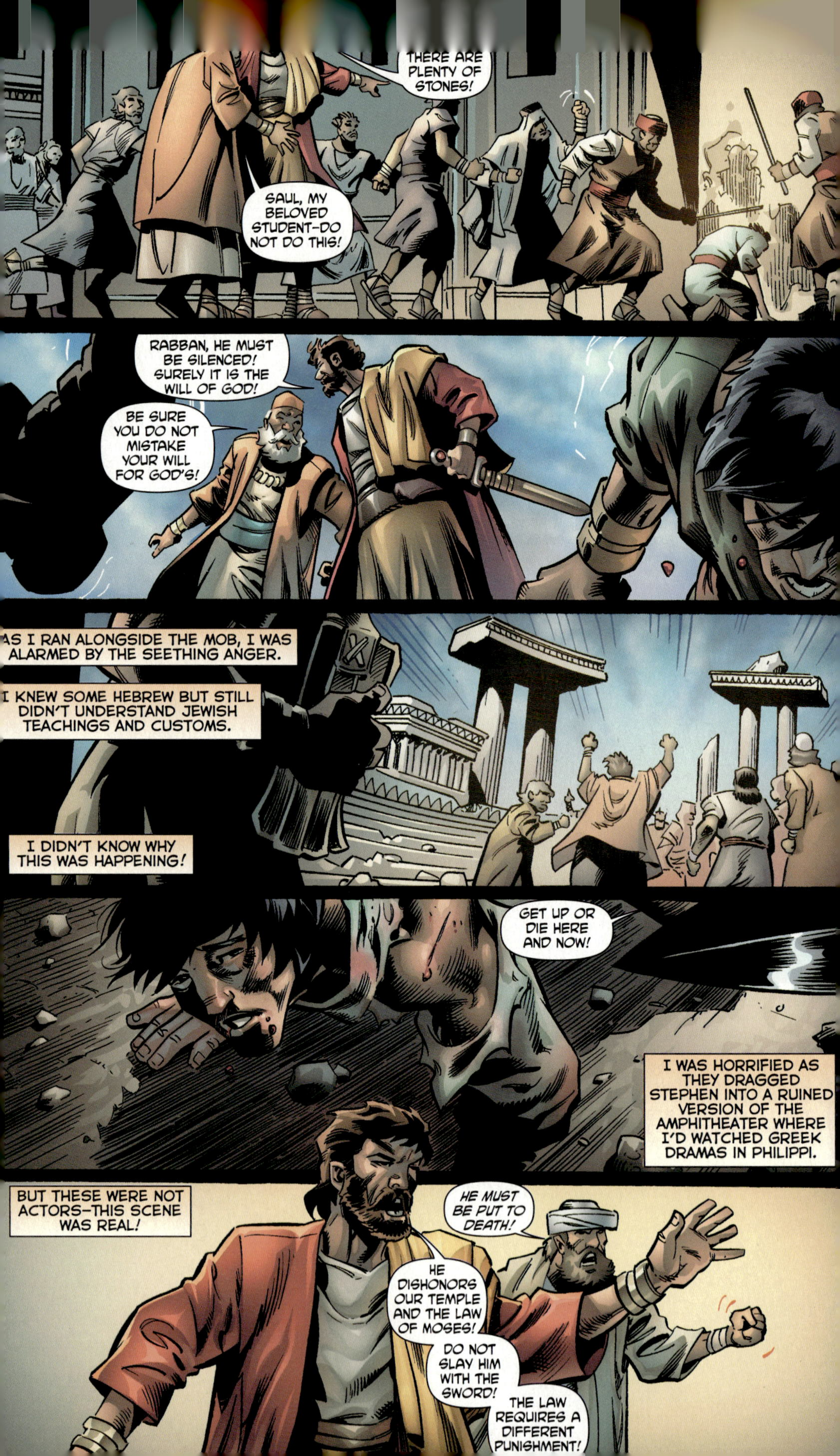
THERE ARE PLENTY OF STONES!
SAUL, MY BELOVED STUDENT–DO NOT DO THIS!
RABBAN, HE MUST BE SILENCED! SURELY IT IS THE WILL OF GOD!
BE SURE YOU DO NOT MISTAKE YOUR WILL FOR GOD'S!
AS I RAN ALONGSIDE THE MOB, I WAS ALARMED BY THE SEETHING ANGER.
I KNEW SOME HEBREW BUT STILL DIDN'T UNDERSTAND JEWISH TEACHINGS AND CUSTOMS.
I DIDN'T KNOW WHY THIS WAS HAPPENING!
GET UP OR DIE HERE AND NOW!
I WAS HORRIFIED AS THEY DRAGGED STEPHEN INTO A RUINED VERSION OF THE AMPHITHEATER WHERE I'D WATCHED GREEK DRAMAS IN PHILIPPI.
BUT THESE WERE NOT ACTORS–THIS SCENE WAS REAL!
HE MUST BE PUT TO DEATH!
HE DISHONORS OUR TEMPLE AND THE LAW OF MOSES!
DO NOT SLAY HIM WITH THE SWORD!
THE LAW REQUIRES A DIFFERENT PUNISHMENT!

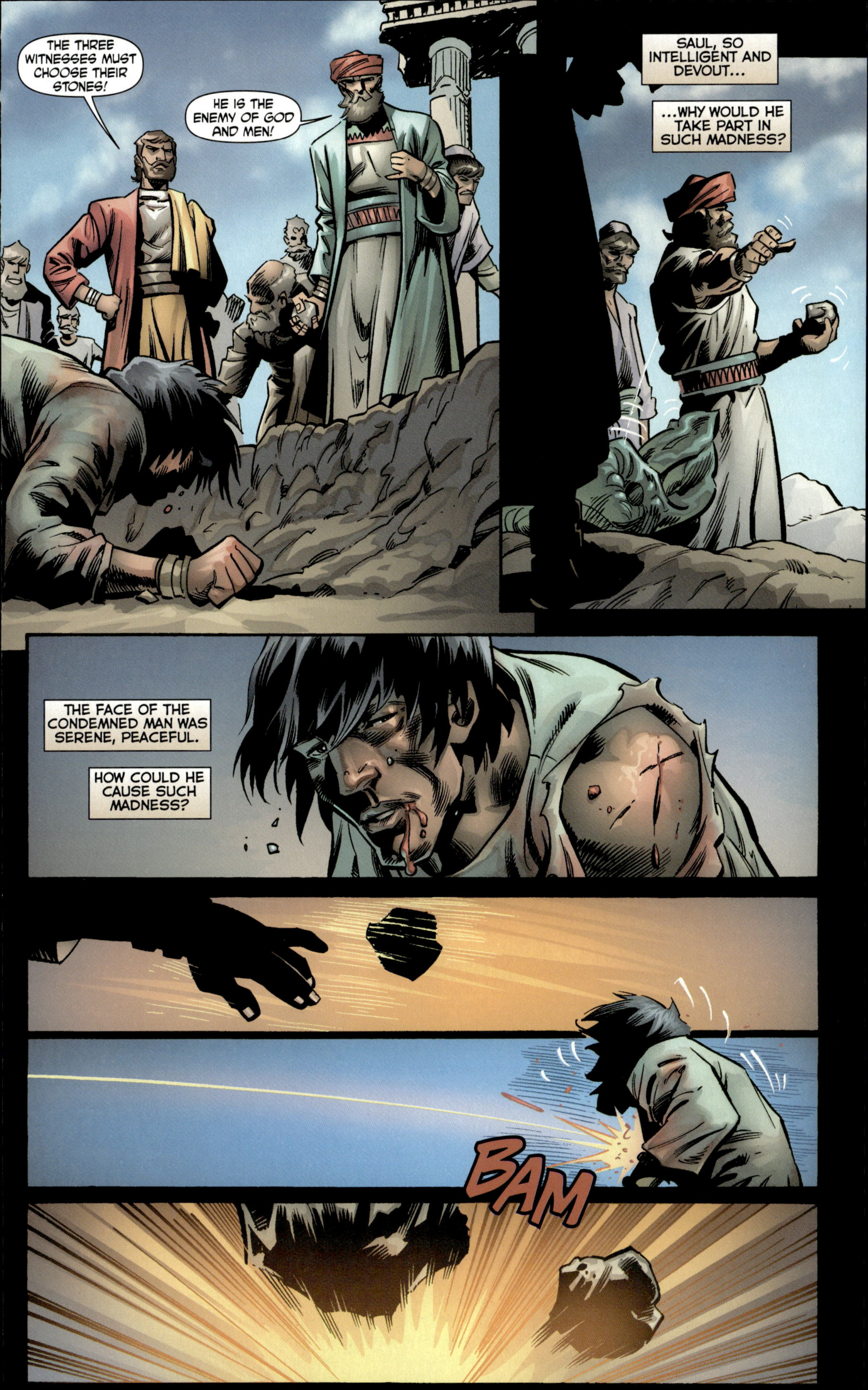
THE THREE WITNESSES MUST CHOOSE THEIR STONES!
HE IS THE ENEMY OF GOD AND MEN!
SAUL, SO INTELLIGENT AND DEVOUT...
...WHY WOULD HE TAKE PART IN SUCH MADNESS?
THE FACE OF THE CONDEMNED MAN WAS SERENE, PEACEFUL.
HOW COULD HE CAUSE SUCH MADNESS?
BAM

ACTS 7:58

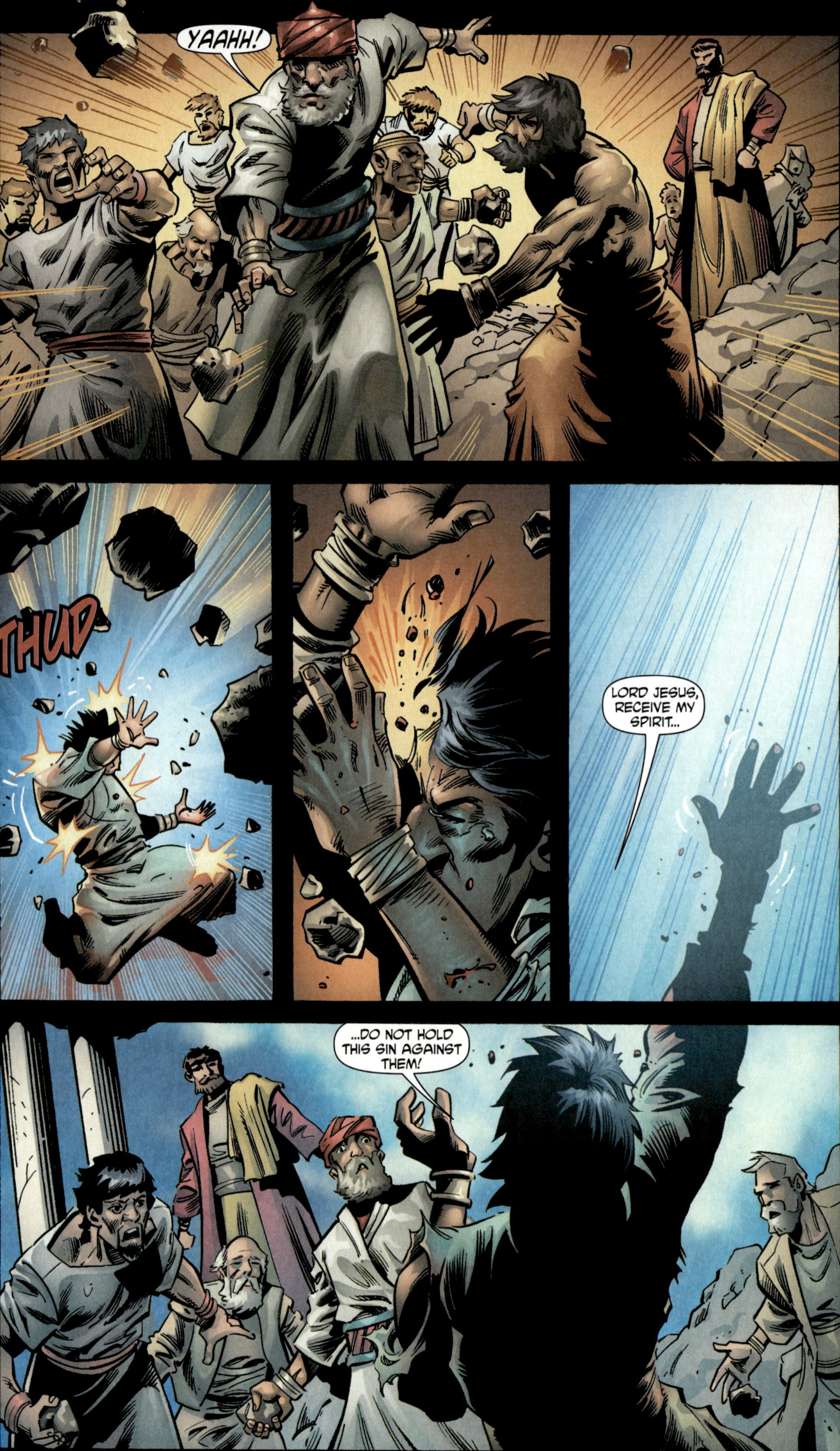
YAAHH!
THUD
LORD JESUS, RECEIVE MY SPIRIT...
...DO NOT HOLD THIS SIN AGAINST THEM!

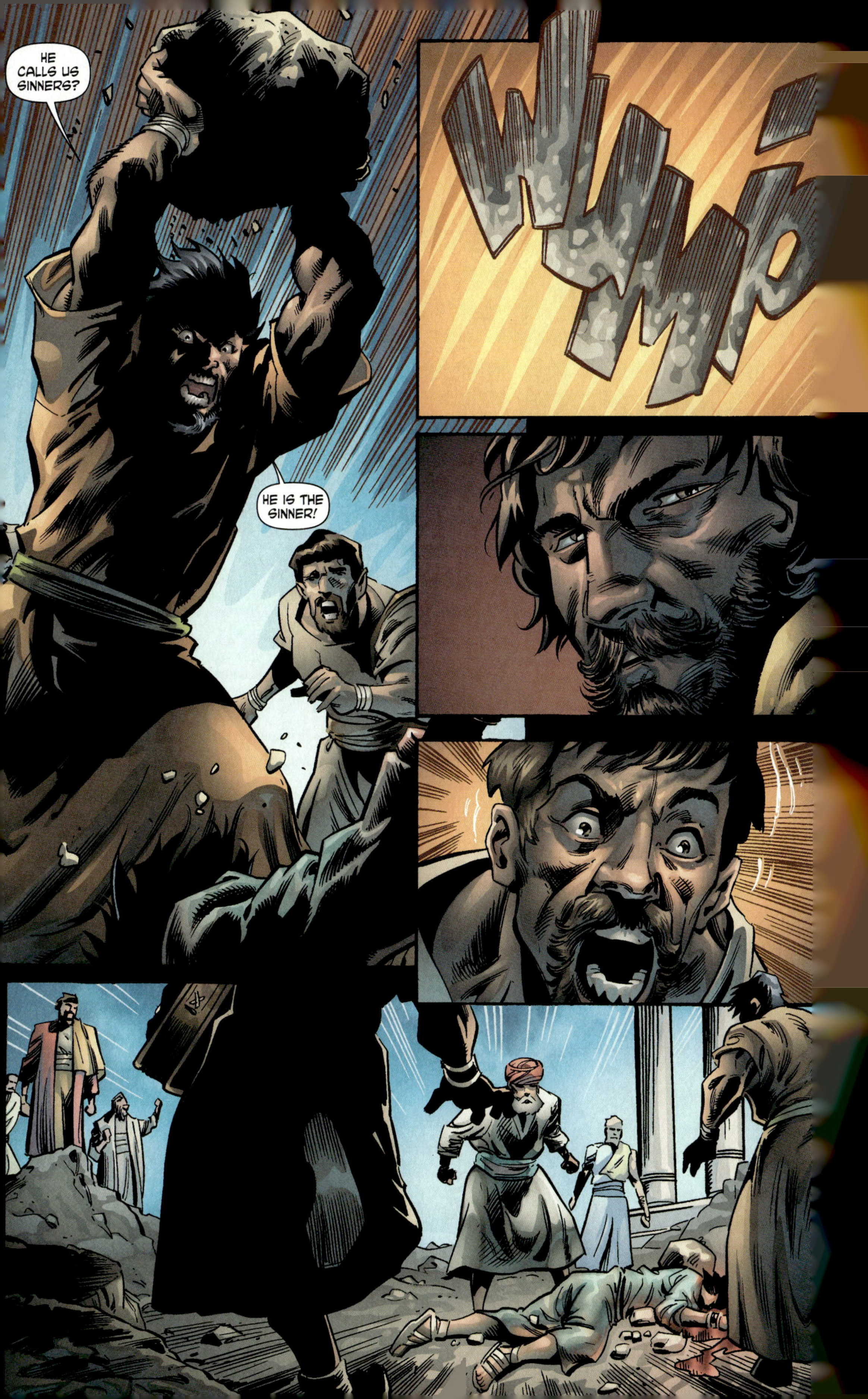
HE CALLS US SINNERS?
HE IS THE SINNER!
WUMP

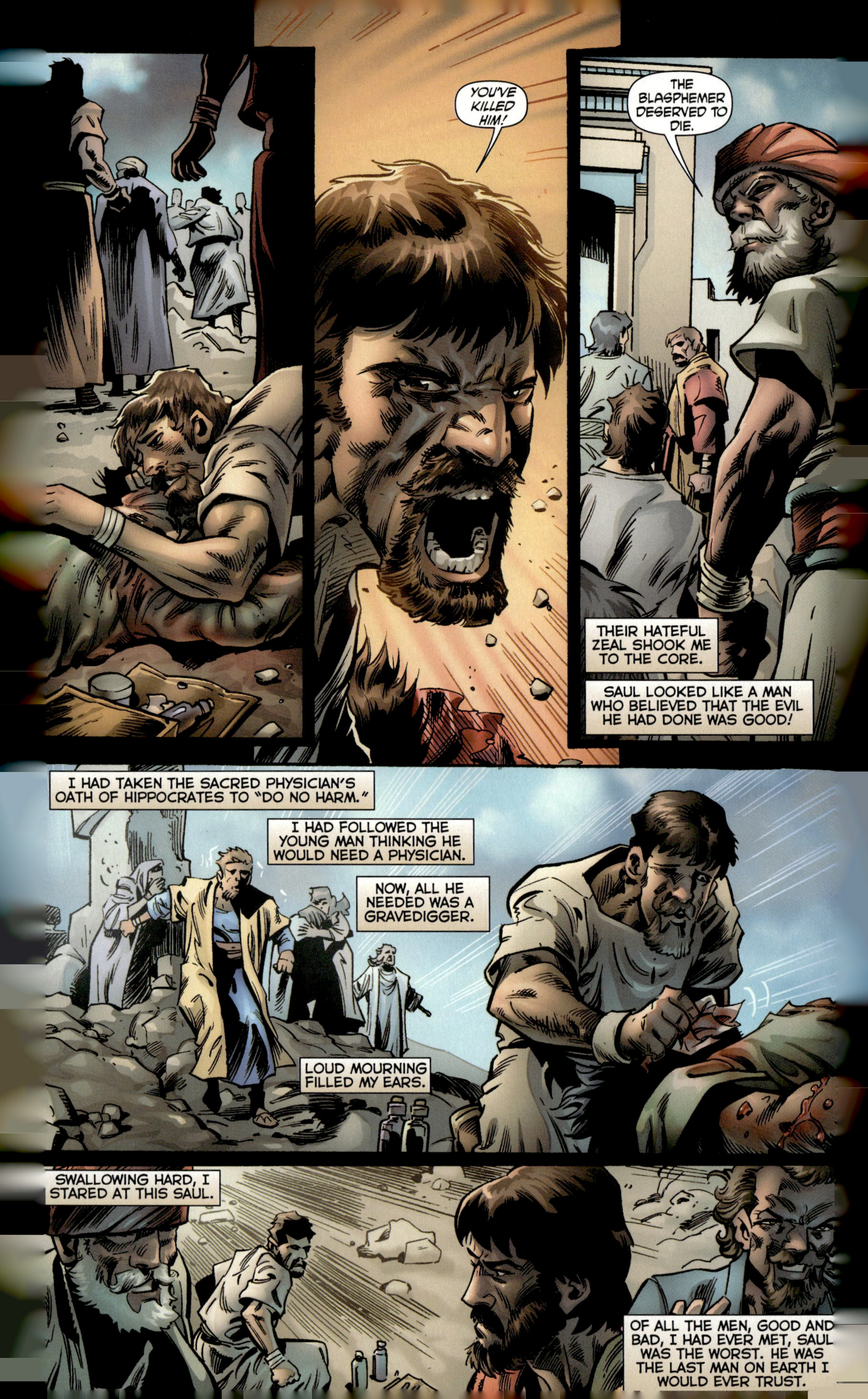
YOU'VE KILLED HIM!
THE BLASPHEMER DESERVED TO DIE.
THEIR HATEFUL ZEAL SHOOK ME TO THE CORE.
SAUL LOOKED LIKE A MAN WHO BELIEVED THAT THE EVIL HE HAD DONE WAS GOOD!
I HAD TAKEN THE SACRED PHYSICIAN'S OATH OF HIPPOCRATES TO "DO NO HARM."
I HAD FOLLOWED THE YOUNG MAN THINKING HE WOULD NEED A PHYSICIAN.
NOW, ALL HE NEEDED WAS A GRAVEDIGGER.
LOUD MOURNING FILLED MY EARS.
SWALLOWING HARD, I STARED AT THIS SAUL.
OF ALL THE MEN, GOOD AND BAD, I HAD EVER MET, SAUL WAS THE WORST. HE WAS THE LAST MAN ON EARTH I WOULD EVER TRUST.

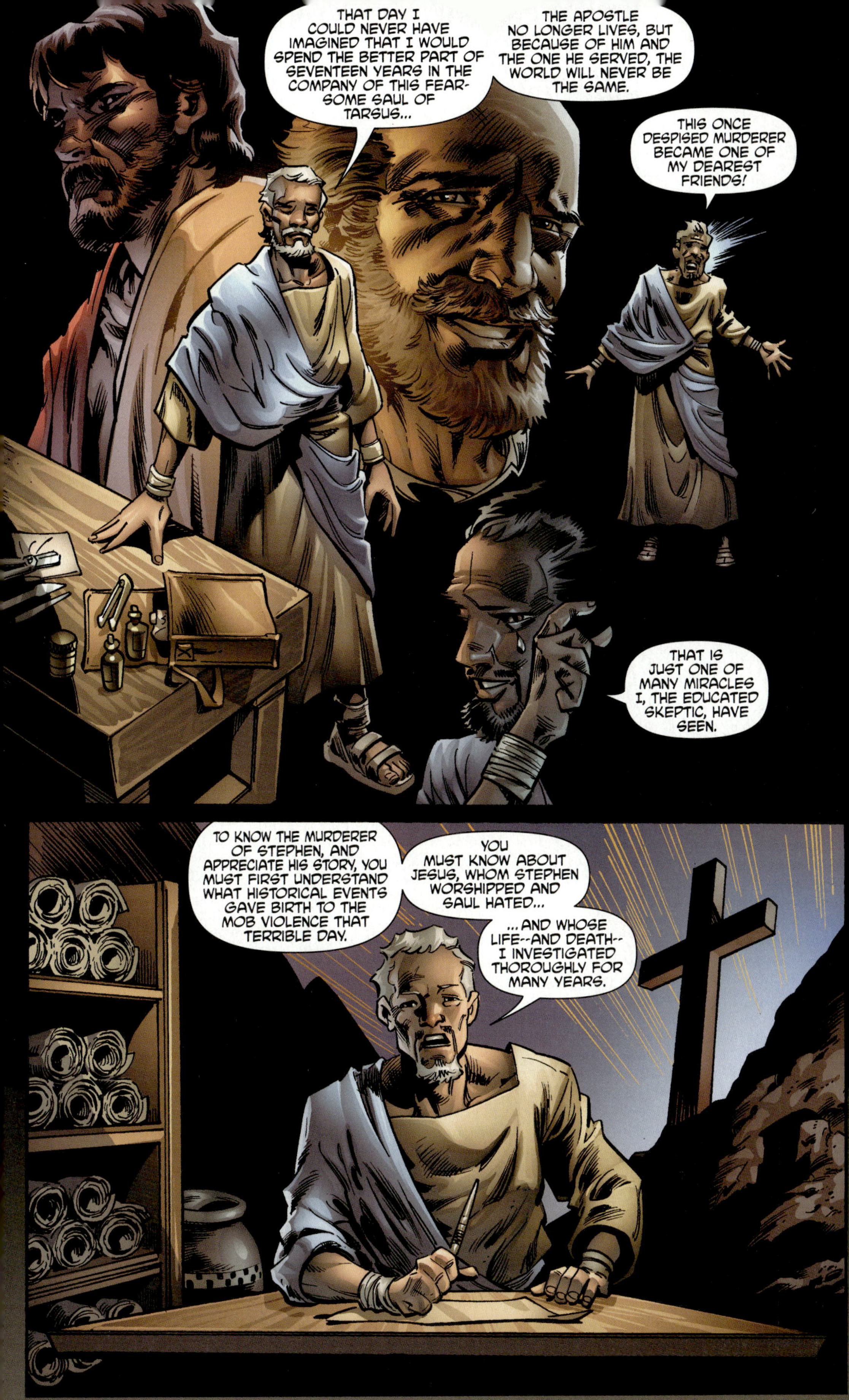
THAT DAY I COULD NEVER HAVE IMAGINED THAT I WOULD SPEND THE BETTER PART OF SEVENTEEN YEARS IN THE COMPANY OF THIS FEAR-SOME SAUL OF TARSUS...
THE APOSTLE NO LONGER LIVES, BUT BECAUSE OF HIM AND THE ONE HE SERVED, THE WORLD WILL NEVER BE THE SAME.
THIS ONCE DESPISED MURDERER BECAME ONE OF MY DEAREST FRIENDS!
THAT IS JUST ONE OF MANY MIRACLES I, THE EDUCATED SKEPTIC, HAVE SEEN.
TO KNOW THE MURDERER OF STEPHEN, AND APPRECIATE HIS STORY, YOU MUST FIRST UNDERSTAND WHAT HISTORICAL EVENTS GAVE BIRTH TO THE MOB VIOLENCE THAT TERRIBLE DAY.
YOU MUST KNOW ABOUT JESUS, WHOM STEPHEN WORSHIPPED AND SAUL HATED...
...AND WHOSE LIFE--AND DEATH--I INVESTIGATED THOROUGHLY FOR MANY YEARS.

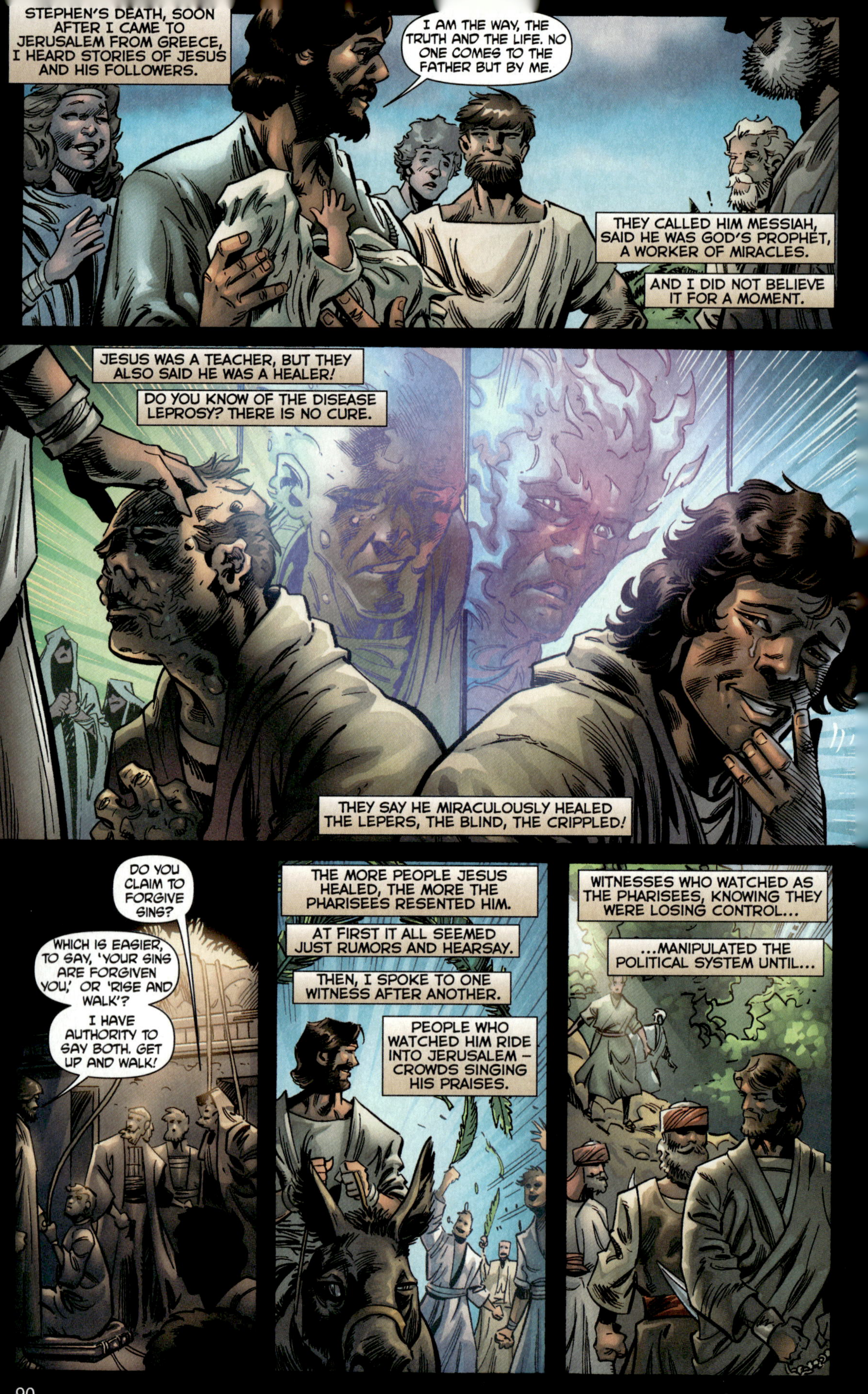
STEPHEN'S DEATH, SOON AFTER I CAME TO JERUSALEM FROM GREECE, I HEARD STORIES OF JESUS AND HIS FOLLOWERS.
I AM THE WAY, THE TRUTH AND THE LIFE. NO ONE COMES TO THE FATHER BUT BY ME.
THEY CALLED HIM MESSIAH, SAID HE WAS GOD'S PROPHET, A WORKER OF MIRACLES.
AND I DID NOT BELIEVE IT FOR A MOMENT.
JESUS WAS A TEACHER, BUT THEY ALSO SAID HE WAS A HEALER!
DO YOU KNOW OF THE DISEASE LEPROSY? THERE IS NO CURE.
THEY SAY HE MIRACULOUSLY HEALED THE LEPERS, THE BLIND, THE CRIPPLED!
DO YOU CLAIM TO FORGIVE SINS?
WHICH IS EASIER, TO SAY, 'YOUR SINS ARE FORGIVEN YOU,' OR 'RISE AND WALK'?
I HAVE AUTHORITY TO SAY BOTH. GET UP AND WALK!
THE MORE PEOPLE JESUS HEALED, THE MORE THE PHARISEES RESENTED HIM.
AT FIRST IT ALL SEEMED JUST RUMORS AND HEARSAY.
THEN, I SPOKE TO ONE WITNESS AFTER ANOTHER.
PEOPLE WHO WATCHED HIM RIDE INTO JERUSALEM – CROWDS SINGING HIS PRAISES.
WITNESSES WHO WATCHED AS THE PHARISEES, KNOWING THEY WERE LOSING CONTROL...
...MANIPULATED THE POLITICAL SYSTEM UNTIL...

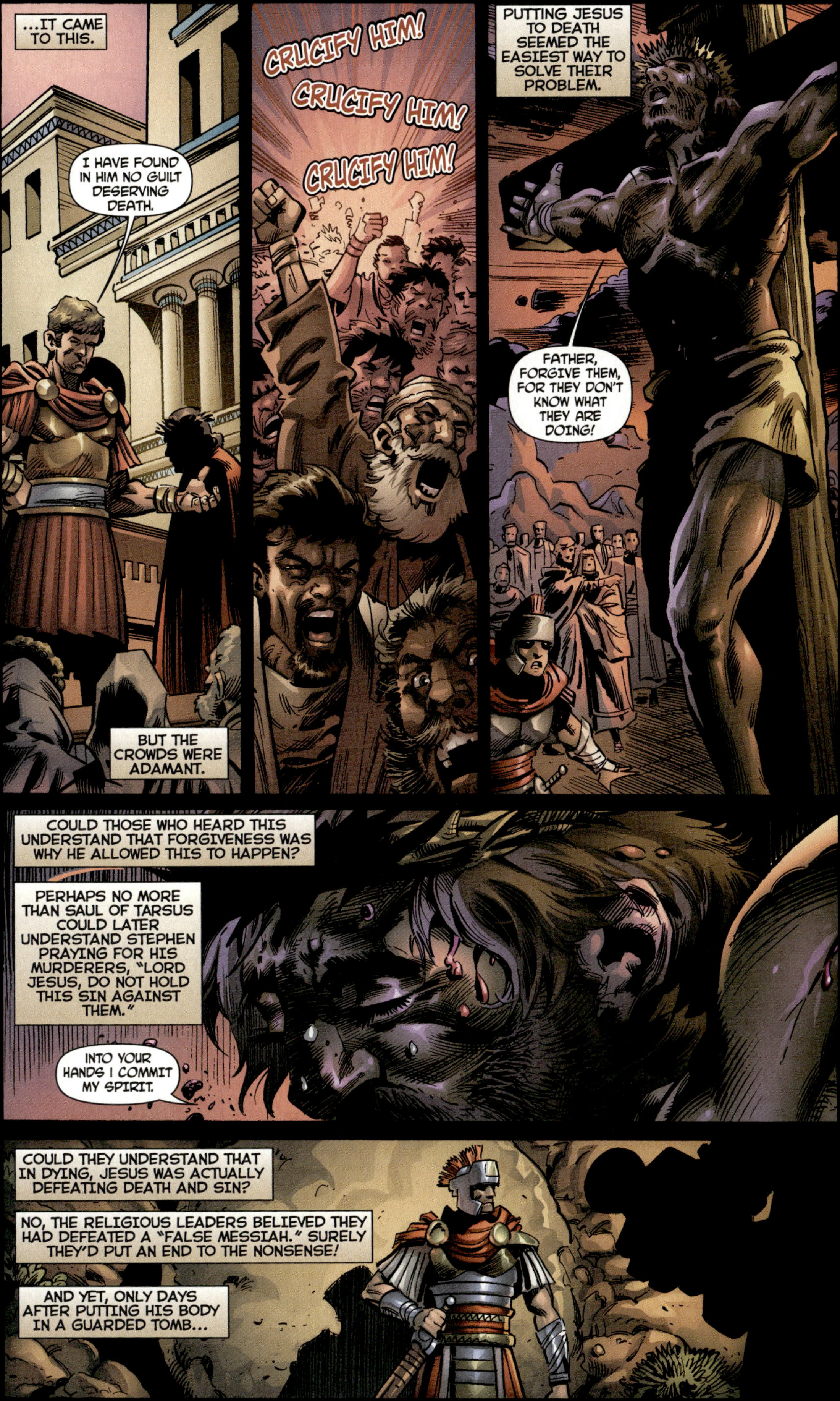
...IT CAME TO THIS.
I HAVE FOUND IN HIM NO GUILT DESERVING DEATH.
BUT THE CROWDS WERE ADAMANT.
CRUCIFY HIM!
CRUCIFY HIM!
CRUCIFY HIM!
PUTTING JESUS TO DEATH SEEMED THE EASIEST WAY TO SOLVE THEIR PROBLEM.
FATHER, FORGIVE THEM, FOR THEY DON'T KNOW WHAT THEY ARE DOING!
COULD THOSE WHO HEARD THIS UNDERSTAND THAT FORGIVENESS WAS WHY HE ALLOWED THIS TO HAPPEN?
PERHAPS NO MORE THAN SAUL OF TARSUS COULD LATER UNDERSTAND STEPHEN PRAYING FOR HIS MURDERERS, "LORD JESUS, DO NOT HOLD THIS SIN AGAINST THEM."
INTO YOUR HANDS I COMMIT MY SPIRIT.
COULD THEY UNDERSTAND THAT IN DYING, JESUS WAS ACTUALLY DEFEATING DEATH AND SIN?
NO, THE RELIGIOUS LEADERS BELIEVED THEY HAD DEFEATED A "FALSE MESSIAH." SURELY THEY'D PUT AN END TO THE NONSENSE!
AND YET, ONLY DAYS AFTER PUTTING HIS BODY IN A GUARDED TOMB...

LUKE 23:1-11, 20-25, 34, 46, 53; MATTHEW 27:65

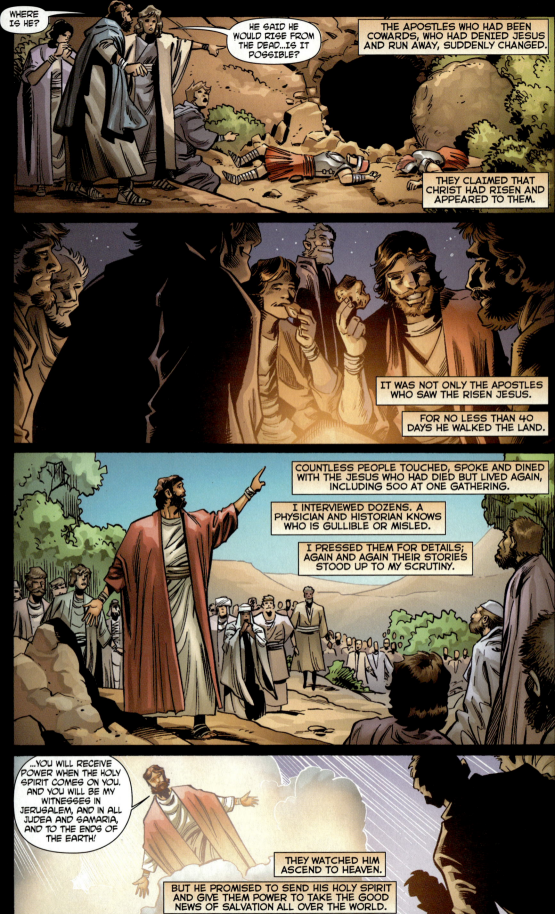

WHERE IS HE?

HE SAID HE WOULD RISE FROM THE DEAD...IS IT POSSIBLE?

THE APOSTLES WHO HAD BEEN COWARDS, WHO HAD DENIED JESUS AND RUN AWAY, SUDDENLY CHANGED.

THEY CLAIMED THAT CHRIST HAD RISEN AND APPEARED TO THEM.

IT WAS NOT ONLY THE APOSTLES WHO SAW THE RISEN JESUS.

FOR NO LESS THAN 40 DAYS HE WALKED THE LAND.

COUNTLESS PEOPLE TOUCHED, SPOKE AND DINED WITH THE JESUS WHO HAD DIED BUT LIVED AGAIN, INCLUDING 500 AT ONE GATHERING.

I INTERVIEWED DOZENS. A PHYSICIAN AND HISTORIAN KNOWS WHO IS GULLIBLE OR MISLED.

I PRESSED THEM FOR DETAILS; AGAIN AND AGAIN THEIR STORIES STOOD UP TO MY SCRUTINY.

...YOU WILL RECEIVE POWER WHEN THE HOLY SPIRIT COMES ON YOU. AND YOU WILL BE MY WITNESSES IN JERUSALEM, AND IN ALL JUDEA AND SAMARIA, AND TO THE ENDS OF THE EARTH!

THEY WATCHED HIM ASCEND TO HEAVEN.

BUT HE PROMISED TO SEND HIS HOLY SPIRIT AND GIVE THEM POWER TO TAKE THE GOOD NEWS OF SALVATION ALL OVER THE WORLD.

LUKE 24:1-12, 33-42; ACTS 1:3; 1 CORINTHIANS 15:6

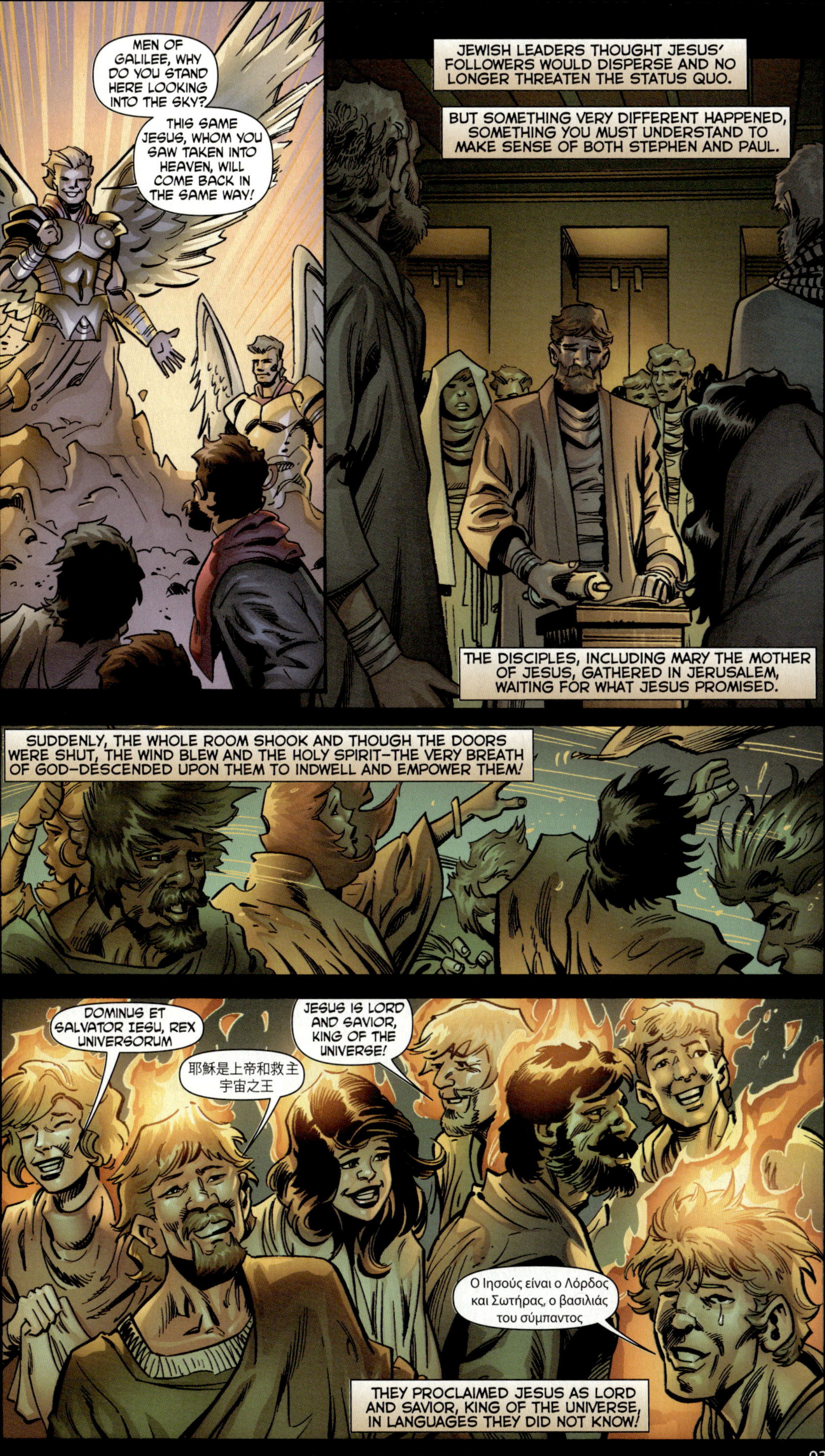
MEN OF GALILEE, WHY DO YOU STAND HERE LOOKING INTO THE SKY?
THIS SAME JESUS, WHOM YOU SAW TAKEN INTO HEAVEN, WILL COME BACK IN THE SAME WAY!
JEWISH LEADERS THOUGHT JESUS' FOLLOWERS WOULD DISPERSE AND NO LONGER THREATEN THE STATUS QUO.
BUT SOMETHING VERY DIFFERENT HAPPENED, SOMETHING YOU MUST UNDERSTAND TO MAKE SENSE OF BOTH STEPHEN AND PAUL.
THE DISCIPLES, INCLUDING MARY THE MOTHER OF JESUS, GATHERED IN JERUSALEM, WAITING FOR WHAT JESUS PROMISED.
SUDDENLY, THE WHOLE ROOM SHOOK AND THOUGH THE DOORS WERE SHUT, THE WIND BLEW AND THE HOLY SPIRIT—THE VERY BREATH OF GOD—DESCENDED UPON THEM TO INDWELL AND EMPOWER THEM!
DOMINUS ET SALVATOR IESU, REX UNIVERSORUM
耶稣是上帝和救主 宇宙之王
JESUS IS LORD AND SAVIOR, KING OF THE UNIVERSE!
Ο Ιησούς είναι ο Λόρδος και Σωτήρας, ο βασιλιάς του σύμπαντος
THEY PROCLAIMED JESUS AS LORD AND SAVIOR, KING OF THE UNIVERSE, IN LANGUAGES THEY DID NOT KNOW!

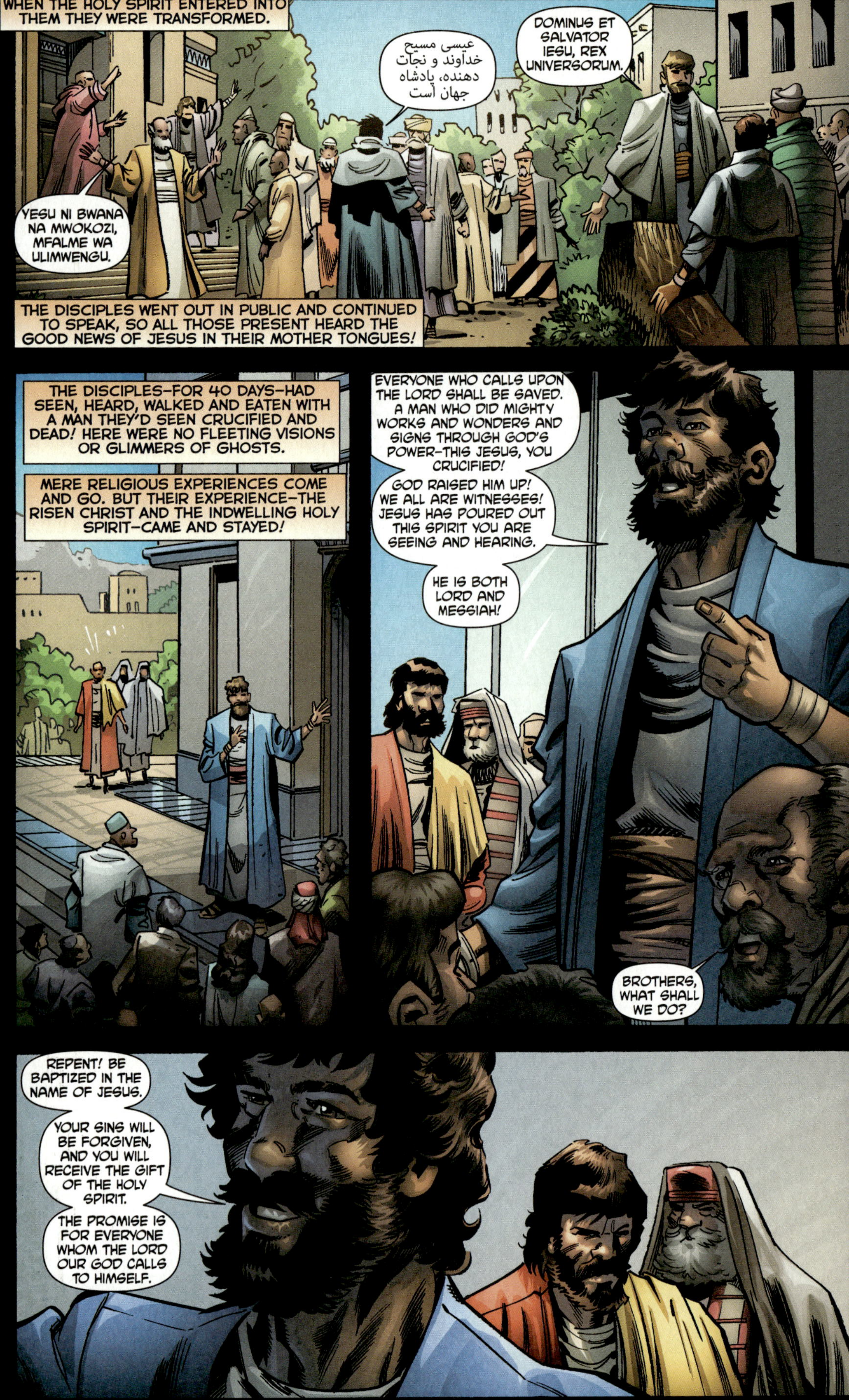
WHEN THE HOLY SPIRIT ENTERED INTO THEM THEY WERE TRANSFORMED.
عیسی مسیح خداوند و نجات دهنده، پادشاه جهان است
DOMINUS ET SALVATOR IESU, REX UNIVERSORUM.
YESU NI BWANA NA MWOKOZI, MFALME WA ULIMWENGU.
THE DISCIPLES WENT OUT IN PUBLIC AND CONTINUED TO SPEAK, SO ALL THOSE PRESENT HEARD THE GOOD NEWS OF JESUS IN THEIR MOTHER TONGUES!
THE DISCIPLES—FOR 40 DAYS—HAD SEEN, HEARD, WALKED AND EATEN WITH A MAN THEY'D SEEN CRUCIFIED AND DEAD! HERE WERE NO FLEETING VISIONS OR GLIMMERS OF GHOSTS.
MERE RELIGIOUS EXPERIENCES COME AND GO. BUT THEIR EXPERIENCE—THE RISEN CHRIST AND THE INDWELLING HOLY SPIRIT—CAME AND STAYED!
EVERYONE WHO CALLS UPON THE LORD SHALL BE SAVED. A MAN WHO DID MIGHTY WORKS AND WONDERS AND SIGNS THROUGH GOD'S POWER—THIS JESUS, YOU CRUCIFIED!
GOD RAISED HIM UP! WE ALL ARE WITNESSES! JESUS HAS POURED OUT THIS SPIRIT YOU ARE SEEING AND HEARING.
HE IS BOTH LORD AND MESSIAH!
BROTHERS, WHAT SHALL WE DO?
REPENT! BE BAPTIZED IN THE NAME OF JESUS.
YOUR SINS WILL BE FORGIVEN, AND YOU WILL RECEIVE THE GIFT OF THE HOLY SPIRIT.
THE PROMISE IS FOR EVERYONE WHOM THE LORD OUR GOD CALLS TO HIMSELF.

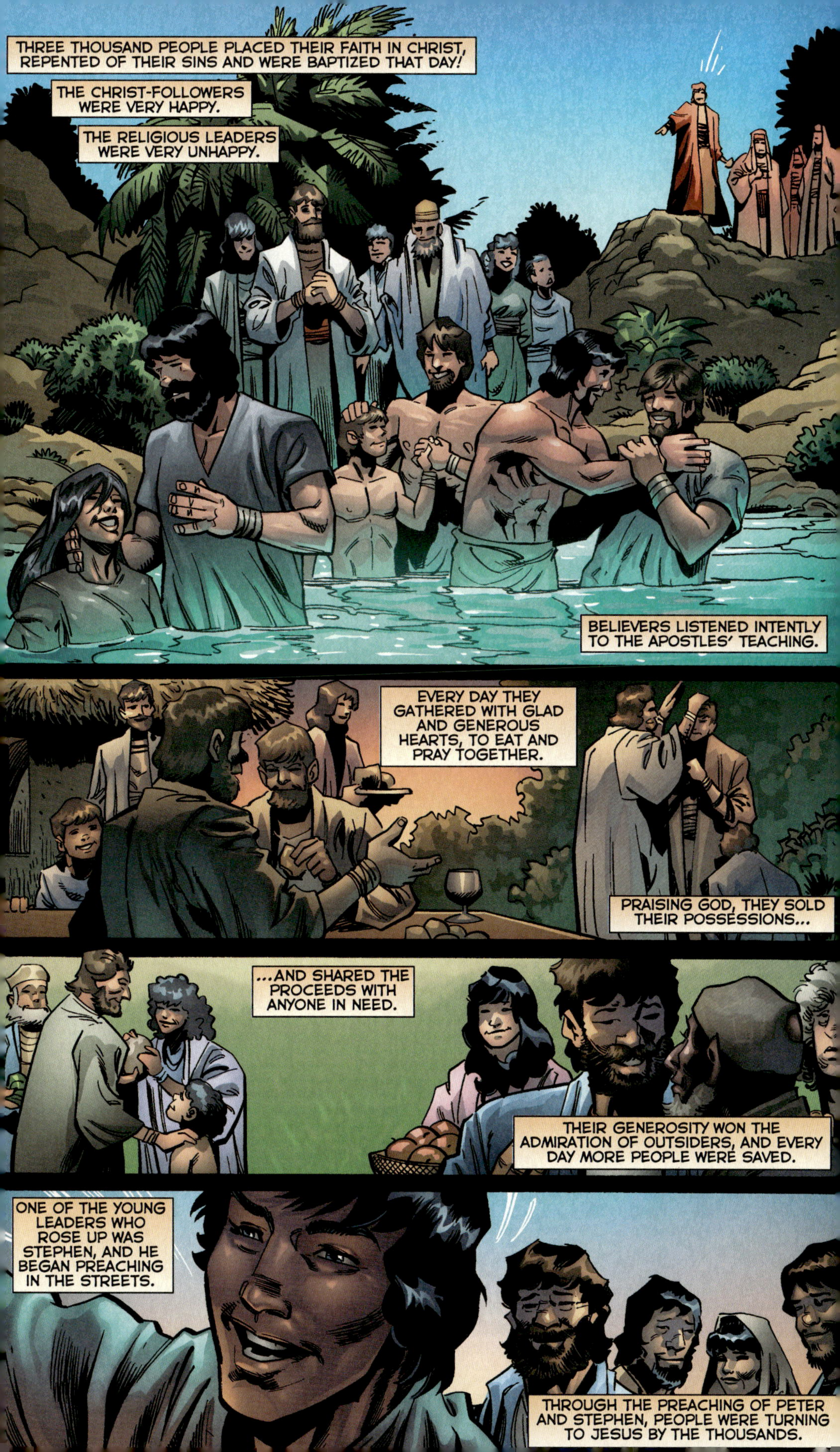
THREE THOUSAND PEOPLE PLACED THEIR FAITH IN CHRIST, REPENTED OF THEIR SINS AND WERE BAPTIZED THAT DAY!
THE CHRIST-FOLLOWERS WERE VERY HAPPY.
THE RELIGIOUS LEADERS WERE VERY UNHAPPY.
BELIEVERS LISTENED INTENTLY TO THE APOSTLES' TEACHING.
EVERY DAY THEY GATHERED WITH GLAD AND GENEROUS HEARTS, TO EAT AND PRAY TOGETHER.
PRAISING GOD, THEY SOLD THEIR POSSESSIONS...
...AND SHARED THE PROCEEDS WITH ANYONE IN NEED.
THEIR GENEROSITY WON THE ADMIRATION OF OUTSIDERS, AND EVERY DAY MORE PEOPLE WERE SAVED.
ONE OF THE YOUNG LEADERS WHO ROSE UP WAS STEPHEN, AND HE BEGAN PREACHING IN THE STREETS.
THROUGH THE PREACHING OF PETER AND STEPHEN, PEOPLE WERE TURNING TO JESUS BY THE THOUSANDS.

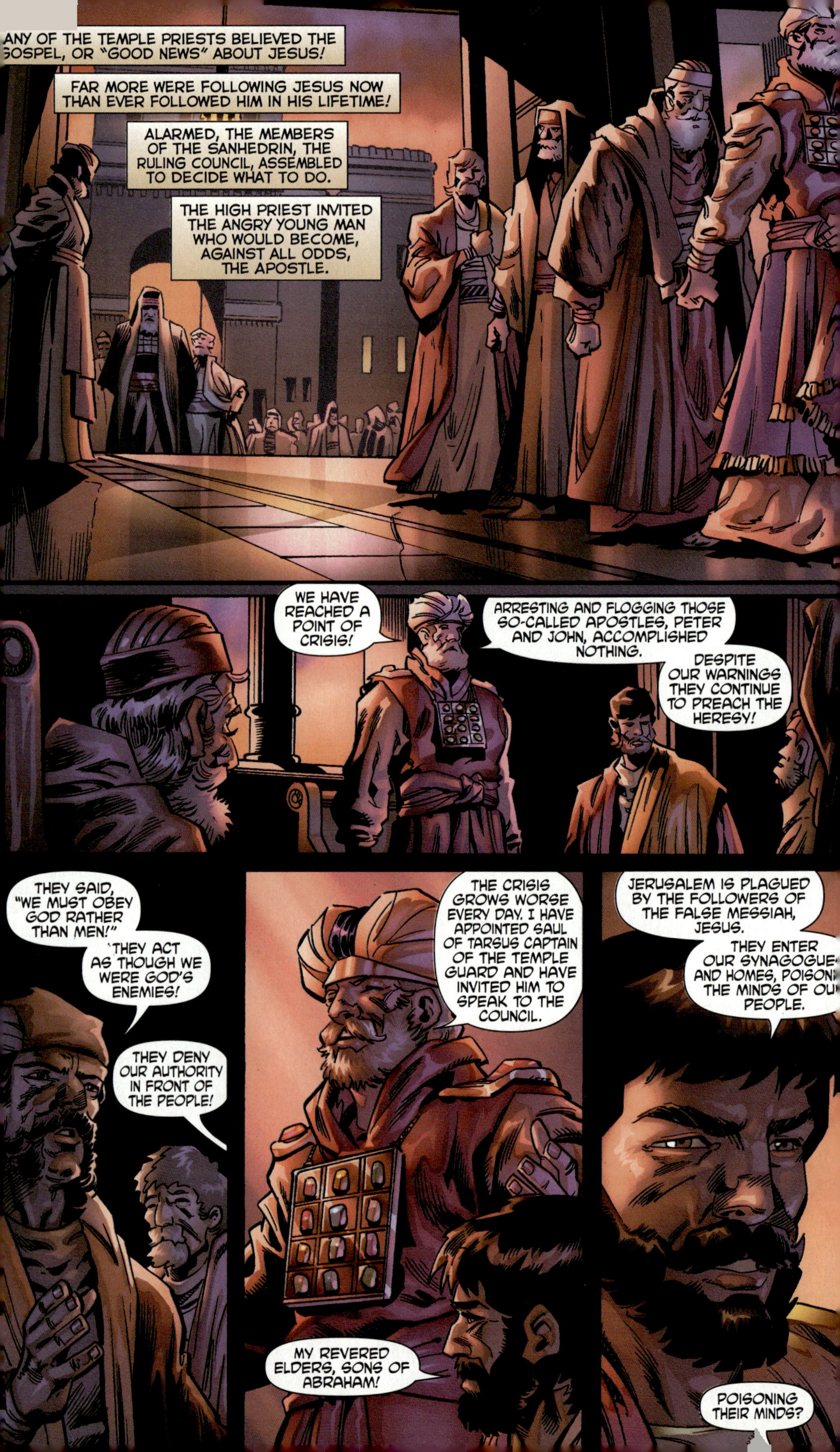

ANY OF THE TEMPLE PRIESTS BELIEVED THE GOSPEL, OR "GOOD NEWS" ABOUT JESUS!
FAR MORE WERE FOLLOWING JESUS NOW THAN EVER FOLLOWED HIM IN HIS LIFETIME!
ALARMED, THE MEMBERS OF THE SANHEDRIN, THE RULING COUNCIL, ASSEMBLED TO DECIDE WHAT TO DO.
THE HIGH PRIEST INVITED THE ANGRY YOUNG MAN WHO WOULD BECOME, AGAINST ALL ODDS, THE APOSTLE.
WE HAVE REACHED A POINT OF CRISIS!
ARRESTING AND FLOGGING THOSE SO-CALLED APOSTLES, PETER AND JOHN, ACCOMPLISHED NOTHING.
DESPITE OUR WARNINGS THEY CONTINUE TO PREACH THE HERESY!
THEY SAID, "WE MUST OBEY GOD RATHER THAN MEN!"
THEY ACT AS THOUGH WE WERE GOD'S ENEMIES!
THEY DENY OUR AUTHORITY IN FRONT OF THE PEOPLE!
THE CRISIS GROWS WORSE EVERY DAY. I HAVE APPOINTED SAUL OF TARSUS CAPTAIN OF THE TEMPLE GUARD AND HAVE INVITED HIM TO SPEAK TO THE COUNCIL.
MY REVERED ELDERS, SONS OF ABRAHAM!
JERUSALEM IS PLAGUED BY THE FOLLOWERS OF THE FALSE MESSIAH, JESUS.
THEY ENTER OUR SYNAGOGUES AND HOMES, POISONI THE MINDS OF OU PEOPLE.
POISONING THEIR MINDS?

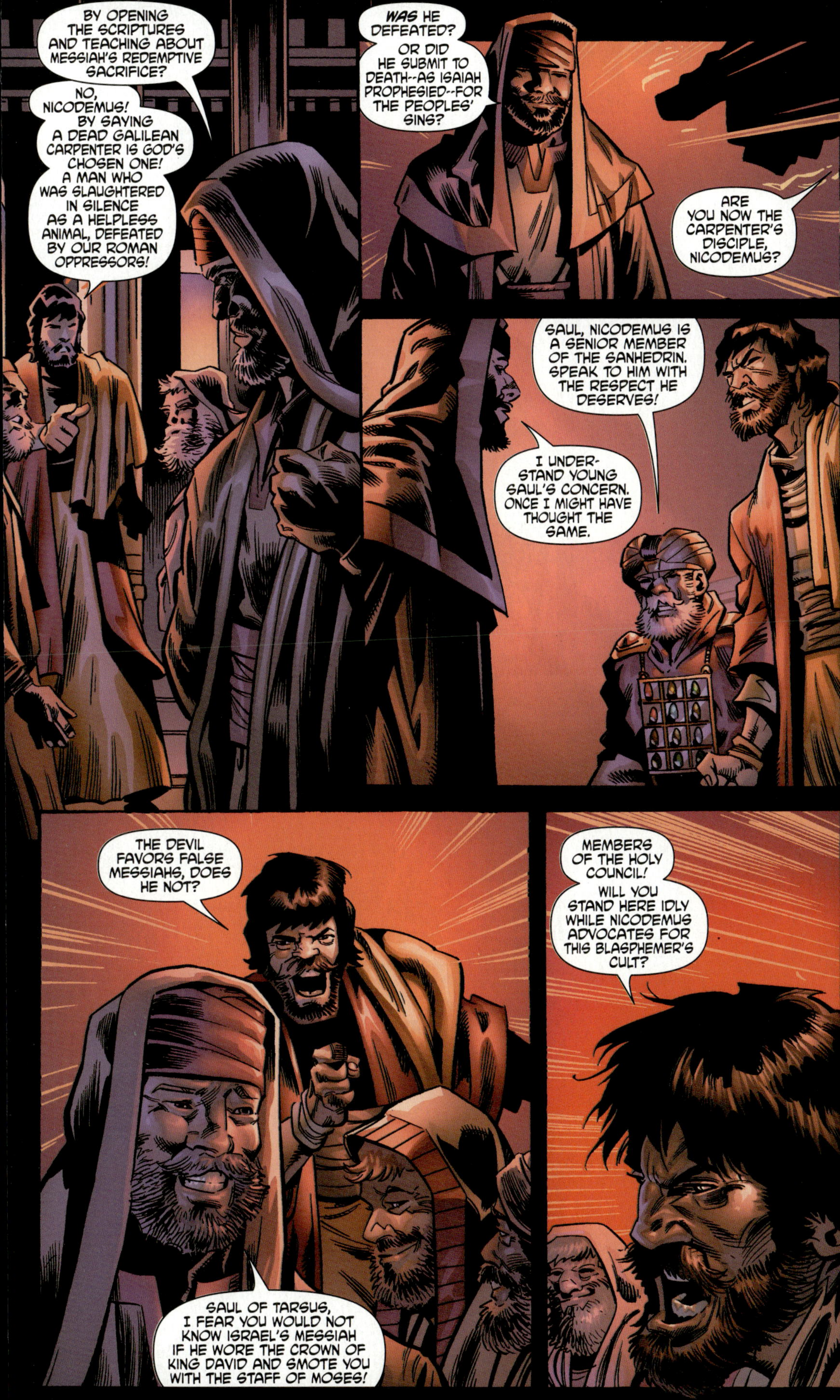
BY OPENING THE SCRIPTURES AND TEACHING ABOUT MESSIAH'S REDEMPTIVE SACRIFICE?
NO, NICODEMUS! BY SAYING A DEAD GALILEAN CARPENTER IS GOD'S CHOSEN ONE! A MAN WHO WAS SLAUGHTERED IN SILENCE AS A HELPLESS ANIMAL, DEFEATED BY OUR ROMAN OPPRESSORS!
WAS HE DEFEATED?
OR DID HE SUBMIT TO DEATH--AS ISAIAH PROPHESIED--FOR THE PEOPLES' SINS?
ARE YOU NOW THE CARPENTER'S DISCIPLE, NICODEMUS?
SAUL, NICODEMUS IS A SENIOR MEMBER OF THE SANHEDRIN. SPEAK TO HIM WITH THE RESPECT HE DESERVES!
I UNDER-STAND YOUNG SAUL'S CONCERN. ONCE I MIGHT HAVE THOUGHT THE SAME.
THE DEVIL FAVORS FALSE MESSIAHS, DOES HE NOT?
SAUL OF TARSUS, I FEAR YOU WOULD NOT KNOW ISRAEL'S MESSIAH IF HE WORE THE CROWN OF KING DAVID AND SMOTE YOU WITH THE STAFF OF MOSES!
MEMBERS OF THE HOLY COUNCIL!
WILL YOU STAND HERE IDLY WHILE NICODEMUS ADVOCATES FOR THIS BLASPHEMER'S CULT?

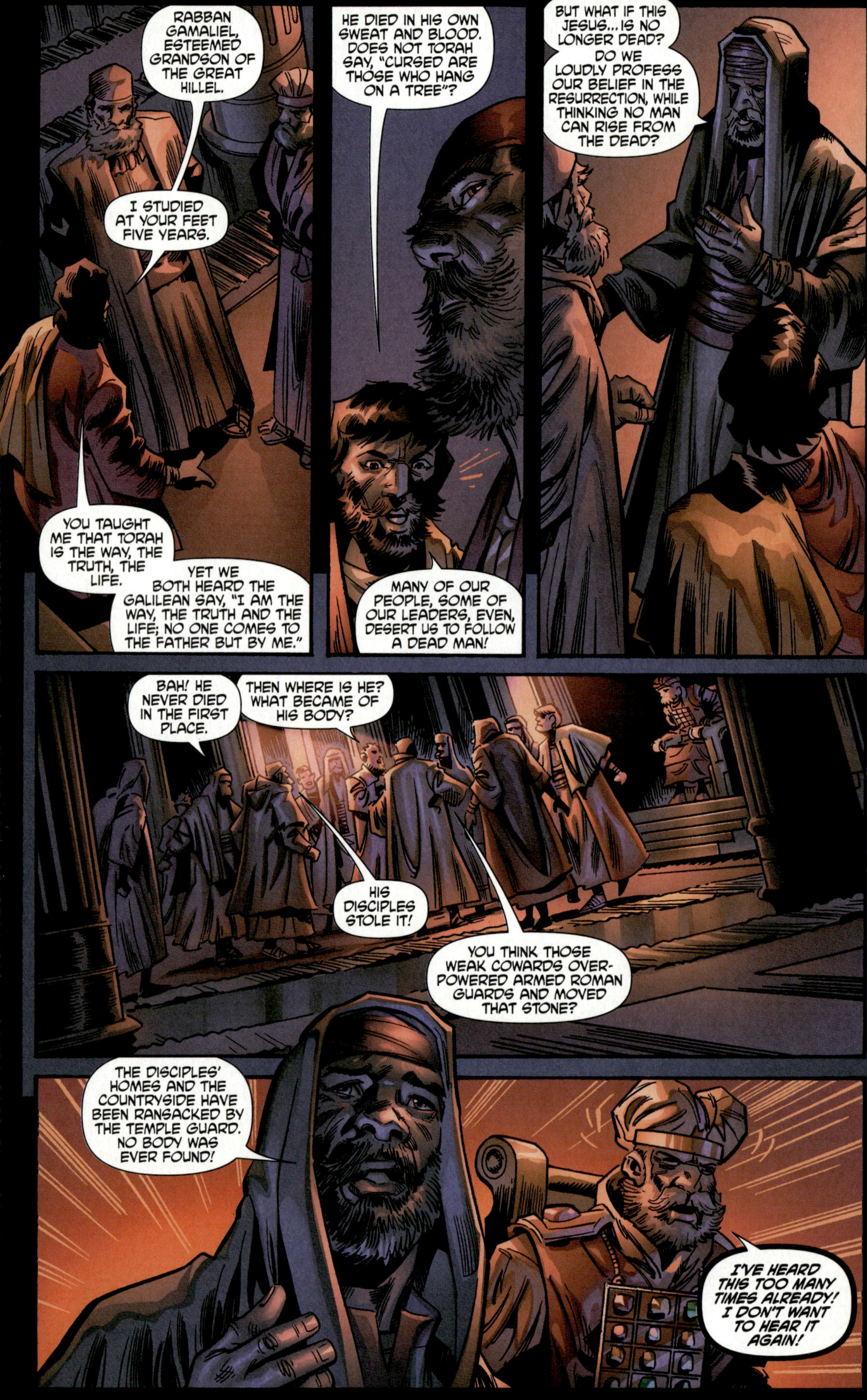
RABBAN GAMALIEL, ESTEEMED GRANDSON OF THE GREAT HILLEL.
I STUDIED AT YOUR FEET FIVE YEARS.
YOU TAUGHT ME THAT TORAH IS THE WAY, THE TRUTH, THE LIFE.
YET WE BOTH HEARD THE GALILEAN SAY, "I AM THE WAY, THE TRUTH AND THE LIFE; NO ONE COMES TO THE FATHER BUT BY ME."
HE DIED IN HIS OWN SWEAT AND BLOOD. DOES NOT TORAH SAY, "CURSED ARE THOSE WHO HANG ON A TREE"?
MANY OF OUR PEOPLE, SOME OF OUR LEADERS, EVEN, DESERT US TO FOLLOW A DEAD MAN!
BUT WHAT IF THIS JESUS... IS NO LONGER DEAD?
DO WE LOUDLY PROFESS OUR BELIEF IN THE RESURRECTION, WHILE THINKING NO MAN CAN RISE FROM THE DEAD?
BAH! HE NEVER DIED IN THE FIRST PLACE.
THEN WHERE IS HE? WHAT BECAME OF HIS BODY?
HIS DISCIPLES STOLE IT!
YOU THINK THOSE WEAK COWARDS OVER-POWERED ARMED ROMAN GUARDS AND MOVED THAT STONE?
THE DISCIPLES' HOMES AND THE COUNTRYSIDE HAVE BEEN RANSACKED BY THE TEMPLE GUARD. NO BODY WAS EVER FOUND!
I'VE HEARD THIS TOO MANY TIMES ALREADY! I DON'T WANT TO HEAR IT AGAIN!

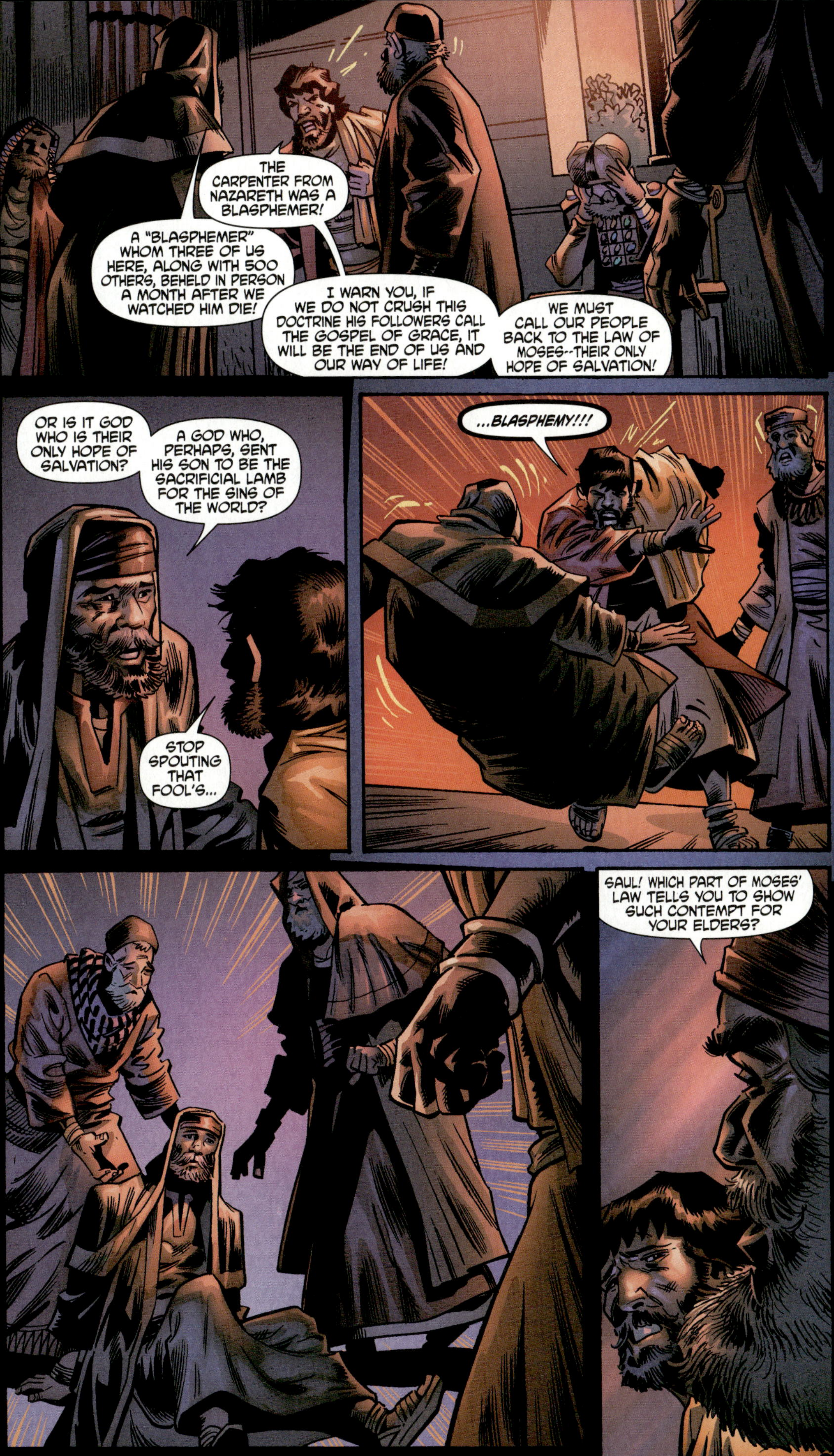
THE CARPENTER FROM NAZARETH WAS A BLASPHEMER!
A "BLASPHEMER" WHOM THREE OF US HERE, ALONG WITH 500 OTHERS, BEHELD IN PERSON A MONTH AFTER WE WATCHED HIM DIE!
I WARN YOU, IF WE DO NOT CRUSH THIS DOCTRINE HIS FOLLOWERS CALL THE GOSPEL OF GRACE, IT WILL BE THE END OF US AND OUR WAY OF LIFE!
WE MUST CALL OUR PEOPLE BACK TO THE LAW OF MOSES--THEIR ONLY HOPE OF SALVATION!
OR IS IT GOD WHO IS THEIR ONLY HOPE OF SALVATION?
A GOD WHO, PERHAPS, SENT HIS SON TO BE THE SACRIFICIAL LAMB FOR THE SINS OF THE WORLD?
STOP SPOUTING THAT FOOL'S...
...BLASPHEMY!!!
SAUL! WHICH PART OF MOSES' LAW TELLS YOU TO SHOW SUCH CONTEMPT FOR YOUR ELDERS?

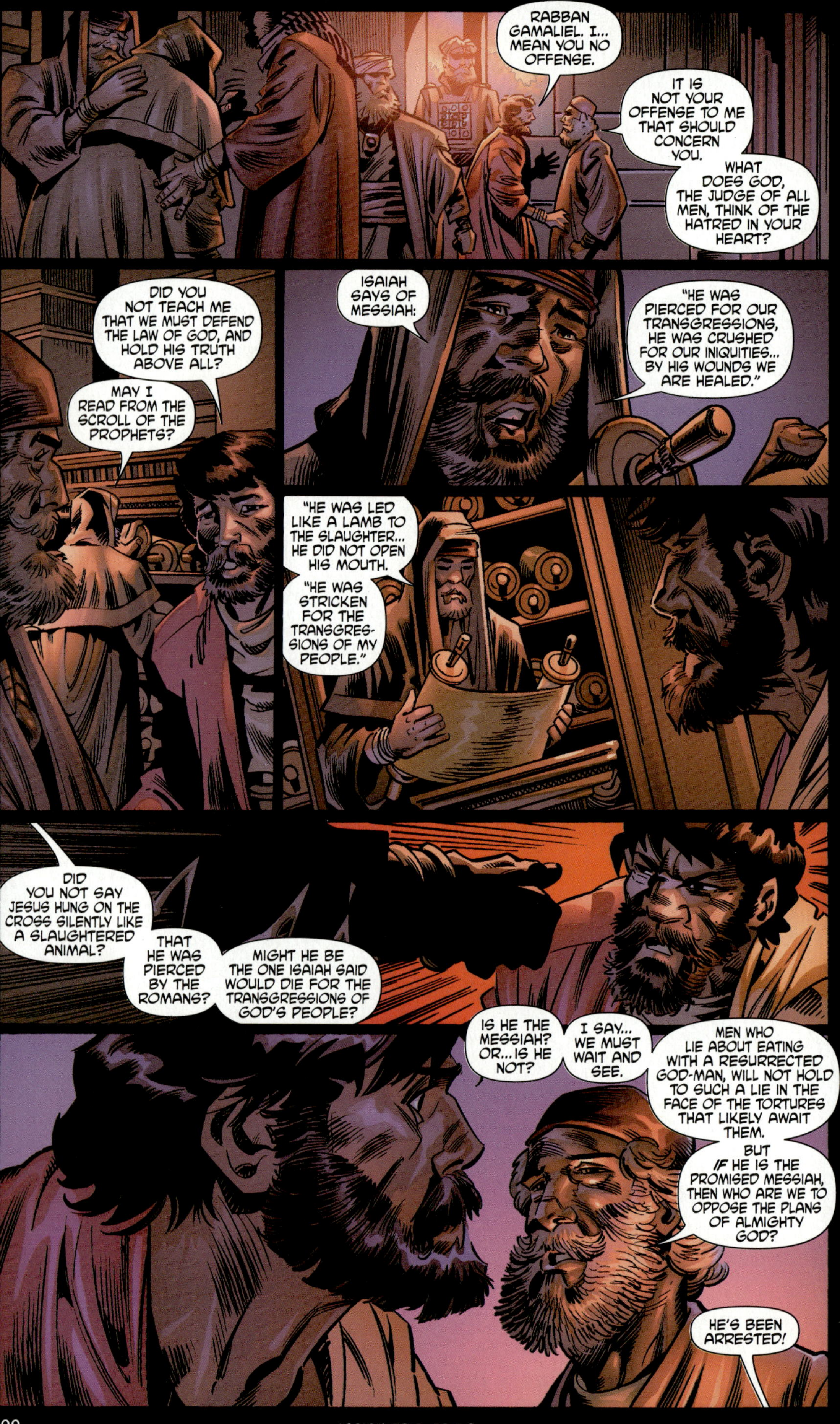
RABBAN GAMALIEL. I... MEAN YOU NO OFFENSE.
IT IS NOT YOUR OFFENSE TO ME THAT SHOULD CONCERN YOU.
WHAT DOES GOD, THE JUDGE OF ALL MEN, THINK OF THE HATRED IN YOUR HEART?
DID YOU NOT TEACH ME THAT WE MUST DEFEND THE LAW OF GOD, AND HOLD HIS TRUTH ABOVE ALL?
MAY I READ FROM THE SCROLL OF THE PROPHETS?
ISAIAH SAYS OF MESSIAH:
"HE WAS PIERCED FOR OUR TRANSGRESSIONS, HE WAS CRUSHED FOR OUR INIQUITIES... BY HIS WOUNDS WE ARE HEALED."
"HE WAS LED LIKE A LAMB TO THE SLAUGHTER... HE DID NOT OPEN HIS MOUTH.
"HE WAS STRICKEN FOR THE TRANSGRES-SIONS OF MY PEOPLE."
DID YOU NOT SAY JESUS HUNG ON THE CROSS SILENTLY LIKE A SLAUGHTERED ANIMAL?
THAT HE WAS PIERCED BY THE ROMANS?
MIGHT HE BE THE ONE ISAIAH SAID WOULD DIE FOR THE TRANSGRESSIONS OF GOD'S PEOPLE?
IS HE THE MESSIAH? OR... IS HE NOT?
I SAY... WE MUST WAIT AND SEE.
MEN WHO LIE ABOUT EATING WITH A RESURRECTED GOD-MAN, WILL NOT HOLD TO SUCH A LIE IN THE FACE OF THE TORTURES THAT LIKELY AWAIT THEM.
BUT *IF* HE IS THE PROMISED MESSIAH, THEN WHO ARE WE TO OPPOSE THE PLANS OF ALMIGHTY GOD?
HE'S BEEN ARRESTED!

ISAIAH 53:5, 53:7-8

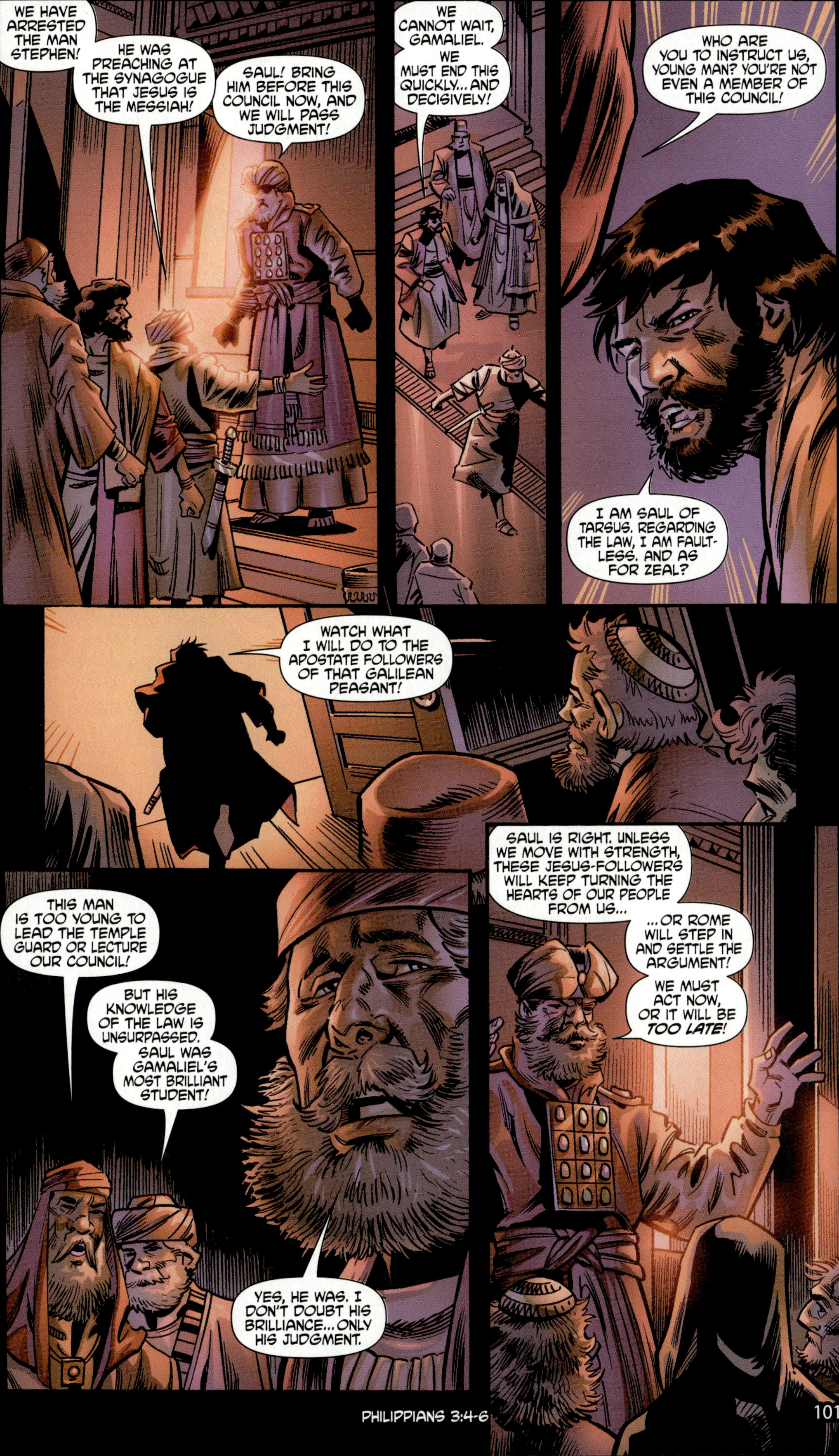
WE HAVE ARRESTED THE MAN STEPHEN!
HE WAS PREACHING AT THE SYNAGOGUE THAT JESUS IS THE MESSIAH!
SAUL! BRING HIM BEFORE THIS COUNCIL NOW, AND WE WILL PASS JUDGMENT!
WE CANNOT WAIT, GAMALIEL.
WE MUST END THIS QUICKLY...AND DECISIVELY!
WHO ARE YOU TO INSTRUCT US, YOUNG MAN? YOU'RE NOT EVEN A MEMBER OF THIS COUNCIL!
I AM SAUL OF TARSUS. REGARDING THE LAW, I AM FAULT-LESS. AND AS FOR ZEAL?
WATCH WHAT I WILL DO TO THE APOSTATE FOLLOWERS OF THAT GALILEAN PEASANT!
THIS MAN IS TOO YOUNG TO LEAD THE TEMPLE GUARD OR LECTURE OUR COUNCIL!
BUT HIS KNOWLEDGE OF THE LAW IS UNSURPASSED.
SAUL WAS GAMALIEL'S MOST BRILLIANT STUDENT!
YES, HE WAS. I DON'T DOUBT HIS BRILLIANCE...ONLY HIS JUDGMENT.
SAUL IS RIGHT. UNLESS WE MOVE WITH STRENGTH, THESE JESUS-FOLLOWERS WILL KEEP TURNING THE HEARTS OF OUR PEOPLE FROM US...
...OR ROME WILL STEP IN AND SETTLE THE ARGUMENT!
WE MUST ACT NOW, OR IT WILL BE *TOO LATE*!
PHILIPPIANS 3:4-6

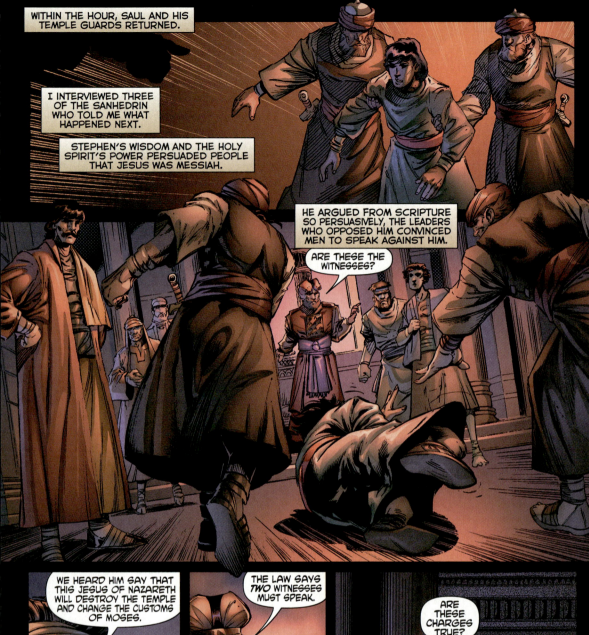

WITHIN THE HOUR, SAUL AND HIS TEMPLE GUARDS RETURNED.

I INTERVIEWED THREE OF THE SANHEDRIN WHO TOLD ME WHAT HAPPENED NEXT.

STEPHEN'S WISDOM AND THE HOLY SPIRIT'S POWER PERSUADED PEOPLE THAT JESUS WAS MESSIAH.

HE ARGUED FROM SCRIPTURE SO PERSUASIVELY, THE LEADERS WHO OPPOSED HIM CONVINCED MEN TO SPEAK AGAINST HIM.

ARE THESE THE WITNESSES?

WE HEARD HIM SAY THAT THIS JESUS OF NAZARETH WILL DESTROY THE TEMPLE AND CHANGE THE CUSTOMS OF MOSES.

THE LAW SAYS *TWO* WITNESSES MUST SPEAK.

UH, WELL... I SAY...WHAT *HE* SAID!

ARE THESE CHARGES TRUE?

YOUNG STEPHEN STOOD, CONFIDENT IN HIS BELIEFS AND OBVIOUSLY MORE RIGHTEOUS THAN HIS ACCUSERS!

DEUTERONOMY 19:15

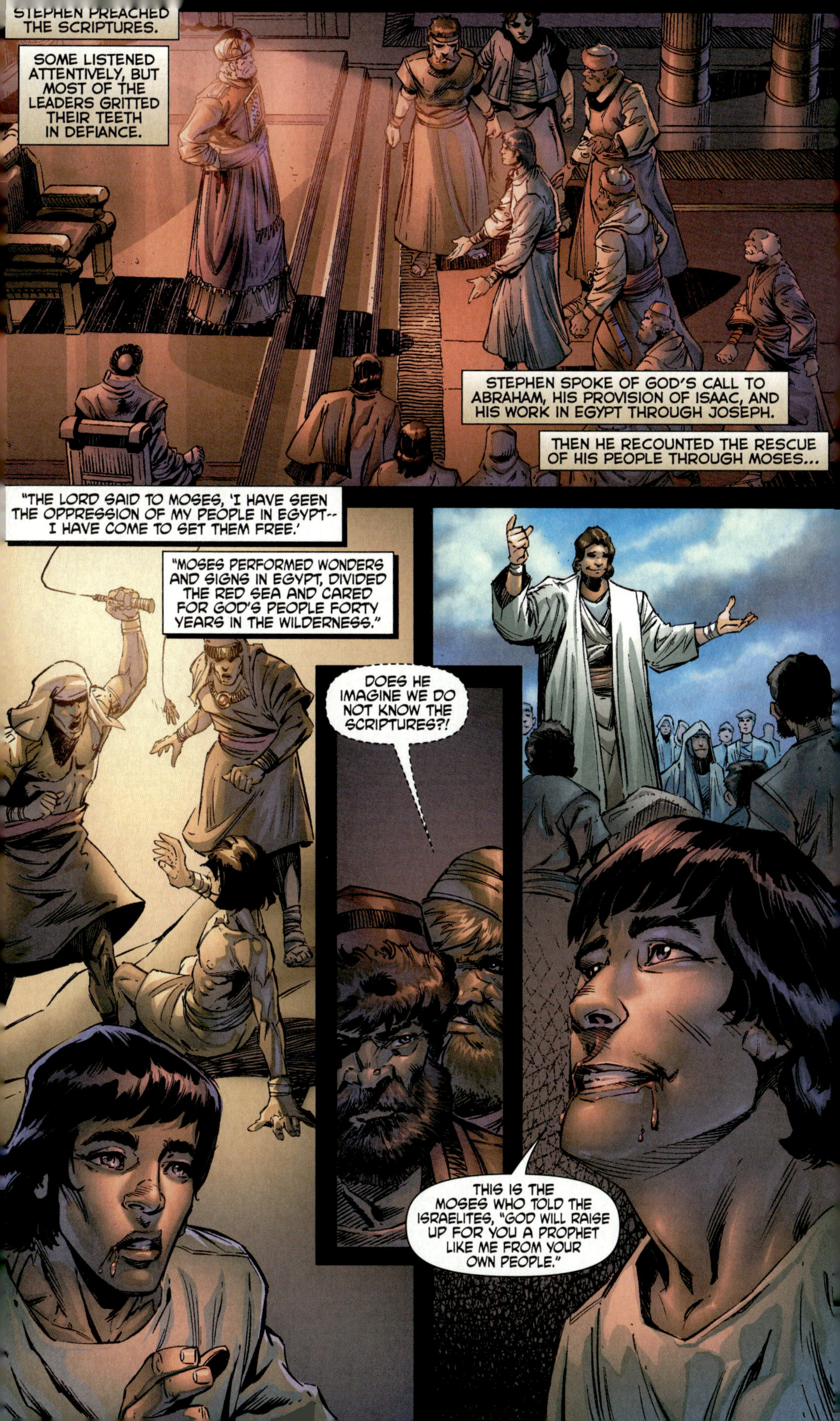
STEPHEN PREACHED THE SCRIPTURES.
SOME LISTENED ATTENTIVELY, BUT MOST OF THE LEADERS GRITTED THEIR TEETH IN DEFIANCE.
STEPHEN SPOKE OF GOD'S CALL TO ABRAHAM, HIS PROVISION OF ISAAC, AND HIS WORK IN EGYPT THROUGH JOSEPH.
THEN HE RECOUNTED THE RESCUE OF HIS PEOPLE THROUGH MOSES...
"THE LORD SAID TO MOSES, 'I HAVE SEEN THE OPPRESSION OF MY PEOPLE IN EGYPT-- I HAVE COME TO SET THEM FREE.'
"MOSES PERFORMED WONDERS AND SIGNS IN EGYPT, DIVIDED THE RED SEA AND CARED FOR GOD'S PEOPLE FORTY YEARS IN THE WILDERNESS."
DOES HE IMAGINE WE DO NOT KNOW THE SCRIPTURES?!
THIS IS THE MOSES WHO TOLD THE ISRAELITES, "GOD WILL RAISE UP FOR YOU A PROPHET LIKE ME FROM YOUR OWN PEOPLE."

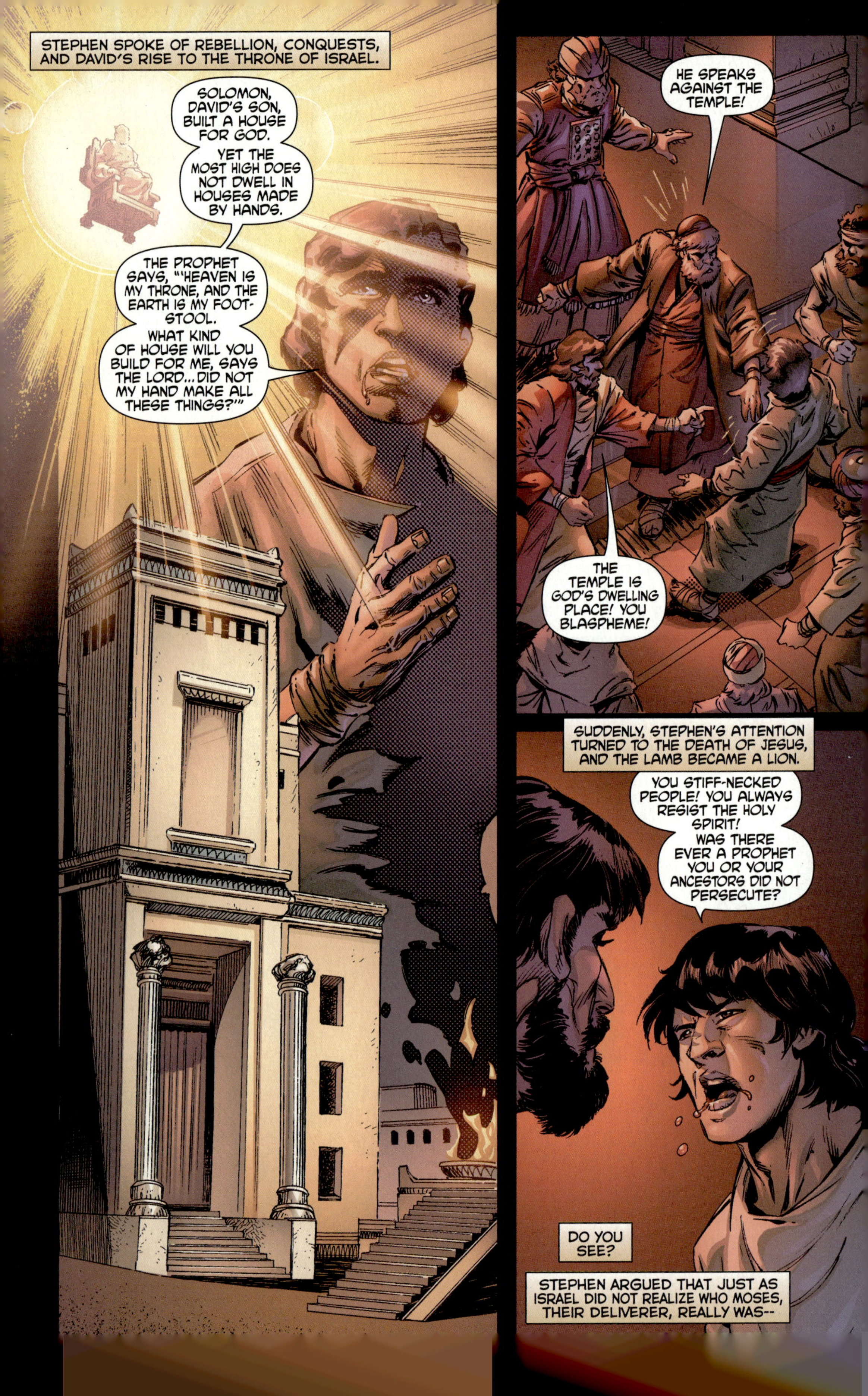
STEPHEN SPOKE OF REBELLION, CONQUESTS, AND DAVID'S RISE TO THE THRONE OF ISRAEL.
SOLOMON, DAVID'S SON, BUILT A HOUSE FOR GOD.
YET THE MOST HIGH DOES NOT DWELL IN HOUSES MADE BY HANDS.
THE PROPHET SAYS, "'HEAVEN IS MY THRONE, AND THE EARTH IS MY FOOT-STOOL.
WHAT KIND OF HOUSE WILL YOU BUILD FOR ME, SAYS THE LORD...DID NOT MY HAND MAKE ALL THESE THINGS?'"
HE SPEAKS AGAINST THE TEMPLE!
THE TEMPLE IS GOD'S DWELLING PLACE! YOU BLASPHEME!
SUDDENLY, STEPHEN'S ATTENTION TURNED TO THE DEATH OF JESUS, AND THE LAMB BECAME A LION.
YOU STIFF-NECKED PEOPLE! YOU ALWAYS RESIST THE HOLY SPIRIT!
WAS THERE EVER A PROPHET YOU OR YOUR ANCESTORS DID NOT PERSECUTE?
DO YOU SEE?
STEPHEN ARGUED THAT JUST AS ISRAEL DID NOT REALIZE WHO MOSES, THEIR DELIVERER, REALLY WAS--

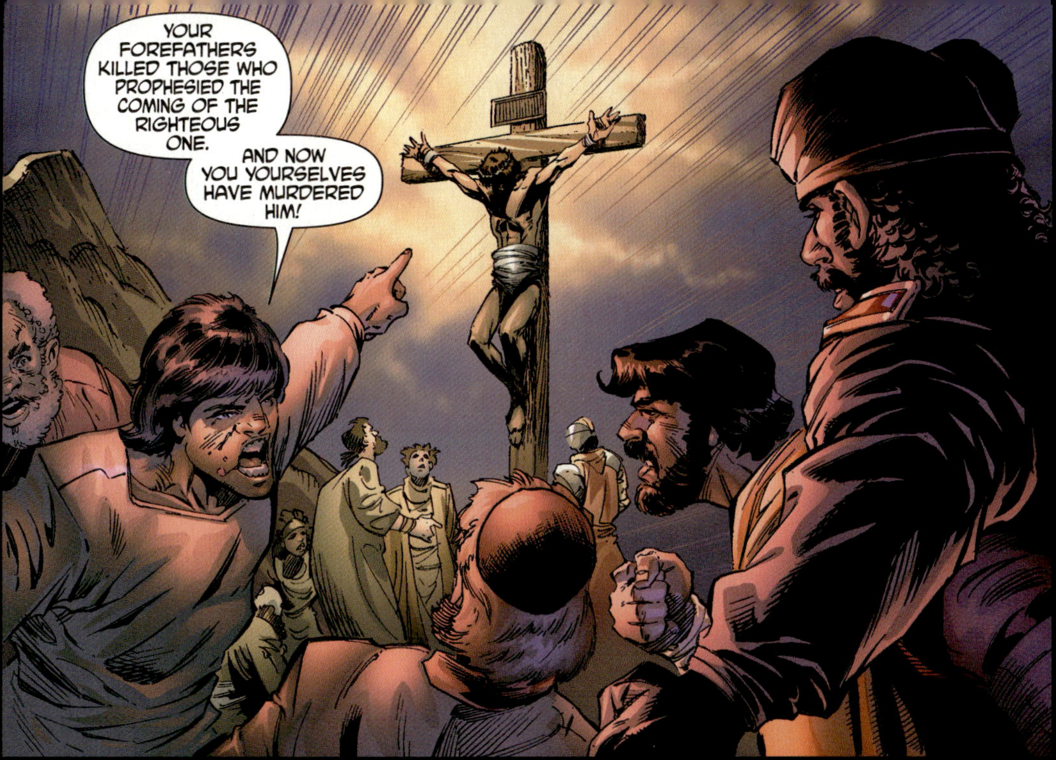
YOUR FOREFATHERS KILLED THOSE WHO PROPHESIED THE COMING OF THE RIGHTEOUS ONE.
AND NOW YOU YOURSELVES HAVE MURDERED HIM!

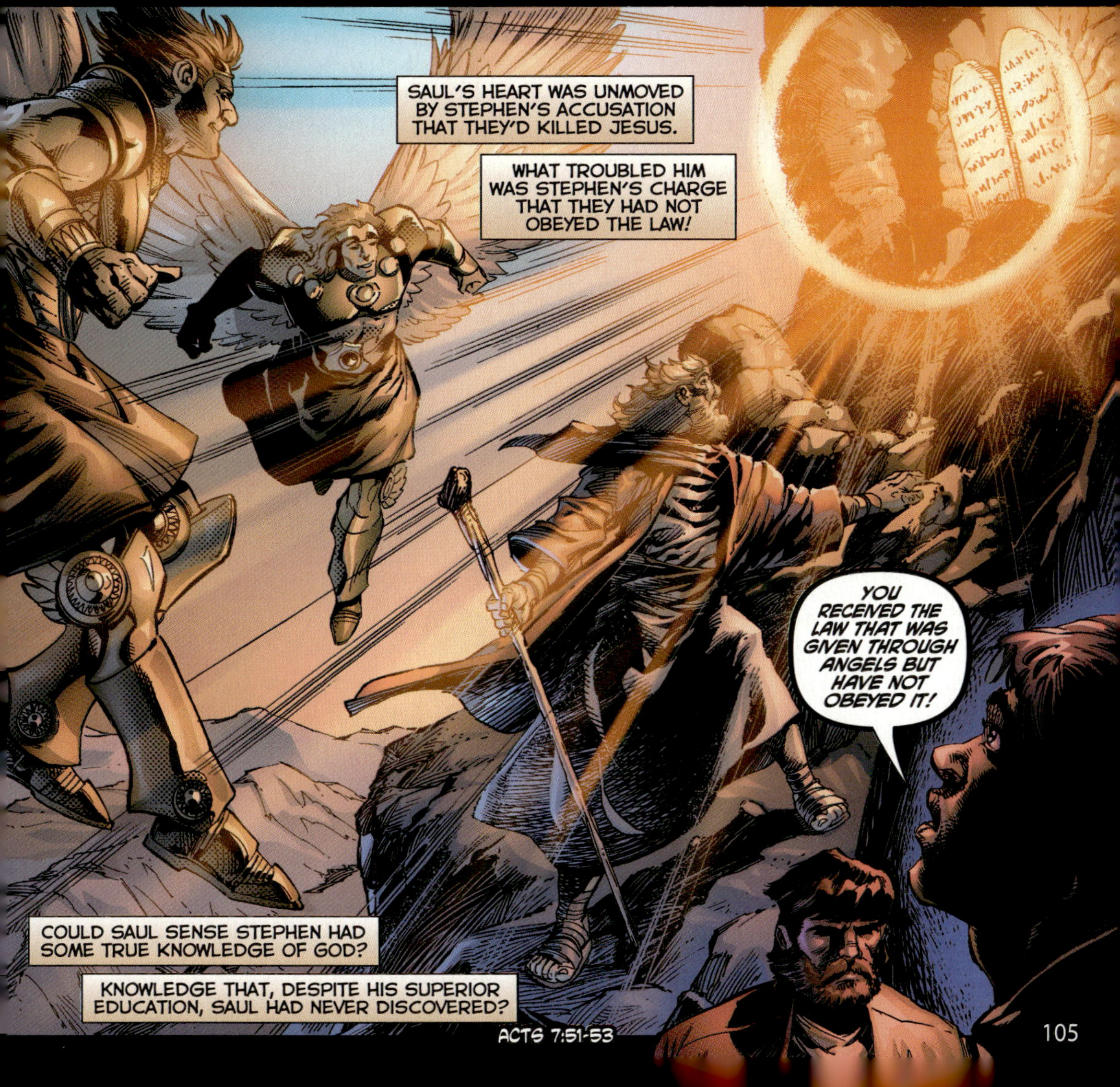
SAUL'S HEART WAS UNMOVED BY STEPHEN'S ACCUSATION THAT THEY'D KILLED JESUS.
WHAT TROUBLED HIM WAS STEPHEN'S CHARGE THAT THEY HAD NOT OBEYED THE LAW!
YOU RECEIVED THE LAW THAT WAS GIVEN THROUGH ANGELS BUT HAVE NOT OBEYED IT!
COULD SAUL SENSE STEPHEN HAD SOME TRUE KNOWLEDGE OF GOD?
KNOWLEDGE THAT, DESPITE HIS SUPERIOR EDUCATION, SAUL HAD NEVER DISCOVERED?
ACTS 7:51-53

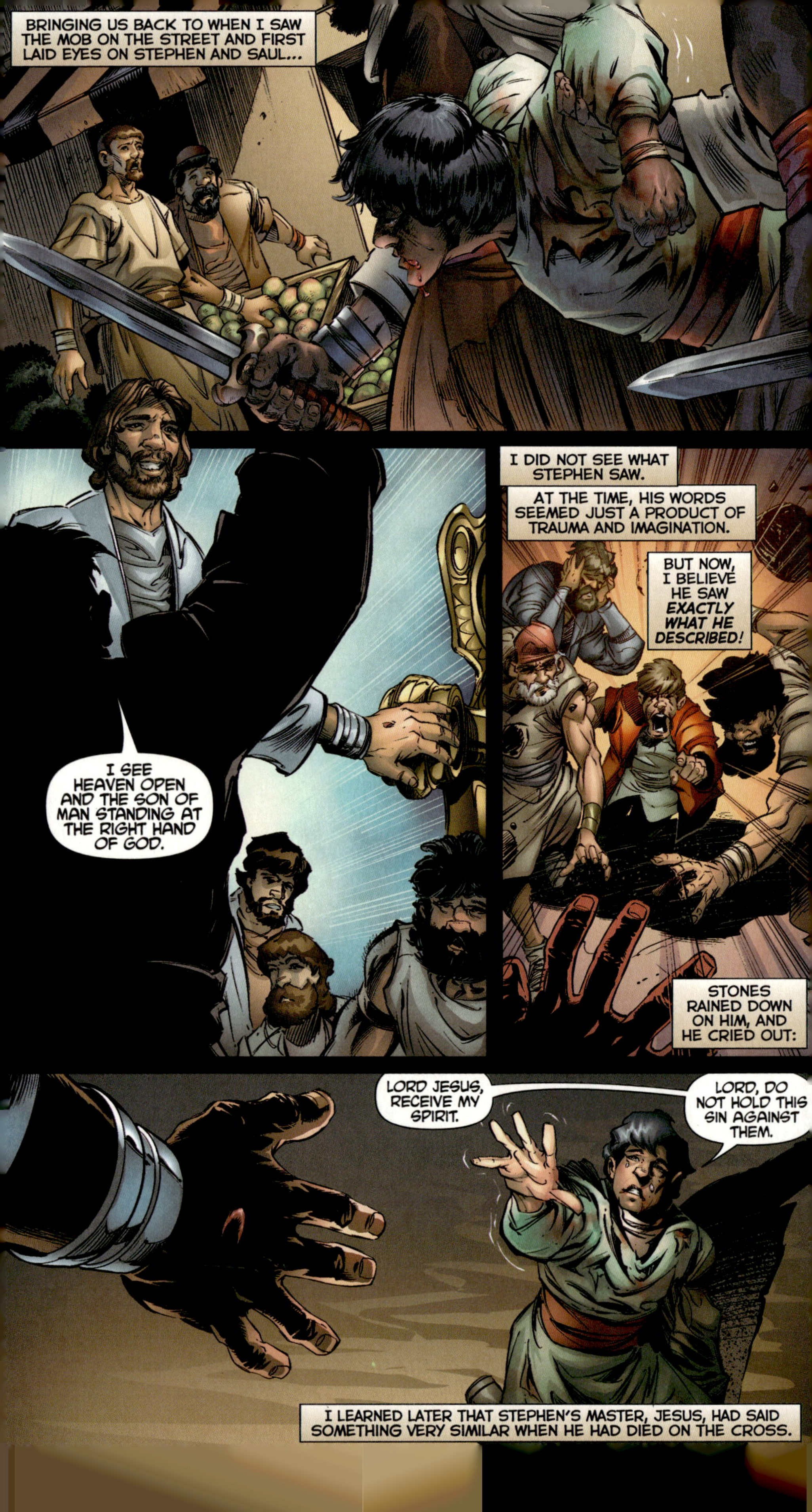

BRINGING US BACK TO WHEN I SAW THE MOB ON THE STREET AND FIRST LAID EYES ON STEPHEN AND SAUL...
I SEE HEAVEN OPEN AND THE SON OF MAN STANDING AT THE RIGHT HAND OF GOD.
I DID NOT SEE WHAT STEPHEN SAW.
AT THE TIME, HIS WORDS SEEMED JUST A PRODUCT OF TRAUMA AND IMAGINATION.
BUT NOW, I BELIEVE HE SAW *EXACTLY WHAT HE DESCRIBED!*
STONES RAINED DOWN ON HIM, AND HE CRIED OUT:
LORD JESUS, RECEIVE MY SPIRIT.
LORD, DO NOT HOLD THIS SIN AGAINST THEM.
I LEARNED LATER THAT STEPHEN'S MASTER, JESUS, HAD SAID SOMETHING VERY SIMILAR WHEN HE HAD DIED ON THE CROSS.

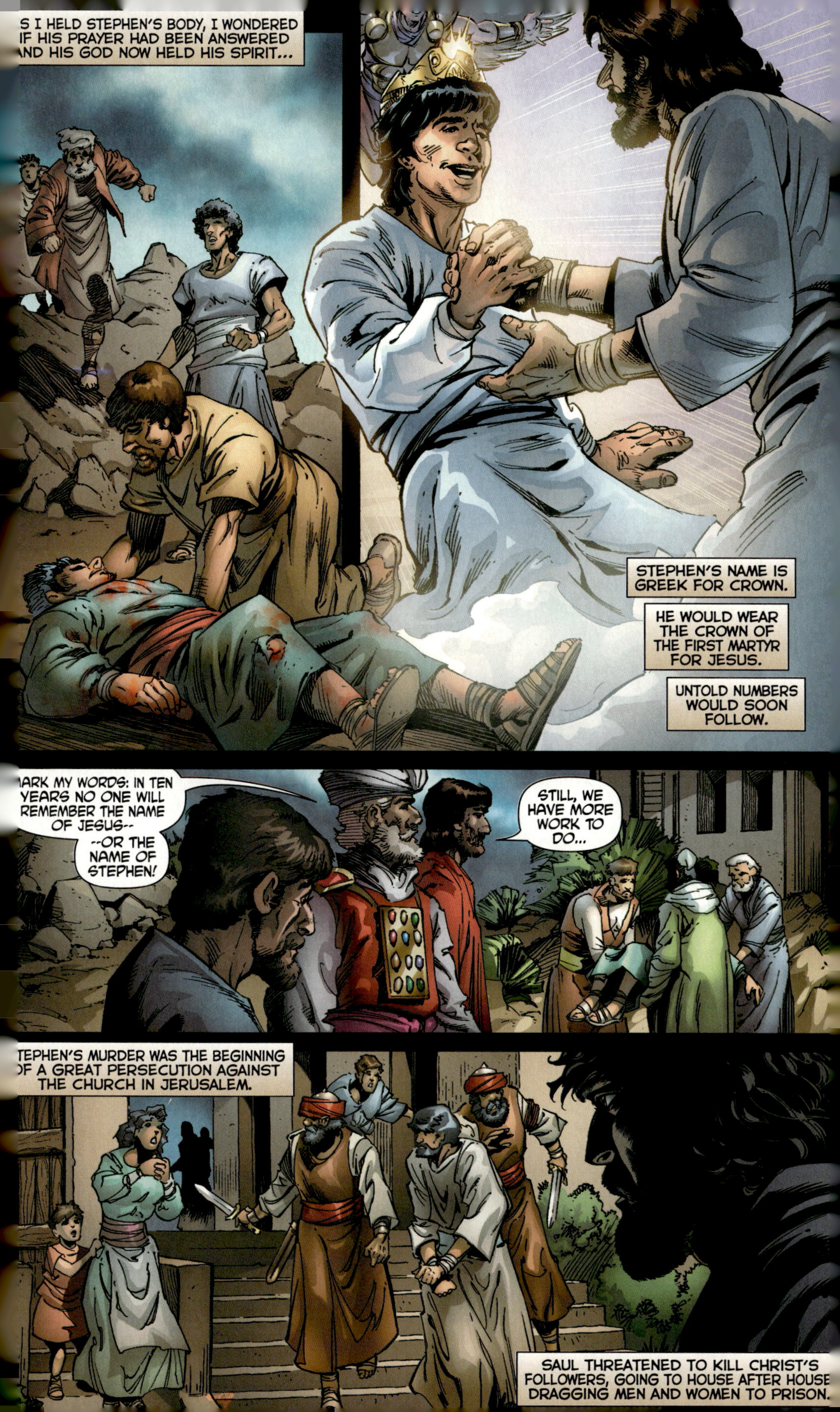

S I HELD STEPHEN'S BODY, I WONDERED IF HIS PRAYER HAD BEEN ANSWERED AND HIS GOD NOW HELD HIS SPIRIT...
STEPHEN'S NAME IS GREEK FOR CROWN.
HE WOULD WEAR THE CROWN OF THE FIRST MARTYR FOR JESUS.
UNTOLD NUMBERS WOULD SOON FOLLOW.
ARK MY WORDS: IN TEN YEARS NO ONE WILL REMEMBER THE NAME OF JESUS--
--OR THE NAME OF STEPHEN!
STILL, WE HAVE MORE WORK TO DO...
TEPHEN'S MURDER WAS THE BEGINNING OF A GREAT PERSECUTION AGAINST THE CHURCH IN JERUSALEM.
SAUL THREATENED TO KILL CHRIST'S FOLLOWERS, GOING TO HOUSE AFTER HOUSE DRAGGING MEN AND WOMEN TO PRISON.

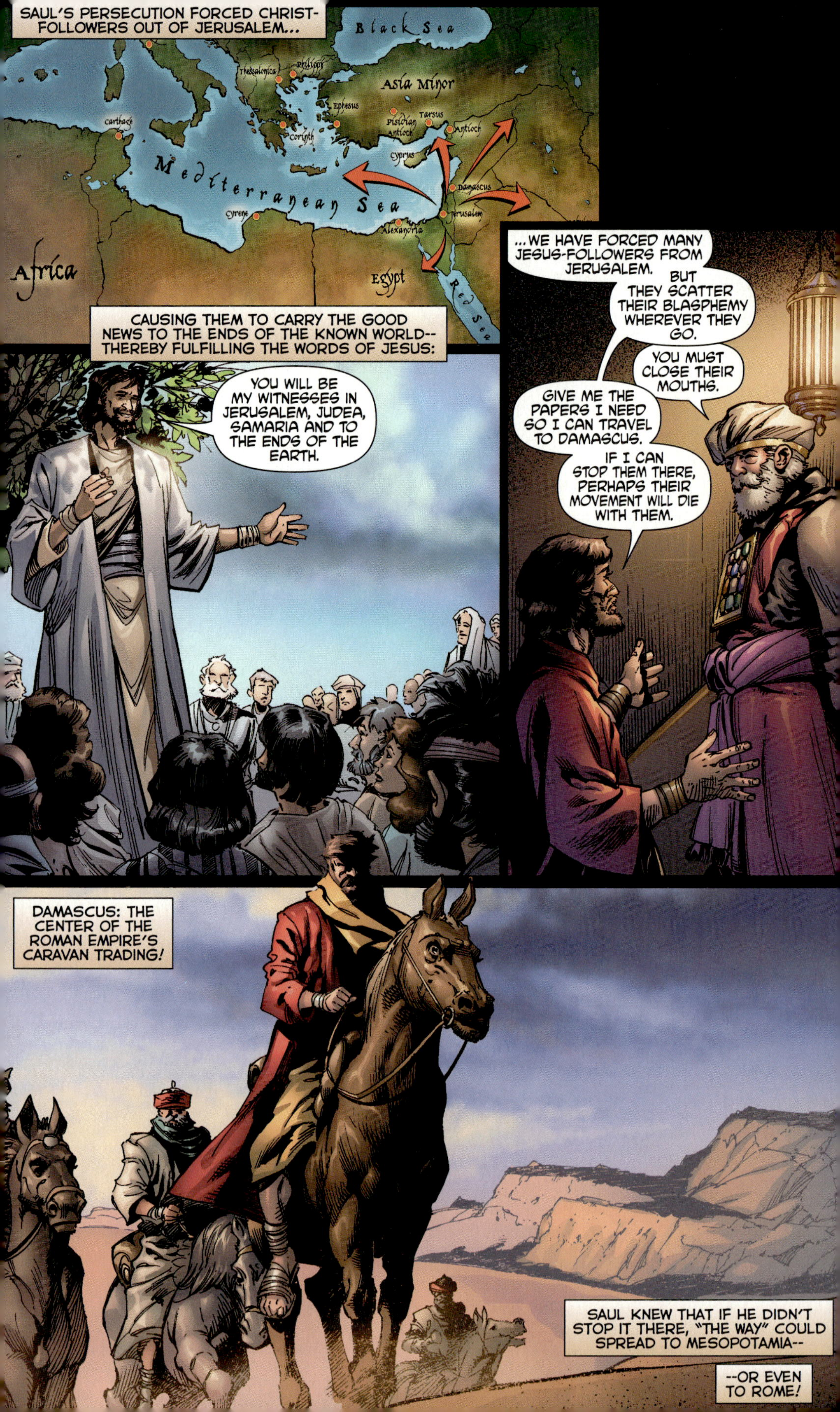
SAUL'S PERSECUTION FORCED CHRIST-FOLLOWERS OUT OF JERUSALEM...
Black Sea
Asia Minor
Thessalonica
Philippi
Ephesus
Pisidian Antioch
Tarsus
Antioch
Carthage
Corinth
Cyprus
Mediterranean Sea
Damascus
Jerusalem
Cyrene
Alexandria
Africa
Egypt
Red Sea
CAUSING THEM TO CARRY THE GOOD NEWS TO THE ENDS OF THE KNOWN WORLD-- THEREBY FULFILLING THE WORDS OF JESUS:
YOU WILL BE MY WITNESSES IN JERUSALEM, JUDEA, SAMARIA AND TO THE ENDS OF THE EARTH.
...WE HAVE FORCED MANY JESUS-FOLLOWERS FROM JERUSALEM.
BUT THEY SCATTER THEIR BLASPHEMY WHEREVER THEY GO.
YOU MUST CLOSE THEIR MOUTHS.
GIVE ME THE PAPERS I NEED SO I CAN TRAVEL TO DAMASCUS.
IF I CAN STOP THEM THERE, PERHAPS THEIR MOVEMENT WILL DIE WITH THEM.
DAMASCUS: THE CENTER OF THE ROMAN EMPIRE'S CARAVAN TRADING!
SAUL KNEW THAT IF HE DIDN'T STOP IT THERE, "THE WAY" COULD SPREAD TO MESOPOTAMIA--
--OR EVEN TO ROME!

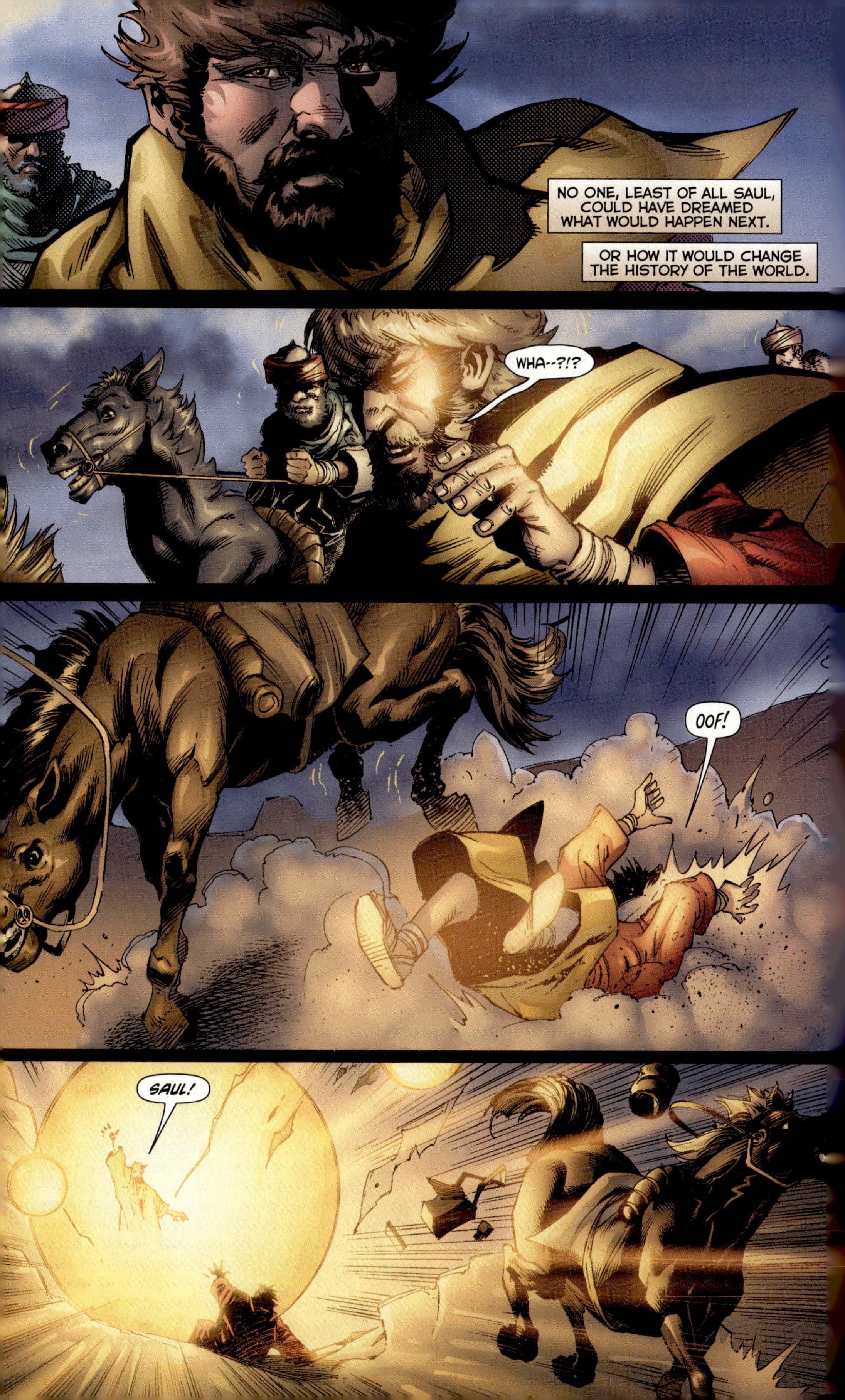
NO ONE, LEAST OF ALL SAUL, COULD HAVE DREAMED WHAT WOULD HAPPEN NEXT.
OR HOW IT WOULD CHANGE THE HISTORY OF THE WORLD.
WHA--?!?
OOF!
SAUL!

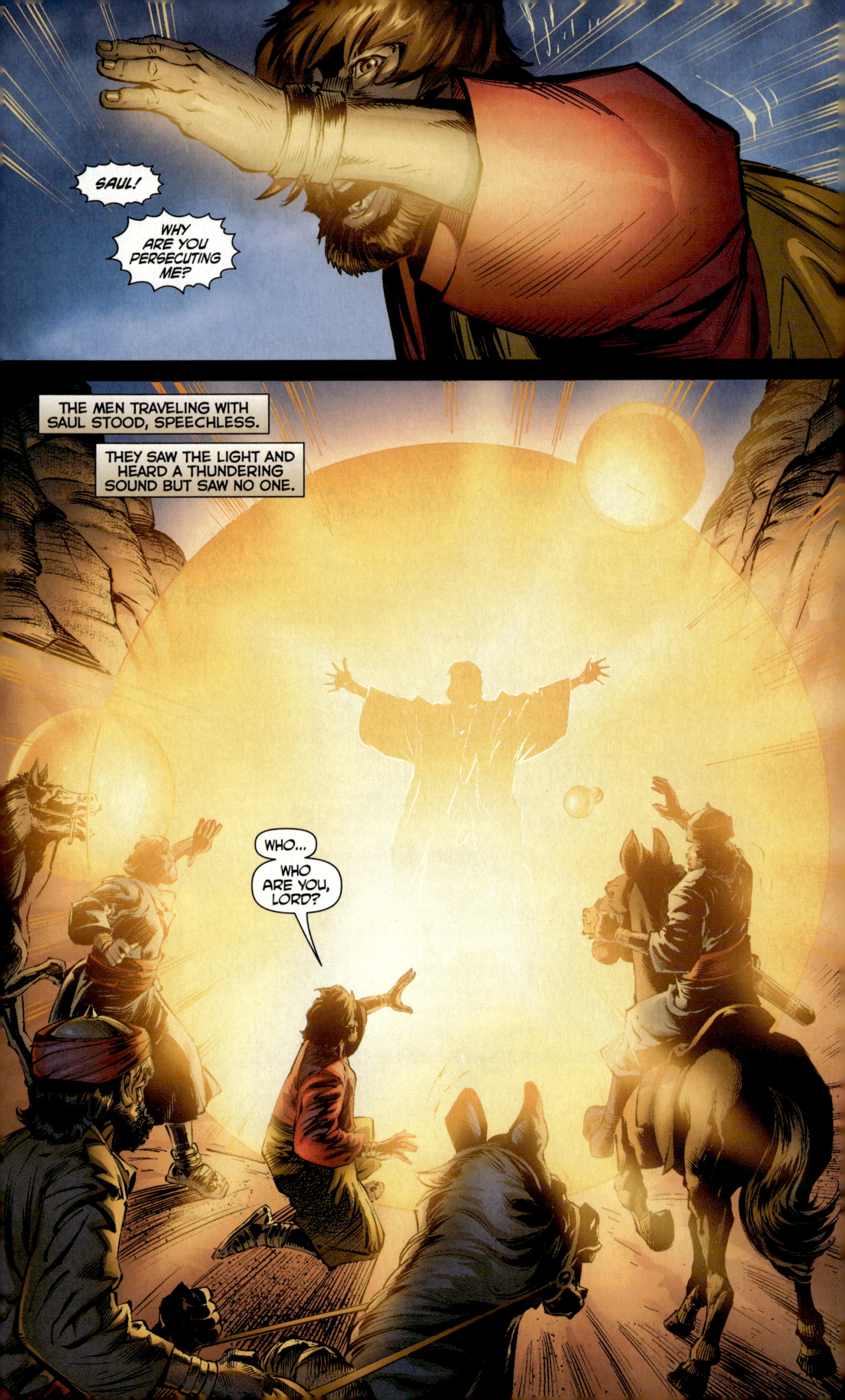
SAUL!
WHY ARE YOU PERSECUTING ME?
THE MEN TRAVELING WITH SAUL STOOD, SPEECHLESS.
THEY SAW THE LIGHT AND HEARD A THUNDERING SOUND BUT SAW NO ONE.
WHO...
WHO ARE YOU, LORD?

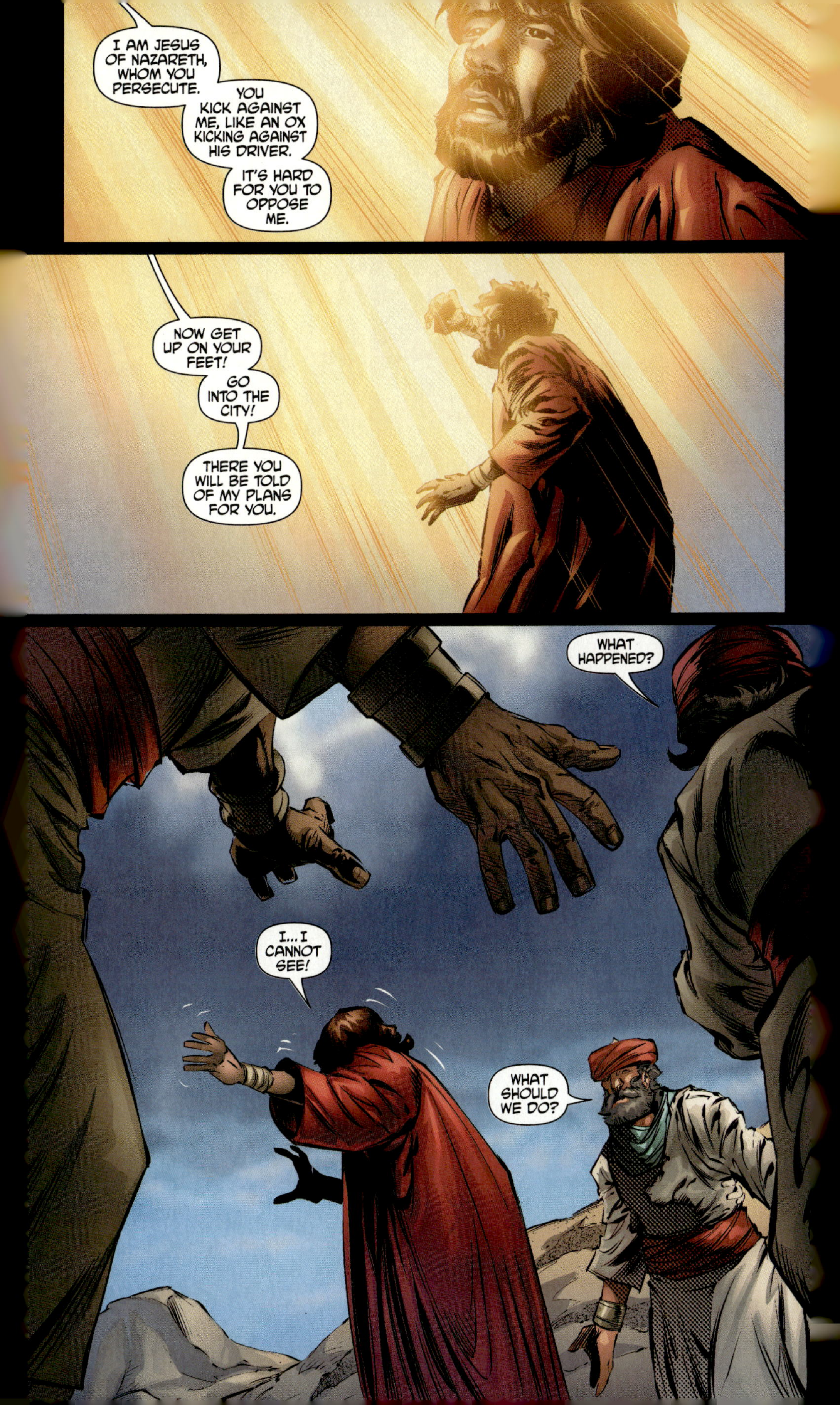
I AM JESUS OF NAZARETH, WHOM YOU PERSECUTE.
YOU KICK AGAINST ME, LIKE AN OX KICKING AGAINST HIS DRIVER.
IT'S HARD FOR YOU TO OPPOSE ME.
NOW GET UP ON YOUR FEET!
GO INTO THE CITY!
THERE YOU WILL BE TOLD OF MY PLANS FOR YOU.
WHAT HAPPENED?
I...I CANNOT SEE!
WHAT SHOULD WE DO?

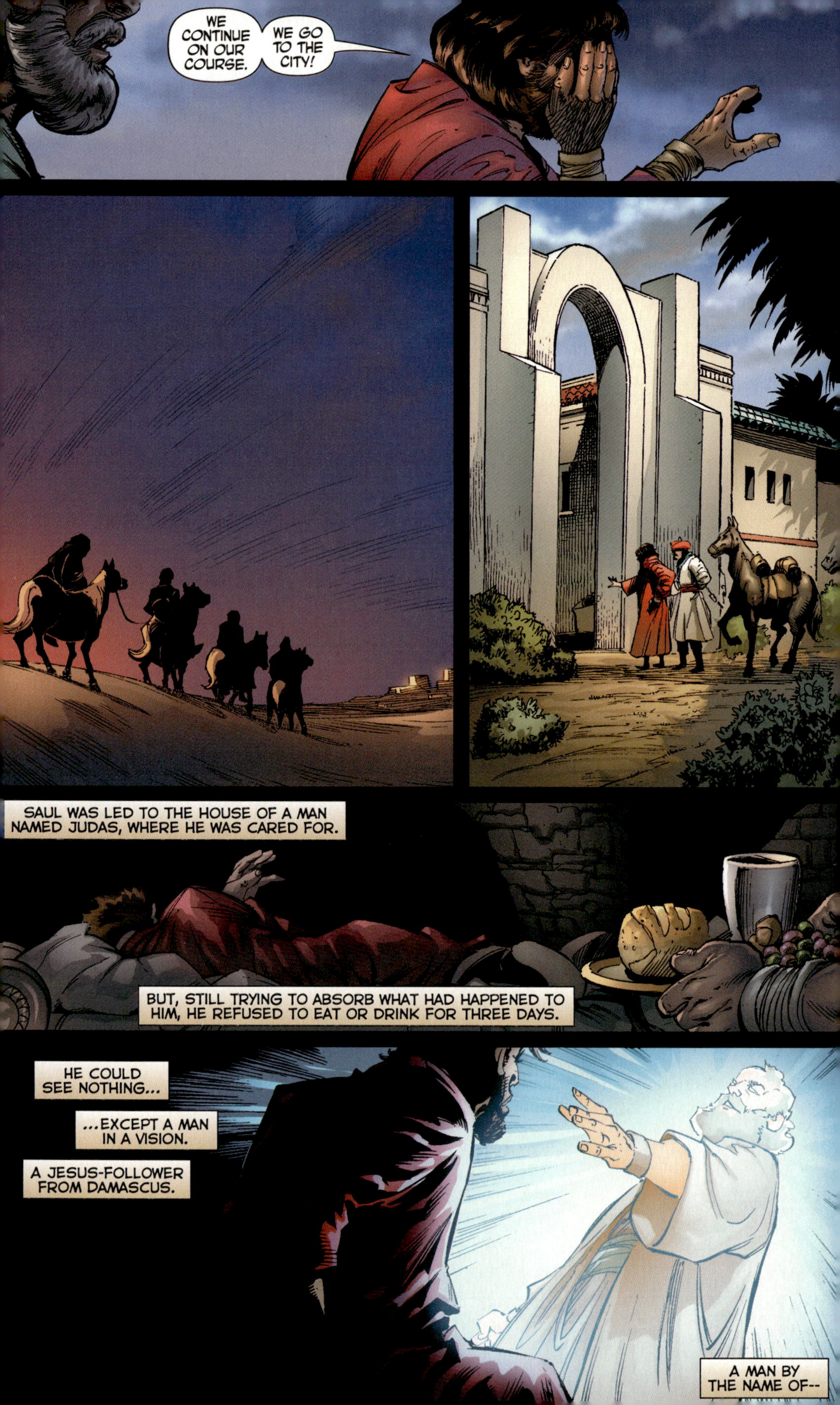
WE CONTINUE ON OUR COURSE.
WE GO TO THE CITY!
SAUL WAS LED TO THE HOUSE OF A MAN NAMED JUDAS, WHERE HE WAS CARED FOR.
BUT, STILL TRYING TO ABSORB WHAT HAD HAPPENED TO HIM, HE REFUSED TO EAT OR DRINK FOR THREE DAYS.
HE COULD SEE NOTHING...
...EXCEPT A MAN IN A VISION.
A JESUS-FOLLOWER FROM DAMASCUS.
A MAN BY THE NAME OF--

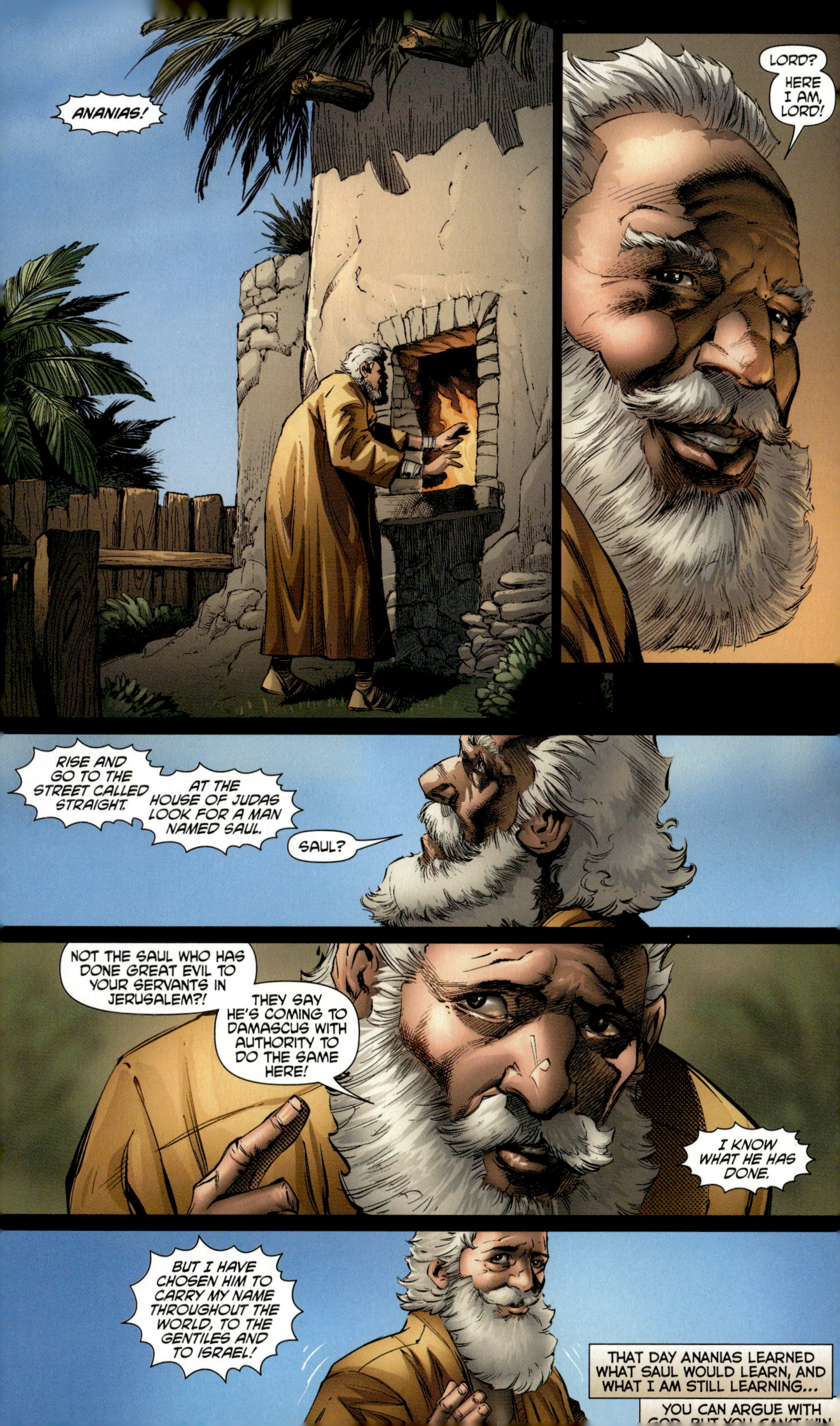
ANANIAS!
LORD? HERE I AM, LORD!
RISE AND GO TO THE STREET CALLED STRAIGHT.
AT THE HOUSE OF JUDAS LOOK FOR A MAN NAMED SAUL.
SAUL?
NOT THE SAUL WHO HAS DONE GREAT EVIL TO YOUR SERVANTS IN JERUSALEM?!
THEY SAY HE'S COMING TO DAMASCUS WITH AUTHORITY TO DO THE SAME HERE!
I KNOW WHAT HE HAS DONE.
BUT I HAVE CHOSEN HIM TO CARRY MY NAME THROUGHOUT THE WORLD, TO THE GENTILES AND TO ISRAEL!
THAT DAY ANANIAS LEARNED WHAT SAUL WOULD LEARN, AND WHAT I AM STILL LEARNING...
YOU CAN ARGUE WITH

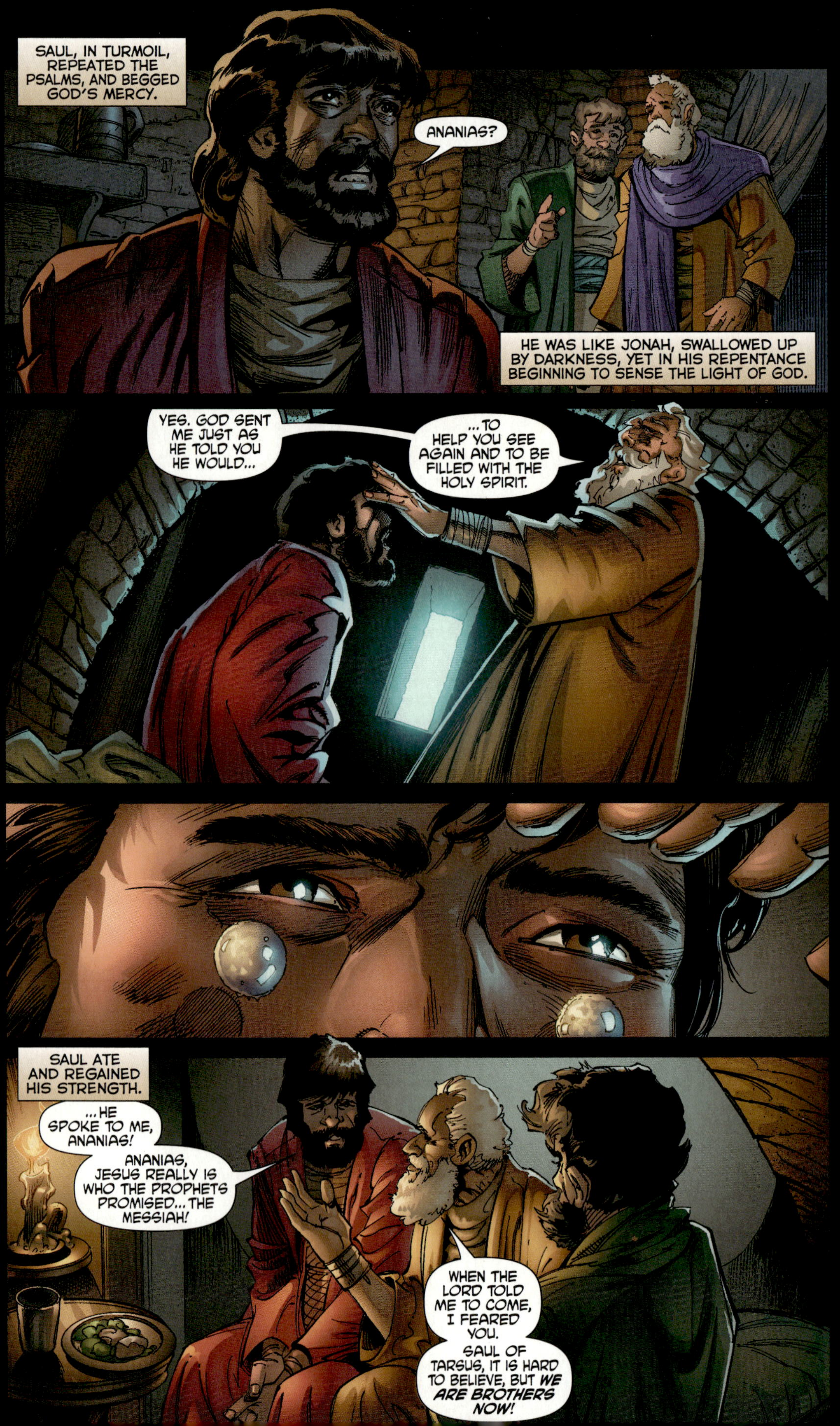
SAUL, IN TURMOIL, REPEATED THE PSALMS, AND BEGGED GOD'S MERCY.
ANANIAS?
HE WAS LIKE JONAH, SWALLOWED UP BY DARKNESS, YET IN HIS REPENTANCE BEGINNING TO SENSE THE LIGHT OF GOD.
YES. GOD SENT ME JUST AS HE TOLD YOU HE WOULD...
...TO HELP YOU SEE AGAIN AND TO BE FILLED WITH THE HOLY SPIRIT.
SAUL ATE AND REGAINED HIS STRENGTH.
...HE SPOKE TO ME, ANANIAS!
ANANIAS, JESUS REALLY IS WHO THE PROPHETS PROMISED... THE MESSIAH!
WHEN THE LORD TOLD ME TO COME, I FEARED YOU.
SAUL OF TARSUS, IT IS HARD TO BELIEVE, BUT ***WE ARE BROTHERS NOW!***

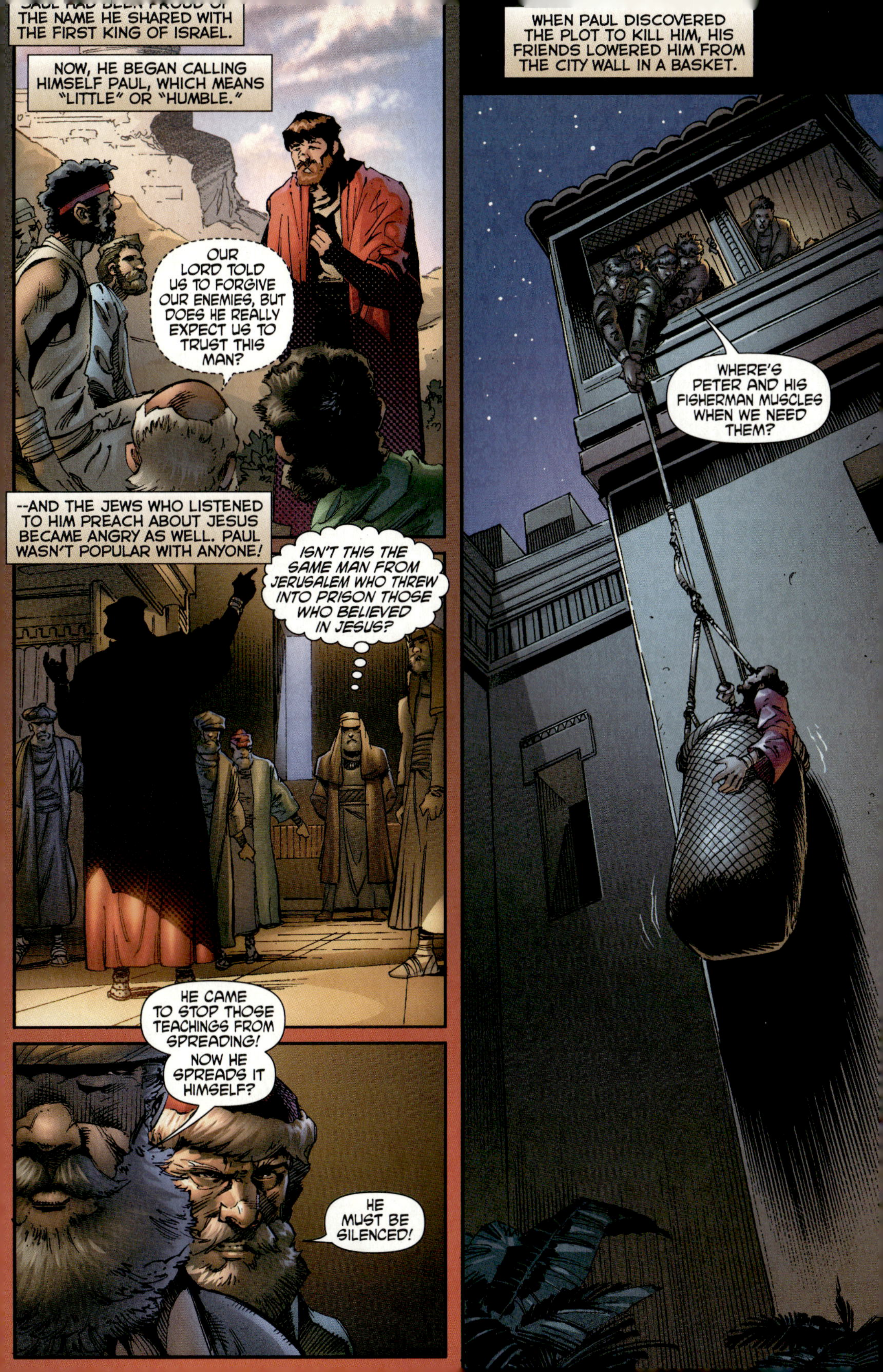
THE NAME HE SHARED WITH THE FIRST KING OF ISRAEL.
NOW, HE BEGAN CALLING HIMSELF PAUL, WHICH MEANS "LITTLE" OR "HUMBLE."
OUR LORD TOLD US TO FORGIVE OUR ENEMIES, BUT DOES HE REALLY EXPECT US TO TRUST THIS MAN?
--AND THE JEWS WHO LISTENED TO HIM PREACH ABOUT JESUS BECAME ANGRY AS WELL. PAUL WASN'T POPULAR WITH ANYONE!
ISN'T THIS THE SAME MAN FROM JERUSALEM WHO THREW INTO PRISON THOSE WHO BELIEVED IN JESUS?
HE CAME TO STOP THOSE TEACHINGS FROM SPREADING!
NOW HE SPREADS IT HIMSELF?
HE MUST BE SILENCED!
WHEN PAUL DISCOVERED THE PLOT TO KILL HIM, HIS FRIENDS LOWERED HIM FROM THE CITY WALL IN A BASKET.
WHERE'S PETER AND HIS FISHERMAN MUSCLES WHEN WE NEED THEM?

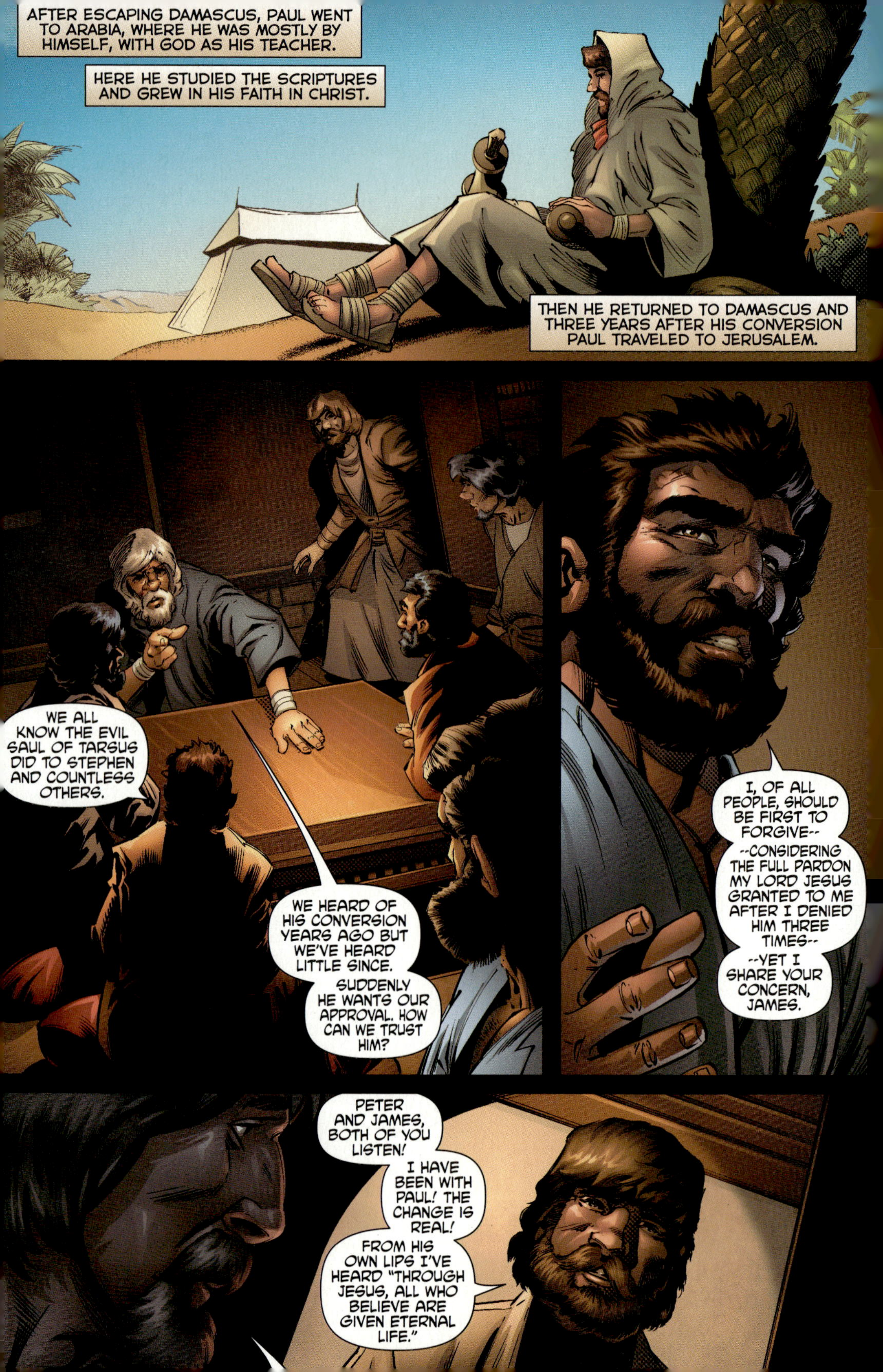
AFTER ESCAPING DAMASCUS, PAUL WENT TO ARABIA, WHERE HE WAS MOSTLY BY HIMSELF, WITH GOD AS HIS TEACHER.
HERE HE STUDIED THE SCRIPTURES AND GREW IN HIS FAITH IN CHRIST.
THEN HE RETURNED TO DAMASCUS AND THREE YEARS AFTER HIS CONVERSION PAUL TRAVELED TO JERUSALEM.
WE ALL KNOW THE EVIL SAUL OF TARSUS DID TO STEPHEN AND COUNTLESS OTHERS.
WE HEARD OF HIS CONVERSION YEARS AGO BUT WE'VE HEARD LITTLE SINCE.
SUDDENLY HE WANTS OUR APPROVAL. HOW CAN WE TRUST HIM?
I, OF ALL PEOPLE, SHOULD BE FIRST TO FORGIVE--
--CONSIDERING THE FULL PARDON MY LORD JESUS GRANTED TO ME AFTER I DENIED HIM THREE TIMES--
--YET I SHARE YOUR CONCERN, JAMES.
PETER AND JAMES, BOTH OF YOU LISTEN!
I HAVE BEEN WITH PAUL! THE CHANGE IS REAL!
FROM HIS OWN LIPS I'VE HEARD "THROUGH JESUS, ALL WHO BELIEVE ARE GIVEN ETERNAL LIFE."

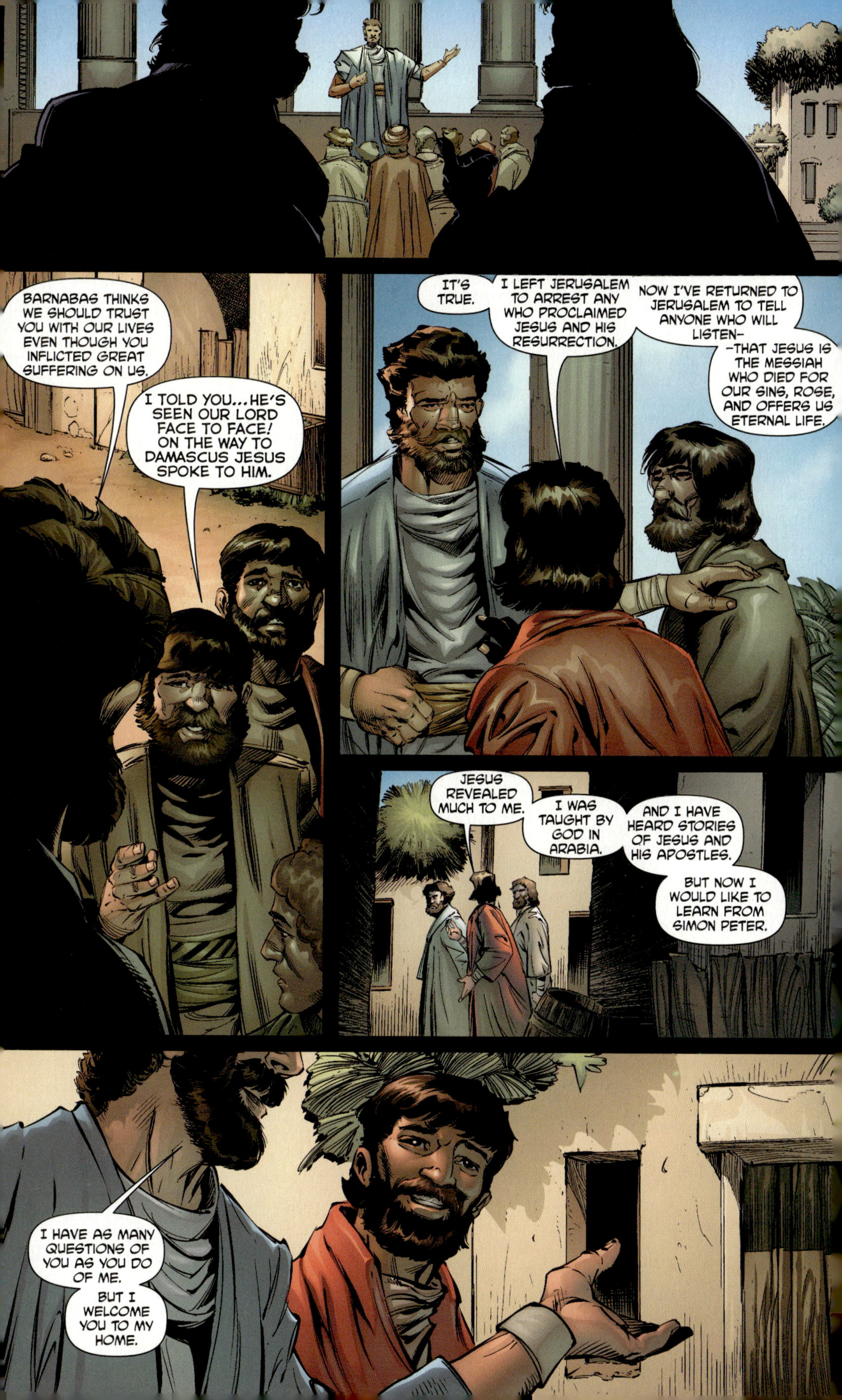
BARNABAS THINKS WE SHOULD TRUST YOU WITH OUR LIVES EVEN THOUGH YOU INFLICTED GREAT SUFFERING ON US.
I TOLD YOU... HE'S SEEN OUR LORD FACE TO FACE! ON THE WAY TO DAMASCUS JESUS SPOKE TO HIM.
IT'S TRUE.
I LEFT JERUSALEM TO ARREST ANY WHO PROCLAIMED JESUS AND HIS RESURRECTION.
NOW I'VE RETURNED TO JERUSALEM TO TELL ANYONE WHO WILL LISTEN–
–THAT JESUS IS THE MESSIAH WHO DIED FOR OUR SINS, ROSE, AND OFFERS US ETERNAL LIFE.
JESUS REVEALED MUCH TO ME.
I WAS TAUGHT BY GOD IN ARABIA.
AND I HAVE HEARD STORIES OF JESUS AND HIS APOSTLES.
BUT NOW I WOULD LIKE TO LEARN FROM SIMON PETER.
I HAVE AS MANY QUESTIONS OF YOU AS YOU DO OF ME.
BUT I WELCOME YOU TO MY HOME.

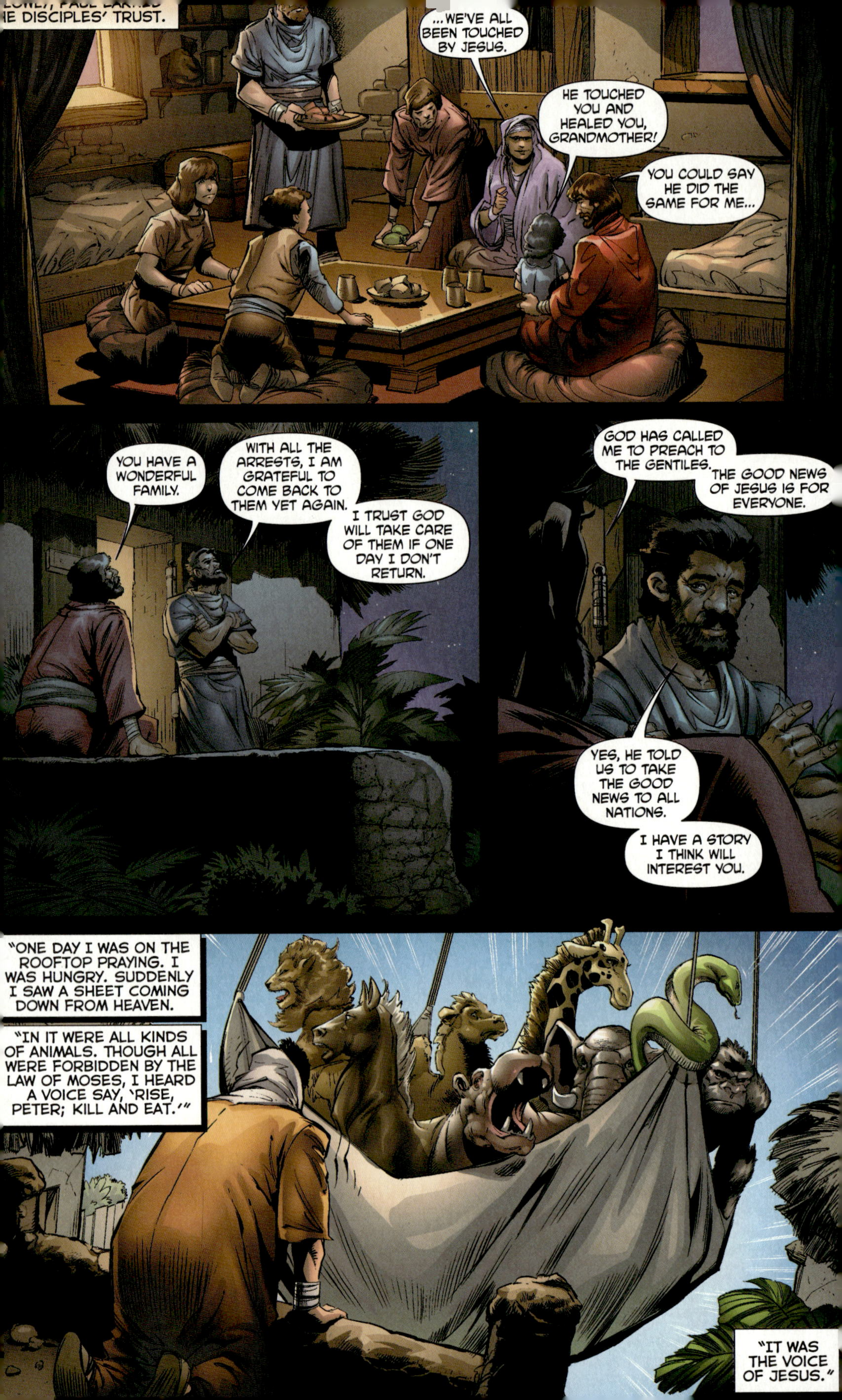

E DISCIPLES' TRUST.
...WE'VE ALL BEEN TOUCHED BY JESUS.
HE TOUCHED YOU AND HEALED YOU, GRANDMOTHER!
YOU COULD SAY HE DID THE SAME FOR ME...
YOU HAVE A WONDERFUL FAMILY.
WITH ALL THE ARRESTS, I AM GRATEFUL TO COME BACK TO THEM YET AGAIN.
I TRUST GOD WILL TAKE CARE OF THEM IF ONE DAY I DON'T RETURN.
GOD HAS CALLED ME TO PREACH TO THE GENTILES.
THE GOOD NEWS OF JESUS IS FOR EVERYONE.
YES, HE TOLD US TO TAKE THE GOOD NEWS TO ALL NATIONS.
I HAVE A STORY I THINK WILL INTEREST YOU.
"ONE DAY I WAS ON THE ROOFTOP PRAYING. I WAS HUNGRY. SUDDENLY I SAW A SHEET COMING DOWN FROM HEAVEN.
"IN IT WERE ALL KINDS OF ANIMALS. THOUGH ALL WERE FORBIDDEN BY THE LAW OF MOSES, I HEARD A VOICE SAY, 'RISE, PETER; KILL AND EAT.'"
"IT WAS THE VOICE OF JESUS."

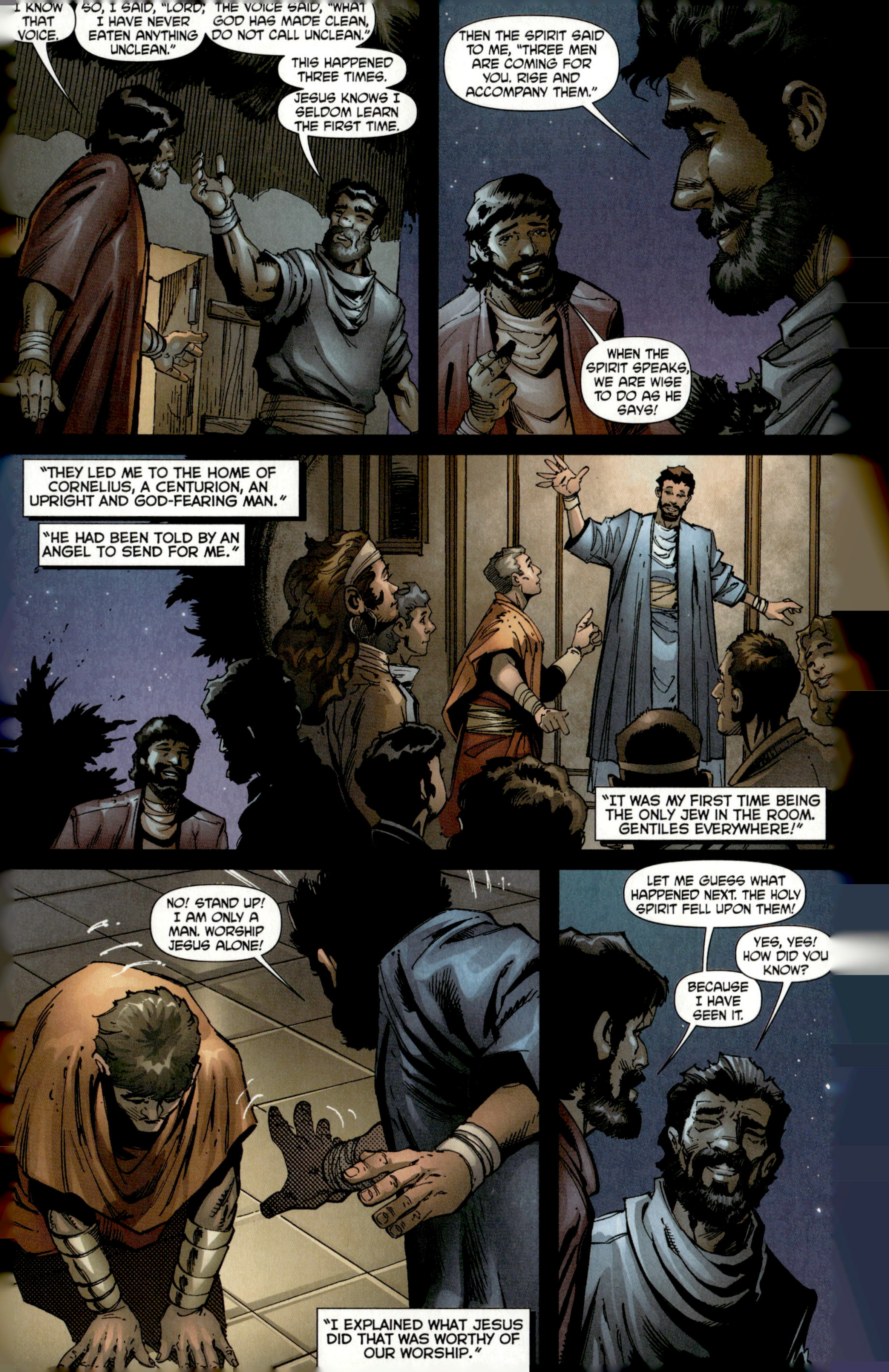
I KNOW THAT VOICE.
SO, I SAID, "LORD; I HAVE NEVER EATEN ANYTHING UNCLEAN."
THE VOICE SAID, "WHAT GOD HAS MADE CLEAN, DO NOT CALL UNCLEAN."
THIS HAPPENED THREE TIMES.
JESUS KNOWS I SELDOM LEARN THE FIRST TIME.
THEN THE SPIRIT SAID TO ME, "THREE MEN ARE COMING FOR YOU. RISE AND ACCOMPANY THEM."
WHEN THE SPIRIT SPEAKS, WE ARE WISE TO DO AS HE SAYS!
"THEY LED ME TO THE HOME OF CORNELIUS, A CENTURION, AN UPRIGHT AND GOD-FEARING MAN."
"HE HAD BEEN TOLD BY AN ANGEL TO SEND FOR ME."
"IT WAS MY FIRST TIME BEING THE ONLY JEW IN THE ROOM. GENTILES EVERYWHERE!"
NO! STAND UP! I AM ONLY A MAN. WORSHIP JESUS ALONE!
"I EXPLAINED WHAT JESUS DID THAT WAS WORTHY OF OUR WORSHIP."
LET ME GUESS WHAT HAPPENED NEXT. THE HOLY SPIRIT FELL UPON THEM!
YES, YES! HOW DID YOU KNOW?
BECAUSE I HAVE SEEN IT.

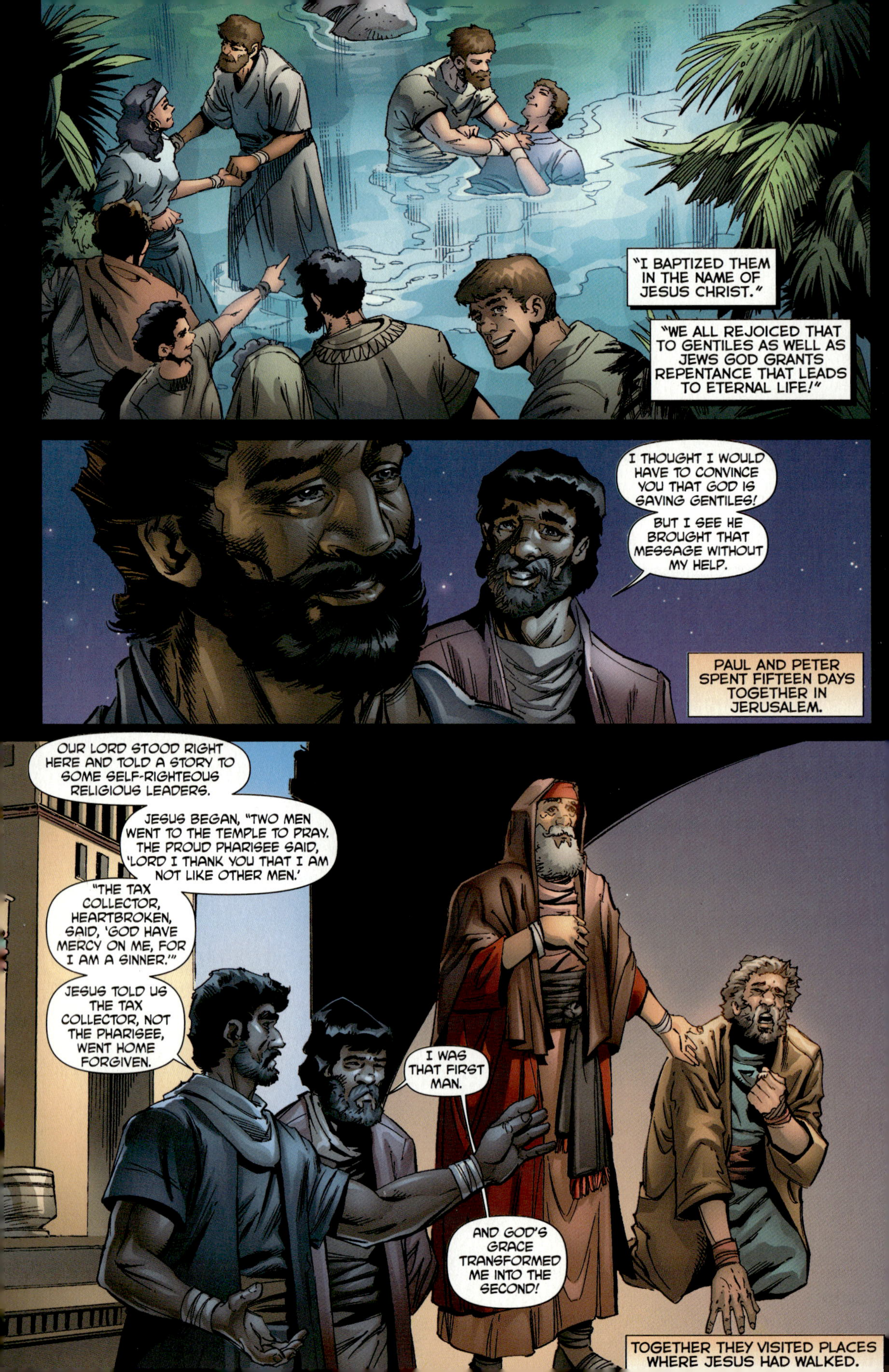
"I BAPTIZED THEM IN THE NAME OF JESUS CHRIST."
"WE ALL REJOICED THAT TO GENTILES AS WELL AS JEWS GOD GRANTS REPENTANCE THAT LEADS TO ETERNAL LIFE!"
I THOUGHT I WOULD HAVE TO CONVINCE YOU THAT GOD IS SAVING GENTILES!
BUT I SEE HE BROUGHT THAT MESSAGE WITHOUT MY HELP.
PAUL AND PETER SPENT FIFTEEN DAYS TOGETHER IN JERUSALEM.
OUR LORD STOOD RIGHT HERE AND TOLD A STORY TO SOME SELF-RIGHTEOUS RELIGIOUS LEADERS.
JESUS BEGAN, "TWO MEN WENT TO THE TEMPLE TO PRAY. THE PROUD PHARISEE SAID, 'LORD I THANK YOU THAT I AM NOT LIKE OTHER MEN.'
"THE TAX COLLECTOR, HEARTBROKEN, SAID, 'GOD HAVE MERCY ON ME, FOR I AM A SINNER.'"
JESUS TOLD US THE TAX COLLECTOR, NOT THE PHARISEE, WENT HOME FORGIVEN.
I WAS THAT FIRST MAN.
AND GOD'S GRACE TRANSFORMED ME INTO THE SECOND!
TOGETHER THEY VISITED PLACES WHERE JESUS HAD WALKED.

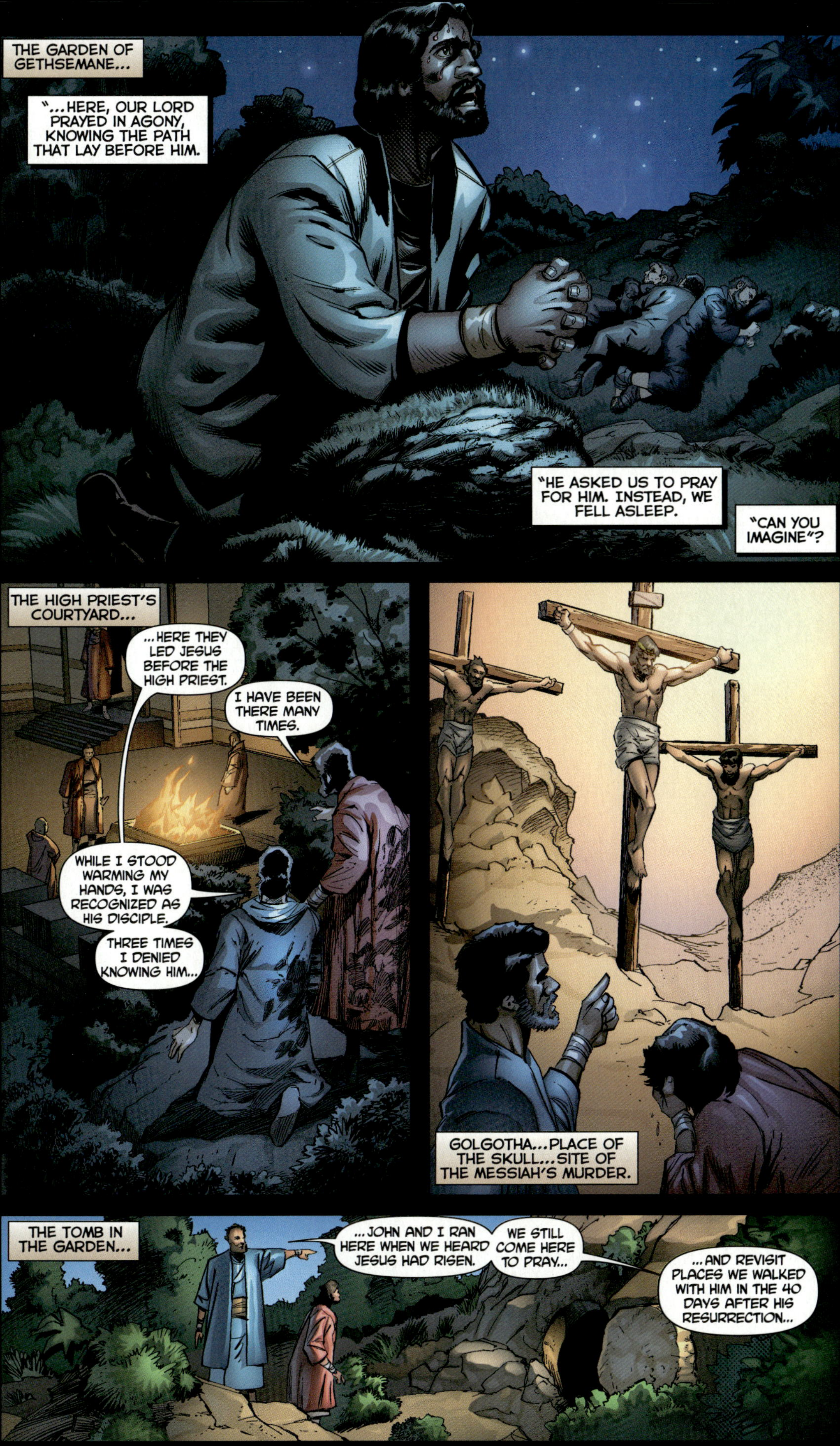

THE GARDEN OF GETHSEMANE...
"...HERE, OUR LORD PRAYED IN AGONY, KNOWING THE PATH THAT LAY BEFORE HIM.
"HE ASKED US TO PRAY FOR HIM. INSTEAD, WE FELL ASLEEP.
"CAN YOU IMAGINE"?
THE HIGH PRIEST'S COURTYARD...
...HERE THEY LED JESUS BEFORE THE HIGH PRIEST.
I HAVE BEEN THERE MANY TIMES.
WHILE I STOOD WARMING MY HANDS, I WAS RECOGNIZED AS HIS DISCIPLE.
THREE TIMES I DENIED KNOWING HIM...
GOLGOTHA...PLACE OF THE SKULL...SITE OF THE MESSIAH'S MURDER.
THE TOMB IN THE GARDEN...
...JOHN AND I RAN HERE WHEN WE HEARD JESUS HAD RISEN.
WE STILL COME HERE TO PRAY...
...AND REVISIT PLACES WE WALKED WITH HIM IN THE 40 DAYS AFTER HIS RESURRECTION...

MARK 14:32-42; 14:66-72; JOHN 20:1-9; ACTS 1:3

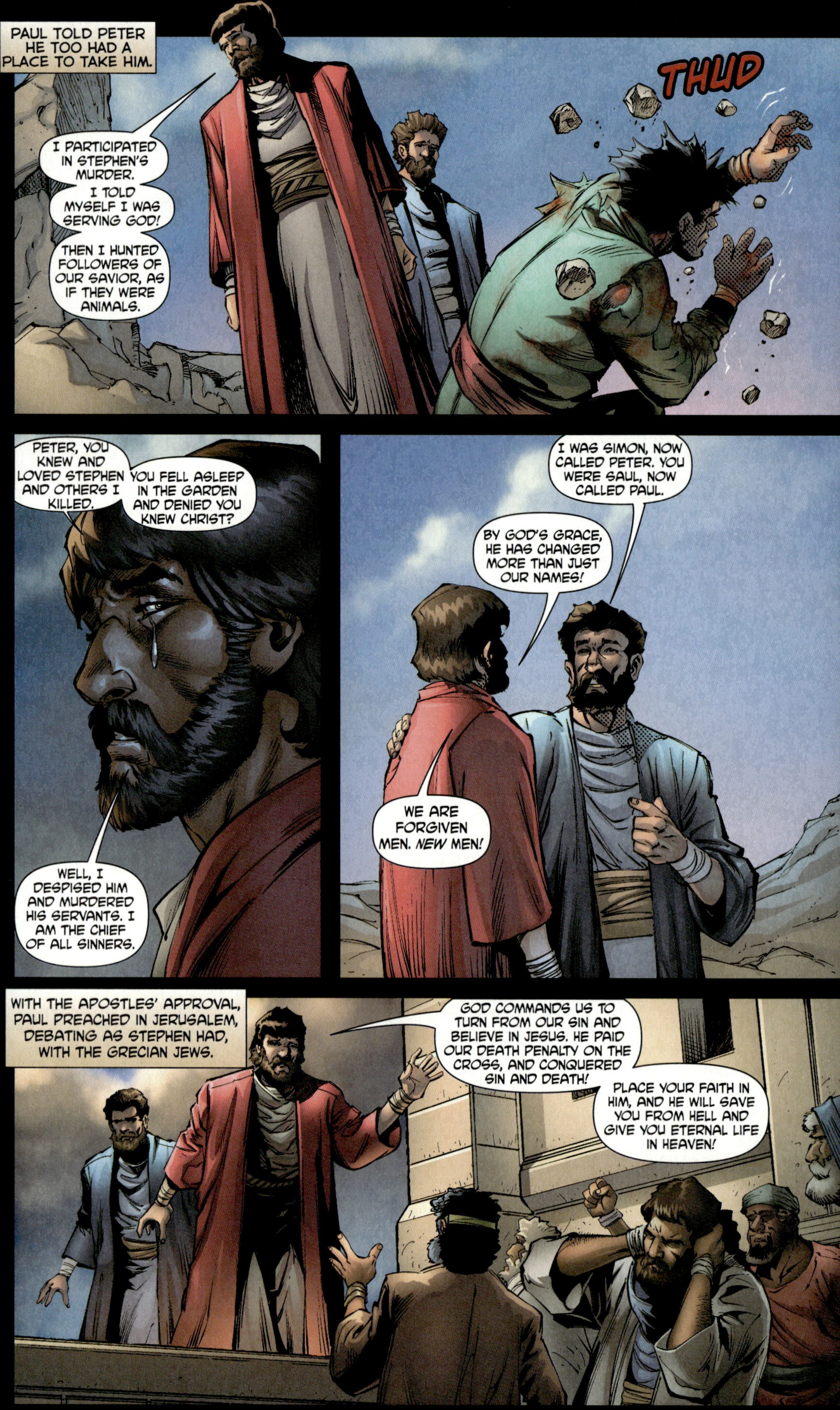
PAUL TOLD PETER HE TOO HAD A PLACE TO TAKE HIM.
I PARTICIPATED IN STEPHEN'S MURDER.
I TOLD MYSELF I WAS SERVING GOD!
THEN I HUNTED FOLLOWERS OF OUR SAVIOR, AS IF THEY WERE ANIMALS.
THUD
PETER, YOU KNEW AND LOVED STEPHEN AND OTHERS I KILLED.
YOU FELL ASLEEP IN THE GARDEN AND DENIED YOU KNEW CHRIST?
WELL, I DESPISED HIM AND MURDERED HIS SERVANTS. I AM THE CHIEF OF ALL SINNERS.
I WAS SIMON, NOW CALLED PETER. YOU WERE SAUL, NOW CALLED PAUL.
BY GOD'S GRACE, HE HAS CHANGED MORE THAN JUST OUR NAMES!
WE ARE FORGIVEN MEN. *NEW* MEN!
WITH THE APOSTLES' APPROVAL, PAUL PREACHED IN JERUSALEM, DEBATING AS STEPHEN HAD, WITH THE GRECIAN JEWS.
GOD COMMANDS US TO TURN FROM OUR SIN AND BELIEVE IN JESUS. HE PAID OUR DEATH PENALTY ON THE CROSS, AND CONQUERED SIN AND DEATH!
PLACE YOUR FAITH IN HIM, AND HE WILL SAVE YOU FROM HELL AND GIVE YOU ETERNAL LIFE IN HEAVEN!

ACTS 9:29

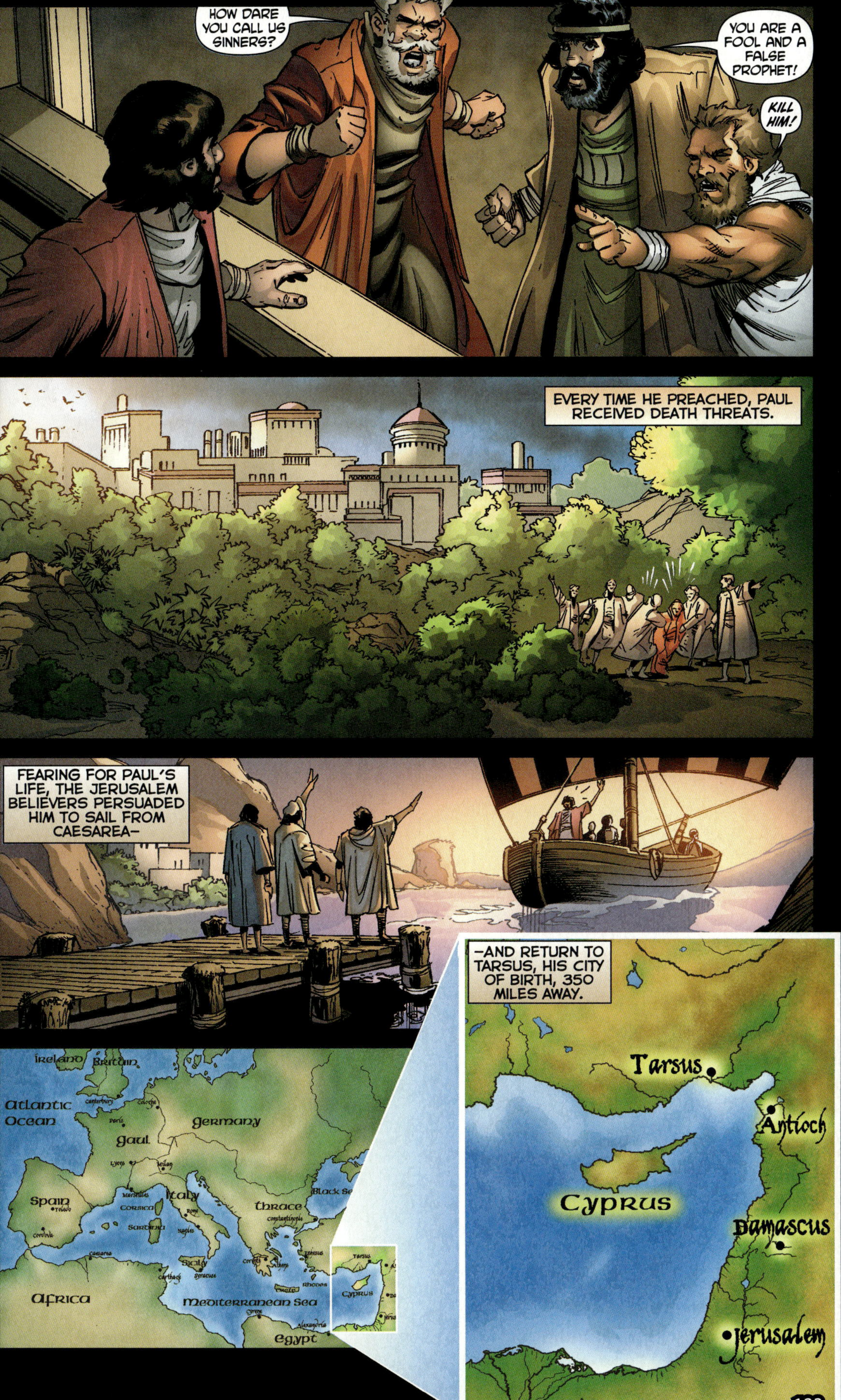

HOW DARE YOU CALL US SINNERS?
YOU ARE A FOOL AND A FALSE PROPHET!
KILL HIM!
EVERY TIME HE PREACHED, PAUL RECEIVED DEATH THREATS.
FEARING FOR PAUL'S LIFE, THE JERUSALEM BELIEVERS PERSUADED HIM TO SAIL FROM CAESAREA–
–AND RETURN TO TARSUS, HIS CITY OF BIRTH, 350 MILES AWAY.
Ireland
Britain
Atlantic Ocean
Germany
Gaul
Spain
Italy
Thrace
Africa
Mediterranean Sea
Egypt
Tarsus
Antioch
Cyprus
Damascus
Jerusalem

ACTS 9:30

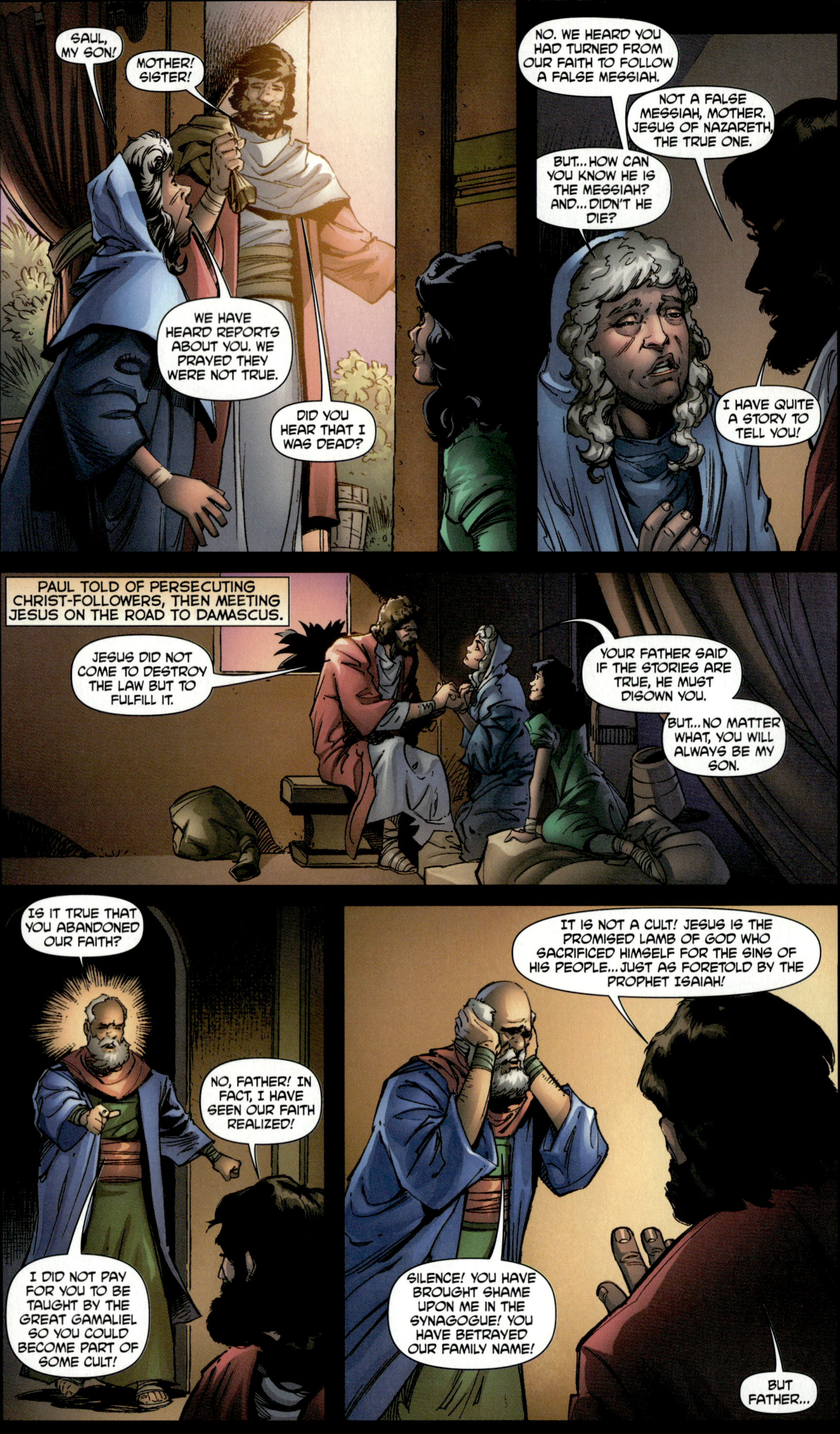
SAUL, MY SON!
MOTHER! SISTER!
WE HAVE HEARD REPORTS ABOUT YOU. WE PRAYED THEY WERE NOT TRUE.
DID YOU HEAR THAT I WAS DEAD?
NO. WE HEARD YOU HAD TURNED FROM OUR FAITH TO FOLLOW A FALSE MESSIAH.
NOT A FALSE MESSIAH, MOTHER. JESUS OF NAZARETH, THE TRUE ONE.
BUT... HOW CAN YOU KNOW HE IS THE MESSIAH? AND... DIDN'T HE DIE?
I HAVE QUITE A STORY TO TELL YOU!
PAUL TOLD OF PERSECUTING CHRIST-FOLLOWERS, THEN MEETING JESUS ON THE ROAD TO DAMASCUS.
JESUS DID NOT COME TO DESTROY THE LAW BUT TO FULFILL IT.
YOUR FATHER SAID IF THE STORIES ARE TRUE, HE MUST DISOWN YOU.
BUT... NO MATTER WHAT, YOU WILL ALWAYS BE MY SON.
IS IT TRUE THAT YOU ABANDONED OUR FAITH?
NO, FATHER! IN FACT, I HAVE SEEN OUR FAITH REALIZED!
I DID NOT PAY FOR YOU TO BE TAUGHT BY THE GREAT GAMALIEL SO YOU COULD BECOME PART OF SOME CULT!
IT IS NOT A CULT! JESUS IS THE PROMISED LAMB OF GOD WHO SACRIFICED HIMSELF FOR THE SINS OF HIS PEOPLE... JUST AS FORETOLD BY THE PROPHET ISAIAH!
SILENCE! YOU HAVE BROUGHT SHAME UPON ME IN THE SYNAGOGUE! YOU HAVE BETRAYED OUR FAMILY NAME!
BUT FATHER...

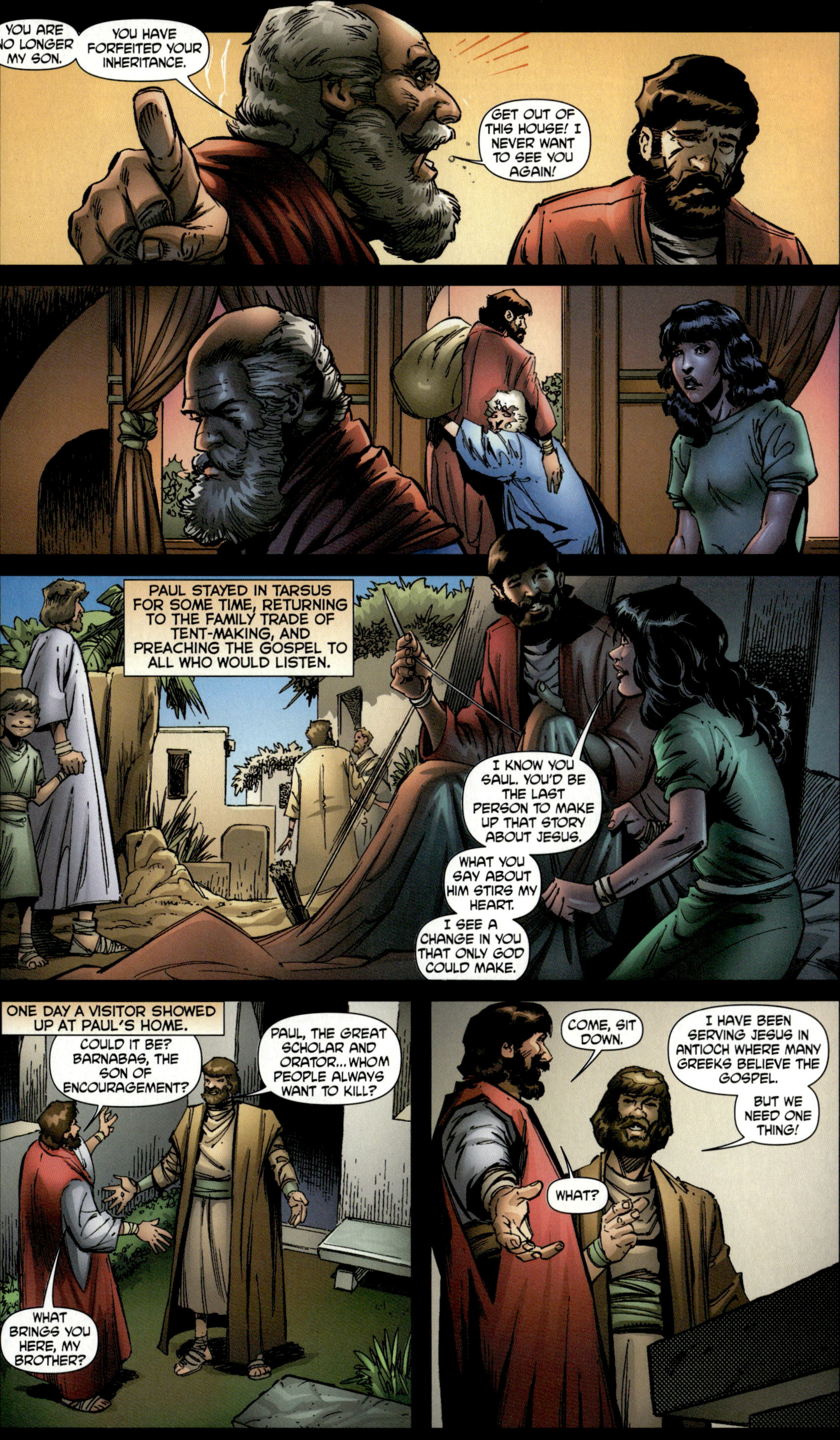
YOU ARE NO LONGER MY SON.
YOU HAVE FORFEITED YOUR INHERITANCE.
GET OUT OF THIS HOUSE! I NEVER WANT TO SEE YOU AGAIN!
PAUL STAYED IN TARSUS FOR SOME TIME, RETURNING TO THE FAMILY TRADE OF TENT-MAKING, AND PREACHING THE GOSPEL TO ALL WHO WOULD LISTEN.
I KNOW YOU SAUL. YOU'D BE THE LAST PERSON TO MAKE UP THAT STORY ABOUT JESUS.
WHAT YOU SAY ABOUT HIM STIRS MY HEART.
I SEE A CHANGE IN YOU THAT ONLY GOD COULD MAKE.
ONE DAY A VISITOR SHOWED UP AT PAUL'S HOME.
COULD IT BE? BARNABAS, THE SON OF ENCOURAGEMENT?
PAUL, THE GREAT SCHOLAR AND ORATOR...WHOM PEOPLE ALWAYS WANT TO KILL?
WHAT BRINGS YOU HERE, MY BROTHER?
COME, SIT DOWN.
I HAVE BEEN SERVING JESUS IN ANTIOCH WHERE MANY GREEKS BELIEVE THE GOSPEL.
BUT WE NEED ONE THING!
WHAT?

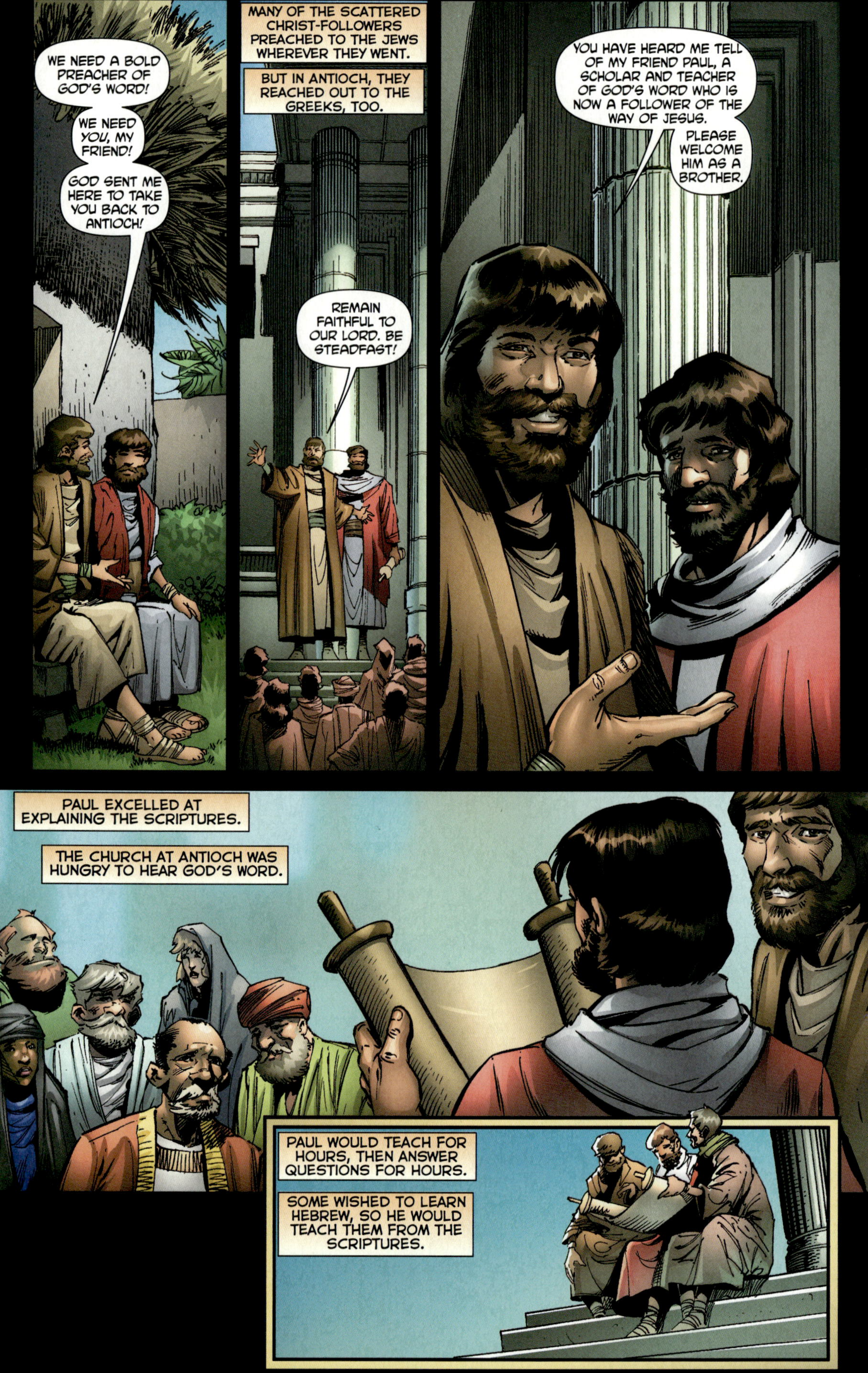

WE NEED A BOLD PREACHER OF GOD'S WORD!
WE NEED YOU, MY FRIEND!
GOD SENT ME HERE TO TAKE YOU BACK TO ANTIOCH!
MANY OF THE SCATTERED CHRIST-FOLLOWERS PREACHED TO THE JEWS WHEREVER THEY WENT.
BUT IN ANTIOCH, THEY REACHED OUT TO THE GREEKS, TOO.
REMAIN FAITHFUL TO OUR LORD. BE STEADFAST!
YOU HAVE HEARD ME TELL OF MY FRIEND PAUL, A SCHOLAR AND TEACHER OF GOD'S WORD WHO IS NOW A FOLLOWER OF THE WAY OF JESUS.
PLEASE WELCOME HIM AS A BROTHER.
PAUL EXCELLED AT EXPLAINING THE SCRIPTURES.
THE CHURCH AT ANTIOCH WAS HUNGRY TO HEAR GOD'S WORD.
PAUL WOULD TEACH FOR HOURS, THEN ANSWER QUESTIONS FOR HOURS.
SOME WISHED TO LEARN HEBREW, SO HE WOULD TEACH THEM FROM THE SCRIPTURES.

ACTS 11:25

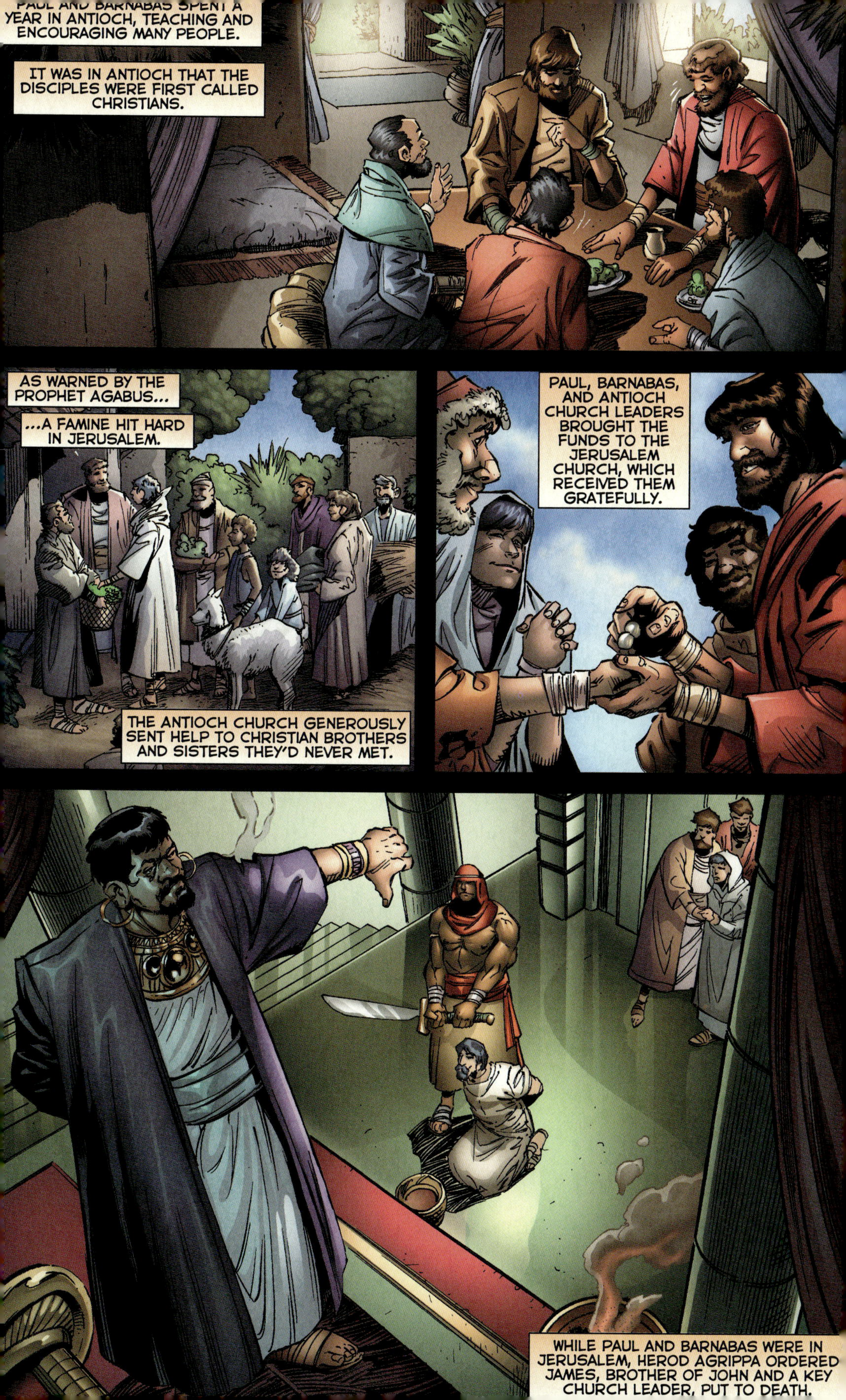
PAUL AND BARNABAS SPENT A YEAR IN ANTIOCH, TEACHING AND ENCOURAGING MANY PEOPLE.
IT WAS IN ANTIOCH THAT THE DISCIPLES WERE FIRST CALLED CHRISTIANS.
AS WARNED BY THE PROPHET AGABUS...
...A FAMINE HIT HARD IN JERUSALEM.
THE ANTIOCH CHURCH GENEROUSLY SENT HELP TO CHRISTIAN BROTHERS AND SISTERS THEY'D NEVER MET.
PAUL, BARNABAS, AND ANTIOCH CHURCH LEADERS BROUGHT THE FUNDS TO THE JERUSALEM CHURCH, WHICH RECEIVED THEM GRATEFULLY.
WHILE PAUL AND BARNABAS WERE IN JERUSALEM, HEROD AGRIPPA ORDERED JAMES, BROTHER OF JOHN AND A KEY CHURCH LEADER, PUT TO DEATH.

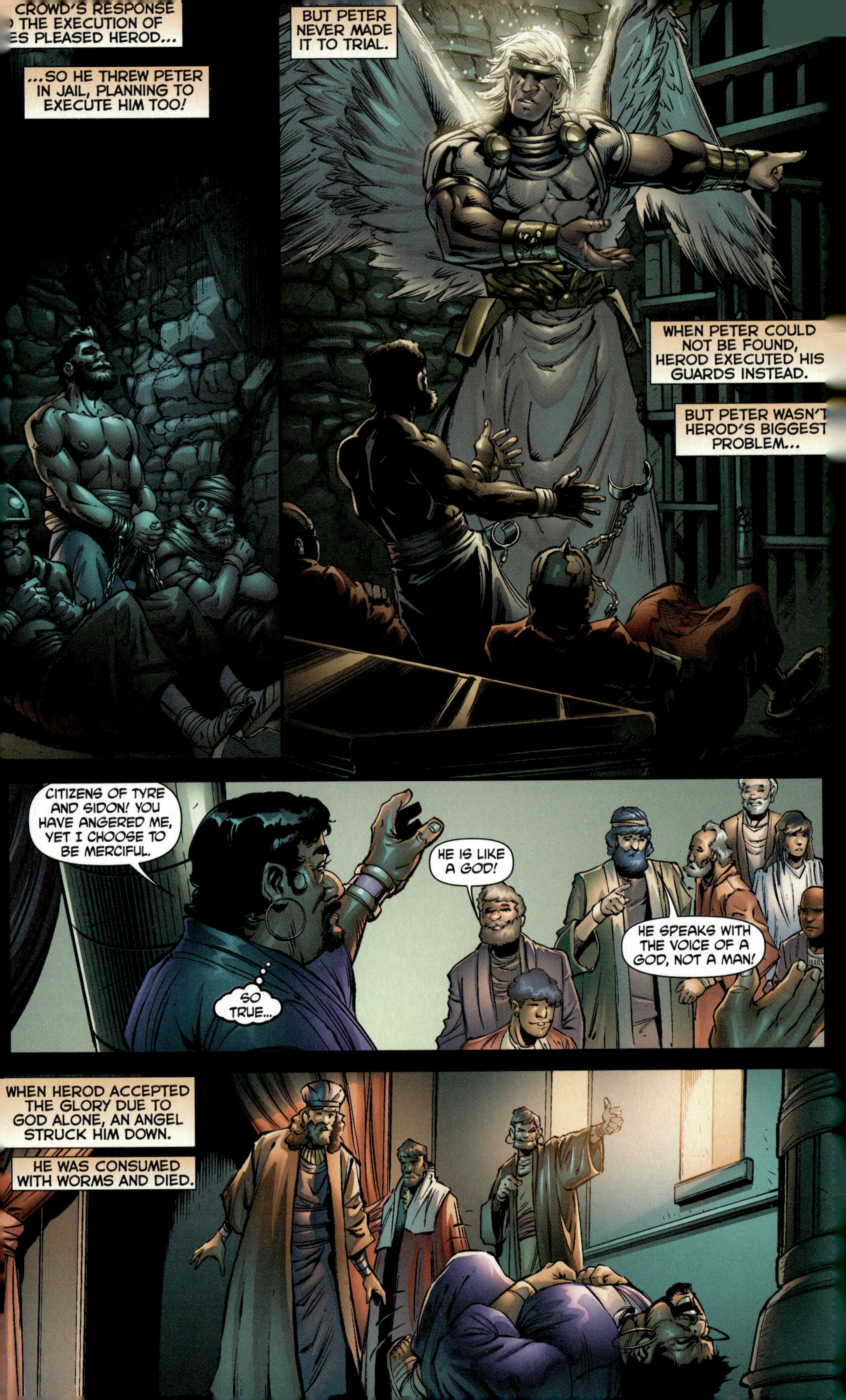

CROWD'S RESPONSE
THE EXECUTION OF
ES PLEASED HEROD...
...SO HE THREW PETER IN JAIL, PLANNING TO EXECUTE HIM TOO!
BUT PETER NEVER MADE IT TO TRIAL.
WHEN PETER COULD NOT BE FOUND, HEROD EXECUTED HIS GUARDS INSTEAD.
BUT PETER WASN'T HEROD'S BIGGEST PROBLEM...
CITIZENS OF TYRE AND SIDON! YOU HAVE ANGERED ME, YET I CHOOSE TO BE MERCIFUL.
HE IS LIKE A GOD!
HE SPEAKS WITH THE VOICE OF A GOD, NOT A MAN!
SO TRUE...
WHEN HEROD ACCEPTED THE GLORY DUE TO GOD ALONE, AN ANGEL STRUCK HIM DOWN.
HE WAS CONSUMED WITH WORMS AND DIED.

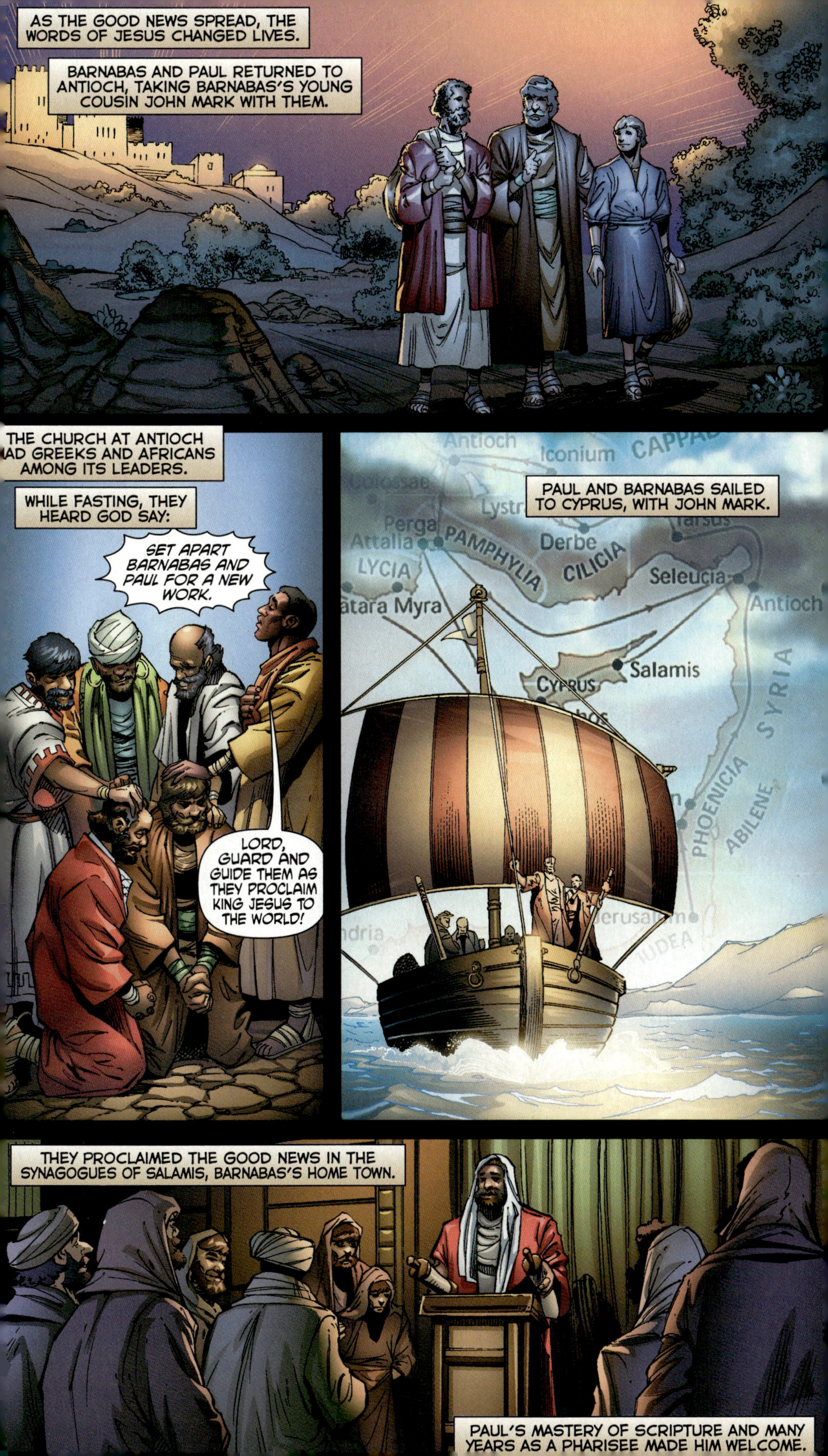

AS THE GOOD NEWS SPREAD, THE WORDS OF JESUS CHANGED LIVES.
BARNABAS AND PAUL RETURNED TO ANTIOCH, TAKING BARNABAS'S YOUNG COUSIN JOHN MARK WITH THEM.
THE CHURCH AT ANTIOCH AD GREEKS AND AFRICANS AMONG ITS LEADERS.
WHILE FASTING, THEY HEARD GOD SAY:
SET APART BARNABAS AND PAUL FOR A NEW WORK.
LORD, GUARD AND GUIDE THEM AS THEY PROCLAIM KING JESUS TO THE WORLD!
PAUL AND BARNABAS SAILED TO CYPRUS, WITH JOHN MARK.
Antioch
Iconium
Lystr
Perga
Attalia
PAMPHYLIA
LYCIA
Derbe
CILICIA
Seleucia
Antioch
Salamis
CYPRUS
SYRIA
PHOENICIA
ABILENE
THEY PROCLAIMED THE GOOD NEWS IN THE SYNAGOGUES OF SALAMIS, BARNABAS'S HOME TOWN.
PAUL'S MASTERY OF SCRIPTURE AND MANY YEARS AS A PHARISEE MADE HIM WELCOME.

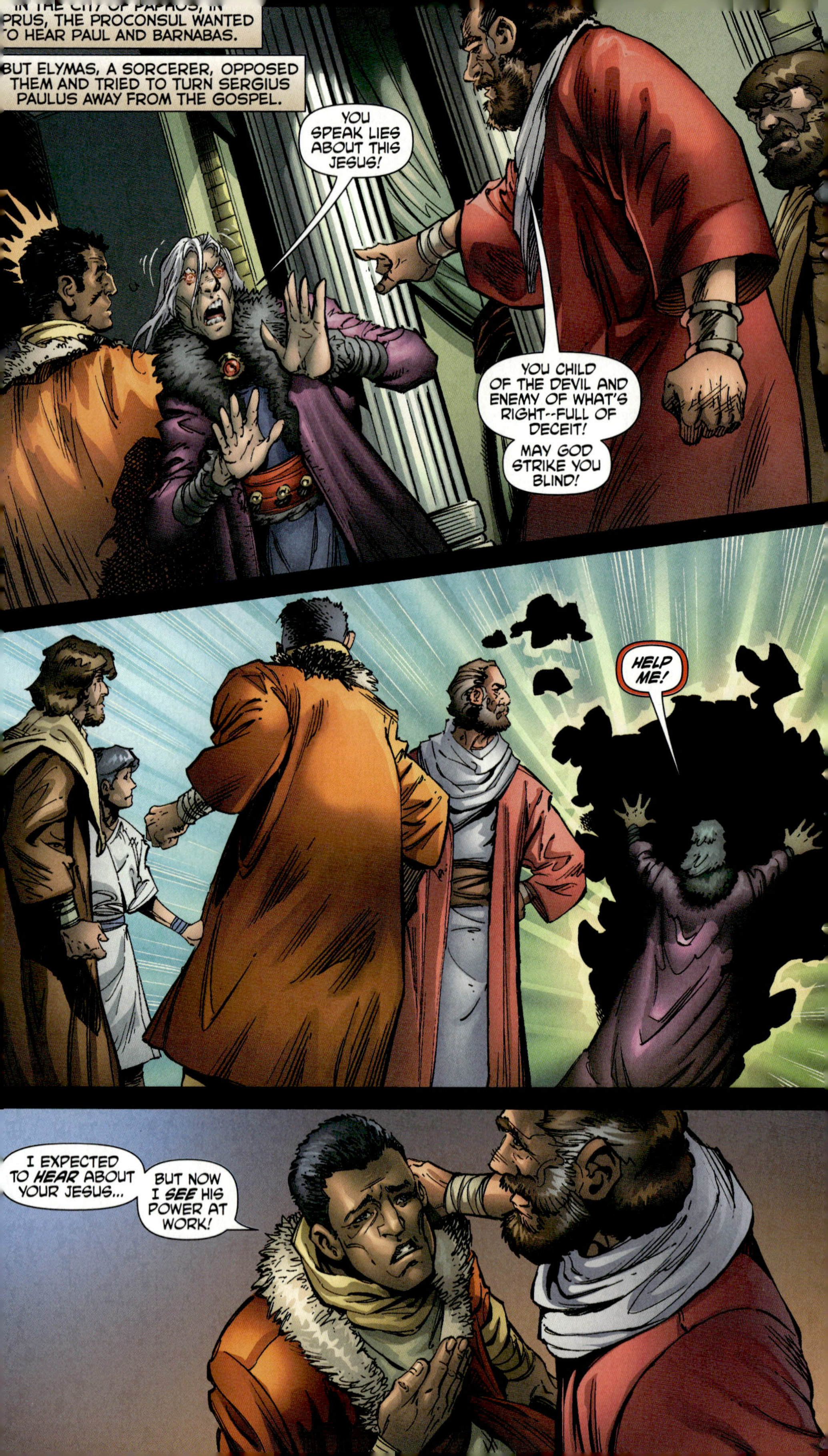
PRUS, THE PROCONSUL WANTED
O HEAR PAUL AND BARNABAS.
BUT ELYMAS, A SORCERER, OPPOSED THEM AND TRIED TO TURN SERGIUS PAULUS AWAY FROM THE GOSPEL.
YOU SPEAK LIES ABOUT THIS JESUS!
YOU CHILD OF THE DEVIL AND ENEMY OF WHAT'S RIGHT--FULL OF DECEIT!
MAY GOD STRIKE YOU BLIND!
HELP ME!
I EXPECTED TO *HEAR* ABOUT YOUR JESUS...
BUT NOW I *SEE* HIS POWER AT WORK!

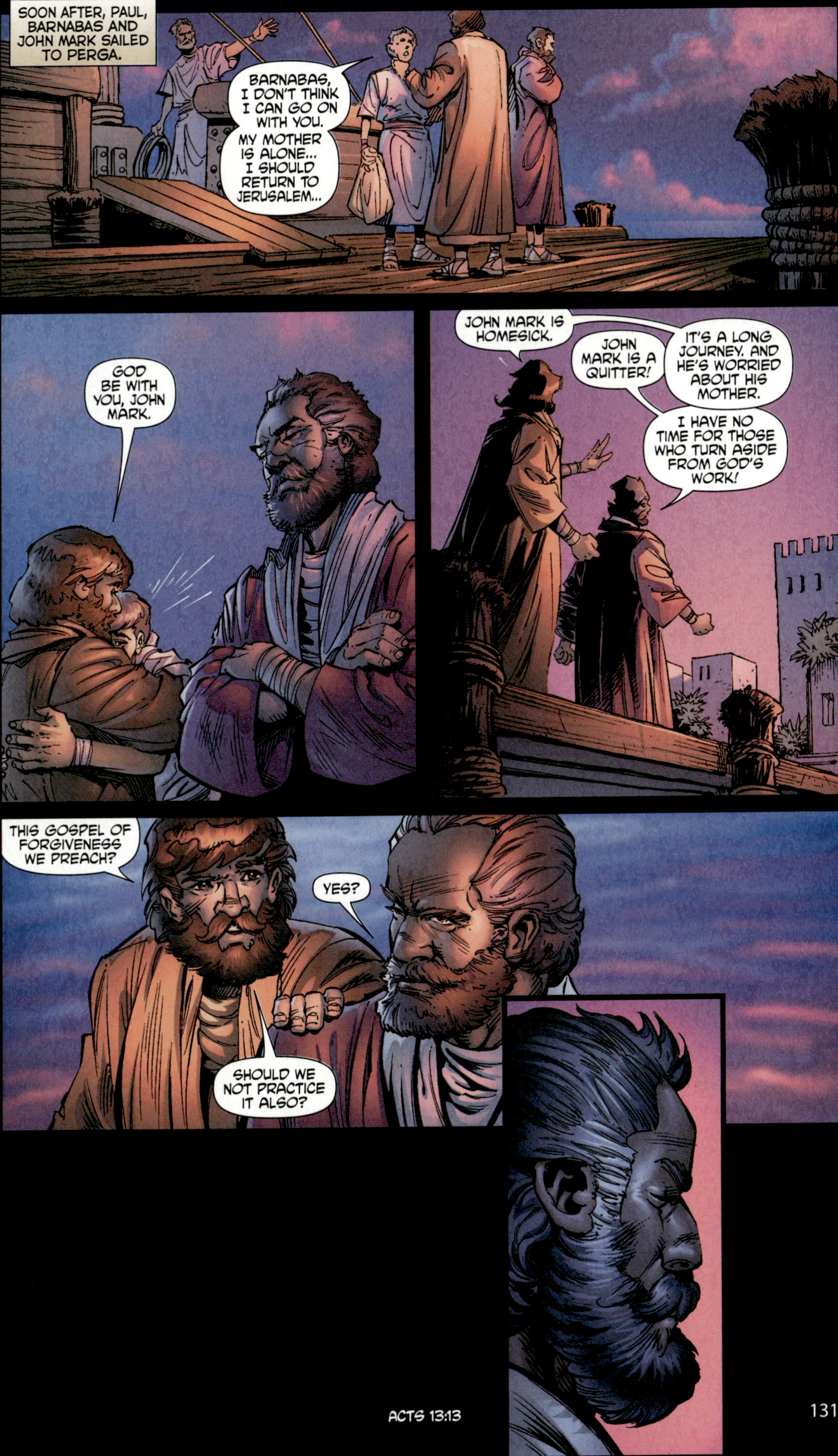
SOON AFTER, PAUL, BARNABAS AND JOHN MARK SAILED TO PERGA.
BARNABAS, I DON'T THINK I CAN GO ON WITH YOU. MY MOTHER IS ALONE... I SHOULD RETURN TO JERUSALEM...
GOD BE WITH YOU, JOHN MARK.
JOHN MARK IS HOMESICK.
JOHN MARK IS A QUITTER!
IT'S A LONG JOURNEY. AND HE'S WORRIED ABOUT HIS MOTHER.
I HAVE NO TIME FOR THOSE WHO TURN ASIDE FROM GOD'S WORK!
THIS GOSPEL OF FORGIVENESS WE PREACH?
YES?
SHOULD WE NOT PRACTICE IT ALSO?

ACTS 13:13

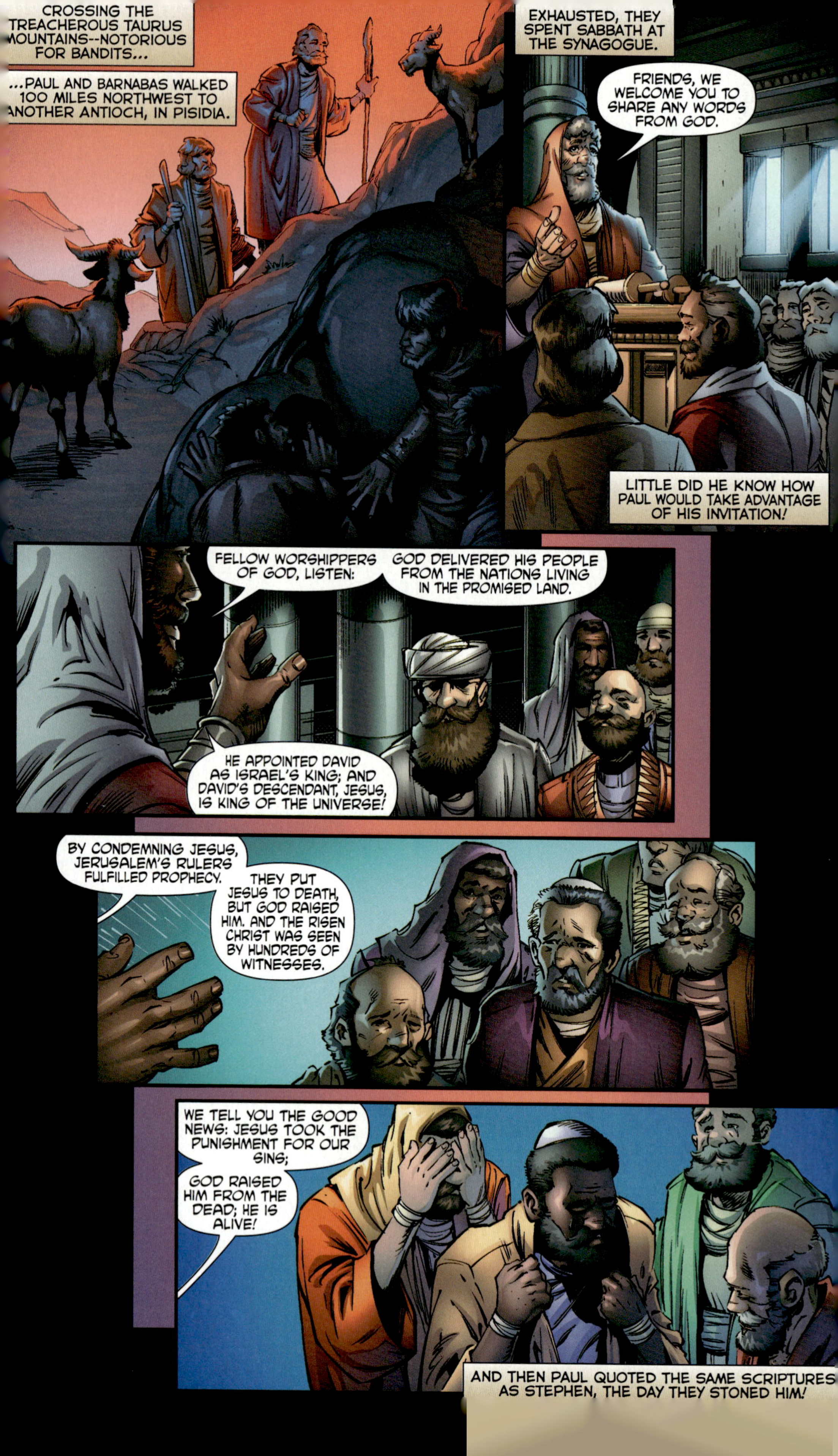
CROSSING THE TREACHEROUS TAURUS MOUNTAINS--NOTORIOUS FOR BANDITS...
...PAUL AND BARNABAS WALKED 100 MILES NORTHWEST TO ANOTHER ANTIOCH, IN PISIDIA.
EXHAUSTED, THEY SPENT SABBATH AT THE SYNAGOGUE.
FRIENDS, WE WELCOME YOU TO SHARE ANY WORDS FROM GOD.
LITTLE DID HE KNOW HOW PAUL WOULD TAKE ADVANTAGE OF HIS INVITATION!
FELLOW WORSHIPPERS OF GOD, LISTEN:
GOD DELIVERED HIS PEOPLE FROM THE NATIONS LIVING IN THE PROMISED LAND.
HE APPOINTED DAVID AS ISRAEL'S KING; AND DAVID'S DESCENDANT, JESUS, IS KING OF THE UNIVERSE!
BY CONDEMNING JESUS, JERUSALEM'S RULERS FULFILLED PROPHECY.
THEY PUT JESUS TO DEATH, BUT GOD RAISED HIM. AND THE RISEN CHRIST WAS SEEN BY HUNDREDS OF WITNESSES.
WE TELL YOU THE GOOD NEWS: JESUS TOOK THE PUNISHMENT FOR OUR SINS;
GOD RAISED HIM FROM THE DEAD; HE IS ALIVE!
AND THEN PAUL QUOTED THE SAME SCRIPTURES AS STEPHEN, THE DAY THEY STONED HIM!

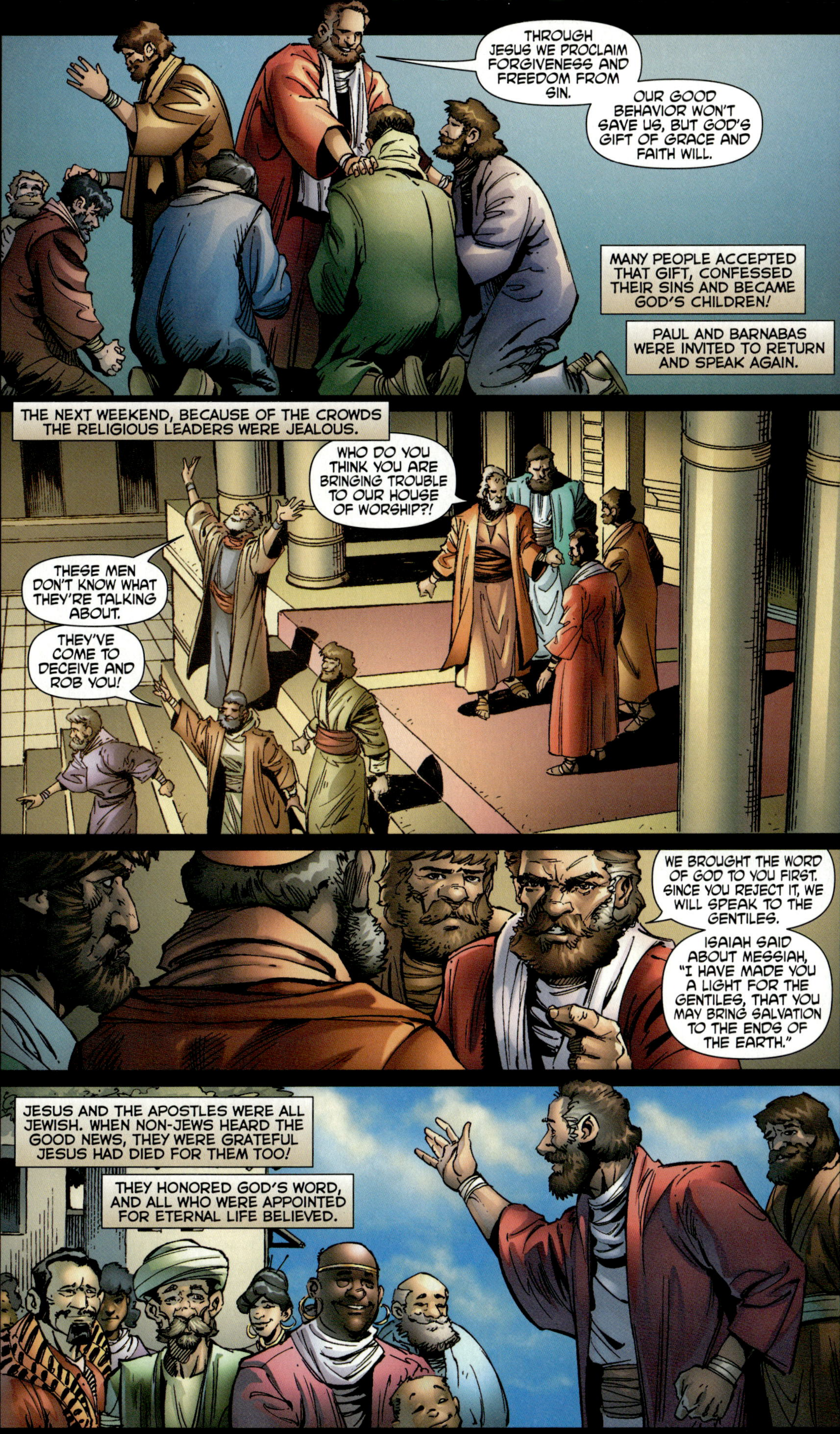
THROUGH JESUS WE PROCLAIM FORGIVENESS AND FREEDOM FROM SIN.
OUR GOOD BEHAVIOR WON'T SAVE US, BUT GOD'S GIFT OF GRACE AND FAITH WILL.
MANY PEOPLE ACCEPTED THAT GIFT, CONFESSED THEIR SINS AND BECAME GOD'S CHILDREN!
PAUL AND BARNABAS WERE INVITED TO RETURN AND SPEAK AGAIN.
THE NEXT WEEKEND, BECAUSE OF THE CROWDS THE RELIGIOUS LEADERS WERE JEALOUS.
WHO DO YOU THINK YOU ARE BRINGING TROUBLE TO OUR HOUSE OF WORSHIP?!
THESE MEN DON'T KNOW WHAT THEY'RE TALKING ABOUT.
THEY'VE COME TO DECEIVE AND ROB YOU!
WE BROUGHT THE WORD OF GOD TO YOU FIRST. SINCE YOU REJECT IT, WE WILL SPEAK TO THE GENTILES.
ISAIAH SAID ABOUT MESSIAH, "I HAVE MADE YOU A LIGHT FOR THE GENTILES, THAT YOU MAY BRING SALVATION TO THE ENDS OF THE EARTH."
JESUS AND THE APOSTLES WERE ALL JEWISH. WHEN NON-JEWS HEARD THE GOOD NEWS, THEY WERE GRATEFUL JESUS HAD DIED FOR THEM TOO!
THEY HONORED GOD'S WORD, AND ALL WHO WERE APPOINTED FOR ETERNAL LIFE BELIEVED.

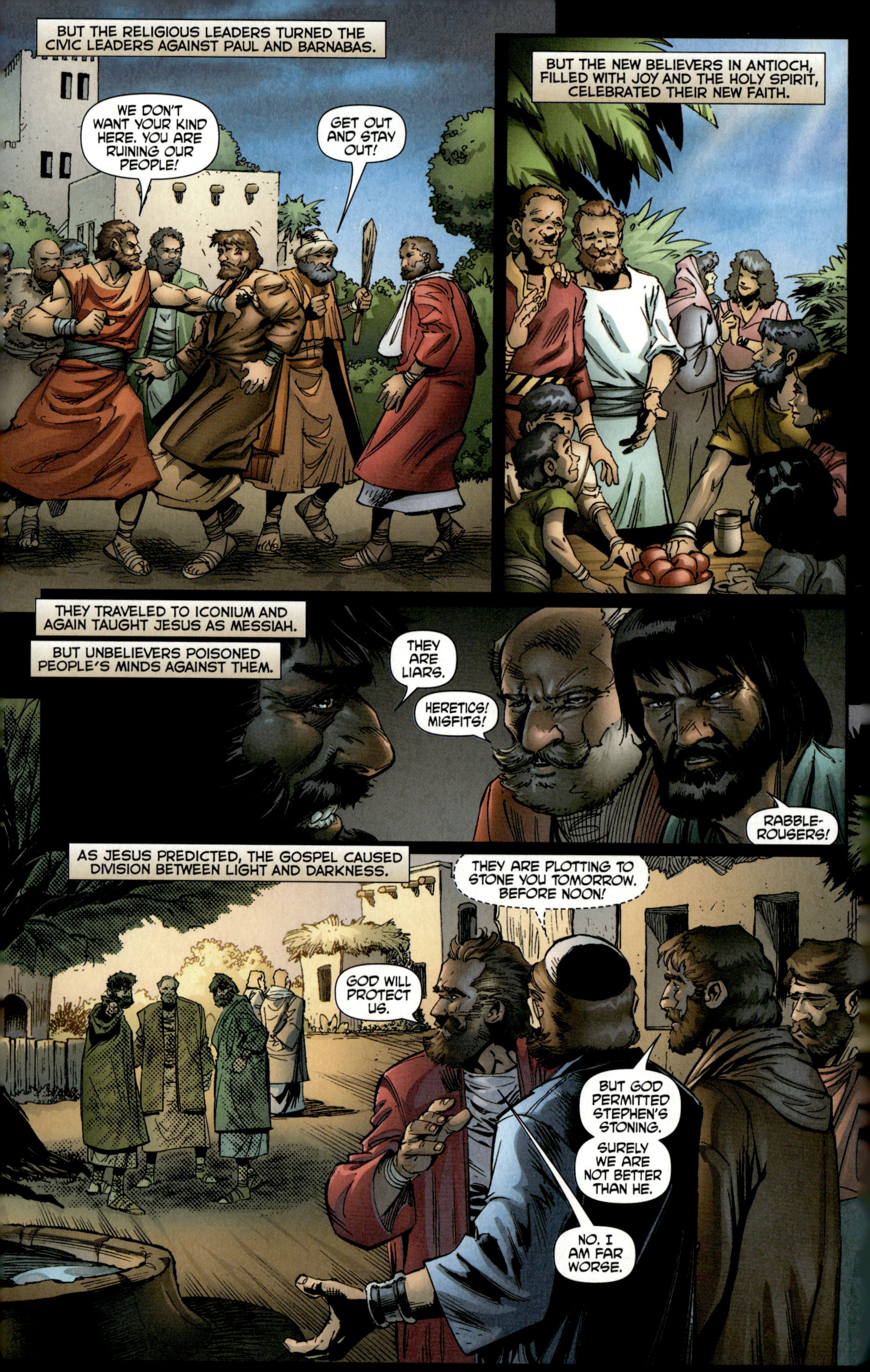
BUT THE RELIGIOUS LEADERS TURNED THE CIVIC LEADERS AGAINST PAUL AND BARNABAS.
WE DON'T WANT YOUR KIND HERE. YOU ARE RUINING OUR PEOPLE!
GET OUT AND STAY OUT!
BUT THE NEW BELIEVERS IN ANTIOCH, FILLED WITH JOY AND THE HOLY SPIRIT, CELEBRATED THEIR NEW FAITH.
THEY TRAVELED TO ICONIUM AND AGAIN TAUGHT JESUS AS MESSIAH.
BUT UNBELIEVERS POISONED PEOPLE'S MINDS AGAINST THEM.
THEY ARE LIARS.
HERETICS! MISFITS!
RABBLE-ROUSERS!
AS JESUS PREDICTED, THE GOSPEL CAUSED DIVISION BETWEEN LIGHT AND DARKNESS.
THEY ARE PLOTTING TO STONE YOU TOMORROW. BEFORE NOON!
GOD WILL PROTECT US.
BUT GOD PERMITTED STEPHEN'S STONING.
SURELY WE ARE NOT BETTER THAN HE.
NO. I AM FAR WORSE.

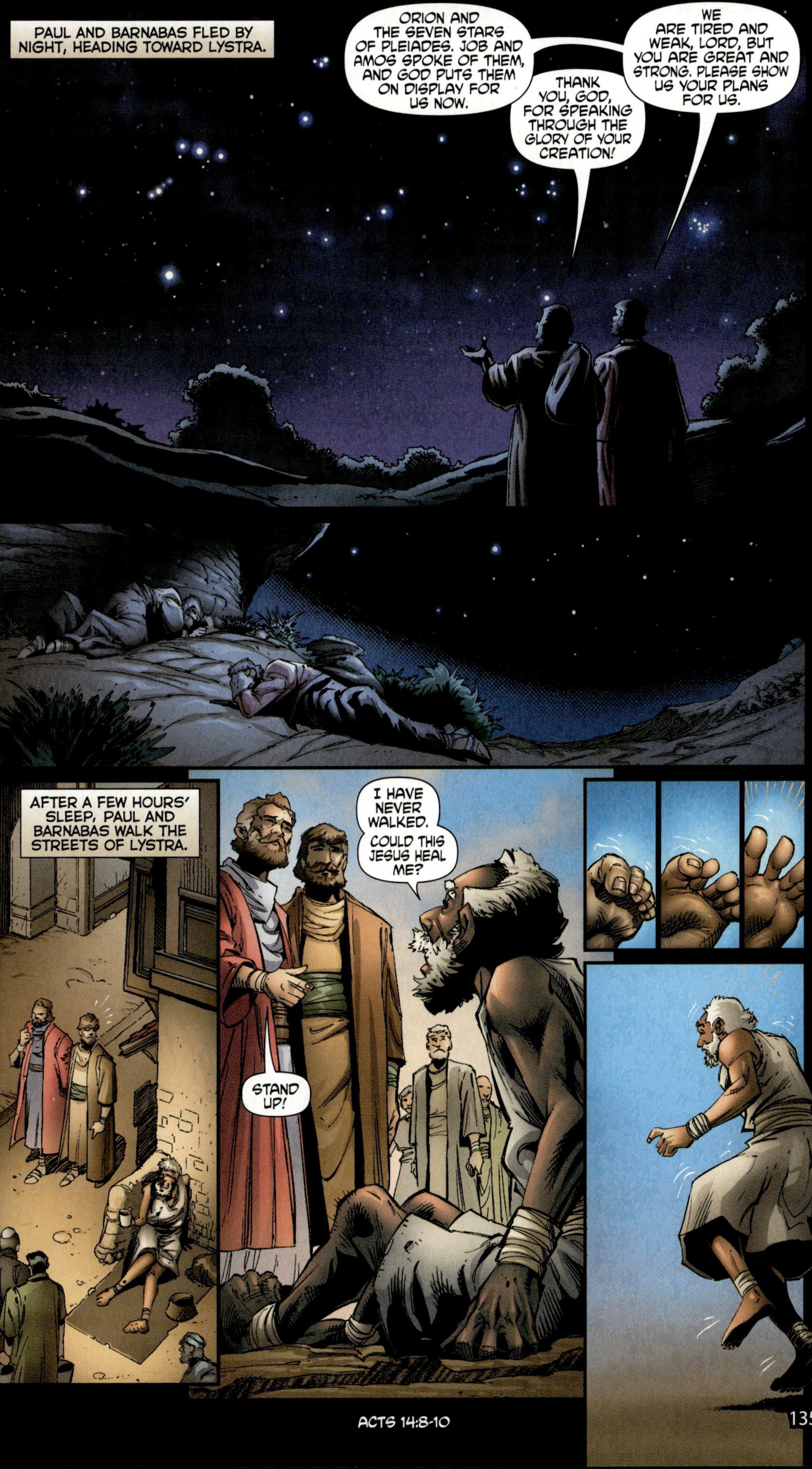

PAUL AND BARNABAS FLED BY NIGHT, HEADING TOWARD LYSTRA.
ORION AND THE SEVEN STARS OF PLEIADES. JOB AND AMOS SPOKE OF THEM, AND GOD PUTS THEM ON DISPLAY FOR US NOW.
WE ARE TIRED AND WEAK, LORD, BUT YOU ARE GREAT AND STRONG. PLEASE SHOW US YOUR PLANS FOR US.
THANK YOU, GOD, FOR SPEAKING THROUGH THE GLORY OF YOUR CREATION!
AFTER A FEW HOURS' SLEEP, PAUL AND BARNABAS WALK THE STREETS OF LYSTRA.
I HAVE NEVER WALKED.
COULD THIS JESUS HEAL ME?
STAND UP!

ACTS 14:8-10

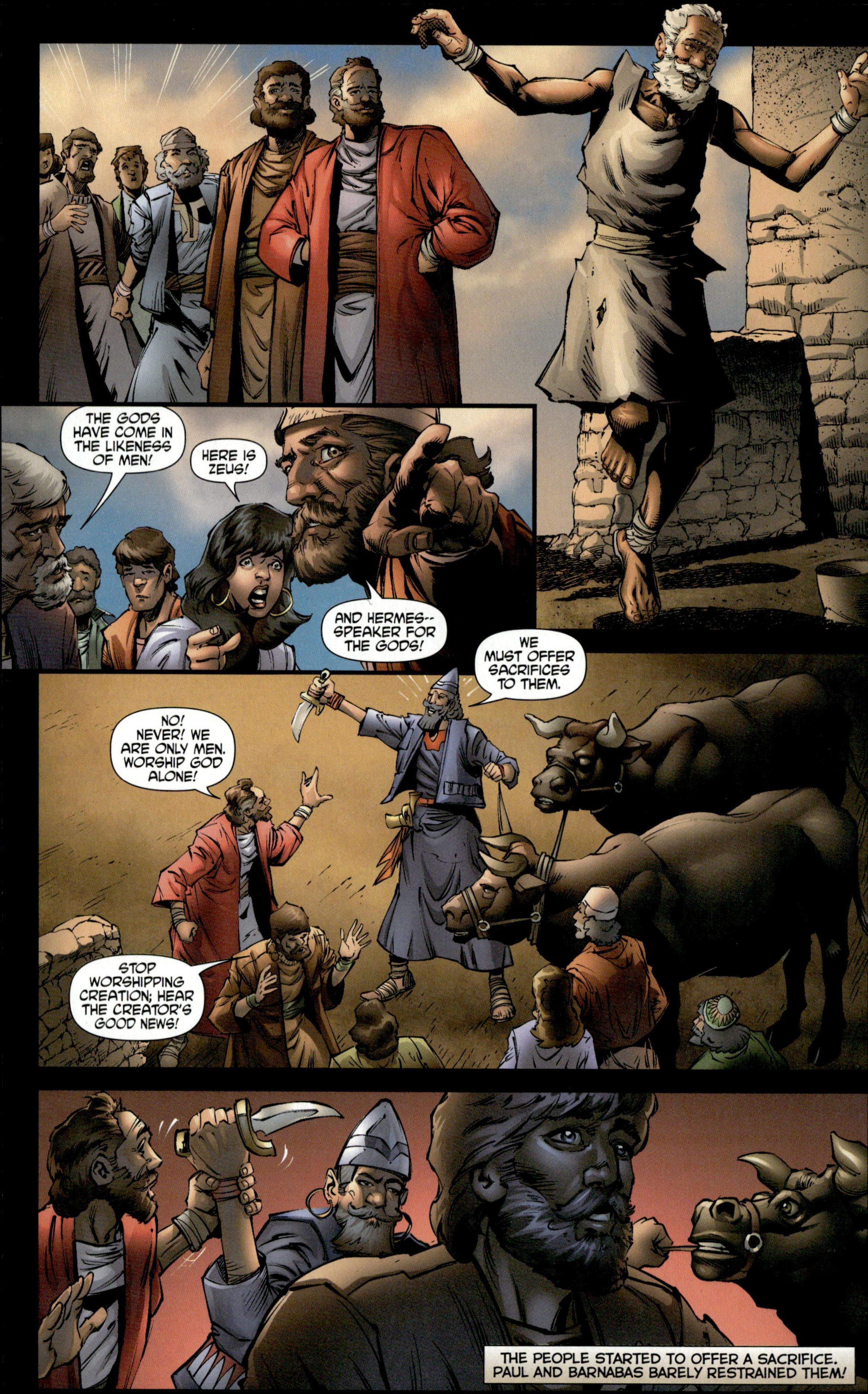
THE GODS HAVE COME IN THE LIKENESS OF MEN!
HERE IS ZEUS!
AND HERMES-- SPEAKER FOR THE GODS!
WE MUST OFFER SACRIFICES TO THEM.
NO! NEVER! WE ARE ONLY MEN. WORSHIP GOD ALONE!
STOP WORSHIPPING CREATION; HEAR THE CREATOR'S GOOD NEWS!
THE PEOPLE STARTED TO OFFER A SACRIFICE. PAUL AND BARNABAS BARELY RESTRAINED THEM!

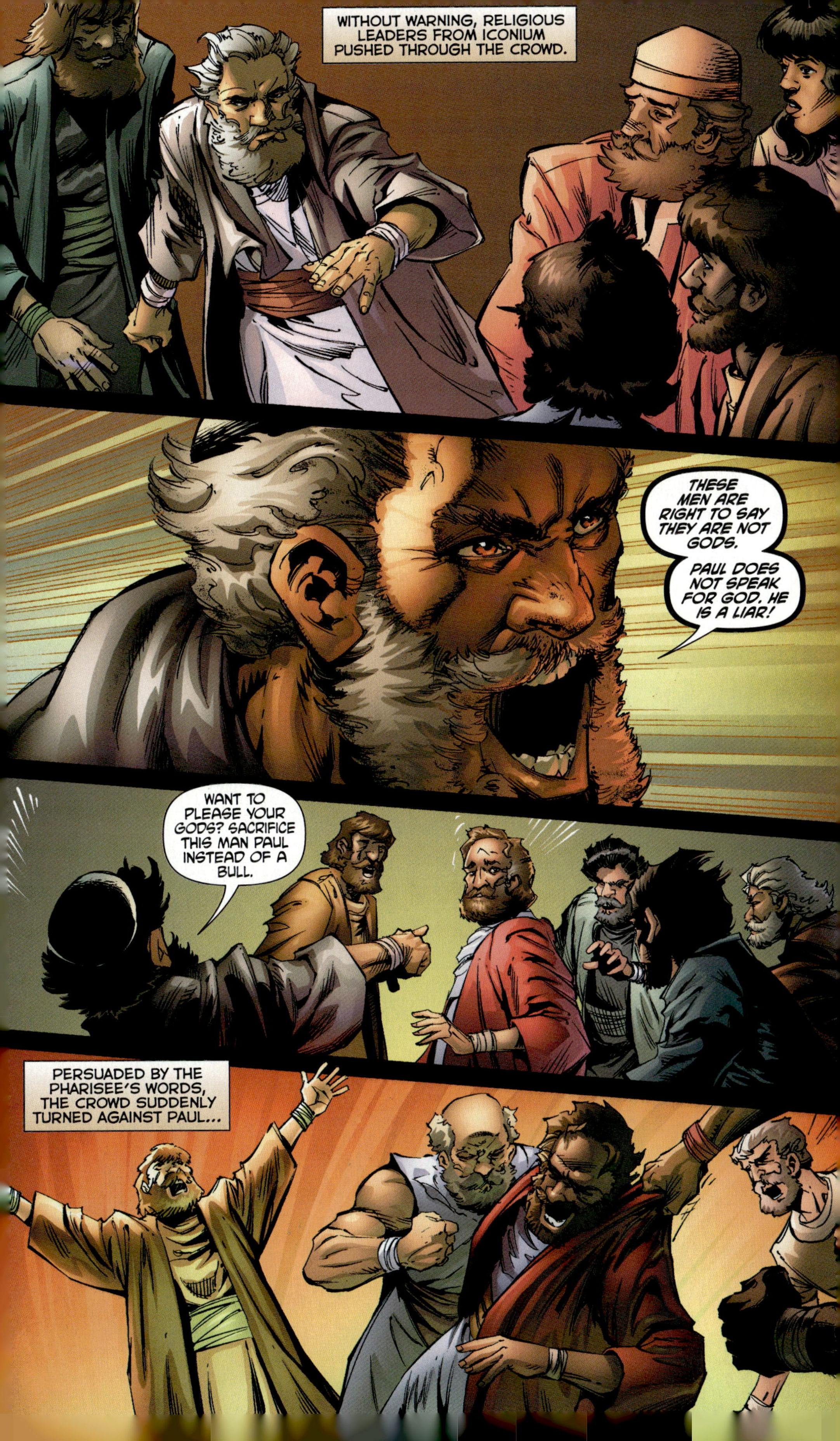
WITHOUT WARNING, RELIGIOUS LEADERS FROM ICONIUM PUSHED THROUGH THE CROWD.
THESE MEN ARE RIGHT TO SAY THEY ARE NOT GODS.
PAUL DOES NOT SPEAK FOR GOD. HE IS A LIAR!
WANT TO PLEASE YOUR GODS? SACRIFICE THIS MAN PAUL INSTEAD OF A BULL.
PERSUADED BY THE PHARISEE'S WORDS, THE CROWD SUDDENLY TURNED AGAINST PAUL...

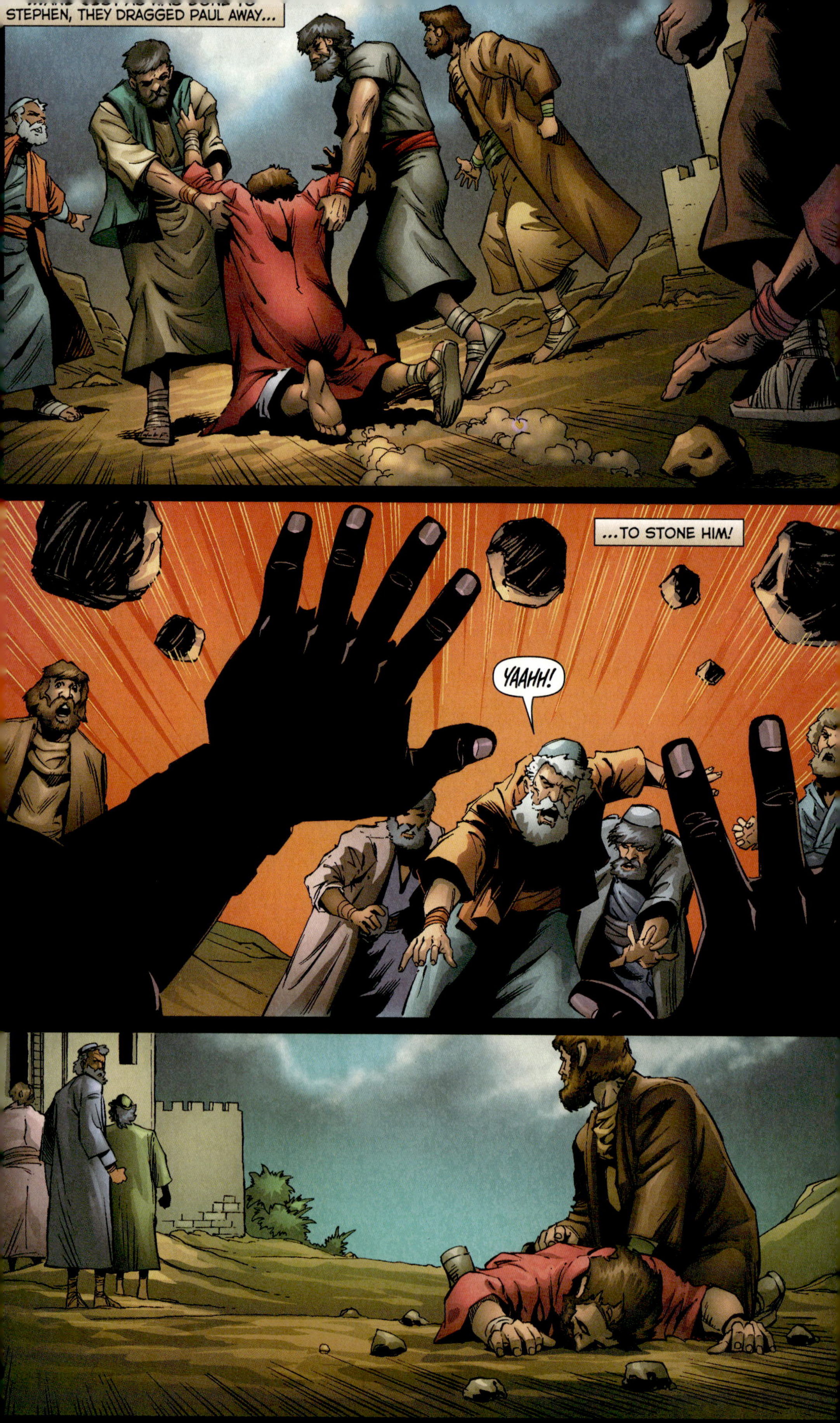
STEPHEN, THEY DRAGGED PAUL AWAY...
...TO STONE HIM!
YAAHH!

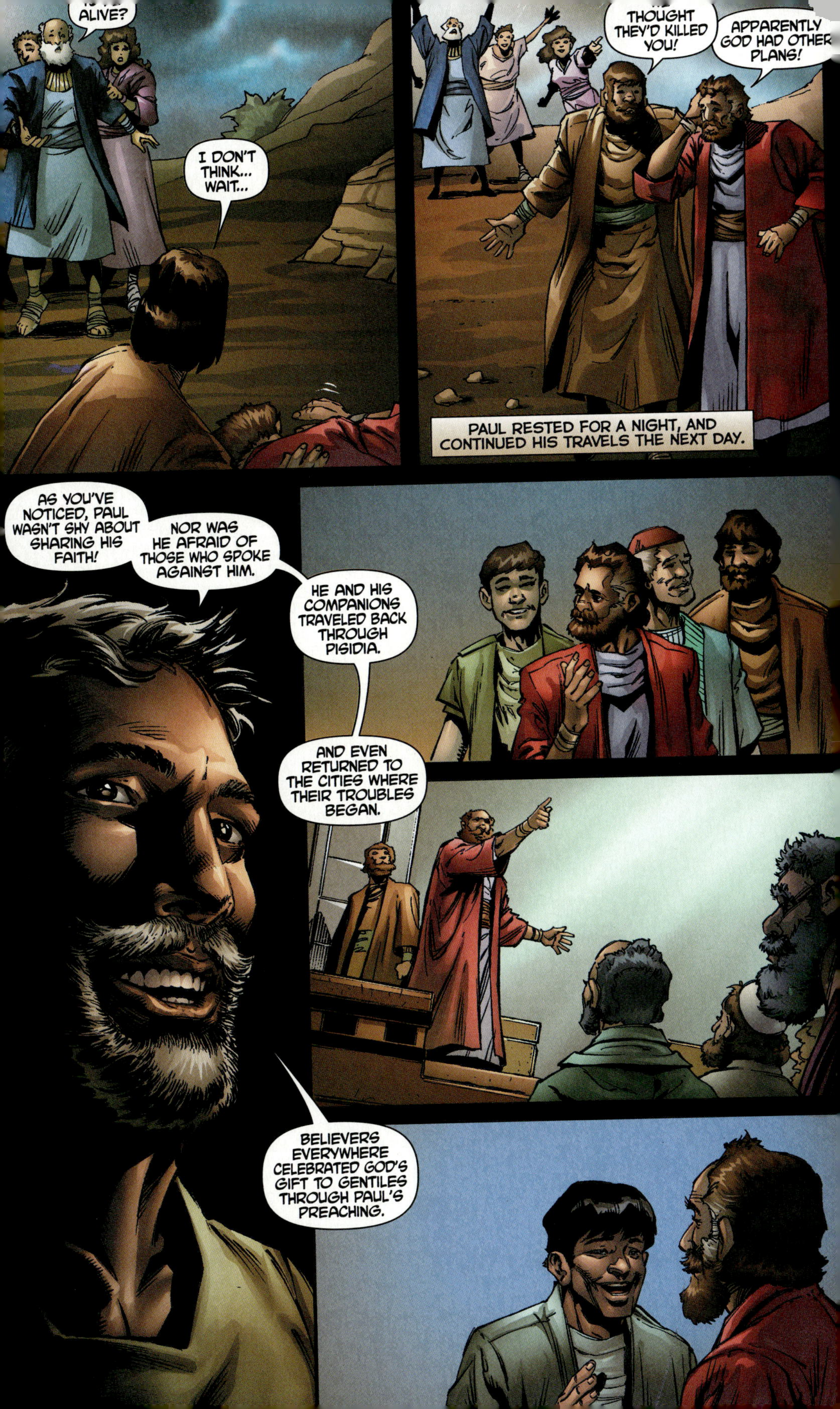
ALIVE?
I DON'T THINK... WAIT...
THOUGHT THEY'D KILLED YOU!
APPARENTLY GOD HAD OTHER PLANS!
PAUL RESTED FOR A NIGHT, AND CONTINUED HIS TRAVELS THE NEXT DAY.
AS YOU'VE NOTICED, PAUL WASN'T SHY ABOUT SHARING HIS FAITH!
NOR WAS HE AFRAID OF THOSE WHO SPOKE AGAINST HIM.
HE AND HIS COMPANIONS TRAVELED BACK THROUGH PISIDIA.
AND EVEN RETURNED TO THE CITIES WHERE THEIR TROUBLES BEGAN.
BELIEVERS EVERYWHERE CELEBRATED GOD'S GIFT TO GENTILES THROUGH PAUL'S PREACHING.

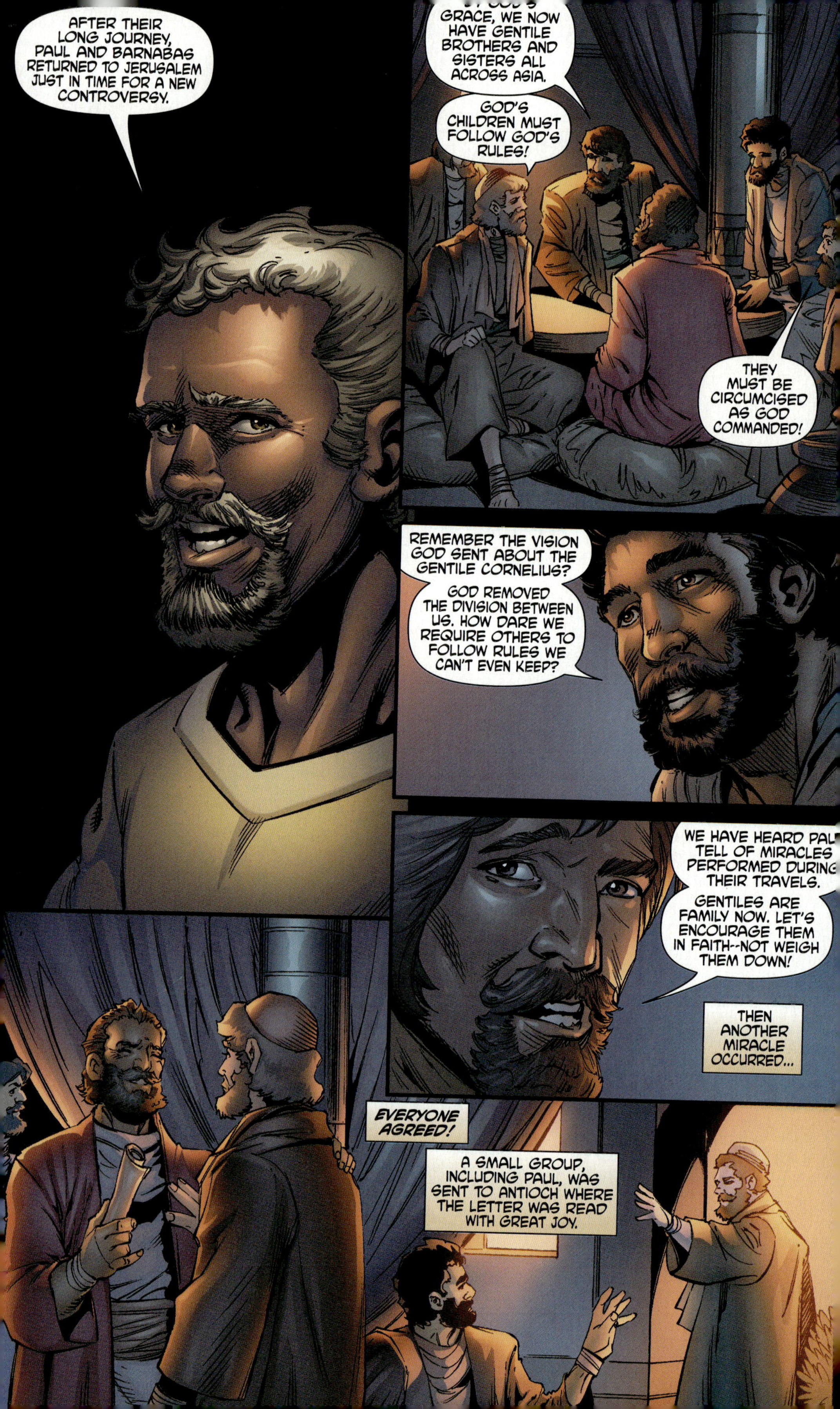
AFTER THEIR LONG JOURNEY, PAUL AND BARNABAS RETURNED TO JERUSALEM JUST IN TIME FOR A NEW CONTROVERSY.
GRACE, WE NOW HAVE GENTILE BROTHERS AND SISTERS ALL ACROSS ASIA.
GOD'S CHILDREN MUST FOLLOW GOD'S RULES!
THEY MUST BE CIRCUMCISED AS GOD COMMANDED!
REMEMBER THE VISION GOD SENT ABOUT THE GENTILE CORNELIUS?
GOD REMOVED THE DIVISION BETWEEN US. HOW DARE WE REQUIRE OTHERS TO FOLLOW RULES WE CAN'T EVEN KEEP?
WE HAVE HEARD PAU TELL OF MIRACLES PERFORMED DURIN THEIR TRAVELS.
GENTILES ARE FAMILY NOW. LET'S ENCOURAGE THEM IN FAITH--NOT WEIGH THEM DOWN!
THEN ANOTHER MIRACLE OCCURRED...
EVERYONE AGREED!
A SMALL GROUP, INCLUDING PAUL, WAS SENT TO ANTIOCH WHERE THE LETTER WAS READ WITH GREAT JOY.

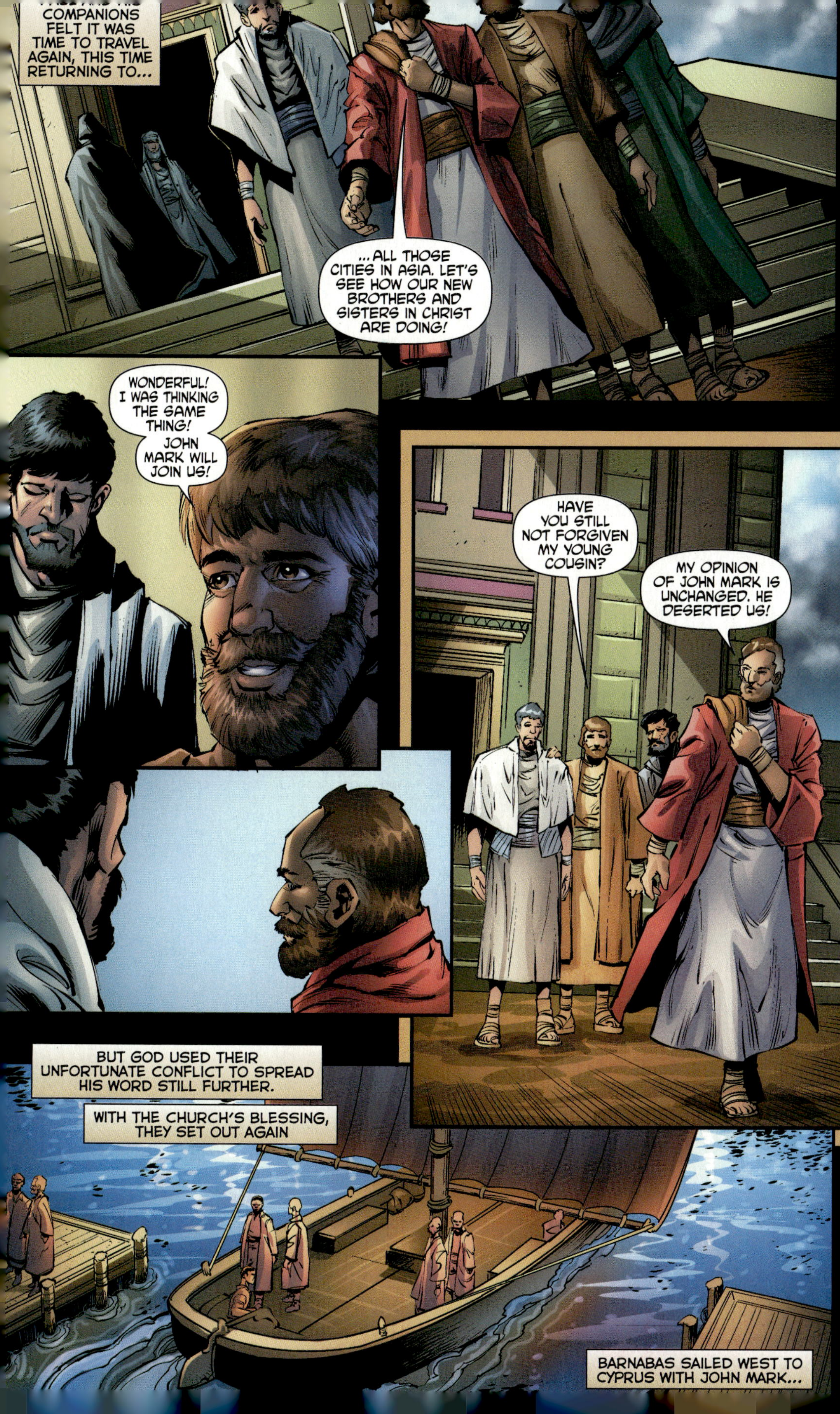
COMPANIONS FELT IT WAS TIME TO TRAVEL AGAIN, THIS TIME RETURNING TO...
...ALL THOSE CITIES IN ASIA. LET'S SEE HOW OUR NEW BROTHERS AND SISTERS IN CHRIST ARE DOING!
WONDERFUL! I WAS THINKING THE SAME THING!
JOHN MARK WILL JOIN US!
HAVE YOU STILL NOT FORGIVEN MY YOUNG COUSIN?
MY OPINION OF JOHN MARK IS UNCHANGED. HE DESERTED US!
BUT GOD USED THEIR UNFORTUNATE CONFLICT TO SPREAD HIS WORD STILL FURTHER.
WITH THE CHURCH'S BLESSING, THEY SET OUT AGAIN
BARNABAS SAILED WEST TO CYPRUS WITH JOHN MARK...

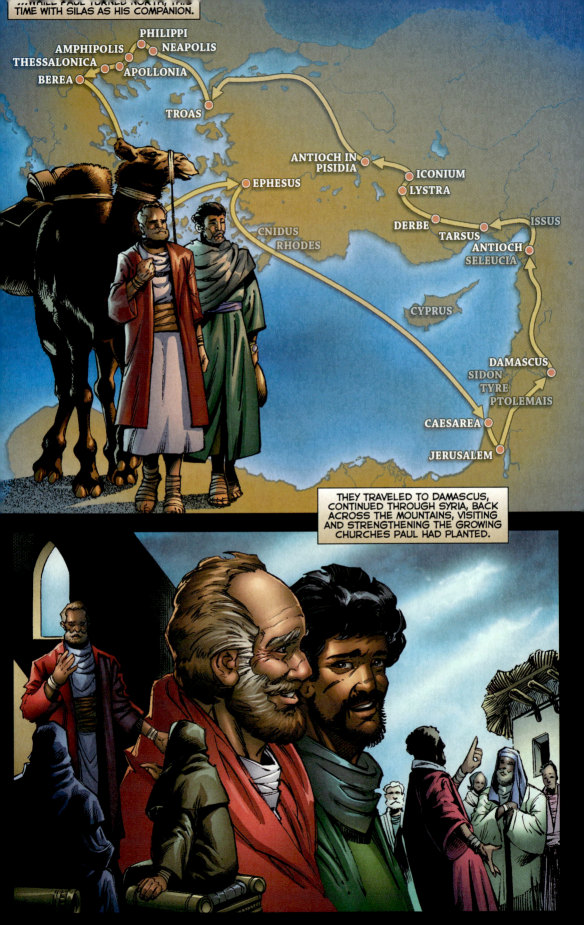

...WHILE PAUL TURNED NORTH, THIS TIME WITH SILAS AS HIS COMPANION.

PHILIPPI
NEAPOLIS
AMPHIPOLIS
THESSALONICA
APOLLONIA
BEREA

TROAS

ANTIOCH IN PISIDIA

ICONIUM
LYSTRA

EPHESUS

CNIDUS
RHODES

DERBE
TARSUS
ISSUS
ANTIOCH
SELEUCIA

CYPRUS

DAMASCUS
SIDON
TYRE
PTOLEMAIS

CAESAREA

JERUSALEM

THEY TRAVELED TO DAMASCUS, CONTINUED THROUGH SYRIA, BACK ACROSS THE MOUNTAINS, VISITING AND STRENGTHENING THE GROWING CHURCHES PAUL HAD PLANTED.

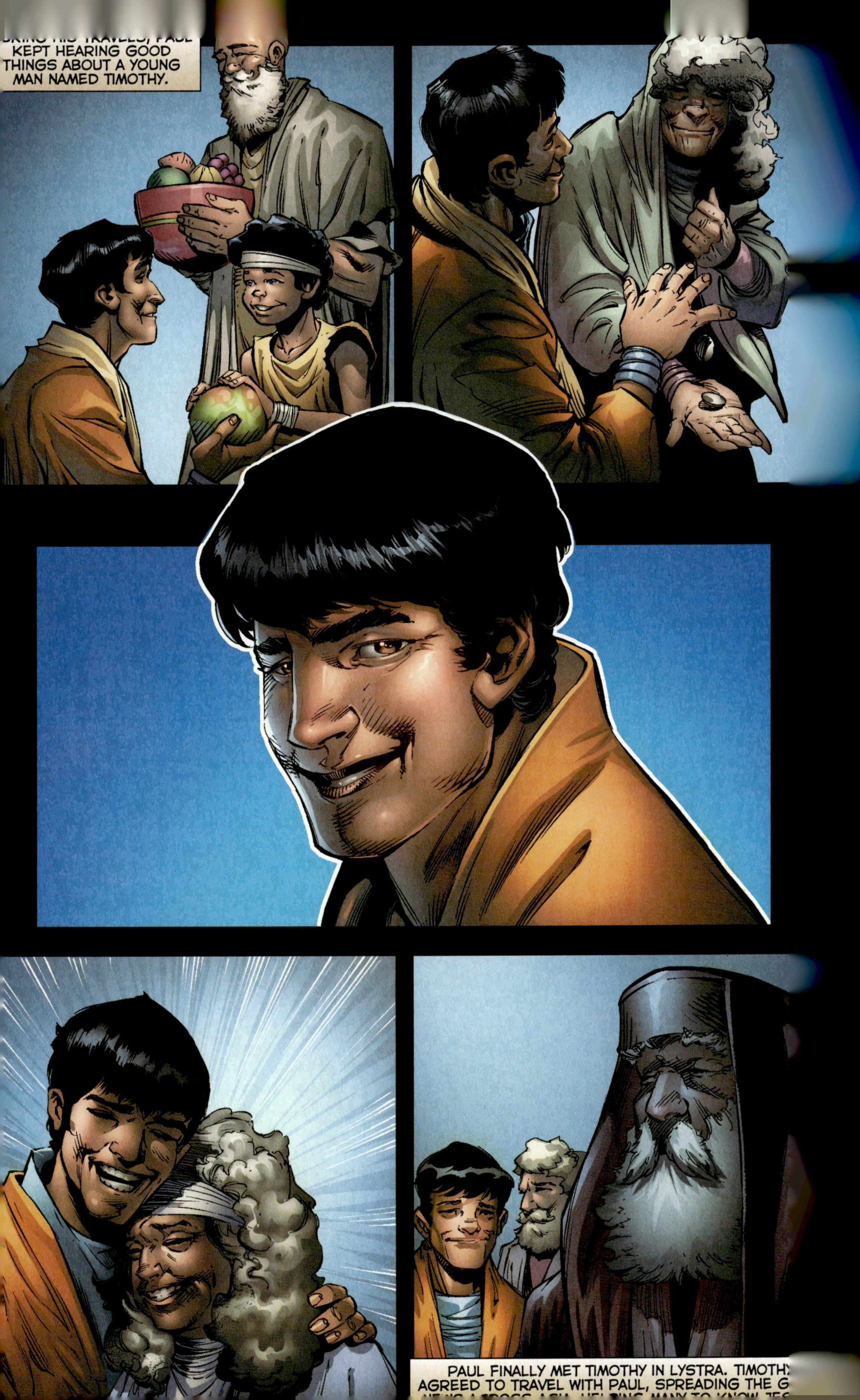
KEPT HEARING GOOD THINGS ABOUT A YOUNG MAN NAMED TIMOTHY.
PAUL FINALLY MET TIMOTHY IN LYSTRA.
AGREED TO TRAVEL WITH PAUL, SPREADING THE

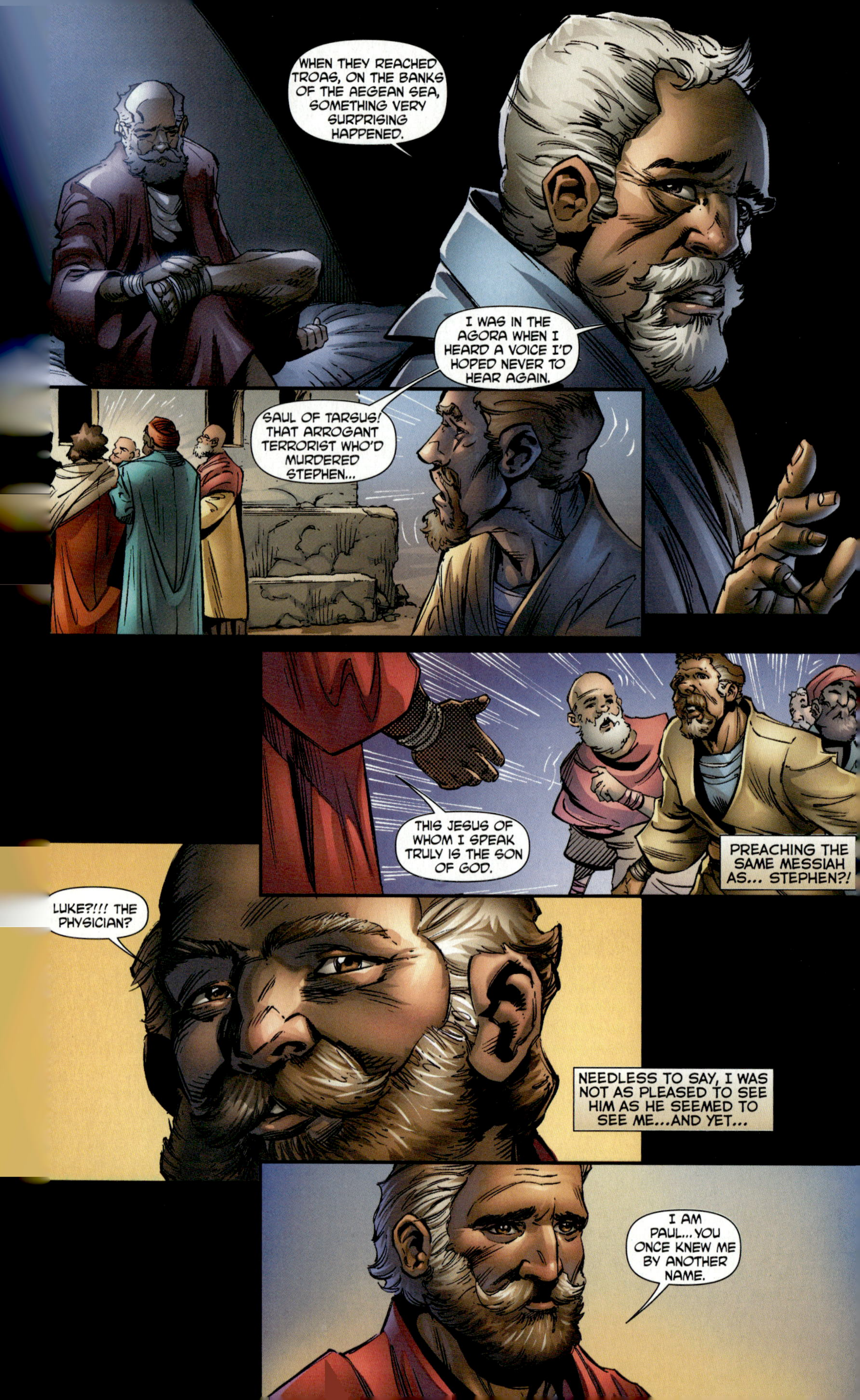
WHEN THEY REACHED TROAS, ON THE BANKS OF THE AEGEAN SEA, SOMETHING VERY SURPRISING HAPPENED.
I WAS IN THE AGORA WHEN I HEARD A VOICE I'D HOPED NEVER TO HEAR AGAIN.
SAUL OF TARSUS! THAT ARROGANT TERRORIST WHO'D MURDERED STEPHEN...
THIS JESUS OF WHOM I SPEAK TRULY IS THE SON OF GOD.
PREACHING THE SAME MESSIAH AS... STEPHEN?!
LUKE?!!! THE PHYSICIAN?
NEEDLESS TO SAY, I WAS NOT AS PLEASED TO SEE HIM AS HE SEEMED TO SEE ME...AND YET...
I AM PAUL...YOU ONCE KNEW ME BY ANOTHER NAME.

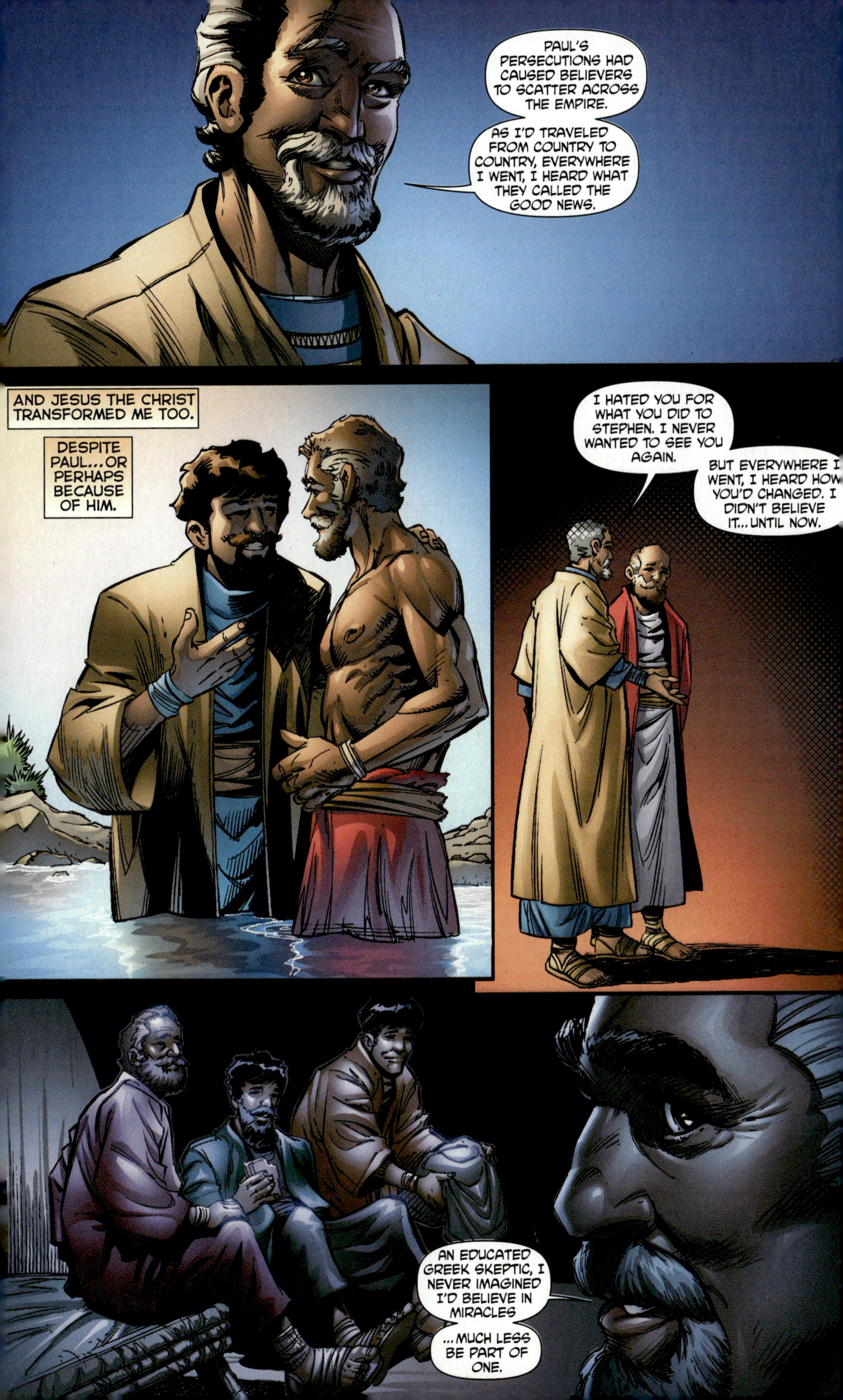
PAUL'S PERSECUTIONS HAD CAUSED BELIEVERS TO SCATTER ACROSS THE EMPIRE.
AS I'D TRAVELED FROM COUNTRY TO COUNTRY, EVERYWHERE I WENT, I HEARD WHAT THEY CALLED THE GOOD NEWS.
AND JESUS THE CHRIST TRANSFORMED ME TOO.
DESPITE PAUL...OR PERHAPS BECAUSE OF HIM.
I HATED YOU FOR WHAT YOU DID TO STEPHEN. I NEVER WANTED TO SEE YOU AGAIN.
BUT EVERYWHERE I WENT, I HEARD HOW YOU'D CHANGED. I DIDN'T BELIEVE IT...UNTIL NOW.
AN EDUCATED GREEK SKEPTIC, I NEVER IMAGINED I'D BELIEVE IN MIRACLES
...MUCH LESS BE PART OF ONE.

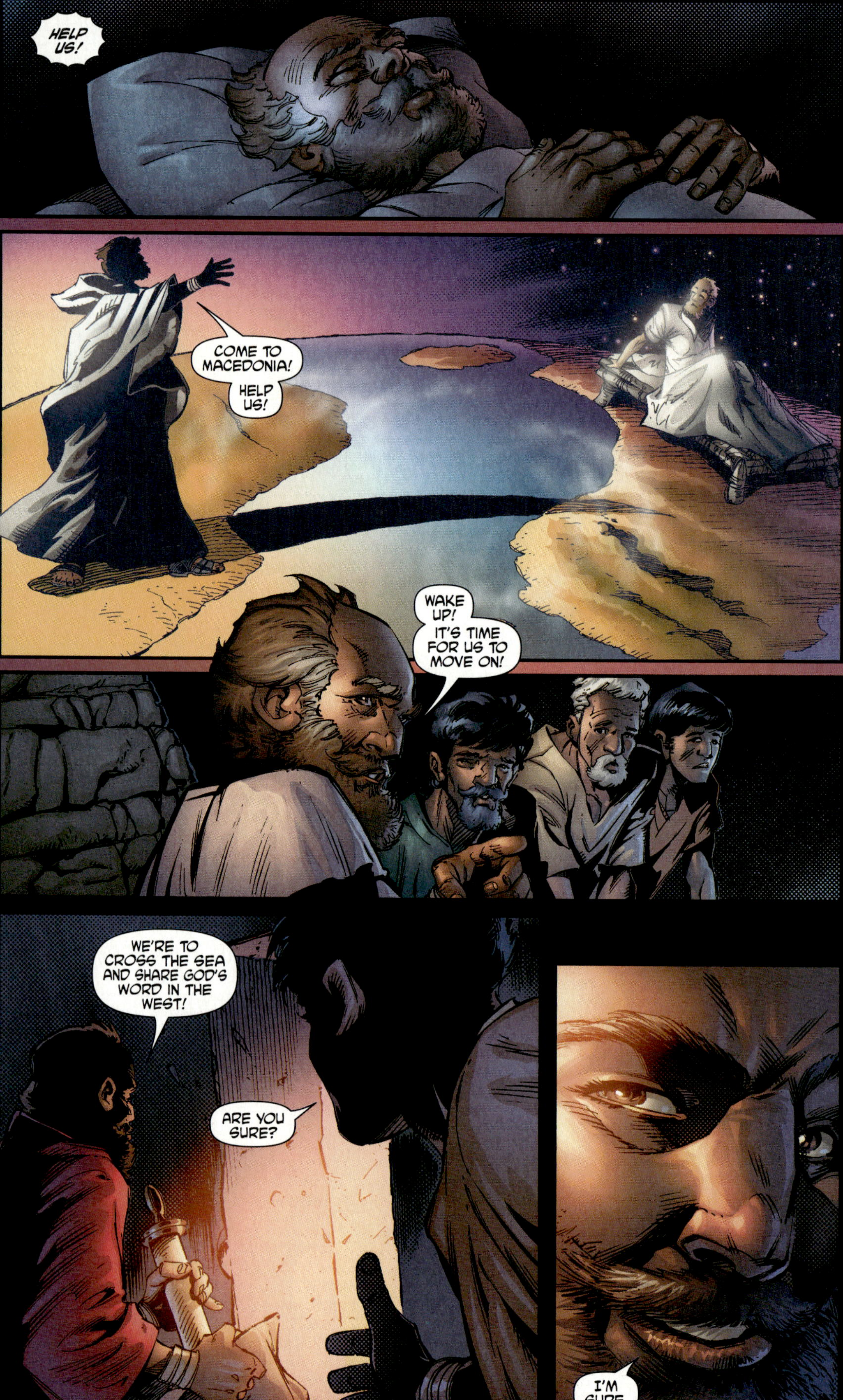
HELP US!
COME TO MACEDONIA!
HELP US!
WAKE UP!
IT'S TIME FOR US TO MOVE ON!
WE'RE TO CROSS THE SEA AND SHARE GOD'S WORD IN THE WEST!
ARE YOU SURE?
I'M

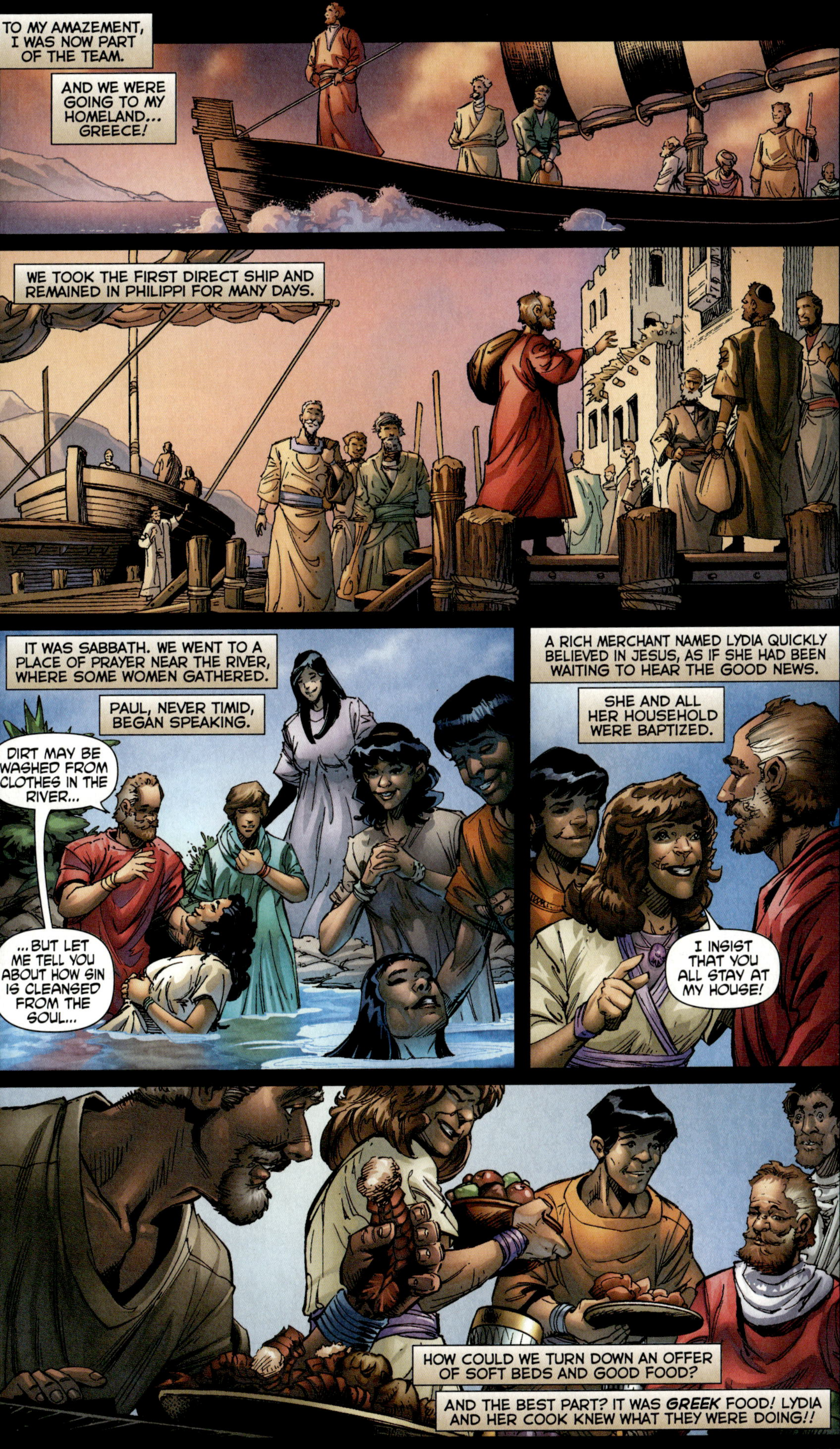
TO MY AMAZEMENT, I WAS NOW PART OF THE TEAM.
AND WE WERE GOING TO MY HOMELAND... GREECE!
WE TOOK THE FIRST DIRECT SHIP AND REMAINED IN PHILIPPI FOR MANY DAYS.
IT WAS SABBATH. WE WENT TO A PLACE OF PRAYER NEAR THE RIVER, WHERE SOME WOMEN GATHERED.
PAUL, NEVER TIMID, BEGAN SPEAKING.
DIRT MAY BE WASHED FROM CLOTHES IN THE RIVER...
...BUT LET ME TELL YOU ABOUT HOW SIN IS CLEANSED FROM THE SOUL...
A RICH MERCHANT NAMED LYDIA QUICKLY BELIEVED IN JESUS, AS IF SHE HAD BEEN WAITING TO HEAR THE GOOD NEWS.
SHE AND ALL HER HOUSEHOLD WERE BAPTIZED.
I INSIST THAT YOU ALL STAY AT MY HOUSE!
HOW COULD WE TURN DOWN AN OFFER OF SOFT BEDS AND GOOD FOOD?
AND THE BEST PART? IT WAS *GREEK* FOOD! LYDIA AND HER COOK KNEW WHAT THEY WERE DOING!!

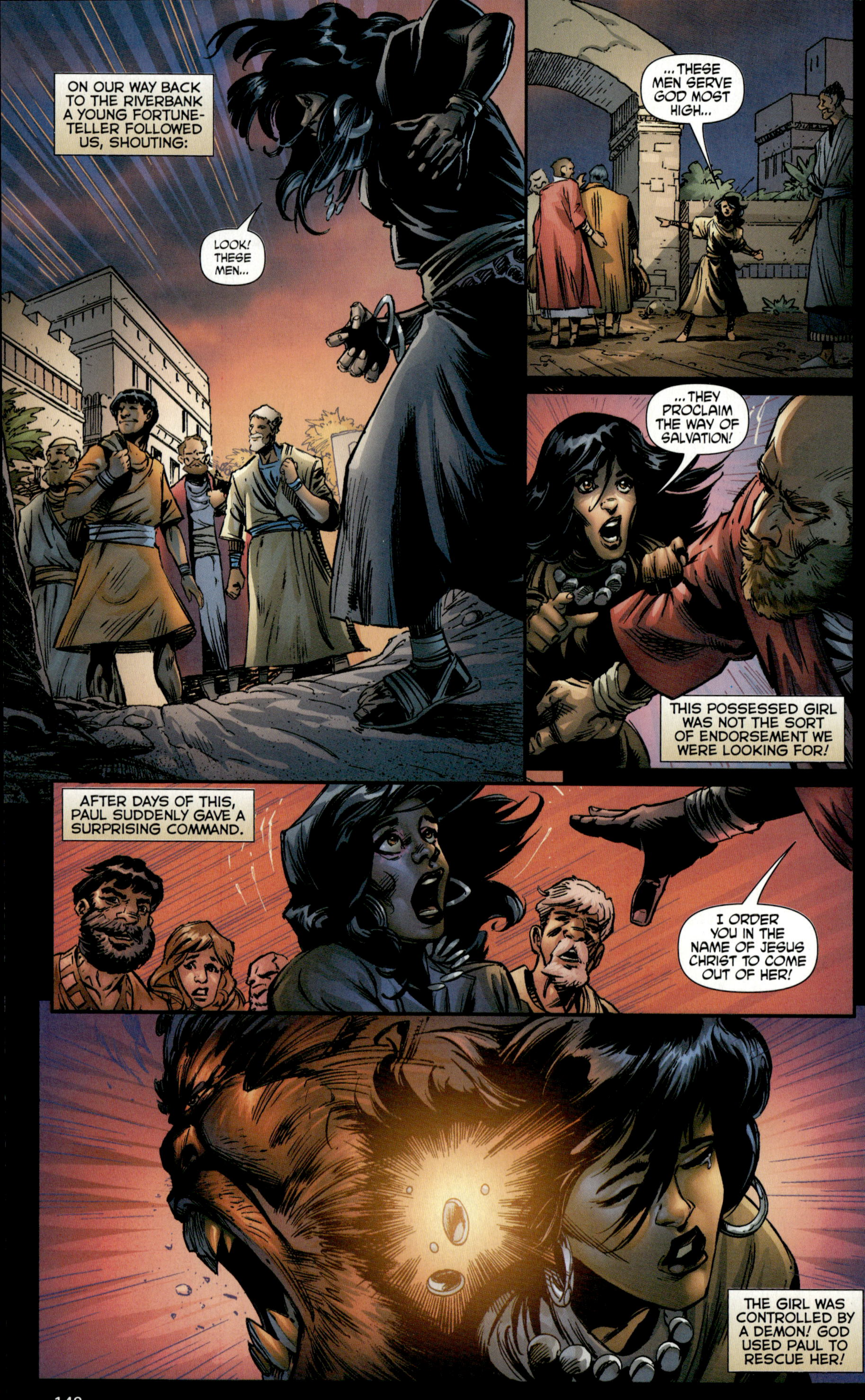
ON OUR WAY BACK TO THE RIVERBANK A YOUNG FORTUNE-TELLER FOLLOWED US, SHOUTING:
LOOK! THESE MEN...
...THESE MEN SERVE GOD MOST HIGH...
...THEY PROCLAIM THE WAY OF SALVATION!
THIS POSSESSED GIRL WAS NOT THE SORT OF ENDORSEMENT WE WERE LOOKING FOR!
AFTER DAYS OF THIS, PAUL SUDDENLY GAVE A SURPRISING COMMAND.
I ORDER YOU IN THE NAME OF JESUS CHRIST TO COME OUT OF HER!
THE GIRL WAS CONTROLLED BY A DEMON! GOD USED PAUL TO RESCUE HER!

ACTS 16:16-18

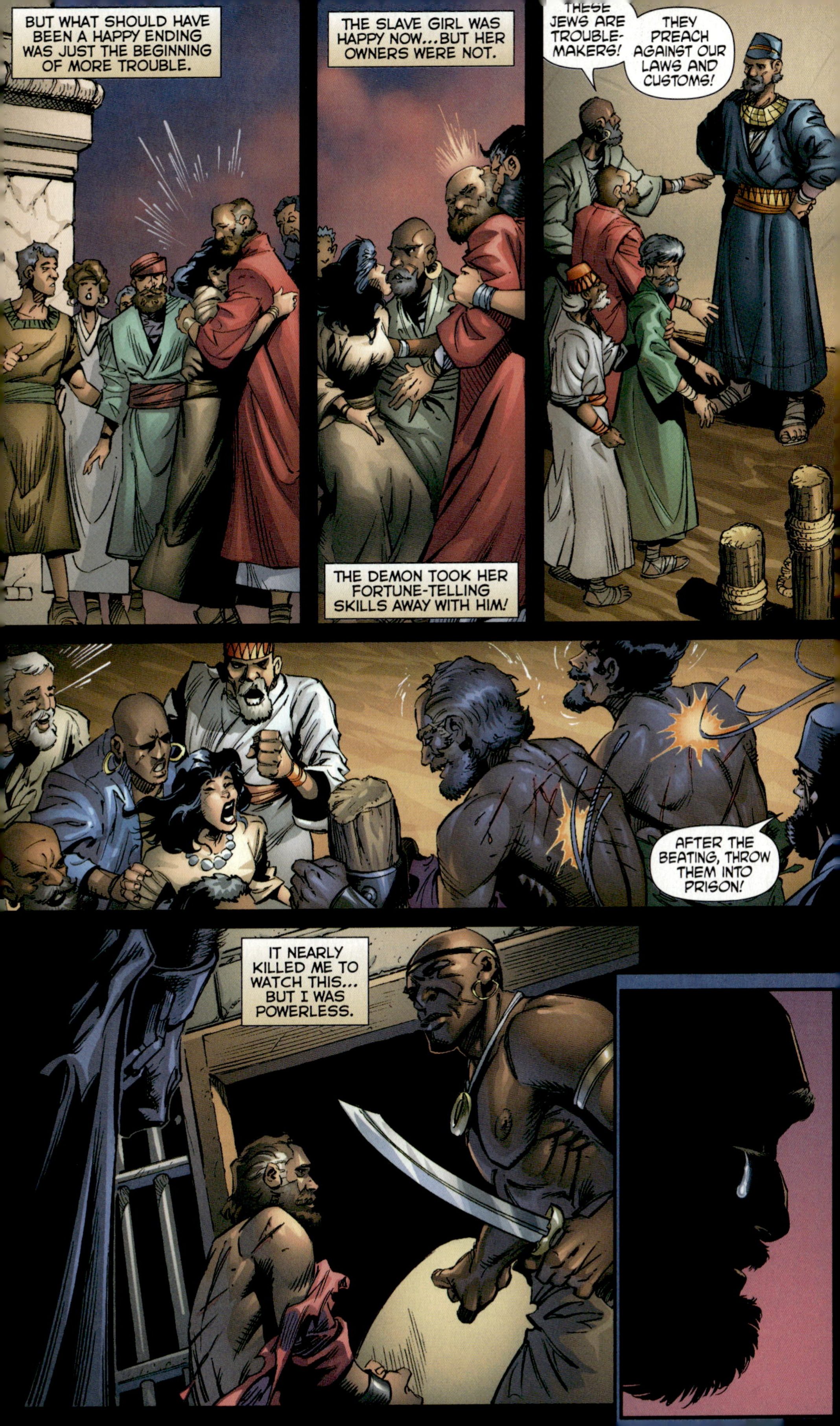
BUT WHAT SHOULD HAVE BEEN A HAPPY ENDING WAS JUST THE BEGINNING OF MORE TROUBLE.
THE SLAVE GIRL WAS HAPPY NOW...BUT HER OWNERS WERE NOT.
THE DEMON TOOK HER FORTUNE-TELLING SKILLS AWAY WITH HIM!
THESE JEWS ARE TROUBLE-MAKERS!
THEY PREACH AGAINST OUR LAWS AND CUSTOMS!
AFTER THE BEATING, THROW THEM INTO PRISON!
IT NEARLY KILLED ME TO WATCH THIS... BUT I WAS POWERLESS.

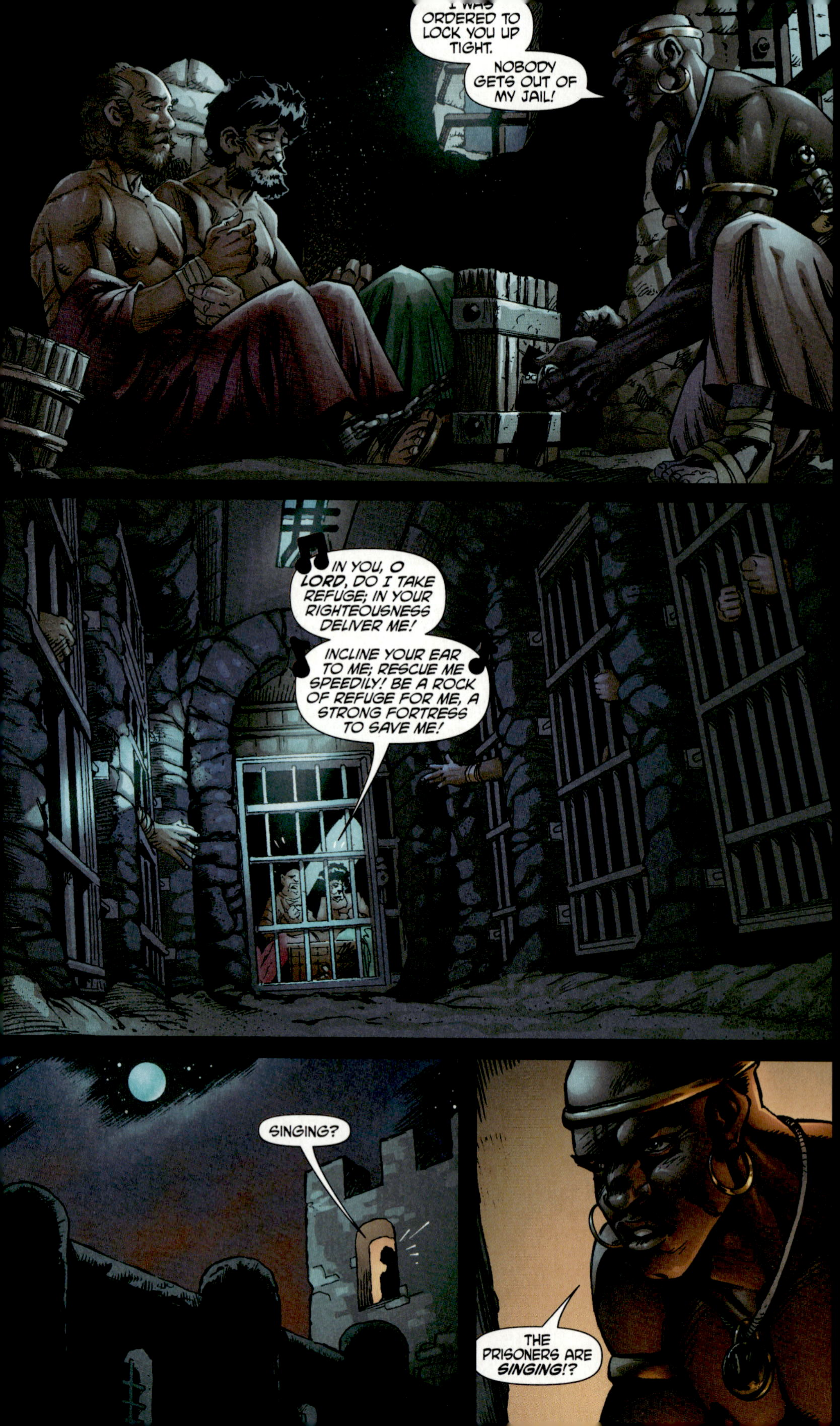

I WAS ORDERED TO LOCK YOU UP TIGHT.
NOBODY GETS OUT OF MY JAIL!
IN YOU, O LORD, DO I TAKE REFUGE; IN YOUR RIGHTEOUSNESS DELIVER ME!
INCLINE YOUR EAR TO ME; RESCUE ME SPEEDILY! BE A ROCK OF REFUGE FOR ME, A STRONG FORTRESS TO SAVE ME!
SINGING?
THE PRISONERS ARE SINGING!?

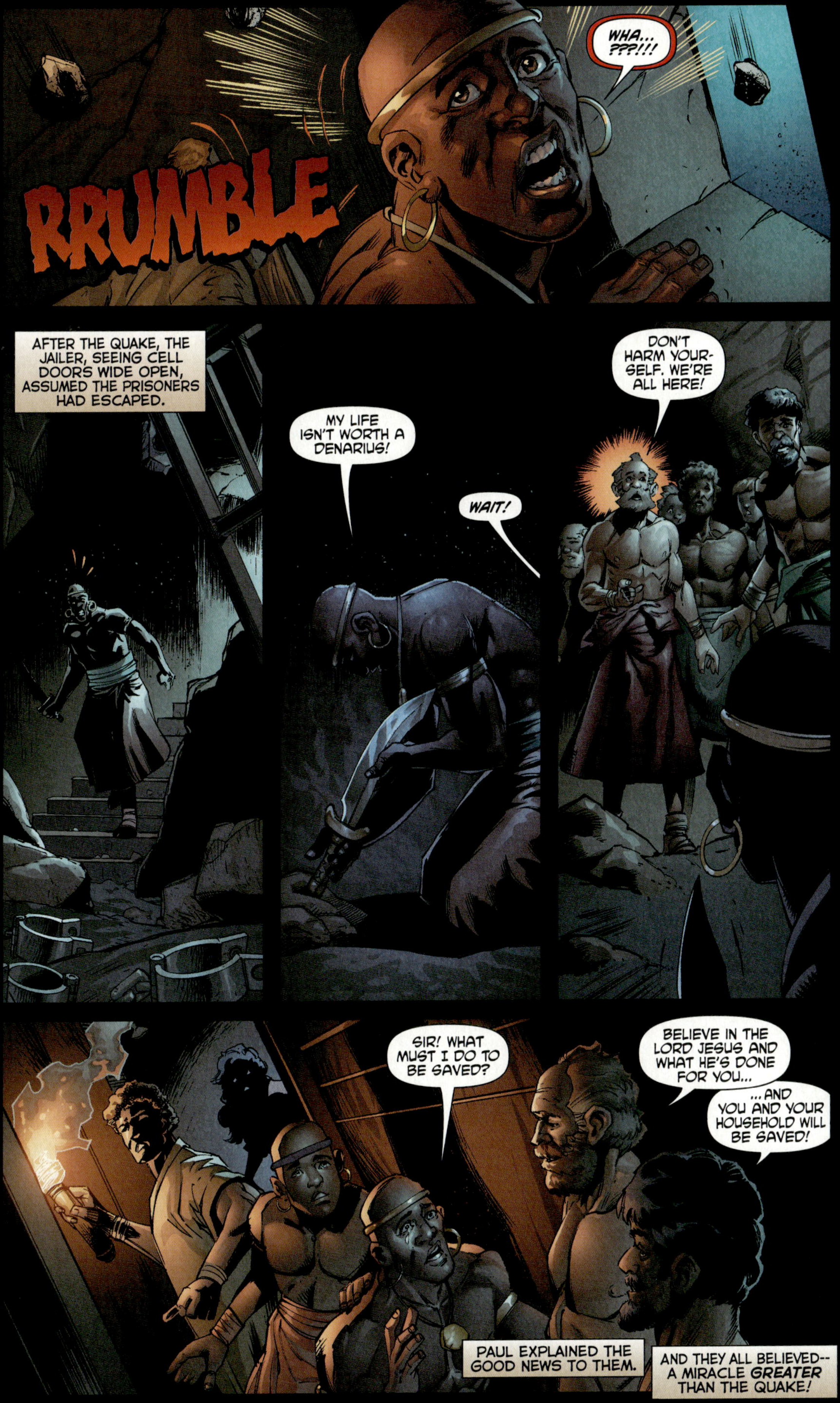

RRUMBLE
WHA... ???!!!
AFTER THE QUAKE, THE JAILER, SEEING CELL DOORS WIDE OPEN, ASSUMED THE PRISONERS HAD ESCAPED.
MY LIFE ISN'T WORTH A DENARIUS!
WAIT!
DON'T HARM YOURSELF. WE'RE ALL HERE!
SIR! WHAT MUST I DO TO BE SAVED?
BELIEVE IN THE LORD JESUS AND WHAT HE'S DONE FOR YOU...
...AND YOU AND YOUR HOUSEHOLD WILL BE SAVED!
PAUL EXPLAINED THE GOOD NEWS TO THEM.
AND THEY ALL BELIEVED-- A MIRACLE GREATER THAN THE QUAKE!

THANK YOU FOR WASHING OUR WOUNDED BODIES.

NOW WE'LL BAPTIZE YOU TO CELEBRATE JESUS' HEALING OF YOUR WOUNDED SOULS.

THANK YOU, GOD, FOR SINGING PRISONERS AND EARTHQUAKES!

RELEASE THE PRISONERS PAUL AND SILAS!

PAUL! THEY'RE LETTING YOU OUT... GO IN PEACE!

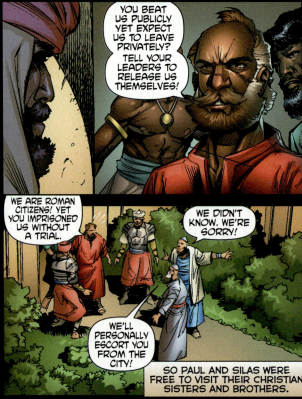

YOU BEAT US PUBLICLY YET EXPECT US TO LEAVE PRIVATELY? TELL YOUR LEADERS TO RELEASE US THEMSELVES!

WE ARE ROMAN CITIZENS! YET YOU IMPRISONED US WITHOUT A TRIAL.

WE DIDN'T KNOW. WE'RE SORRY!

WE'LL PERSONALLY ESCORT YOU FROM THE CITY!

SO PAUL AND SILAS WERE FREE TO VISIT THEIR CHRISTIAN SISTERS AND BROTHERS.

152

ACTS 16:33-40

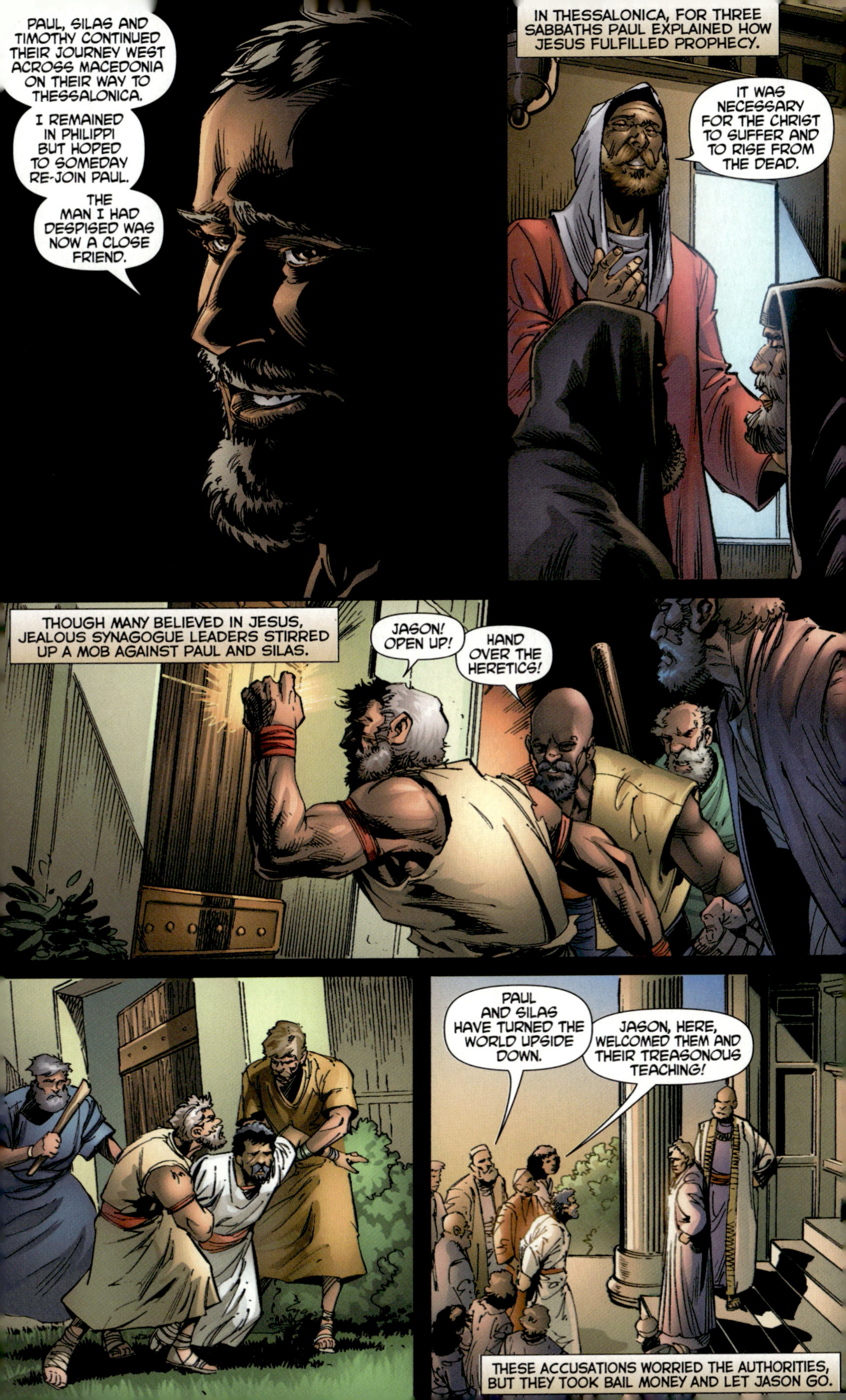

PAUL, SILAS AND TIMOTHY CONTINUED THEIR JOURNEY WEST ACROSS MACEDONIA ON THEIR WAY TO THESSALONICA.
I REMAINED IN PHILIPPI BUT HOPED TO SOMEDAY RE-JOIN PAUL.
THE MAN I HAD DESPISED WAS NOW A CLOSE FRIEND.
IN THESSALONICA, FOR THREE SABBATHS PAUL EXPLAINED HOW JESUS FULFILLED PROPHECY.
IT WAS NECESSARY FOR THE CHRIST TO SUFFER AND TO RISE FROM THE DEAD.
THOUGH MANY BELIEVED IN JESUS, JEALOUS SYNAGOGUE LEADERS STIRRED UP A MOB AGAINST PAUL AND SILAS.
JASON! OPEN UP!
HAND OVER THE HERETICS!
PAUL AND SILAS HAVE TURNED THE WORLD UPSIDE DOWN.
JASON, HERE, WELCOMED THEM AND THEIR TREASONOUS TEACHING!
THESE ACCUSATIONS WORRIED THE AUTHORITIES, BUT THEY TOOK BAIL MONEY AND LET JASON GO.

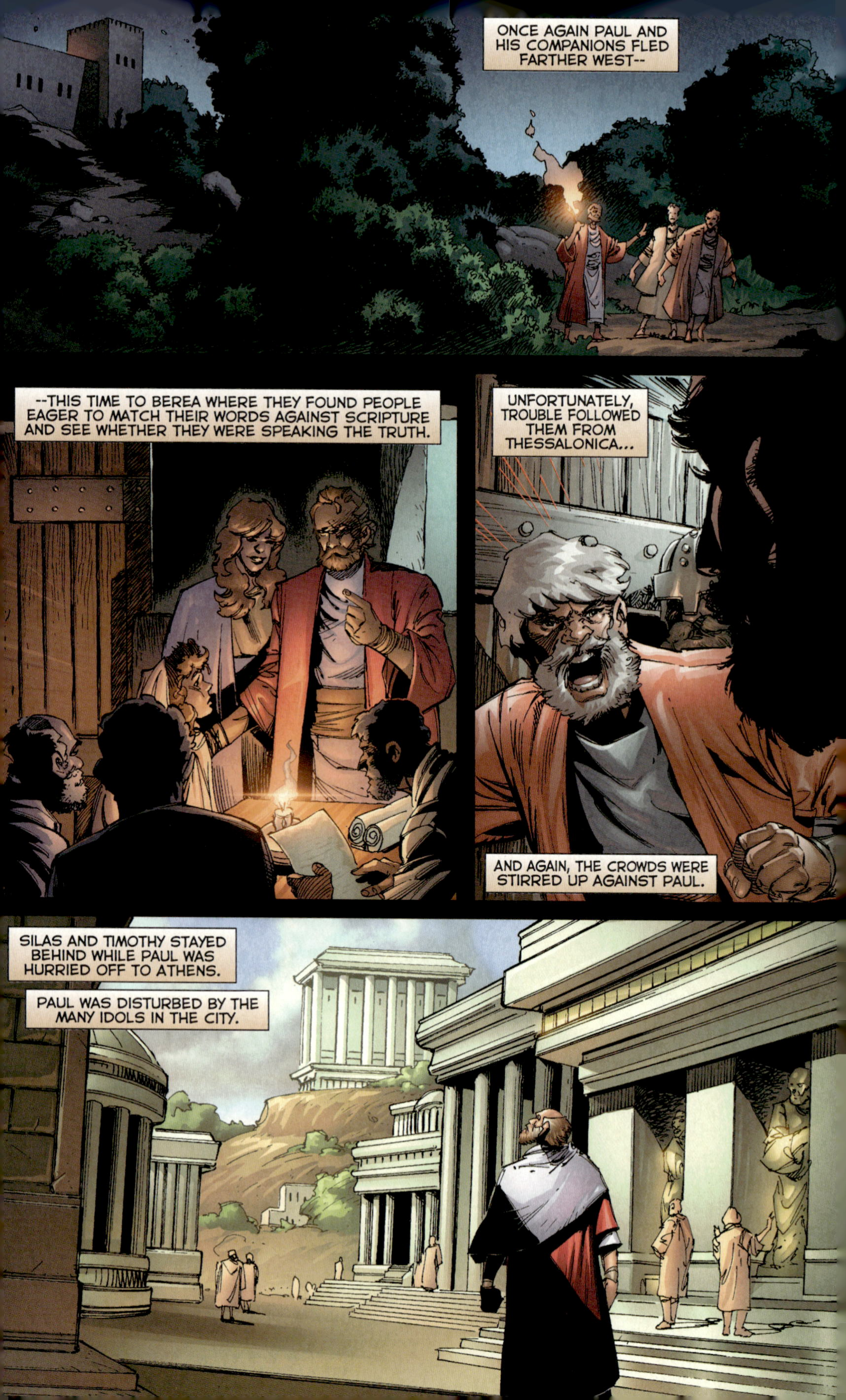
ONCE AGAIN PAUL AND HIS COMPANIONS FLED FARTHER WEST--
--THIS TIME TO BEREA WHERE THEY FOUND PEOPLE EAGER TO MATCH THEIR WORDS AGAINST SCRIPTURE AND SEE WHETHER THEY WERE SPEAKING THE TRUTH.
UNFORTUNATELY, TROUBLE FOLLOWED THEM FROM THESSALONICA...
AND AGAIN, THE CROWDS WERE STIRRED UP AGAINST PAUL.
SILAS AND TIMOTHY STAYED BEHIND WHILE PAUL WAS HURRIED OFF TO ATHENS.
PAUL WAS DISTURBED BY THE MANY IDOLS IN THE CITY.

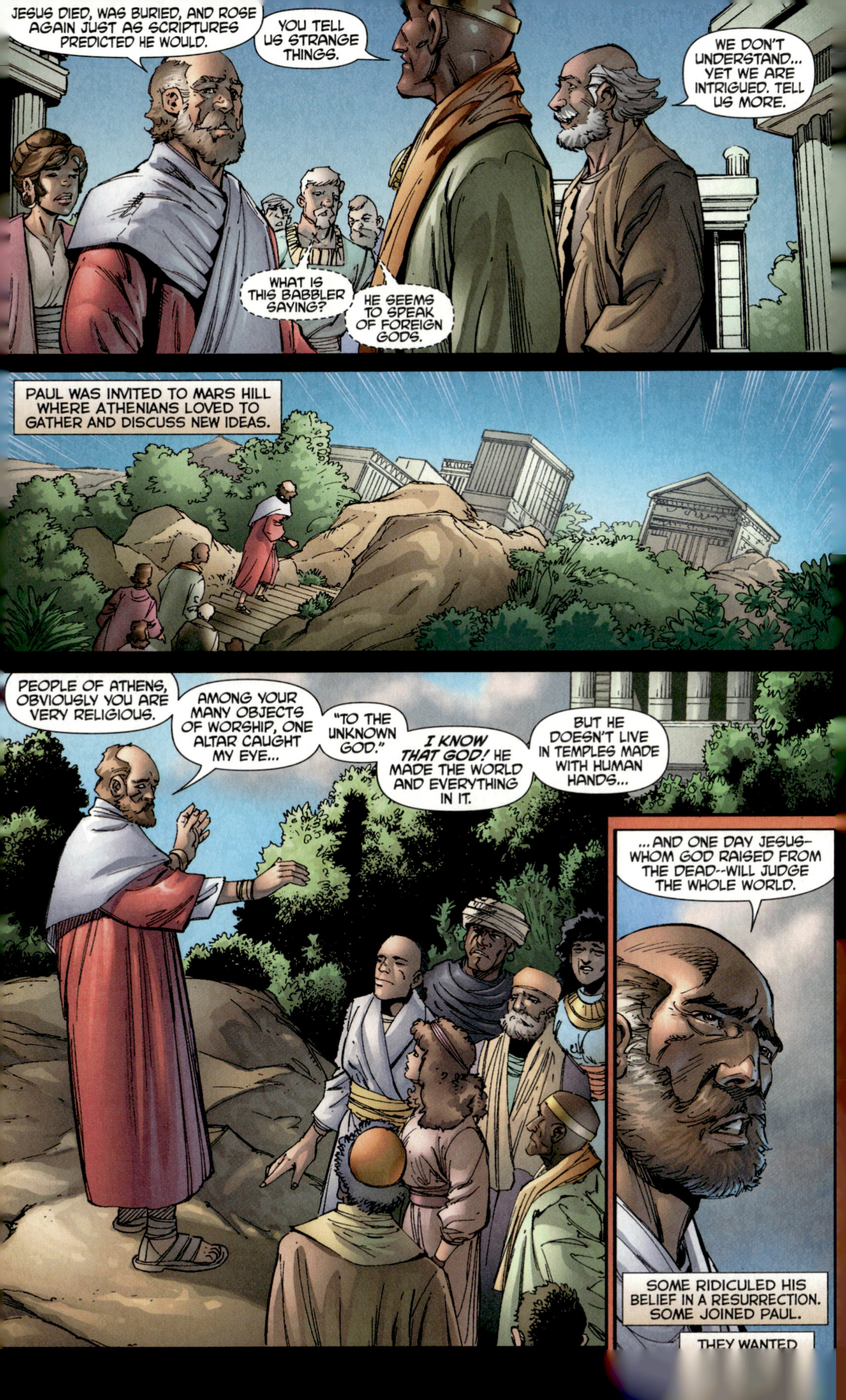
JESUS DIED, WAS BURIED, AND ROSE AGAIN JUST AS SCRIPTURES PREDICTED HE WOULD.
YOU TELL US STRANGE THINGS.
WE DON'T UNDERSTAND... YET WE ARE INTRIGUED. TELL US MORE.
WHAT IS THIS BABBLER SAYING?
HE SEEMS TO SPEAK OF FOREIGN GODS.
PAUL WAS INVITED TO MARS HILL WHERE ATHENIANS LOVED TO GATHER AND DISCUSS NEW IDEAS.
PEOPLE OF ATHENS, OBVIOUSLY YOU ARE VERY RELIGIOUS.
AMONG YOUR MANY OBJECTS OF WORSHIP, ONE ALTAR CAUGHT MY EYE...
"TO THE UNKNOWN GOD."
I KNOW THAT GOD! HE MADE THE WORLD AND EVERYTHING IN IT.
BUT HE DOESN'T LIVE IN TEMPLES MADE WITH HUMAN HANDS...
...AND ONE DAY JESUS--WHOM GOD RAISED FROM THE DEAD--WILL JUDGE THE WHOLE WORLD.
SOME RIDICULED HIS BELIEF IN A RESURRECTION. SOME JOINED PAUL.
THEY WANTED

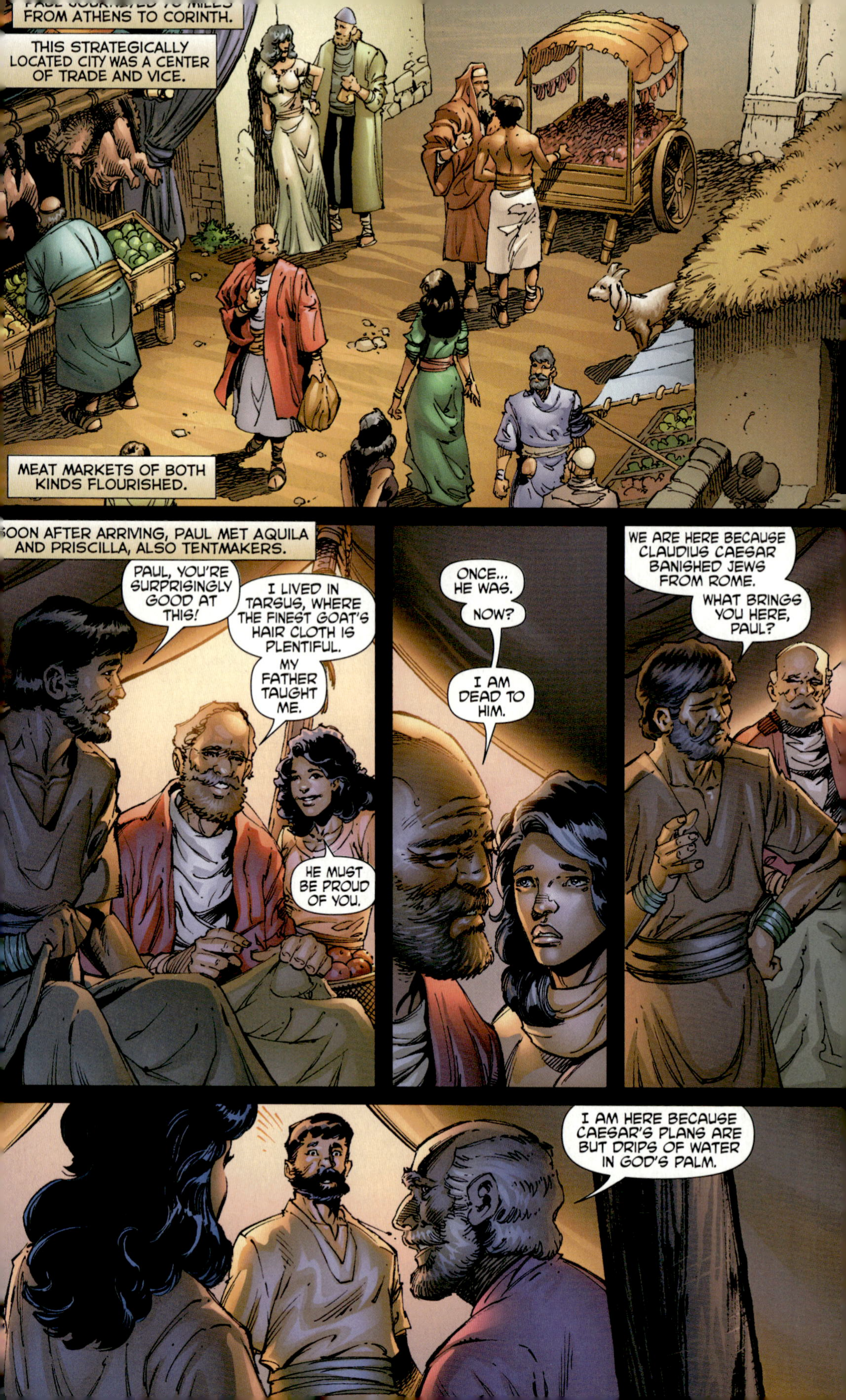

FROM ATHENS TO CORINTH.
THIS STRATEGICALLY LOCATED CITY WAS A CENTER OF TRADE AND VICE.
MEAT MARKETS OF BOTH KINDS FLOURISHED.
SOON AFTER ARRIVING, PAUL MET AQUILA AND PRISCILLA, ALSO TENTMAKERS.
PAUL, YOU'RE SURPRISINGLY GOOD AT THIS!
I LIVED IN TARSUS, WHERE THE FINEST GOAT'S HAIR CLOTH IS PLENTIFUL.
MY FATHER TAUGHT ME.
HE MUST BE PROUD OF YOU.
ONCE... HE WAS.
NOW?
I AM DEAD TO HIM.
WE ARE HERE BECAUSE CLAUDIUS CAESAR BANISHED JEWS FROM ROME.
WHAT BRINGS YOU HERE, PAUL?
I AM HERE BECAUSE CAESAR'S PLANS ARE BUT DRIPS OF WATER IN GOD'S PALM.

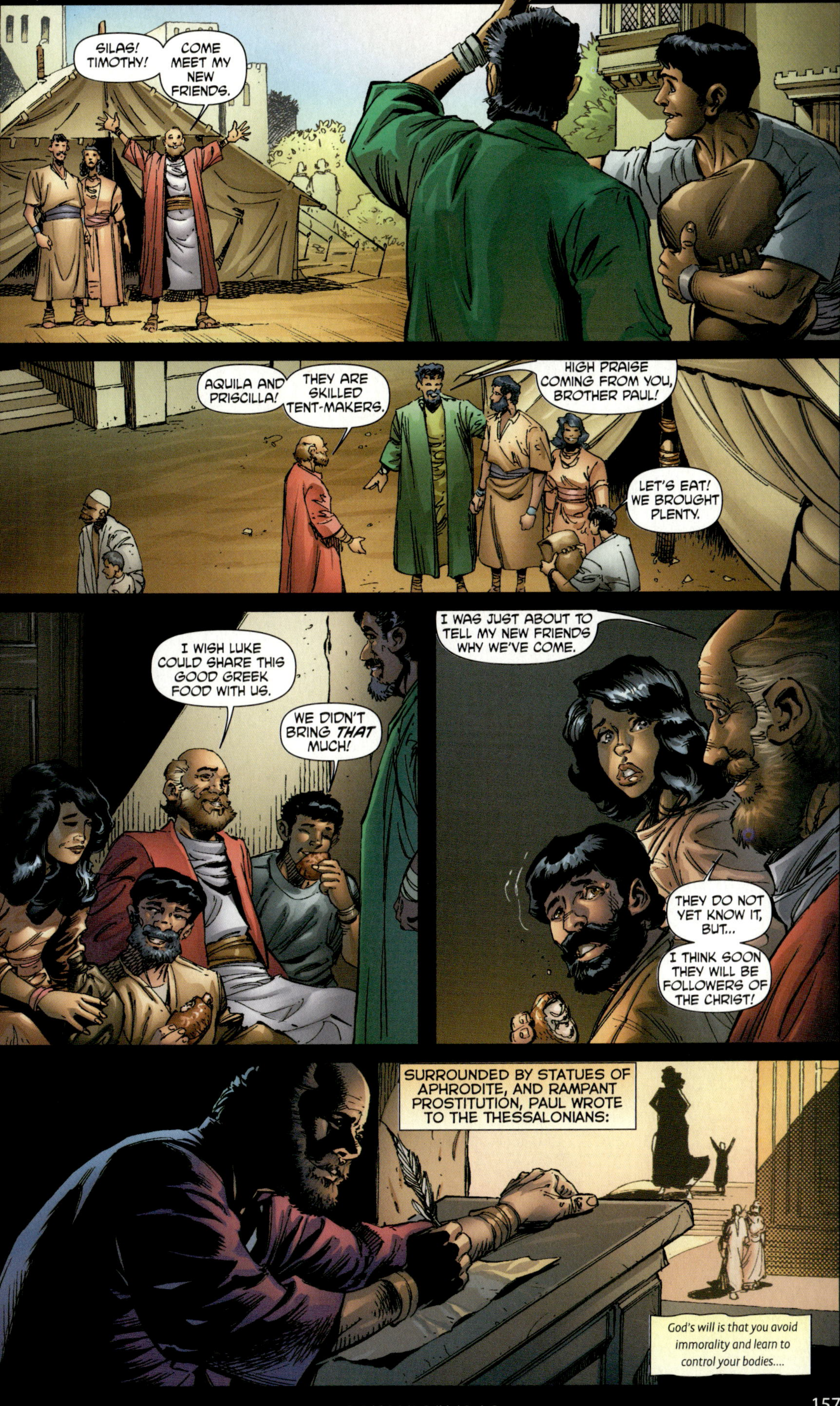
SILAS! TIMOTHY!
COME MEET MY NEW FRIENDS.
AQUILA AND PRISCILLA!
THEY ARE SKILLED TENT-MAKERS.
HIGH PRAISE COMING FROM YOU, BROTHER PAUL!
LET'S EAT! WE BROUGHT PLENTY.
I WISH LUKE COULD SHARE THIS GOOD GREEK FOOD WITH US.
WE DIDN'T BRING *THAT* MUCH!
I WAS JUST ABOUT TO TELL MY NEW FRIENDS WHY WE'VE COME.
THEY DO NOT YET KNOW IT, BUT...
I THINK SOON THEY WILL BE FOLLOWERS OF THE CHRIST!
SURROUNDED BY STATUES OF APHRODITE, AND RAMPANT PROSTITUTION, PAUL WROTE TO THE THESSALONIANS:
God's will is that you avoid immorality and learn to control your bodies....

I THESSALONIANS 4:3

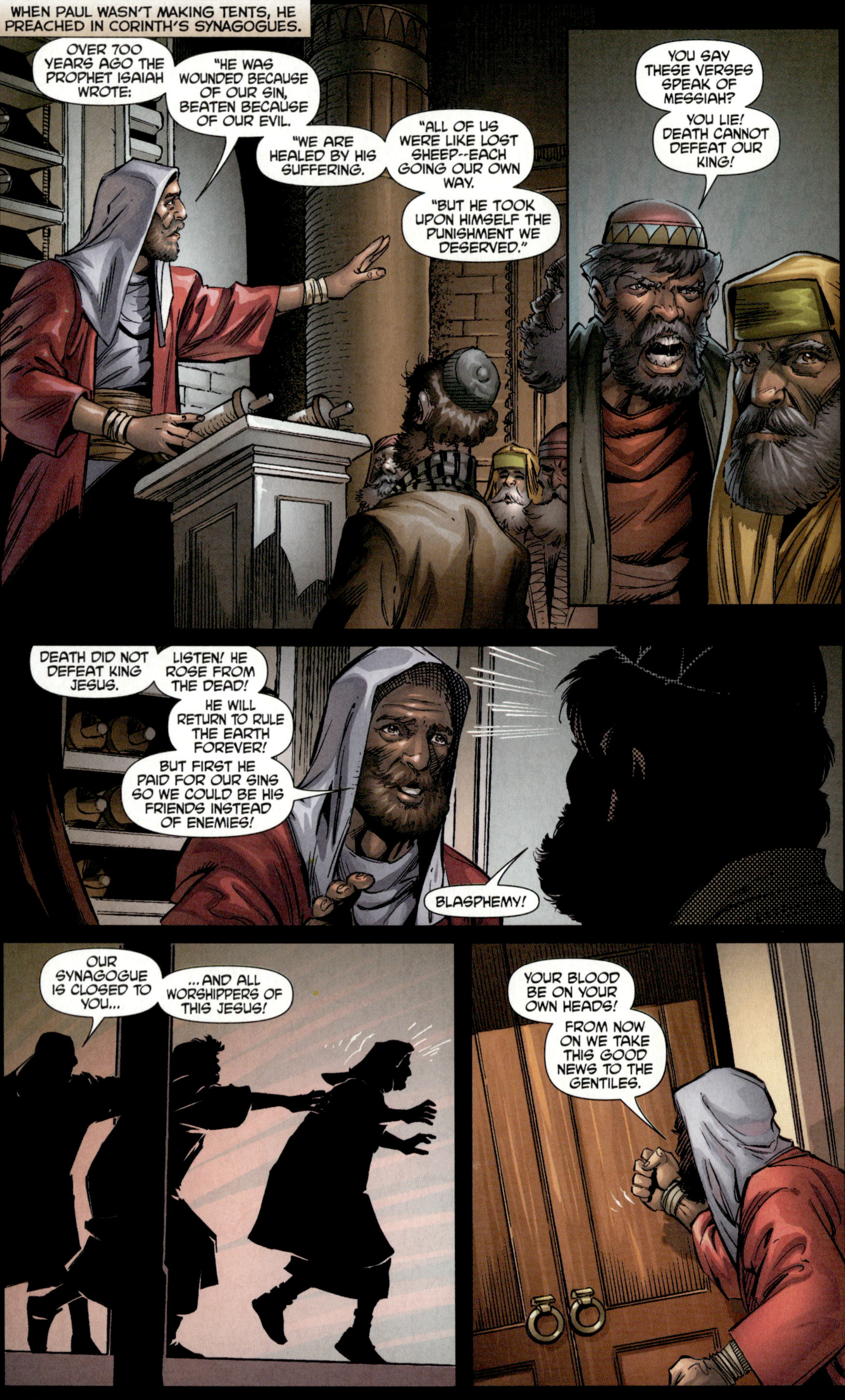
WHEN PAUL WASN'T MAKING TENTS, HE PREACHED IN CORINTH'S SYNAGOGUES.
OVER 700 YEARS AGO THE PROPHET ISAIAH WROTE:
"HE WAS WOUNDED BECAUSE OF OUR SIN, BEATEN BECAUSE OF OUR EVIL.
"WE ARE HEALED BY HIS SUFFERING.
"ALL OF US WERE LIKE LOST SHEEP--EACH GOING OUR OWN WAY.
"BUT HE TOOK UPON HIMSELF THE PUNISHMENT WE DESERVED."
YOU SAY THESE VERSES SPEAK OF MESSIAH?
YOU LIE! DEATH CANNOT DEFEAT OUR KING!
DEATH DID NOT DEFEAT KING JESUS.
LISTEN! HE ROSE FROM THE DEAD!
HE WILL RETURN TO RULE THE EARTH FOREVER!
BUT FIRST HE PAID FOR OUR SINS SO WE COULD BE HIS FRIENDS INSTEAD OF ENEMIES!
BLASPHEMY!
OUR SYNAGOGUE IS CLOSED TO YOU...
...AND ALL WORSHIPPERS OF THIS JESUS!
YOUR BLOOD BE ON YOUR OWN HEADS!
FROM NOW ON WE TAKE THIS GOOD NEWS TO THE GENTILES.

ISAIAH 53:5-6; ACTS 18:7

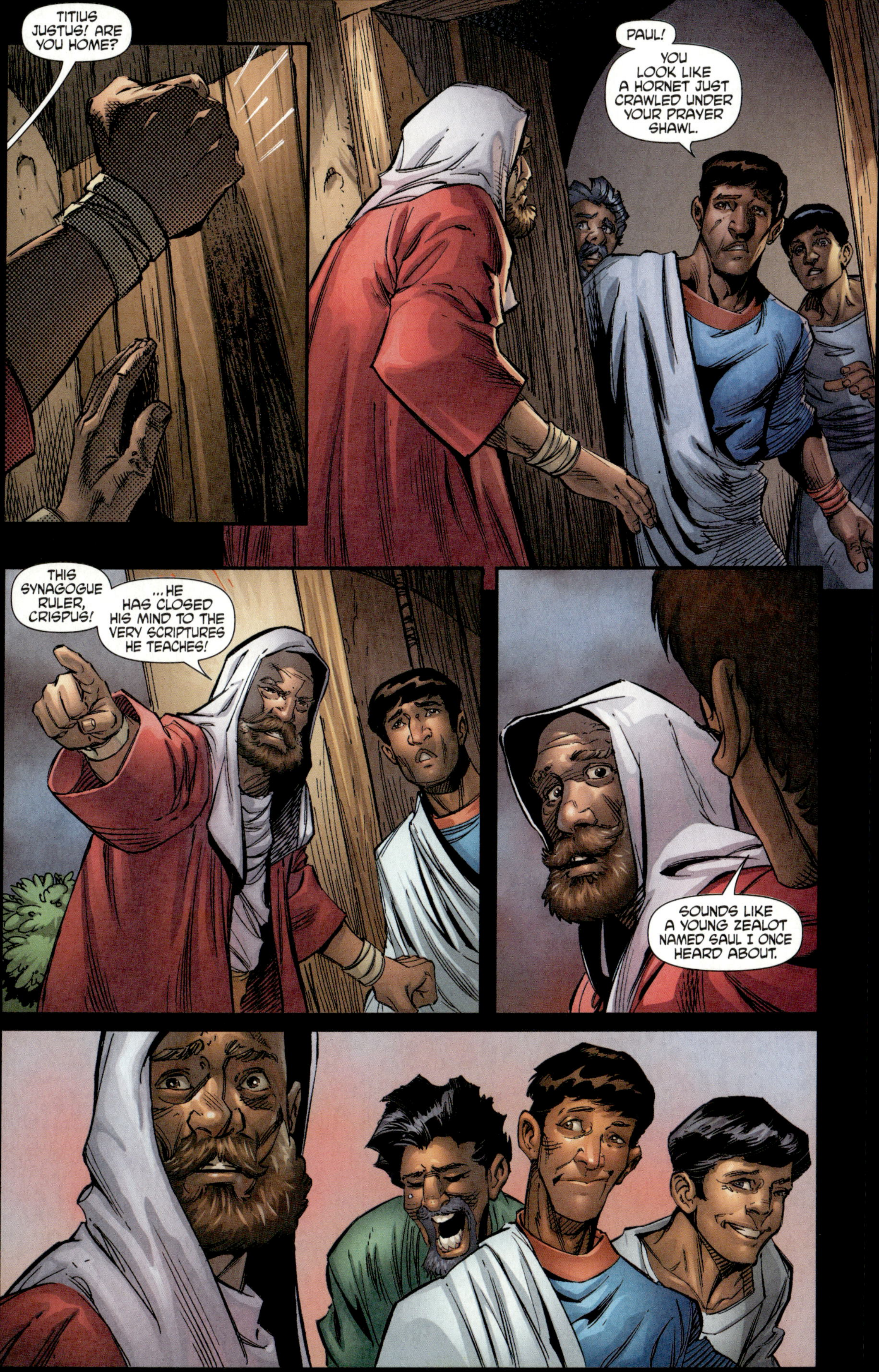
TITIUS JUSTUS! ARE YOU HOME?
PAUL!
YOU LOOK LIKE A HORNET JUST CRAWLED UNDER YOUR PRAYER SHAWL.
THIS SYNAGOGUE RULER, CRISPUS!
...HE HAS CLOSED HIS MIND TO THE VERY SCRIPTURES HE TEACHES!
SOUNDS LIKE A YOUNG ZEALOT NAMED SAUL I ONCE HEARD ABOUT.

THAT NIGHT.

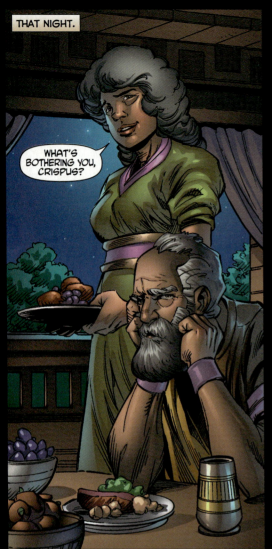

WHAT'S BOTHERING YOU, CRISPUS?

A CURSE UPON THIS PAUL! THE WORDS OF ISAIAH TORTURE ME.

TELL ME, WHY DOES A SYNAGOGUE RULER FIND SCRIPTURE DISTURBING?

COULD... COULD JESUS BE THE PROMISED MESSIAH?

I THINK WE SHOULD TALK TO THIS MAN PAUL...

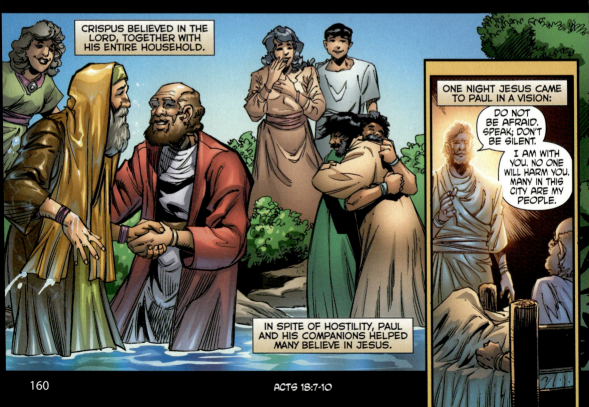

CRISPUS BELIEVED IN THE LORD, TOGETHER WITH HIS ENTIRE HOUSEHOLD.

ONE NIGHT JESUS CAME TO PAUL IN A VISION:

DO NOT BE AFRAID. SPEAK; DON'T BE SILENT. I AM WITH YOU. NO ONE WILL HARM YOU. MANY IN THIS CITY ARE MY PEOPLE.

IN SPITE OF HOSTILITY, PAUL AND HIS COMPANIONS HELPED MANY BELIEVE IN JESUS.

ACTS 18:7-10

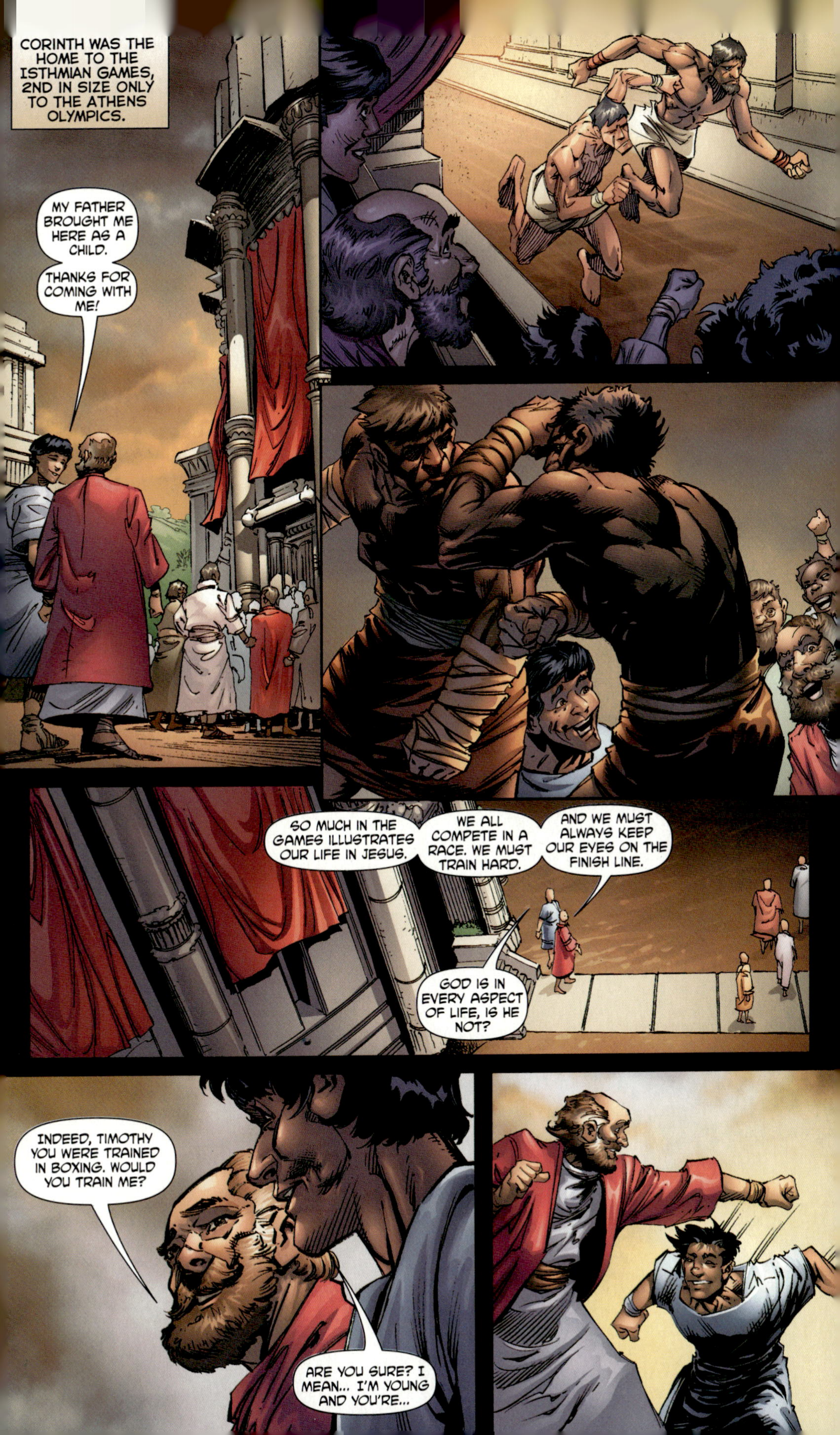

CORINTH WAS THE HOME TO THE ISTHMIAN GAMES, 2ND IN SIZE ONLY TO THE ATHENS OLYMPICS.
MY FATHER BROUGHT ME HERE AS A CHILD.
THANKS FOR COMING WITH ME!
SO MUCH IN THE GAMES ILLUSTRATES OUR LIFE IN JESUS.
WE ALL COMPETE IN A RACE. WE MUST TRAIN HARD.
AND WE MUST ALWAYS KEEP OUR EYES ON THE FINISH LINE.
GOD IS IN EVERY ASPECT OF LIFE, IS HE NOT?
INDEED, TIMOTHY YOU WERE TRAINED IN BOXING. WOULD YOU TRAIN ME?
ARE YOU SURE? I MEAN... I'M YOUNG AND YOU'RE...

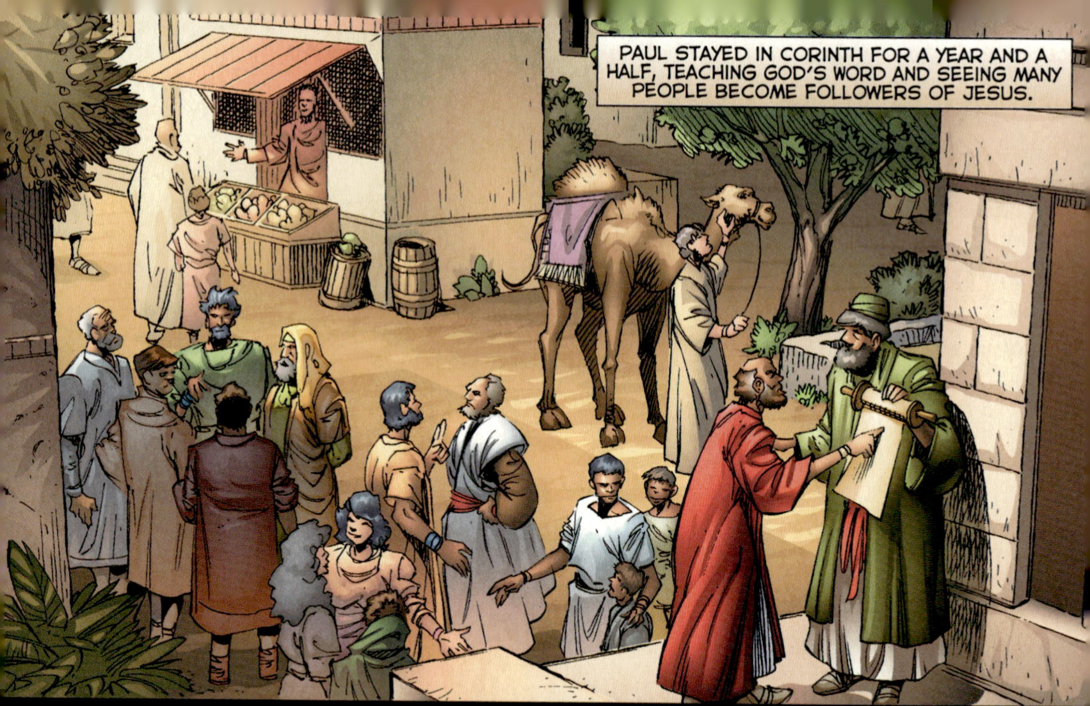
PAUL STAYED IN CORINTH FOR A YEAR AND A HALF, TEACHING GOD'S WORD AND SEEING MANY PEOPLE BECOME FOLLOWERS OF JESUS.

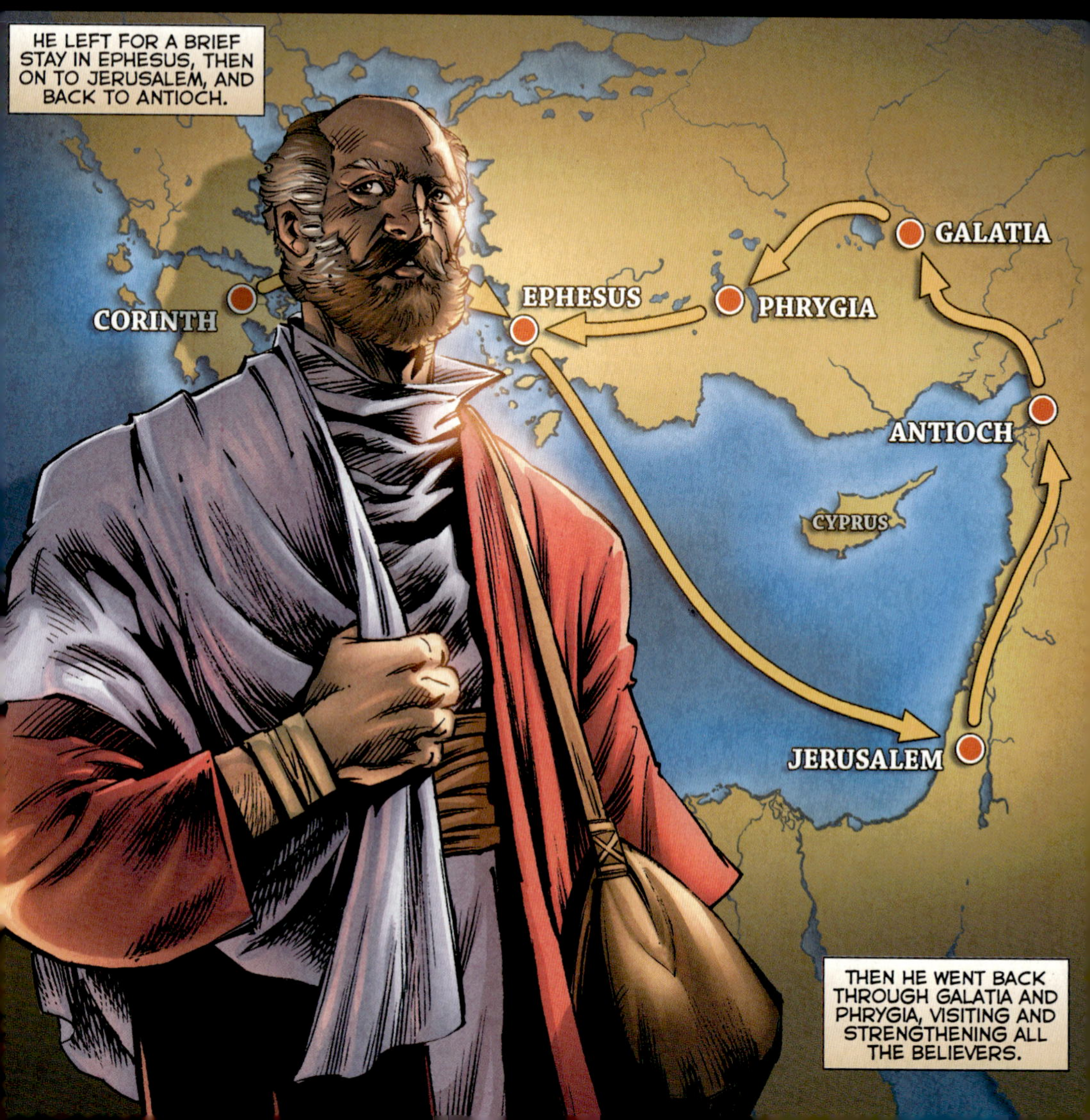
HE LEFT FOR A BRIEF STAY IN EPHESUS, THEN ON TO JERUSALEM, AND BACK TO ANTIOCH.
CORINTH
EPHESUS
PHRYGIA
GALATIA
ANTIOCH
CYPRUS
JERUSALEM
THEN HE WENT BACK THROUGH GALATIA AND PHRYGIA, VISITING AND STRENGTHENING ALL THE BELIEVERS.

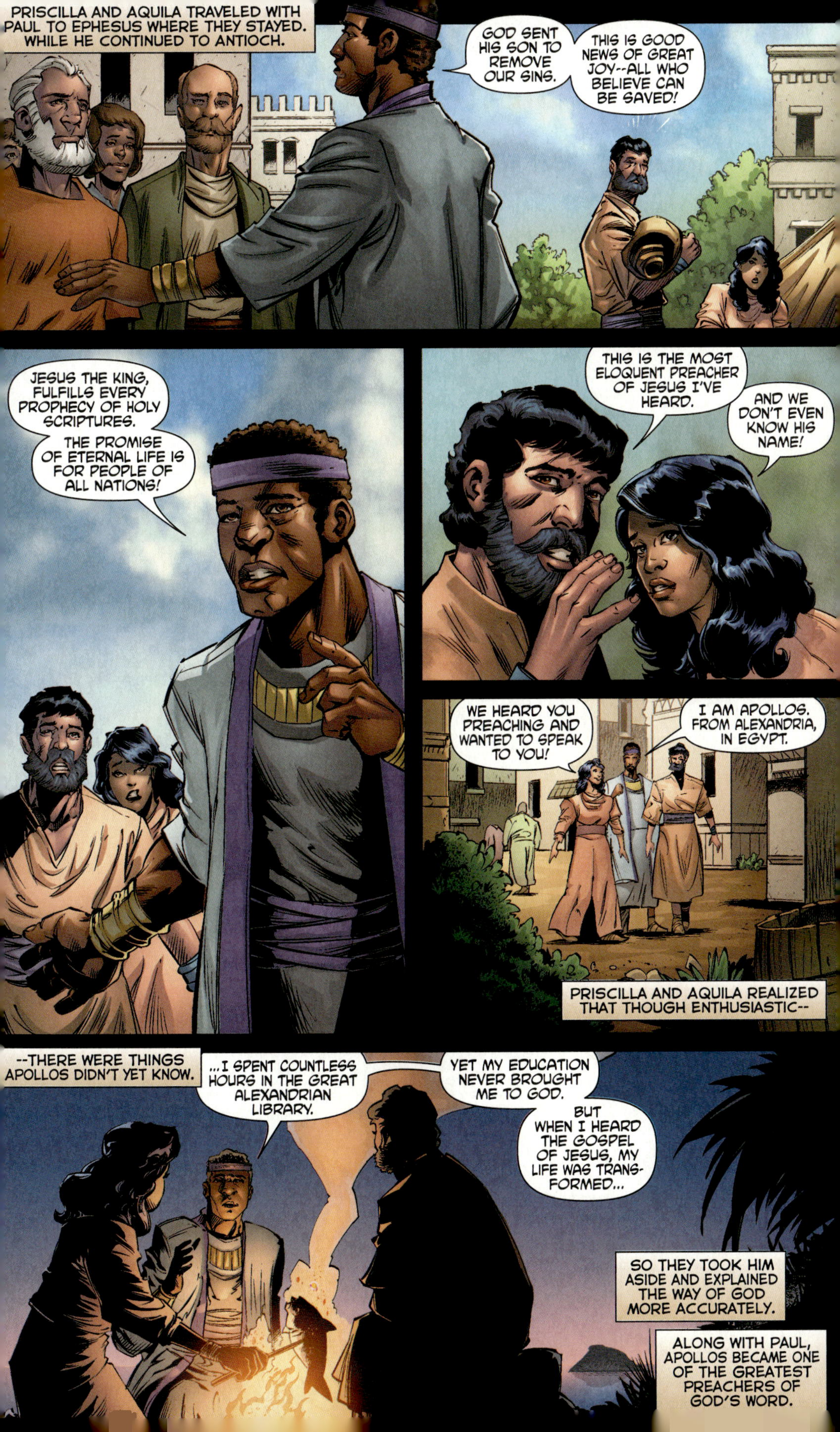
PRISCILLA AND AQUILA TRAVELED WITH PAUL TO EPHESUS WHERE THEY STAYED. WHILE HE CONTINUED TO ANTIOCH.
GOD SENT HIS SON TO REMOVE OUR SINS.
THIS IS GOOD NEWS OF GREAT JOY--ALL WHO BELIEVE CAN BE SAVED!
JESUS THE KING, FULFILLS EVERY PROPHECY OF HOLY SCRIPTURES.
THE PROMISE OF ETERNAL LIFE IS FOR PEOPLE OF ALL NATIONS!
THIS IS THE MOST ELOQUENT PREACHER OF JESUS I'VE HEARD.
AND WE DON'T EVEN KNOW HIS NAME!
WE HEARD YOU PREACHING AND WANTED TO SPEAK TO YOU!
I AM APOLLOS. FROM ALEXANDRIA, IN EGYPT.
PRISCILLA AND AQUILA REALIZED THAT THOUGH ENTHUSIASTIC--
--THERE WERE THINGS APOLLOS DIDN'T YET KNOW.
...I SPENT COUNTLESS HOURS IN THE GREAT ALEXANDRIAN LIBRARY.
YET MY EDUCATION NEVER BROUGHT ME TO GOD.
BUT WHEN I HEARD THE GOSPEL OF JESUS, MY LIFE WAS TRANS-FORMED...
SO THEY TOOK HIM ASIDE AND EXPLAINED THE WAY OF GOD MORE ACCURATELY.
ALONG WITH PAUL, APOLLOS BECAME ONE OF THE GREATEST PREACHERS OF GOD'S WORD.

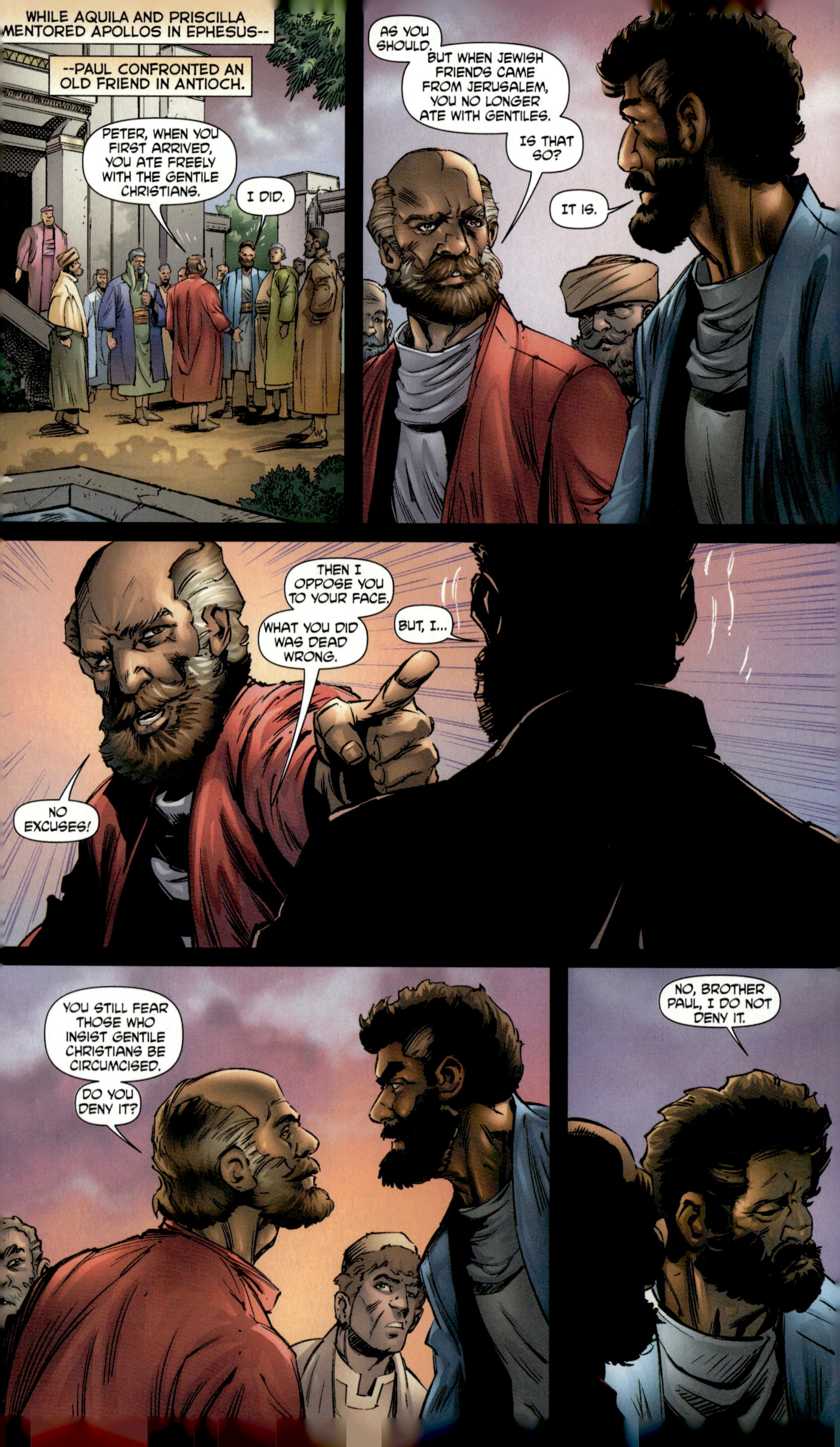
WHILE AQUILA AND PRISCILLA MENTORED APOLLOS IN EPHESUS--
--PAUL CONFRONTED AN OLD FRIEND IN ANTIOCH.
PETER, WHEN YOU FIRST ARRIVED, YOU ATE FREELY WITH THE GENTILE CHRISTIANS.
I DID.
AS YOU SHOULD.
BUT WHEN JEWISH FRIENDS CAME FROM JERUSALEM, YOU NO LONGER ATE WITH GENTILES.
IS THAT SO?
IT IS.
THEN I OPPOSE YOU TO YOUR FACE.
WHAT YOU DID WAS DEAD WRONG.
BUT, I...
NO EXCUSES!
YOU STILL FEAR THOSE WHO INSIST GENTILE CHRISTIANS BE CIRCUMCISED.
DO YOU DENY IT?
NO, BROTHER PAUL, I DO NOT DENY IT.

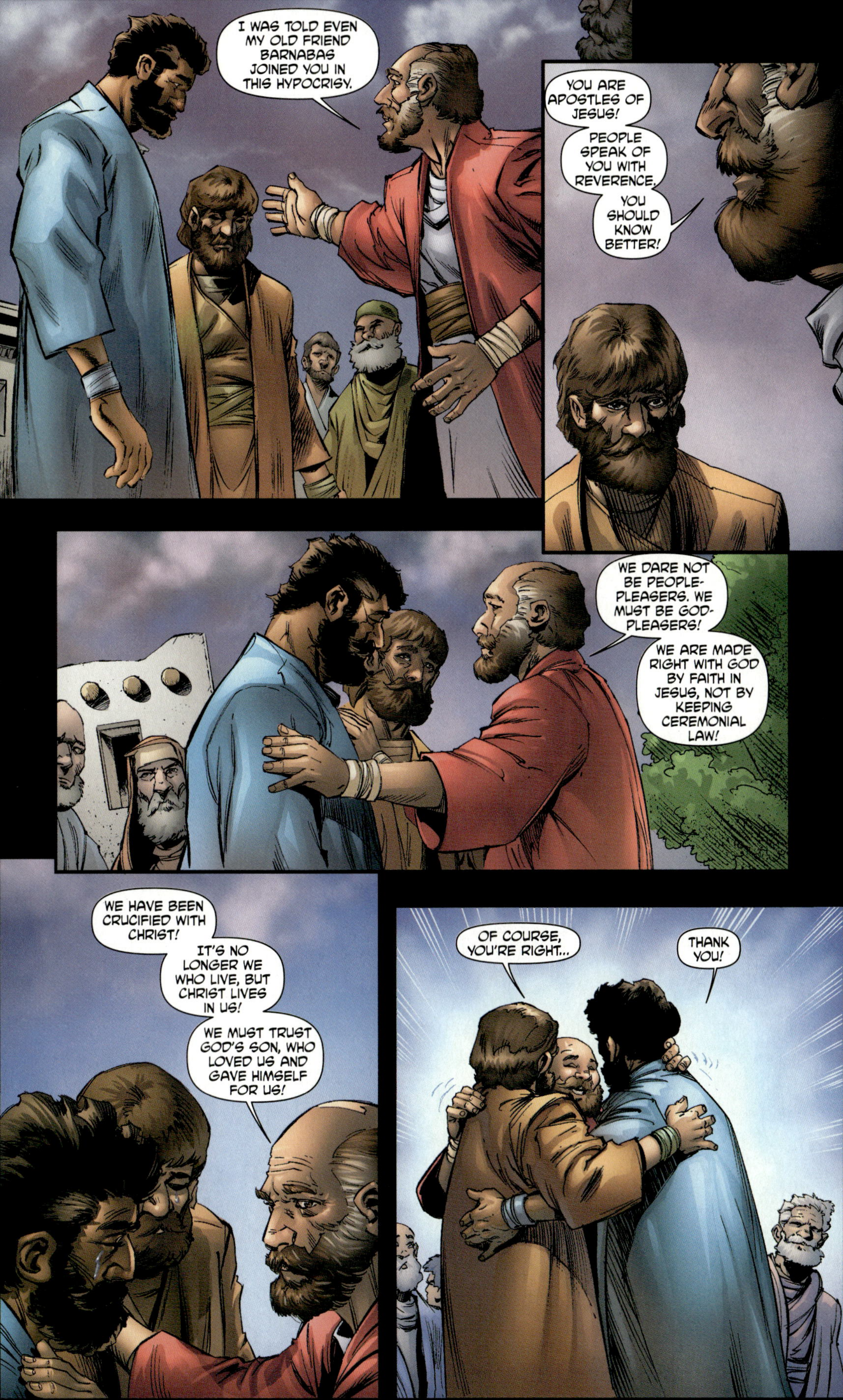
I WAS TOLD EVEN MY OLD FRIEND BARNABAS JOINED YOU IN THIS HYPOCRISY.
YOU ARE APOSTLES OF JESUS!
PEOPLE SPEAK OF YOU WITH REVERENCE.
YOU SHOULD KNOW BETTER!
WE DARE NOT BE PEOPLE-PLEASERS. WE MUST BE GOD-PLEASERS!
WE ARE MADE RIGHT WITH GOD BY FAITH IN JESUS, NOT BY KEEPING CEREMONIAL LAW!
WE HAVE BEEN CRUCIFIED WITH CHRIST!
IT'S NO LONGER WE WHO LIVE, BUT CHRIST LIVES IN US!
WE MUST TRUST GOD'S SON, WHO LOVED US AND GAVE HIMSELF FOR US!
OF COURSE, YOU'RE RIGHT...
THANK YOU!

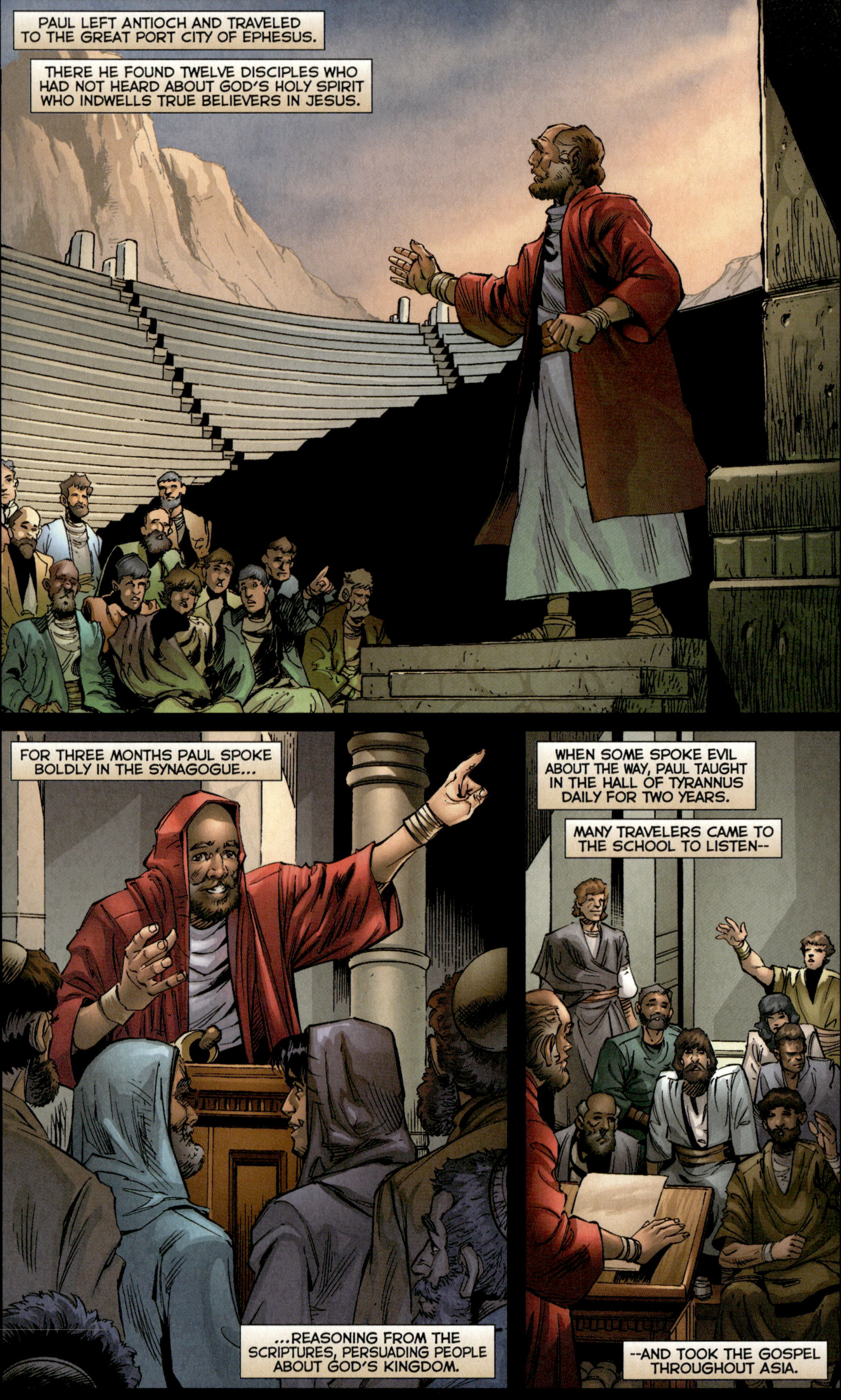
PAUL LEFT ANTIOCH AND TRAVELED TO THE GREAT PORT CITY OF EPHESUS.
THERE HE FOUND TWELVE DISCIPLES WHO HAD NOT HEARD ABOUT GOD'S HOLY SPIRIT WHO INDWELLS TRUE BELIEVERS IN JESUS.
FOR THREE MONTHS PAUL SPOKE BOLDLY IN THE SYNAGOGUE...
...REASONING FROM THE SCRIPTURES, PERSUADING PEOPLE ABOUT GOD'S KINGDOM.
WHEN SOME SPOKE EVIL ABOUT THE WAY, PAUL TAUGHT IN THE HALL OF TYRANNUS DAILY FOR TWO YEARS.
MANY TRAVELERS CAME TO THE SCHOOL TO LISTEN--
--AND TOOK THE GOSPEL THROUGHOUT ASIA.

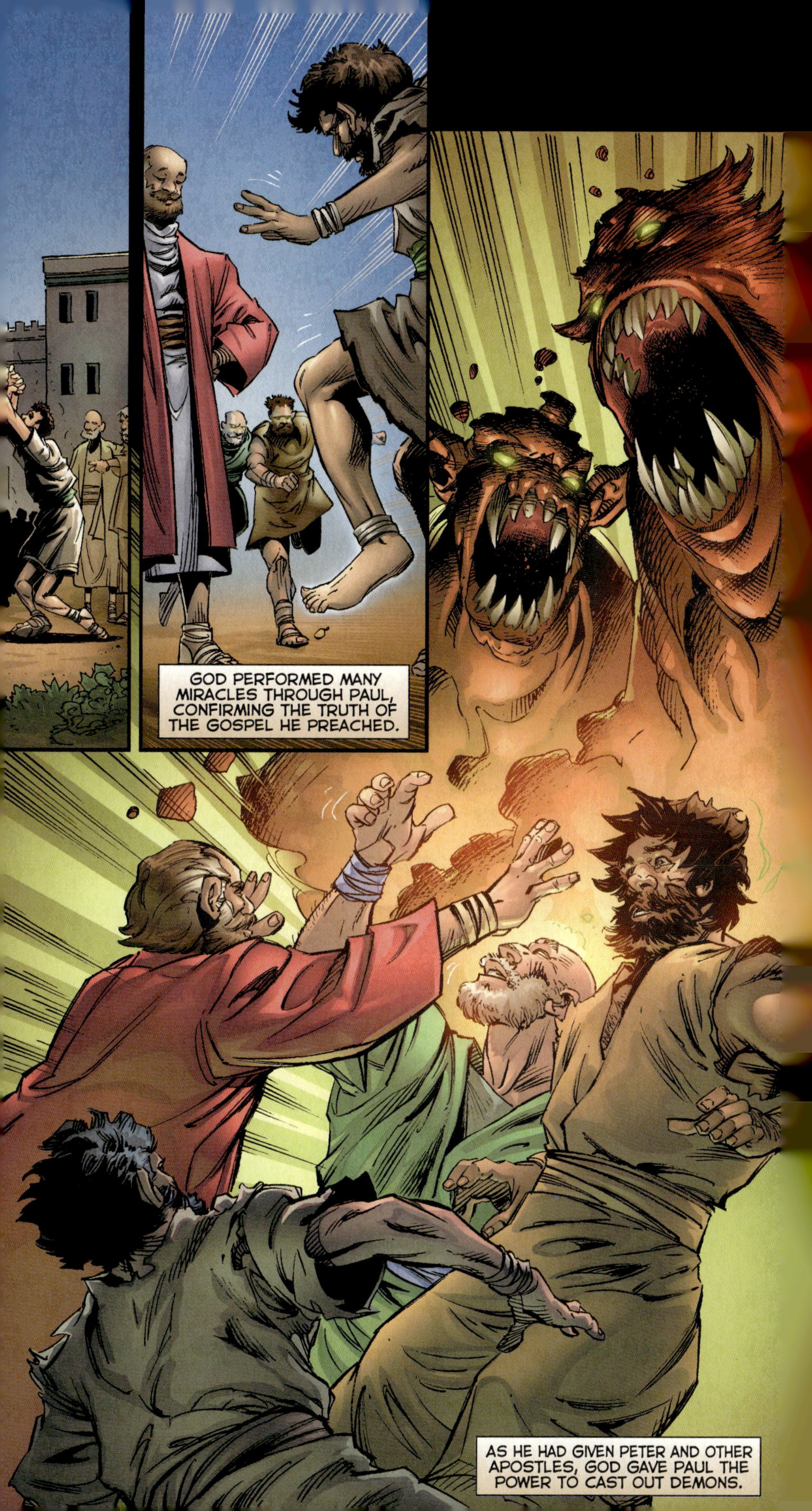
GOD PERFORMED MANY MIRACLES THROUGH PAUL, CONFIRMING THE TRUTH OF THE GOSPEL HE PREACHED.
AS HE HAD GIVEN PETER AND OTHER APOSTLES, GOD GAVE PAUL THE POWER TO CAST OUT DEMONS.

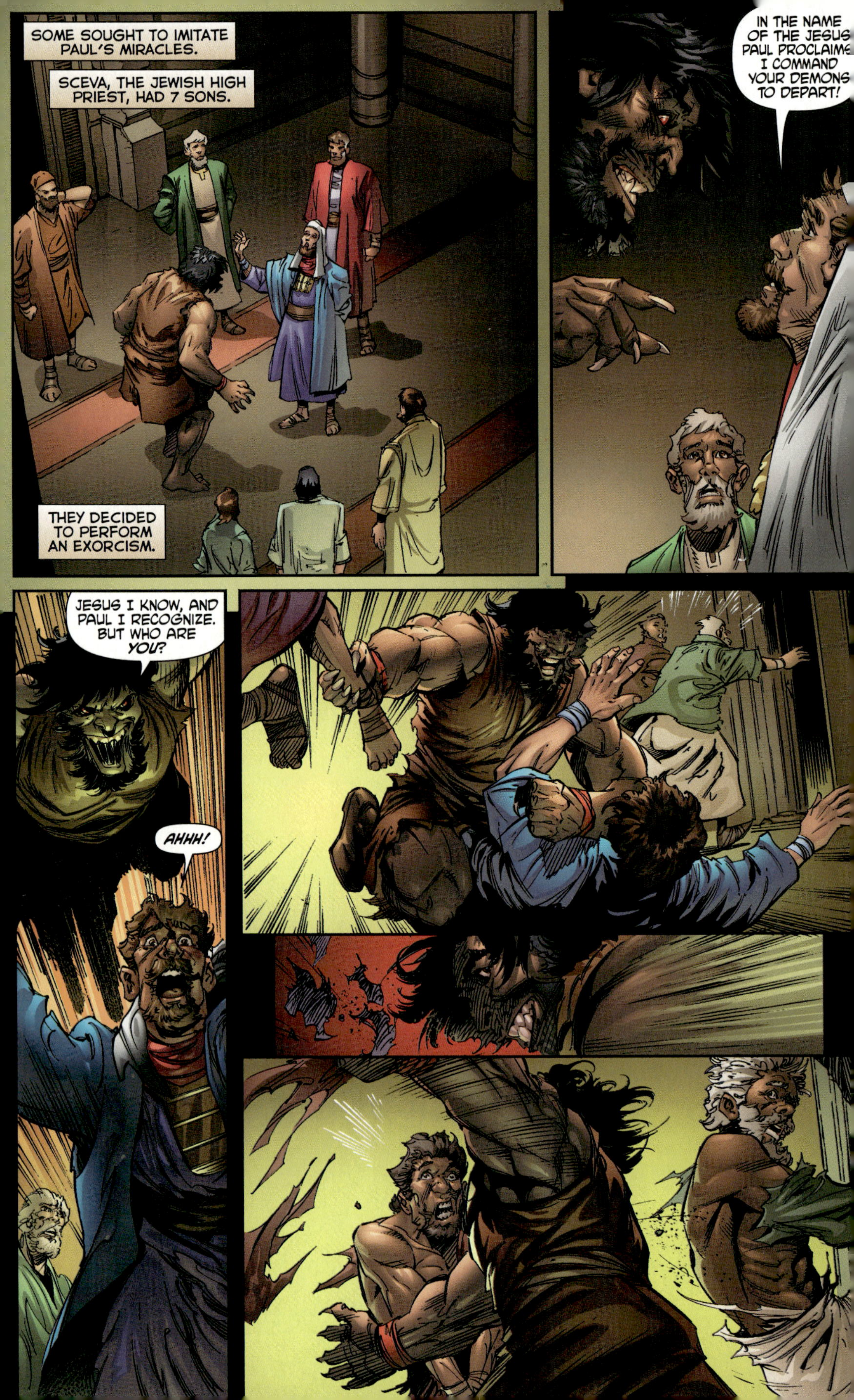

SOME SOUGHT TO IMITATE PAUL'S MIRACLES.
SCEVA, THE JEWISH HIGH PRIEST, HAD 7 SONS.
THEY DECIDED TO PERFORM AN EXORCISM.
IN THE NAME OF THE JESUS PAUL PROCLAIMS I COMMAND YOUR DEMONS TO DEPART!
JESUS I KNOW, AND PAUL I RECOGNIZE. BUT WHO ARE *YOU*?
AHHH!

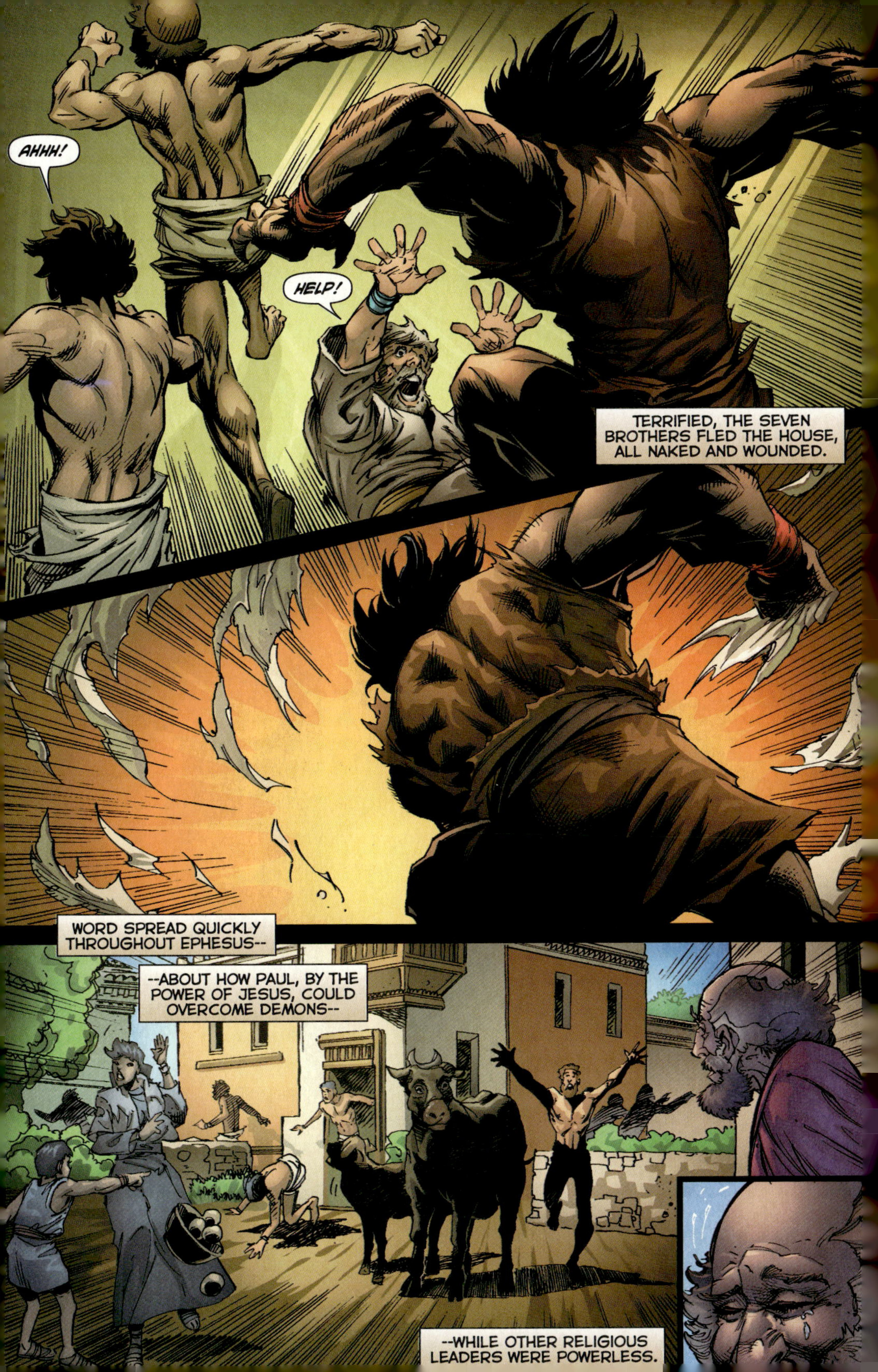

AHHH!
HELP!
TERRIFIED, THE SEVEN BROTHERS FLED THE HOUSE, ALL NAKED AND WOUNDED.
WORD SPREAD QUICKLY THROUGHOUT EPHESUS--
--ABOUT HOW PAUL, BY THE POWER OF JESUS, COULD OVERCOME DEMONS--
--WHILE OTHER RELIGIOUS LEADERS WERE POWERLESS.

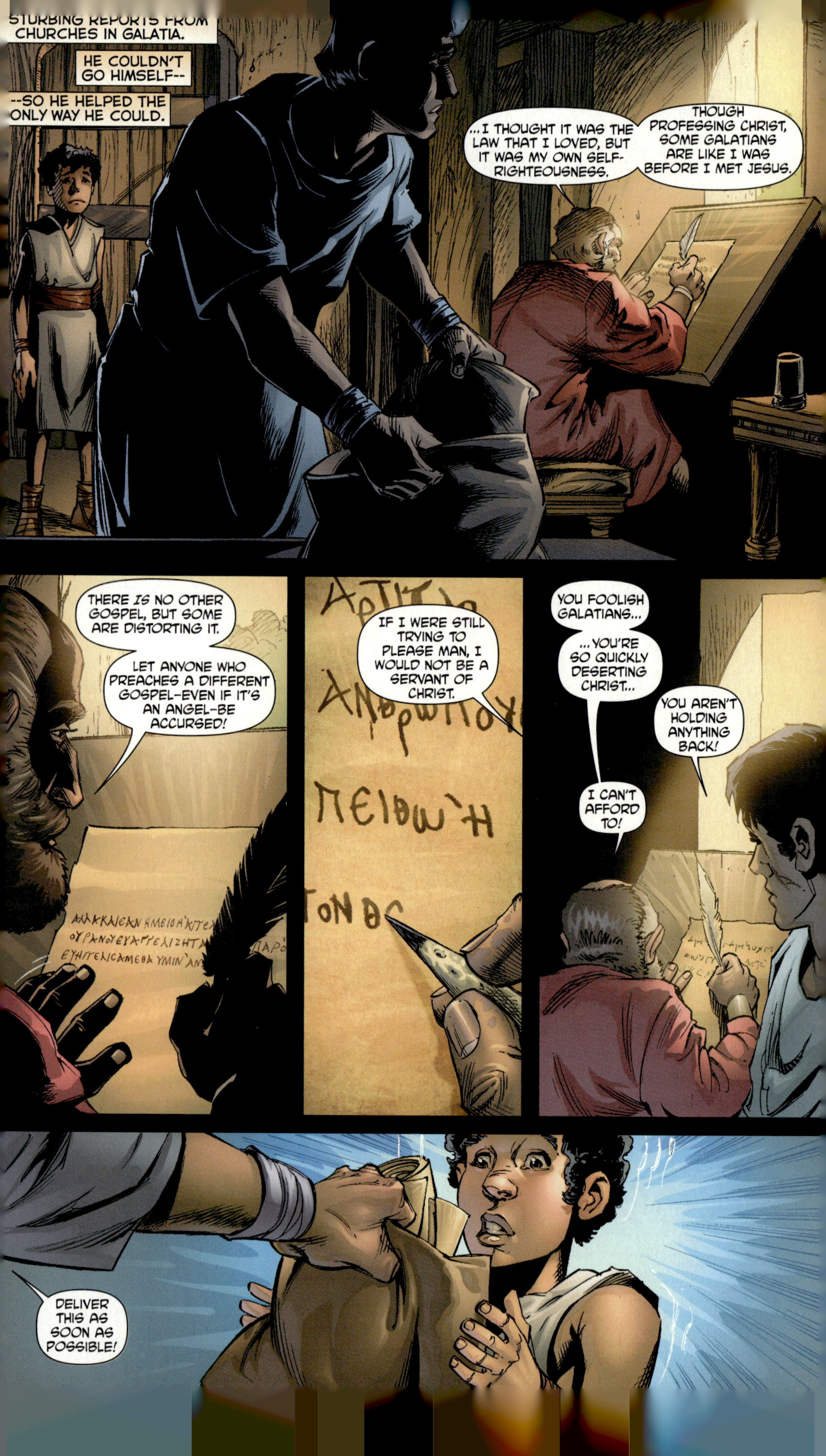
STURBING REPORTS FROM CHURCHES IN GALATIA.
HE COULDN'T GO HIMSELF--
--SO HE HELPED THE ONLY WAY HE COULD.
THOUGH PROFESSING CHRIST, SOME GALATIANS ARE LIKE I WAS BEFORE I MET JESUS.
...I THOUGHT IT WAS THE LAW THAT I LOVED, BUT IT WAS MY OWN SELF-RIGHTEOUSNESS.
THERE IS NO OTHER GOSPEL, BUT SOME ARE DISTORTING IT.
LET ANYONE WHO PREACHES A DIFFERENT GOSPEL—EVEN IF IT'S AN ANGEL—BE ACCURSED!
IF I WERE STILL TRYING TO PLEASE MAN, I WOULD NOT BE A SERVANT OF CHRIST.
YOU FOOLISH GALATIANS...
...YOU'RE SO QUICKLY DESERTING CHRIST...
YOU AREN'T HOLDING ANYTHING BACK!
I CAN'T AFFORD TO!
DELIVER THIS AS SOON AS POSSIBLE!

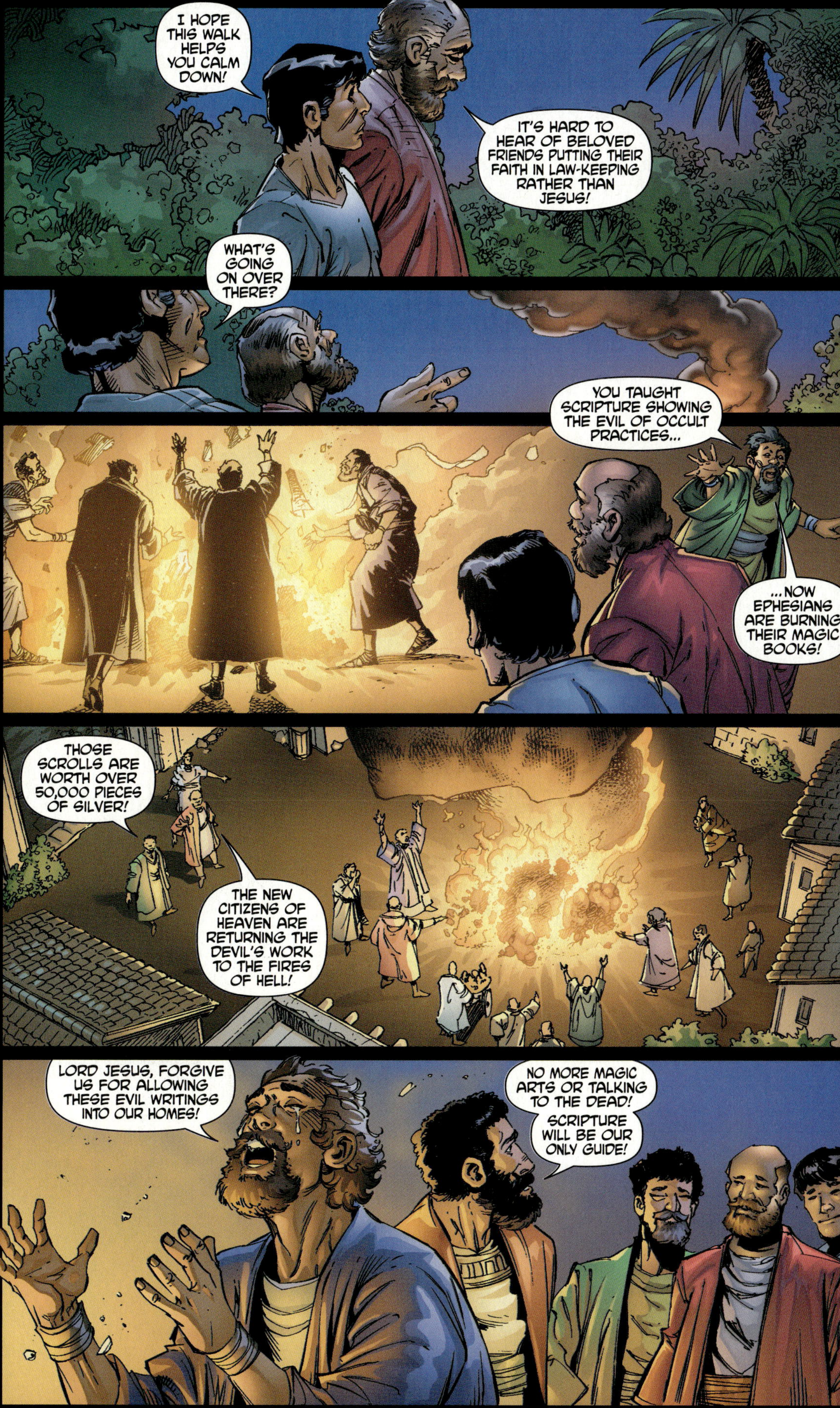
I HOPE THIS WALK HELPS YOU CALM DOWN!
IT'S HARD TO HEAR OF BELOVED FRIENDS PUTTING THEIR FAITH IN LAW-KEEPING RATHER THAN JESUS!
WHAT'S GOING ON OVER THERE?
YOU TAUGHT SCRIPTURE SHOWING THE EVIL OF OCCULT PRACTICES...
...NOW EPHESIANS ARE BURNING THEIR MAGIC BOOKS!
THOSE SCROLLS ARE WORTH OVER 50,000 PIECES OF SILVER!
THE NEW CITIZENS OF HEAVEN ARE RETURNING THE DEVIL'S WORK TO THE FIRES OF HELL!
LORD JESUS, FORGIVE US FOR ALLOWING THESE EVIL WRITINGS INTO OUR HOMES!
NO MORE MAGIC ARTS OR TALKING TO THE DEAD!
SCRIPTURE WILL BE OUR ONLY GUIDE!

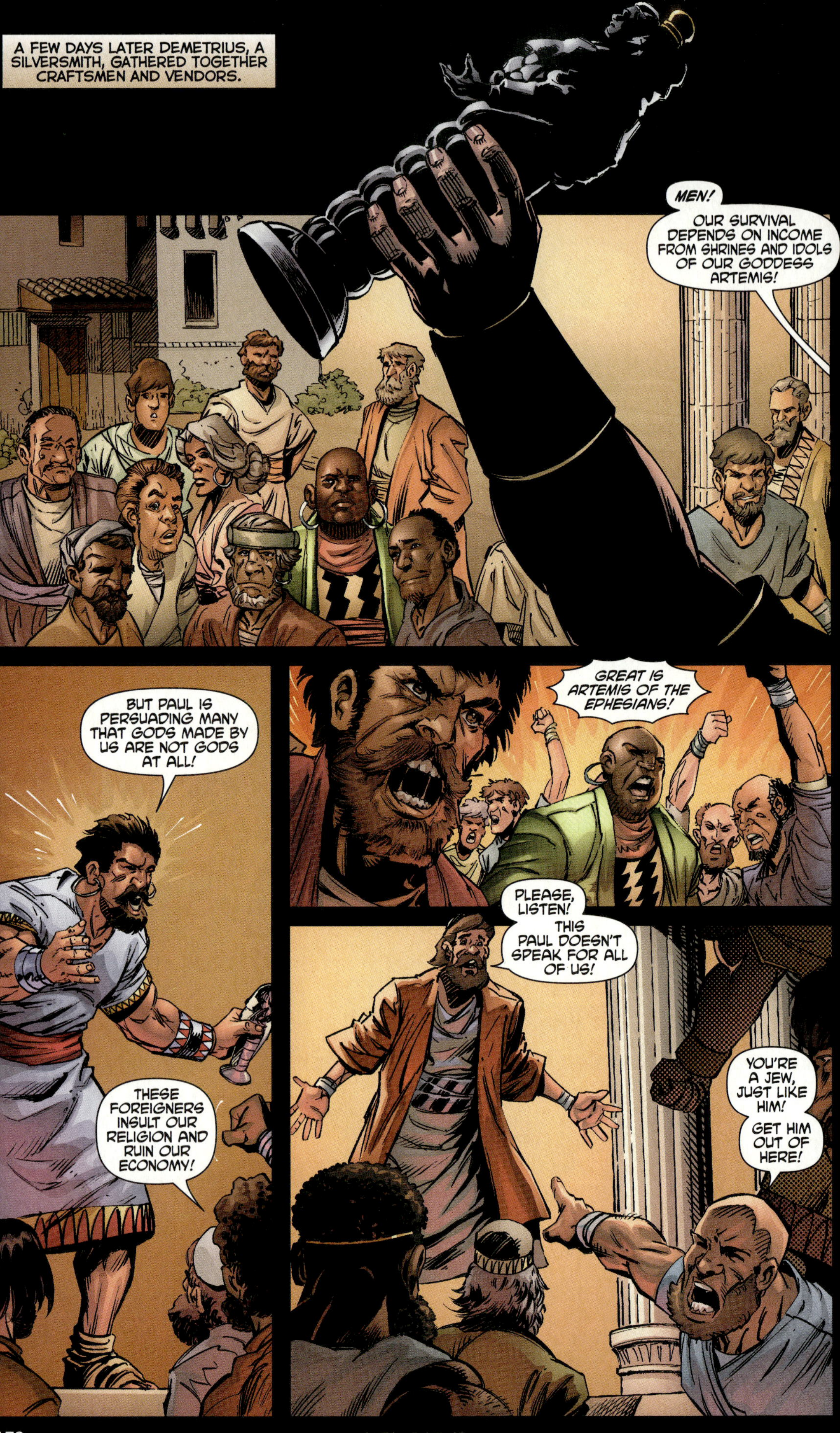
A FEW DAYS LATER DEMETRIUS, A SILVERSMITH, GATHERED TOGETHER CRAFTSMEN AND VENDORS.
MEN!
OUR SURVIVAL DEPENDS ON INCOME FROM SHRINES AND IDOLS OF OUR GODDESS ARTEMIS!
BUT PAUL IS PERSUADING MANY THAT GODS MADE BY US ARE NOT GODS AT ALL!
THESE FOREIGNERS INSULT OUR RELIGION AND RUIN OUR ECONOMY!
GREAT IS ARTEMIS OF THE EPHESIANS!
PLEASE, LISTEN!
THIS PAUL DOESN'T SPEAK FOR ALL OF US!
YOU'RE A JEW, JUST LIKE HIM!
GET HIM OUT OF HERE!

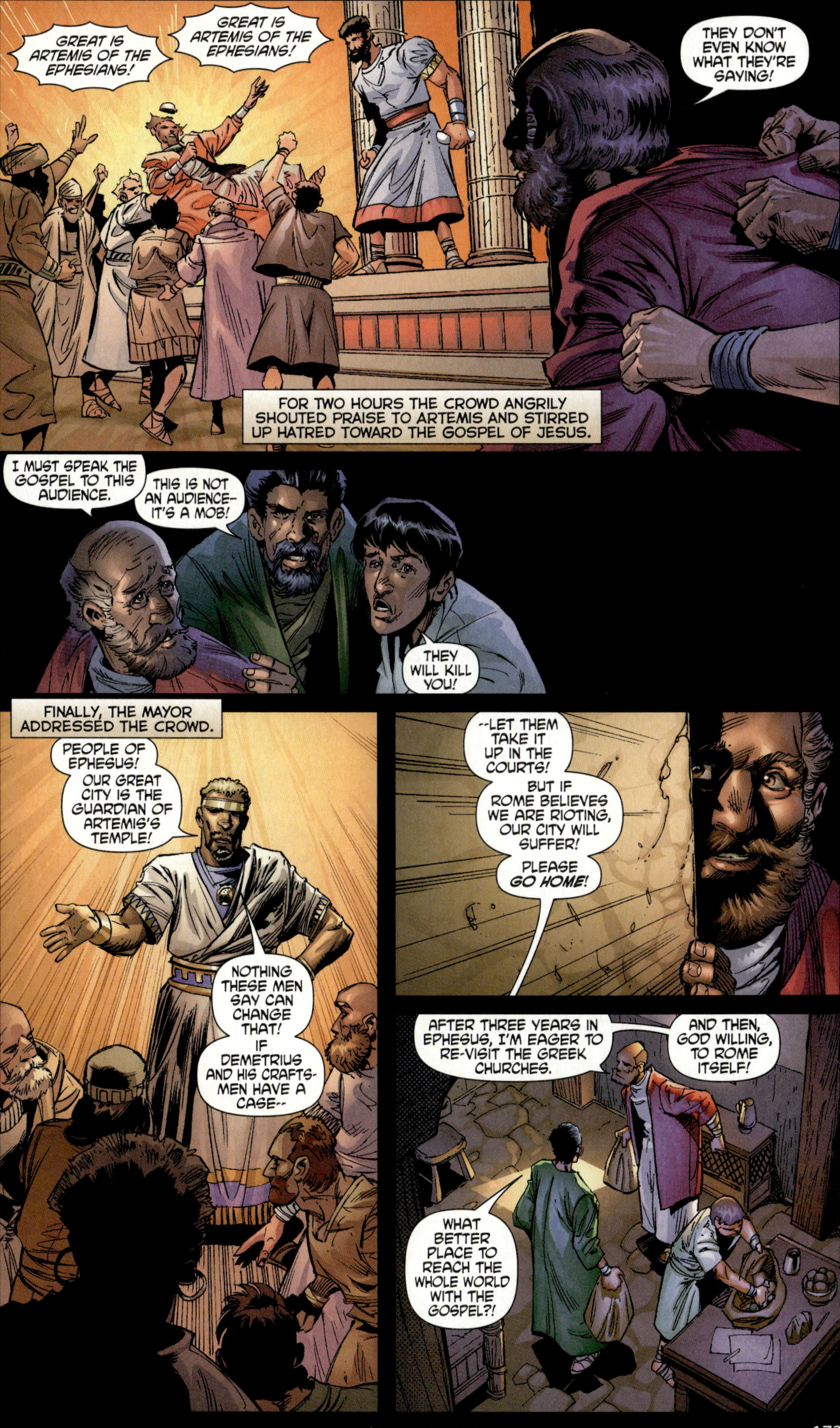
GREAT IS ARTEMIS OF THE EPHESIANS!
GREAT IS ARTEMIS OF THE EPHESIANS!
THEY DON'T EVEN KNOW WHAT THEY'RE SAYING!
FOR TWO HOURS THE CROWD ANGRILY SHOUTED PRAISE TO ARTEMIS AND STIRRED UP HATRED TOWARD THE GOSPEL OF JESUS.
I MUST SPEAK THE GOSPEL TO THIS AUDIENCE.
THIS IS NOT AN AUDIENCE-IT'S A MOB!
THEY WILL KILL YOU!
FINALLY, THE MAYOR ADDRESSED THE CROWD.
PEOPLE OF EPHESUS! OUR GREAT CITY IS THE GUARDIAN OF ARTEMIS'S TEMPLE!
NOTHING THESE MEN SAY CAN CHANGE THAT! IF DEMETRIUS AND HIS CRAFTS-MEN HAVE A CASE--
--LET THEM TAKE IT UP IN THE COURTS! BUT IF ROME BELIEVES WE ARE RIOTING, OUR CITY WILL SUFFER! PLEASE *GO HOME*!
AFTER THREE YEARS IN EPHESUS, I'M EAGER TO RE-VISIT THE GREEK CHURCHES.
AND THEN, GOD WILLING, TO ROME ITSELF!
WHAT BETTER PLACE TO REACH THE WHOLE WORLD WITH THE GOSPEL?!

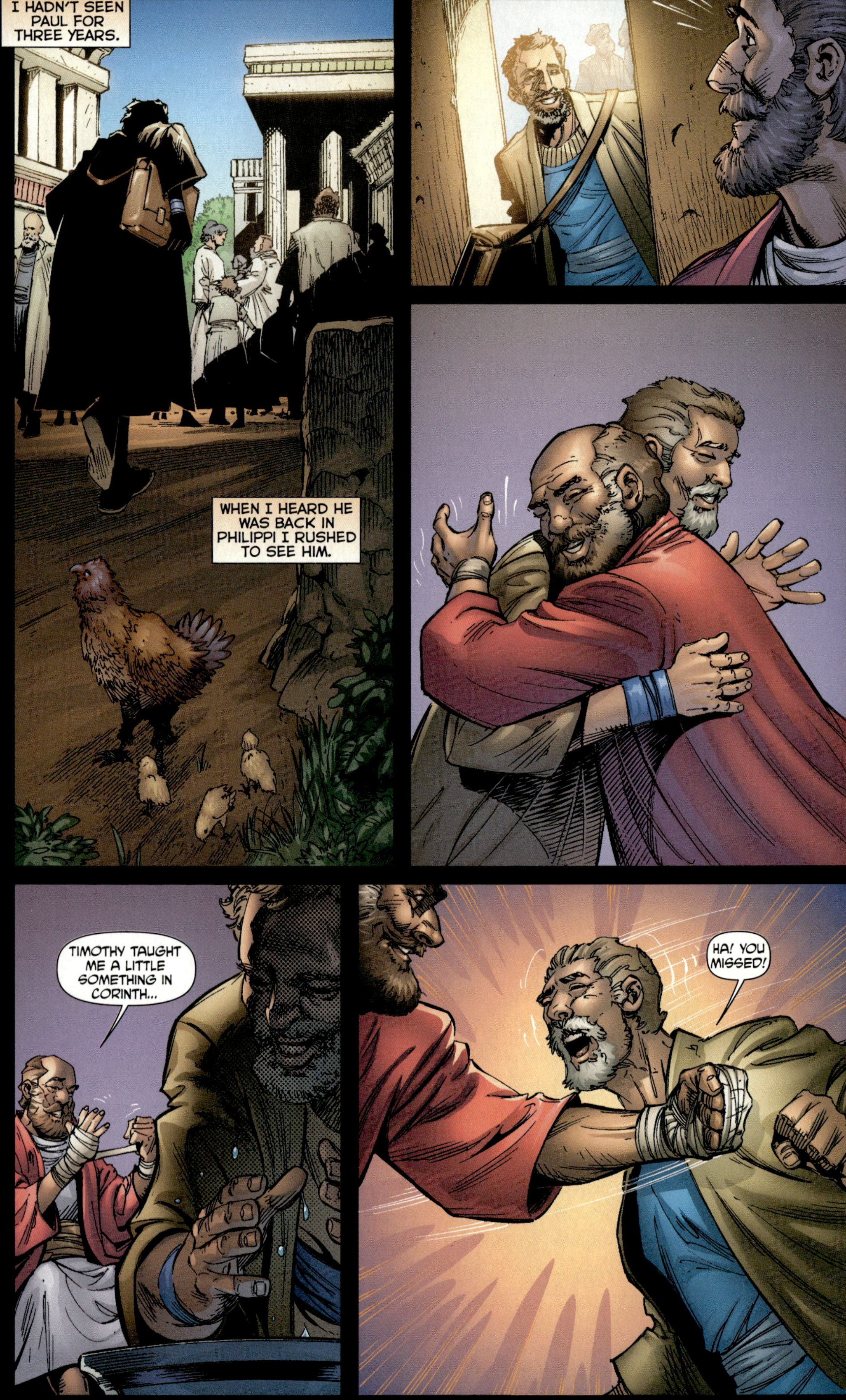
I HADN'T SEEN PAUL FOR THREE YEARS.
WHEN I HEARD HE WAS BACK IN PHILIPPI I RUSHED TO SEE HIM.
TIMOTHY TAUGHT ME A LITTLE SOMETHING IN CORINTH...
HA! YOU MISSED!

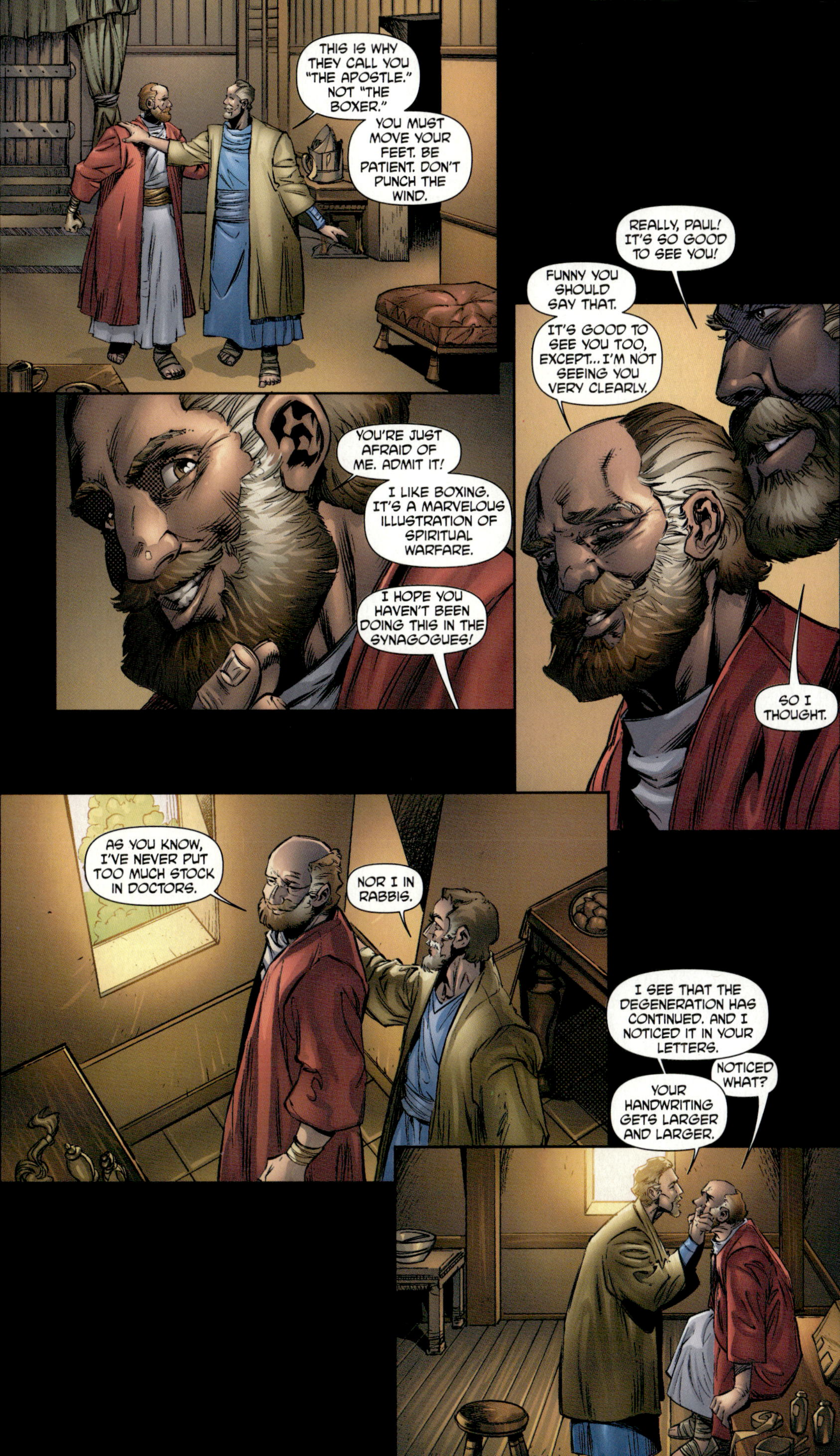
THIS IS WHY THEY CALL YOU "THE APOSTLE." NOT "THE BOXER."
YOU MUST MOVE YOUR FEET. BE PATIENT. DON'T PUNCH THE WIND.
REALLY, PAUL! IT'S SO GOOD TO SEE YOU!
FUNNY YOU SHOULD SAY THAT.
IT'S GOOD TO SEE YOU TOO, EXCEPT... I'M NOT SEEING YOU VERY CLEARLY.
YOU'RE JUST AFRAID OF ME. ADMIT IT!
I LIKE BOXING. IT'S A MARVELOUS ILLUSTRATION OF SPIRITUAL WARFARE.
I HOPE YOU HAVEN'T BEEN DOING THIS IN THE SYNAGOGUES!
SO I THOUGHT.
AS YOU KNOW, I'VE NEVER PUT TOO MUCH STOCK IN DOCTORS.
NOR I IN RABBIS.
I SEE THAT THE DEGENERATION HAS CONTINUED. AND I NOTICED IT IN YOUR LETTERS.
NOTICED WHAT?
YOUR HANDWRITING GETS LARGER AND LARGER.

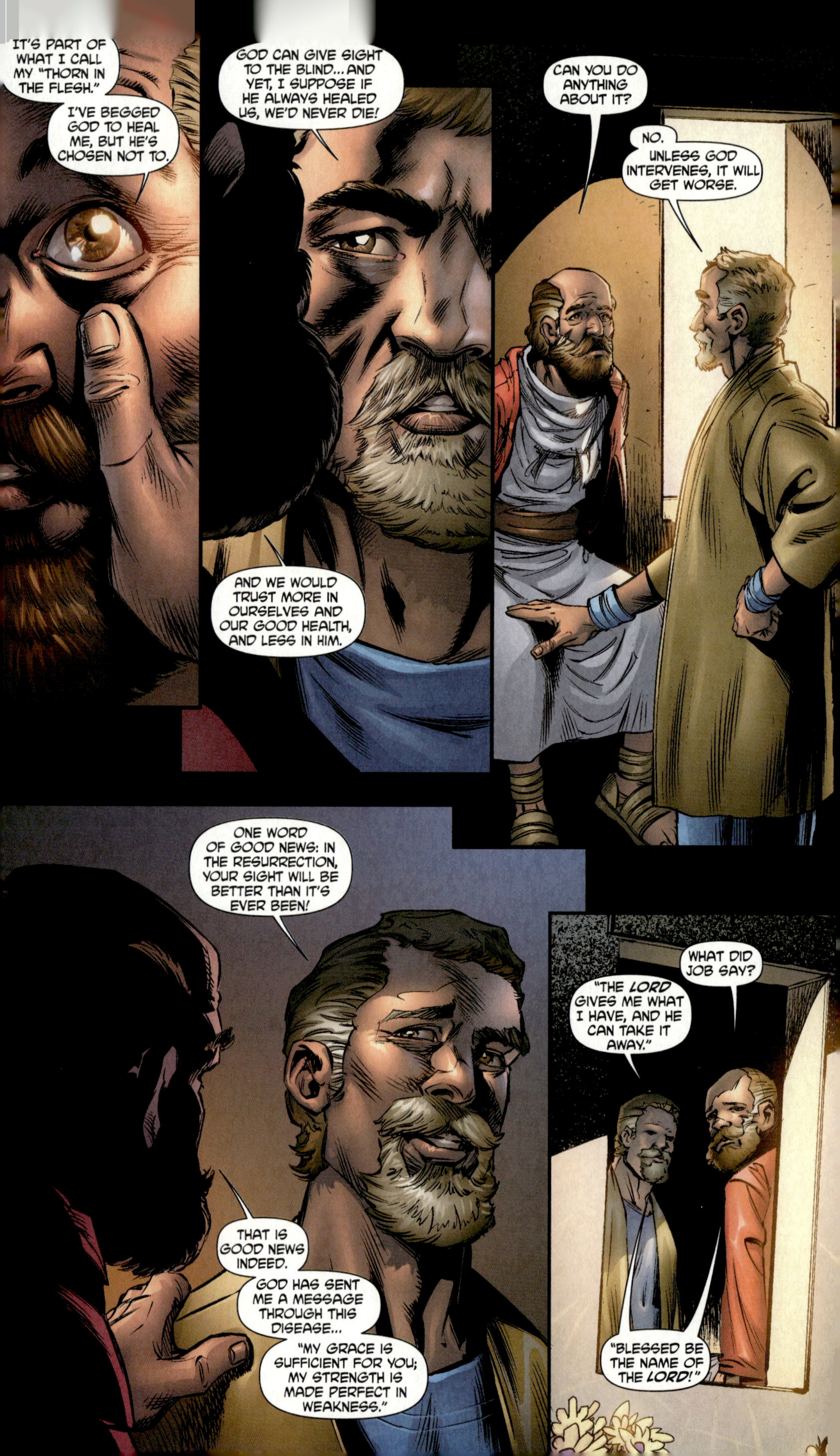
IT'S PART OF WHAT I CALL MY "THORN IN THE FLESH."
I'VE BEGGED GOD TO HEAL ME, BUT HE'S CHOSEN NOT TO.
GOD CAN GIVE SIGHT TO THE BLIND... AND YET, I SUPPOSE IF HE ALWAYS HEALED US, WE'D NEVER DIE!
AND WE WOULD TRUST MORE IN OURSELVES AND OUR GOOD HEALTH, AND LESS IN HIM.
CAN YOU DO ANYTHING ABOUT IT?
NO.
UNLESS GOD INTERVENES, IT WILL GET WORSE.
ONE WORD OF GOOD NEWS: IN THE RESURRECTION, YOUR SIGHT WILL BE BETTER THAN IT'S EVER BEEN!
THAT IS GOOD NEWS INDEED.
GOD HAS SENT ME A MESSAGE THROUGH THIS DISEASE...
"MY GRACE IS SUFFICIENT FOR YOU; MY STRENGTH IS MADE PERFECT IN WEAKNESS."
WHAT DID JOB SAY?
"THE *LORD* GIVES ME WHAT I HAVE, AND HE CAN TAKE IT AWAY."
"BLESSED BE THE NAME OF THE *LORD*!"

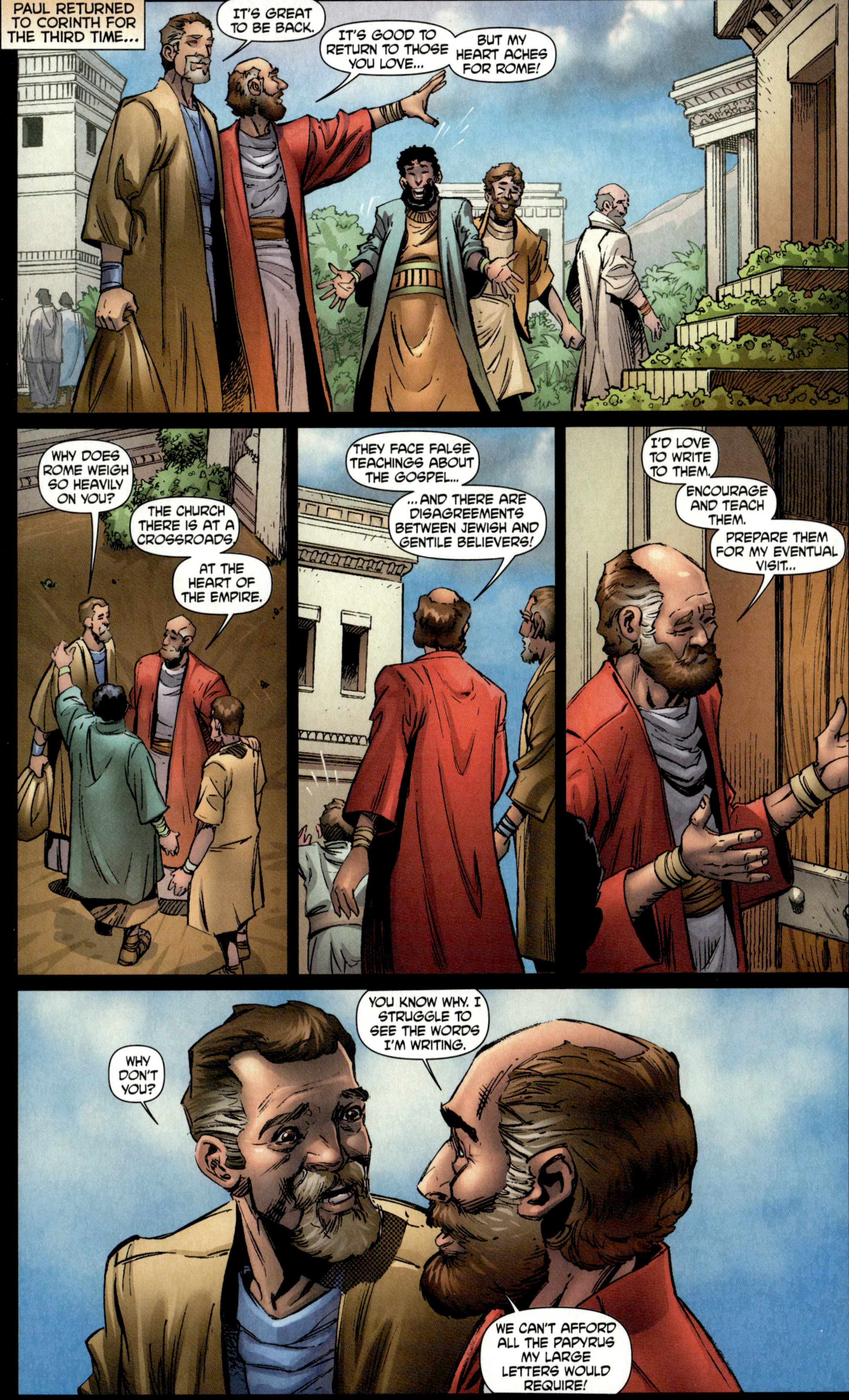
PAUL RETURNED TO CORINTH FOR THE THIRD TIME...
IT'S GREAT TO BE BACK.
IT'S GOOD TO RETURN TO THOSE YOU LOVE...
BUT MY HEART ACHES FOR ROME!
WHY DOES ROME WEIGH SO HEAVILY ON YOU?
THE CHURCH THERE IS AT A CROSSROADS.
AT THE HEART OF THE EMPIRE.
THEY FACE FALSE TEACHINGS ABOUT THE GOSPEL...
...AND THERE ARE DISAGREEMENTS BETWEEN JEWISH AND GENTILE BELIEVERS!
I'D LOVE TO WRITE TO THEM.
ENCOURAGE AND TEACH THEM.
PREPARE THEM FOR MY EVENTUAL VISIT...
WHY DON'T YOU?
YOU KNOW WHY. I STRUGGLE TO SEE THE WORDS I'M WRITING.
WE CAN'T AFFORD ALL THE PAPYRUS MY LARGE LETTERS WOULD REQUIRE!

ACTS 20:3

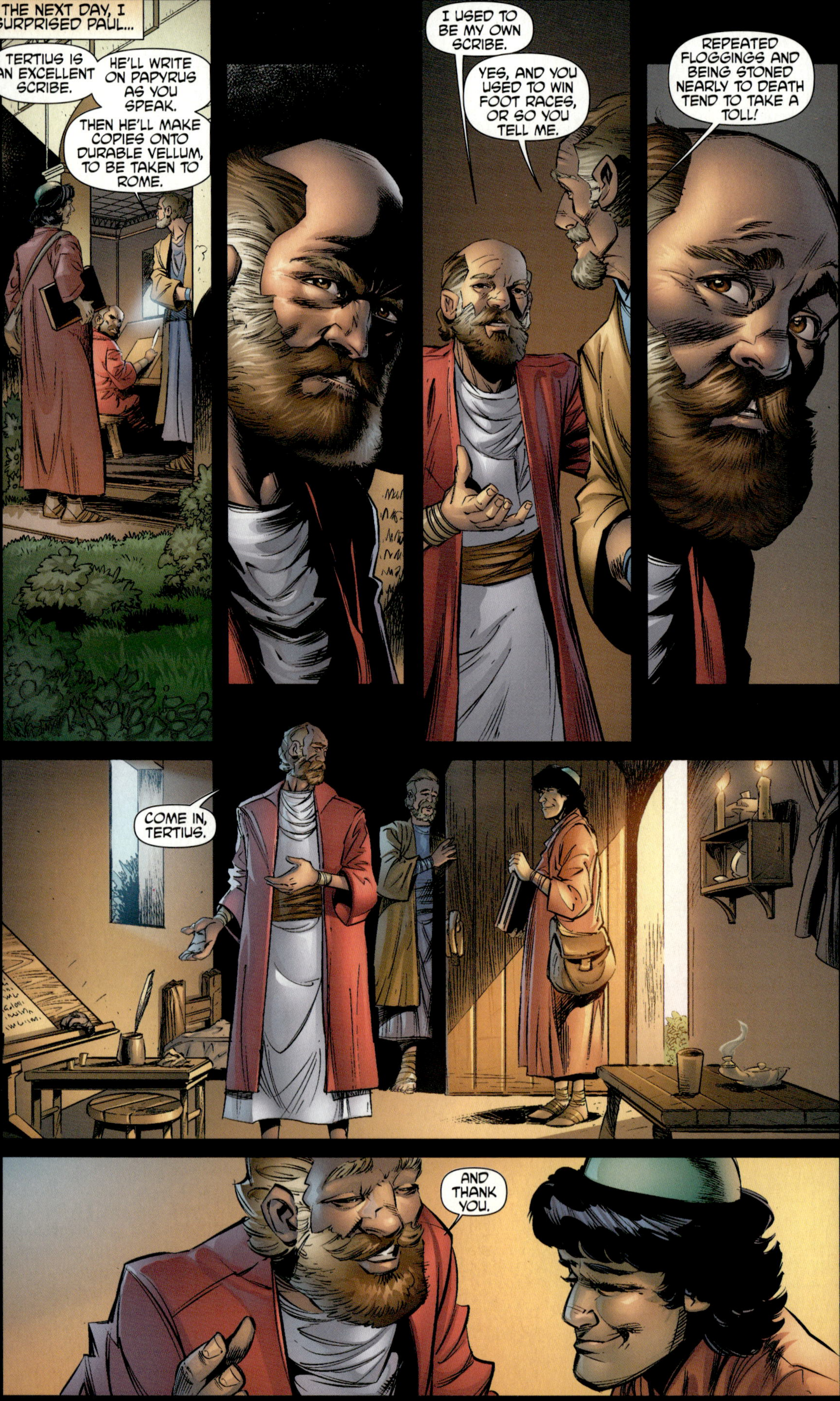
THE NEXT DAY, I SURPRISED PAUL...
TERTIUS IS AN EXCELLENT SCRIBE.
HE'LL WRITE ON PAPYRUS AS YOU SPEAK.
THEN HE'LL MAKE COPIES ONTO DURABLE VELLUM, TO BE TAKEN TO ROME.
I USED TO BE MY OWN SCRIBE.
YES, AND YOU USED TO WIN FOOT RACES, OR SO YOU TELL ME.
REPEATED FLOGGINGS AND BEING STONED NEARLY TO DEATH TEND TO TAKE A TOLL!
COME IN, TERTIUS.
AND THANK YOU.

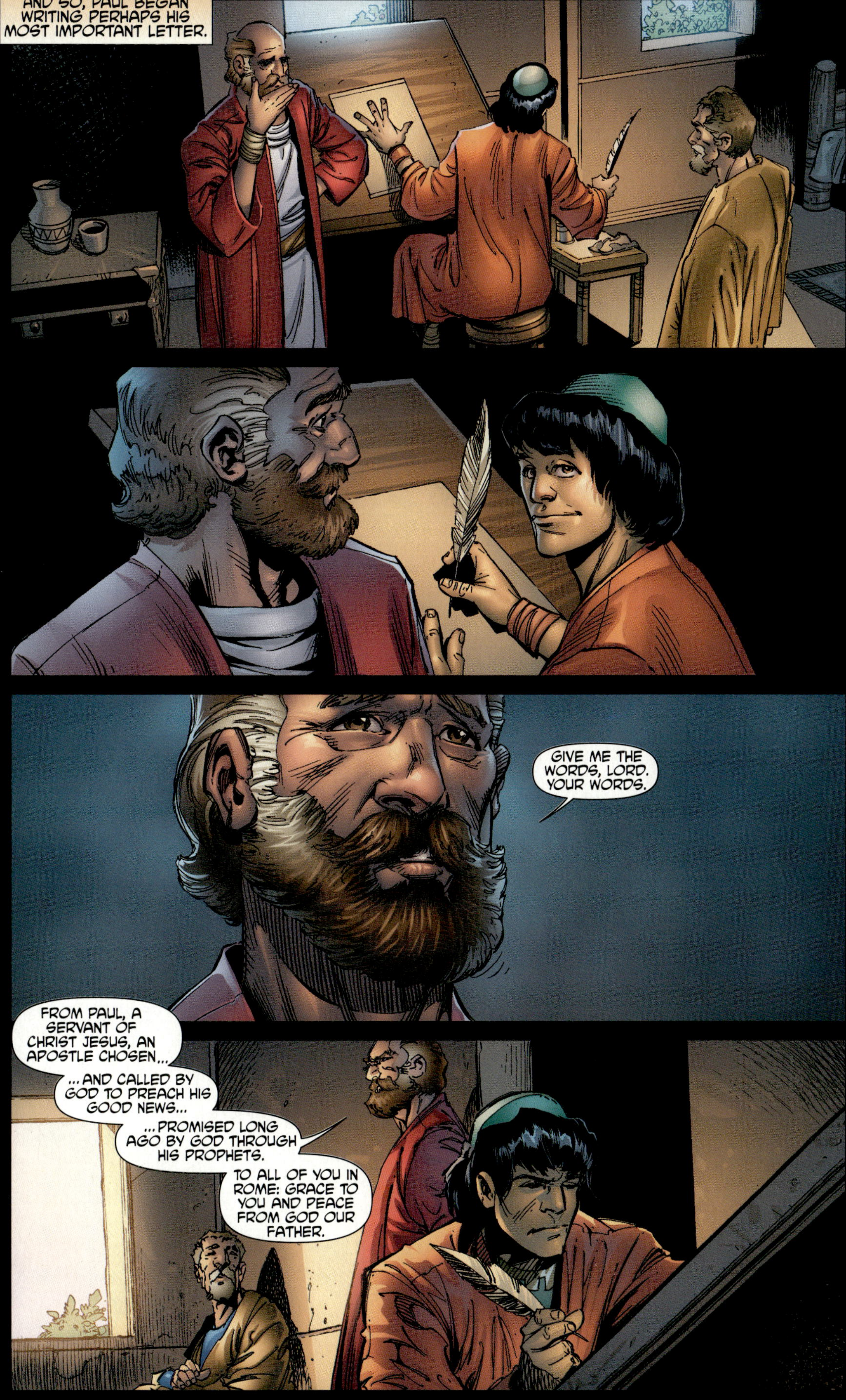
AND SO, PAUL BEGAN WRITING PERHAPS HIS MOST IMPORTANT LETTER.
GIVE ME THE WORDS, LORD. YOUR WORDS.
FROM PAUL, A SERVANT OF CHRIST JESUS, AN APOSTLE CHOSEN...
...AND CALLED BY GOD TO PREACH HIS GOOD NEWS...
...PROMISED LONG AGO BY GOD THROUGH HIS PROPHETS.
TO ALL OF YOU IN ROME: GRACE TO YOU AND PEACE FROM GOD OUR FATHER.

ROMANS 1:1-7

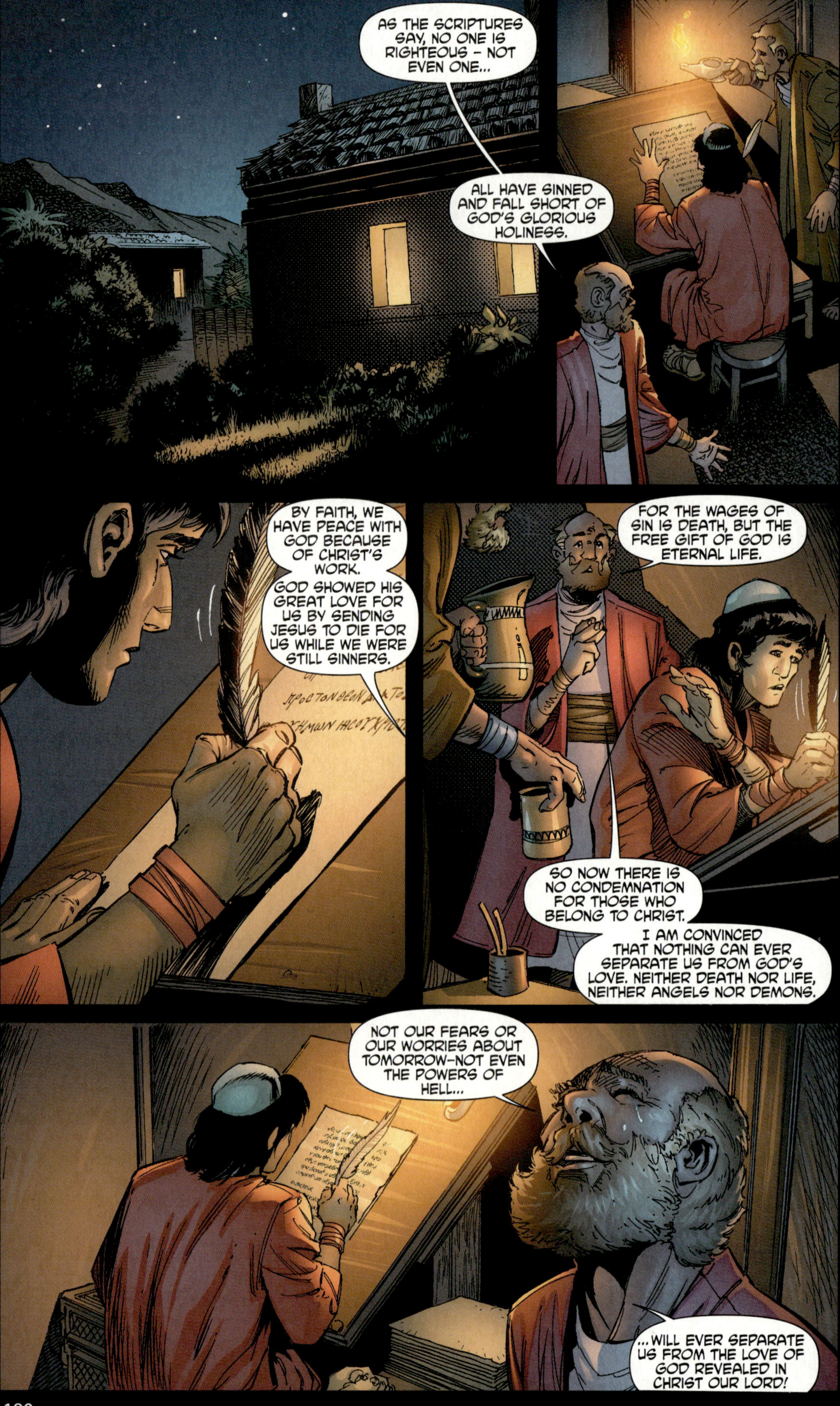
AS THE SCRIPTURES SAY, NO ONE IS RIGHTEOUS – NOT EVEN ONE...
ALL HAVE SINNED AND FALL SHORT OF GOD'S GLORIOUS HOLINESS.
BY FAITH, WE HAVE PEACE WITH GOD BECAUSE OF CHRIST'S WORK.
GOD SHOWED HIS GREAT LOVE FOR US BY SENDING JESUS TO DIE FOR US WHILE WE WERE STILL SINNERS.
FOR THE WAGES OF SIN IS DEATH, BUT THE FREE GIFT OF GOD IS ETERNAL LIFE.
SO NOW THERE IS NO CONDEMNATION FOR THOSE WHO BELONG TO CHRIST.
I AM CONVINCED THAT NOTHING CAN EVER SEPARATE US FROM GOD'S LOVE. NEITHER DEATH NOR LIFE, NEITHER ANGELS NOR DEMONS.
NOT OUR FEARS OR OUR WORRIES ABOUT TOMORROW–NOT EVEN THE POWERS OF HELL...
...WILL EVER SEPARATE US FROM THE LOVE OF GOD REVEALED IN CHRIST OUR LORD!

ROMANS 5:1, 5:8, 6:23, 8:1, 8:39

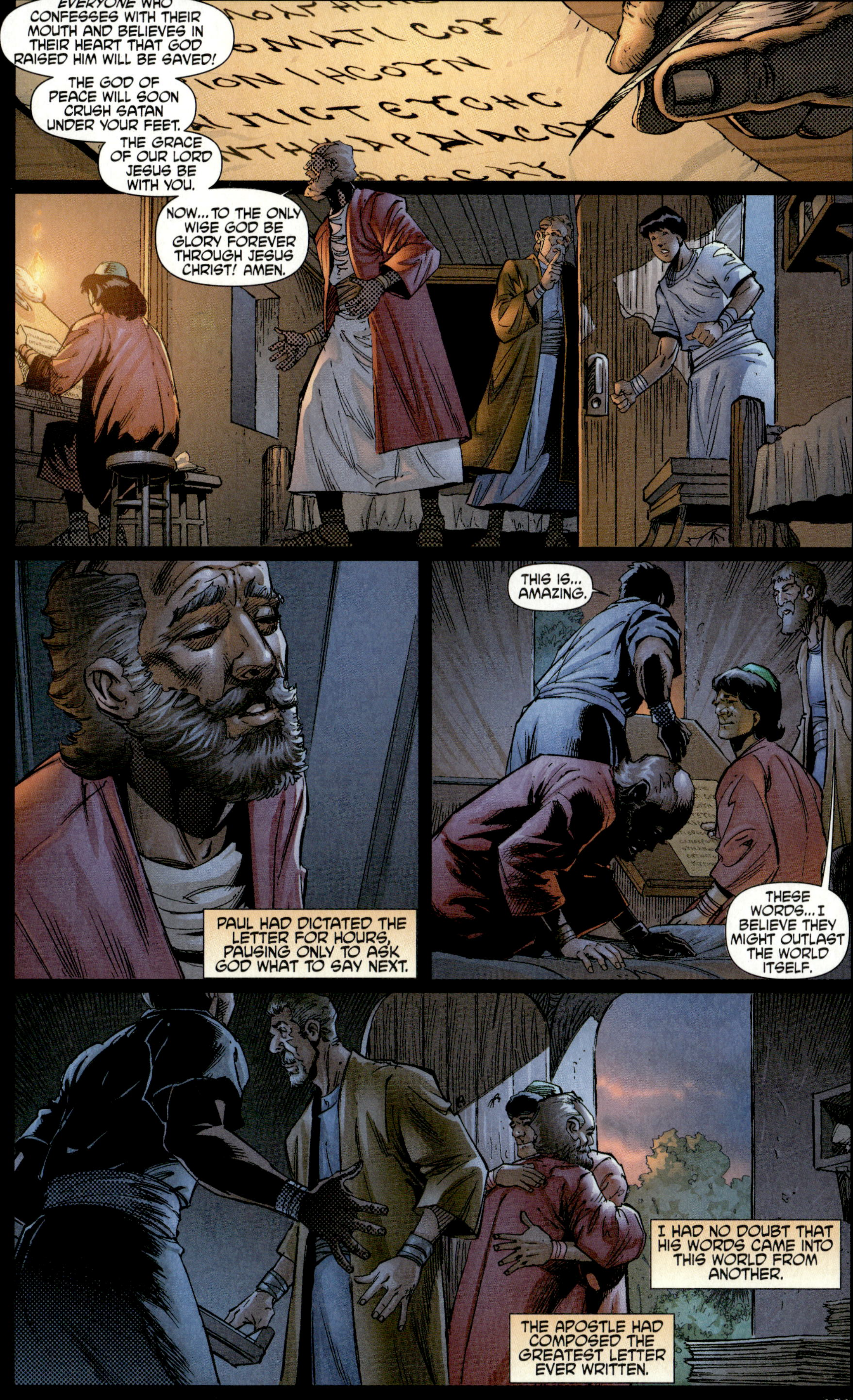
EVERYONE WHO CONFESSES WITH THEIR MOUTH AND BELIEVES IN THEIR HEART THAT GOD RAISED HIM WILL BE SAVED!
THE GOD OF PEACE WILL SOON CRUSH SATAN UNDER YOUR FEET.
THE GRACE OF OUR LORD JESUS BE WITH YOU.
NOW... TO THE ONLY WISE GOD BE GLORY FOREVER THROUGH JESUS CHRIST! AMEN.
PAUL HAD DICTATED THE LETTER FOR HOURS, PAUSING ONLY TO ASK GOD WHAT TO SAY NEXT.
THIS IS... AMAZING.
THESE WORDS... I BELIEVE THEY MIGHT OUTLAST THE WORLD ITSELF.
I HAD NO DOUBT THAT HIS WORDS CAME INTO THIS WORLD FROM ANOTHER.
THE APOSTLE HAD COMPOSED THE GREATEST LETTER EVER WRITTEN.

ROMANS 10:9-10, 13; 16:20-27

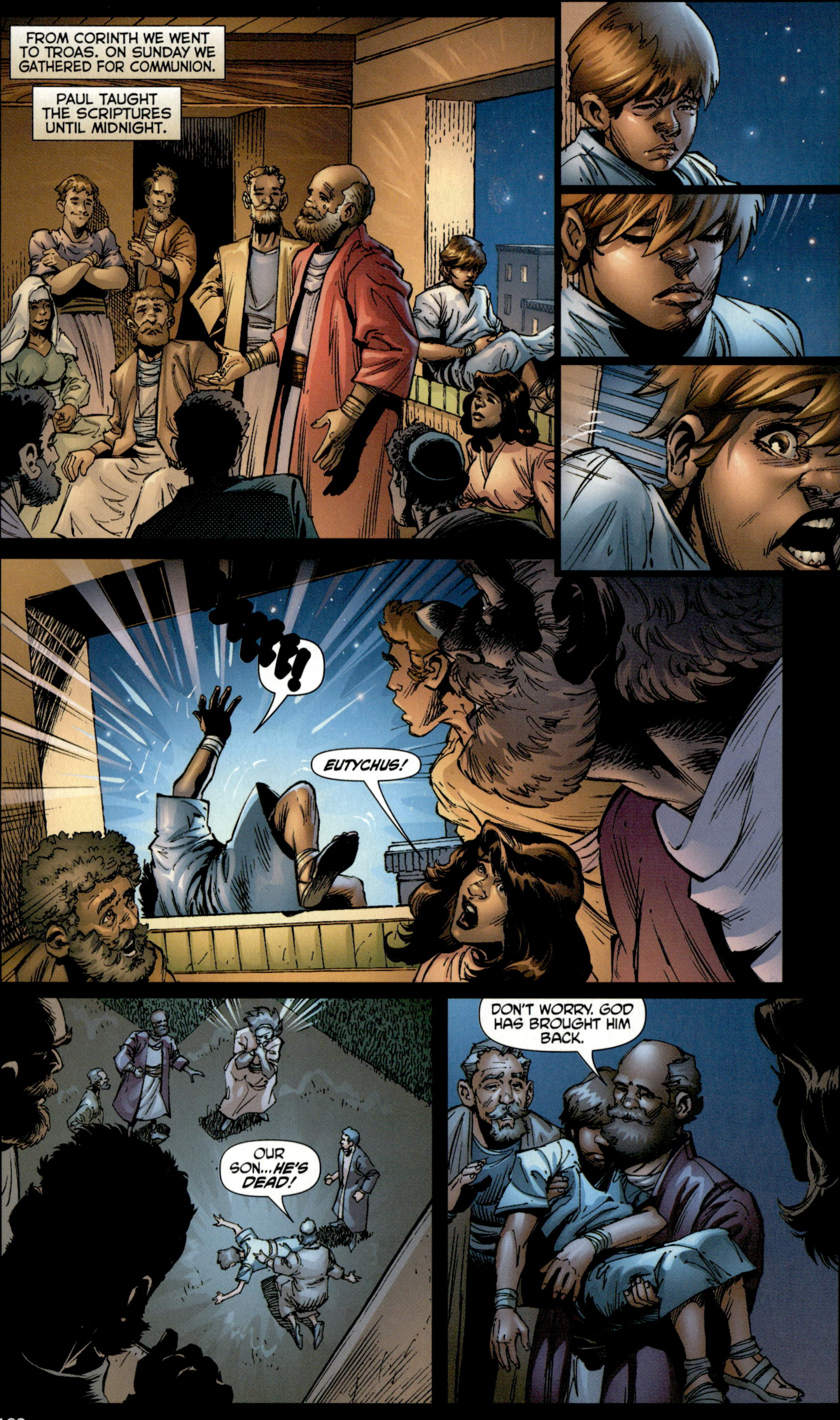
FROM CORINTH WE WENT TO TROAS. ON SUNDAY WE GATHERED FOR COMMUNION.
PAUL TAUGHT THE SCRIPTURES UNTIL MIDNIGHT.
EUTYCHUS!
OUR SON...HE'S DEAD!
DON'T WORRY. GOD HAS BROUGHT HIM BACK.

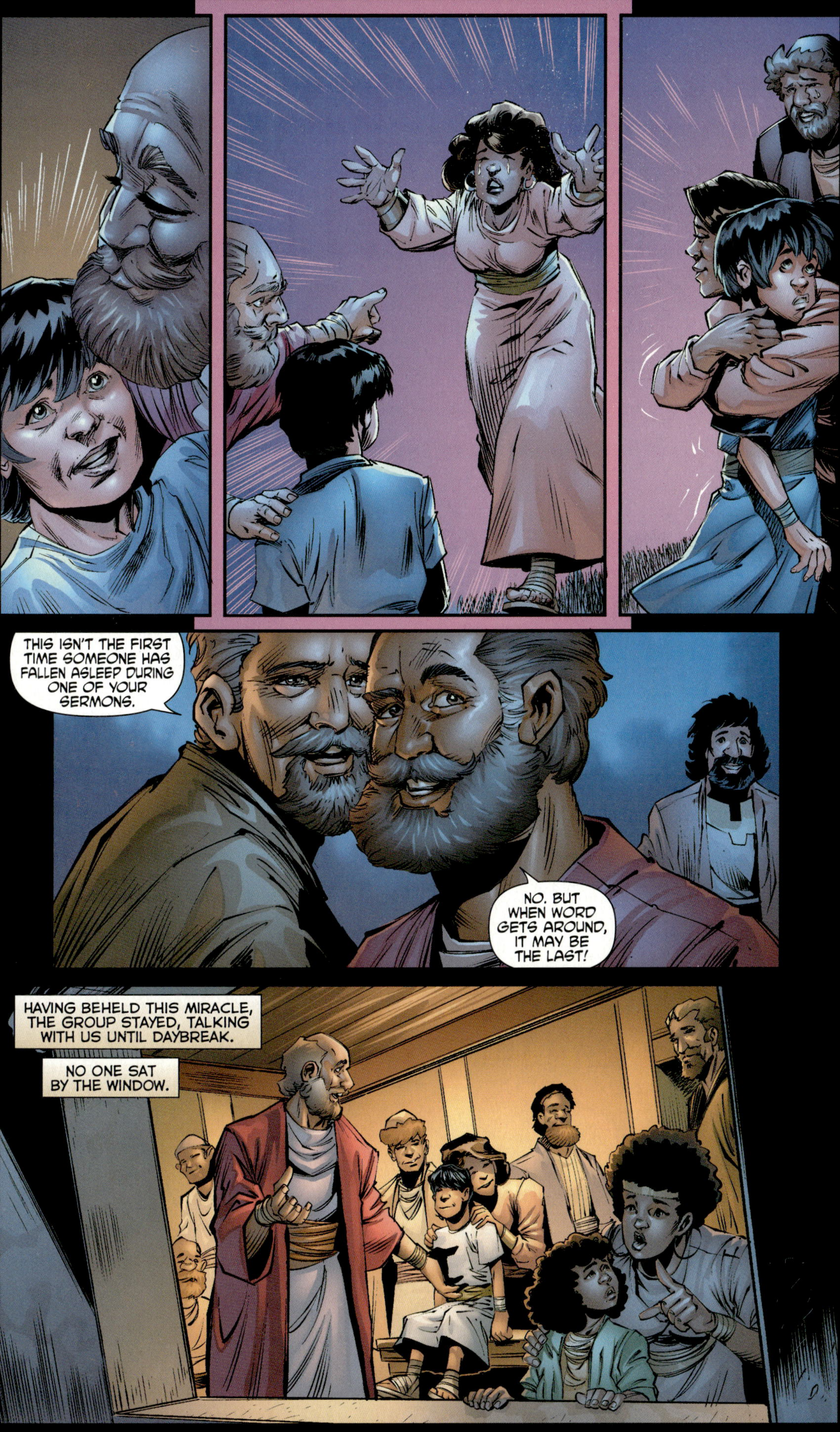

THIS ISN'T THE FIRST TIME SOMEONE HAS FALLEN ASLEEP DURING ONE OF YOUR SERMONS.
NO. BUT WHEN WORD GETS AROUND, IT MAY BE THE LAST!
HAVING BEHELD THIS MIRACLE, THE GROUP STAYED, TALKING WITH US UNTIL DAYBREAK.
NO ONE SAT BY THE WINDOW.

ACTS 20:11-12

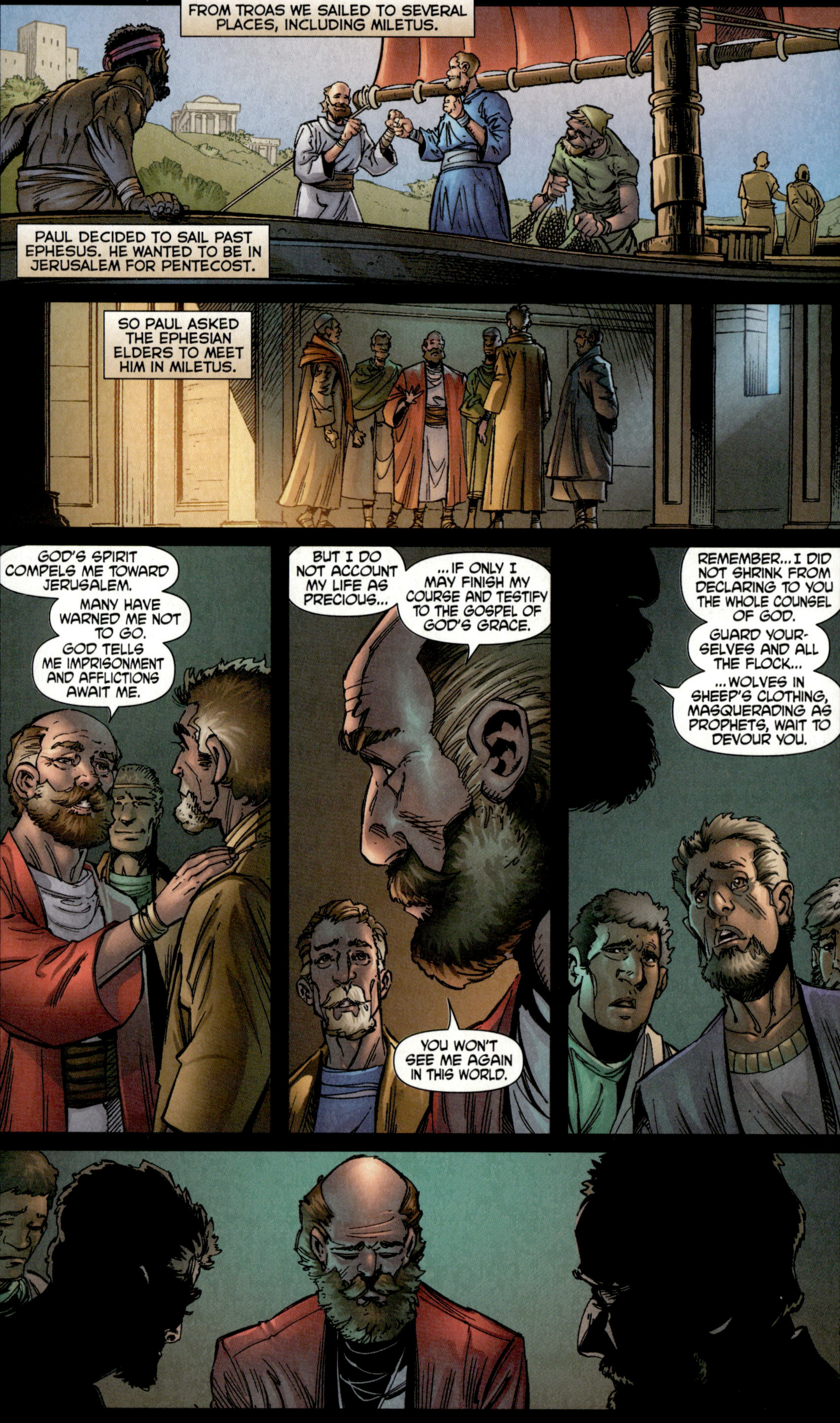
FROM TROAS WE SAILED TO SEVERAL PLACES, INCLUDING MILETUS.
PAUL DECIDED TO SAIL PAST EPHESUS. HE WANTED TO BE IN JERUSALEM FOR PENTECOST.
SO PAUL ASKED THE EPHESIAN ELDERS TO MEET HIM IN MILETUS.
GOD'S SPIRIT COMPELS ME TOWARD JERUSALEM.
MANY HAVE WARNED ME NOT TO GO.
GOD TELLS ME IMPRISONMENT AND AFFLICTIONS AWAIT ME.
BUT I DO NOT ACCOUNT MY LIFE AS PRECIOUS...
...IF ONLY I MAY FINISH MY COURSE AND TESTIFY TO THE GOSPEL OF GOD'S GRACE.
YOU WON'T SEE ME AGAIN IN THIS WORLD.
REMEMBER...I DID NOT SHRINK FROM DECLARING TO YOU THE WHOLE COUNSEL OF GOD.
GUARD YOURSELVES AND ALL THE FLOCK...
...WOLVES IN SHEEP'S CLOTHING, MASQUERADING AS PROPHETS, WAIT TO DEVOUR YOU.

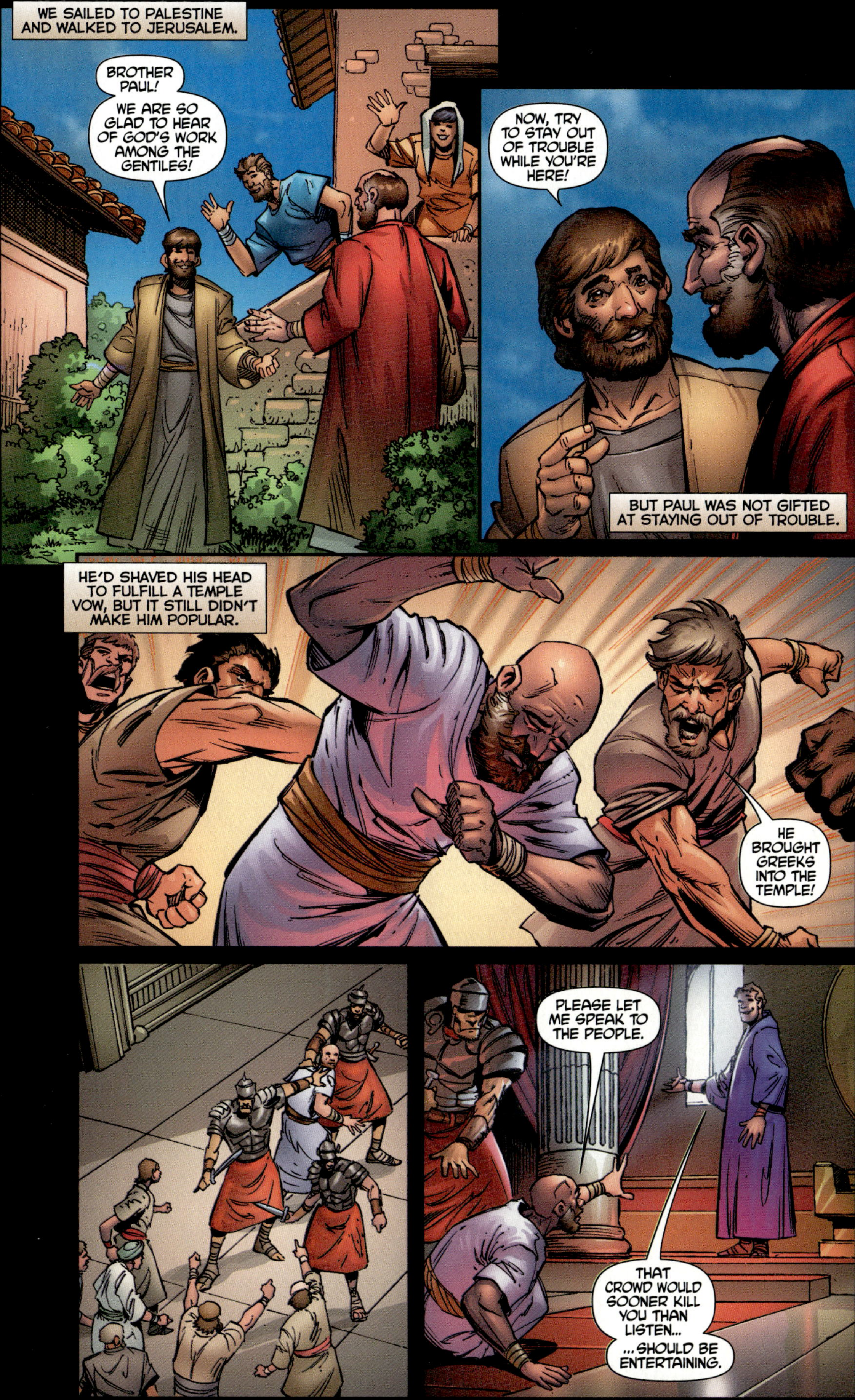

WE SAILED TO PALESTINE AND WALKED TO JERUSALEM.
BROTHER PAUL!
WE ARE SO GLAD TO HEAR OF GOD'S WORK AMONG THE GENTILES!
NOW, TRY TO STAY OUT OF TROUBLE WHILE YOU'RE HERE!
BUT PAUL WAS NOT GIFTED AT STAYING OUT OF TROUBLE.
HE'D SHAVED HIS HEAD TO FULFILL A TEMPLE VOW, BUT IT STILL DIDN'T MAKE HIM POPULAR.
HE BROUGHT GREEKS INTO THE TEMPLE!
PLEASE LET ME SPEAK TO THE PEOPLE.
THAT CROWD WOULD SOONER KILL YOU THAN LISTEN...
...SHOULD BE ENTERTAINING.

ACTS 21:27-28, 37-40

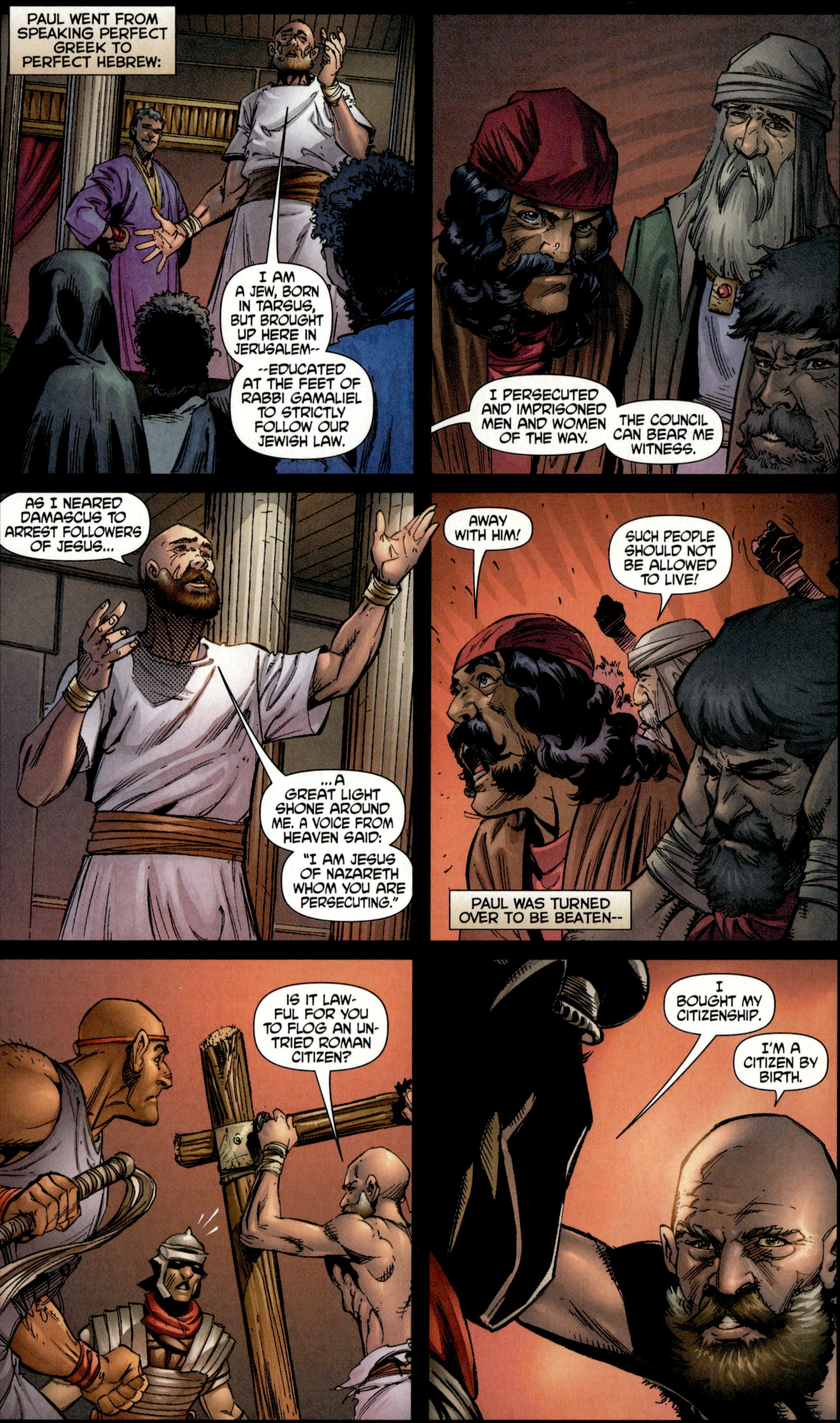
PAUL WENT FROM SPEAKING PERFECT GREEK TO PERFECT HEBREW:
I AM A JEW, BORN IN TARSUS, BUT BROUGHT UP HERE IN JERUSALEM--
--EDUCATED AT THE FEET OF RABBI GAMALIEL TO STRICTLY FOLLOW OUR JEWISH LAW.
I PERSECUTED AND IMPRISONED MEN AND WOMEN OF THE WAY.
THE COUNCIL CAN BEAR ME WITNESS.
AS I NEARED DAMASCUS TO ARREST FOLLOWERS OF JESUS...
...A GREAT LIGHT SHONE AROUND ME. A VOICE FROM HEAVEN SAID:
"I AM JESUS OF NAZARETH WHOM YOU ARE PERSECUTING."
AWAY WITH HIM!
SUCH PEOPLE SHOULD NOT BE ALLOWED TO LIVE!
PAUL WAS TURNED OVER TO BE BEATEN--
IS IT LAWFUL FOR YOU TO FLOG AN UNTRIED ROMAN CITIZEN?
I BOUGHT MY CITIZENSHIP.
I'M A CITIZEN BY BIRTH.

ACTS 22:6-8, 22:22-29

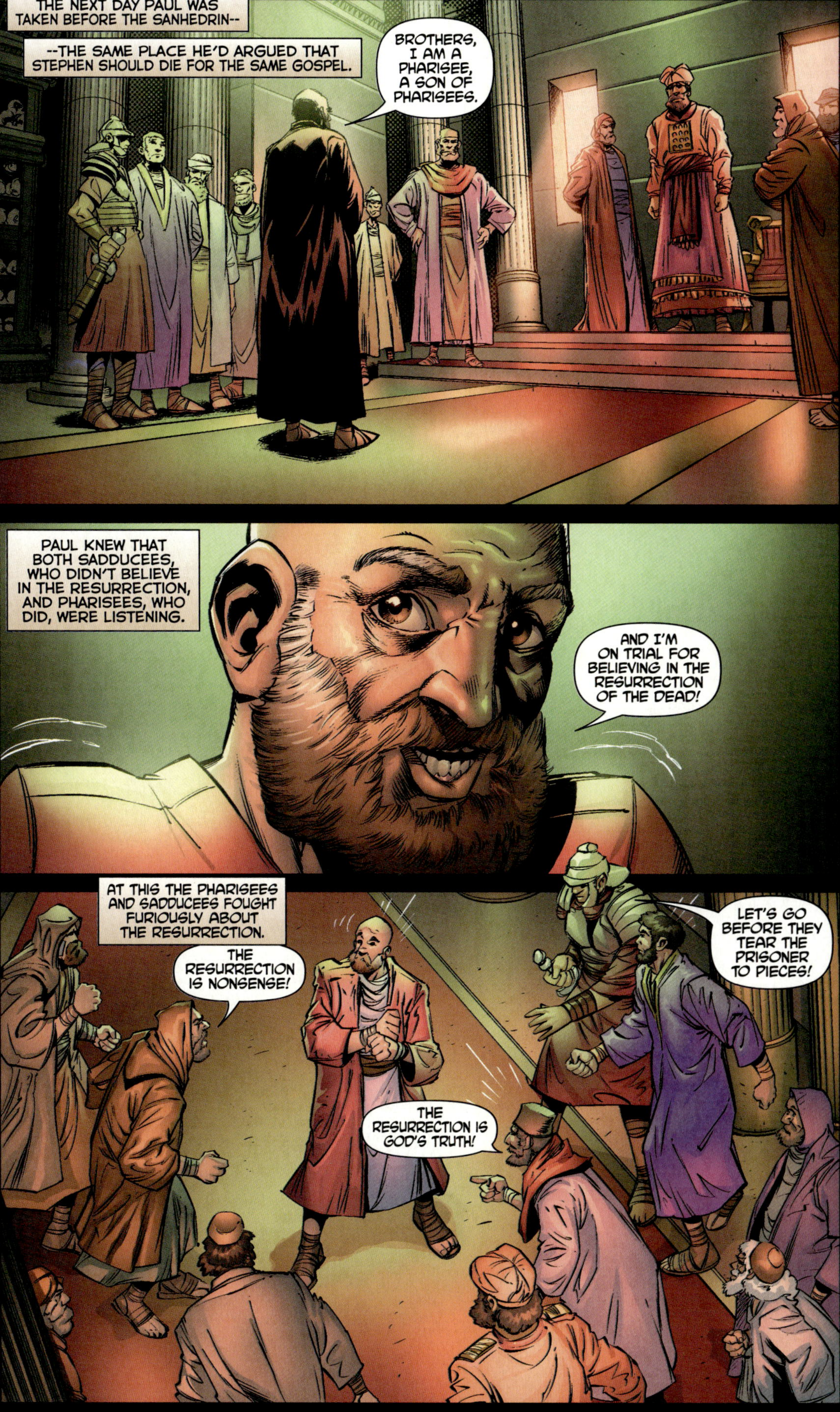
THE NEXT DAY PAUL WAS TAKEN BEFORE THE SANHEDRIN--
--THE SAME PLACE HE'D ARGUED THAT STEPHEN SHOULD DIE FOR THE SAME GOSPEL.
BROTHERS, I AM A PHARISEE, A SON OF PHARISEES.
PAUL KNEW THAT BOTH SADDUCEES, WHO DIDN'T BELIEVE IN THE RESURRECTION, AND PHARISEES, WHO DID, WERE LISTENING.
AND I'M ON TRIAL FOR BELIEVING IN THE RESURRECTION OF THE DEAD!
AT THIS THE PHARISEES AND SADDUCEES FOUGHT FURIOUSLY ABOUT THE RESURRECTION.
THE RESURRECTION IS NONSENSE!
LET'S GO BEFORE THEY TEAR THE PRISONER TO PIECES!
THE RESURRECTION IS GOD'S TRUTH!

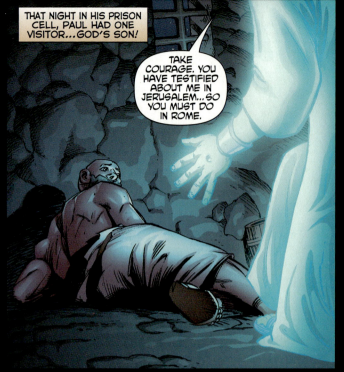

THAT NIGHT IN HIS PRISON CELL, PAUL HAD ONE VISITOR...GOD'S SON!

TAKE COURAGE. YOU HAVE TESTIFIED ABOUT ME IN JERUSALEM...SO YOU MUST DO IN ROME.

...AND THEN ANOTHER.

YOUR NEPHEW?

YES! IT'S BEEN SO LONG SINCE I'VE SEEN YOU!

I WISH I HAD GOOD NEWS... ...I OVERHEARD MEN TALKING TO THE TEMPLE LEADERS!

THEY SAID...

...WE HAVE MADE A VOW!

WE WILL NOT EAT OR DRINK UNTIL PAUL IS DEAD!

AND WE ARE WILLING TO KILL HIM OURSELVES!

ACTS 23:11-16

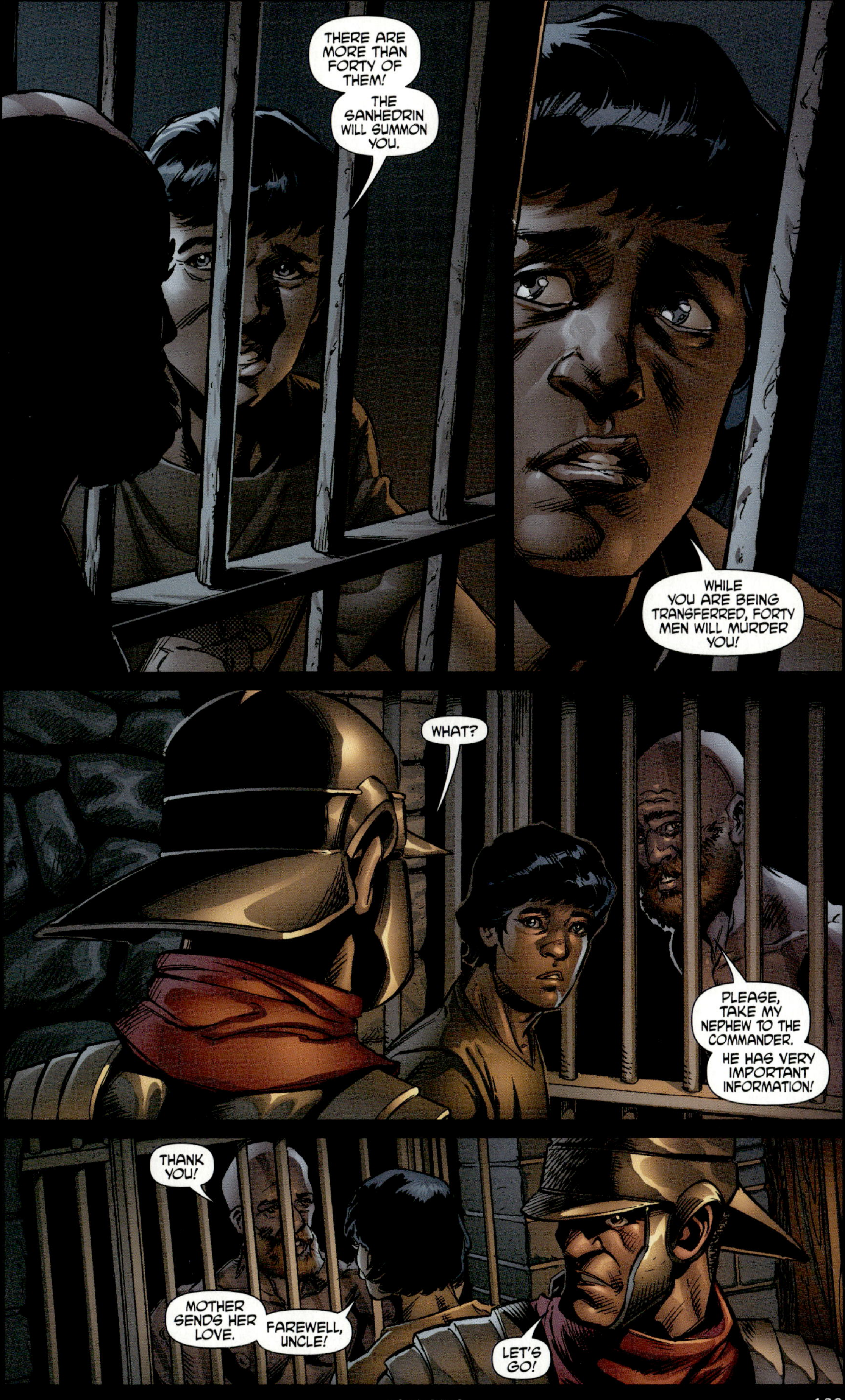
THERE ARE MORE THAN FORTY OF THEM!
THE SANHEDRIN WILL SUMMON YOU.
WHILE YOU ARE BEING TRANSFERRED, FORTY MEN WILL MURDER YOU!
WHAT?
PLEASE, TAKE MY NEPHEW TO THE COMMANDER.
HE HAS VERY IMPORTANT INFORMATION!
THANK YOU!
MOTHER SENDS HER LOVE.
FAREWELL, UNCLE!
LET'S GO!

ACTS 23:18

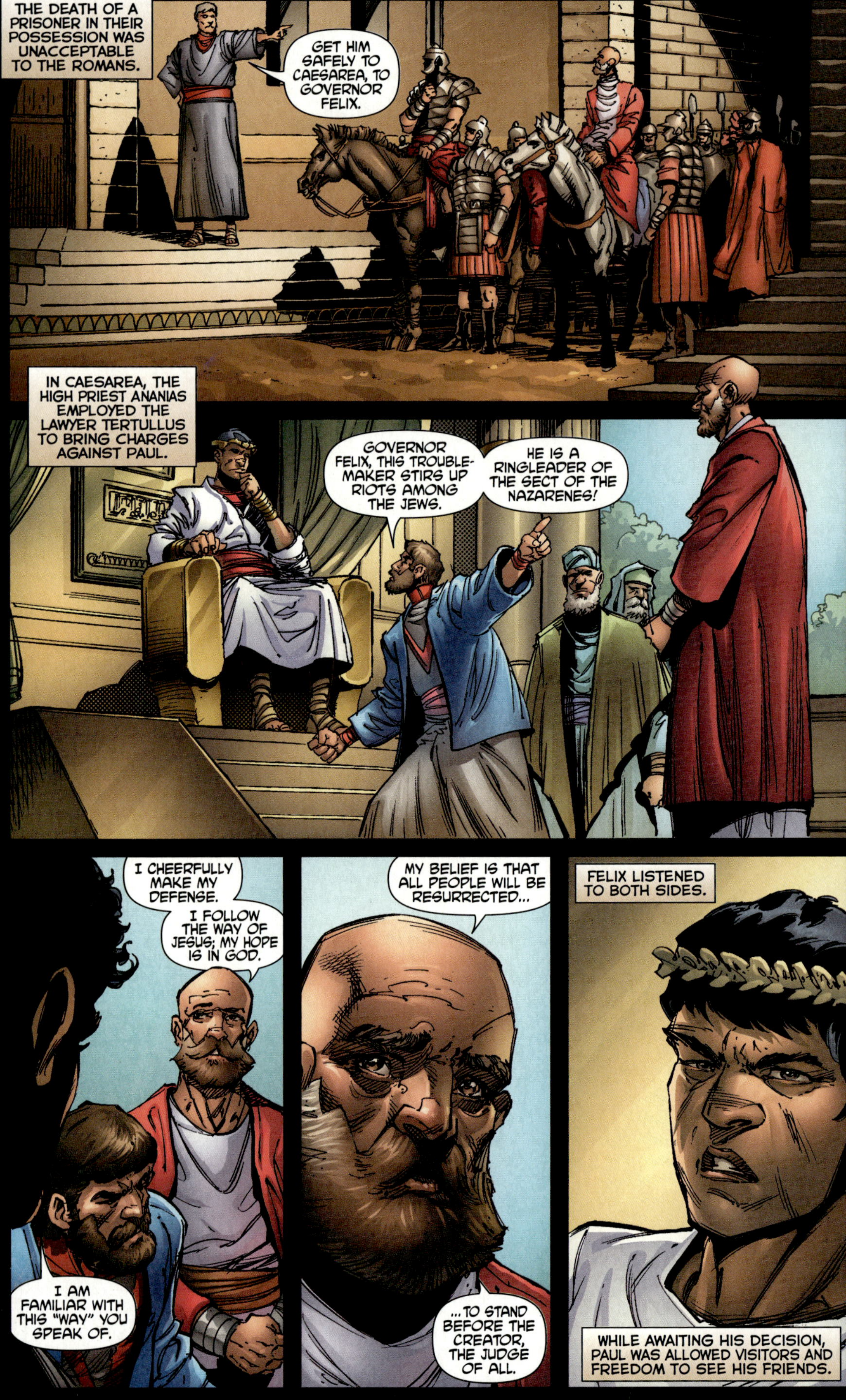
THE DEATH OF A PRISONER IN THEIR POSSESSION WAS UNACCEPTABLE TO THE ROMANS.
GET HIM SAFELY TO CAESAREA, TO GOVERNOR FELIX.
IN CAESAREA, THE HIGH PRIEST ANANIAS EMPLOYED THE LAWYER TERTULLUS TO BRING CHARGES AGAINST PAUL.
GOVERNOR FELIX, THIS TROUBLE-MAKER STIRS UP RIOTS AMONG THE JEWS.
HE IS A RINGLEADER OF THE SECT OF THE NAZARENES!
I CHEERFULLY MAKE MY DEFENSE.
I FOLLOW THE WAY OF JESUS; MY HOPE IS IN GOD.
I AM FAMILIAR WITH THIS "WAY" YOU SPEAK OF.
MY BELIEF IS THAT ALL PEOPLE WILL BE RESURRECTED...
...TO STAND BEFORE THE CREATOR, THE JUDGE OF ALL.
FELIX LISTENED TO BOTH SIDES.
WHILE AWAITING HIS DECISION, PAUL WAS ALLOWED VISITORS AND FREEDOM TO SEE HIS FRIENDS.

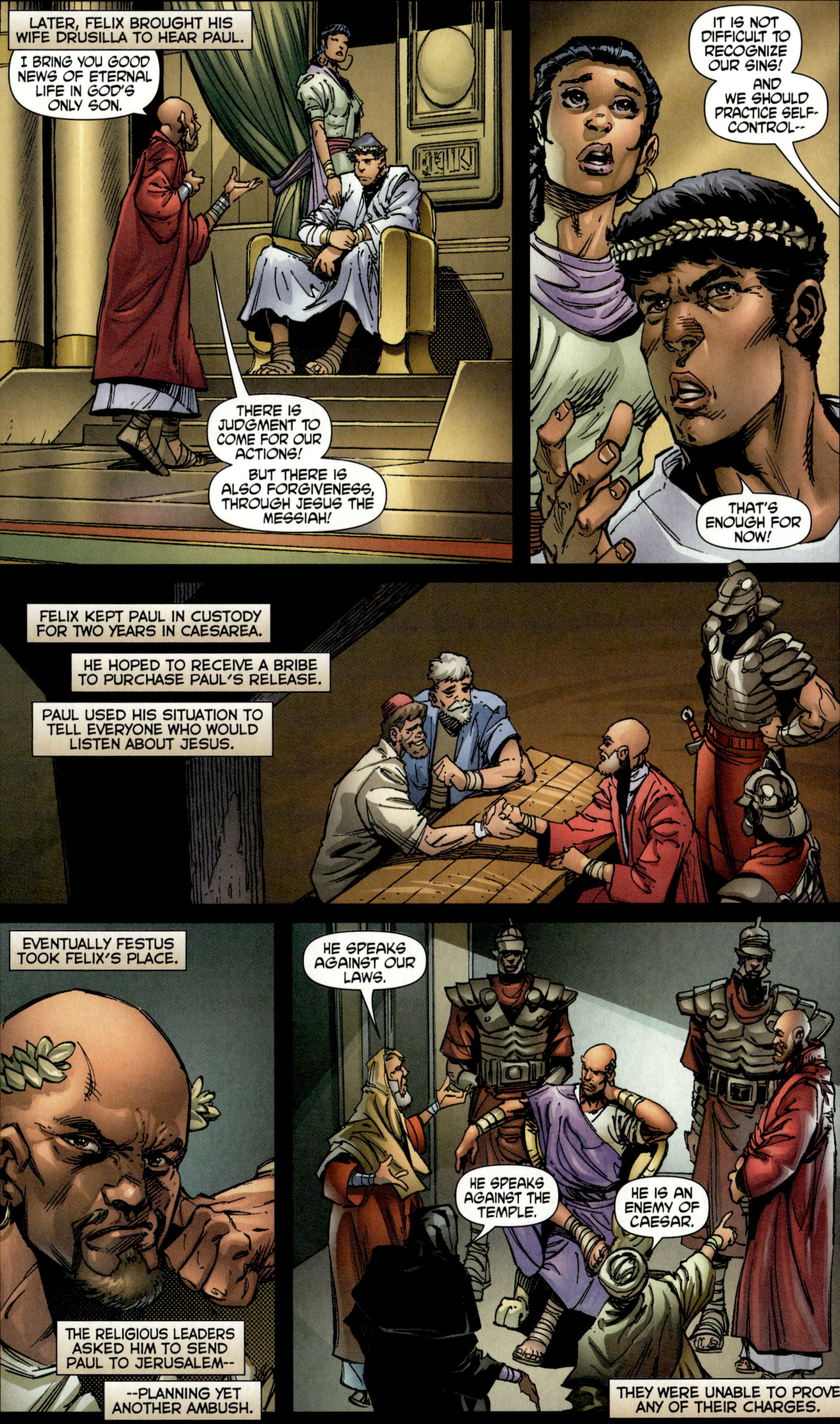
LATER, FELIX BROUGHT HIS WIFE DRUSILLA TO HEAR PAUL.
I BRING YOU GOOD NEWS OF ETERNAL LIFE IN GOD'S ONLY SON.
THERE IS JUDGMENT TO COME FOR OUR ACTIONS!
BUT THERE IS ALSO FORGIVENESS, THROUGH JESUS THE MESSIAH!
IT IS NOT DIFFICULT TO RECOGNIZE OUR SINS!
AND WE SHOULD PRACTICE SELF-CONTROL--
THAT'S ENOUGH FOR NOW!
FELIX KEPT PAUL IN CUSTODY FOR TWO YEARS IN CAESAREA.
HE HOPED TO RECEIVE A BRIBE TO PURCHASE PAUL'S RELEASE.
PAUL USED HIS SITUATION TO TELL EVERYONE WHO WOULD LISTEN ABOUT JESUS.
EVENTUALLY FESTUS TOOK FELIX'S PLACE.
THE RELIGIOUS LEADERS ASKED HIM TO SEND PAUL TO JERUSALEM--
--PLANNING YET ANOTHER AMBUSH.
HE SPEAKS AGAINST OUR LAWS.
HE SPEAKS AGAINST THE TEMPLE.
HE IS AN ENEMY OF CAESAR.
THEY WERE UNABLE TO PROVE ANY OF THEIR CHARGES.

ACTS 24:24-25:7

SO ON RETURNING TO CAESAREA, FESTUS HAD PAUL BROUGHT BEFORE HIM.

DO YOU WISH TO GO TO JERUSALEM AND BE TRIED ON THESE CHARGES BEFORE ME?

YOU KNOW THEIR CHARGES ARE BASELESS.

I APPEAL TO CAESAR HIMSELF!

YOU ARE A ROMAN CITIZEN.

TO CAESAR YOU HAVE APPEALED; TO CAESAR YOU SHALL GO!

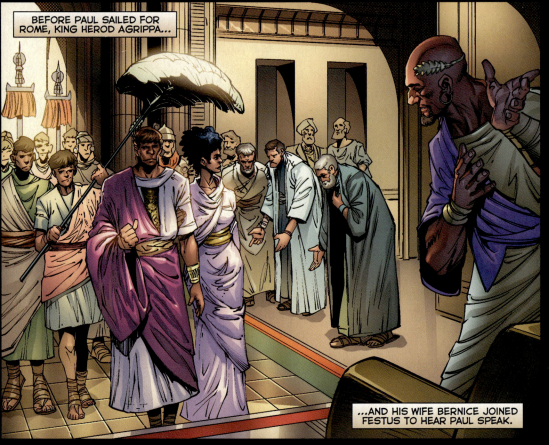

BEFORE PAUL SAILED FOR ROME, KING HEROD AGRIPPA...

...AND HIS WIFE BERNICE JOINED FESTUS TO HEAR PAUL SPEAK.

ACTS 25:1-26:1

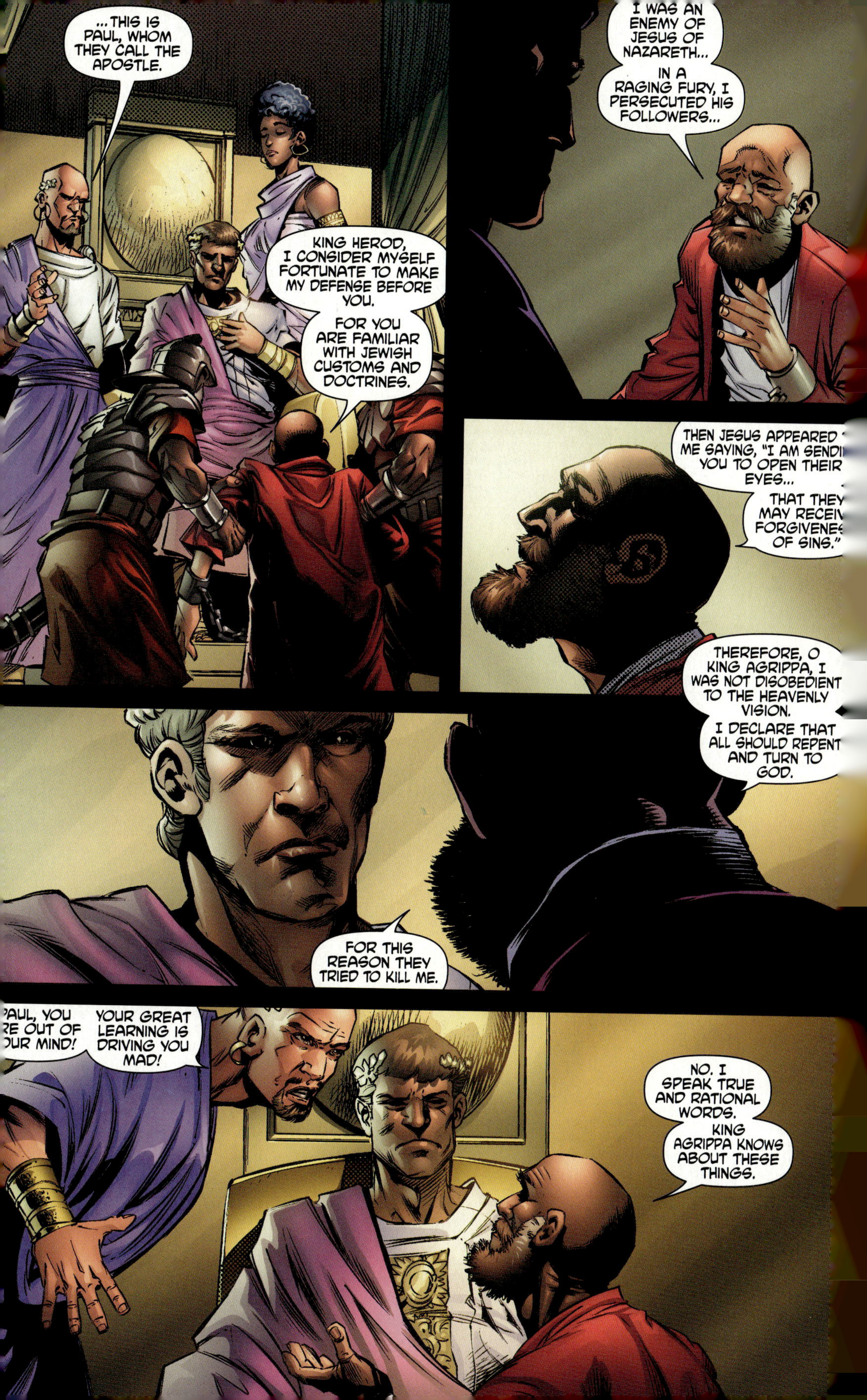
...THIS IS PAUL, WHOM THEY CALL THE APOSTLE.
KING HEROD, I CONSIDER MYSELF FORTUNATE TO MAKE MY DEFENSE BEFORE YOU.
FOR YOU ARE FAMILIAR WITH JEWISH CUSTOMS AND DOCTRINES.
I WAS AN ENEMY OF JESUS OF NAZARETH...
IN A RAGING FURY, I PERSECUTED HIS FOLLOWERS...
THEN JESUS APPEARED ME SAYING, "I AM SENDI YOU TO OPEN THEIR EYES...
THAT THEY MAY RECEIV FORGIVENES OF SINS."
THEREFORE, O KING AGRIPPA, I WAS NOT DISOBEDIENT TO THE HEAVENLY VISION.
I DECLARE THAT ALL SHOULD REPENT AND TURN TO GOD.
FOR THIS REASON THEY TRIED TO KILL ME.
PAUL, YOU RE OUT OF UR MIND!
YOUR GREAT LEARNING IS DRIVING YOU MAD!
NO. I SPEAK TRUE AND RATIONAL WORDS.
KING AGRIPPA KNOWS ABOUT THESE THINGS.

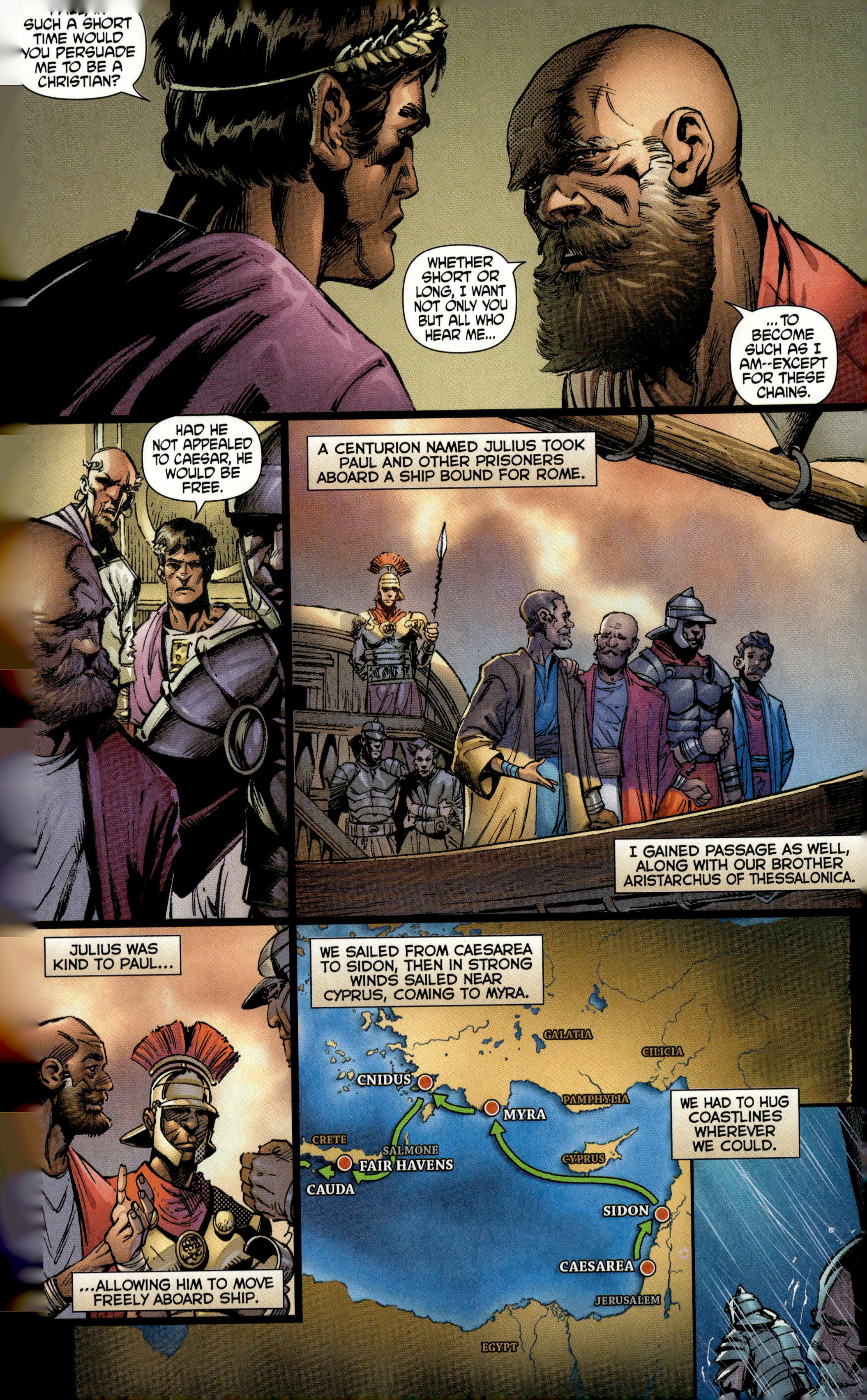
SUCH A SHORT TIME WOULD YOU PERSUADE ME TO BE A CHRISTIAN?
WHETHER SHORT OR LONG, I WANT NOT ONLY YOU BUT ALL WHO HEAR ME...
...TO BECOME SUCH AS I AM--EXCEPT FOR THESE CHAINS.
HAD HE NOT APPEALED TO CAESAR, HE WOULD BE FREE.
A CENTURION NAMED JULIUS TOOK PAUL AND OTHER PRISONERS ABOARD A SHIP BOUND FOR ROME.
I GAINED PASSAGE AS WELL, ALONG WITH OUR BROTHER ARISTARCHUS OF THESSALONICA.
JULIUS WAS KIND TO PAUL...
...ALLOWING HIM TO MOVE FREELY ABOARD SHIP.
WE SAILED FROM CAESAREA TO SIDON, THEN IN STRONG WINDS SAILED NEAR CYPRUS, COMING TO MYRA.
GALATIA
CILICIA
CNIDUS
PAMPHYLIA
MYRA
CRETE
SALMONE
FAIR HAVENS
CAUDA
CYPRUS
SIDON
CAESAREA
JERUSALEM
EGYPT
WE HAD TO HUG COASTLINES WHEREVER WE COULD.

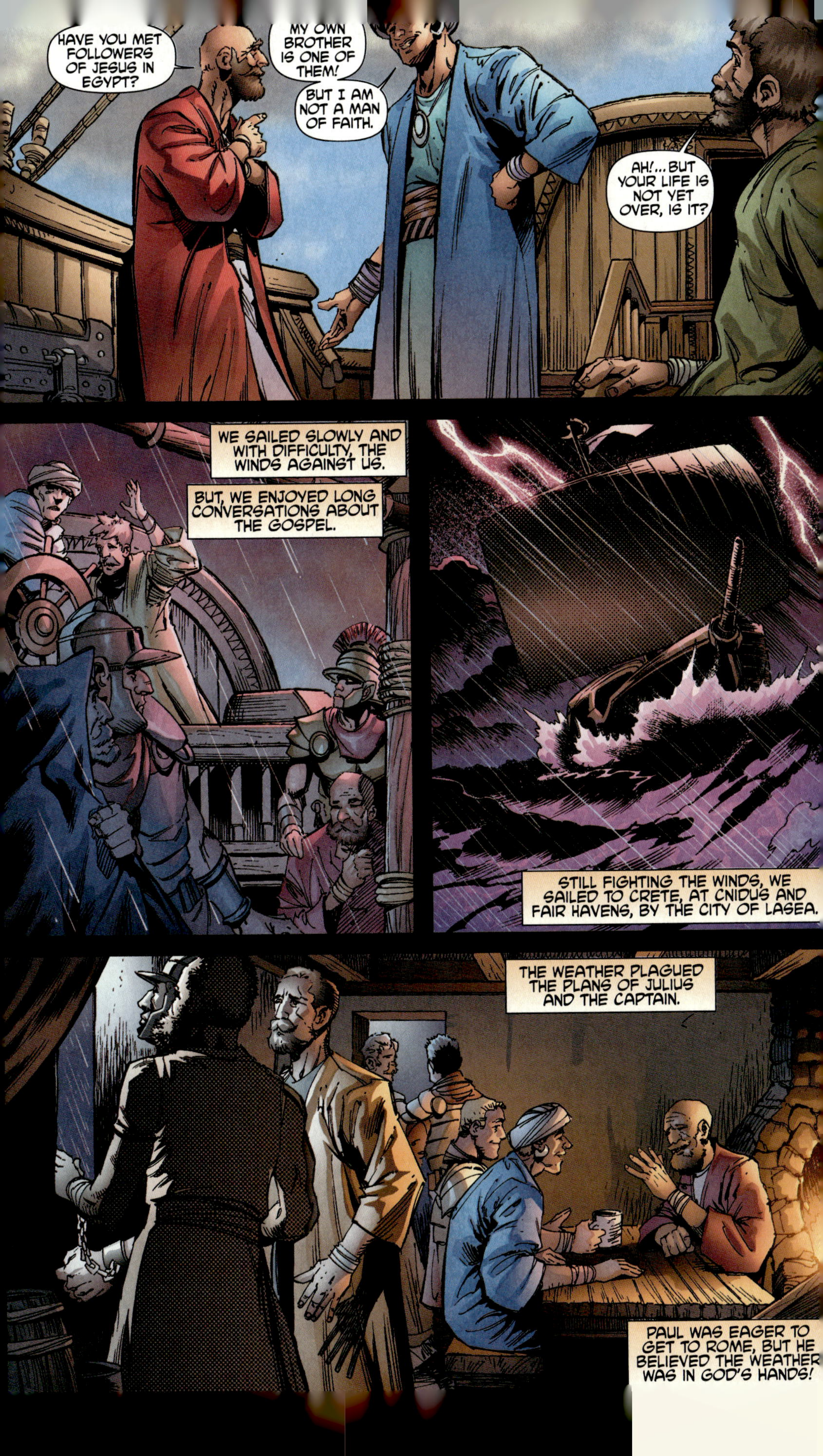
HAVE YOU MET FOLLOWERS OF JESUS IN EGYPT?
MY OWN BROTHER IS ONE OF THEM!
BUT I AM NOT A MAN OF FAITH.
AH!... BUT YOUR LIFE IS NOT YET OVER, IS IT?
WE SAILED SLOWLY AND WITH DIFFICULTY, THE WINDS AGAINST US.
BUT, WE ENJOYED LONG CONVERSATIONS ABOUT THE GOSPEL.
STILL FIGHTING THE WINDS, WE SAILED TO CRETE, AT CNIDUS AND FAIR HAVENS, BY THE CITY OF LASEA.
THE WEATHER PLAGUED THE PLANS OF JULIUS AND THE CAPTAIN.
PAUL WAS EAGER TO GET TO ROME, BUT HE BELIEVED THE WEATHER WAS IN GOD'S HANDS!

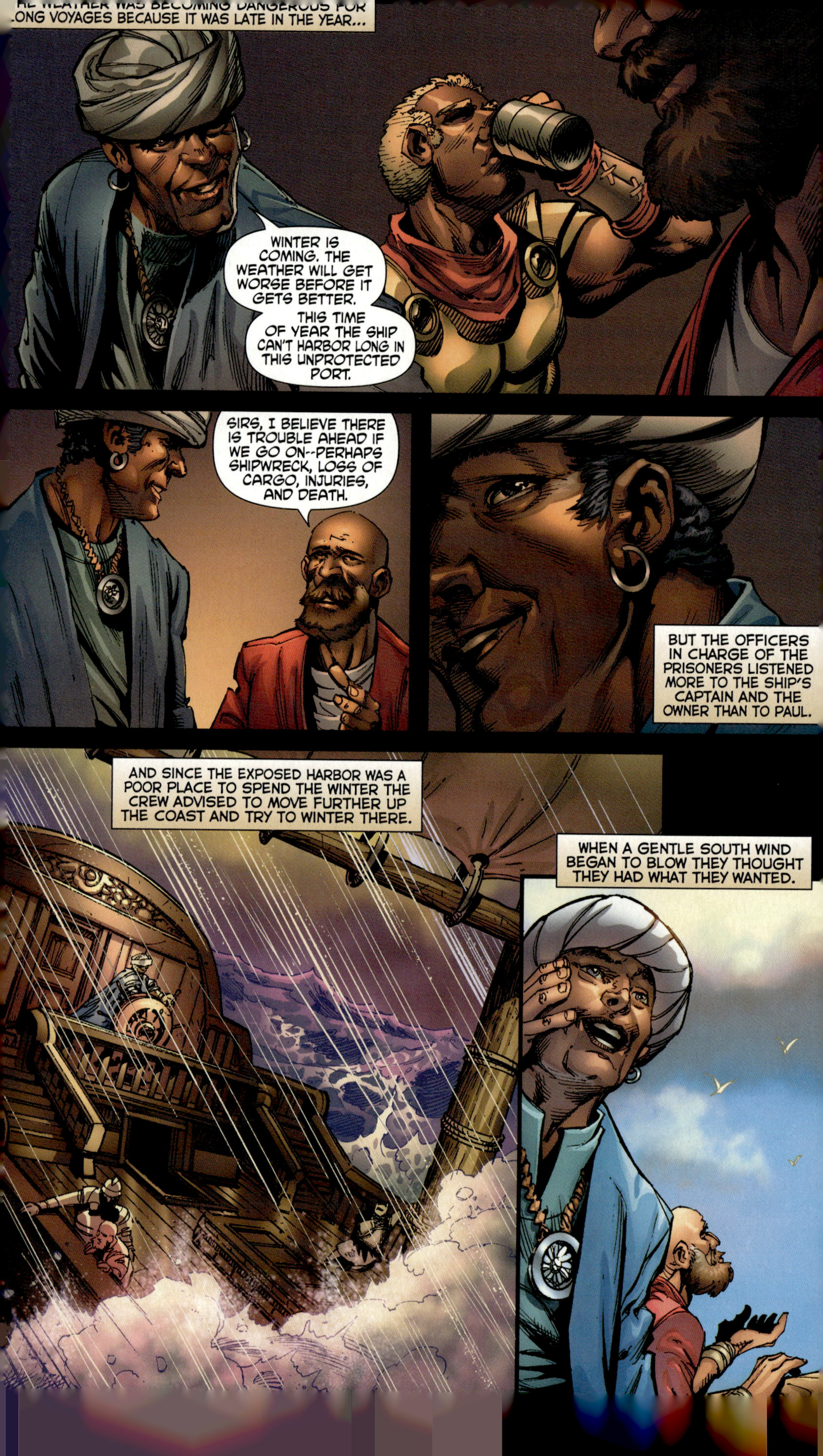
HE WEATHER WAS BECOMING DANGEROUS FOR
ONG VOYAGES BECAUSE IT WAS LATE IN THE YEAR...
WINTER IS COMING. THE WEATHER WILL GET WORSE BEFORE IT GETS BETTER.
THIS TIME OF YEAR THE SHIP CAN'T HARBOR LONG IN THIS UNPROTECTED PORT.
SIRS, I BELIEVE THERE IS TROUBLE AHEAD IF WE GO ON--PERHAPS SHIPWRECK, LOSS OF CARGO, INJURIES, AND DEATH.
BUT THE OFFICERS IN CHARGE OF THE PRISONERS LISTENED MORE TO THE SHIP'S CAPTAIN AND THE OWNER THAN TO PAUL.
AND SINCE THE EXPOSED HARBOR WAS A POOR PLACE TO SPEND THE WINTER THE CREW ADVISED TO MOVE FURTHER UP THE COAST AND TRY TO WINTER THERE.
WHEN A GENTLE SOUTH WIND BEGAN TO BLOW THEY THOUGHT THEY HAD WHAT THEY WANTED.

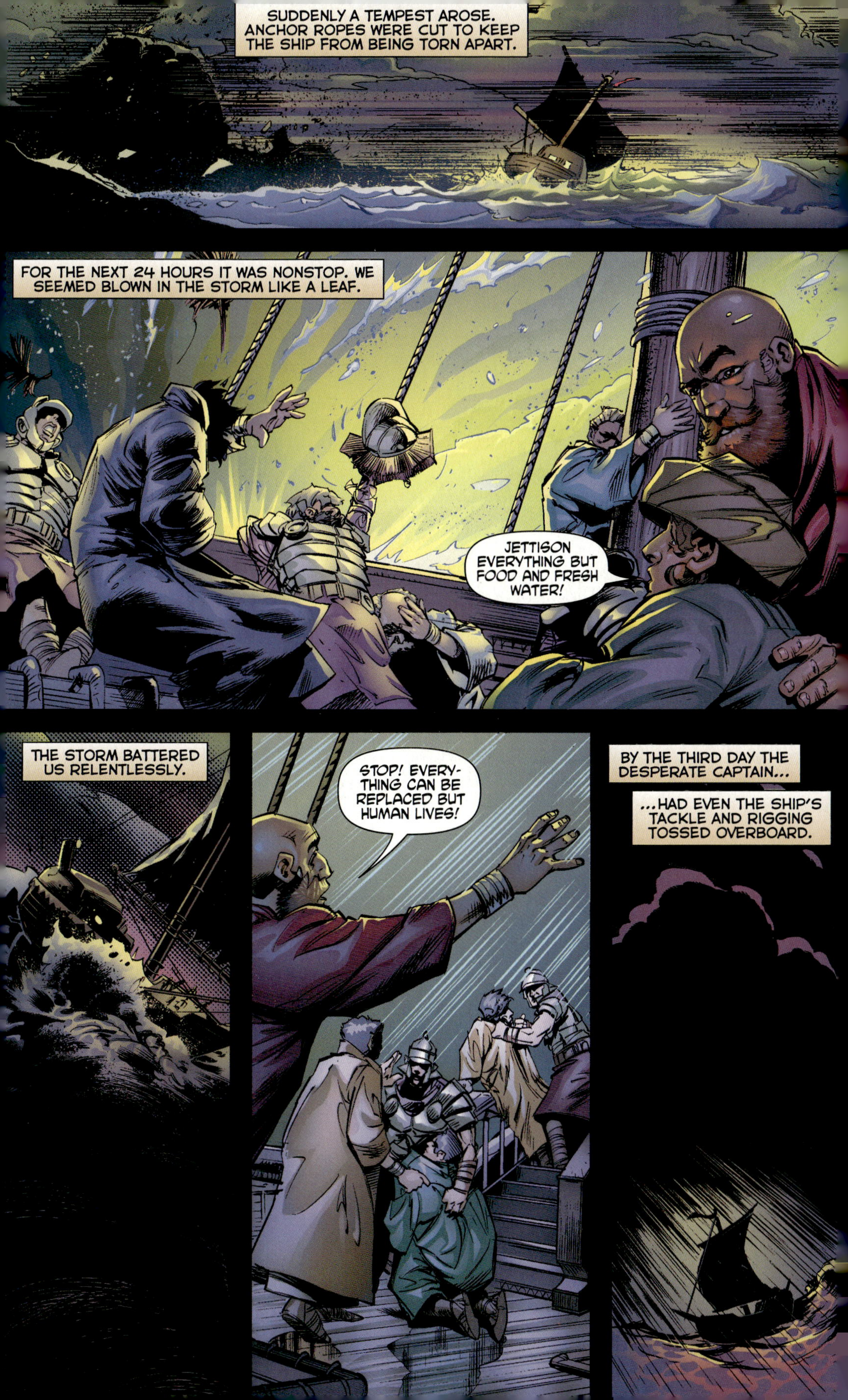
SUDDENLY A TEMPEST AROSE. ANCHOR ROPES WERE CUT TO KEEP THE SHIP FROM BEING TORN APART.
FOR THE NEXT 24 HOURS IT WAS NONSTOP. WE SEEMED BLOWN IN THE STORM LIKE A LEAF.
JETTISON EVERYTHING BUT FOOD AND FRESH WATER!
THE STORM BATTERED US RELENTLESSLY.
STOP! EVERY-THING CAN BE REPLACED BUT HUMAN LIVES!
BY THE THIRD DAY THE DESPERATE CAPTAIN...
...HAD EVEN THE SHIP'S TACKLE AND RIGGING TOSSED OVERBOARD.

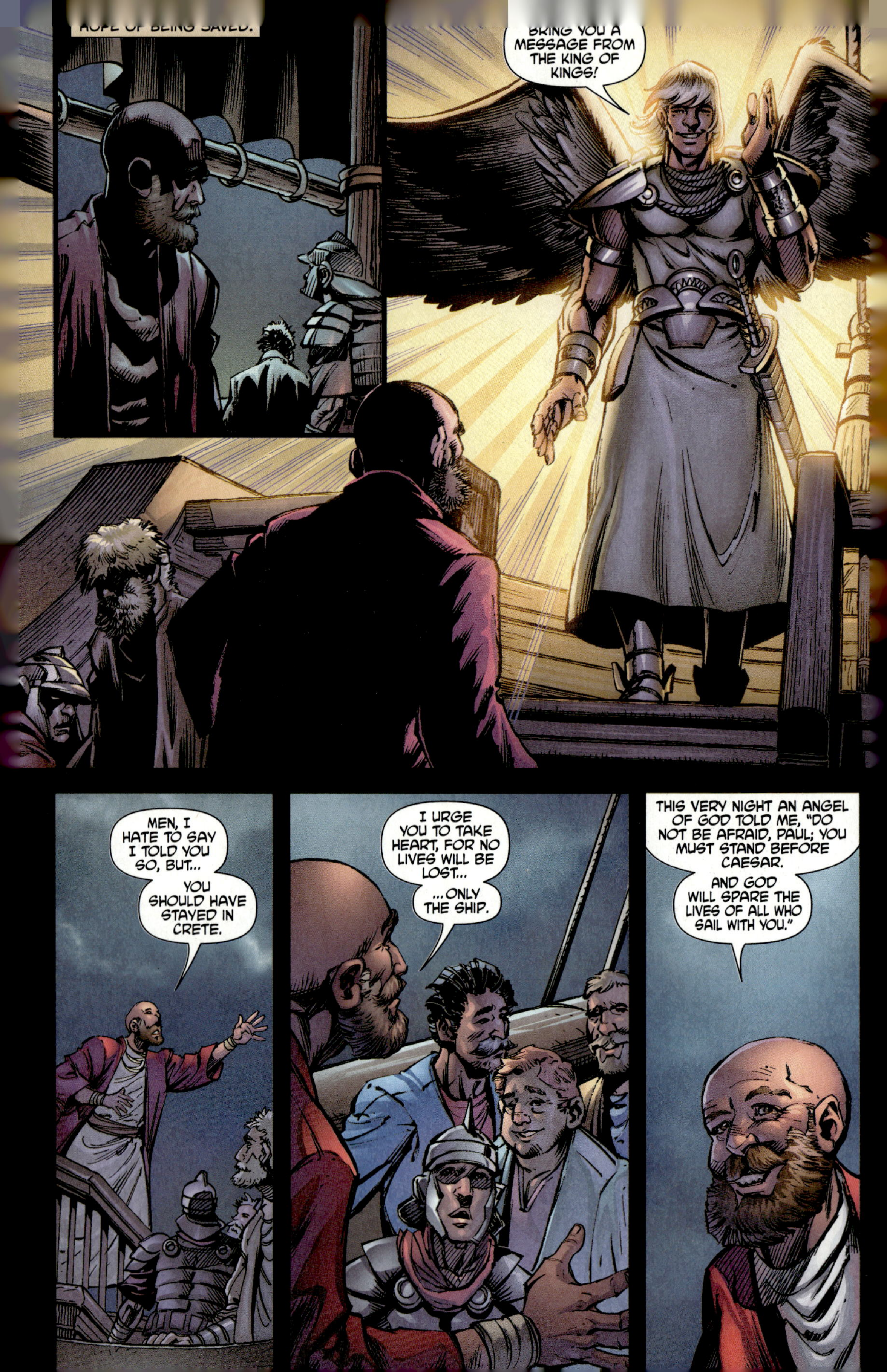
HOPE OF BEING SAVED.
BRING YOU A MESSAGE FROM THE KING OF KINGS!
MEN, I HATE TO SAY I TOLD YOU SO, BUT...
YOU SHOULD HAVE STAYED IN CRETE.
I URGE YOU TO TAKE HEART, FOR NO LIVES WILL BE LOST...
...ONLY THE SHIP.
THIS VERY NIGHT AN ANGEL OF GOD TOLD ME, "DO NOT BE AFRAID, PAUL; YOU MUST STAND BEFORE CAESAR.
AND GOD WILL SPARE THE LIVES OF ALL WHO SAIL WITH YOU."

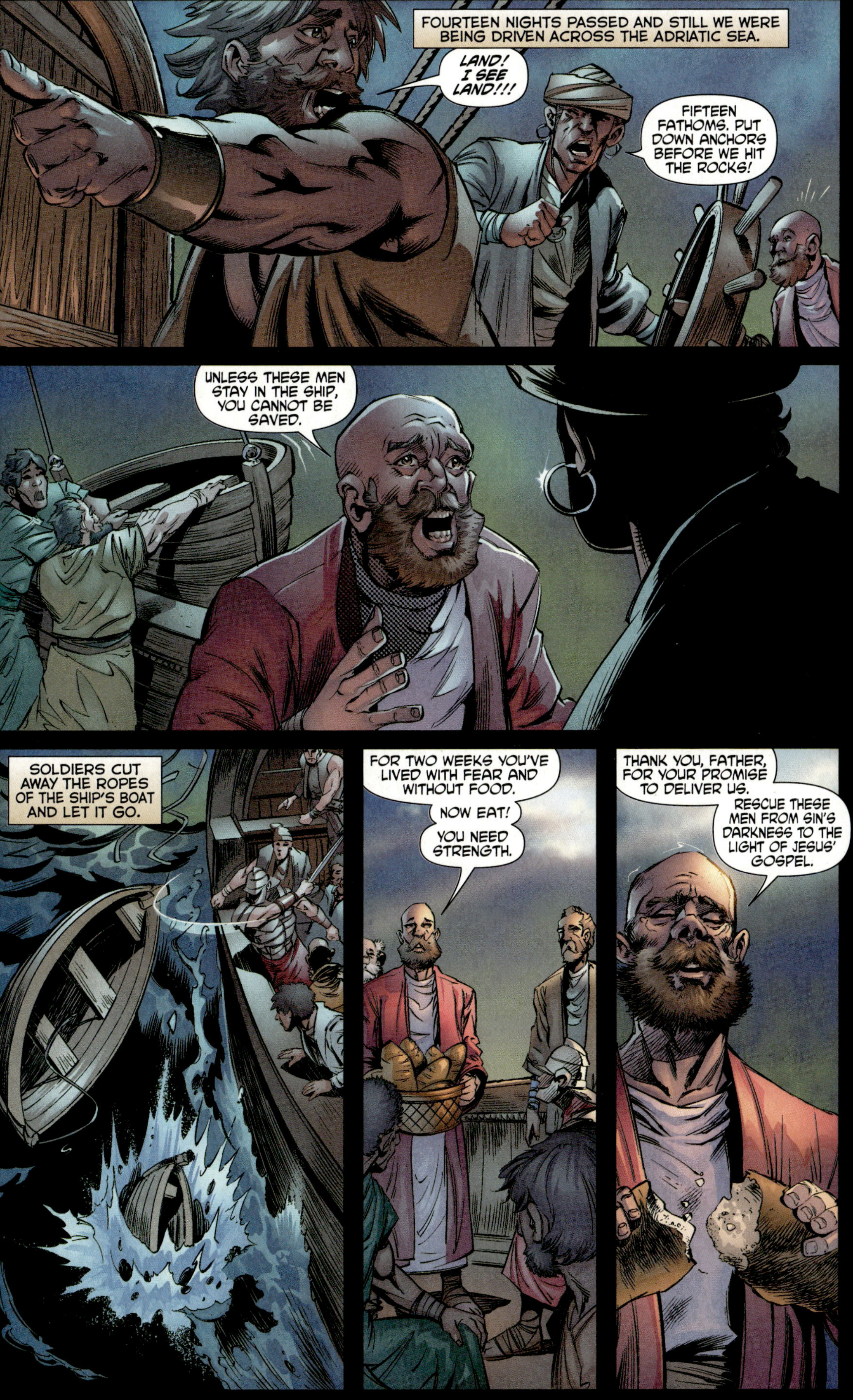
FOURTEEN NIGHTS PASSED AND STILL WE WERE BEING DRIVEN ACROSS THE ADRIATIC SEA.
LAND! I SEE LAND!!!
FIFTEEN FATHOMS. PUT DOWN ANCHORS BEFORE WE HIT THE ROCKS!
UNLESS THESE MEN STAY IN THE SHIP, YOU CANNOT BE SAVED.
SOLDIERS CUT AWAY THE ROPES OF THE SHIP'S BOAT AND LET IT GO.
FOR TWO WEEKS YOU'VE LIVED WITH FEAR AND WITHOUT FOOD.
NOW EAT!
YOU NEED STRENGTH.
THANK YOU, FATHER, FOR YOUR PROMISE TO DELIVER US.
RESCUE THESE MEN FROM SIN'S DARKNESS TO THE LIGHT OF JESUS' GOSPEL.

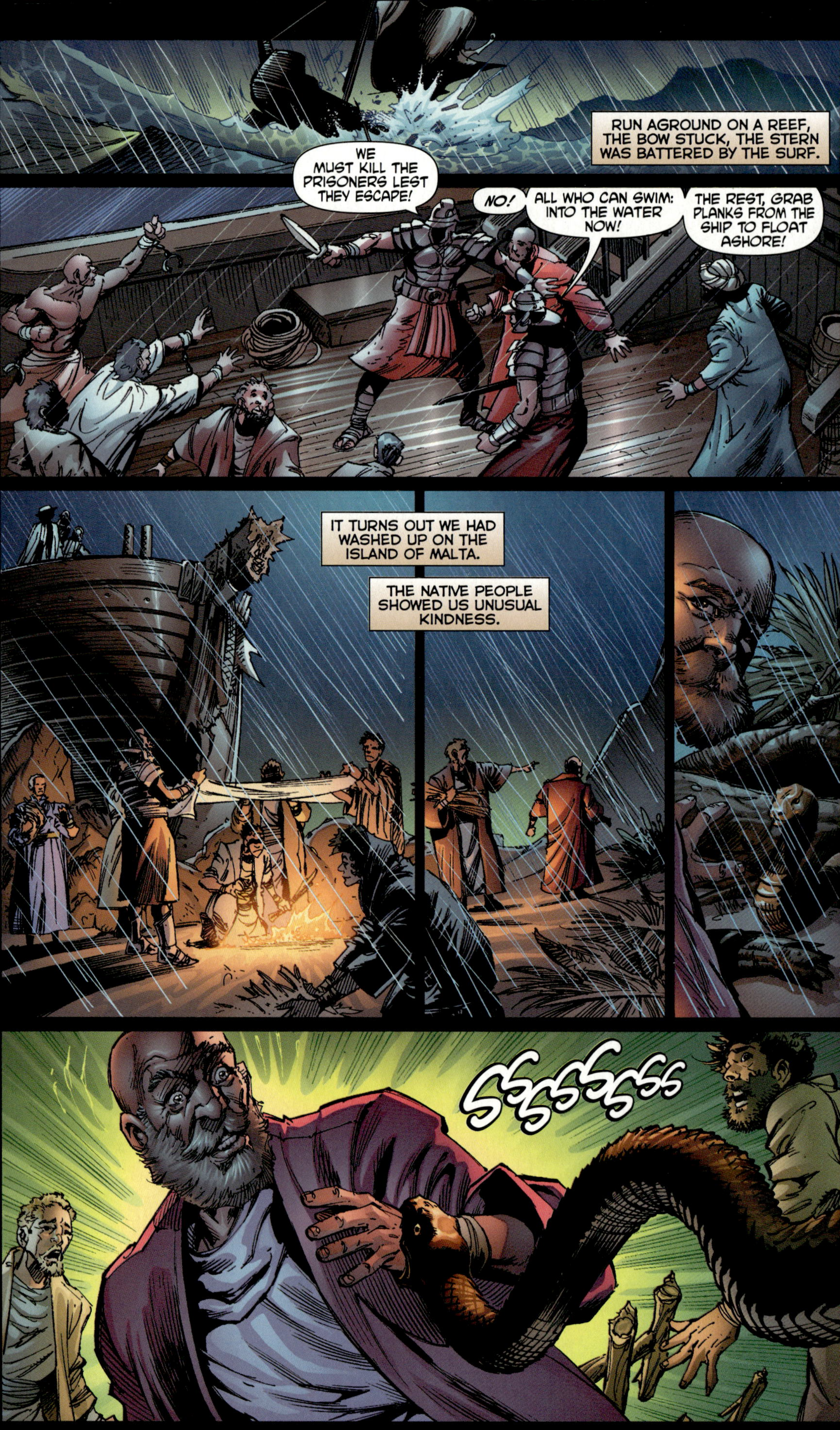
RUN AGROUND ON A REEF, THE BOW STUCK, THE STERN WAS BATTERED BY THE SURF.
WE MUST KILL THE PRISONERS LEST THEY ESCAPE!
NO!
ALL WHO CAN SWIM: INTO THE WATER NOW!
THE REST, GRAB PLANKS FROM THE SHIP TO FLOAT ASHORE!
IT TURNS OUT WE HAD WASHED UP ON THE ISLAND OF MALTA.
THE NATIVE PEOPLE SHOWED US UNUSUAL KINDNESS.
SSSSSSSS

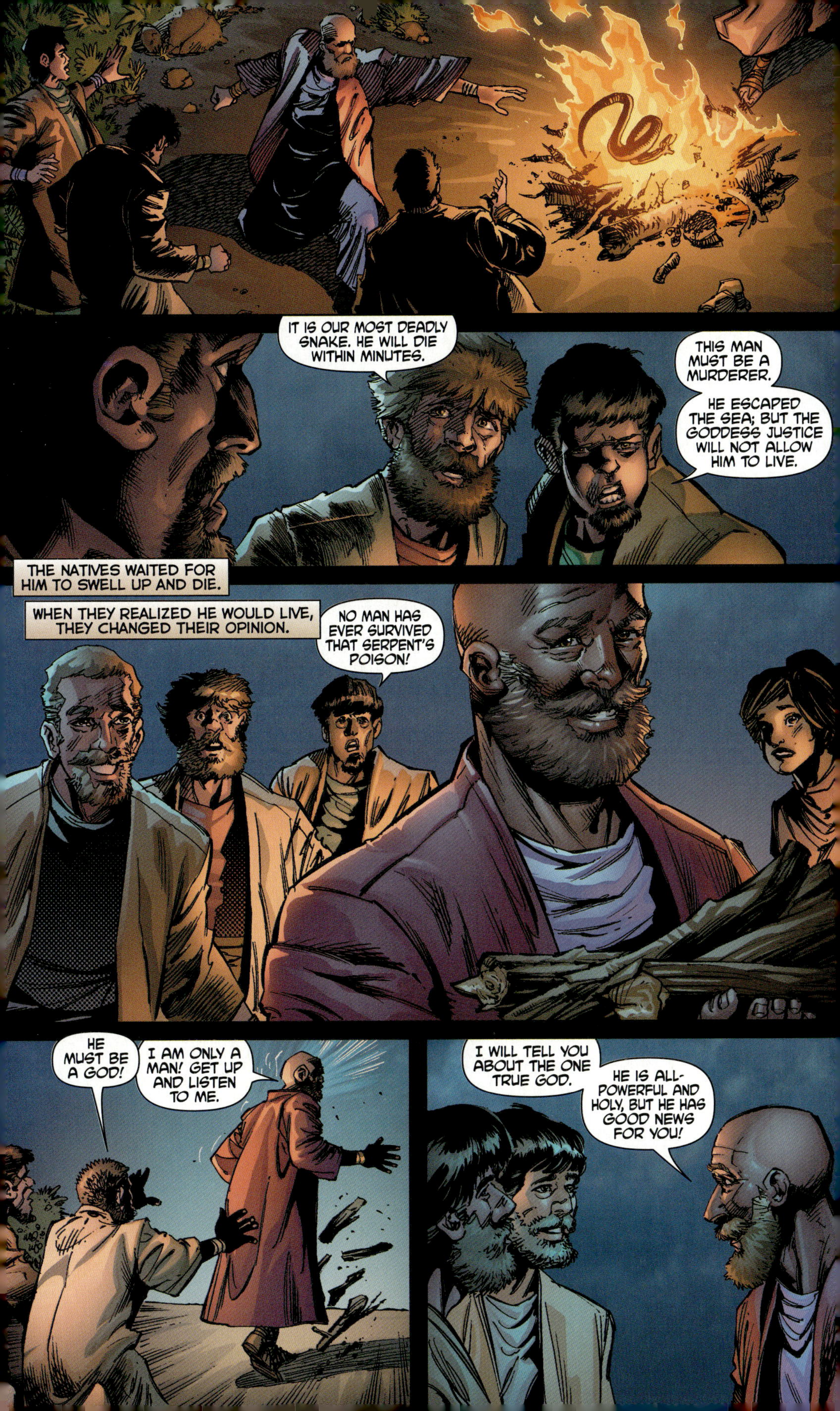

IT IS OUR MOST DEADLY SNAKE. HE WILL DIE WITHIN MINUTES.
THIS MAN MUST BE A MURDERER.
HE ESCAPED THE SEA; BUT THE GODDESS JUSTICE WILL NOT ALLOW HIM TO LIVE.
THE NATIVES WAITED FOR HIM TO SWELL UP AND DIE.
WHEN THEY REALIZED HE WOULD LIVE, THEY CHANGED THEIR OPINION.
NO MAN HAS EVER SURVIVED THAT SERPENT'S POISON!
HE MUST BE A GOD!
I AM ONLY A MAN! GET UP AND LISTEN TO ME.
I WILL TELL YOU ABOUT THE ONE TRUE GOD.
HE IS ALL-POWERFUL AND HOLY, BUT HE HAS GOOD NEWS FOR YOU!

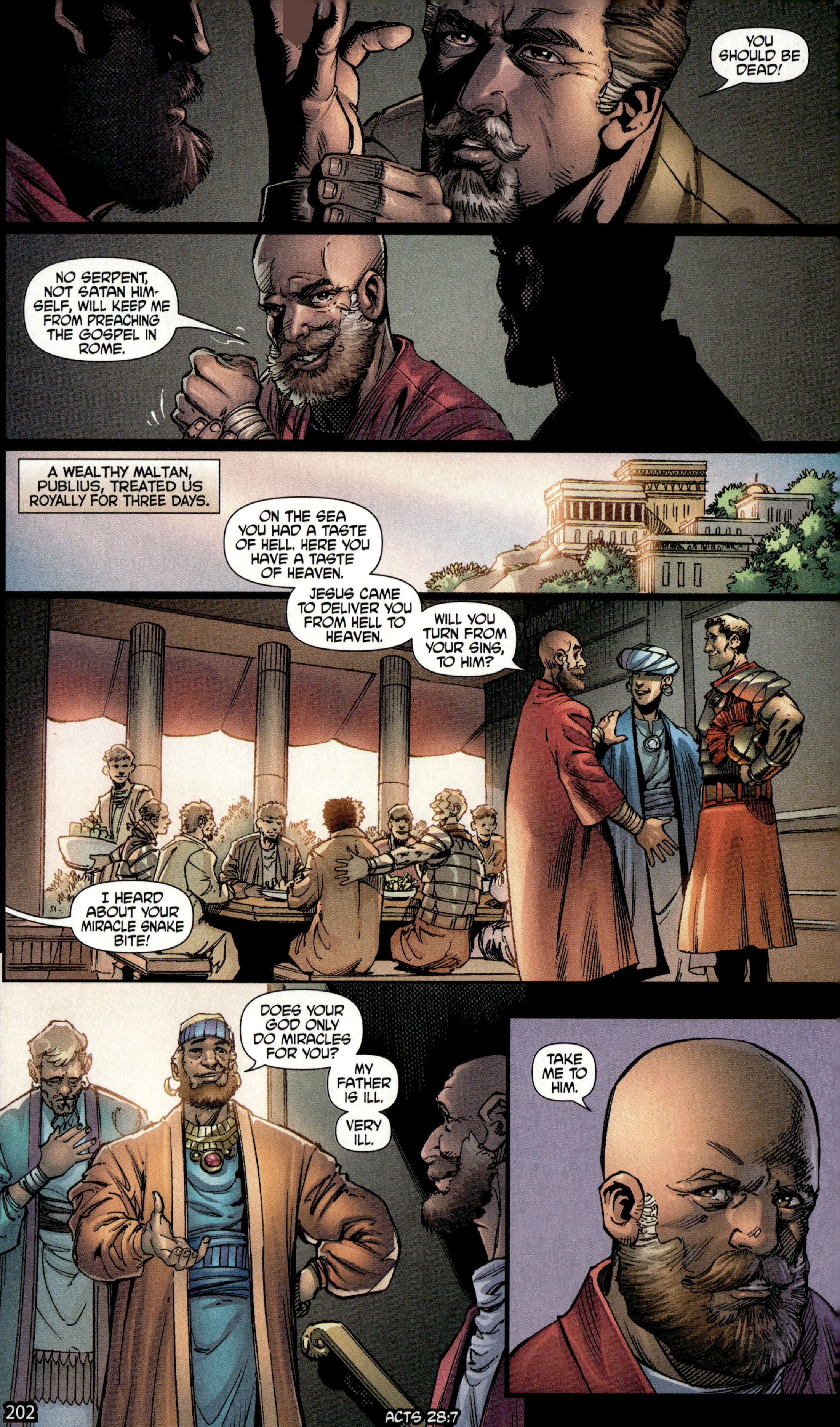
YOU SHOULD BE DEAD!
NO SERPENT, NOT SATAN HIMSELF, WILL KEEP ME FROM PREACHING THE GOSPEL IN ROME.
A WEALTHY MALTAN, PUBLIUS, TREATED US ROYALLY FOR THREE DAYS.
ON THE SEA YOU HAD A TASTE OF HELL. HERE YOU HAVE A TASTE OF HEAVEN.
JESUS CAME TO DELIVER YOU FROM HELL TO HEAVEN.
WILL YOU TURN FROM YOUR SINS, TO HIM?
I HEARD ABOUT YOUR MIRACLE SNAKE BITE!
DOES YOUR GOD ONLY DO MIRACLES FOR YOU?
MY FATHER IS ILL.
VERY ILL.
TAKE ME TO HIM.
ACTS 28:7

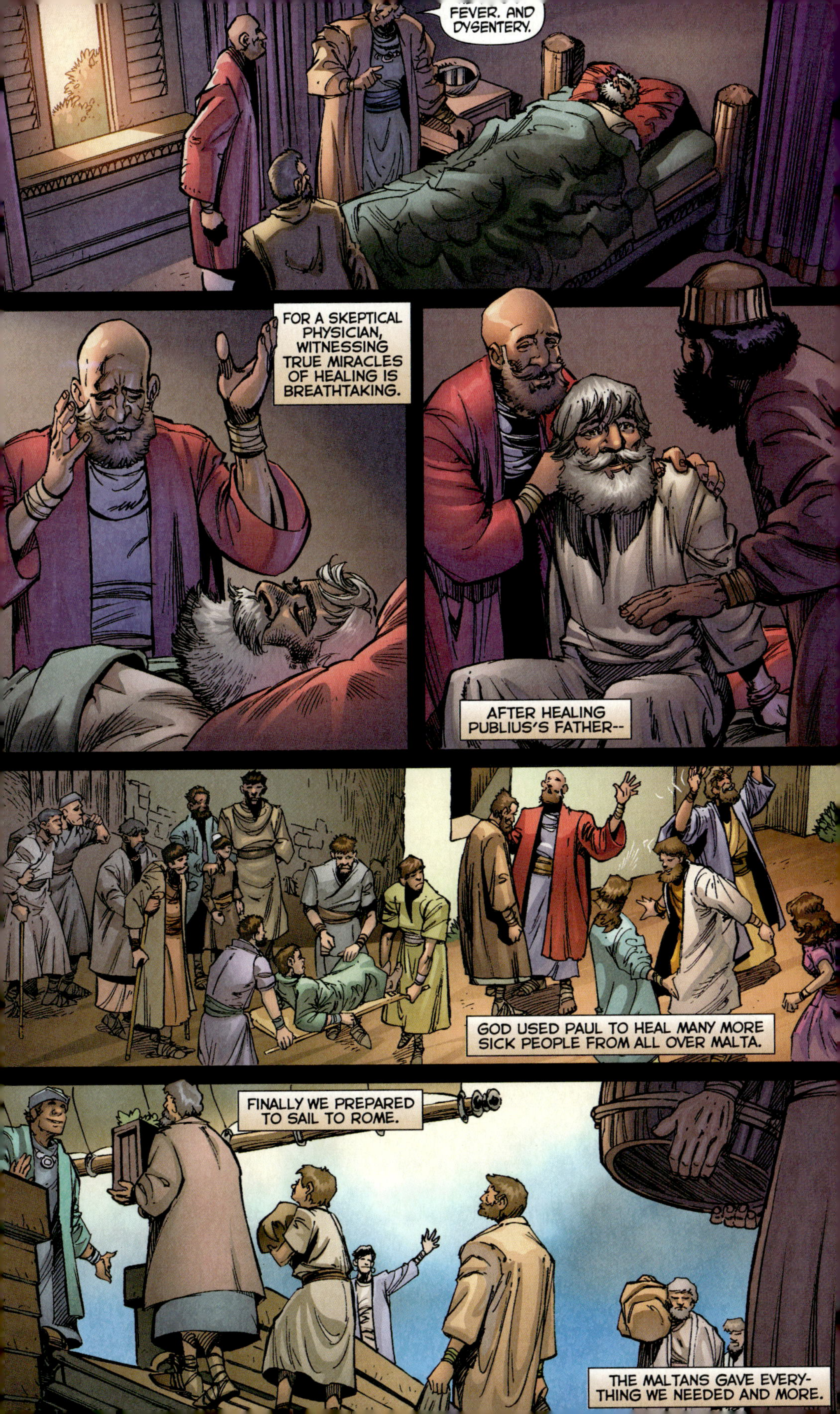
FEVER. AND DYSENTERY.
FOR A SKEPTICAL PHYSICIAN, WITNESSING TRUE MIRACLES OF HEALING IS BREATHTAKING.
AFTER HEALING PUBLIUS'S FATHER--
GOD USED PAUL TO HEAL MANY MORE SICK PEOPLE FROM ALL OVER MALTA.
FINALLY WE PREPARED TO SAIL TO ROME.
THE MALTANS GAVE EVERY-THING WE NEEDED AND MORE.

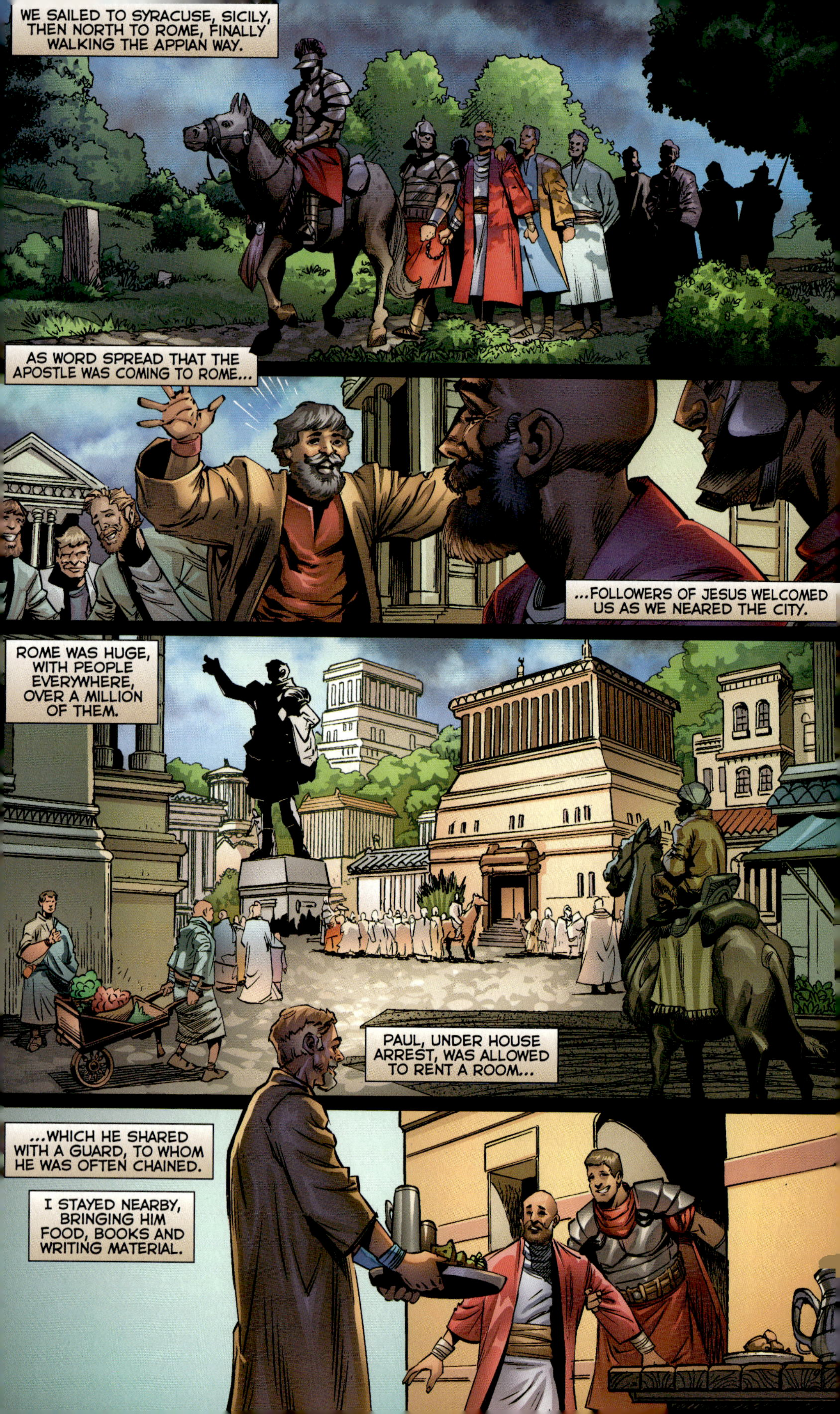
WE SAILED TO SYRACUSE, SICILY, THEN NORTH TO ROME, FINALLY WALKING THE APPIAN WAY.
AS WORD SPREAD THAT THE APOSTLE WAS COMING TO ROME...
...FOLLOWERS OF JESUS WELCOMED US AS WE NEARED THE CITY.
ROME WAS HUGE, WITH PEOPLE EVERYWHERE, OVER A MILLION OF THEM.
PAUL, UNDER HOUSE ARREST, WAS ALLOWED TO RENT A ROOM...
...WHICH HE SHARED WITH A GUARD, TO WHOM HE WAS OFTEN CHAINED.
I STAYED NEARBY, BRINGING HIM FOOD, BOOKS AND WRITING MATERIAL.

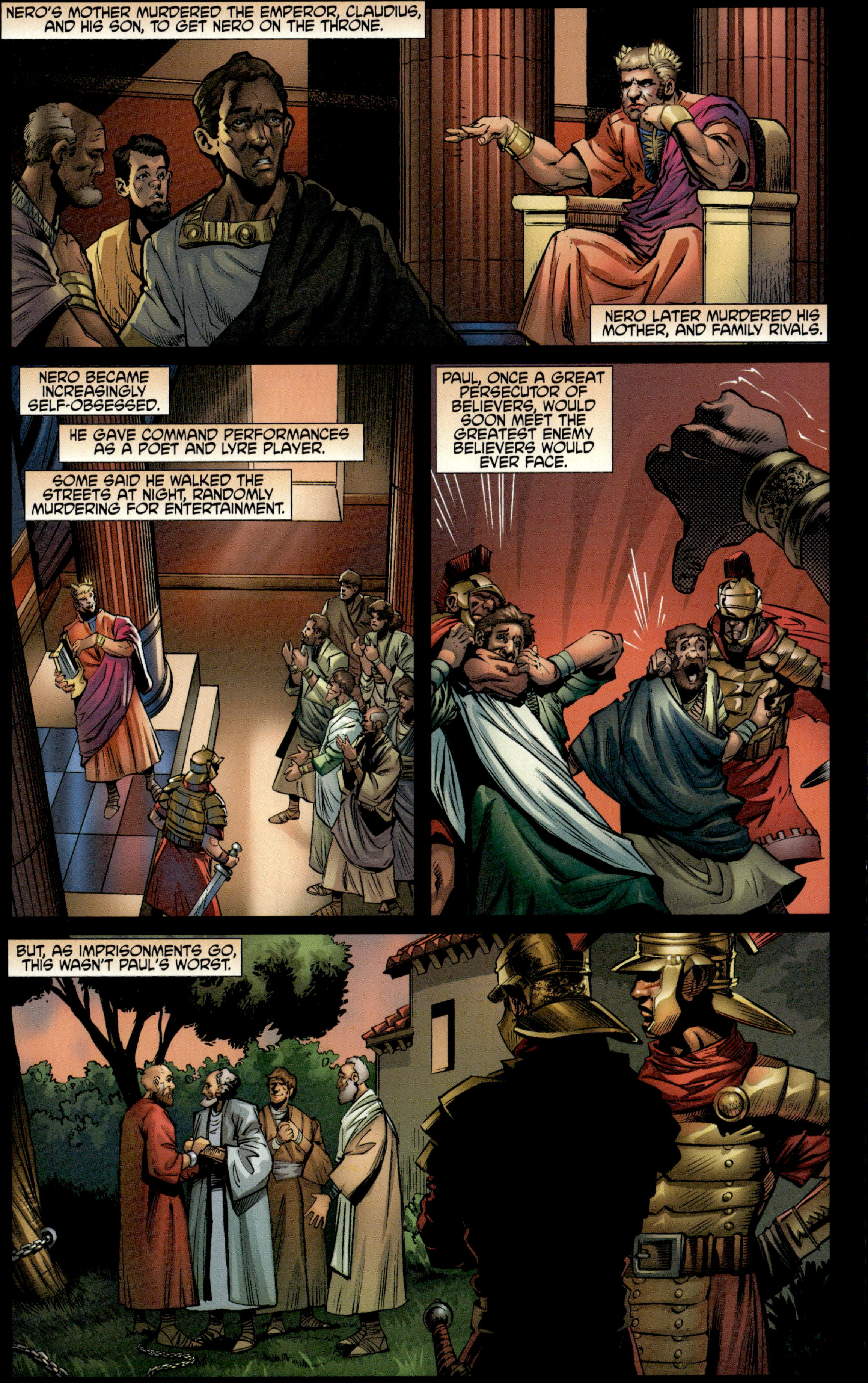
NERO'S MOTHER MURDERED THE EMPEROR, CLAUDIUS, AND HIS SON, TO GET NERO ON THE THRONE.
NERO LATER MURDERED HIS MOTHER, AND FAMILY RIVALS.
NERO BECAME INCREASINGLY SELF-OBSESSED.
HE GAVE COMMAND PERFORMANCES AS A POET AND LYRE PLAYER.
SOME SAID HE WALKED THE STREETS AT NIGHT, RANDOMLY MURDERING FOR ENTERTAINMENT.
PAUL, ONCE A GREAT PERSECUTOR OF BELIEVERS, WOULD SOON MEET THE GREATEST ENEMY BELIEVERS WOULD EVER FACE.
BUT, AS IMPRISONMENTS GO, THIS WASN'T PAUL'S WORST.

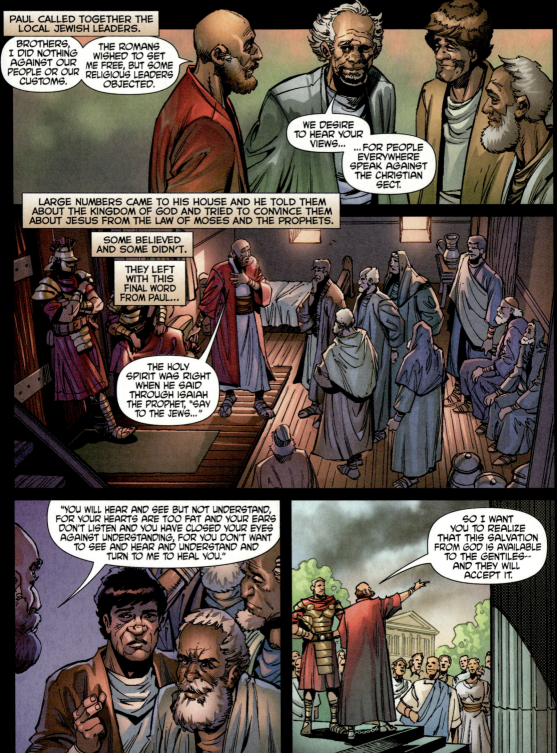

PAUL CALLED TOGETHER THE LOCAL JEWISH LEADERS.

BROTHERS, I DID NOTHING AGAINST OUR PEOPLE OR OUR CUSTOMS.

THE ROMANS WISHED TO SET ME FREE, BUT SOME RELIGIOUS LEADERS OBJECTED.

WE DESIRE TO HEAR YOUR VIEWS...

...FOR PEOPLE EVERYWHERE SPEAK AGAINST THE CHRISTIAN SECT.

LARGE NUMBERS CAME TO HIS HOUSE AND HE TOLD THEM ABOUT THE KINGDOM OF GOD AND TRIED TO CONVINCE THEM ABOUT JESUS FROM THE LAW OF MOSES AND THE PROPHETS.

SOME BELIEVED AND SOME DIDN'T.

THEY LEFT WITH THIS FINAL WORD FROM PAUL...

THE HOLY SPIRIT WAS RIGHT WHEN HE SAID THROUGH ISAIAH THE PROPHET, "SAY TO THE JEWS..."

"YOU WILL HEAR AND SEE BUT NOT UNDERSTAND, FOR YOUR HEARTS ARE TOO FAT AND YOUR EARS DON'T LISTEN AND YOU HAVE CLOSED YOUR EYES AGAINST UNDERSTANDING, FOR YOU DON'T WANT TO SEE AND HEAR AND UNDERSTAND AND TURN TO ME TO HEAL YOU."

SO I WANT YOU TO REALIZE THAT THIS SALVATION FROM GOD IS AVAILABLE TO THE GENTILES-- AND THEY WILL ACCEPT IT.

PAUL LIVED FOR THE NEXT TWO YEARS IN HIS RENTED HOUSE AND WELCOMED ALL WHO VISITED HIM, TELLING THEM WITH ALL BOLDNESS ABOUT THE KINGDOM OF GOD AND ABOUT THE LORD JESUS CHRIST; AND NO ONE TRIED TO STOP HIM.

ACTS 28:17-31

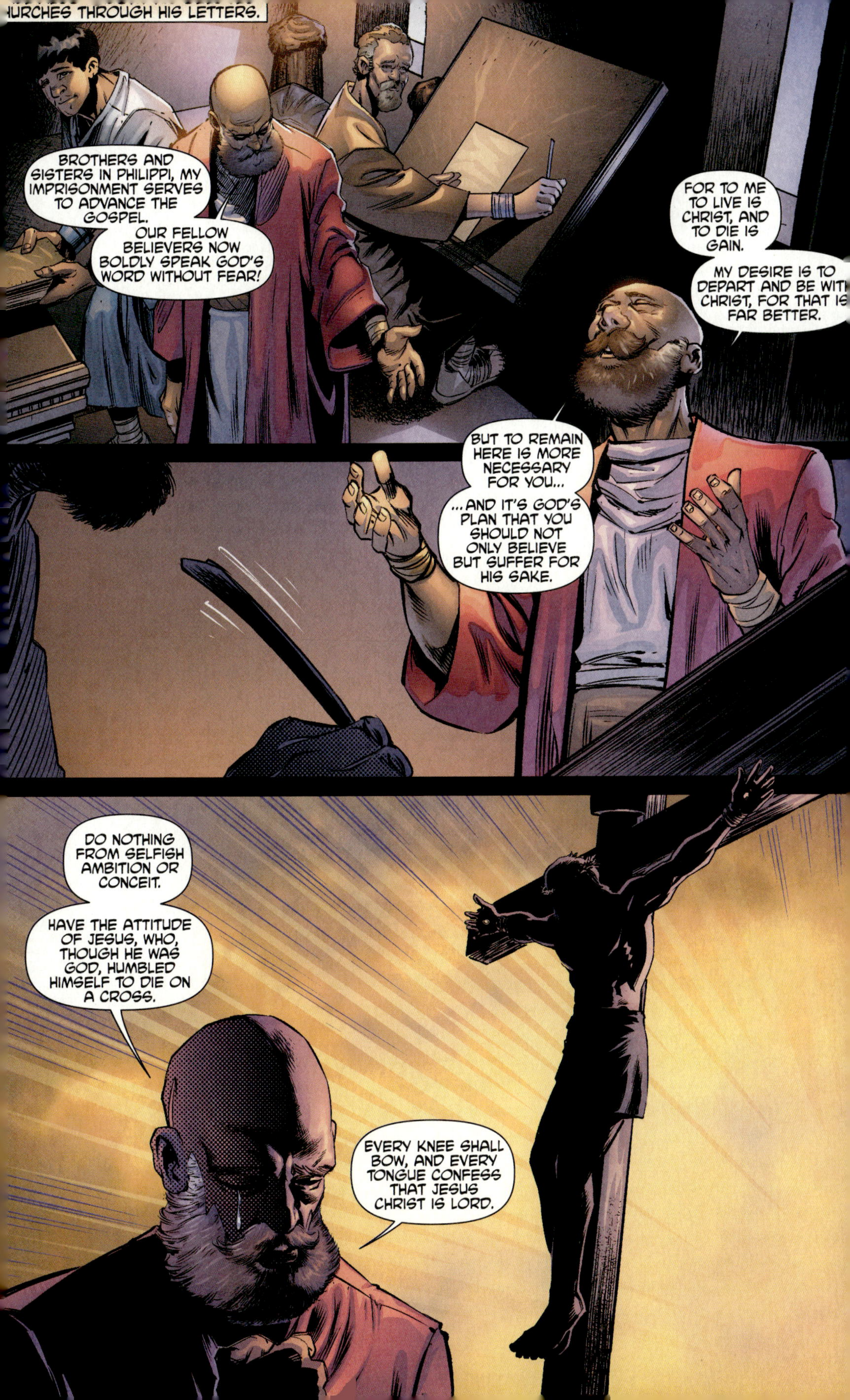
URCHES THROUGH HIS LETTERS.
BROTHERS AND SISTERS IN PHILIPPI, MY IMPRISONMENT SERVES TO ADVANCE THE GOSPEL.
OUR FELLOW BELIEVERS NOW BOLDLY SPEAK GOD'S WORD WITHOUT FEAR!
FOR TO ME TO LIVE IS CHRIST, AND TO DIE IS GAIN.
MY DESIRE IS TO DEPART AND BE WIT CHRIST, FOR THAT IS FAR BETTER.
BUT TO REMAIN HERE IS MORE NECESSARY FOR YOU...
...AND IT'S GOD'S PLAN THAT YOU SHOULD NOT ONLY BELIEVE BUT SUFFER FOR HIS SAKE.
DO NOTHING FROM SELFISH AMBITION OR CONCEIT.
HAVE THE ATTITUDE OF JESUS, WHO, THOUGH HE WAS GOD, HUMBLED HIMSELF TO DIE ON A CROSS.
EVERY KNEE SHALL BOW, AND EVERY TONGUE CONFESS THAT JESUS CHRIST IS LORD.

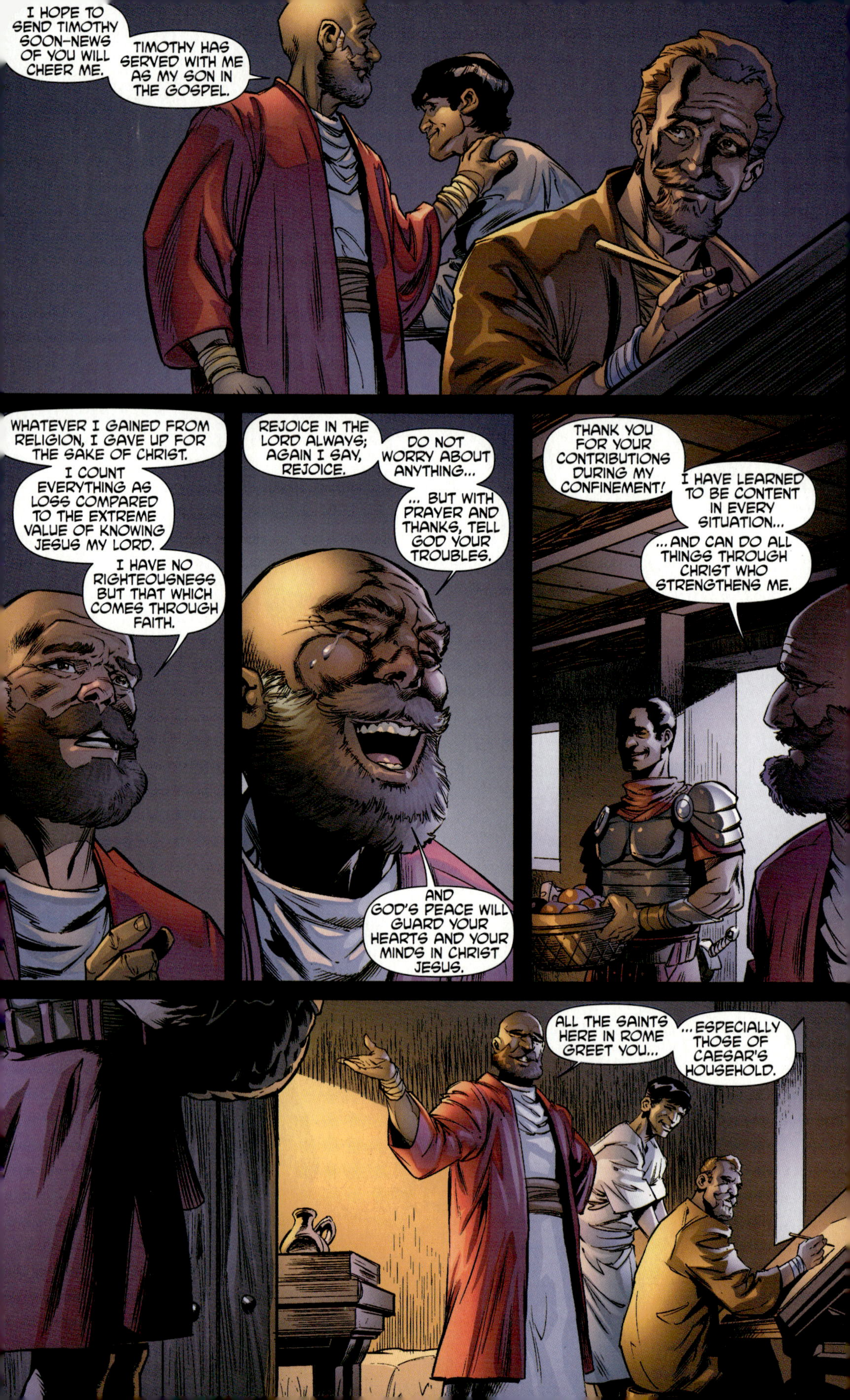

I HOPE TO SEND TIMOTHY SOON–NEWS OF YOU WILL CHEER ME.
TIMOTHY HAS SERVED WITH ME AS MY SON IN THE GOSPEL.
WHATEVER I GAINED FROM RELIGION, I GAVE UP FOR THE SAKE OF CHRIST.
I COUNT EVERYTHING AS LOSS COMPARED TO THE EXTREME VALUE OF KNOWING JESUS MY LORD.
I HAVE NO RIGHTEOUSNESS BUT THAT WHICH COMES THROUGH FAITH.
REJOICE IN THE LORD ALWAYS; AGAIN I SAY, REJOICE.
DO NOT WORRY ABOUT ANYTHING...
... BUT WITH PRAYER AND THANKS, TELL GOD YOUR TROUBLES.
AND GOD'S PEACE WILL GUARD YOUR HEARTS AND YOUR MINDS IN CHRIST JESUS.
THANK YOU FOR YOUR CONTRIBUTIONS DURING MY CONFINEMENT!
I HAVE LEARNED TO BE CONTENT IN EVERY SITUATION...
...AND CAN DO ALL THINGS THROUGH CHRIST WHO STRENGTHENS ME.
ALL THE SAINTS HERE IN ROME GREET YOU...
...ESPECIALLY THOSE OF CAESAR'S HOUSEHOLD.

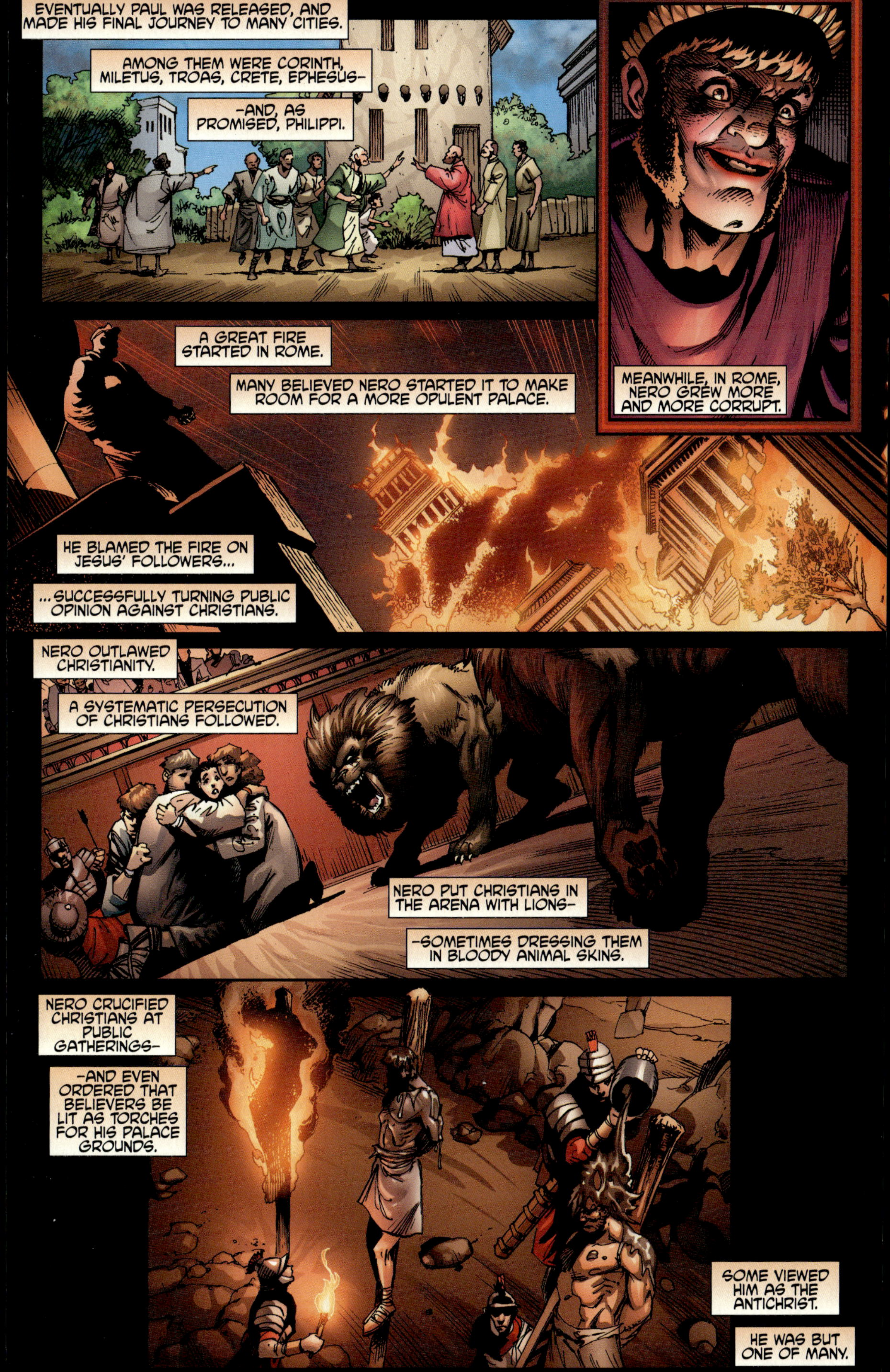
EVENTUALLY PAUL WAS RELEASED, AND MADE HIS FINAL JOURNEY TO MANY CITIES.
AMONG THEM WERE CORINTH, MILETUS, TROAS, CRETE, EPHESUS–
–AND, AS PROMISED, PHILIPPI.
MEANWHILE, IN ROME, NERO GREW MORE AND MORE CORRUPT.
A GREAT FIRE STARTED IN ROME.
MANY BELIEVED NERO STARTED IT TO MAKE ROOM FOR A MORE OPULENT PALACE.
HE BLAMED THE FIRE ON JESUS' FOLLOWERS...
...SUCCESSFULLY TURNING PUBLIC OPINION AGAINST CHRISTIANS.
NERO OUTLAWED CHRISTIANITY.
A SYSTEMATIC PERSECUTION OF CHRISTIANS FOLLOWED.
NERO PUT CHRISTIANS IN THE ARENA WITH LIONS–
–SOMETIMES DRESSING THEM IN BLOODY ANIMAL SKINS.
NERO CRUCIFIED CHRISTIANS AT PUBLIC GATHERINGS–
–AND EVEN ORDERED THAT BELIEVERS BE LIT AS TORCHES FOR HIS PALACE GROUNDS.
SOME VIEWED HIM AS THE ANTICHRIST.
HE WAS BUT ONE OF MANY.

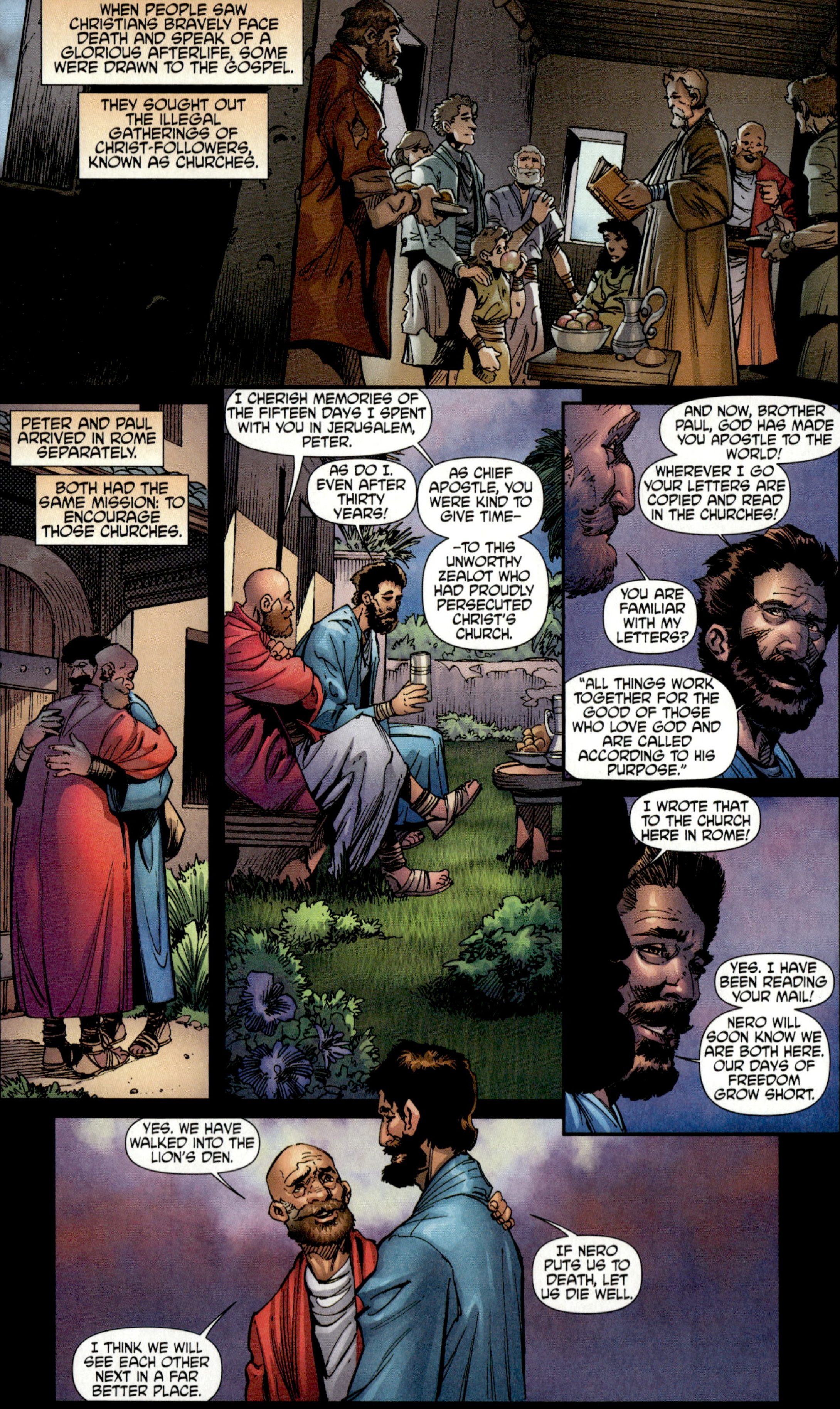
WHEN PEOPLE SAW CHRISTIANS BRAVELY FACE DEATH AND SPEAK OF A GLORIOUS AFTERLIFE, SOME WERE DRAWN TO THE GOSPEL.
THEY SOUGHT OUT THE ILLEGAL GATHERINGS OF CHRIST-FOLLOWERS, KNOWN AS CHURCHES.
PETER AND PAUL ARRIVED IN ROME SEPARATELY.
BOTH HAD THE SAME MISSION: TO ENCOURAGE THOSE CHURCHES.
I CHERISH MEMORIES OF THE FIFTEEN DAYS I SPENT WITH YOU IN JERUSALEM, PETER.
AS DO I. EVEN AFTER THIRTY YEARS!
AS CHIEF APOSTLE, YOU WERE KIND TO GIVE TIME–
–TO THIS UNWORTHY ZEALOT WHO HAD PROUDLY PERSECUTED CHRIST'S CHURCH.
AND NOW, BROTHER PAUL, GOD HAS MADE YOU APOSTLE TO THE WORLD!
WHEREVER I GO YOUR LETTERS ARE COPIED AND READ IN THE CHURCHES!
YOU ARE FAMILIAR WITH MY LETTERS?
"ALL THINGS WORK TOGETHER FOR THE GOOD OF THOSE WHO LOVE GOD AND ARE CALLED ACCORDING TO HIS PURPOSE."
I WROTE THAT TO THE CHURCH HERE IN ROME!
YES. I HAVE BEEN READING YOUR MAIL!
NERO WILL SOON KNOW WE ARE BOTH HERE. OUR DAYS OF FREEDOM GROW SHORT.
YES. WE HAVE WALKED INTO THE LION'S DEN.
IF NERO PUTS US TO DEATH, LET US DIE WELL.
I THINK WE WILL SEE EACH OTHER NEXT IN A FAR BETTER PLACE.

2 PETER 3:15-16

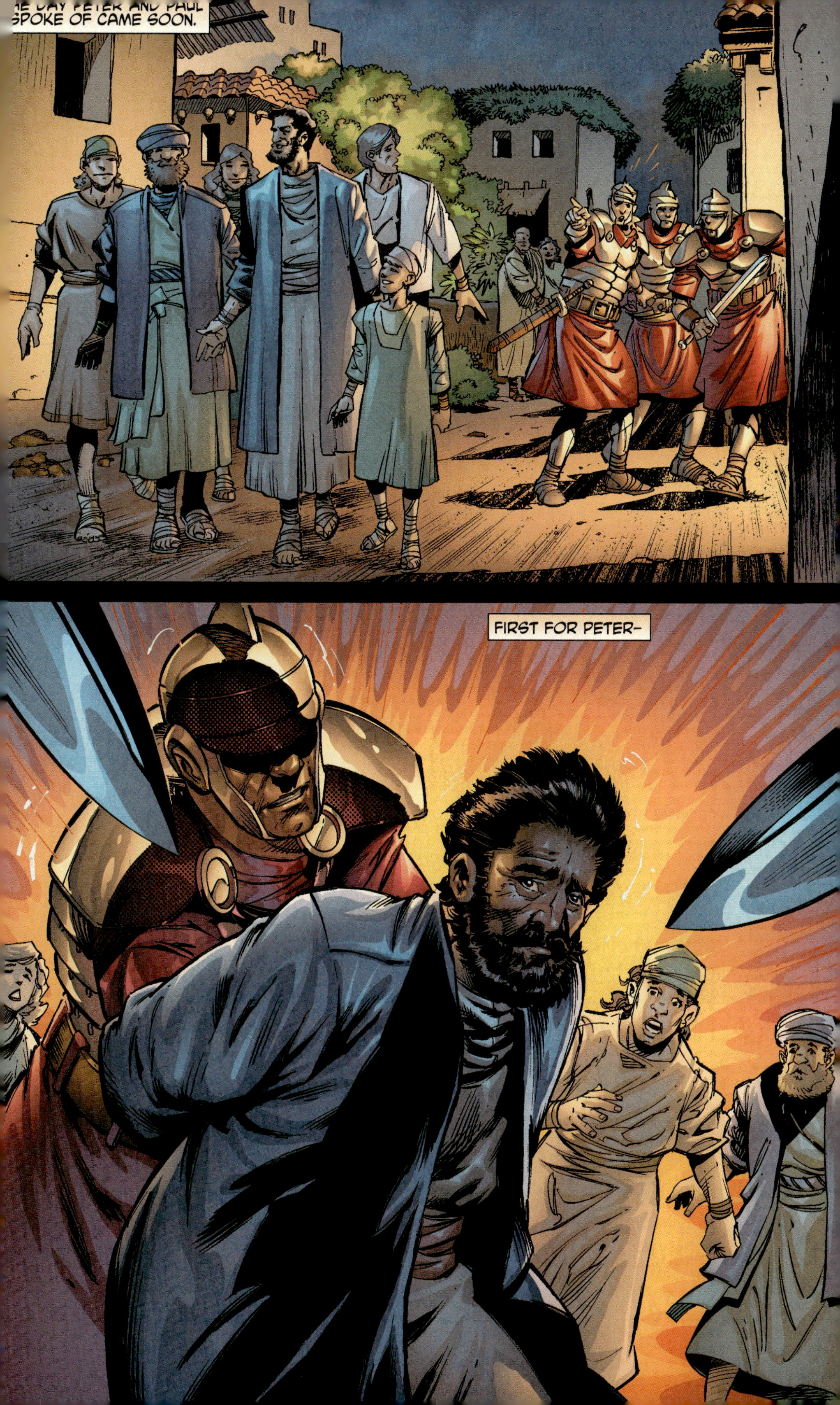
DAY PETER AND PAUL SPOKE OF CAME SOON.
FIRST FOR PETER-

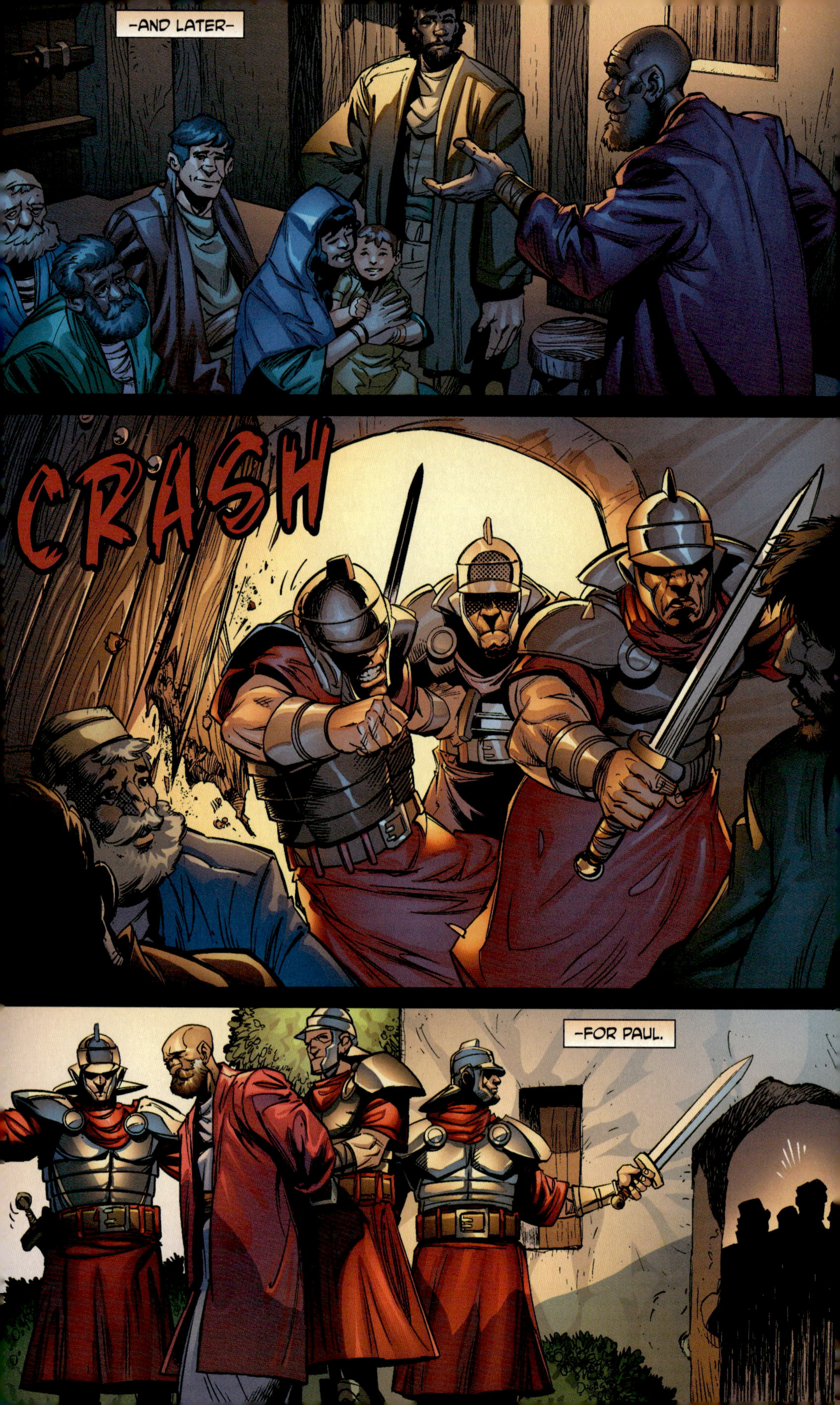
-AND LATER-
CRASH
-FOR PAUL.

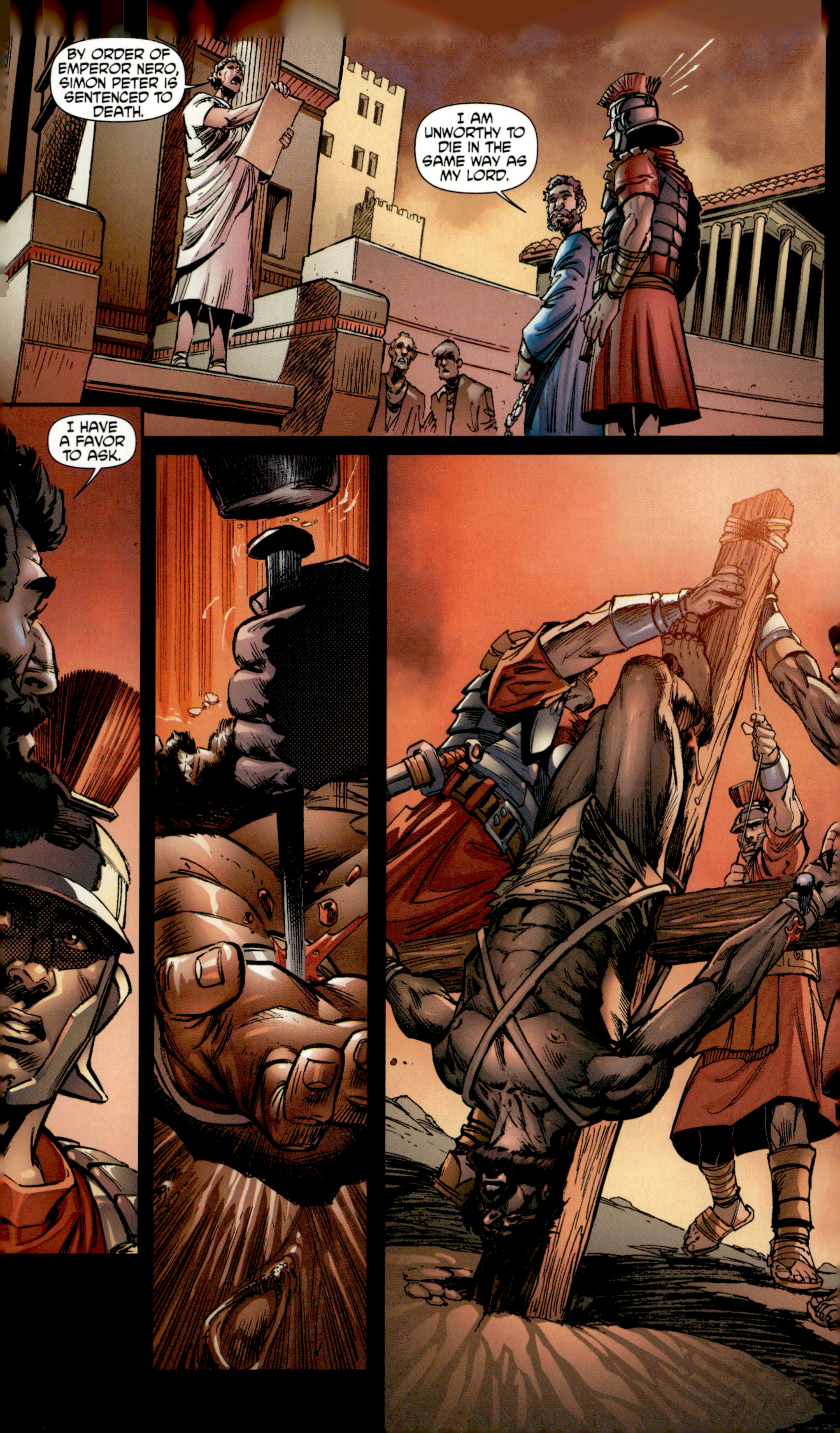
BY ORDER OF EMPEROR NERO, SIMON PETER IS SENTENCED TO DEATH.
I AM UNWORTHY TO DIE IN THE SAME WAY AS MY LORD.
I HAVE A FAVOR TO ASK.

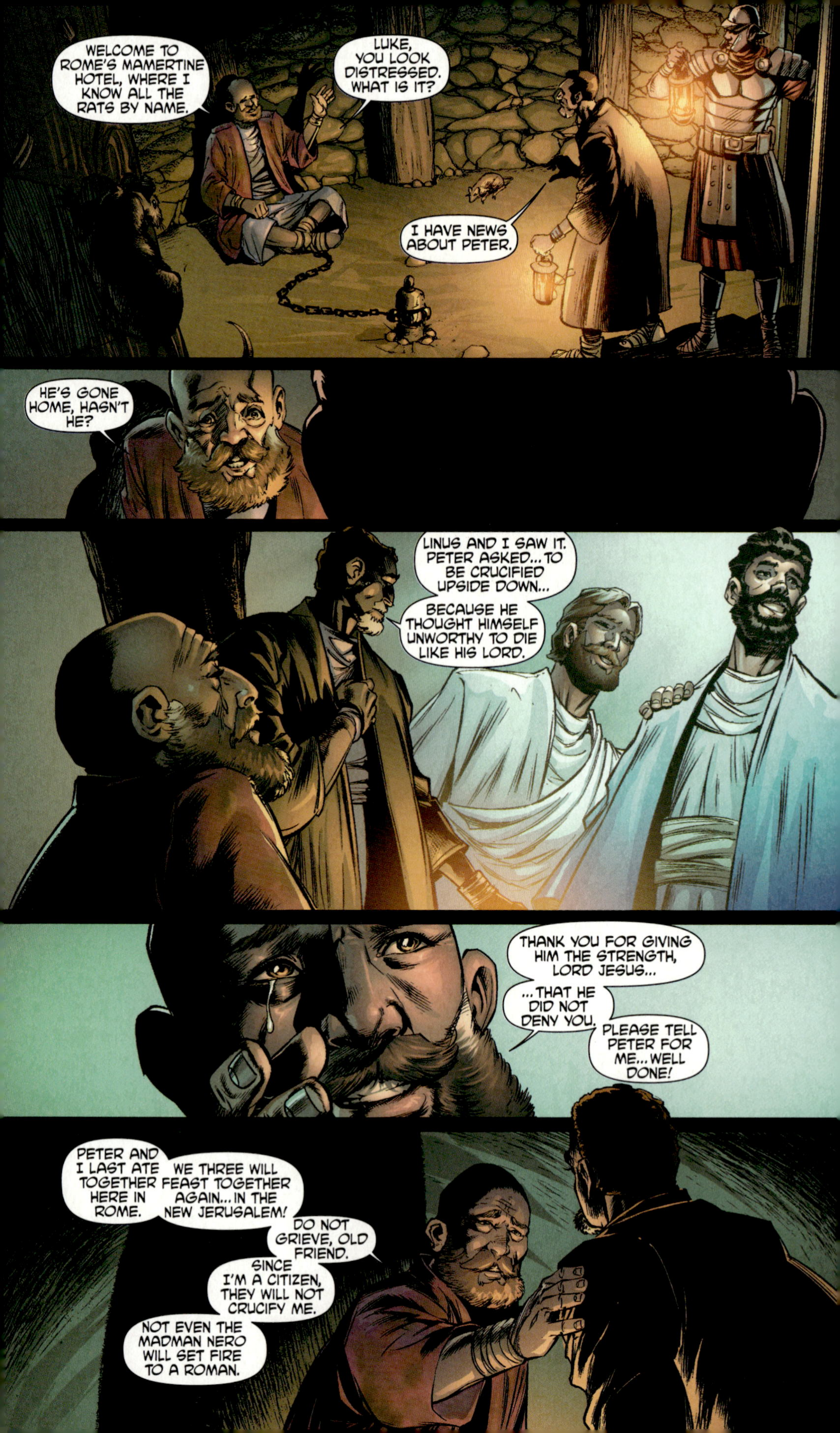
WELCOME TO ROME'S MAMERTINE HOTEL, WHERE I KNOW ALL THE RATS BY NAME.
LUKE, YOU LOOK DISTRESSED. WHAT IS IT?
I HAVE NEWS ABOUT PETER.
HE'S GONE HOME, HASN'T HE?
LINUS AND I SAW IT. PETER ASKED... TO BE CRUCIFIED UPSIDE DOWN...
BECAUSE HE THOUGHT HIMSELF UNWORTHY TO DIE LIKE HIS LORD.
THANK YOU FOR GIVING HIM THE STRENGTH, LORD JESUS...
...THAT HE DID NOT DENY YOU.
PLEASE TELL PETER FOR ME... WELL DONE!
PETER AND I LAST ATE TOGETHER HERE IN ROME.
WE THREE WILL FEAST TOGETHER AGAIN... IN THE NEW JERUSALEM!
DO NOT GRIEVE, OLD FRIEND.
SINCE I'M A CITIZEN, THEY WILL NOT CRUCIFY ME.
NOT EVEN THE MADMAN NERO WILL SET FIRE TO A ROMAN.

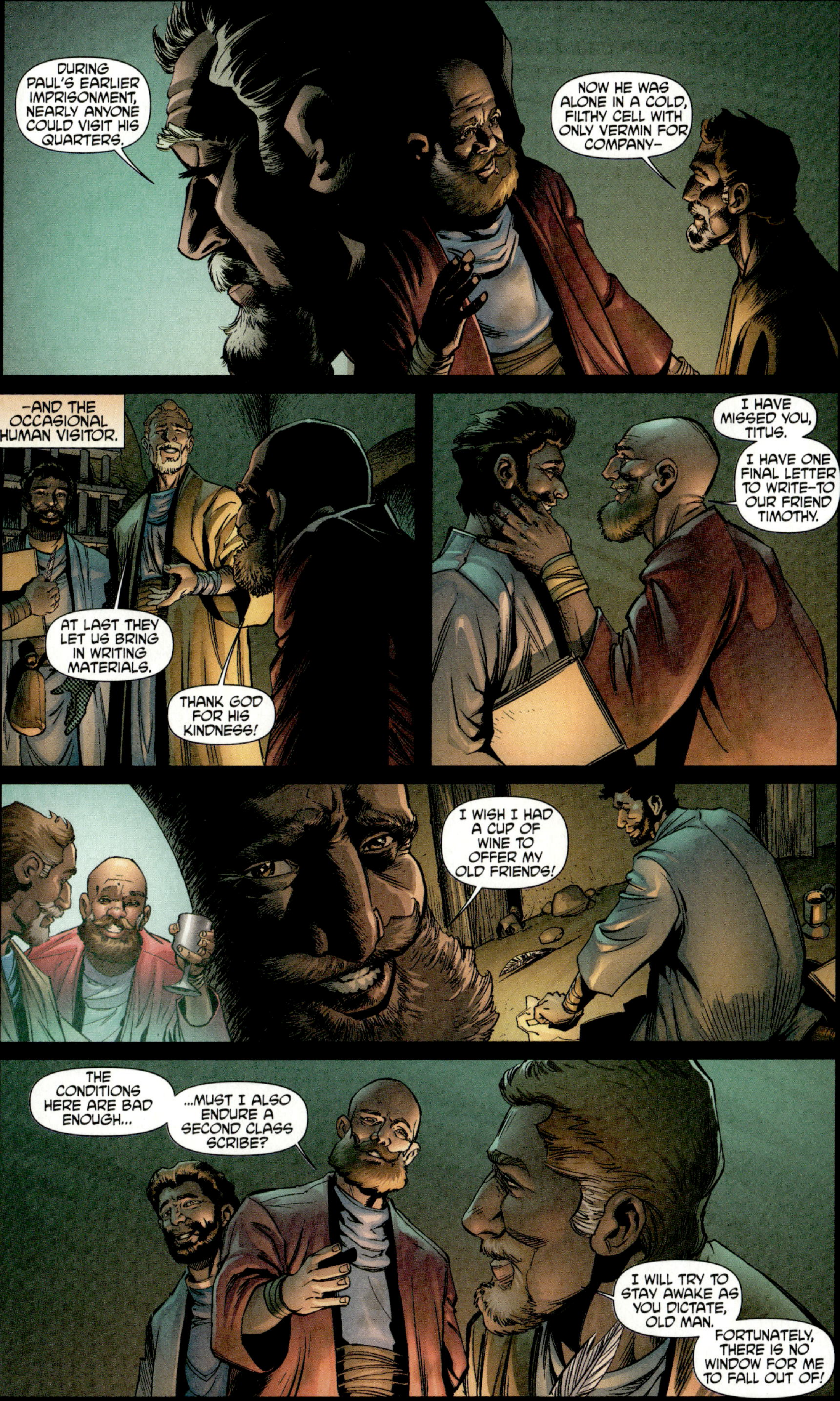
DURING PAUL'S EARLIER IMPRISONMENT, NEARLY ANYONE COULD VISIT HIS QUARTERS.
NOW HE WAS ALONE IN A COLD, FILTHY CELL WITH ONLY VERMIN FOR COMPANY–
–AND THE OCCASIONAL HUMAN VISITOR.
AT LAST THEY LET US BRING IN WRITING MATERIALS.
THANK GOD FOR HIS KINDNESS!
I HAVE MISSED YOU, TITUS.
I HAVE ONE FINAL LETTER TO WRITE–TO OUR FRIEND TIMOTHY.
I WISH I HAD A CUP OF WINE TO OFFER MY OLD FRIENDS!
THE CONDITIONS HERE ARE BAD ENOUGH...
...MUST I ALSO ENDURE A SECOND CLASS SCRIBE?
I WILL TRY TO STAY AWAKE AS YOU DICTATE, OLD MAN.
FORTUNATELY, THERE IS NO WINDOW FOR ME TO FALL OUT OF!

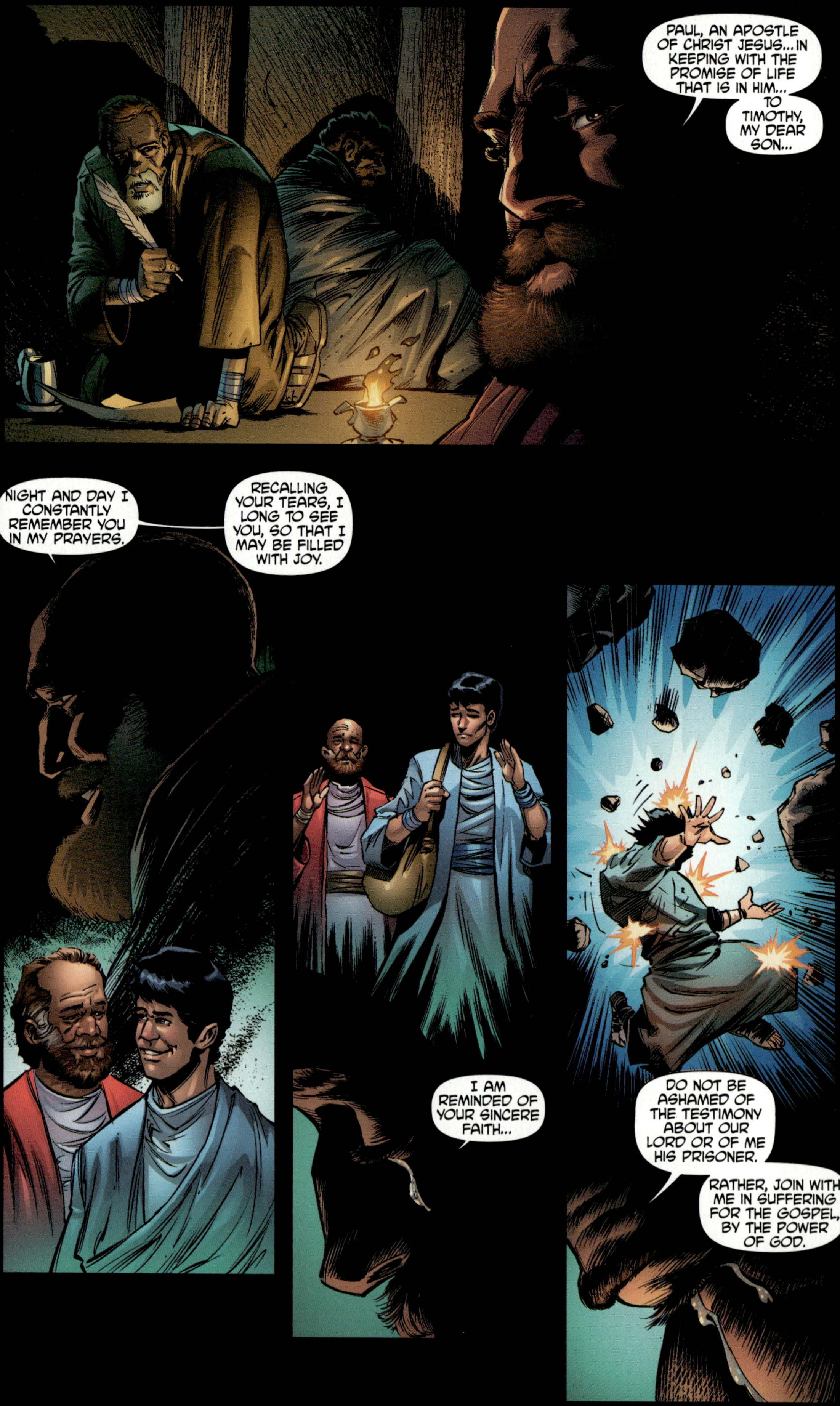
PAUL, AN APOSTLE OF CHRIST JESUS... IN KEEPING WITH THE PROMISE OF LIFE THAT IS IN HIM...
TO TIMOTHY, MY DEAR SON...
NIGHT AND DAY I CONSTANTLY REMEMBER YOU IN MY PRAYERS.
RECALLING YOUR TEARS, I LONG TO SEE YOU, SO THAT I MAY BE FILLED WITH JOY.
I AM REMINDED OF YOUR SINCERE FAITH...
DO NOT BE ASHAMED OF THE TESTIMONY ABOUT OUR LORD OR OF ME HIS PRISONER.
RATHER, JOIN WITH ME IN SUFFERING FOR THE GOSPEL, BY THE POWER OF GOD.

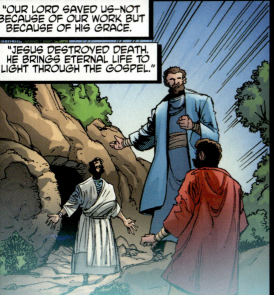

"OUR LORD SAVED US—NOT BECAUSE OF OUR WORK BUT BECAUSE OF HIS GRACE.

"JESUS DESTROYED DEATH. HE BRINGS ETERNAL LIFE TO LIGHT THROUGH THE GOSPEL."

"I WAS APPOINTED A HERALD AND AN APOSTLE OF THIS GOSPEL."

I KNOW THE ONE I BELIEVE IN, AND I AM SURE THAT HE WILL GUARD WHAT HE ENTRUSTED TO ME.

"JOIN WITH ME IN SUFFERING, LIKE A GOOD SOLDIER OF CHRIST JESUS."

ATHLETES RECEIVE THE VICTOR'S CROWN ONLY WHEN THEY COMPETE ACCORDING TO THE RULES.

I MAY BE CHAINED, BUT GOD'S WORD IS NOT CHAINED!

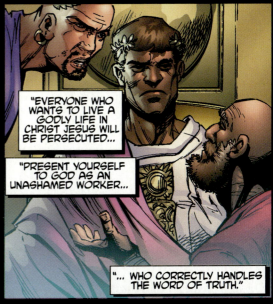

"EVERYONE WHO WANTS TO LIVE A GODLY LIFE IN CHRIST JESUS WILL BE PERSECUTED...

"PRESENT YOURSELF TO GOD AS AN UNASHAMED WORKER...

"... WHO CORRECTLY HANDLES THE WORD OF TRUTH."

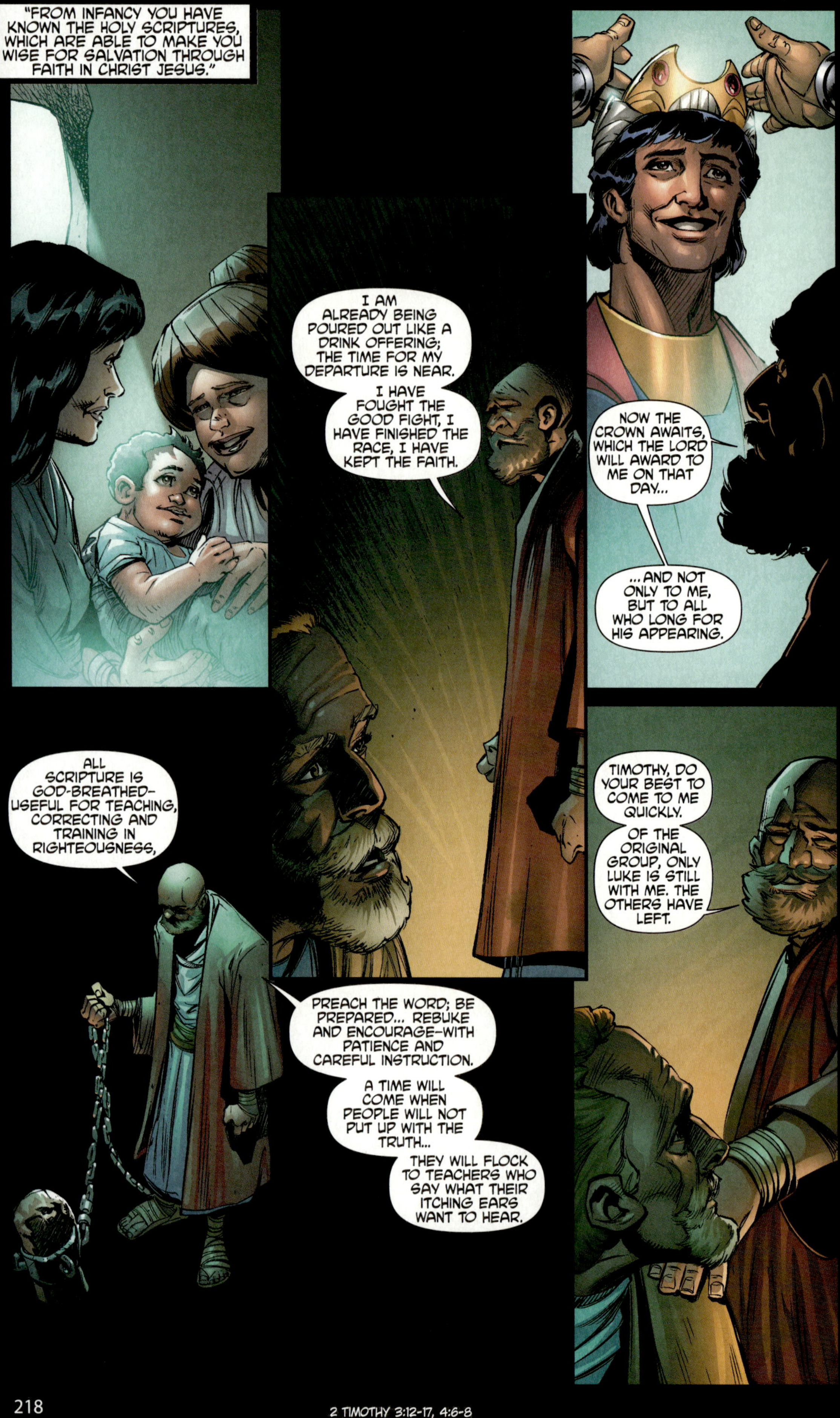
"FROM INFANCY YOU HAVE KNOWN THE HOLY SCRIPTURES, WHICH ARE ABLE TO MAKE YOU WISE FOR SALVATION THROUGH FAITH IN CHRIST JESUS."
I AM ALREADY BEING POURED OUT LIKE A DRINK OFFERING; THE TIME FOR MY DEPARTURE IS NEAR.
I HAVE FOUGHT THE GOOD FIGHT, I HAVE FINISHED THE RACE, I HAVE KEPT THE FAITH.
NOW THE CROWN AWAITS, WHICH THE LORD WILL AWARD TO ME ON THAT DAY...
...AND NOT ONLY TO ME, BUT TO ALL WHO LONG FOR HIS APPEARING.
ALL SCRIPTURE IS GOD-BREATHED–USEFUL FOR TEACHING, CORRECTING AND TRAINING IN RIGHTEOUSNESS,
PREACH THE WORD; BE PREPARED... REBUKE AND ENCOURAGE–WITH PATIENCE AND CAREFUL INSTRUCTION.
A TIME WILL COME WHEN PEOPLE WILL NOT PUT UP WITH THE TRUTH...
THEY WILL FLOCK TO TEACHERS WHO SAY WHAT THEIR ITCHING EARS WANT TO HEAR.
TIMOTHY, DO YOUR BEST TO COME TO ME QUICKLY.
OF THE ORIGINAL GROUP, ONLY LUKE IS STILL WITH ME. THE OTHERS HAVE LEFT.

2 TIMOTHY 3:12-17, 4:6-8

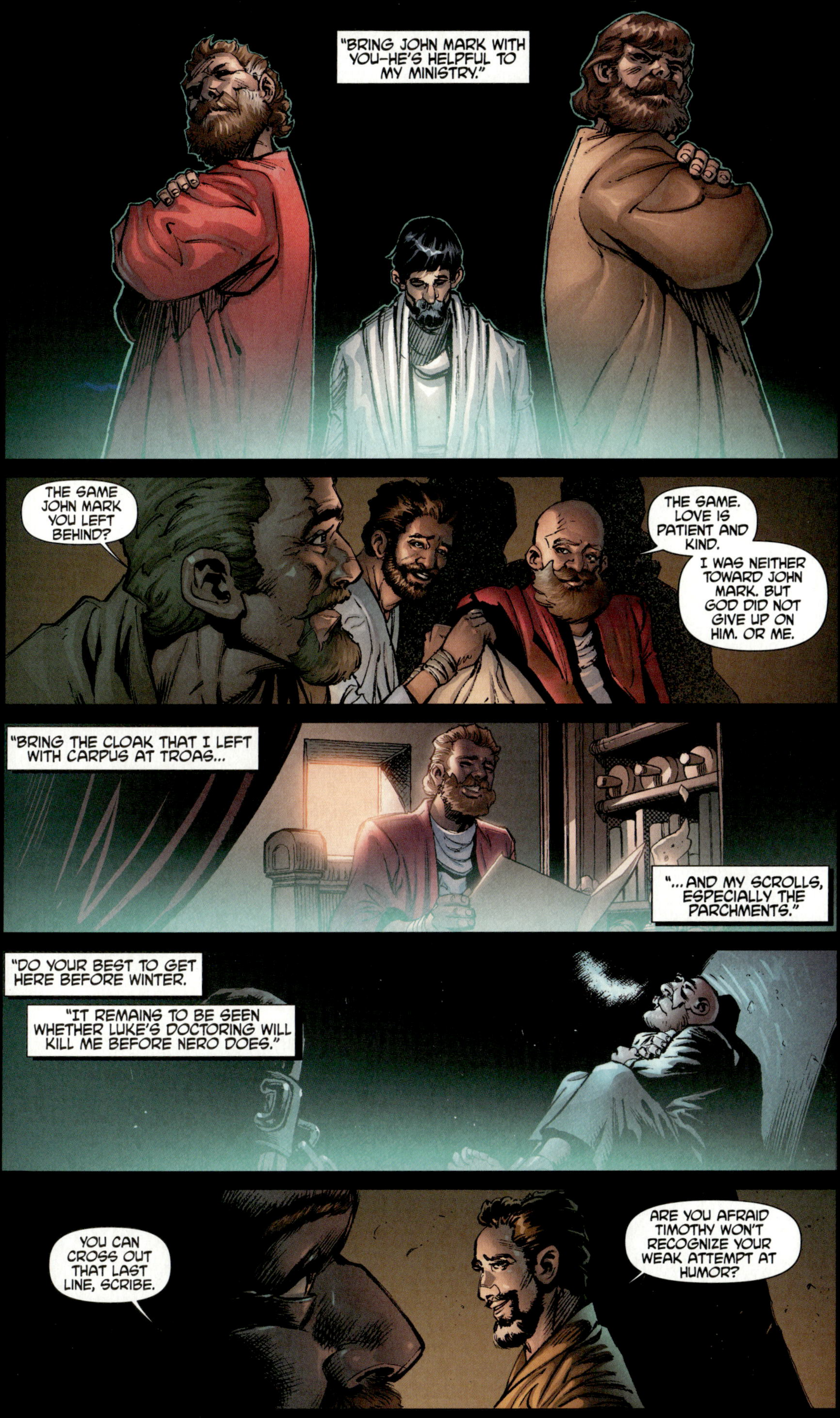
"BRING JOHN MARK WITH YOU—HE'S HELPFUL TO MY MINISTRY."
THE SAME JOHN MARK YOU LEFT BEHIND?
THE SAME. LOVE IS PATIENT AND KIND.
I WAS NEITHER TOWARD JOHN MARK. BUT GOD DID NOT GIVE UP ON HIM. OR ME.
"BRING THE CLOAK THAT I LEFT WITH CARPUS AT TROAS...
"...AND MY SCROLLS, ESPECIALLY THE PARCHMENTS."
"DO YOUR BEST TO GET HERE BEFORE WINTER.
"IT REMAINS TO BE SEEN WHETHER LUKE'S DOCTORING WILL KILL ME BEFORE NERO DOES."
YOU CAN CROSS OUT THAT LAST LINE, SCRIBE.
ARE YOU AFRAID TIMOTHY WON'T RECOGNIZE YOUR WEAK ATTEMPT AT HUMOR?

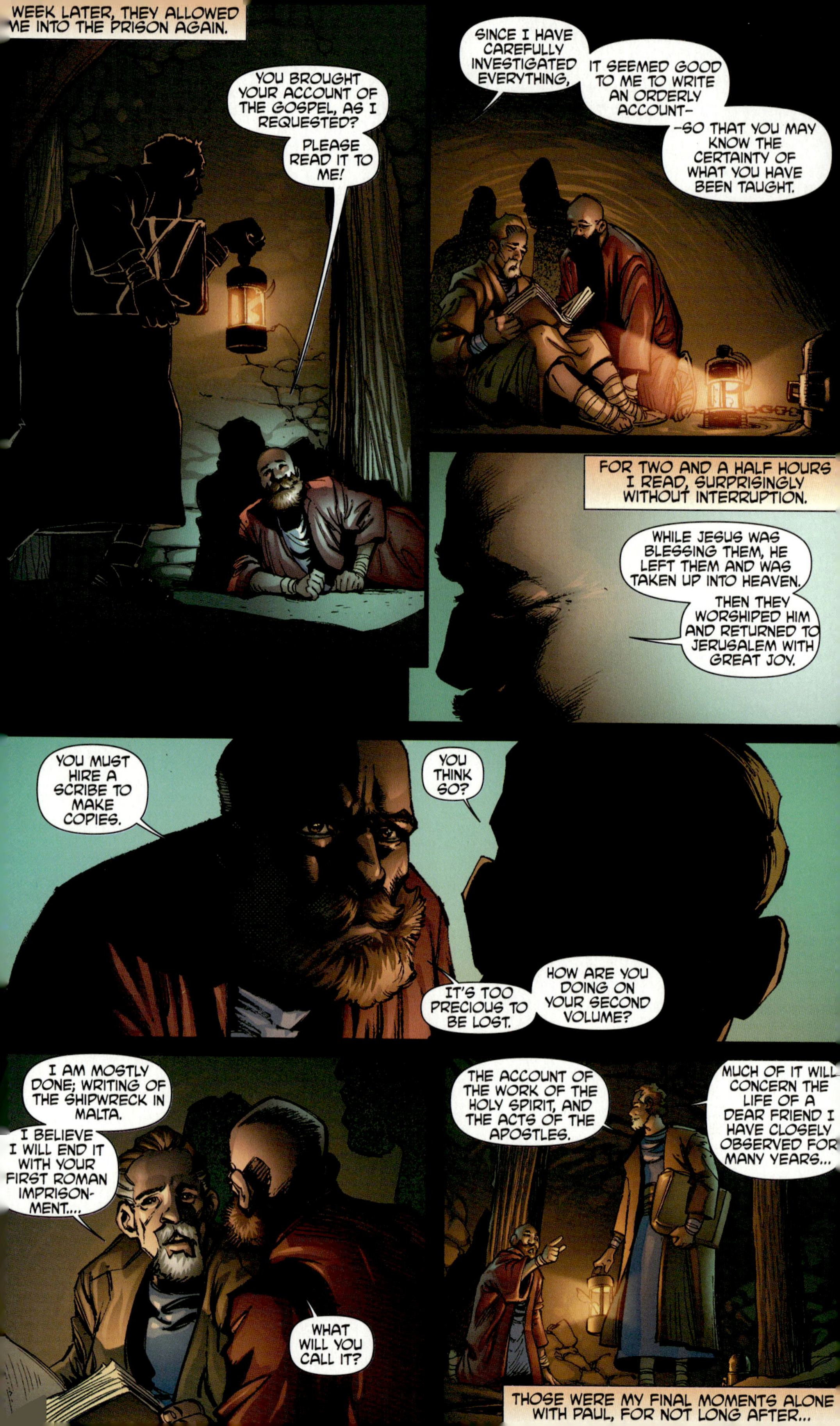
WEEK LATER, THEY ALLOWED ME INTO THE PRISON AGAIN.
YOU BROUGHT YOUR ACCOUNT OF THE GOSPEL, AS I REQUESTED?
PLEASE READ IT TO ME!
SINCE I HAVE CAREFULLY INVESTIGATED EVERYTHING,
IT SEEMED GOOD TO ME TO WRITE AN ORDERLY ACCOUNT–
–SO THAT YOU MAY KNOW THE CERTAINTY OF WHAT YOU HAVE BEEN TAUGHT.
FOR TWO AND A HALF HOURS I READ, SURPRISINGLY WITHOUT INTERRUPTION.
WHILE JESUS WAS BLESSING THEM, HE LEFT THEM AND WAS TAKEN UP INTO HEAVEN.
THEN THEY WORSHIPED HIM AND RETURNED TO JERUSALEM WITH GREAT JOY.
YOU MUST HIRE A SCRIBE TO MAKE COPIES.
YOU THINK SO?
IT'S TOO PRECIOUS TO BE LOST.
HOW ARE YOU DOING ON YOUR SECOND VOLUME?
I AM MOSTLY DONE; WRITING OF THE SHIPWRECK IN MALTA.
I BELIEVE I WILL END IT WITH YOUR FIRST ROMAN IMPRISON-MENT....
WHAT WILL YOU CALL IT?
THE ACCOUNT OF THE WORK OF THE HOLY SPIRIT, AND THE ACTS OF THE APOSTLES.
MUCH OF IT WILL CONCERN THE LIFE OF A DEAR FRIEND I HAVE CLOSELY OBSERVED FOR MANY YEARS...
THOSE WERE MY FINAL MOMENTS ALONE WITH PAUL, FOR NOT LONG AFTER...

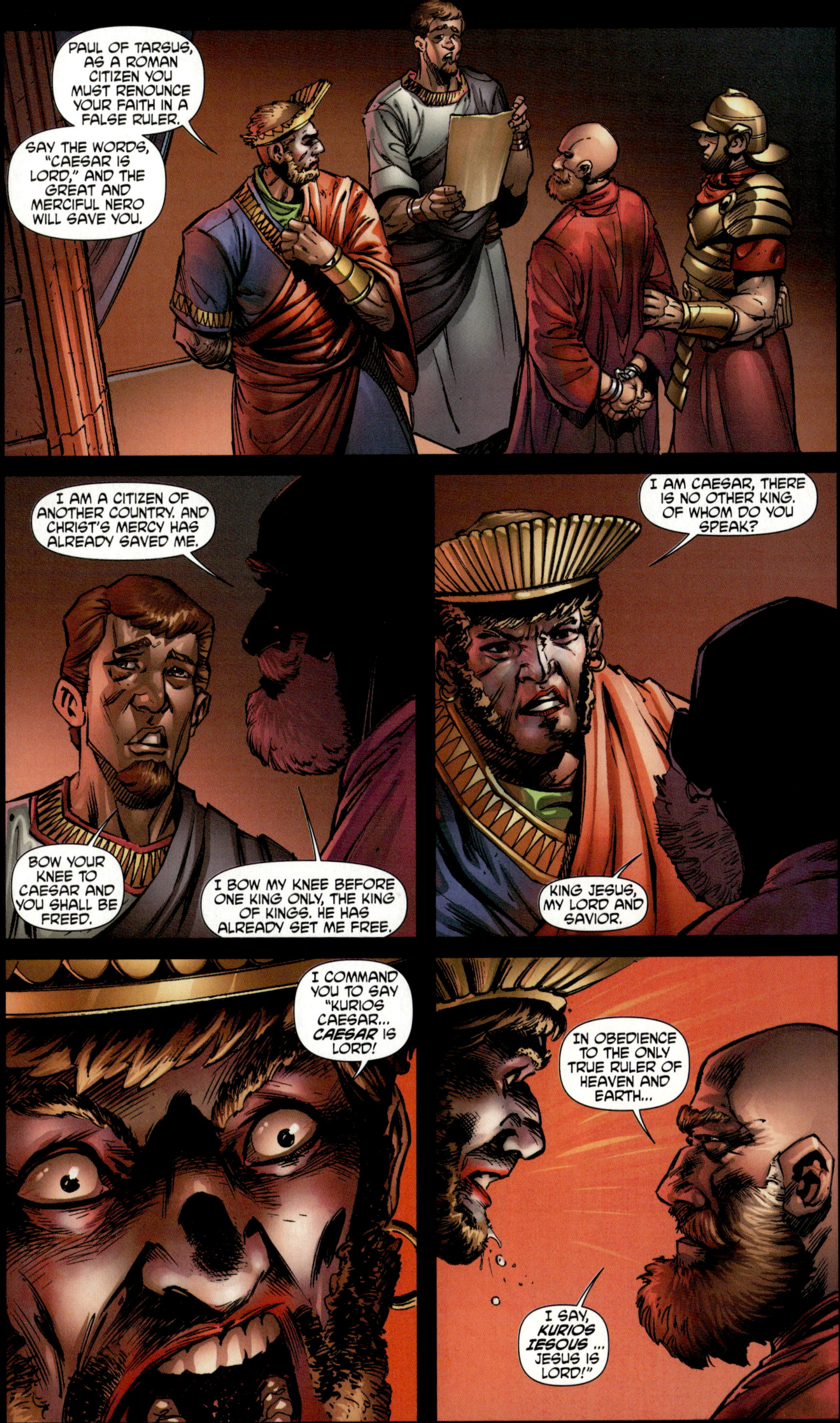
PAUL OF TARSUS, AS A ROMAN CITIZEN YOU MUST RENOUNCE YOUR FAITH IN A FALSE RULER.
SAY THE WORDS, "CAESAR IS LORD," AND THE GREAT AND MERCIFUL NERO WILL SAVE YOU.
I AM A CITIZEN OF ANOTHER COUNTRY. AND CHRIST'S MERCY HAS ALREADY SAVED ME.
BOW YOUR KNEE TO CAESAR AND YOU SHALL BE FREED.
I BOW MY KNEE BEFORE ONE KING ONLY, THE KING OF KINGS. HE HAS ALREADY SET ME FREE.
I AM CAESAR, THERE IS NO OTHER KING. OF WHOM DO YOU SPEAK?
KING JESUS, MY LORD AND SAVIOR.
I COMMAND YOU TO SAY "KURIOS CAESAR... *CAESAR* IS LORD!
IN OBEDIENCE TO THE ONLY TRUE RULER OF HEAVEN AND EARTH...
I SAY, *KURIOS IESOUS* ... JESUS IS LORD!"

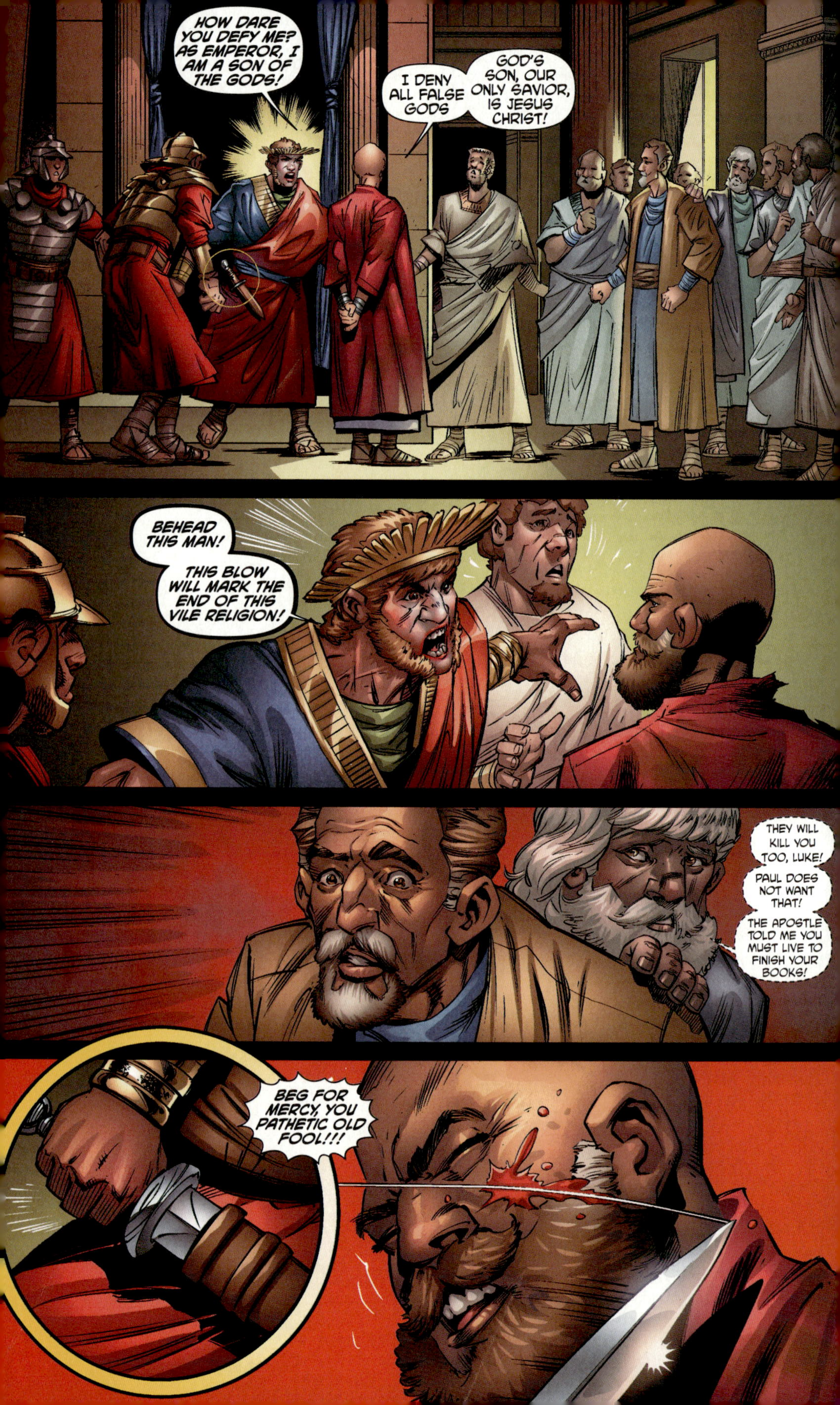
HOW DARE YOU DEFY ME? AS EMPEROR, I AM A SON OF THE GODS!
I DENY ALL FALSE GODS
GOD'S SON, OUR ONLY SAVIOR, IS JESUS CHRIST!
BEHEAD THIS MAN!
THIS BLOW WILL MARK THE END OF THIS VILE RELIGION!
THEY WILL KILL YOU TOO, LUKE!
PAUL DOES NOT WANT THAT!
THE APOSTLE TOLD ME YOU MUST LIVE TO FINISH YOUR BOOKS!
BEG FOR MERCY, YOU PATHETIC OLD FOOL!!!

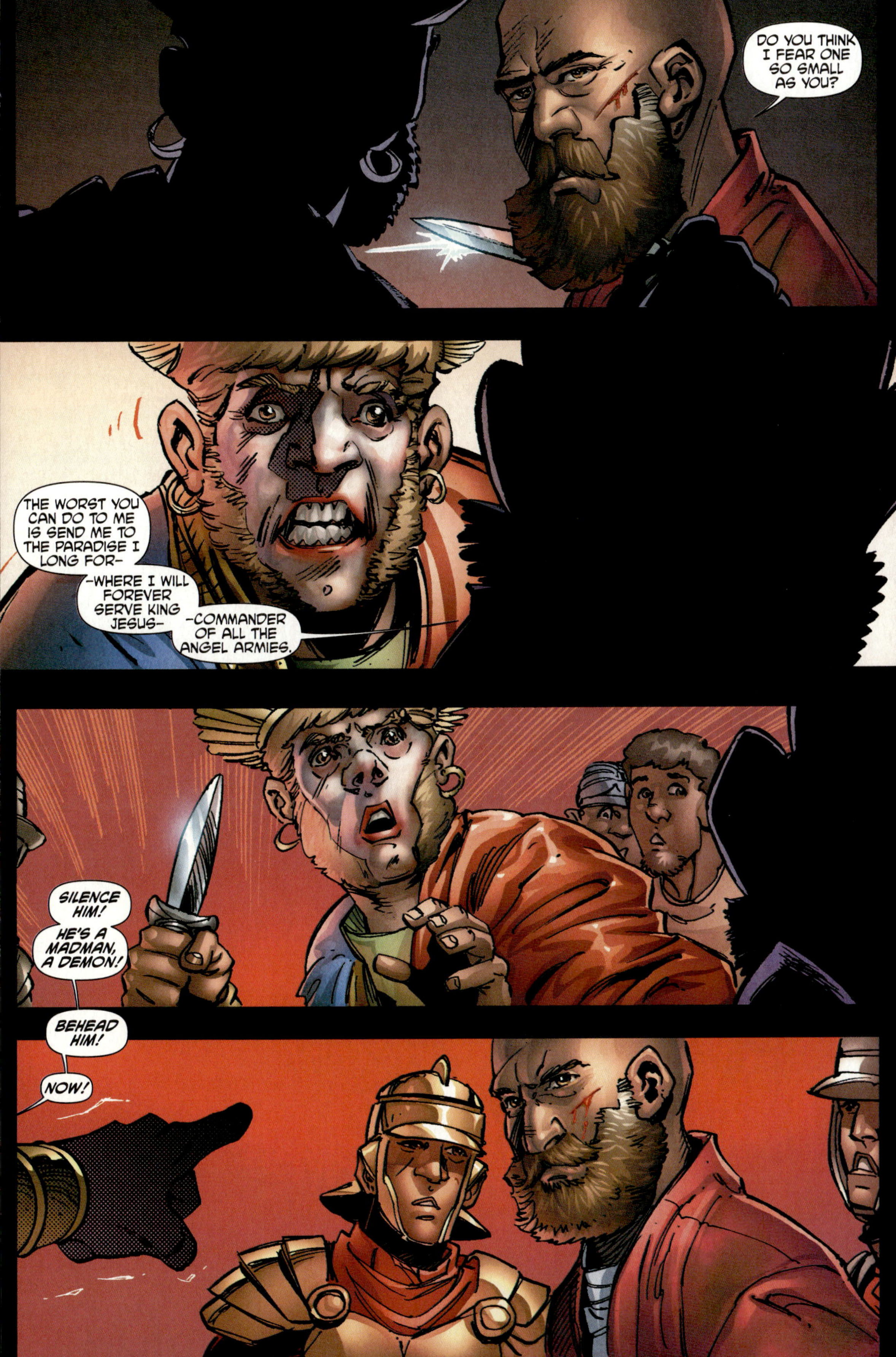
DO YOU THINK I FEAR ONE SO SMALL AS YOU?
THE WORST YOU CAN DO TO ME IS SEND ME TO THE PARADISE I LONG FOR-
-WHERE I WILL FOREVER SERVE KING JESUS-
-COMMANDER OF ALL THE ANGEL ARMIES.
SILENCE HIM!
HE'S A MADMAN, A DEMON!
BEHEAD HIM!
NOW!

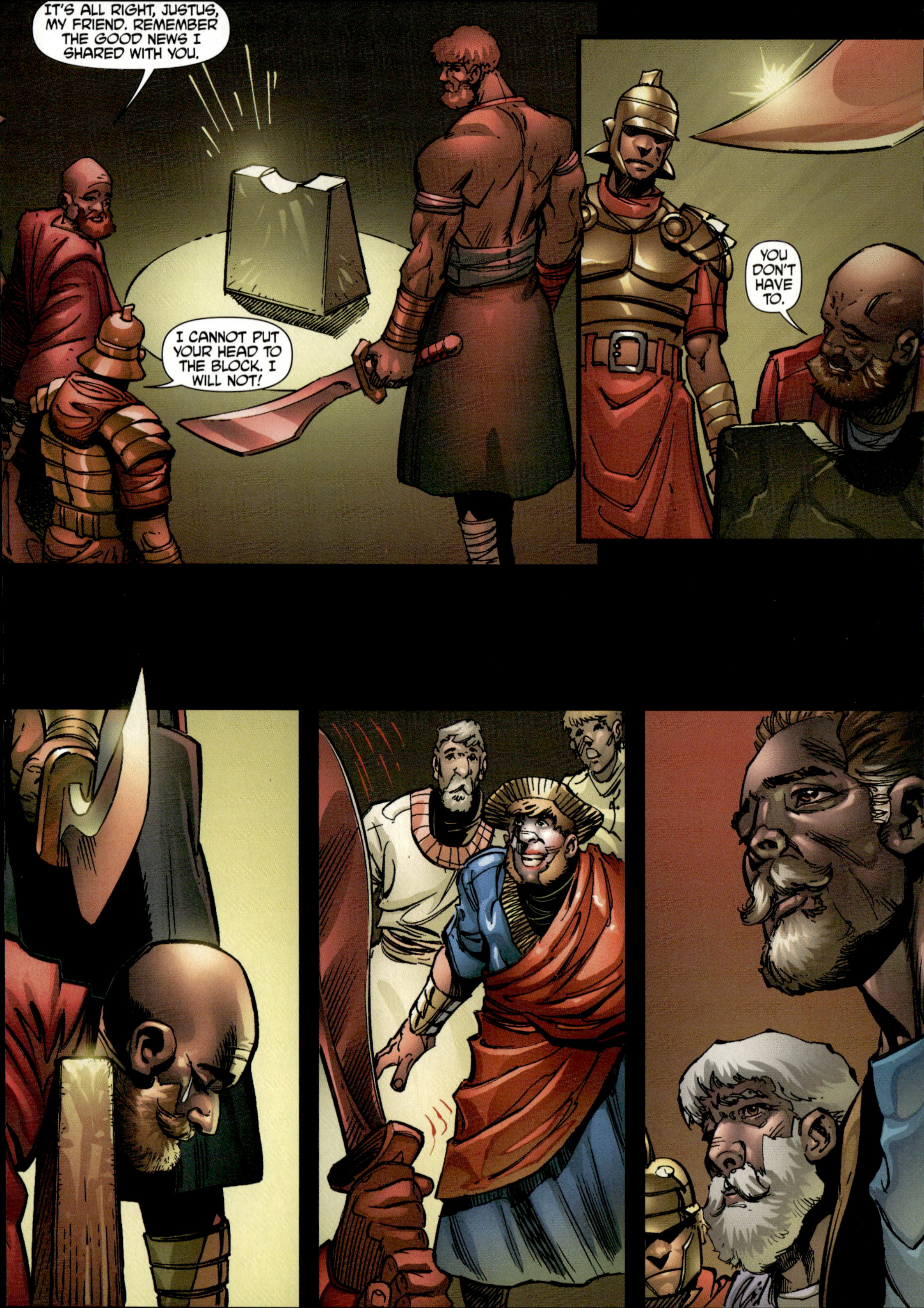
IT'S ALL RIGHT, JUSTUS, MY FRIEND. REMEMBER THE GOOD NEWS I SHARED WITH YOU.
I CANNOT PUT YOUR HEAD TO THE BLOCK. I WILL NOT!
YOU DON'T HAVE TO.

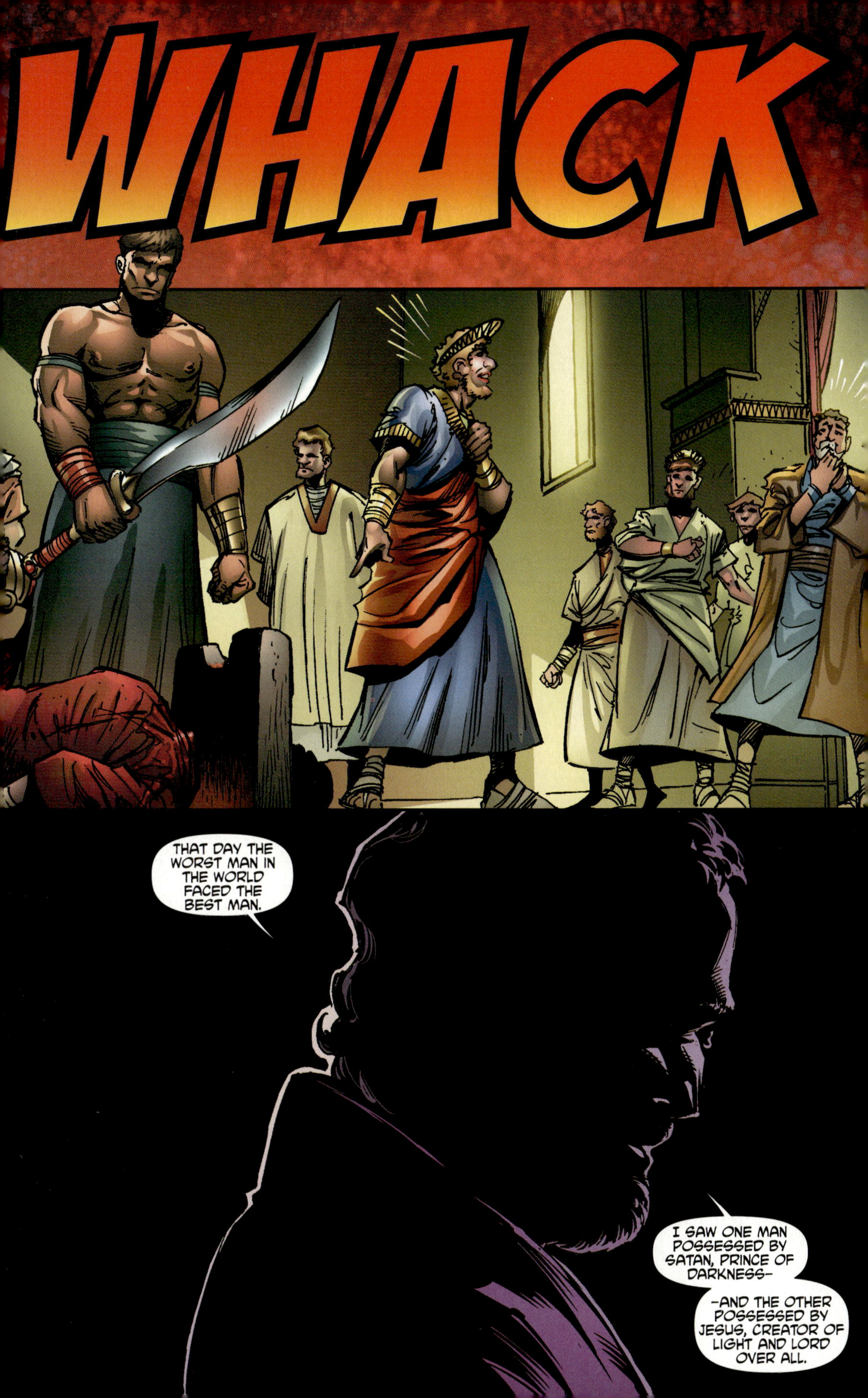
WHACK
THAT DAY THE WORST MAN IN THE WORLD FACED THE BEST MAN.
I SAW ONE MAN POSSESSED BY SATAN, PRINCE OF DARKNESS–
–AND THE OTHER POSSESSED BY JESUS, CREATOR OF LIGHT AND LORD OVER ALL.

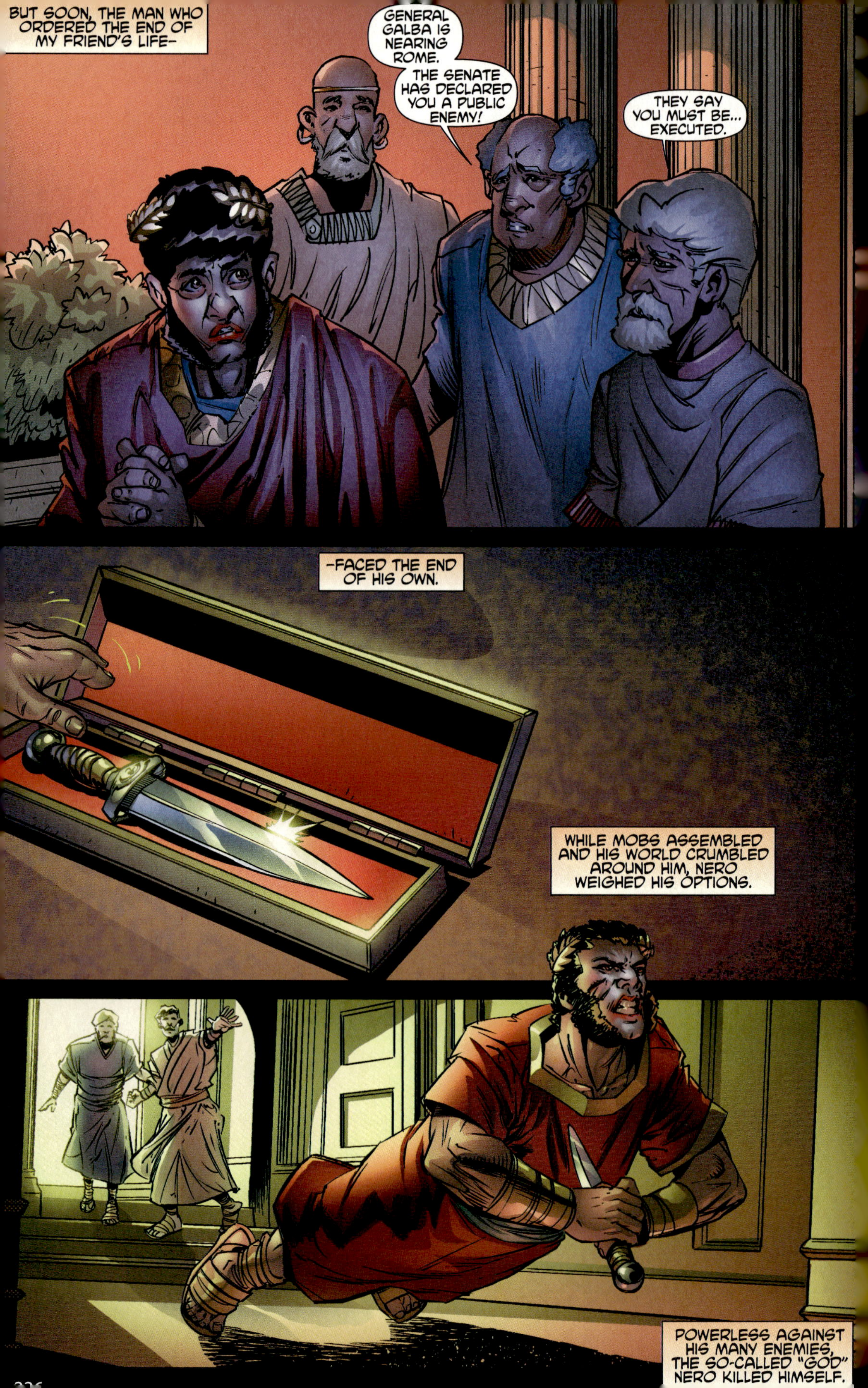
BUT SOON, THE MAN WHO ORDERED THE END OF MY FRIEND'S LIFE-
GENERAL GALBA IS NEARING ROME.
THE SENATE HAS DECLARED YOU A PUBLIC ENEMY!
THEY SAY YOU MUST BE... EXECUTED.
-FACED THE END OF HIS OWN.
WHILE MOBS ASSEMBLED AND HIS WORLD CRUMBLED AROUND HIM, NERO WEIGHED HIS OPTIONS.
POWERLESS AGAINST HIS MANY ENEMIES, THE SO-CALLED "GOD" NERO KILLED HIMSELF.

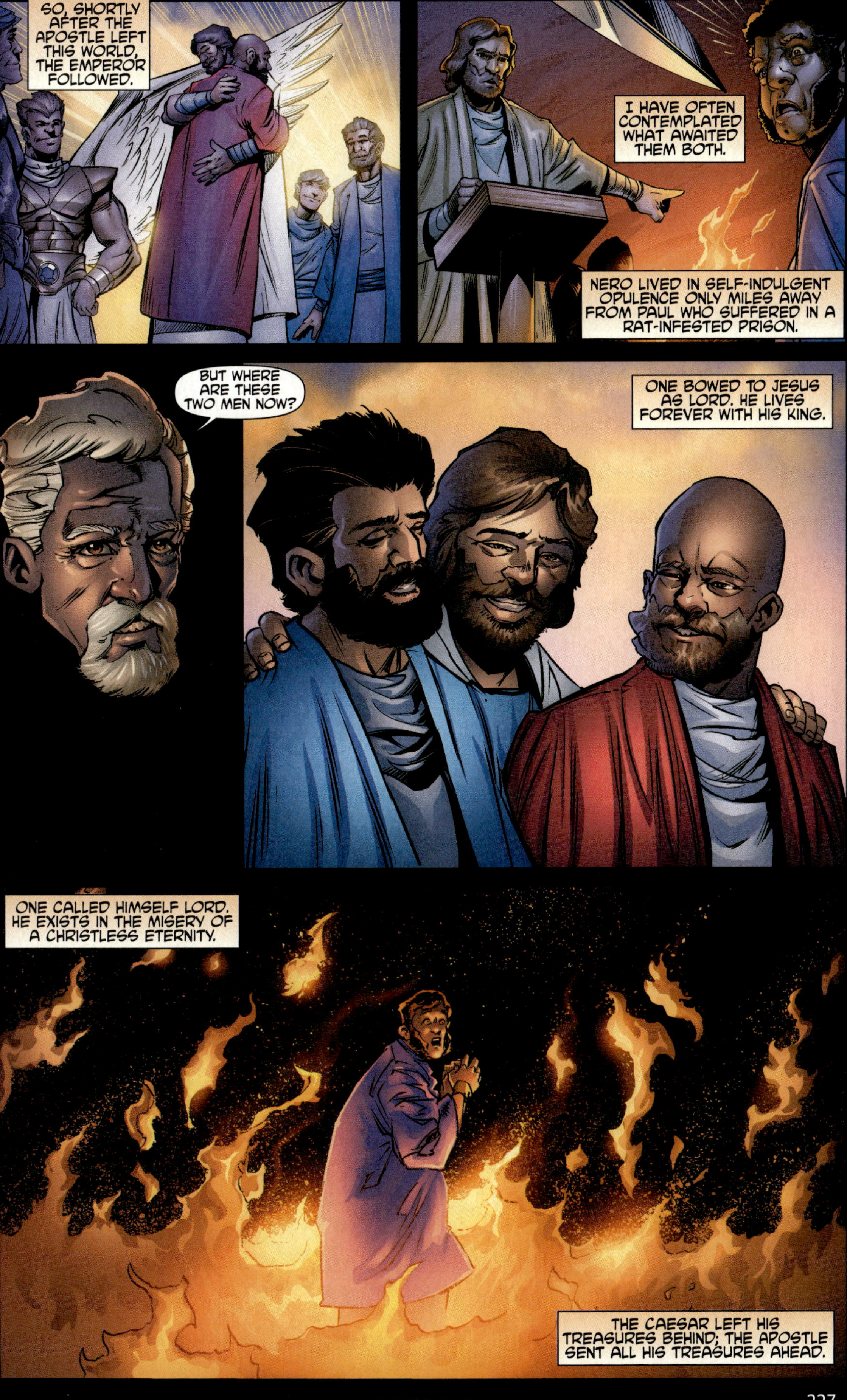
SO, SHORTLY AFTER THE APOSTLE LEFT THIS WORLD, THE EMPEROR FOLLOWED.
I HAVE OFTEN CONTEMPLATED WHAT AWAITED THEM BOTH.
NERO LIVED IN SELF-INDULGENT OPULENCE ONLY MILES AWAY FROM PAUL WHO SUFFERED IN A RAT-INFESTED PRISON.
BUT WHERE ARE THESE TWO MEN NOW?
ONE BOWED TO JESUS AS LORD. HE LIVES FOREVER WITH HIS KING.
ONE CALLED HIMSELF LORD. HE EXISTS IN THE MISERY OF A CHRISTLESS ETERNITY.
THE CAESAR LEFT HIS TREASURES BEHIND; THE APOSTLE SENT ALL HIS TREASURES AHEAD.

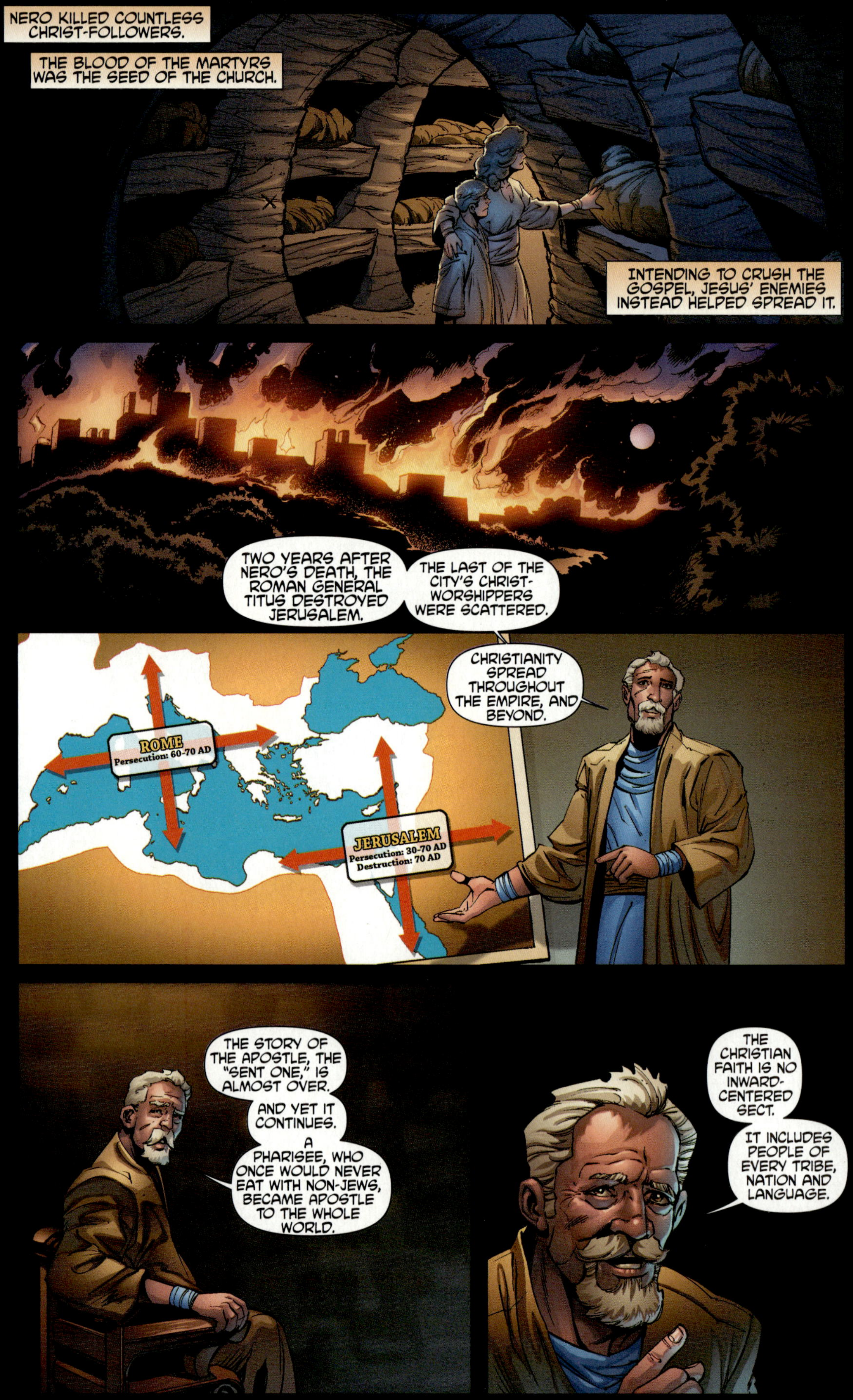

NERO KILLED COUNTLESS CHRIST-FOLLOWERS.
THE BLOOD OF THE MARTYRS WAS THE SEED OF THE CHURCH.
INTENDING TO CRUSH THE GOSPEL, JESUS' ENEMIES INSTEAD HELPED SPREAD IT.
TWO YEARS AFTER NERO'S DEATH, THE ROMAN GENERAL TITUS DESTROYED JERUSALEM.
THE LAST OF THE CITY'S CHRIST-WORSHIPPERS WERE SCATTERED.
CHRISTIANITY SPREAD THROUGHOUT THE EMPIRE, AND BEYOND.
ROME
Persecution: 60-70 AD
JERUSALEM
Persecution: 30-70 AD
Destruction: 70 AD
THE STORY OF THE APOSTLE, THE "SENT ONE," IS ALMOST OVER.
AND YET IT CONTINUES.
A PHARISEE, WHO ONCE WOULD NEVER EAT WITH NON-JEWS, BECAME APOSTLE TO THE WHOLE WORLD.
THE CHRISTIAN FAITH IS NO INWARD-CENTERED SECT.
IT INCLUDES PEOPLE OF EVERY TRIBE, NATION AND LANGUAGE.

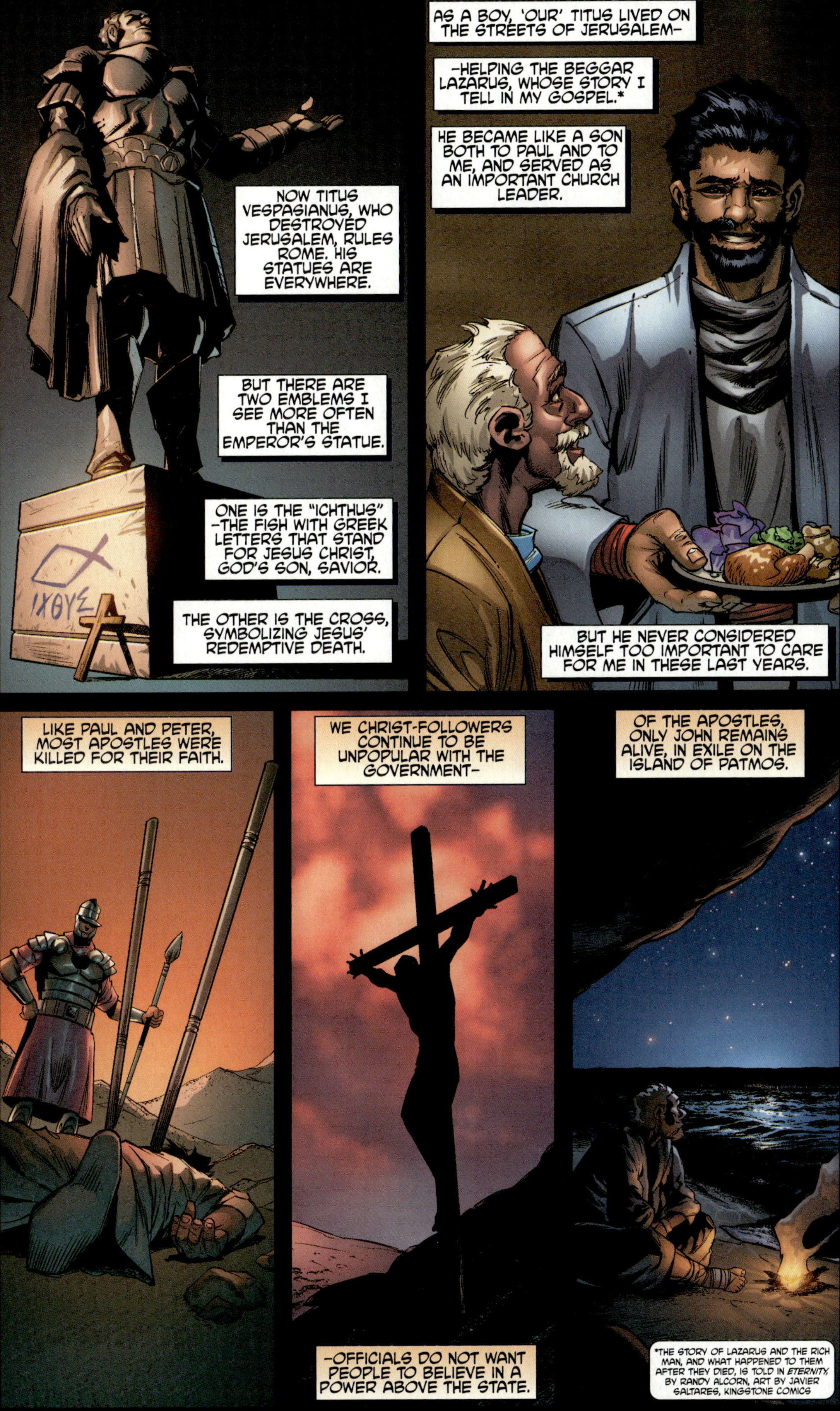

NOW TITUS VESPASIANUS, WHO DESTROYED JERUSALEM, RULES ROME. HIS STATUES ARE EVERYWHERE.
BUT THERE ARE TWO EMBLEMS I SEE MORE OFTEN THAN THE EMPEROR'S STATUE.
ONE IS THE "ICHTHUS" -THE FISH WITH GREEK LETTERS THAT STAND FOR JESUS CHRIST, GOD'S SON, SAVIOR.
ΙΧΘΥΣ
THE OTHER IS THE CROSS, SYMBOLIZING JESUS' REDEMPTIVE DEATH.
AS A BOY, 'OUR' TITUS LIVED ON THE STREETS OF JERUSALEM-
-HELPING THE BEGGAR LAZARUS, WHOSE STORY I TELL IN MY GOSPEL.*
HE BECAME LIKE A SON BOTH TO PAUL AND TO ME, AND SERVED AS AN IMPORTANT CHURCH LEADER.
BUT HE NEVER CONSIDERED HIMSELF TOO IMPORTANT TO CARE FOR ME IN THESE LAST YEARS.
LIKE PAUL AND PETER, MOST APOSTLES WERE KILLED FOR THEIR FAITH.
WE CHRIST-FOLLOWERS CONTINUE TO BE UNPOPULAR WITH THE GOVERNMENT-
-OFFICIALS DO NOT WANT PEOPLE TO BELIEVE IN A POWER ABOVE THE STATE.
OF THE APOSTLES, ONLY JOHN REMAINS ALIVE, IN EXILE ON THE ISLAND OF PATMOS.
*THE STORY OF LAZARUS AND THE RICH MAN, AND WHAT HAPPENED TO THEM AFTER THEY DIED, IS TOLD IN *ETERNITY*, BY RANDY ALCORN, ART BY JAVIER SALTARES, KINGSTONE COMICS

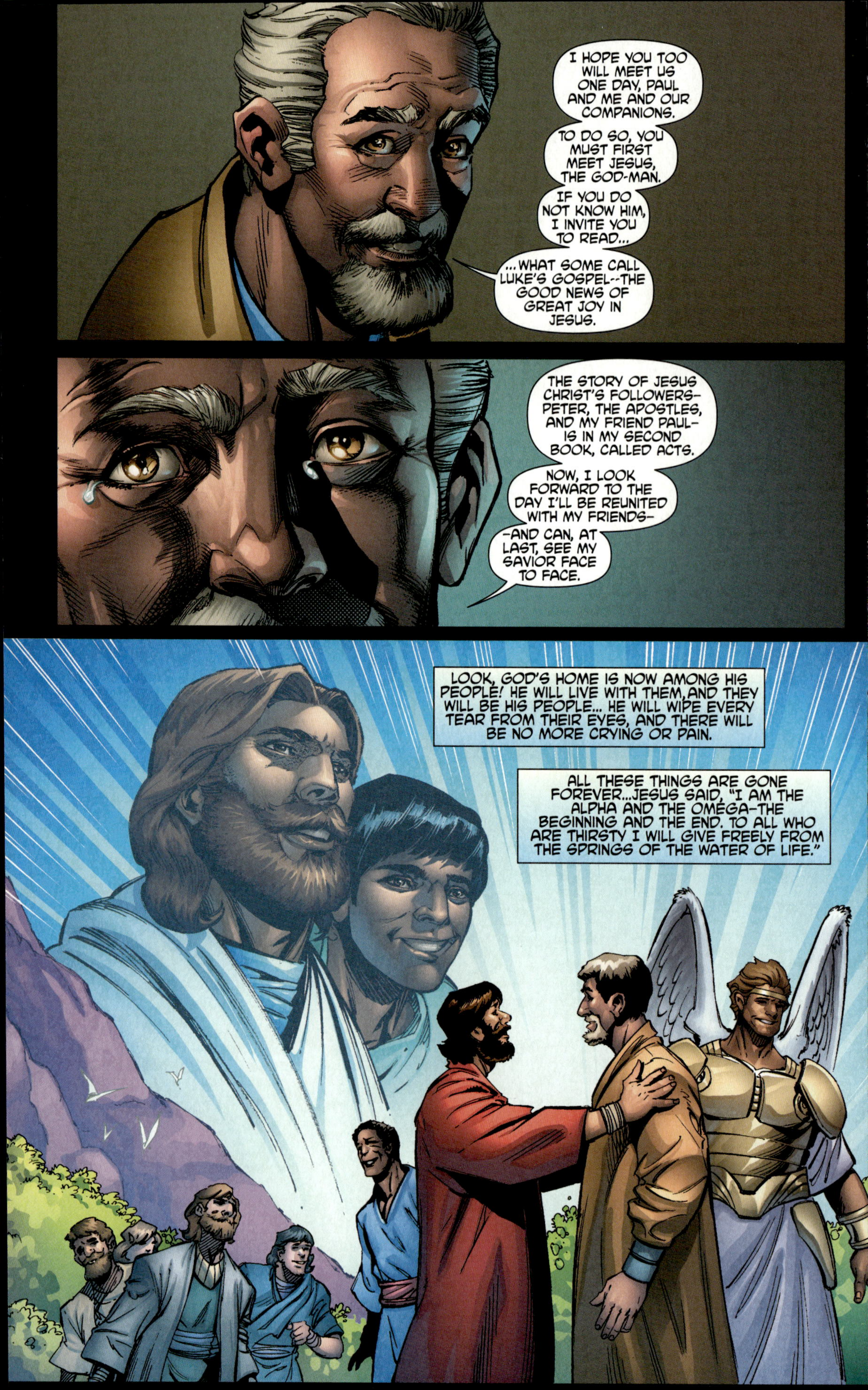
I HOPE YOU TOO WILL MEET US ONE DAY, PAUL AND ME AND OUR COMPANIONS.
TO DO SO, YOU MUST FIRST MEET JESUS, THE GOD-MAN.
IF YOU DO NOT KNOW HIM, I INVITE YOU TO READ...
...WHAT SOME CALL LUKE'S GOSPEL--THE GOOD NEWS OF GREAT JOY IN JESUS.
THE STORY OF JESUS CHRIST'S FOLLOWERS-PETER, THE APOSTLES, AND MY FRIEND PAUL-IS IN MY SECOND BOOK, CALLED ACTS.
NOW, I LOOK FORWARD TO THE DAY I'LL BE REUNITED WITH MY FRIENDS-
-AND CAN, AT LAST, SEE MY SAVIOR FACE TO FACE.
LOOK, GOD'S HOME IS NOW AMONG HIS PEOPLE! HE WILL LIVE WITH THEM, AND THEY WILL BE HIS PEOPLE... HE WILL WIPE EVERY TEAR FROM THEIR EYES, AND THERE WILL BE NO MORE CRYING OR PAIN.
ALL THESE THINGS ARE GONE FOREVER...JESUS SAID, "I AM THE ALPHA AND THE OMEGA-THE BEGINNING AND THE END. TO ALL WHO ARE THIRSTY I WILL GIVE FREELY FROM THE SPRINGS OF THE WATER OF LIFE."

REVELATION 21:3-4, 6

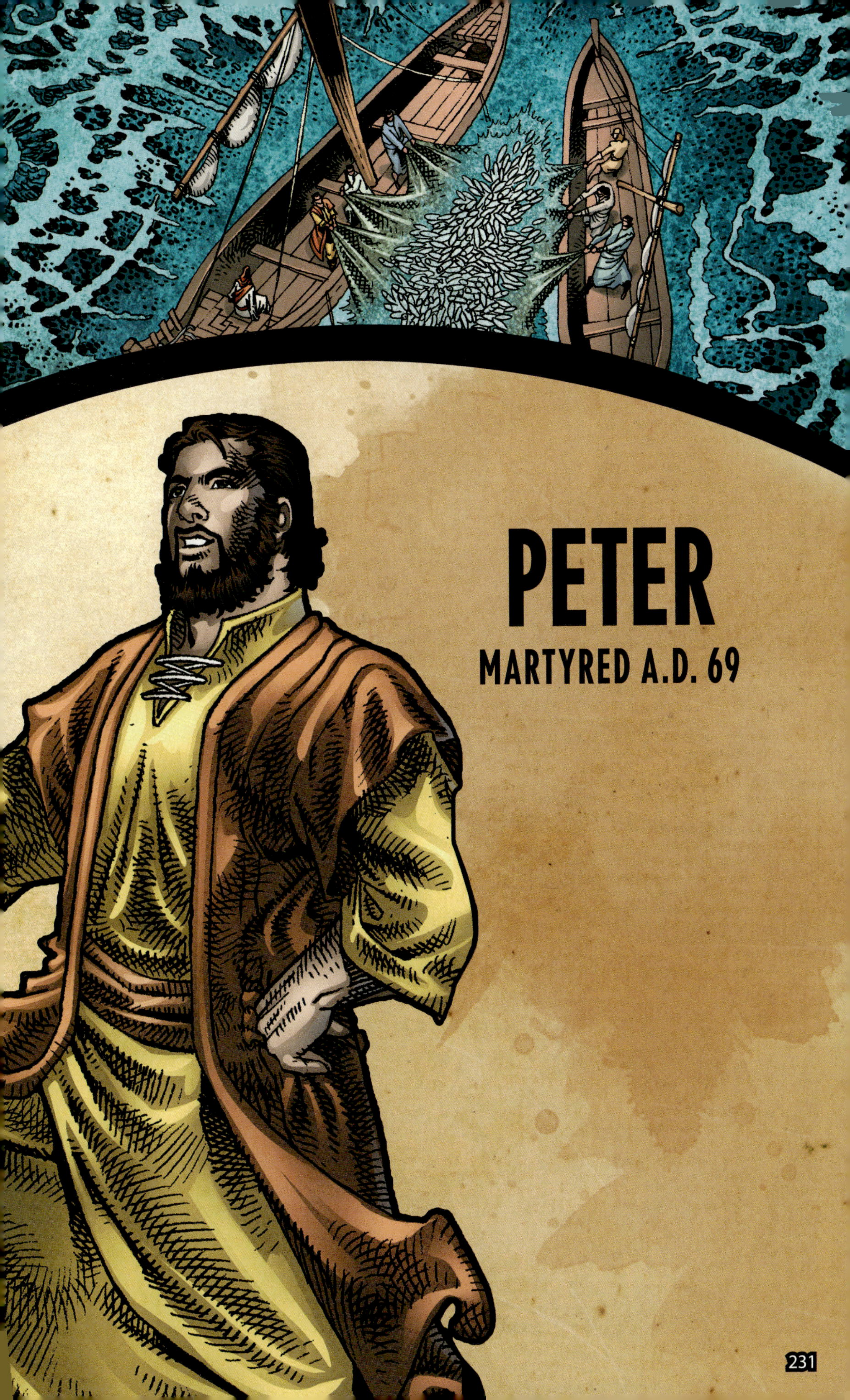

PETER

MARTYRED A.D. 69

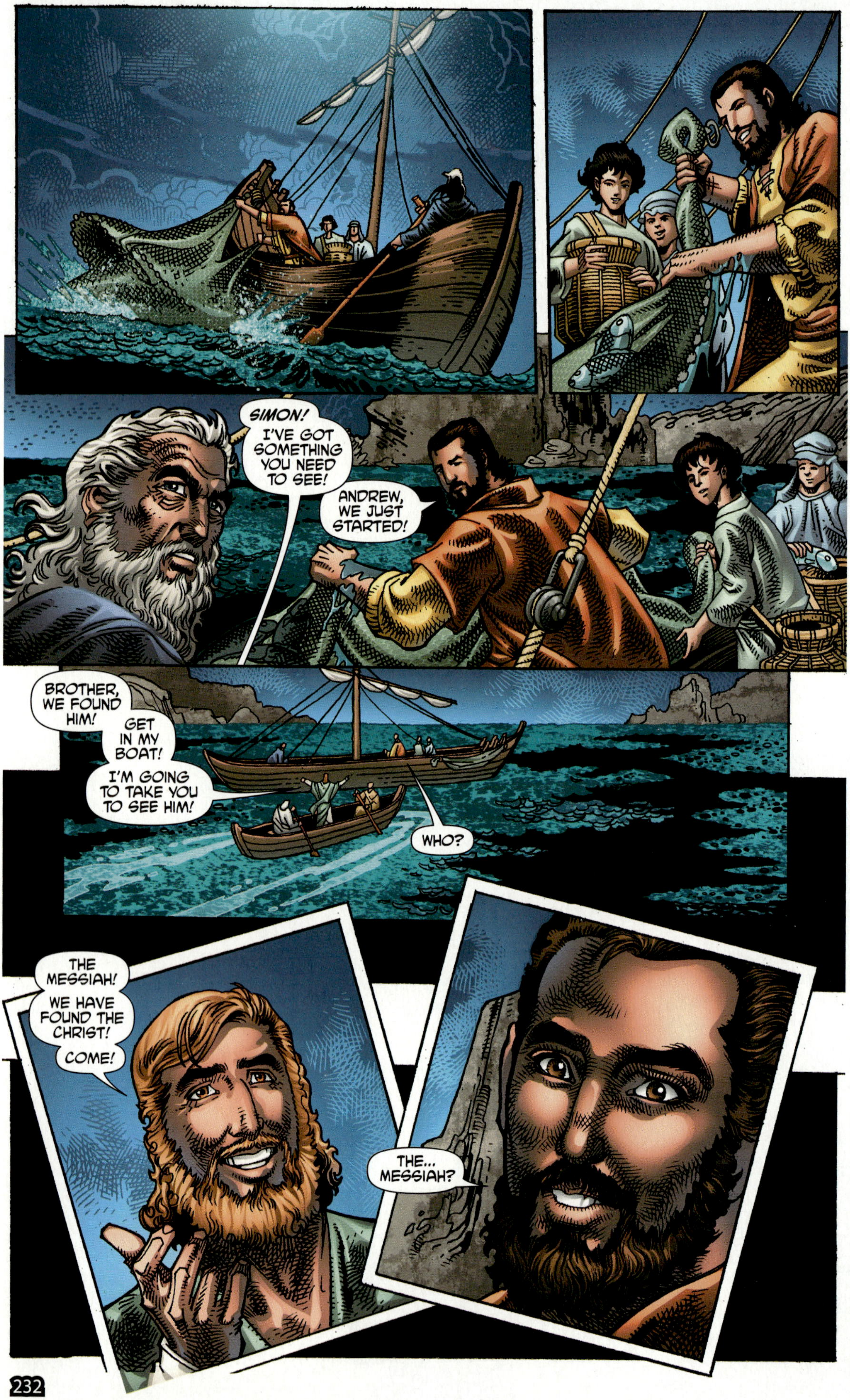
SIMON!
I'VE GOT SOMETHING YOU NEED TO SEE!
ANDREW, WE JUST STARTED!
BROTHER, WE FOUND HIM!
GET IN MY BOAT!
I'M GOING TO TAKE YOU TO SEE HIM!
WHO?
THE MESSIAH!
WE HAVE FOUND THE CHRIST!
COME!
THE... MESSIAH?

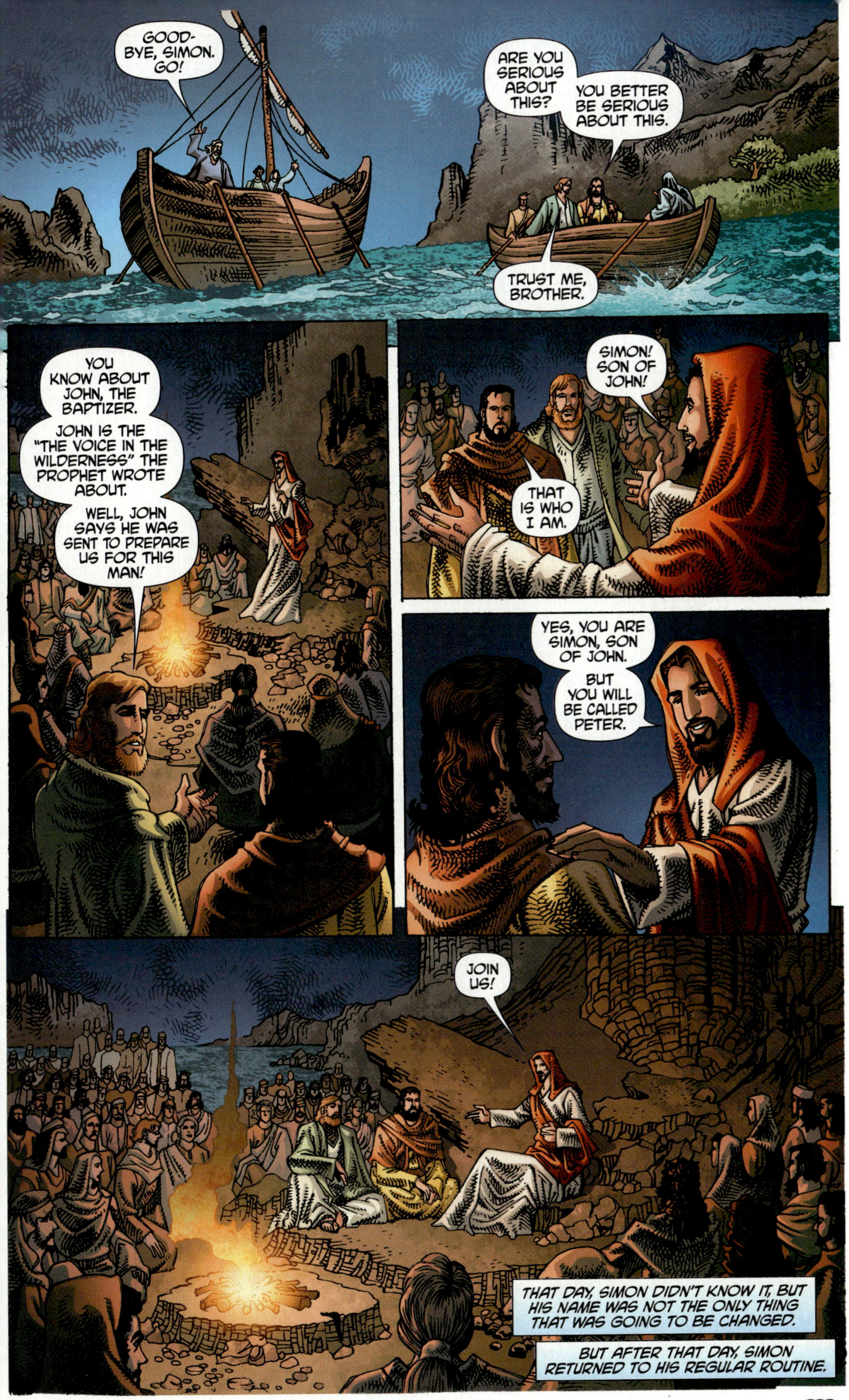
GOOD-BYE, SIMON. GO!
ARE YOU SERIOUS ABOUT THIS?
YOU BETTER BE SERIOUS ABOUT THIS.
TRUST ME, BROTHER.
YOU KNOW ABOUT JOHN, THE BAPTIZER.
JOHN IS THE "THE VOICE IN THE WILDERNESS" THE PROPHET WROTE ABOUT.
WELL, JOHN SAYS HE WAS SENT TO PREPARE US FOR THIS MAN!
SIMON! SON OF JOHN!
THAT IS WHO I AM.
YES, YOU ARE SIMON, SON OF JOHN.
BUT YOU WILL BE CALLED PETER.
JOIN US!
THAT DAY, SIMON DIDN'T KNOW IT, BUT HIS NAME WAS NOT THE ONLY THING THAT WAS GOING TO BE CHANGED.
BUT AFTER THAT DAY, SIMON RETURNED TO HIS REGULAR ROUTINE.

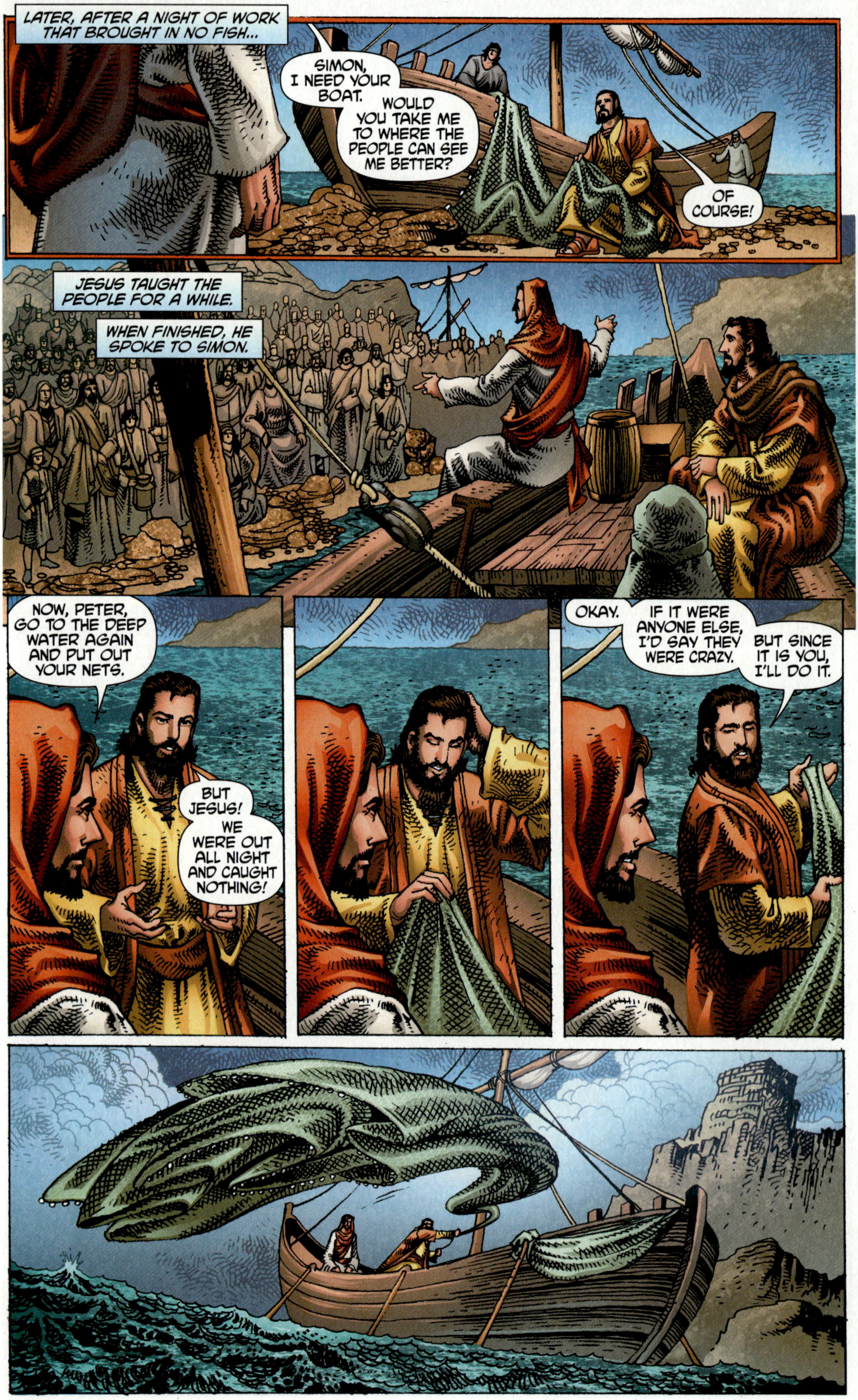
LATER, AFTER A NIGHT OF WORK THAT BROUGHT IN NO FISH...
SIMON, I NEED YOUR BOAT.
WOULD YOU TAKE ME TO WHERE THE PEOPLE CAN SEE ME BETTER?
OF COURSE!
JESUS TAUGHT THE PEOPLE FOR A WHILE.
WHEN FINISHED, HE SPOKE TO SIMON.
NOW, PETER, GO TO THE DEEP WATER AGAIN AND PUT OUT YOUR NETS.
BUT JESUS! WE WERE OUT ALL NIGHT AND CAUGHT NOTHING!
OKAY.
IF IT WERE ANYONE ELSE, I'D SAY THEY WERE CRAZY.
BUT SINCE IT IS YOU, I'LL DO IT.

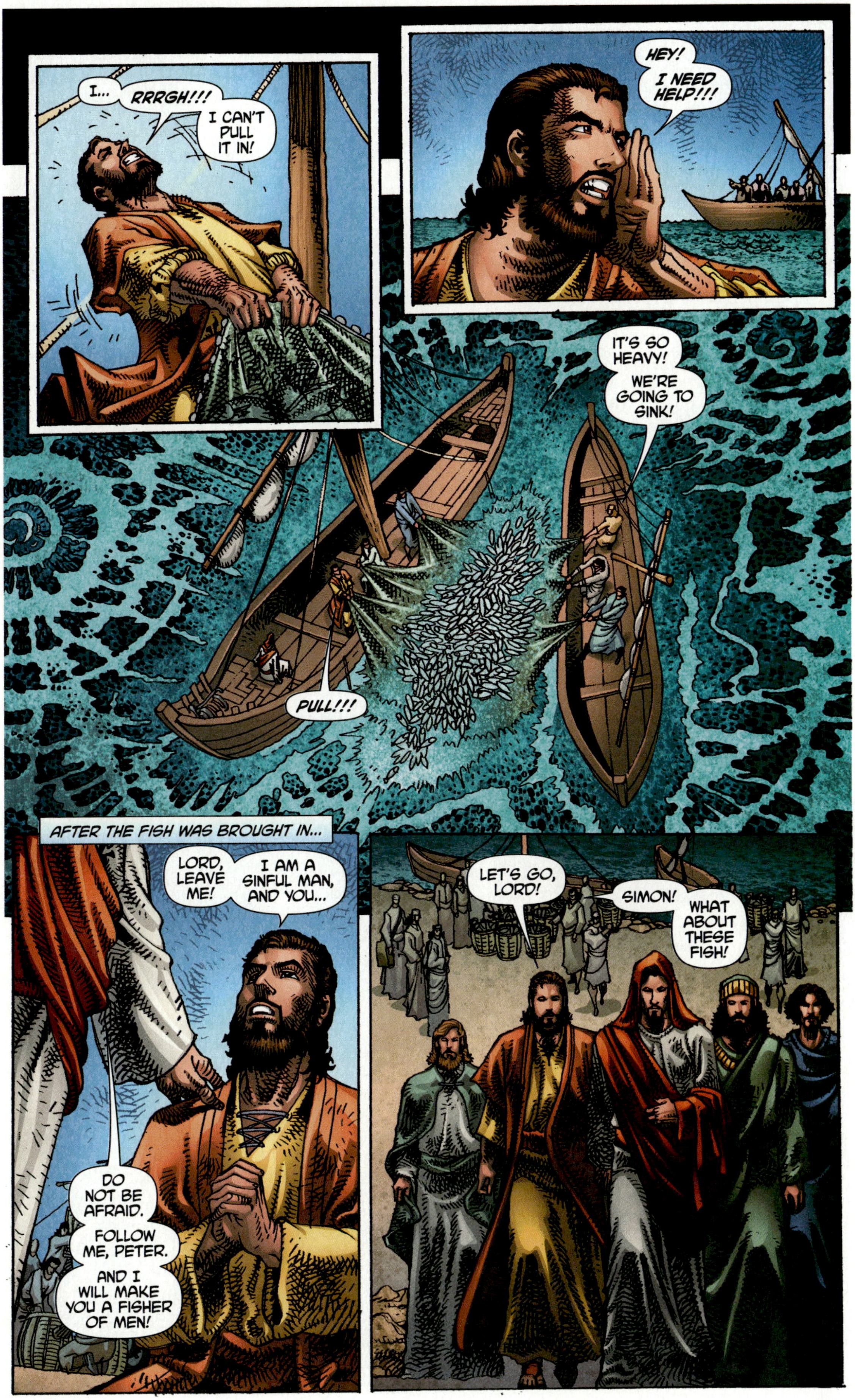
I...
RRRGH!!!
I CAN'T PULL IT IN!
HEY! I NEED HELP!!!
IT'S SO HEAVY!
WE'RE GOING TO SINK!
PULL!!!
AFTER THE FISH WAS BROUGHT IN...
LORD, LEAVE ME!
I AM A SINFUL MAN, AND YOU...
DO NOT BE AFRAID.
FOLLOW ME, PETER.
AND I WILL MAKE YOU A FISHER OF MEN!
LET'S GO, LORD!
SIMON!
WHAT ABOUT THESE FISH!

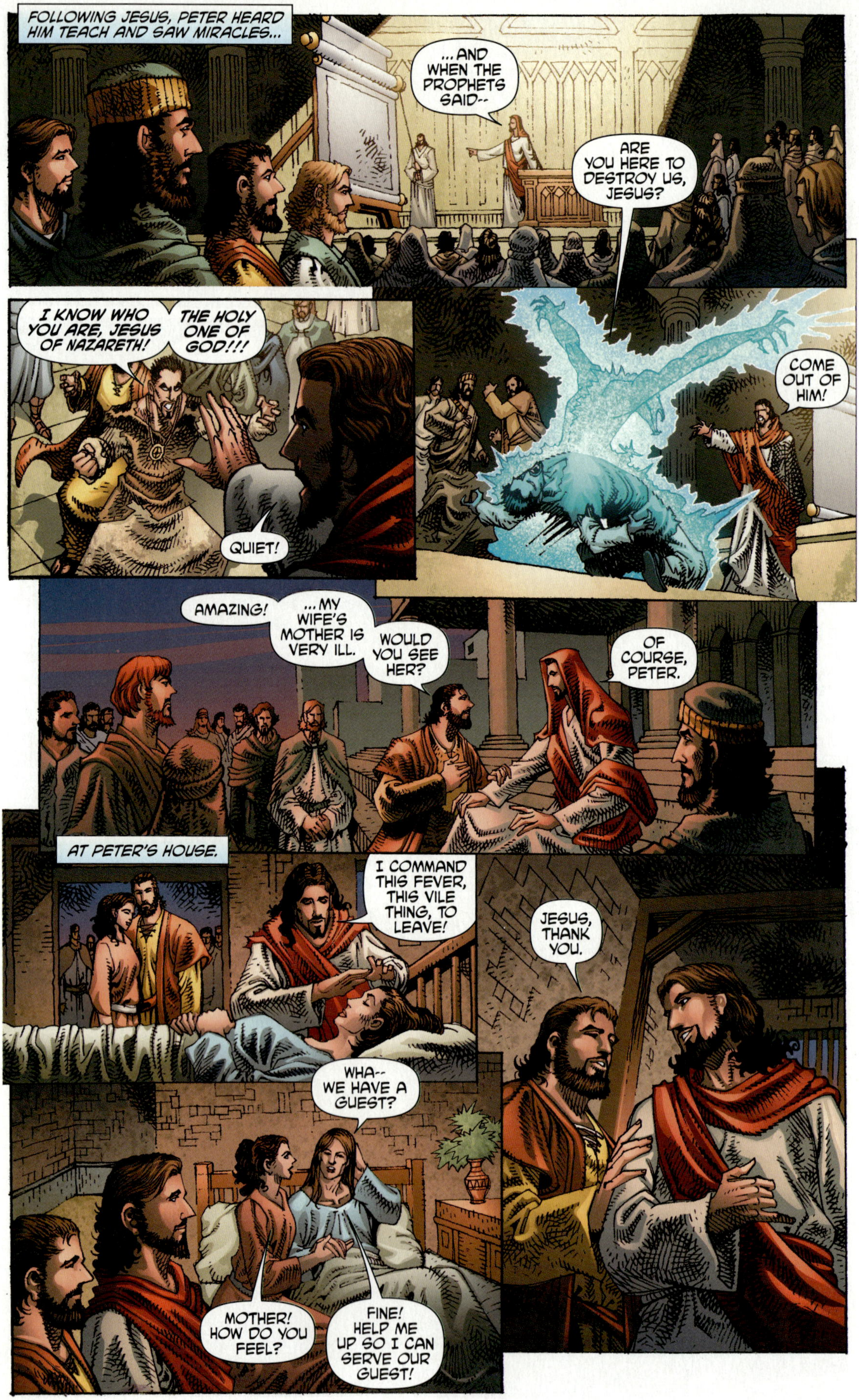
FOLLOWING JESUS, PETER HEARD HIM TEACH AND SAW MIRACLES...
...AND WHEN THE PROPHETS SAID--
ARE YOU HERE TO DESTROY US, JESUS?
I KNOW WHO YOU ARE, JESUS OF NAZARETH!
THE HOLY ONE OF GOD!!!
QUIET!
COME OUT OF HIM!
AMAZING!
...MY WIFE'S MOTHER IS VERY ILL.
WOULD YOU SEE HER?
OF COURSE, PETER.
AT PETER'S HOUSE.
I COMMAND THIS FEVER, THIS VILE THING, TO LEAVE!
WHA-- WE HAVE A GUEST?
MOTHER! HOW DO YOU FEEL?
FINE! HELP ME UP SO I CAN SERVE OUR GUEST!
JESUS, THANK YOU.

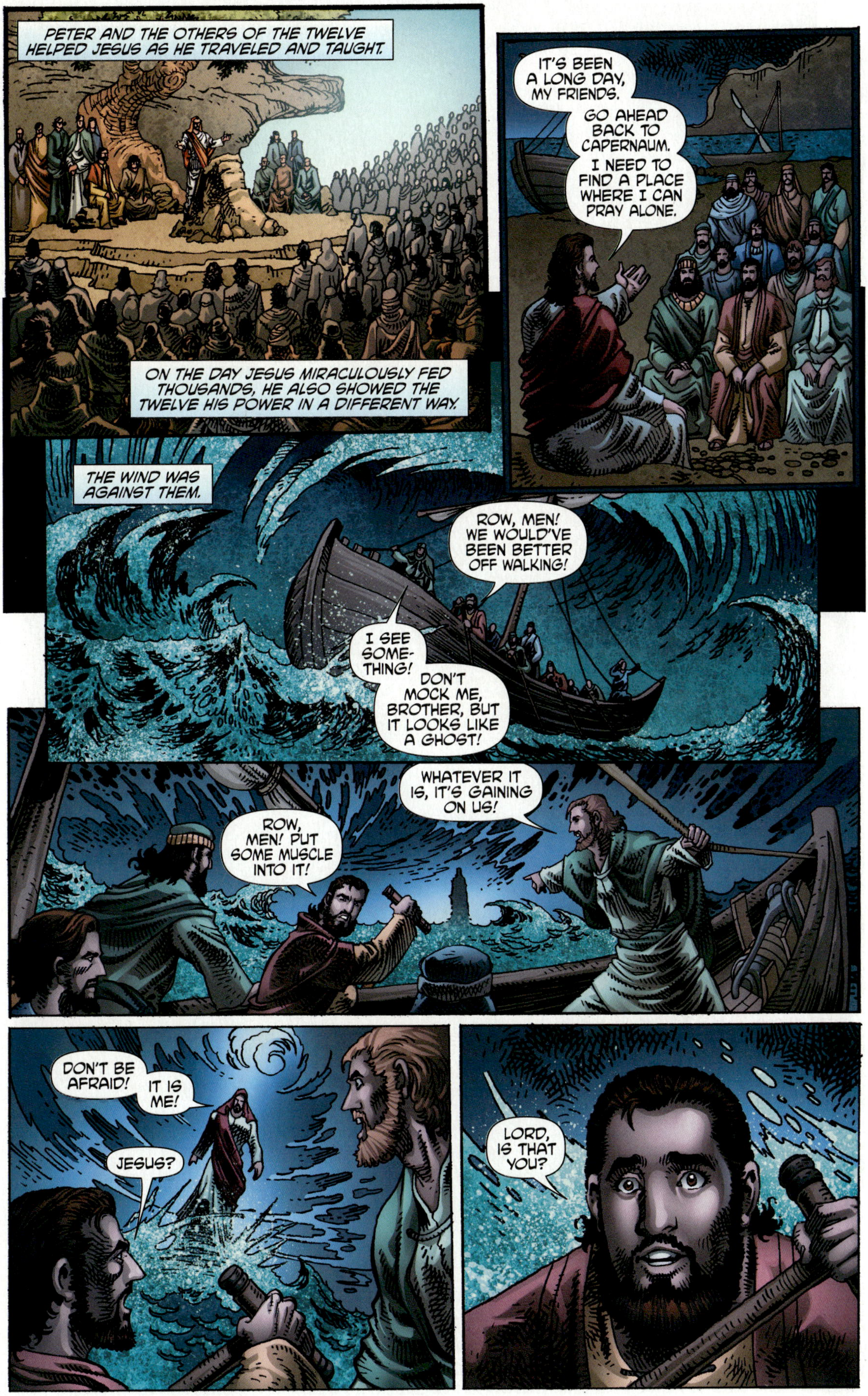

PETER AND THE OTHERS OF THE TWELVE HELPED JESUS AS HE TRAVELED AND TAUGHT.
ON THE DAY JESUS MIRACULOUSLY FED THOUSANDS, HE ALSO SHOWED THE TWELVE HIS POWER IN A DIFFERENT WAY.
IT'S BEEN A LONG DAY, MY FRIENDS.
GO AHEAD BACK TO CAPERNAUM.
I NEED TO FIND A PLACE WHERE I CAN PRAY ALONE.
THE WIND WAS AGAINST THEM.
ROW, MEN! WE WOULD'VE BEEN BETTER OFF WALKING!
I SEE SOME-THING!
DON'T MOCK ME, BROTHER, BUT IT LOOKS LIKE A GHOST!
ROW, MEN! PUT SOME MUSCLE INTO IT!
WHATEVER IT IS, IT'S GAINING ON US!
DON'T BE AFRAID!
IT IS ME!
JESUS?
LORD, IS THAT YOU?

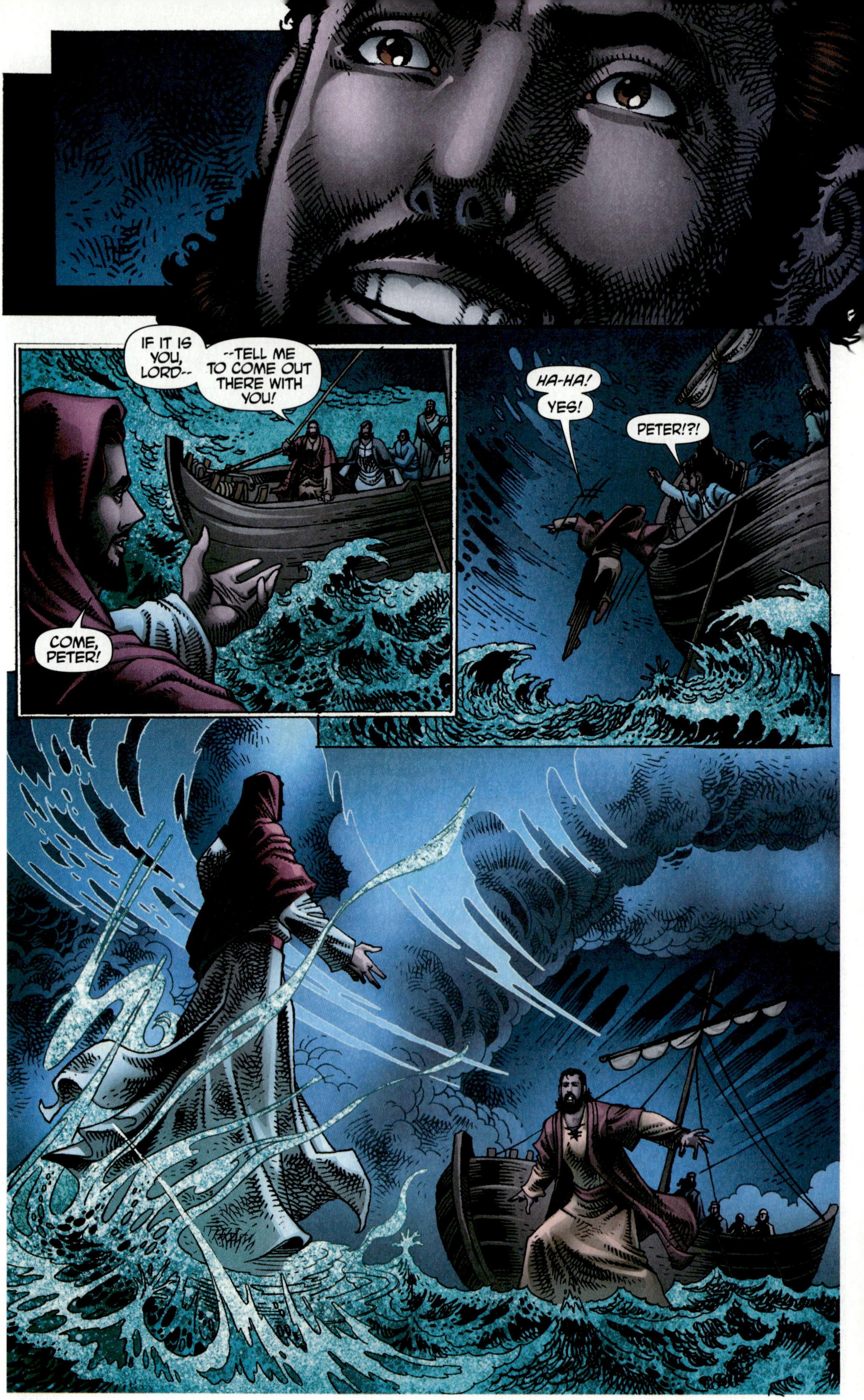
IF IT IS YOU, LORD--
--TELL ME TO COME OUT THERE WITH YOU!
COME, PETER!
HA-HA! YES!
PETER!?!

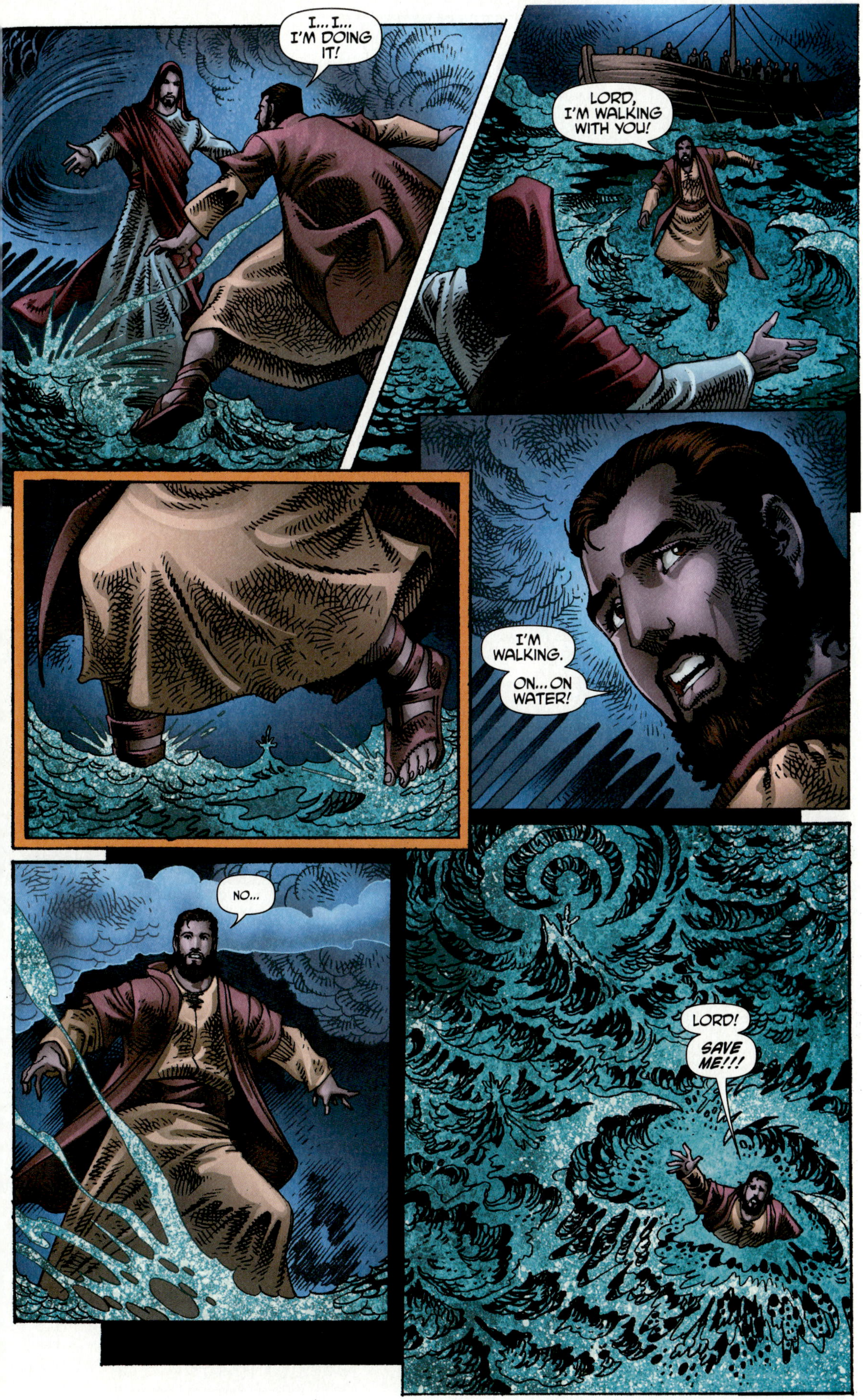
I... I... I'M DOING IT!
LORD, I'M WALKING WITH YOU!
I'M WALKING.
ON... ON WATER!
NO...
LORD!
SAVE ME!!!

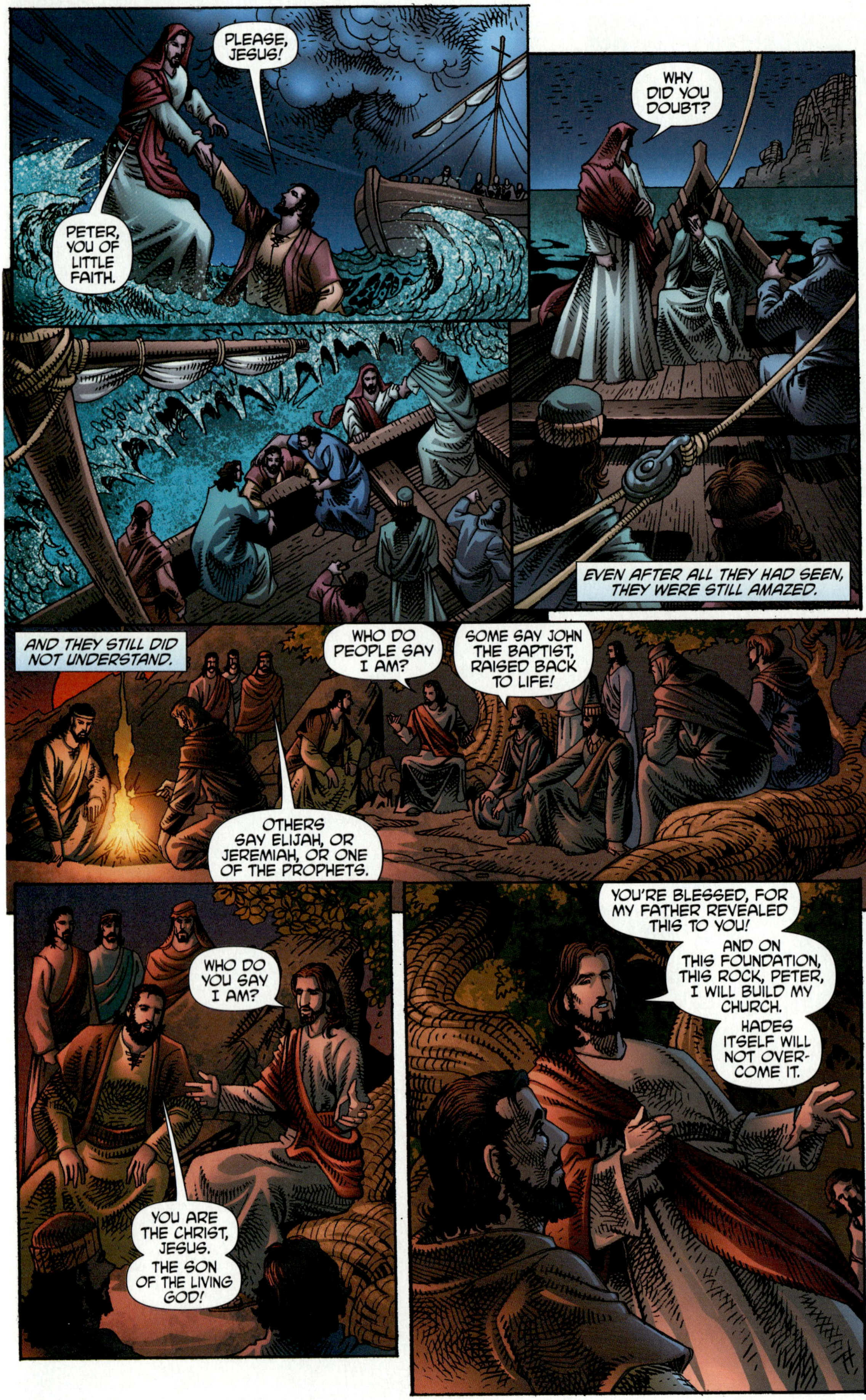
PLEASE, JESUS!
PETER, YOU OF LITTLE FAITH.
WHY DID YOU DOUBT?
EVEN AFTER ALL THEY HAD SEEN, THEY WERE STILL AMAZED.
AND THEY STILL DID NOT UNDERSTAND.
WHO DO PEOPLE SAY I AM?
SOME SAY JOHN THE BAPTIST, RAISED BACK TO LIFE!
OTHERS SAY ELIJAH, OR JEREMIAH, OR ONE OF THE PROPHETS.
WHO DO YOU SAY I AM?
YOU ARE THE CHRIST, JESUS.
THE SON OF THE LIVING GOD!
YOU'RE BLESSED, FOR MY FATHER REVEALED THIS TO YOU!
AND ON THIS FOUNDATION, THIS ROCK, PETER, I WILL BUILD MY CHURCH.
HADES ITSELF WILL NOT OVER-COME IT.

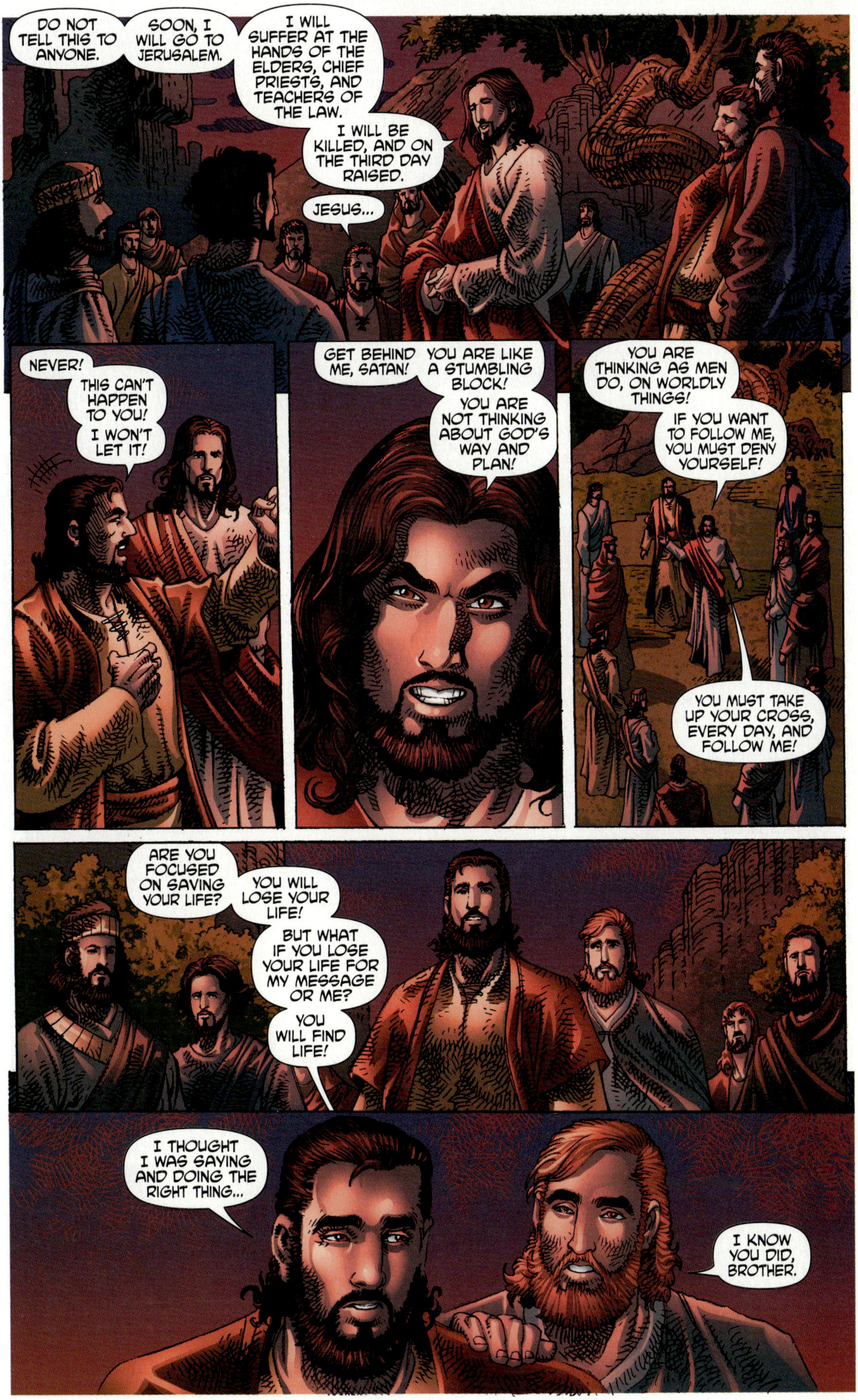
DO NOT TELL THIS TO ANYONE.
SOON, I WILL GO TO JERUSALEM.
I WILL SUFFER AT THE HANDS OF THE ELDERS, CHIEF PRIESTS, AND TEACHERS OF THE LAW.
I WILL BE KILLED, AND ON THE THIRD DAY RAISED.
JESUS...
NEVER!
THIS CAN'T HAPPEN TO YOU!
I WON'T LET IT!
GET BEHIND ME, SATAN!
YOU ARE LIKE A STUMBLING BLOCK!
YOU ARE NOT THINKING ABOUT GOD'S WAY AND PLAN!
YOU ARE THINKING AS MEN DO, ON WORLDLY THINGS!
IF YOU WANT TO FOLLOW ME, YOU MUST DENY YOURSELF!
YOU MUST TAKE UP YOUR CROSS, EVERY DAY, AND FOLLOW ME!
ARE YOU FOCUSED ON SAVING YOUR LIFE?
YOU WILL LOSE YOUR LIFE!
BUT WHAT IF YOU LOSE YOUR LIFE FOR MY MESSAGE OR ME?
YOU WILL FIND LIFE!
I THOUGHT I WAS SAYING AND DOING THE RIGHT THING...
I KNOW YOU DID, BROTHER.

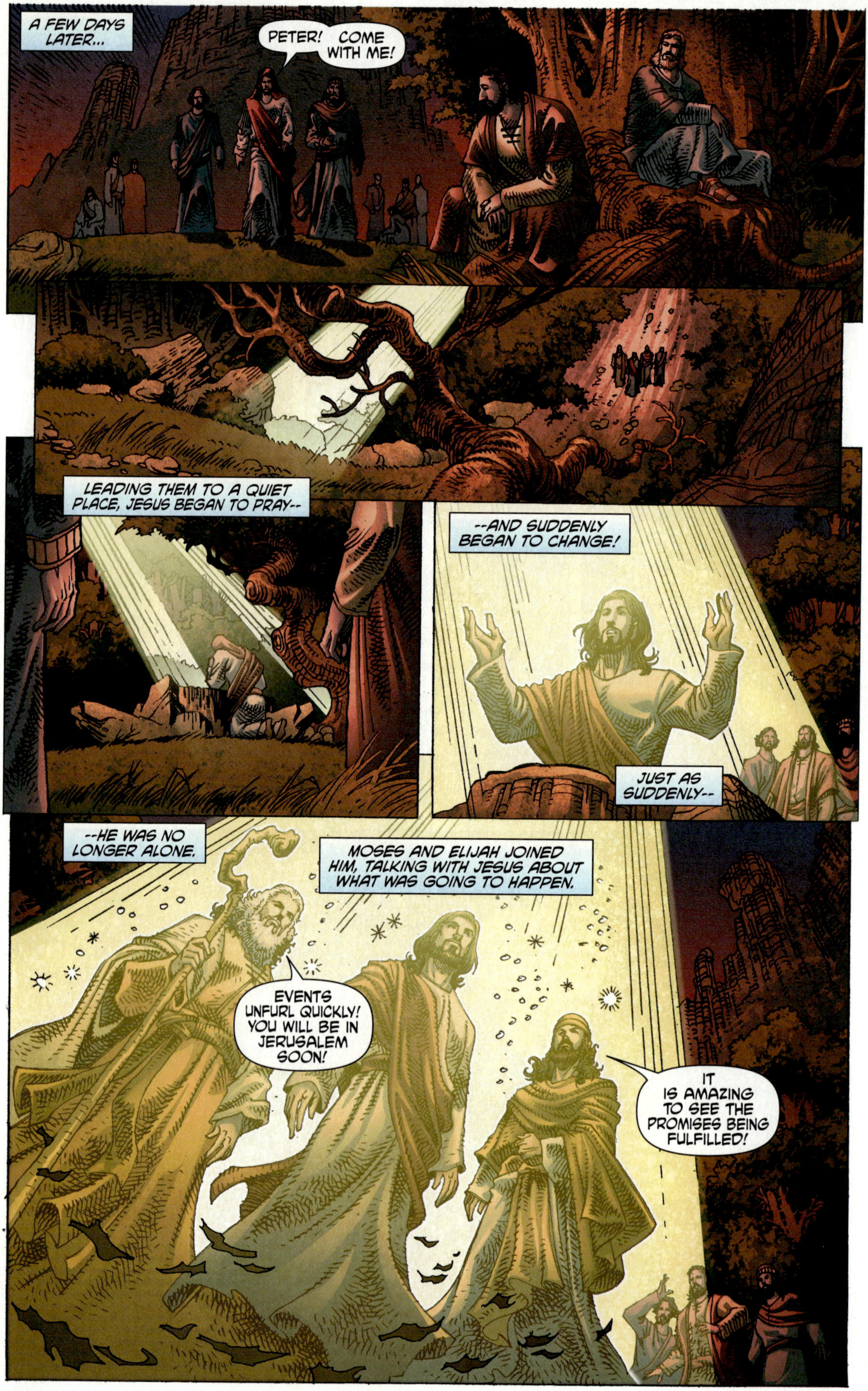
A FEW DAYS LATER...
PETER! COME WITH ME!
LEADING THEM TO A QUIET PLACE, JESUS BEGAN TO PRAY--
--AND SUDDENLY BEGAN TO CHANGE!
JUST AS SUDDENLY--
--HE WAS NO LONGER ALONE.
MOSES AND ELIJAH JOINED HIM, TALKING WITH JESUS ABOUT WHAT WAS GOING TO HAPPEN.
EVENTS UNFURL QUICKLY! YOU WILL BE IN JERUSALEM SOON!
IT IS AMAZING TO SEE THE PROMISES BEING FULFILLED!

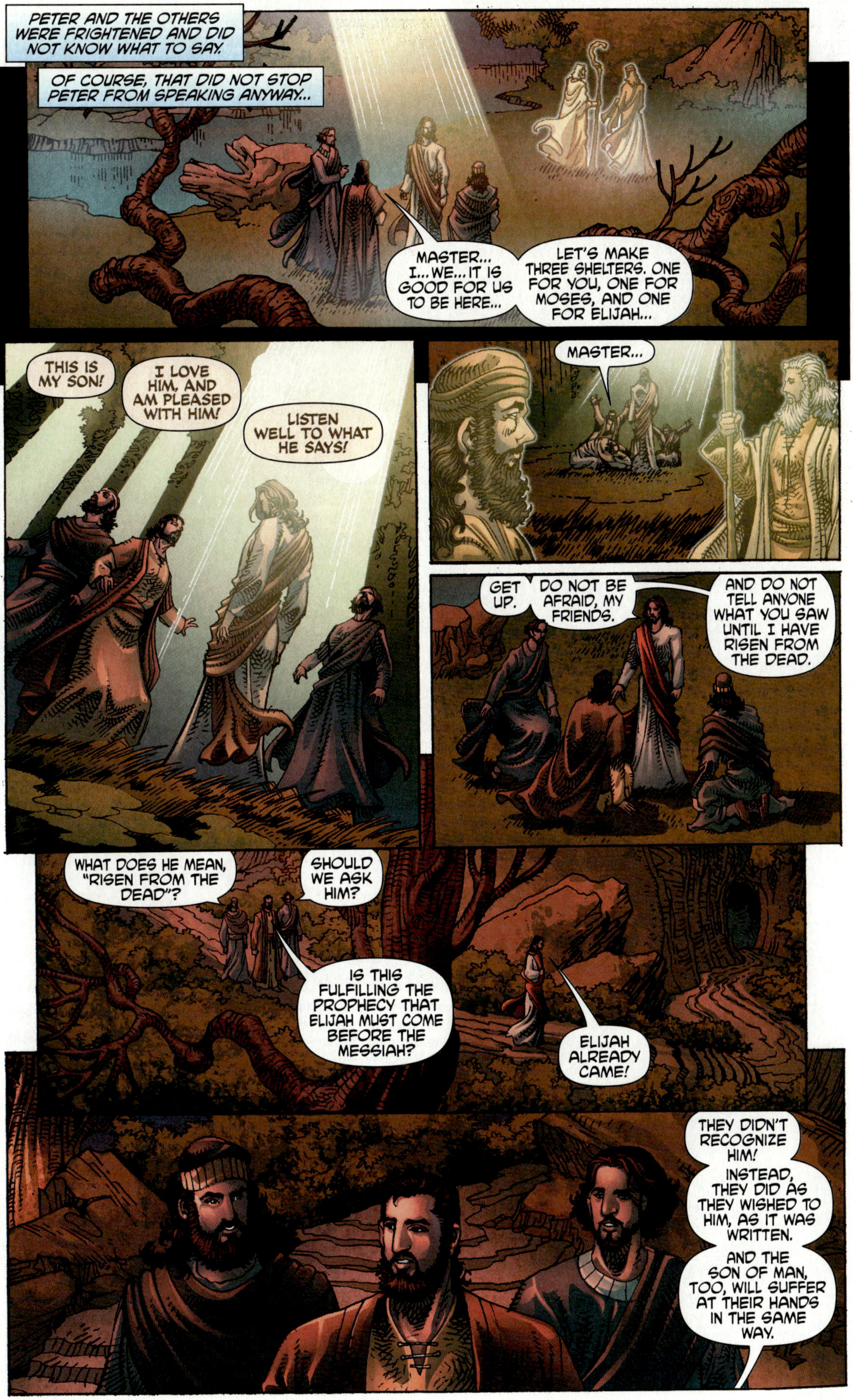
PETER AND THE OTHERS WERE FRIGHTENED AND DID NOT KNOW WHAT TO SAY.
OF COURSE, THAT DID NOT STOP PETER FROM SPEAKING ANYWAY...
MASTER... I...WE...IT IS GOOD FOR US TO BE HERE...
LET'S MAKE THREE SHELTERS. ONE FOR YOU, ONE FOR MOSES, AND ONE FOR ELIJAH...
THIS IS MY SON!
I LOVE HIM, AND AM PLEASED WITH HIM!
LISTEN WELL TO WHAT HE SAYS!
MASTER...
GET UP.
DO NOT BE AFRAID, MY FRIENDS.
AND DO NOT TELL ANYONE WHAT YOU SAW UNTIL I HAVE RISEN FROM THE DEAD.
WHAT DOES HE MEAN, "RISEN FROM THE DEAD"?
SHOULD WE ASK HIM?
IS THIS FULFILLING THE PROPHECY THAT ELIJAH MUST COME BEFORE THE MESSIAH?
ELIJAH ALREADY CAME!
THEY DIDN'T RECOGNIZE HIM!
INSTEAD, THEY DID AS THEY WISHED TO HIM, AS IT WAS WRITTEN.
AND THE SON OF MAN, TOO, WILL SUFFER AT THEIR HANDS IN THE SAME WAY.

...MY LOVE, SO GOOD TO SEE Y--

I COLLECT THE TEMPLE TAX. DOES YOUR RABBI PAY THAT TAX?

OF COURSE HE DOES!

HMMM. VERY WELL!

I...UH... I NEED TO TALK TO JESUS...

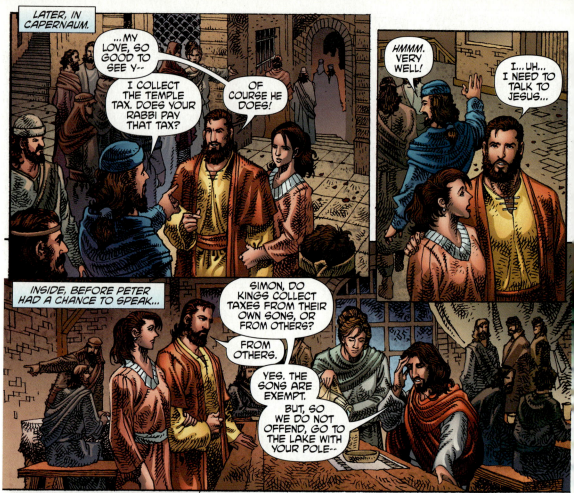

INSIDE, BEFORE PETER HAD A CHANCE TO SPEAK...

SIMON, DO KINGS COLLECT TAXES FROM THEIR OWN SONS, OR FROM OTHERS?

FROM OTHERS.

YES. THE SONS ARE EXEMPT.

BUT, SO WE DO NOT OFFEND, GO TO THE LAKE WITH YOUR POLE--

"--AND CAST YOUR LINE.

"TAKE THE FIRST FISH YOU CATCH.

"OPEN ITS MOUTH. INSIDE, YOU WILL FIND--

"--A FOUR DRACHMA COIN.

"TAKE IT AND PAY MY TEMPLE TAX AND YOURS."

JUST AS HE SAID...

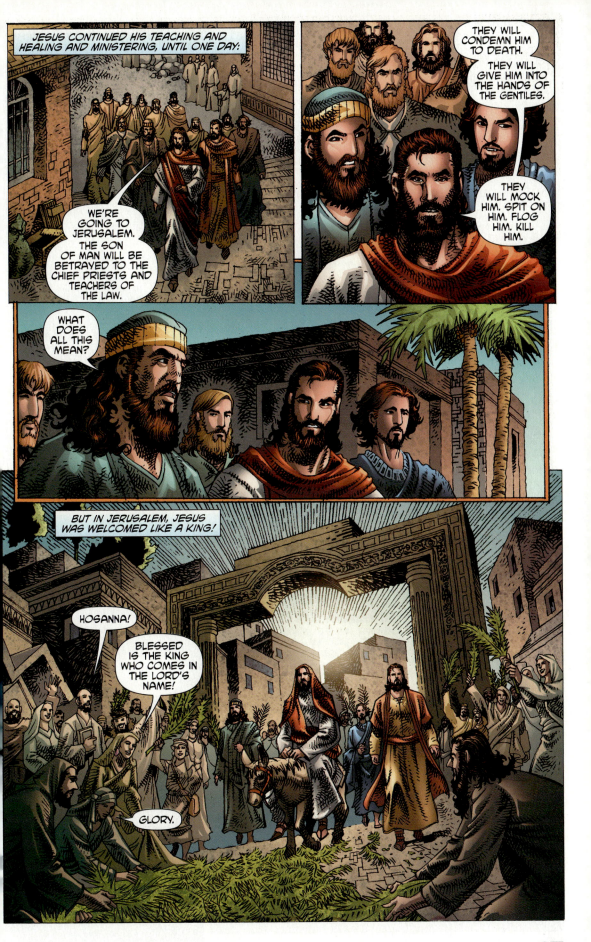

JESUS CONTINUED HIS TEACHING AND HEALING AND MINISTERING, UNTIL ONE DAY:

WE'RE GOING TO JERUSALEM. THE SON OF MAN WILL BE BETRAYED TO THE CHIEF PRIESTS AND TEACHERS OF THE LAW.

THEY WILL CONDEMN HIM TO DEATH.

THEY WILL GIVE HIM INTO THE HANDS OF THE GENTILES.

THEY WILL MOCK HIM. SPIT ON HIM. FLOG HIM. KILL HIM.

WHAT DOES ALL THIS MEAN?

BUT IN JERUSALEM, JESUS WAS WELCOMED LIKE A KING!

HOSANNA!

BLESSED IS THE KING WHO COMES IN THE LORD'S NAME!

GLORY.

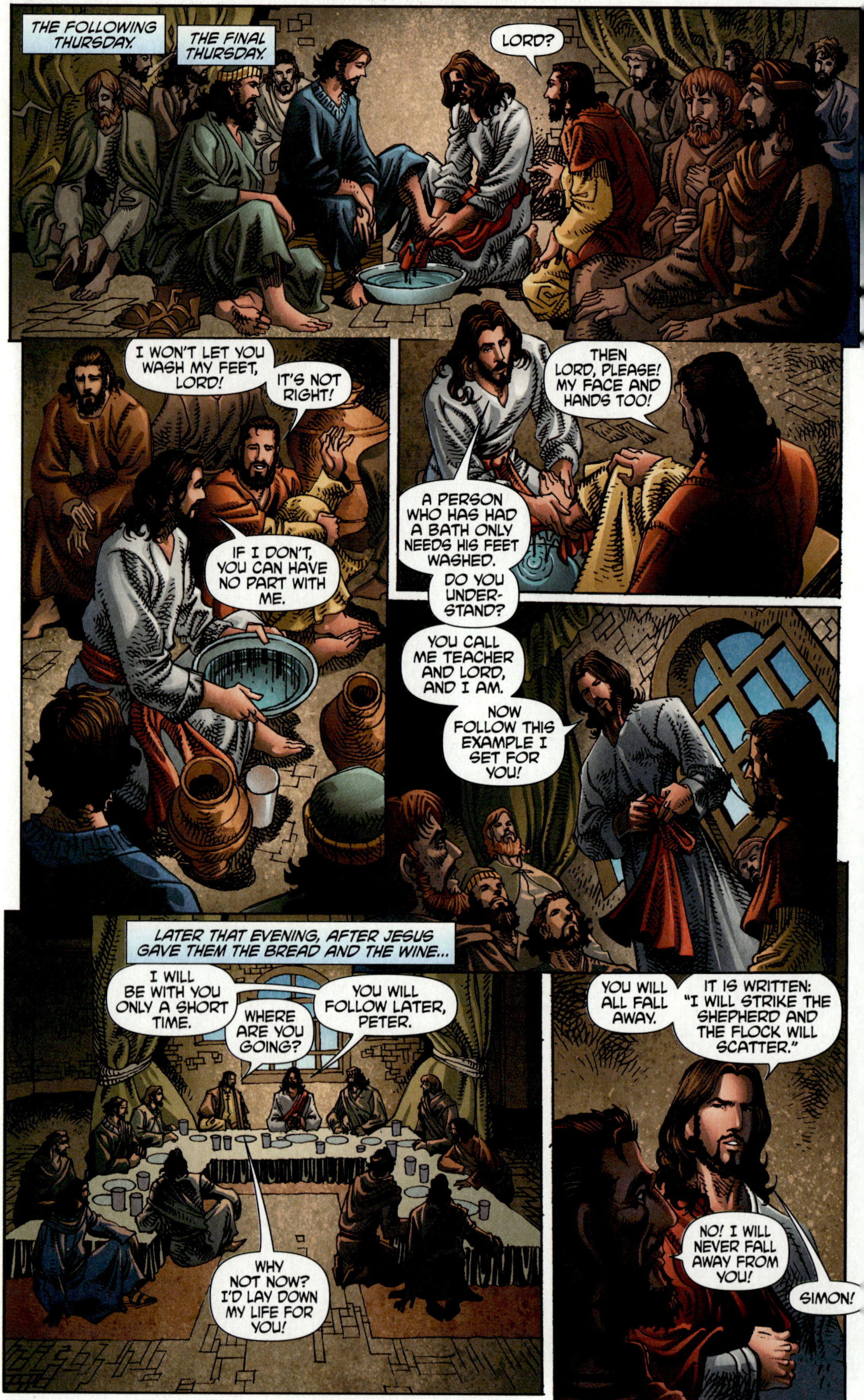

THE FOLLOWING THURSDAY.
THE FINAL THURSDAY.
LORD?
I WON'T LET YOU WASH MY FEET, LORD!
IT'S NOT RIGHT!
IF I DON'T, YOU CAN HAVE NO PART WITH ME.
THEN LORD, PLEASE! MY FACE AND HANDS TOO!
A PERSON WHO HAS HAD A BATH ONLY NEEDS HIS FEET WASHED.
DO YOU UNDER-STAND?
YOU CALL ME TEACHER AND LORD, AND I AM.
NOW FOLLOW THIS EXAMPLE I SET FOR YOU!
LATER THAT EVENING, AFTER JESUS GAVE THEM THE BREAD AND THE WINE...
I WILL BE WITH YOU ONLY A SHORT TIME.
WHERE ARE YOU GOING?
YOU WILL FOLLOW LATER, PETER.
WHY NOT NOW? I'D LAY DOWN MY LIFE FOR YOU!
YOU WILL ALL FALL AWAY.
IT IS WRITTEN: "I WILL STRIKE THE SHEPHERD AND THE FLOCK WILL SCATTER."
NO! I WILL NEVER FALL AWAY FROM YOU!
SIMON!

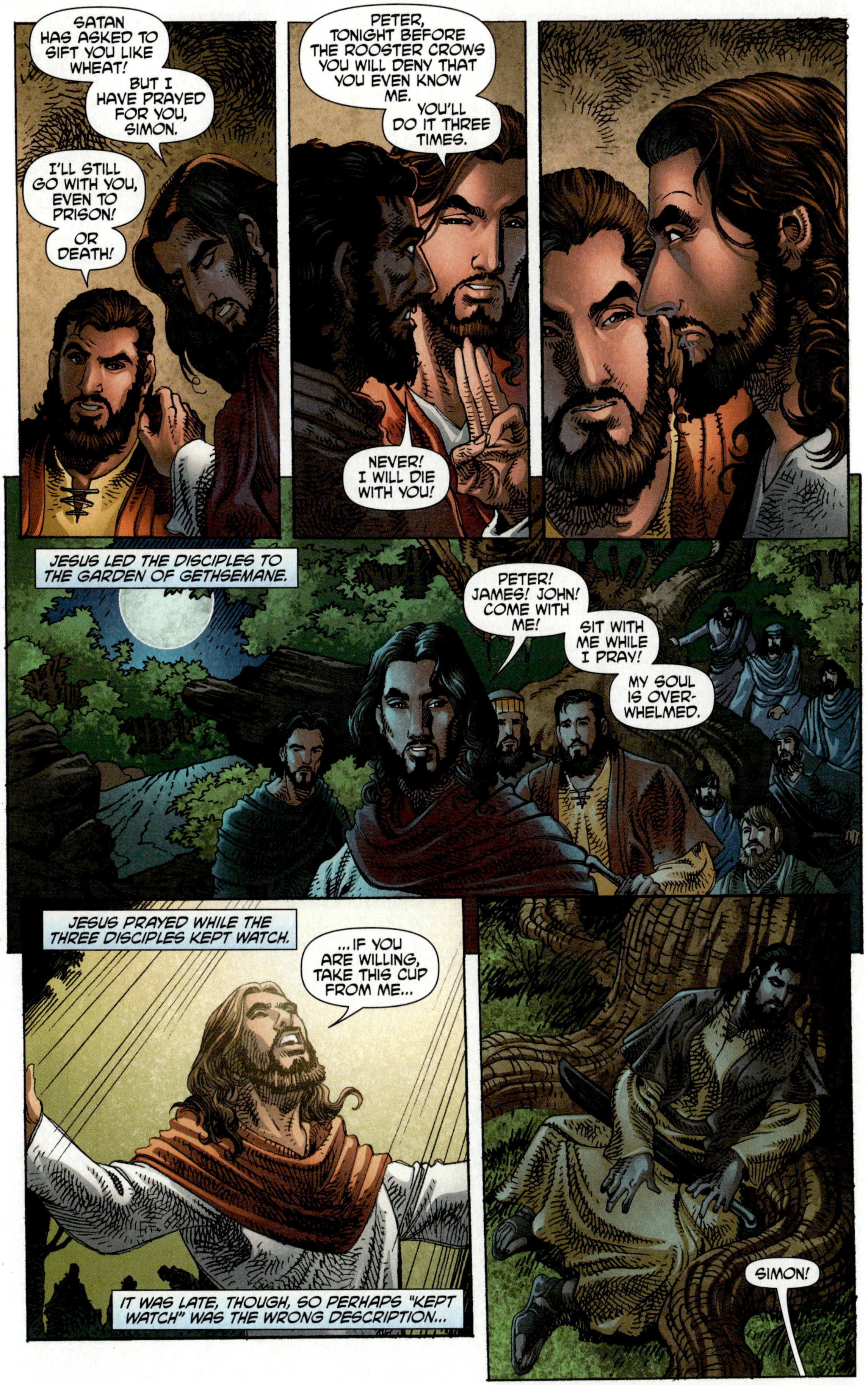
SATAN HAS ASKED TO SIFT YOU LIKE WHEAT!
BUT I HAVE PRAYED FOR YOU, SIMON.
I'LL STILL GO WITH YOU, EVEN TO PRISON!
OR DEATH!
PETER, TONIGHT BEFORE THE ROOSTER CROWS YOU WILL DENY THAT YOU EVEN KNOW ME.
YOU'LL DO IT THREE TIMES.
NEVER! I WILL DIE WITH YOU!
JESUS LED THE DISCIPLES TO THE GARDEN OF GETHSEMANE.
PETER! JAMES! JOHN! COME WITH ME!
SIT WITH ME WHILE I PRAY!
MY SOUL IS OVER-WHELMED.
JESUS PRAYED WHILE THE THREE DISCIPLES KEPT WATCH.
...IF YOU ARE WILLING, TAKE THIS CUP FROM ME...
IT WAS LATE, THOUGH, SO PERHAPS "KEPT WATCH" WAS THE WRONG DESCRIPTION...
SIMON!

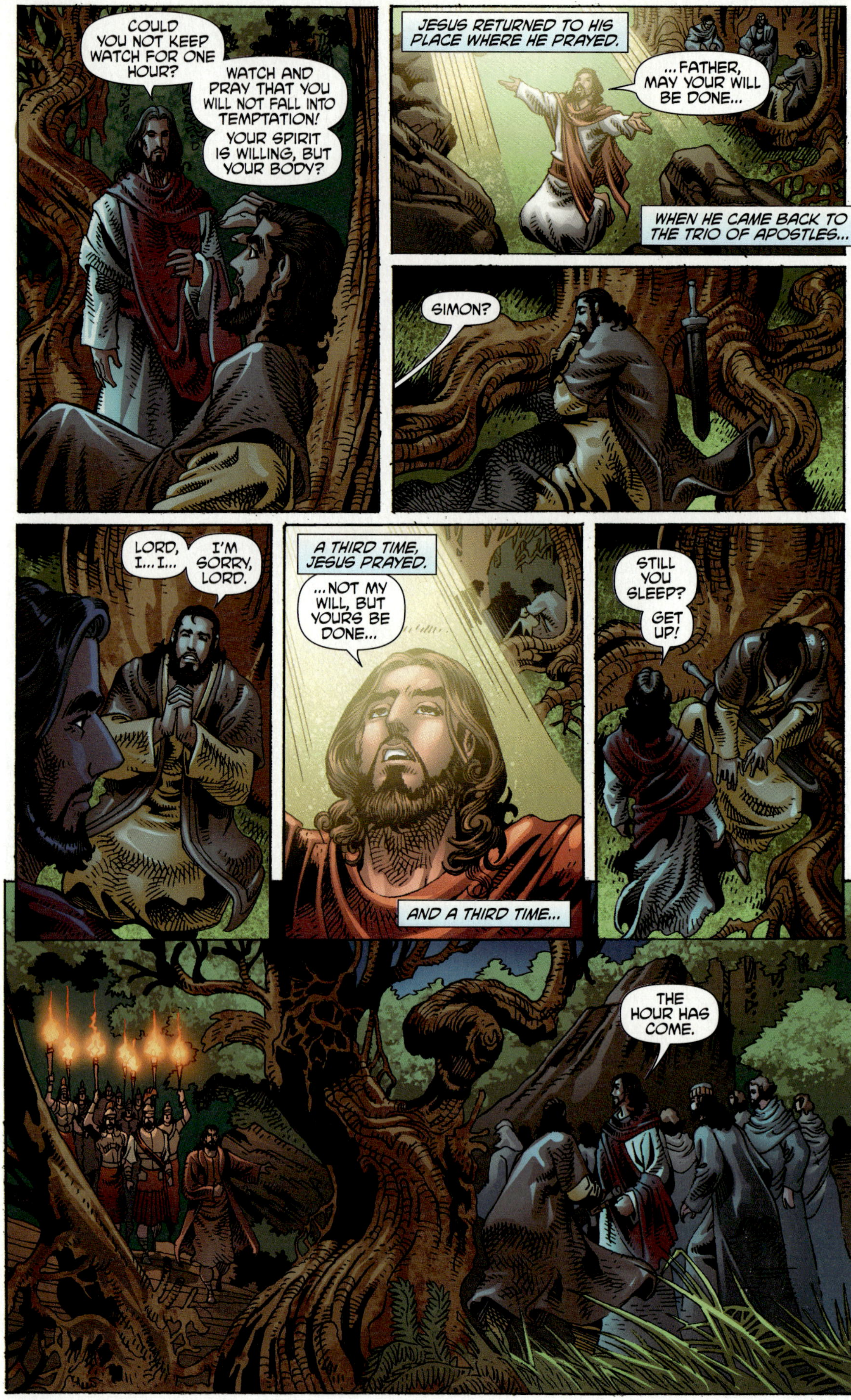
COULD YOU NOT KEEP WATCH FOR ONE HOUR?
WATCH AND PRAY THAT YOU WILL NOT FALL INTO TEMPTATION! YOUR SPIRIT IS WILLING, BUT YOUR BODY?
JESUS RETURNED TO HIS PLACE WHERE HE PRAYED.
...FATHER, MAY YOUR WILL BE DONE...
WHEN HE CAME BACK TO THE TRIO OF APOSTLES...
SIMON?
LORD, I...I...
I'M SORRY, LORD.
A THIRD TIME, JESUS PRAYED.
...NOT MY WILL, BUT YOURS BE DONE...
AND A THIRD TIME...
STILL YOU SLEEP?
GET UP!
THE HOUR HAS COME.

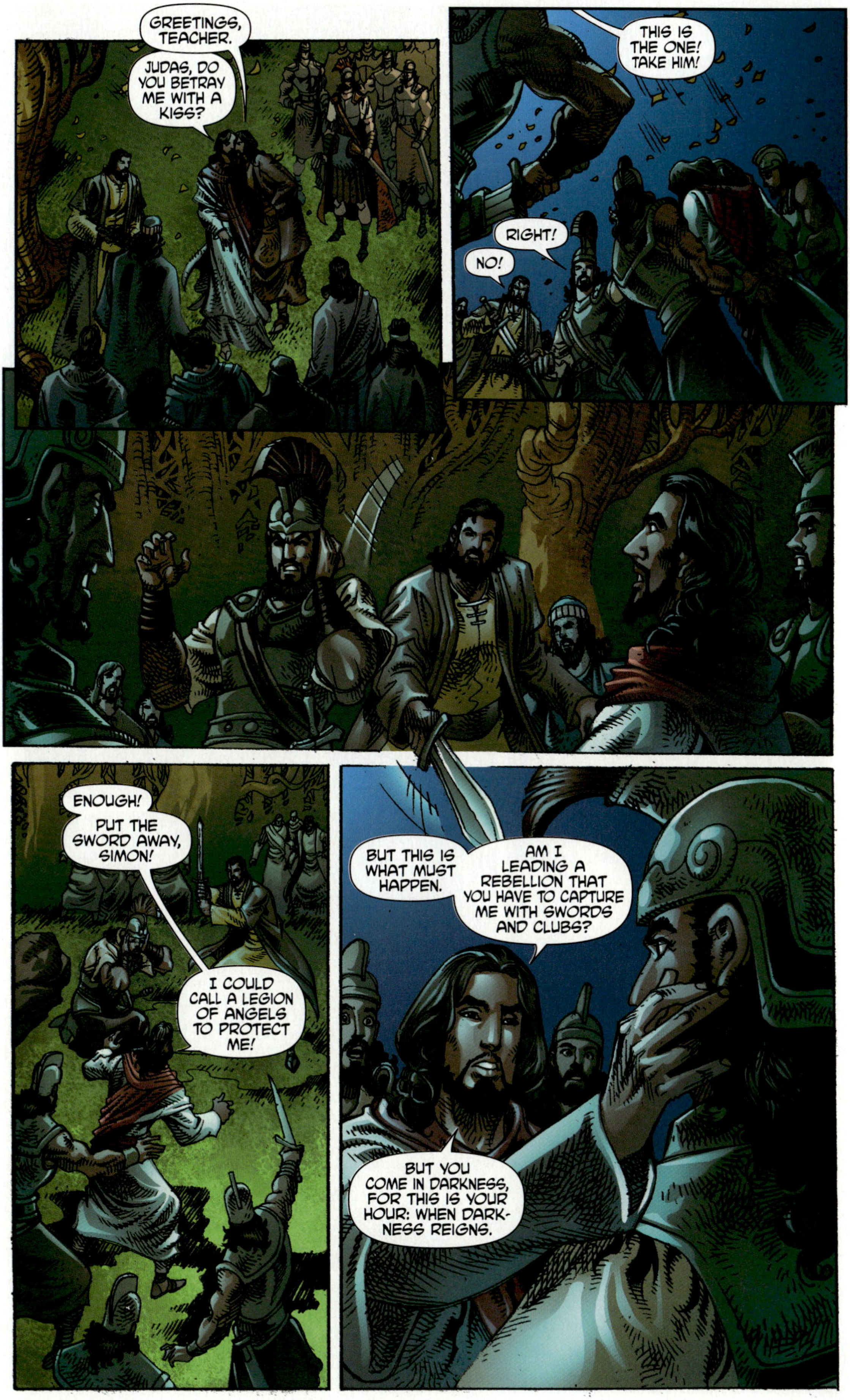
GREETINGS, TEACHER.
JUDAS, DO YOU BETRAY ME WITH A KISS?
THIS IS THE ONE! TAKE HIM!
RIGHT!
NO!
ENOUGH!
PUT THE SWORD AWAY, SIMON!
I COULD CALL A LEGION OF ANGELS TO PROTECT ME!
AM I LEADING A REBELLION THAT YOU HAVE TO CAPTURE ME WITH SWORDS AND CLUBS?
BUT THIS IS WHAT MUST HAPPEN.
BUT YOU COME IN DARKNESS, FOR THIS IS YOUR HOUR: WHEN DARKNESS REIGNS.

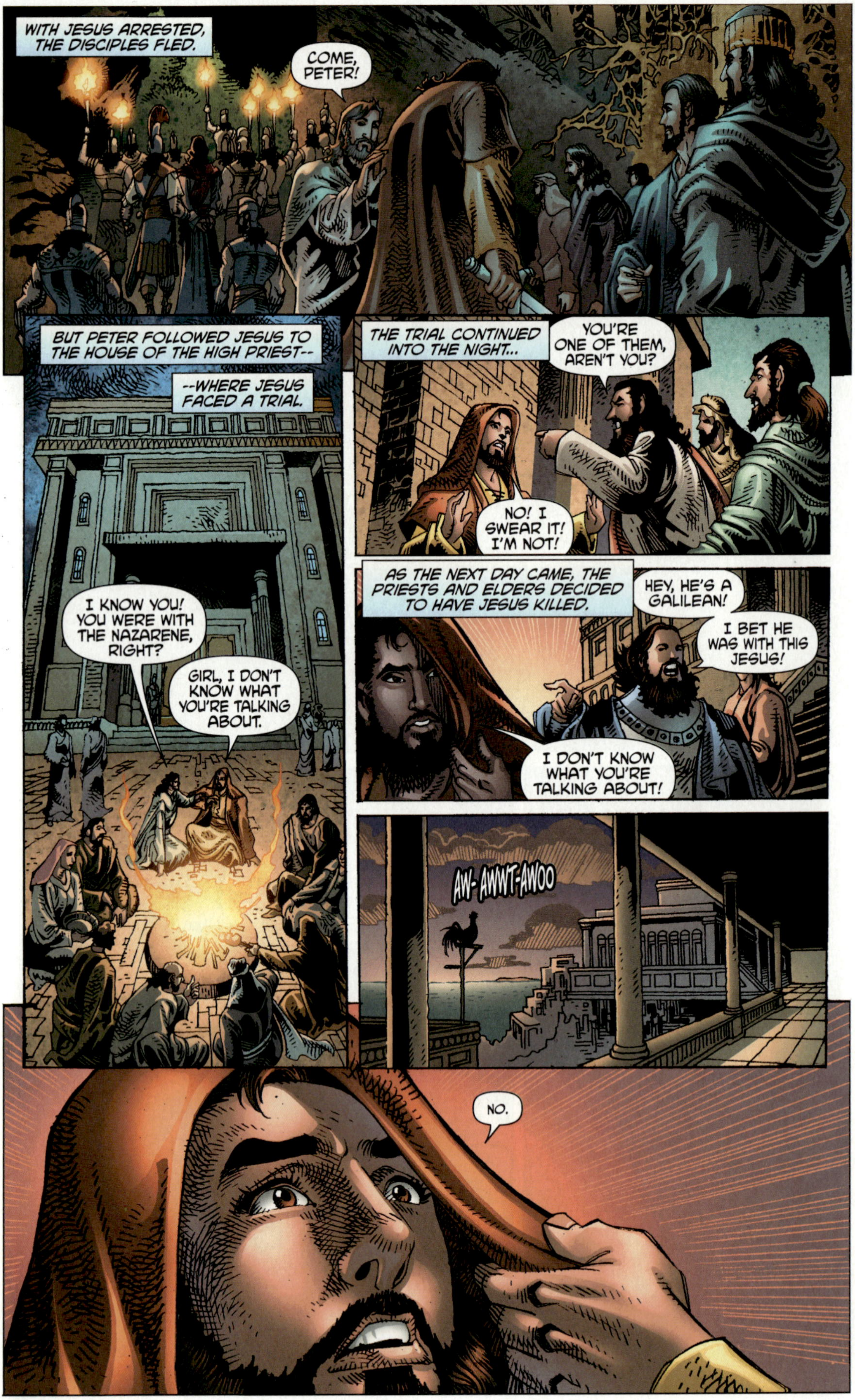

WITH JESUS ARRESTED, THE DISCIPLES FLED.
COME, PETER!
BUT PETER FOLLOWED JESUS TO THE HOUSE OF THE HIGH PRIEST--
--WHERE JESUS FACED A TRIAL.
I KNOW YOU! YOU WERE WITH THE NAZARENE, RIGHT?
GIRL, I DON'T KNOW WHAT YOU'RE TALKING ABOUT.
THE TRIAL CONTINUED INTO THE NIGHT...
YOU'RE ONE OF THEM, AREN'T YOU?
NO! I SWEAR IT! I'M NOT!
AS THE NEXT DAY CAME, THE PRIESTS AND ELDERS DECIDED TO HAVE JESUS KILLED.
HEY, HE'S A GALILEAN!
I BET HE WAS WITH THIS JESUS!
I DON'T KNOW WHAT YOU'RE TALKING ABOUT!
AW- AWWT-AWOO
NO.

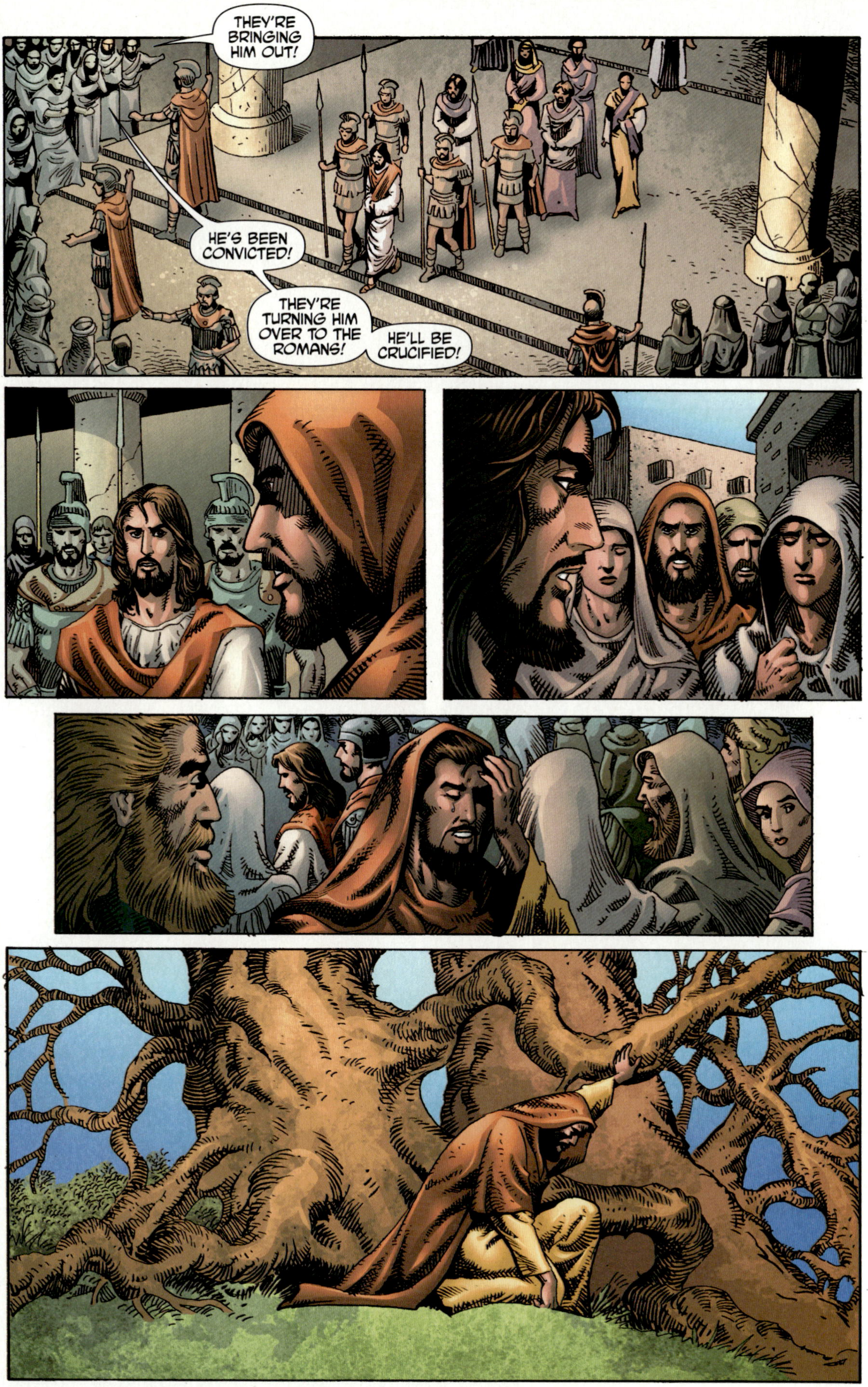
THEY'RE BRINGING HIM OUT!
HE'S BEEN CONVICTED!
THEY'RE TURNING HIM OVER TO THE ROMANS!
HE'LL BE CRUCIFIED!

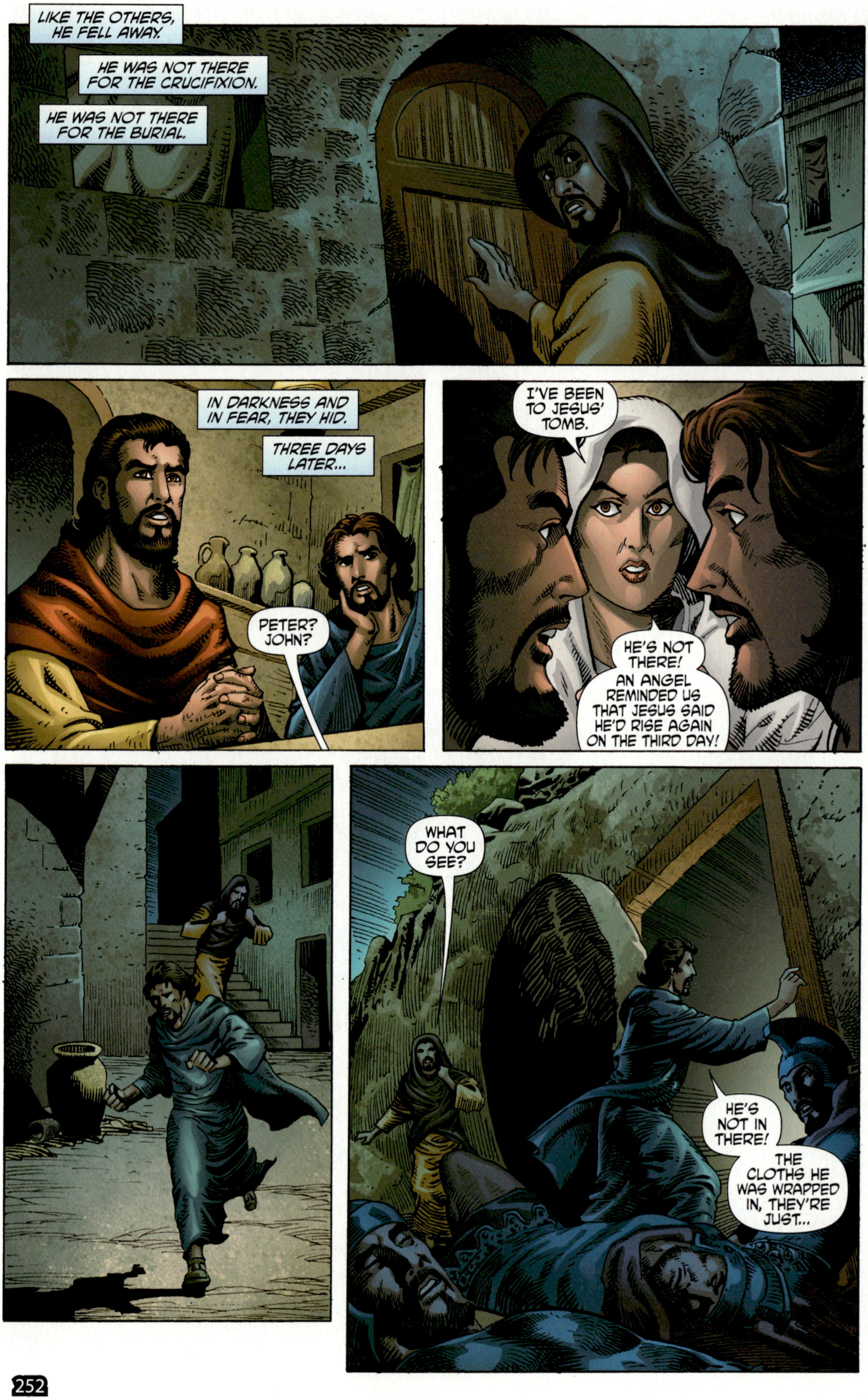
LIKE THE OTHERS, HE FELL AWAY.
HE WAS NOT THERE FOR THE CRUCIFIXION.
HE WAS NOT THERE FOR THE BURIAL.
IN DARKNESS AND IN FEAR, THEY HID.
THREE DAYS LATER...
PETER? JOHN?
I'VE BEEN TO JESUS' TOMB.
HE'S NOT THERE!
AN ANGEL REMINDED US THAT JESUS SAID HE'D RISE AGAIN ON THE THIRD DAY!
WHAT DO YOU SEE?
HE'S NOT IN THERE!
THE CLOTHS HE WAS WRAPPED IN, THEY'RE JUST...

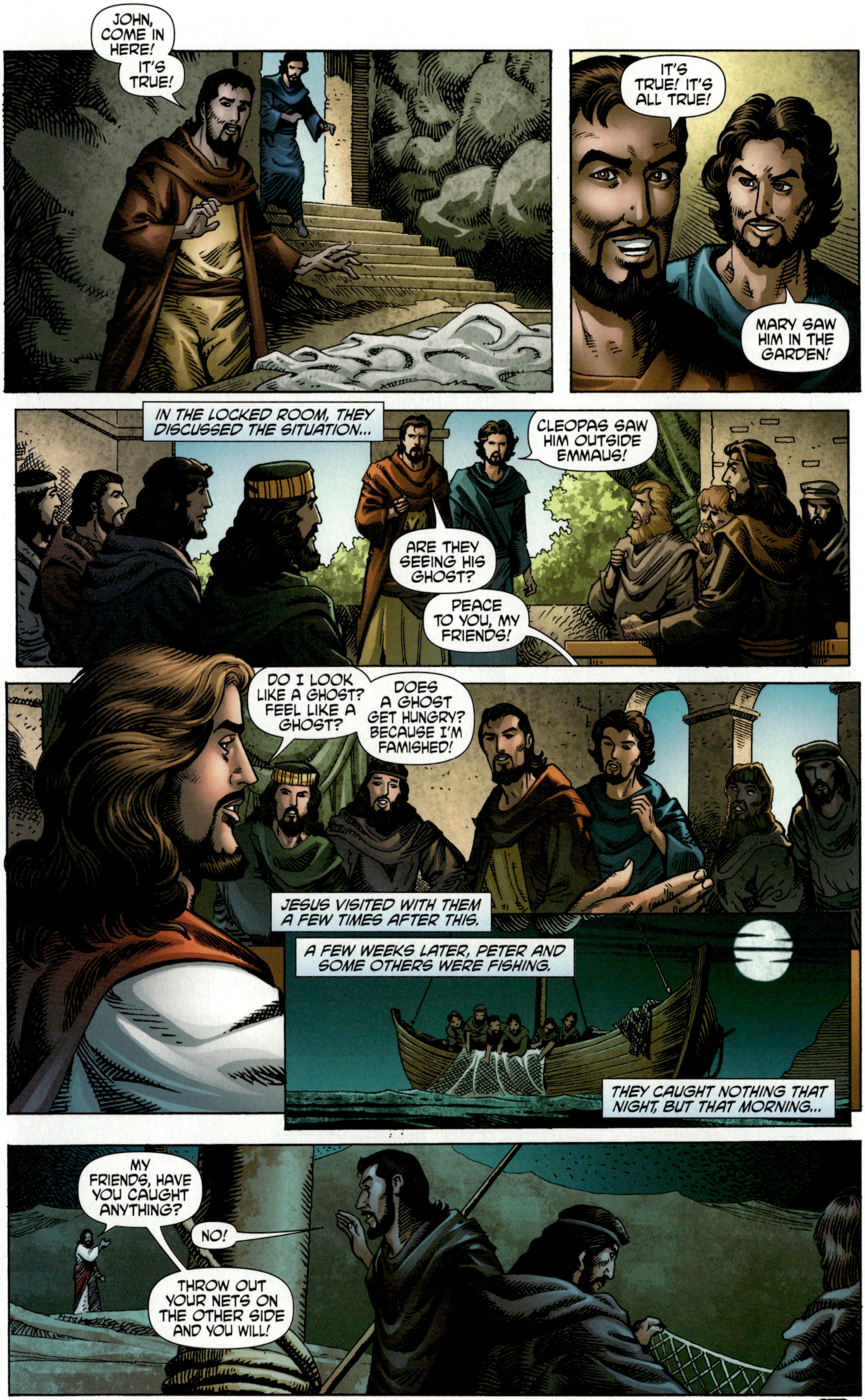
JOHN, COME IN HERE! IT'S TRUE!
IT'S TRUE! IT'S ALL TRUE!
MARY SAW HIM IN THE GARDEN!
IN THE LOCKED ROOM, THEY DISCUSSED THE SITUATION...
CLEOPAS SAW HIM OUTSIDE EMMAUS!
ARE THEY SEEING HIS GHOST?
PEACE TO YOU, MY FRIENDS!
DO I LOOK LIKE A GHOST? FEEL LIKE A GHOST?
DOES A GHOST GET HUNGRY? BECAUSE I'M FAMISHED!
JESUS VISITED WITH THEM A FEW TIMES AFTER THIS.
A FEW WEEKS LATER, PETER AND SOME OTHERS WERE FISHING.
THEY CAUGHT NOTHING THAT NIGHT, BUT THAT MORNING...
MY FRIENDS, HAVE YOU CAUGHT ANYTHING?
NO!
THROW OUT YOUR NETS ON THE OTHER SIDE AND YOU WILL!

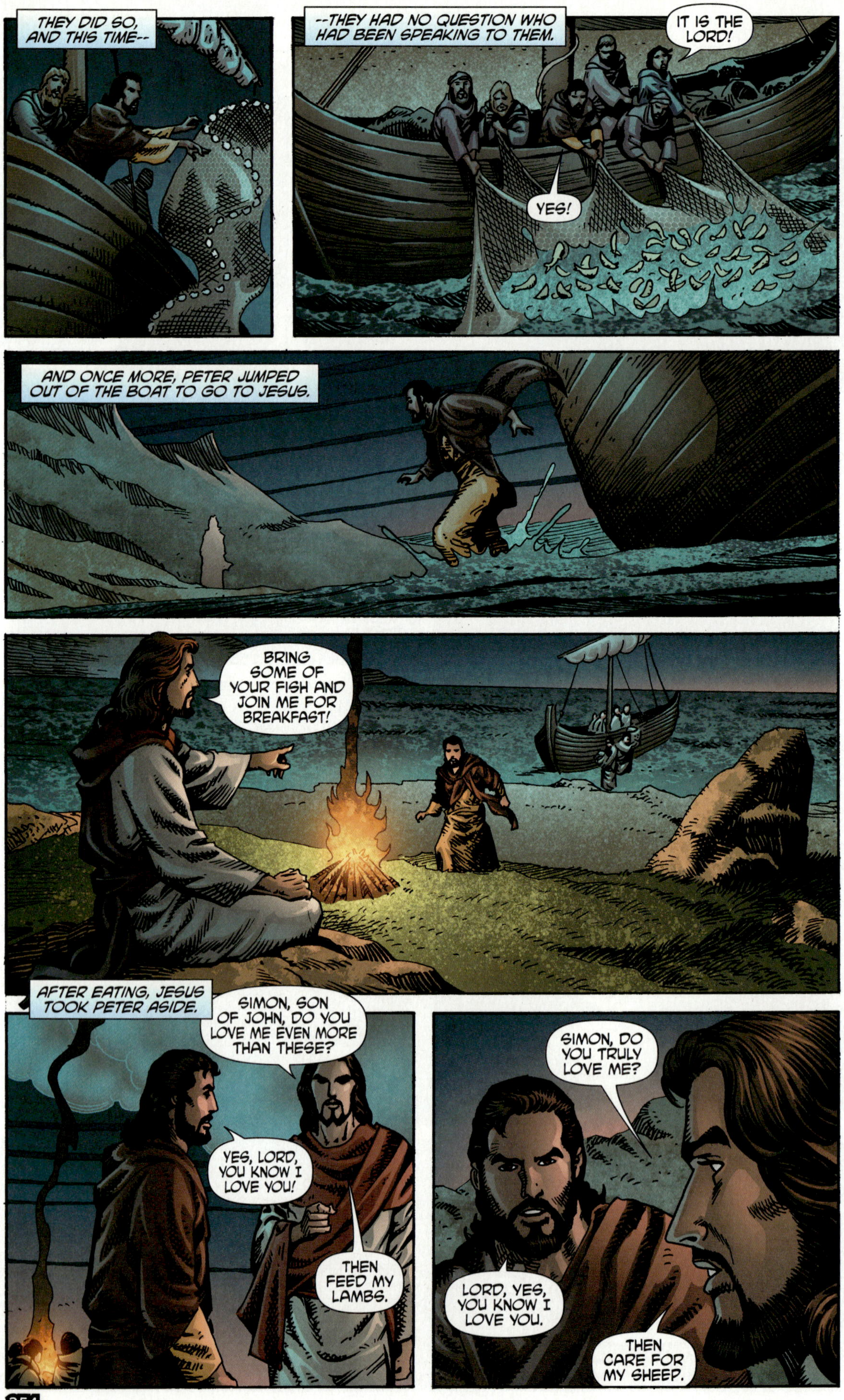
THEY DID SO, AND THIS TIME--
--THEY HAD NO QUESTION WHO HAD BEEN SPEAKING TO THEM.
IT IS THE LORD!
YES!
AND ONCE MORE, PETER JUMPED OUT OF THE BOAT TO GO TO JESUS.
BRING SOME OF YOUR FISH AND JOIN ME FOR BREAKFAST!
AFTER EATING, JESUS TOOK PETER ASIDE.
SIMON, SON OF JOHN, DO YOU LOVE ME EVEN MORE THAN THESE?
YES, LORD, YOU KNOW I LOVE YOU!
THEN FEED MY LAMBS.
SIMON, DO YOU TRULY LOVE ME?
LORD, YES, YOU KNOW I LOVE YOU.
THEN CARE FOR MY SHEEP.

SIMON, SON OF JOHN, DO YOU LOVE ME?

YOU KNOW EVERYTHING, MY LORD. YOU *KNOW* THAT I LOVE YOU!

THEN FEED MY SHEEP.

PETER, IN YOUR YOUTH, YOU DID AS YOU CHOSE.

YOU DRESSED YOURSELF, AND WENT WHERE YOU PLEASED.

BUT IN YOUR AGE, YOU WILL STRETCH OUT YOUR HAND.

OTHERS WILL DRESS YOU AND YOU WILL GO WHERE THEY TAKE YOU.

...AS I SAID, EVERYTHING WRITTEN ABOUT ME IN THE LAW, PROPHETS, AND PSALMS MUST BE FULFILLED...

JESUS SPENT TIME WITH THEM, UNTIL THE TIME HE ASCENDED INTO HEAVEN.

JESUS TOLD THEM TO WAIT IN JERUSALEM UNTIL THEY WERE FILLED WITH THE HOLY SPIRIT.

WHEN THE HOLY SPIRIT CAME ON THEM, THEY BEGAN TO SPEAK IN TONGUES.

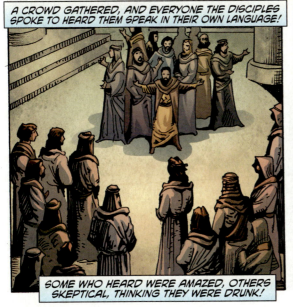

A CROWD GATHERED, AND EVERYONE THE DISCIPLES SPOKE TO HEARD THEM SPEAK IN THEIR OWN LANGUAGE!

SOME WHO HEARD WERE AMAZED, OTHERS SKEPTICAL, THINKING THEY WERE DRUNK!

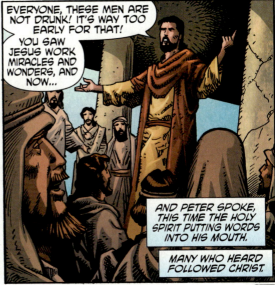

EVERYONE, THESE MEN ARE NOT DRUNK! IT'S WAY TOO EARLY FOR THAT!

YOU SAW JESUS WORK MIRACLES AND WONDERS, AND NOW...

AND PETER SPOKE, THIS TIME THE HOLY SPIRIT PUTTING WORDS INTO HIS MOUTH.

MANY WHO HEARD FOLLOWED CHRIST.

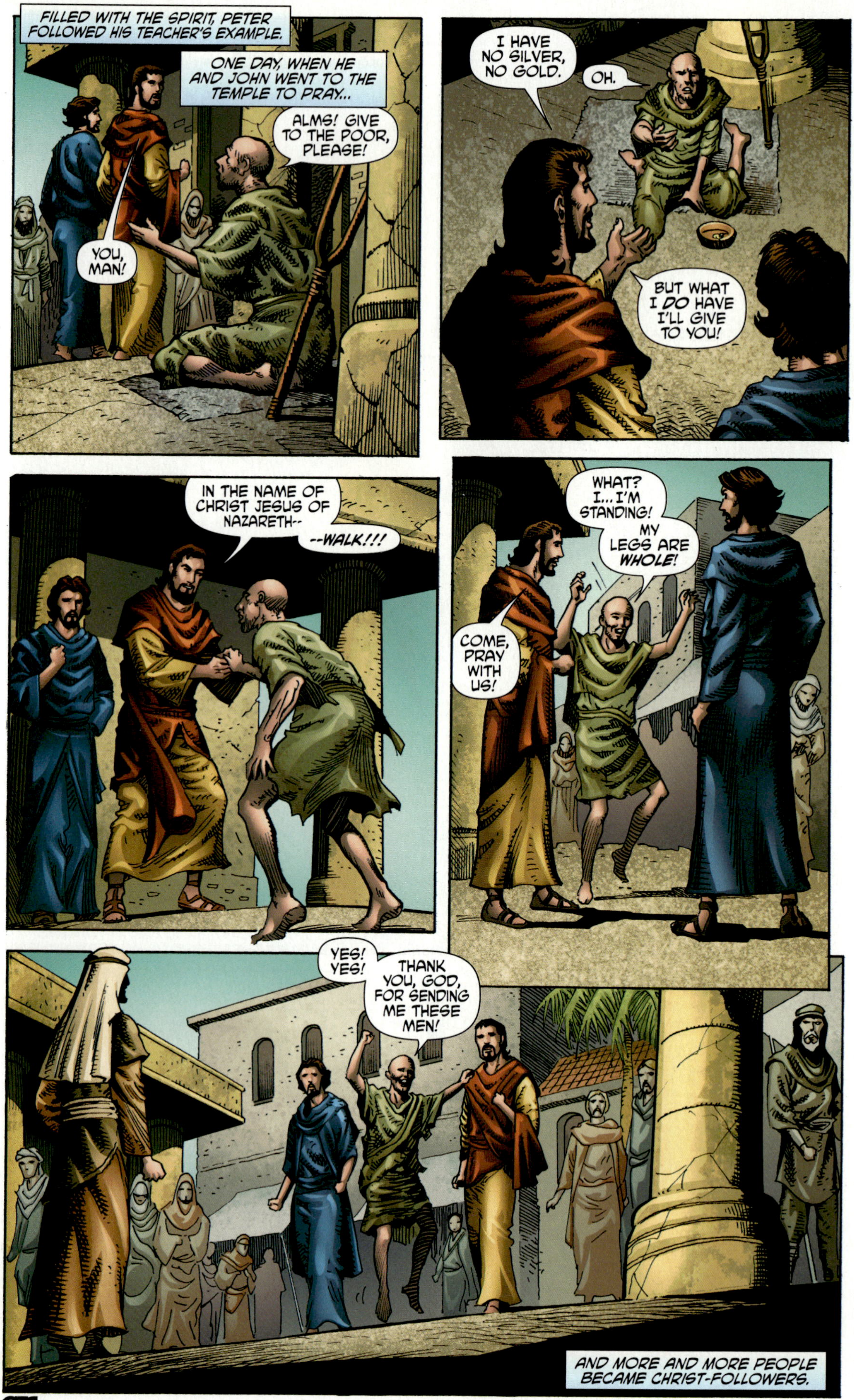
FILLED WITH THE SPIRIT, PETER FOLLOWED HIS TEACHER'S EXAMPLE.
ONE DAY, WHEN HE AND JOHN WENT TO THE TEMPLE TO PRAY...
ALMS! GIVE TO THE POOR, PLEASE!
YOU, MAN!
I HAVE NO SILVER, NO GOLD.
OH.
BUT WHAT I DO HAVE I'LL GIVE TO YOU!
IN THE NAME OF CHRIST JESUS OF NAZARETH--
--WALK!!!
WHAT? I... I'M STANDING! MY LEGS ARE WHOLE!
COME, PRAY WITH US!
YES! YES!
THANK YOU, GOD, FOR SENDING ME THESE MEN!
AND MORE AND MORE PEOPLE BECAME CHRIST-FOLLOWERS.

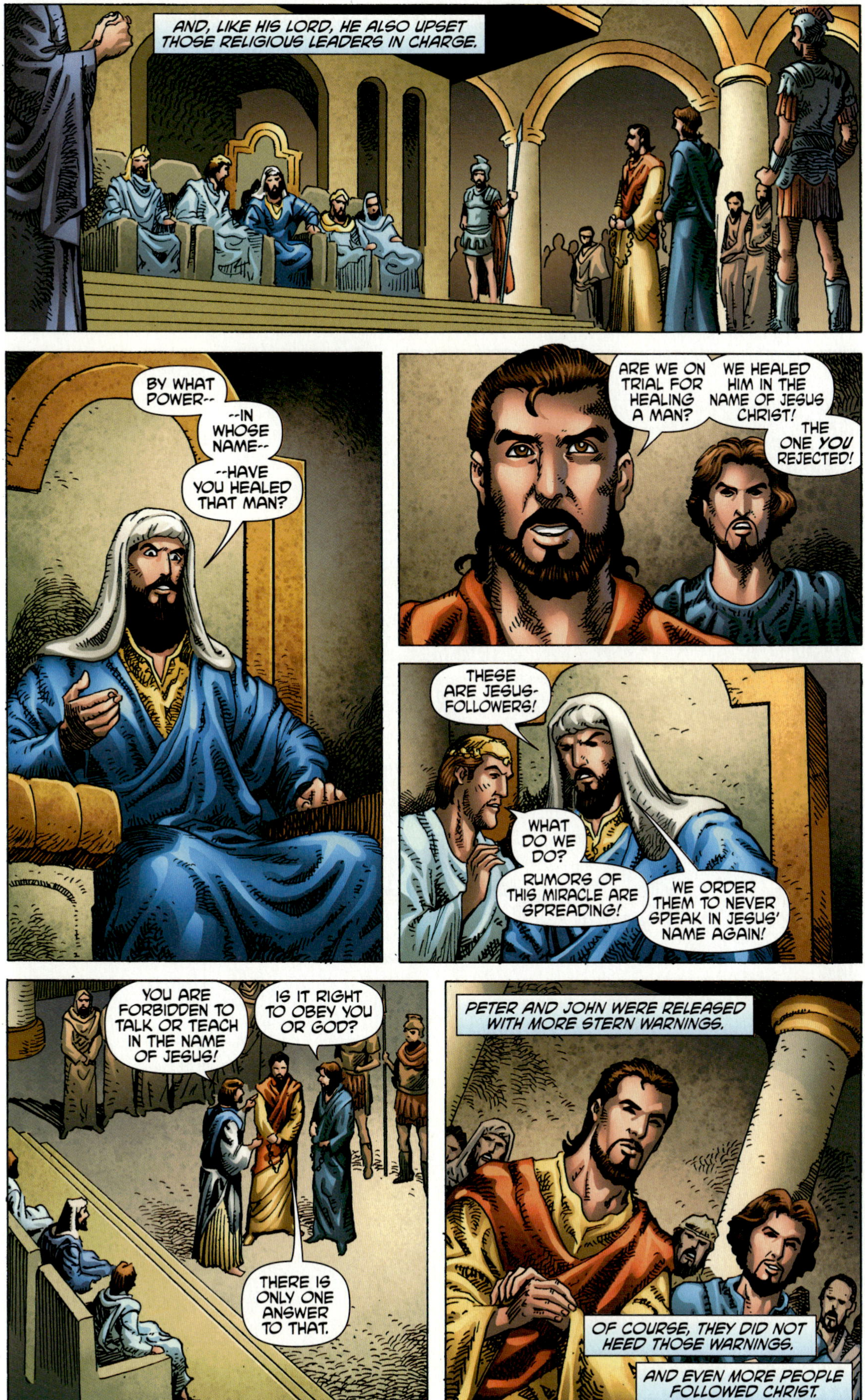
AND, LIKE HIS LORD, HE ALSO UPSET THOSE RELIGIOUS LEADERS IN CHARGE.
BY WHAT POWER--
--IN WHOSE NAME--
--HAVE YOU HEALED THAT MAN?
ARE WE ON TRIAL FOR HEALING A MAN?
WE HEALED HIM IN THE NAME OF JESUS CHRIST!
THE ONE YOU REJECTED!
THESE ARE JESUS-FOLLOWERS!
WHAT DO WE DO?
RUMORS OF THIS MIRACLE ARE SPREADING!
WE ORDER THEM TO NEVER SPEAK IN JESUS' NAME AGAIN!
YOU ARE FORBIDDEN TO TALK OR TEACH IN THE NAME OF JESUS!
IS IT RIGHT TO OBEY YOU OR GOD?
THERE IS ONLY ONE ANSWER TO THAT.
PETER AND JOHN WERE RELEASED WITH MORE STERN WARNINGS.
OF COURSE, THEY DID NOT HEED THOSE WARNINGS.
AND EVEN MORE PEOPLE FOLLOWED CHRIST.

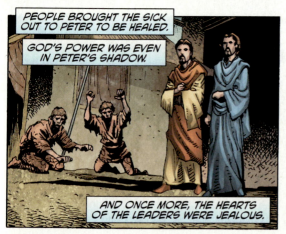

PEOPLE BROUGHT THE SICK OUT TO PETER TO BE HEALED.

GOD'S POWER WAS EVEN IN PETER'S SHADOW.

AND ONCE MORE, THE HEARTS OF THE LEADERS WERE JEALOUS.

THEY HAD THE APOSTLES ARRESTED.

BUT THIS TIME, THERE WAS NO TRIAL.

INSTEAD...

COME OUT!

GO PREACH IN THE TEMPLE COURTS!

THAT MORNING...

...YOU HUNG HIM FROM A CROSS, BUT GOD RAISED HIM FROM THE DEAD!

HOW DID THEY GET OUT?

ARREST THEM!

THEY WERE FLOGGED, AND WERE ONCE MORE WARNED NOT TO PREACH ABOUT JESUS.

ONCE MORE, THEY IGNORED IT.

PETER TRAVELED TO SAMARIA AND MANY OTHER PLACES, HEALING AND LAYING HANDS ON PEOPLE.

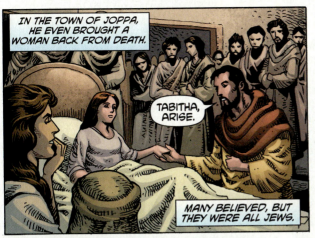

IN THE TOWN OF JOPPA, HE EVEN BROUGHT A WOMAN BACK FROM DEATH.

TABITHA, ARISE.

MANY BELIEVED, BUT THEY WERE ALL JEWS.

THEN, ONE DAY ABOUT NOON PETER WAS PRAYING.

HE WAS HUNGRY, AND FOOD WAS BEING PREPARED, BUT HE FELL INTO A TRANCE.

PETER, GET UP, KILL, AND EAT.

BUT LORD, NO! I HAVE NEVER EATEN ANYTHING THAT IS UNCLEAN OR IMPURE!

WHAT GOD HAS MADE CLEAN, DO NOT CONSIDER IMPURE OR UNHOLY!

NOW, THREE MEN ARE LOOKING FOR YOU.

I SENT THEM TO YOU MYSELF. GO WITH THEM.

GREETINGS! I BELIEVE YOU ARE LOOKING FOR ME!

MY COMMANDER, CORNELIUS, PRAYS TO YOUR GOD.

AN ANGEL TOLD HIM TO SEND FOR YOU.

PLEASE, COME TO HIS HOME AND GIVE HIM A MESSAGE.

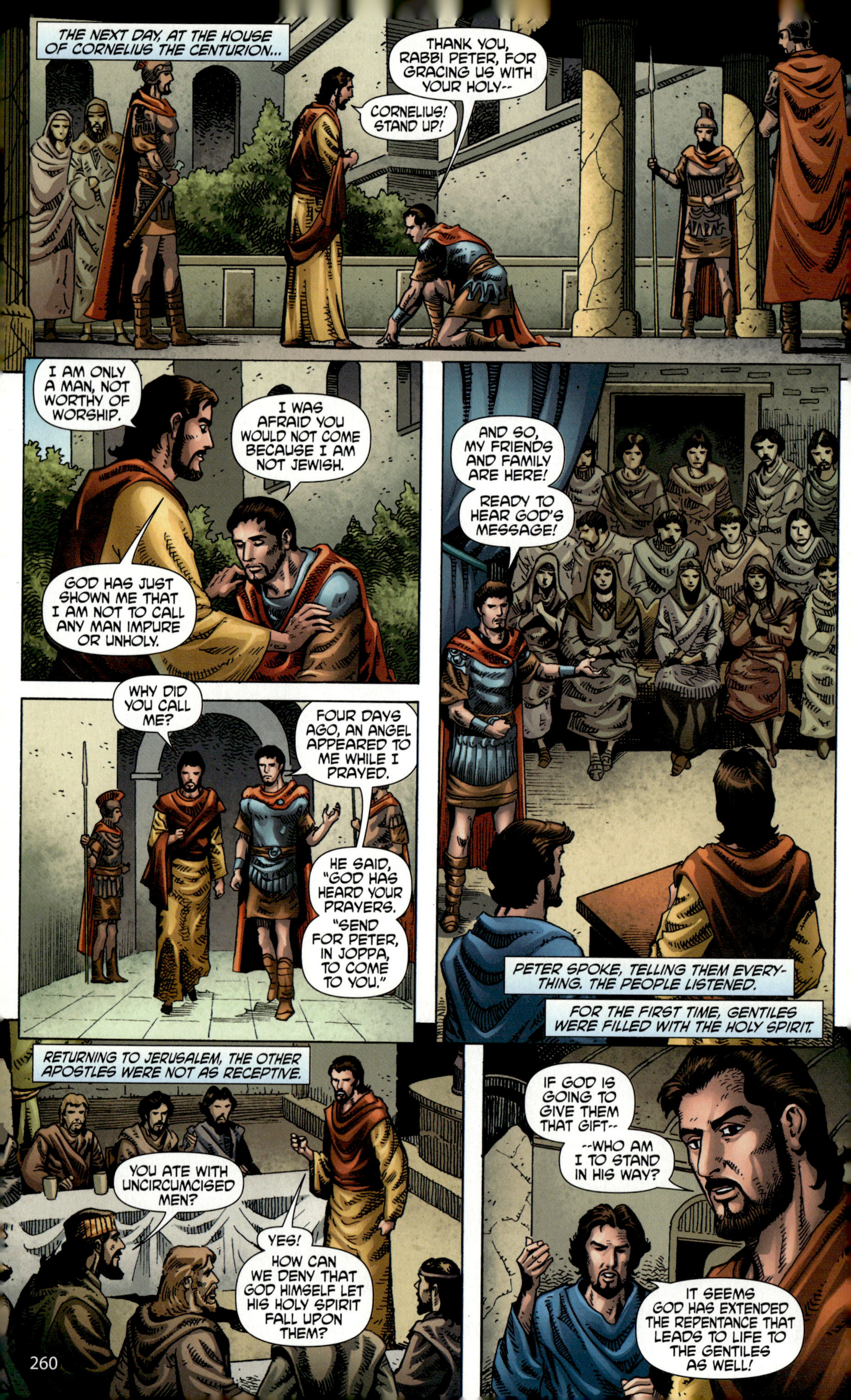
THE NEXT DAY, AT THE HOUSE OF CORNELIUS THE CENTURION...
THANK YOU, RABBI PETER, FOR GRACING US WITH YOUR HOLY--
CORNELIUS! STAND UP!
I AM ONLY A MAN, NOT WORTHY OF WORSHIP.
I WAS AFRAID YOU WOULD NOT COME BECAUSE I AM NOT JEWISH.
GOD HAS JUST SHOWN ME THAT I AM NOT TO CALL ANY MAN IMPURE OR UNHOLY.
WHY DID YOU CALL ME?
FOUR DAYS AGO, AN ANGEL APPEARED TO ME WHILE I PRAYED.
HE SAID, "GOD HAS HEARD YOUR PRAYERS.
"SEND FOR PETER, IN JOPPA, TO COME TO YOU."
AND SO, MY FRIENDS AND FAMILY ARE HERE!
READY TO HEAR GOD'S MESSAGE!
PETER SPOKE, TELLING THEM EVERY-THING. THE PEOPLE LISTENED.
FOR THE FIRST TIME, GENTILES WERE FILLED WITH THE HOLY SPIRIT.
RETURNING TO JERUSALEM, THE OTHER APOSTLES WERE NOT AS RECEPTIVE.
YOU ATE WITH UNCIRCUMCISED MEN?
YES!
HOW CAN WE DENY THAT GOD HIMSELF LET HIS HOLY SPIRIT FALL UPON THEM?
IF GOD IS GOING TO GIVE THEM THAT GIFT--
--WHO AM I TO STAND IN HIS WAY?
IT SEEMS GOD HAS EXTENDED THE REPENTANCE THAT LEADS TO LIFE TO THE GENTILES AS WELL!

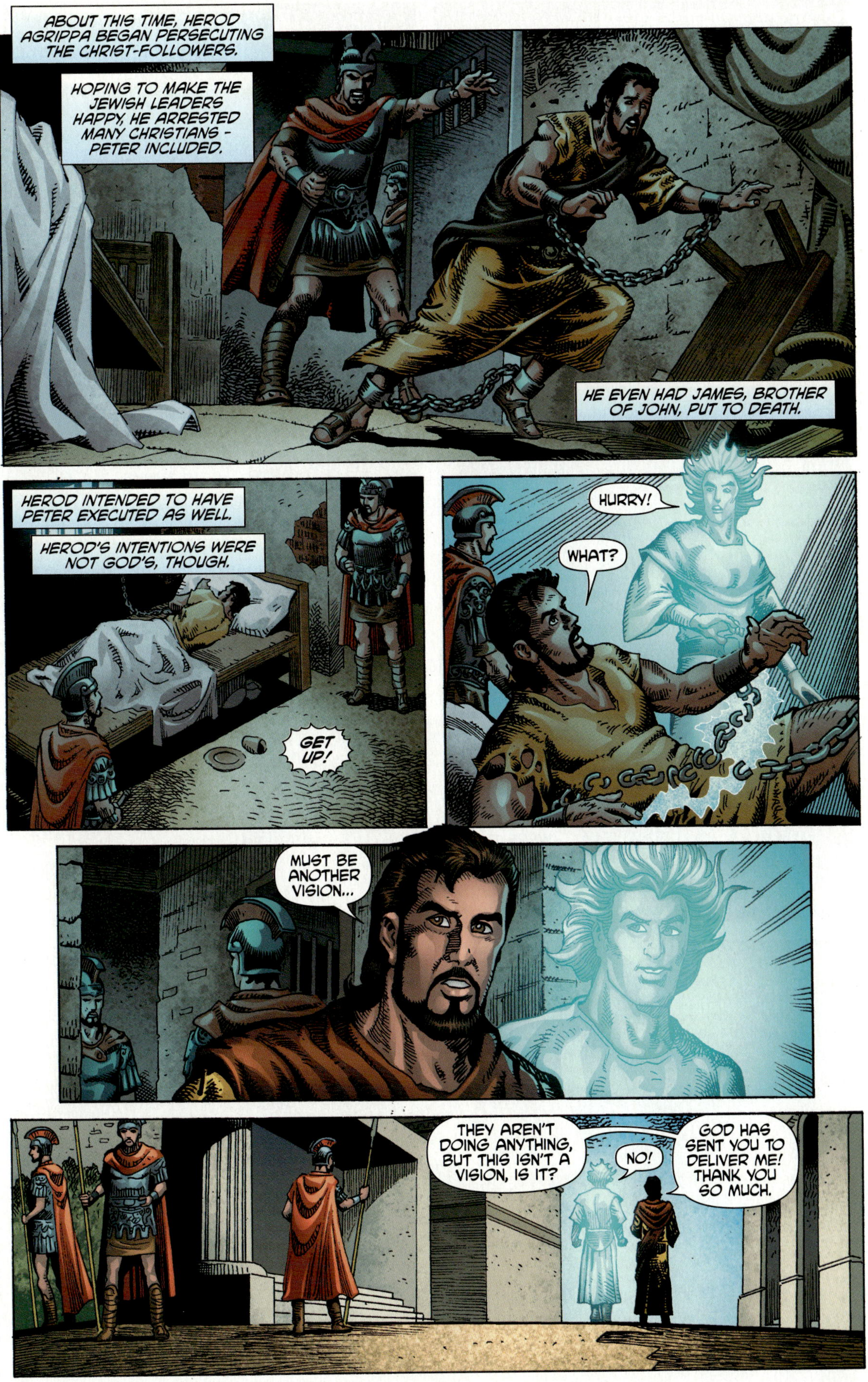
ABOUT THIS TIME, HEROD AGRIPPA BEGAN PERSECUTING THE CHRIST-FOLLOWERS.
HOPING TO MAKE THE JEWISH LEADERS HAPPY, HE ARRESTED MANY CHRISTIANS - PETER INCLUDED.
HE EVEN HAD JAMES, BROTHER OF JOHN, PUT TO DEATH.
HEROD INTENDED TO HAVE PETER EXECUTED AS WELL.
HEROD'S INTENTIONS WERE NOT GOD'S, THOUGH.
GET UP!
HURRY!
WHAT?
MUST BE ANOTHER VISION...
THEY AREN'T DOING ANYTHING, BUT THIS ISN'T A VISION, IS IT?
NO!
GOD HAS SENT YOU TO DELIVER ME! THANK YOU SO MUCH.

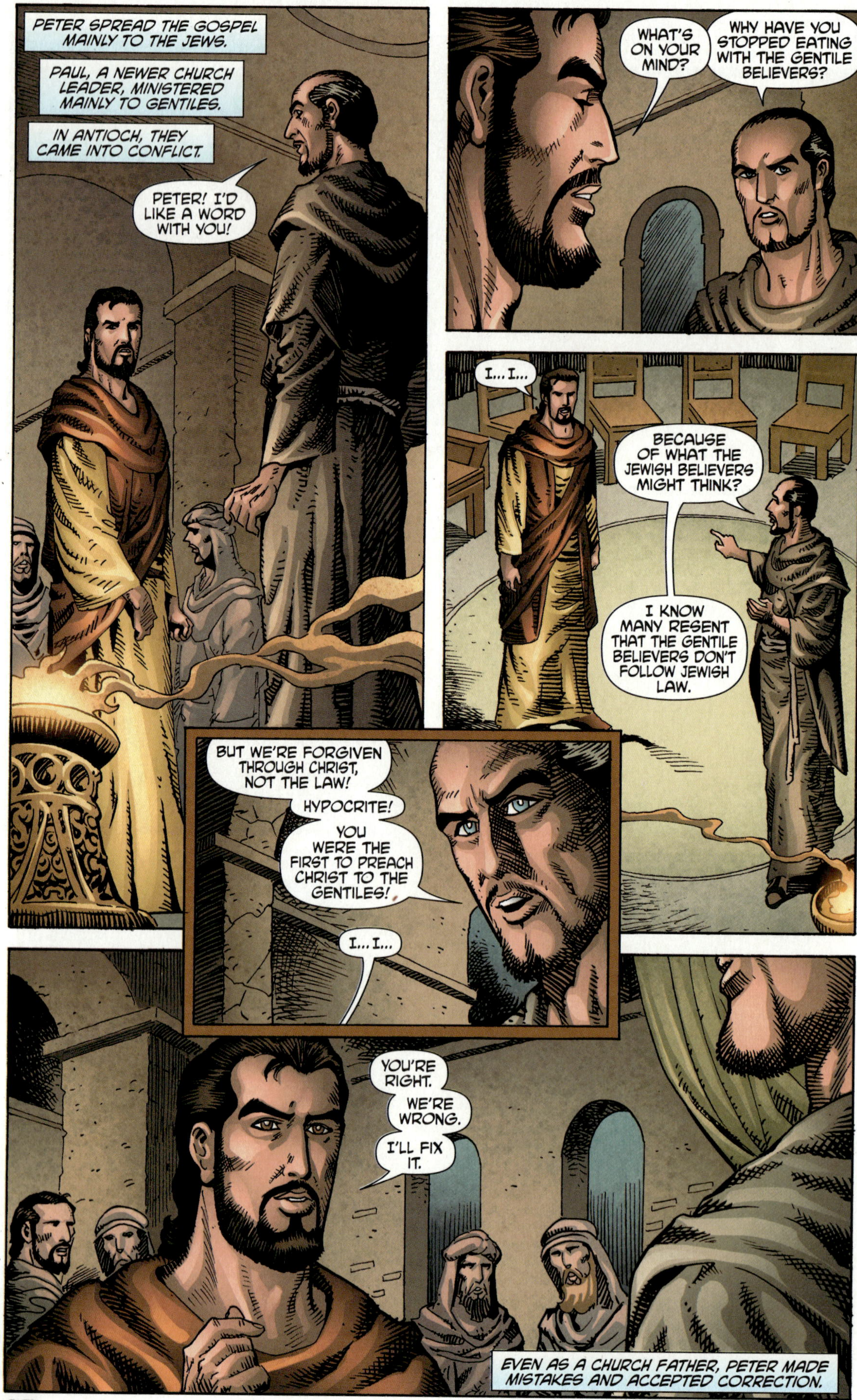
PETER SPREAD THE GOSPEL MAINLY TO THE JEWS.
PAUL, A NEWER CHURCH LEADER, MINISTERED MAINLY TO GENTILES.
IN ANTIOCH, THEY CAME INTO CONFLICT.
PETER! I'D LIKE A WORD WITH YOU!
WHAT'S ON YOUR MIND?
WHY HAVE YOU STOPPED EATING WITH THE GENTILE BELIEVERS?
I... I...
BECAUSE OF WHAT THE JEWISH BELIEVERS MIGHT THINK?
I KNOW MANY RESENT THAT THE GENTILE BELIEVERS DON'T FOLLOW JEWISH LAW.
BUT WE'RE FORGIVEN THROUGH CHRIST, NOT THE LAW!
HYPOCRITE!
YOU WERE THE FIRST TO PREACH CHRIST TO THE GENTILES!
I... I...
YOU'RE RIGHT.
WE'RE WRONG.
I'LL FIX IT.
EVEN AS A CHURCH FATHER, PETER MADE MISTAKES AND ACCEPTED CORRECTION.

AFTER THIS, LITTLE IS KNOWN ABOUT PETER'S ACTIVITIES. IT IS BELIEVED THAT MARK WROTE HIS GOSPEL BASED ON PETER'S RECOLLECTIONS.

...AND HE SAID, "PEACE, BE STILL," AND THE WIND AND WAVES STOPPED...

PETER WROTE TWO LETTERS THAT WERE COLLECTED INTO THE NEW TESTAMENT.

TO GOD'S CHOSEN PEOPLE, EXILES THROUGHOUT PONTUS, GALATIA, CAPPADOCIA...

BECAUSE OF SOME DIFFERENCES IN THE WAY THE TWO LETTERS ARE WORDED--

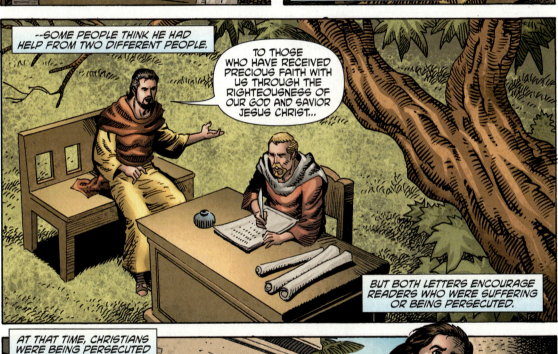

--SOME PEOPLE THINK HE HAD HELP FROM TWO DIFFERENT PEOPLE.

TO THOSE WHO HAVE RECEIVED PRECIOUS FAITH WITH US THROUGH THE RIGHTEOUSNESS OF OUR GOD AND SAVIOR JESUS CHRIST...

BUT BOTH LETTERS ENCOURAGE READERS WHO WERE SUFFERING OR BEING PERSECUTED.

AT THAT TIME, CHRISTIANS WERE BEING PERSECUTED BY GOVERNMENT AND RELIGIOUS LEADERS.

IN HIS FIRST LETTER, HE WROTE:

"...REJOICE THOUGH YOU HAVE SUFFERED GRIEF IN ALL KINDS OF TRIALS.

"...THEY PROVE THE GENUINENESS OF YOUR FAITH..."

AND ALSO, "DEAR FRIENDS, DO NOT BE SURPRISED AT YOUR FIERY TRIALS...

"...AS IF SOMETHING STRANGE WAS HAPPENING TO YOU...

"...BUT REJOICE BECAUSE YOU PARTICIPATE IN CHRIST'S SUFFERINGS..."

HE ENCOURAGED THEM TO NEVER GIVE UP HOPE, NO MATTER WHAT.

IN HIS SECOND LETTER, HE ALSO WANTED TO GIVE HOPE.

"...WE LOOK FORWARD TO A NEW HEAVEN AND EARTH, WHERE THERE WILL BE ONLY RIGHTEOUSNESS.

"DEAR FRIENDS, WHILE WAITING FOR THESE THINGS TO COME... LIVE LIVES THAT ARE PEACEFUL, PURE, AND BLAMELESS...

AND HE WANTED TO ENCOURAGE BELIEVERS TO LIVE RIGHTEOUS LIVES.

"--BUT GROW IN THE GRACE AND KNOWLEDGE OF OUR LORD AND SAVIOR JESUS CHRIST.

"TO HIM BE THE GLORY, BOTH NOW AND UNTIL ETERNITY! AMEN."

THANK YOU, MY FRIEND!

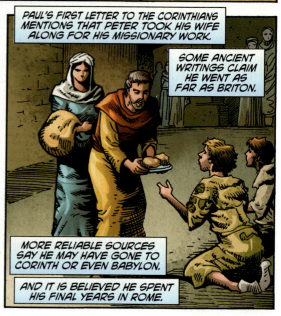

PAUL'S FIRST LETTER TO THE CORINTHIANS MENTIONS THAT PETER TOOK HIS WIFE ALONG FOR HIS MISSIONARY WORK.

SOME ANCIENT WRITINGS CLAIM HE WENT AS FAR AS BRITON.

MORE RELIABLE SOURCES SAY HE MAY HAVE GONE TO CORINTH OR EVEN BABYLON.

AND IT IS BELIEVED HE SPENT HIS FINAL YEARS IN ROME.

BUT ROME WAS NOT A SAFE PLACE FOR CHRISTIANS AT THAT TIME.

IT IS COMMONLY BELIEVED PETER, AND POSSIBLY HIS WIFE, WERE ARRESTED.

VICTIMS OF THE ROMAN EMPEROR NERO'S PERSECUTION OF CHRISTIANS.

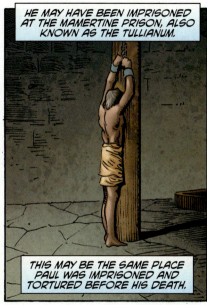

HE MAY HAVE BEEN IMPRISONED AT THE MAMERTINE PRISON, ALSO KNOWN AS THE TULLIANUM.

THIS MAY BE THE SAME PLACE PAUL WAS IMPRISONED AND TORTURED BEFORE HIS DEATH.

SOME SOURCES SAY PETER'S WIFE WAS KILLED BEFORE HIM AND THAT HE MAY HAVE BEEN WITNESS TO IT.

SOME SOURCES SAY HE WAS HELD AND BEATEN AT TULLIANUM FOR AS LONG AS NINE MONTHS.

EVEN IF THE EXACT DETAILS OF PETER'S DEATH ARE NOT KNOWN--

--THEY DO FIT THE ACCOUNT OF PETER'S DEATH THAT JESUS SPOKE:

"IN YOUR YOUTH, YOU DID AS YOU CHOSE.

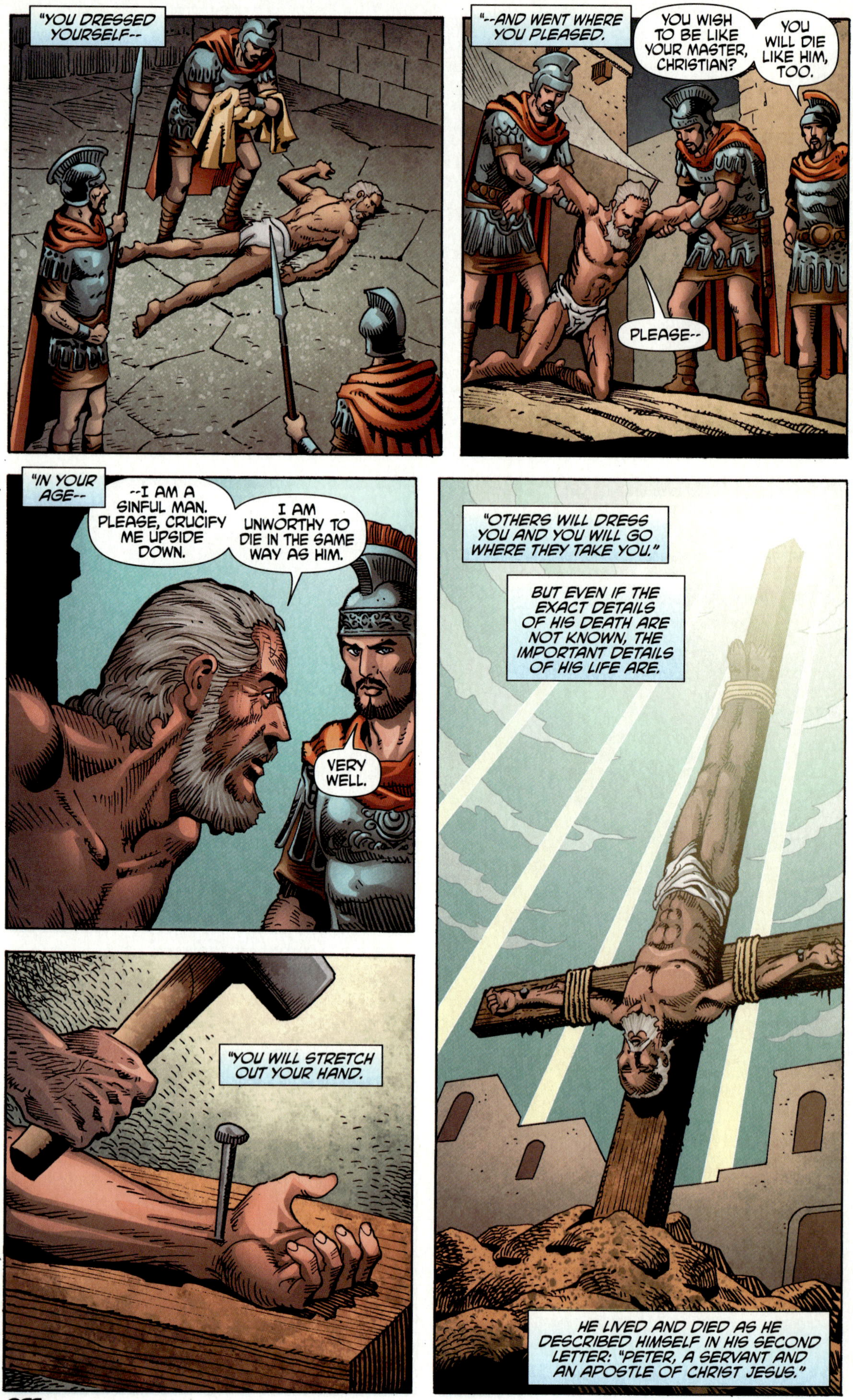
"YOU DRESSED YOURSELF--
"--AND WENT WHERE YOU PLEASED.
YOU WISH TO BE LIKE YOUR MASTER, CHRISTIAN?
YOU WILL DIE LIKE HIM, TOO.
PLEASE--
"IN YOUR AGE--
--I AM A SINFUL MAN. PLEASE, CRUCIFY ME UPSIDE DOWN.
I AM UNWORTHY TO DIE IN THE SAME WAY AS HIM.
VERY WELL.
"YOU WILL STRETCH OUT YOUR HAND.
"OTHERS WILL DRESS YOU AND YOU WILL GO WHERE THEY TAKE YOU."
BUT EVEN IF THE EXACT DETAILS OF HIS DEATH ARE NOT KNOWN, THE IMPORTANT DETAILS OF HIS LIFE ARE.
HE LIVED AND DIED AS HE DESCRIBED HIMSELF IN HIS SECOND LETTER: "PETER, A SERVANT AND AN APOSTLE OF CHRIST JESUS."

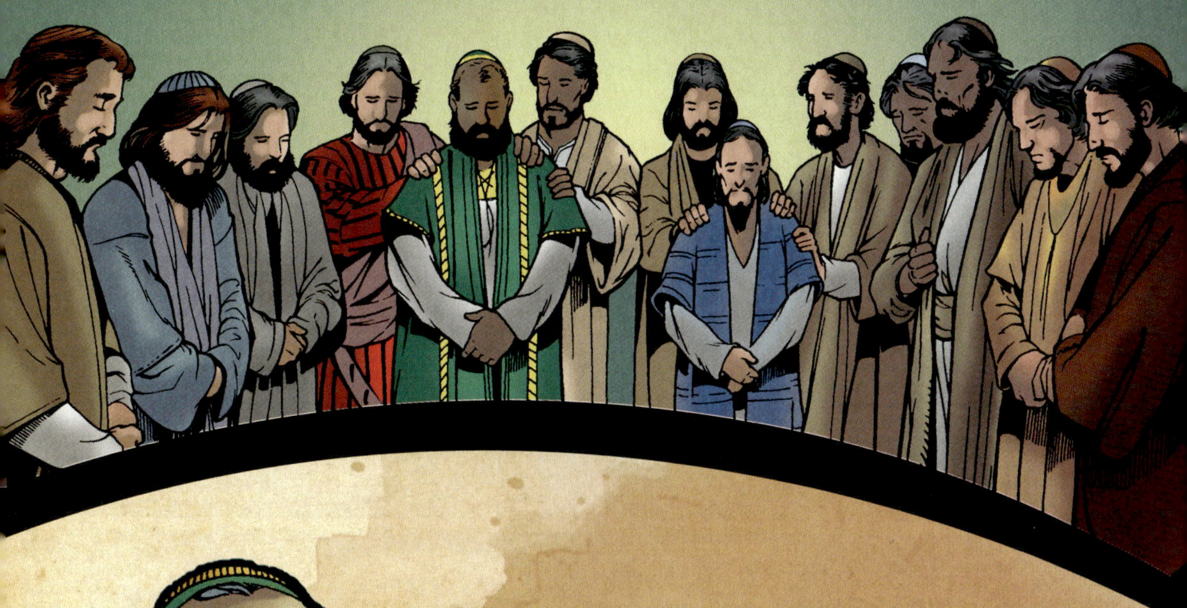

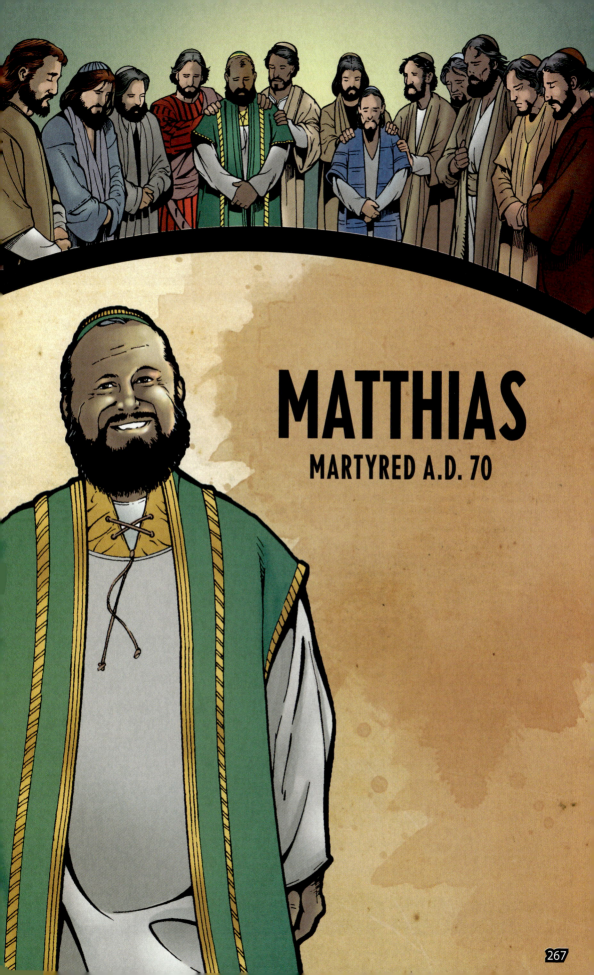

MATTHIAS

MARTYRED A.D. 70

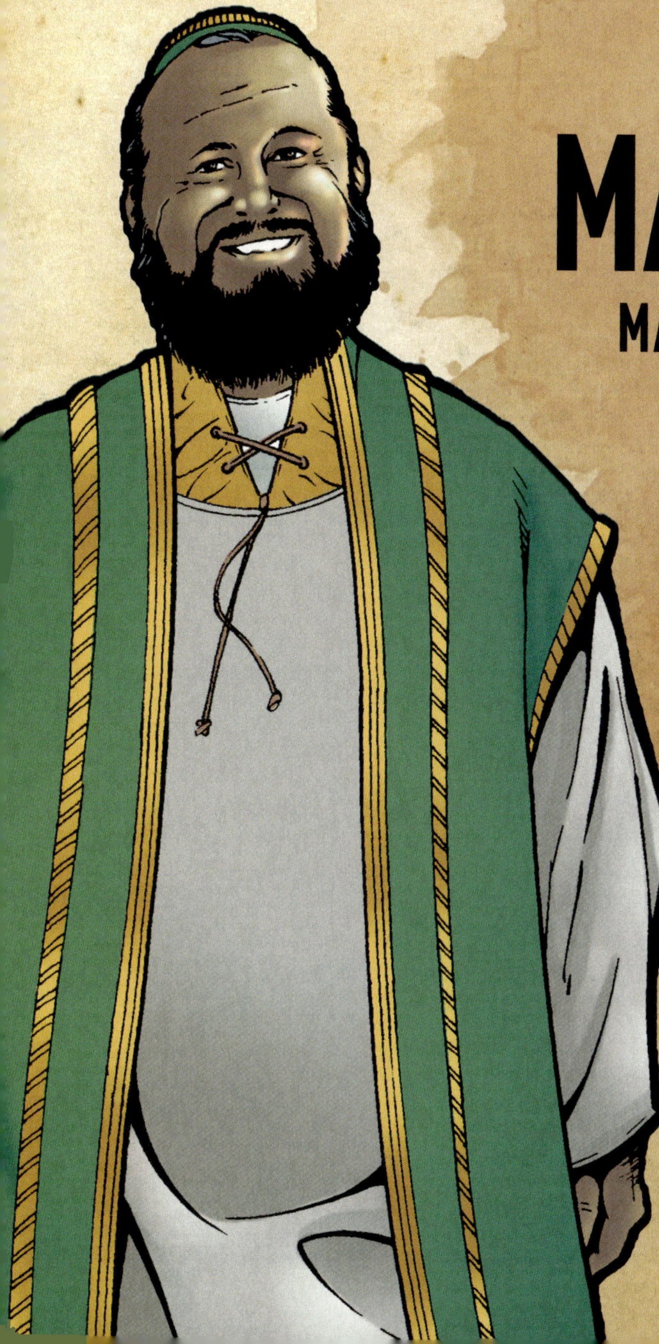

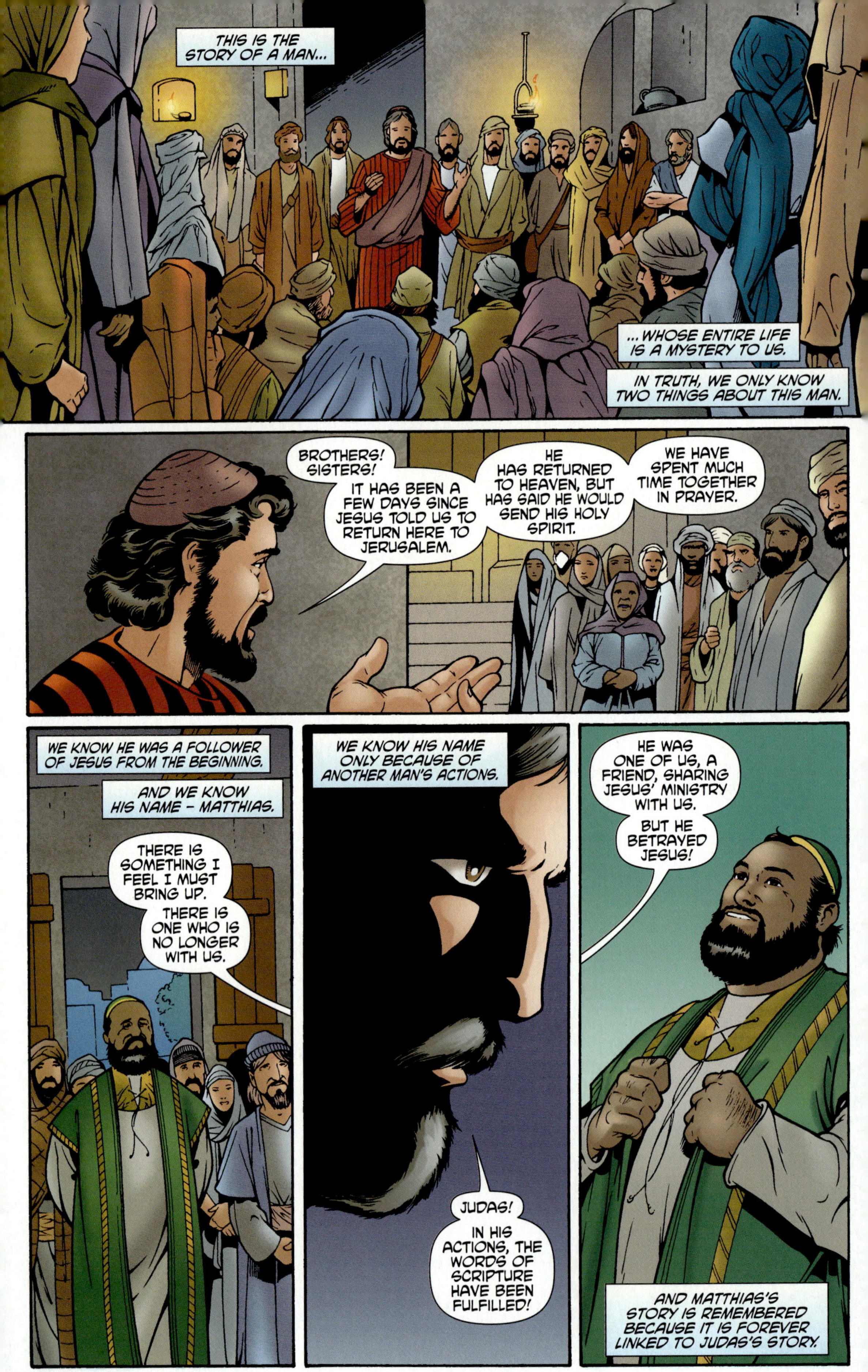

THIS IS THE STORY OF A MAN...
...WHOSE ENTIRE LIFE IS A MYSTERY TO US.
IN TRUTH, WE ONLY KNOW TWO THINGS ABOUT THIS MAN.
BROTHERS! SISTERS!
IT HAS BEEN A FEW DAYS SINCE JESUS TOLD US TO RETURN HERE TO JERUSALEM.
HE HAS RETURNED TO HEAVEN, BUT HAS SAID HE WOULD SEND HIS HOLY SPIRIT.
WE HAVE SPENT MUCH TIME TOGETHER IN PRAYER.
WE KNOW HE WAS A FOLLOWER OF JESUS FROM THE BEGINNING.
AND WE KNOW HIS NAME – MATTHIAS.
THERE IS SOMETHING I FEEL I MUST BRING UP.
THERE IS ONE WHO IS NO LONGER WITH US.
WE KNOW HIS NAME ONLY BECAUSE OF ANOTHER MAN'S ACTIONS.
JUDAS!
IN HIS ACTIONS, THE WORDS OF SCRIPTURE HAVE BEEN FULFILLED!
HE WAS ONE OF US, A FRIEND, SHARING JESUS' MINISTRY WITH US.
BUT HE BETRAYED JESUS!
AND MATTHIAS'S STORY IS REMEMBERED BECAUSE IT IS FOREVER LINKED TO JUDAS'S STORY.

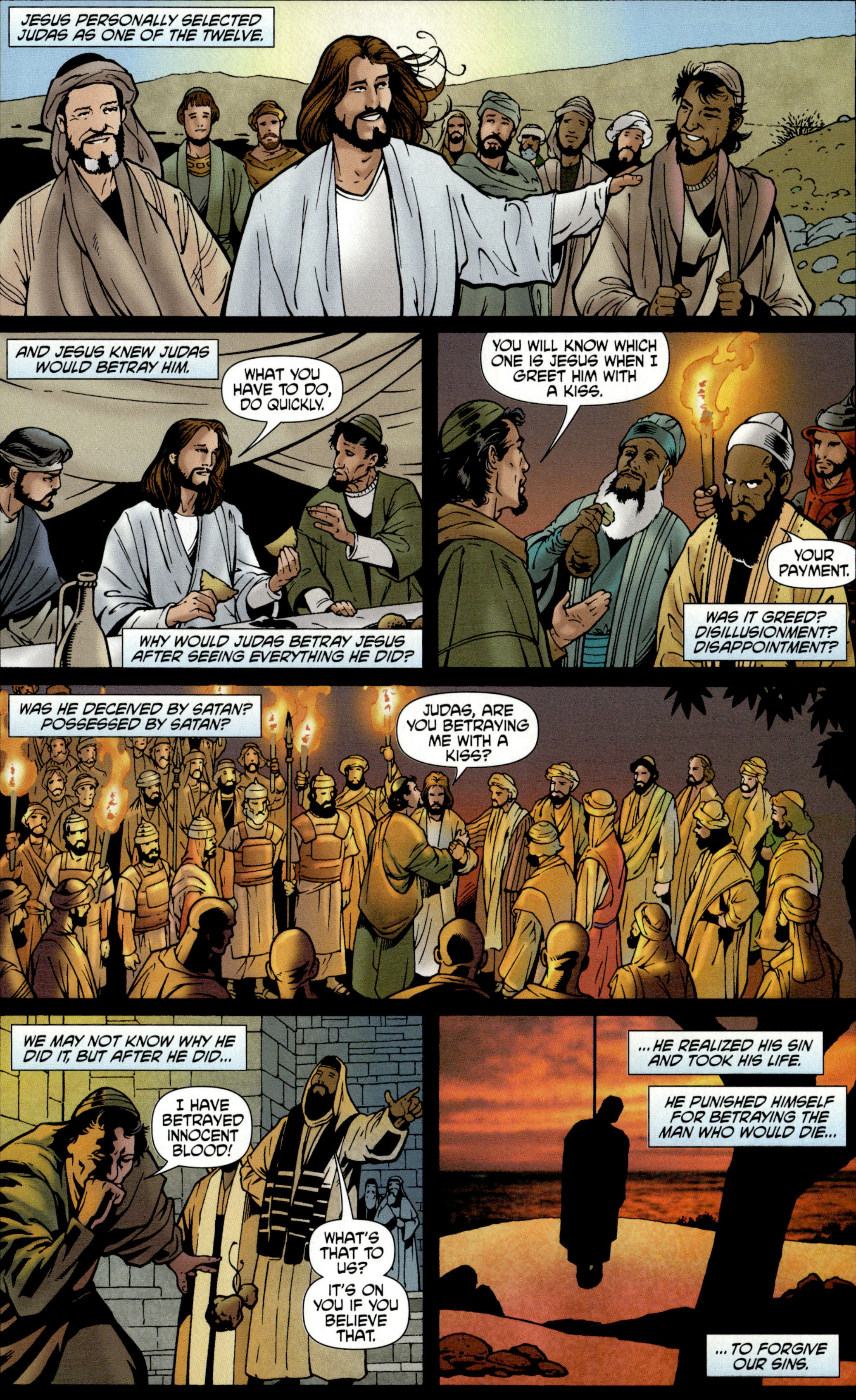
JESUS PERSONALLY SELECTED JUDAS AS ONE OF THE TWELVE.
AND JESUS KNEW JUDAS WOULD BETRAY HIM.
WHAT YOU HAVE TO DO, DO QUICKLY.
WHY WOULD JUDAS BETRAY JESUS AFTER SEEING EVERYTHING HE DID?
YOU WILL KNOW WHICH ONE IS JESUS WHEN I GREET HIM WITH A KISS.
YOUR PAYMENT.
WAS IT GREED? DISILLUSIONMENT? DISAPPOINTMENT?
WAS HE DECEIVED BY SATAN? POSSESSED BY SATAN?
JUDAS, ARE YOU BETRAYING ME WITH A KISS?
WE MAY NOT KNOW WHY HE DID IT, BUT AFTER HE DID...
I HAVE BETRAYED INNOCENT BLOOD!
WHAT'S THAT TO US?
IT'S ON YOU IF YOU BELIEVE THAT.
...HE REALIZED HIS SIN AND TOOK HIS LIFE.
HE PUNISHED HIMSELF FOR BETRAYING THE MAN WHO WOULD DIE...
...TO FORGIVE OUR SINS.

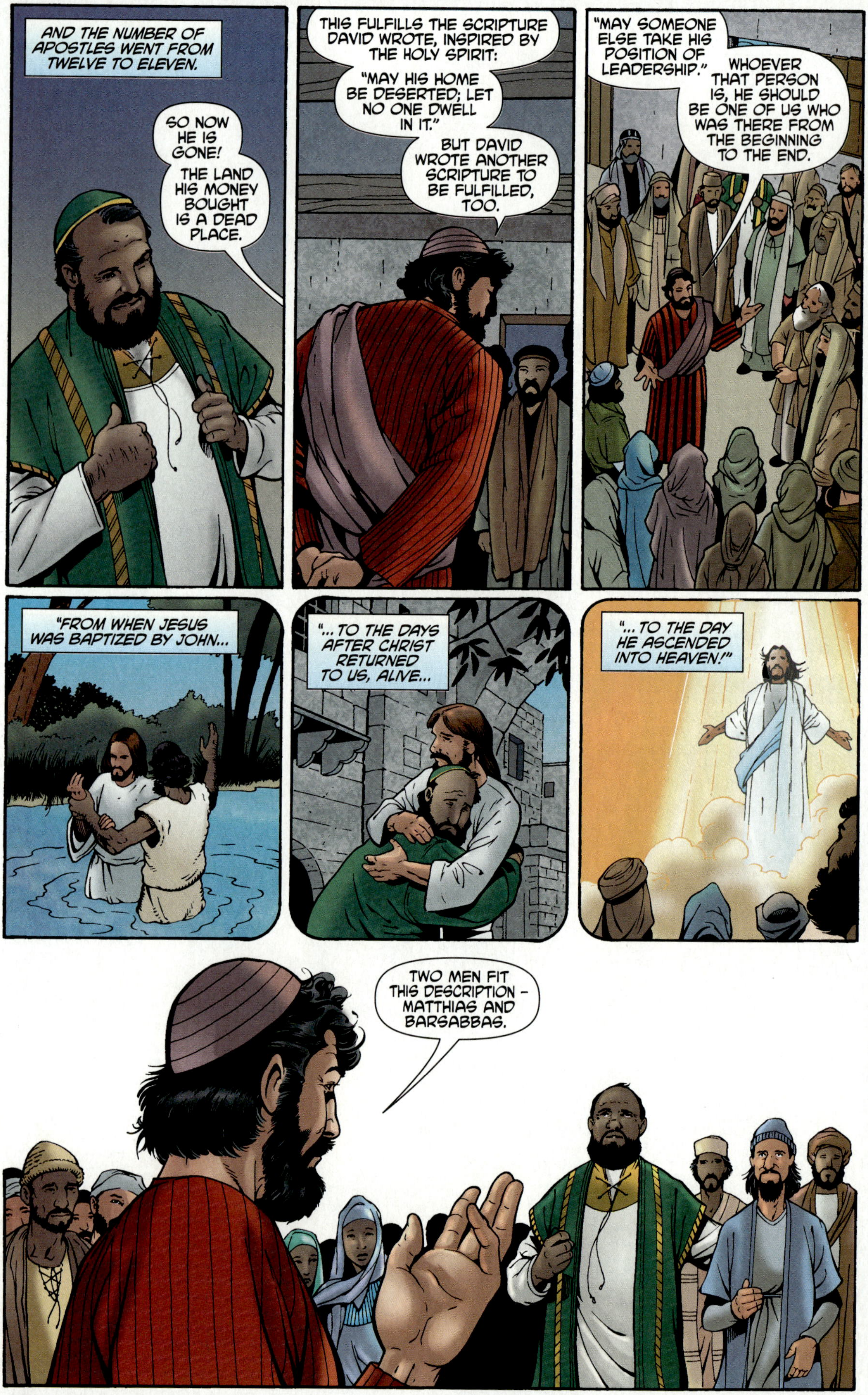
AND THE NUMBER OF APOSTLES WENT FROM TWELVE TO ELEVEN.
SO NOW HE IS GONE!
THE LAND HIS MONEY BOUGHT IS A DEAD PLACE.
THIS FULFILLS THE SCRIPTURE DAVID WROTE, INSPIRED BY THE HOLY SPIRIT:
"MAY HIS HOME BE DESERTED; LET NO ONE DWELL IN IT."
BUT DAVID WROTE ANOTHER SCRIPTURE TO BE FULFILLED, TOO.
"MAY SOMEONE ELSE TAKE HIS POSITION OF LEADERSHIP."
WHOEVER THAT PERSON IS, HE SHOULD BE ONE OF US WHO WAS THERE FROM THE BEGINNING TO THE END.
"FROM WHEN JESUS WAS BAPTIZED BY JOHN...
"...TO THE DAYS AFTER CHRIST RETURNED TO US, ALIVE...
"...TO THE DAY HE ASCENDED INTO HEAVEN!"
TWO MEN FIT THIS DESCRIPTION - MATTHIAS AND BARSABBAS.

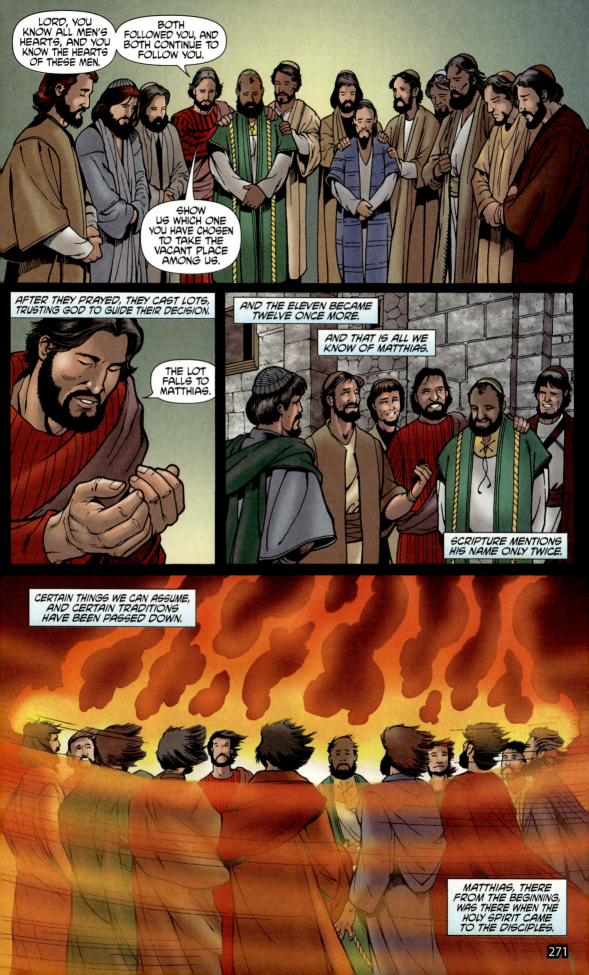

LORD, YOU KNOW ALL MEN'S HEARTS, AND YOU KNOW THE HEARTS OF THESE MEN.

BOTH FOLLOWED YOU, AND BOTH CONTINUE TO FOLLOW YOU.

SHOW US WHICH ONE YOU HAVE CHOSEN TO TAKE THE VACANT PLACE AMONG US.

AFTER THEY PRAYED, THEY CAST LOTS, TRUSTING GOD TO GUIDE THEIR DECISION.

THE LOT FALLS TO MATTHIAS.

AND THE ELEVEN BECAME TWELVE ONCE MORE.

AND THAT IS ALL WE KNOW OF MATTHIAS.

SCRIPTURE MENTIONS HIS NAME ONLY TWICE.

CERTAIN THINGS WE CAN ASSUME, AND CERTAIN TRADITIONS HAVE BEEN PASSED DOWN.

MATTHIAS, THERE FROM THE BEGINNING, WAS THERE WHEN THE HOLY SPIRIT CAME TO THE DISCIPLES.

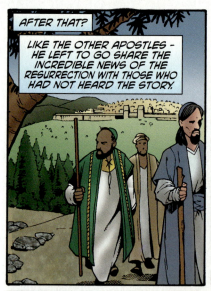

AFTER THAT?

LIKE THE OTHER APOSTLES – HE LEFT TO GO SHARE THE INCREDIBLE NEWS OF THE RESURRECTION WITH THOSE WHO HAD NOT HEARD THE STORY.

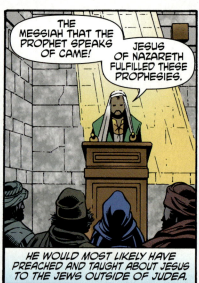

THE MESSIAH THAT THE PROPHET SPEAKS OF CAME!

JESUS OF NAZARETH FULFILLED THESE PROPHESIES.

HE WOULD MOST LIKELY HAVE PREACHED AND TAUGHT ABOUT JESUS TO THE JEWS OUTSIDE OF JUDEA.

TRADITIONS GIVE DIFFERENT ACCOUNTS OF HIS DEATH.

THE MOST RELIABLE SUGGEST THAT HE RETURNED TO JERUSALEM.

IN JERUSALEM, HE UPSET THE RELIGIOUS LEADERS BY SPREADING THE GOSPEL.

THE DIFFERENT TRADITIONS MAY NOT AGREE ABOUT WHERE OR HOW...

...BUT THEY AGREE THAT LIKE THE OTHER ELEVEN, HE DEDICATED HIS LIFE TO CHRIST.

AND HE DIED FOR CHRIST, TOO.

TWO MEN. TWO STORIES WITH THE SAME BEGINNING – FOLLOWING CHRIST.

ONE MAN DIED IN SERVICE TO HIMSELF...

...THE OTHER, IN SERVICE TO CHRIST.

TWO STORIES WITH TWO VERY DIFFERENT ENDINGS.

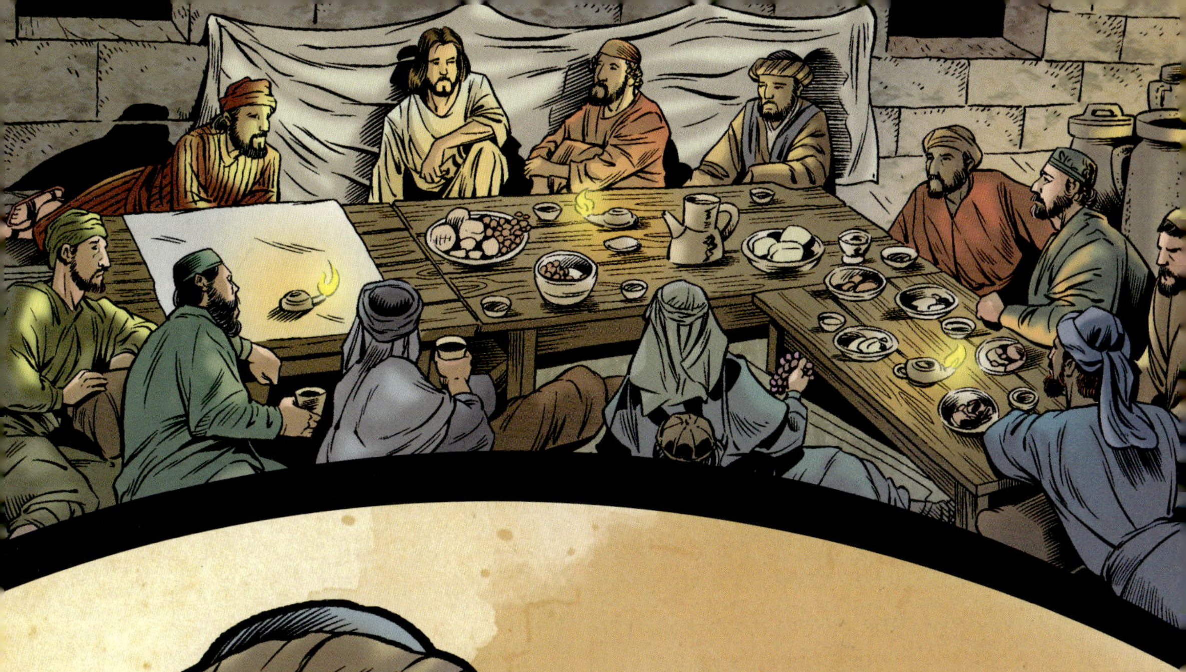

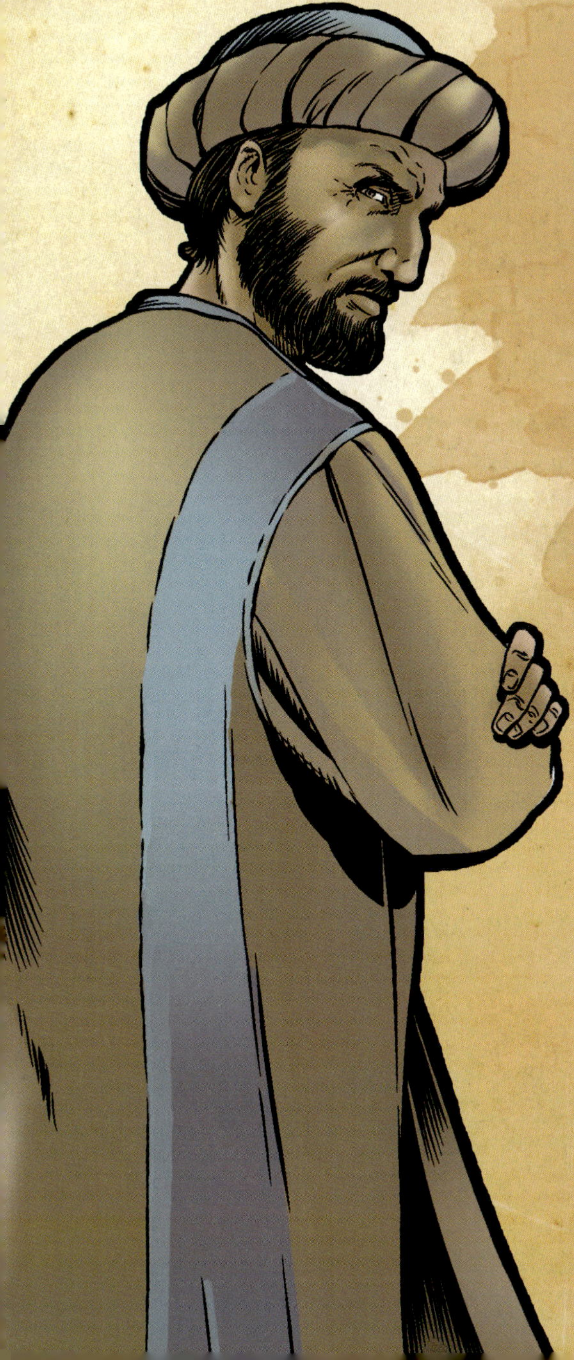

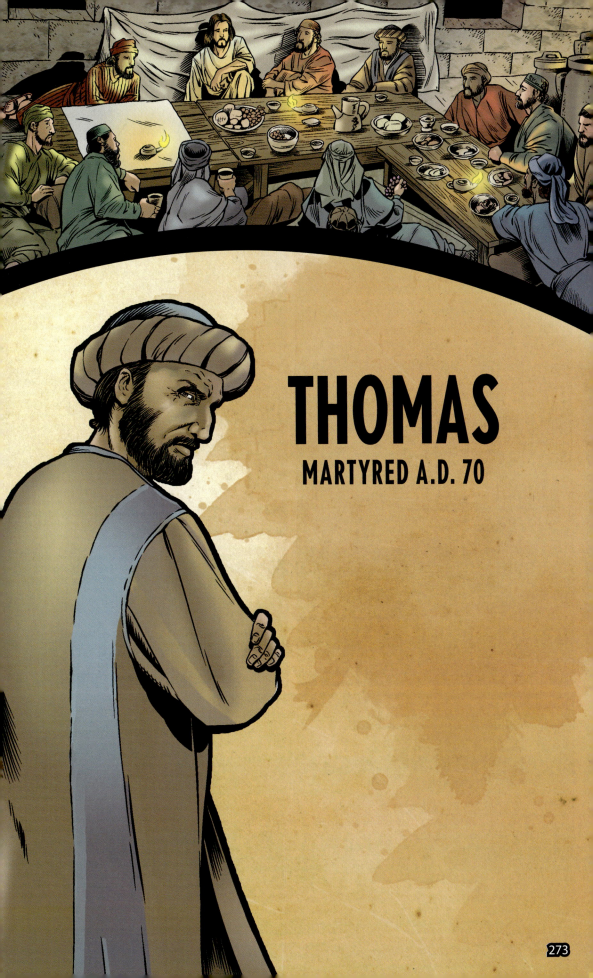

THOMAS

MARTYRED A.D. 70

WE CALL HIM "THOMAS THE DOUBTER" OR "DOUBTING THOMAS"...

...BUT THAT'S NOT COMPLETELY FAIR.

WE DO NOT KNOW WHAT THOMAS WAS DOING WHEN HE MET JESUS.

IT IS LIKELY THAT HE WAS A FISHERMAN FROM THE SAME AREA AS THE OTHERS.

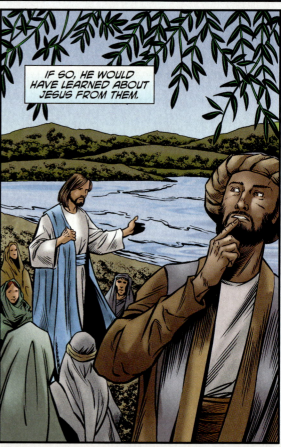

IF SO, HE WOULD HAVE LEARNED ABOUT JESUS FROM THEM.

WE DO NOT KNOW WHEN THOMAS BEGAN TO FOLLOW JESUS...

...BUT WE DO KNOW THAT HE WAS ONE OF THE 12 DISCIPLES JESUS CHOSE.

AND HE DID NOT DOUBT.

HE TRUSTED JESUS ENOUGH TO DROP EVERYTHING AND FOLLOW HIM.

WOULD "THOMAS THE DEDICATED" BE ANOTHER NAME WE COULD GIVE HIM?

CONSIDER HIS LOYALTY WHEN JESUS WAS PERSECUTED.

IN JERUSALEM, IN THE AREA OF THE TEMPLE, SOME JEWS CONFRONTED JESUS:

IF YOU'RE THE CHRIST – THE MESSIAH – JUST SAY IT!

I DID, BUT YOU WOULD NOT BELIEVE.

MY FATHER IS GREATER THAN ALL.

I HAVE DONE MIRACLES IN MY FATHER'S NAME.

I AND THE FATHER ARE ONE.

THEY INTENDED TO SEIZE JESUS AND STONE HIM.

I HAVE SHOWN YOU MANY MIRACLES FROM THE FATHER.

WHICH MIRACLE ARE YOU STONING ME FOR?

IT'S NOT FOR THE MIRACLES. IT'S FOR THE BLASPHEMY!

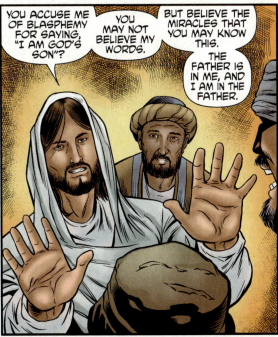

YOU ACCUSE ME OF BLASPHEMY FOR SAYING, "I AM GOD'S SON"?

YOU MAY NOT BELIEVE MY WORDS.

BUT BELIEVE THE MIRACLES THAT YOU MAY KNOW THIS.

THE FATHER IS IN ME, AND I AM IN THE FATHER.

JESUS LEFT THAT AREA.

AND EVEN THOUGH JESUS MADE THESE BOLD STATEMENTS THAT MANY DID NOT BELIEVE...

...THOMAS FOLLOWED HIM. HE DID NOT DOUBT JESUS' MESSAGE.

275

MAYBE ANOTHER NAME FOR HIM COULD BE "THOMAS THE DUTIFUL."

JESUS! MARY AND MARTHA HAVE SENT US!

THEIR BROTHER, LAZARUS, IS DEATHLY ILL.

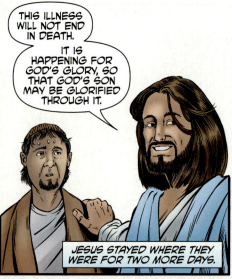

THIS ILLNESS WILL NOT END IN DEATH.

IT IS HAPPENING FOR GOD'S GLORY, SO THAT GOD'S SON MAY BE GLORIFIED THROUGH IT.

JESUS STAYED WHERE THEY WERE FOR TWO MORE DAYS.

AND THEN...

IT IS TIME FOR US TO RETURN TO JUDEA.

BUT MASTER, YOU KNOW THEY WANT TO KILL YOU THERE! AND YOU WANT TO GO BACK?

OUR FRIEND LAZARUS HAS FALLEN ASLEEP.

I AM GOING THERE TO WAKE HIM UP.

IF HE'S SLEEPING, THEN HE'LL WAKE UP ON HIS OWN.

HE'LL GET BETTER.

WHY PUT YOURSELF AND US IN DANGER?

LAZARUS IS DEAD, MY FRIENDS.

AND I AM GLAD I WAS NOT THERE, SO YOU MAY BELIEVE.

COME, LET US GO TO HIM.

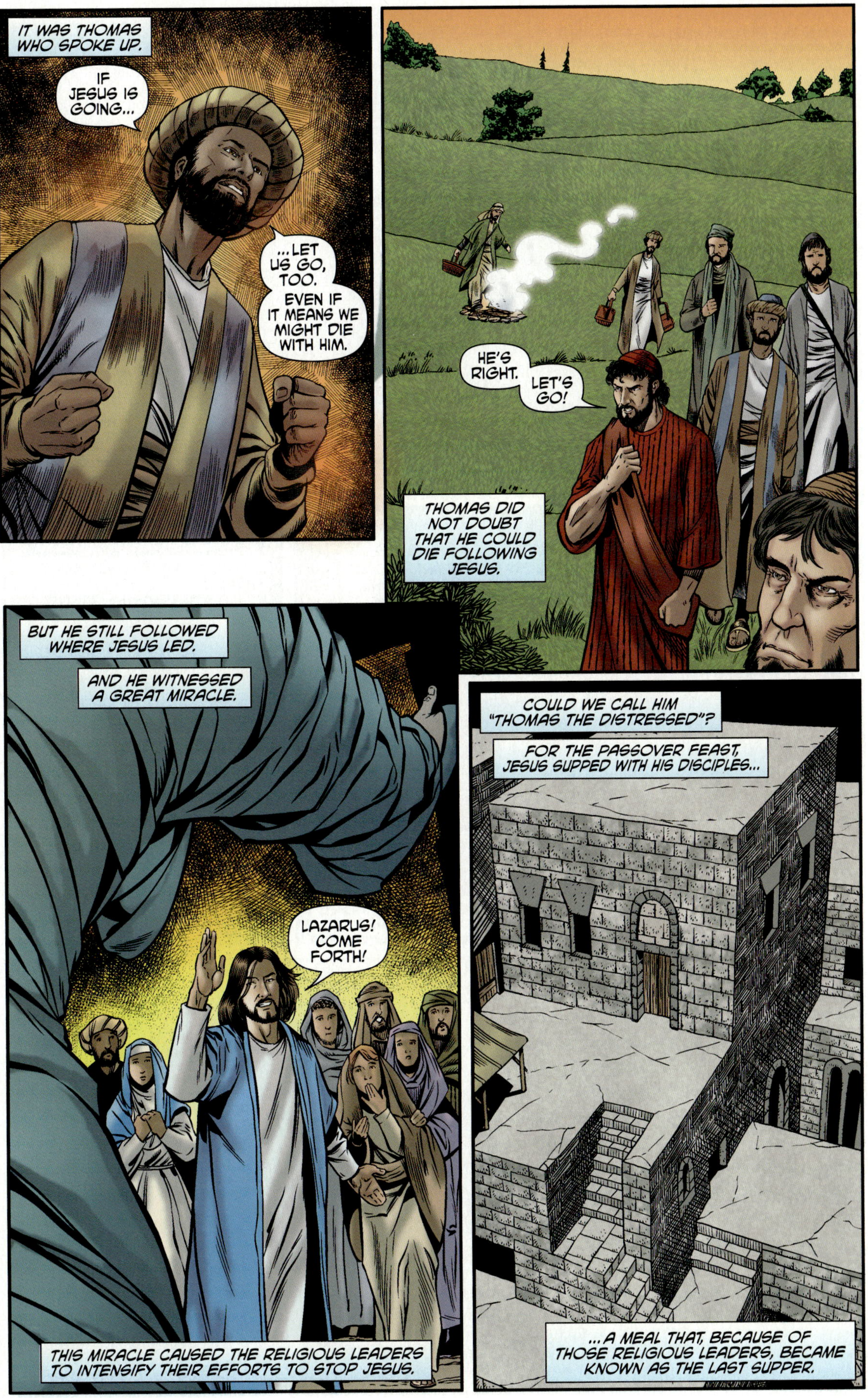
IT WAS THOMAS WHO SPOKE UP.
IF JESUS IS GOING...
...LET US GO, TOO.
EVEN IF IT MEANS WE MIGHT DIE WITH HIM.
HE'S RIGHT.
LET'S GO!
THOMAS DID NOT DOUBT THAT HE COULD DIE FOLLOWING JESUS.
BUT HE STILL FOLLOWED WHERE JESUS LED.
AND HE WITNESSED A GREAT MIRACLE.
LAZARUS! COME FORTH!
THIS MIRACLE CAUSED THE RELIGIOUS LEADERS TO INTENSIFY THEIR EFFORTS TO STOP JESUS.
COULD WE CALL HIM "THOMAS THE DISTRESSED"?
FOR THE PASSOVER FEAST, JESUS SUPPED WITH HIS DISCIPLES...
...A MEAL THAT, BECAUSE OF THOSE RELIGIOUS LEADERS, BECAME KNOWN AS THE LAST SUPPER.

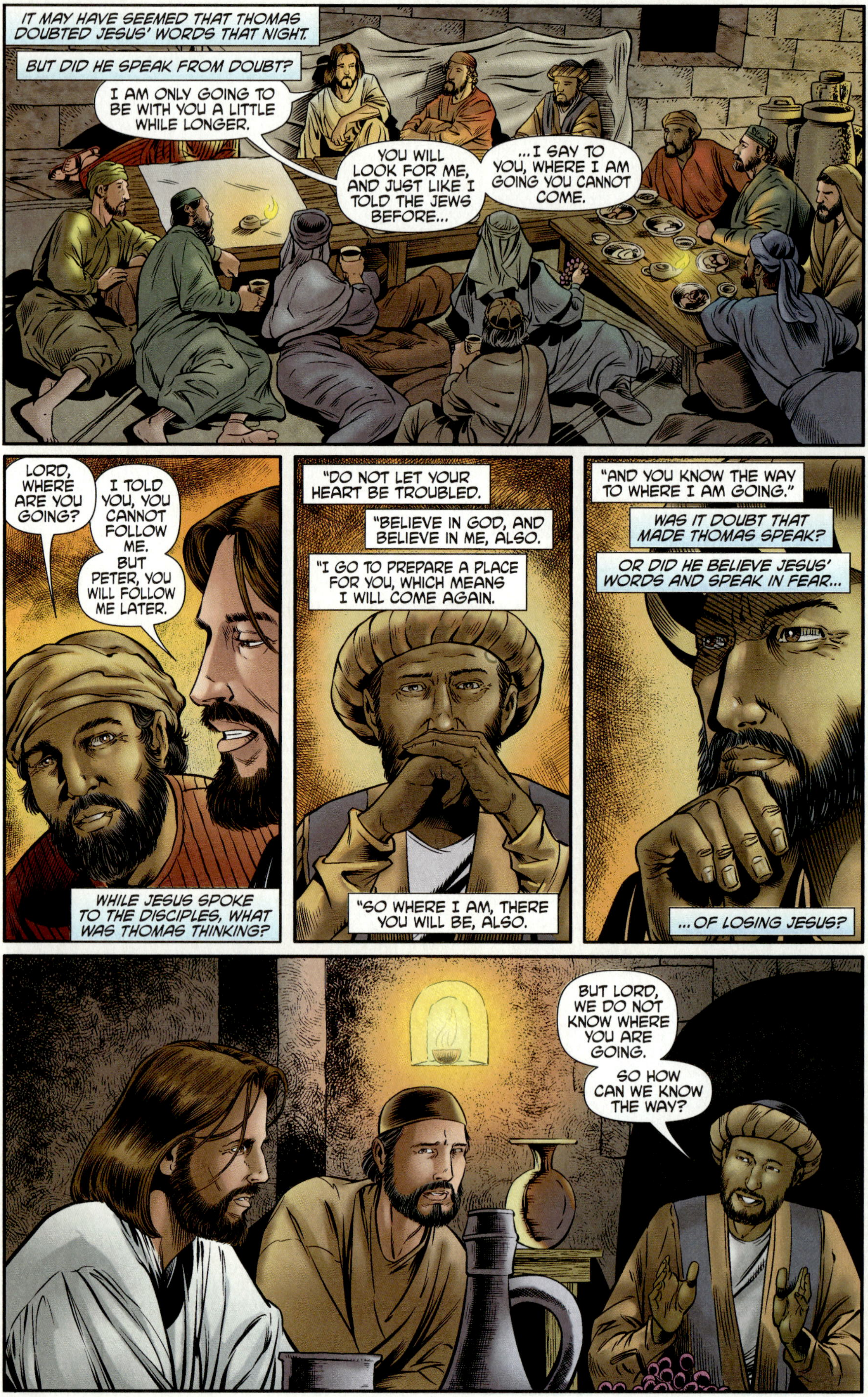

IT MAY HAVE SEEMED THAT THOMAS DOUBTED JESUS' WORDS THAT NIGHT.
BUT DID HE SPEAK FROM DOUBT?
I AM ONLY GOING TO BE WITH YOU A LITTLE WHILE LONGER.
YOU WILL LOOK FOR ME, AND JUST LIKE I TOLD THE JEWS BEFORE...
...I SAY TO YOU, WHERE I AM GOING YOU CANNOT COME.
LORD, WHERE ARE YOU GOING?
I TOLD YOU, YOU CANNOT FOLLOW ME.
BUT PETER, YOU WILL FOLLOW ME LATER.
WHILE JESUS SPOKE TO THE DISCIPLES, WHAT WAS THOMAS THINKING?
"DO NOT LET YOUR HEART BE TROUBLED.
"BELIEVE IN GOD, AND BELIEVE IN ME, ALSO.
"I GO TO PREPARE A PLACE FOR YOU, WHICH MEANS I WILL COME AGAIN.
"SO WHERE I AM, THERE YOU WILL BE, ALSO.
"AND YOU KNOW THE WAY TO WHERE I AM GOING."
WAS IT DOUBT THAT MADE THOMAS SPEAK?
OR DID HE BELIEVE JESUS' WORDS AND SPEAK IN FEAR...
...OF LOSING JESUS?
BUT LORD, WE DO NOT KNOW WHERE YOU ARE GOING.
SO HOW CAN WE KNOW THE WAY?

I AM. THE WAY. I AM THE TRUTH AND THE LIFE.

NO ONE COMES TO THE FATHER EXCEPT THROUGH ME. YOU HAVE KNOWN ME AND YOU HAVE SEEN ME...

...THEREFORE, YOU HAVE KNOWN THE FATHER AND HAVE SEEN THE FATHER.

JESUS SAID MANY THINGS THE DISCIPLES DID NOT UNDERSTAND.

BUT THOMAS UNDERSTOOD THAT JESUS WAS LEAVING THEM.

HE DID NOT DOUBT JESUS WOULD LEAVE THEM...

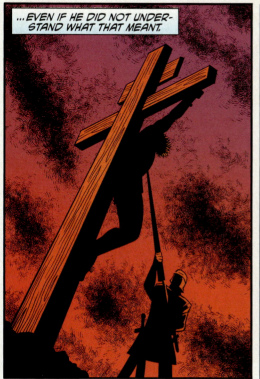

...EVEN IF HE DID NOT UNDERSTAND WHAT THAT MEANT.

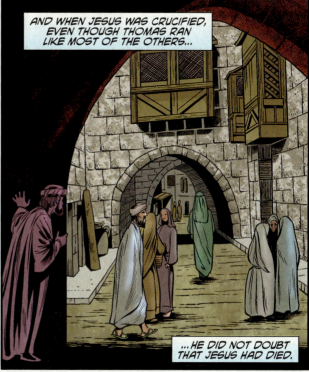

AND WHEN JESUS WAS CRUCIFIED, EVEN THOUGH THOMAS RAN LIKE MOST OF THE OTHERS...

...HE DID NOT DOUBT THAT JESUS HAD DIED.

AFTER THAT DAY, THE DISCIPLES GATHERED AGAIN...

...IN A DARK, LOCKED ROOM, HIDING LIKE SCARED ANIMALS.

BUT THOMAS WAS NOT THERE FOR PART OF THAT TIME.

WHO'S THERE?

IT'S ME! THOMAS!

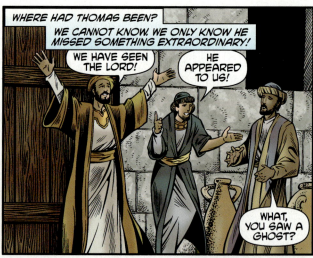

WHERE HAD THOMAS BEEN? WE CANNOT KNOW. WE ONLY KNOW HE MISSED SOMETHING EXTRAORDINARY!

WE HAVE SEEN THE LORD!

HE APPEARED TO US!

WHAT, YOU SAW A GHOST?

NO. HE WAS ALIVE!

HE CAME INTO THIS ROOM EVEN THOUGH THE DOOR AND WINDOWS WERE SEALED.

AND HE WAS ALIVE!

THEN CAME THOMAS'S DEFINING MOMENT.

THIS IS HOW HE BECAME KNOWN AS "DOUBTING THOMAS."

NO. YOU EXPECT ME TO BELIEVE THIS?

NOT UNTIL I CAN SEE HIS HANDS, WITH THE NAIL MARKS!

NOT UNTIL I...I TOUCH THE HOLES THOSE NAILS MADE WITH MY OWN FINGERS!

NOT UNTIL I PUT MY HAND IN HIS SIDE, WHERE THE SPEAR PIERCED HIM!

A WEEK PASSED.

THE DISCIPLES STILL USED THAT ROOM AS THEIR MEETING PLACE.

AND EVEN THOUGH HE DID NOT BELIEVE THEM, THOMAS CONTINUED TO BE WITH THEM.

THEN THEY WERE JOINED BY ANOTHER...

PEACE, FRIENDS!

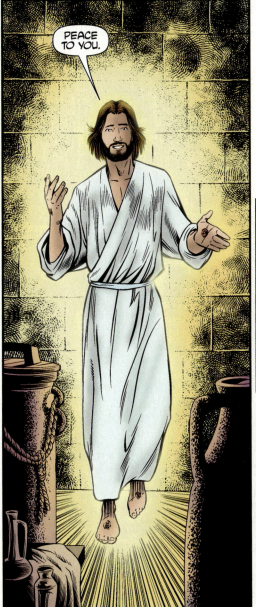

PEACE TO YOU.

HELLO, THOMAS.

SEE, HERE, MY HANDS.

FEEL MY FLESH AND MY WOUNDS WITH YOUR OWN HANDS. LOOK, THOMAS...

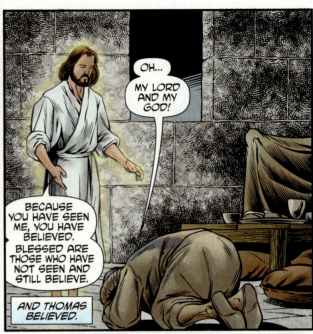

LOOK, THOMAS, THE WOUND IN MY SIDE.

REACH OUT YOUR HAND.

THOMAS, IT IS TIME TO STOP DOUBTING.

BELIEVE.

OH... MY LORD AND MY GOD!

BECAUSE YOU HAVE SEEN ME, YOU HAVE BELIEVED. BLESSED ARE THOSE WHO HAVE NOT SEEN AND STILL BELIEVE.

AND THOMAS BELIEVED.

PERHAPS THE BEST NAME FOR HIM WOULD BE "THOMAS THE DISCIPLE."

WHEN JESUS LEFT, HE TOLD THEM TO GO TO ALL THE WORLD.

THOMAS TOOK THAT COMMAND SERIOUSLY.

IT IS SAID THAT THOMAS CARRIED CHRIST'S MESSAGE AS FAR AWAY AS INDIA!

WHY WOULD HE NOT?

THOMAS MAY HAVE DOUBTED HIS FRIENDS...

...BUT HE DID NOT DOUBT HIS LORD AND HIS GOD.

AND MANY STORIES AGREE ABOUT THE WAY HE DIED.

A KING RECRUITED MEN TO KILL THOMAS.

THEY KILLED HIM WITH A SPEAR.

THE DISCIPLE WHO HAD ONCE PUT HIS HAND WHERE A SPEAR PIERCED HIS MASTER'S SIDE...

...WAS STRUCK DOWN BY A SPEAR HIMSELF.

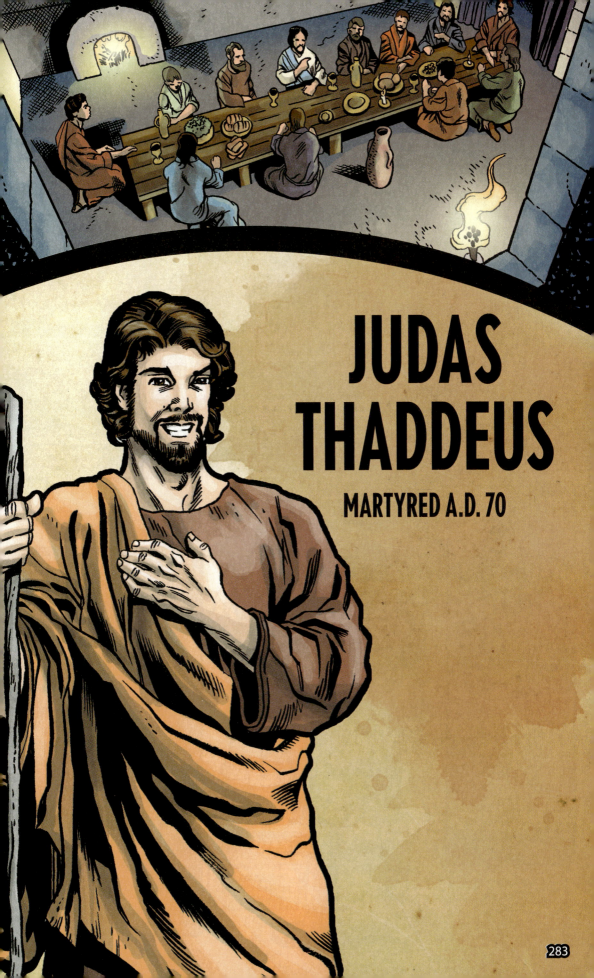

JUDAS THADDEUS

MARTYRED A.D. 70

HIS NAME WAS JUDAS. AN HONORABLE NAME, WHEN HE WAS GIVEN IT--

--BUT ANOTHER MAN DISHONORED IT.

BUT THEY SUGGEST MUCH ABOUT HIS CHARACTER.

SO HE WAS CALLED OTHER NAMES: JUDAS, NOT ISCARIOT; JUDE, SON OF JAMES; LEBBAEUS; AND THADDAEUS.

HIS NAMES AND ONE QUESTION THAT HE ASKED JESUS ARE ALL THAT IS KNOWN ABOUT HIM.

"JUDAS, NOT ISCARIOT": TO AVOID CONFUSION WITH JESUS' BETRAYER.

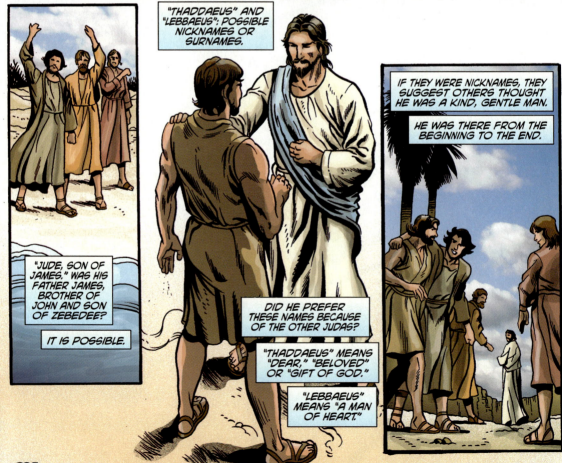

"THADDAEUS" AND "LEBBAEUS": POSSIBLE NICKNAMES OR SURNAMES.

IF THEY WERE NICKNAMES, THEY SUGGEST OTHERS THOUGHT HE WAS A KIND, GENTLE MAN.

HE WAS THERE FROM THE BEGINNING TO THE END.

"JUDE, SON OF JAMES." WAS HIS FATHER JAMES, BROTHER OF JOHN AND SON OF ZEBEDEE?

IT IS POSSIBLE.

DID HE PREFER THESE NAMES BECAUSE OF THE OTHER JUDAS?

"THADDAEUS" MEANS "DEAR," "BELOVED" OR "GIFT OF GOD."

"LEBBAEUS" MEANS "A MAN OF HEART."

HE WAS THERE IN THE UPPER ROOM, WHERE HE ASKED HIS QUESTION.

...SOON I WILL LEAVE, BUT I WILL NOT LEAVE YOU ALONE.

THE FATHER WILL GIVE YOU A COUNSELOR: THE SPIRIT OF TRUTH.

THE WORLD DOES NOT SEE OR KNOW HIM.

BUT YOU KNOW THE SPIRIT--

--BECAUSE HE IS WITH YOU AND WILL BE IN YOU.

YOU SEE, I AM IN MY FATHER, AND YOU ARE IN ME.

TO YOU WHO LOVE ME, I WILL LOVE AND REVEAL MYSELF.

AND THEN JUDAS SPOKE.

HIS ONLY RECORDED WORDS, REVEALING A TENDER, GENTLE HEART.

BUT LORD, WHY DO YOU REVEAL YOURSELF TO US ONLY?

WHY NOT TO THE WORLD?

I TEACH YOU WHILE I AM WITH YOU.

THE HOLY SPIRIT WILL BRING MY TEACHINGS BACK TO YOU.

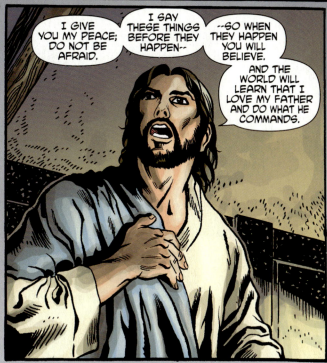

I GIVE YOU MY PEACE; DO NOT BE AFRAID.

I SAY THESE THINGS BEFORE THEY HAPPEN--

--SO WHEN THEY HAPPEN YOU WILL BELIEVE.

AND THE WORLD WILL LEARN THAT I LOVE MY FATHER AND DO WHAT HE COMMANDS.

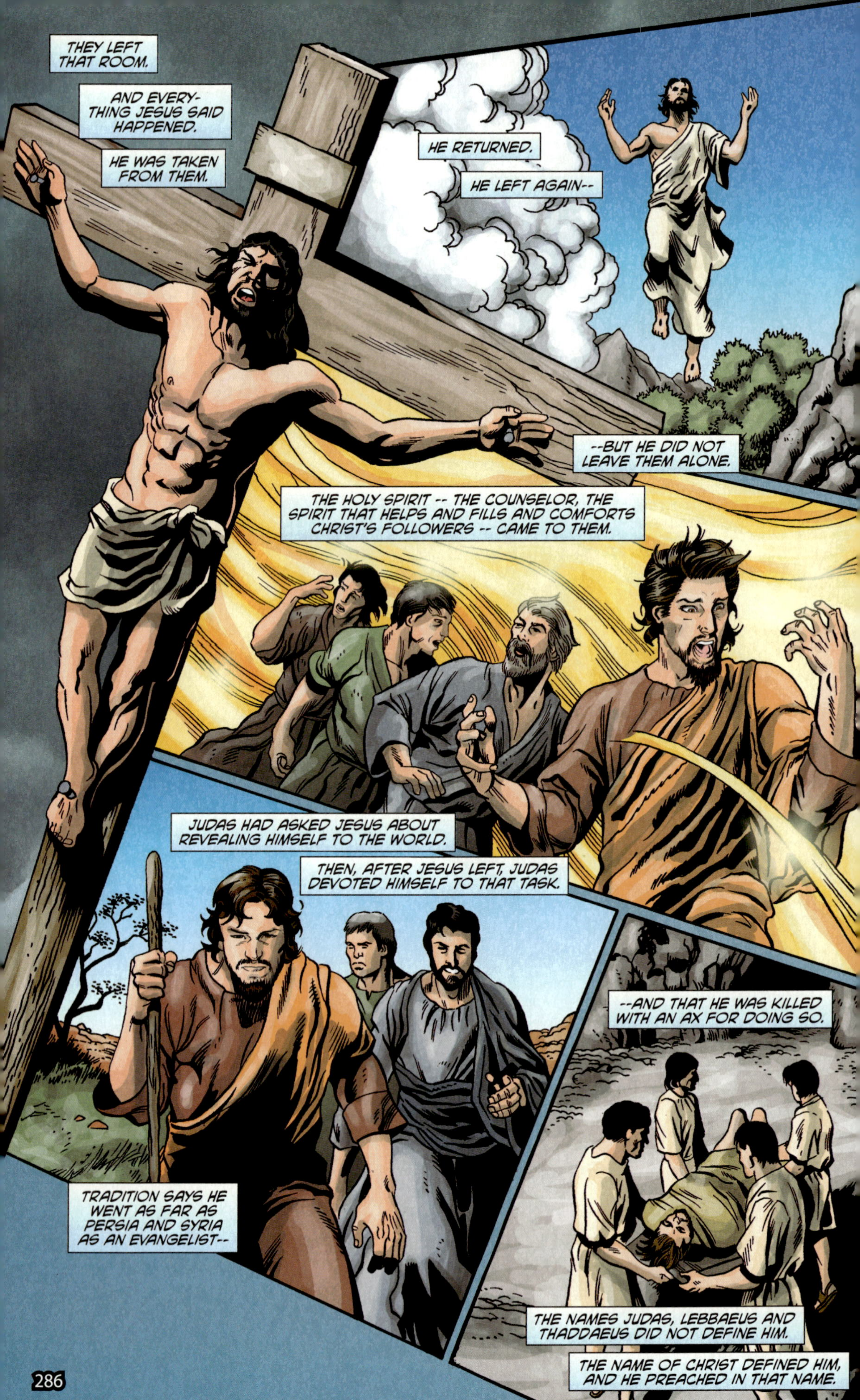
THEY LEFT THAT ROOM.
AND EVERY-THING JESUS SAID HAPPENED.
HE WAS TAKEN FROM THEM.
HE RETURNED.
HE LEFT AGAIN--
--BUT HE DID NOT LEAVE THEM ALONE.
THE HOLY SPIRIT -- THE COUNSELOR, THE SPIRIT THAT HELPS AND FILLS AND COMFORTS CHRIST'S FOLLOWERS -- CAME TO THEM.
JUDAS HAD ASKED JESUS ABOUT REVEALING HIMSELF TO THE WORLD.
THEN, AFTER JESUS LEFT, JUDAS DEVOTED HIMSELF TO THAT TASK.
TRADITION SAYS HE WENT AS FAR AS PERSIA AND SYRIA AS AN EVANGELIST--
--AND THAT HE WAS KILLED WITH AN AX FOR DOING SO.
THE NAMES JUDAS, LEBBAEUS AND THADDAEUS DID NOT DEFINE HIM.
THE NAME OF CHRIST DEFINED HIM, AND HE PREACHED IN THAT NAME.

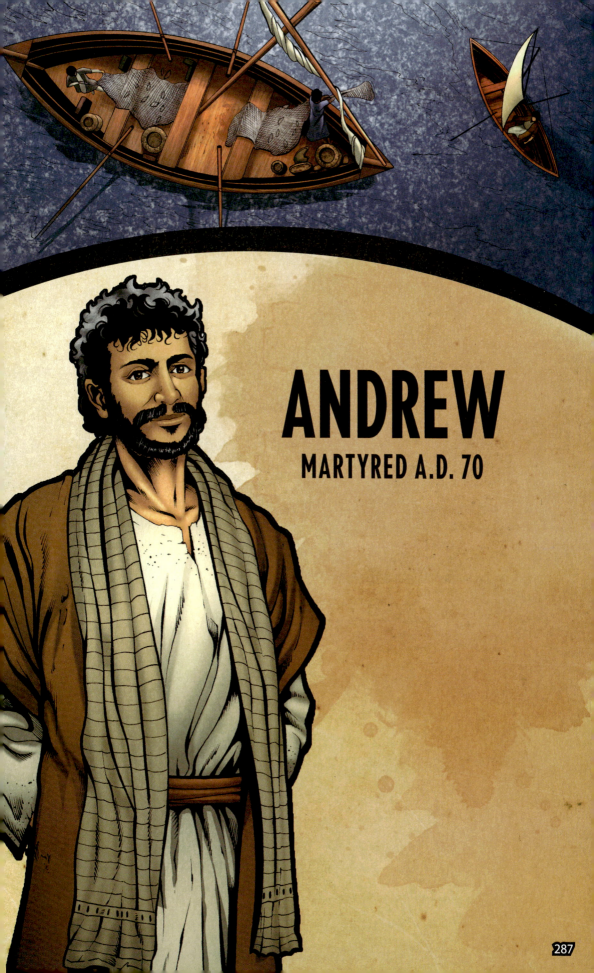

ANDREW

MARTYRED A.D. 70

SIMON, I WON'T BE GOING HOME WITH YOU TODAY.

WHY NOT, BROTHER? AREN'T YOU TIRED?

I WANT TO HEAR THIS BAPTIZER FROM THE JORDAN RIVER.

THEY SAY HE SPEAKS POWERFULLY, WITH THE SPIRIT OF ELIJAH.

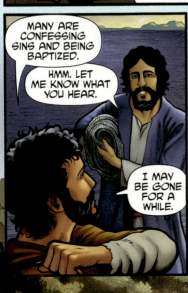

MANY ARE CONFESSING SINS AND BEING BAPTIZED.

HMM. LET ME KNOW WHAT YOU HEAR.

I MAY BE GONE FOR A WHILE.

WE'LL MANAGE WITHOUT YOU SOMEHOW.

OH, I'M SURE YOU WILL, BROTHER. I'LL BE BACK IN A FEW DAYS, MAYBE A WEEK.

ANDREW, LIKE MANY YOUNG JEWISH MEN OF THE TIME...

...AWAITED THE SAVIOR PROMISED BY GOD THROUGH THE PROPHETS CENTURIES AGO.

THEY AWAITED A SAVIOR WHO WOULD RESCUE THEIR PEOPLE FROM BONDAGE.

DON'T JUST REPENT.

PRODUCE THE FRUIT THAT GOES WITH TRUE REPENTANCE.

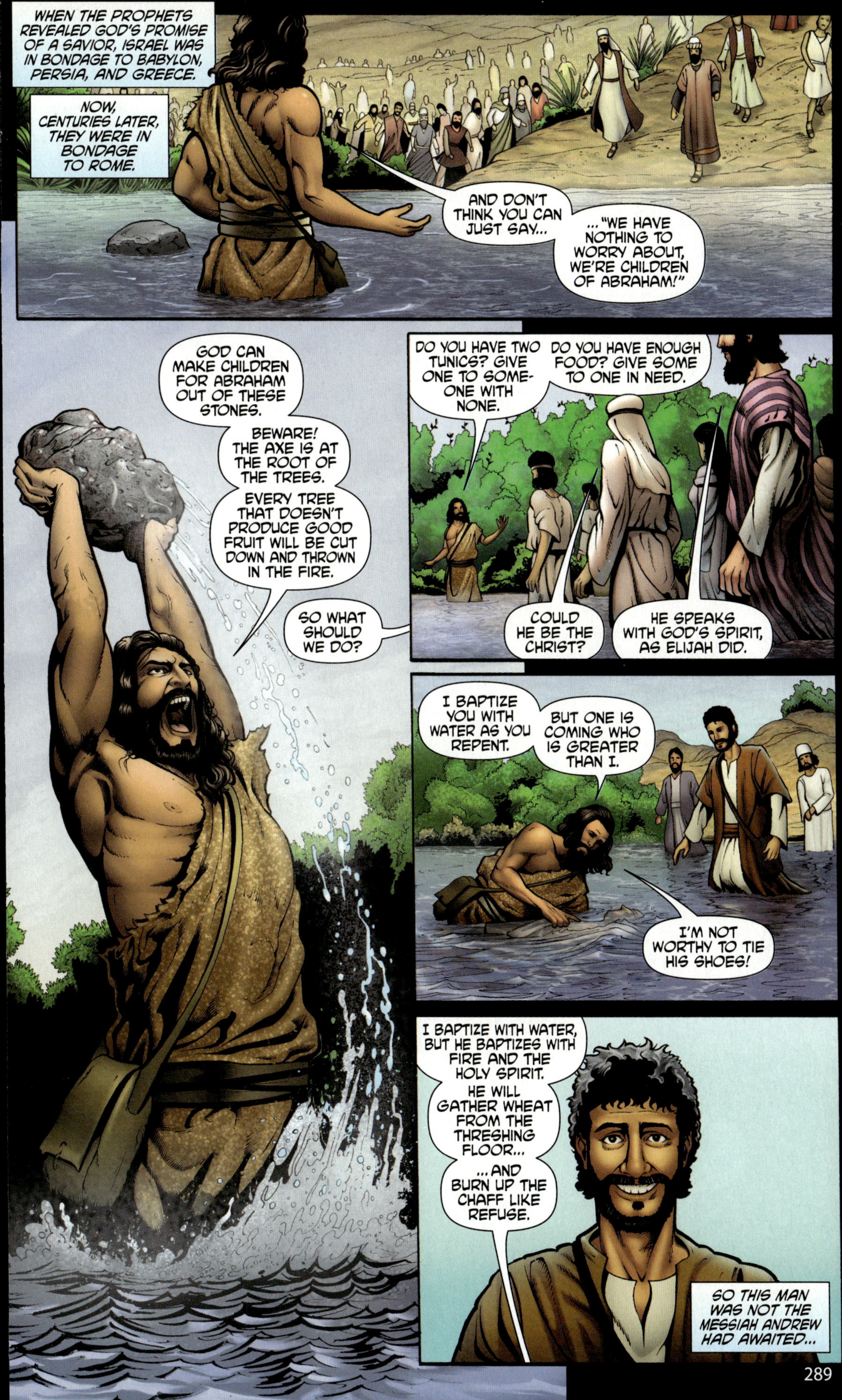

WHEN THE PROPHETS REVEALED GOD'S PROMISE OF A SAVIOR, ISRAEL WAS IN BONDAGE TO BABYLON, PERSIA, AND GREECE.
NOW, CENTURIES LATER, THEY WERE IN BONDAGE TO ROME.
AND DON'T THINK YOU CAN JUST SAY...
..."WE HAVE NOTHING TO WORRY ABOUT, WE'RE CHILDREN OF ABRAHAM!"
GOD CAN MAKE CHILDREN FOR ABRAHAM OUT OF THESE STONES.
BEWARE! THE AXE IS AT THE ROOT OF THE TREES.
EVERY TREE THAT DOESN'T PRODUCE GOOD FRUIT WILL BE CUT DOWN AND THROWN IN THE FIRE.
SO WHAT SHOULD WE DO?
DO YOU HAVE TWO TUNICS? GIVE ONE TO SOME-ONE WITH NONE.
DO YOU HAVE ENOUGH FOOD? GIVE SOME TO ONE IN NEED.
COULD HE BE THE CHRIST?
HE SPEAKS WITH GOD'S SPIRIT, AS ELIJAH DID.
I BAPTIZE YOU WITH WATER AS YOU REPENT.
BUT ONE IS COMING WHO IS GREATER THAN I.
I'M NOT WORTHY TO TIE HIS SHOES!
I BAPTIZE WITH WATER, BUT HE BAPTIZES WITH FIRE AND THE HOLY SPIRIT.
HE WILL GATHER WHEAT FROM THE THRESHING FLOOR...
...AND BURN UP THE CHAFF LIKE REFUSE.
SO THIS MAN WAS NOT THE MESSIAH ANDREW HAD AWAITED...

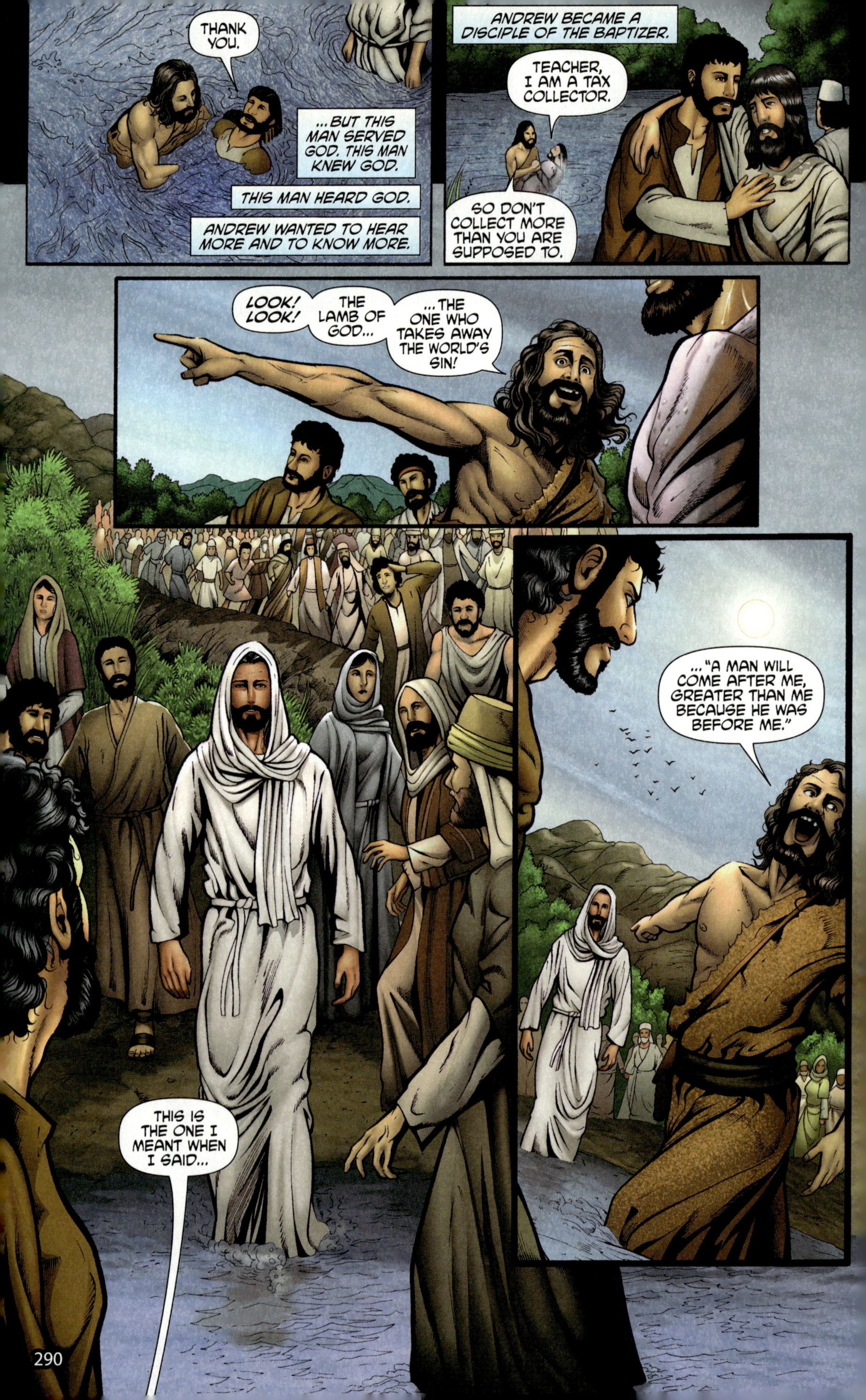
THANK YOU.
...BUT THIS MAN SERVED GOD. THIS MAN KNEW GOD.
THIS MAN HEARD GOD.
ANDREW WANTED TO HEAR MORE AND TO KNOW MORE.
ANDREW BECAME A DISCIPLE OF THE BAPTIZER.
TEACHER, I AM A TAX COLLECTOR.
SO DON'T COLLECT MORE THAN YOU ARE SUPPOSED TO.
LOOK! LOOK!
THE LAMB OF GOD...
...THE ONE WHO TAKES AWAY THE WORLD'S SIN!
THIS IS THE ONE I MEANT WHEN I SAID...
..."A MAN WILL COME AFTER ME, GREATER THAN ME BECAUSE HE WAS BEFORE ME."

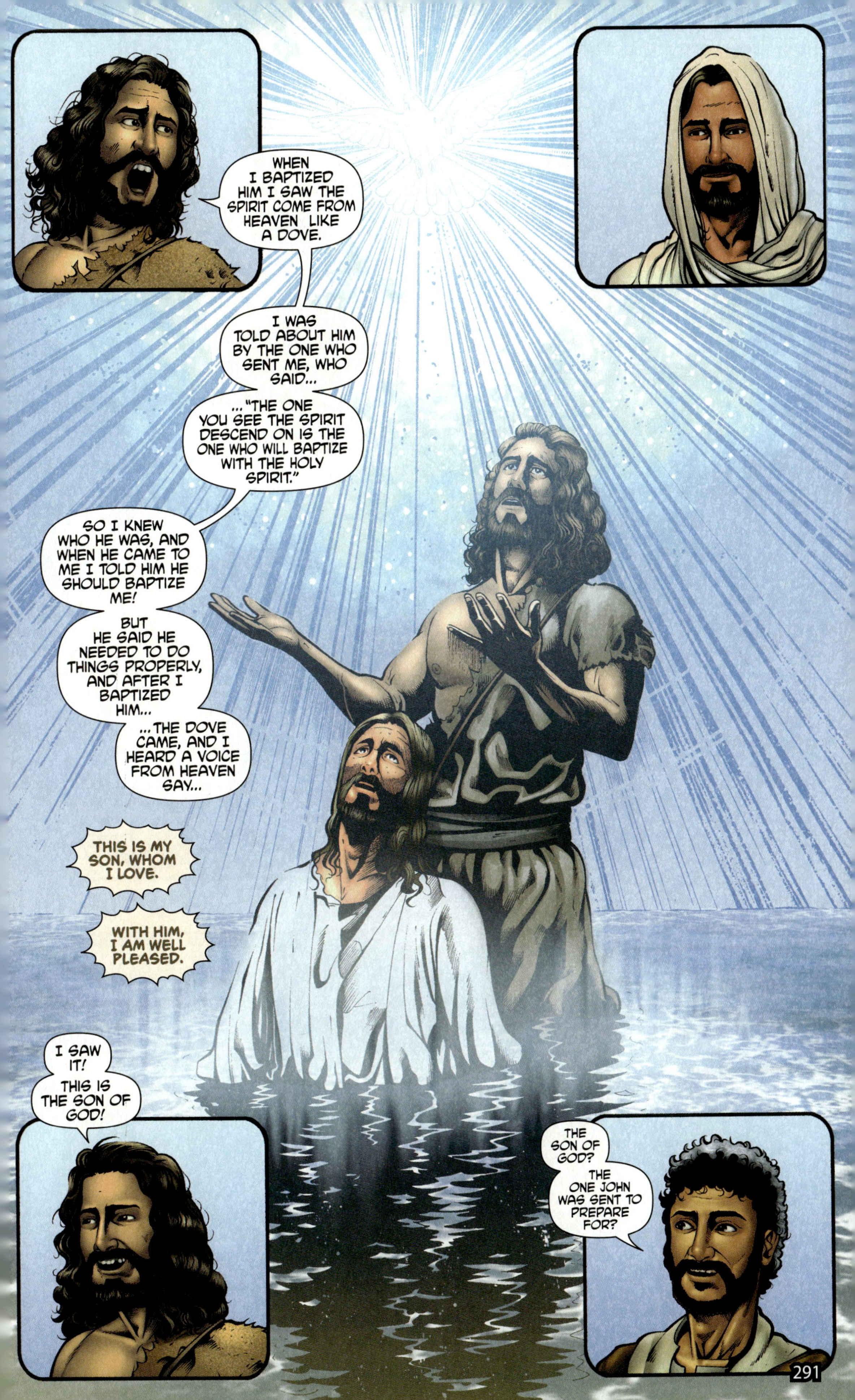
WHEN I BAPTIZED HIM I SAW THE SPIRIT COME FROM HEAVEN LIKE A DOVE.
I WAS TOLD ABOUT HIM BY THE ONE WHO SENT ME, WHO SAID...
..."THE ONE YOU SEE THE SPIRIT DESCEND ON IS THE ONE WHO WILL BAPTIZE WITH THE HOLY SPIRIT."
SO I KNEW WHO HE WAS, AND WHEN HE CAME TO ME I TOLD HIM HE SHOULD BAPTIZE ME!
BUT HE SAID HE NEEDED TO DO THINGS PROPERLY, AND AFTER I BAPTIZED HIM...
...THE DOVE CAME, AND I HEARD A VOICE FROM HEAVEN SAY...
THIS IS MY SON, WHOM I LOVE.
WITH HIM, I AM WELL PLEASED.
I SAW IT!
THIS IS THE SON OF GOD!
THE SON OF GOD?
THE ONE JOHN WAS SENT TO PREPARE FOR?

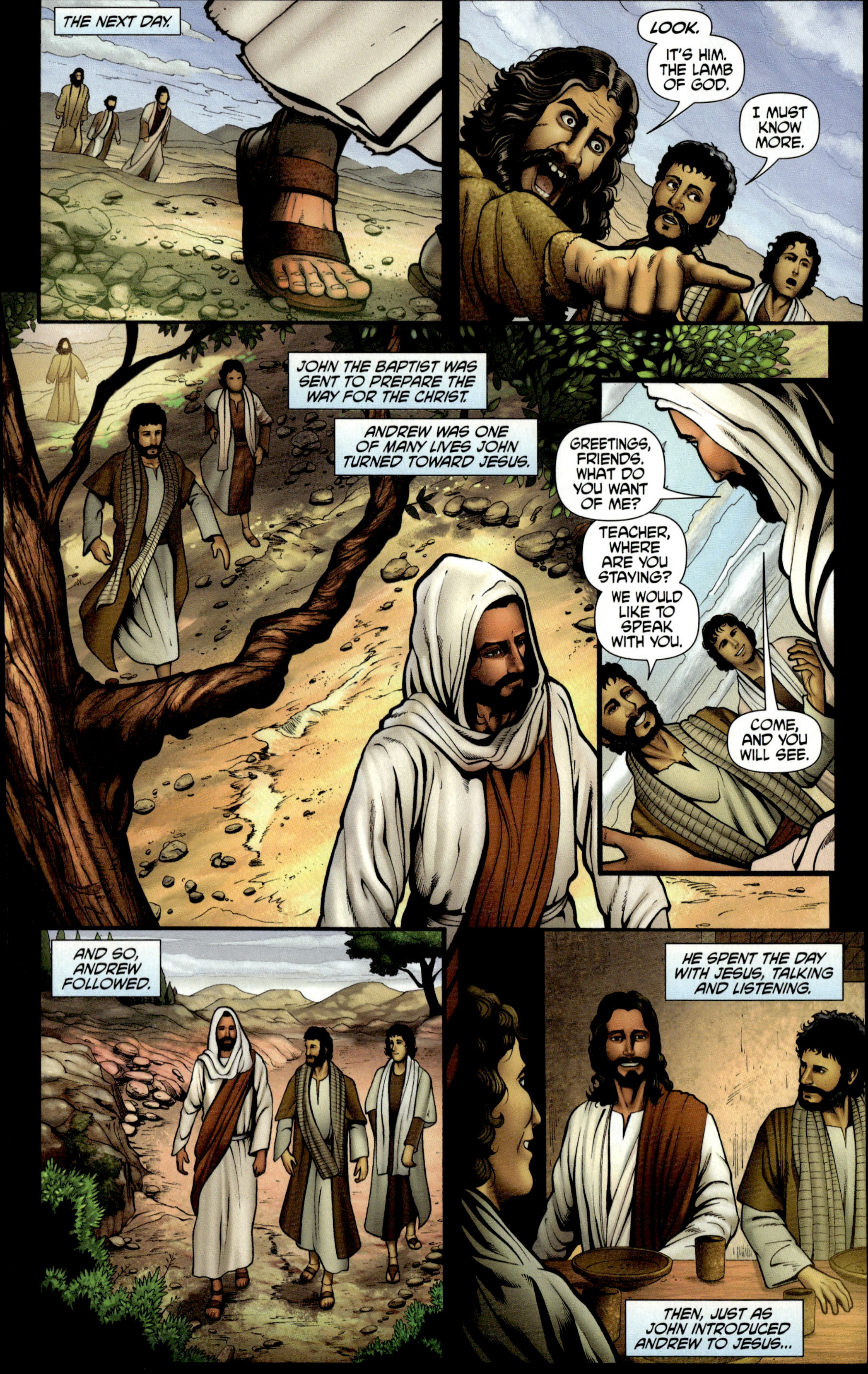

THE NEXT DAY.
LOOK.
IT'S HIM. THE LAMB OF GOD.
I MUST KNOW MORE.
JOHN THE BAPTIST WAS SENT TO PREPARE THE WAY FOR THE CHRIST.
ANDREW WAS ONE OF MANY LIVES JOHN TURNED TOWARD JESUS.
GREETINGS, FRIENDS. WHAT DO YOU WANT OF ME?
TEACHER, WHERE ARE YOU STAYING?
WE WOULD LIKE TO SPEAK WITH YOU.
COME, AND YOU WILL SEE.
AND SO, ANDREW FOLLOWED.
HE SPENT THE DAY WITH JESUS, TALKING AND LISTENING.
THEN, JUST AS JOHN INTRODUCED ANDREW TO JESUS...

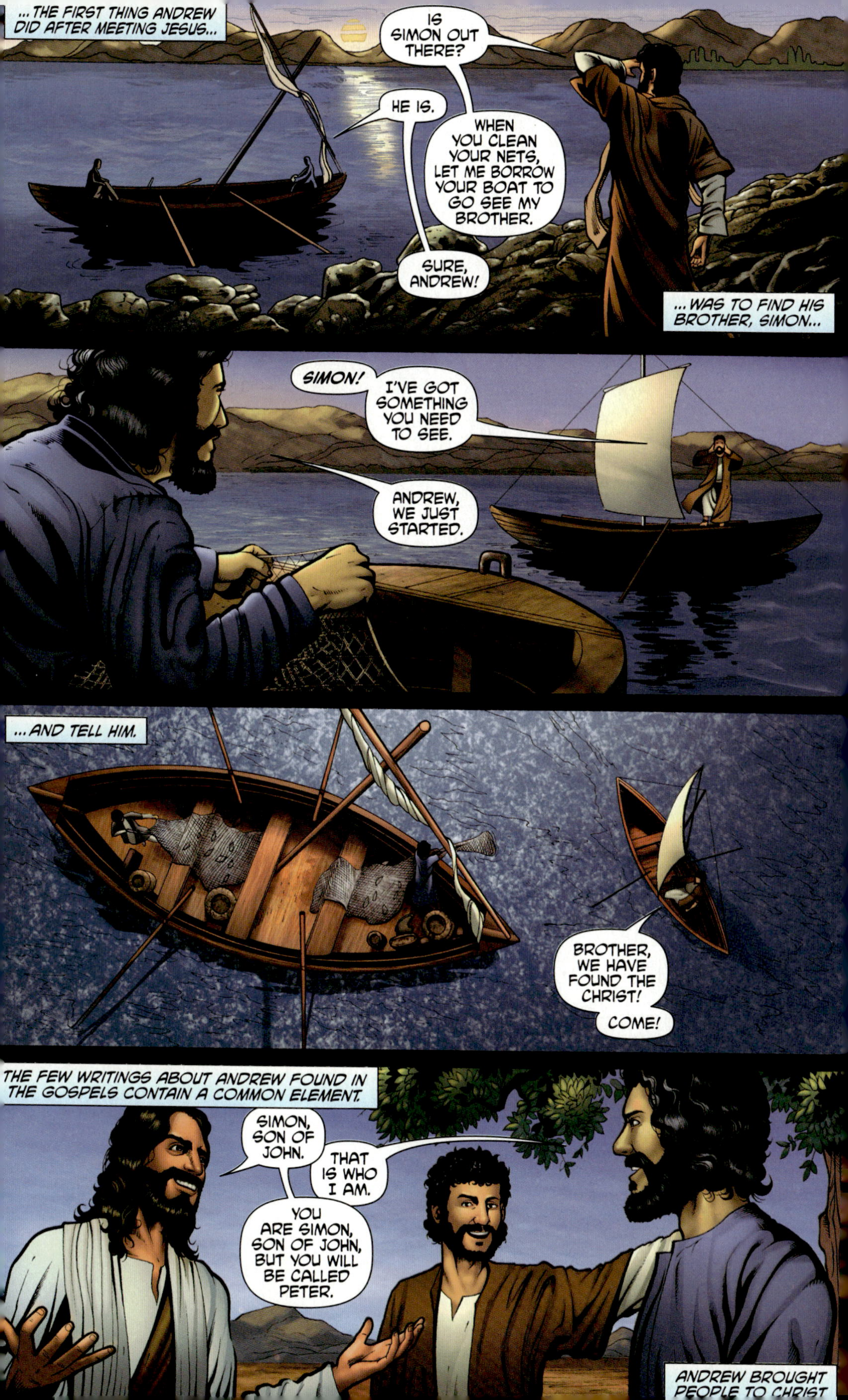
...THE FIRST THING ANDREW DID AFTER MEETING JESUS...
IS SIMON OUT THERE?
HE IS.
WHEN YOU CLEAN YOUR NETS, LET ME BORROW YOUR BOAT TO GO SEE MY BROTHER.
SURE, ANDREW!
...WAS TO FIND HIS BROTHER, SIMON...
SIMON! I'VE GOT SOMETHING YOU NEED TO SEE.
ANDREW, WE JUST STARTED.
...AND TELL HIM.
BROTHER, WE HAVE FOUND THE CHRIST!
COME!
THE FEW WRITINGS ABOUT ANDREW FOUND IN THE GOSPELS CONTAIN A COMMON ELEMENT.
SIMON, SON OF JOHN.
THAT IS WHO I AM.
YOU ARE SIMON, SON OF JOHN, BUT YOU WILL BE CALLED PETER.
ANDREW BROUGHT PEOPLE TO CHRIST

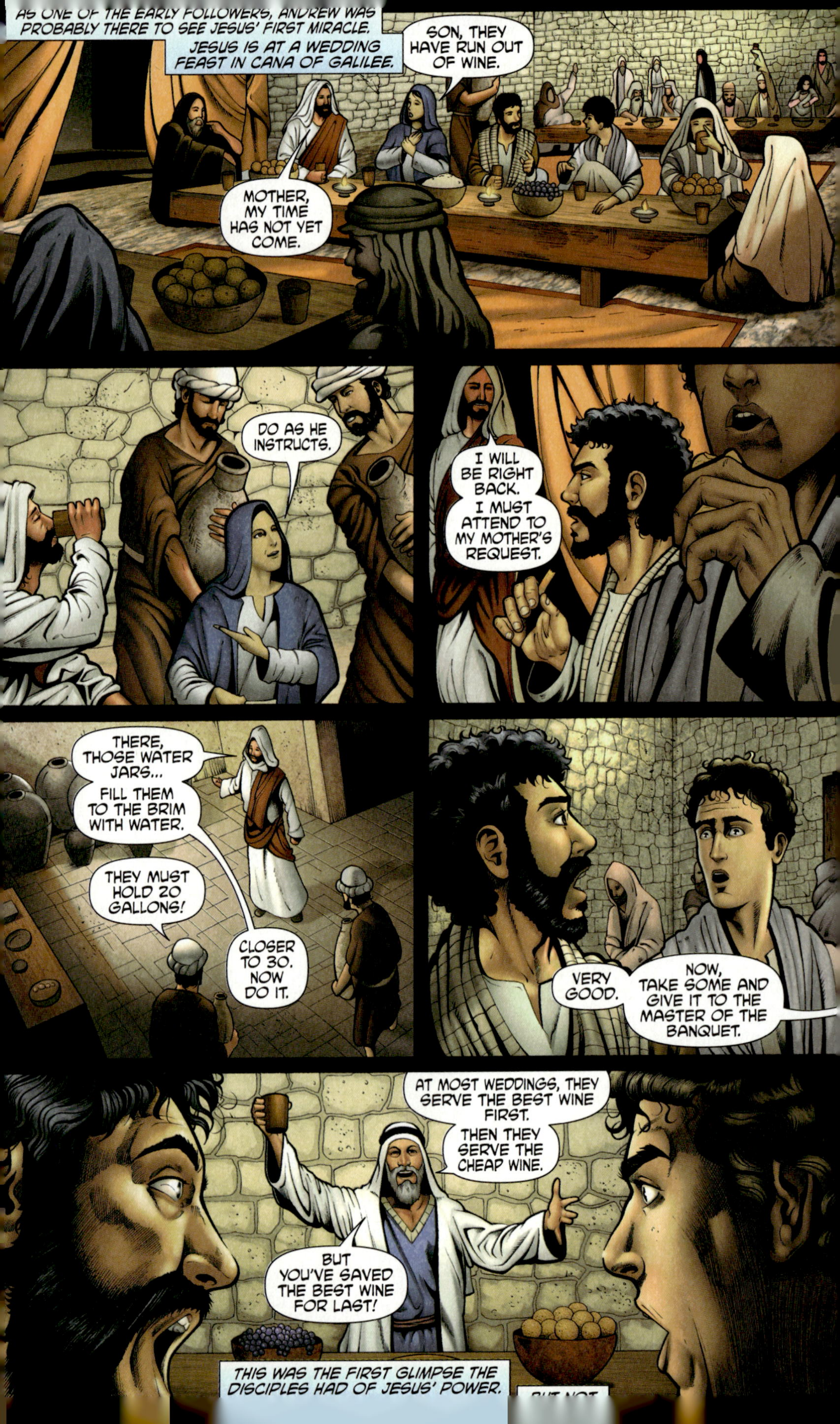
AS ONE OF THE EARLY FOLLOWERS, ANDREW WAS PROBABLY THERE TO SEE JESUS' FIRST MIRACLE.
JESUS IS AT A WEDDING FEAST IN CANA OF GALILEE.
SON, THEY HAVE RUN OUT OF WINE.
MOTHER, MY TIME HAS NOT YET COME.
DO AS HE INSTRUCTS.
I WILL BE RIGHT BACK.
I MUST ATTEND TO MY MOTHER'S REQUEST.
THERE, THOSE WATER JARS...
FILL THEM TO THE BRIM WITH WATER.
THEY MUST HOLD 20 GALLONS!
CLOSER TO 30. NOW DO IT.
VERY GOOD.
NOW, TAKE SOME AND GIVE IT TO THE MASTER OF THE BANQUET.
AT MOST WEDDINGS, THEY SERVE THE BEST WINE FIRST.
THEN THEY SERVE THE CHEAP WINE.
BUT YOU'VE SAVED THE BEST WINE FOR LAST!
THIS WAS THE FIRST GLIMPSE THE DISCIPLES HAD OF JESUS' POWER.

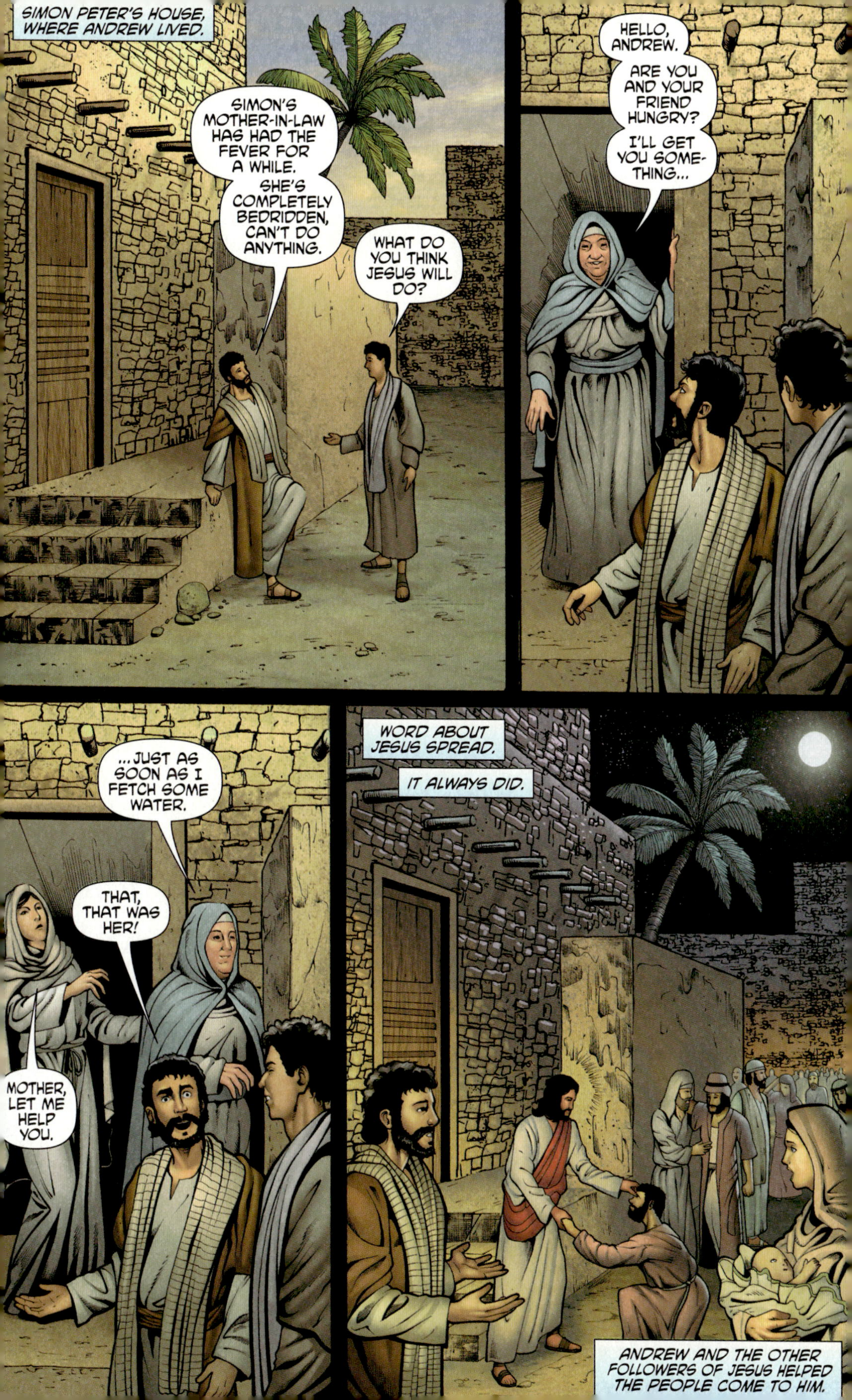
SIMON PETER'S HOUSE, WHERE ANDREW LIVED.
SIMON'S MOTHER-IN-LAW HAS HAD THE FEVER FOR A WHILE.
SHE'S COMPLETELY BEDRIDDEN, CAN'T DO ANYTHING.
WHAT DO YOU THINK JESUS WILL DO?
HELLO, ANDREW.
ARE YOU AND YOUR FRIEND HUNGRY?
I'LL GET YOU SOMETHING...
...JUST AS SOON AS I FETCH SOME WATER.
THAT, THAT WAS HER!
MOTHER, LET ME HELP YOU.
WORD ABOUT JESUS SPREAD.
IT ALWAYS DID.
ANDREW AND THE OTHER FOLLOWERS OF JESUS HELPED THE PEOPLE COME TO HIM.

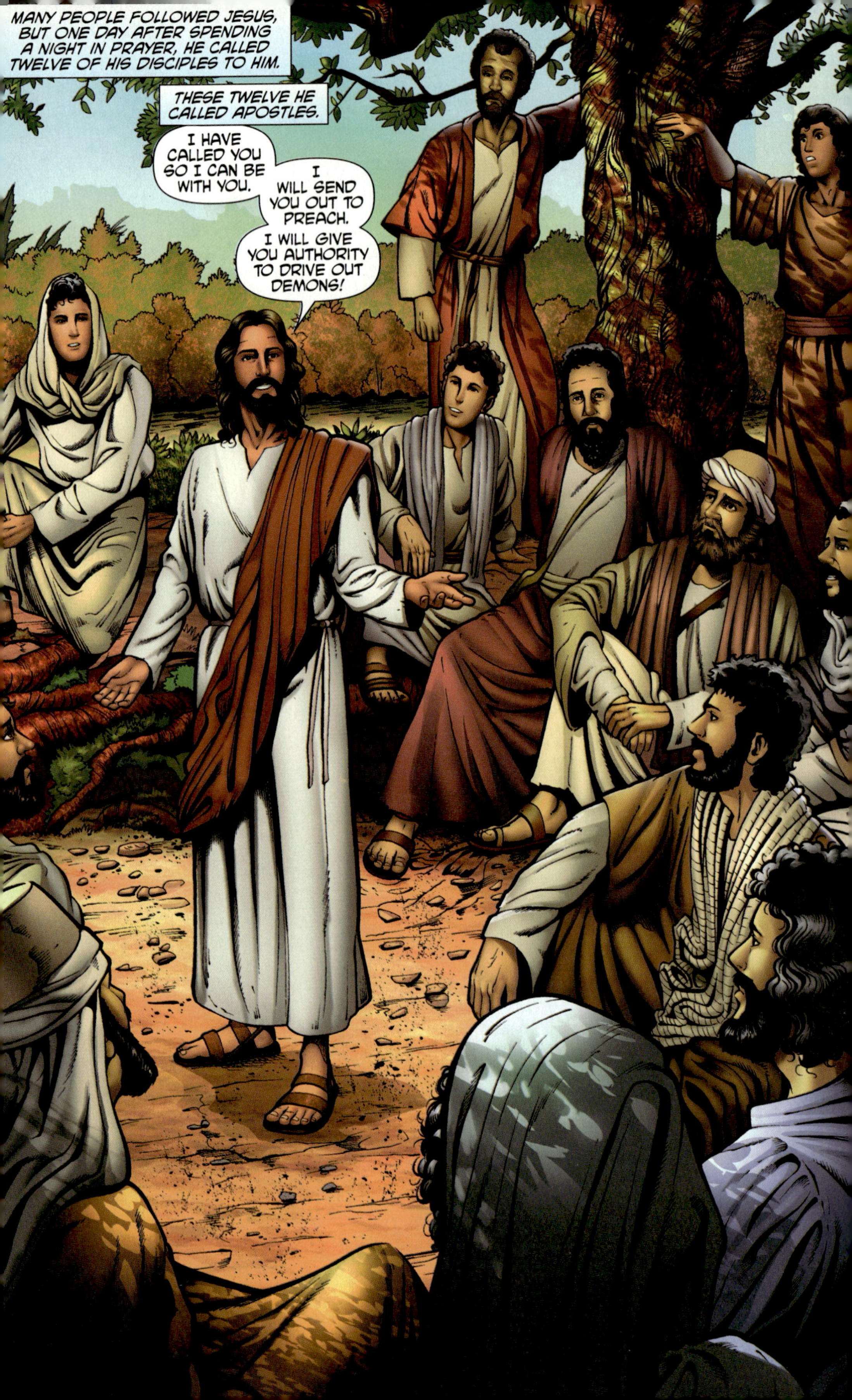
MANY PEOPLE FOLLOWED JESUS, BUT ONE DAY AFTER SPENDING A NIGHT IN PRAYER, HE CALLED TWELVE OF HIS DISCIPLES TO HIM.
THESE TWELVE HE CALLED APOSTLES.
I HAVE CALLED YOU SO I CAN BE WITH YOU.
I WILL SEND YOU OUT TO PREACH.
I WILL GIVE YOU AUTHORITY TO DRIVE OUT DEMONS!

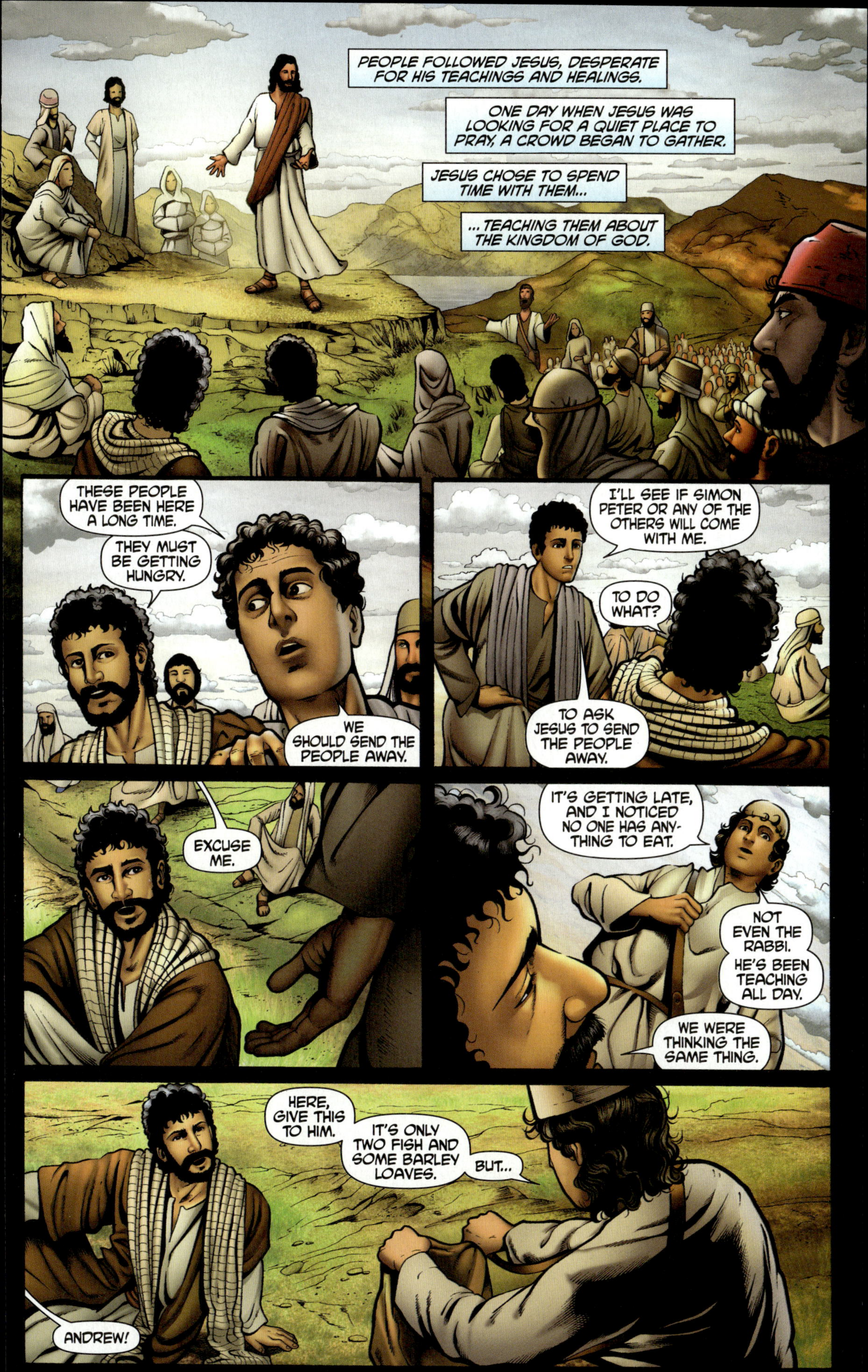
PEOPLE FOLLOWED JESUS, DESPERATE FOR HIS TEACHINGS AND HEALINGS.
ONE DAY WHEN JESUS WAS LOOKING FOR A QUIET PLACE TO PRAY, A CROWD BEGAN TO GATHER.
JESUS CHOSE TO SPEND TIME WITH THEM...
...TEACHING THEM ABOUT THE KINGDOM OF GOD.
THESE PEOPLE HAVE BEEN HERE A LONG TIME.
THEY MUST BE GETTING HUNGRY.
WE SHOULD SEND THE PEOPLE AWAY.
I'LL SEE IF SIMON PETER OR ANY OF THE OTHERS WILL COME WITH ME.
TO DO WHAT?
TO ASK JESUS TO SEND THE PEOPLE AWAY.
EXCUSE ME.
IT'S GETTING LATE, AND I NOTICED NO ONE HAS ANY-THING TO EAT.
NOT EVEN THE RABBI.
HE'S BEEN TEACHING ALL DAY.
WE WERE THINKING THE SAME THING.
HERE, GIVE THIS TO HIM.
IT'S ONLY TWO FISH AND SOME BARLEY LOAVES.
BUT...
ANDREW!

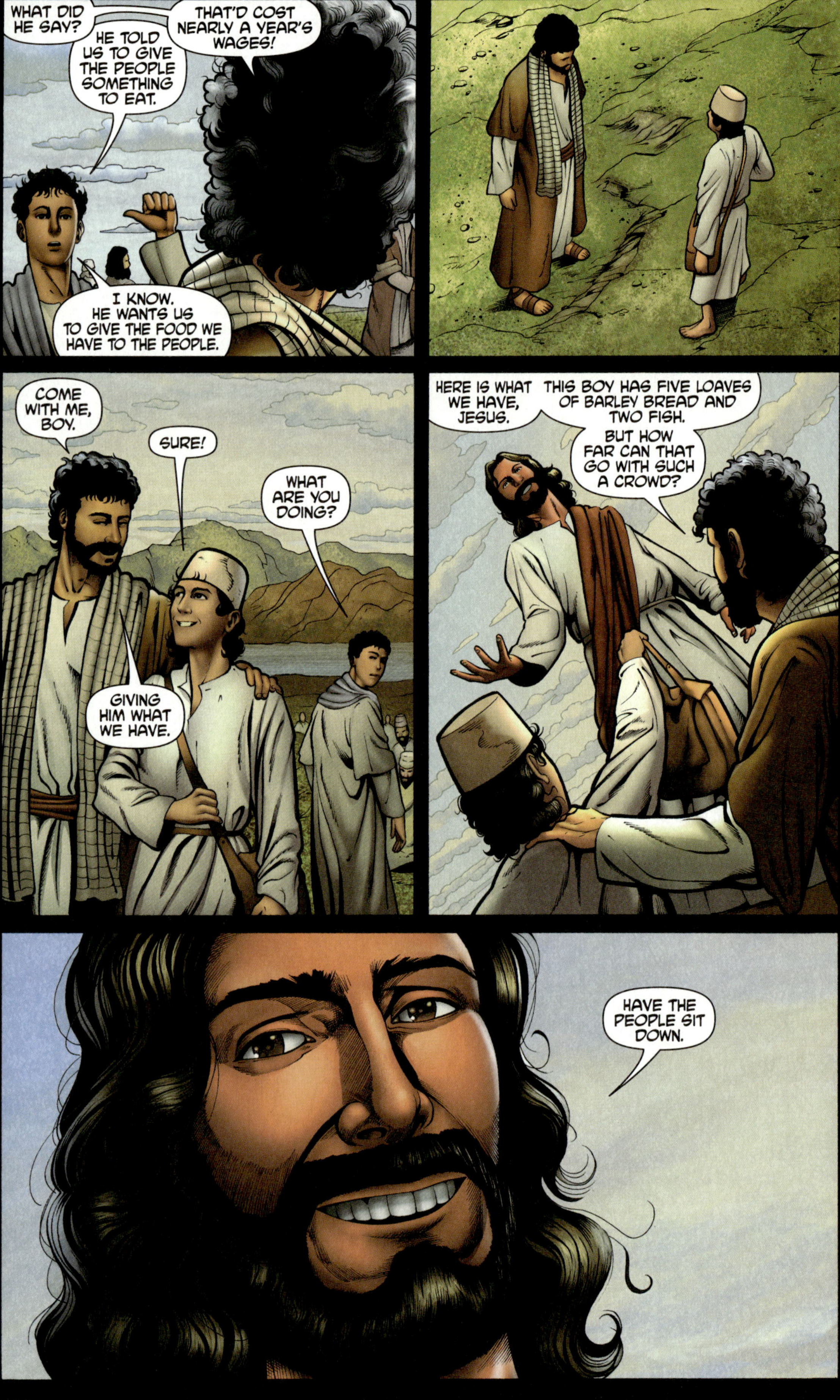
WHAT DID HE SAY?
HE TOLD US TO GIVE THE PEOPLE SOMETHING TO EAT.
THAT'D COST NEARLY A YEAR'S WAGES!
I KNOW. HE WANTS US TO GIVE THE FOOD WE HAVE TO THE PEOPLE.
COME WITH ME, BOY.
SURE!
WHAT ARE YOU DOING?
GIVING HIM WHAT WE HAVE.
HERE IS WHAT WE HAVE, JESUS.
THIS BOY HAS FIVE LOAVES OF BARLEY BREAD AND TWO FISH.
BUT HOW FAR CAN THAT GO WITH SUCH A CROWD?
HAVE THE PEOPLE SIT DOWN.

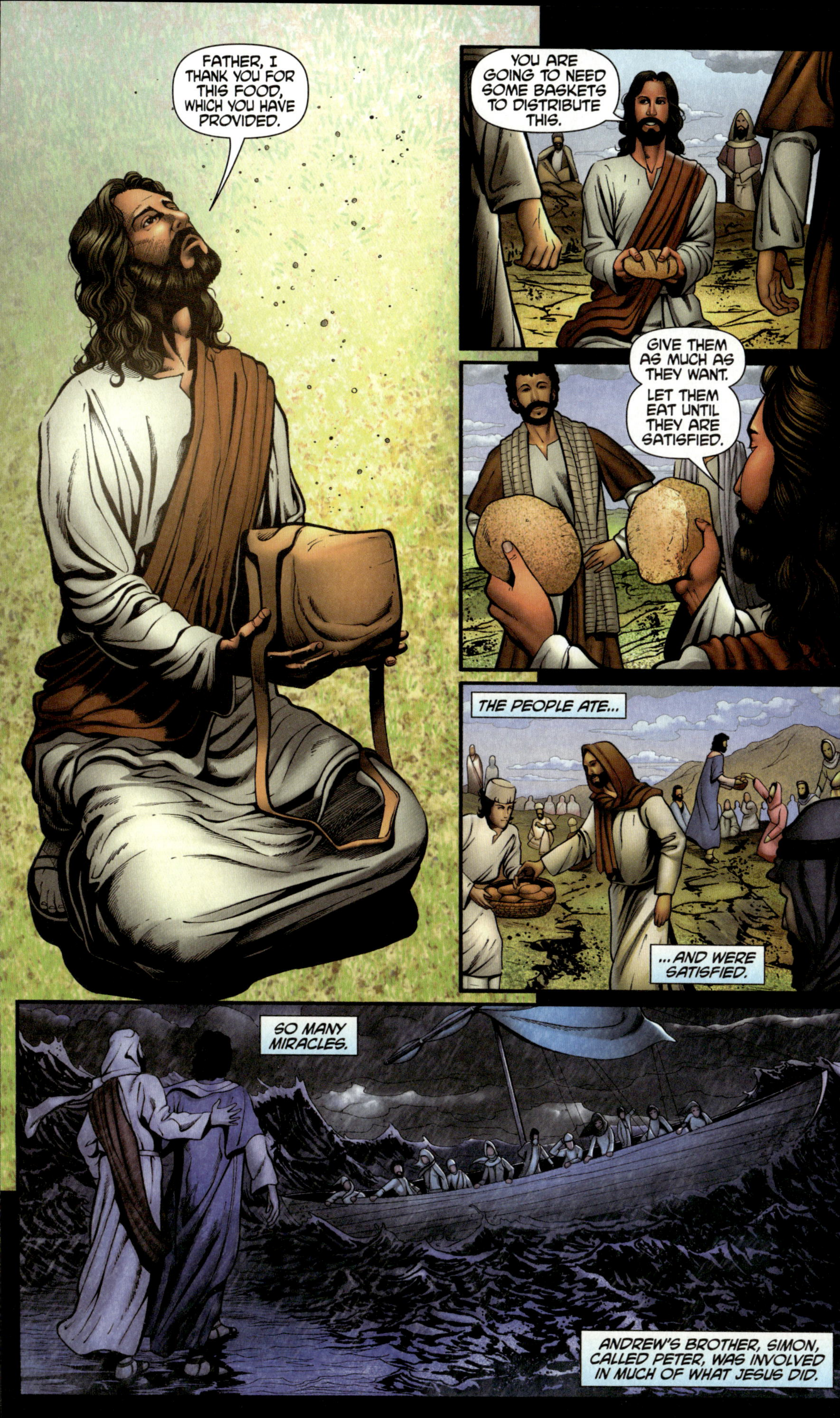
FATHER, I THANK YOU FOR THIS FOOD, WHICH YOU HAVE PROVIDED.
YOU ARE GOING TO NEED SOME BASKETS TO DISTRIBUTE THIS.
GIVE THEM AS MUCH AS THEY WANT.
LET THEM EAT UNTIL THEY ARE SATISFIED.
THE PEOPLE ATE...
...AND WERE SATISFIED.
SO MANY MIRACLES.
ANDREW'S BROTHER, SIMON, CALLED PETER, WAS INVOLVED IN MUCH OF WHAT JESUS DID.

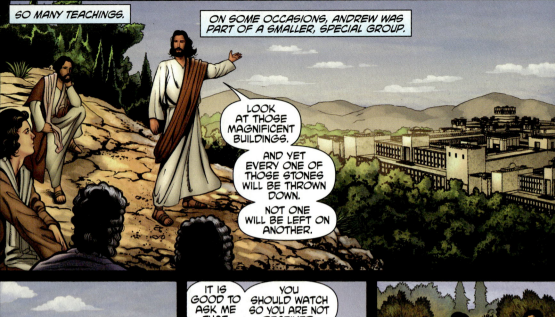

SO MANY TEACHINGS.

ON SOME OCCASIONS, ANDREW WAS PART OF A SMALLER, SPECIAL GROUP.

LOOK AT THOSE MAGNIFICENT BUILDINGS.

AND YET EVERY ONE OF THOSE STONES WILL BE THROWN DOWN.

NOT ONE WILL BE LEFT ON ANOTHER.

WHEN WILL THAT HAPPEN?

AND BY WHAT SIGN CAN WE KNOW YOUR WORDS ARE ABOUT TO TAKE PLACE?

IT IS GOOD TO ASK ME THAT.

YOU SHOULD WATCH SO YOU ARE NOT DECEIVED.

MANY WILL COME IN MY NAME AND SAY THEY ARE THE CHRIST.

THEY WILL SAY THE TIME IS NEAR.

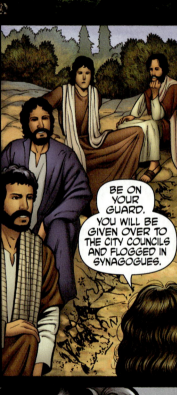

BE ON YOUR GUARD.

YOU WILL BE GIVEN OVER TO THE CITY COUNCILS AND FLOGGED IN SYNAGOGUES.

OTHER TIMES, THE SMALL GROUP WAS ONLY THREE--

JAMES, JOHN, AND ANDREW'S BROTHER, SIMON PETER.

THESE THREE HAD WITNESSED THE TRANSFIGURATION.

THEY HAD BEEN IN THE ROOM WHEN JESUS RAISED JAIRUS'S DAUGHTER FROM THE DEAD.

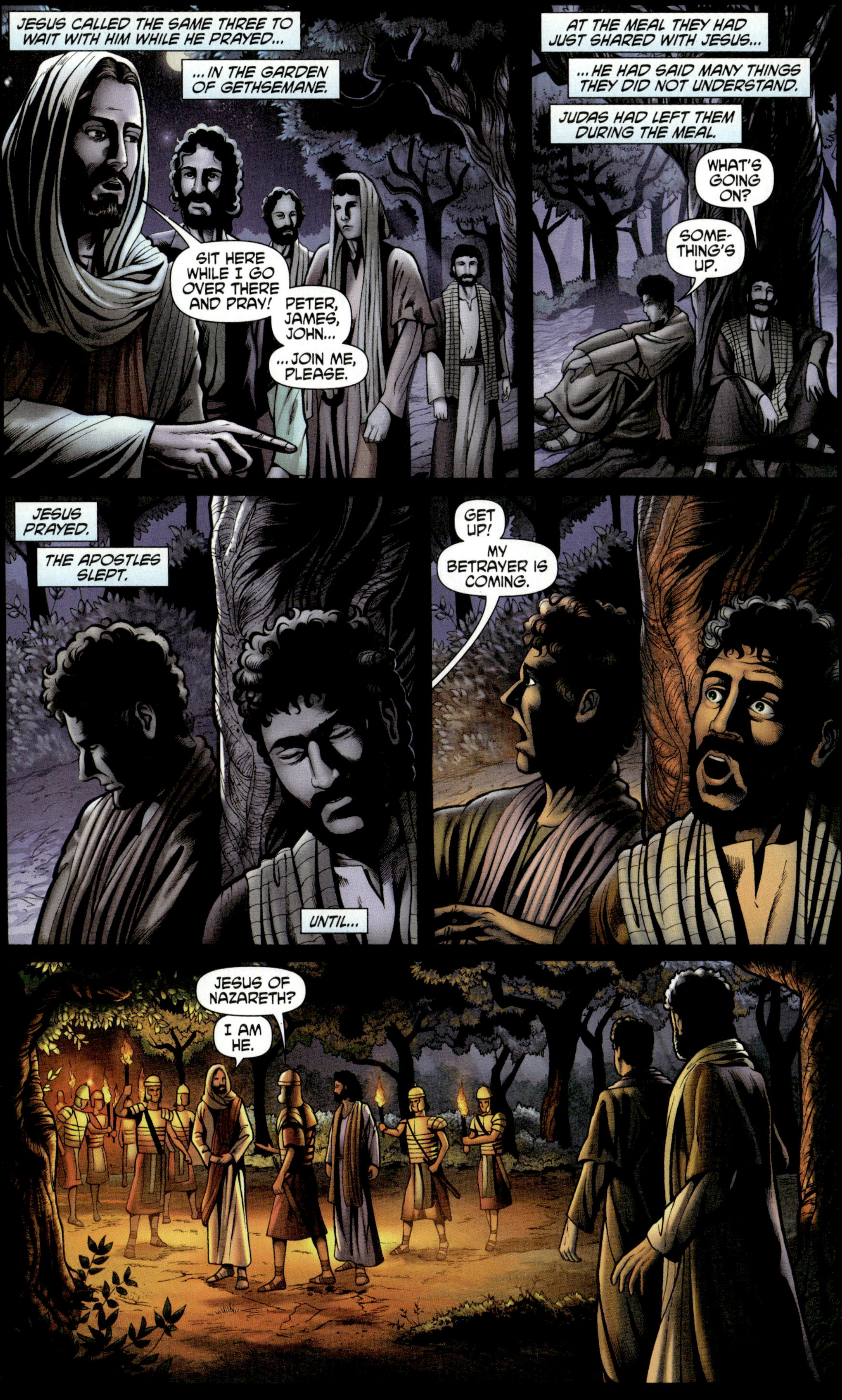
JESUS CALLED THE SAME THREE TO WAIT WITH HIM WHILE HE PRAYED...
...IN THE GARDEN OF GETHSEMANE.
SIT HERE WHILE I GO OVER THERE AND PRAY!
PETER, JAMES, JOHN...
...JOIN ME, PLEASE.
AT THE MEAL THEY HAD JUST SHARED WITH JESUS...
...HE HAD SAID MANY THINGS THEY DID NOT UNDERSTAND.
JUDAS HAD LEFT THEM DURING THE MEAL.
WHAT'S GOING ON?
SOME-THING'S UP.
JESUS PRAYED.
THE APOSTLES SLEPT.
UNTIL...
GET UP!
MY BETRAYER IS COMING.
JESUS OF NAZARETH?
I AM HE.

AFTER JESUS' ARREST...

...THE APOSTLES FLED.

THE APOSTLES WENT INTO HIDING.

IT'S JOHN!

LET HIM IN.

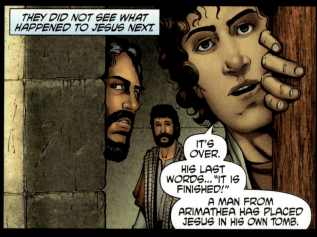

THEY DID NOT SEE WHAT HAPPENED TO JESUS NEXT.

IT'S OVER.

HIS LAST WORDS... "IT IS FINISHED!"

A MAN FROM ARIMATHEA HAS PLACED JESUS IN HIS OWN TOMB.

THEY WAITED...

...IN FEAR...

...IN MOURNING...

...IN HOPE-LESSNESS.

UNTIL...

IT'S EMPTY!

JESUS' TOMB IS EMPTY!

COME SEE!

CAN IT BE?

JOHN HAD INVESTIGATED...

IT'S EMPTY, JUST AS MARY SAID.

EXCEPT FOR HIS BURIAL LINEN.

MY FRIENDS!

HAVE NO FEAR.

PEACE BE WITH YOU.

IT'S TRUE. IT'S HIM.

JESUS SPENT MORE TIME WITH THEM AFTER HE RETURNED.

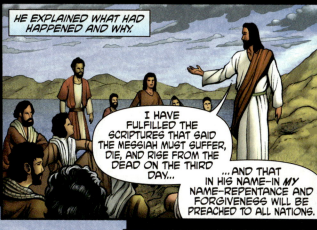

HE EXPLAINED WHAT HAD HAPPENED AND WHY.

I HAVE FULFILLED THE SCRIPTURES THAT SAID THE MESSIAH MUST SUFFER, DIE, AND RISE FROM THE DEAD ON THE THIRD DAY...

...AND THAT IN HIS NAME—IN MY NAME—REPENTANCE AND FORGIVENESS WILL BE PREACHED TO ALL NATIONS.

JESUS ASCENDED INTO HEAVEN.

HIS NAME WAS ANDREW.

LIKE MANY YOUNG JEWISH MEN OF THE TIME...

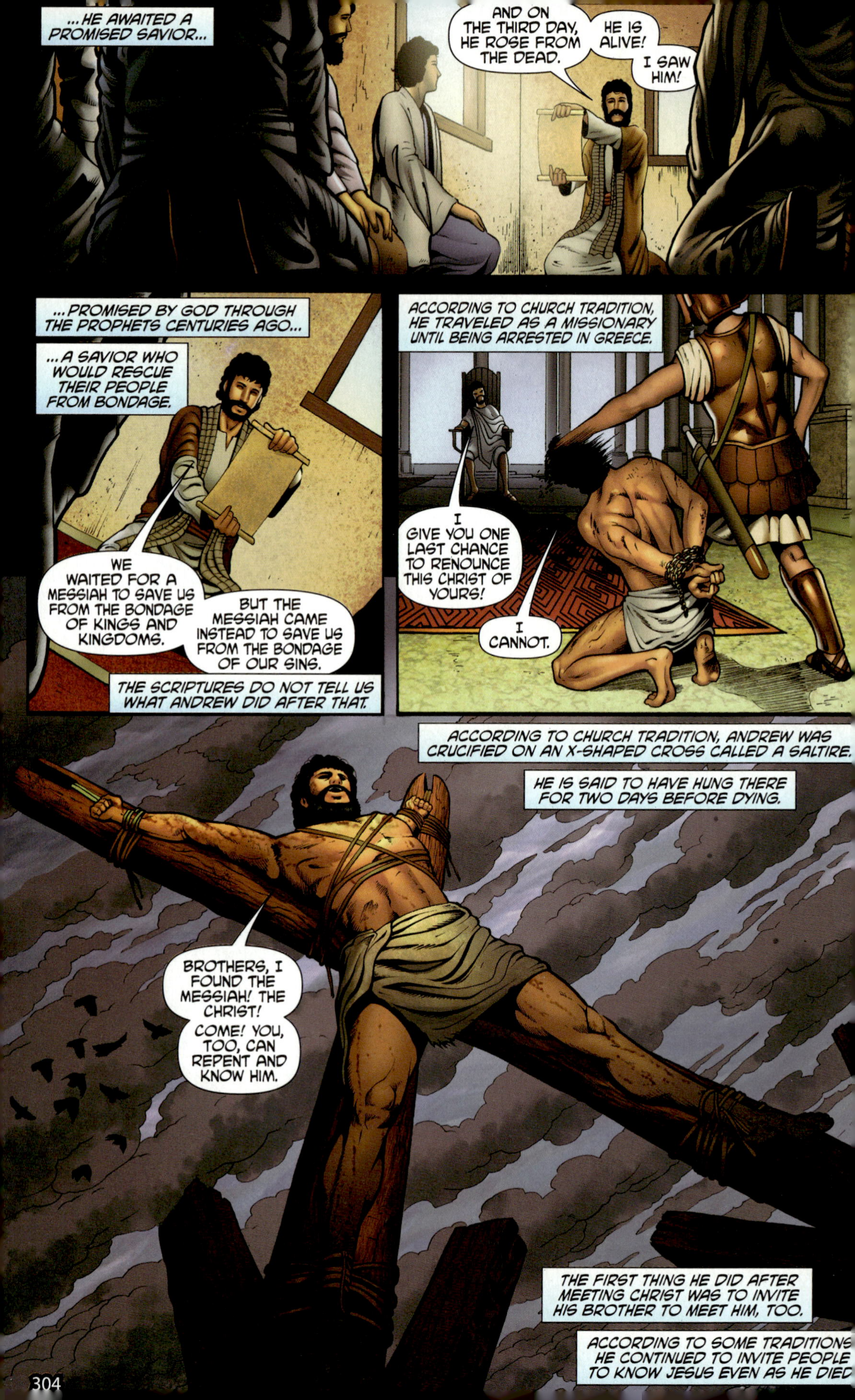

...HE AWAITED A PROMISED SAVIOR...
AND ON THE THIRD DAY, HE ROSE FROM THE DEAD.
HE IS ALIVE!
I SAW HIM!
...PROMISED BY GOD THROUGH THE PROPHETS CENTURIES AGO...
...A SAVIOR WHO WOULD RESCUE THEIR PEOPLE FROM BONDAGE.
WE WAITED FOR A MESSIAH TO SAVE US FROM THE BONDAGE OF KINGS AND KINGDOMS.
BUT THE MESSIAH CAME INSTEAD TO SAVE US FROM THE BONDAGE OF OUR SINS.
THE SCRIPTURES DO NOT TELL US WHAT ANDREW DID AFTER THAT.
ACCORDING TO CHURCH TRADITION, HE TRAVELED AS A MISSIONARY UNTIL BEING ARRESTED IN GREECE.
I GIVE YOU ONE LAST CHANCE TO RENOUNCE THIS CHRIST OF YOURS!
I CANNOT.
ACCORDING TO CHURCH TRADITION, ANDREW WAS CRUCIFIED ON AN X-SHAPED CROSS CALLED A SALTIRE.
HE IS SAID TO HAVE HUNG THERE FOR TWO DAYS BEFORE DYING.
BROTHERS, I FOUND THE MESSIAH! THE CHRIST!
COME! YOU, TOO, CAN REPENT AND KNOW HIM.
THE FIRST THING HE DID AFTER MEETING CHRIST WAS TO INVITE HIS BROTHER TO MEET HIM, TOO.
ACCORDING TO SOME TRADITIONS HE CONTINUED TO INVITE PEOPLE TO KNOW JESUS EVEN AS HE DIED

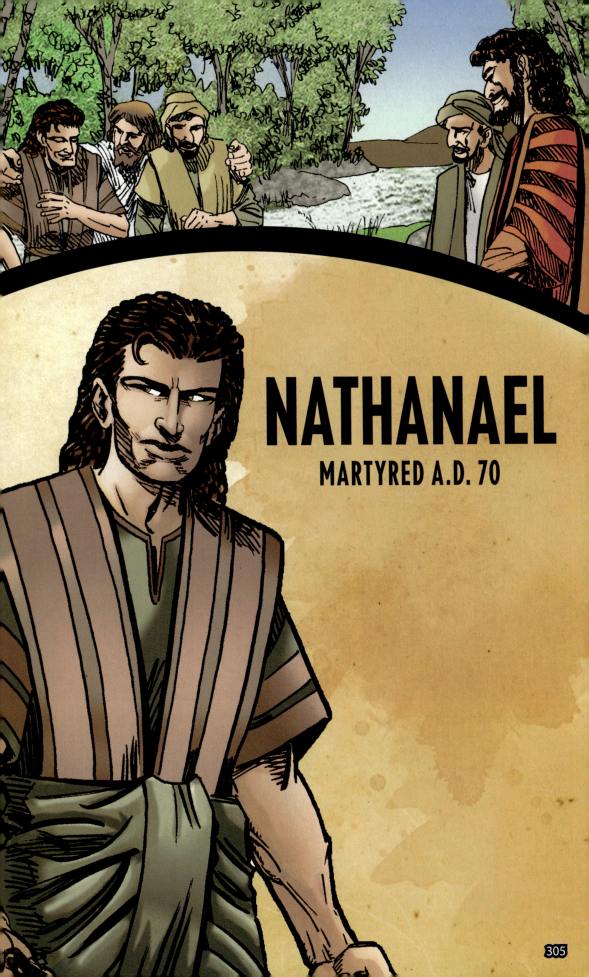

NATHANAEL

MARTYRED A.D. 70

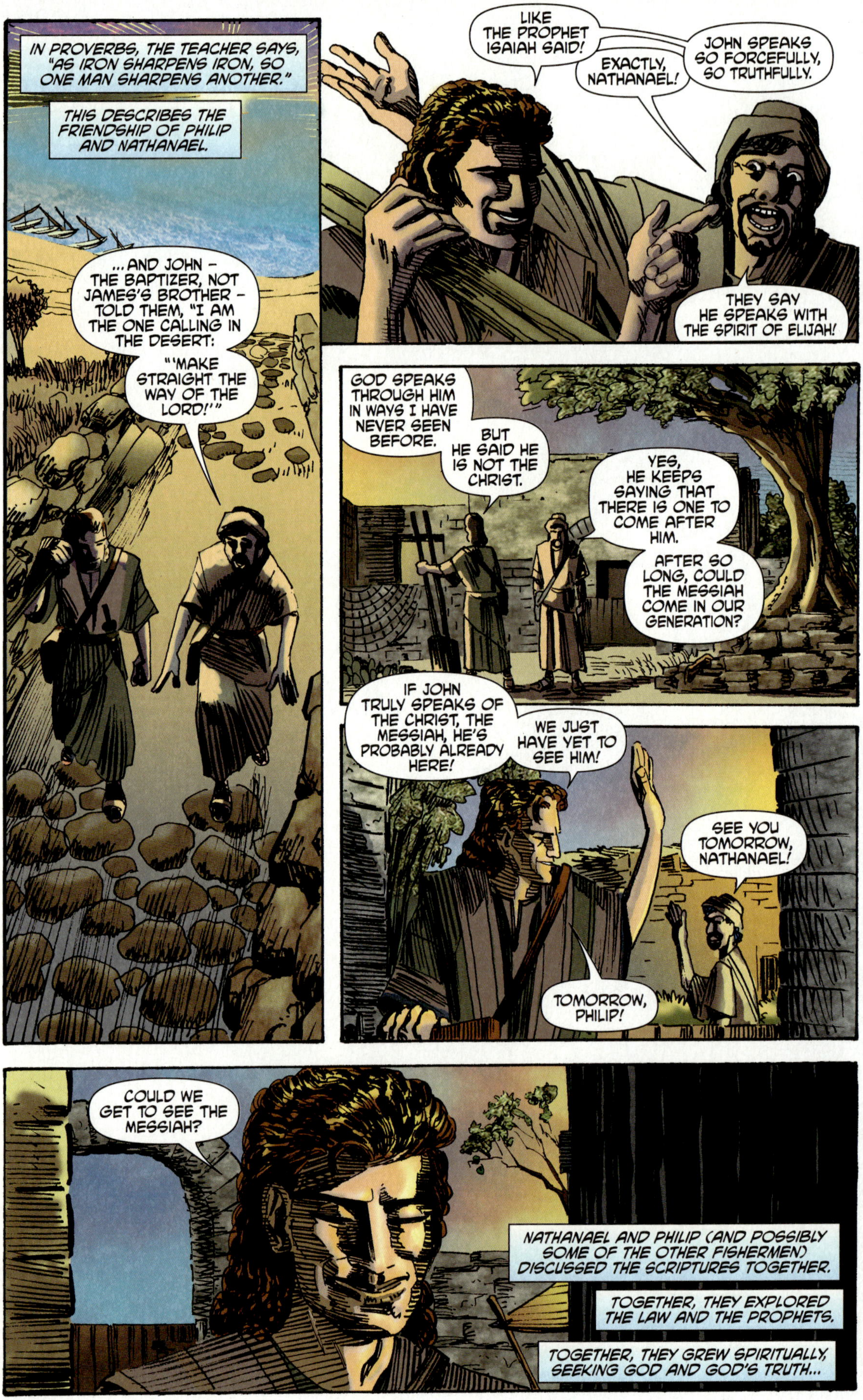
IN PROVERBS, THE TEACHER SAYS, "AS IRON SHARPENS IRON, SO ONE MAN SHARPENS ANOTHER."
THIS DESCRIBES THE FRIENDSHIP OF PHILIP AND NATHANAEL.
...AND JOHN - THE BAPTIZER, NOT JAMES'S BROTHER - TOLD THEM, "I AM THE ONE CALLING IN THE DESERT:
"'MAKE STRAIGHT THE WAY OF THE LORD!'"
LIKE THE PROPHET ISAIAH SAID!
EXACTLY, NATHANAEL!
JOHN SPEAKS SO FORCEFULLY, SO TRUTHFULLY.
THEY SAY HE SPEAKS WITH THE SPIRIT OF ELIJAH!
GOD SPEAKS THROUGH HIM IN WAYS I HAVE NEVER SEEN BEFORE.
BUT HE SAID HE IS NOT THE CHRIST.
YES, HE KEEPS SAYING THAT THERE IS ONE TO COME AFTER HIM.
AFTER SO LONG, COULD THE MESSIAH COME IN OUR GENERATION?
IF JOHN TRULY SPEAKS OF THE CHRIST, THE MESSIAH, HE'S PROBABLY ALREADY HERE!
WE JUST HAVE YET TO SEE HIM!
SEE YOU TOMORROW, NATHANAEL!
TOMORROW, PHILIP!
COULD WE GET TO SEE THE MESSIAH?
NATHANAEL AND PHILIP (AND POSSIBLY SOME OF THE OTHER FISHERMEN) DISCUSSED THE SCRIPTURES TOGETHER.
TOGETHER, THEY EXPLORED THE LAW AND THE PROPHETS.
TOGETHER, THEY GREW SPIRITUALLY, SEEKING GOD AND GOD'S TRUTH...

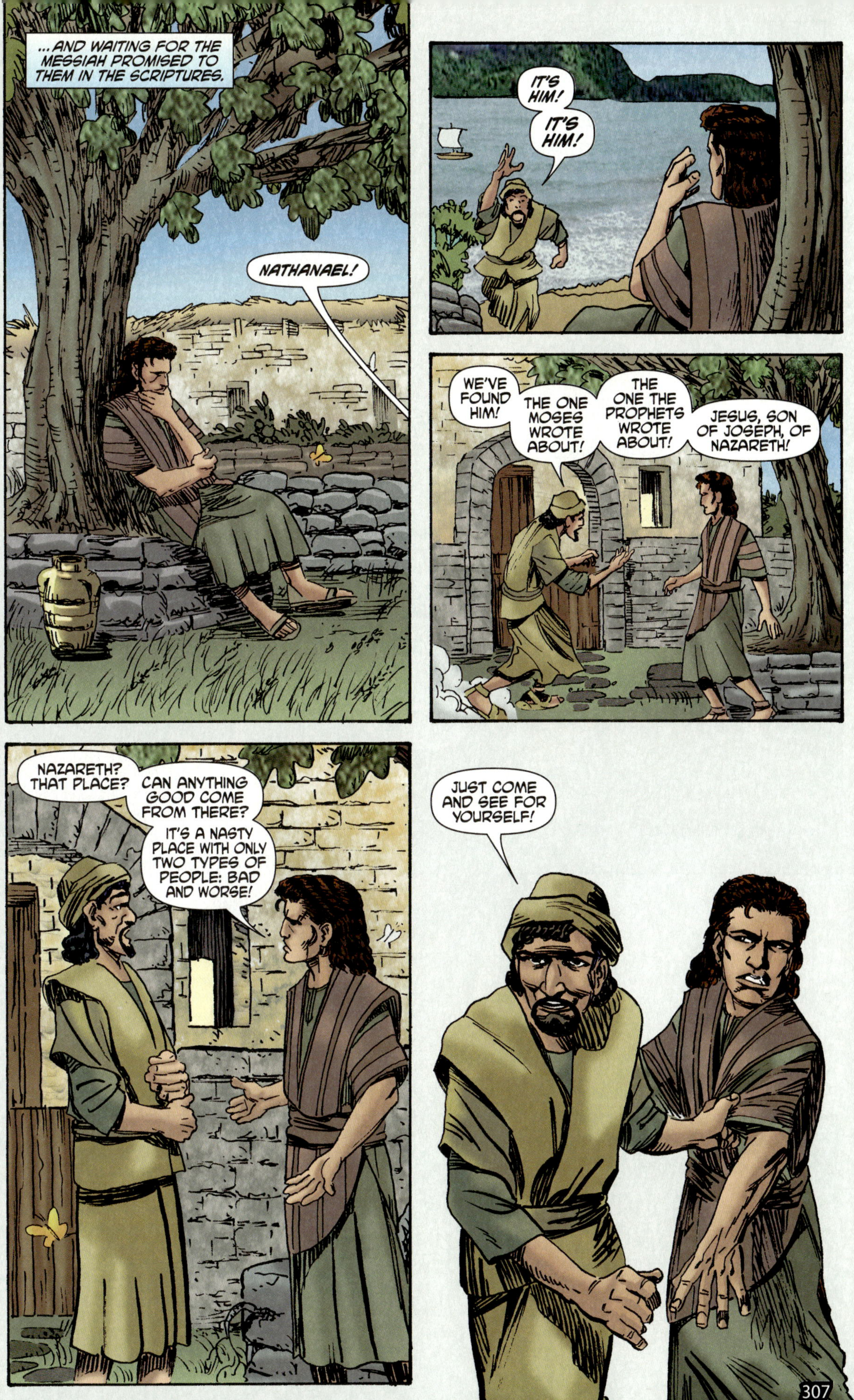
...AND WAITING FOR THE MESSIAH PROMISED TO THEM IN THE SCRIPTURES.
NATHANAEL!
IT'S HIM!
IT'S HIM!
WE'VE FOUND HIM!
THE ONE MOSES WROTE ABOUT!
THE ONE THE PROPHETS WROTE ABOUT!
JESUS, SON OF JOSEPH, OF NAZARETH!
NAZARETH? THAT PLACE?
CAN ANYTHING GOOD COME FROM THERE?
IT'S A NASTY PLACE WITH ONLY TWO TYPES OF PEOPLE: BAD AND WORSE!
JUST COME AND SEE FOR YOURSELF!

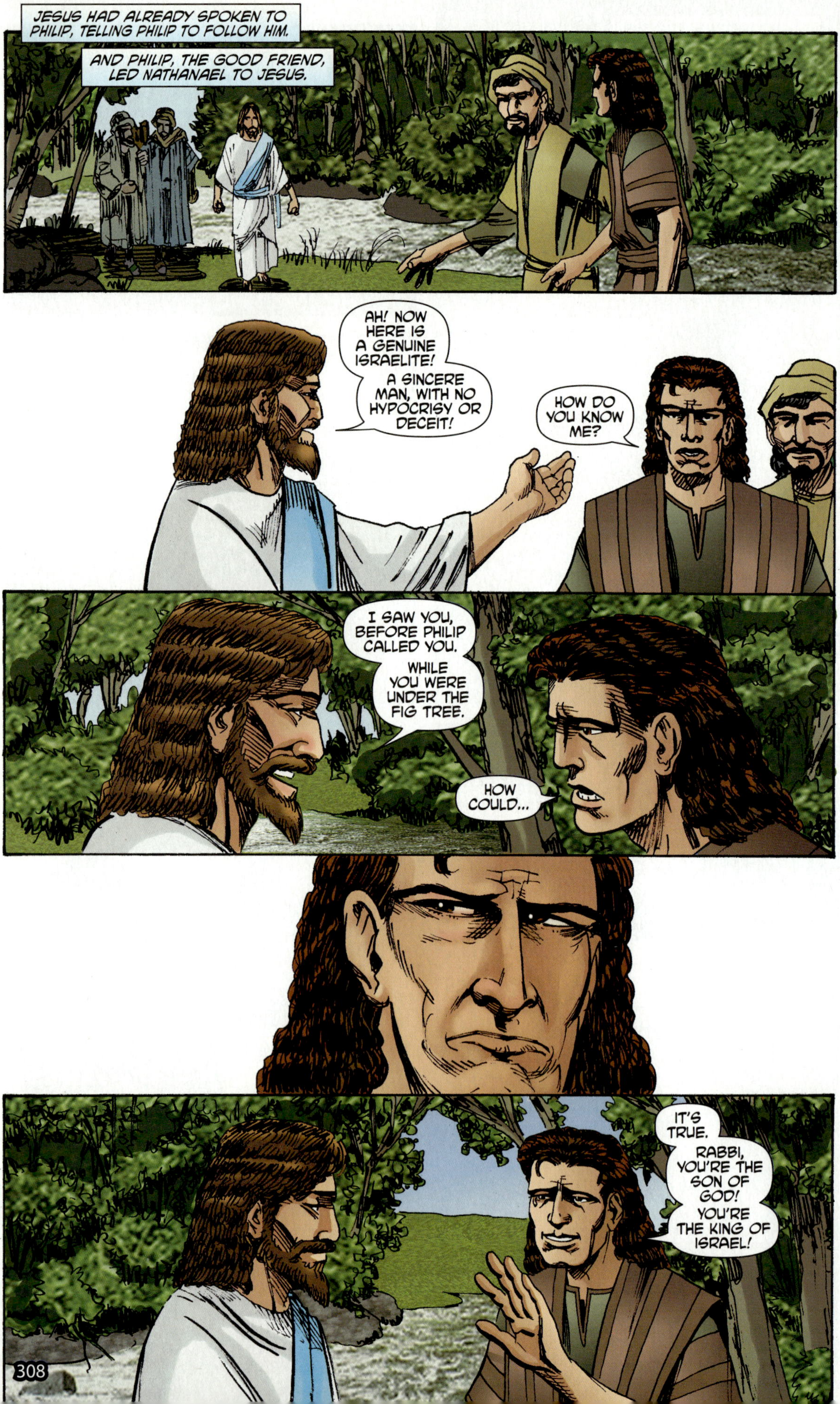
JESUS HAD ALREADY SPOKEN TO PHILIP, TELLING PHILIP TO FOLLOW HIM.
AND PHILIP, THE GOOD FRIEND, LED NATHANAEL TO JESUS.
AH! NOW HERE IS A GENUINE ISRAELITE!
A SINCERE MAN, WITH NO HYPOCRISY OR DECEIT!
HOW DO YOU KNOW ME?
I SAW YOU, BEFORE PHILIP CALLED YOU.
WHILE YOU WERE UNDER THE FIG TREE.
HOW COULD...
IT'S TRUE.
RABBI, YOU'RE THE SON OF GOD!
YOU'RE THE KING OF ISRAEL!

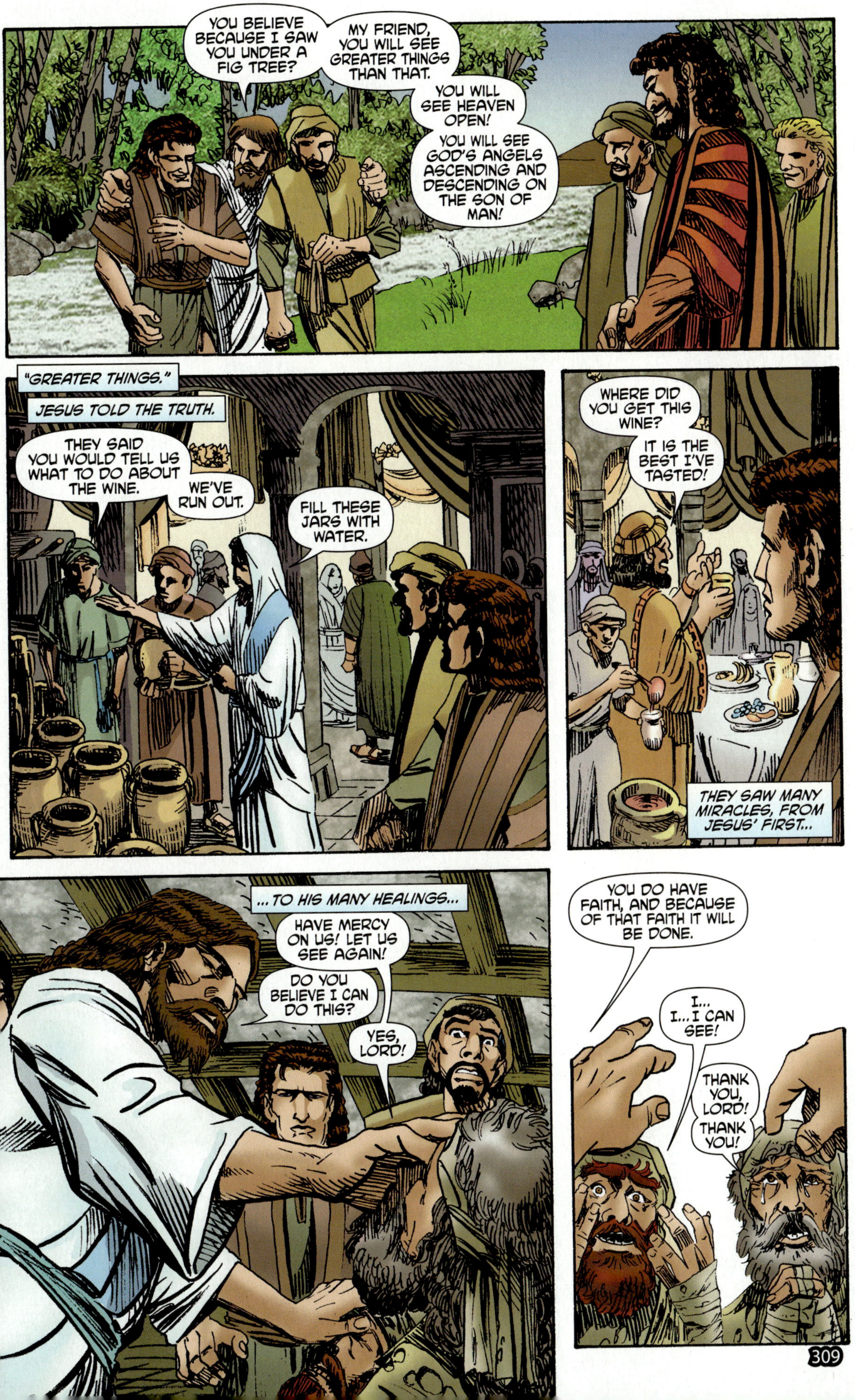
YOU BELIEVE BECAUSE I SAW YOU UNDER A FIG TREE?
MY FRIEND, YOU WILL SEE GREATER THINGS THAN THAT.
YOU WILL SEE HEAVEN OPEN!
YOU WILL SEE GOD'S ANGELS ASCENDING AND DESCENDING ON THE SON OF MAN!
"GREATER THINGS."
JESUS TOLD THE TRUTH.
THEY SAID YOU WOULD TELL US WHAT TO DO ABOUT THE WINE.
WE'VE RUN OUT.
FILL THESE JARS WITH WATER.
WHERE DID YOU GET THIS WINE?
IT IS THE BEST I'VE TASTED!
THEY SAW MANY MIRACLES, FROM JESUS' FIRST...
...TO HIS MANY HEALINGS...
HAVE MERCY ON US! LET US SEE AGAIN!
DO YOU BELIEVE I CAN DO THIS?
YES, LORD!
YOU DO HAVE FAITH, AND BECAUSE OF THAT FAITH IT WILL BE DONE.
I... I...I CAN SEE!
THANK YOU, LORD!
THANK YOU!

...TO HIS GREATEST MIRACLE...

...THE MIRACLE OF HIS MISSION HERE ON EARTH...

...TO HIS FINAL MIRACLE, ASCENDING INTO HEAVEN...

GO, AND MAKE DISCIPLES OF ALL NATIONS.

...AFTER WHICH, JUST AS HE SAID...

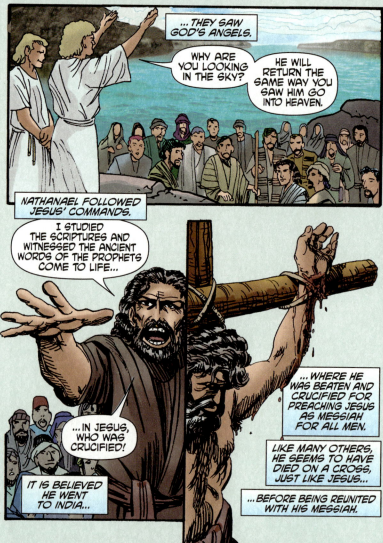

...THEY SAW GOD'S ANGELS.

WHY ARE YOU LOOKING IN THE SKY?

HE WILL RETURN THE SAME WAY YOU SAW HIM GO INTO HEAVEN.

NATHANAEL FOLLOWED JESUS' COMMANDS.

I STUDIED THE SCRIPTURES AND WITNESSED THE ANCIENT WORDS OF THE PROPHETS COME TO LIFE...

...IN JESUS, WHO WAS CRUCIFIED!

IT IS BELIEVED HE WENT TO INDIA...

...WHERE HE WAS BEATEN AND CRUCIFIED FOR PREACHING JESUS AS MESSIAH FOR ALL MEN.

LIKE MANY OTHERS, HE SEEMS TO HAVE DIED ON A CROSS, JUST LIKE JESUS...

...BEFORE BEING REUNITED WITH HIS MESSIAH.

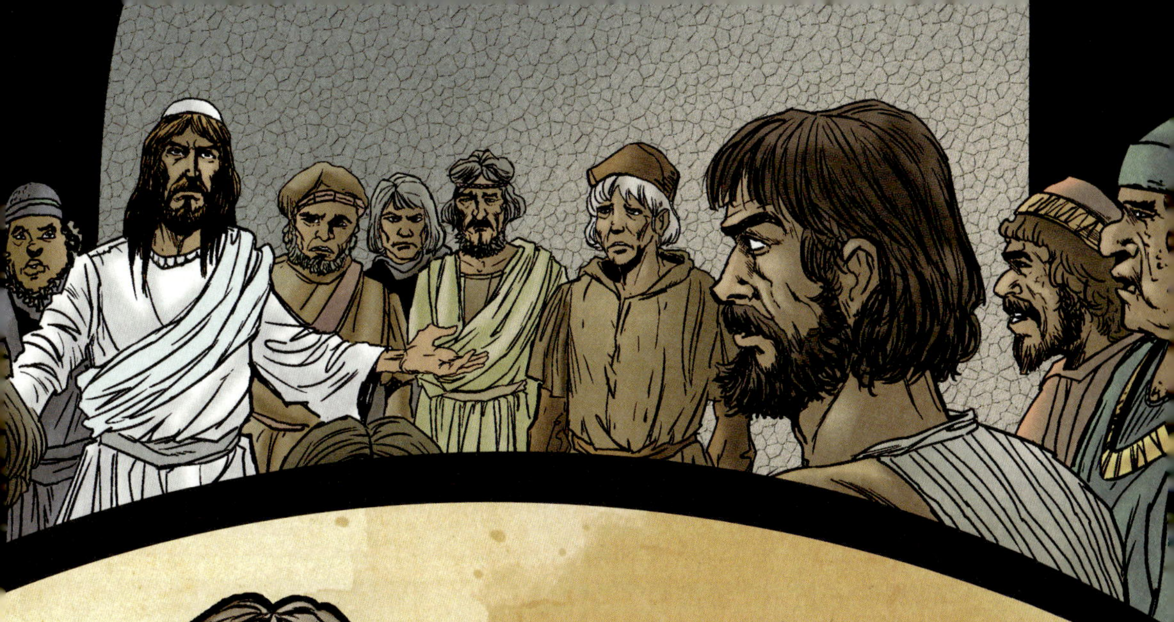

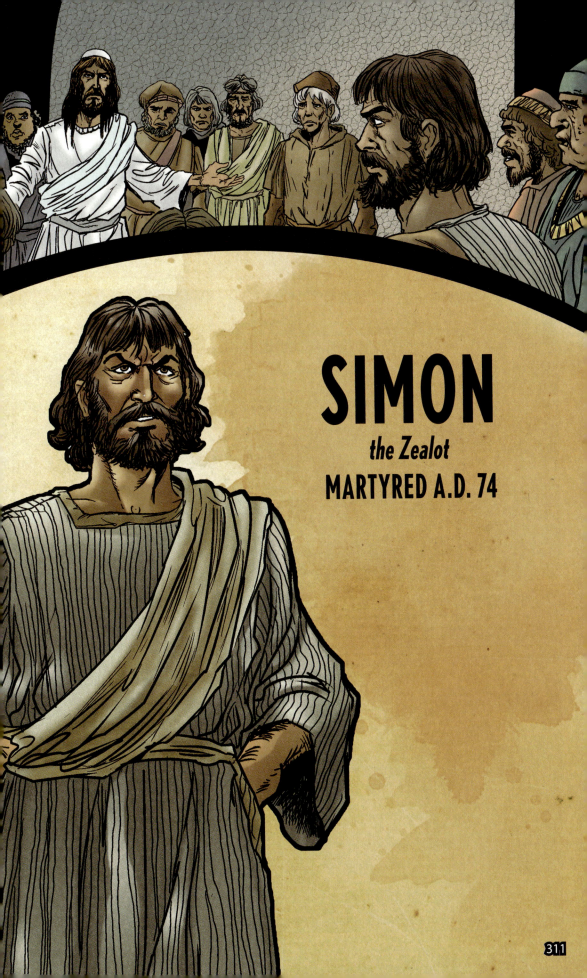

SIMON

the Zealot

MARTYRED A.D. 74

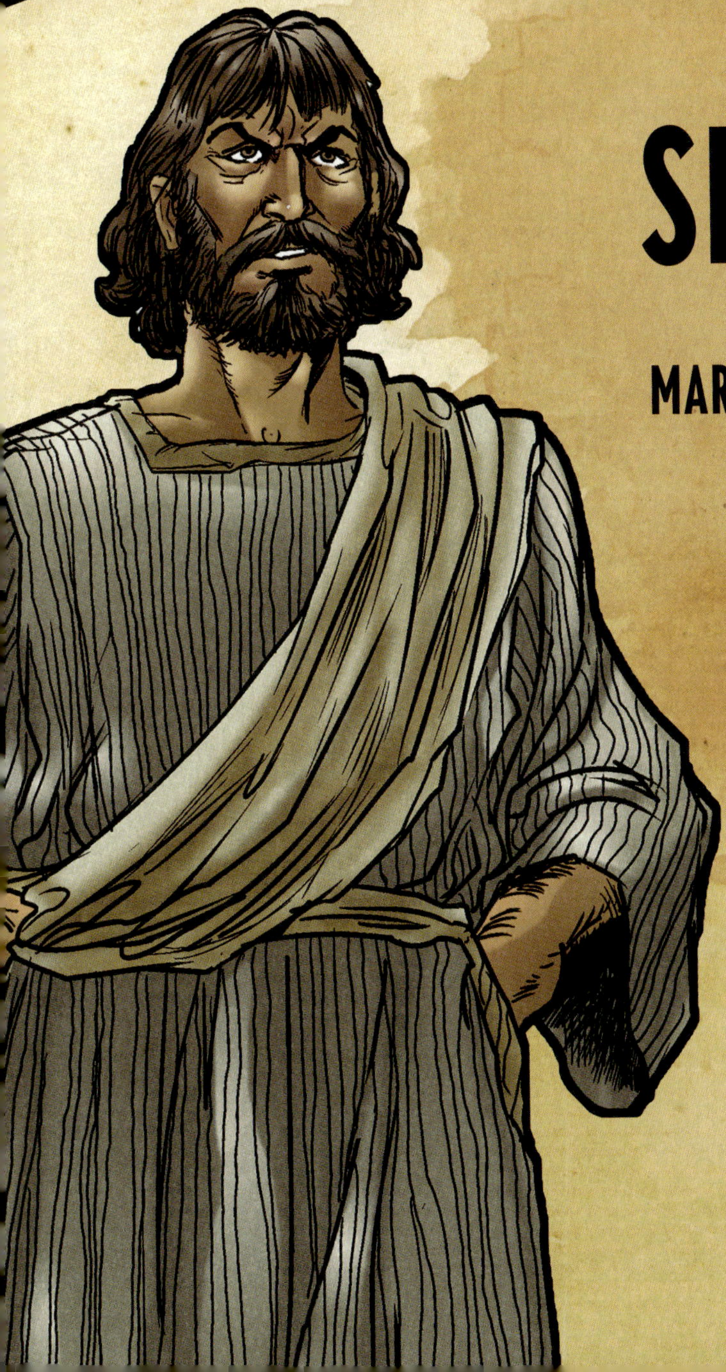

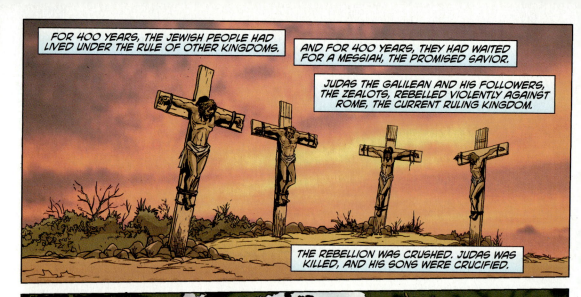

FOR 400 YEARS, THE JEWISH PEOPLE HAD LIVED UNDER THE RULE OF OTHER KINGDOMS.

AND FOR 400 YEARS, THEY HAD WAITED FOR A MESSIAH, THE PROMISED SAVIOR.

JUDAS THE GALILEAN AND HIS FOLLOWERS, THE ZEALOTS, REBELLED VIOLENTLY AGAINST ROME, THE CURRENT RULING KINGDOM.

THE REBELLION WAS CRUSHED. JUDAS WAS KILLED, AND HIS SONS WERE CRUCIFIED.

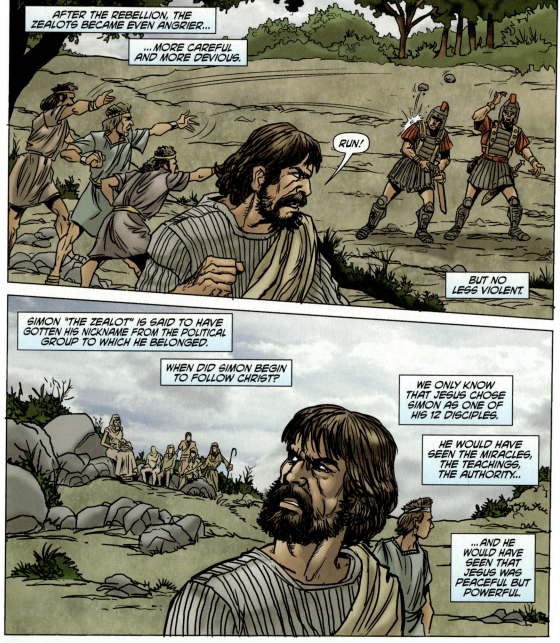

AFTER THE REBELLION, THE ZEALOTS BECAME EVEN ANGRIER...

...MORE CAREFUL AND MORE DEVIOUS.

RUN!

BUT NO LESS VIOLENT.

SIMON "THE ZEALOT" IS SAID TO HAVE GOTTEN HIS NICKNAME FROM THE POLITICAL GROUP TO WHICH HE BELONGED.

WHEN DID SIMON BEGIN TO FOLLOW CHRIST?

WE ONLY KNOW THAT JESUS CHOSE SIMON AS ONE OF HIS 12 DISCIPLES.

HE WOULD HAVE SEEN THE MIRACLES, THE TEACHINGS, THE AUTHORITY...

...AND HE WOULD HAVE SEEN THAT JESUS WAS PEACEFUL BUT POWERFUL.

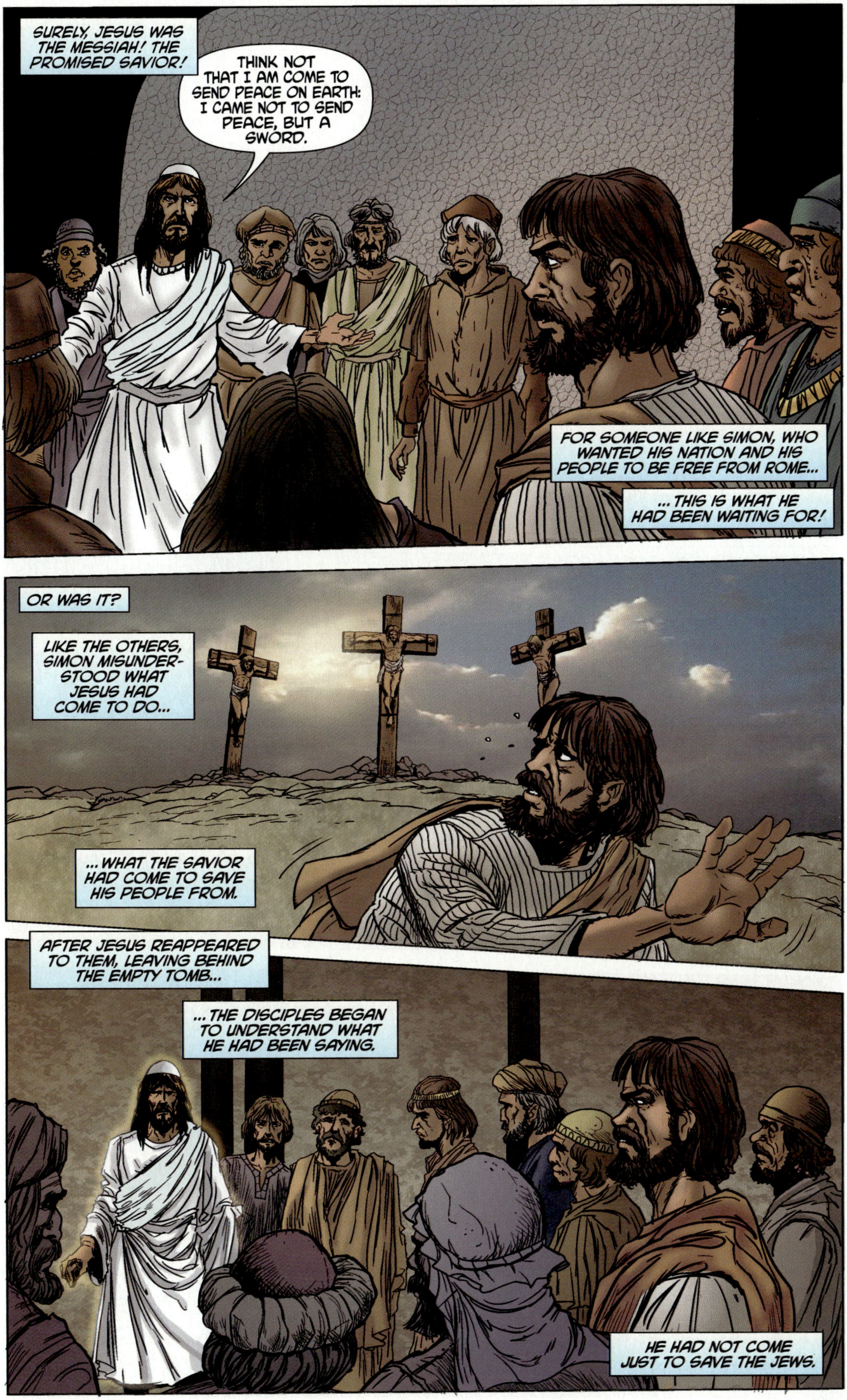
SURELY, JESUS WAS THE MESSIAH! THE PROMISED SAVIOR!
THINK NOT THAT I AM COME TO SEND PEACE ON EARTH: I CAME NOT TO SEND PEACE, BUT A SWORD.
FOR SOMEONE LIKE SIMON, WHO WANTED HIS NATION AND HIS PEOPLE TO BE FREE FROM ROME...
...THIS IS WHAT HE HAD BEEN WAITING FOR!
OR WAS IT?
LIKE THE OTHERS, SIMON MISUNDER-STOOD WHAT JESUS HAD COME TO DO...
...WHAT THE SAVIOR HAD COME TO SAVE HIS PEOPLE FROM.
AFTER JESUS REAPPEARED TO THEM, LEAVING BEHIND THE EMPTY TOMB...
...THE DISCIPLES BEGAN TO UNDERSTAND WHAT HE HAD BEEN SAYING.
HE HAD NOT COME JUST TO SAVE THE JEWS.

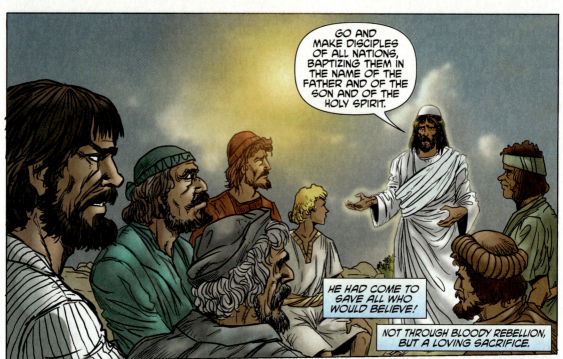

GO AND MAKE DISCIPLES OF ALL NATIONS, BAPTIZING THEM IN THE NAME OF THE FATHER AND OF THE SON AND OF THE HOLY SPIRIT.

HE HAD COME TO SAVE ALL WHO WOULD BELIEVE!

NOT THROUGH BLOODY REBELLION, BUT A LOVING SACRIFICE.

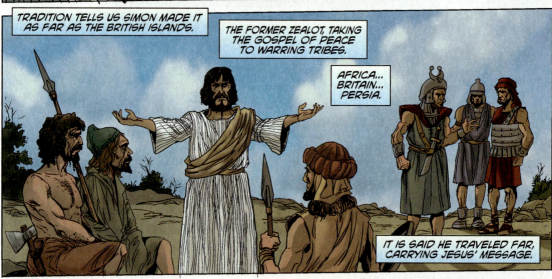

TRADITION TELLS US SIMON MADE IT AS FAR AS THE BRITISH ISLANDS.

THE FORMER ZEALOT, TAKING THE GOSPEL OF PEACE TO WARRING TRIBES.

AFRICA... BRITAIN... PERSIA.

IT IS SAID HE TRAVELED FAR, CARRYING JESUS' MESSAGE.

IT IS ALSO SAID THAT HE DIED IN PERSIA, CRUCIFIED FOR HIS PREACHING.

BUT THIS FORMER ZEALOT TOUCHED MANY LIVES.

HE TOLD JESUS' STORY OF SACRIFICE AND HOPE TO MANY PEOPLE IN MANY PLACES.

AND HIS OWN STORY ENDED ON A CROSS.

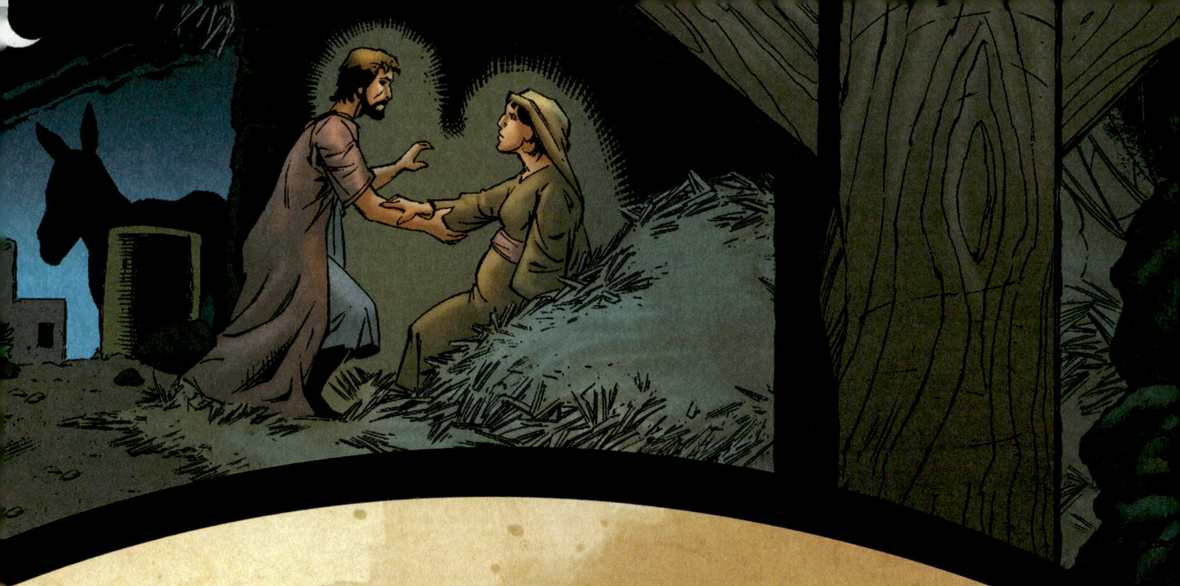

MARY

the Mother of Jesus

DATE OF DEATH UNKNOWN

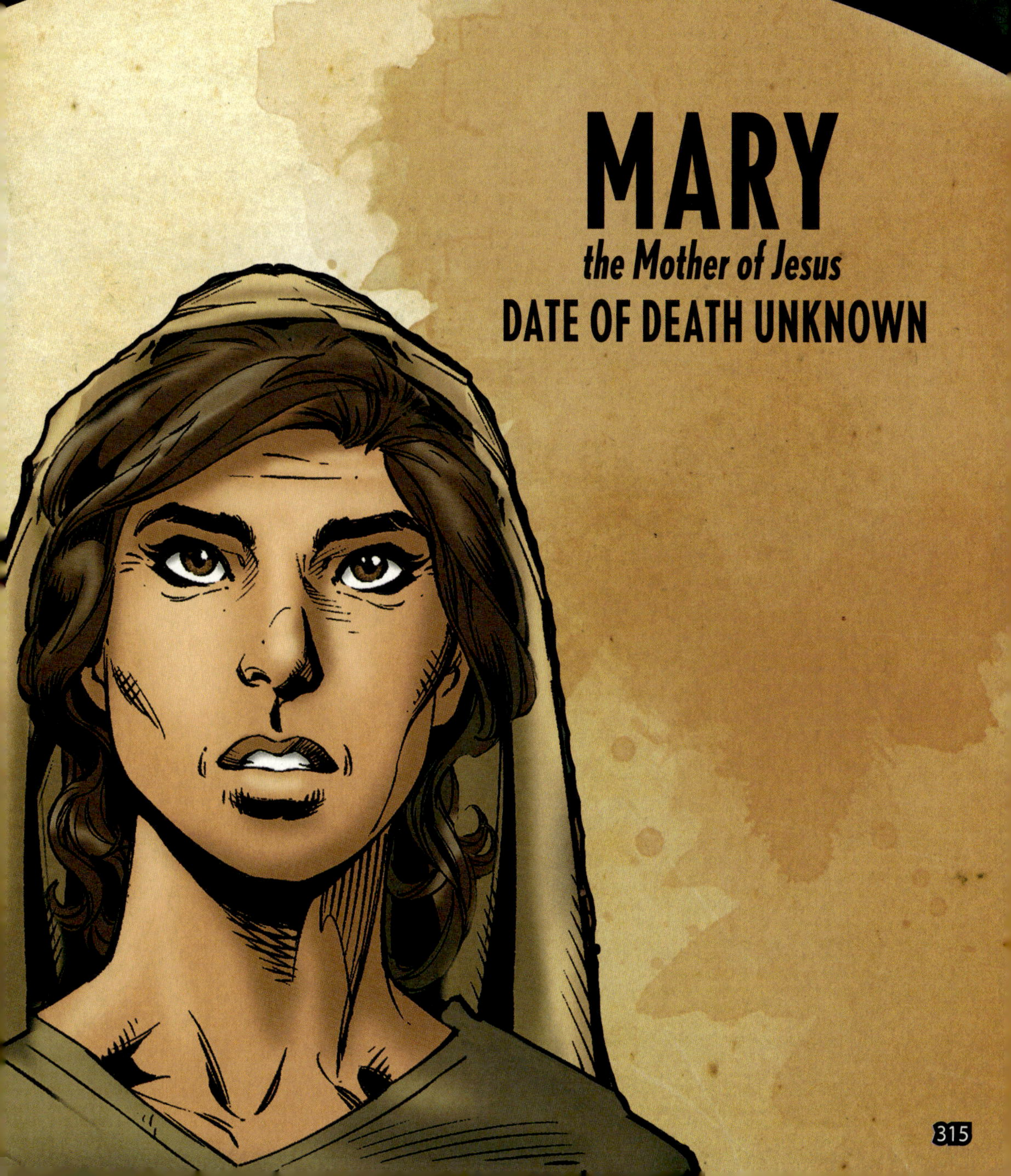

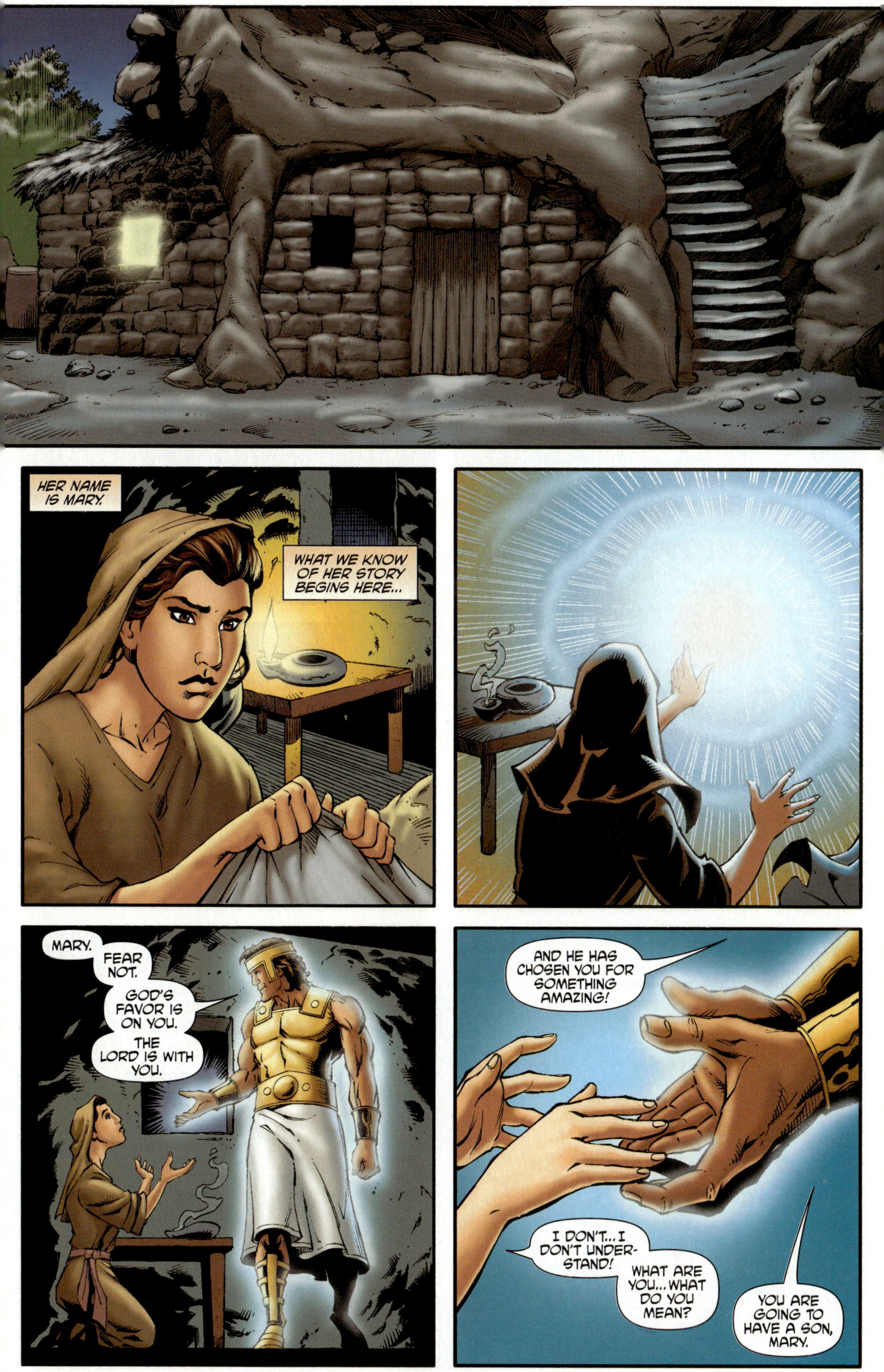
HER NAME IS MARY.
WHAT WE KNOW OF HER STORY BEGINS HERE...
MARY.
FEAR NOT.
GOD'S FAVOR IS ON YOU.
THE LORD IS WITH YOU.
AND HE HAS CHOSEN YOU FOR SOMETHING AMAZING!
I DON'T... I DON'T UNDERSTAND!
WHAT ARE YOU... WHAT DO YOU MEAN?
YOU ARE GOING TO HAVE A SON, MARY.

LUKE 1:26-31

HE WILL BE NO ORDINARY CHILD!

HE WILL BE CALLED SON OF THE MOST HIGH GOD!

I AM PLEDGED TO BE JOSEPH'S WIFE AND AM STILL A VIRGIN!

THE POWER OF THE HOLY SPIRIT WILL CAUSE THE CHILD TO BE IN YOUR WOMB.

I... I...

HE WILL HAVE THE THRONE OF KING DAVID, HIS FOREFATHER!

BUT THIS CANNOT HAPPEN!

I... I AM GOD'S SERVANT. MAY GOD'S WORD BE FULFILLED.

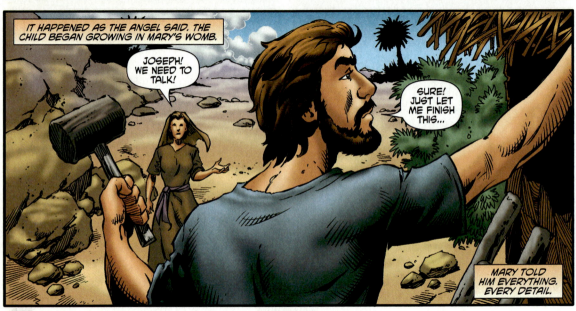

IT HAPPENED AS THE ANGEL SAID. THE CHILD BEGAN GROWING IN MARY'S WOMB.

JOSEPH! WE NEED TO TALK!

SURE! JUST LET ME FINISH THIS...

MARY TOLD HIM EVERYTHING. EVERY DETAIL.

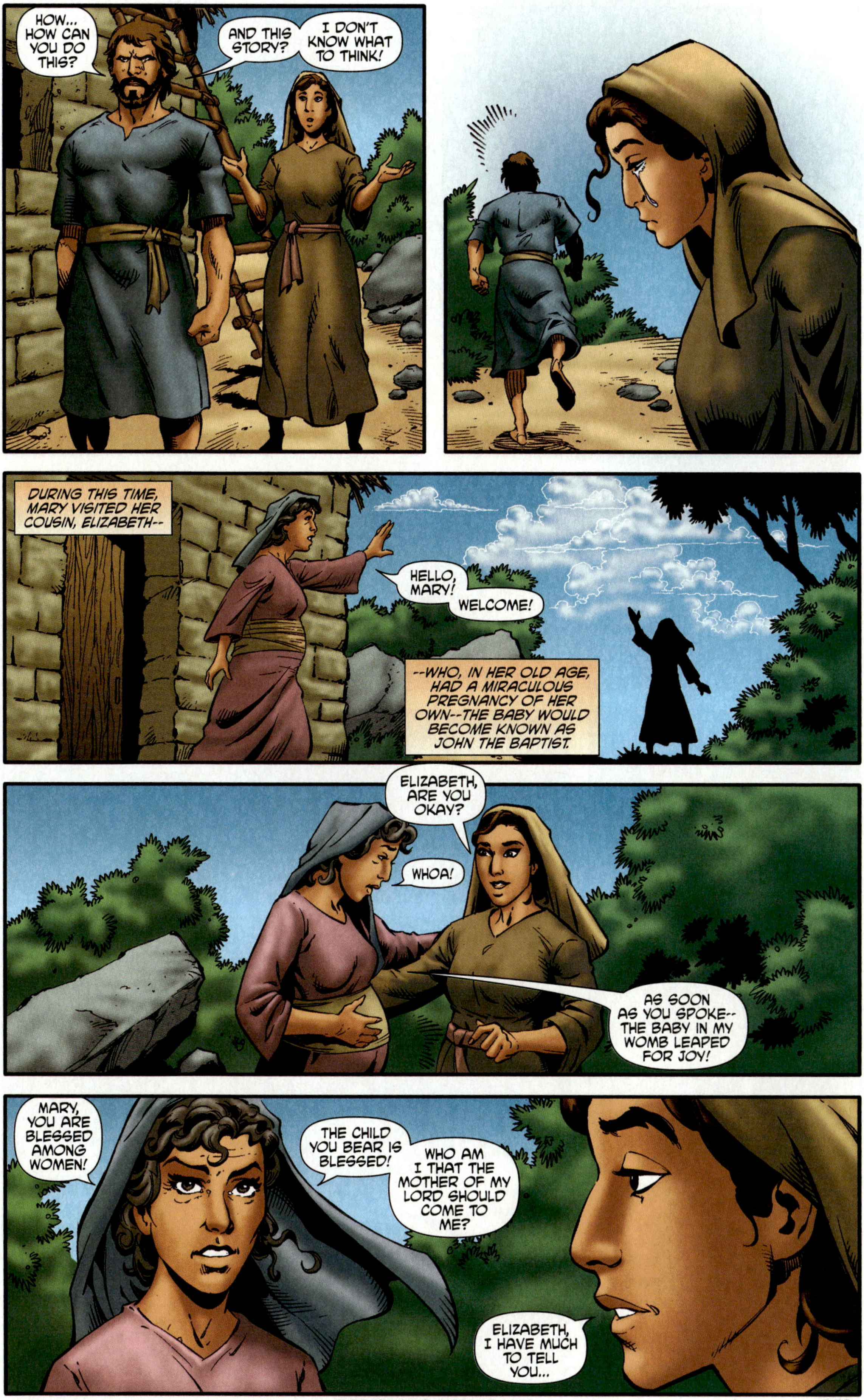
HOW... HOW CAN YOU DO THIS?
AND THIS STORY?
I DON'T KNOW WHAT TO THINK!
DURING THIS TIME, MARY VISITED HER COUSIN, ELIZABETH--
HELLO, MARY!
WELCOME!
--WHO, IN HER OLD AGE, HAD A MIRACULOUS PREGNANCY OF HER OWN--THE BABY WOULD BECOME KNOWN AS JOHN THE BAPTIST.
ELIZABETH, ARE YOU OKAY?
WHOA!
AS SOON AS YOU SPOKE-- THE BABY IN MY WOMB LEAPED FOR JOY!
MARY, YOU ARE BLESSED AMONG WOMEN!
THE CHILD YOU BEAR IS BLESSED!
WHO AM I THAT THE MOTHER OF MY LORD SHOULD COME TO ME?
ELIZABETH, I HAVE MUCH TO TELL YOU...

MATTHEW 1:18; LUKE 1:39-45

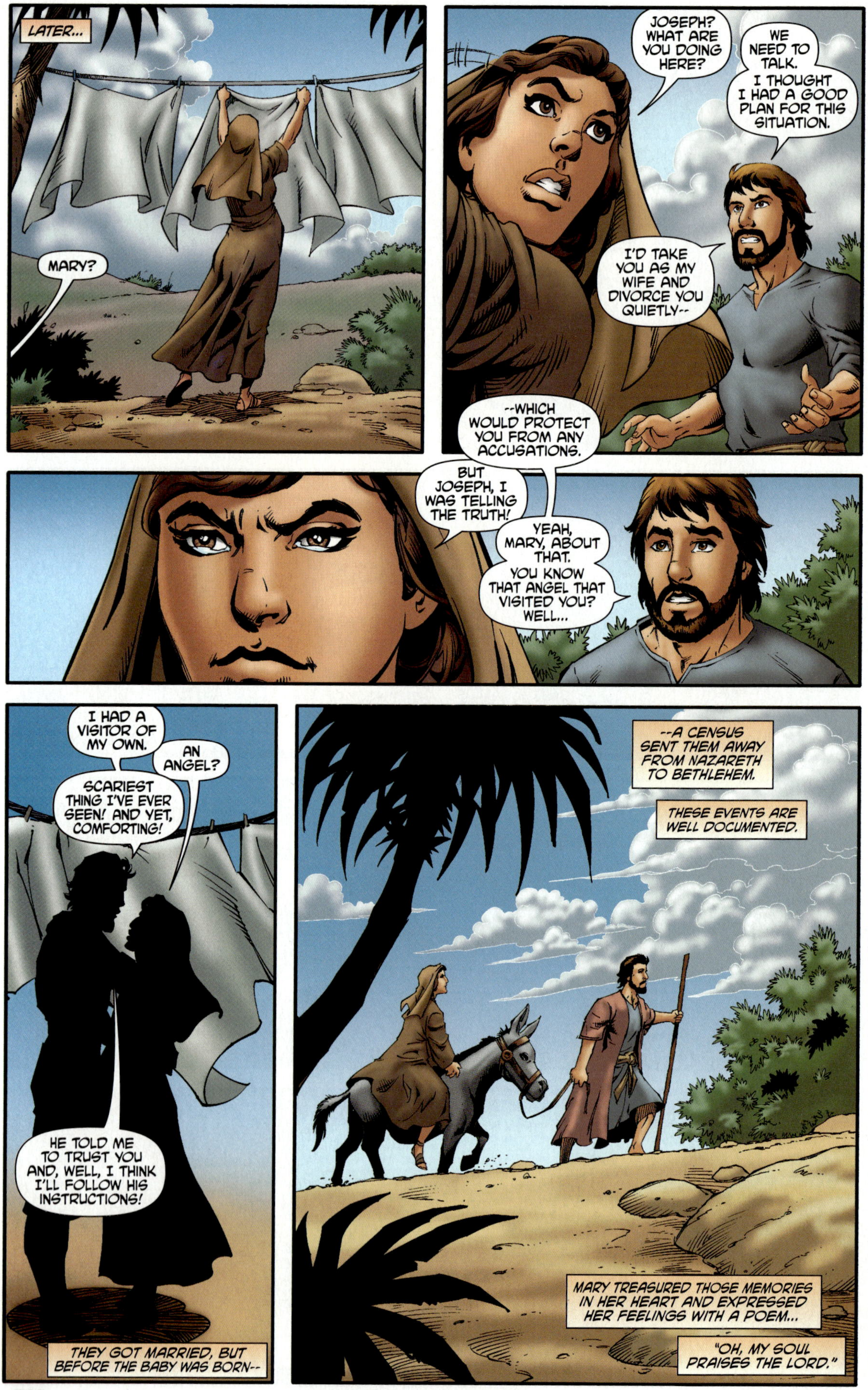
LATER...
MARY?
JOSEPH? WHAT ARE YOU DOING HERE?
WE NEED TO TALK. I THOUGHT I HAD A GOOD PLAN FOR THIS SITUATION.
I'D TAKE YOU AS MY WIFE AND DIVORCE YOU QUIETLY--
--WHICH WOULD PROTECT YOU FROM ANY ACCUSATIONS.
BUT JOSEPH, I WAS TELLING THE TRUTH!
YEAH, MARY, ABOUT THAT. YOU KNOW THAT ANGEL THAT VISITED YOU? WELL...
I HAD A VISITOR OF MY OWN.
AN ANGEL?
SCARIEST THING I'VE EVER SEEN! AND YET, COMFORTING!
HE TOLD ME TO TRUST YOU AND, WELL, I THINK I'LL FOLLOW HIS INSTRUCTIONS!
THEY GOT MARRIED, BUT BEFORE THE BABY WAS BORN--
--A CENSUS SENT THEM AWAY FROM NAZARETH TO BETHLEHEM.
THESE EVENTS ARE WELL DOCUMENTED.
MARY TREASURED THOSE MEMORIES IN HER HEART AND EXPRESSED HER FEELINGS WITH A POEM...
"OH, MY SOUL PRAISES THE LORD."

MATTHEW 1:19-25; LUKE 2:1-4

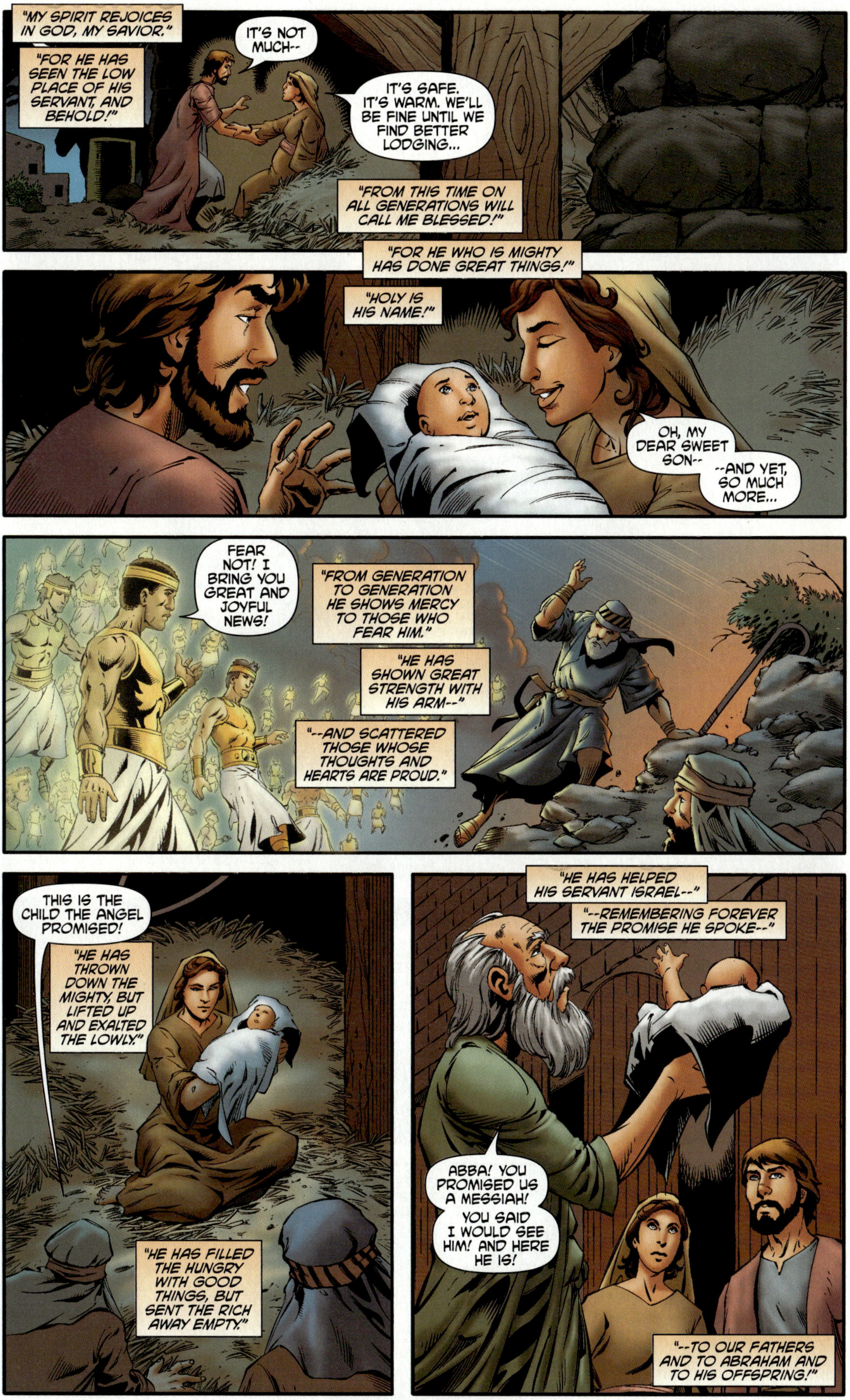

"MY SPIRIT REJOICES IN GOD, MY SAVIOR."
"FOR HE HAS SEEN THE LOW PLACE OF HIS SERVANT, AND BEHOLD!"
IT'S NOT MUCH--
IT'S SAFE. IT'S WARM. WE'LL BE FINE UNTIL WE FIND BETTER LODGING...
"FROM THIS TIME ON ALL GENERATIONS WILL CALL ME BLESSED!"
"FOR HE WHO IS MIGHTY HAS DONE GREAT THINGS!"
"HOLY IS HIS NAME!"
OH, MY DEAR SWEET SON--
--AND YET, SO MUCH MORE...
FEAR NOT! I BRING YOU GREAT AND JOYFUL NEWS!
"FROM GENERATION TO GENERATION HE SHOWS MERCY TO THOSE WHO FEAR HIM."
"HE HAS SHOWN GREAT STRENGTH WITH HIS ARM--"
"--AND SCATTERED THOSE WHOSE THOUGHTS AND HEARTS ARE PROUD."
THIS IS THE CHILD THE ANGEL PROMISED!
"HE HAS THROWN DOWN THE MIGHTY, BUT LIFTED UP AND EXALTED THE LOWLY."
"HE HAS FILLED THE HUNGRY WITH GOOD THINGS, BUT SENT THE RICH AWAY EMPTY."
"HE HAS HELPED HIS SERVANT ISRAEL--"
"--REMEMBERING FOREVER THE PROMISE HE SPOKE--"
ABBA! YOU PROMISED US A MESSIAH!
YOU SAID I WOULD SEE HIM! AND HERE HE IS!
"--TO OUR FATHERS AND TO ABRAHAM AND TO HIS OFFSPRING!"

LUKE 1:46-55; LUKE 2:4-32

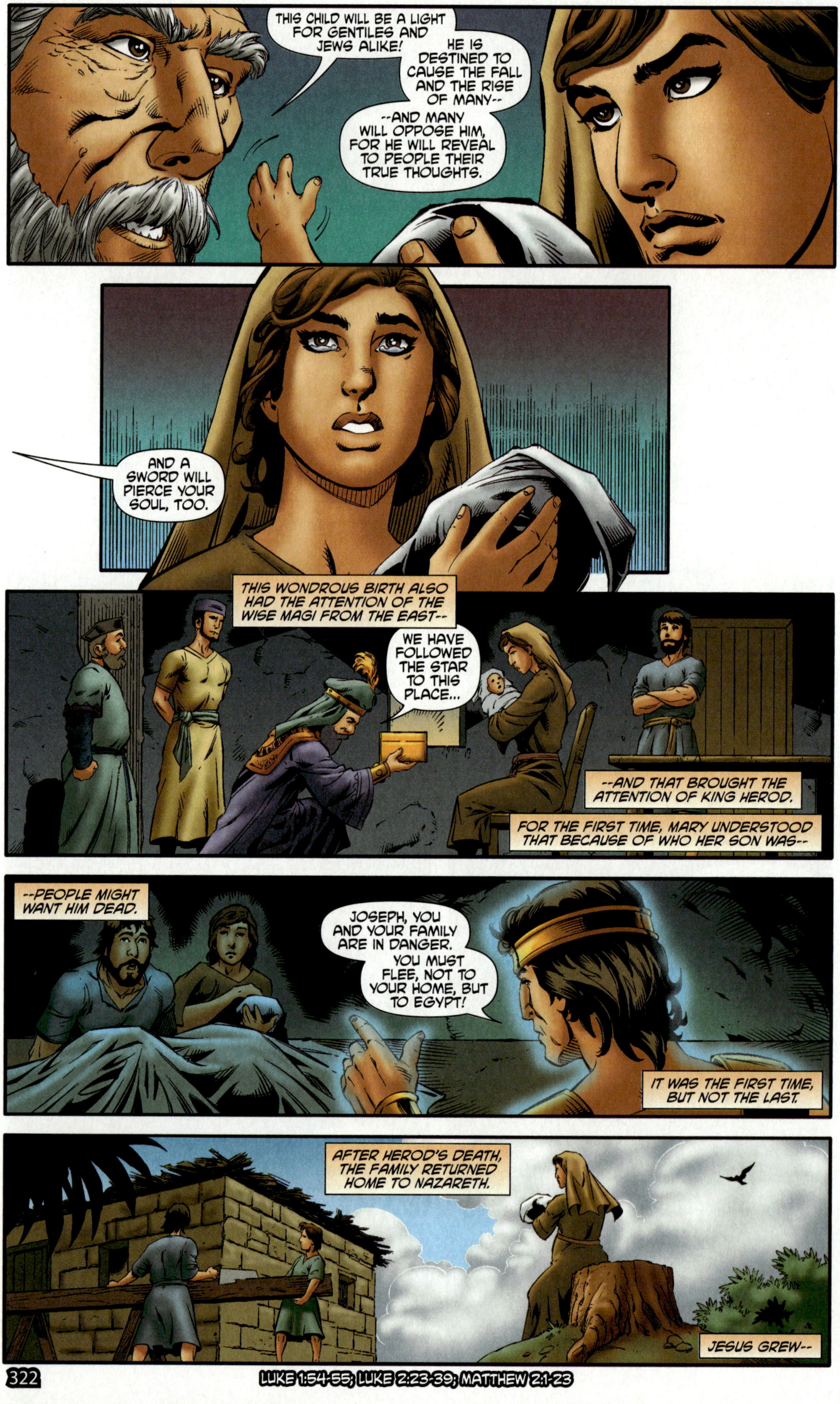
THIS CHILD WILL BE A LIGHT FOR GENTILES AND JEWS ALIKE!
HE IS DESTINED TO CAUSE THE FALL AND THE RISE OF MANY--
--AND MANY WILL OPPOSE HIM, FOR HE WILL REVEAL TO PEOPLE THEIR TRUE THOUGHTS.
AND A SWORD WILL PIERCE YOUR SOUL, TOO.
THIS WONDROUS BIRTH ALSO HAD THE ATTENTION OF THE WISE MAGI FROM THE EAST--
WE HAVE FOLLOWED THE STAR TO THIS PLACE...
--AND THAT BROUGHT THE ATTENTION OF KING HEROD.
FOR THE FIRST TIME, MARY UNDERSTOOD THAT BECAUSE OF WHO HER SON WAS--
--PEOPLE MIGHT WANT HIM DEAD.
JOSEPH, YOU AND YOUR FAMILY ARE IN DANGER.
YOU MUST FLEE, NOT TO YOUR HOME, BUT TO EGYPT!
IT WAS THE FIRST TIME, BUT NOT THE LAST.
AFTER HEROD'S DEATH, THE FAMILY RETURNED HOME TO NAZARETH.
JESUS GREW--

LUKE 1:54-55; LUKE 2:23-39; MATTHEW 2:1-23

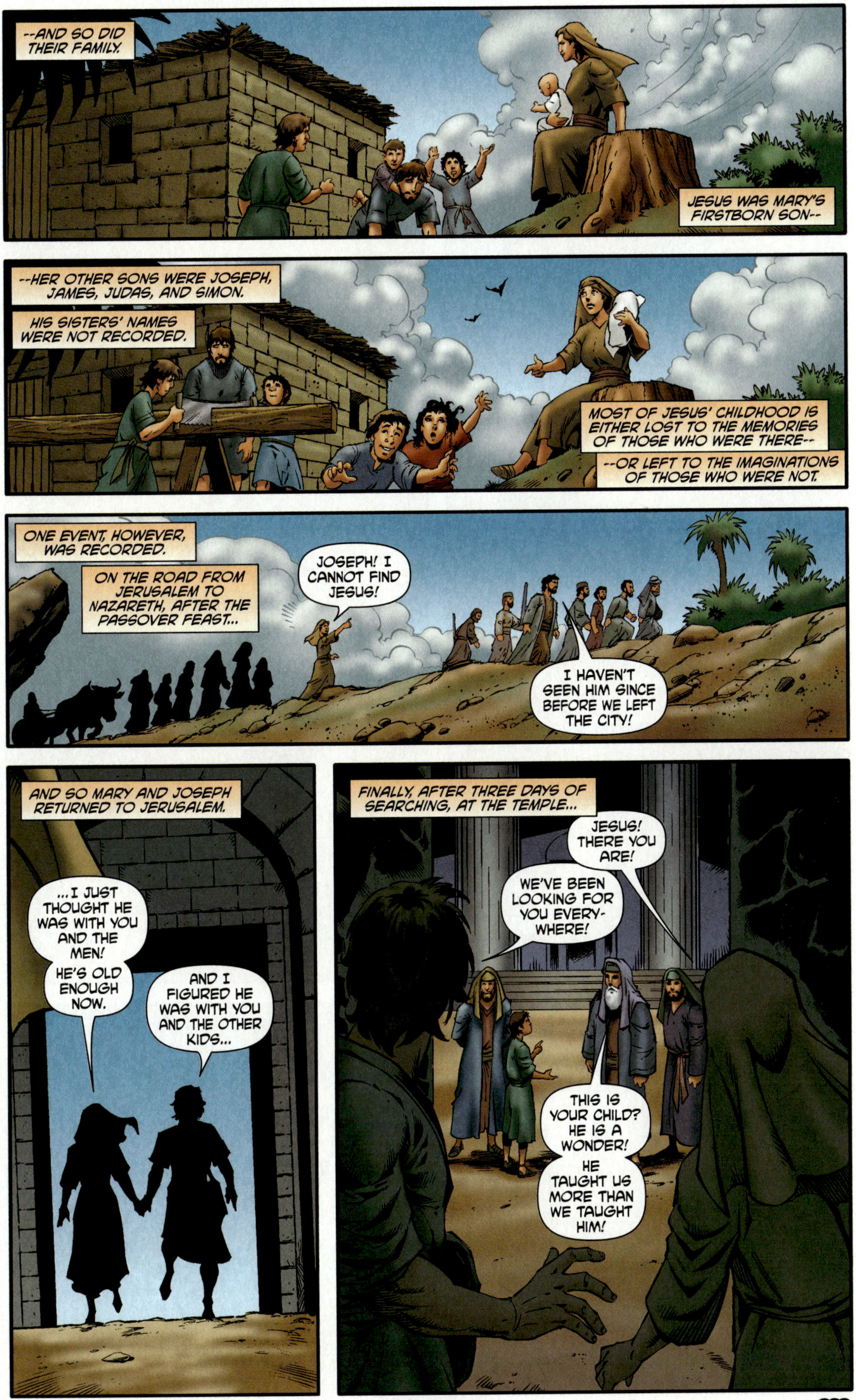
--AND SO DID THEIR FAMILY.
JESUS WAS MARY'S FIRSTBORN SON--
--HER OTHER SONS WERE JOSEPH, JAMES, JUDAS, AND SIMON.
HIS SISTERS' NAMES WERE NOT RECORDED.
MOST OF JESUS' CHILDHOOD IS EITHER LOST TO THE MEMORIES OF THOSE WHO WERE THERE--
--OR LEFT TO THE IMAGINATIONS OF THOSE WHO WERE NOT.
ONE EVENT, HOWEVER, WAS RECORDED.
ON THE ROAD FROM JERUSALEM TO NAZARETH, AFTER THE PASSOVER FEAST...
JOSEPH! I CANNOT FIND JESUS!
I HAVEN'T SEEN HIM SINCE BEFORE WE LEFT THE CITY!
AND SO MARY AND JOSEPH RETURNED TO JERUSALEM.
...I JUST THOUGHT HE WAS WITH YOU AND THE MEN!
HE'S OLD ENOUGH NOW.
AND I FIGURED HE WAS WITH YOU AND THE OTHER KIDS...
FINALLY, AFTER THREE DAYS OF SEARCHING, AT THE TEMPLE...
JESUS! THERE YOU ARE!
WE'VE BEEN LOOKING FOR YOU EVERY-WHERE!
THIS IS YOUR CHILD? HE IS A WONDER!
HE TAUGHT US MORE THAN WE TAUGHT HIM!

LUKE 2:40-47

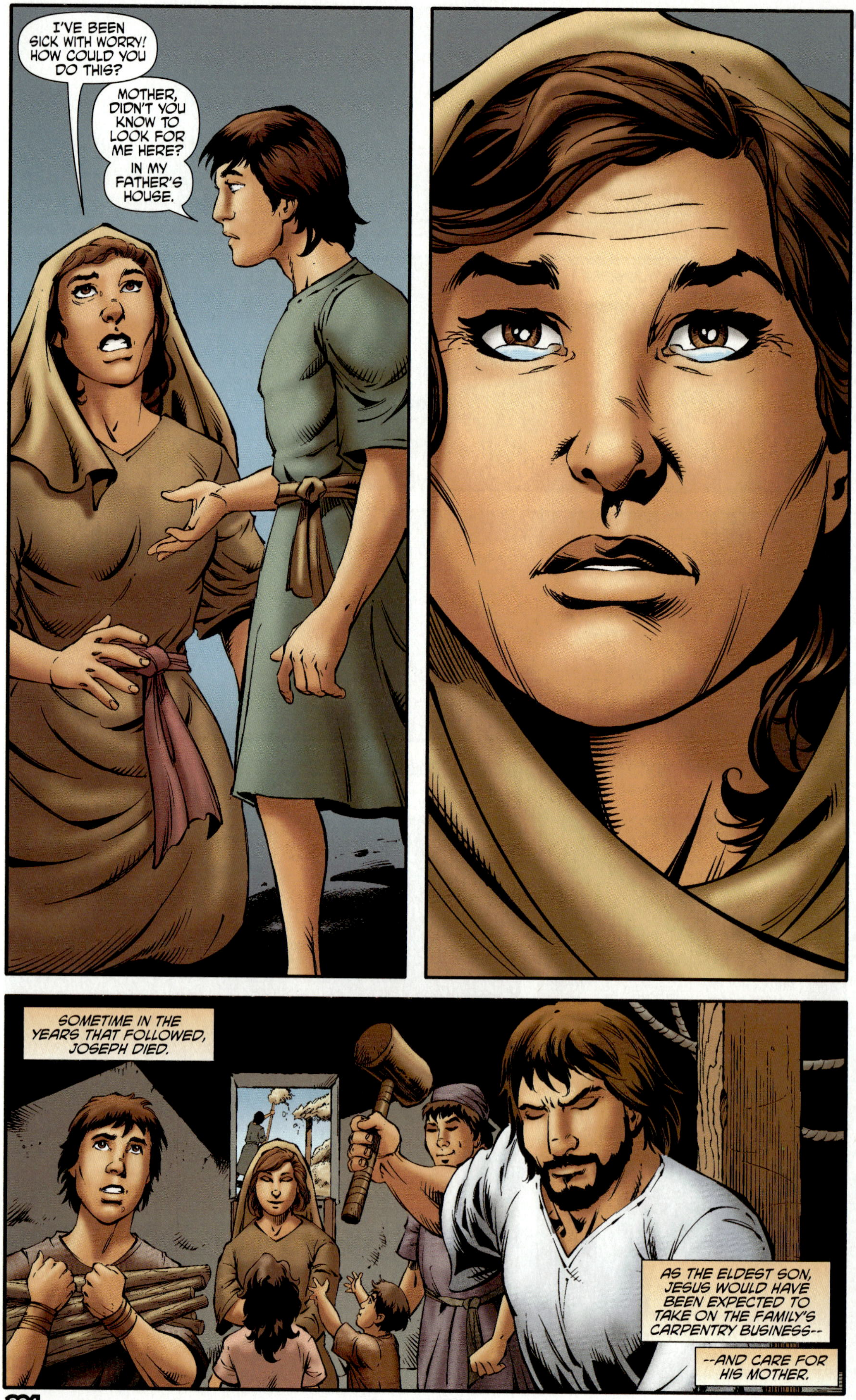
I'VE BEEN SICK WITH WORRY! HOW COULD YOU DO THIS?
MOTHER, DIDN'T YOU KNOW TO LOOK FOR ME HERE?
IN MY FATHER'S HOUSE.
SOMETIME IN THE YEARS THAT FOLLOWED, JOSEPH DIED.
AS THE ELDEST SON, JESUS WOULD HAVE BEEN EXPECTED TO TAKE ON THE FAMILY'S CARPENTRY BUSINESS--
--AND CARE FOR HIS MOTHER.

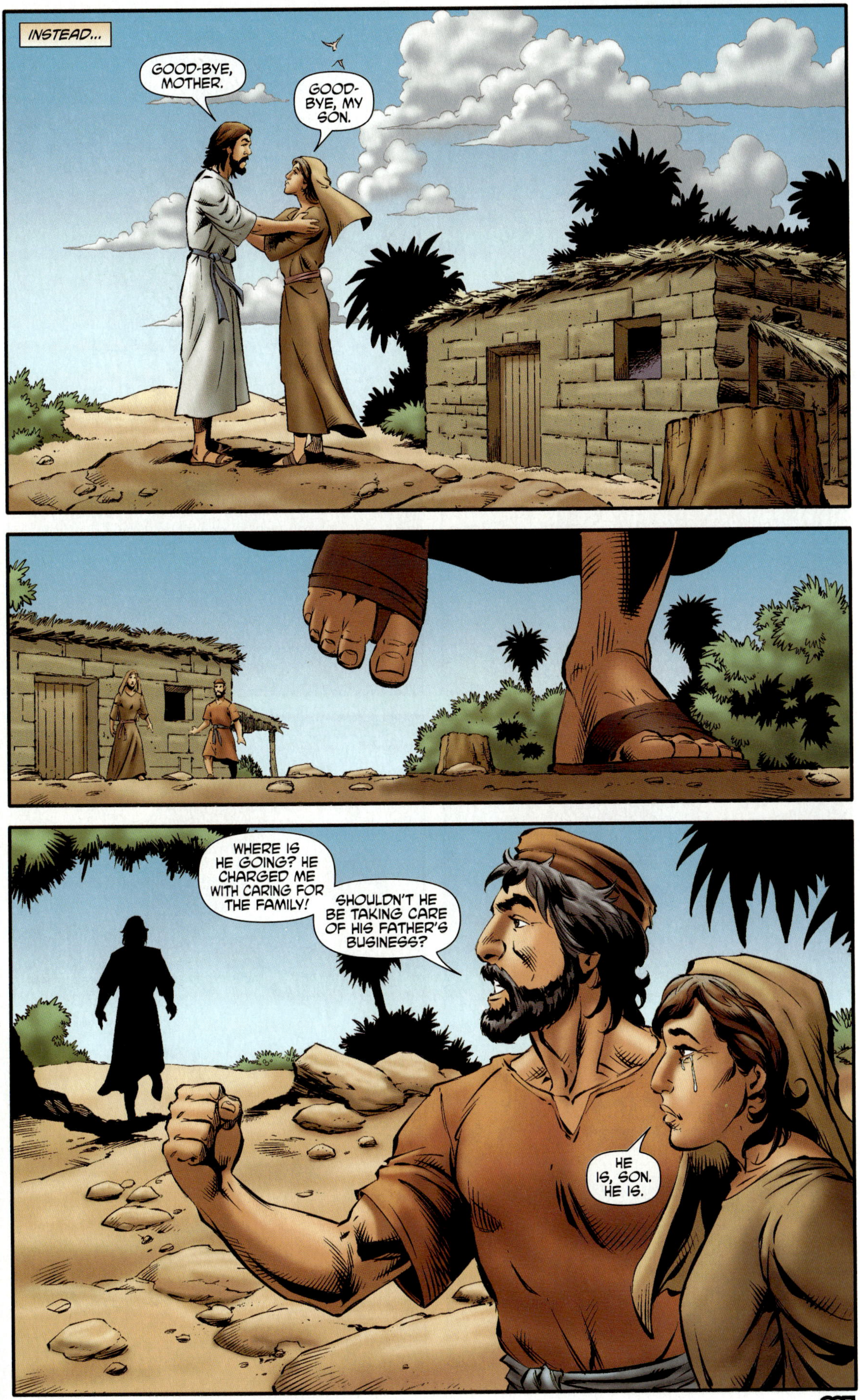
INSTEAD...
GOOD-BYE, MOTHER.
GOOD-BYE, MY SON.
WHERE IS HE GOING? HE CHARGED ME WITH CARING FOR THE FAMILY!
SHOULDN'T HE BE TAKING CARE OF HIS FATHER'S BUSINESS?
HE IS, SON. HE IS.

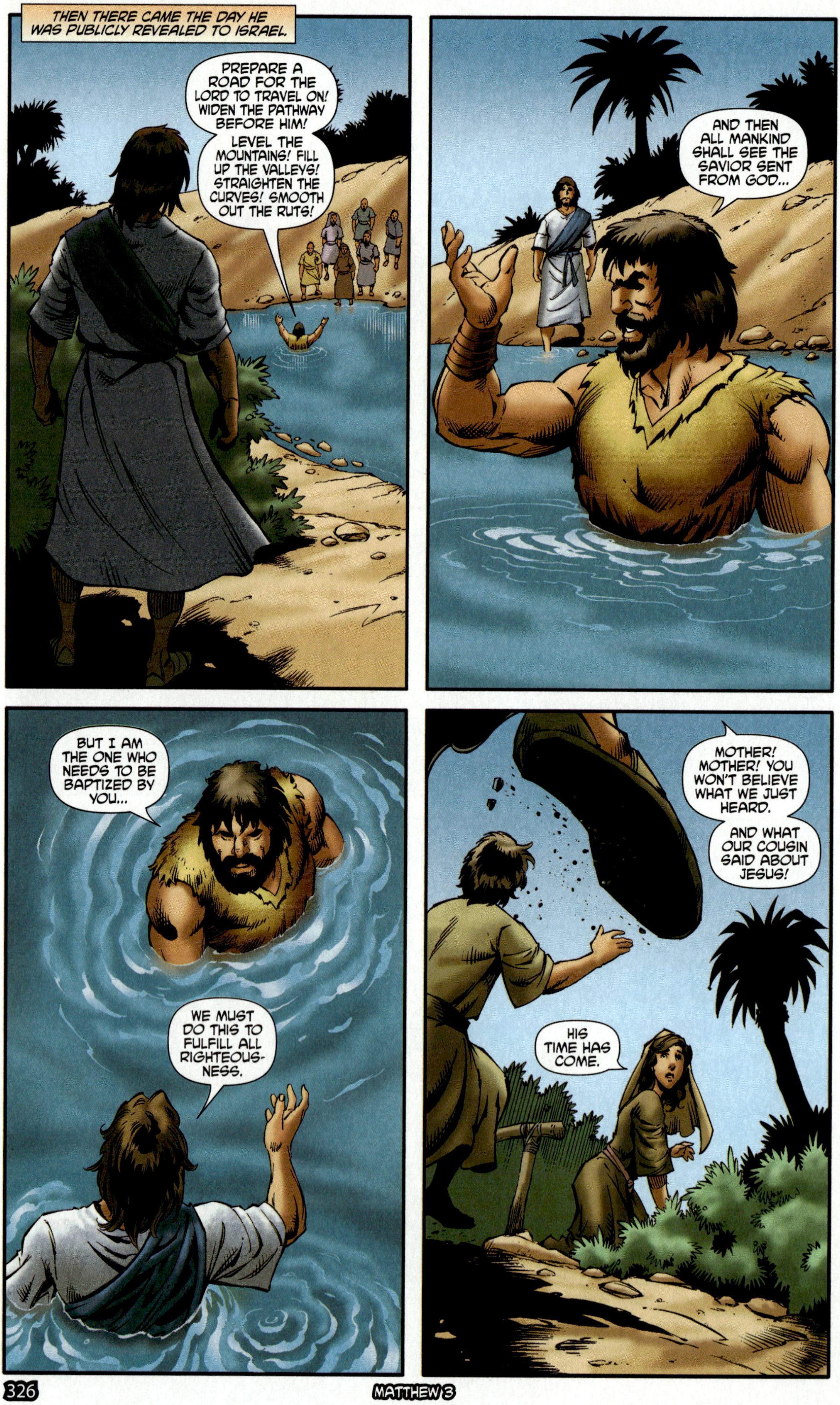
THEN THERE CAME THE DAY HE WAS PUBLICLY REVEALED TO ISRAEL.
PREPARE A ROAD FOR THE LORD TO TRAVEL ON! WIDEN THE PATHWAY BEFORE HIM!
LEVEL THE MOUNTAINS! FILL UP THE VALLEYS! STRAIGHTEN THE CURVES! SMOOTH OUT THE RUTS!
AND THEN ALL MANKIND SHALL SEE THE SAVIOR SENT FROM GOD...
BUT I AM THE ONE WHO NEEDS TO BE BAPTIZED BY YOU...
WE MUST DO THIS TO FULFILL ALL RIGHTEOUS-NESS.
MOTHER! MOTHER! YOU WON'T BELIEVE WHAT WE JUST HEARD.
AND WHAT OUR COUSIN SAID ABOUT JESUS!
HIS TIME HAS COME.

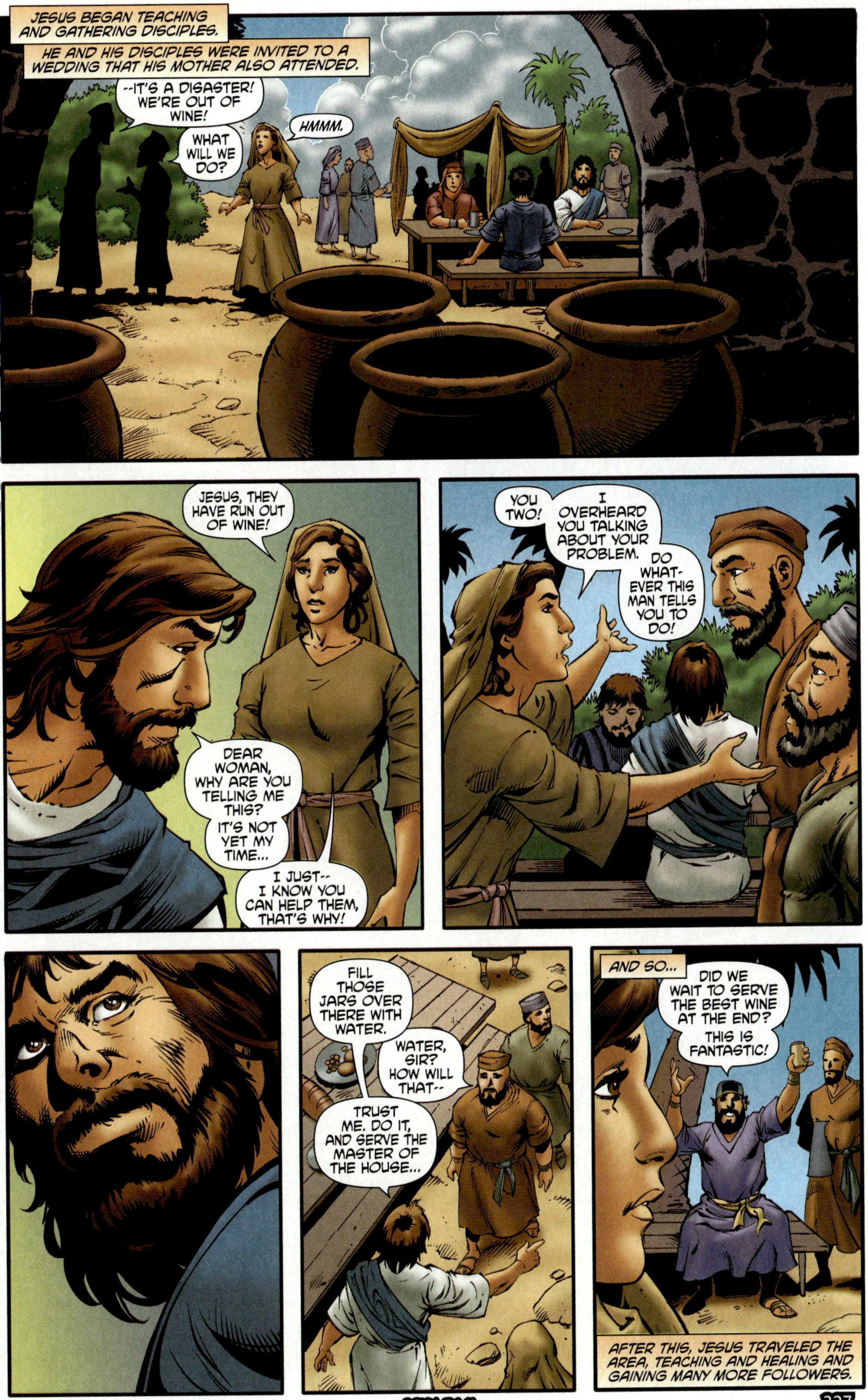
JESUS BEGAN TEACHING AND GATHERING DISCIPLES.
HE AND HIS DISCIPLES WERE INVITED TO A WEDDING THAT HIS MOTHER ALSO ATTENDED.
--IT'S A DISASTER! WE'RE OUT OF WINE!
WHAT WILL WE DO?
HMMM.
JESUS, THEY HAVE RUN OUT OF WINE!
DEAR WOMAN, WHY ARE YOU TELLING ME THIS?
IT'S NOT YET MY TIME...
I JUST-- I KNOW YOU CAN HELP THEM, THAT'S WHY!
YOU TWO!
I OVERHEARD YOU TALKING ABOUT YOUR PROBLEM.
DO WHAT-EVER THIS MAN TELLS YOU TO DO!
FILL THOSE JARS OVER THERE WITH WATER.
WATER, SIR? HOW WILL THAT--
TRUST ME. DO IT, AND SERVE THE MASTER OF THE HOUSE...
AND SO...
DID WE WAIT TO SERVE THE BEST WINE AT THE END?
THIS IS FANTASTIC!
AFTER THIS, JESUS TRAVELED THE AREA, TEACHING AND HEALING AND GAINING MANY MORE FOLLOWERS.

JOHN 2:1-11

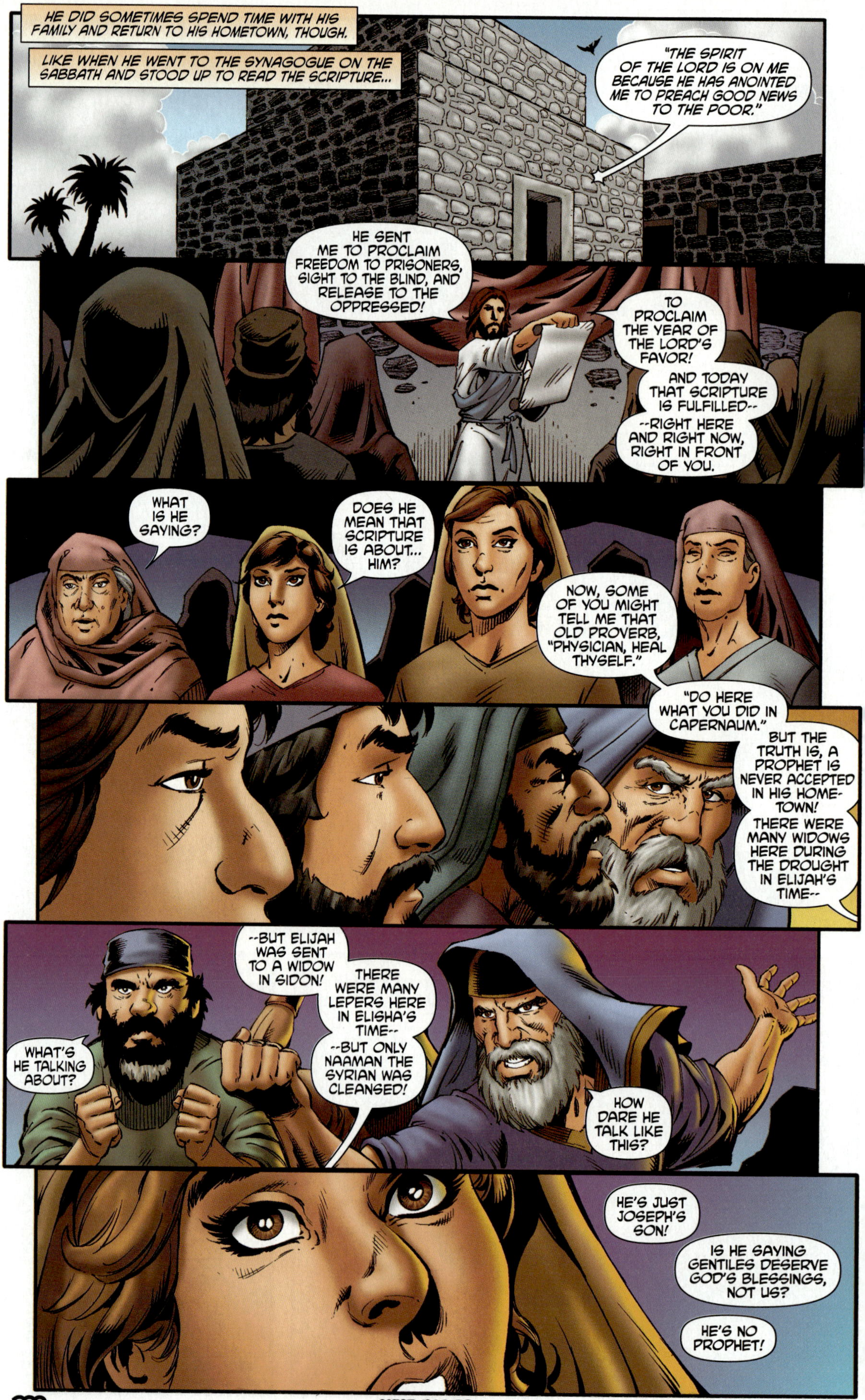
HE DID SOMETIMES SPEND TIME WITH HIS FAMILY AND RETURN TO HIS HOMETOWN, THOUGH.
LIKE WHEN HE WENT TO THE SYNAGOGUE ON THE SABBATH AND STOOD UP TO READ THE SCRIPTURE...
"THE SPIRIT OF THE LORD IS ON ME BECAUSE HE HAS ANOINTED ME TO PREACH GOOD NEWS TO THE POOR."
HE SENT ME TO PROCLAIM FREEDOM TO PRISONERS, SIGHT TO THE BLIND, AND RELEASE TO THE OPPRESSED!
TO PROCLAIM THE YEAR OF THE LORD'S FAVOR!
AND TODAY THAT SCRIPTURE IS FULFILLED--
--RIGHT HERE AND RIGHT NOW, RIGHT IN FRONT OF YOU.
WHAT IS HE SAYING?
DOES HE MEAN THAT SCRIPTURE IS ABOUT... HIM?
NOW, SOME OF YOU MIGHT TELL ME THAT OLD PROVERB, "PHYSICIAN, HEAL THYSELF."
"DO HERE WHAT YOU DID IN CAPERNAUM."
BUT THE TRUTH IS, A PROPHET IS NEVER ACCEPTED IN HIS HOME-TOWN!
THERE WERE MANY WIDOWS HERE DURING THE DROUGHT IN ELIJAH'S TIME--
--BUT ELIJAH WAS SENT TO A WIDOW IN SIDON!
THERE WERE MANY LEPERS HERE IN ELISHA'S TIME--
--BUT ONLY NAAMAN THE SYRIAN WAS CLEANSED!
WHAT'S HE TALKING ABOUT?
HOW DARE HE TALK LIKE THIS?
HE'S JUST JOSEPH'S SON!
IS HE SAYING GENTILES DESERVE GOD'S BLESSINGS, NOT US?
HE'S NO PROPHET!

LUKE 4:16-28

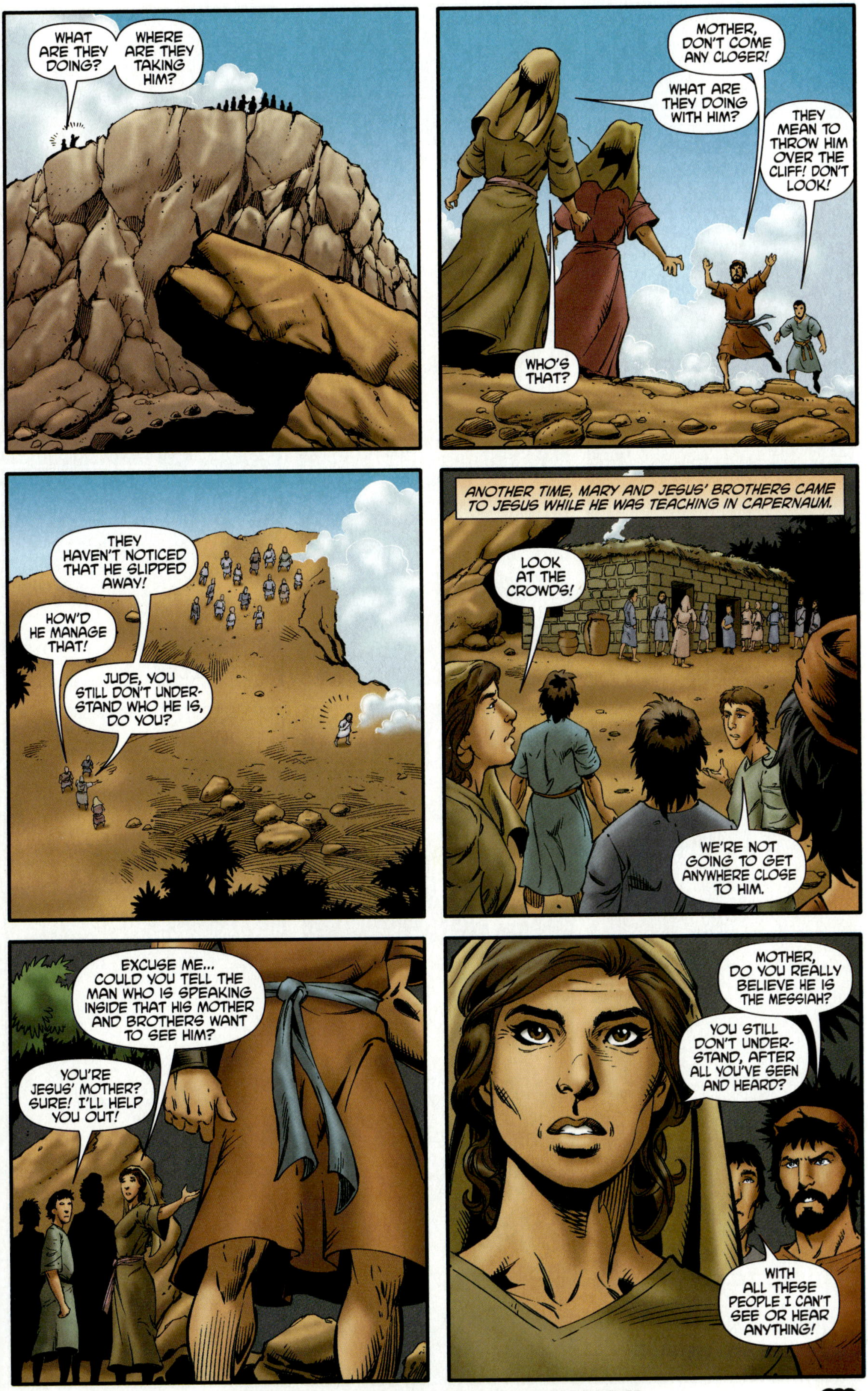
WHAT ARE THEY DOING?
WHERE ARE THEY TAKING HIM?
MOTHER, DON'T COME ANY CLOSER!
WHAT ARE THEY DOING WITH HIM?
THEY MEAN TO THROW HIM OVER THE CLIFF! DON'T LOOK!
WHO'S THAT?
THEY HAVEN'T NOTICED THAT HE SLIPPED AWAY!
HOW'D HE MANAGE THAT!
JUDE, YOU STILL DON'T UNDER-STAND WHO HE IS, DO YOU?
ANOTHER TIME, MARY AND JESUS' BROTHERS CAME TO JESUS WHILE HE WAS TEACHING IN CAPERNAUM.
LOOK AT THE CROWDS!
WE'RE NOT GOING TO GET ANYWHERE CLOSE TO HIM.
EXCUSE ME... COULD YOU TELL THE MAN WHO IS SPEAKING INSIDE THAT HIS MOTHER AND BROTHERS WANT TO SEE HIM?
YOU'RE JESUS' MOTHER? SURE! I'LL HELP YOU OUT!
MOTHER, DO YOU REALLY BELIEVE HE IS THE MESSIAH?
YOU STILL DON'T UNDER-STAND, AFTER ALL YOU'VE SEEN AND HEARD?
WITH ALL THESE PEOPLE I CAN'T SEE OR HEAR ANYTHING!

LUKE 4:29-30, 8:19-20; MATTHEW 12:46-47; MARK 3:31-32

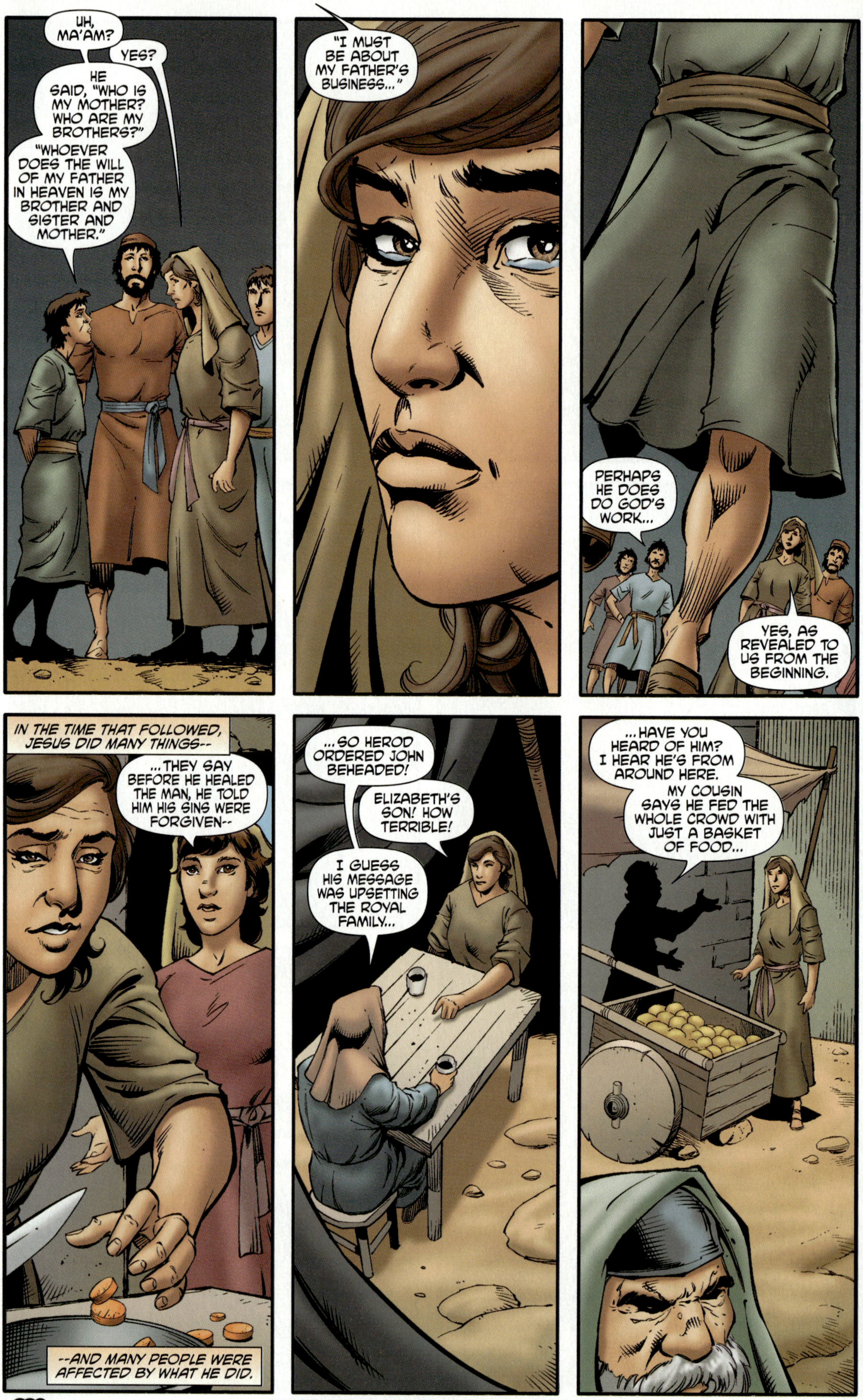
UH, MA'AM?
YES?
HE SAID, "WHO IS MY MOTHER? WHO ARE MY BROTHERS?"
"WHOEVER DOES THE WILL OF MY FATHER IN HEAVEN IS MY BROTHER AND SISTER AND MOTHER."
"I MUST BE ABOUT MY FATHER'S BUSINESS..."
PERHAPS HE DOES DO GOD'S WORK...
YES, AS REVEALED TO US FROM THE BEGINNING.
IN THE TIME THAT FOLLOWED, JESUS DID MANY THINGS--
...THEY SAY BEFORE HE HEALED THE MAN, HE TOLD HIM HIS SINS WERE FORGIVEN--
--AND MANY PEOPLE WERE AFFECTED BY WHAT HE DID.
...SO HEROD ORDERED JOHN BEHEADED!
ELIZABETH'S SON! HOW TERRIBLE!
I GUESS HIS MESSAGE WAS UPSETTING THE ROYAL FAMILY...
...HAVE YOU HEARD OF HIM? I HEAR HE'S FROM AROUND HERE.
MY COUSIN SAYS HE FED THE WHOLE CROWD WITH JUST A BASKET OF FOOD...

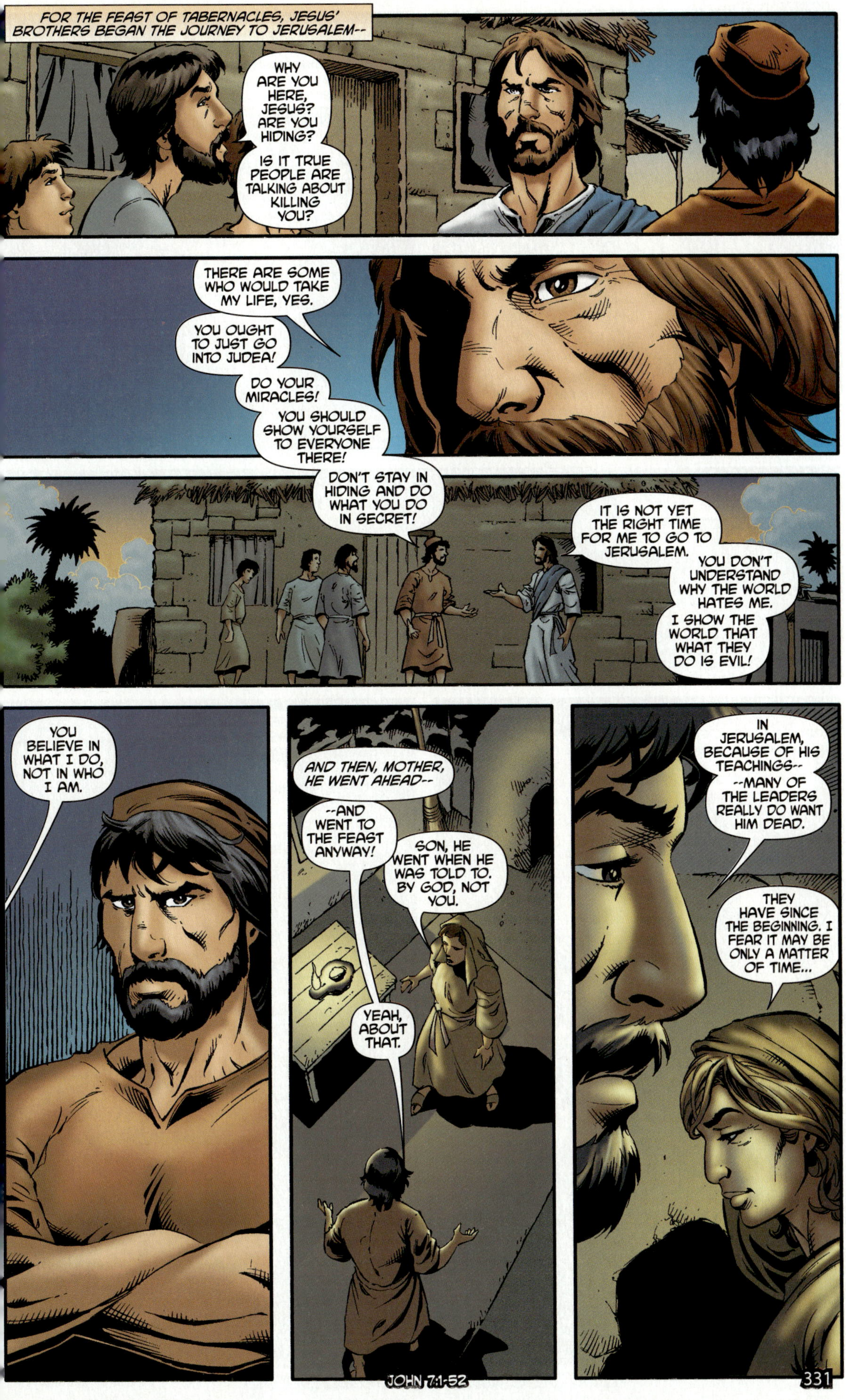

FOR THE FEAST OF TABERNACLES, JESUS' BROTHERS BEGAN THE JOURNEY TO JERUSALEM--
WHY ARE YOU HERE, JESUS? ARE YOU HIDING?
IS IT TRUE PEOPLE ARE TALKING ABOUT KILLING YOU?
THERE ARE SOME WHO WOULD TAKE MY LIFE, YES.
YOU OUGHT TO JUST GO INTO JUDEA!
DO YOUR MIRACLES!
YOU SHOULD SHOW YOURSELF TO EVERYONE THERE!
DON'T STAY IN HIDING AND DO WHAT YOU DO IN SECRET!
IT IS NOT YET THE RIGHT TIME FOR ME TO GO TO JERUSALEM.
YOU DON'T UNDERSTAND WHY THE WORLD HATES ME.
I SHOW THE WORLD THAT WHAT THEY DO IS EVIL!
YOU BELIEVE IN WHAT I DO, NOT IN WHO I AM.
AND THEN, MOTHER, HE WENT AHEAD--
--AND WENT TO THE FEAST ANYWAY!
SON, HE WENT WHEN HE WAS TOLD TO. BY GOD, NOT YOU.
YEAH, ABOUT THAT.
IN JERUSALEM, BECAUSE OF HIS TEACHINGS--
--MANY OF THE LEADERS REALLY DO WANT HIM DEAD.
THEY HAVE SINCE THE BEGINNING. I FEAR IT MAY BE ONLY A MATTER OF TIME...
JOHN 7:1-52

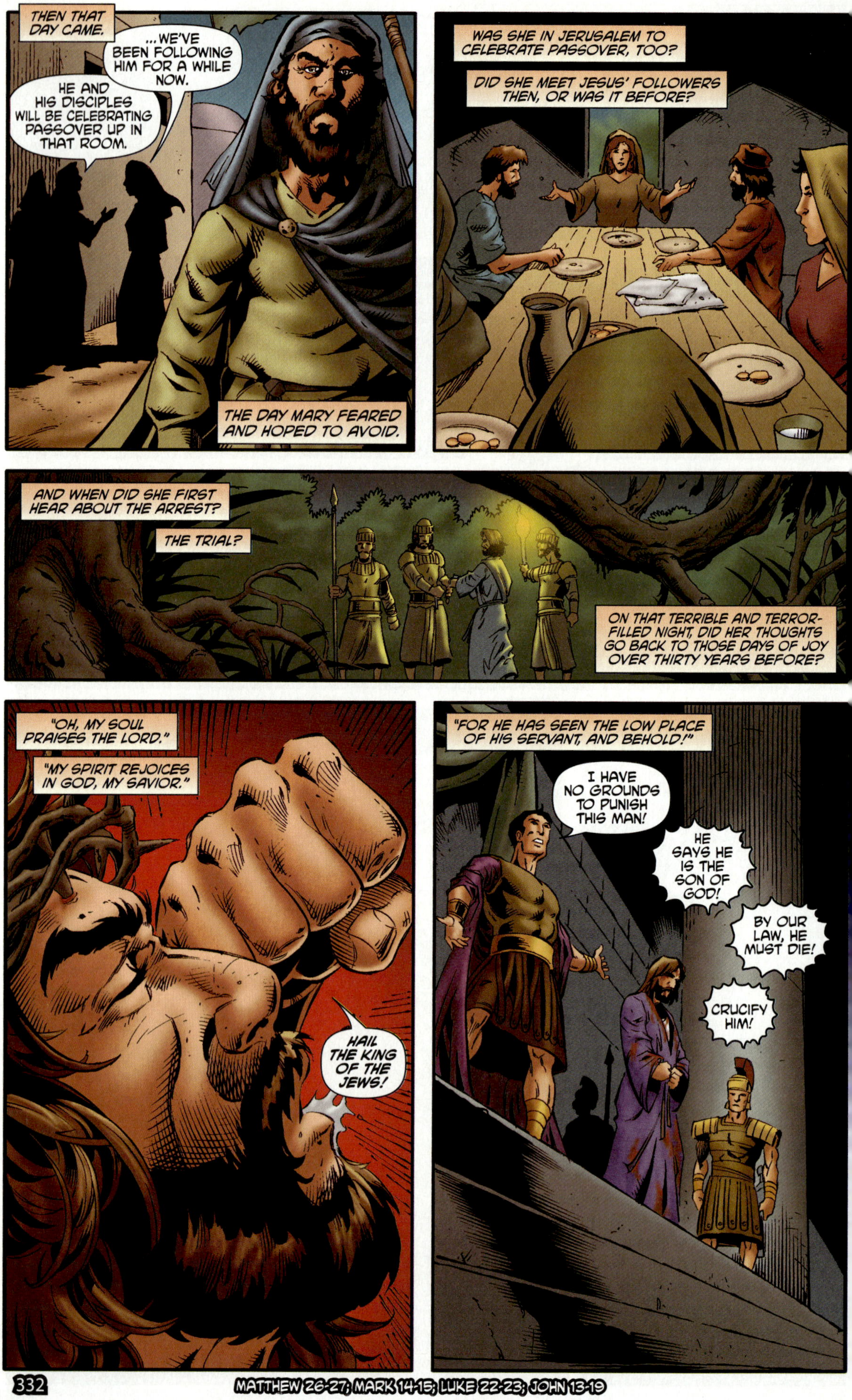
THEN THAT DAY CAME.
...WE'VE BEEN FOLLOWING HIM FOR A WHILE NOW.
HE AND HIS DISCIPLES WILL BE CELEBRATING PASSOVER UP IN THAT ROOM.
THE DAY MARY FEARED AND HOPED TO AVOID.
WAS SHE IN JERUSALEM TO CELEBRATE PASSOVER, TOO?
DID SHE MEET JESUS' FOLLOWERS THEN, OR WAS IT BEFORE?
AND WHEN DID SHE FIRST HEAR ABOUT THE ARREST?
THE TRIAL?
ON THAT TERRIBLE AND TERROR-FILLED NIGHT, DID HER THOUGHTS GO BACK TO THOSE DAYS OF JOY OVER THIRTY YEARS BEFORE?
"OH, MY SOUL PRAISES THE LORD."
"MY SPIRIT REJOICES IN GOD, MY SAVIOR."
HAIL THE KING OF THE JEWS!
"FOR HE HAS SEEN THE LOW PLACE OF HIS SERVANT, AND BEHOLD!"
I HAVE NO GROUNDS TO PUNISH THIS MAN!
HE SAYS HE IS THE SON OF GOD!
BY OUR LAW, HE MUST DIE!
CRUCIFY HIM!

MATTHEW 26-27; MARK 14-15; LUKE 22-23; JOHN 13-19

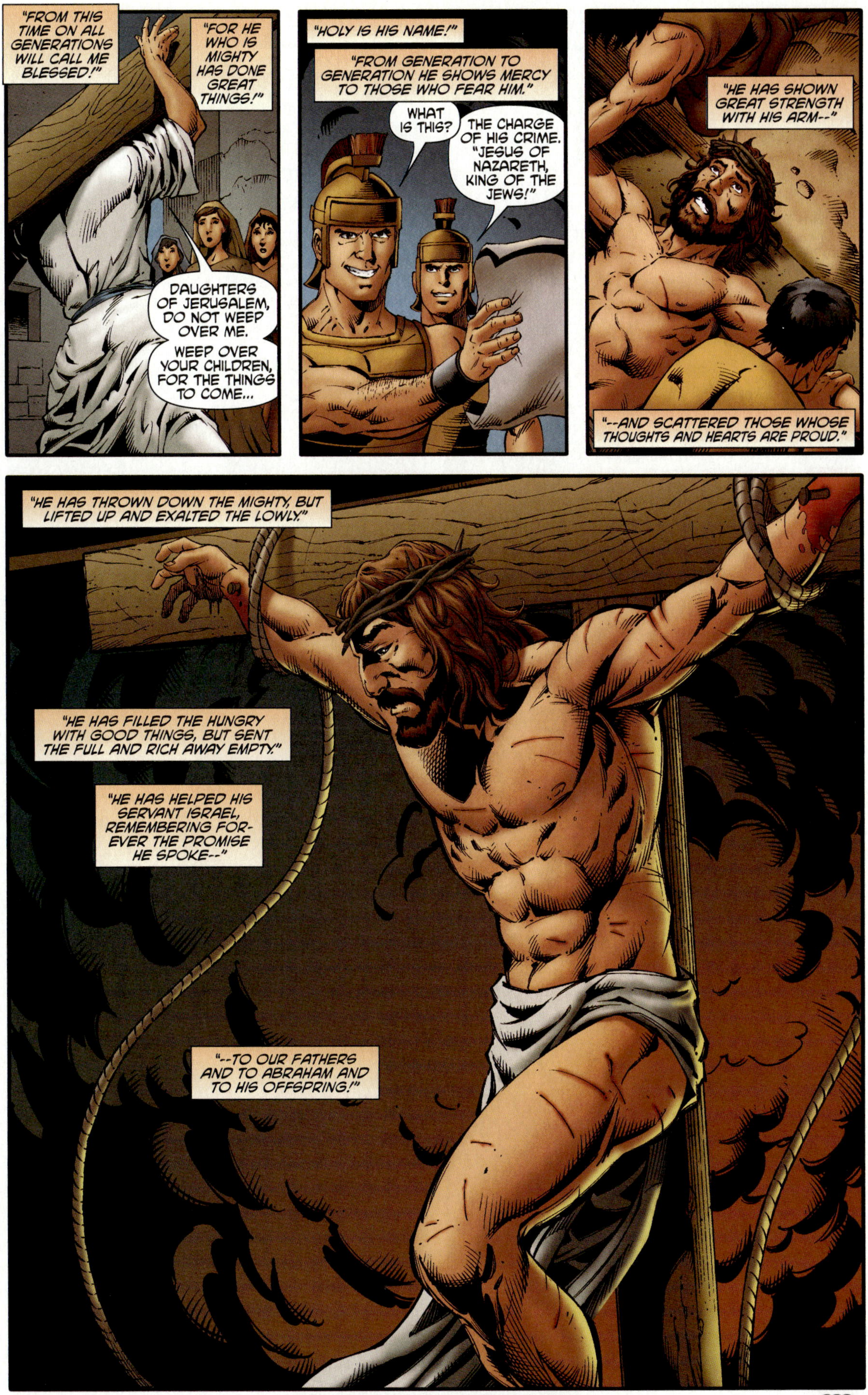
"FROM THIS TIME ON ALL GENERATIONS WILL CALL ME BLESSED!"
"FOR HE WHO IS MIGHTY HAS DONE GREAT THINGS!"
DAUGHTERS OF JERUSALEM, DO NOT WEEP OVER ME.
WEEP OVER YOUR CHILDREN, FOR THE THINGS TO COME...
"HOLY IS HIS NAME!"
"FROM GENERATION TO GENERATION HE SHOWS MERCY TO THOSE WHO FEAR HIM."
WHAT IS THIS?
THE CHARGE OF HIS CRIME. "JESUS OF NAZARETH, KING OF THE JEWS!"
"HE HAS SHOWN GREAT STRENGTH WITH HIS ARM--"
"--AND SCATTERED THOSE WHOSE THOUGHTS AND HEARTS ARE PROUD."
"HE HAS THROWN DOWN THE MIGHTY, BUT LIFTED UP AND EXALTED THE LOWLY."
"HE HAS FILLED THE HUNGRY WITH GOOD THINGS, BUT SENT THE FULL AND RICH AWAY EMPTY."
"HE HAS HELPED HIS SERVANT ISRAEL, REMEMBERING FOR-EVER THE PROMISE HE SPOKE--"
"--TO OUR FATHERS AND TO ABRAHAM AND TO HIS OFFSPRING."

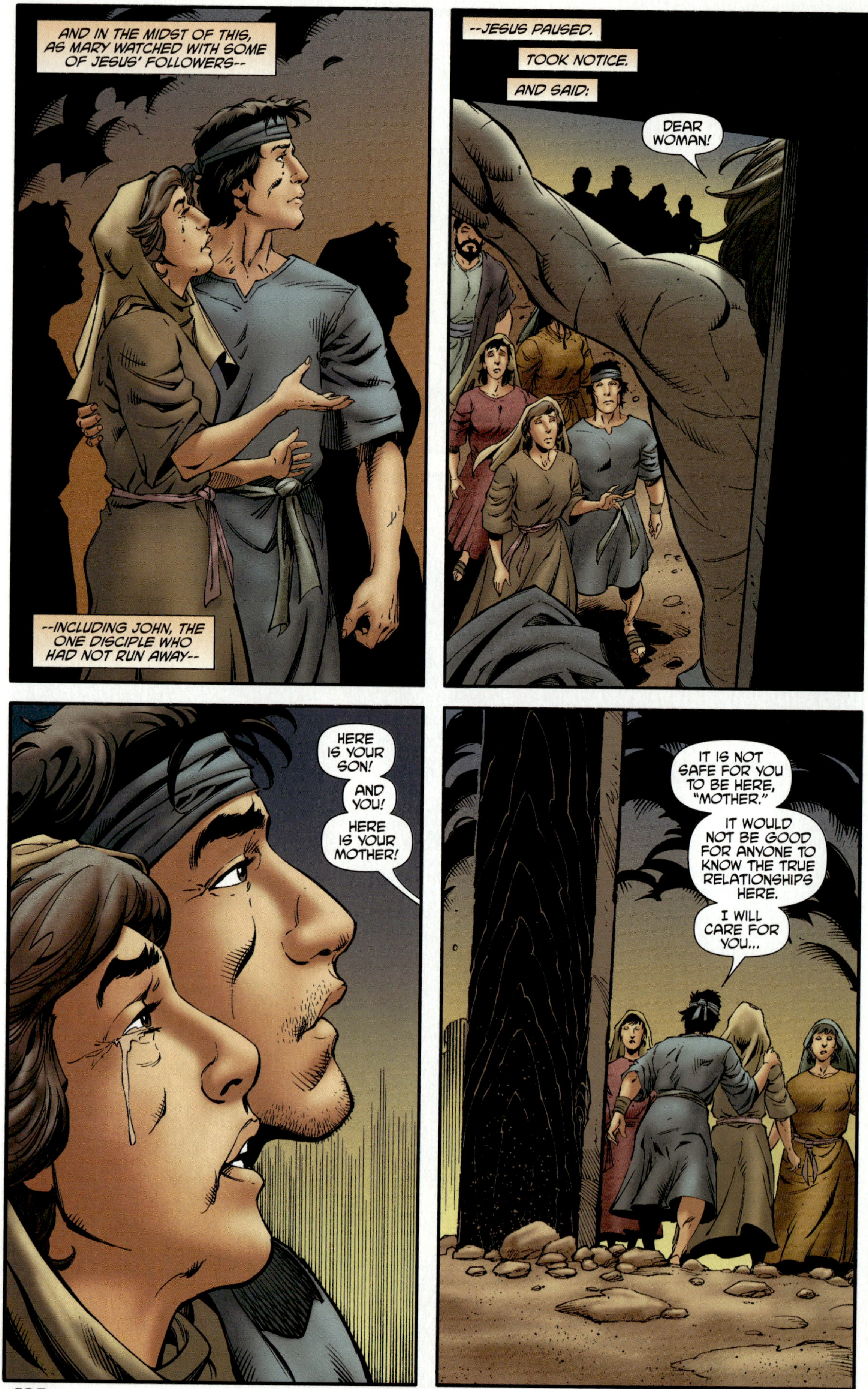
AND IN THE MIDST OF THIS, AS MARY WATCHED WITH SOME OF JESUS' FOLLOWERS--
--INCLUDING JOHN, THE ONE DISCIPLE WHO HAD NOT RUN AWAY--
--JESUS PAUSED.
TOOK NOTICE.
AND SAID:
DEAR WOMAN!
HERE IS YOUR SON!
AND YOU!
HERE IS YOUR MOTHER!
IT IS NOT SAFE FOR YOU TO BE HERE, "MOTHER."
IT WOULD NOT BE GOOD FOR ANYONE TO KNOW THE TRUE RELATIONSHIPS HERE.
I WILL CARE FOR YOU...

JOHN 19:25-27

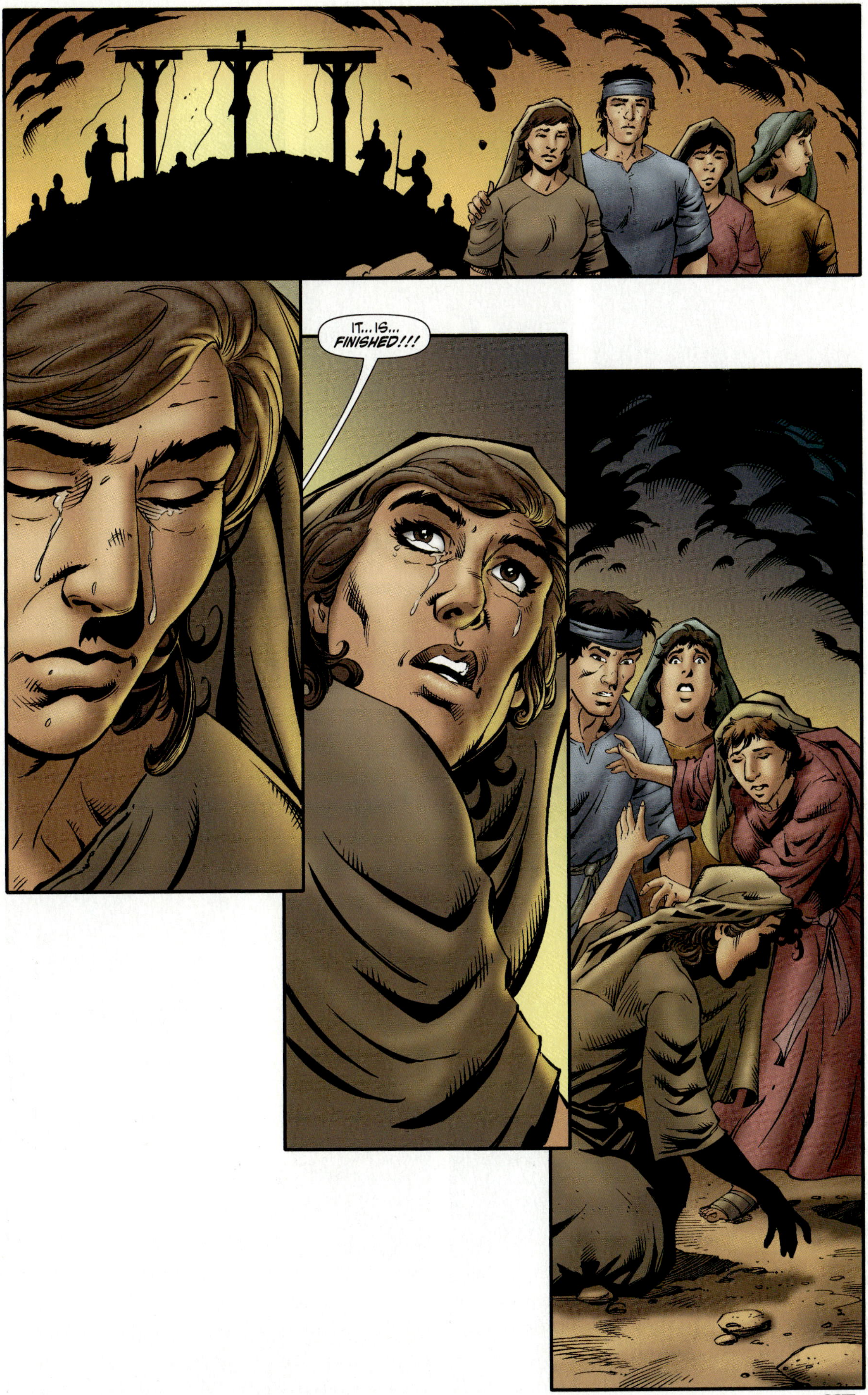
IT... IS... FINISHED!!!

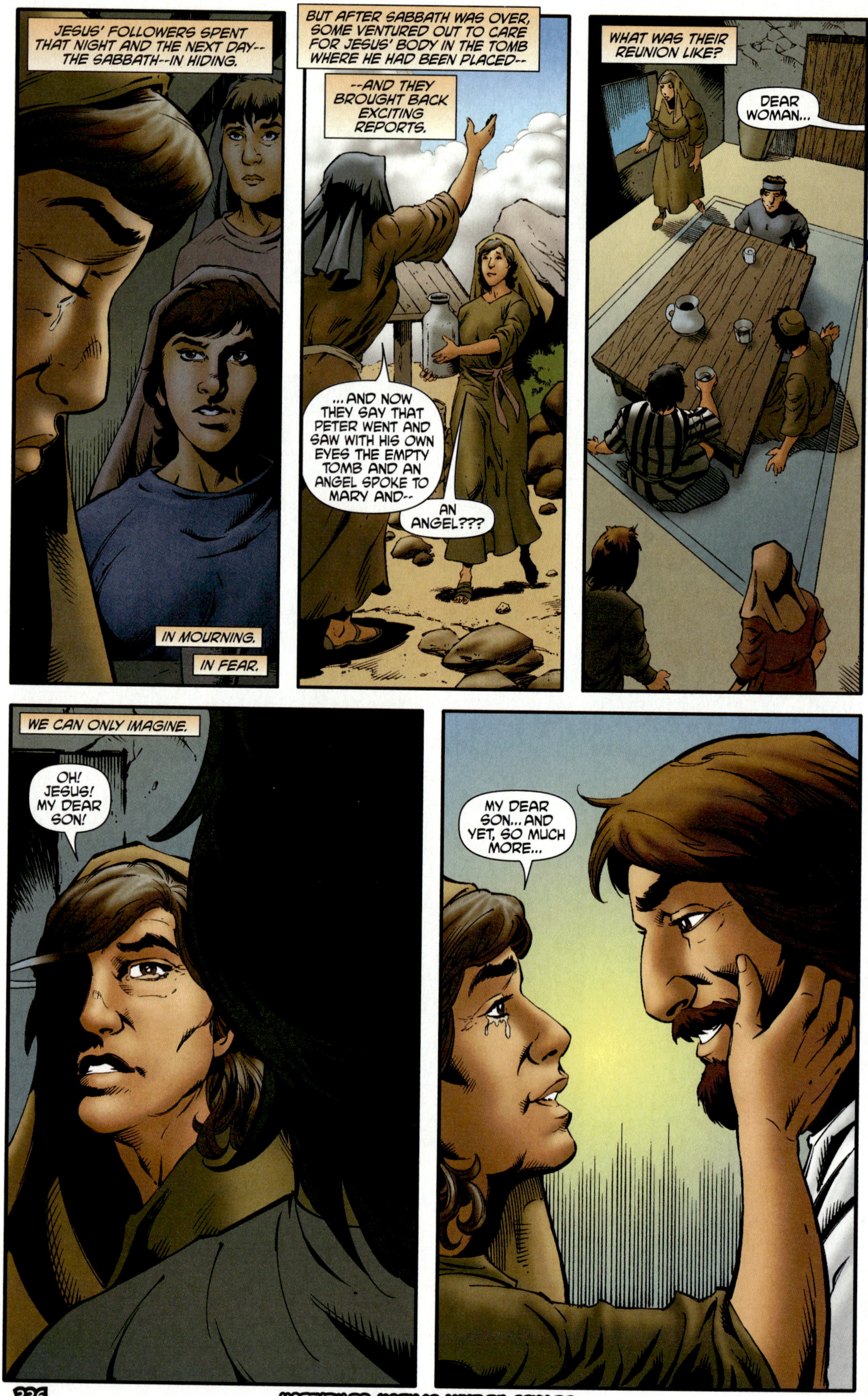
JESUS' FOLLOWERS SPENT THAT NIGHT AND THE NEXT DAY-- THE SABBATH--IN HIDING.
IN MOURNING.
IN FEAR.
BUT AFTER SABBATH WAS OVER, SOME VENTURED OUT TO CARE FOR JESUS' BODY IN THE TOMB WHERE HE HAD BEEN PLACED--
--AND THEY BROUGHT BACK EXCITING REPORTS.
...AND NOW THEY SAY THAT PETER WENT AND SAW WITH HIS OWN EYES THE EMPTY TOMB AND AN ANGEL SPOKE TO MARY AND--
AN ANGEL???
WHAT WAS THEIR REUNION LIKE?
DEAR WOMAN...
WE CAN ONLY IMAGINE.
OH! JESUS! MY DEAR SON!
MY DEAR SON... AND YET, SO MUCH MORE...

MATTHEW 28; MARK 16; LUKE 24; JOHN 20

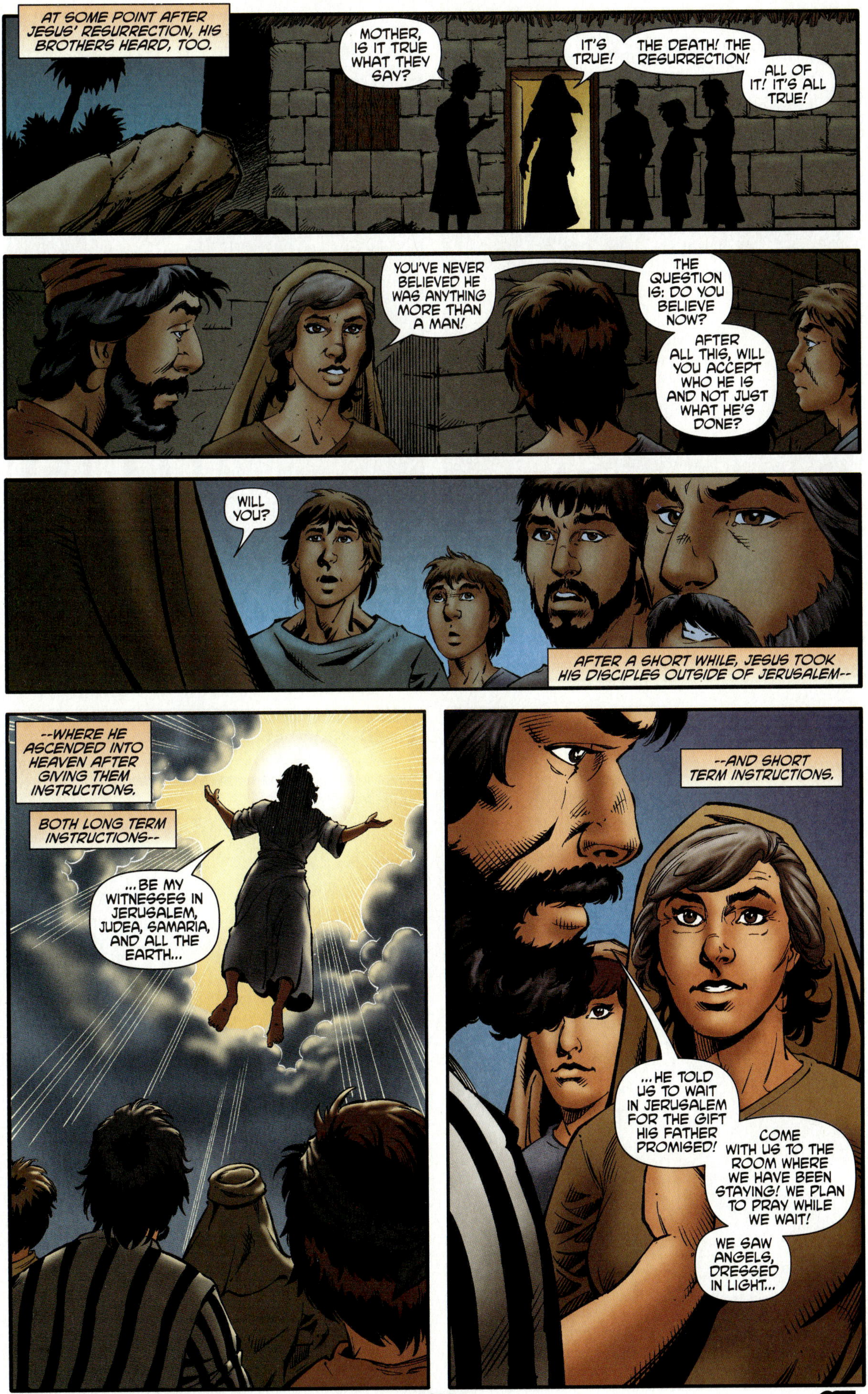

AT SOME POINT AFTER JESUS' RESURRECTION, HIS BROTHERS HEARD, TOO.
MOTHER, IS IT TRUE WHAT THEY SAY?
IT'S TRUE!
THE DEATH! THE RESURRECTION!
ALL OF IT! IT'S ALL TRUE!
YOU'VE NEVER BELIEVED HE WAS ANYTHING MORE THAN A MAN!
THE QUESTION IS: DO YOU BELIEVE NOW?
AFTER ALL THIS, WILL YOU ACCEPT WHO HE IS AND NOT JUST WHAT HE'S DONE?
WILL YOU?
AFTER A SHORT WHILE, JESUS TOOK HIS DISCIPLES OUTSIDE OF JERUSALEM--
--WHERE HE ASCENDED INTO HEAVEN AFTER GIVING THEM INSTRUCTIONS.
BOTH LONG TERM INSTRUCTIONS--
...BE MY WITNESSES IN JERUSALEM, JUDEA, SAMARIA, AND ALL THE EARTH...
--AND SHORT TERM INSTRUCTIONS.
...HE TOLD US TO WAIT IN JERUSALEM FOR THE GIFT HIS FATHER PROMISED!
COME WITH US TO THE ROOM WHERE WE HAVE BEEN STAYING! WE PLAN TO PRAY WHILE WE WAIT!
WE SAW ANGELS, DRESSED IN LIGHT...

HER NAME IS MARY.

AND WHAT WE KNOW OF HER STORY ENDS HERE.

ONCE MORE WITH ANGELS AND A PROMISE OF A GREAT GIFT FROM GOD.

WE NEED A REPLACEMENT FOR THE ONE WHO BETRAYED JESUS.

IT SHOULD BE SOMEONE WHO WAS WITH US FROM THE BEGINNING!

FROM THE BAPTISM WITH JOHN TO THE RESURRECTION OF JESUS TO NOW!

THE BEGINNING...

WE DON'T KNOW WHEN HER OTHER SONS BECAME FOLLOWERS OF THEIR BROTHER--

--BUT THEY, TOO, WERE IN THAT ROOM, WAITING AND PRAYING.

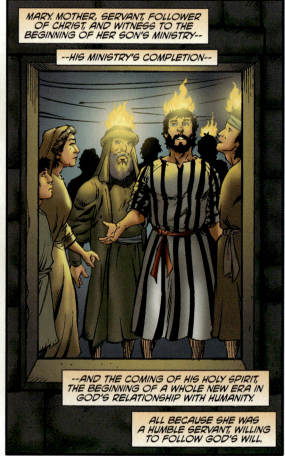

MARY. MOTHER, SERVANT, FOLLOWER OF CHRIST, AND WITNESS TO THE BEGINNING OF HER SON'S MINISTRY--

--HIS MINISTRY'S COMPLETION--

--AND THE COMING OF HIS HOLY SPIRIT, THE BEGINNING OF A WHOLE NEW ERA IN GOD'S RELATIONSHIP WITH HUMANITY.

ALL BECAUSE SHE WAS A HUMBLE SERVANT, WILLING TO FOLLOW GOD'S WILL.

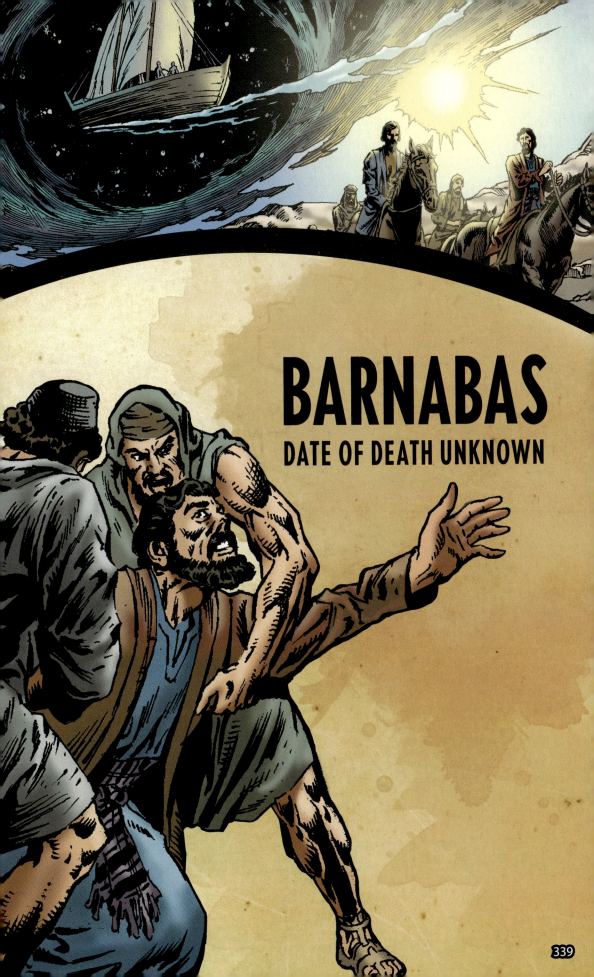

BARNABAS

DATE OF DEATH UNKNOWN

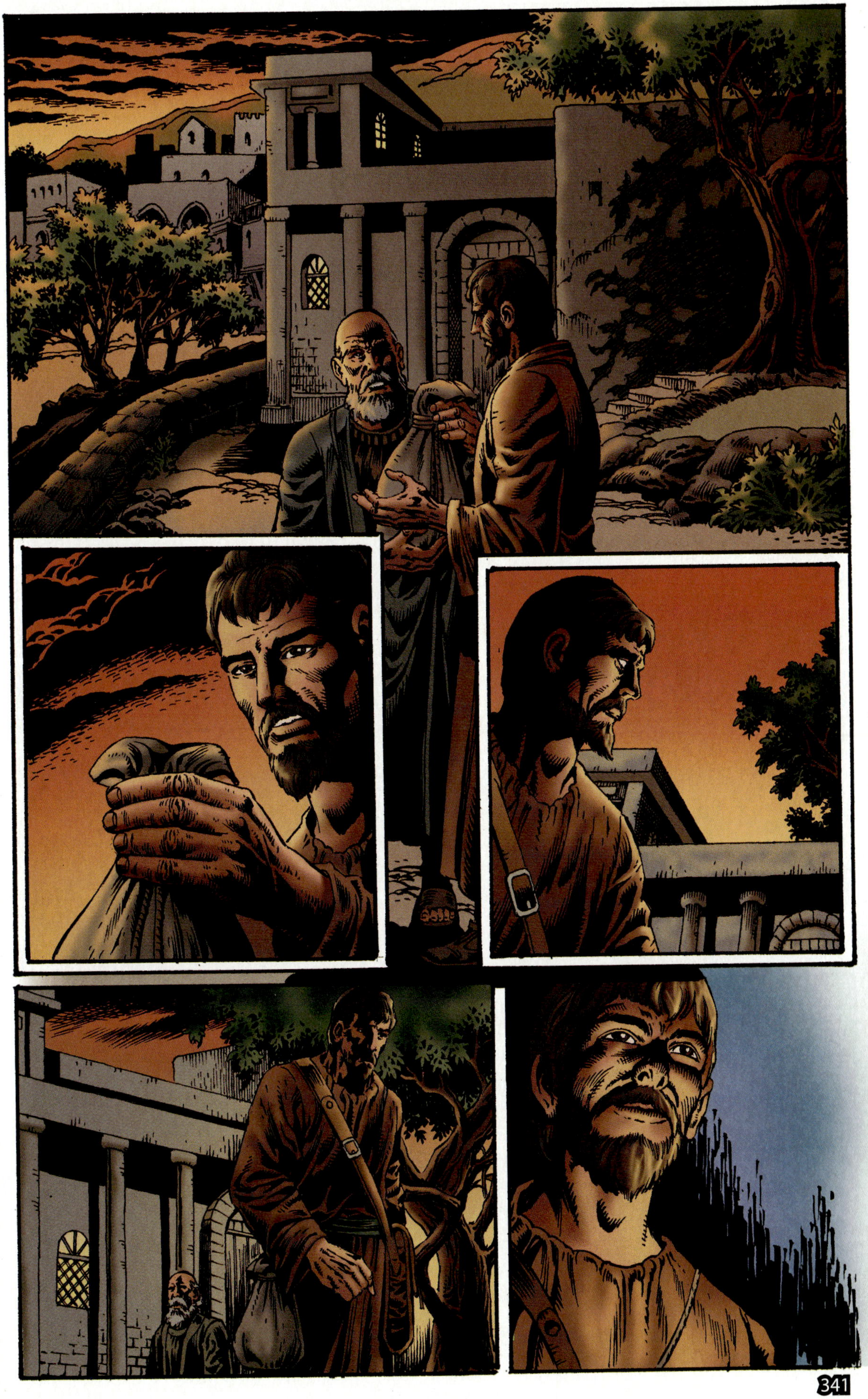

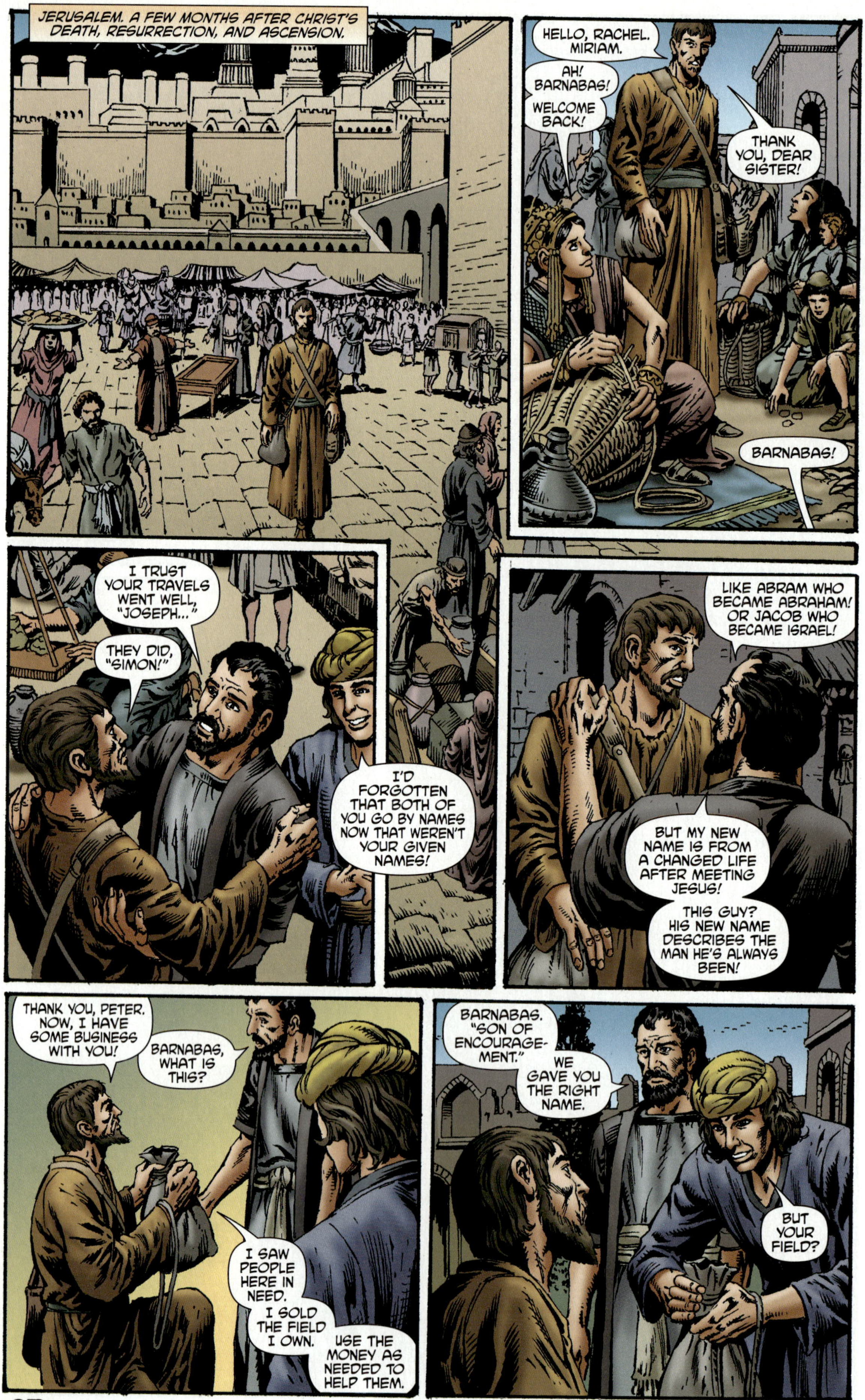
JERUSALEM. A FEW MONTHS AFTER CHRIST'S DEATH, RESURRECTION, AND ASCENSION.
HELLO, RACHEL. MIRIAM.
AH! BARNABAS!
WELCOME BACK!
THANK YOU, DEAR SISTER!
BARNABAS!
I TRUST YOUR TRAVELS WENT WELL, "JOSEPH..."
THEY DID, "SIMON!"
I'D FORGOTTEN THAT BOTH OF YOU GO BY NAMES NOW THAT WEREN'T YOUR GIVEN NAMES!
LIKE ABRAM WHO BECAME ABRAHAM! OR JACOB WHO BECAME ISRAEL!
BUT MY NEW NAME IS FROM A CHANGED LIFE AFTER MEETING JESUS!
THIS GUY? HIS NEW NAME DESCRIBES THE MAN HE'S ALWAYS BEEN!
THANK YOU, PETER. NOW, I HAVE SOME BUSINESS WITH YOU!
BARNABAS, WHAT IS THIS?
I SAW PEOPLE HERE IN NEED. I SOLD THE FIELD I OWN.
USE THE MONEY AS NEEDED TO HELP THEM.
BARNABAS. "SON OF ENCOURAGE-MENT."
WE GAVE YOU THE RIGHT NAME.
BUT YOUR FIELD?

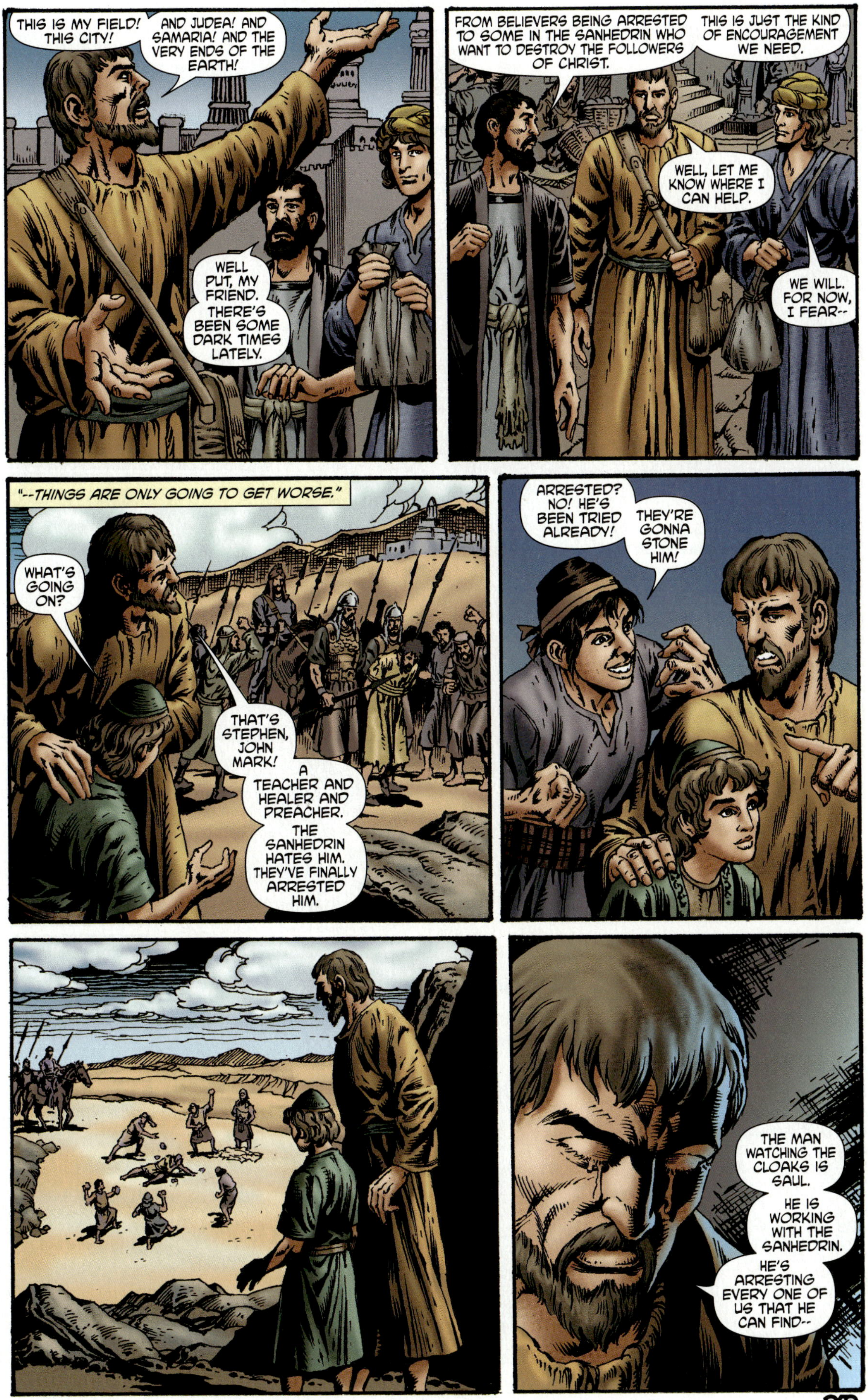
THIS IS MY FIELD! THIS CITY!
AND JUDEA! AND SAMARIA! AND THE VERY ENDS OF THE EARTH!
WELL PUT, MY FRIEND. THERE'S BEEN SOME DARK TIMES LATELY.
FROM BELIEVERS BEING ARRESTED TO SOME IN THE SANHEDRIN WHO WANT TO DESTROY THE FOLLOWERS OF CHRIST.
THIS IS JUST THE KIND OF ENCOURAGEMENT WE NEED.
WELL, LET ME KNOW WHERE I CAN HELP.
WE WILL. FOR NOW, I FEAR--
"--THINGS ARE ONLY GOING TO GET WORSE."
WHAT'S GOING ON?
THAT'S STEPHEN, JOHN MARK!
A TEACHER AND HEALER AND PREACHER.
THE SANHEDRIN HATES HIM. THEY'VE FINALLY ARRESTED HIM.
ARRESTED? NO! HE'S BEEN TRIED ALREADY!
THEY'RE GONNA STONE HIM!
THE MAN WATCHING THE CLOAKS IS SAUL.
HE IS WORKING WITH THE SANHEDRIN.
HE'S ARRESTING EVERY ONE OF US THAT HE CAN FIND--

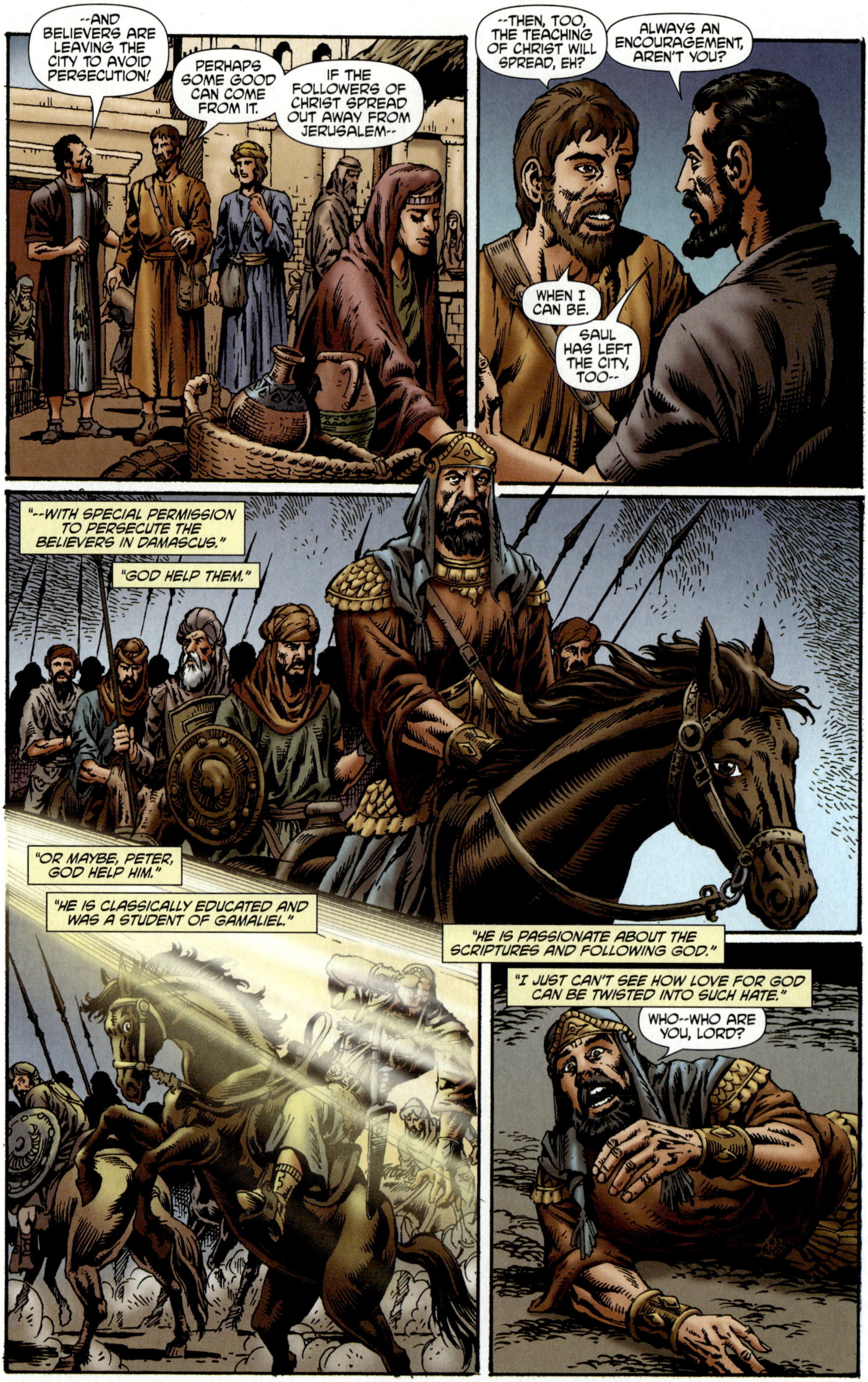
--AND BELIEVERS ARE LEAVING THE CITY TO AVOID PERSECUTION!
PERHAPS SOME GOOD CAN COME FROM IT.
IF THE FOLLOWERS OF CHRIST SPREAD OUT AWAY FROM JERUSALEM--
--THEN, TOO, THE TEACHING OF CHRIST WILL SPREAD, EH?
ALWAYS AN ENCOURAGEMENT, AREN'T YOU?
WHEN I CAN BE.
SAUL HAS LEFT THE CITY, TOO--
"--WITH SPECIAL PERMISSION TO PERSECUTE THE BELIEVERS IN DAMASCUS."
"GOD HELP THEM."
"OR MAYBE, PETER, GOD HELP HIM."
"HE IS CLASSICALLY EDUCATED AND WAS A STUDENT OF GAMALIEL."
"HE IS PASSIONATE ABOUT THE SCRIPTURES AND FOLLOWING GOD."
"I JUST CAN'T SEE HOW LOVE FOR GOD CAN BE TWISTED INTO SUCH HATE."
WHO--WHO ARE YOU, LORD?

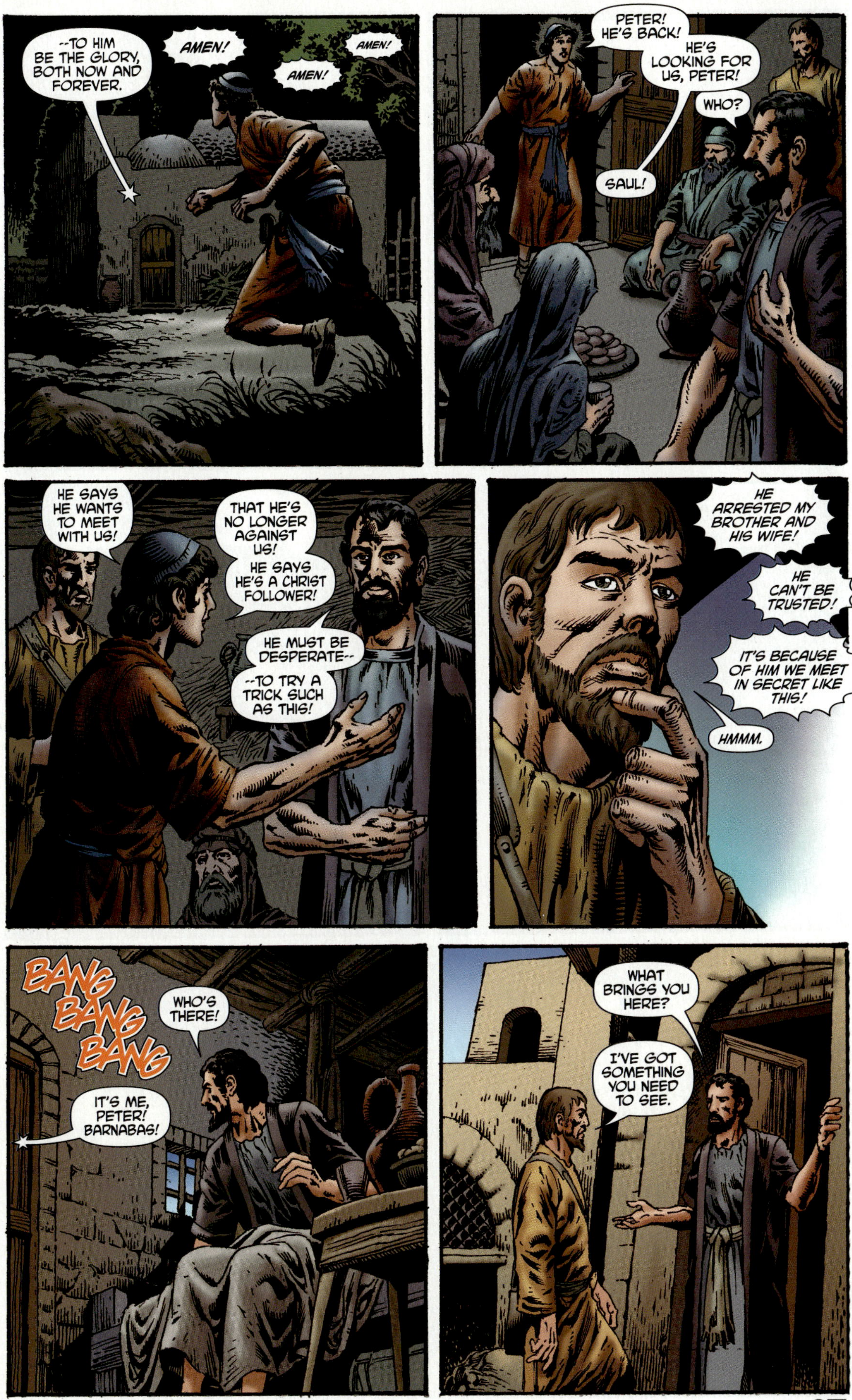
--TO HIM BE THE GLORY, BOTH NOW AND FOREVER.
AMEN!
AMEN!
AMEN!
PETER! HE'S BACK!
HE'S LOOKING FOR US, PETER!
WHO?
SAUL!
HE SAYS HE WANTS TO MEET WITH US!
THAT HE'S NO LONGER AGAINST US!
HE SAYS HE'S A CHRIST FOLLOWER!
HE MUST BE DESPERATE--
--TO TRY A TRICK SUCH AS THIS!
HE ARRESTED MY BROTHER AND HIS WIFE!
HE CAN'T BE TRUSTED!
IT'S BECAUSE OF HIM WE MEET IN SECRET LIKE THIS!
HMMM.
BANG BANG BANG
WHO'S THERE!
IT'S ME, PETER! BARNABAS!
WHAT BRINGS YOU HERE?
I'VE GOT SOMETHING YOU NEED TO SEE.

WHAT? BARNABAS!
HAVE YOU LOST YOUR MIND BRINGING HIM HERE!?!
I LISTENED TO HIM, PETER.
YOU SHOULD, TOO.
HE HAS SEEN JESUS.
OUR LORD SCOLDED HIM FOR PERSECUTING US.
HE WAS BLINDED AND WENT INTO DAMASCUS.
ANANIAS, ONE OF THE CHRISTIANS SAUL WOULD HAVE PERSECUTED, HAD A VISION--
--TELLING HIM TO COME TO ME! HE LAID HANDS ON ME AND HEALED ME!
AND SOON AFTER, SAUL WAS IN THE STREETS, NOT PERSECUTING CHRISTIANS--
--BUT PREACHING CHRIST!
YOU SHOULD'VE STAYED THERE!
I COULDN'T. THEY DIDN'T LIKE MY PREACHING.
THEY PLANNED TO KILL ME.
HAHAHA! THAT'S TOO PERFECT!
PETER!
I BELIEVE WE SHOULD LET HIM SPEAK TO THE APOSTLES.
ARE YOU JOKING?
PETER... OR "SIMON?"
YOU YOURSELF WERE CHANGED BY CHRIST!
IF WE BELIEVE CHRIST CAN FORGIVE SINS AND CHANGE PEOPLE'S LIVES--
--THEN WE MUST BELIEVE THAT APPLIES EVEN TO ONE SUCH AS HIM!
LET HIM COME BEFORE THE APOSTLES.
I DON'T KNOW...

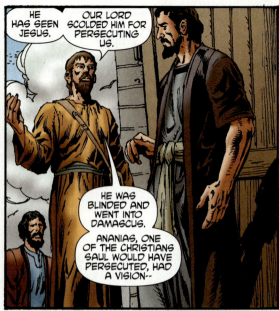

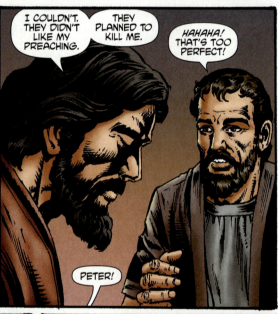

--AND I PREACHED WHAT I KNEW OF CHRIST IN DAMASCUS.

UNTIL THEY CHASED ME OUT.

THE THINGS YOU HAVE DONE TO US...HOW DO WE KNOW THIS ISN'T A TRICK?

YOU HAVE TORN FAMILIES APART AND IMPRISONED INNOCENT PEOPLE!

ENOUGH!

IF WE BELIEVE CHRIST CAN FORGIVE SINS AND CHANGE PEOPLE'S LIVES--

--THEN WE MUST BELIEVE THAT APPLIES EVEN TO ONE SUCH AS HIM!

THE APOSTLES LET SAUL PREACH...

...IN CHRIST, THERE IS NO JEW OR GREEK! WE ARE ALL ONE...

BUT SAUL'S FERVENT PREACHING MADE ENEMIES IN JERUSALEM.

HE WAS SENT TO SERVE IN TARSUS, WHERE HE HAD FAMILY.

SOME TIME LATER.

BARNABAS, THE APOSTLES HAVE A MISSION FOR YOU.

A MISSION?

YES. I'D PREFER YOU STAY HERE, BUT YOU ARE NEEDED--

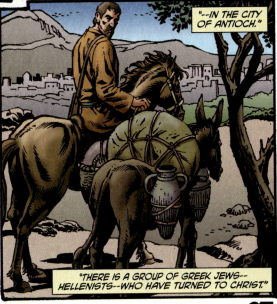

"--IN THE CITY OF ANTIOCH."

"THERE IS A GROUP OF GREEK JEWS-- HELLENISTS--WHO HAVE TURNED TO CHRIST."

347

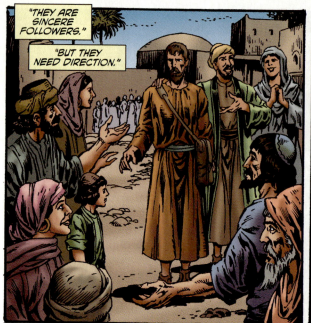

"THEY ARE SINCERE FOLLOWERS."

"BUT THEY NEED DIRECTION."

"YOU ARE FROM CYPRESS SO THEY SHOULD RELATE TO YOU."

"YOU ALSO HEARD CHRIST'S WORDS FROM HIS OWN MOUTH."

"AND YOU LIVE OUT CHRIST'S MESSAGE IN EVERYTHING YOU DO."

"YOU ARE THE PERFECT SHEPHERD FOR THIS SMALL COMMUNITY."

"WILL YOU GO AND HELP THEM?"

"YES, OF COURSE."

AFTER YEARS OF WORK IN ANTIOCH...

BARNABAS, THANK YOU SO MUCH FOR ALL YOU HAVE DONE!

WE KNOW IT IS A DIFFICULT LOAD TO BEAR.

WE THINK IT MIGHT BE WISE IF YOU HAD SOME HELP!

SOME HELP?

YOU MAY BE RIGHT.

AND I KNOW JUST THE PERSON!

SAUL!

BARNABAS! WHAT BRINGS YOU TO TARSUS?

I'VE COME FOR YOU, MY FRIEND!

WHAT HAVE YOU BEEN DOING HERE?

MY WORK. MAKING AND REPAIRING TENTS!

WELL--

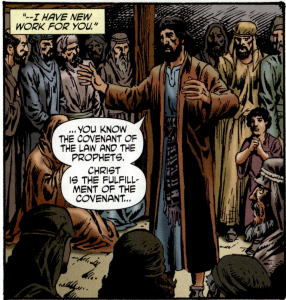

"--I HAVE NEW WORK FOR YOU."

...YOU KNOW THE COVENANT OF THE LAW AND THE PROPHETS.

CHRIST IS THE FULFILL-MENT OF THE COVENANT...

...I CAN UNDERSTAND YOU WOULD BE SKEPTICAL, AND I WAS TOO!

I KEPT ALL THE COMMANDMENTS, BUT IT MEANT NOTHING...

WHY DO YOU HELP US?

IF YOU REALLY WANT TO KNOW, IT IS BECAUSE OF OUR LORD, CHRIST.

HE GAVE EVERYTHING FOR US.

AH, YOU ARE ONE OF THOSE CHRISTIANS!

"CHRISTIAN?" LITTLE CHRIST? IS THAT WHAT THEY CALL US?

PERHAPS IT IS MEANT AS AN INSULT.

BUT I THINK THE NAME DESCRIBES US WELL.

I RATHER LIKE IT.

AFTER SERVING TOGETHER IN TARSUS FOR A WHILE...

THE LORD HAS SHOWN ME THAT A FAMINE IS COMING--

--THAT WILL STRIKE OUR BROTHERS AND SISTERS IN JERUSALEM ESPECIALLY HARD!

MANY THERE WILL HAVE GREAT AND DIRE NEED!

I THINK WE ALL AGREE ON WHAT WE MUST DO--

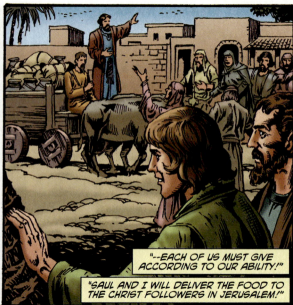

"--EACH OF US MUST GIVE ACCORDING TO OUR ABILITY!"

"SAUL AND I WILL DELIVER THE FOOD TO THE CHRIST FOLLOWERS IN JERUSALEM!"

THERE WAS A TIME WHEN, IF SAUL WAS COMING TO YOU, YOU WOULD HIDE!

BUT NOW, YOU COME BEARING FOOD IN OUR TIME OF GREATEST NEED!

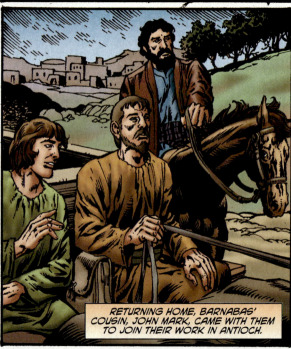

RETURNING HOME, BARNABAS' COUSIN, JOHN MARK, CAME WITH THEM TO JOIN THEIR WORK IN ANTIOCH.

BUT THAT WORK DID NOT LAST MUCH LONGER...

WE HAVE HEARD THE LORD SPEAK CLEARLY.

HIS HOLY SPIRIT HAS TOLD US TO SET THESE MEN APART FOR GOD'S WORK.

THE WORK HE HAS CALLED THEM TO.

AND SO, WE MOVE FARTHER AWAY FROM JERUSALEM WITH JESUS' MESSAGE.

I'D LIKE TO BE CALLED PAUL, A NAME FROM MY FAMILY'S GREEK BACKGROUND.

YES. WE'RE GOING TO BE AROUND GREEKS AND ROMANS AND HELLENIST JEWS MORE AND MORE.

I'VE BEEN THINKING ABOUT A NAME CHANGE.

CHANGING YOUR NAME TO REFLECT YOUR MISSION?

A GREAT THOUGHT!

THEY TRAVELED AROUND, PREACHING THE WORD OF GOD IN SYNAGOGUES--

...ADAM BROUGHT DEATH INTO THIS WORLD--

--AND CHRIST CAME TO BRING LIFE...

--AND TO MANY WHO WANTED TO HEAR MORE OF THE WAY OF CHRIST.

...AND THIS CHRIST DIED EVEN FOR ME?

EVEN FOR YOU, PROCONSUL SERGIUS PAULUS.

BAH! DO NOT LISTEN TO THEM!

MY SORCERY IS MORE POWERFUL THAN THIS JESUS!

YOU, SORCERER, ARE A CHILD OF THE DEVIL!

YOUR "POWERS" ARE TRICKS AND LIES!

THE HAND OF THE TRUE LORD IS AGAINST YOU!

YOU TRY TO BLIND OTHERS FROM THE TRUTH--

--SO NOW, FOR A TIME, YOU WILL BE BLINDED FROM ALL LIGHT!

WHAT... WHAT... HELP ME! PLEASE!

I'M SORRY, COUSIN, I CAN'T CONTINUE WITH YOU.

PEOPLE ARE HEARING THE MESSAGE AND CHANGING THEIR LIVES!

AND OTHER PEOPLE HEAR THE MESSAGE AND WANT TO TAKE OUR LIVES!

DON'T LET FEAR DRIVE YOU AWAY!

YOU ARE A GREAT HELP TO US!

EVERY-WHERE WE GO IT SEEMS WE MAKE ENEMIES! IT'S TOO DANGEROUS! I'M GOING HOME...

IT'S GOOD HE SHOWS US HIS TRUE CHARACTER NOW.

BECAUSE HE'S RIGHT.

EVERYWHERE WE GO PEOPLE ACCEPT THE MESSAGE--

"--AND OTHER PEOPLE HATE IT AND PLOT AGAINST US."

I HAVE HEARD YOU SPEAK OF THE CHRIST AND MY SOUL IS STIRRED.

I SEE YOU HAVE FAITH TO BE HEALED.

I DO.

WELL, THEN, STAND UP!

I... I... LOOK AT ME!

IT'S THE GODS!

THE GODS HAVE COME TO US DISGUISED AS HUMANS!

THE STRONG SILENT ONE MUST BE ZEUS! THE TALKATIVE ONE IS HERMES, HIS MESSENGER!

WHY DO YOU GET CALLED ZEUS?

THEY KNOW A LEADER WHEN THEY SEE ONE!

VERY FUNNY. WHAT NOW?

COME WITH US!

NO! WHY ARE YOU DOING THIS?

WE WISH TO OFFER THIS SACRIFICE TO YOU!

EVERYONE! STOP THIS! NOW!

WE ARE ONLY HUMAN, LIKE YOU, PROCLAIMING THE GOOD NEWS OF THE LIVING GOD!

GOD CALLS YOU TO TURN AWAY FROM THIS KIND OF WORTHLESS WORSHIP!

HE MADE EVERYTHING AND HAS GIVEN YOU EVERYTHING AND LOVES YOU!

SO THEY PRETEND TO BE GODS, THEN?

THEY MUST BE PUNISHED!

HE MUST BE SILENCED!

STONE HIM! STONE HIM!

NO...

"PAUL! PLEASE ANSWER ME--"

--CAN YOU SPEAK? THEY LEFT YOU FOR DEAD!

I'M... ALIVE... BUT I THINK IT'S TIME TO MOVE ON FROM HERE...

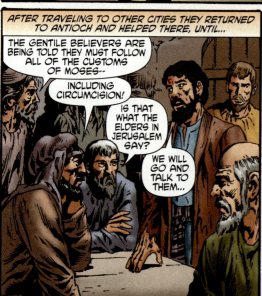

AFTER TRAVELING TO OTHER CITIES THEY RETURNED TO ANTIOCH AND HELPED THERE, UNTIL...

THE GENTILE BELIEVERS ARE BEING TOLD THEY MUST FOLLOW ALL OF THE CUSTOMS OF MOSES--

INCLUDING CIRCUMCISION!

IS THAT WHAT THE ELDERS IN JERUSALEM SAY?

WE WILL GO AND TALK TO THEM...

JERUSALEM.

--THE GENTILES ARE HEARING CHRIST'S MESSAGE AND FOLLOWING IT!

BUT CHRIST'S MESSAGE DID NOT REQUIRE CIRCUMCISION!

DON'T PUT A WALL IN THEIR WAY THAT OUR LORD DID NOT INTEND!

BUT ARE WE JUST ABANDONING THE LAW OF MOSES, THEN?

THAT'S NOT WHAT PAUL IS SAYING.

GOD HAS GIVEN HIS HOLY SPIRIT TO THE GENTILES.

NOT BECAUSE OF CIRCUMCISION, BUT BECAUSE OF FAITH!

I AGREE! WE SHOULD NOT MAKE IT DIFFICULT!

WE SHOULD WRITE A LETTER WITH GUIDELINES TO THE GENTILES...

THIS IS GOING TO TAKE A WHILE.

THAT'S GOOD. IT MEANS THEY ARE TRULY THINKING ABOUT IT.

AFTER MUCH DISCUSSION AND DEBATE.

TAKE THIS TO THE PEOPLE IN ANTIOCH.

IT CONFIRMS WE WILL NOT REQUIRE CIRCUMCISION OF GENTILES.

AND IT ASKS GENTILES TO FOLLOW MORAL GUIDELINES.

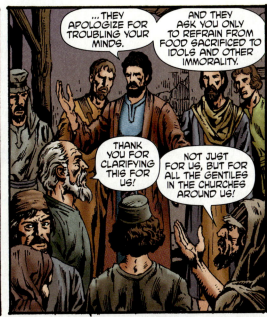

...THEY APOLOGIZE FOR TROUBLING YOUR MINDS.

AND THEY ASK YOU ONLY TO REFRAIN FROM FOOD SACRIFICED TO IDOLS AND OTHER IMMORALITY.

THANK YOU FOR CLARIFYING THIS FOR US!

NOT JUST FOR US, BUT FOR ALL THE GENTILES IN THE CHURCHES AROUND US!

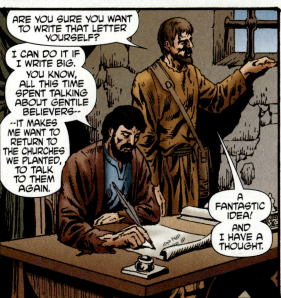

ARE YOU SURE YOU WANT TO WRITE THAT LETTER YOURSELF?

I CAN DO IT IF I WRITE BIG.

YOU KNOW, ALL THIS TIME SPENT TALKING ABOUT GENTILE BELIEVERS--

--IT MAKES ME WANT TO RETURN TO THE CHURCHES WE PLANTED, TO TALK TO THEM AGAIN.

A FANTASTIC IDEA!

AND I HAVE A THOUGHT.

I WOULD LIKE TO HAVE JOHN MARK JOIN US AGAIN.

WHAT? NO!

HE'S A DIFFERENT MAN NOW!

WE SHOULD GIVE HIM A SECOND CHANCE!

HE DESERTED US ONCE! WHAT IF HE DOES IT AGAIN? THOSE JOURNEYS ARE TOO DANGEROUS AND IMPORTANT TO RISK THAT!

PAUL...YOU OF ALL PEOPLE UNDERSTAND WHAT IT MEANS TO CHANGE!

TO BECOME SOMEONE NEW!

TO RECEIVE A SECOND CHANCE!

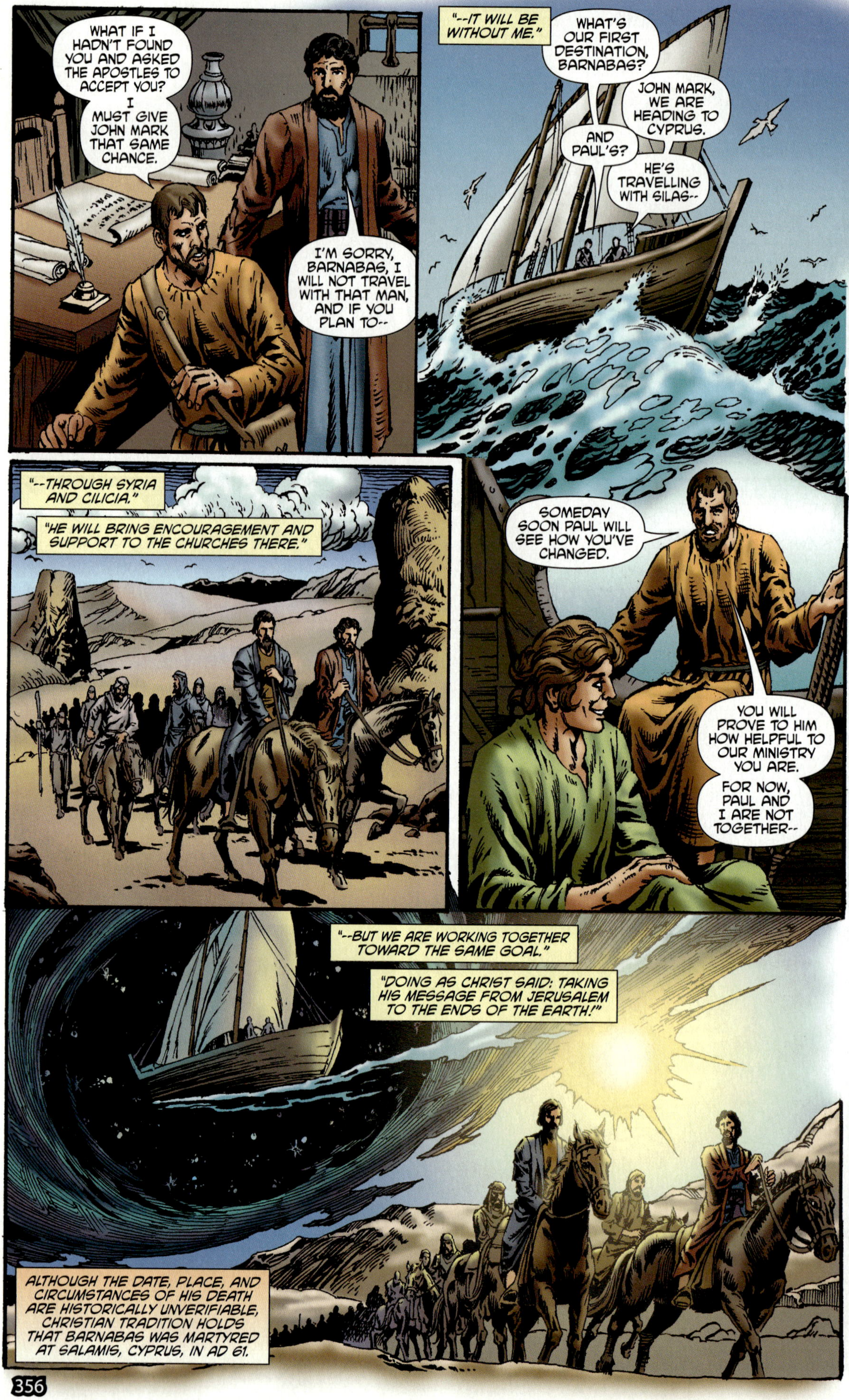

WHAT IF I HADN'T FOUND YOU AND ASKED THE APOSTLES TO ACCEPT YOU?
I MUST GIVE JOHN MARK THAT SAME CHANCE.
I'M SORRY, BARNABAS, I WILL NOT TRAVEL WITH THAT MAN, AND IF YOU PLAN TO--
"--IT WILL BE WITHOUT ME."
WHAT'S OUR FIRST DESTINATION, BARNABAS?
JOHN MARK, WE ARE HEADING TO CYPRUS.
AND PAUL'S?
HE'S TRAVELLING WITH SILAS--
"--THROUGH SYRIA AND CILICIA."
"HE WILL BRING ENCOURAGEMENT AND SUPPORT TO THE CHURCHES THERE."
SOMEDAY SOON PAUL WILL SEE HOW YOU'VE CHANGED.
YOU WILL PROVE TO HIM HOW HELPFUL TO OUR MINISTRY YOU ARE.
FOR NOW, PAUL AND I ARE NOT TOGETHER--
"--BUT WE ARE WORKING TOGETHER TOWARD THE SAME GOAL."
"DOING AS CHRIST SAID: TAKING HIS MESSAGE FROM JERUSALEM TO THE ENDS OF THE EARTH!"
ALTHOUGH THE DATE, PLACE, AND CIRCUMSTANCES OF HIS DEATH ARE HISTORICALLY UNVERIFIABLE, CHRISTIAN TRADITION HOLDS THAT BARNABAS WAS MARTYRED AT SALAMIS, CYPRUS, IN AD 61.

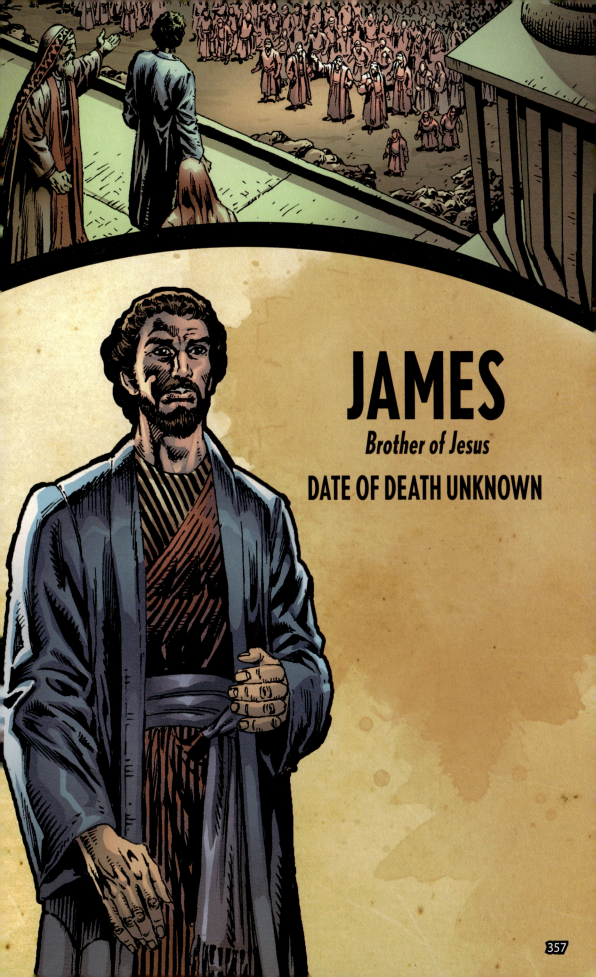

JAMES
Brother of Jesus

DATE OF DEATH UNKNOWN

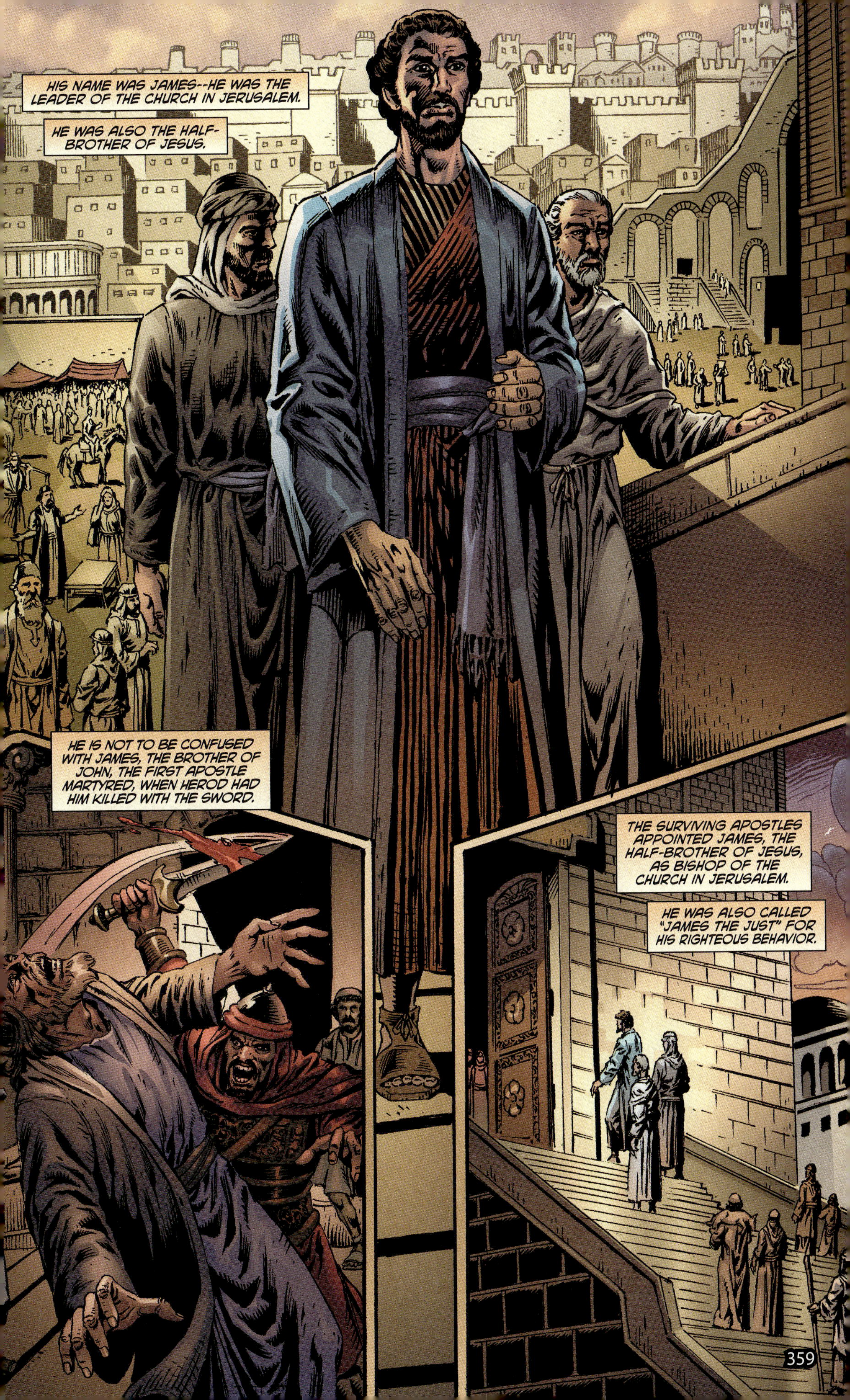
HIS NAME WAS JAMES--HE WAS THE LEADER OF THE CHURCH IN JERUSALEM.
HE WAS ALSO THE HALF-BROTHER OF JESUS.
HE IS NOT TO BE CONFUSED WITH JAMES, THE BROTHER OF JOHN, THE FIRST APOSTLE MARTYRED, WHEN HEROD HAD HIM KILLED WITH THE SWORD.
THE SURVIVING APOSTLES APPOINTED JAMES, THE HALF-BROTHER OF JESUS, AS BISHOP OF THE CHURCH IN JERUSALEM.
HE WAS ALSO CALLED "JAMES THE JUST" FOR HIS RIGHTEOUS BEHAVIOR.

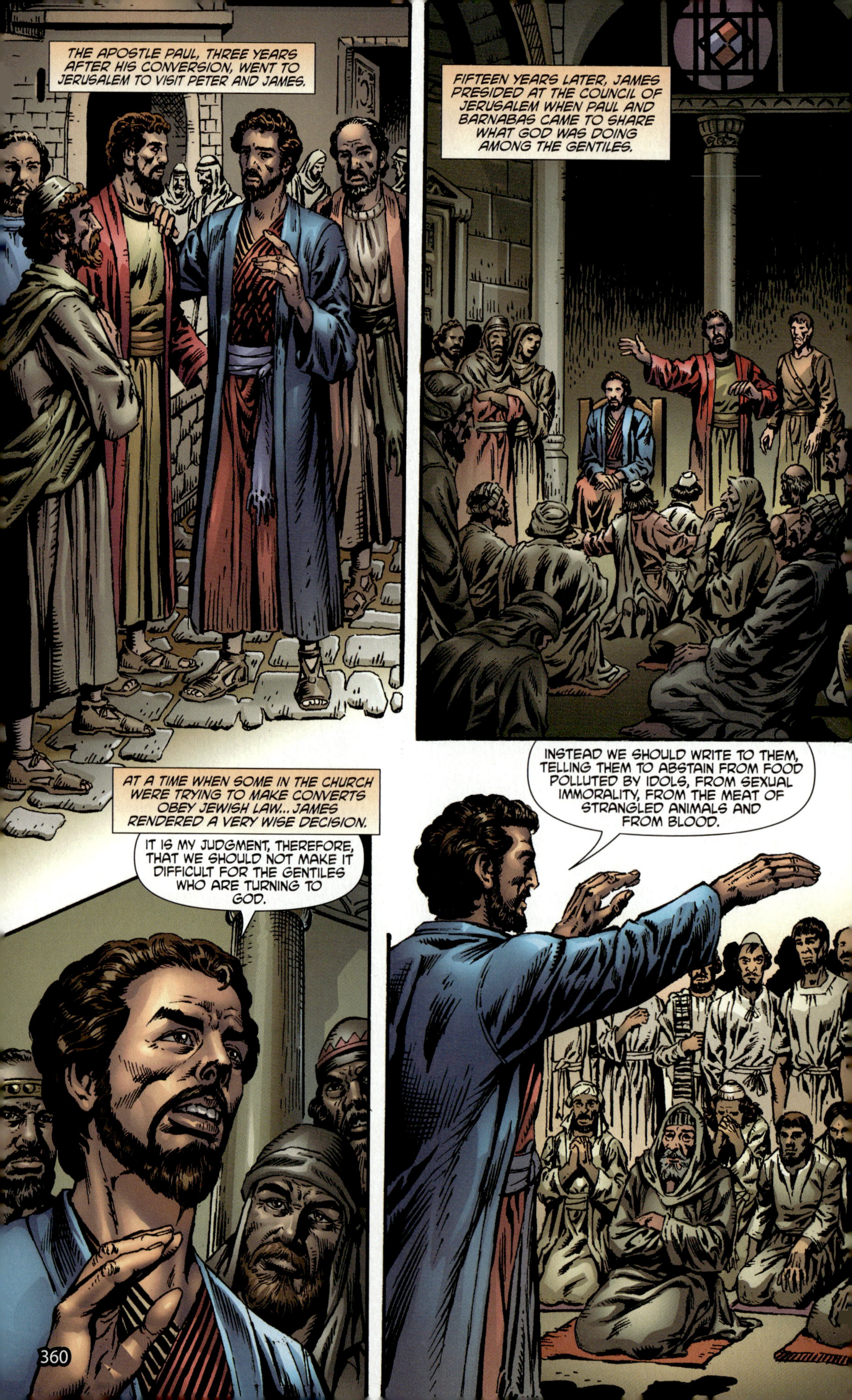
THE APOSTLE PAUL, THREE YEARS AFTER HIS CONVERSION, WENT TO JERUSALEM TO VISIT PETER AND JAMES.
FIFTEEN YEARS LATER, JAMES PRESIDED AT THE COUNCIL OF JERUSALEM WHEN PAUL AND BARNABAS CAME TO SHARE WHAT GOD WAS DOING AMONG THE GENTILES.
AT A TIME WHEN SOME IN THE CHURCH WERE TRYING TO MAKE CONVERTS OBEY JEWISH LAW... JAMES RENDERED A VERY WISE DECISION.
IT IS MY JUDGMENT, THEREFORE, THAT WE SHOULD NOT MAKE IT DIFFICULT FOR THE GENTILES WHO ARE TURNING TO GOD.
INSTEAD WE SHOULD WRITE TO THEM, TELLING THEM TO ABSTAIN FROM FOOD POLLUTED BY IDOLS, FROM SEXUAL IMMORALITY, FROM THE MEAT OF STRANGLED ANIMALS AND FROM BLOOD.

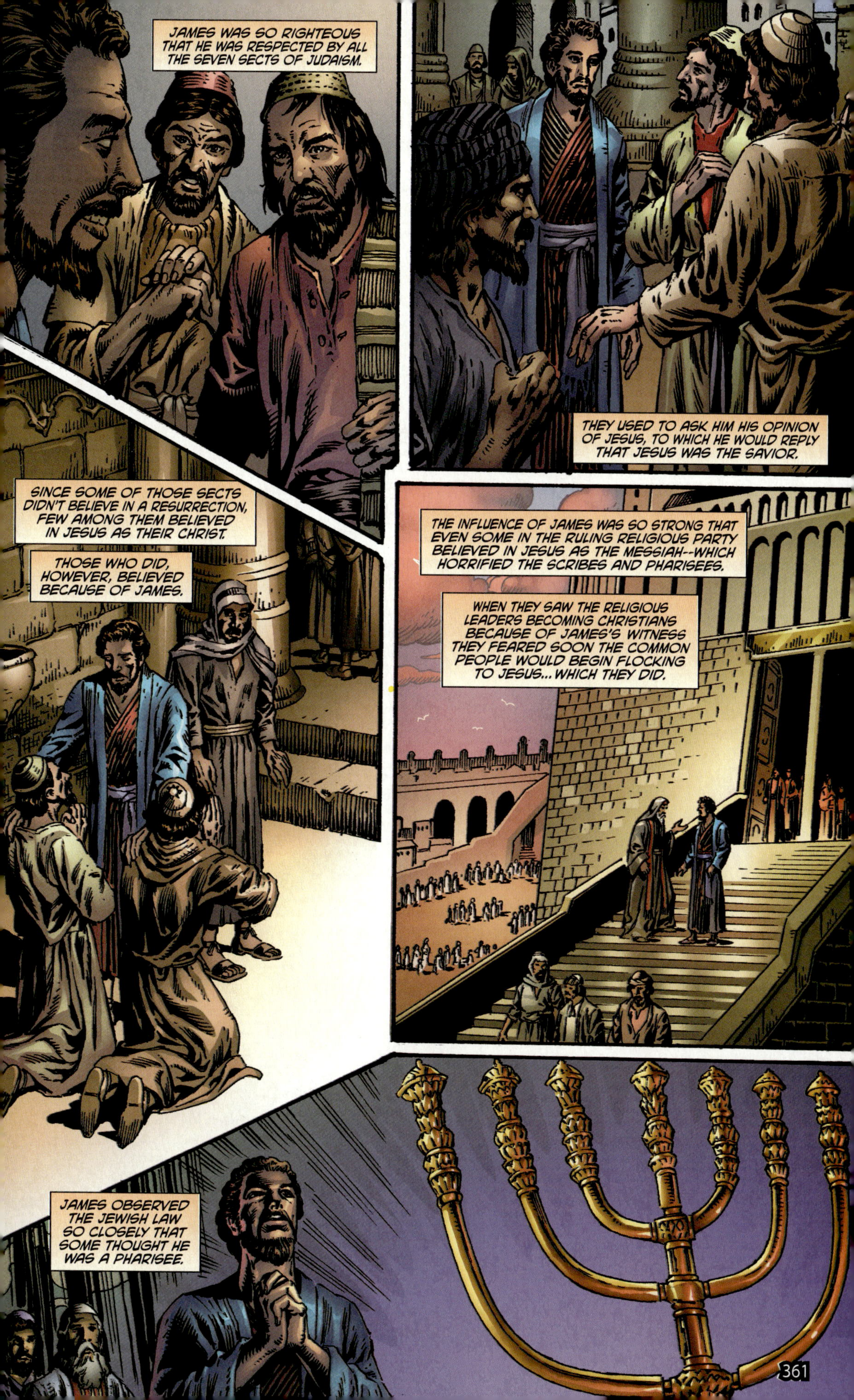
JAMES WAS SO RIGHTEOUS THAT HE WAS RESPECTED BY ALL THE SEVEN SECTS OF JUDAISM.
THEY USED TO ASK HIM HIS OPINION OF JESUS, TO WHICH HE WOULD REPLY THAT JESUS WAS THE SAVIOR.
SINCE SOME OF THOSE SECTS DIDN'T BELIEVE IN A RESURRECTION, FEW AMONG THEM BELIEVED IN JESUS AS THEIR CHRIST.
THOSE WHO DID, HOWEVER, BELIEVED BECAUSE OF JAMES.
THE INFLUENCE OF JAMES WAS SO STRONG THAT EVEN SOME IN THE RULING RELIGIOUS PARTY BELIEVED IN JESUS AS THE MESSIAH--WHICH HORRIFIED THE SCRIBES AND PHARISEES.
WHEN THEY SAW THE RELIGIOUS LEADERS BECOMING CHRISTIANS BECAUSE OF JAMES'S WITNESS THEY FEARED SOON THE COMMON PEOPLE WOULD BEGIN FLOCKING TO JESUS... WHICH THEY DID.
JAMES OBSERVED THE JEWISH LAW SO CLOSELY THAT SOME THOUGHT HE WAS A PHARISEE.

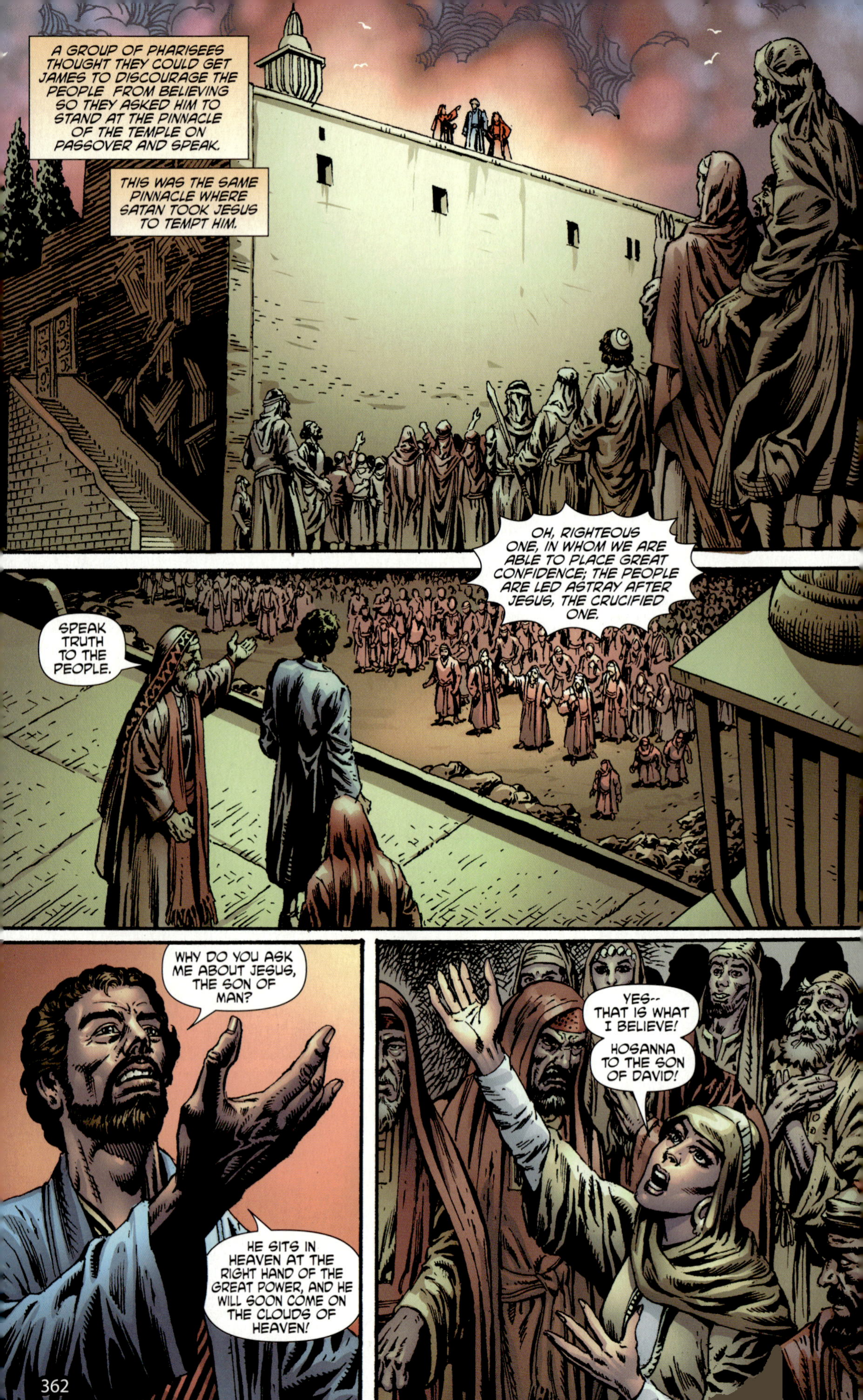
A GROUP OF PHARISEES THOUGHT THEY COULD GET JAMES TO DISCOURAGE THE PEOPLE FROM BELIEVING SO THEY ASKED HIM TO STAND AT THE PINNACLE OF THE TEMPLE ON PASSOVER AND SPEAK.
THIS WAS THE SAME PINNACLE WHERE SATAN TOOK JESUS TO TEMPT HIM.
OH, RIGHTEOUS ONE, IN WHOM WE ARE ABLE TO PLACE GREAT CONFIDENCE; THE PEOPLE ARE LED ASTRAY AFTER JESUS, THE CRUCIFIED ONE.
SPEAK TRUTH TO THE PEOPLE.
WHY DO YOU ASK ME ABOUT JESUS, THE SON OF MAN?
HE SITS IN HEAVEN AT THE RIGHT HAND OF THE GREAT POWER, AND HE WILL SOON COME ON THE CLOUDS OF HEAVEN!
YES-- THAT IS WHAT I BELIEVE!
HOSANNA TO THE SON OF DAVID!

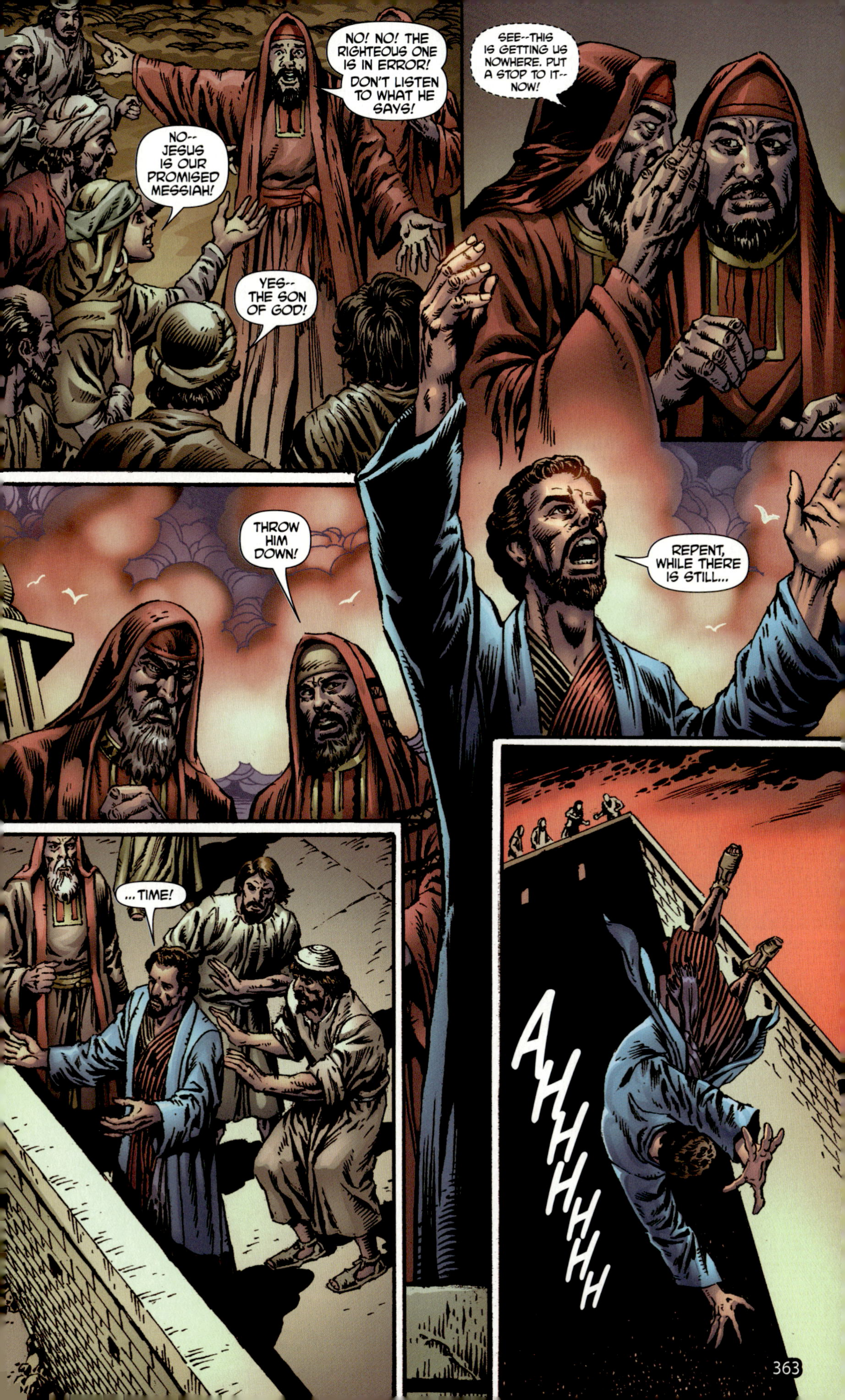
NO! NO! THE RIGHTEOUS ONE IS IN ERROR! DON'T LISTEN TO WHAT HE SAYS!
NO-- JESUS IS OUR PROMISED MESSIAH!
YES-- THE SON OF GOD!
SEE--THIS IS GETTING US NOWHERE. PUT A STOP TO IT-- NOW!
THROW HIM DOWN!
REPENT, WHILE THERE IS STILL...
...TIME!
AHHHHHH

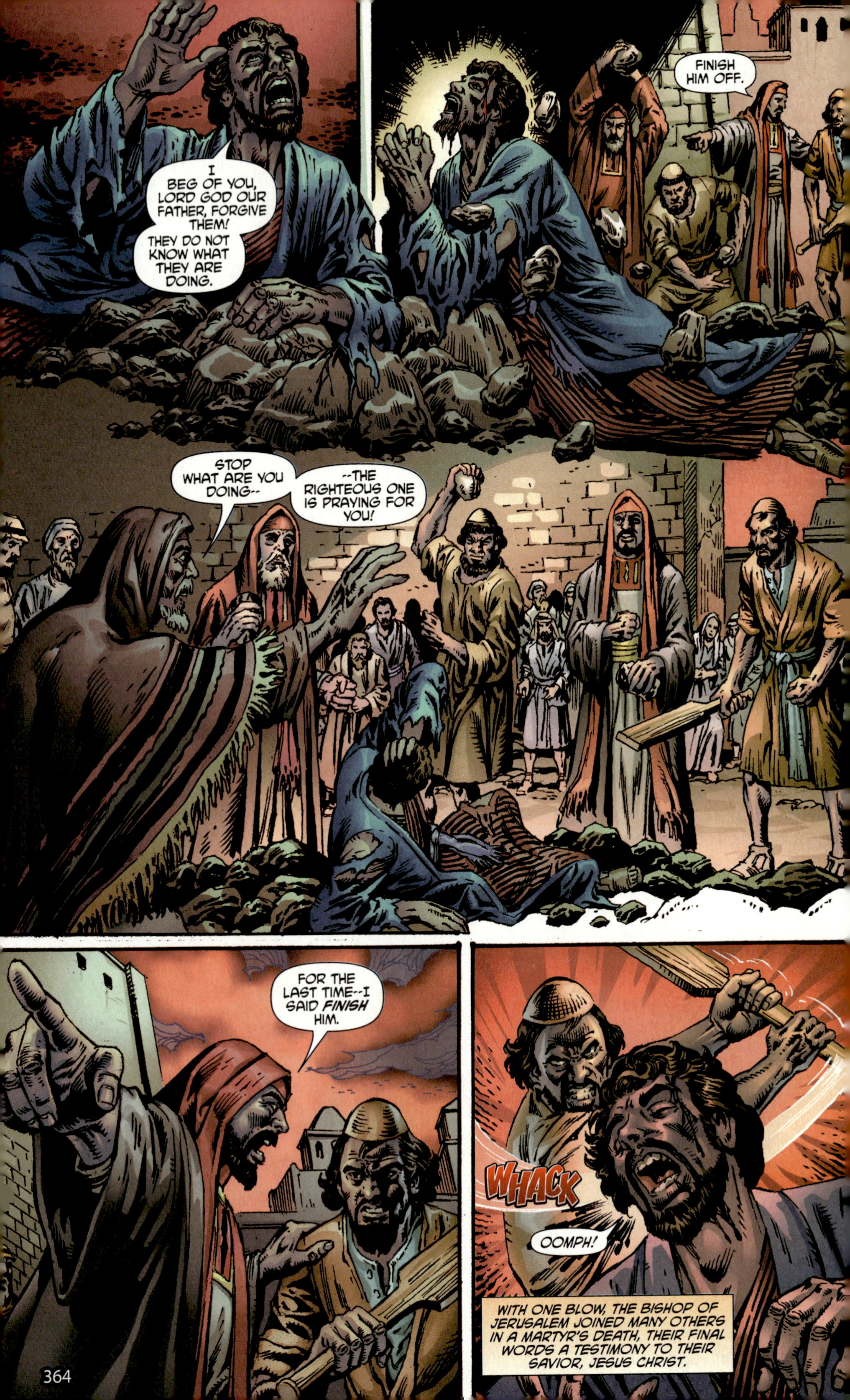
I BEG OF YOU, LORD GOD OUR FATHER, FORGIVE THEM!
THEY DO NOT KNOW WHAT THEY ARE DOING.
FINISH HIM OFF.
STOP WHAT ARE YOU DOING--
--THE RIGHTEOUS ONE IS PRAYING FOR YOU!
FOR THE LAST TIME--I SAID *FINISH* HIM.
WHACK
OOMPH!
WITH ONE BLOW, THE BISHOP OF JERUSALEM JOINED MANY OTHERS IN A MARTYR'S DEATH, THEIR FINAL WORDS A TESTIMONY TO THEIR SAVIOR, JESUS CHRIST.

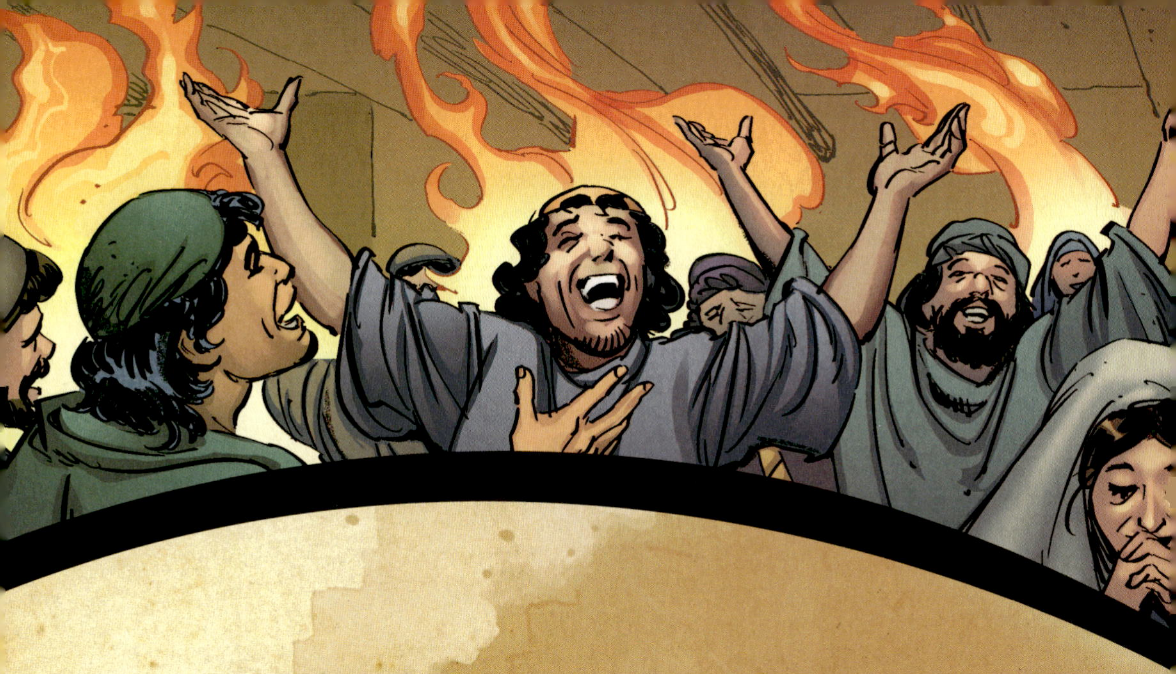

JUDE

Brother of Jesus

DATE OF DEATH UNKNOWN

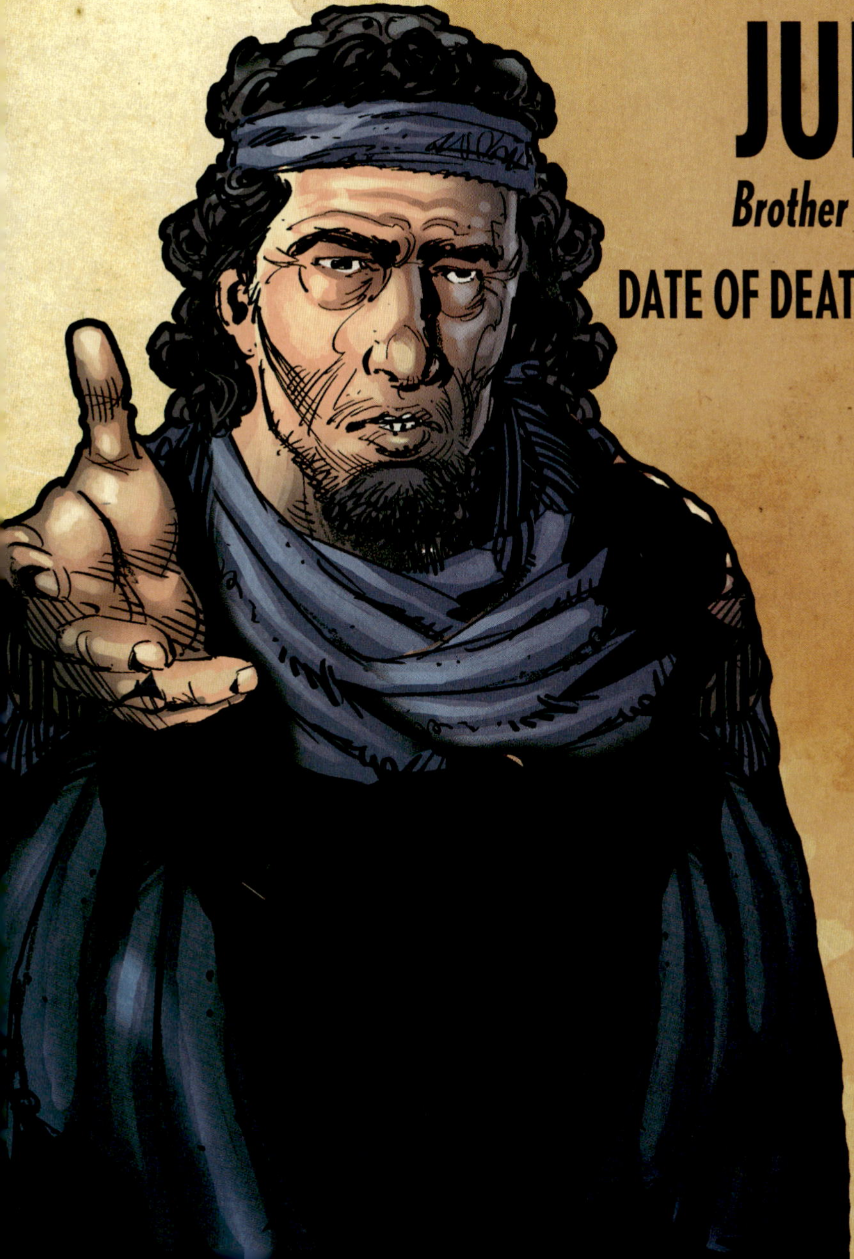

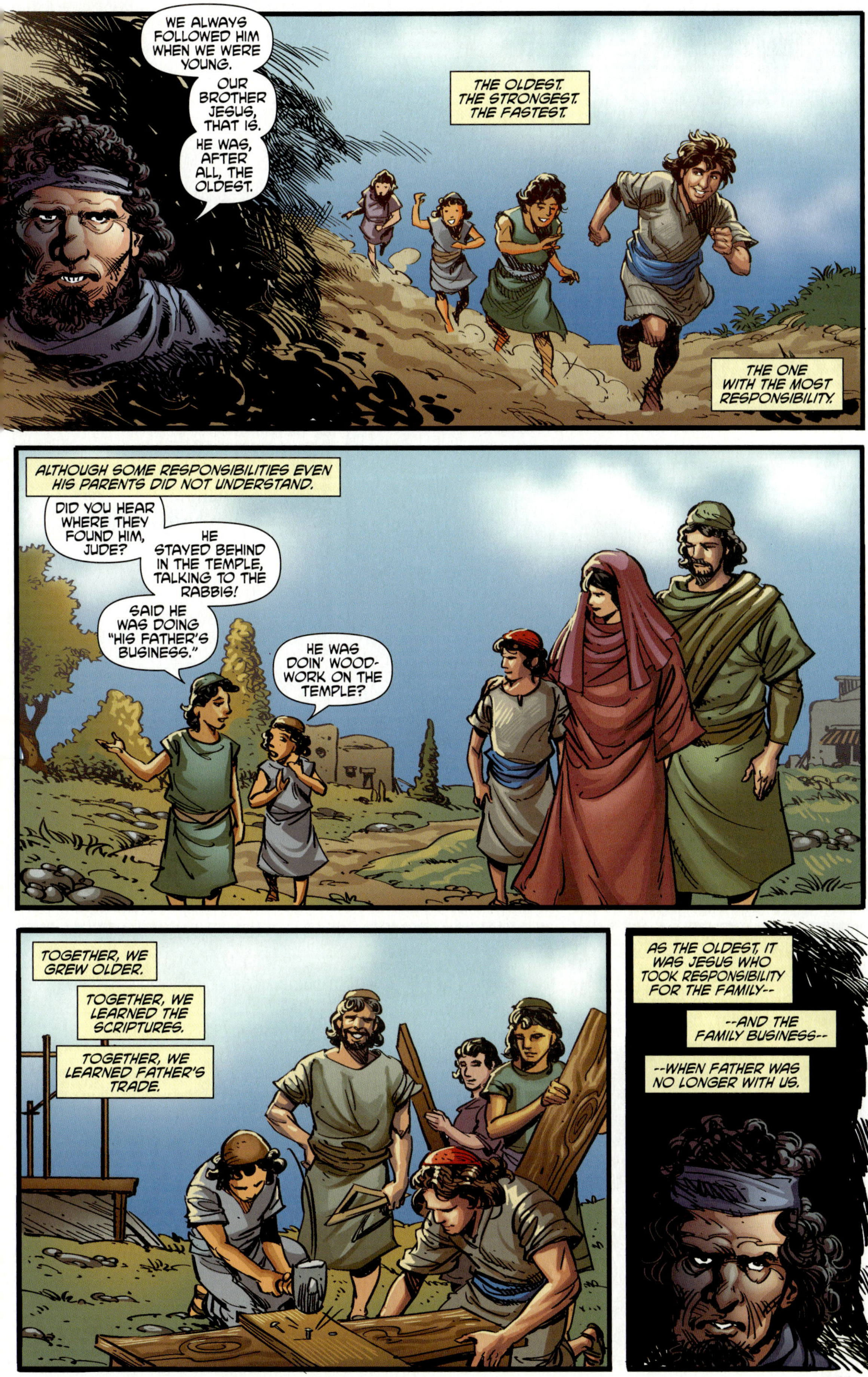
WE ALWAYS FOLLOWED HIM WHEN WE WERE YOUNG.
OUR BROTHER JESUS, THAT IS.
HE WAS, AFTER ALL, THE OLDEST.
THE OLDEST. THE STRONGEST. THE FASTEST.
THE ONE WITH THE MOST RESPONSIBILITY.
ALTHOUGH SOME RESPONSIBILITIES EVEN HIS PARENTS DID NOT UNDERSTAND.
DID YOU HEAR WHERE THEY FOUND HIM, JUDE?
HE STAYED BEHIND IN THE TEMPLE, TALKING TO THE RABBIS!
SAID HE WAS DOING "HIS FATHER'S BUSINESS."
HE WAS DOIN' WOOD-WORK ON THE TEMPLE?
TOGETHER, WE GREW OLDER.
TOGETHER, WE LEARNED THE SCRIPTURES.
TOGETHER, WE LEARNED FATHER'S TRADE.
AS THE OLDEST, IT WAS JESUS WHO TOOK RESPONSIBILITY FOR THE FAMILY--
--AND THE FAMILY BUSINESS--
--WHEN FATHER WAS NO LONGER WITH US.

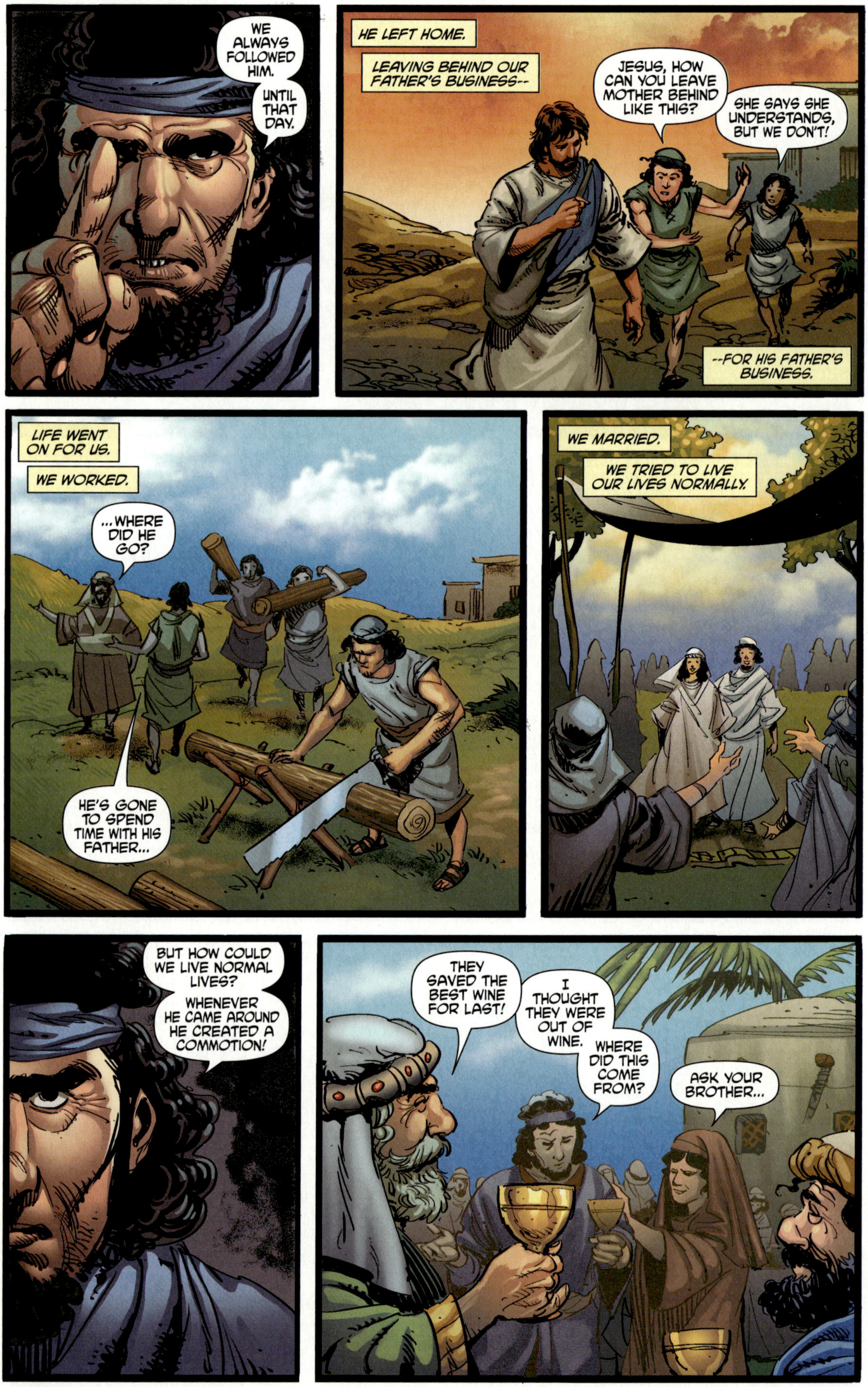

WE ALWAYS FOLLOWED HIM.
UNTIL THAT DAY.
HE LEFT HOME.
LEAVING BEHIND OUR FATHER'S BUSINESS--
JESUS, HOW CAN YOU LEAVE MOTHER BEHIND LIKE THIS?
SHE SAYS SHE UNDERSTANDS, BUT WE DON'T!
--FOR HIS FATHER'S BUSINESS.
LIFE WENT ON FOR US.
WE WORKED.
...WHERE DID HE GO?
HE'S GONE TO SPEND TIME WITH HIS FATHER...
WE MARRIED.
WE TRIED TO LIVE OUR LIVES NORMALLY.
BUT HOW COULD WE LIVE NORMAL LIVES?
WHENEVER HE CAME AROUND HE CREATED A COMMOTION!
THEY SAVED THE BEST WINE FOR LAST!
I THOUGHT THEY WERE OUT OF WINE.
WHERE DID THIS COME FROM?
ASK YOUR BROTHER...

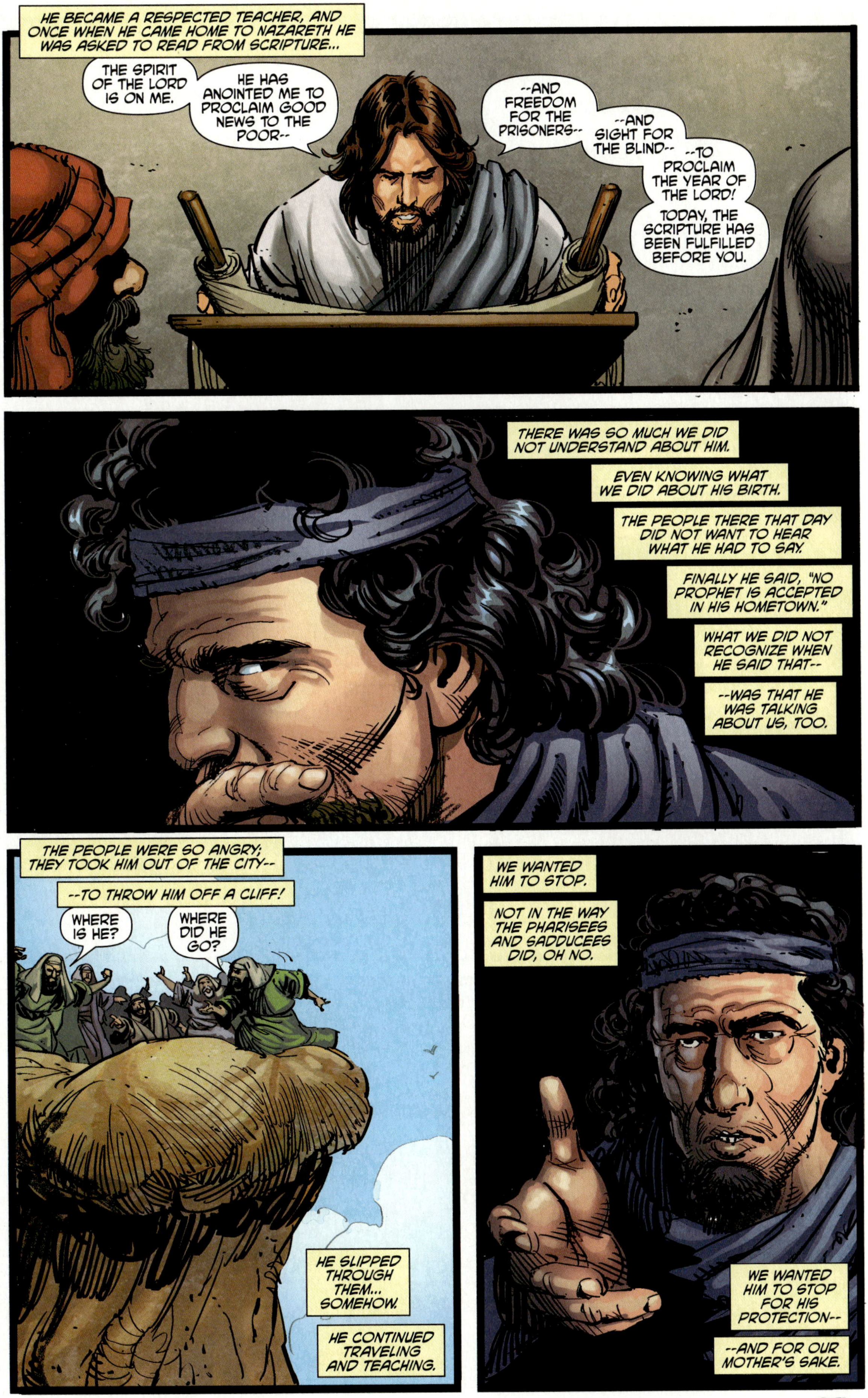

HE BECAME A RESPECTED TEACHER, AND ONCE WHEN HE CAME HOME TO NAZARETH HE WAS ASKED TO READ FROM SCRIPTURE...
THE SPIRIT OF THE LORD IS ON ME.
HE HAS ANOINTED ME TO PROCLAIM GOOD NEWS TO THE POOR--
--AND FREEDOM FOR THE PRISONERS--
--AND SIGHT FOR THE BLIND--
--TO PROCLAIM THE YEAR OF THE LORD!
TODAY, THE SCRIPTURE HAS BEEN FULFILLED BEFORE YOU.
THERE WAS SO MUCH WE DID NOT UNDERSTAND ABOUT HIM.
EVEN KNOWING WHAT WE DID ABOUT HIS BIRTH.
THE PEOPLE THERE THAT DAY DID NOT WANT TO HEAR WHAT HE HAD TO SAY.
FINALLY HE SAID, "NO PROPHET IS ACCEPTED IN HIS HOMETOWN."
WHAT WE DID NOT RECOGNIZE WHEN HE SAID THAT--
--WAS THAT HE WAS TALKING ABOUT US, TOO.
THE PEOPLE WERE SO ANGRY; THEY TOOK HIM OUT OF THE CITY--
--TO THROW HIM OFF A CLIFF!
WHERE IS HE?
WHERE DID HE GO?
HE SLIPPED THROUGH THEM... SOMEHOW.
HE CONTINUED TRAVELING AND TEACHING.
WE WANTED HIM TO STOP.
NOT IN THE WAY THE PHARISEES AND SADDUCEES DID, OH NO.
WE WANTED HIM TO STOP FOR HIS PROTECTION--
--AND FOR OUR MOTHER'S SAKE.

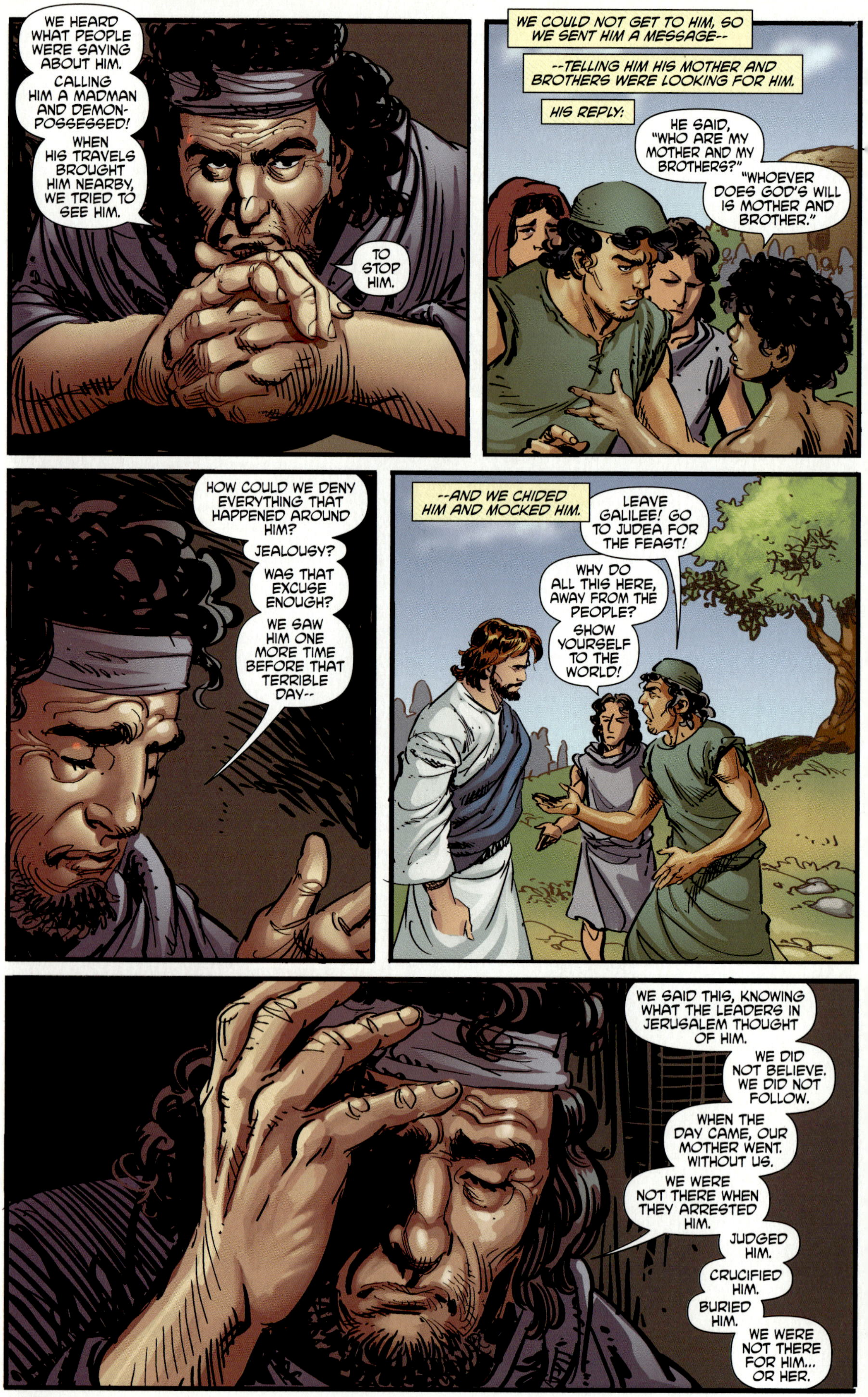
WE HEARD WHAT PEOPLE WERE SAYING ABOUT HIM.
CALLING HIM A MADMAN AND DEMON-POSSESSED!
WHEN HIS TRAVELS BROUGHT HIM NEARBY, WE TRIED TO SEE HIM.
TO STOP HIM.
WE COULD NOT GET TO HIM, SO WE SENT HIM A MESSAGE--
--TELLING HIM HIS MOTHER AND BROTHERS WERE LOOKING FOR HIM.
HIS REPLY:
HE SAID, "WHO ARE MY MOTHER AND MY BROTHERS?"
"WHOEVER DOES GOD'S WILL IS MOTHER AND BROTHER."
HOW COULD WE DENY EVERYTHING THAT HAPPENED AROUND HIM?
JEALOUSY?
WAS THAT EXCUSE ENOUGH?
WE SAW HIM ONE MORE TIME BEFORE THAT TERRIBLE DAY--
--AND WE CHIDED HIM AND MOCKED HIM.
LEAVE GALILEE! GO TO JUDEA FOR THE FEAST!
WHY DO ALL THIS HERE, AWAY FROM THE PEOPLE?
SHOW YOURSELF TO THE WORLD!
WE SAID THIS, KNOWING WHAT THE LEADERS IN JERUSALEM THOUGHT OF HIM.
WE DID NOT BELIEVE. WE DID NOT FOLLOW.
WHEN THE DAY CAME, OUR MOTHER WENT. WITHOUT US.
WE WERE NOT THERE WHEN THEY ARRESTED HIM.
JUDGED HIM.
CRUCIFIED HIM.
BURIED HIM.
WE WERE NOT THERE FOR HIM... OR HER.

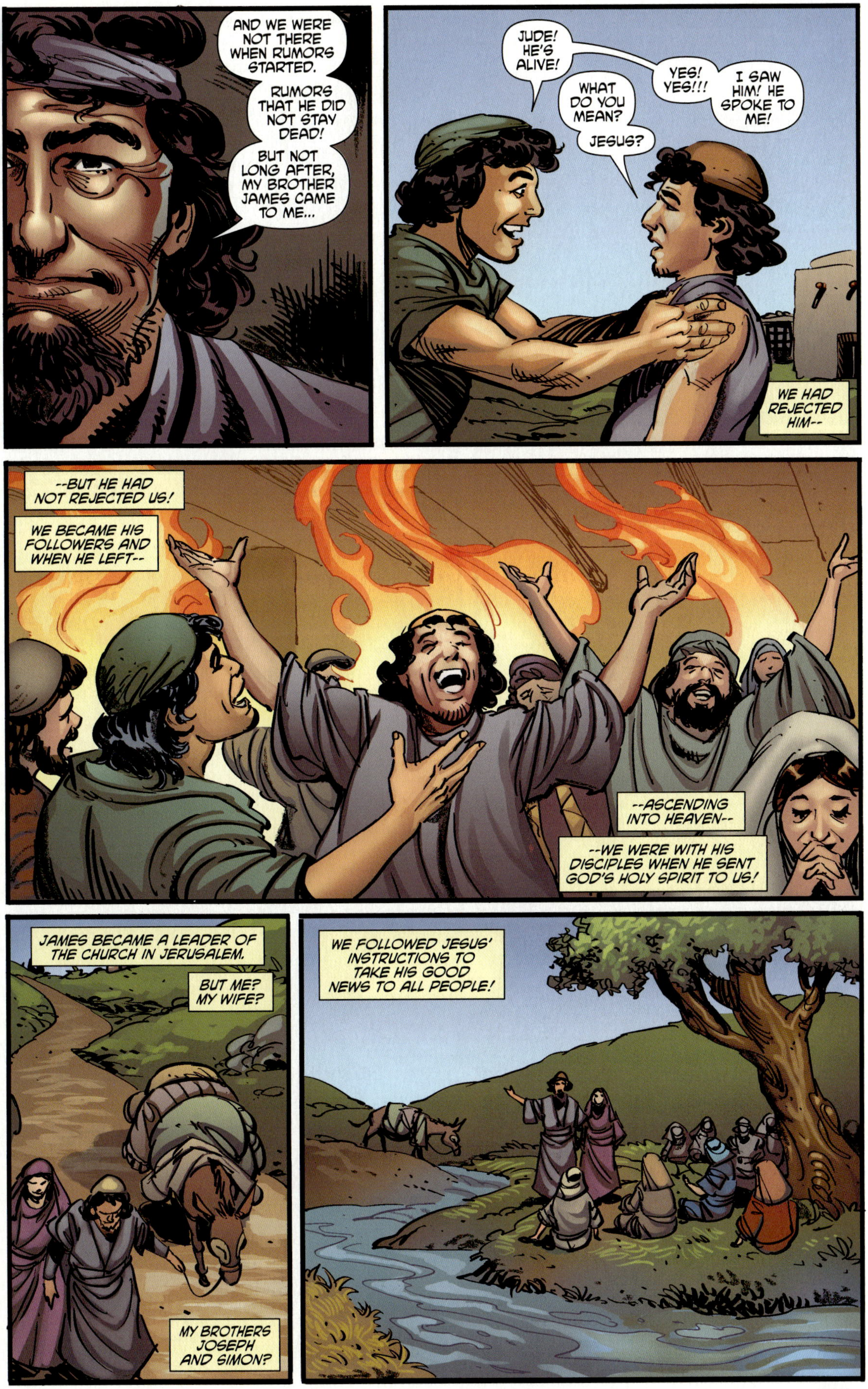
AND WE WERE NOT THERE WHEN RUMORS STARTED.
RUMORS THAT HE DID NOT STAY DEAD!
BUT NOT LONG AFTER, MY BROTHER JAMES CAME TO ME...
JUDE! HE'S ALIVE!
WHAT DO YOU MEAN?
JESUS?
YES! YES!!!
I SAW HIM! HE SPOKE TO ME!
WE HAD REJECTED HIM--
--BUT HE HAD NOT REJECTED US!
WE BECAME HIS FOLLOWERS AND WHEN HE LEFT--
--ASCENDING INTO HEAVEN--
--WE WERE WITH HIS DISCIPLES WHEN HE SENT GOD'S HOLY SPIRIT TO US!
JAMES BECAME A LEADER OF THE CHURCH IN JERUSALEM.
BUT ME? MY WIFE?
MY BROTHERS JOSEPH AND SIMON?
WE FOLLOWED JESUS' INSTRUCTIONS TO TAKE HIS GOOD NEWS TO ALL PEOPLE!

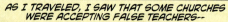

AS I TRAVELED, I SAW THAT SOME CHURCHES WERE ACCEPTING FALSE TEACHERS--

--AND FALSE TEACHINGS.

...YOU CANNOT LISTEN TO PEOPLE DEVOID OF THE SPIRIT!

THEY CAUSE DIVISIONS AMONG US!

THEY ARE LIKE WATERLESS CLOUDS BLOWN BY THE WIND...

I WROTE A LETTER OF MY OWN, WARNING THE CHURCHES AGAINST THIS.

...BUT YOU, BELOVED, BUILD YOURSELF UP ON YOUR HOLY FAITH--

--AND PRAY IN THE HOLY SPIRIT...

AND ENCOURAGING THEM TO REMEMBER THE APOSTLES' TEACHINGS.

"NOW TO HIM WHO IS ABLE TO KEEP YOU FROM FALLING..."

"...TO THE ONLY GOD OUR SAVIOR, THROUGH JESUS CHRIST OUR LORD..."

"...BE ALL GLORY, MAJESTY, AND AUTHORITY FOREVER AND EVER, AMEN."

MANY OF US WERE PUT TO DEATH IN THOSE DAYS.

STEPHEN. PHILIP, PETER. AND EVEN...

...THERE WAS A TRIAL.

THE RESULT WAS NEVER IN QUESTION.

THEY... THEY...

THEY EXECUTED JAMES...

MY BROTHER. KILLED, AS THEY KILLED OUR LORD.

KILLED FOR FOLLOWING OUR LORD.

FOR YOU SEE, WE HAD FINALLY ACCEPTED HIM.

FINALLY FOLLOWED HIM.

NOT AS BROTHERS, BUT, AS JAMES PUT IT IN HIS LETTER:

"SERVANTS OF OUR LORD JESUS CHRIST!"

THIS STORY WAS BASED ON HINTS AND SUGGESTIONS FOUND IN THE BIBLE (AND OTHER DOCUMENTS) ABOUT JESUS' FAMILY, PARTICULARLY: MATTHEW 12; MARK 6 & MATTHEW 13; JOHN 7; AND GALATIANS 1:9. AND, OF COURSE, THE BOOK OF JUDE, WHICH ARE JUDE'S OWN WORDS!

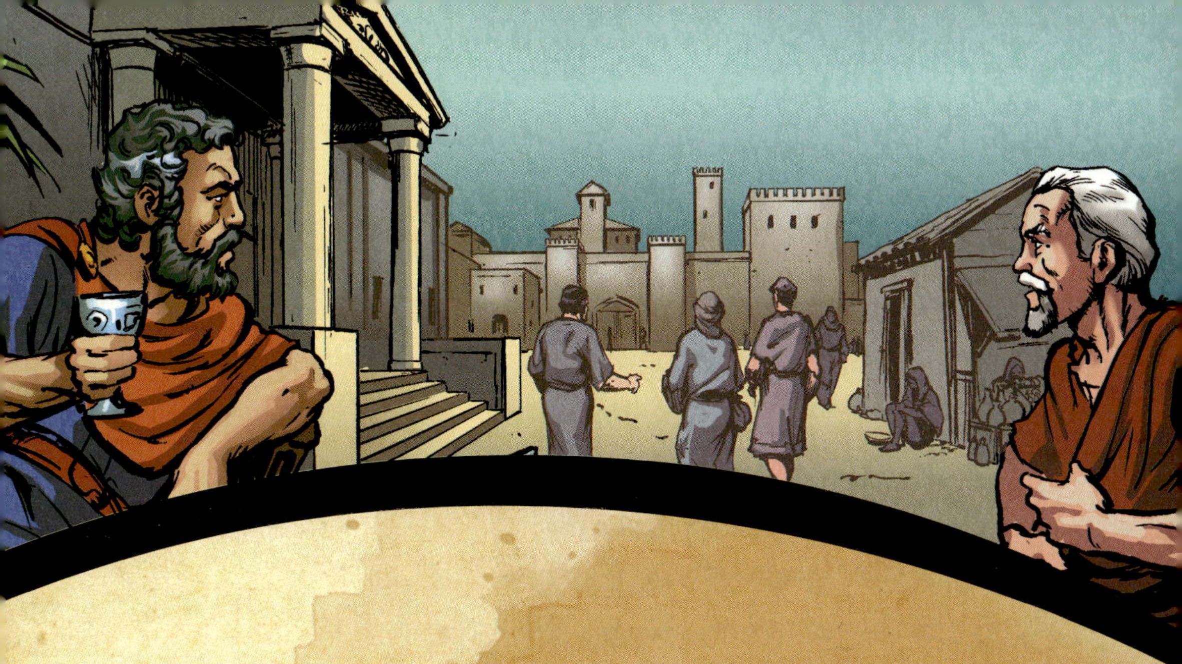

LUKE

MARTYRED A.D. 93

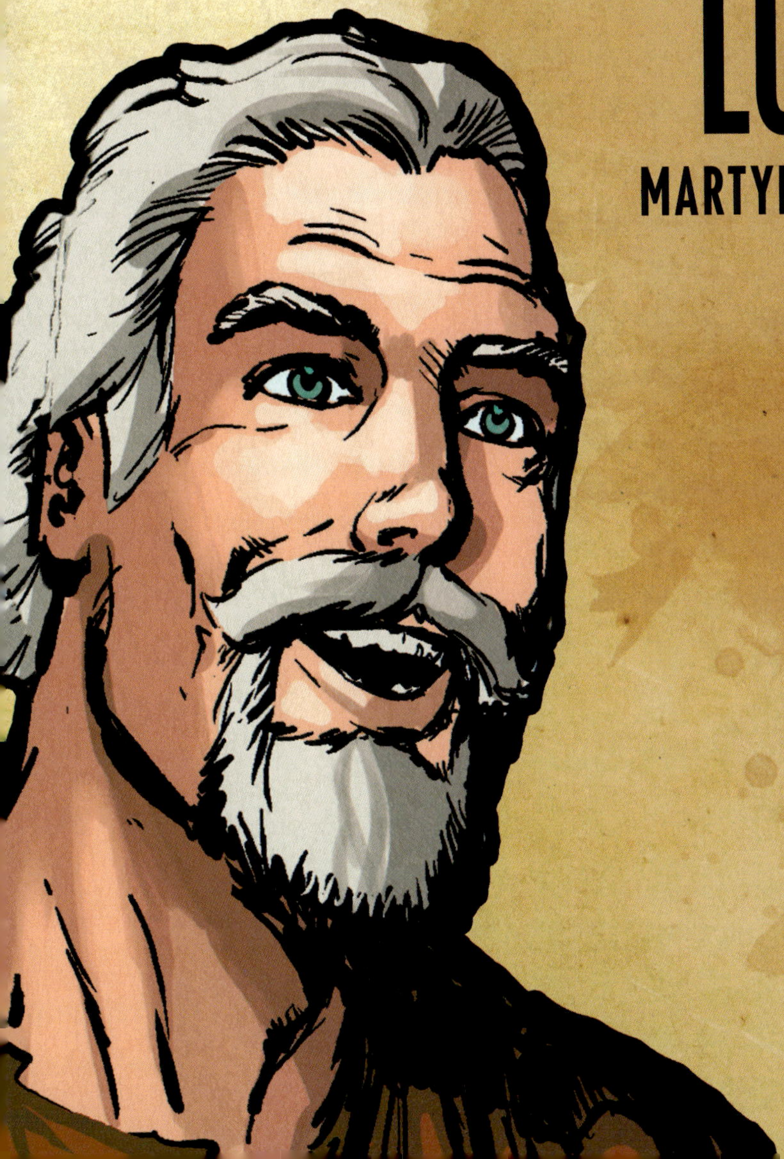

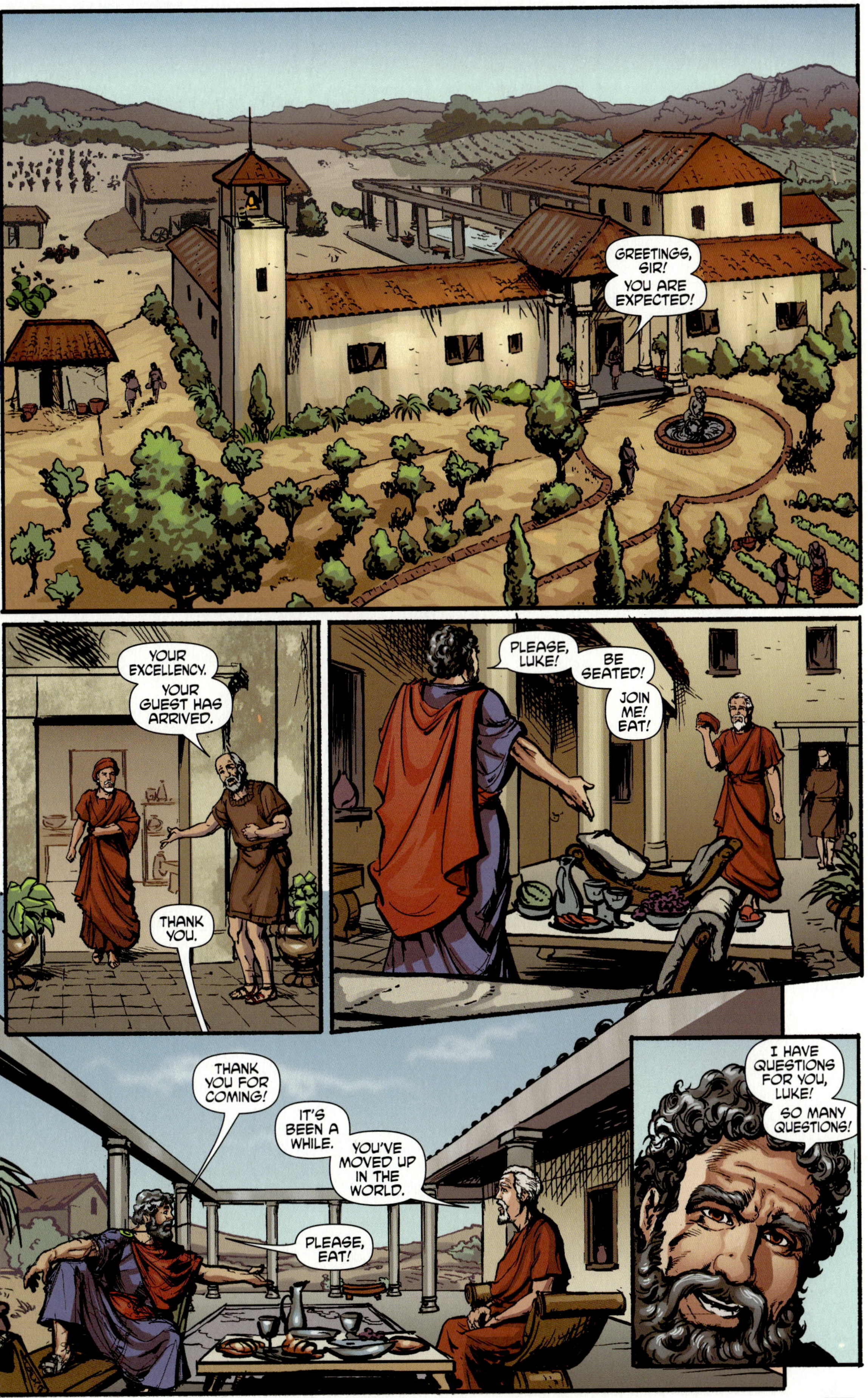
GREETINGS, SIR! YOU ARE EXPECTED!
YOUR EXCELLENCY. YOUR GUEST HAS ARRIVED.
THANK YOU.
PLEASE, LUKE!
BE SEATED!
JOIN ME! EAT!
THANK YOU FOR COMING!
IT'S BEEN A WHILE.
YOU'VE MOVED UP IN THE WORLD.
PLEASE, EAT!
I HAVE QUESTIONS FOR YOU, LUKE!
SO MANY QUESTIONS!

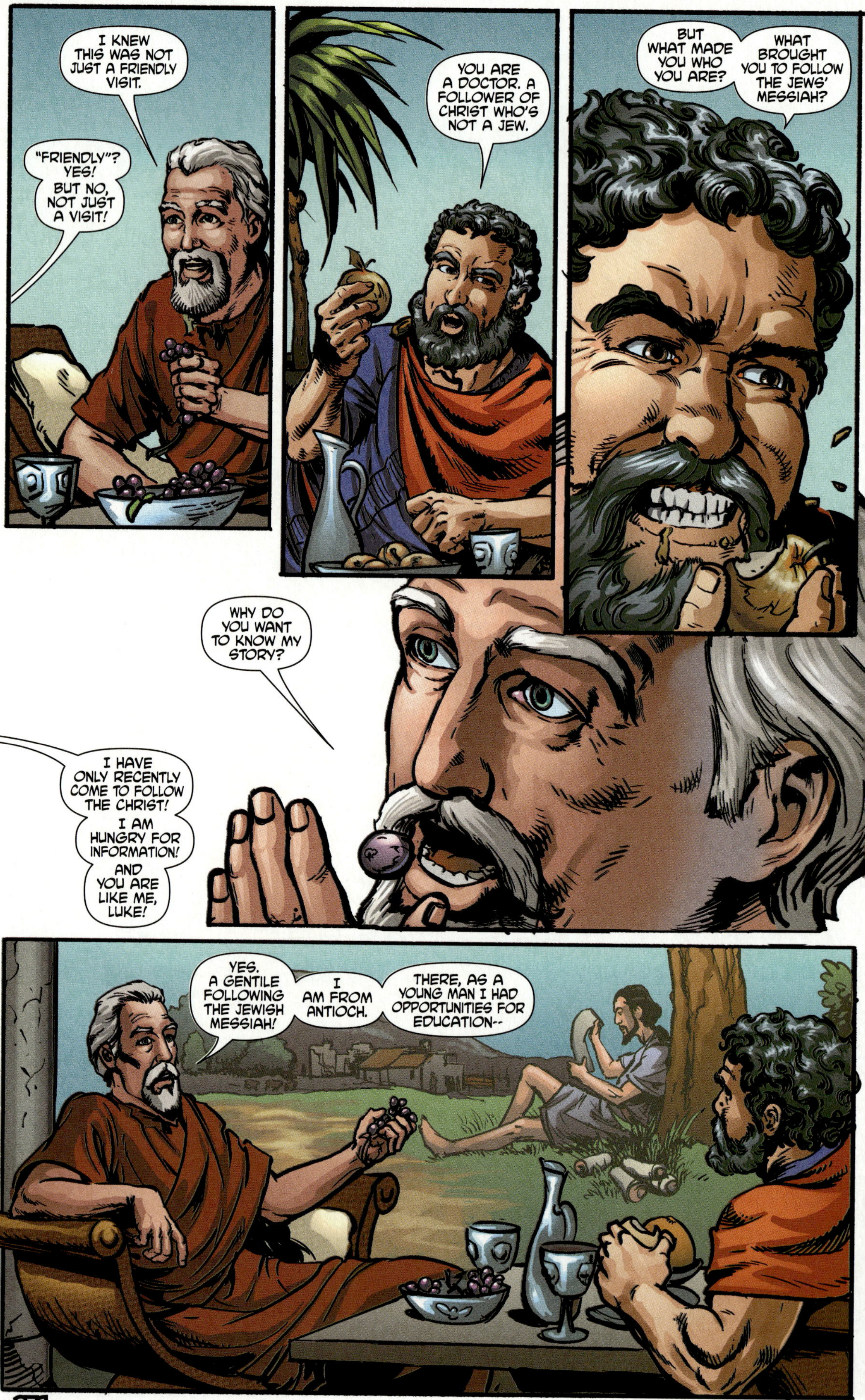
I KNEW THIS WAS NOT JUST A FRIENDLY VISIT.
"FRIENDLY"? YES! BUT NO, NOT JUST A VISIT!
YOU ARE A DOCTOR. A FOLLOWER OF CHRIST WHO'S NOT A JEW.
BUT WHAT MADE YOU WHO YOU ARE?
WHAT BROUGHT YOU TO FOLLOW THE JEWS' MESSIAH?
WHY DO YOU WANT TO KNOW MY STORY?
I HAVE ONLY RECENTLY COME TO FOLLOW THE CHRIST!
I AM HUNGRY FOR INFORMATION!
AND YOU ARE LIKE ME, LUKE!
YES. A GENTILE FOLLOWING THE JEWISH MESSIAH!
I AM FROM ANTIOCH.
THERE, AS A YOUNG MAN I HAD OPPORTUNITIES FOR EDUCATION--

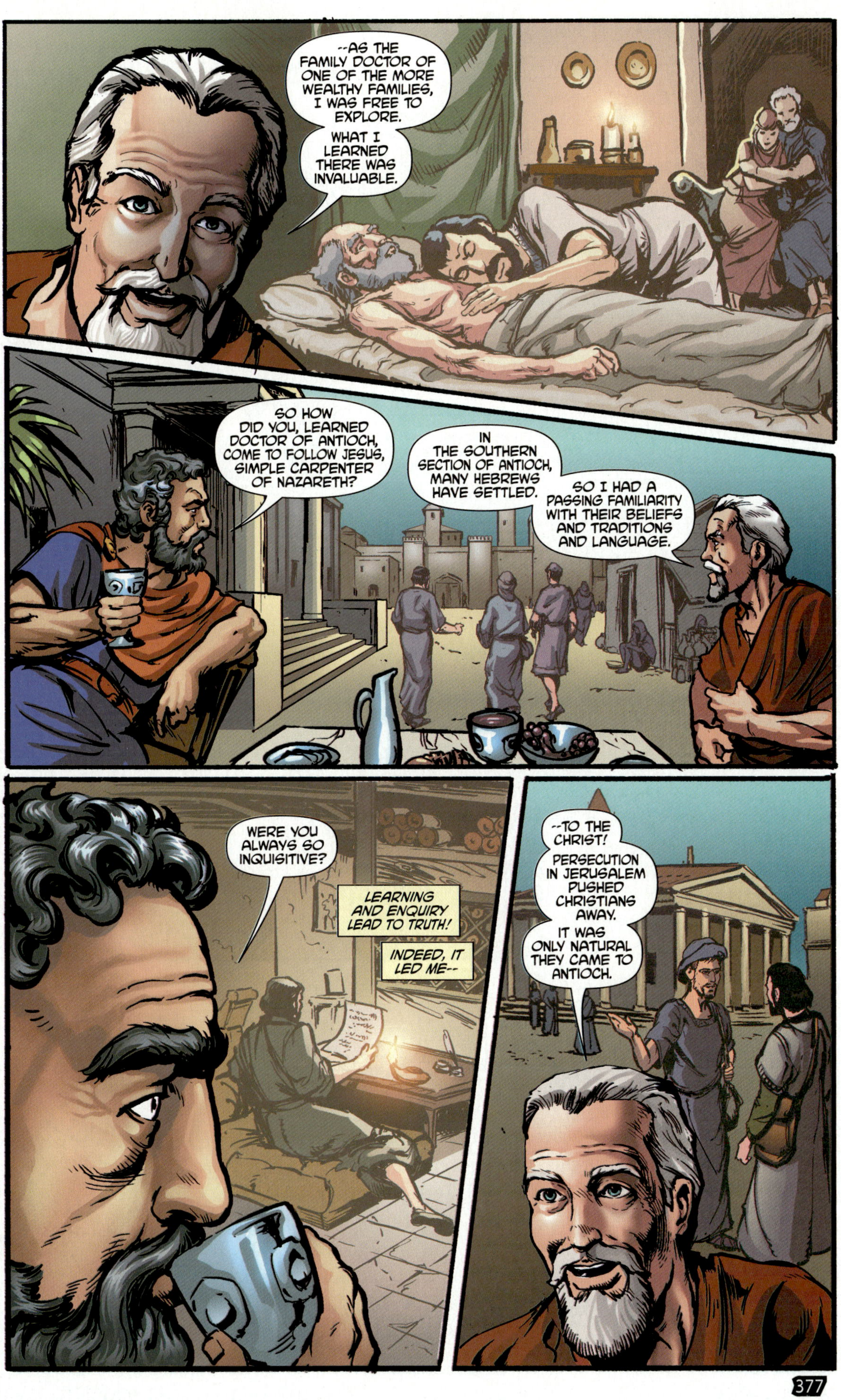
--AS THE FAMILY DOCTOR OF ONE OF THE MORE WEALTHY FAMILIES, I WAS FREE TO EXPLORE.
WHAT I LEARNED THERE WAS INVALUABLE.
SO HOW DID YOU, LEARNED DOCTOR OF ANTIOCH, COME TO FOLLOW JESUS, SIMPLE CARPENTER OF NAZARETH?
IN THE SOUTHERN SECTION OF ANTIOCH, MANY HEBREWS HAVE SETTLED.
SO I HAD A PASSING FAMILIARITY WITH THEIR BELIEFS AND TRADITIONS AND LANGUAGE.
WERE YOU ALWAYS SO INQUISITIVE?
LEARNING AND ENQUIRY LEAD TO TRUTH!
INDEED, IT LED ME--
--TO THE CHRIST!
PERSECUTION IN JERUSALEM PUSHED CHRISTIANS AWAY.
IT WAS ONLY NATURAL THEY CAME TO ANTIOCH.

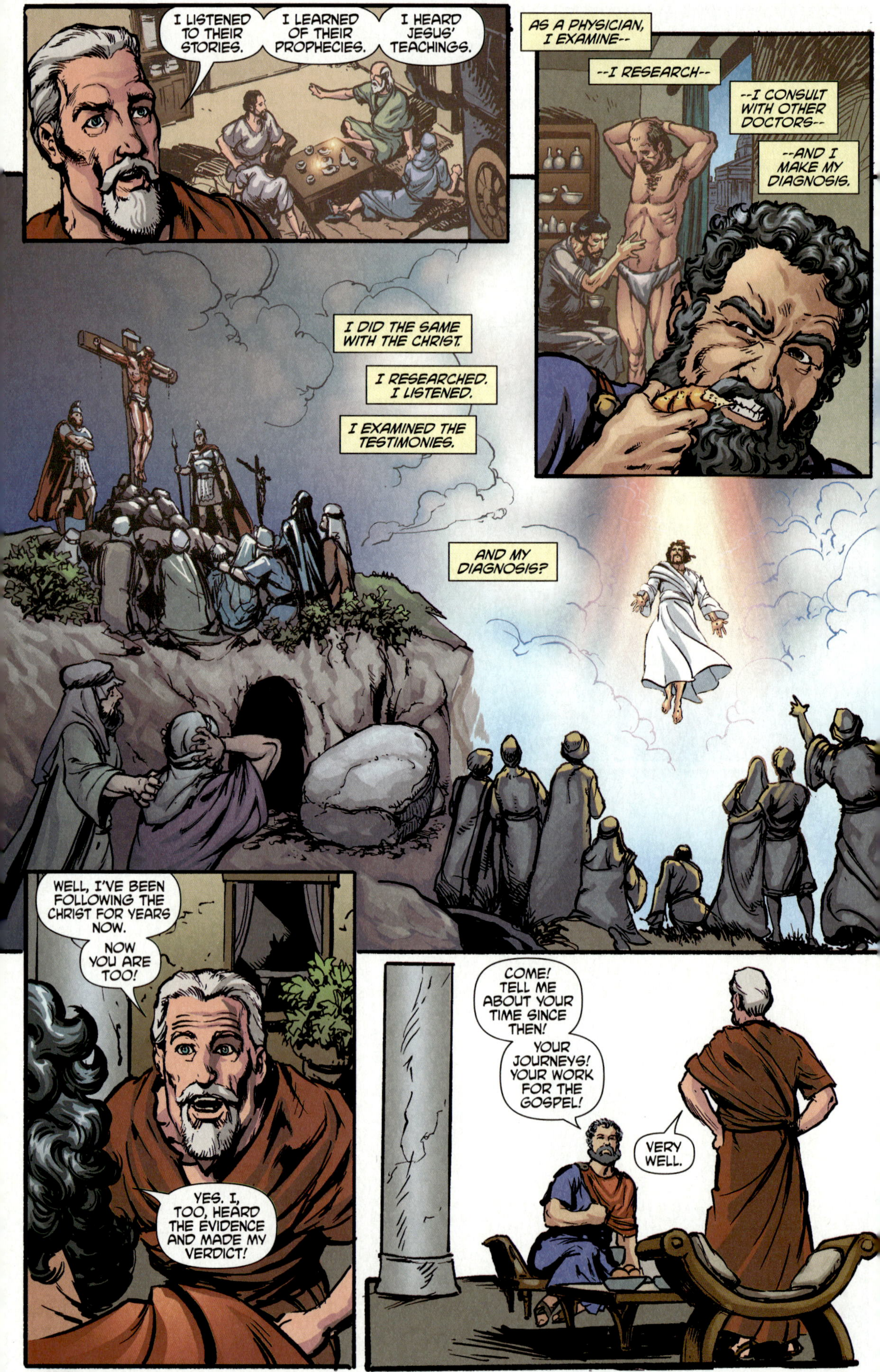
I LISTENED TO THEIR STORIES.
I LEARNED OF THEIR PROPHECIES.
I HEARD JESUS' TEACHINGS.
AS A PHYSICIAN, I EXAMINE--
--I RESEARCH--
--I CONSULT WITH OTHER DOCTORS--
--AND I MAKE MY DIAGNOSIS.
I DID THE SAME WITH THE CHRIST.
I RESEARCHED. I LISTENED.
I EXAMINED THE TESTIMONIES.
AND MY DIAGNOSIS?
WELL, I'VE BEEN FOLLOWING THE CHRIST FOR YEARS NOW.
NOW YOU ARE TOO!
YES. I, TOO, HEARD THE EVIDENCE AND MADE MY VERDICT!
COME! TELL ME ABOUT YOUR TIME SINCE THEN!
YOUR JOURNEYS! YOUR WORK FOR THE GOSPEL!
VERY WELL.

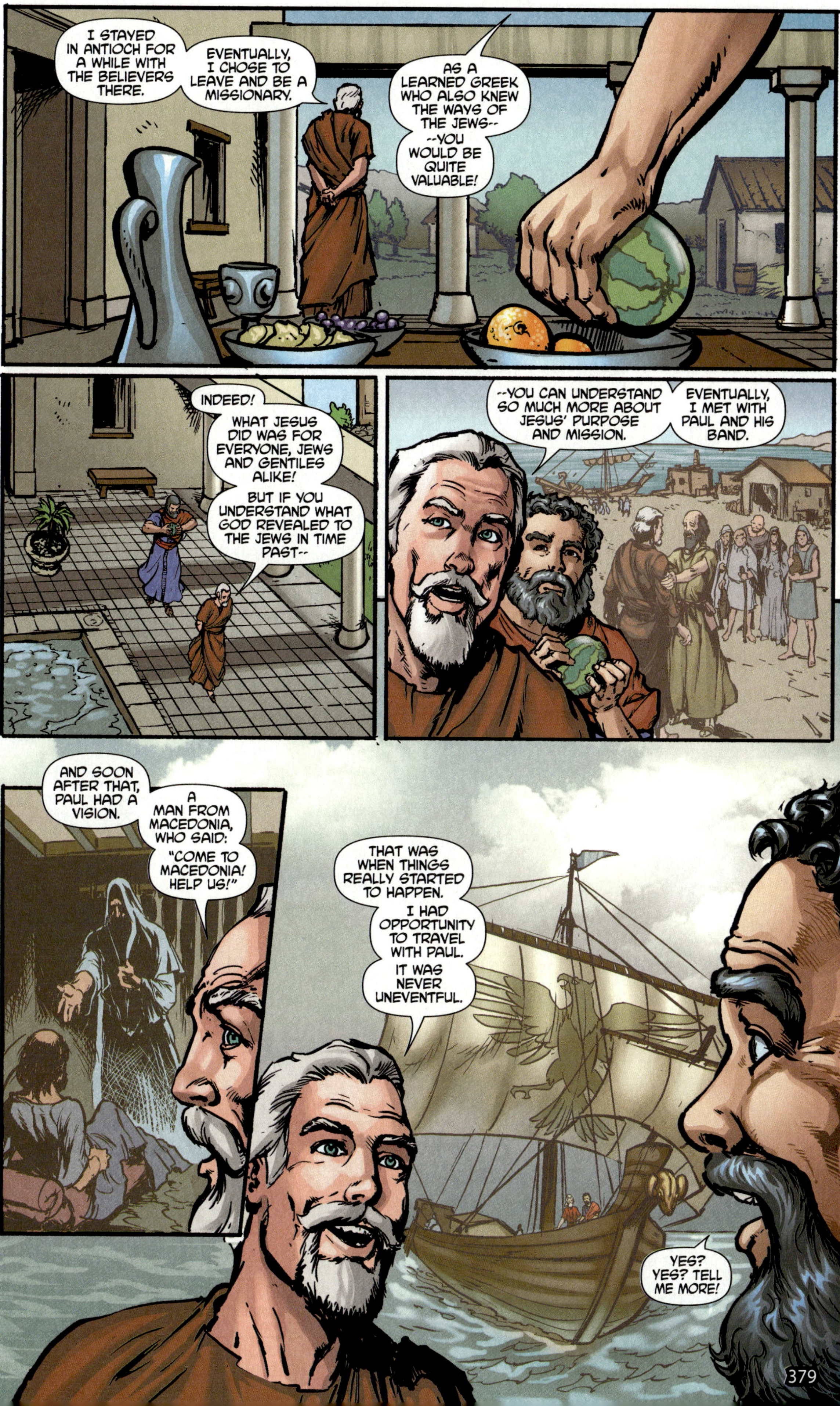

I STAYED IN ANTIOCH FOR A WHILE WITH THE BELIEVERS THERE.
EVENTUALLY, I CHOSE TO LEAVE AND BE A MISSIONARY.
AS A LEARNED GREEK WHO ALSO KNEW THE WAYS OF THE JEWS--
--YOU WOULD BE QUITE VALUABLE!
INDEED!
WHAT JESUS DID WAS FOR EVERYONE, JEWS AND GENTILES ALIKE!
BUT IF YOU UNDERSTAND WHAT GOD REVEALED TO THE JEWS IN TIME PAST--
--YOU CAN UNDERSTAND SO MUCH MORE ABOUT JESUS' PURPOSE AND MISSION.
EVENTUALLY, I MET WITH PAUL AND HIS BAND.
AND SOON AFTER THAT, PAUL HAD A VISION.
A MAN FROM MACEDONIA, WHO SAID:
"COME TO MACEDONIA! HELP US!"
THAT WAS WHEN THINGS REALLY STARTED TO HAPPEN.
I HAD OPPORTUNITY TO TRAVEL WITH PAUL.
IT WAS NEVER UNEVENTFUL.
YES? YES? TELL ME MORE!

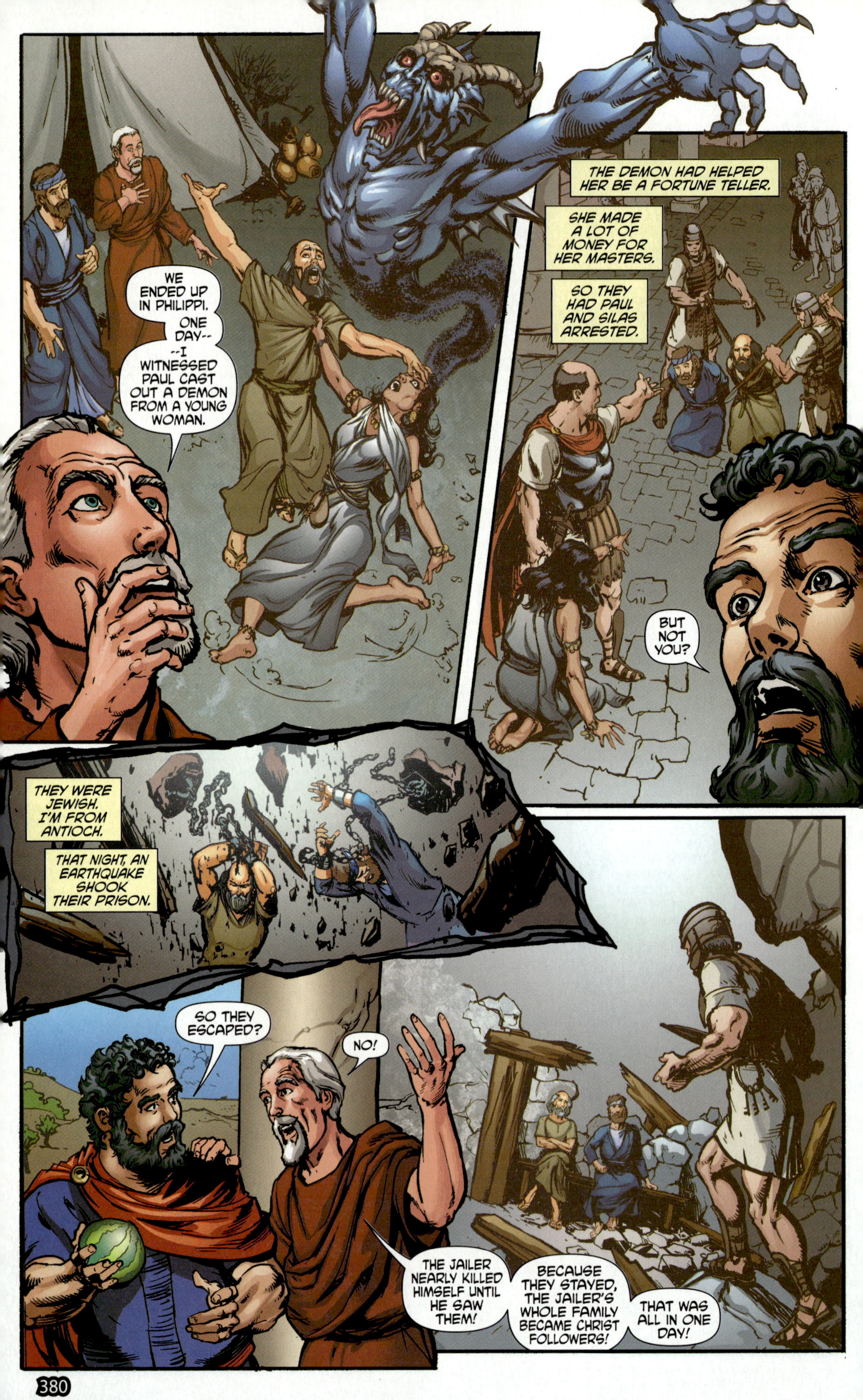
WE ENDED UP IN PHILIPPI.
ONE DAY--
--I WITNESSED PAUL CAST OUT A DEMON FROM A YOUNG WOMAN.
THE DEMON HAD HELPED HER BE A FORTUNE TELLER.
SHE MADE A LOT OF MONEY FOR HER MASTERS.
SO THEY HAD PAUL AND SILAS ARRESTED.
BUT NOT YOU?
THEY WERE JEWISH. I'M FROM ANTIOCH.
THAT NIGHT, AN EARTHQUAKE SHOOK THEIR PRISON.
SO THEY ESCAPED?
NO!
THE JAILER NEARLY KILLED HIMSELF UNTIL HE SAW THEM!
BECAUSE THEY STAYED, THE JAILER'S WHOLE FAMILY BECAME CHRIST FOLLOWERS!
THAT WAS ALL IN ONE DAY!

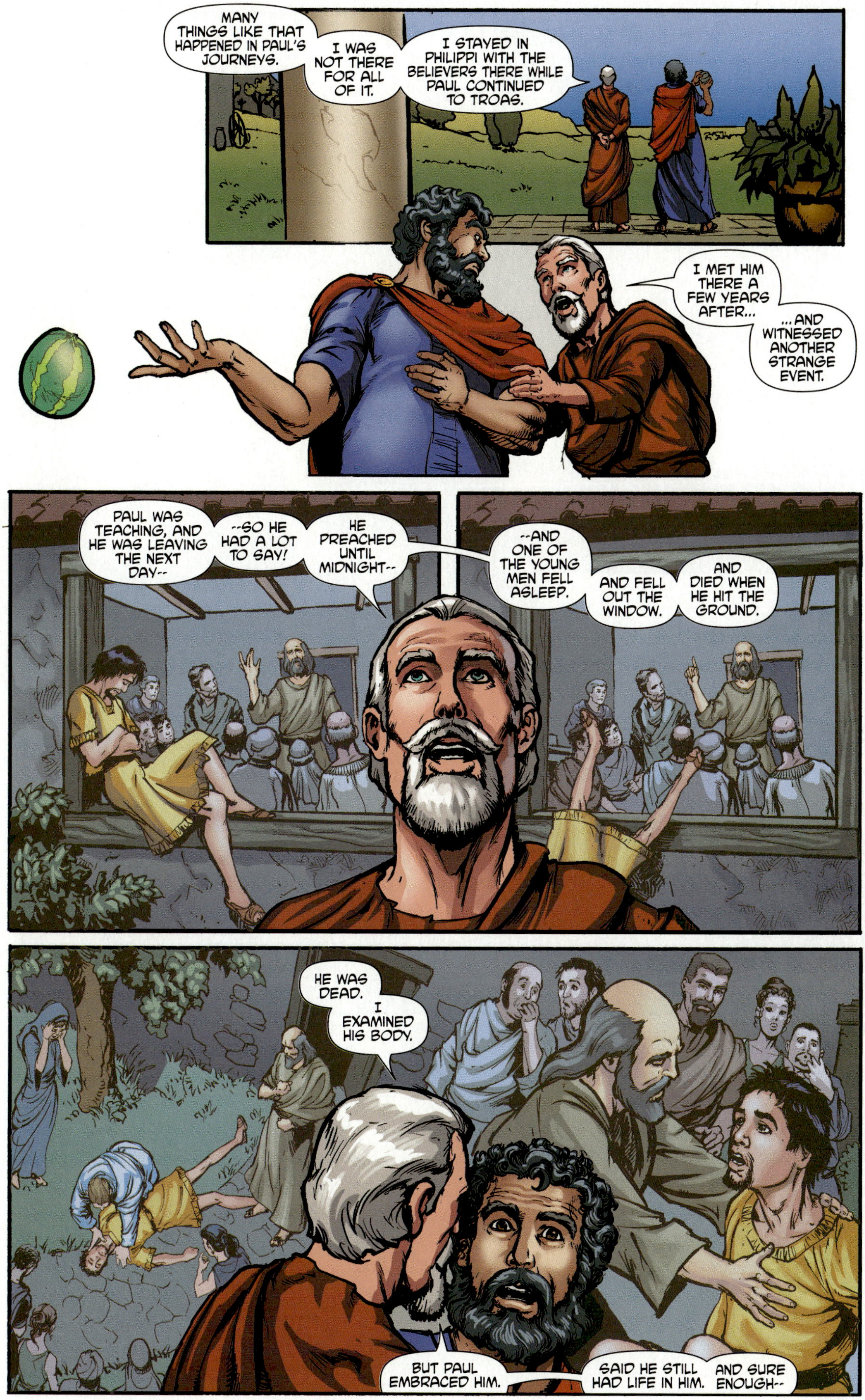
MANY THINGS LIKE THAT HAPPENED IN PAUL'S JOURNEYS.
I WAS NOT THERE FOR ALL OF IT.
I STAYED IN PHILIPPI WITH THE BELIEVERS THERE WHILE PAUL CONTINUED TO TROAS.
I MET HIM THERE A FEW YEARS AFTER...
...AND WITNESSED ANOTHER STRANGE EVENT.
PAUL WAS TEACHING, AND HE WAS LEAVING THE NEXT DAY--
--SO HE HAD A LOT TO SAY!
HE PREACHED UNTIL MIDNIGHT--
--AND ONE OF THE YOUNG MEN FELL ASLEEP.
AND FELL OUT THE WINDOW.
AND DIED WHEN HE HIT THE GROUND.
HE WAS DEAD.
I EXAMINED HIS BODY.
BUT PAUL EMBRACED HIM.
SAID HE STILL HAD LIFE IN HIM.
AND SURE ENOUGH--

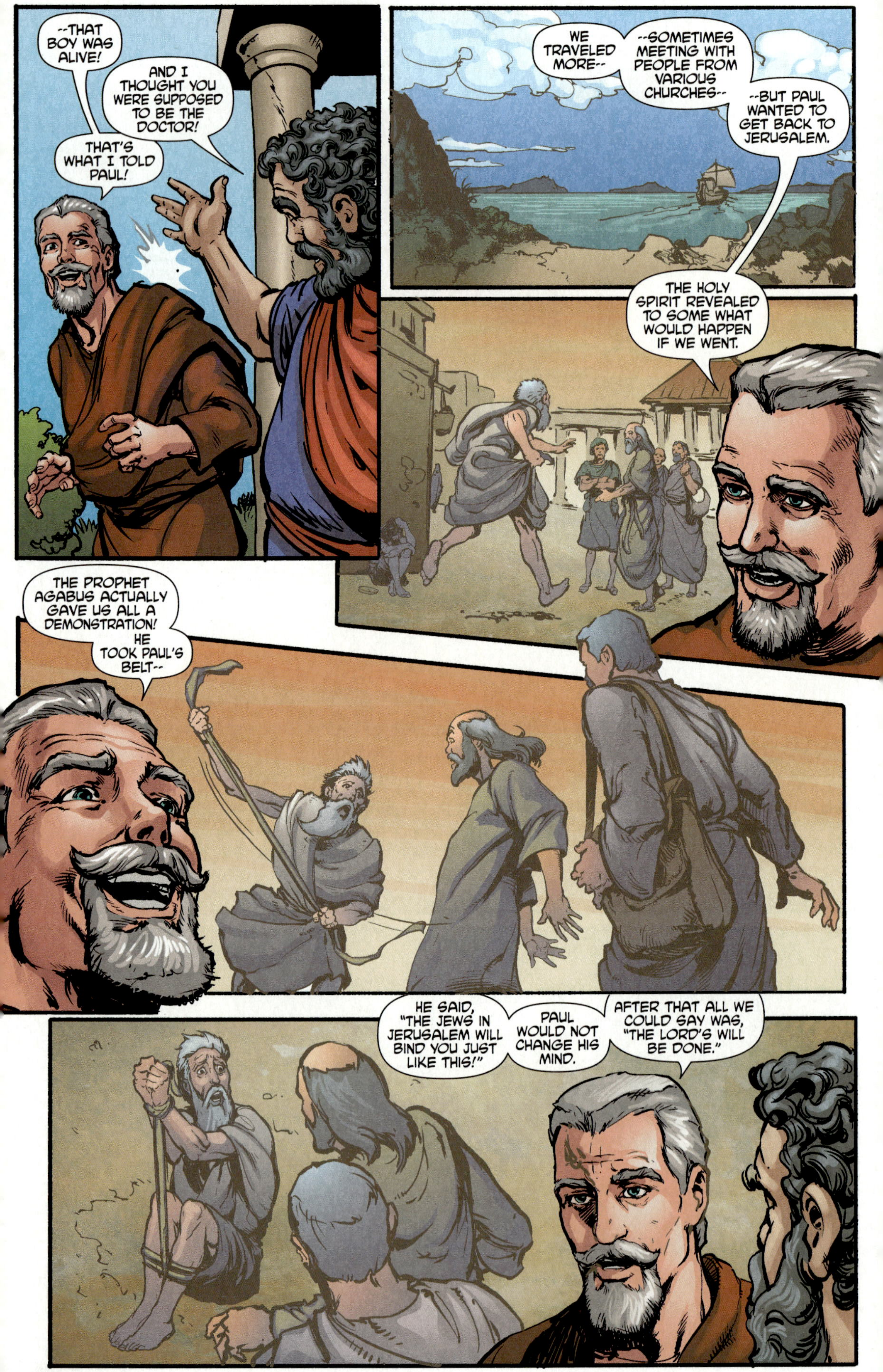
--THAT BOY WAS ALIVE!
AND I THOUGHT YOU WERE SUPPOSED TO BE THE DOCTOR!
THAT'S WHAT I TOLD PAUL!
WE TRAVELED MORE--
--SOMETIMES MEETING WITH PEOPLE FROM VARIOUS CHURCHES--
--BUT PAUL WANTED TO GET BACK TO JERUSALEM.
THE HOLY SPIRIT REVEALED TO SOME WHAT WOULD HAPPEN IF WE WENT.
THE PROPHET AGABUS ACTUALLY GAVE US ALL A DEMONSTRATION!
HE TOOK PAUL'S BELT--
HE SAID, "THE JEWS IN JERUSALEM WILL BIND YOU JUST LIKE THIS!"
PAUL WOULD NOT CHANGE HIS MIND.
AFTER THAT ALL WE COULD SAY WAS, "THE LORD'S WILL BE DONE."

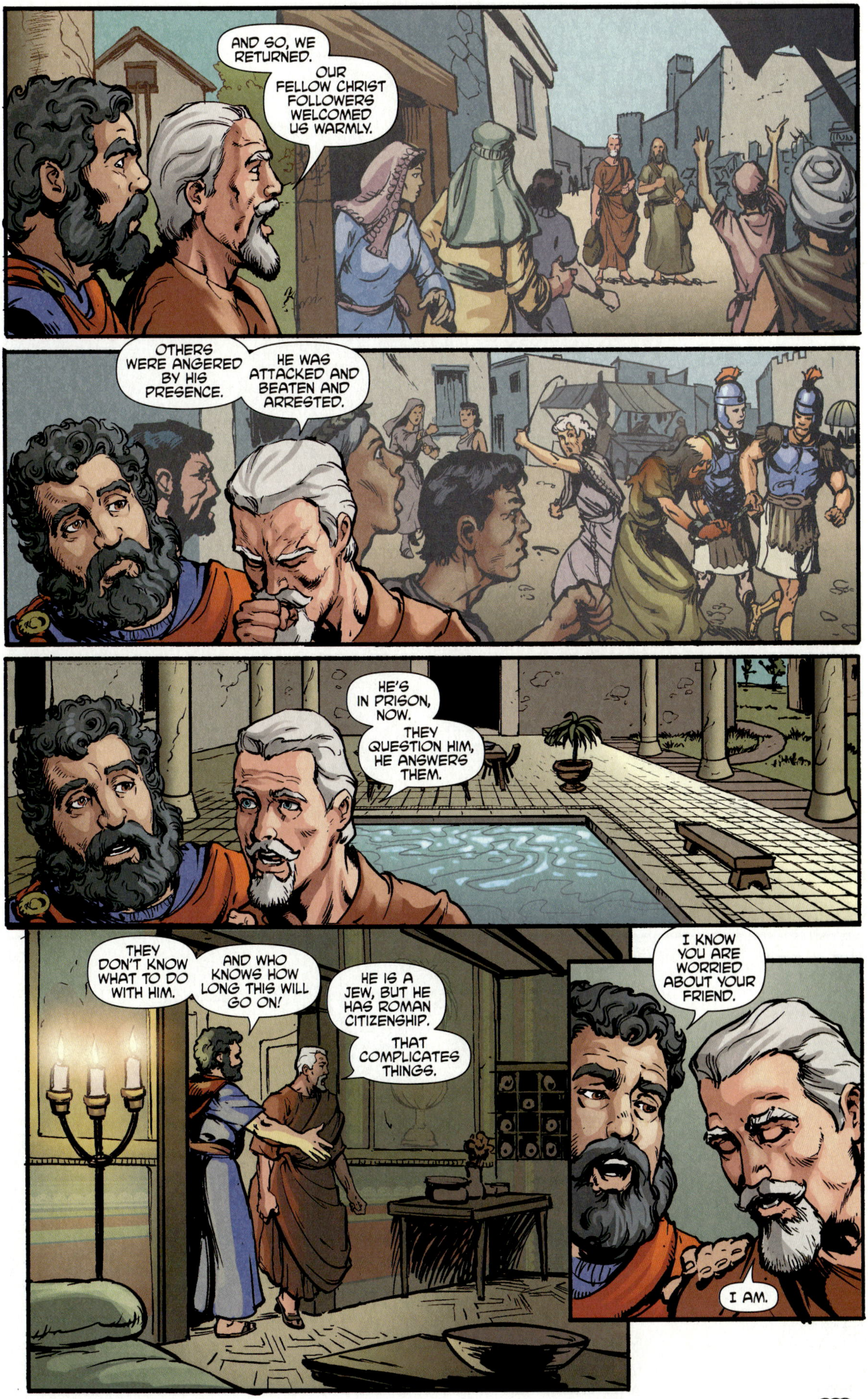
AND SO, WE RETURNED.
OUR FELLOW CHRIST FOLLOWERS WELCOMED US WARMLY.
OTHERS WERE ANGERED BY HIS PRESENCE.
HE WAS ATTACKED AND BEATEN AND ARRESTED.
HE'S IN PRISON, NOW.
THEY QUESTION HIM, HE ANSWERS THEM.
THEY DON'T KNOW WHAT TO DO WITH HIM.
AND WHO KNOWS HOW LONG THIS WILL GO ON!
HE IS A JEW, BUT HE HAS ROMAN CITIZENSHIP.
THAT COMPLICATES THINGS.
I KNOW YOU ARE WORRIED ABOUT YOUR FRIEND.
I AM.

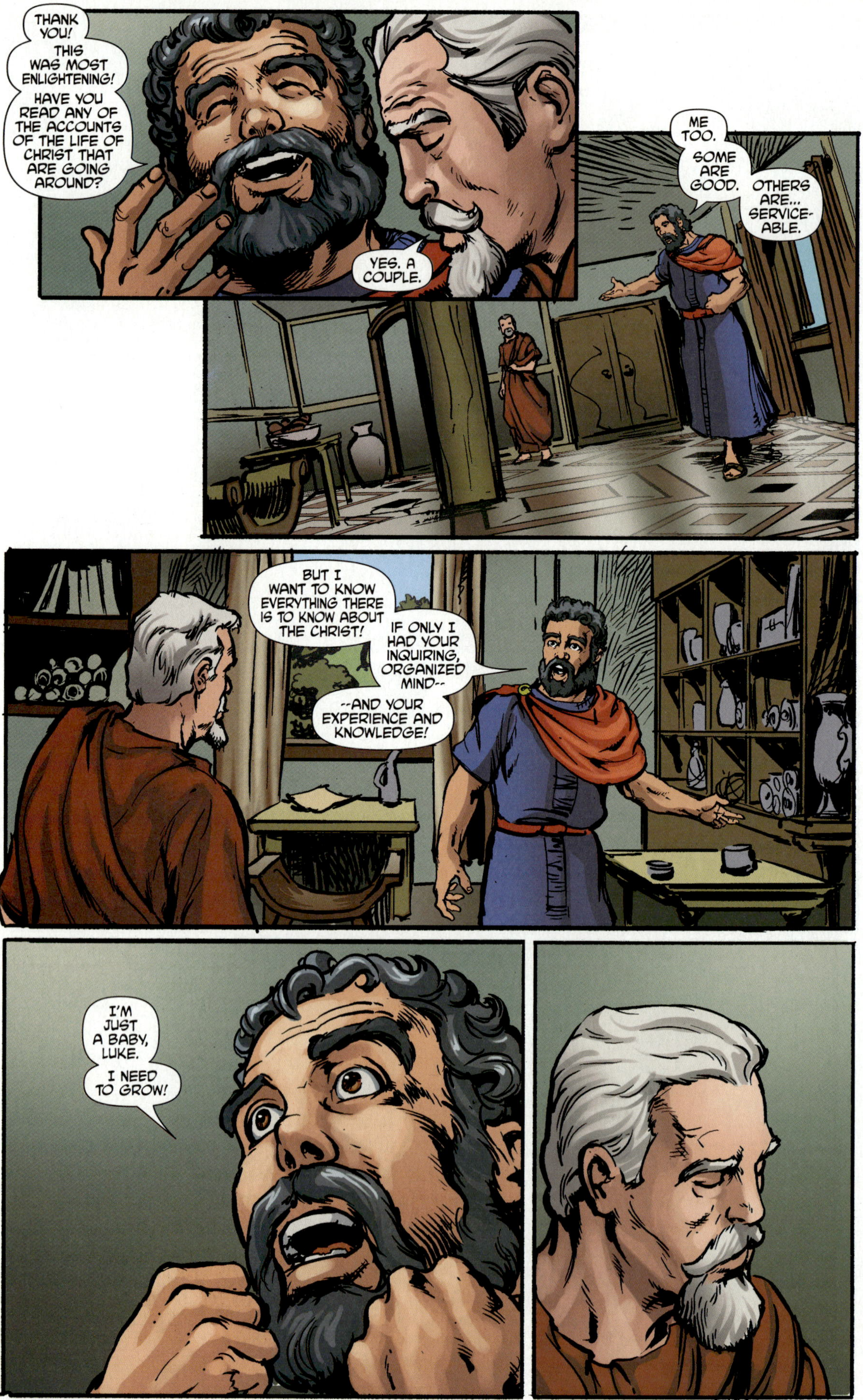
THANK YOU!
THIS WAS MOST ENLIGHTENING!
HAVE YOU READ ANY OF THE ACCOUNTS OF THE LIFE OF CHRIST THAT ARE GOING AROUND?
YES. A COUPLE.
ME TOO.
SOME ARE GOOD.
OTHERS ARE... SERVICE-ABLE.
BUT I WANT TO KNOW EVERYTHING THERE IS TO KNOW ABOUT THE CHRIST!
IF ONLY I HAD YOUR INQUIRING, ORGANIZED MIND--
--AND YOUR EXPERIENCE AND KNOWLEDGE!
I'M JUST A BABY, LUKE.
I NEED TO GROW!

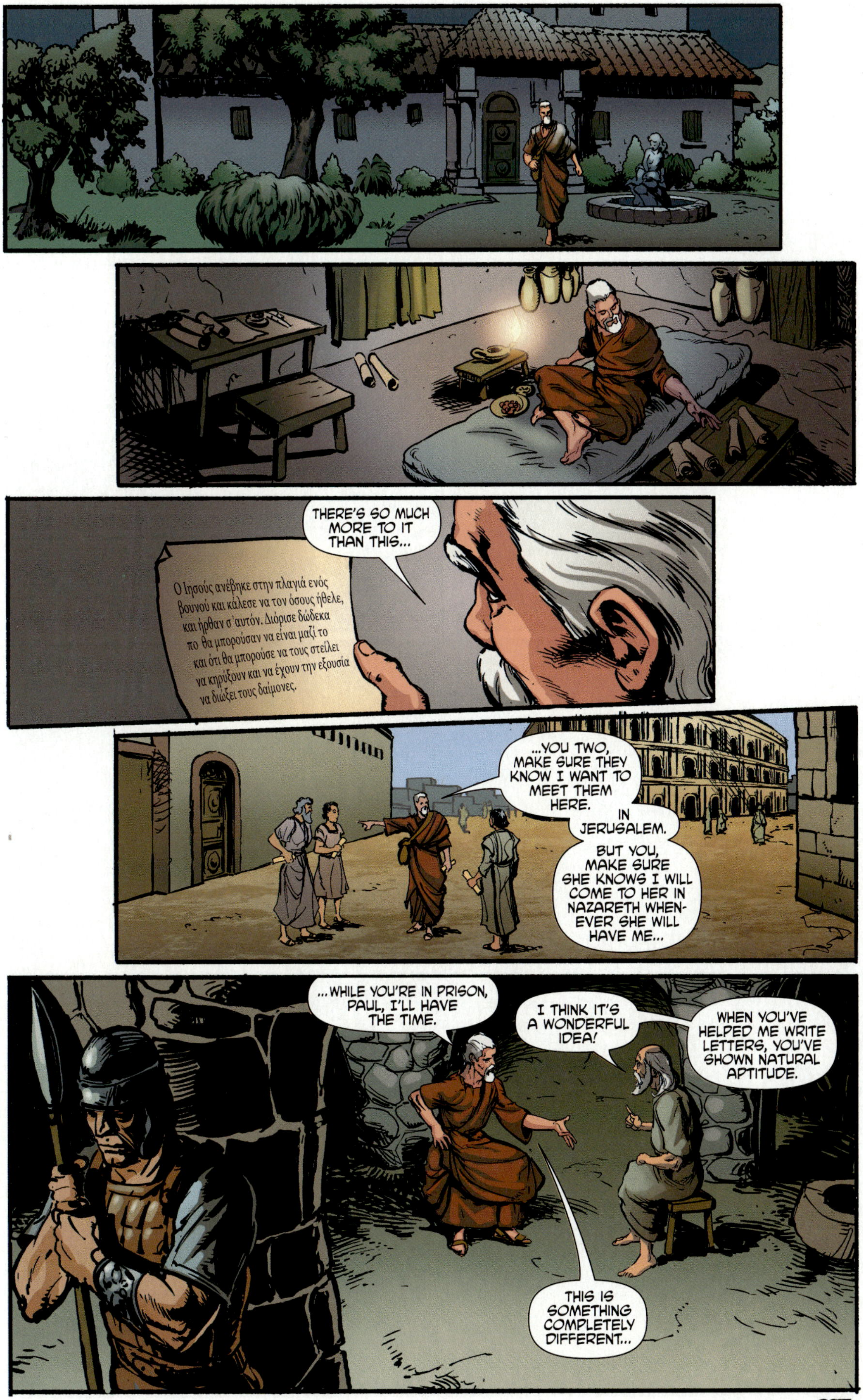
THERE'S SO MUCH MORE TO IT THAN THIS...
Ο Ιησούς ανέβηκε στην πλαγιά ενός
βουνού και κάλεσε να τον όσους ήθελε,
και ήρθαν σ'αυτόν. Διόρισε δώδεκα
πο θα μπορούσαν να είναι μαζί το
και ότι θα μπορούσε να τους στείλει
να κηρύξουν και να έχουν την εξουσία
να διώξει τους δαίμονες.
...YOU TWO, MAKE SURE THEY KNOW I WANT TO MEET THEM HERE.
IN JERUSALEM.
BUT YOU, MAKE SURE SHE KNOWS I WILL COME TO HER IN NAZARETH WHEN-EVER SHE WILL HAVE ME...
...WHILE YOU'RE IN PRISON, PAUL, I'LL HAVE THE TIME.
I THINK IT'S A WONDERFUL IDEA!
WHEN YOU'VE HELPED ME WRITE LETTERS, YOU'VE SHOWN NATURAL APTITUDE.
THIS IS SOMETHING COMPLETELY DIFFERENT...

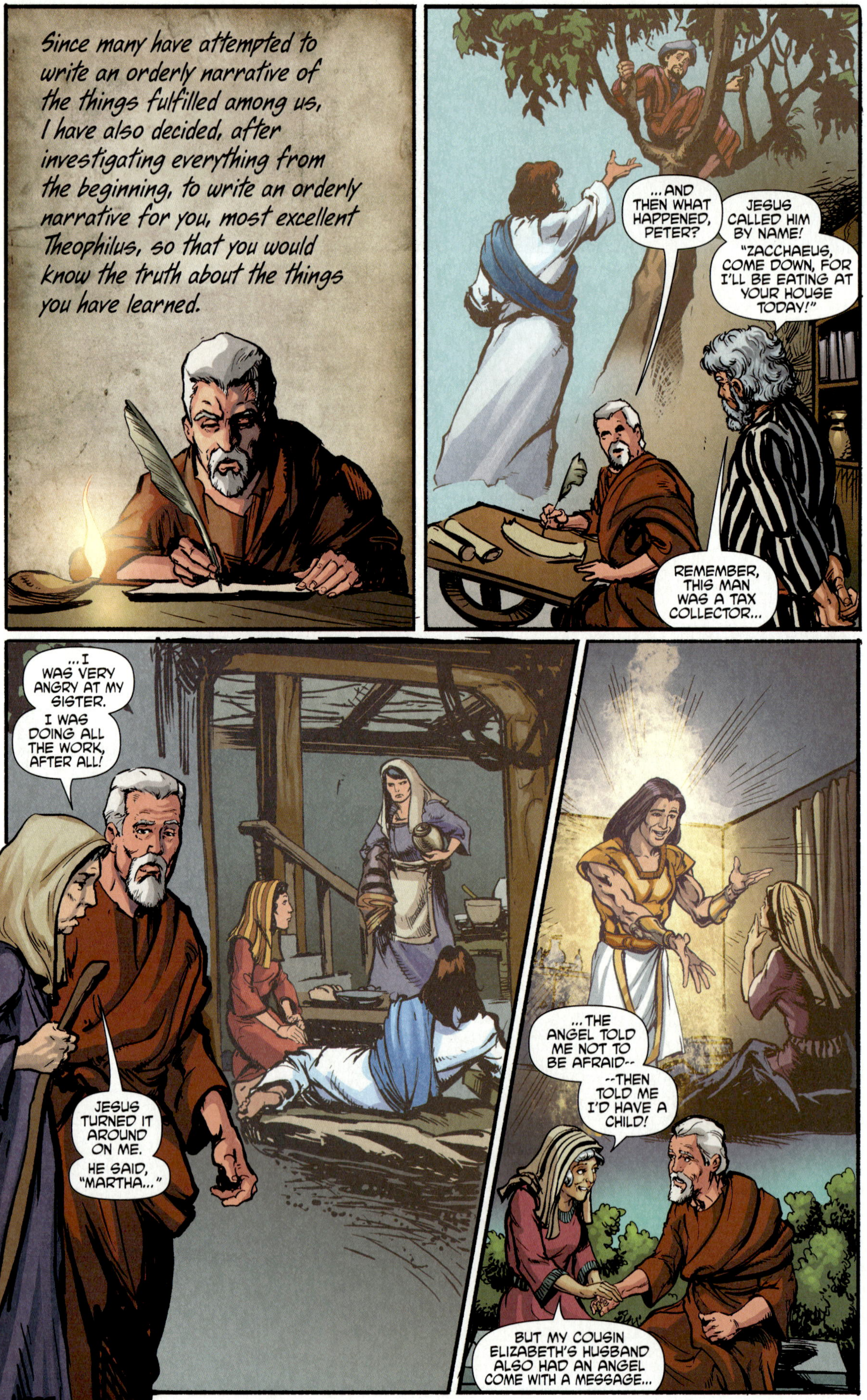
Since many have attempted to write an orderly narrative of the things fulfilled among us, I have also decided, after investigating everything from the beginning, to write an orderly narrative for you, most excellent Theophilus, so that you would know the truth about the things you have learned.
...AND THEN WHAT HAPPENED, PETER?
JESUS CALLED HIM BY NAME! "ZACCHAEUS, COME DOWN, FOR I'LL BE EATING AT YOUR HOUSE TODAY!"
REMEMBER, THIS MAN WAS A TAX COLLECTOR...
...I WAS VERY ANGRY AT MY SISTER.
I WAS DOING ALL THE WORK, AFTER ALL!
JESUS TURNED IT AROUND ON ME.
HE SAID, "MARTHA..."
...THE ANGEL TOLD ME NOT TO BE AFRAID--
--THEN TOLD ME I'D HAVE A CHILD!
BUT MY COUSIN ELIZABETH'S HUSBAND ALSO HAD AN ANGEL COME WITH A MESSAGE...

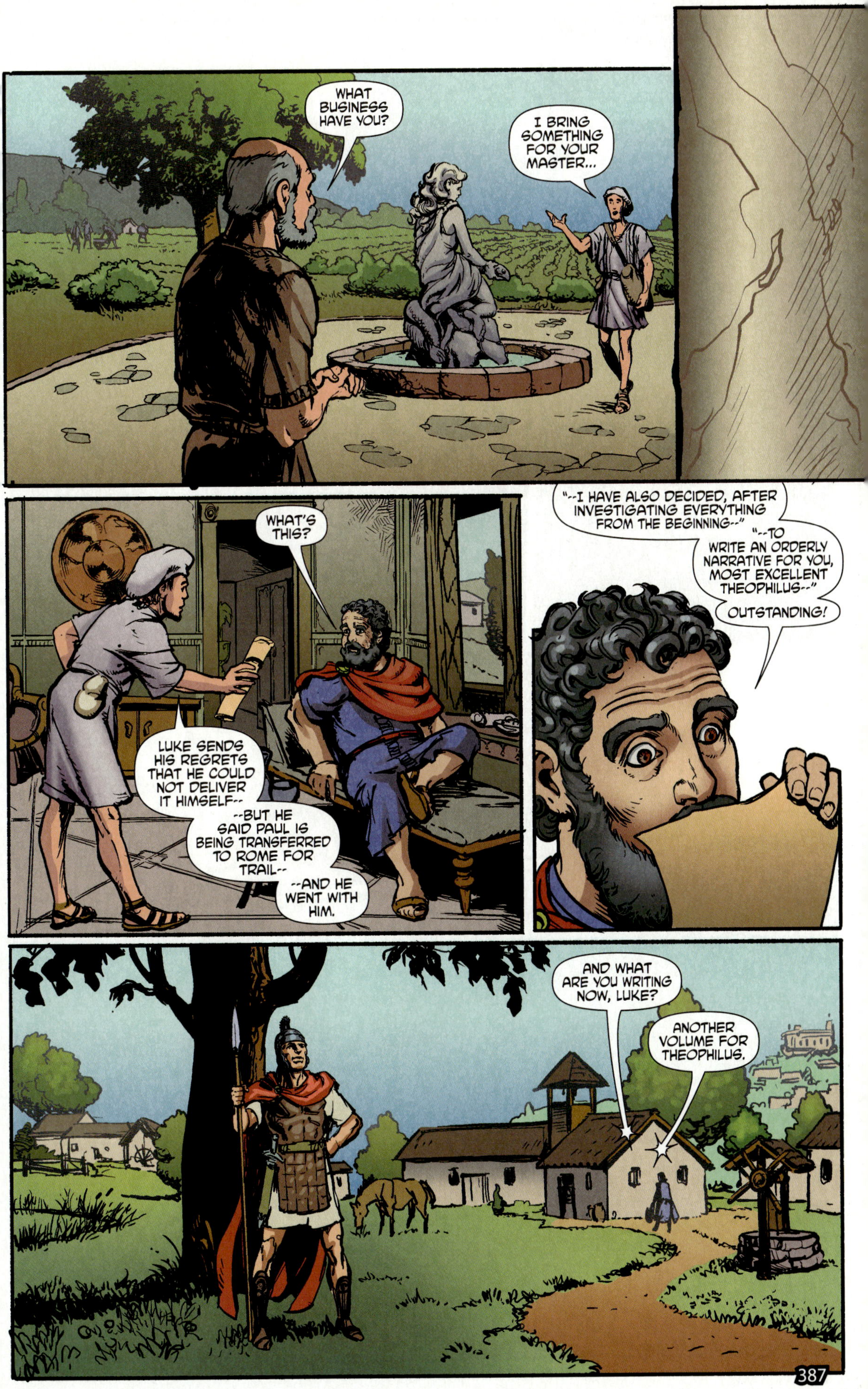
WHAT BUSINESS HAVE YOU?
I BRING SOMETHING FOR YOUR MASTER...
WHAT'S THIS?
LUKE SENDS HIS REGRETS THAT HE COULD NOT DELIVER IT HIMSELF--
--BUT HE SAID PAUL IS BEING TRANSFERRED TO ROME FOR TRAIL--
--AND HE WENT WITH HIM.
"--I HAVE ALSO DECIDED, AFTER INVESTIGATING EVERYTHING FROM THE BEGINNING--"
"--TO WRITE AN ORDERLY NARRATIVE FOR YOU, MOST EXCELLENT THEOPHILUS--"
OUTSTANDING!
AND WHAT ARE YOU WRITING NOW, LUKE?
ANOTHER VOLUME FOR THEOPHILUS.

THIS ONE ABOUT THE FOLLOWERS OF THE CHRIST SINCE HE LEFT!

THERE ARE SOME AMAZING THINGS TO RECOUNT!

LIKE THE COMING OF THE HOLY SPIRIT AT PENTECOST!

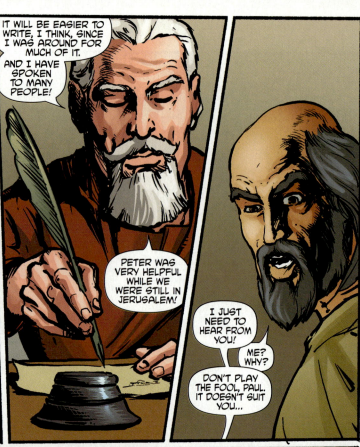

IT WILL BE EASIER TO WRITE, I THINK, SINCE I WAS AROUND FOR MUCH OF IT. AND I HAVE SPOKEN TO MANY PEOPLE!

PETER WAS VERY HELPFUL WHILE WE WERE STILL IN JERUSALEM!

I JUST NEED TO HEAR FROM YOU!

ME? WHY?

DON'T PLAY THE FOOL, PAUL. IT DOESN'T SUIT YOU...

I HAVE ACCOUNTS OF THE SPREADING OF THE MESSAGE EARLY ON.

AND PETER'S VISION AND CALLING TO THE GENTILES!

NOW I WANT TO HEAR FROM YOU ABOUT WHEN YOU SAW THE CHRIST!

AND WHERE YOU WENT TO BRING THE CHRIST TO THE WORLD!

I CAN FILL IN SOME OF THE DETAILS. LIKE OUR SHIPWRECK WHEN WE WERE COMING HERE FROM JERUSALEM!

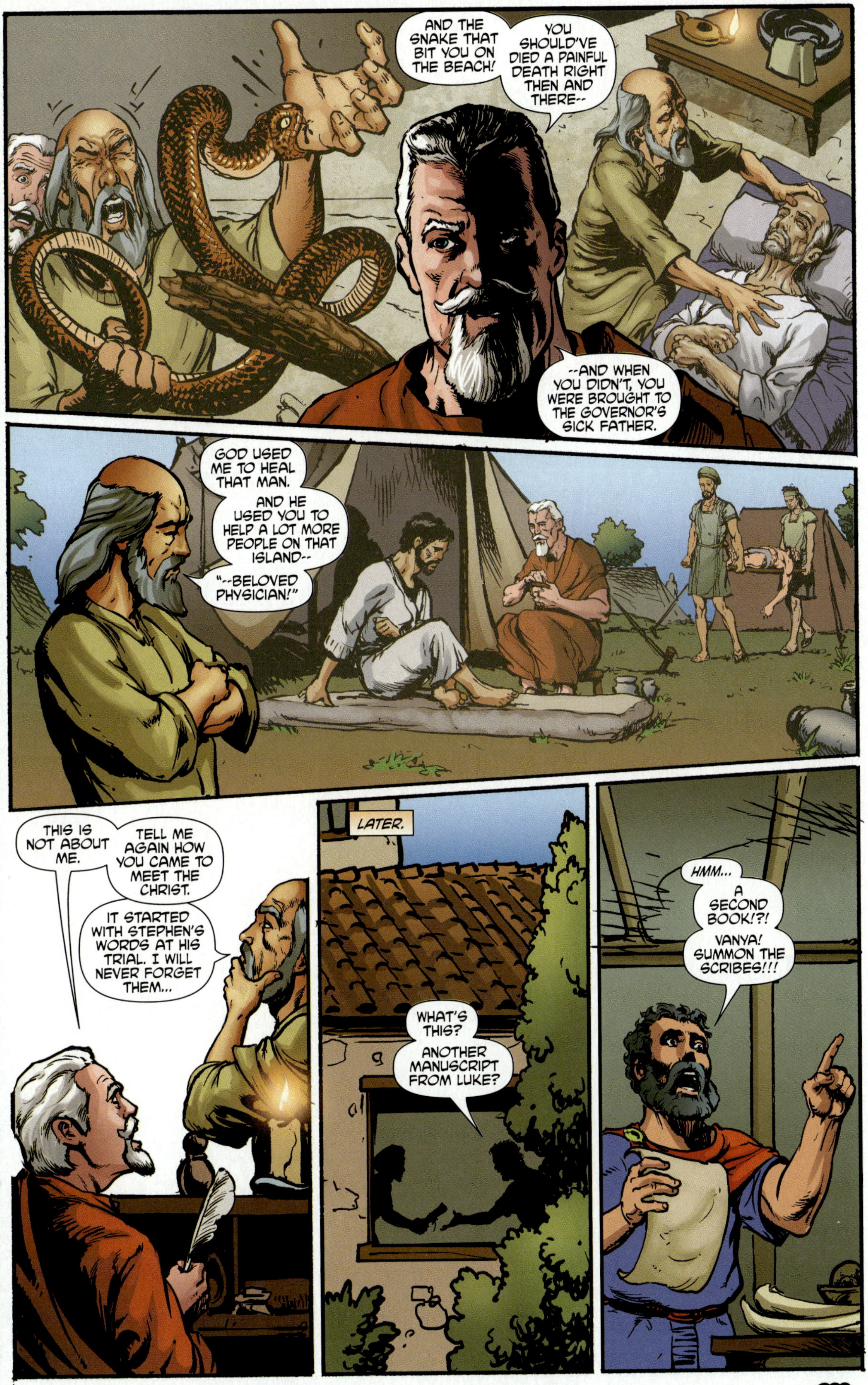

AND THE SNAKE THAT BIT YOU ON THE BEACH!
YOU SHOULD'VE DIED A PAINFUL DEATH RIGHT THEN AND THERE--
--AND WHEN YOU DIDN'T, YOU WERE BROUGHT TO THE GOVERNOR'S SICK FATHER.
GOD USED ME TO HEAL THAT MAN.
AND HE USED YOU TO HELP A LOT MORE PEOPLE ON THAT ISLAND--
"--BELOVED PHYSICIAN!"
THIS IS NOT ABOUT ME.
TELL ME AGAIN HOW YOU CAME TO MEET THE CHRIST.
IT STARTED WITH STEPHEN'S WORDS AT HIS TRIAL. I WILL NEVER FORGET THEM...
LATER.
WHAT'S THIS?
ANOTHER MANUSCRIPT FROM LUKE?
HMM...
A SECOND BOOK!?!
VANYA! SUMMON THE SCRIBES!!!

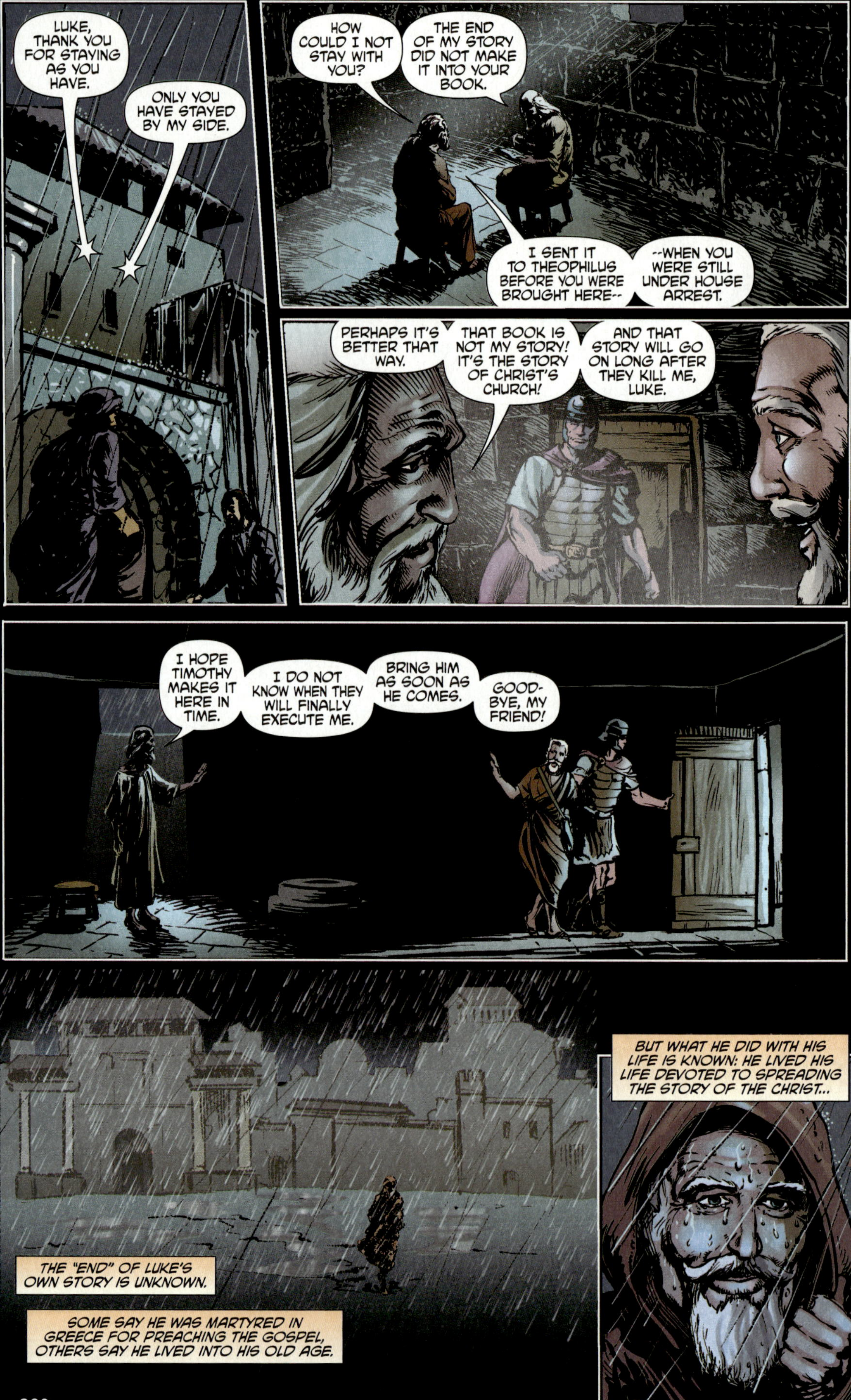
LUKE, THANK YOU FOR STAYING AS YOU HAVE.
ONLY YOU HAVE STAYED BY MY SIDE.
HOW COULD I NOT STAY WITH YOU?
THE END OF MY STORY DID NOT MAKE IT INTO YOUR BOOK.
I SENT IT TO THEOPHILUS BEFORE YOU WERE BROUGHT HERE--
--WHEN YOU WERE STILL UNDER HOUSE ARREST.
PERHAPS IT'S BETTER THAT WAY.
THAT BOOK IS NOT MY STORY! IT'S THE STORY OF CHRIST'S CHURCH!
AND THAT STORY WILL GO ON LONG AFTER THEY KILL ME, LUKE.
I HOPE TIMOTHY MAKES IT HERE IN TIME.
I DO NOT KNOW WHEN THEY WILL FINALLY EXECUTE ME.
BRING HIM AS SOON AS HE COMES.
GOOD-BYE, MY FRIEND!
THE "END" OF LUKE'S OWN STORY IS UNKNOWN.
SOME SAY HE WAS MARTYRED IN GREECE FOR PREACHING THE GOSPEL, OTHERS SAY HE LIVED INTO HIS OLD AGE.
BUT WHAT HE DID WITH HIS LIFE IS KNOWN: HE LIVED HIS LIFE DEVOTED TO SPREADING THE STORY OF THE CHRIST...

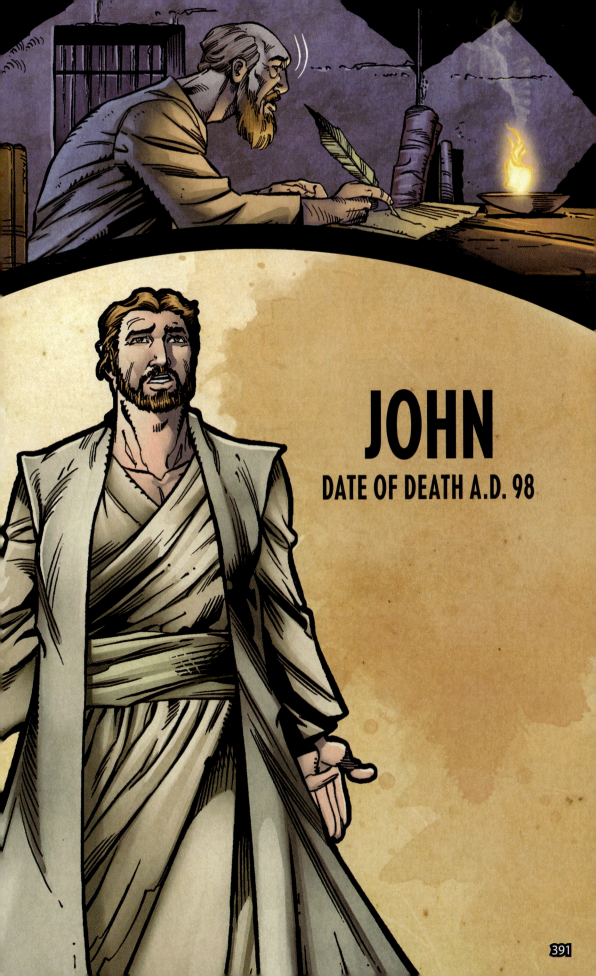

JOHN

DATE OF DEATH A.D. 98

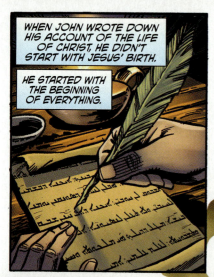

WHEN JOHN WROTE DOWN HIS ACCOUNT OF THE LIFE OF CHRIST, HE DIDN'T START WITH JESUS' BIRTH.

HE STARTED WITH THE BEGINNING OF EVERYTHING.

"IN THE BEGINNING WAS THE WORD.

"AND THE WORD WAS WITH GOD.

"AND THE WORD WAS GOD.

"THE WORD BECAME FLESH.

"AND DWELLED AMONG US.

"WE HAVE WITNESSED HIS GLORY.

"THE GLORY OF THE ONLY SON.

"THE SON WHO CAME FROM THE FATHER, FULL OF GRACE AND TRUTH.

"OUT OF HIS FULLNESS WE HAVE ALL RECEIVED GRACE.

"NO ONE HAS SEEN GOD BUT THE SON.

"AND THROUGH THE SON, THE FATHER HAS BEEN MADE KNOWN."

JOHN. THE YOUNGER BROTHER OF JAMES.

ONE OF JESUS' TRIO OF CLOSE DISCIPLES.

AN EYE WITNESS TO JESUS' LIFE...

...AND A WRITER OF JESUS' LIFE STORY.

LIKE ANDREW, JOHN WAS FIRST A DISCIPLE OF JOHN THE BAPTIST.

ABOUT THE BAPTIST, JOHN WROTE:

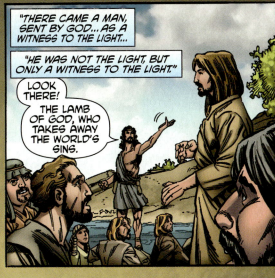

"THERE CAME A MAN, SENT BY GOD... AS A WITNESS TO THE LIGHT...

"HE WAS NOT THE LIGHT, BUT ONLY A WITNESS TO THE LIGHT."

LOOK THERE! THE LAMB OF GOD, WHO TAKES AWAY THE WORLD'S SINS.

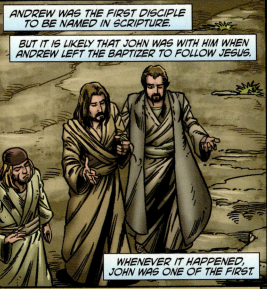

ANDREW WAS THE FIRST DISCIPLE TO BE NAMED IN SCRIPTURE.

BUT IT IS LIKELY THAT JOHN WAS WITH HIM WHEN ANDREW LEFT THE BAPTIZER TO FOLLOW JESUS.

WHENEVER IT HAPPENED, JOHN WAS ONE OF THE FIRST.

LIKE ANDREW, HE TOLD HIS OLDER BROTHER ABOUT JESUS.

HE SPOKE WITH SUCH WISDOM! WISDOM THAT CAME FROM TRUTH AND KNOWLEDGE.

SIMON, HOW WAS YOUR CATCH?

WE CAUGHT NOTHING, ZEBEDEE.

LATER THAT DAY...

HELP! THERE'S TOO MUCH!

THAT'S SIMON...

WHAT'S GOING ON?

THEY'VE PUT OUT THEIR NETS.

AT THIS HOUR?

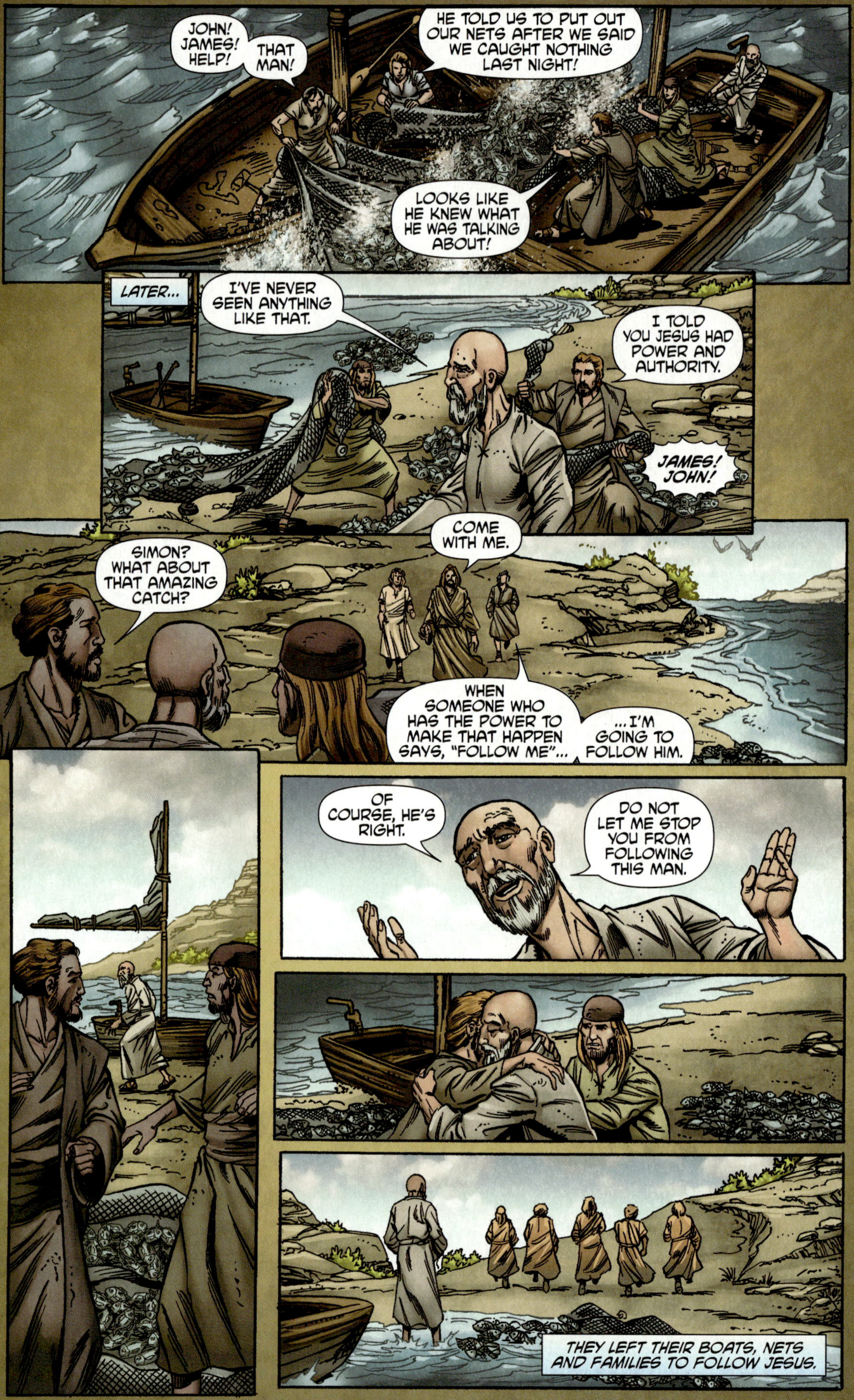

JOHN! JAMES! HELP!
THAT MAN!
HE TOLD US TO PUT OUT OUR NETS AFTER WE SAID WE CAUGHT NOTHING LAST NIGHT!
LOOKS LIKE HE KNEW WHAT HE WAS TALKING ABOUT!
LATER...
I'VE NEVER SEEN ANYTHING LIKE THAT.
I TOLD YOU JESUS HAD POWER AND AUTHORITY.
JAMES! JOHN!
SIMON? WHAT ABOUT THAT AMAZING CATCH?
COME WITH ME.
WHEN SOMEONE WHO HAS THE POWER TO MAKE THAT HAPPEN SAYS, "FOLLOW ME"...
...I'M GOING TO FOLLOW HIM.
OF COURSE, HE'S RIGHT.
DO NOT LET ME STOP YOU FROM FOLLOWING THIS MAN.
THEY LEFT THEIR BOATS, NETS AND FAMILIES TO FOLLOW JESUS.

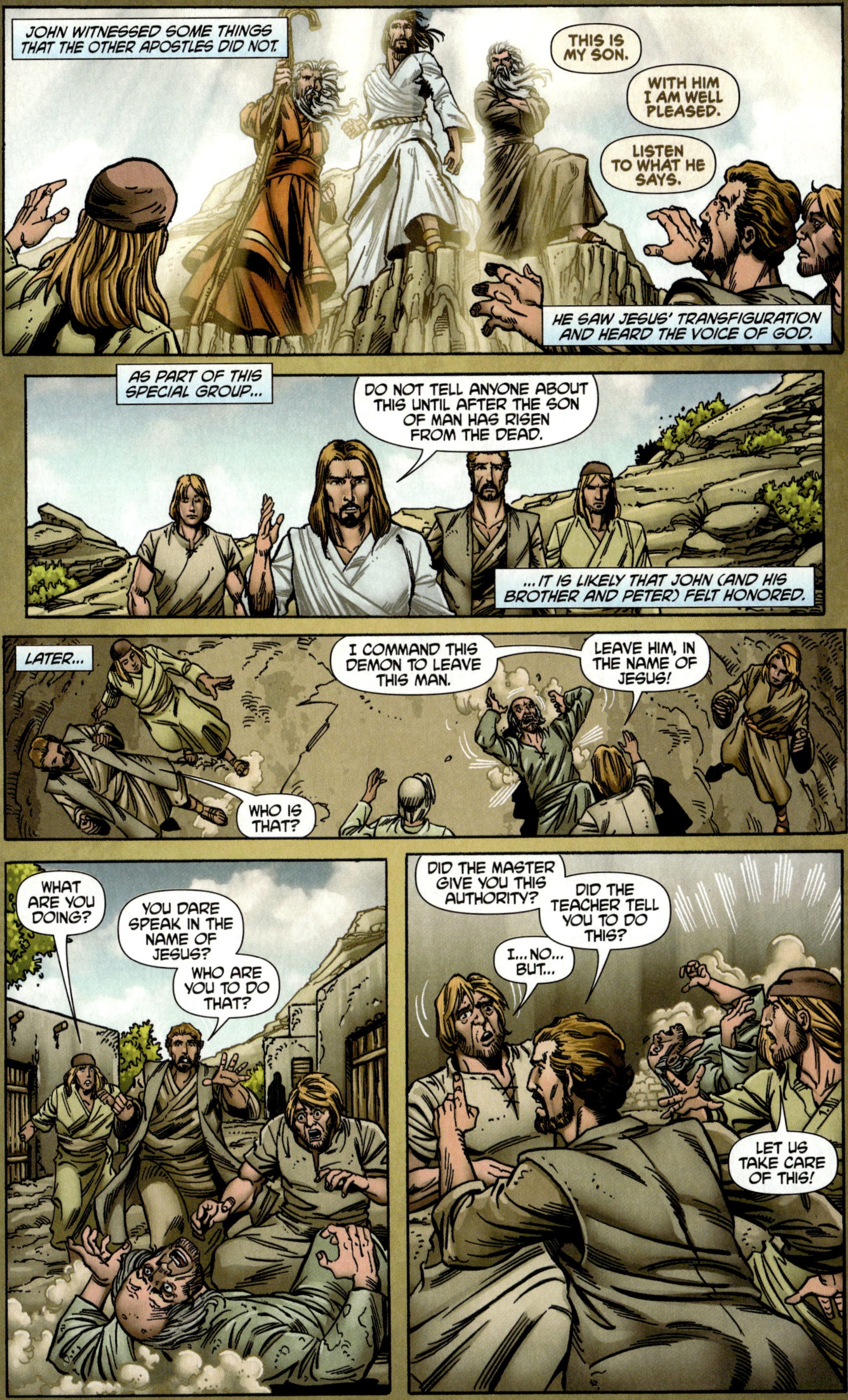
JOHN WITNESSED SOME THINGS THAT THE OTHER APOSTLES DID NOT.
THIS IS MY SON.
WITH HIM I AM WELL PLEASED.
LISTEN TO WHAT HE SAYS.
HE SAW JESUS' TRANSFIGURATION AND HEARD THE VOICE OF GOD.
AS PART OF THIS SPECIAL GROUP...
DO NOT TELL ANYONE ABOUT THIS UNTIL AFTER THE SON OF MAN HAS RISEN FROM THE DEAD.
...IT IS LIKELY THAT JOHN (AND HIS BROTHER AND PETER) FELT HONORED.
LATER...
I COMMAND THIS DEMON TO LEAVE THIS MAN.
LEAVE HIM, IN THE NAME OF JESUS!
WHO IS THAT?
WHAT ARE YOU DOING?
YOU DARE SPEAK IN THE NAME OF JESUS?
WHO ARE YOU TO DO THAT?
DID THE MASTER GIVE YOU THIS AUTHORITY?
DID THE TEACHER TELL YOU TO DO THIS?
I... NO... BUT...
LET US TAKE CARE OF THIS!

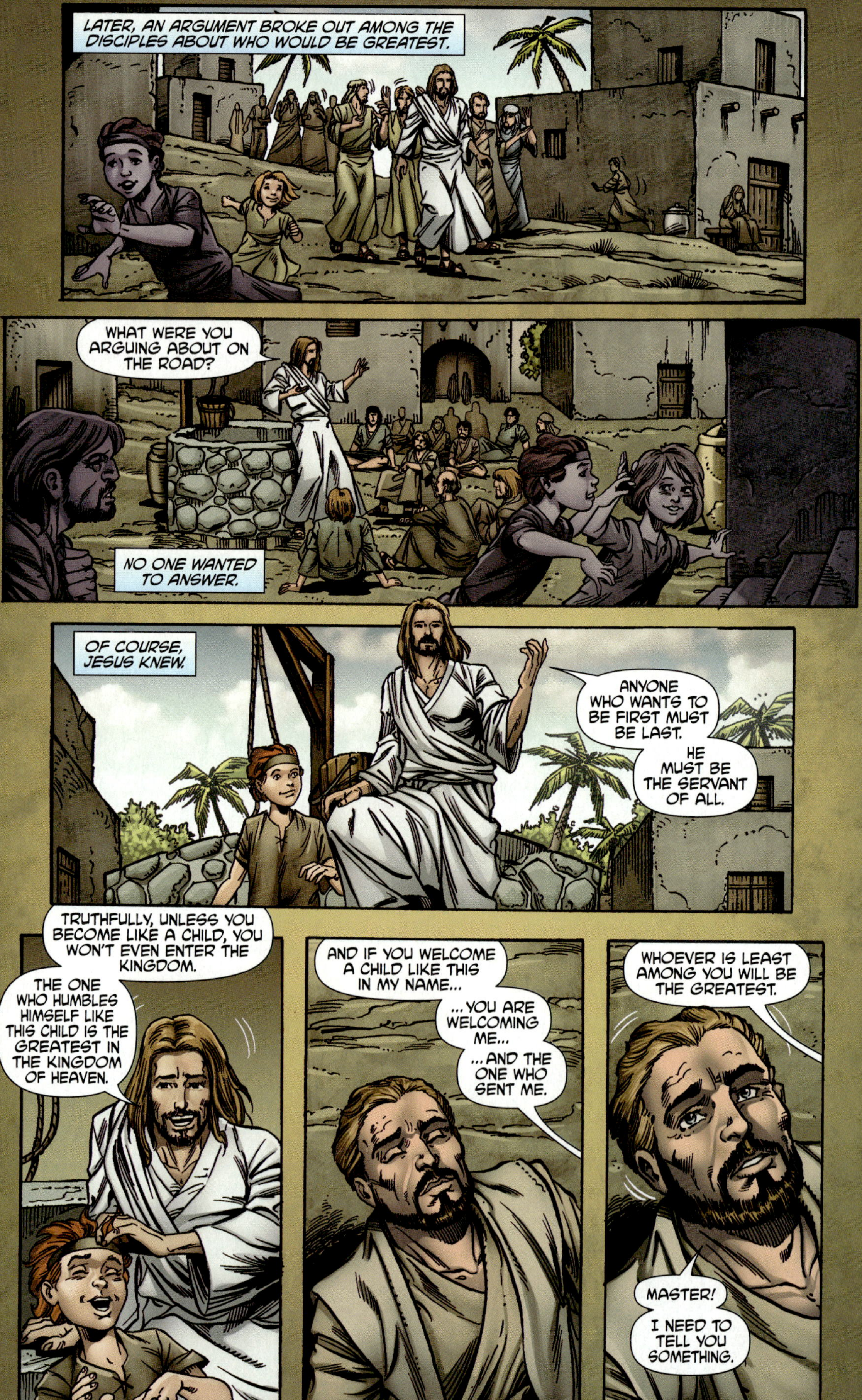
LATER, AN ARGUMENT BROKE OUT AMONG THE DISCIPLES ABOUT WHO WOULD BE GREATEST.
WHAT WERE YOU ARGUING ABOUT ON THE ROAD?
NO ONE WANTED TO ANSWER.
OF COURSE, JESUS KNEW.
ANYONE WHO WANTS TO BE FIRST MUST BE LAST.
HE MUST BE THE SERVANT OF ALL.
TRUTHFULLY, UNLESS YOU BECOME LIKE A CHILD, YOU WON'T EVEN ENTER THE KINGDOM.
THE ONE WHO HUMBLES HIMSELF LIKE THIS CHILD IS THE GREATEST IN THE KINGDOM OF HEAVEN.
AND IF YOU WELCOME A CHILD LIKE THIS IN MY NAME...
...YOU ARE WELCOMING ME...
...AND THE ONE WHO SENT ME.
WHOEVER IS LEAST AMONG YOU WILL BE THE GREATEST.
MASTER!
I NEED TO TELL YOU SOMETHING.

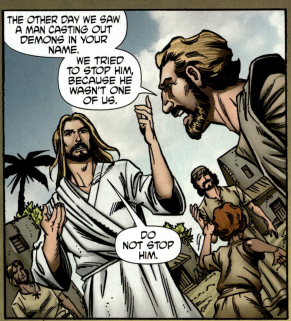

THE OTHER DAY WE SAW A MAN CASTING OUT DEMONS IN YOUR NAME.

WE TRIED TO STOP HIM, BECAUSE HE WASN'T ONE OF US.

DO NOT STOP HIM.

NO ONE WHO DOES A MIRACLE IN MY NAME IS AGAINST ME.

ANYONE WHO IS NOT AGAINST US IS FOR US.

ANYONE WHO GIVES YOU A CUP OF WATER IN MY NAME WILL NOT LOSE HIS REWARD!

THAT WAS NOT THE FIRST TIME THE DISCIPLES HAD HEARD A SURPRISING LESSON ABOUT "GREATNESS" IN GOD'S KINGDOM...

...AND IT WAS NOT THE LAST.

THE TOWN HAS NO PLACE FOR YOU TO STAY!

DO YOU WANT US TO CALL DOWN FIRE ON THEM LIKE ELIJAH DID?

DO YOU KNOW WHAT YOU ARE SAYING?

THE SON OF MAN COMES NOT TO DESTROY MEN'S LIVES, BUT TO SAVE THEM.

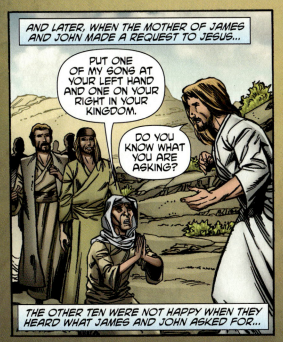

AND LATER, WHEN THE MOTHER OF JAMES AND JOHN MADE A REQUEST TO JESUS...

PUT ONE OF MY SONS AT YOUR LEFT HAND AND ONE ON YOUR RIGHT IN YOUR KINGDOM.

DO YOU KNOW WHAT YOU ARE ASKING?

THE OTHER TEN WERE NOT HAPPY WHEN THEY HEARD WHAT JAMES AND JOHN ASKED FOR...

...SO ONCE MORE JESUS EXPLAINED WHAT IT MEANT TO BE IN HIS KINGDOM.

WHOEVER WANTS TO BE GREAT MUST BE A SERVANT.

THE SON OF MAN DID NOT COME TO BE SERVED.

I CAME TO SERVE OTHERS AND TO GIVE MY LIFE AS THE RANSOM FOR MANY!

NOT LONG AFTERWARD, THE TWELVE LEARNED WHAT HE MEANT.

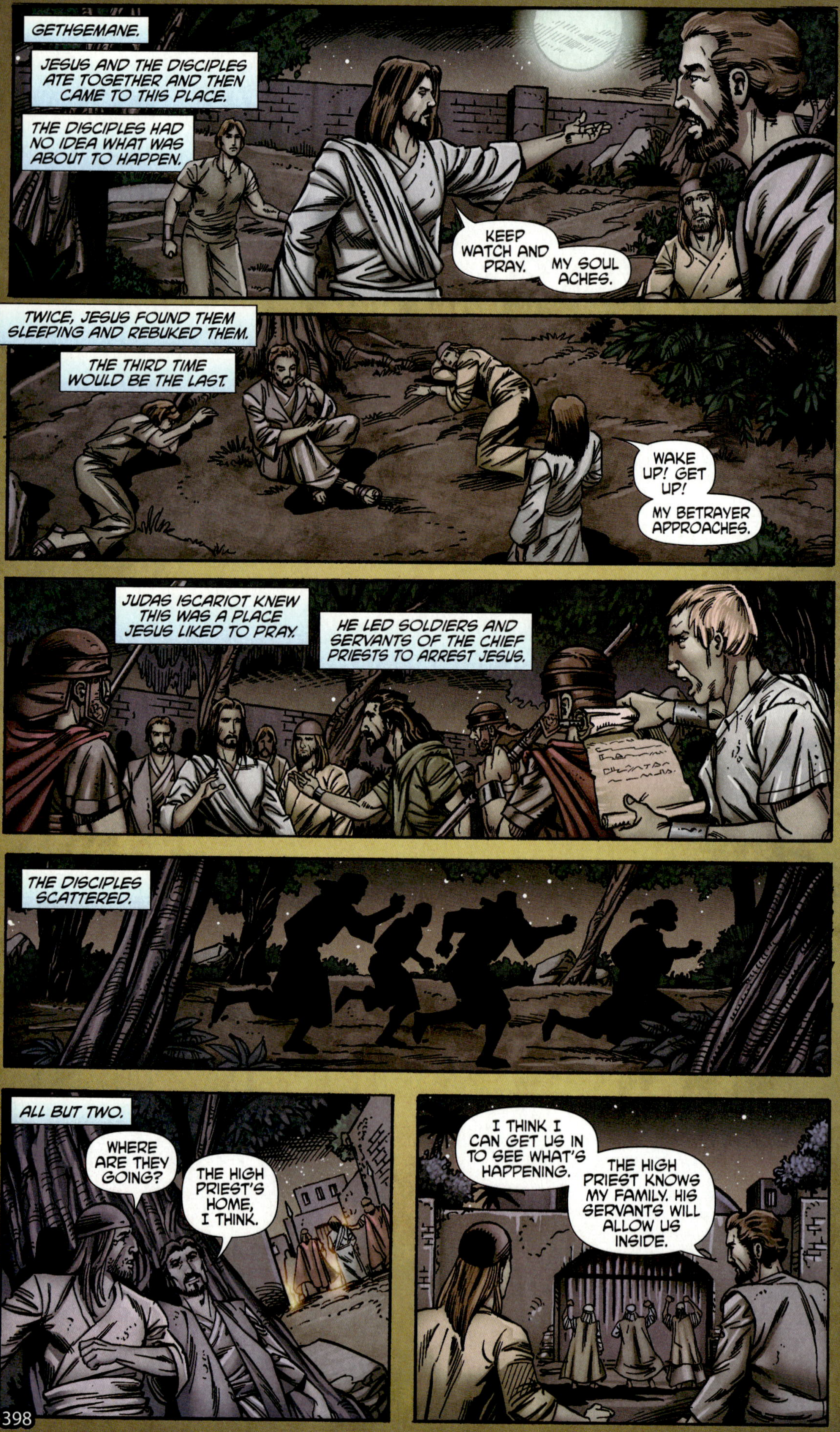
GETHSEMANE.
JESUS AND THE DISCIPLES ATE TOGETHER AND THEN CAME TO THIS PLACE.
THE DISCIPLES HAD NO IDEA WHAT WAS ABOUT TO HAPPEN.
KEEP WATCH AND PRAY.
MY SOUL ACHES.
TWICE, JESUS FOUND THEM SLEEPING AND REBUKED THEM.
THE THIRD TIME WOULD BE THE LAST.
WAKE UP! GET UP!
MY BETRAYER APPROACHES.
JUDAS ISCARIOT KNEW THIS WAS A PLACE JESUS LIKED TO PRAY.
HE LED SOLDIERS AND SERVANTS OF THE CHIEF PRIESTS TO ARREST JESUS.
THE DISCIPLES SCATTERED.
ALL BUT TWO.
WHERE ARE THEY GOING?
THE HIGH PRIEST'S HOME, I THINK.
I THINK I CAN GET US IN TO SEE WHAT'S HAPPENING.
THE HIGH PRIEST KNOWS MY FAMILY. HIS SERVANTS WILL ALLOW US INSIDE.

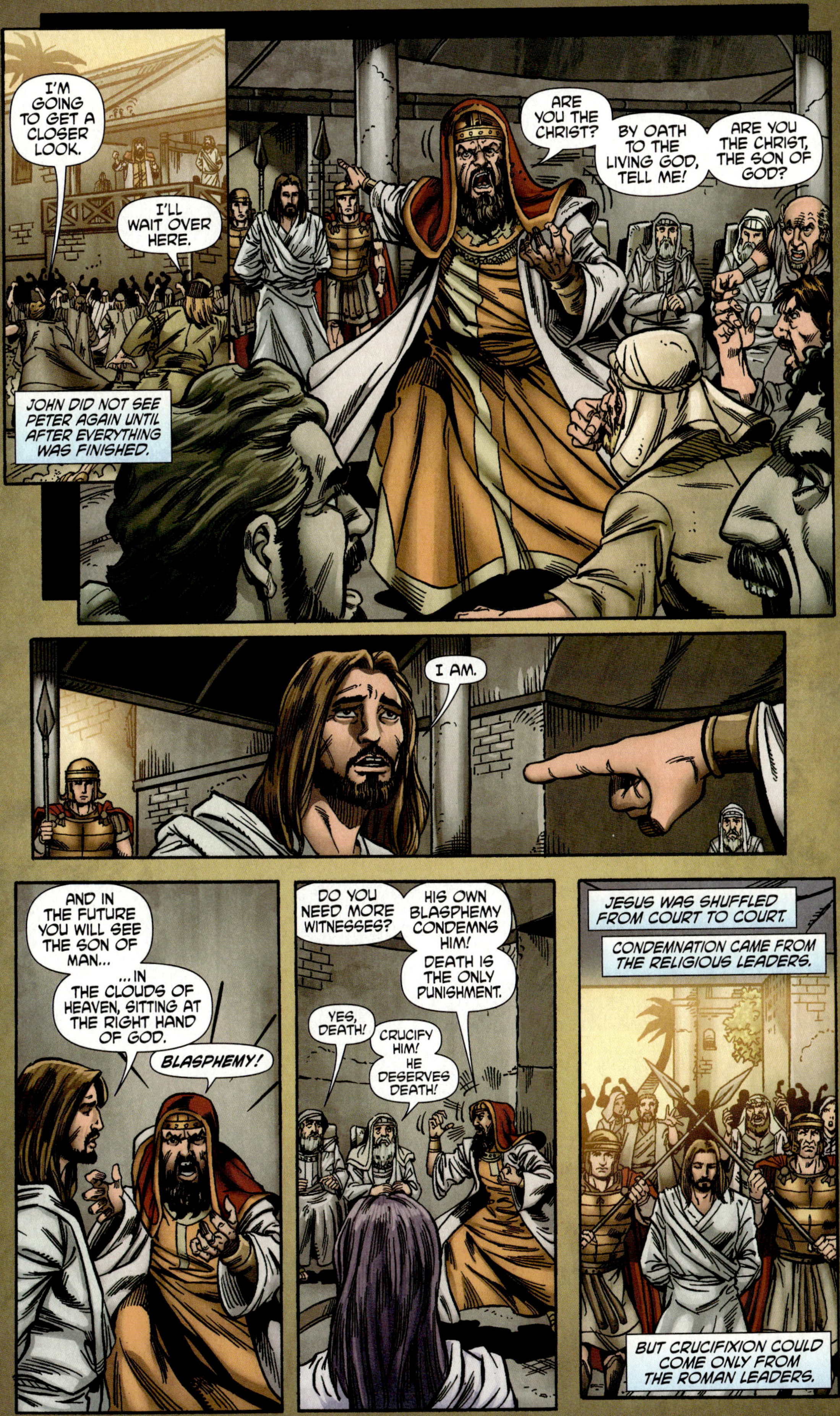
I'M GOING TO GET A CLOSER LOOK.
I'LL WAIT OVER HERE.
JOHN DID NOT SEE PETER AGAIN UNTIL AFTER EVERYTHING WAS FINISHED.
ARE YOU THE CHRIST?
BY OATH TO THE LIVING GOD, TELL ME!
ARE YOU THE CHRIST, THE SON OF GOD?
I AM.
AND IN THE FUTURE YOU WILL SEE THE SON OF MAN...
...IN THE CLOUDS OF HEAVEN, SITTING AT THE RIGHT HAND OF GOD.
BLASPHEMY!
DO YOU NEED MORE WITNESSES?
HIS OWN BLASPHEMY CONDEMNS HIM!
DEATH IS THE ONLY PUNISHMENT.
YES, DEATH!
CRUCIFY HIM!
HE DESERVES DEATH!
JESUS WAS SHUFFLED FROM COURT TO COURT.
CONDEMNATION CAME FROM THE RELIGIOUS LEADERS.
BUT CRUCIFIXION COULD COME ONLY FROM THE ROMAN LEADERS.

FINALLY, JESUS WAS BROUGHT BEFORE PILATE, THE ROMAN GOVERNOR.

AFTER A LENGTHY TRIAL PROCESS...

WHAT WOULD YOU HAVE ME DO WITH THIS MAN YOU SAY CLAIMS TO BE "KING OF THE JEWS"?

CRUCIFY HIM!

NO.

CRUCIFY HIM!

EVENTUALLY, PILATE GAVE IN.

THE ROMANS BEAT AND MOCKED JESUS, AND THEN HAD HIM CARRY HIS OWN CROSS.

THIS CAN'T BE HAPPENING!

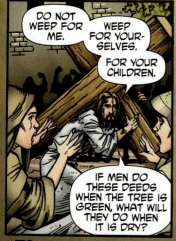

DO NOT WEEP FOR ME.

WEEP FOR YOUR-SELVES.

FOR YOUR CHILDREN.

IF MEN DO THESE DEEDS WHEN THE TREE IS GREEN, WHAT WILL THEY DO WHEN IT IS DRY?

MARY!

YOU SHOULD NOT SEE THIS.

HE IS MY SON!

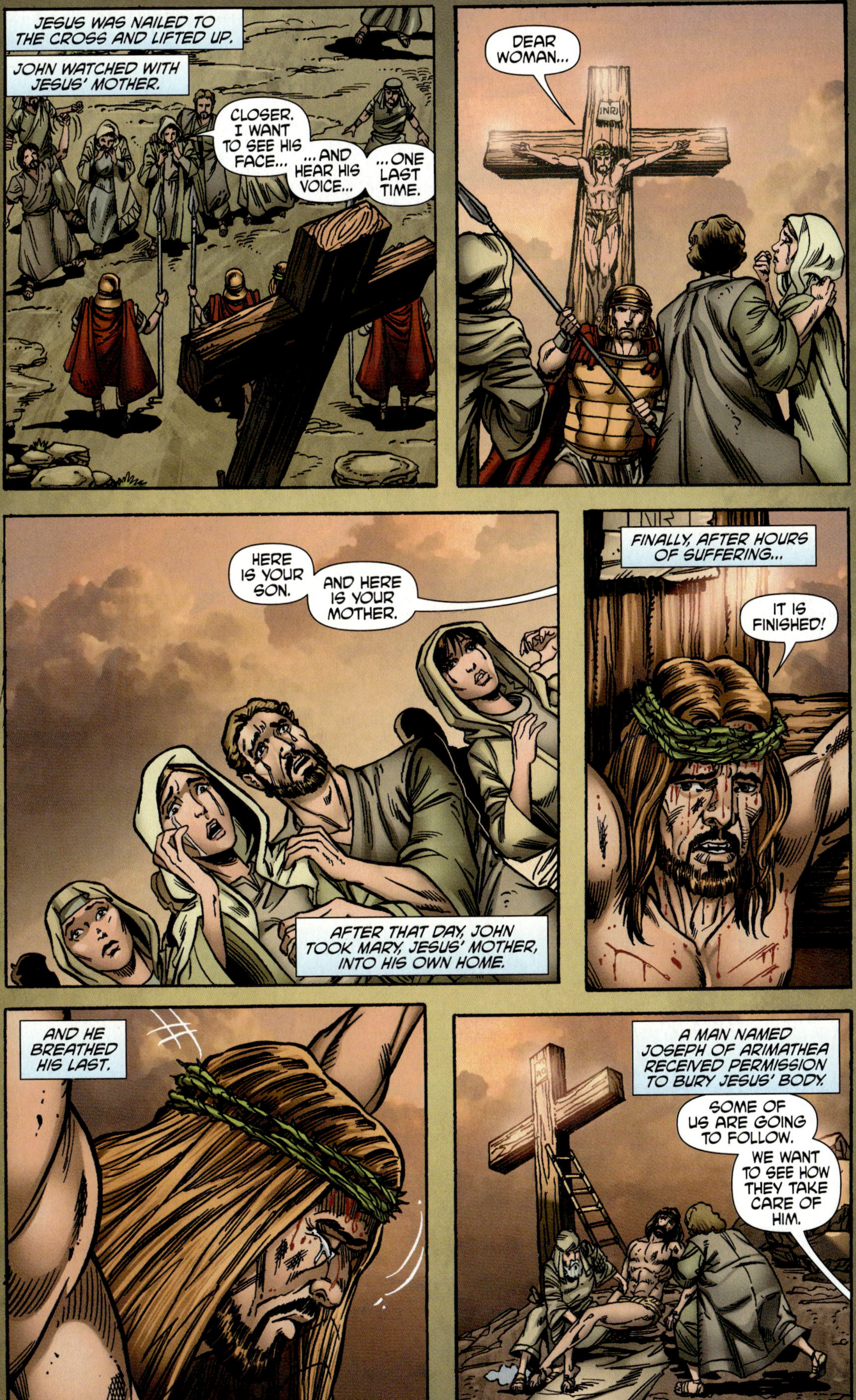

JESUS WAS NAILED TO THE CROSS AND LIFTED UP.
JOHN WATCHED WITH JESUS' MOTHER.
CLOSER. I WANT TO SEE HIS FACE...
...AND HEAR HIS VOICE...
...ONE LAST TIME.
DEAR WOMAN...
INRI
HERE IS YOUR SON.
AND HERE IS YOUR MOTHER.
AFTER THAT DAY, JOHN TOOK MARY, JESUS' MOTHER, INTO HIS OWN HOME.
FINALLY, AFTER HOURS OF SUFFERING...
IT IS FINISHED!
AND HE BREATHED HIS LAST.
A MAN NAMED JOSEPH OF ARIMATHEA RECEIVED PERMISSION TO BURY JESUS' BODY.
SOME OF US ARE GOING TO FOLLOW.
WE WANT TO SEE HOW THEY TAKE CARE OF HIM.

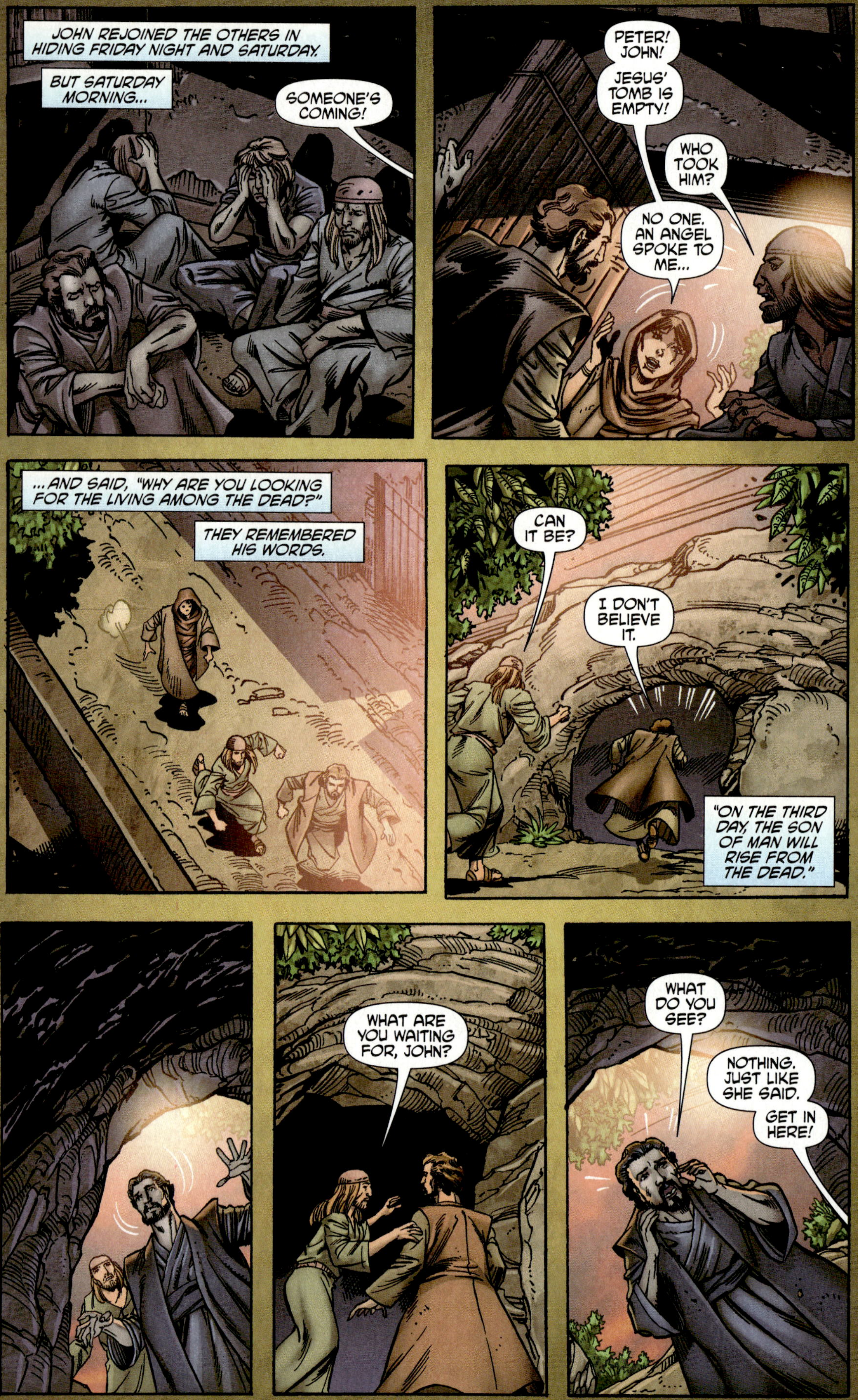
JOHN REJOINED THE OTHERS IN HIDING FRIDAY NIGHT AND SATURDAY.
BUT SATURDAY MORNING...
SOMEONE'S COMING!
PETER! JOHN!
JESUS' TOMB IS EMPTY!
WHO TOOK HIM?
NO ONE. AN ANGEL SPOKE TO ME...
...AND SAID, "WHY ARE YOU LOOKING FOR THE LIVING AMONG THE DEAD?"
THEY REMEMBERED HIS WORDS.
CAN IT BE?
I DON'T BELIEVE IT.
"ON THE THIRD DAY, THE SON OF MAN WILL RISE FROM THE DEAD."
WHAT ARE YOU WAITING FOR, JOHN?
WHAT DO YOU SEE?
NOTHING. JUST LIKE SHE SAID.
GET IN HERE!

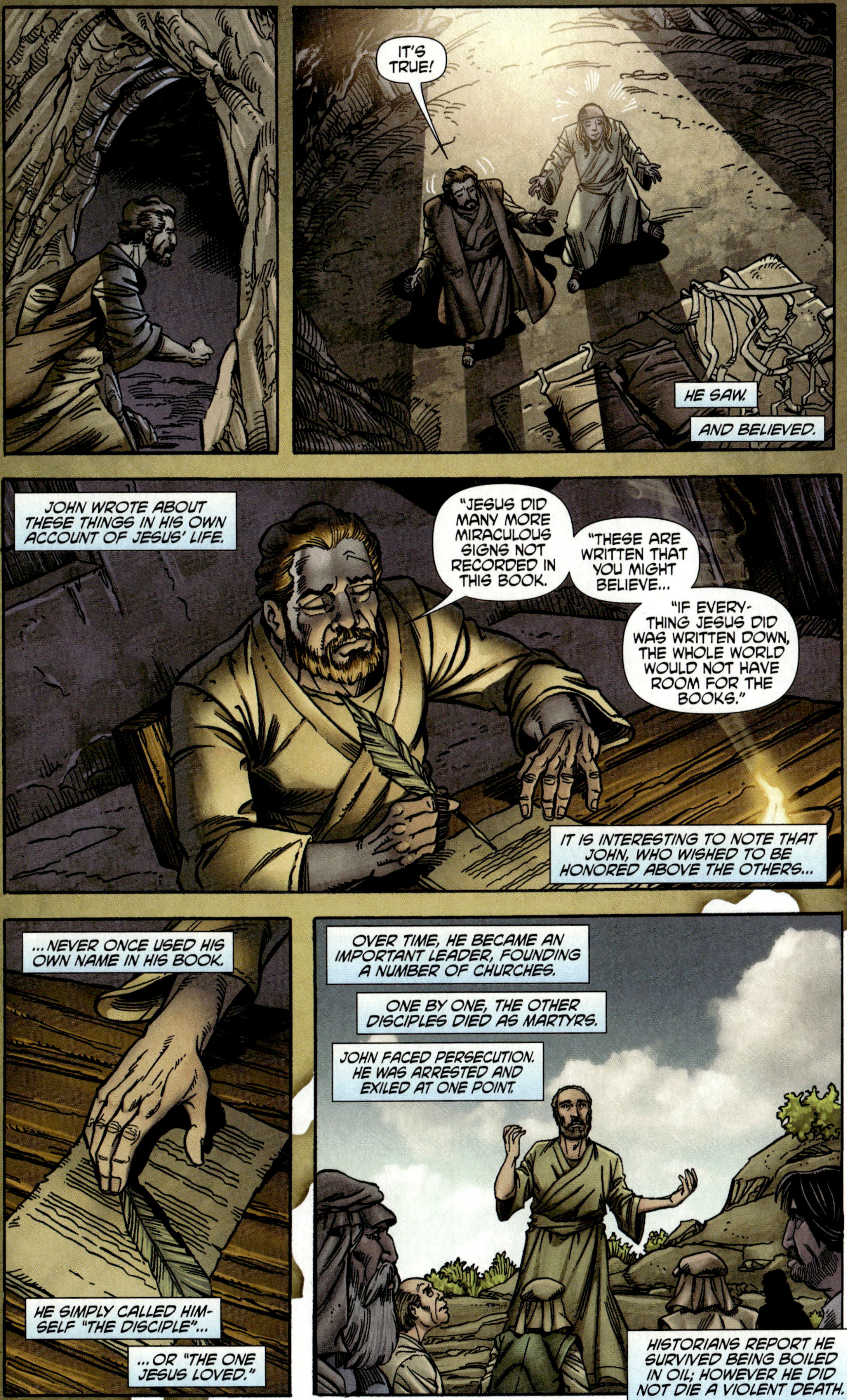

IT'S TRUE!
HE SAW.
AND BELIEVED.
JOHN WROTE ABOUT THESE THINGS IN HIS OWN ACCOUNT OF JESUS' LIFE.
"JESUS DID MANY MORE MIRACULOUS SIGNS NOT RECORDED IN THIS BOOK.
"THESE ARE WRITTEN THAT YOU MIGHT BELIEVE...
"IF EVERYTHING JESUS DID WAS WRITTEN DOWN, THE WHOLE WORLD WOULD NOT HAVE ROOM FOR THE BOOKS."
IT IS INTERESTING TO NOTE THAT JOHN, WHO WISHED TO BE HONORED ABOVE THE OTHERS...
...NEVER ONCE USED HIS OWN NAME IN HIS BOOK.
HE SIMPLY CALLED HIMSELF "THE DISCIPLE"...
...OR "THE ONE JESUS LOVED."
OVER TIME, HE BECAME AN IMPORTANT LEADER, FOUNDING A NUMBER OF CHURCHES.
ONE BY ONE, THE OTHER DISCIPLES DIED AS MARTYRS.
JOHN FACED PERSECUTION. HE WAS ARRESTED AND EXILED AT ONE POINT.
HISTORIANS REPORT HE SURVIVED BEING BOILED IN OIL; HOWEVER HE DID NOT DIE A VIOLENT DEATH.

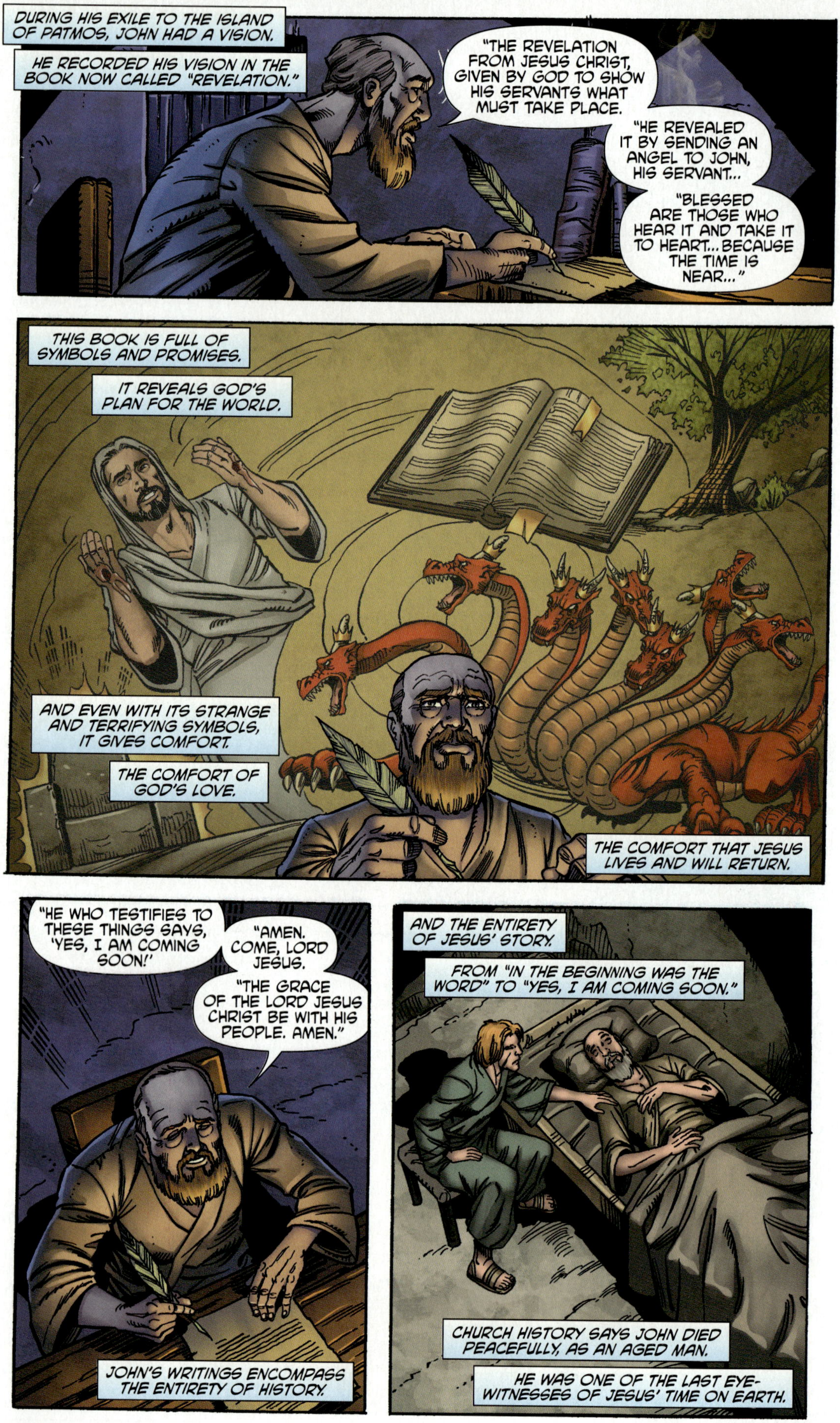
DURING HIS EXILE TO THE ISLAND OF PATMOS, JOHN HAD A VISION.
HE RECORDED HIS VISION IN THE BOOK NOW CALLED "REVELATION."
"THE REVELATION FROM JESUS CHRIST, GIVEN BY GOD TO SHOW HIS SERVANTS WHAT MUST TAKE PLACE.
"HE REVEALED IT BY SENDING AN ANGEL TO JOHN, HIS SERVANT...
"BLESSED ARE THOSE WHO HEAR IT AND TAKE IT TO HEART...BECAUSE THE TIME IS NEAR..."
THIS BOOK IS FULL OF SYMBOLS AND PROMISES.
IT REVEALS GOD'S PLAN FOR THE WORLD.
AND EVEN WITH ITS STRANGE AND TERRIFYING SYMBOLS, IT GIVES COMFORT.
THE COMFORT OF GOD'S LOVE.
THE COMFORT THAT JESUS LIVES AND WILL RETURN.
"HE WHO TESTIFIES TO THESE THINGS SAYS, 'YES, I AM COMING SOON!'
"AMEN. COME, LORD JESUS.
"THE GRACE OF THE LORD JESUS CHRIST BE WITH HIS PEOPLE. AMEN."
JOHN'S WRITINGS ENCOMPASS THE ENTIRETY OF HISTORY.
AND THE ENTIRETY OF JESUS' STORY.
FROM "IN THE BEGINNING WAS THE WORD" TO "YES, I AM COMING SOON."
CHURCH HISTORY SAYS JOHN DIED PEACEFULLY, AS AN AGED MAN.
HE WAS ONE OF THE LAST EYE-WITNESSES OF JESUS' TIME ON EARTH.

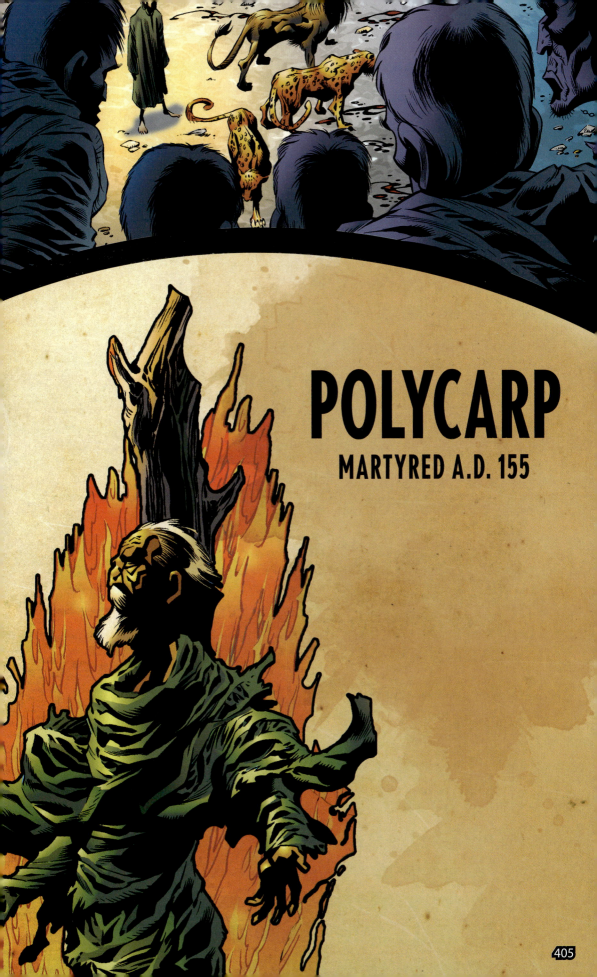

POLYCARP

MARTYRED A.D. 155

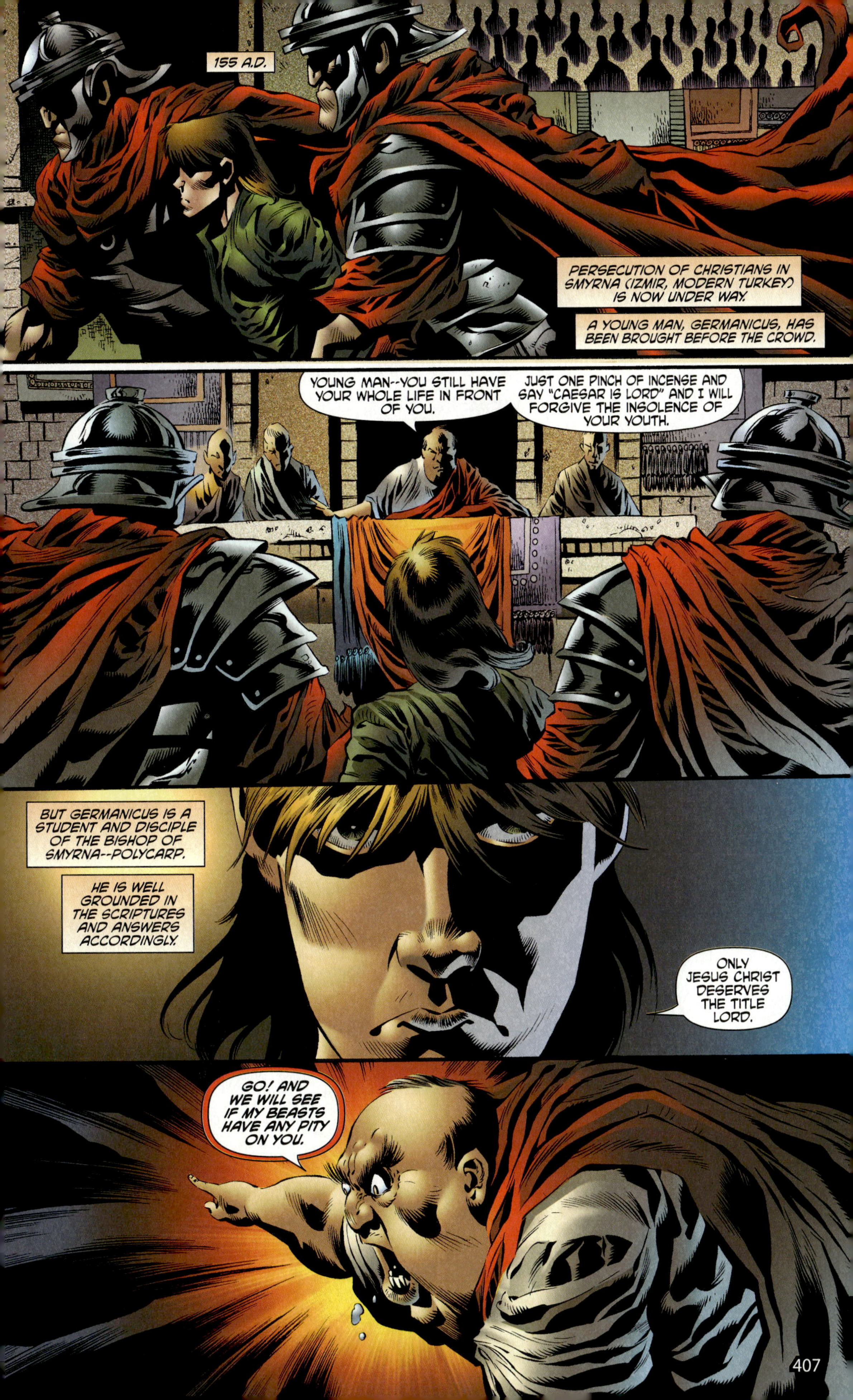
155 A.D.
PERSECUTION OF CHRISTIANS IN SMYRNA (IZMIR, MODERN TURKEY) IS NOW UNDER WAY.
A YOUNG MAN, GERMANICUS, HAS BEEN BROUGHT BEFORE THE CROWD.
YOUNG MAN--YOU STILL HAVE YOUR WHOLE LIFE IN FRONT OF YOU.
JUST ONE PINCH OF INCENSE AND SAY "CAESAR IS LORD" AND I WILL FORGIVE THE INSOLENCE OF YOUR YOUTH.
BUT GERMANICUS IS A STUDENT AND DISCIPLE OF THE BISHOP OF SMYRNA--POLYCARP.
HE IS WELL GROUNDED IN THE SCRIPTURES AND ANSWERS ACCORDINGLY.
ONLY JESUS CHRIST DESERVES THE TITLE LORD.
GO! AND WE WILL SEE IF MY BEASTS HAVE ANY PITY ON YOU.

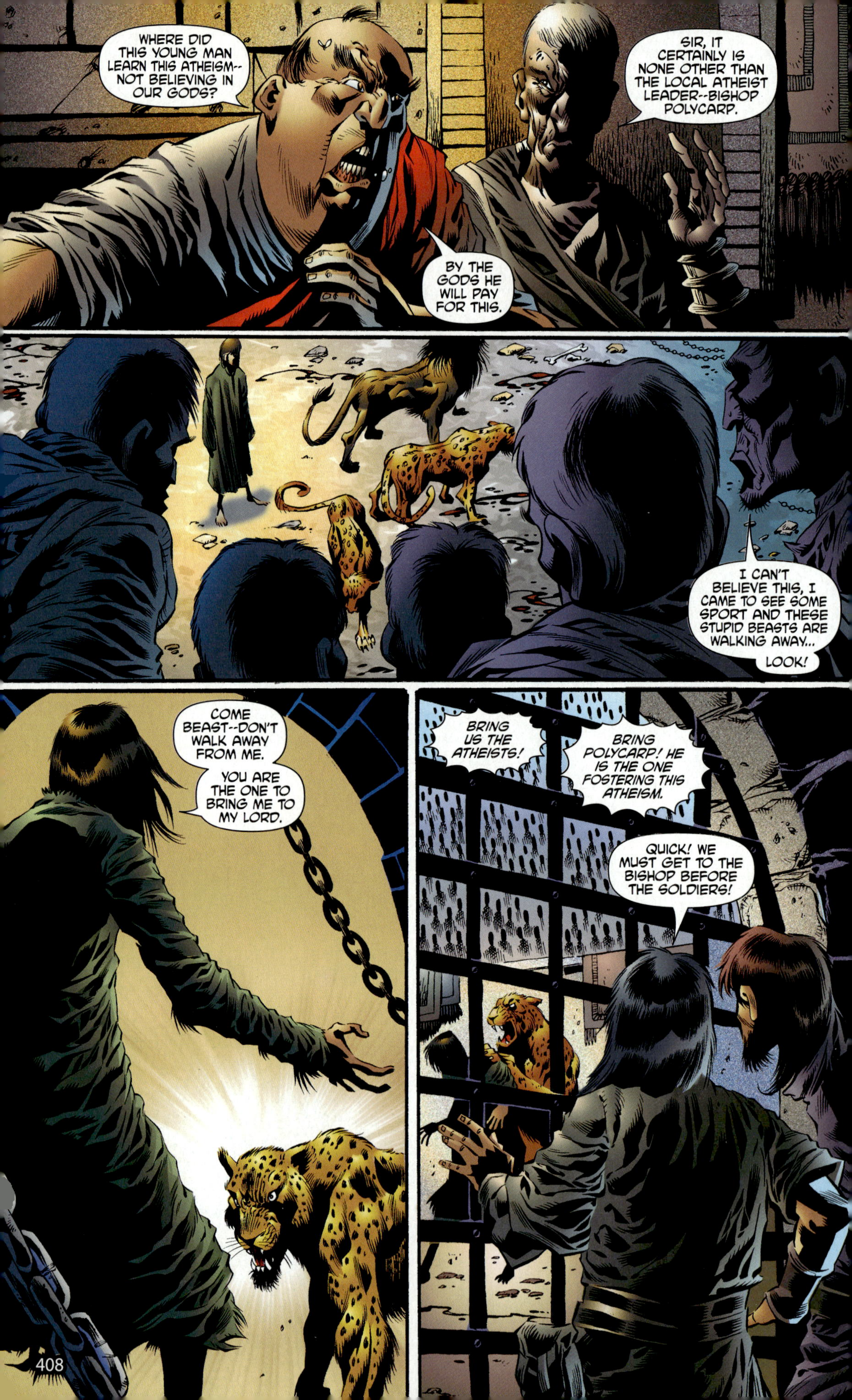
WHERE DID THIS YOUNG MAN LEARN THIS ATHEISM--NOT BELIEVING IN OUR GODS?
SIR, IT CERTAINLY IS NONE OTHER THAN THE LOCAL ATHEIST LEADER--BISHOP POLYCARP.
BY THE GODS HE WILL PAY FOR THIS.
I CAN'T BELIEVE THIS, I CAME TO SEE SOME SPORT AND THESE STUPID BEASTS ARE WALKING AWAY...
LOOK!
COME BEAST--DON'T WALK AWAY FROM ME.
YOU ARE THE ONE TO BRING ME TO MY LORD.
BRING US THE ATHEISTS!
BRING POLYCARP! HE IS THE ONE FOSTERING THIS ATHEISM.
QUICK! WE MUST GET TO THE BISHOP BEFORE THE SOLDIERS!

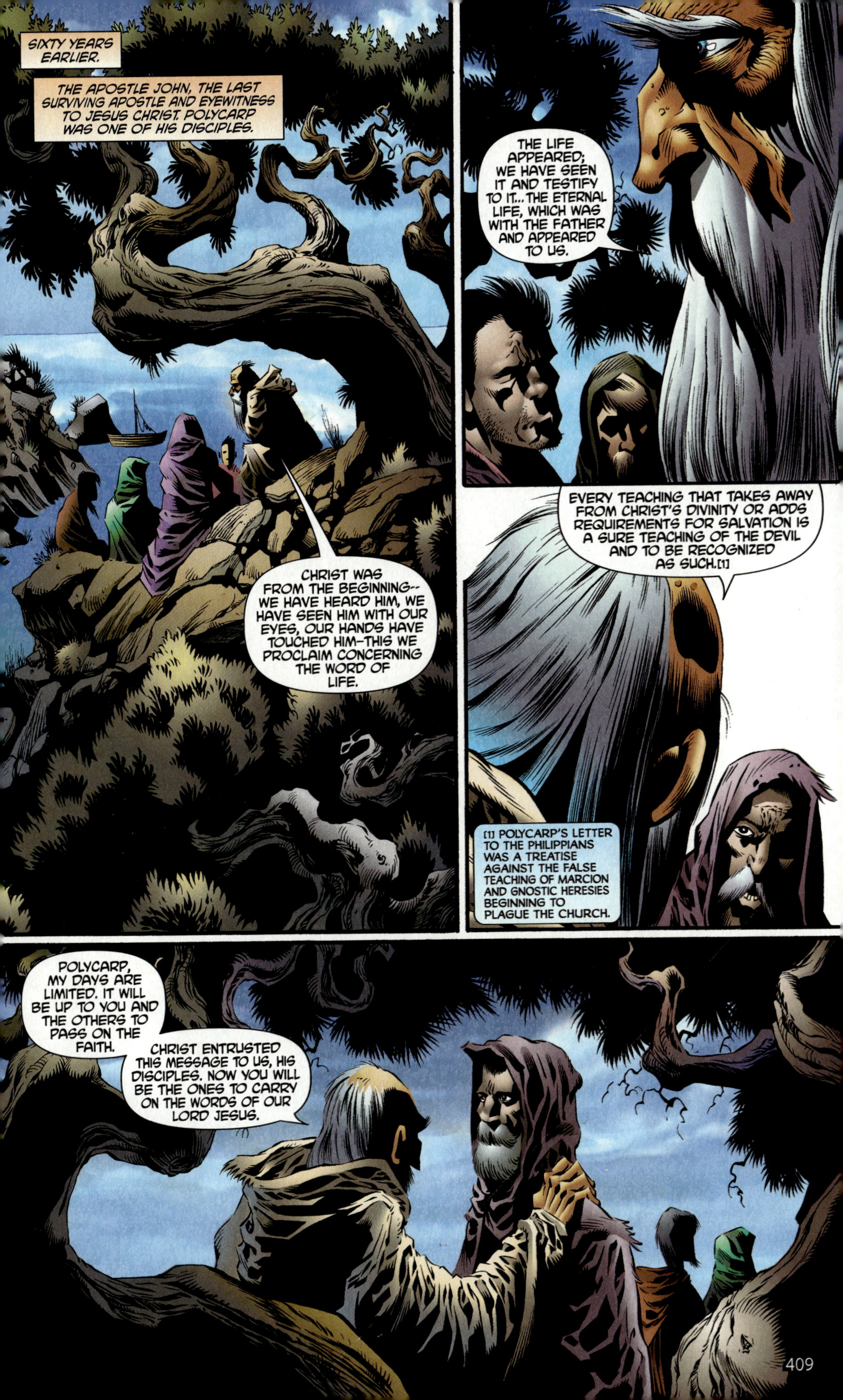
SIXTY YEARS EARLIER.
THE APOSTLE JOHN, THE LAST SURVIVING APOSTLE AND EYEWITNESS TO JESUS CHRIST. POLYCARP WAS ONE OF HIS DISCIPLES.
CHRIST WAS FROM THE BEGINNING-- WE HAVE HEARD HIM, WE HAVE SEEN HIM WITH OUR EYES, OUR HANDS HAVE TOUCHED HIM--THIS WE PROCLAIM CONCERNING THE WORD OF LIFE.
THE LIFE APPEARED; WE HAVE SEEN IT AND TESTIFY TO IT... THE ETERNAL LIFE, WHICH WAS WITH THE FATHER AND APPEARED TO US.
EVERY TEACHING THAT TAKES AWAY FROM CHRIST'S DIVINITY OR ADDS REQUIREMENTS FOR SALVATION IS A SURE TEACHING OF THE DEVIL AND TO BE RECOGNIZED AS SUCH.[1]
[1] POLYCARP'S LETTER TO THE PHILIPPIANS WAS A TREATISE AGAINST THE FALSE TEACHING OF MARCION AND GNOSTIC HERESIES BEGINNING TO PLAGUE THE CHURCH.
POLYCARP, MY DAYS ARE LIMITED. IT WILL BE UP TO YOU AND THE OTHERS TO PASS ON THE FAITH.
CHRIST ENTRUSTED THIS MESSAGE TO US, HIS DISCIPLES. NOW YOU WILL BE THE ONES TO CARRY ON THE WORDS OF OUR LORD JESUS.

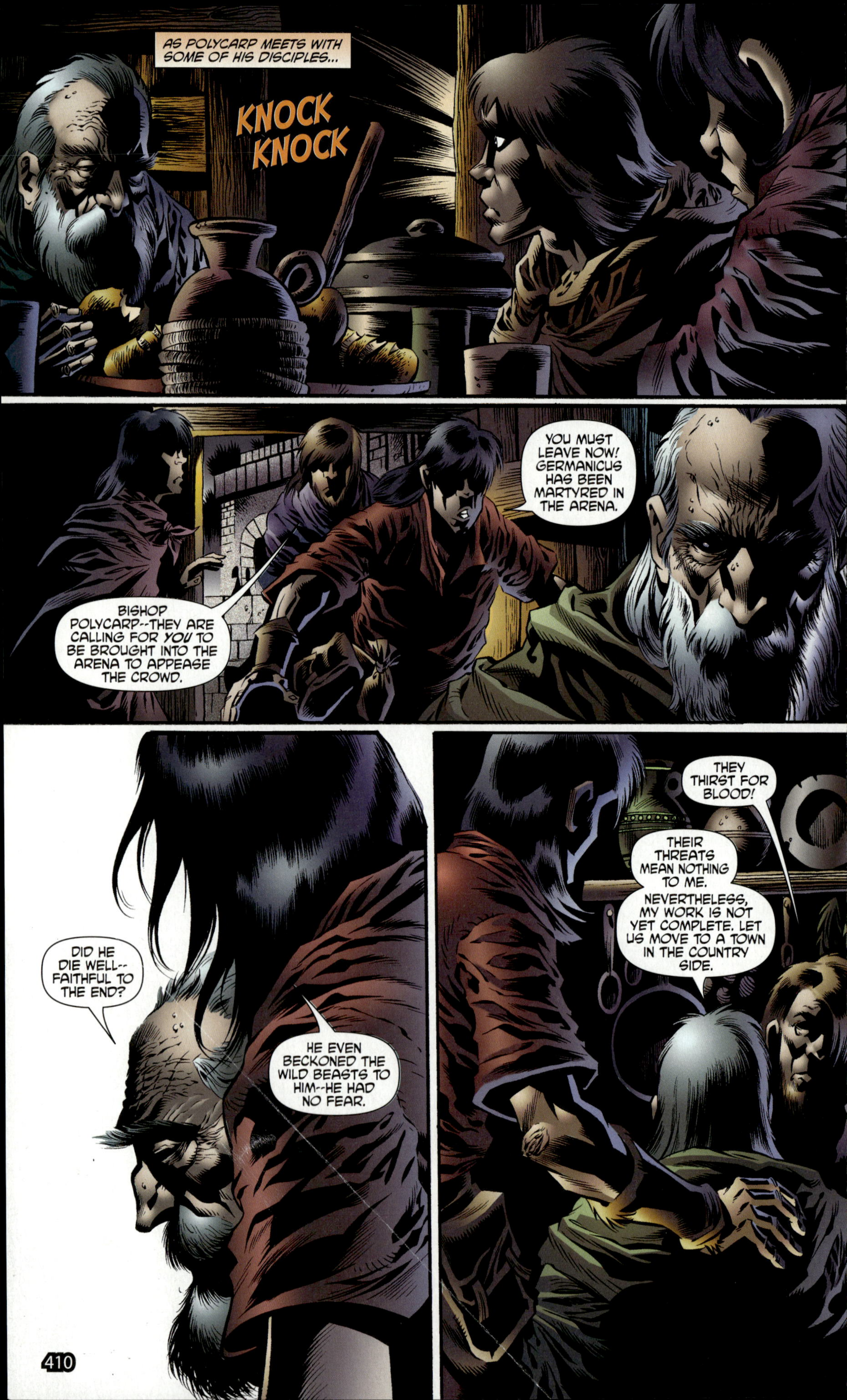
AS POLYCARP MEETS WITH SOME OF HIS DISCIPLES...
KNOCK KNOCK
YOU MUST LEAVE NOW! GERMANICUS HAS BEEN MARTYRED IN THE ARENA.
BISHOP POLYCARP--THEY ARE CALLING FOR YOU TO BE BROUGHT INTO THE ARENA TO APPEASE THE CROWD.
DID HE DIE WELL--FAITHFUL TO THE END?
HE EVEN BECKONED THE WILD BEASTS TO HIM--HE HAD NO FEAR.
THEY THIRST FOR BLOOD!
THEIR THREATS MEAN NOTHING TO ME.
NEVERTHELESS, MY WORK IS NOT YET COMPLETE. LET US MOVE TO A TOWN IN THE COUNTRY SIDE.

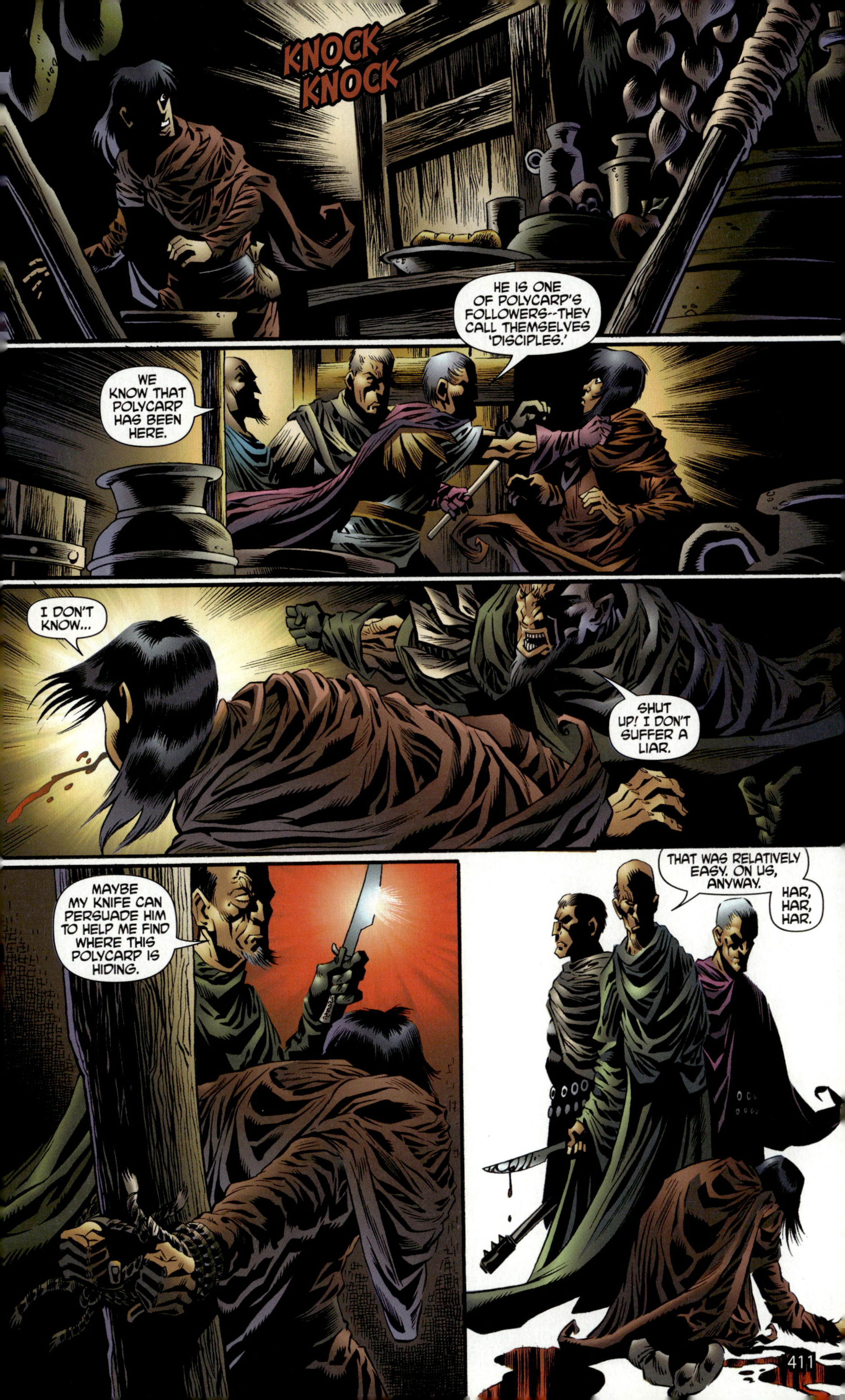
KNOCK KNOCK
HE IS ONE OF POLYCARP'S FOLLOWERS--THEY CALL THEMSELVES 'DISCIPLES.'
WE KNOW THAT POLYCARP HAS BEEN HERE.
I DON'T KNOW...
SHUT UP! I DON'T SUFFER A LIAR.
MAYBE MY KNIFE CAN PERSUADE HIM TO HELP ME FIND WHERE THIS POLYCARP IS HIDING.
THAT WAS RELATIVELY EASY. ON US, ANYWAY.
HAR, HAR, HAR.

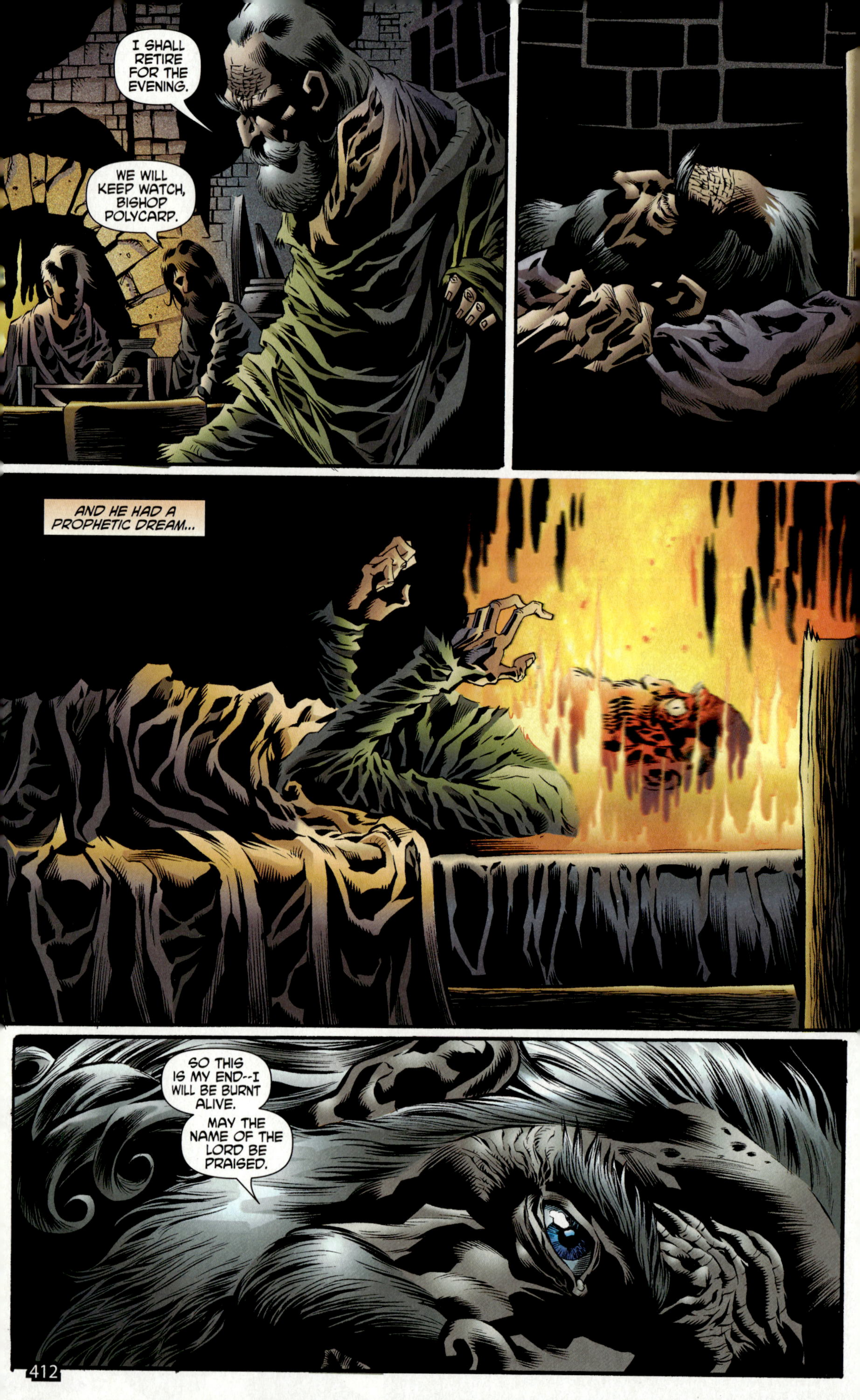
I SHALL RETIRE FOR THE EVENING.
WE WILL KEEP WATCH, BISHOP POLYCARP.
AND HE HAD A PROPHETIC DREAM...
SO THIS IS MY END--I WILL BE BURNT ALIVE.
MAY THE NAME OF THE LORD BE PRAISED.

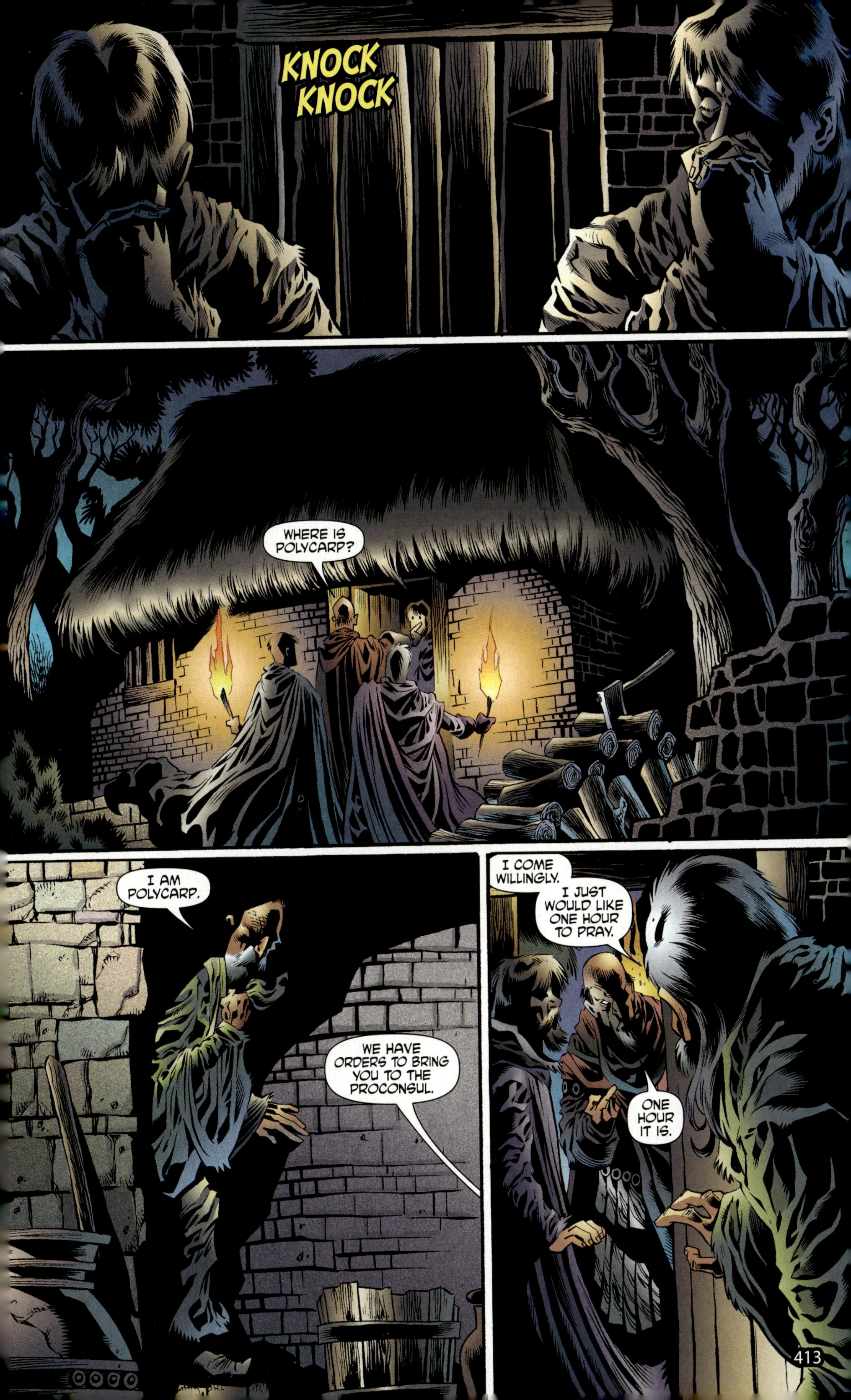
KNOCK KNOCK
WHERE IS POLYCARP?
I AM POLYCARP.
WE HAVE ORDERS TO BRING YOU TO THE PROCONSUL.
I COME WILLINGLY.
I JUST WOULD LIKE ONE HOUR TO PRAY.
ONE HOUR IT IS.

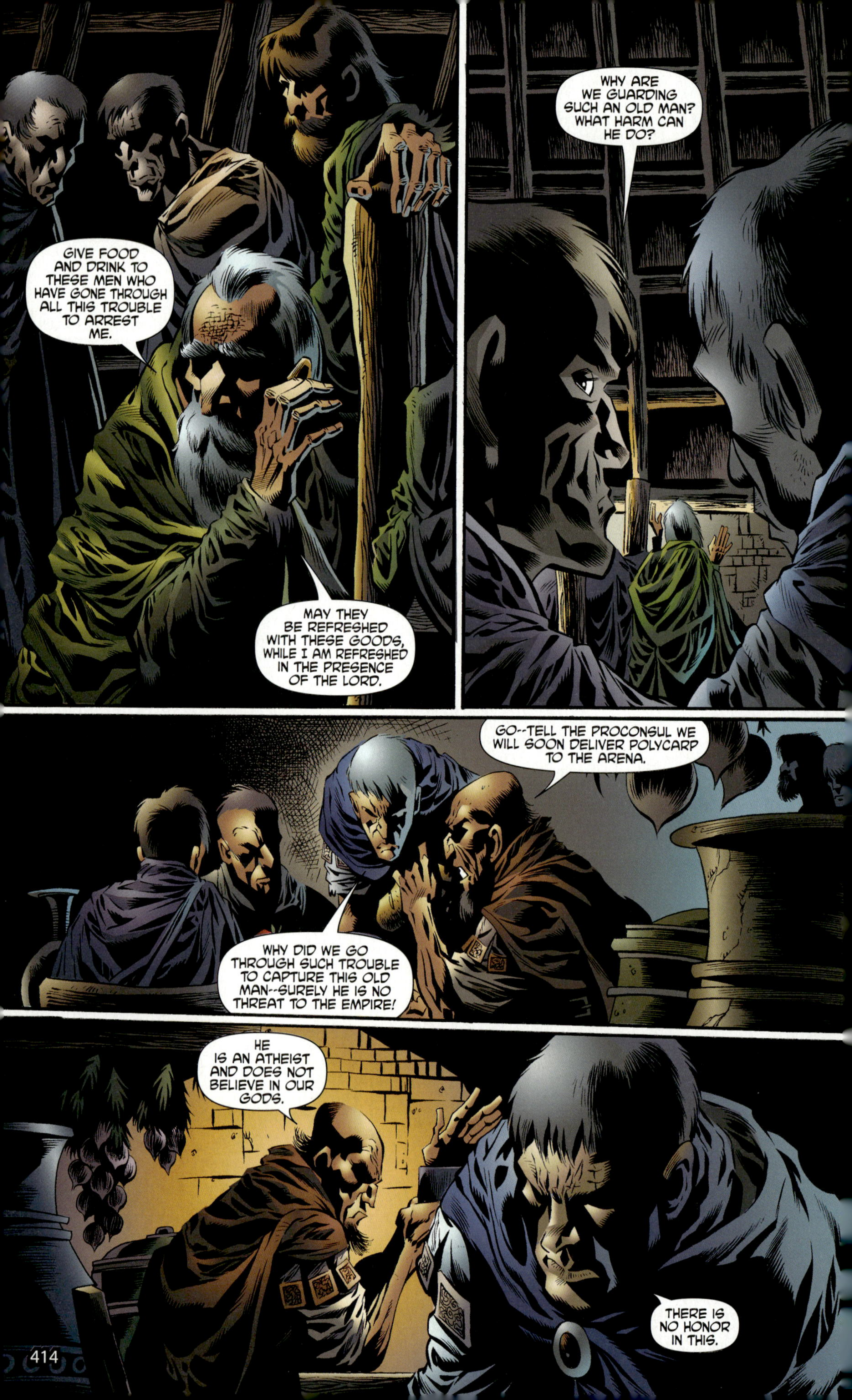
GIVE FOOD AND DRINK TO THESE MEN WHO HAVE GONE THROUGH ALL THIS TROUBLE TO ARREST ME.
MAY THEY BE REFRESHED WITH THESE GOODS, WHILE I AM REFRESHED IN THE PRESENCE OF THE LORD.
WHY ARE WE GUARDING SUCH AN OLD MAN? WHAT HARM CAN HE DO?
GO--TELL THE PROCONSUL WE WILL SOON DELIVER POLYCARP TO THE ARENA.
WHY DID WE GO THROUGH SUCH TROUBLE TO CAPTURE THIS OLD MAN--SURELY HE IS NO THREAT TO THE EMPIRE!
HE IS AN ATHEIST AND DOES NOT BELIEVE IN OUR GODS.
THERE IS NO HONOR IN THIS.

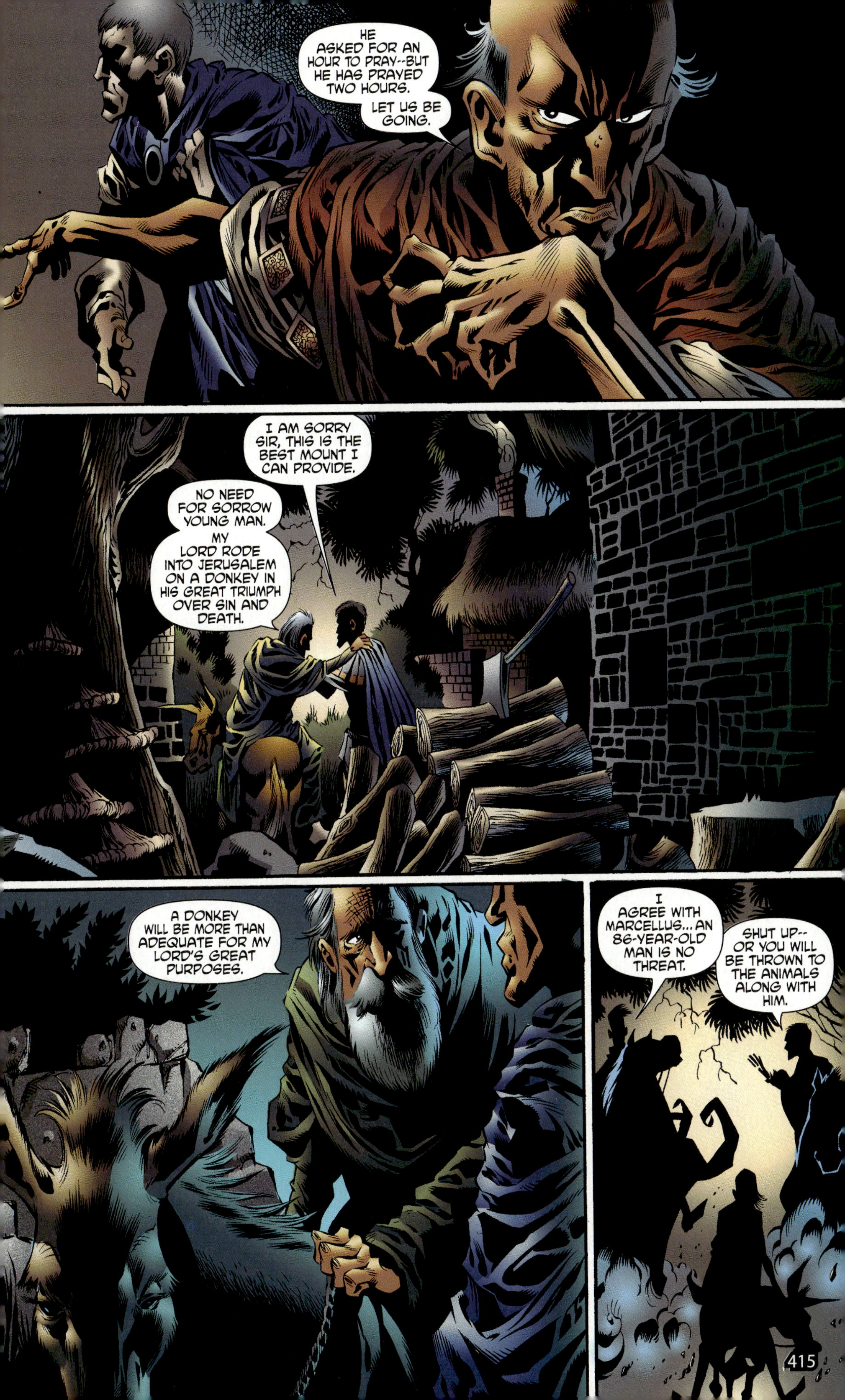
HE ASKED FOR AN HOUR TO PRAY--BUT HE HAS PRAYED TWO HOURS.
LET US BE GOING.
I AM SORRY SIR, THIS IS THE BEST MOUNT I CAN PROVIDE.
NO NEED FOR SORROW YOUNG MAN.
MY LORD RODE INTO JERUSALEM ON A DONKEY IN HIS GREAT TRIUMPH OVER SIN AND DEATH.
A DONKEY WILL BE MORE THAN ADEQUATE FOR MY LORD'S GREAT PURPOSES.
I AGREE WITH MARCELLUS... AN 86-YEAR-OLD MAN IS NO THREAT.
SHUT UP-- OR YOU WILL BE THROWN TO THE ANIMALS ALONG WITH HIM.

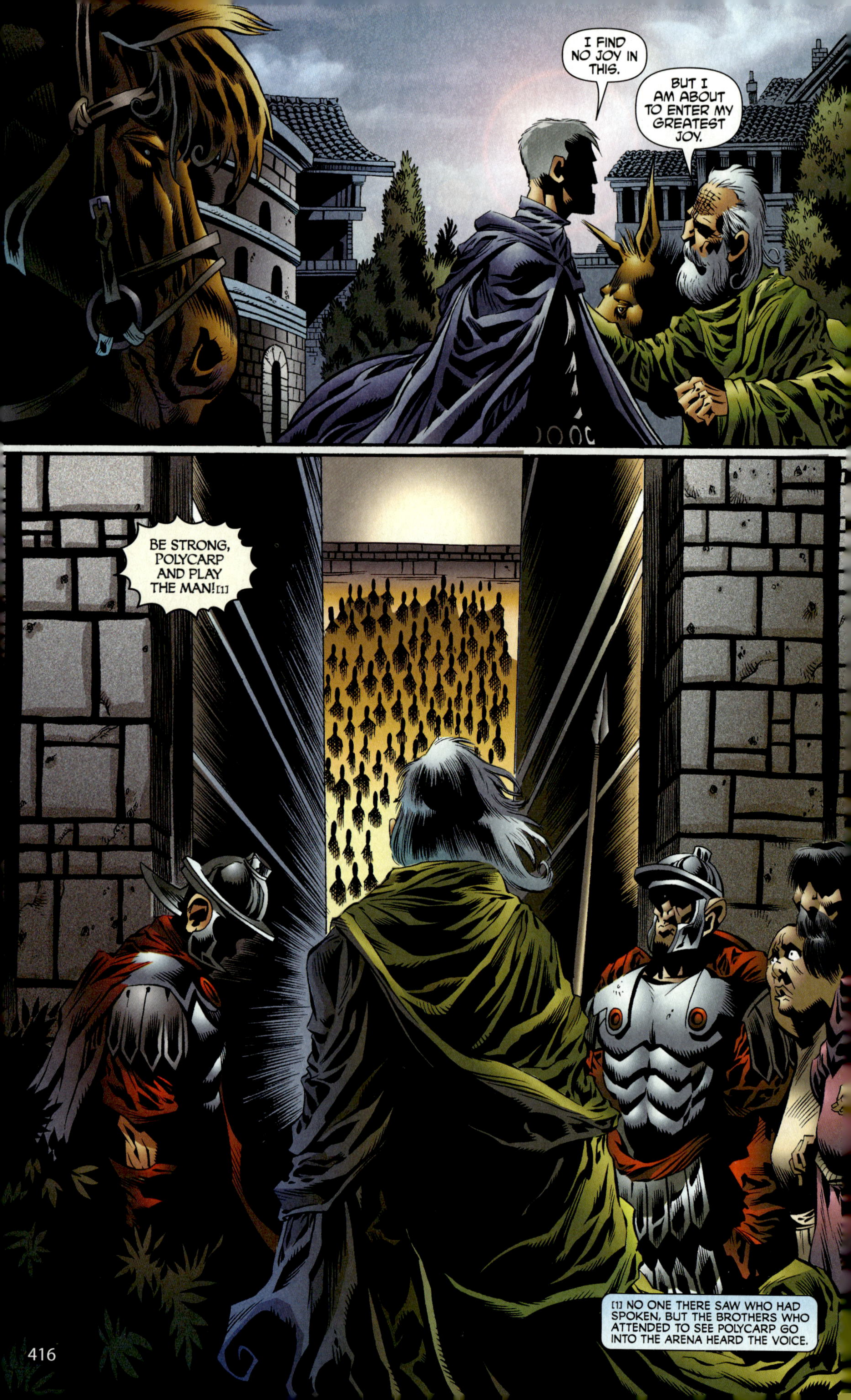
I FIND NO JOY IN THIS.
BUT I AM ABOUT TO ENTER MY GREATEST JOY.
BE STRONG, POLYCARP AND PLAY THE MAN![1]
[1] NO ONE THERE SAW WHO HAD SPOKEN, BUT THE BROTHERS WHO ATTENDED TO SEE POLYCARP GO INTO THE ARENA HEARD THE VOICE.

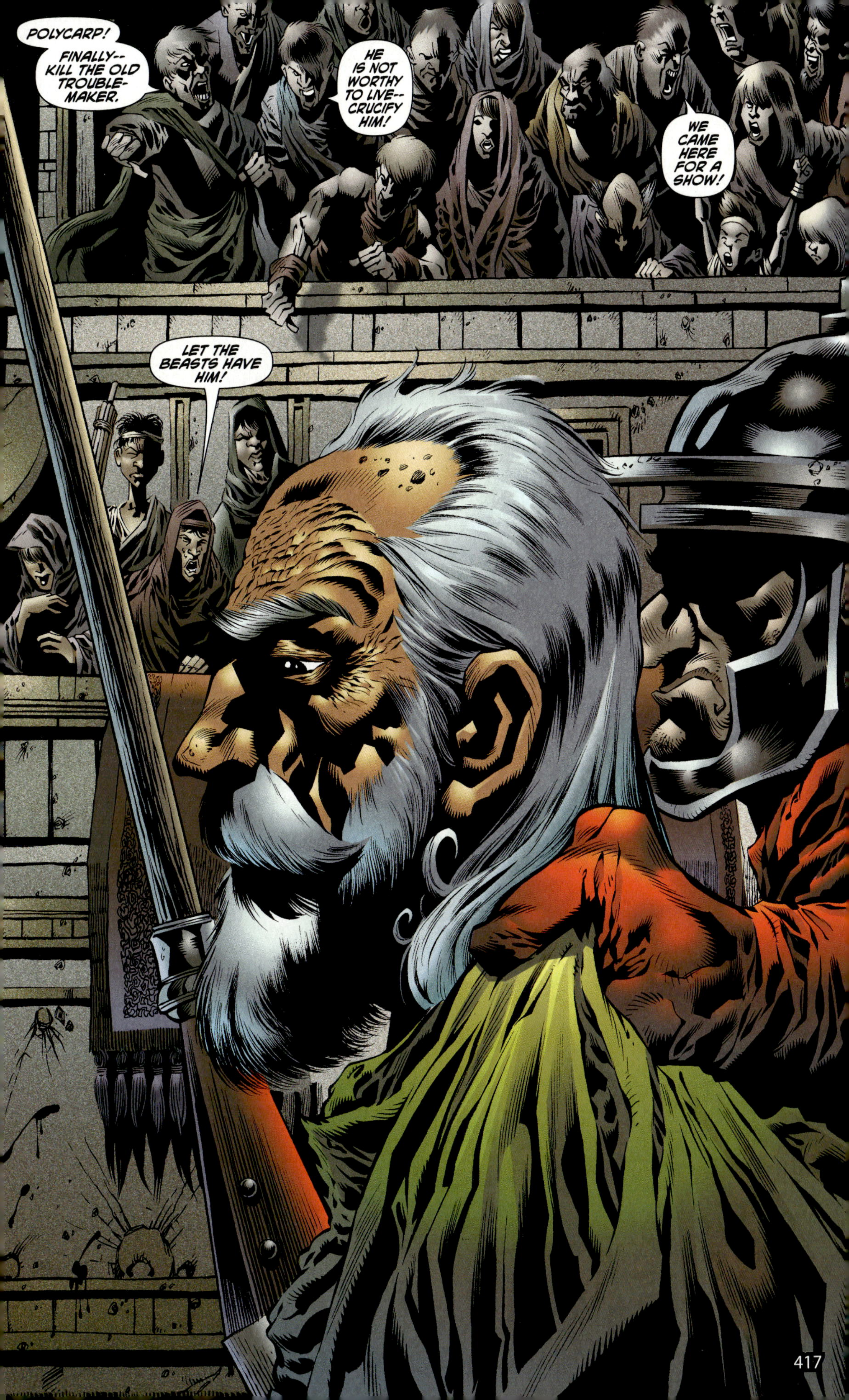
POLYCARP!
FINALLY-- KILL THE OLD TROUBLE-MAKER.
HE IS NOT WORTHY TO LIVE-- CRUCIFY HIM!
WE CAME HERE FOR A SHOW!
LET THE BEASTS HAVE HIM!

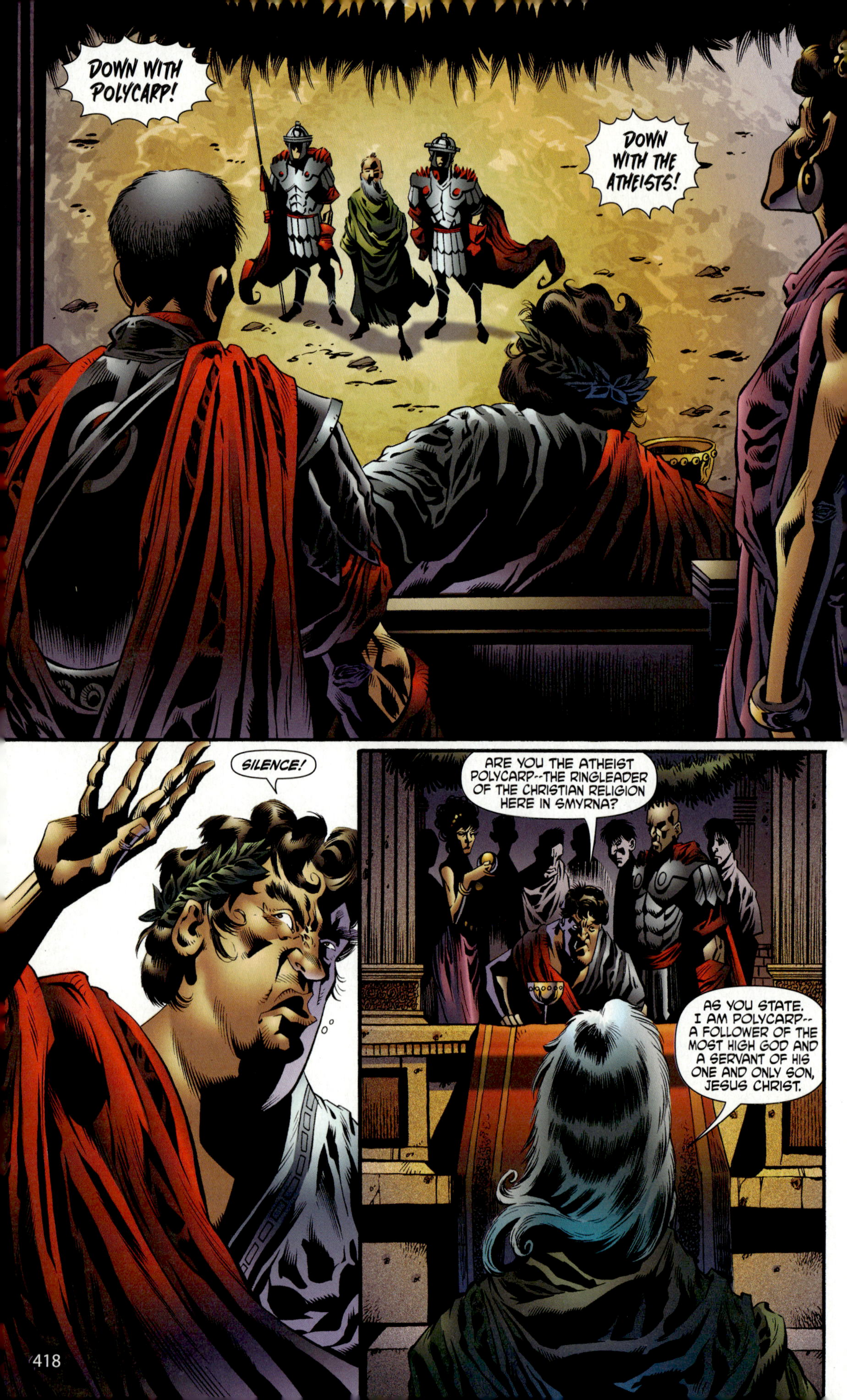
DOWN WITH POLYCARP!
DOWN WITH THE ATHEISTS!
SILENCE!
ARE YOU THE ATHEIST POLYCARP--THE RINGLEADER OF THE CHRISTIAN RELIGION HERE IN SMYRNA?
AS YOU STATE. I AM POLYCARP-- A FOLLOWER OF THE MOST HIGH GOD AND A SERVANT OF HIS ONE AND ONLY SON, JESUS CHRIST.

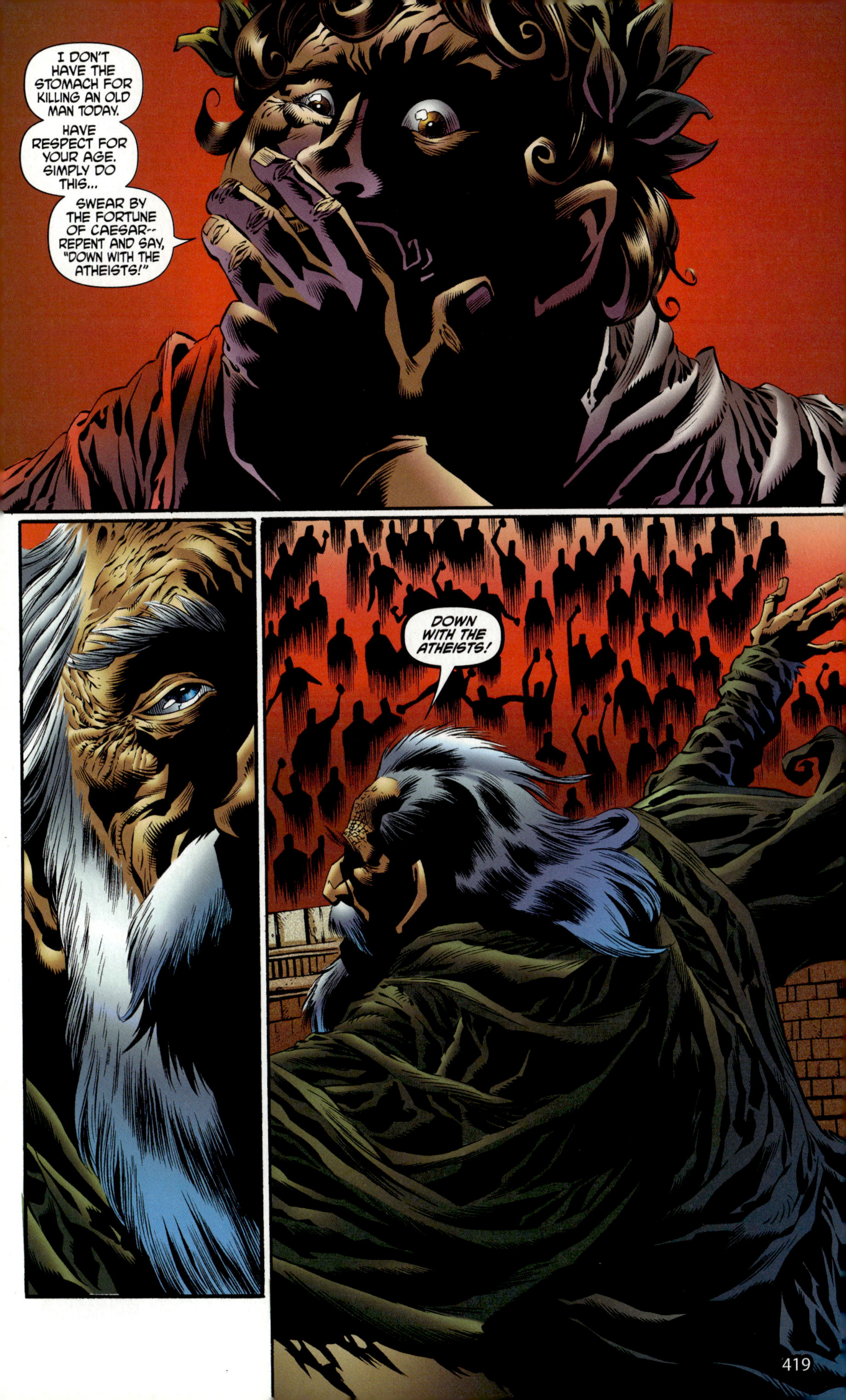
I DON'T HAVE THE STOMACH FOR KILLING AN OLD MAN TODAY.
HAVE RESPECT FOR YOUR AGE. SIMPLY DO THIS...
SWEAR BY THE FORTUNE OF CAESAR-- REPENT AND SAY, "DOWN WITH THE ATHEISTS!"
DOWN WITH THE ATHEISTS!

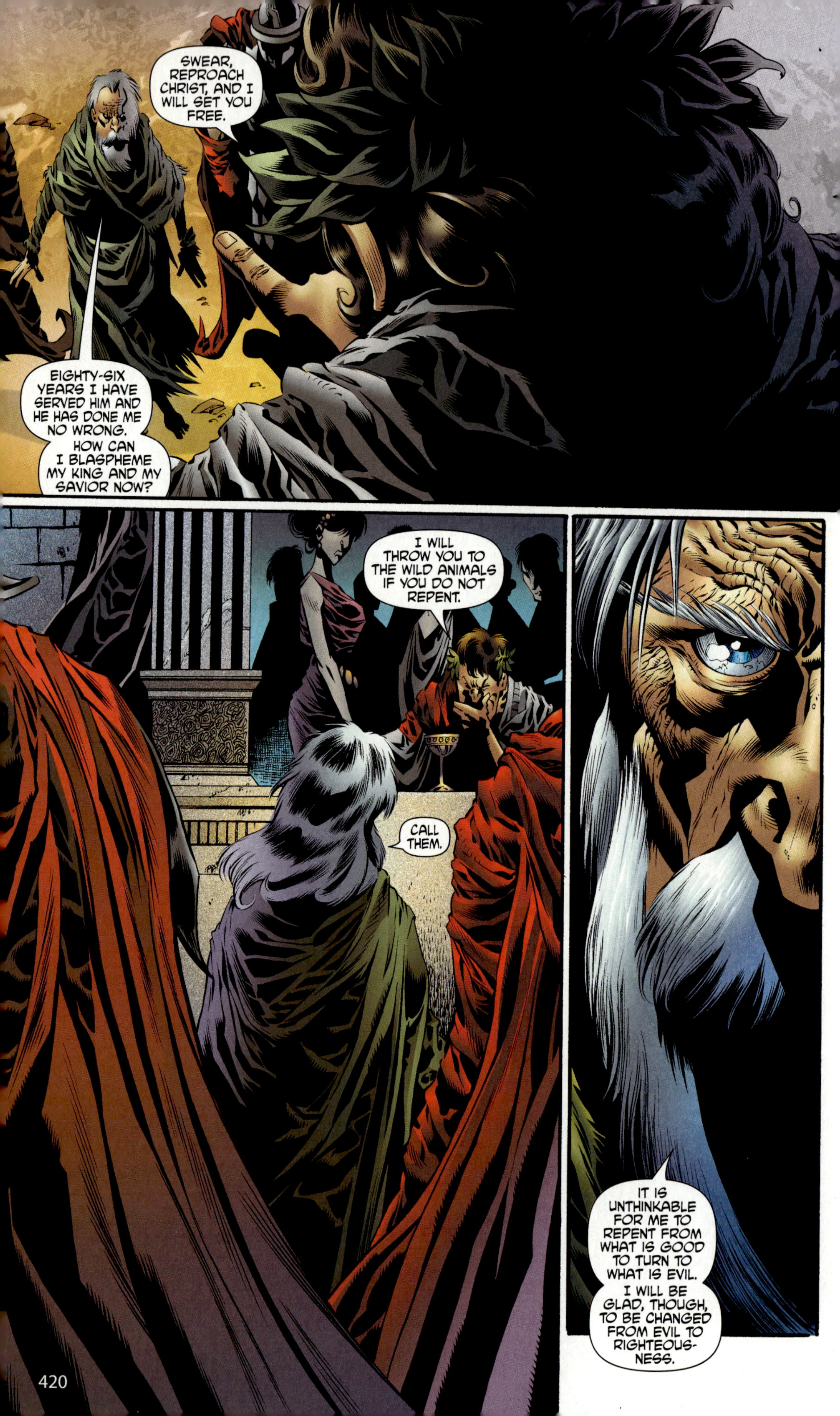
SWEAR, REPROACH CHRIST, AND I WILL SET YOU FREE.
EIGHTY-SIX YEARS I HAVE SERVED HIM AND HE HAS DONE ME NO WRONG. HOW CAN I BLASPHEME MY KING AND MY SAVIOR NOW?
I WILL THROW YOU TO THE WILD ANIMALS IF YOU DO NOT REPENT.
CALL THEM.
IT IS UNTHINKABLE FOR ME TO REPENT FROM WHAT IS GOOD TO TURN TO WHAT IS EVIL. I WILL BE GLAD, THOUGH, TO BE CHANGED FROM EVIL TO RIGHTEOUS-NESS.

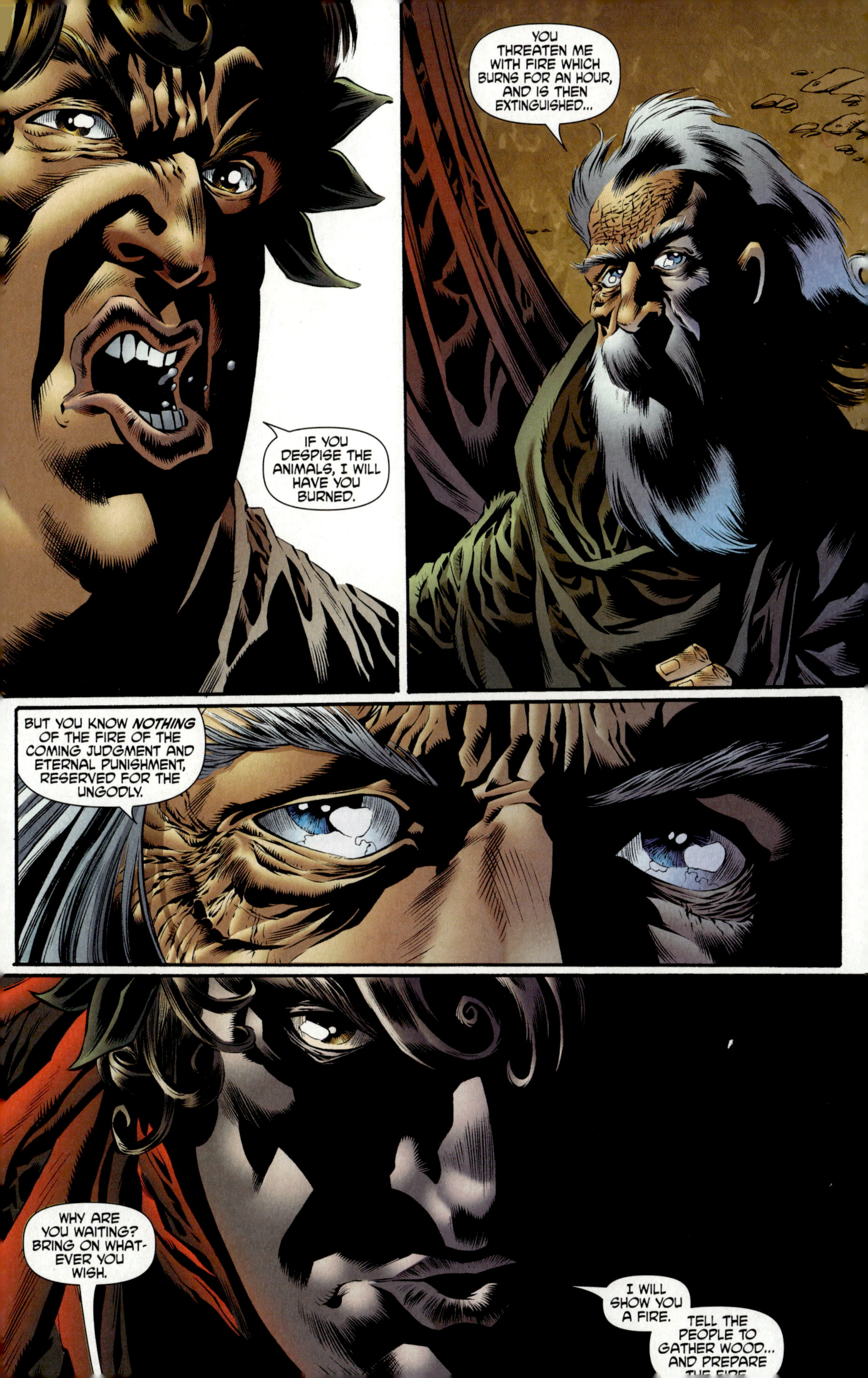
IF YOU DESPISE THE ANIMALS, I WILL HAVE YOU BURNED.
YOU THREATEN ME WITH FIRE WHICH BURNS FOR AN HOUR, AND IS THEN EXTINGUISHED...
BUT YOU KNOW *NOTHING* OF THE FIRE OF THE COMING JUDGMENT AND ETERNAL PUNISHMENT, RESERVED FOR THE UNGODLY.
WHY ARE YOU WAITING? BRING ON WHATEVER YOU WISH.
I WILL SHOW YOU A FIRE.
TELL THE PEOPLE TO GATHER WOOD... AND PREPARE

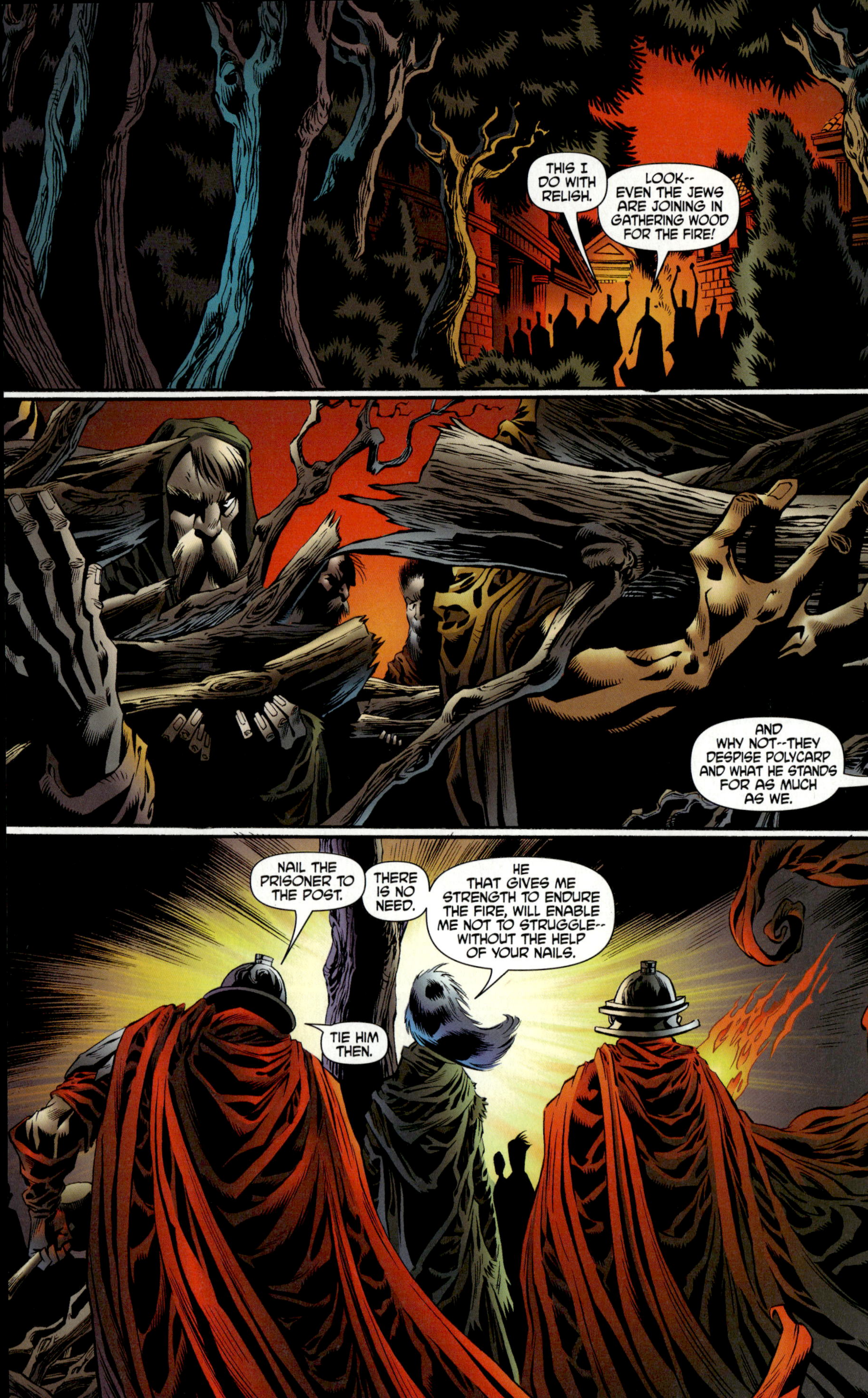
THIS I DO WITH RELISH.
LOOK-- EVEN THE JEWS ARE JOINING IN GATHERING WOOD FOR THE FIRE!
AND WHY NOT--THEY DESPISE POLYCARP AND WHAT HE STANDS FOR AS MUCH AS WE.
NAIL THE PRISONER TO THE POST.
THERE IS NO NEED.
HE THAT GIVES ME STRENGTH TO ENDURE THE FIRE, WILL ENABLE ME NOT TO STRUGGLE-- WITHOUT THE HELP OF YOUR NAILS.
TIE HIM THEN.

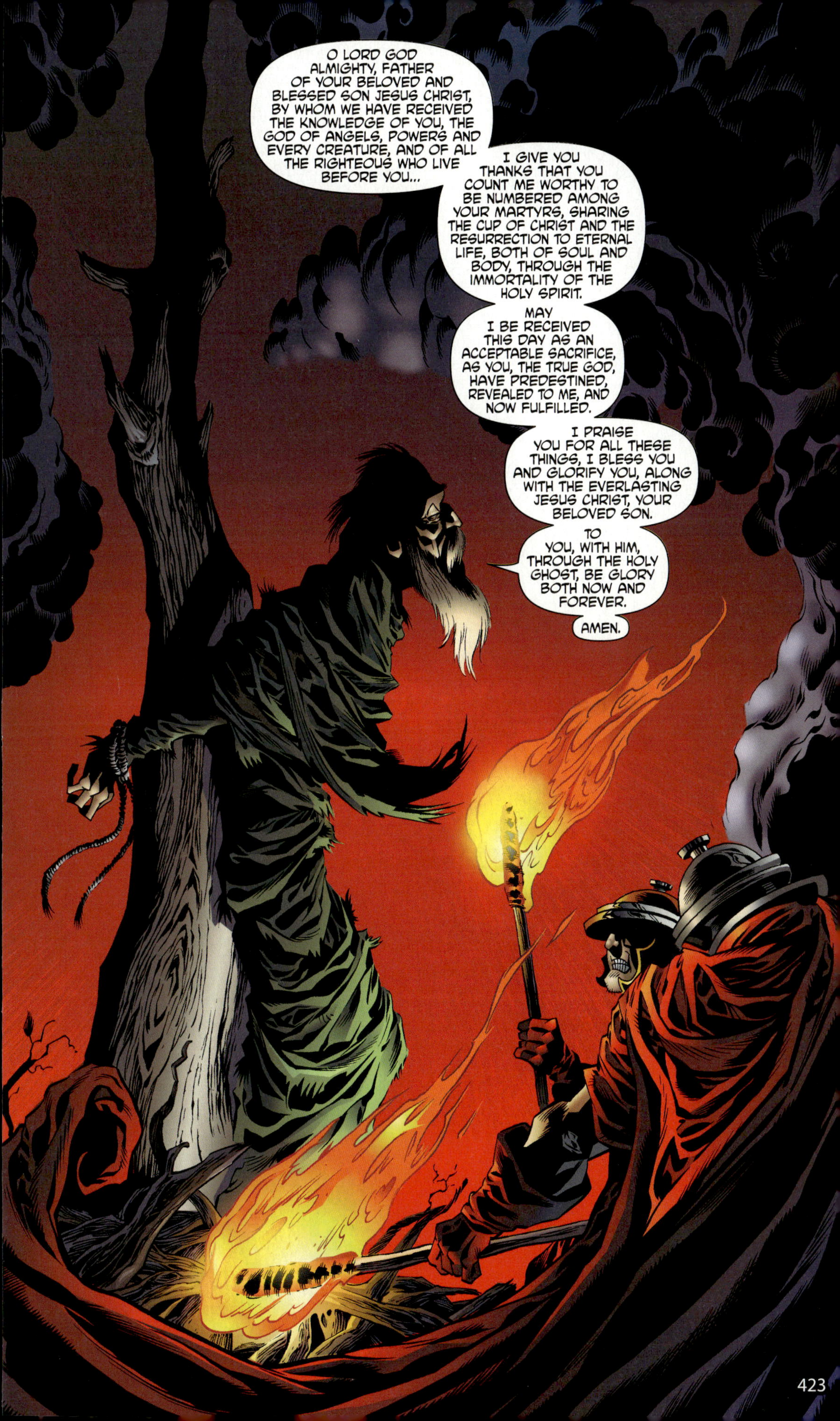
O LORD GOD ALMIGHTY, FATHER OF YOUR BELOVED AND BLESSED SON JESUS CHRIST, BY WHOM WE HAVE RECEIVED THE KNOWLEDGE OF YOU, THE GOD OF ANGELS, POWERS AND EVERY CREATURE, AND OF ALL THE RIGHTEOUS WHO LIVE BEFORE YOU...
I GIVE YOU THANKS THAT YOU COUNT ME WORTHY TO BE NUMBERED AMONG YOUR MARTYRS, SHARING THE CUP OF CHRIST AND THE RESURRECTION TO ETERNAL LIFE, BOTH OF SOUL AND BODY, THROUGH THE IMMORTALITY OF THE HOLY SPIRIT.
MAY I BE RECEIVED THIS DAY AS AN ACCEPTABLE SACRIFICE, AS YOU, THE TRUE GOD, HAVE PREDESTINED, REVEALED TO ME, AND NOW FULFILLED.
I PRAISE YOU FOR ALL THESE THINGS, I BLESS YOU AND GLORIFY YOU, ALONG WITH THE EVERLASTING JESUS CHRIST, YOUR BELOVED SON.
TO YOU, WITH HIM, THROUGH THE HOLY GHOST, BE GLORY BOTH NOW AND FOREVER.
AMEN.

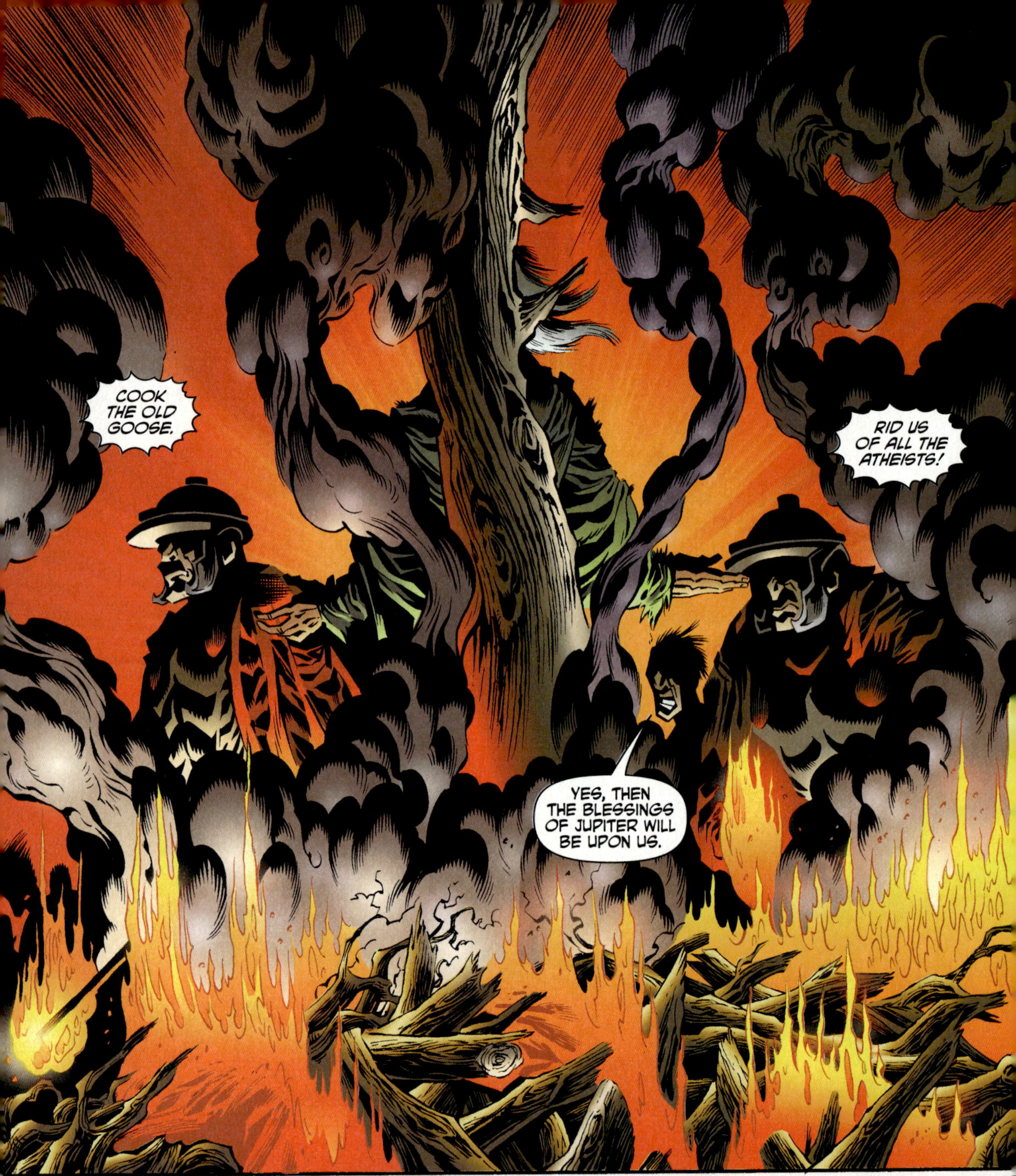
COOK THE OLD GOOSE.
RID US OF ALL THE ATHEISTS!
YES, THEN THE BLESSINGS OF JUPITER WILL BE UPON US.

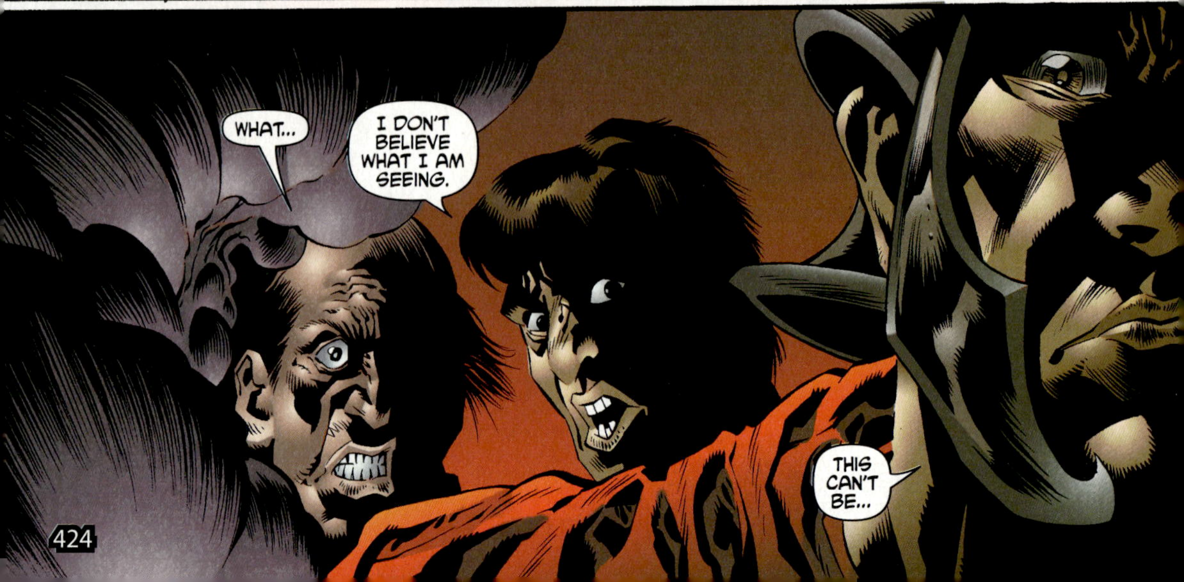
WHAT...
I DON'T BELIEVE WHAT I AM SEEING.
THIS CAN'T BE...

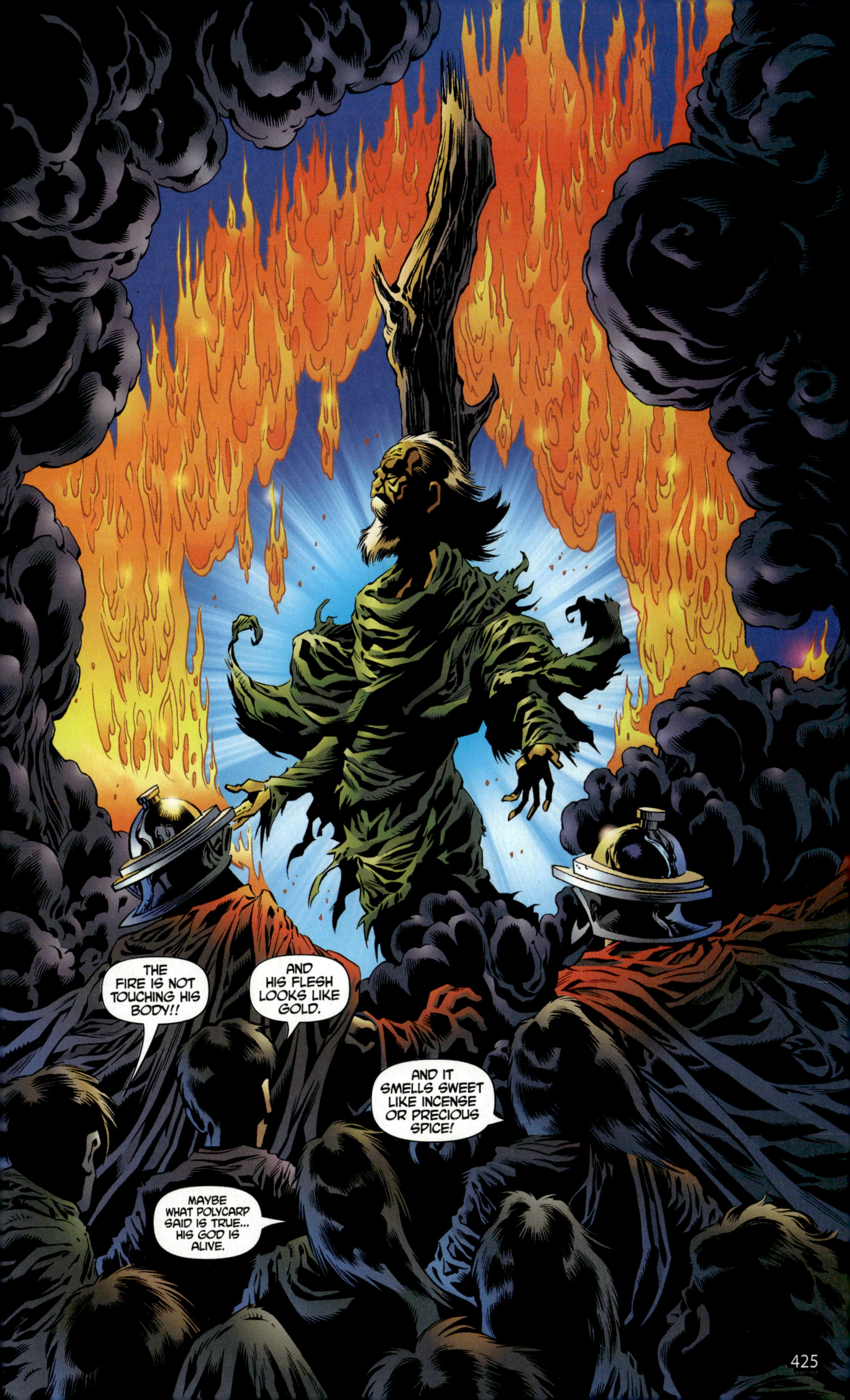
THE FIRE IS NOT TOUCHING HIS BODY!!
AND HIS FLESH LOOKS LIKE GOLD.
AND IT SMELLS SWEET LIKE INCENSE OR PRECIOUS SPICE!
MAYBE WHAT POLYCARP SAID IS TRUE... HIS GOD IS ALIVE.

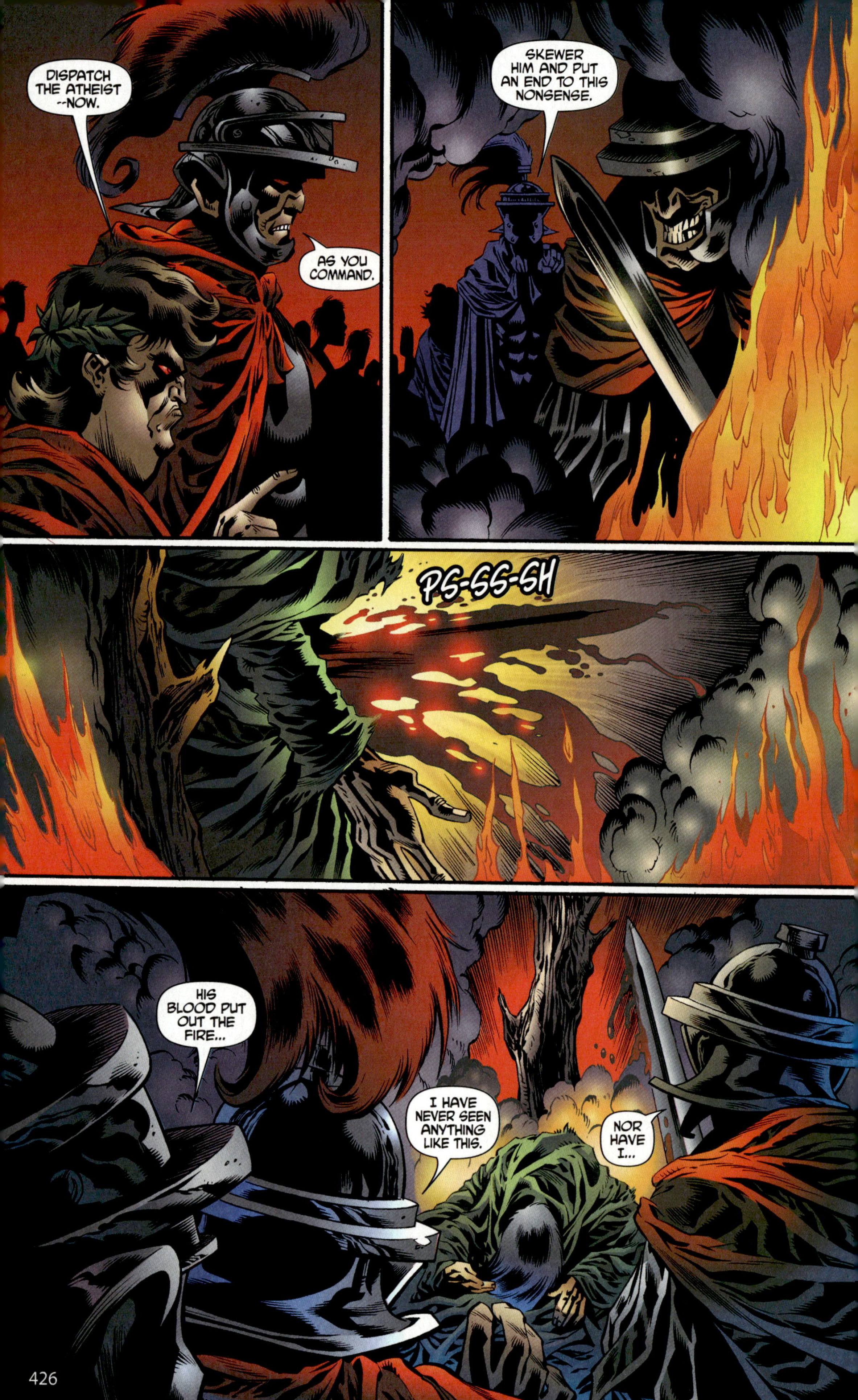
DISPATCH THE ATHEIST --NOW.
AS YOU COMMAND.
SKEWER HIM AND PUT AN END TO THIS NONSENSE.
PS-SS-SH
HIS BLOOD PUT OUT THE FIRE...
I HAVE NEVER SEEN ANYTHING LIKE THIS.
NOR HAVE I...

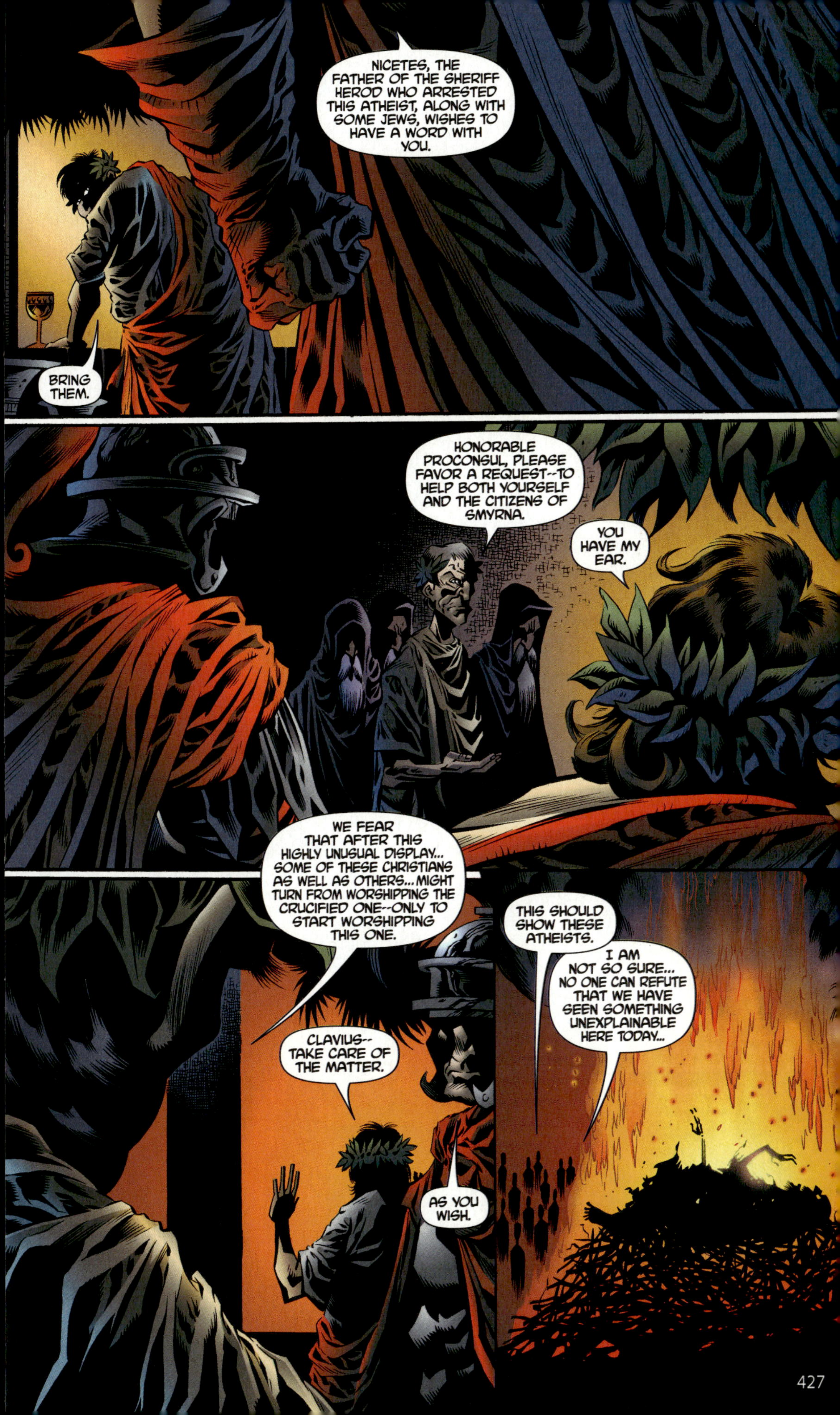
NICETES, THE FATHER OF THE SHERIFF HEROD WHO ARRESTED THIS ATHEIST, ALONG WITH SOME JEWS, WISHES TO HAVE A WORD WITH YOU.
BRING THEM.
HONORABLE PROCONSUL, PLEASE FAVOR A REQUEST--TO HELP BOTH YOURSELF AND THE CITIZENS OF SMYRNA.
YOU HAVE MY EAR.
WE FEAR THAT AFTER THIS HIGHLY UNUSUAL DISPLAY... SOME OF THESE CHRISTIANS AS WELL AS OTHERS... MIGHT TURN FROM WORSHIPPING THE CRUCIFIED ONE--ONLY TO START WORSHIPPING THIS ONE.
CLAVIUS--TAKE CARE OF THE MATTER.
AS YOU WISH.
THIS SHOULD SHOW THESE ATHEISTS.
I AM NOT SO SURE... NO ONE CAN REFUTE THAT WE HAVE SEEN SOMETHING UNEXPLAINABLE HERE TODAY...

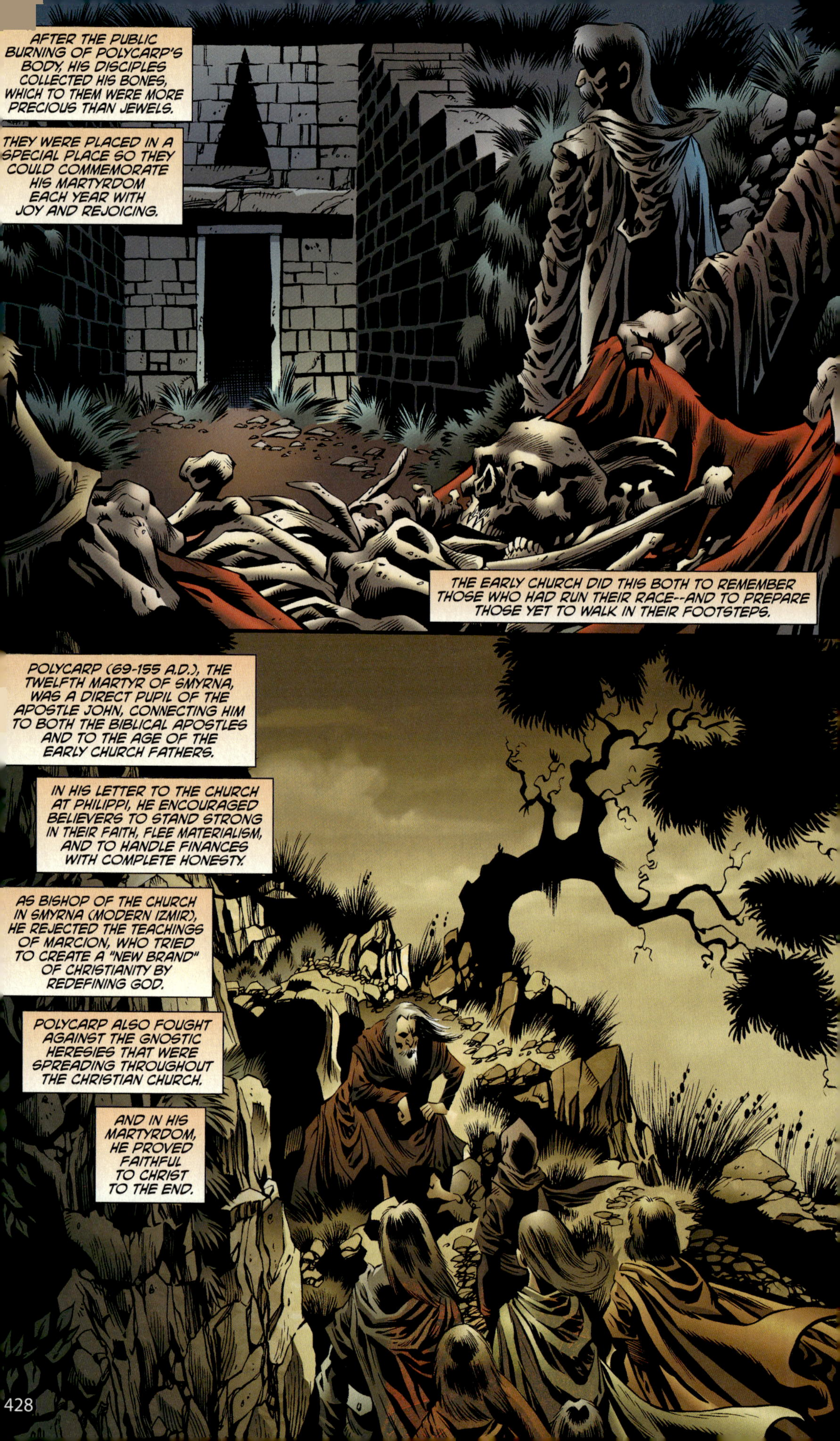
AFTER THE PUBLIC BURNING OF POLYCARP'S BODY, HIS DISCIPLES COLLECTED HIS BONES, WHICH TO THEM WERE MORE PRECIOUS THAN JEWELS.
THEY WERE PLACED IN A SPECIAL PLACE SO THEY COULD COMMEMORATE HIS MARTYRDOM EACH YEAR WITH JOY AND REJOICING.
THE EARLY CHURCH DID THIS BOTH TO REMEMBER THOSE WHO HAD RUN THEIR RACE--AND TO PREPARE THOSE YET TO WALK IN THEIR FOOTSTEPS.
POLYCARP (69-155 A.D.), THE TWELFTH MARTYR OF SMYRNA, WAS A DIRECT PUPIL OF THE APOSTLE JOHN, CONNECTING HIM TO BOTH THE BIBLICAL APOSTLES AND TO THE AGE OF THE EARLY CHURCH FATHERS.
IN HIS LETTER TO THE CHURCH AT PHILIPPI, HE ENCOURAGED BELIEVERS TO STAND STRONG IN THEIR FAITH, FLEE MATERIALISM, AND TO HANDLE FINANCES WITH COMPLETE HONESTY.
AS BISHOP OF THE CHURCH IN SMYRNA (MODERN IZMIR), HE REJECTED THE TEACHINGS OF MARCION, WHO TRIED TO CREATE A "NEW BRAND" OF CHRISTIANITY BY REDEFINING GOD.
POLYCARP ALSO FOUGHT AGAINST THE GNOSTIC HERESIES THAT WERE SPREADING THROUGHOUT THE CHRISTIAN CHURCH.
AND IN HIS MARTYRDOM, HE PROVED FAITHFUL TO CHRIST TO THE END.

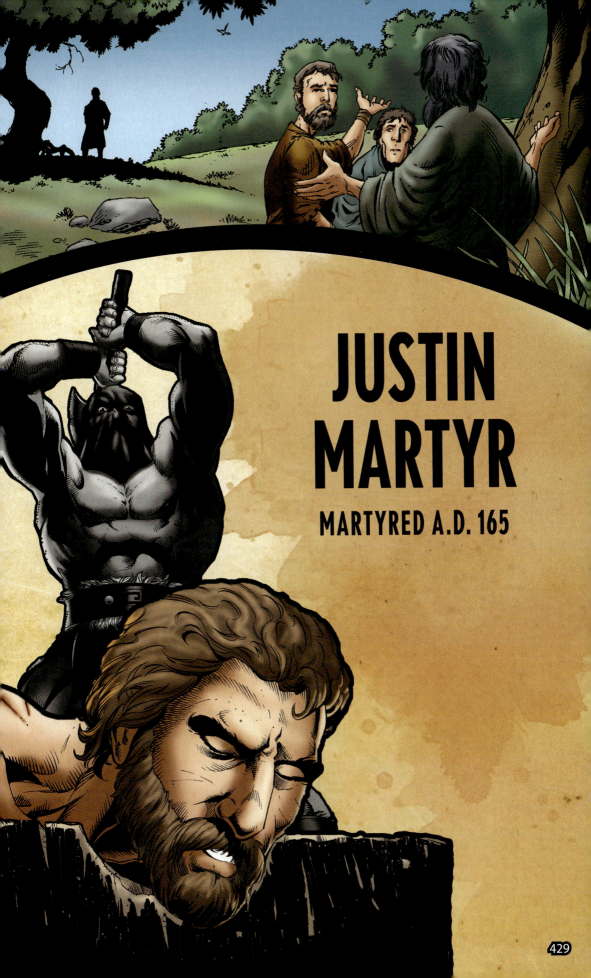

JUSTIN
MARTYR

MARTYRED A.D. 165

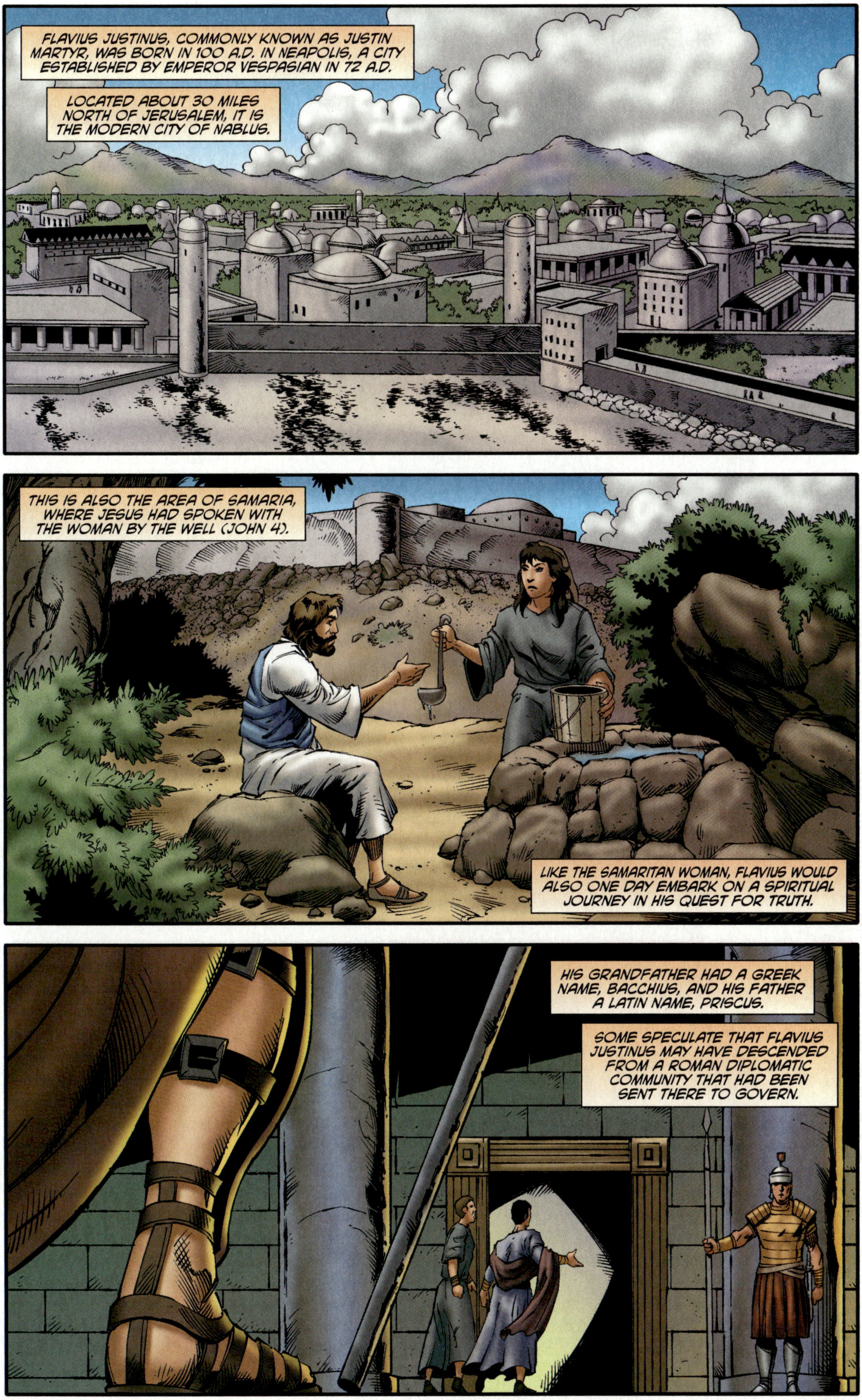
FLAVIUS JUSTINUS, COMMONLY KNOWN AS JUSTIN MARTYR, WAS BORN IN 100 A.D. IN NEAPOLIS, A CITY ESTABLISHED BY EMPEROR VESPASIAN IN 72 A.D.
LOCATED ABOUT 30 MILES NORTH OF JERUSALEM, IT IS THE MODERN CITY OF NABLUS.
THIS IS ALSO THE AREA OF SAMARIA, WHERE JESUS HAD SPOKEN WITH THE WOMAN BY THE WELL (JOHN 4).
LIKE THE SAMARITAN WOMAN, FLAVIUS WOULD ALSO ONE DAY EMBARK ON A SPIRITUAL JOURNEY IN HIS QUEST FOR TRUTH.
HIS GRANDFATHER HAD A GREEK NAME, BACCHIUS, AND HIS FATHER A LATIN NAME, PRISCUS.
SOME SPECULATE THAT FLAVIUS JUSTINUS MAY HAVE DESCENDED FROM A ROMAN DIPLOMATIC COMMUNITY THAT HAD BEEN SENT THERE TO GOVERN.

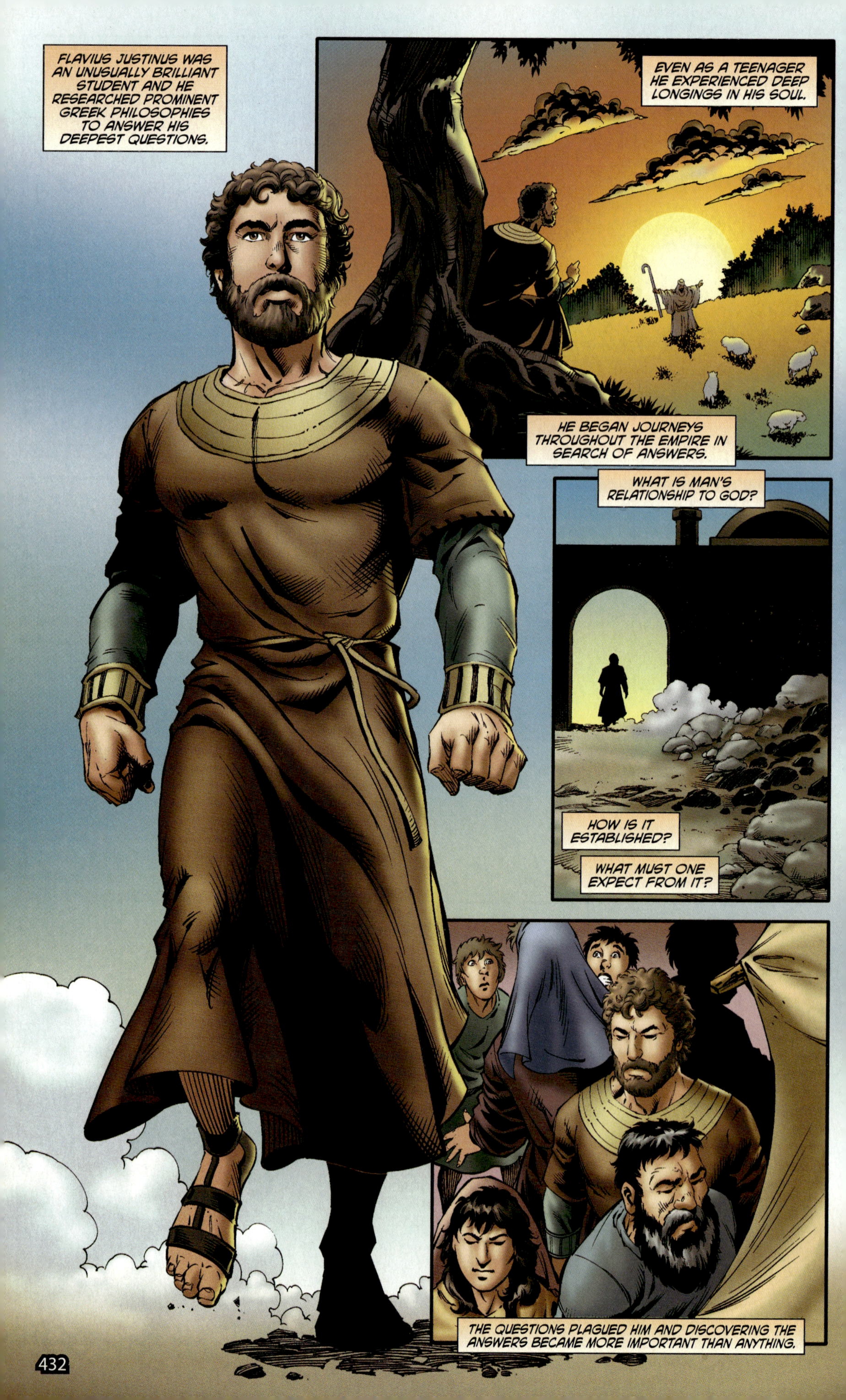
FLAVIUS JUSTINUS WAS AN UNUSUALLY BRILLIANT STUDENT AND HE RESEARCHED PROMINENT GREEK PHILOSOPHIES TO ANSWER HIS DEEPEST QUESTIONS.
EVEN AS A TEENAGER HE EXPERIENCED DEEP LONGINGS IN HIS SOUL.
HE BEGAN JOURNEYS THROUGHOUT THE EMPIRE IN SEARCH OF ANSWERS.
WHAT IS MAN'S RELATIONSHIP TO GOD?
HOW IS IT ESTABLISHED?
WHAT MUST ONE EXPECT FROM IT?
THE QUESTIONS PLAGUED HIM AND DISCOVERING THE ANSWERS BECAME MORE IMPORTANT THAN ANYTHING.

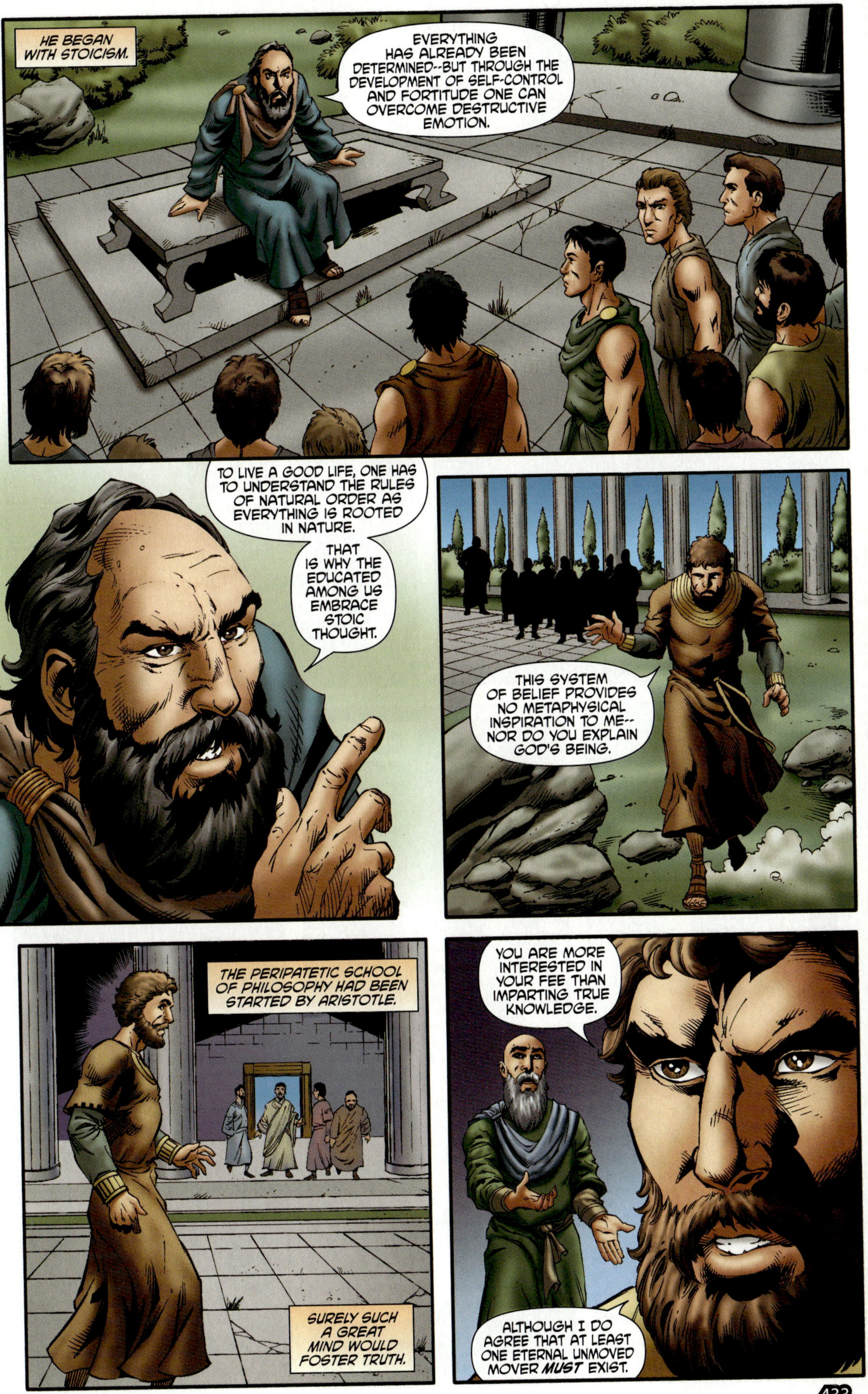
HE BEGAN WITH STOICISM.
EVERYTHING HAS ALREADY BEEN DETERMINED--BUT THROUGH THE DEVELOPMENT OF SELF-CONTROL AND FORTITUDE ONE CAN OVERCOME DESTRUCTIVE EMOTION.
TO LIVE A GOOD LIFE, ONE HAS TO UNDERSTAND THE RULES OF NATURAL ORDER AS EVERYTHING IS ROOTED IN NATURE.
THAT IS WHY THE EDUCATED AMONG US EMBRACE STOIC THOUGHT.
THIS SYSTEM OF BELIEF PROVIDES NO METAPHYSICAL INSPIRATION TO ME--NOR DO YOU EXPLAIN GOD'S BEING.
THE PERIPATETIC SCHOOL OF PHILOSOPHY HAD BEEN STARTED BY ARISTOTLE.
SURELY SUCH A GREAT MIND WOULD FOSTER TRUTH.
YOU ARE MORE INTERESTED IN YOUR FEE THAN IMPARTING TRUE KNOWLEDGE.
ALTHOUGH I DO AGREE THAT AT LEAST ONE ETERNAL UNMOVED MOVER MUST EXIST.

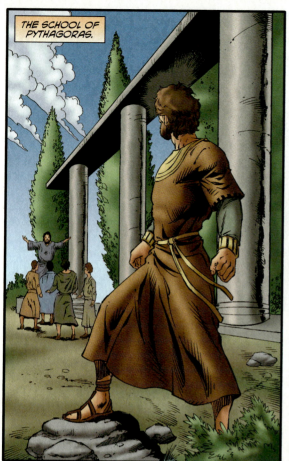

THE SCHOOL OF PYTHAGORAS.

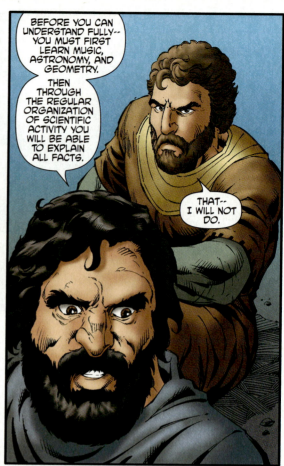

BEFORE YOU CAN UNDERSTAND FULLY-- YOU MUST FIRST LEARN MUSIC, ASTRONOMY, AND GEOMETRY.

THEN THROUGH THE REGULAR ORGANIZATION OF SCIENTIFIC ACTIVITY YOU WILL BE ABLE TO EXPLAIN ALL FACTS.

THAT-- I WILL NOT DO.

BUT IN THE TEACHING OF PLATO, FLAVIUS JUSTINUS FELT HE FOUND VESTIGES OF TRUTH.

HE WAS TO LATER SAY...

THE PERCEPTION OF IMMATERIAL THINGS QUITE OVER-POWERED ME, AND THE CONTEMPLATION OF IDEAS FURNISHED MY MIND WITH WINGS... I SUPPOSED THAT I HAD BECOME WISE; AND SUCH WAS MY STUPIDITY.

I EXPECTED FORTHWITH TO LOOK UPON GOD, FOR THIS IS THE END OF PLATO'S PHILOSOPHY.

NOW I CAN WITHDRAW FAR FROM THE TURMOIL OF THE WORLD--

--AND IN PERFECT SELF-COLLECTION GIVE MYSELF TO MY OWN CONTEMPLA-TIONS.

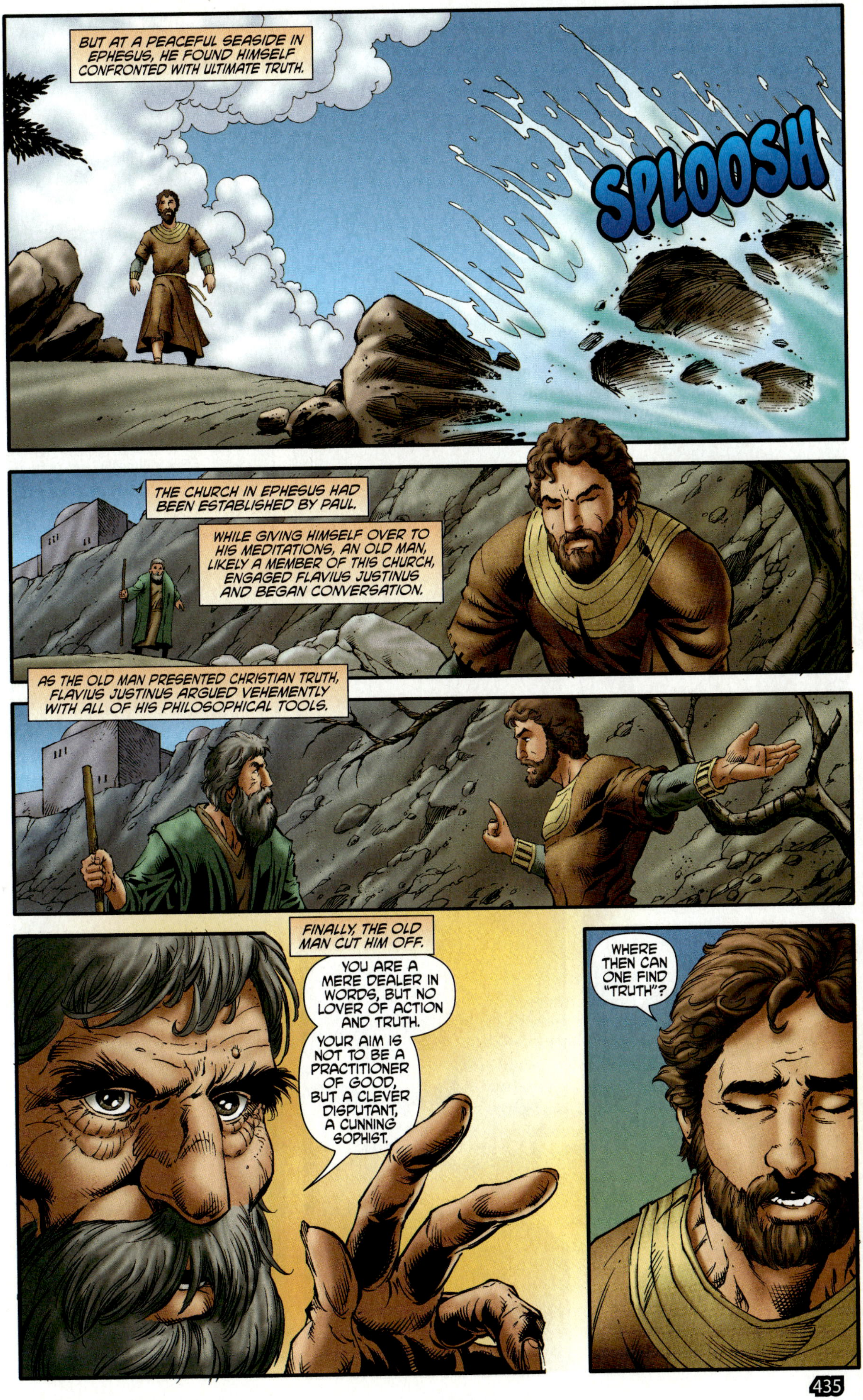
BUT AT A PEACEFUL SEASIDE IN EPHESUS, HE FOUND HIMSELF CONFRONTED WITH ULTIMATE TRUTH.
SPLOOSH
THE CHURCH IN EPHESUS HAD BEEN ESTABLISHED BY PAUL.
WHILE GIVING HIMSELF OVER TO HIS MEDITATIONS, AN OLD MAN, LIKELY A MEMBER OF THIS CHURCH, ENGAGED FLAVIUS JUSTINUS AND BEGAN CONVERSATION.
AS THE OLD MAN PRESENTED CHRISTIAN TRUTH, FLAVIUS JUSTINUS ARGUED VEHEMENTLY WITH ALL OF HIS PHILOSOPHICAL TOOLS.
FINALLY, THE OLD MAN CUT HIM OFF.
YOU ARE A MERE DEALER IN WORDS, BUT NO LOVER OF ACTION AND TRUTH.
YOUR AIM IS NOT TO BE A PRACTITIONER OF GOOD, BUT A CLEVER DISPUTANT, A CUNNING SOPHIST.
WHERE THEN CAN ONE FIND "TRUTH"?

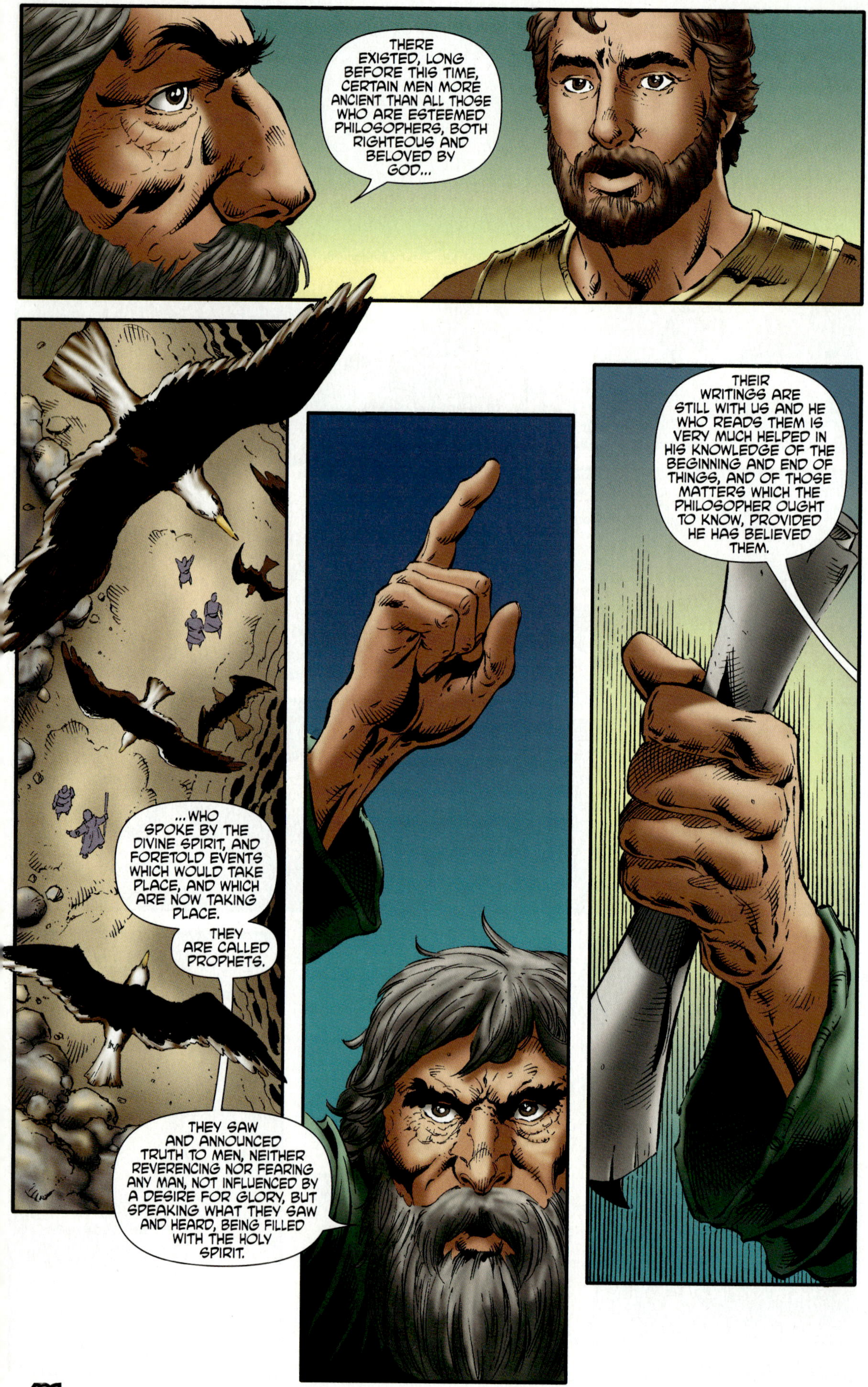
THERE EXISTED, LONG BEFORE THIS TIME, CERTAIN MEN MORE ANCIENT THAN ALL THOSE WHO ARE ESTEEMED PHILOSOPHERS, BOTH RIGHTEOUS AND BELOVED BY GOD...
...WHO SPOKE BY THE DIVINE SPIRIT, AND FORETOLD EVENTS WHICH WOULD TAKE PLACE, AND WHICH ARE NOW TAKING PLACE.
THEY ARE CALLED PROPHETS.
THEY SAW AND ANNOUNCED TRUTH TO MEN, NEITHER REVERENCING NOR FEARING ANY MAN, NOT INFLUENCED BY A DESIRE FOR GLORY, BUT SPEAKING WHAT THEY SAW AND HEARD, BEING FILLED WITH THE HOLY SPIRIT.
THEIR WRITINGS ARE STILL WITH US AND HE WHO READS THEM IS VERY MUCH HELPED IN HIS KNOWLEDGE OF THE BEGINNING AND END OF THINGS, AND OF THOSE MATTERS WHICH THE PHILOSOPHER OUGHT TO KNOW, PROVIDED HE HAS BELIEVED THEM.

"...THESE WERE WITNESSES TO THE TRUTH AND WORTHY OF BELIEF...ASSENT TO THE UTTERANCES MADE BY THEM."

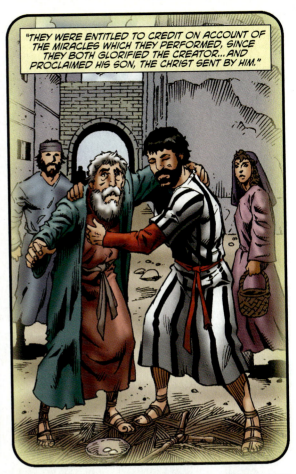

"THEY WERE ENTITLED TO CREDIT ON ACCOUNT OF THE MIRACLES WHICH THEY PERFORMED, SINCE THEY BOTH GLORIFIED THE CREATOR...AND PROCLAIMED HIS SON, THE CHRIST SENT BY HIM."

THE FALSE PROPHETS ARE FILLED WITH THE LYING UNCLEAN SPIRIT AND VENTURE TO WORK WONDERFUL DEEDS FOR THE PURPOSE OF ASTONISHING MEN, AND GLORIFY THE SPIRITS AND DEMONS OF ERROR.

SEARCH THE SCRIPTURES AND PRAY...FOR NONE CAN PERCEIVE AND COMPREHEND THESE THINGS EXCEPT GOD AND HIS CHRIST GRANT THEM UNDERSTANDING.

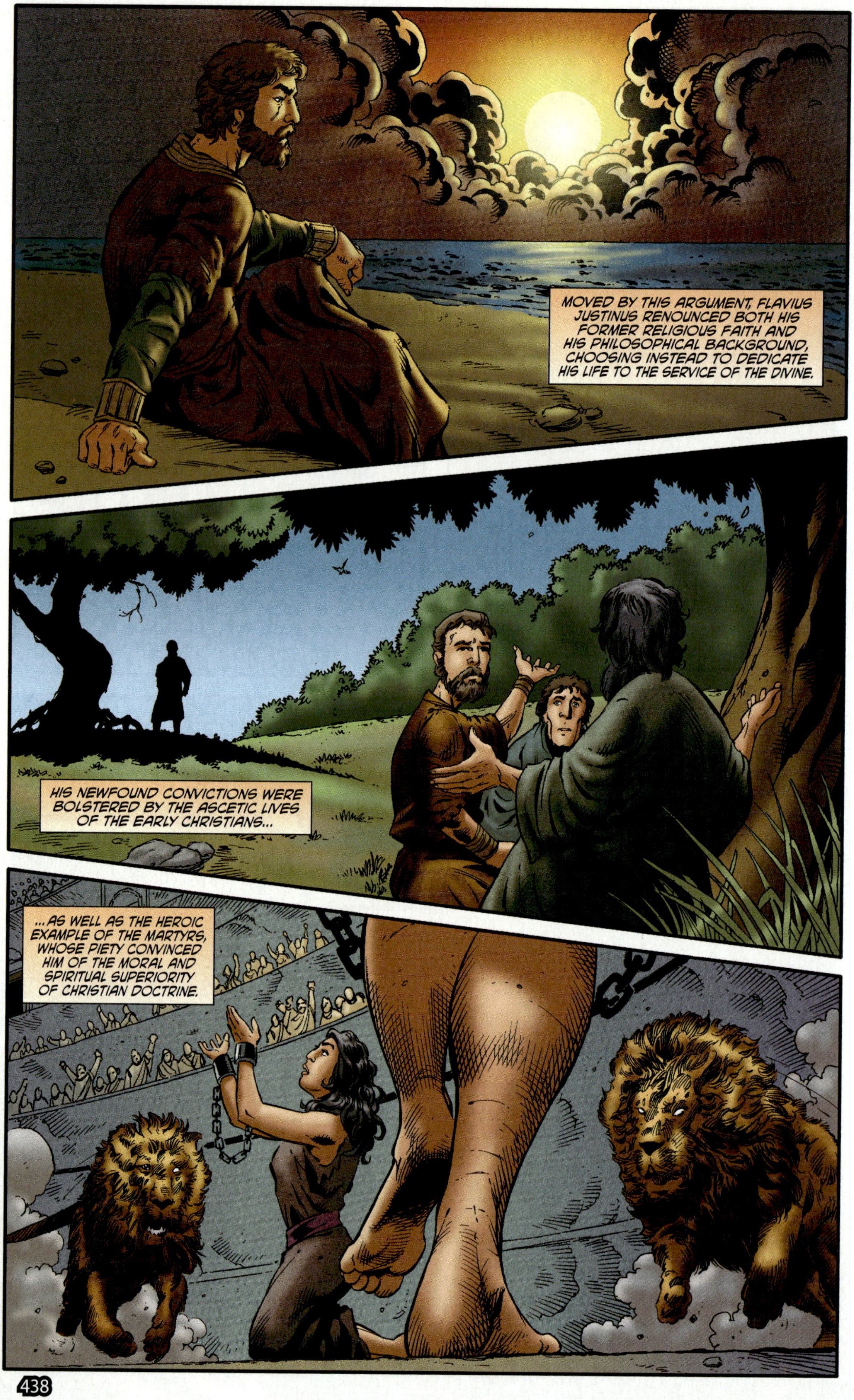
MOVED BY THIS ARGUMENT, FLAVIUS JUSTINUS RENOUNCED BOTH HIS FORMER RELIGIOUS FAITH AND HIS PHILOSOPHICAL BACKGROUND, CHOOSING INSTEAD TO DEDICATE HIS LIFE TO THE SERVICE OF THE DIVINE.
HIS NEWFOUND CONVICTIONS WERE BOLSTERED BY THE ASCETIC LIVES OF THE EARLY CHRISTIANS...
...AS WELL AS THE HEROIC EXAMPLE OF THE MARTYRS, WHOSE PIETY CONVINCED HIM OF THE MORAL AND SPIRITUAL SUPERIORITY OF CHRISTIAN DOCTRINE.

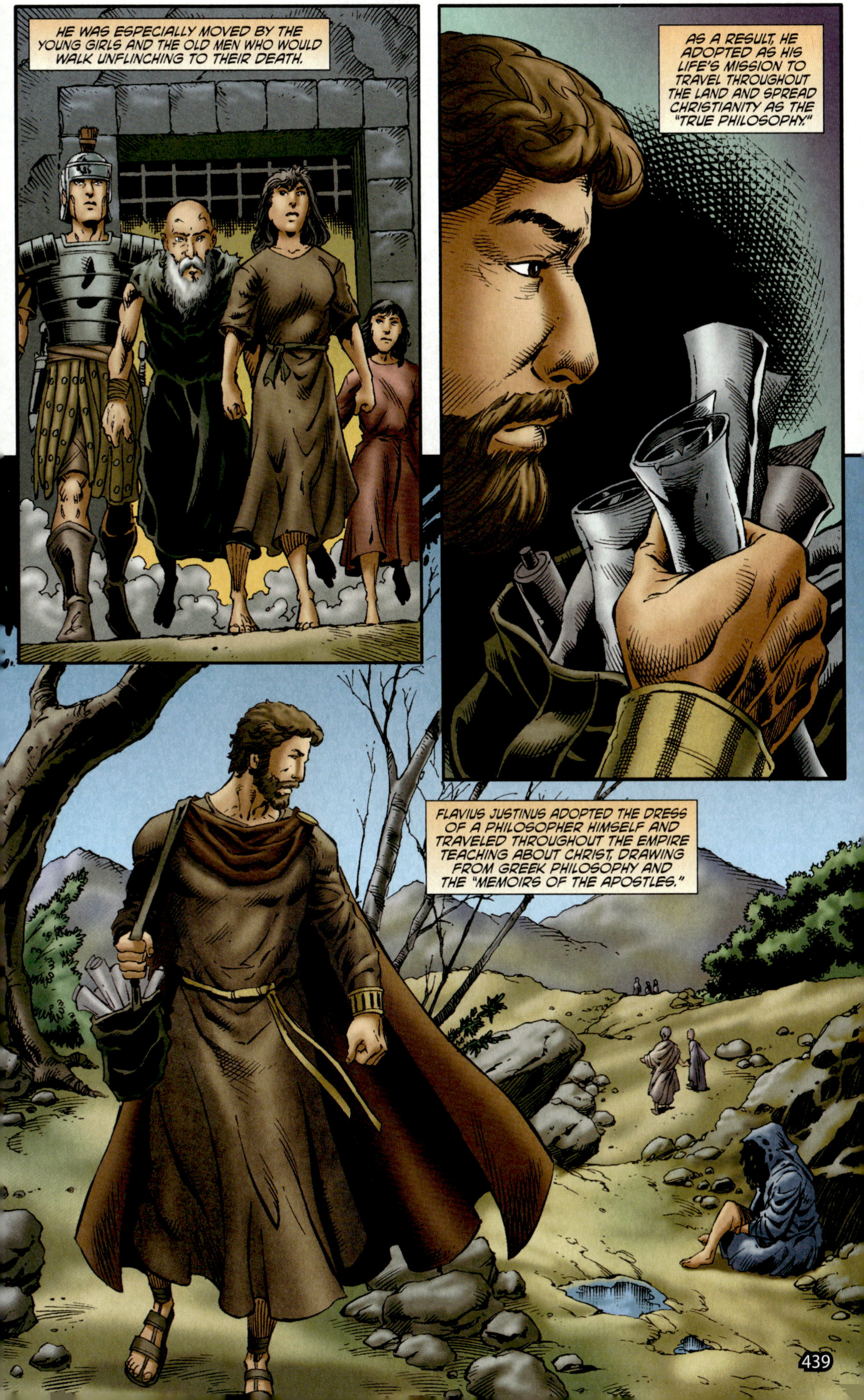
HE WAS ESPECIALLY MOVED BY THE YOUNG GIRLS AND THE OLD MEN WHO WOULD WALK UNFLINCHING TO THEIR DEATH.
AS A RESULT, HE ADOPTED AS HIS LIFE'S MISSION TO TRAVEL THROUGHOUT THE LAND AND SPREAD CHRISTIANITY AS THE "TRUE PHILOSOPHY."
FLAVIUS JUSTINUS ADOPTED THE DRESS OF A PHILOSOPHER HIMSELF AND TRAVELED THROUGHOUT THE EMPIRE TEACHING ABOUT CHRIST, DRAWING FROM GREEK PHILOSOPHY AND THE "MEMOIRS OF THE APOSTLES."

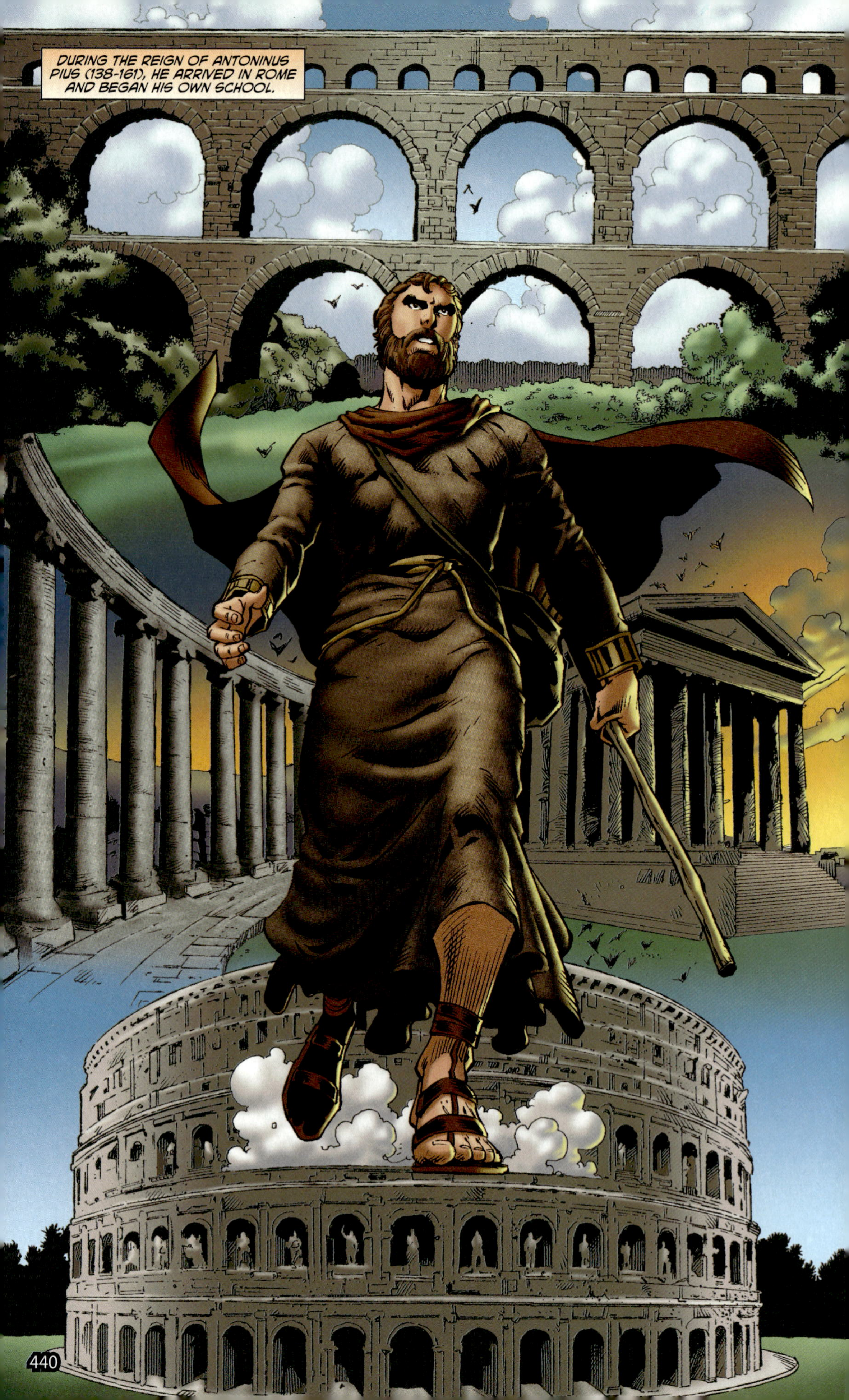
DURING THE REIGN OF ANTONINUS PIUS (138-161), HE ARRIVED IN ROME AND BEGAN HIS OWN SCHOOL.

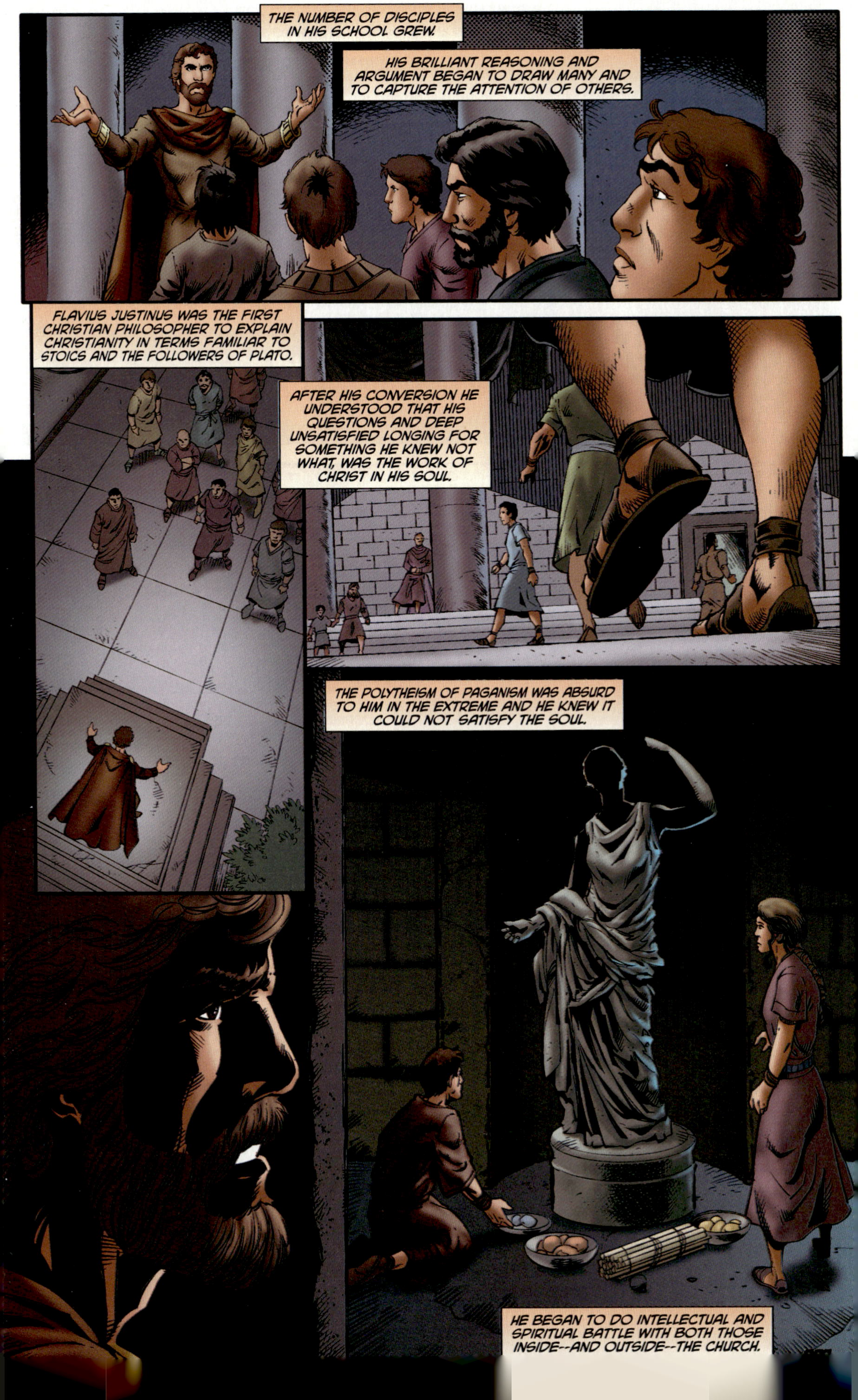
THE NUMBER OF DISCIPLES IN HIS SCHOOL GREW.
HIS BRILLIANT REASONING AND ARGUMENT BEGAN TO DRAW MANY AND TO CAPTURE THE ATTENTION OF OTHERS.
FLAVIUS JUSTINUS WAS THE FIRST CHRISTIAN PHILOSOPHER TO EXPLAIN CHRISTIANITY IN TERMS FAMILIAR TO STOICS AND THE FOLLOWERS OF PLATO.
AFTER HIS CONVERSION HE UNDERSTOOD THAT HIS QUESTIONS AND DEEP UNSATISFIED LONGING FOR SOMETHING HE KNEW NOT WHAT, WAS THE WORK OF CHRIST IN HIS SOUL.
THE POLYTHEISM OF PAGANISM WAS ABSURD TO HIM IN THE EXTREME AND HE KNEW IT COULD NOT SATISFY THE SOUL.
HE BEGAN TO DO INTELLECTUAL AND SPIRITUAL BATTLE WITH BOTH THOSE INSIDE--AND OUTSIDE--THE CHURCH.

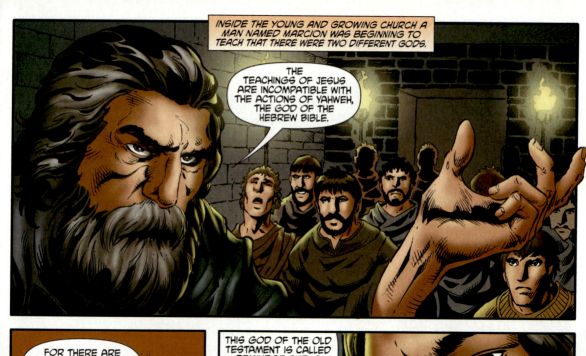

INSIDE THE YOUNG AND GROWING CHURCH A MAN NAMED MARCION WAS BEGINNING TO TEACH THAT THERE WERE TWO DIFFERENT GODS.

THE TEACHINGS OF JESUS ARE INCOMPATIBLE WITH THE ACTIONS OF YAHWEH, THE GOD OF THE HEBREW BIBLE.

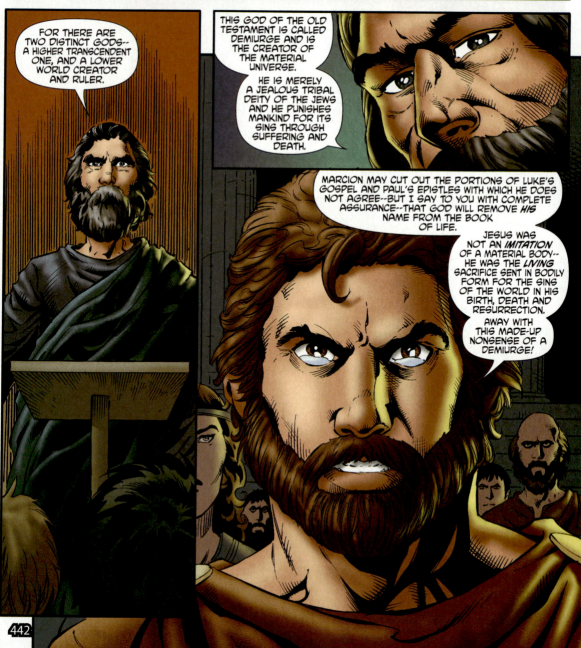

FOR THERE ARE TWO DISTINCT GODS-- A HIGHER TRANSCENDENT ONE, AND A LOWER WORLD CREATOR AND RULER.

THIS GOD OF THE OLD TESTAMENT IS CALLED DEMIURGE AND IS THE CREATOR OF THE MATERIAL UNIVERSE.

HE IS MERELY A JEALOUS TRIBAL DEITY OF THE JEWS AND HE PUNISHES MANKIND FOR ITS SINS THROUGH SUFFERING AND DEATH.

MARCION MAY CUT OUT THE PORTIONS OF LUKE'S GOSPEL AND PAUL'S EPISTLES WITH WHICH HE DOES NOT AGREE--BUT I SAY TO YOU WITH COMPLETE ASSURANCE--THAT GOD WILL REMOVE *HIS* NAME FROM THE BOOK OF LIFE.

JESUS WAS NOT AN *IMITATION* OF A MATERIAL BODY-- HE WAS THE *LIVING* SACRIFICE SENT IN BODILY FORM FOR THE SINS OF THE WORLD IN HIS BIRTH, DEATH AND RESURRECTION.

AWAY WITH THIS MADE-UP NONSENSE OF A DEMIURGE!

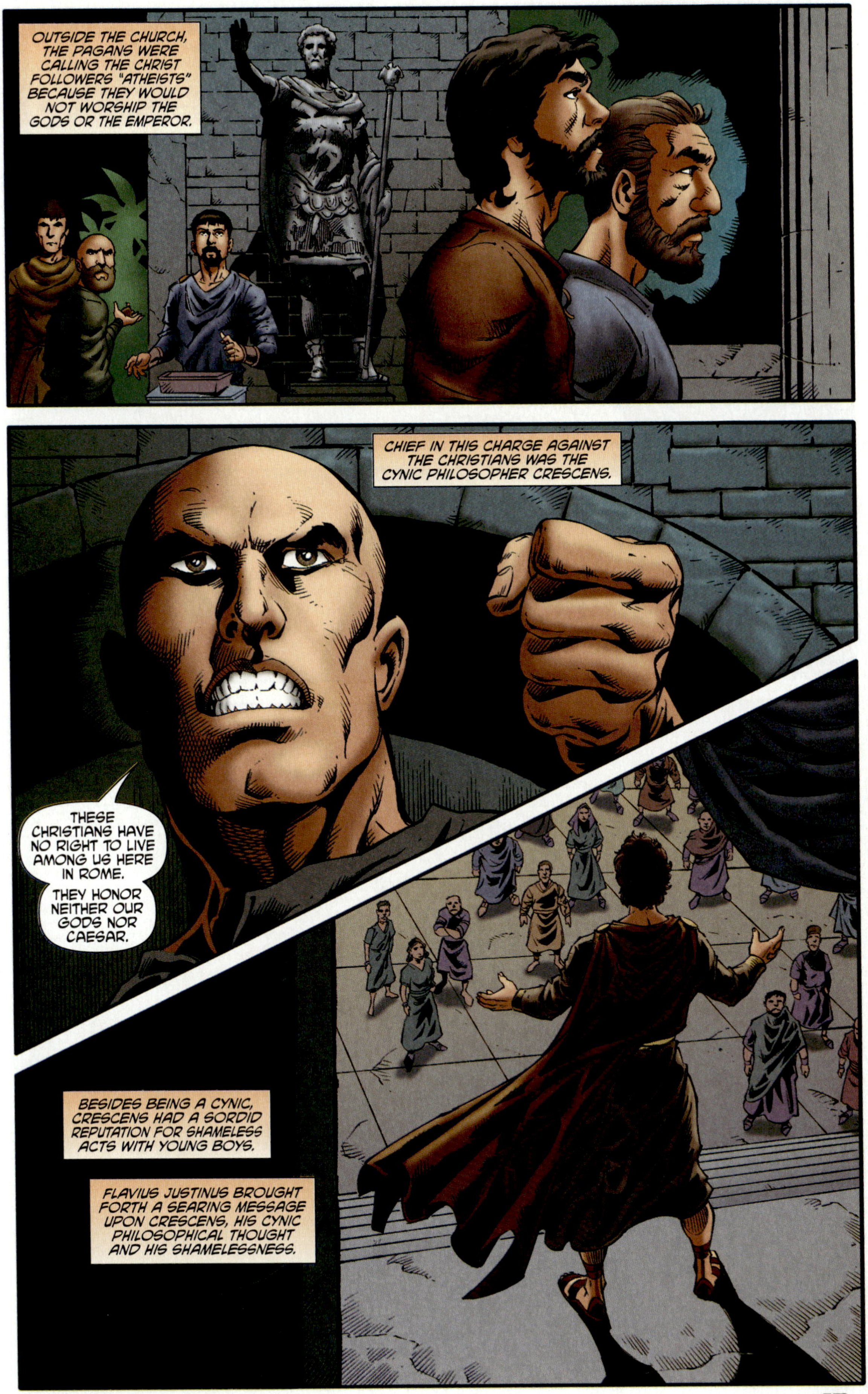
OUTSIDE THE CHURCH, THE PAGANS WERE CALLING THE CHRIST FOLLOWERS "ATHEISTS" BECAUSE THEY WOULD NOT WORSHIP THE GODS OR THE EMPEROR.
CHIEF IN THIS CHARGE AGAINST THE CHRISTIANS WAS THE CYNIC PHILOSOPHER CRESCENS.
THESE CHRISTIANS HAVE NO RIGHT TO LIVE AMONG US HERE IN ROME.
THEY HONOR NEITHER OUR GODS NOR CAESAR.
BESIDES BEING A CYNIC, CRESCENS HAD A SORDID REPUTATION FOR SHAMELESS ACTS WITH YOUNG BOYS.
FLAVIUS JUSTINUS BROUGHT FORTH A SEARING MESSAGE UPON CRESCENS, HIS CYNIC PHILOSOPHICAL THOUGHT AND HIS SHAMELESSNESS.

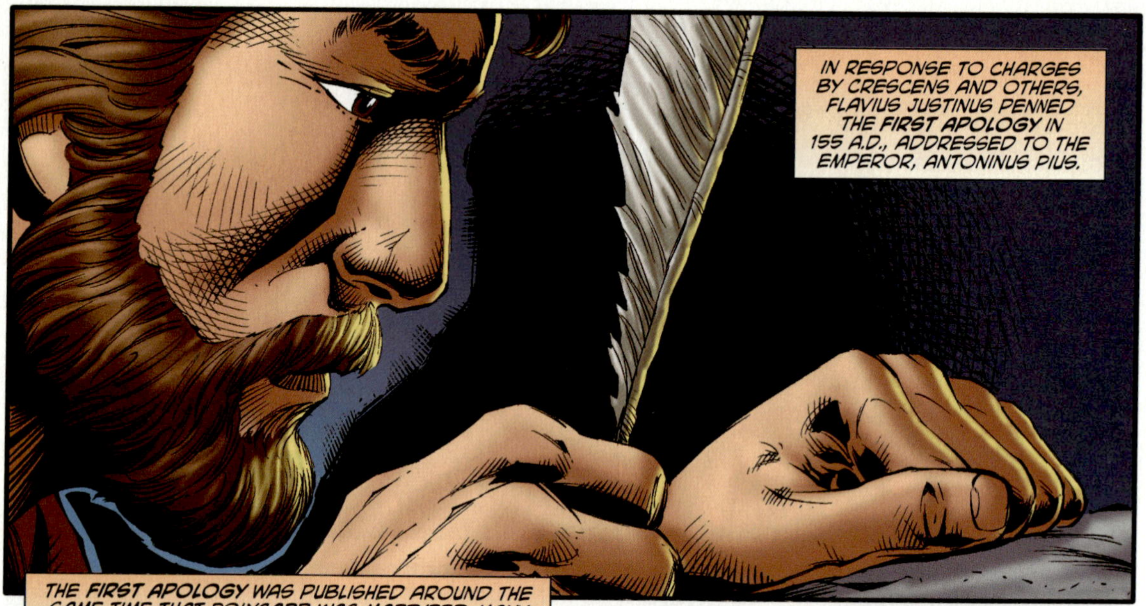
IN RESPONSE TO CHARGES BY CRESCENS AND OTHERS, FLAVIUS JUSTINUS PENNED THE **FIRST APOLOGY** IN 155 A.D., ADDRESSED TO THE EMPEROR, ANTONINUS PIUS.

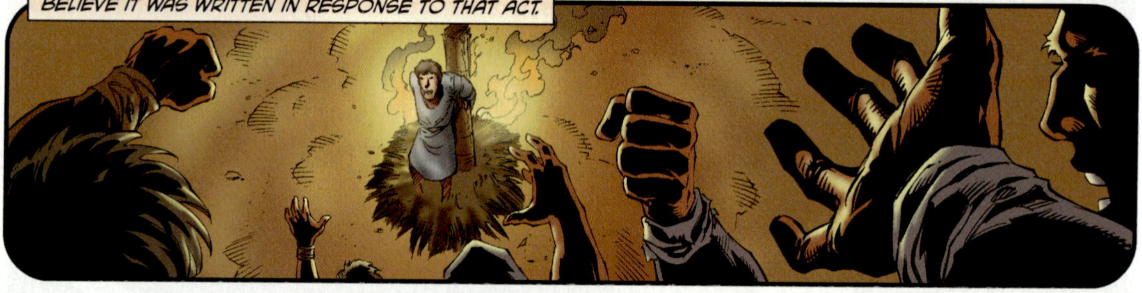
THE **FIRST APOLOGY** WAS PUBLISHED AROUND THE SAME TIME THAT POLYCARP WAS MARTYRED. MANY BELIEVE IT WAS WRITTEN IN RESPONSE TO THAT ACT.

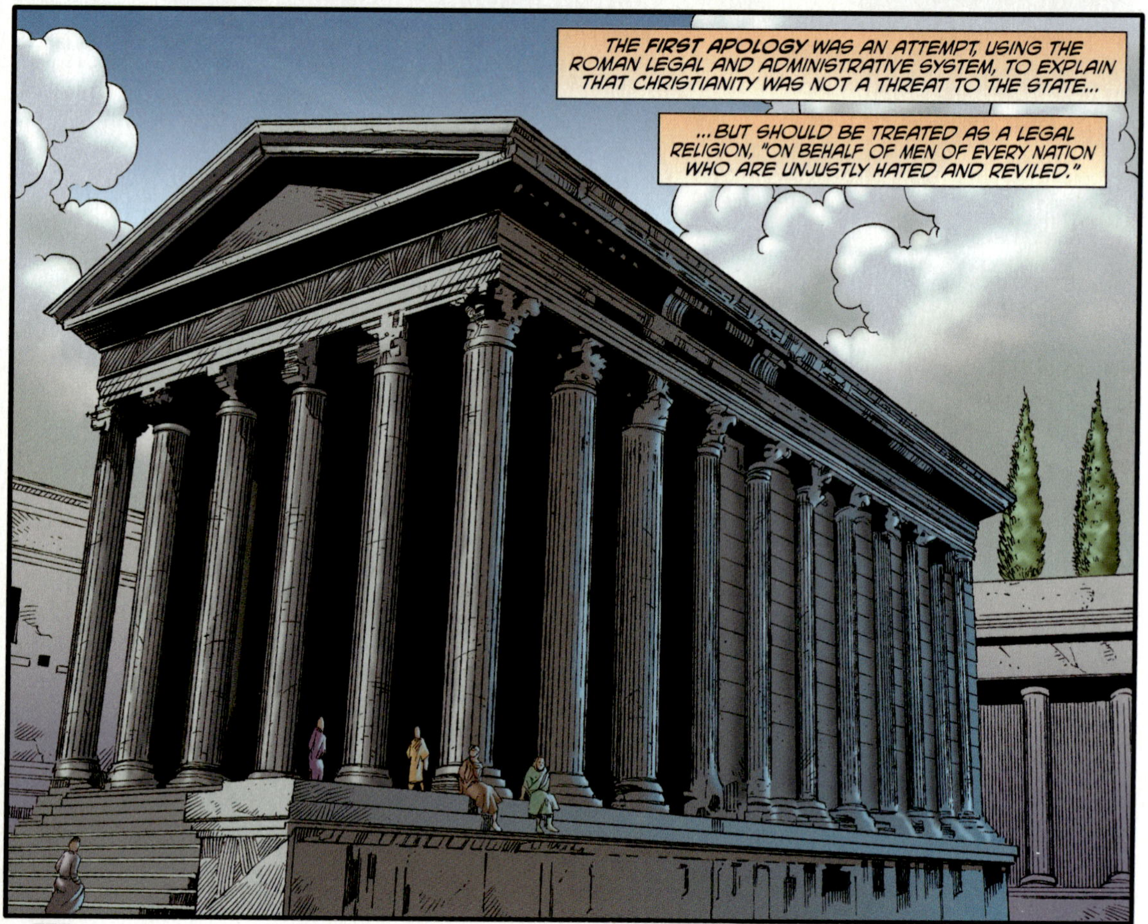
THE **FIRST APOLOGY** WAS AN ATTEMPT, USING THE ROMAN LEGAL AND ADMINISTRATIVE SYSTEM, TO EXPLAIN THAT CHRISTIANITY WAS NOT A THREAT TO THE STATE...
...BUT SHOULD BE TREATED AS A LEGAL RELIGION, "ON BEHALF OF MEN OF EVERY NATION WHO ARE UNJUSTLY HATED AND REVILED."

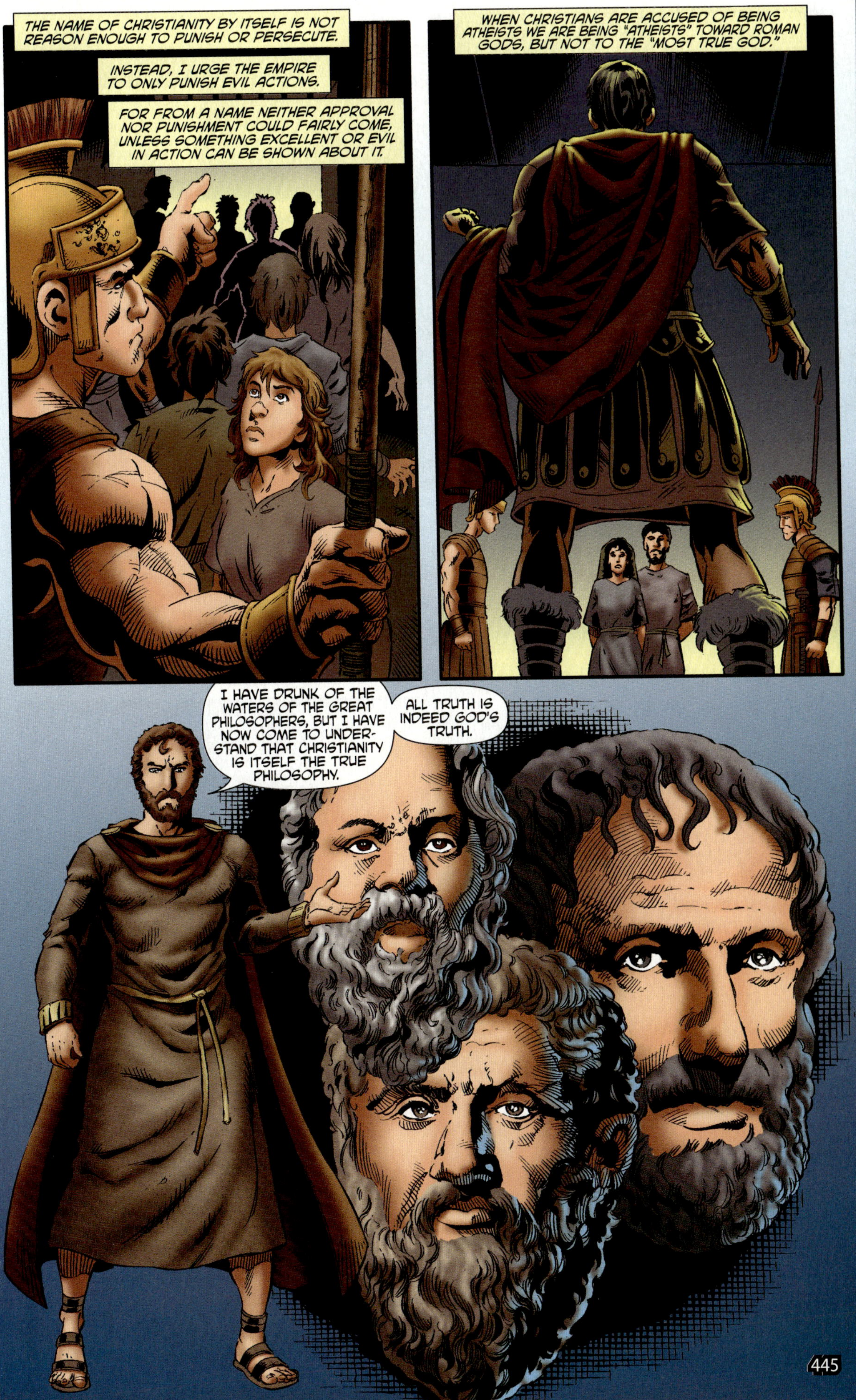
THE NAME OF CHRISTIANITY BY ITSELF IS NOT REASON ENOUGH TO PUNISH OR PERSECUTE.
INSTEAD, I URGE THE EMPIRE TO ONLY PUNISH EVIL ACTIONS.
FOR FROM A NAME NEITHER APPROVAL NOR PUNISHMENT COULD FAIRLY COME, UNLESS SOMETHING EXCELLENT OR EVIL IN ACTION CAN BE SHOWN ABOUT IT.
WHEN CHRISTIANS ARE ACCUSED OF BEING ATHEISTS WE ARE BEING "ATHEISTS" TOWARD ROMAN GODS, BUT NOT TO THE "MOST TRUE GOD."
I HAVE DRUNK OF THE WATERS OF THE GREAT PHILOSOPHERS, BUT I HAVE NOW COME TO UNDER-STAND THAT CHRISTIANITY IS ITSELF THE TRUE PHILOSOPHY.
ALL TRUTH IS INDEED GOD'S TRUTH.

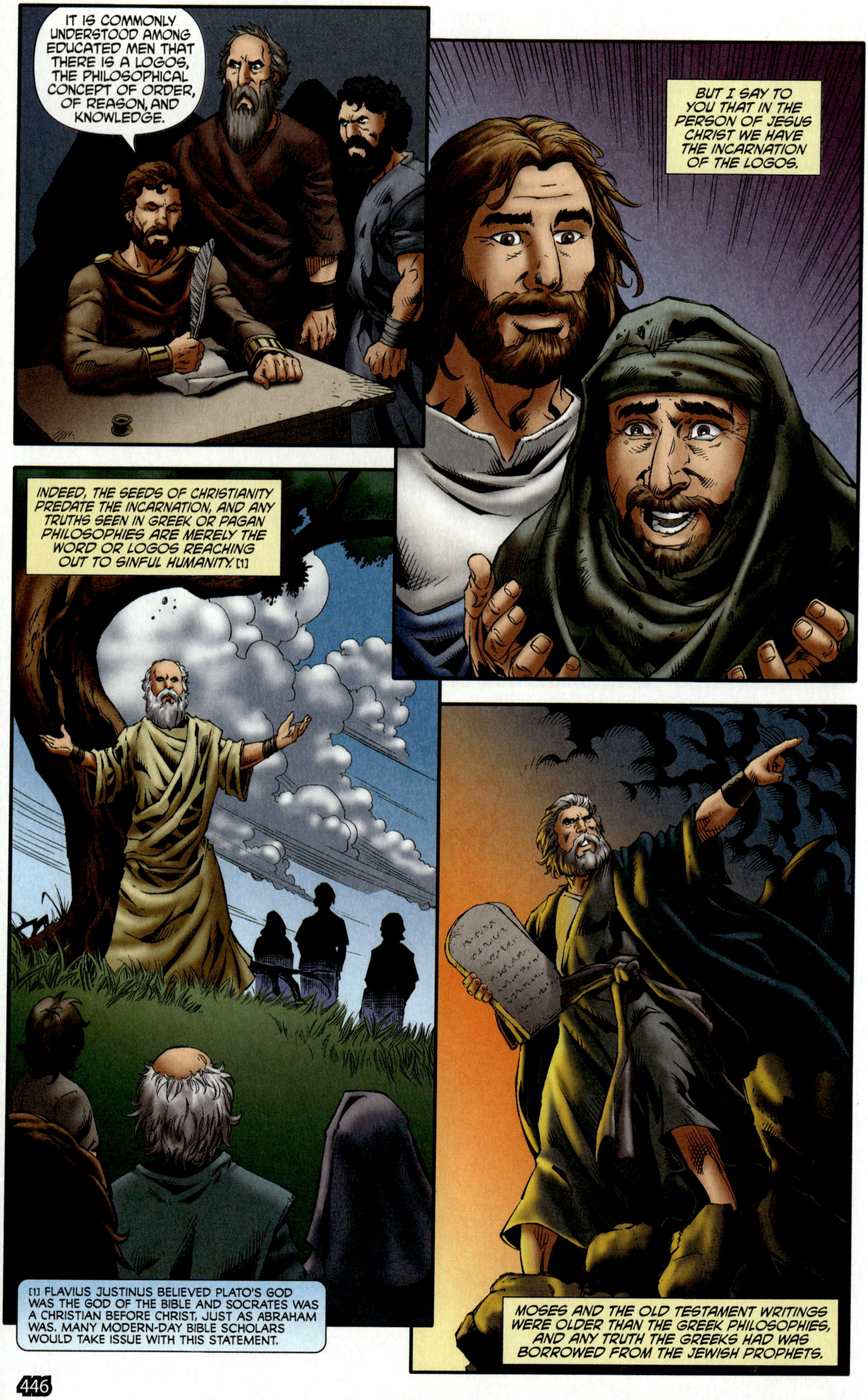
IT IS COMMONLY UNDERSTOOD AMONG EDUCATED MEN THAT THERE IS A LOGOS, THE PHILOSOPHICAL CONCEPT OF ORDER, OF REASON, AND KNOWLEDGE.
BUT I SAY TO YOU THAT IN THE PERSON OF JESUS CHRIST WE HAVE THE INCARNATION OF THE LOGOS.
INDEED, THE SEEDS OF CHRISTIANITY PREDATE THE INCARNATION, AND ANY TRUTHS SEEN IN GREEK OR PAGAN PHILOSOPHIES ARE MERELY THE WORD OR LOGOS REACHING OUT TO SINFUL HUMANITY. [1]
MOSES AND THE OLD TESTAMENT WRITINGS WERE OLDER THAN THE GREEK PHILOSOPHIES, AND ANY TRUTH THE GREEKS HAD WAS BORROWED FROM THE JEWISH PROPHETS.

[1] FLAVIUS JUSTINUS BELIEVED PLATO'S GOD WAS THE GOD OF THE BIBLE AND SOCRATES WAS A CHRISTIAN BEFORE CHRIST, JUST AS ABRAHAM WAS. MANY MODERN-DAY BIBLE SCHOLARS WOULD TAKE ISSUE WITH THIS STATEMENT.

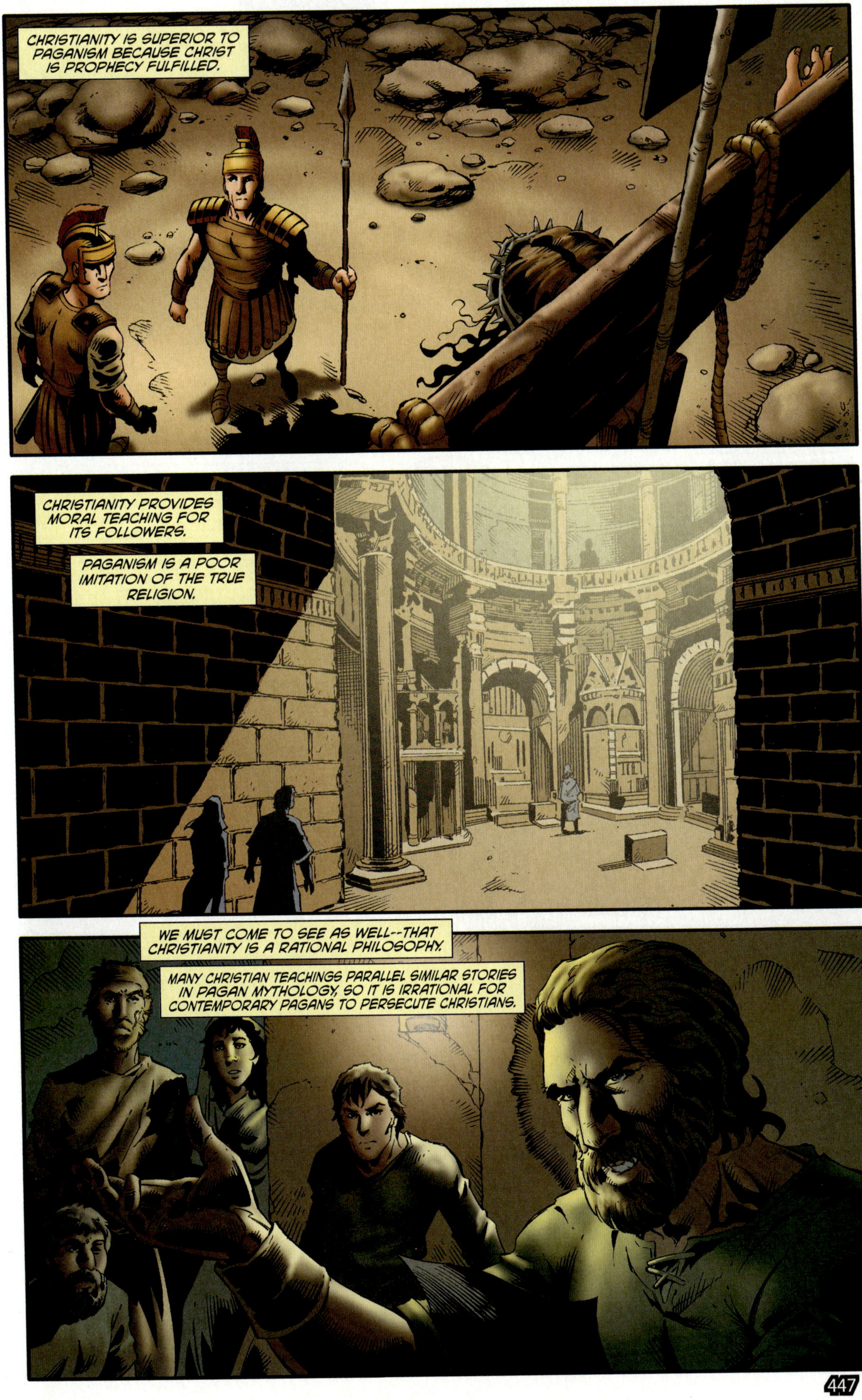
CHRISTIANITY IS SUPERIOR TO PAGANISM BECAUSE CHRIST IS PROPHECY FULFILLED.
CHRISTIANITY PROVIDES MORAL TEACHING FOR ITS FOLLOWERS.
PAGANISM IS A POOR IMITATION OF THE TRUE RELIGION.
WE MUST COME TO SEE AS WELL--THAT CHRISTIANITY IS A RATIONAL PHILOSOPHY.
MANY CHRISTIAN TEACHINGS PARALLEL SIMILAR STORIES IN PAGAN MYTHOLOGY, SO IT IS IRRATIONAL FOR CONTEMPORARY PAGANS TO PERSECUTE CHRISTIANS.

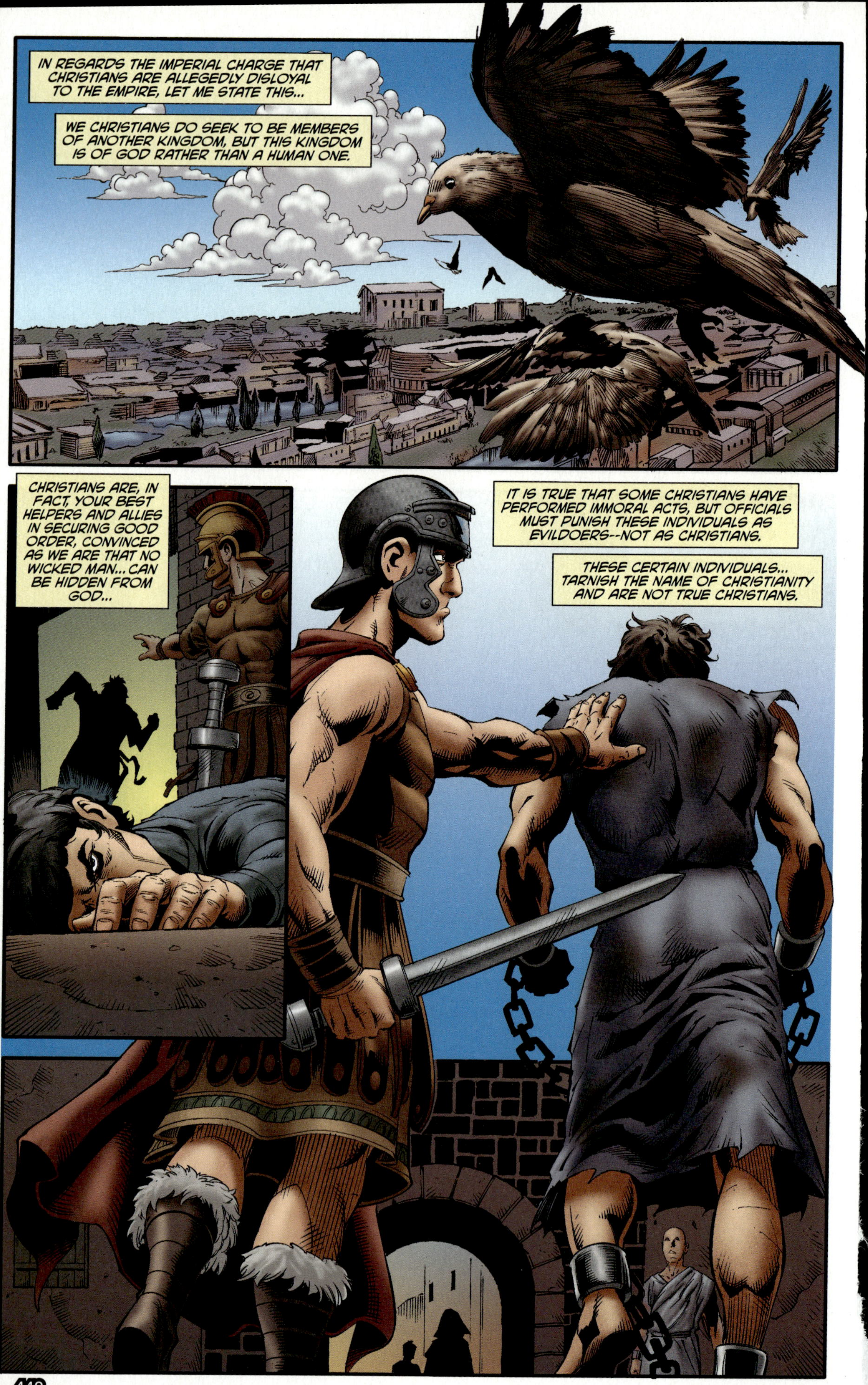
IN REGARDS THE IMPERIAL CHARGE THAT CHRISTIANS ARE ALLEGEDLY DISLOYAL TO THE EMPIRE, LET ME STATE THIS...
WE CHRISTIANS DO SEEK TO BE MEMBERS OF ANOTHER KINGDOM, BUT THIS KINGDOM IS OF GOD RATHER THAN A HUMAN ONE.
CHRISTIANS ARE, IN FACT, YOUR BEST HELPERS AND ALLIES IN SECURING GOOD ORDER, CONVINCED AS WE ARE THAT NO WICKED MAN... CAN BE HIDDEN FROM GOD...
IT IS TRUE THAT SOME CHRISTIANS HAVE PERFORMED IMMORAL ACTS, BUT OFFICIALS MUST PUNISH THESE INDIVIDUALS AS EVILDOERS--NOT AS CHRISTIANS.
THESE CERTAIN INDIVIDUALS... TARNISH THE NAME OF CHRISTIANITY AND ARE NOT TRUE CHRISTIANS.

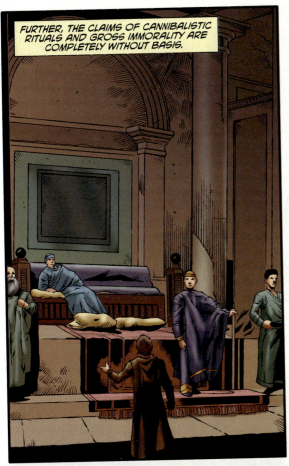

FURTHER, THE CLAIMS OF CANNIBALISTIC RITUALS AND GROSS IMMORALITY ARE COMPLETELY WITHOUT BASIS.

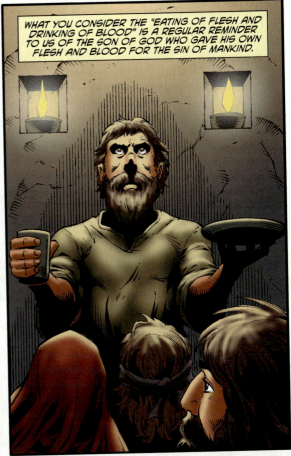

WHAT YOU CONSIDER THE "EATING OF FLESH AND DRINKING OF BLOOD" IS A REGULAR REMINDER TO US OF THE SON OF GOD WHO GAVE HIS OWN FLESH AND BLOOD FOR THE SIN OF MANKIND.

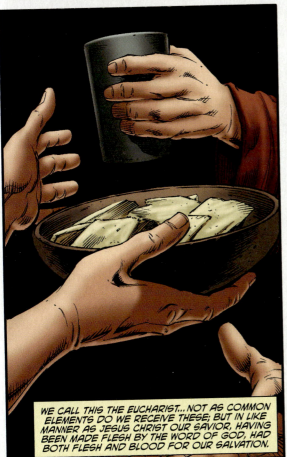

WE CALL THIS THE EUCHARIST... NOT AS COMMON ELEMENTS DO WE RECEIVE THESE; BUT IN LIKE MANNER AS JESUS CHRIST OUR SAVIOR, HAVING BEEN MADE FLESH BY THE WORD OF GOD, HAD BOTH FLESH AND BLOOD FOR OUR SALVATION.

OUR LOVE FEASTS ARE... A FILIAL GATHERING OF THE PEOPLE OF CHRIST WHO GATHER IN HIS HOLY NAME.

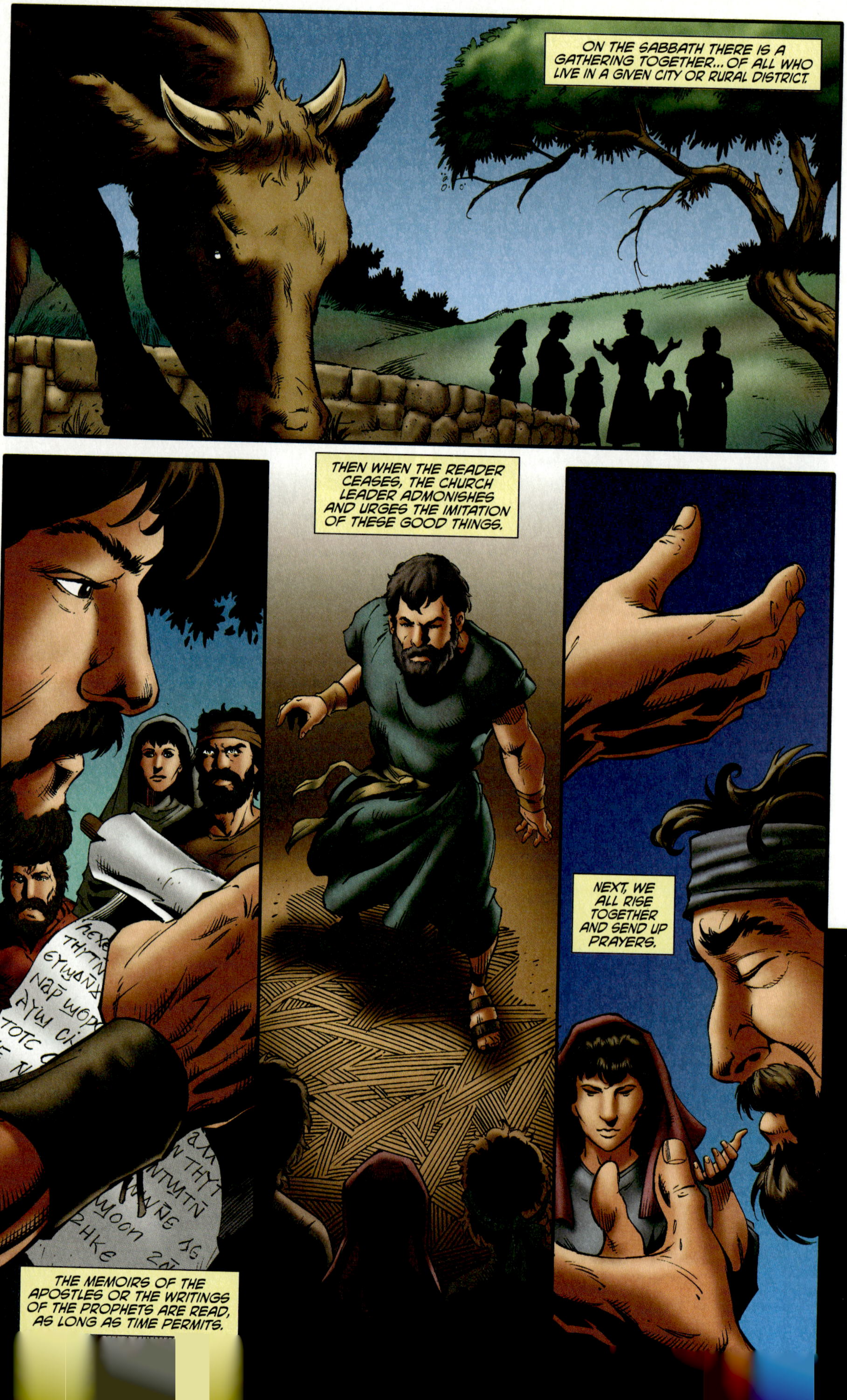
ON THE SABBATH THERE IS A GATHERING TOGETHER... OF ALL WHO LIVE IN A GIVEN CITY OR RURAL DISTRICT.
THE MEMOIRS OF THE APOSTLES OR THE WRITINGS OF THE PROPHETS ARE READ, AS LONG AS TIME PERMITS.
THEN WHEN THE READER CEASES, THE CHURCH LEADER ADMONISHES AND URGES THE IMITATION OF THESE GOOD THINGS.
NEXT, WE ALL RISE TOGETHER AND SEND UP PRAYERS.

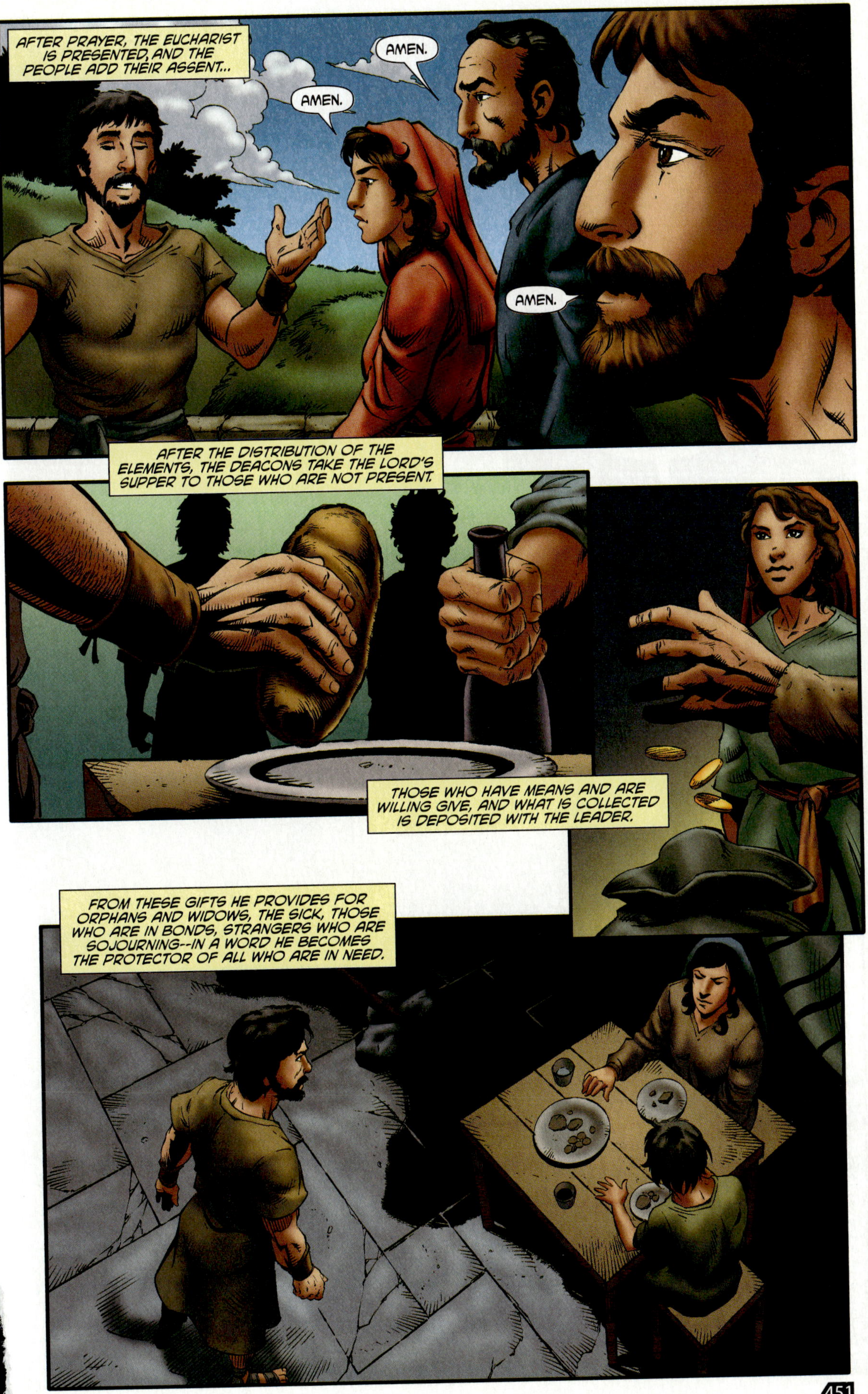
AFTER PRAYER, THE EUCHARIST IS PRESENTED, AND THE PEOPLE ADD THEIR ASSENT...
AMEN.
AMEN.
AMEN.
AFTER THE DISTRIBUTION OF THE ELEMENTS, THE DEACONS TAKE THE LORD'S SUPPER TO THOSE WHO ARE NOT PRESENT.
THOSE WHO HAVE MEANS AND ARE WILLING GIVE, AND WHAT IS COLLECTED IS DEPOSITED WITH THE LEADER.
FROM THESE GIFTS HE PROVIDES FOR ORPHANS AND WIDOWS, THE SICK, THOSE WHO ARE IN BONDS, STRANGERS WHO ARE SOJOURNING--IN A WORD HE BECOMES THE PROTECTOR OF ALL WHO ARE IN NEED.

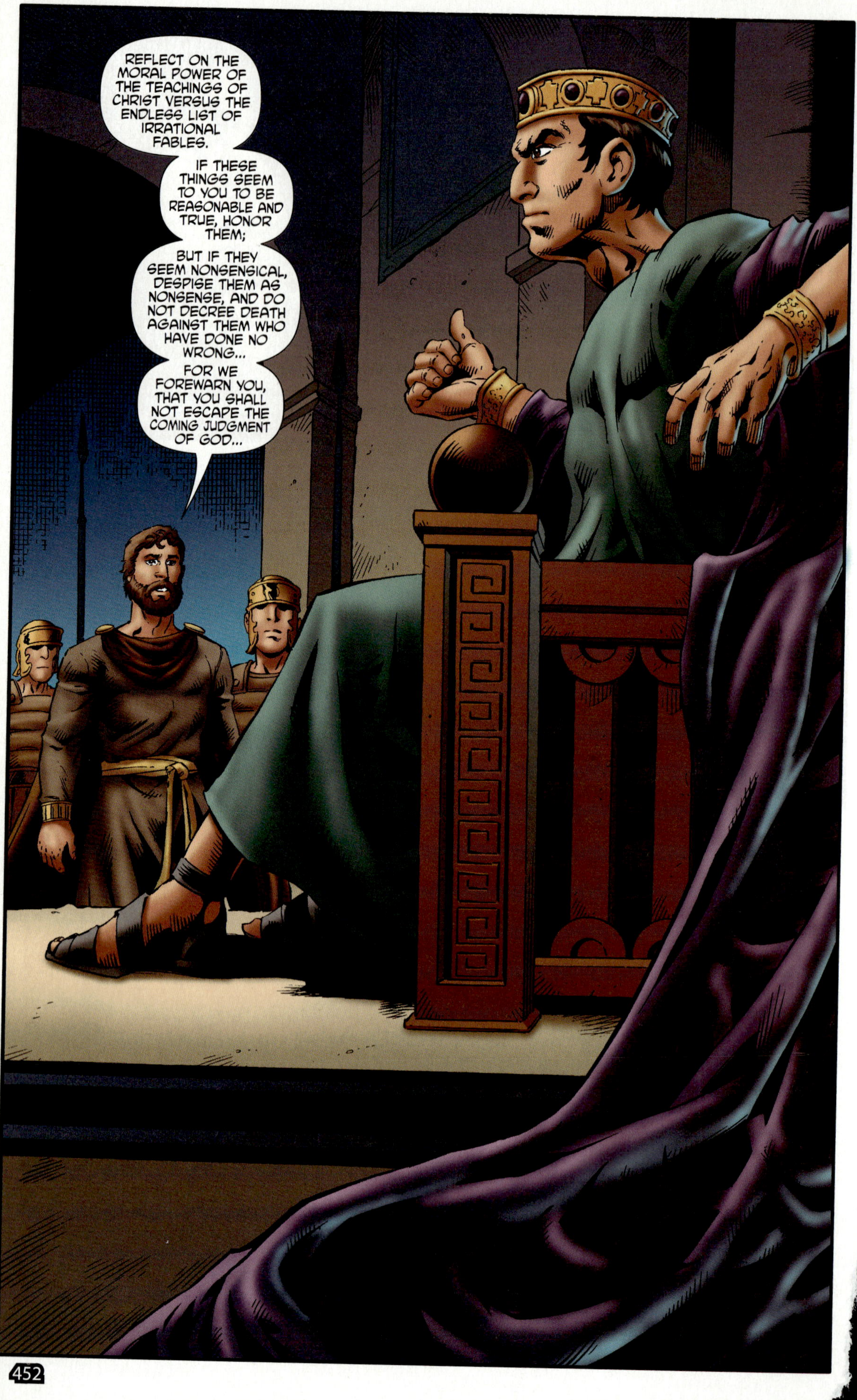
REFLECT ON THE MORAL POWER OF THE TEACHINGS OF CHRIST VERSUS THE ENDLESS LIST OF IRRATIONAL FABLES.
IF THESE THINGS SEEM TO YOU TO BE REASONABLE AND TRUE, HONOR THEM;
BUT IF THEY SEEM NONSENSICAL, DESPISE THEM AS NONSENSE, AND DO NOT DECREE DEATH AGAINST THEM WHO HAVE DONE NO WRONG...
FOR WE FOREWARN YOU, THAT YOU SHALL NOT ESCAPE THE COMING JUDGMENT OF GOD...

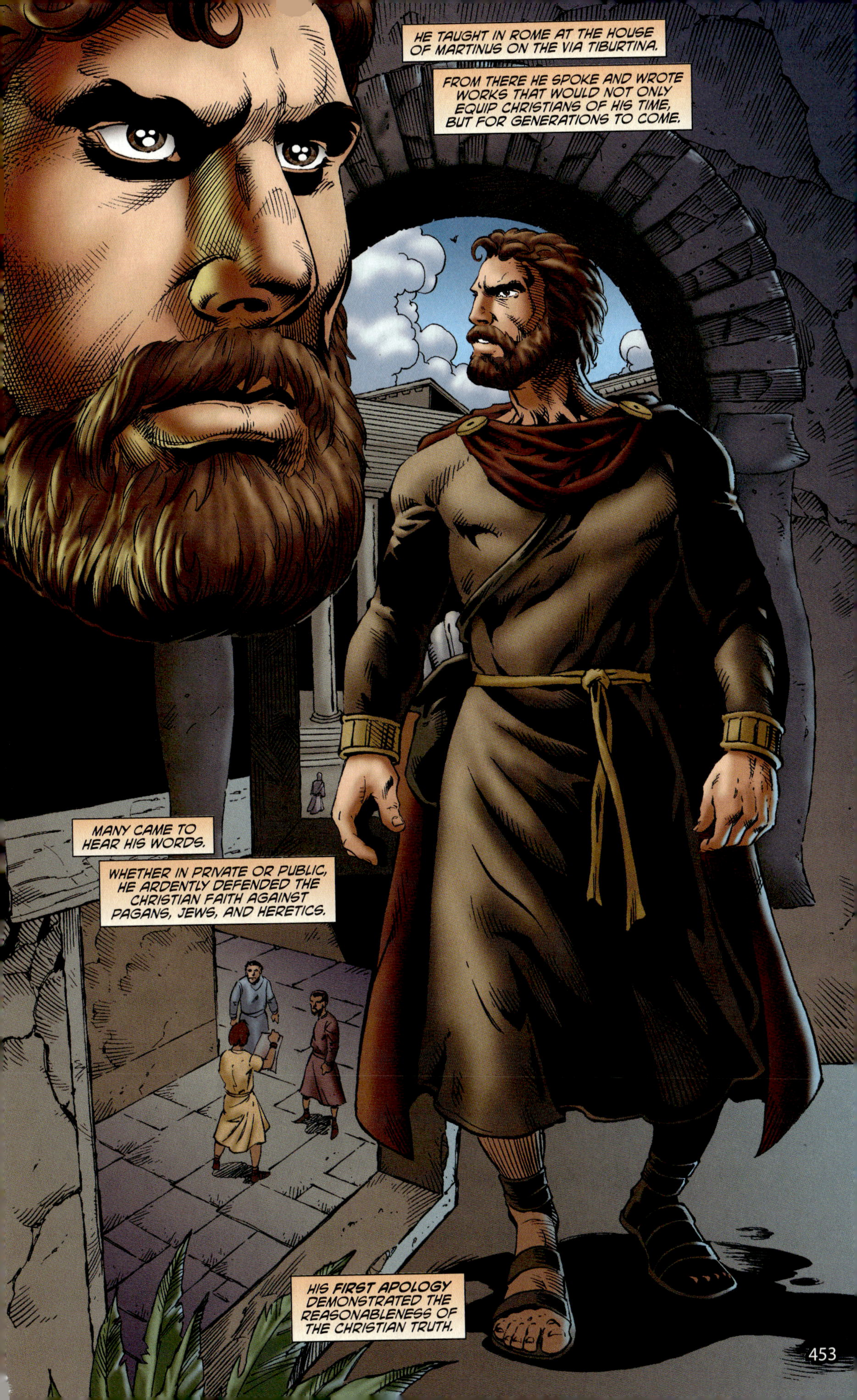
HE TAUGHT IN ROME AT THE HOUSE OF MARTINUS ON THE VIA TIBURTINA.
FROM THERE HE SPOKE AND WROTE WORKS THAT WOULD NOT ONLY EQUIP CHRISTIANS OF HIS TIME, BUT FOR GENERATIONS TO COME.
MANY CAME TO HEAR HIS WORDS.
WHETHER IN PRIVATE OR PUBLIC, HE ARDENTLY DEFENDED THE CHRISTIAN FAITH AGAINST PAGANS, JEWS, AND HERETICS.
HIS FIRST APOLOGY DEMONSTRATED THE REASONABLENESS OF THE CHRISTIAN TRUTH.

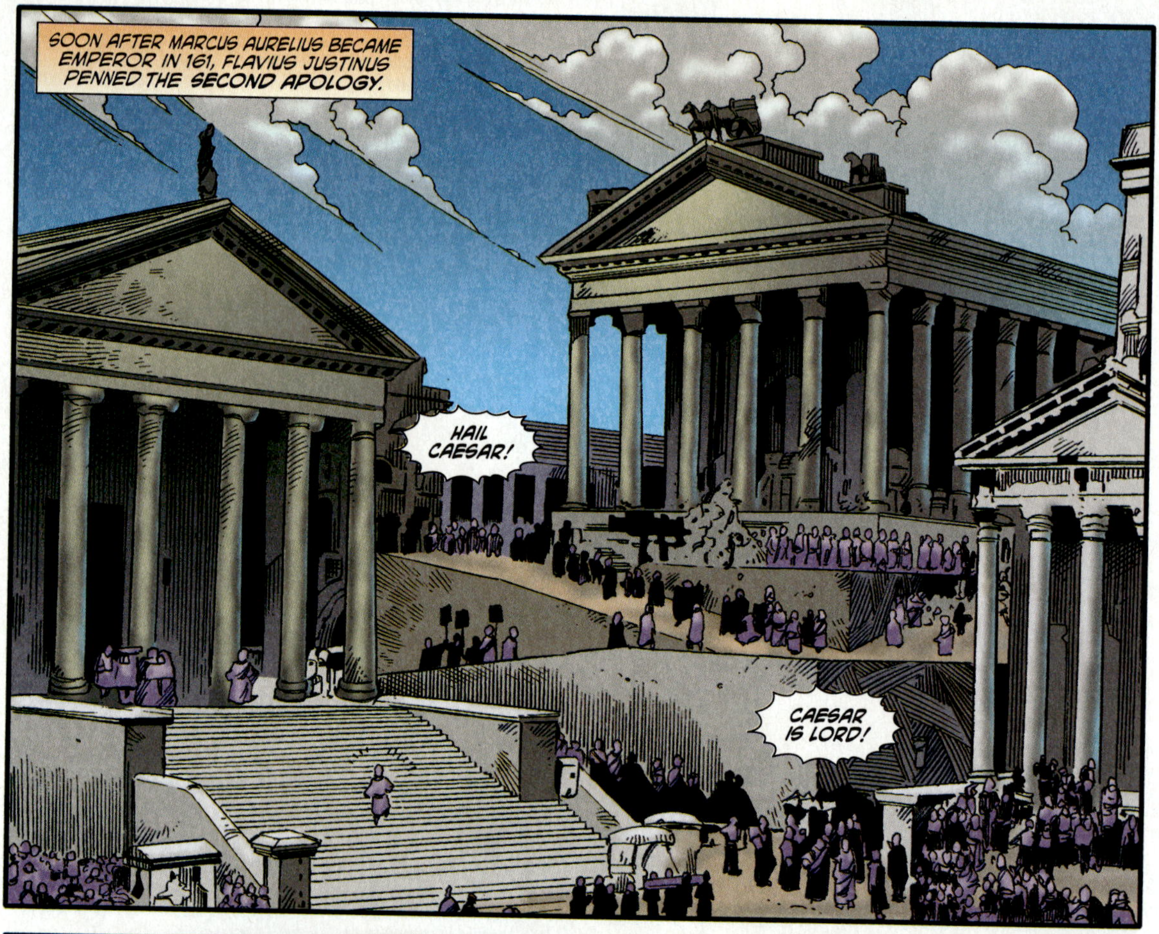
SOON AFTER MARCUS AURELIUS BECAME EMPEROR IN 161, FLAVIUS JUSTINUS PENNED THE SECOND APOLOGY.
HAIL CAESAR!
CAESAR IS LORD!

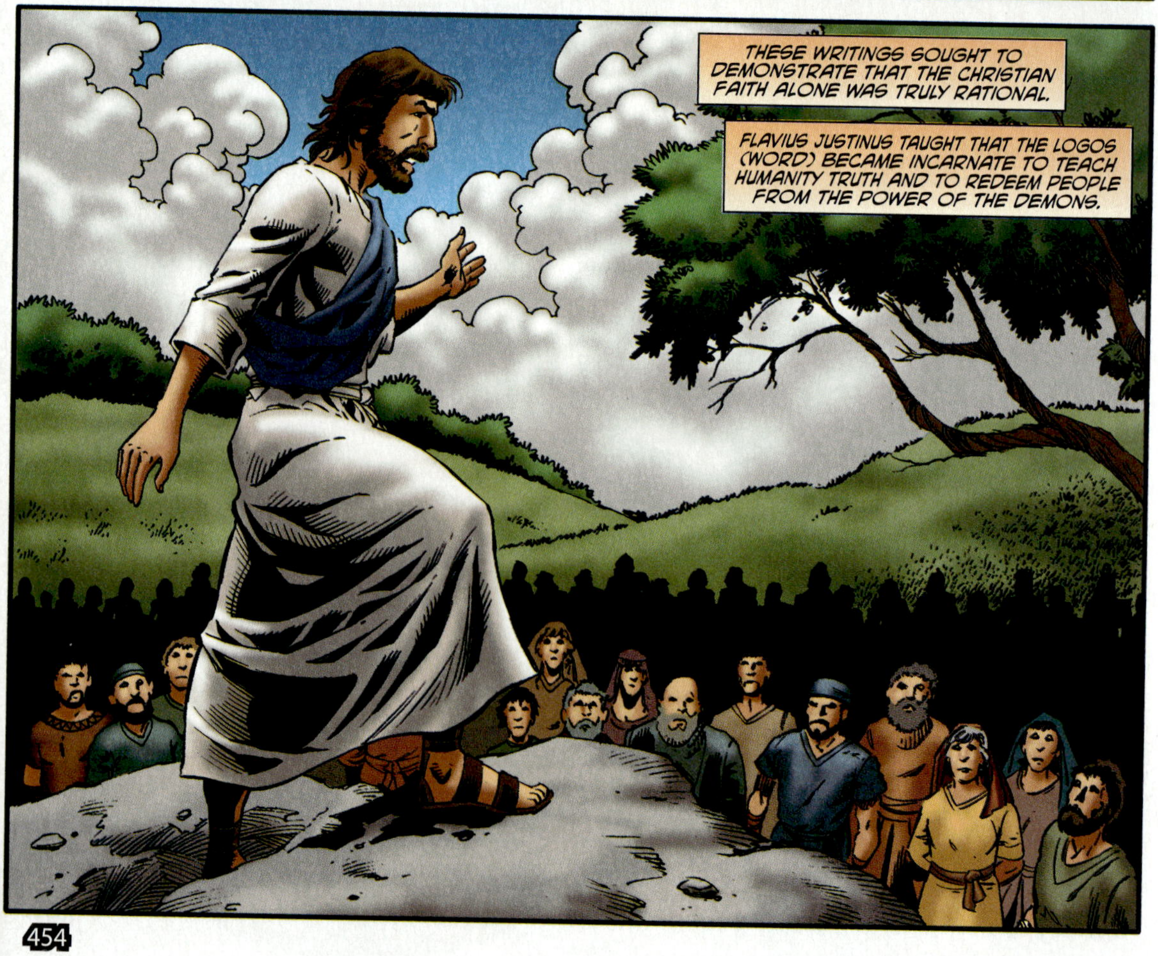
THESE WRITINGS SOUGHT TO DEMONSTRATE THAT THE CHRISTIAN FAITH ALONE WAS TRULY RATIONAL.
FLAVIUS JUSTINUS TAUGHT THAT THE LOGOS (WORD) BECAME INCARNATE TO TEACH HUMANITY TRUTH AND TO REDEEM PEOPLE FROM THE POWER OF THE DEMONS.

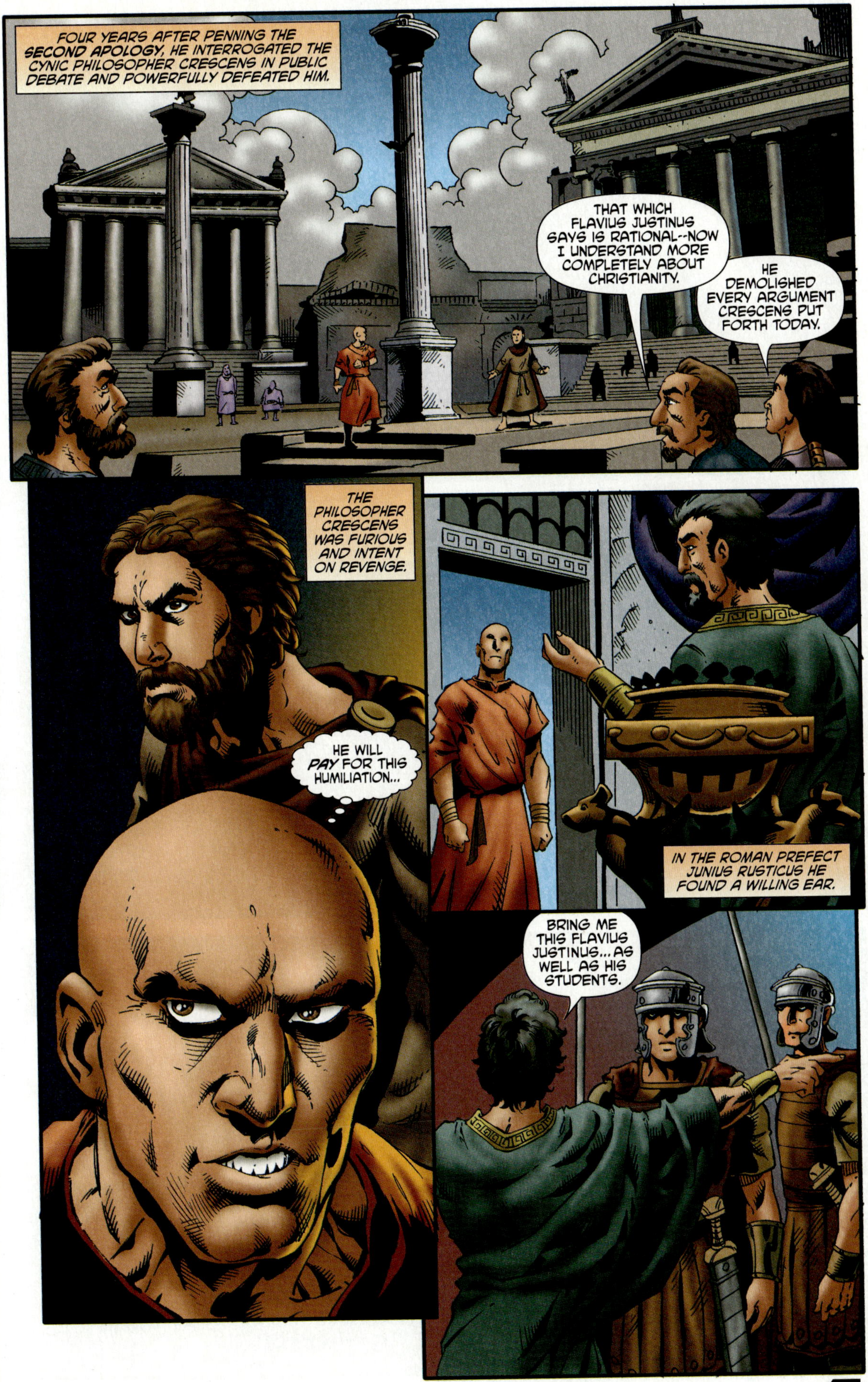
FOUR YEARS AFTER PENNING THE SECOND APOLOGY, HE INTERROGATED THE CYNIC PHILOSOPHER CRESCENS IN PUBLIC DEBATE AND POWERFULLY DEFEATED HIM.
THAT WHICH FLAVIUS JUSTINUS SAYS IS RATIONAL--NOW I UNDERSTAND MORE COMPLETELY ABOUT CHRISTIANITY.
HE DEMOLISHED EVERY ARGUMENT CRESCENS PUT FORTH TODAY.
THE PHILOSOPHER CRESCENS WAS FURIOUS AND INTENT ON REVENGE.
HE WILL PAY FOR THIS HUMILIATION...
IN THE ROMAN PREFECT JUNIUS RUSTICUS HE FOUND A WILLING EAR.
BRING ME THIS FLAVIUS JUSTINUS...AS WELL AS HIS STUDENTS.

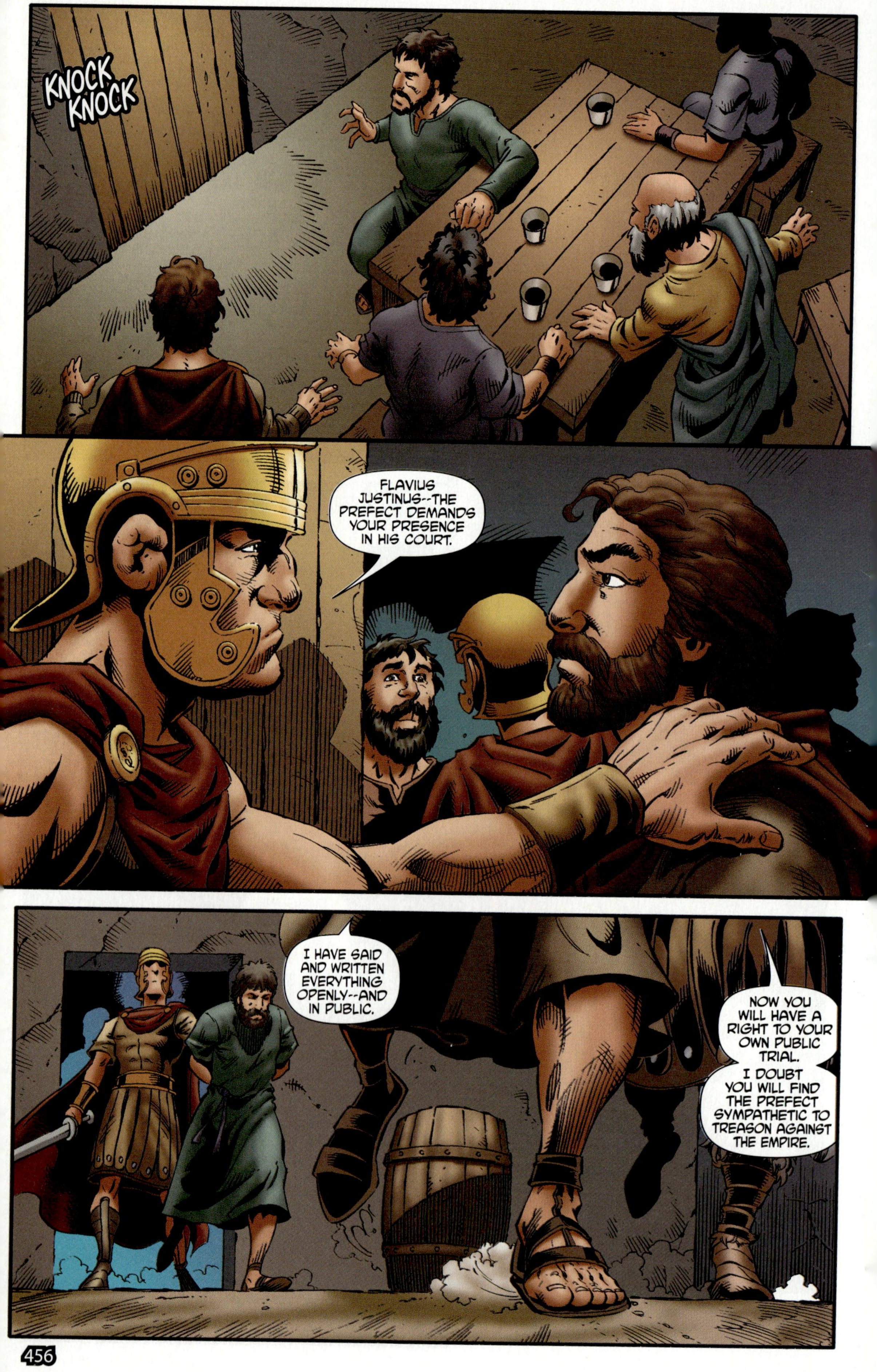
KNOCK KNOCK
FLAVIUS JUSTINUS--THE PREFECT DEMANDS YOUR PRESENCE IN HIS COURT.
I HAVE SAID AND WRITTEN EVERYTHING OPENLY--AND IN PUBLIC.
NOW YOU WILL HAVE A RIGHT TO YOUR OWN PUBLIC TRIAL.
I DOUBT YOU WILL FIND THE PREFECT SYMPATHETIC TO TREASON AGAINST THE EMPIRE.

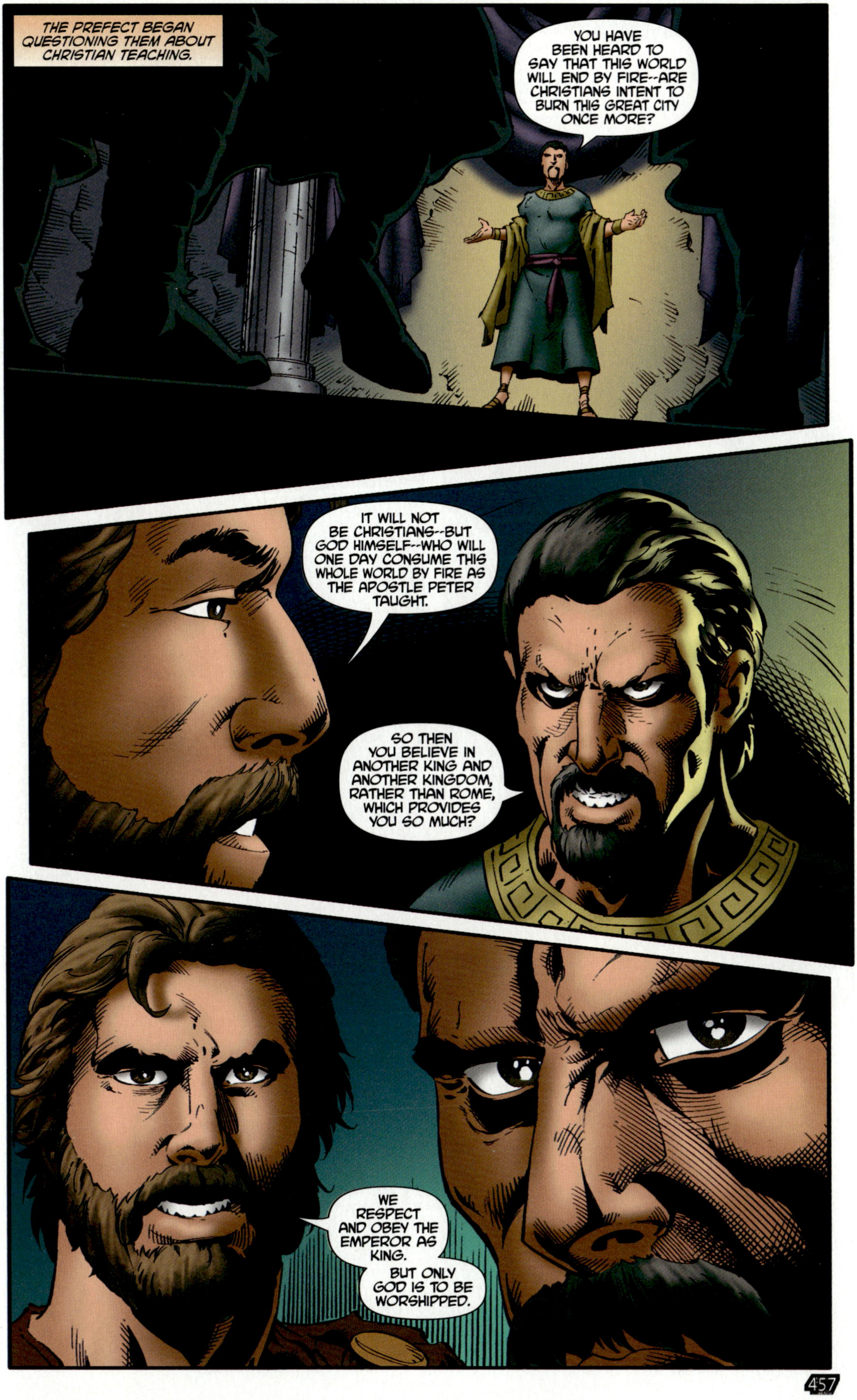

THE PREFECT BEGAN QUESTIONING THEM ABOUT CHRISTIAN TEACHING.
YOU HAVE BEEN HEARD TO SAY THAT THIS WORLD WILL END BY FIRE--ARE CHRISTIANS INTENT TO BURN THIS GREAT CITY ONCE MORE?
IT WILL NOT BE CHRISTIANS--BUT GOD HIMSELF--WHO WILL ONE DAY CONSUME THIS WHOLE WORLD BY FIRE AS THE APOSTLE PETER TAUGHT.
SO THEN YOU BELIEVE IN ANOTHER KING AND ANOTHER KINGDOM, RATHER THAN ROME, WHICH PROVIDES YOU SO MUCH?
WE RESPECT AND OBEY THE EMPEROR AS KING.
BUT ONLY GOD IS TO BE WORSHIPPED.

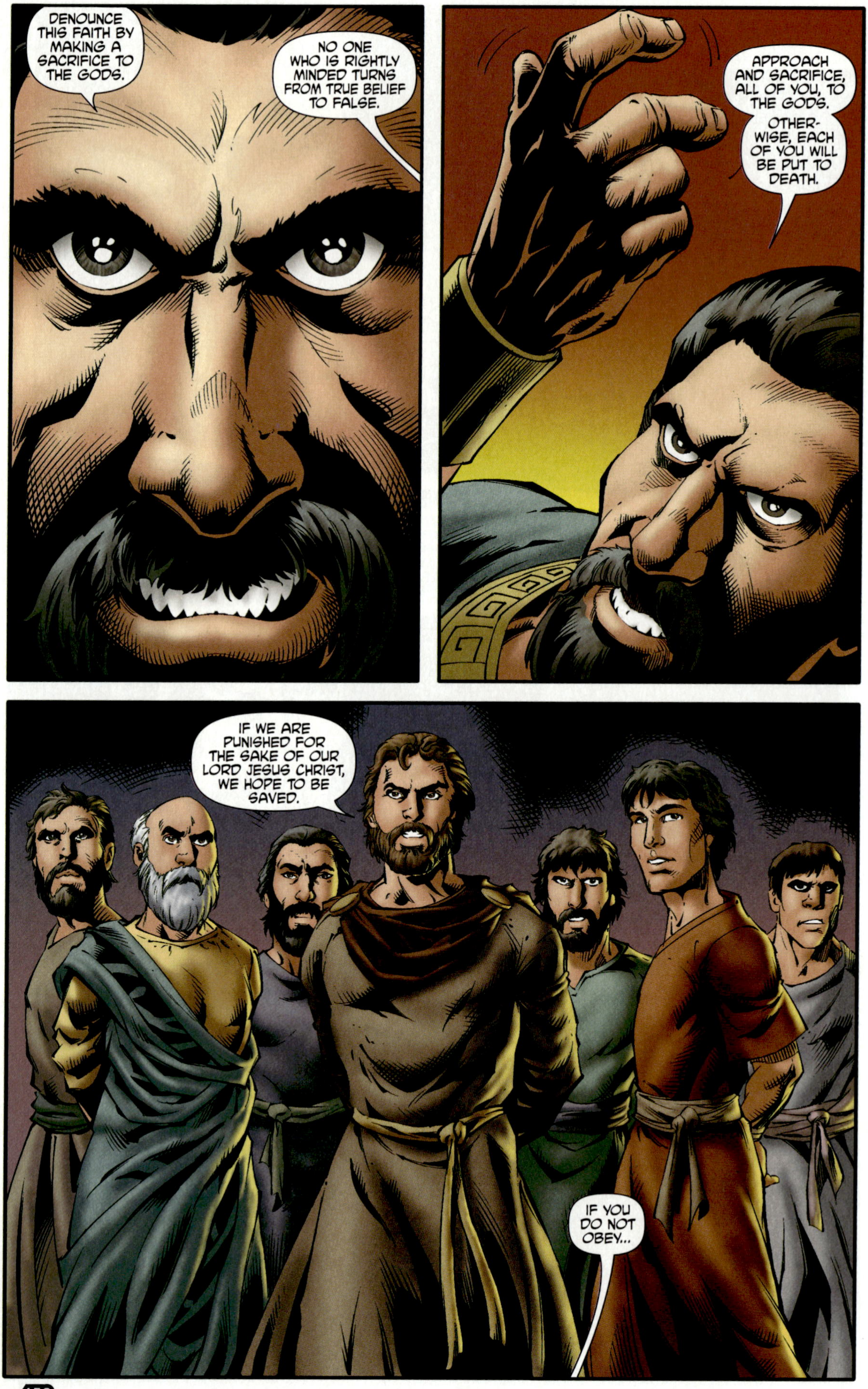
DENOUNCE THIS FAITH BY MAKING A SACRIFICE TO THE GODS.
NO ONE WHO IS RIGHTLY MINDED TURNS FROM TRUE BELIEF TO FALSE.
APPROACH AND SACRIFICE, ALL OF YOU, TO THE GODS.
OTHER-WISE, EACH OF YOU WILL BE PUT TO DEATH.
IF WE ARE PUNISHED FOR THE SAKE OF OUR LORD JESUS CHRIST, WE HOPE TO BE SAVED.
IF YOU DO NOT OBEY...

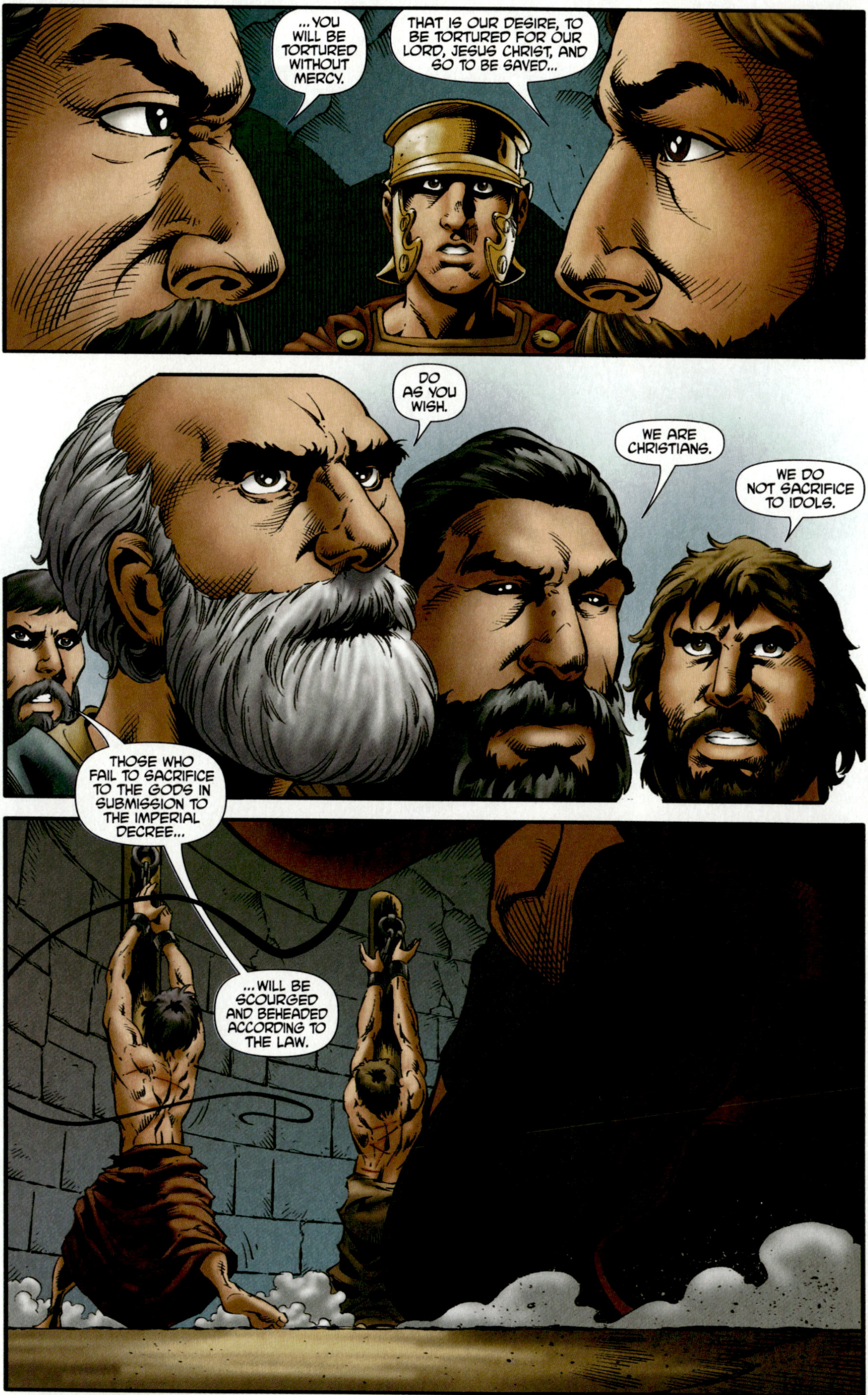
...YOU WILL BE TORTURED WITHOUT MERCY.
THAT IS OUR DESIRE, TO BE TORTURED FOR OUR LORD, JESUS CHRIST, AND SO TO BE SAVED...
DO AS YOU WISH.
WE ARE CHRISTIANS.
WE DO NOT SACRIFICE TO IDOLS.
THOSE WHO FAIL TO SACRIFICE TO THE GODS IN SUBMISSION TO THE IMPERIAL DECREE...
...WILL BE SCOURGED AND BEHEADED ACCORDING TO THE LAW.

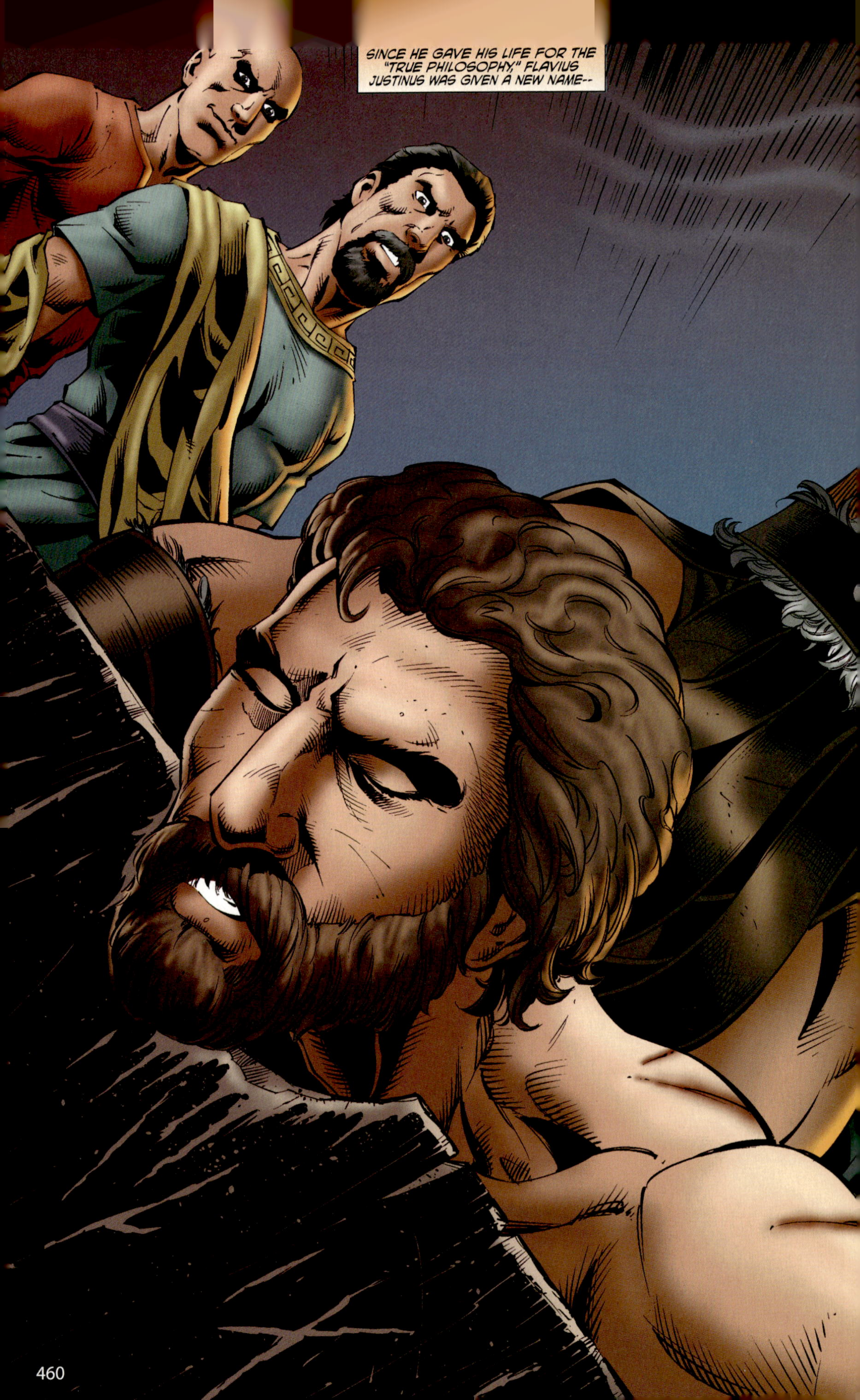
SINCE HE GAVE HIS LIFE FOR THE "TRUE PHILOSOPHY," FLAVIUS JUSTINUS WAS GIVEN A NEW NAME--

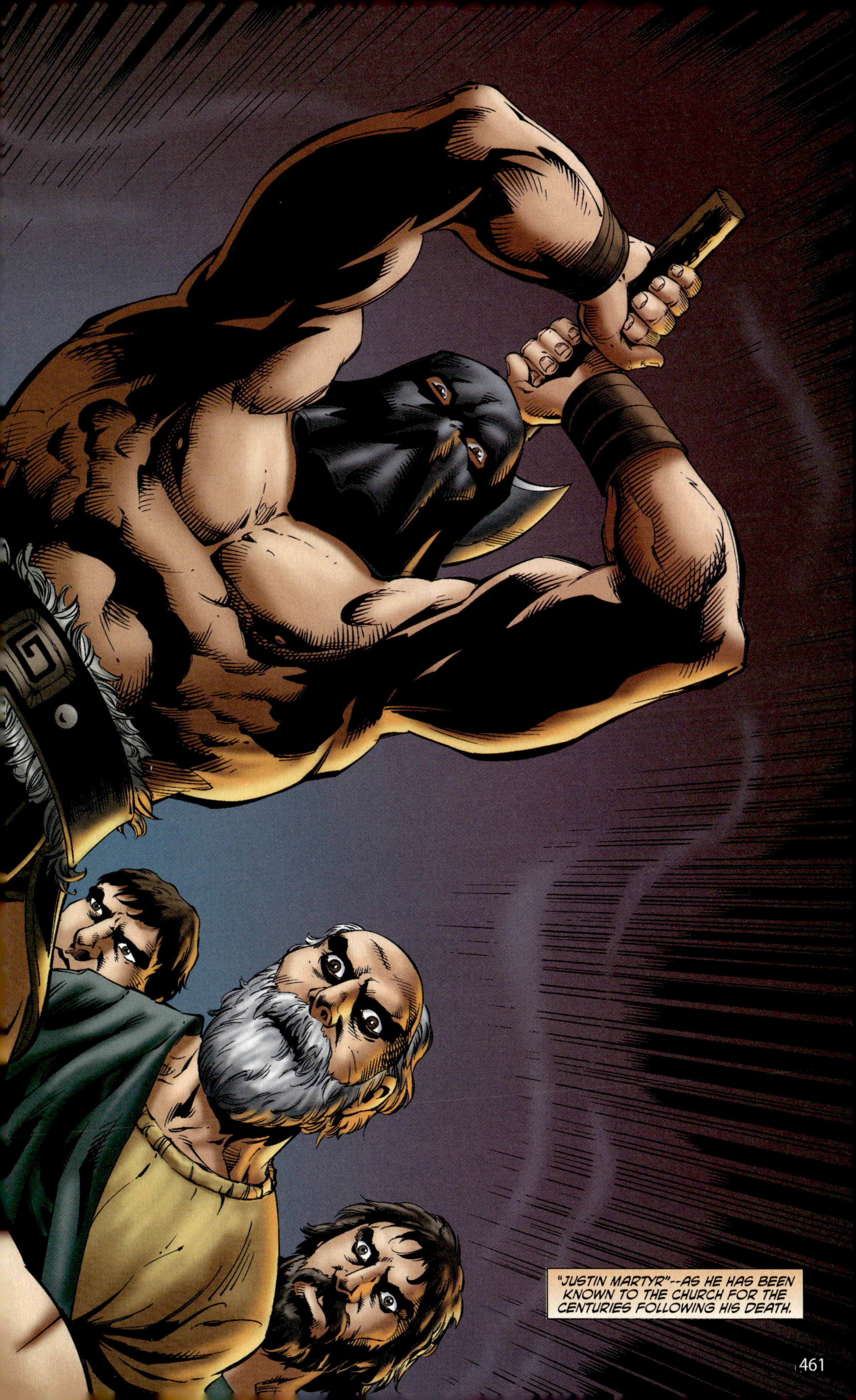
"JUSTIN MARTYR"--AS HE HAS BEEN KNOWN TO THE CHURCH FOR THE CENTURIES FOLLOWING HIS DEATH.

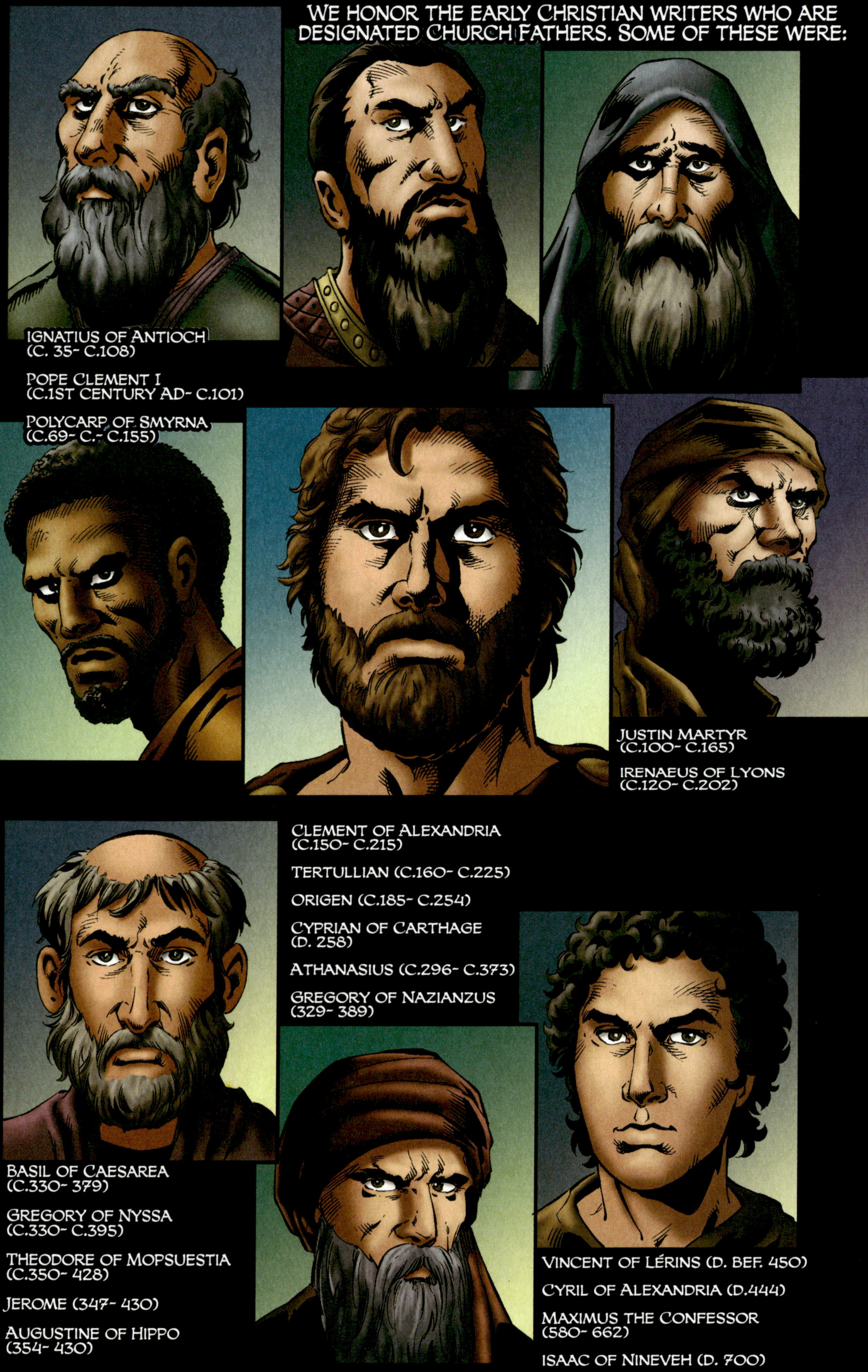
WE HONOR THE EARLY CHRISTIAN WRITERS WHO ARE DESIGNATED CHURCH FATHERS. SOME OF THESE WERE:
IGNATIUS OF ANTIOCH (C. 35- C.108)
POPE CLEMENT I (C.1ST CENTURY AD- C.101)
POLYCARP OF SMYRNA (C.69- C.- C.155)
JUSTIN MARTYR (C.100- C.165)
IRENAEUS OF LYONS (C.120- C.202)
CLEMENT OF ALEXANDRIA (C.150- C.215)
TERTULLIAN (C.160- C.225)
ORIGEN (C.185- C.254)
CYPRIAN OF CARTHAGE (D. 258)
ATHANASIUS (C.296- C.373)
GREGORY OF NAZIANZUS (329- 389)
BASIL OF CAESAREA (C.330- 379)
GREGORY OF NYSSA (C.330- C.395)
THEODORE OF MOPSUESTIA (C.350- 428)
JEROME (347- 430)
AUGUSTINE OF HIPPO (354- 430)
VINCENT OF LÉRINS (D. BEF. 450)
CYRIL OF ALEXANDRIA (D.444)
MAXIMUS THE CONFESSOR (580- 662)
ISAAC OF NINEVEH (D. 700)

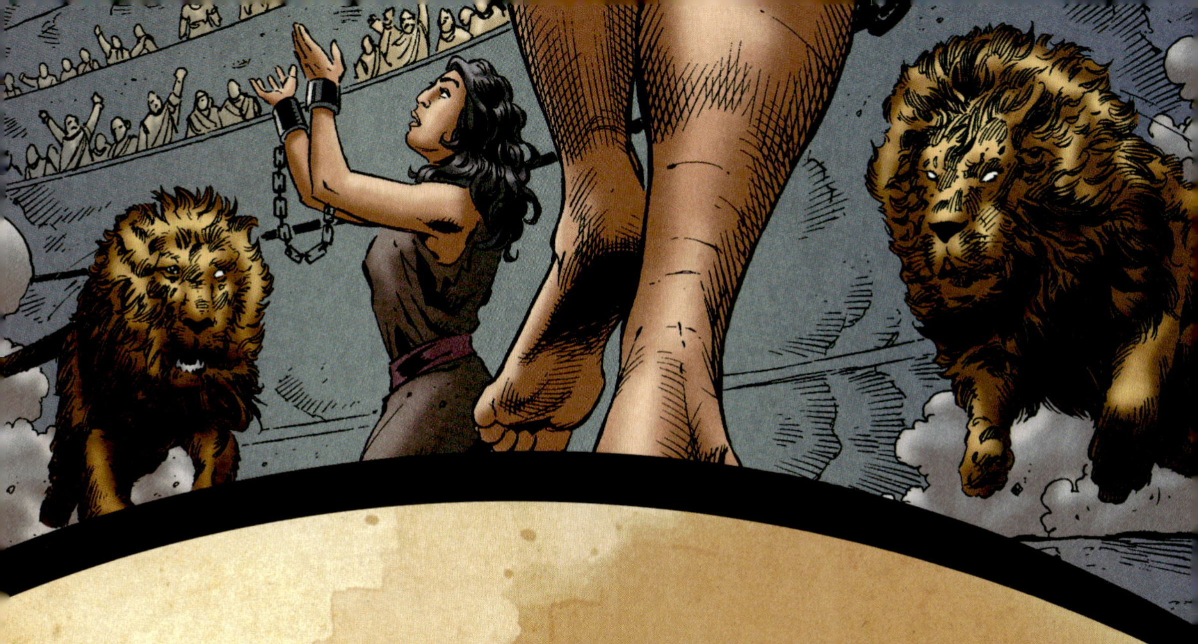

PERPETUA

MARTYRED A.D. 203

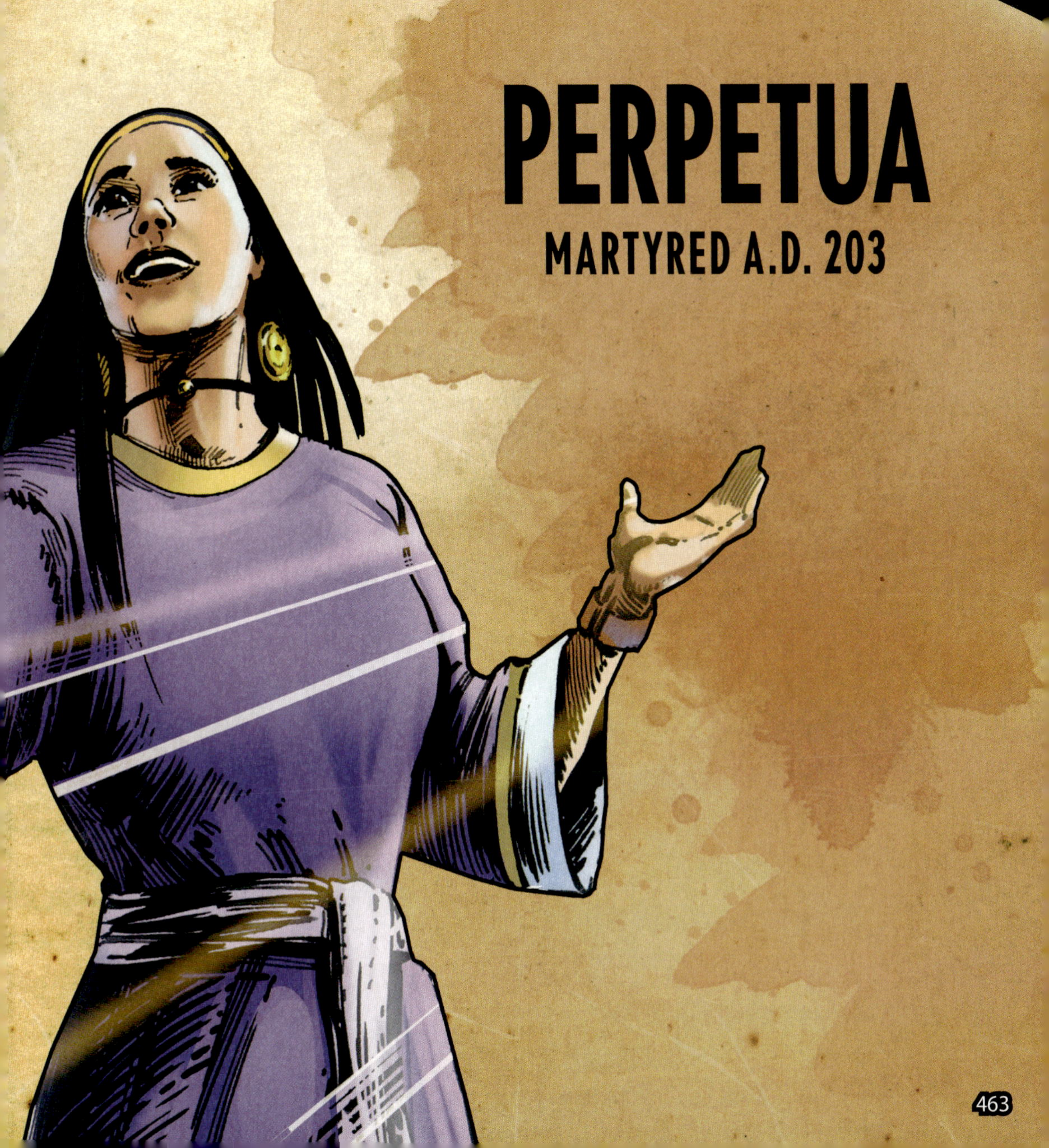

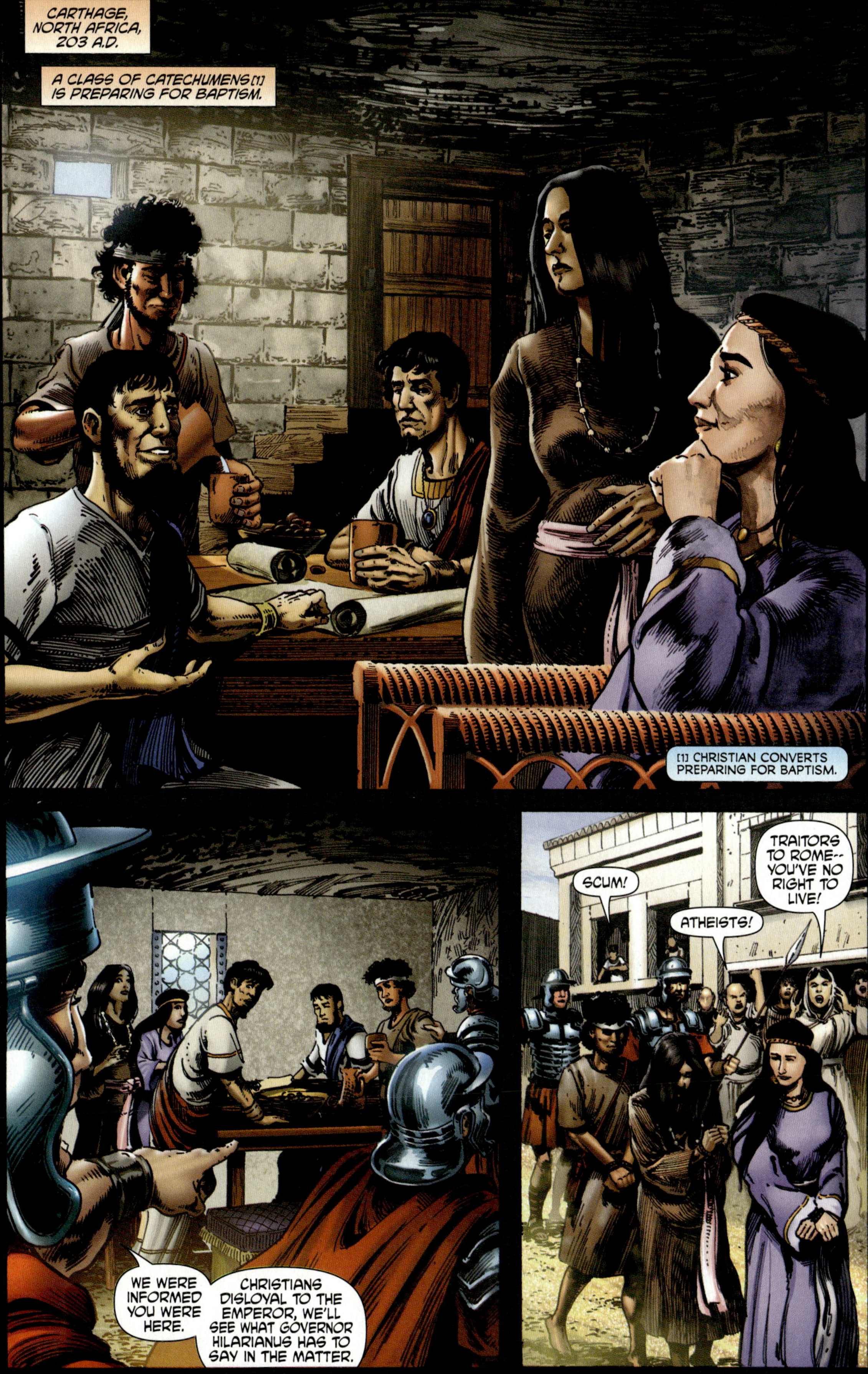
CARTHAGE, NORTH AFRICA, 203 A.D.
A CLASS OF CATECHUMENS[1] IS PREPARING FOR BAPTISM.
[1] CHRISTIAN CONVERTS PREPARING FOR BAPTISM.
WE WERE INFORMED YOU WERE HERE.
CHRISTIANS DISLOYAL TO THE EMPEROR, WE'LL SEE WHAT GOVERNOR HILARIANUS HAS TO SAY IN THE MATTER.
SCUM!
TRAITORS TO ROME-- YOU'VE NO RIGHT TO LIVE!
ATHEISTS!

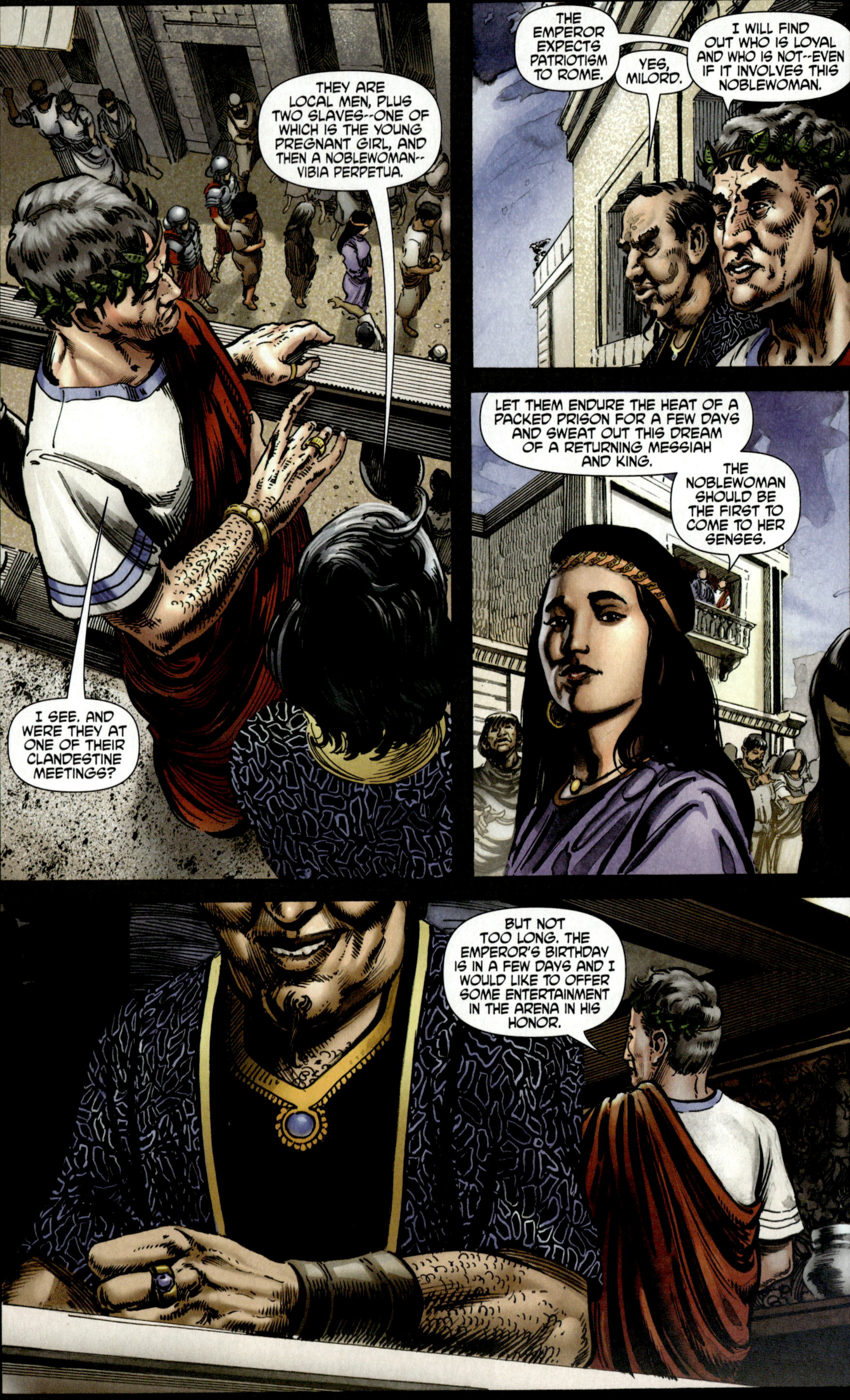

THEY ARE LOCAL MEN, PLUS TWO SLAVES--ONE OF WHICH IS THE YOUNG PREGNANT GIRL, AND THEN A NOBLEWOMAN--VIBIA PERPETUA.
I SEE. AND WERE THEY AT ONE OF THEIR CLANDESTINE MEETINGS?
THE EMPEROR EXPECTS PATRIOTISM TO ROME.
YES, MILORD.
I WILL FIND OUT WHO IS LOYAL AND WHO IS NOT--EVEN IF IT INVOLVES THIS NOBLEWOMAN.
LET THEM ENDURE THE HEAT OF A PACKED PRISON FOR A FEW DAYS AND SWEAT OUT THIS DREAM OF A RETURNING MESSIAH AND KING.
THE NOBLEWOMAN SHOULD BE THE FIRST TO COME TO HER SENSES.
BUT NOT TOO LONG. THE EMPEROR'S BIRTHDAY IS IN A FEW DAYS AND I WOULD LIKE TO OFFER SOME ENTERTAINMENT IN THE ARENA IN HIS HONOR.

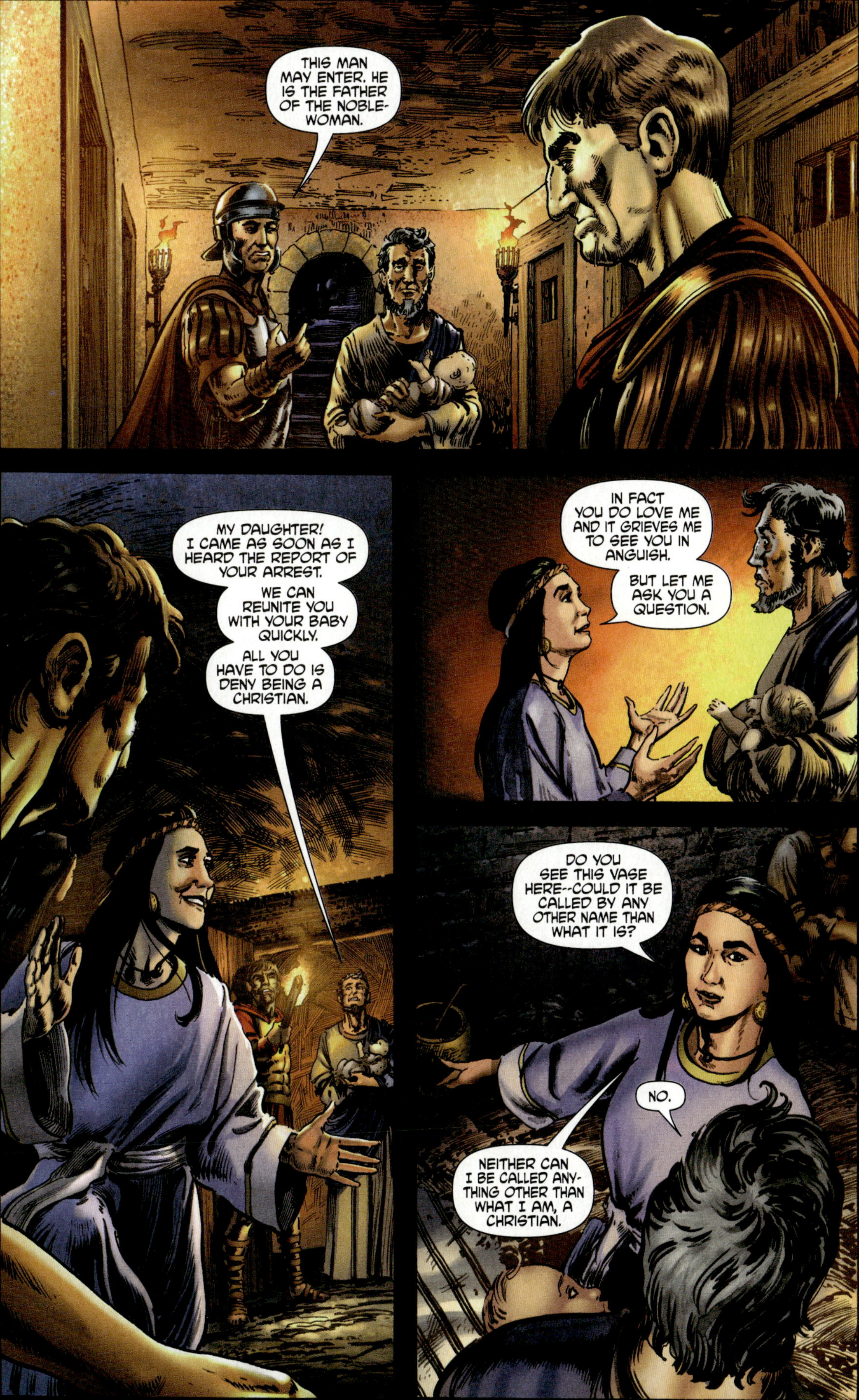
THIS MAN MAY ENTER. HE IS THE FATHER OF THE NOBLE-WOMAN.
MY DAUGHTER! I CAME AS SOON AS I HEARD THE REPORT OF YOUR ARREST.
WE CAN REUNITE YOU WITH YOUR BABY QUICKLY.
ALL YOU HAVE TO DO IS DENY BEING A CHRISTIAN.
IN FACT YOU DO LOVE ME AND IT GRIEVES ME TO SEE YOU IN ANGUISH.
BUT LET ME ASK YOU A QUESTION.
DO YOU SEE THIS VASE HERE--COULD IT BE CALLED BY ANY OTHER NAME THAN WHAT IT IS?
NO.
NEITHER CAN I BE CALLED ANY-THING OTHER THAN WHAT I AM, A CHRISTIAN.

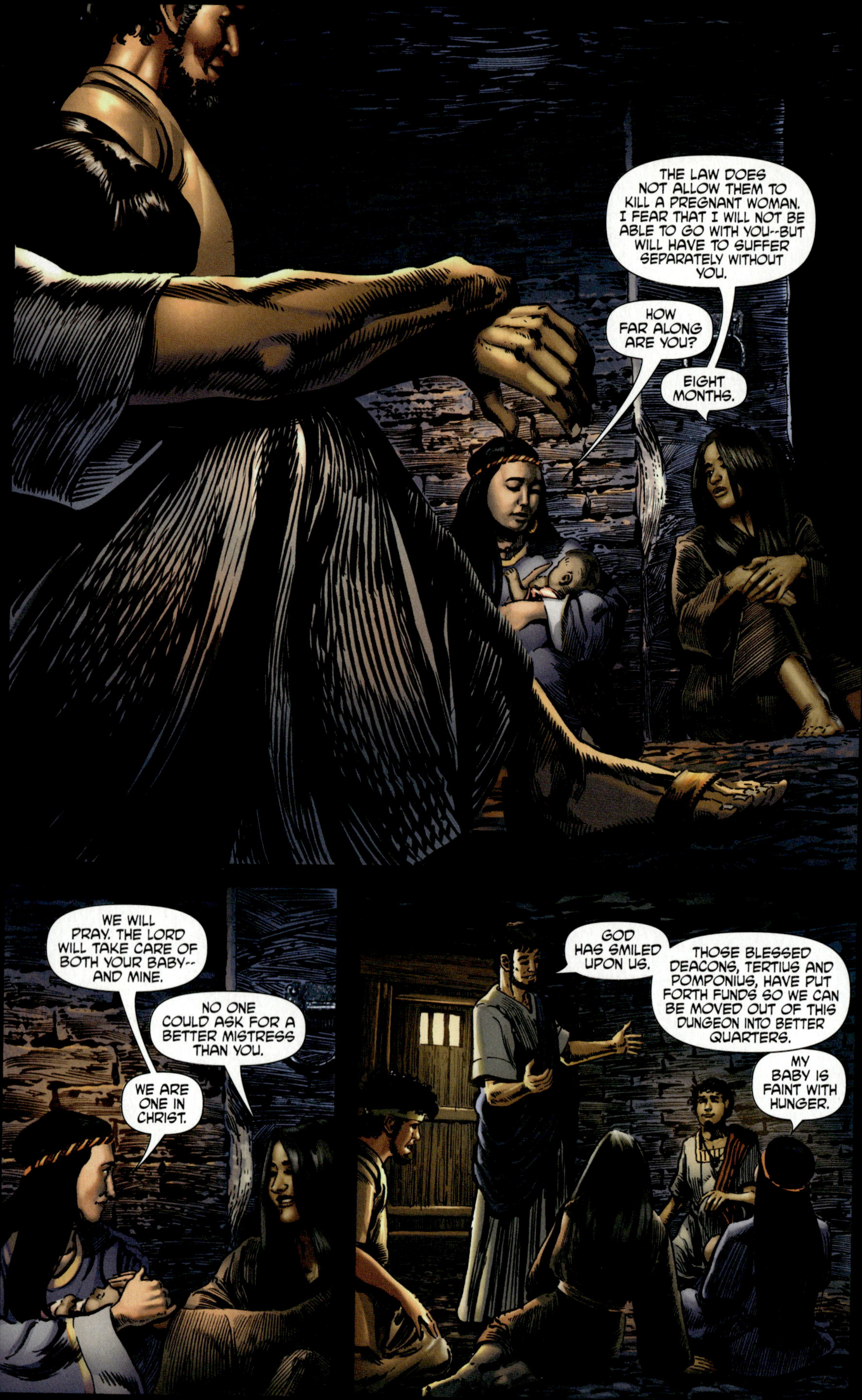

THE LAW DOES NOT ALLOW THEM TO KILL A PREGNANT WOMAN. I FEAR THAT I WILL NOT BE ABLE TO GO WITH YOU--BUT WILL HAVE TO SUFFER SEPARATELY WITHOUT YOU.
HOW FAR ALONG ARE YOU?
EIGHT MONTHS.
WE WILL PRAY. THE LORD WILL TAKE CARE OF BOTH YOUR BABY--AND MINE.
NO ONE COULD ASK FOR A BETTER MISTRESS THAN YOU.
WE ARE ONE IN CHRIST.
GOD HAS SMILED UPON US.
THOSE BLESSED DEACONS, TERTIUS AND POMPONIUS, HAVE PUT FORTH FUNDS SO WE CAN BE MOVED OUT OF THIS DUNGEON INTO BETTER QUARTERS.
MY BABY IS FAINT WITH HUNGER.

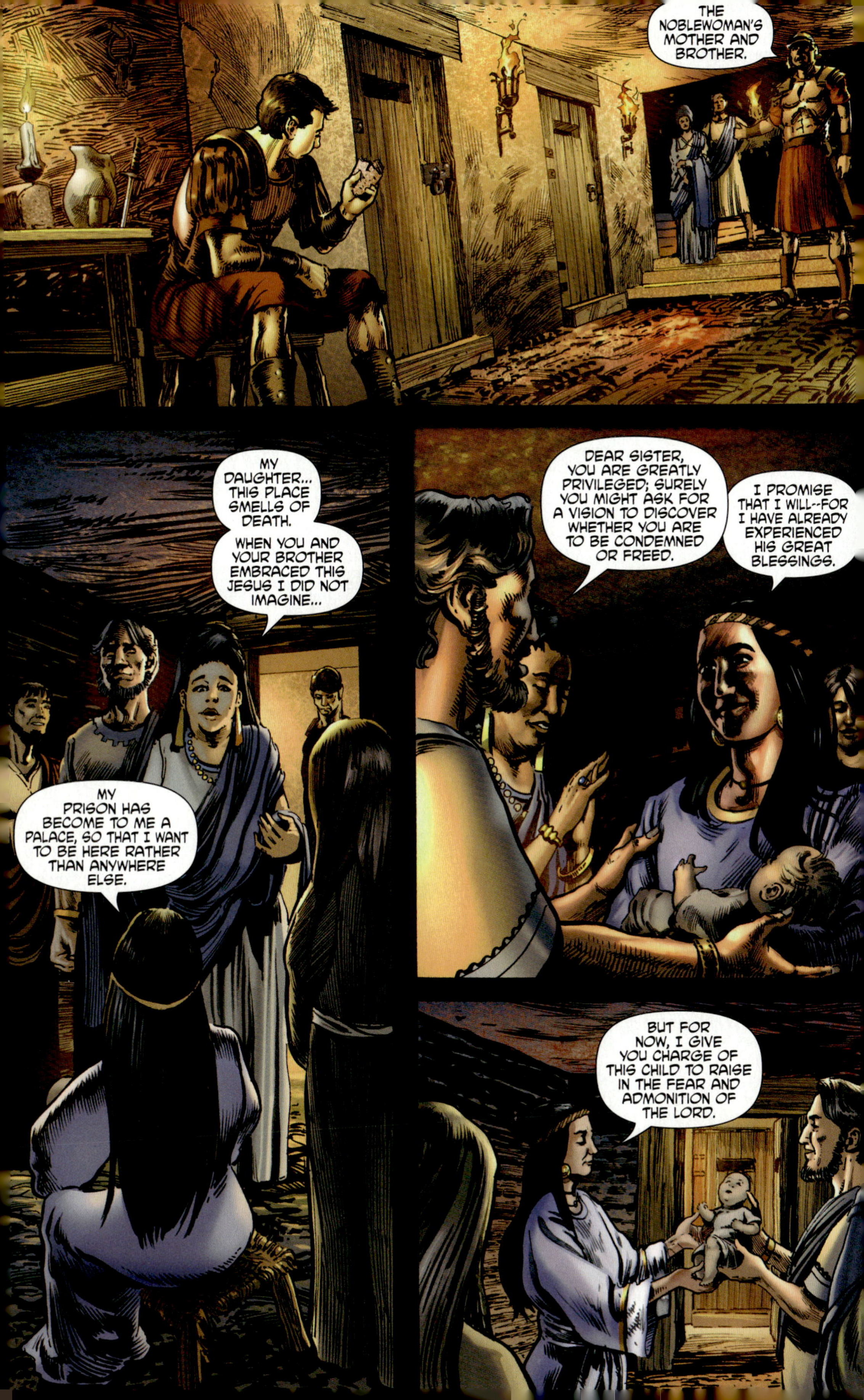
THE NOBLEWOMAN'S MOTHER AND BROTHER.
MY DAUGHTER... THIS PLACE SMELLS OF DEATH.
WHEN YOU AND YOUR BROTHER EMBRACED THIS JESUS I DID NOT IMAGINE...
MY PRISON HAS BECOME TO ME A PALACE, SO THAT I WANT TO BE HERE RATHER THAN ANYWHERE ELSE.
DEAR SISTER, YOU ARE GREATLY PRIVILEGED; SURELY YOU MIGHT ASK FOR A VISION TO DISCOVER WHETHER YOU ARE TO BE CONDEMNED OR FREED.
I PROMISE THAT I WILL--FOR I HAVE ALREADY EXPERIENCED HIS GREAT BLESSINGS.
BUT FOR NOW, I GIVE YOU CHARGE OF THIS CHILD TO RAISE IN THE FEAR AND ADMONITION OF THE LORD.

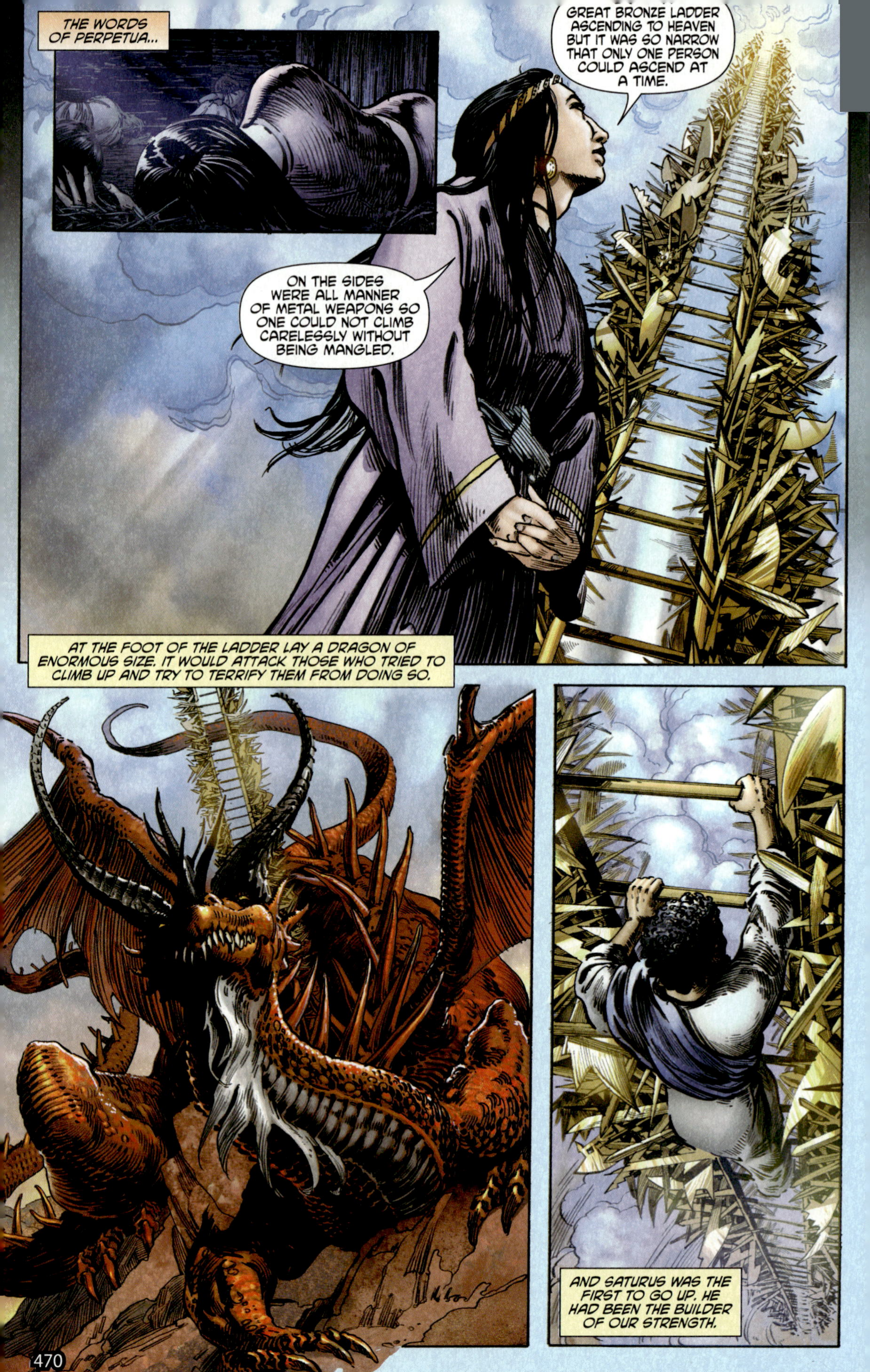
THE WORDS OF PERPETUA...
GREAT BRONZE LADDER ASCENDING TO HEAVEN BUT IT WAS SO NARROW THAT ONLY ONE PERSON COULD ASCEND AT A TIME.
ON THE SIDES WERE ALL MANNER OF METAL WEAPONS SO ONE COULD NOT CLIMB CARELESSLY WITHOUT BEING MANGLED.
AT THE FOOT OF THE LADDER LAY A DRAGON OF ENORMOUS SIZE. IT WOULD ATTACK THOSE WHO TRIED TO CLIMB UP AND TRY TO TERRIFY THEM FROM DOING SO.
AND SATURUS WAS THE FIRST TO GO UP. HE HAD BEEN THE BUILDER OF OUR STRENGTH.

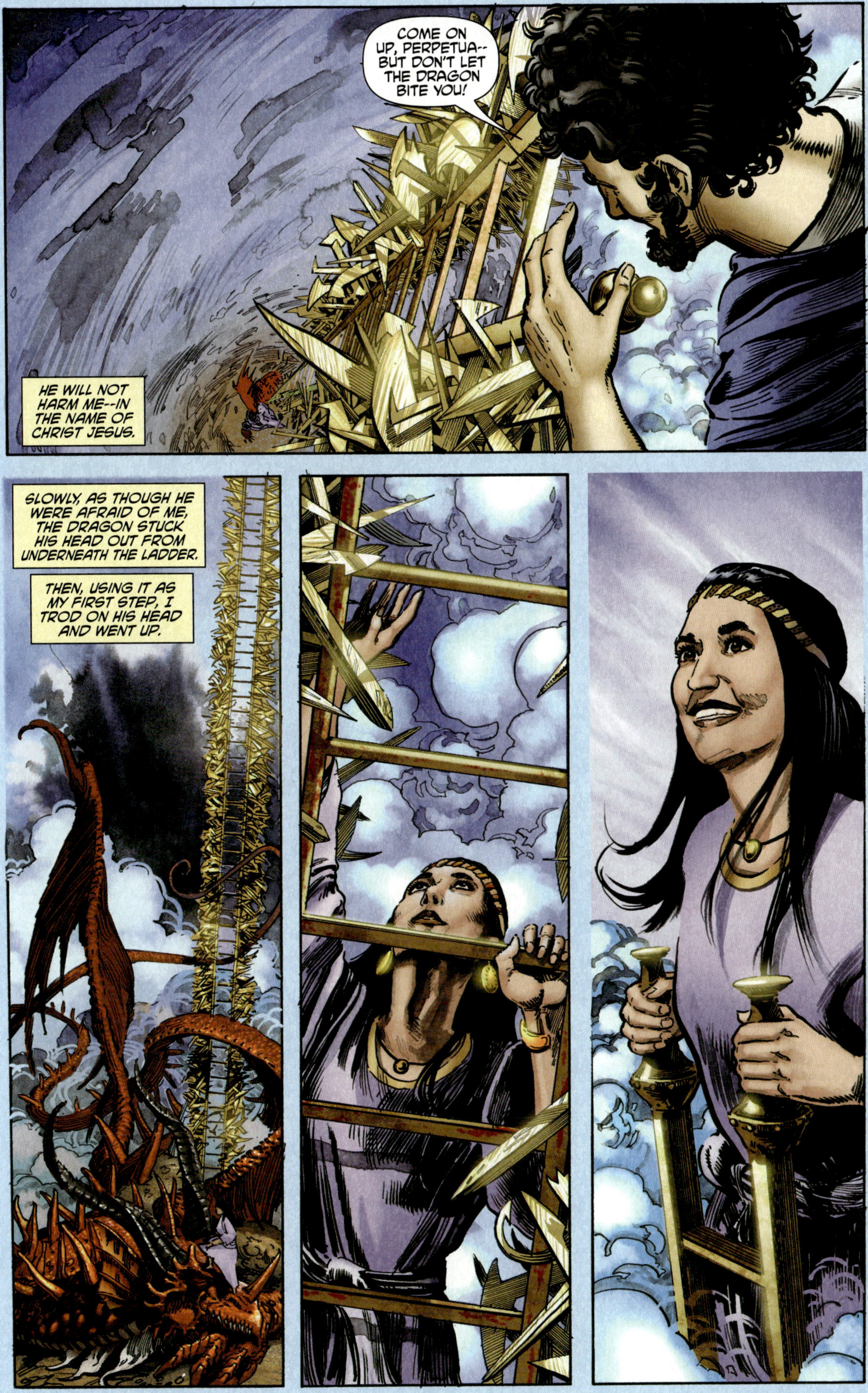
COME ON UP, PERPETUA-- BUT DON'T LET THE DRAGON BITE YOU!
HE WILL NOT HARM ME--IN THE NAME OF CHRIST JESUS.
SLOWLY, AS THOUGH HE WERE AFRAID OF ME, THE DRAGON STUCK HIS HEAD OUT FROM UNDERNEATH THE LADDER.
THEN, USING IT AS MY FIRST STEP, I TROD ON HIS HEAD AND WENT UP.

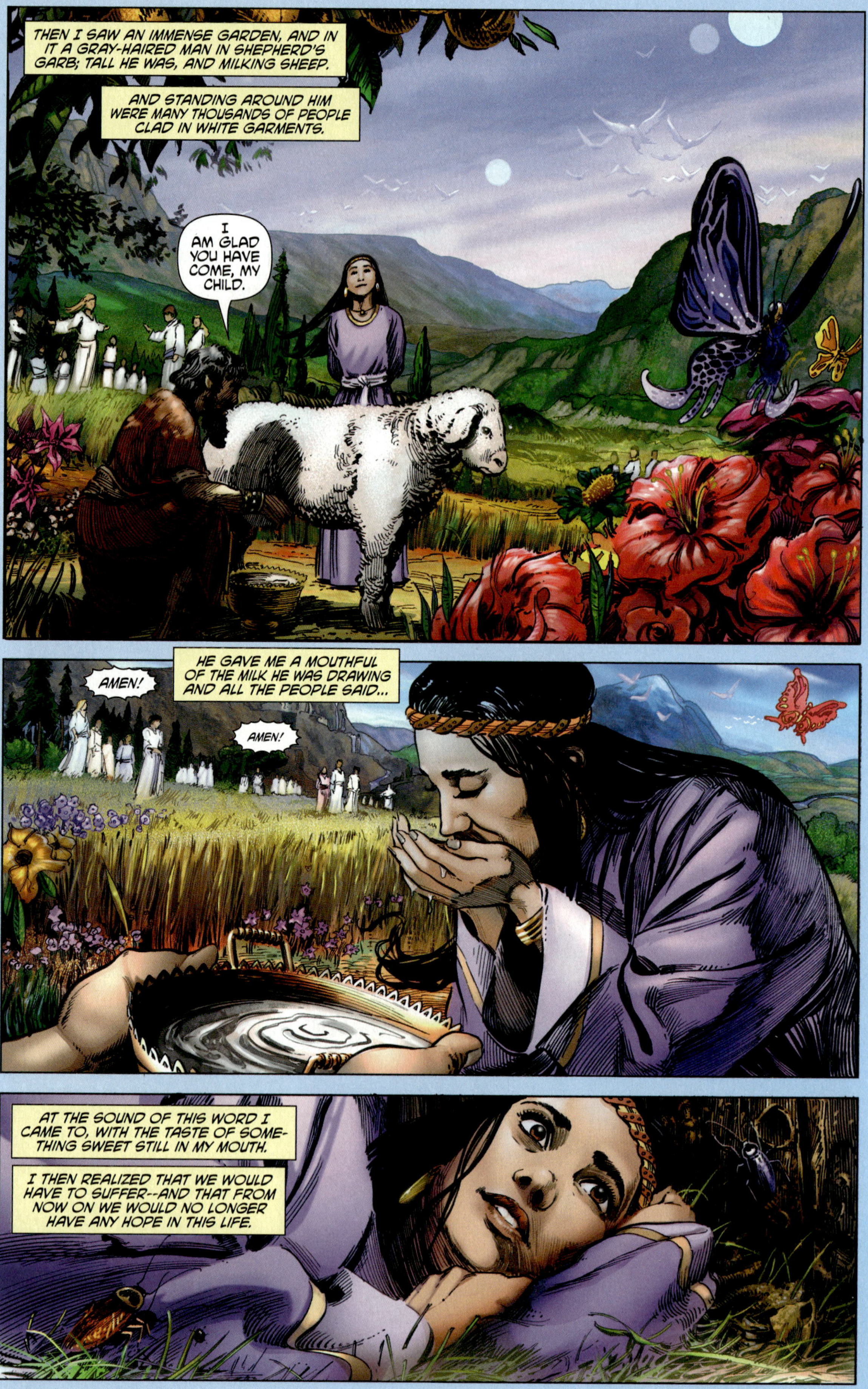
THEN I SAW AN IMMENSE GARDEN, AND IN IT A GRAY-HAIRED MAN IN SHEPHERD'S GARB; TALL HE WAS, AND MILKING SHEEP.
AND STANDING AROUND HIM WERE MANY THOUSANDS OF PEOPLE CLAD IN WHITE GARMENTS.
I AM GLAD YOU HAVE COME, MY CHILD.
HE GAVE ME A MOUTHFUL OF THE MILK HE WAS DRAWING AND ALL THE PEOPLE SAID...
AMEN!
AMEN!
AT THE SOUND OF THIS WORD I CAME TO, WITH THE TASTE OF SOMETHING SWEET STILL IN MY MOUTH.
I THEN REALIZED THAT WE WOULD HAVE TO SUFFER--AND THAT FROM NOW ON WE WOULD NO LONGER HAVE ANY HOPE IN THIS LIFE.

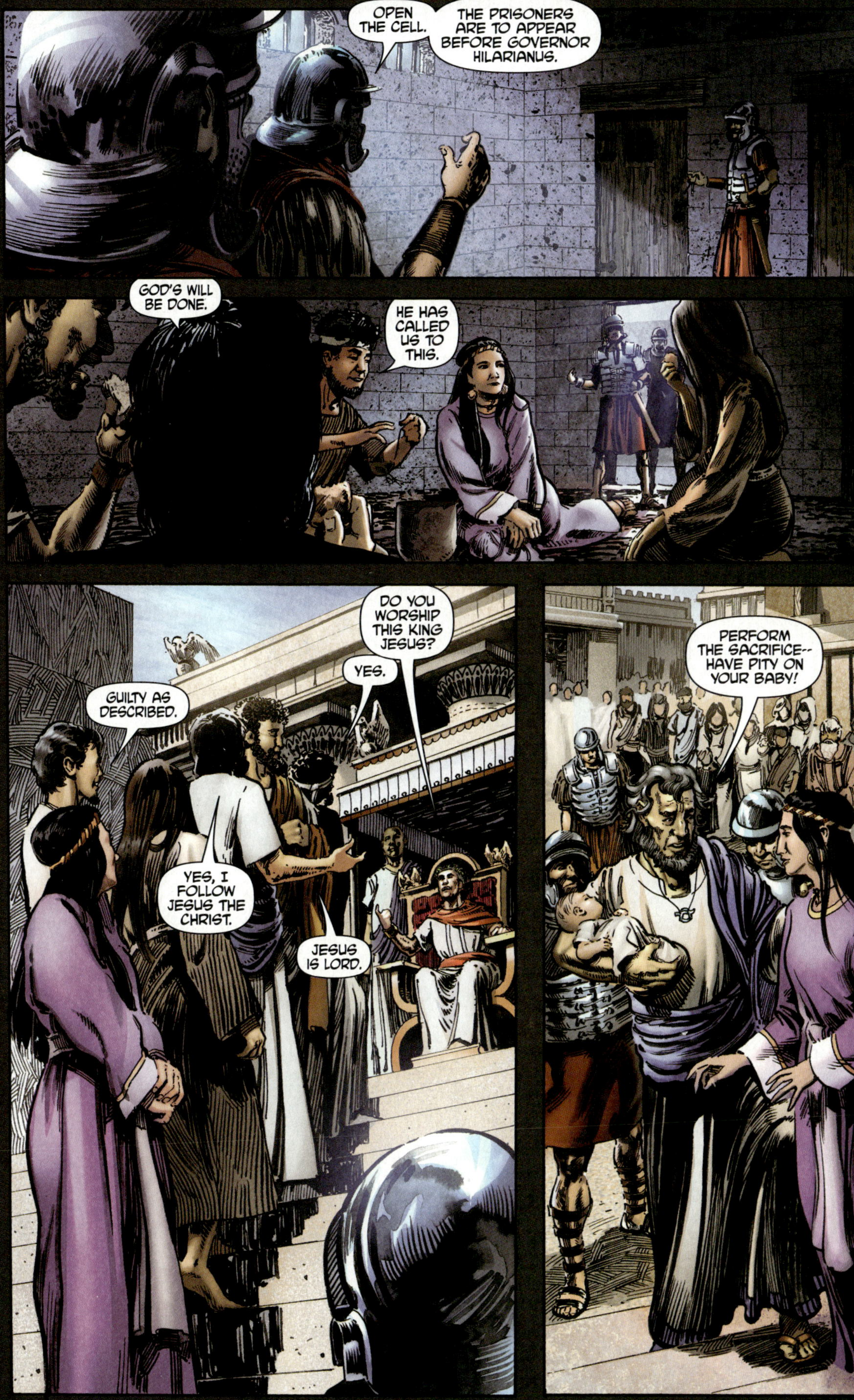
OPEN THE CELL.
THE PRISONERS ARE TO APPEAR BEFORE GOVERNOR HILARIANUS.
GOD'S WILL BE DONE.
HE HAS CALLED US TO THIS.
DO YOU WORSHIP THIS KING JESUS?
YES.
GUILTY AS DESCRIBED.
YES, I FOLLOW JESUS THE CHRIST.
JESUS IS LORD.
PERFORM THE SACRIFICE-- HAVE PITY ON YOUR BABY!

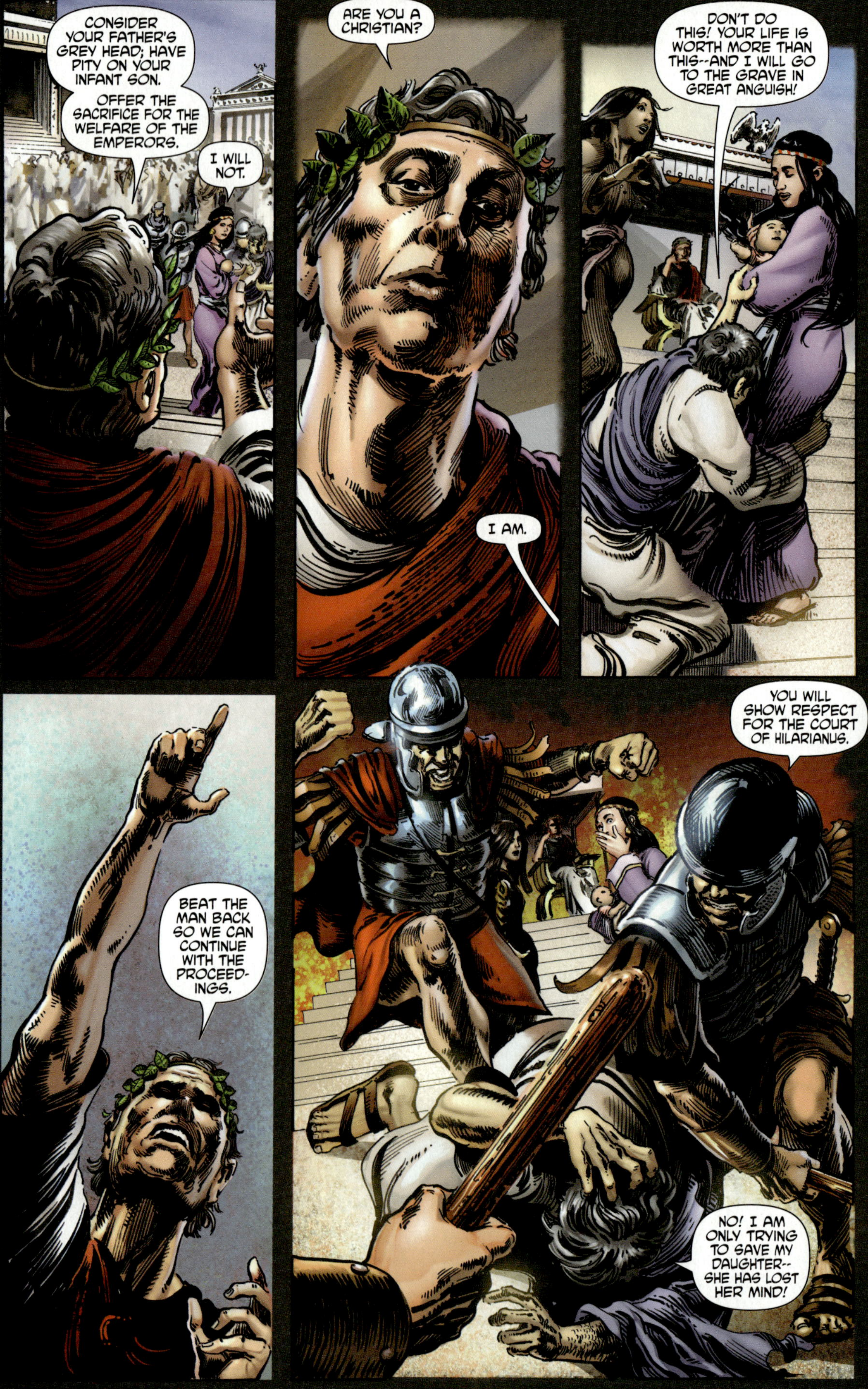
CONSIDER YOUR FATHER'S GREY HEAD; HAVE PITY ON YOUR INFANT SON.
OFFER THE SACRIFICE FOR THE WELFARE OF THE EMPERORS.
I WILL NOT.
ARE YOU A CHRISTIAN?
I AM.
DON'T DO THIS! YOUR LIFE IS WORTH MORE THAN THIS--AND I WILL GO TO THE GRAVE IN GREAT ANGUISH!
BEAT THE MAN BACK SO WE CAN CONTINUE WITH THE PROCEED-INGS.
YOU WILL SHOW RESPECT FOR THE COURT OF HILARIANUS.
NO! I AM ONLY TRYING TO SAVE MY DAUGHTER-- SHE HAS LOST HER MIND!

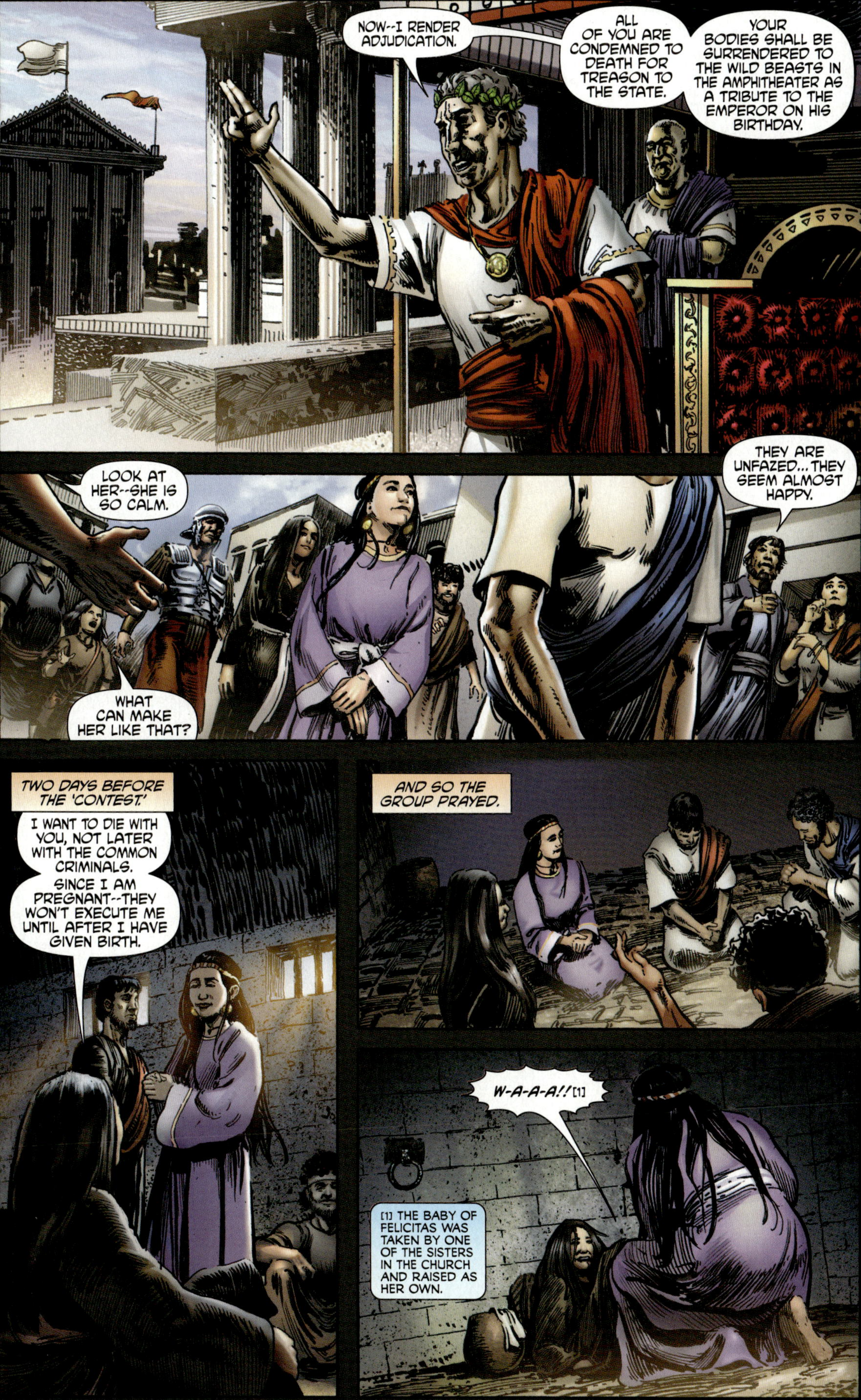
NOW--I RENDER ADJUDICATION.
ALL OF YOU ARE CONDEMNED TO DEATH FOR TREASON TO THE STATE.
YOUR BODIES SHALL BE SURRENDERED TO THE WILD BEASTS IN THE AMPHITHEATER AS A TRIBUTE TO THE EMPEROR ON HIS BIRTHDAY.
LOOK AT HER--SHE IS SO CALM.
WHAT CAN MAKE HER LIKE THAT?
THEY ARE UNFAZED... THEY SEEM ALMOST HAPPY.
TWO DAYS BEFORE THE 'CONTEST.'
I WANT TO DIE WITH YOU, NOT LATER WITH THE COMMON CRIMINALS.
SINCE I AM PREGNANT--THEY WON'T EXECUTE ME UNTIL AFTER I HAVE GIVEN BIRTH.
AND SO THE GROUP PRAYED.
W-A-A-A!! [1]
[1] THE BABY OF FELICITAS WAS TAKEN BY ONE OF THE SISTERS IN THE CHURCH AND RAISED AS HER OWN.

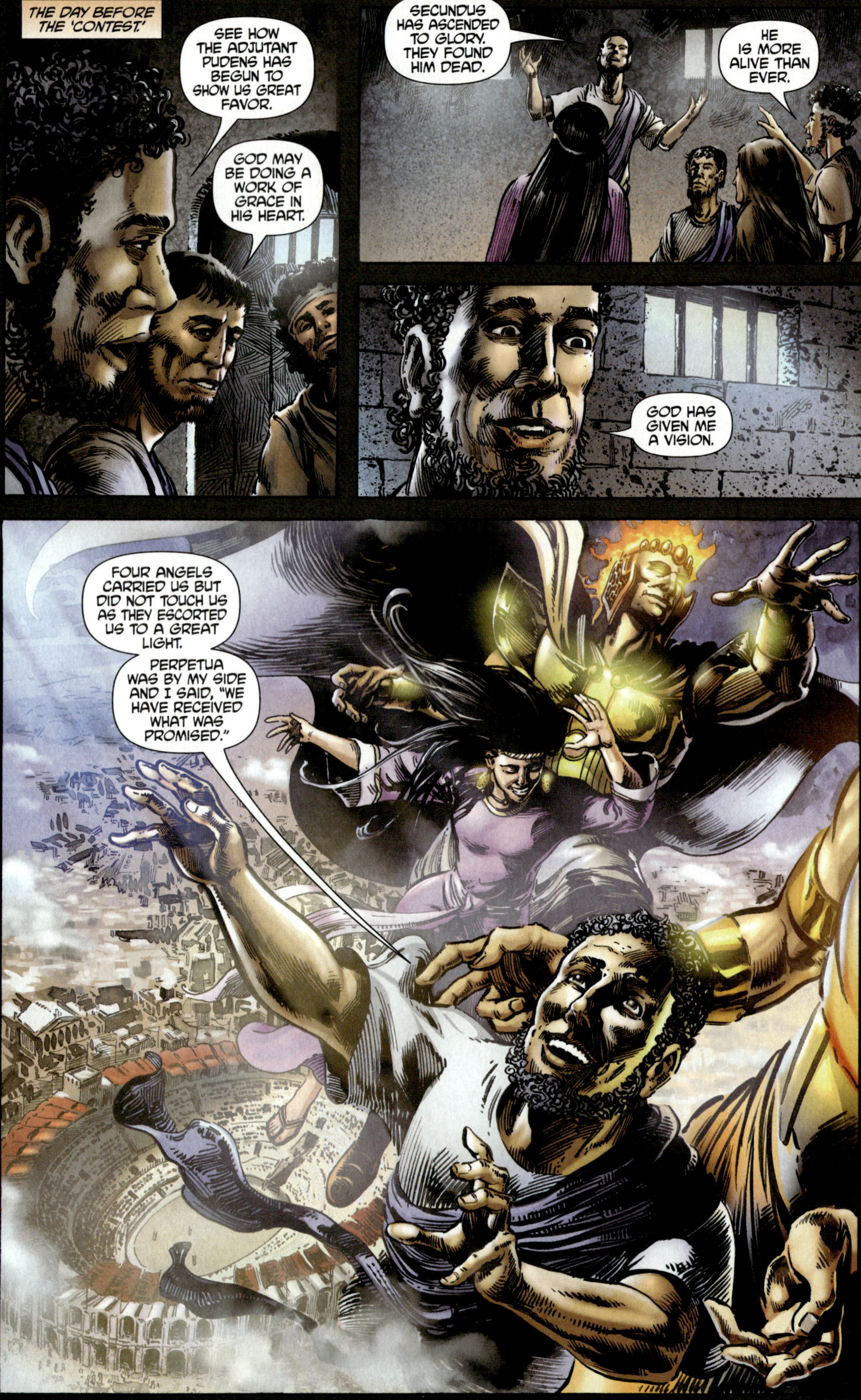
THE DAY BEFORE THE 'CONTEST.'
SEE HOW THE ADJUTANT PUDENS HAS BEGUN TO SHOW US GREAT FAVOR.
GOD MAY BE DOING A WORK OF GRACE IN HIS HEART.
SECUNDUS HAS ASCENDED TO GLORY. THEY FOUND HIM DEAD.
HE IS MORE ALIVE THAN EVER.
GOD HAS GIVEN ME A VISION.
FOUR ANGELS CARRIED US BUT DID NOT TOUCH US AS THEY ESCORTED US TO A GREAT LIGHT.
PERPETUA WAS BY MY SIDE AND I SAID, "WE HAVE RECEIVED WHAT WAS PROMISED."

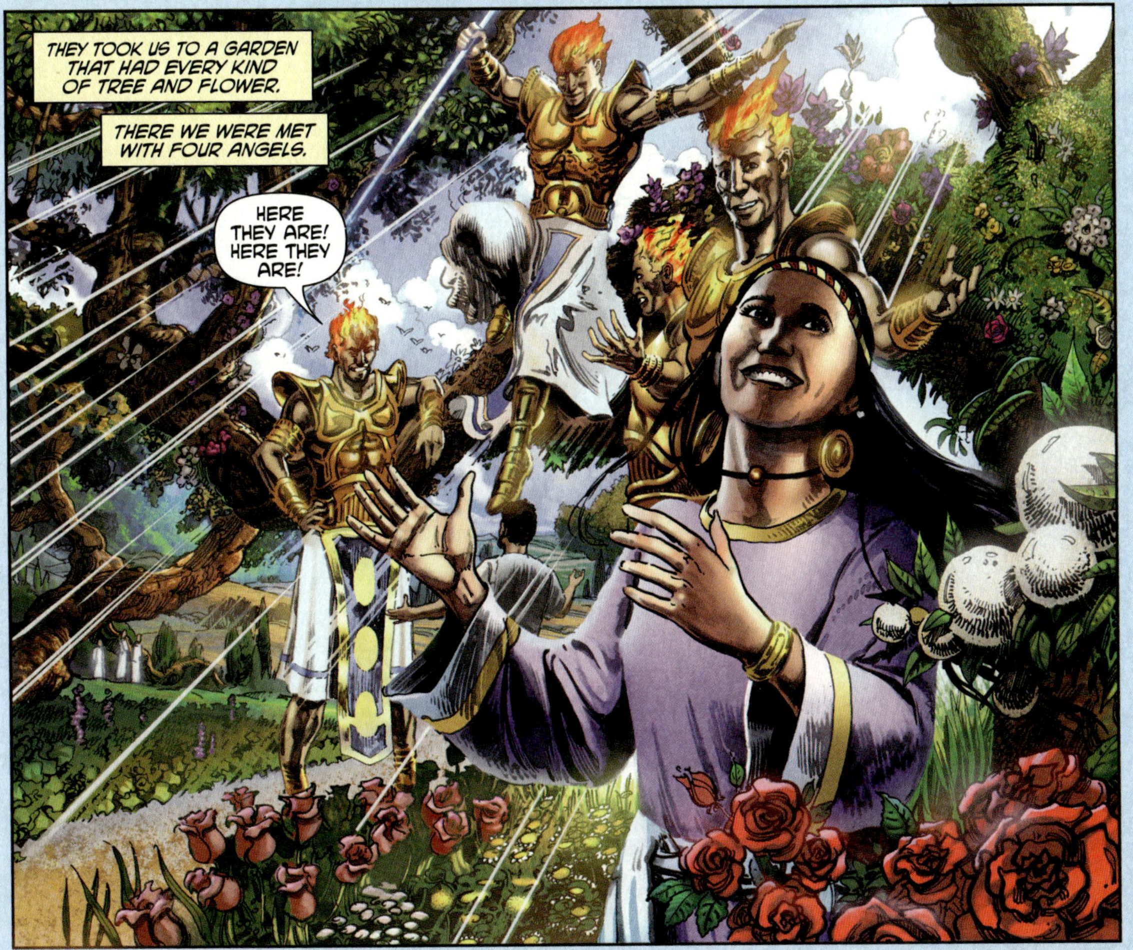
THEY TOOK US TO A GARDEN THAT HAD EVERY KIND OF TREE AND FLOWER.
THERE WE WERE MET WITH FOUR ANGELS.
HERE THEY ARE! HERE THEY ARE!

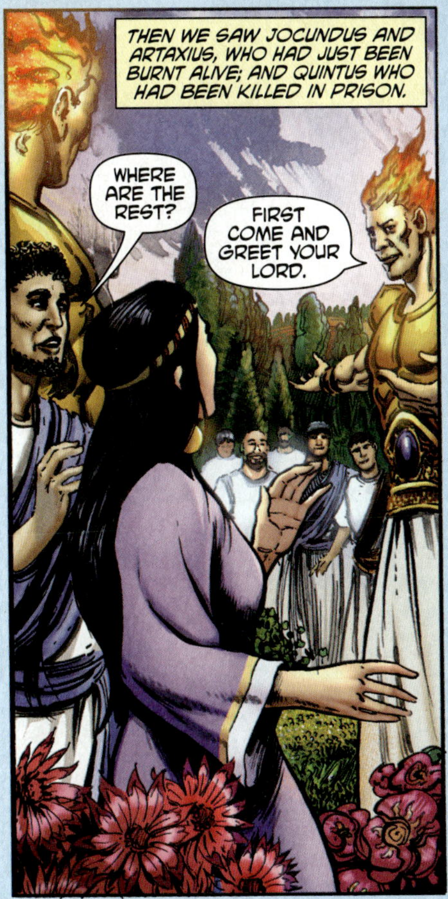
THEN WE SAW JOCUNDUS AND ARTAXIUS, WHO HAD JUST BEEN BURNT ALIVE; AND QUINTUS WHO HAD BEEN KILLED IN PRISON.
WHERE ARE THE REST?
FIRST COME AND GREET YOUR LORD.

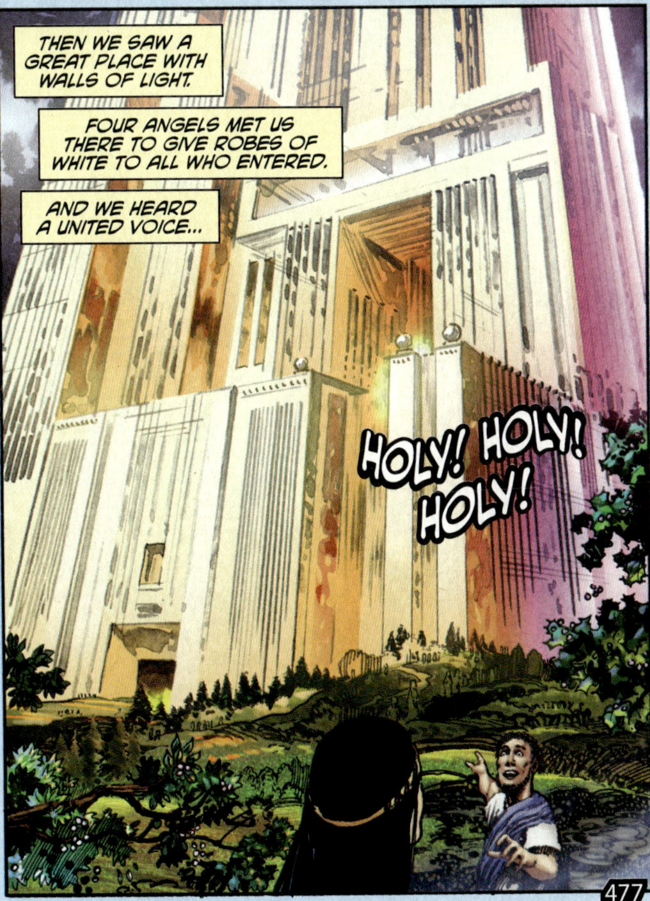
THEN WE SAW A GREAT PLACE WITH WALLS OF LIGHT.
FOUR ANGELS MET US THERE TO GIVE ROBES OF WHITE TO ALL WHO ENTERED.
AND WE HEARD A UNITED VOICE...
HOLY! HOLY! HOLY!

AND WE SAW A MAN WITH A YOUTHFUL COUNTENANCE HAVING SNOW-WHITE HAIR.

AND ON HIS RIGHT HAND AND ON HIS LEFT WERE FOUR-AND-TWENTY ELDERS, AND BEHIND THEM A GREAT MANY OTHERS WERE STANDING.

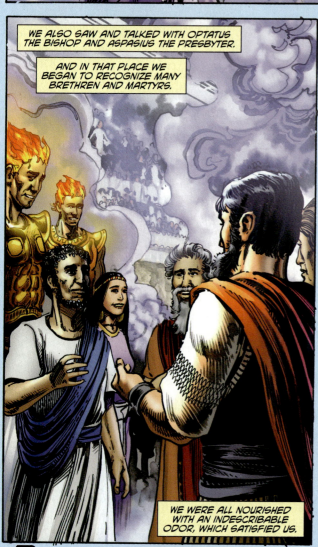

WE ALSO SAW AND TALKED WITH OPTATUS THE BISHOP AND ASPASIUS THE PRESBYTER.

AND IN THAT PLACE WE BEGAN TO RECOGNIZE MANY BRETHREN AND MARTYRS.

WE WERE ALL NOURISHED WITH AN INDESCRIBABLE ODOR, WHICH SATISFIED US.

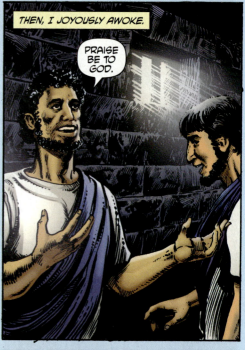

THEN, I JOYOUSLY AWOKE.

PRAISE BE TO GOD.

I ALSO HAD A VISION...

478

IN MY VISION, THE DEACON POMPONIUS MET ME AT THE PRISON GATES.

HE TOOK ME TO THE AMPHITHEATER.

DO NOT BE AFRAID. I AM HERE, STRUGGLING WITH YOU.

THEN HE LEFT.

I LOOKED AT THE ENORMOUS CROWD WHO WATCHED IN ASTONISHMENT.

I WAS SURPRISED THAT NO BEASTS WERE LET LOOSE ON ME; FOR I KNEW THAT I WAS CONDEMNED TO DIE BY THE BEASTS.

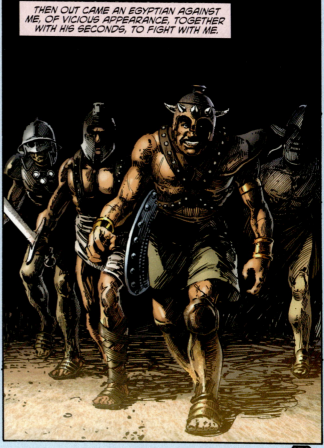

THEN OUT CAME AN EGYPTIAN AGAINST ME, OF VICIOUS APPEARANCE, TOGETHER WITH HIS SECONDS, TO FIGHT WITH ME.

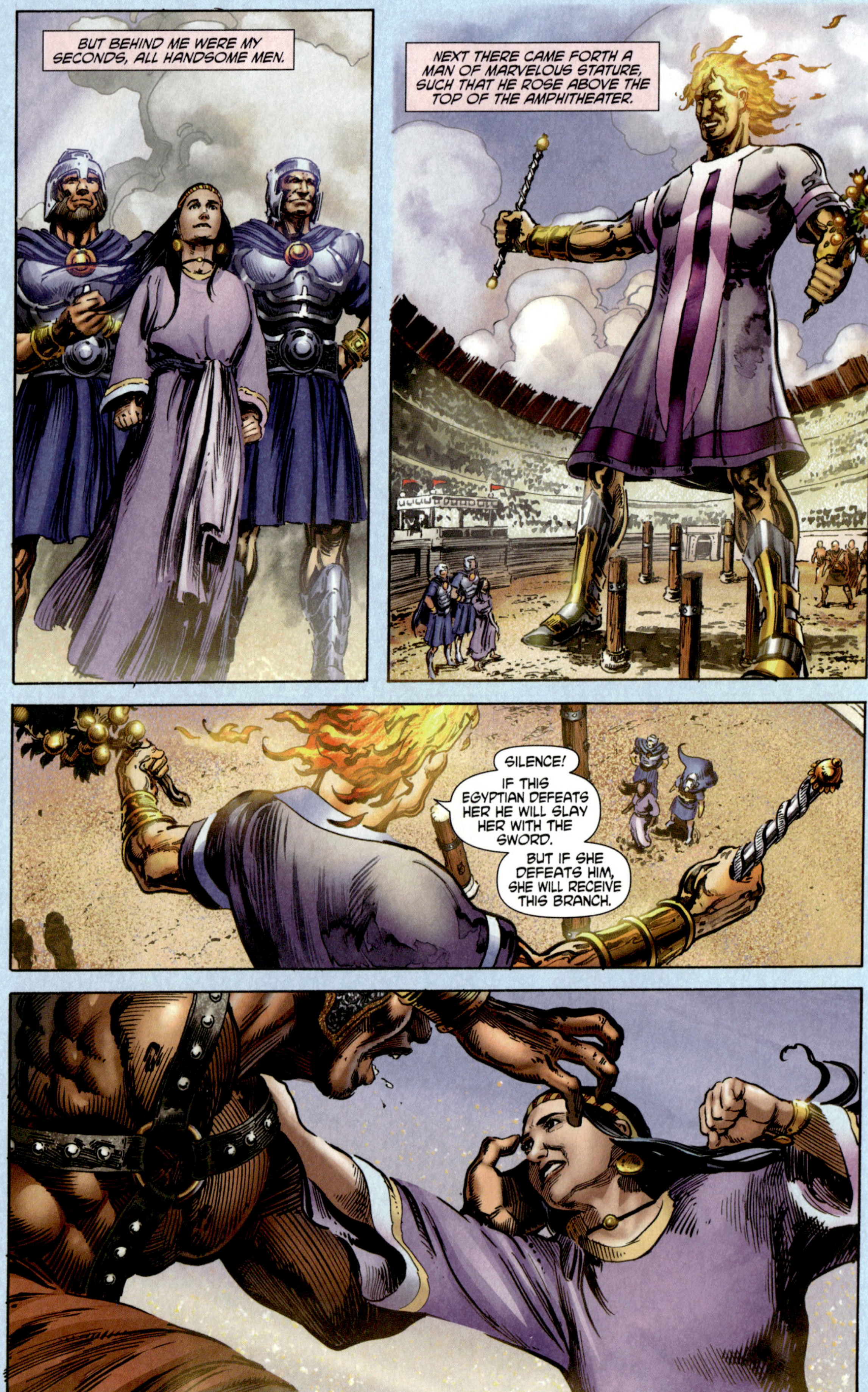
BUT BEHIND ME WERE MY SECONDS, ALL HANDSOME MEN.
NEXT THERE CAME FORTH A MAN OF MARVELOUS STATURE, SUCH THAT HE ROSE ABOVE THE TOP OF THE AMPHITHEATER.
SILENCE!
IF THIS EGYPTIAN DEFEATS HER HE WILL SLAY HER WITH THE SWORD.
BUT IF SHE DEFEATS HIM, SHE WILL RECEIVE THIS BRANCH.

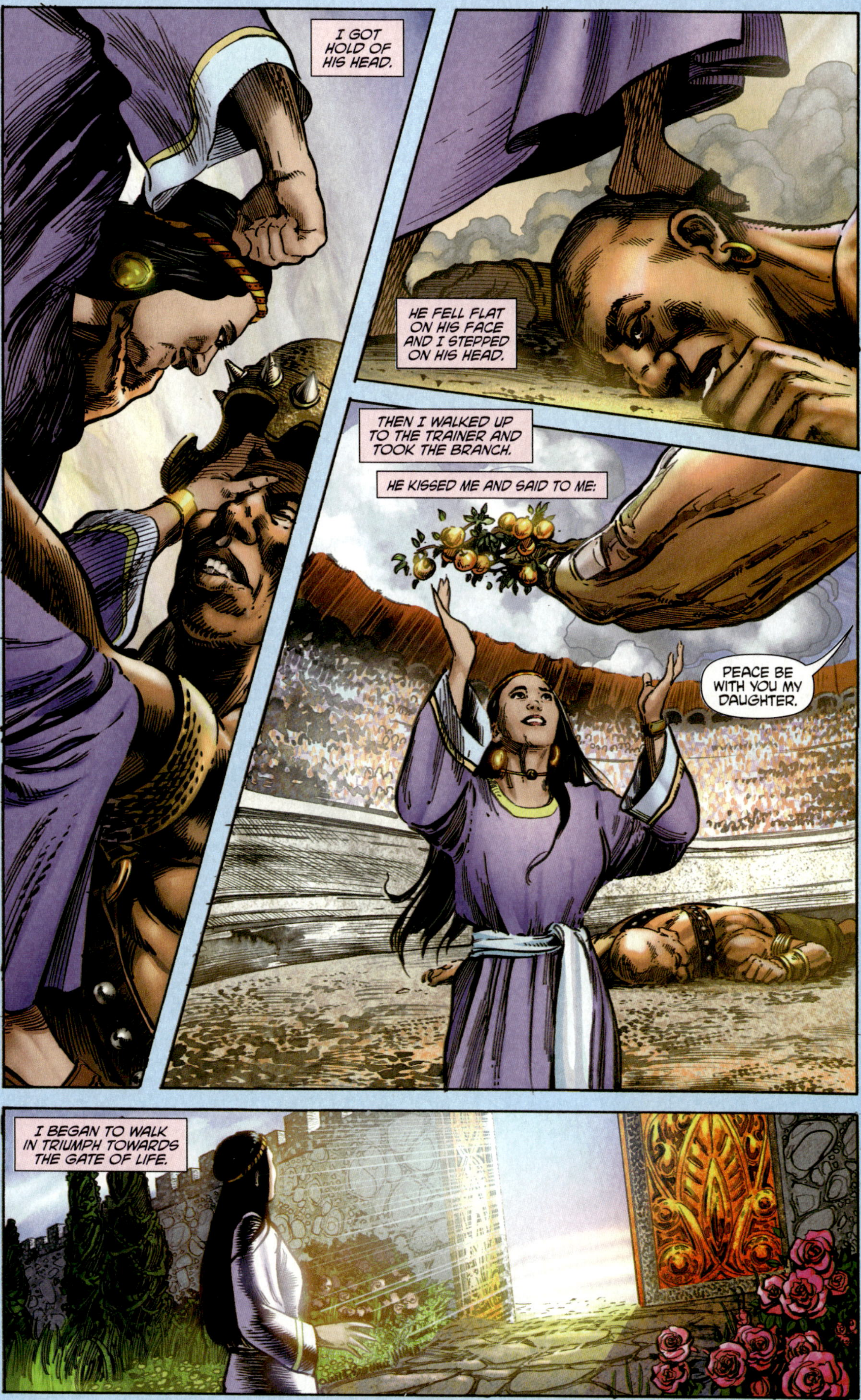
I GOT HOLD OF HIS HEAD.
HE FELL FLAT ON HIS FACE AND I STEPPED ON HIS HEAD.
THEN I WALKED UP TO THE TRAINER AND TOOK THE BRANCH.
HE KISSED ME AND SAID TO ME:
PEACE BE WITH YOU MY DAUGHTER.
I BEGAN TO WALK IN TRIUMPH TOWARDS THE GATE OF LIFE.

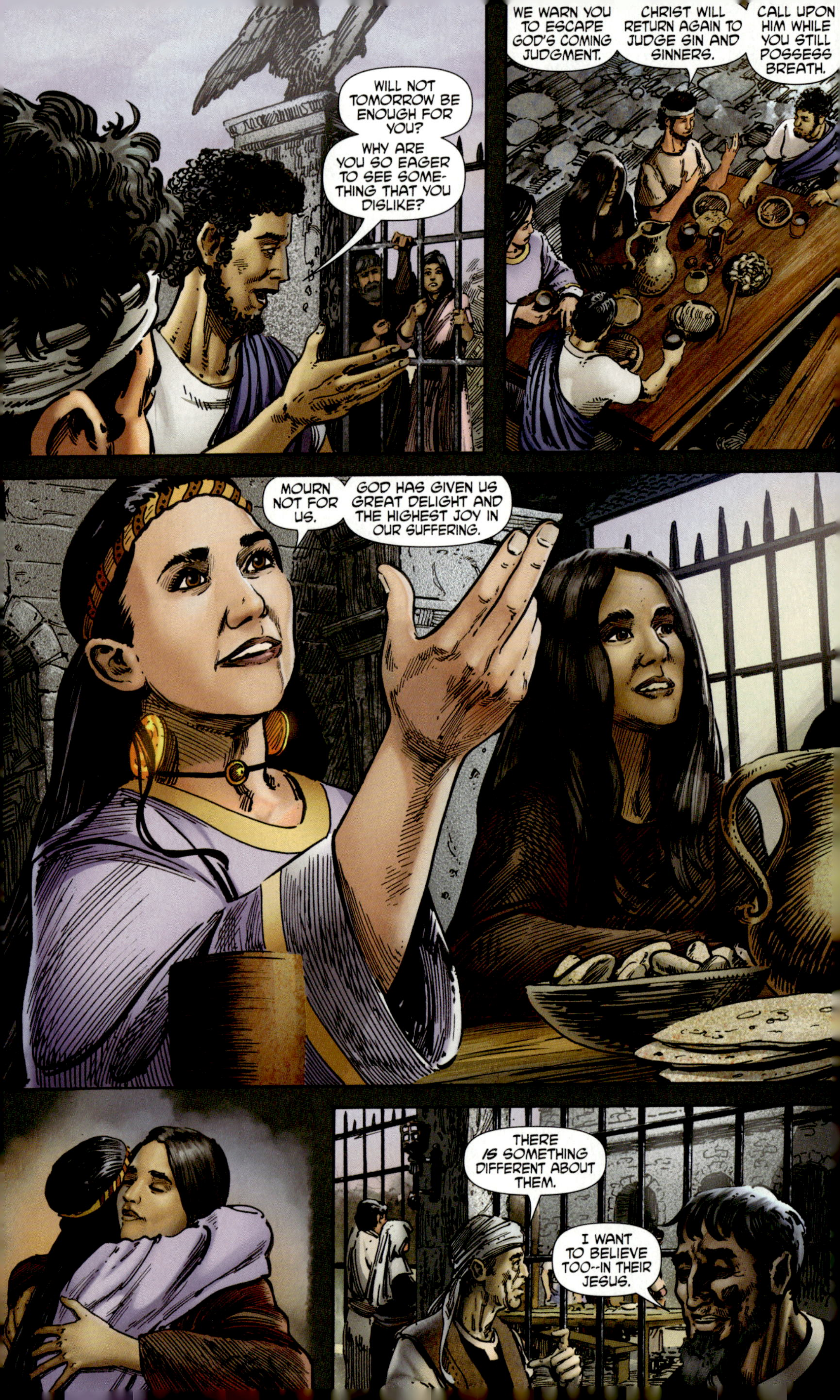
WILL NOT TOMORROW BE ENOUGH FOR YOU?
WHY ARE YOU SO EAGER TO SEE SOMETHING THAT YOU DISLIKE?
WE WARN YOU TO ESCAPE GOD'S COMING JUDGMENT.
CHRIST WILL RETURN AGAIN TO JUDGE SIN AND SINNERS.
CALL UPON HIM WHILE YOU STILL POSSESS BREATH.
MOURN NOT FOR US.
GOD HAS GIVEN US GREAT DELIGHT AND THE HIGHEST JOY IN OUR SUFFERING.
THERE *IS* SOMETHING DIFFERENT ABOUT THEM.
I WANT TO BELIEVE TOO--IN THEIR JESUS.

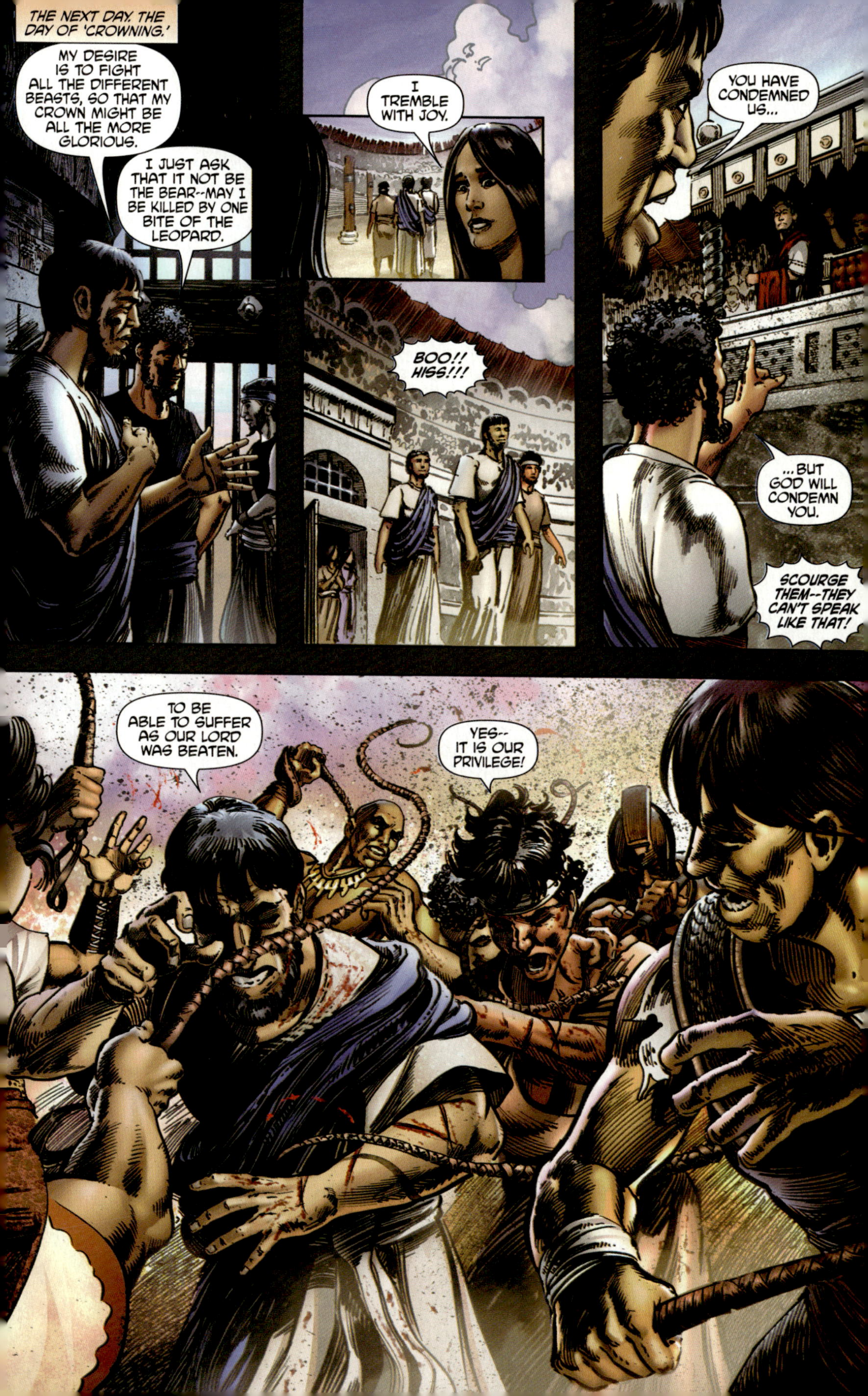
THE NEXT DAY. THE DAY OF 'CROWNING.'
MY DESIRE IS TO FIGHT ALL THE DIFFERENT BEASTS, SO THAT MY CROWN MIGHT BE ALL THE MORE GLORIOUS.
I JUST ASK THAT IT NOT BE THE BEAR--MAY I BE KILLED BY ONE BITE OF THE LEOPARD.
I TREMBLE WITH JOY.
BOO!! HISS!!!
YOU HAVE CONDEMNED US...
...BUT GOD WILL CONDEMN YOU.
SCOURGE THEM--THEY CAN'T SPEAK LIKE THAT!
TO BE ABLE TO SUFFER AS OUR LORD WAS BEATEN.
YES-- IT IS OUR PRIVILEGE!

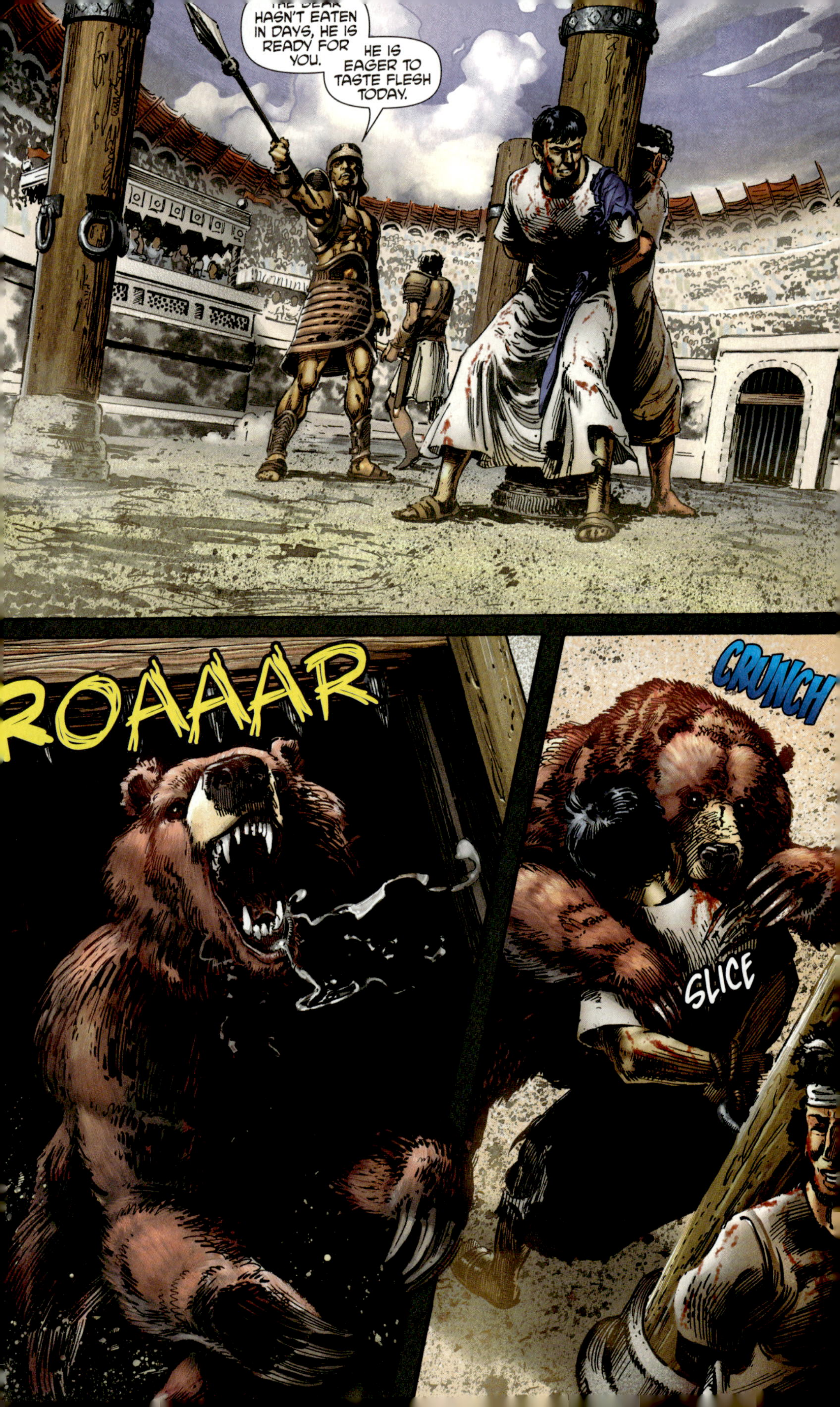
HASN'T EATEN IN DAYS, HE IS READY FOR YOU.
HE IS EAGER TO TASTE FLESH TODAY.
ROAAAR
CRUNCH
SLICE

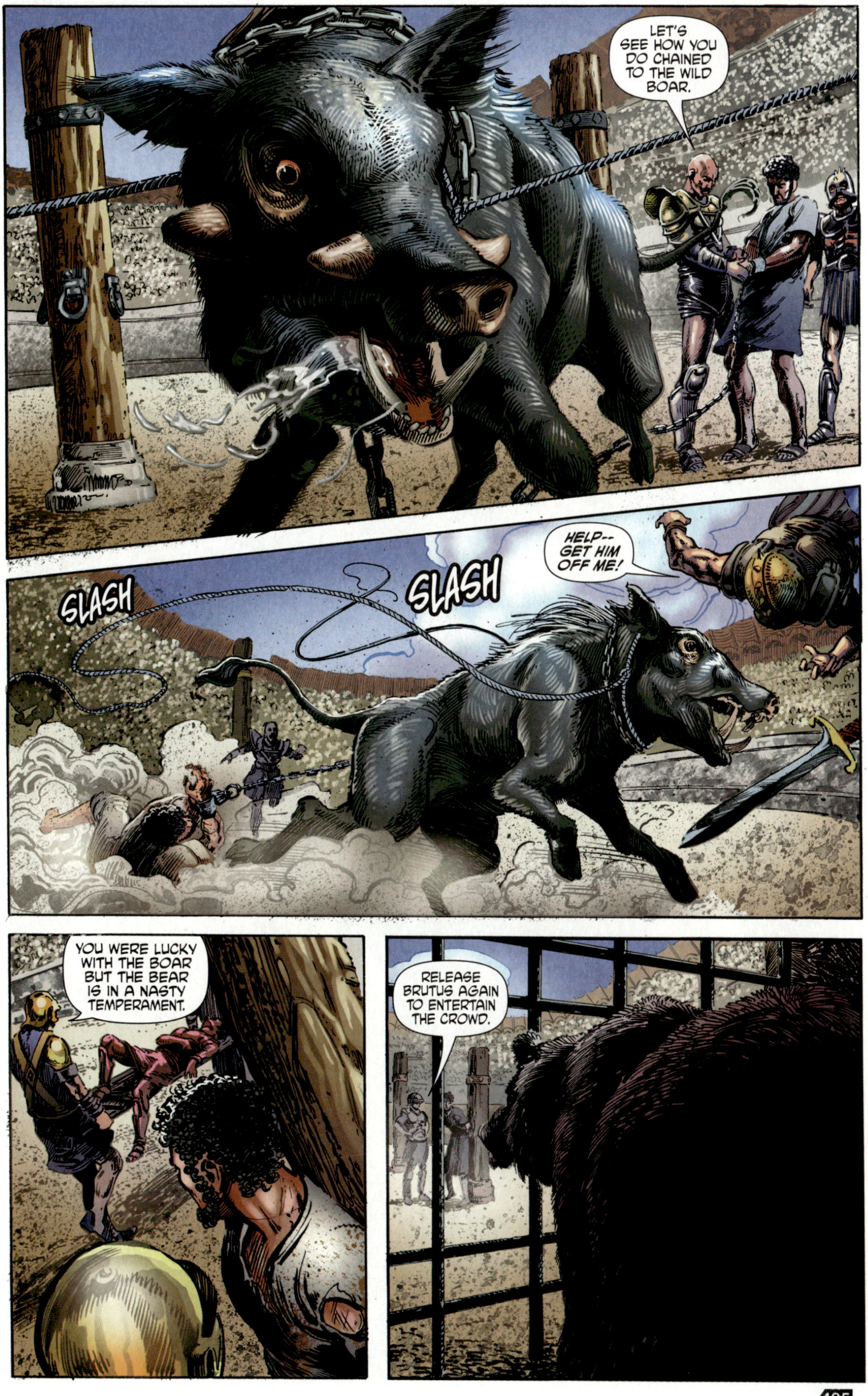
LET'S SEE HOW YOU DO CHAINED TO THE WILD BOAR.
SLASH
SLASH
HELP-- GET HIM OFF ME!
YOU WERE LUCKY WITH THE BOAR BUT THE BEAR IS IN A NASTY TEMPERAMENT.
RELEASE BRUTUS AGAIN TO ENTERTAIN THE CROWD.

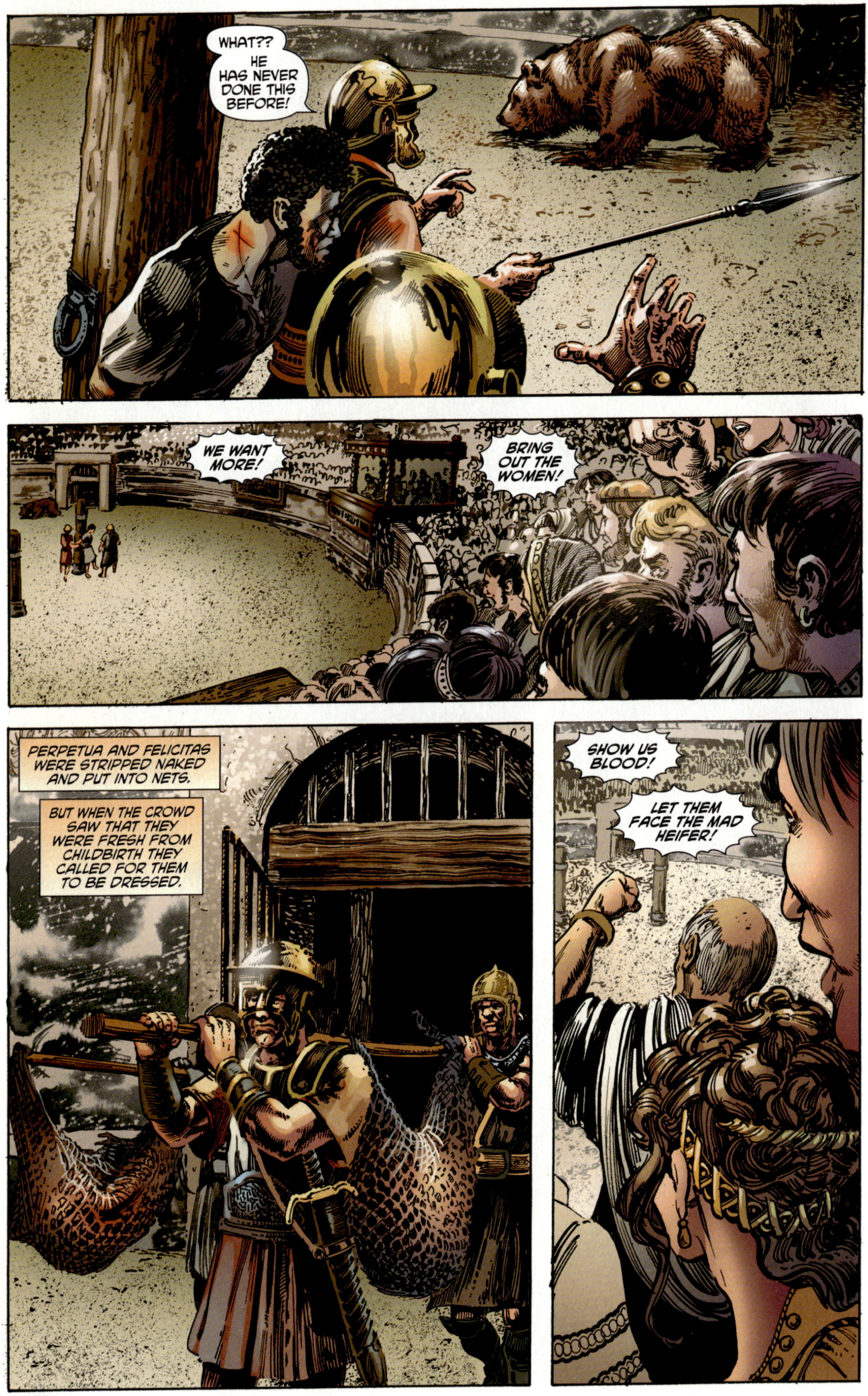
WHAT?? HE HAS NEVER DONE THIS BEFORE!
WE WANT MORE!
BRING OUT THE WOMEN!
PERPETUA AND FELICITAS WERE STRIPPED NAKED AND PUT INTO NETS.
BUT WHEN THE CROWD SAW THAT THEY WERE FRESH FROM CHILDBIRTH THEY CALLED FOR THEM TO BE DRESSED.
SHOW US BLOOD!
LET THEM FACE THE MAD HEIFER!

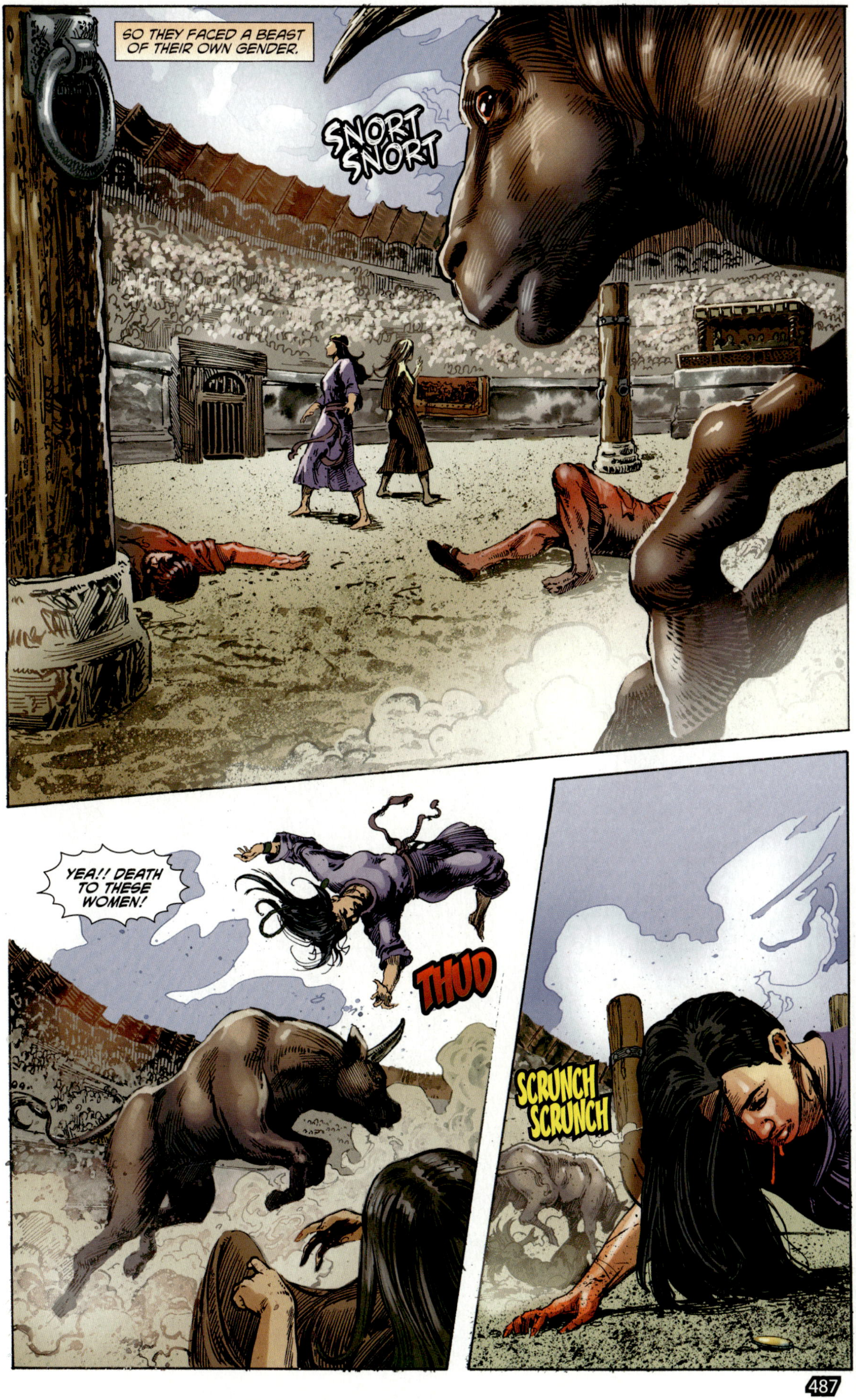
SO THEY FACED A BEAST OF THEIR OWN GENDER.
SNORT SNORT
YEA!! DEATH TO THESE WOMEN!
THUD
SCRUNCH SCRUNCH

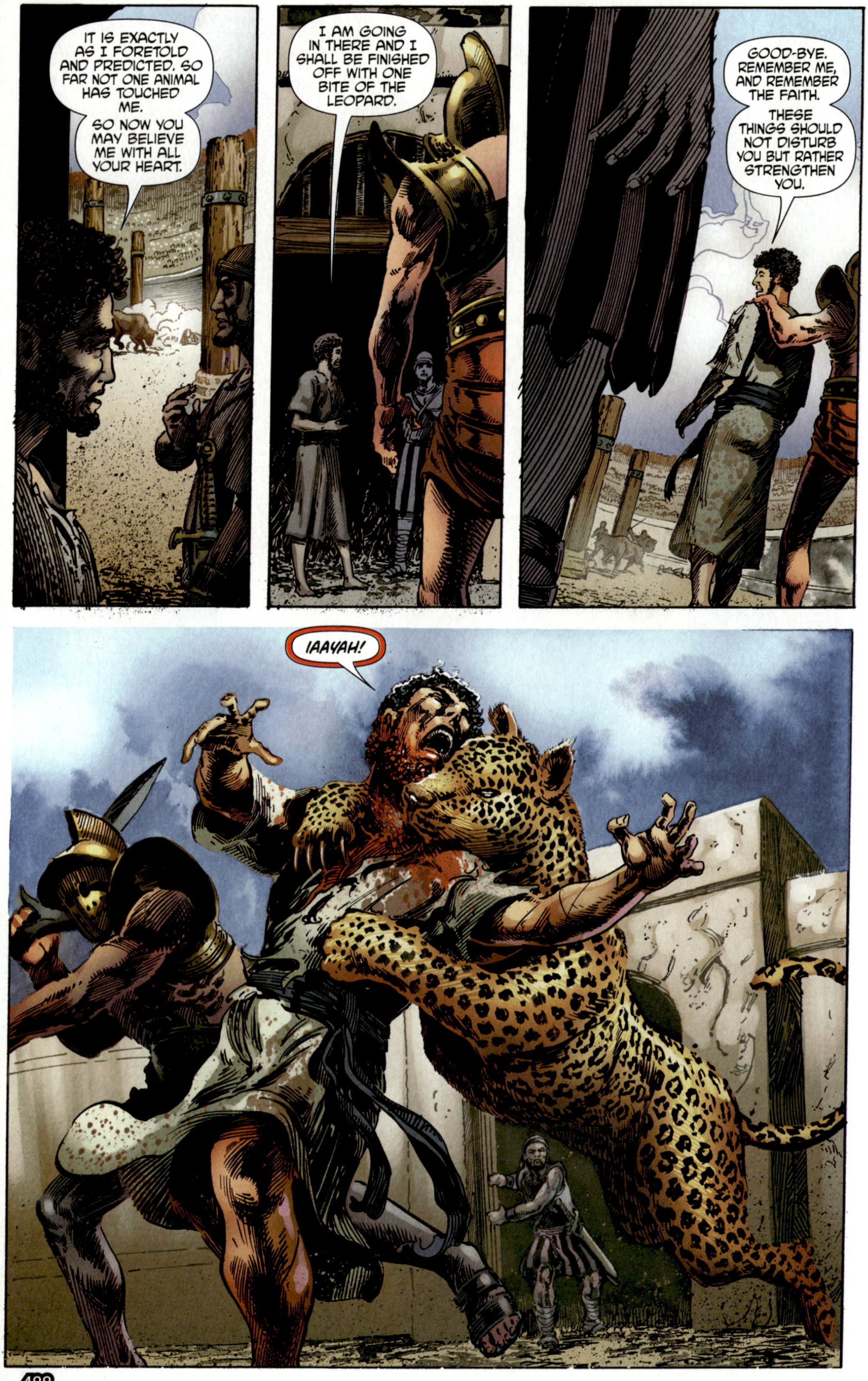
IT IS EXACTLY AS I FORETOLD AND PREDICTED. SO FAR NOT ONE ANIMAL HAS TOUCHED ME.
SO NOW YOU MAY BELIEVE ME WITH ALL YOUR HEART.
I AM GOING IN THERE AND I SHALL BE FINISHED OFF WITH ONE BITE OF THE LEOPARD.
GOOD-BYE. REMEMBER ME, AND REMEMBER THE FAITH.
THESE THINGS SHOULD NOT DISTURB YOU BUT RATHER STRENGTHEN YOU.
¡AAYAH!

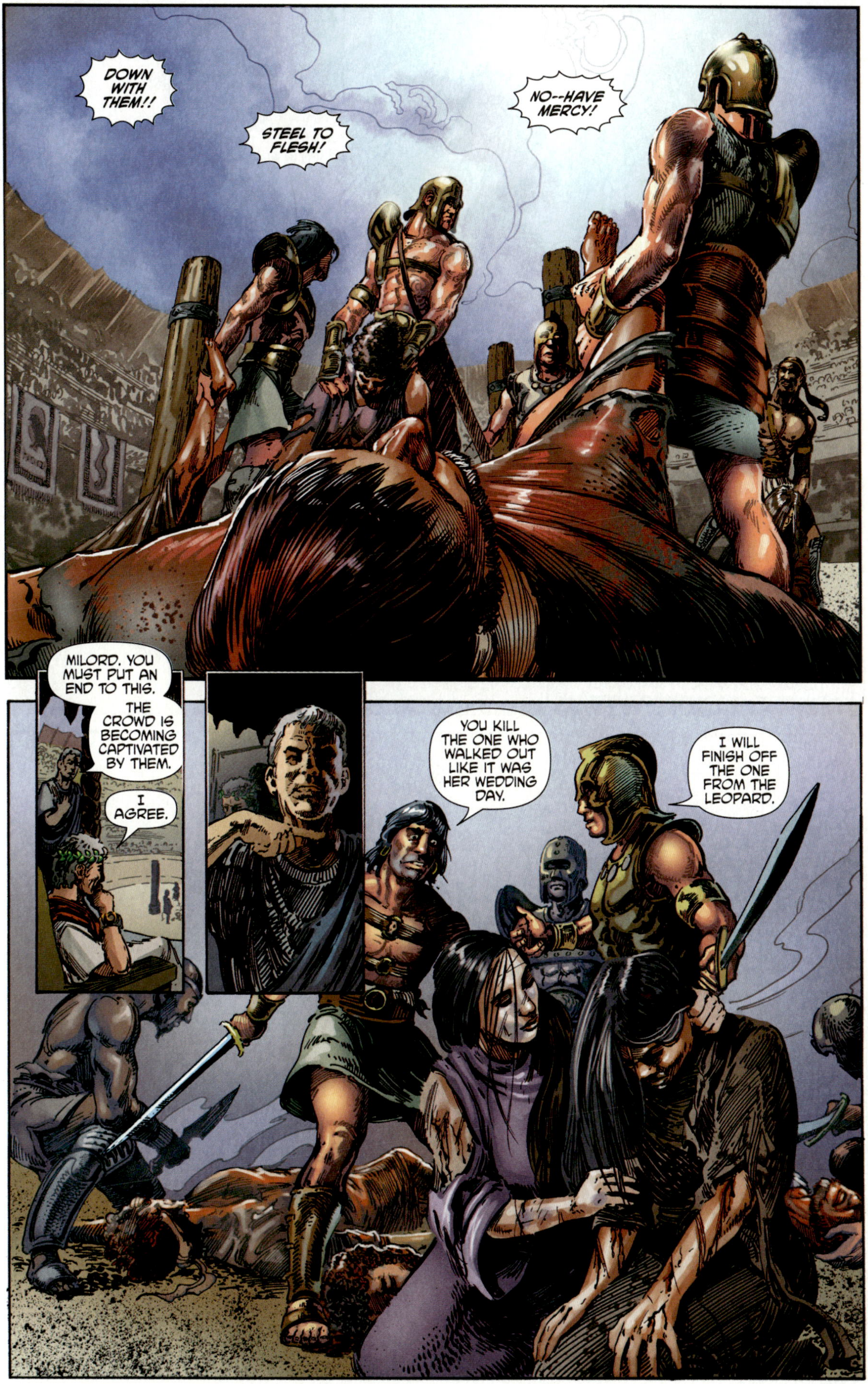
DOWN WITH THEM!!
STEEL TO FLESH!
NO--HAVE MERCY!
MILORD. YOU MUST PUT AN END TO THIS.
THE CROWD IS BECOMING CAPTIVATED BY THEM.
I AGREE.
YOU KILL THE ONE WHO WALKED OUT LIKE IT WAS HER WEDDING DAY.
I WILL FINISH OFF THE ONE FROM THE LEOPARD.

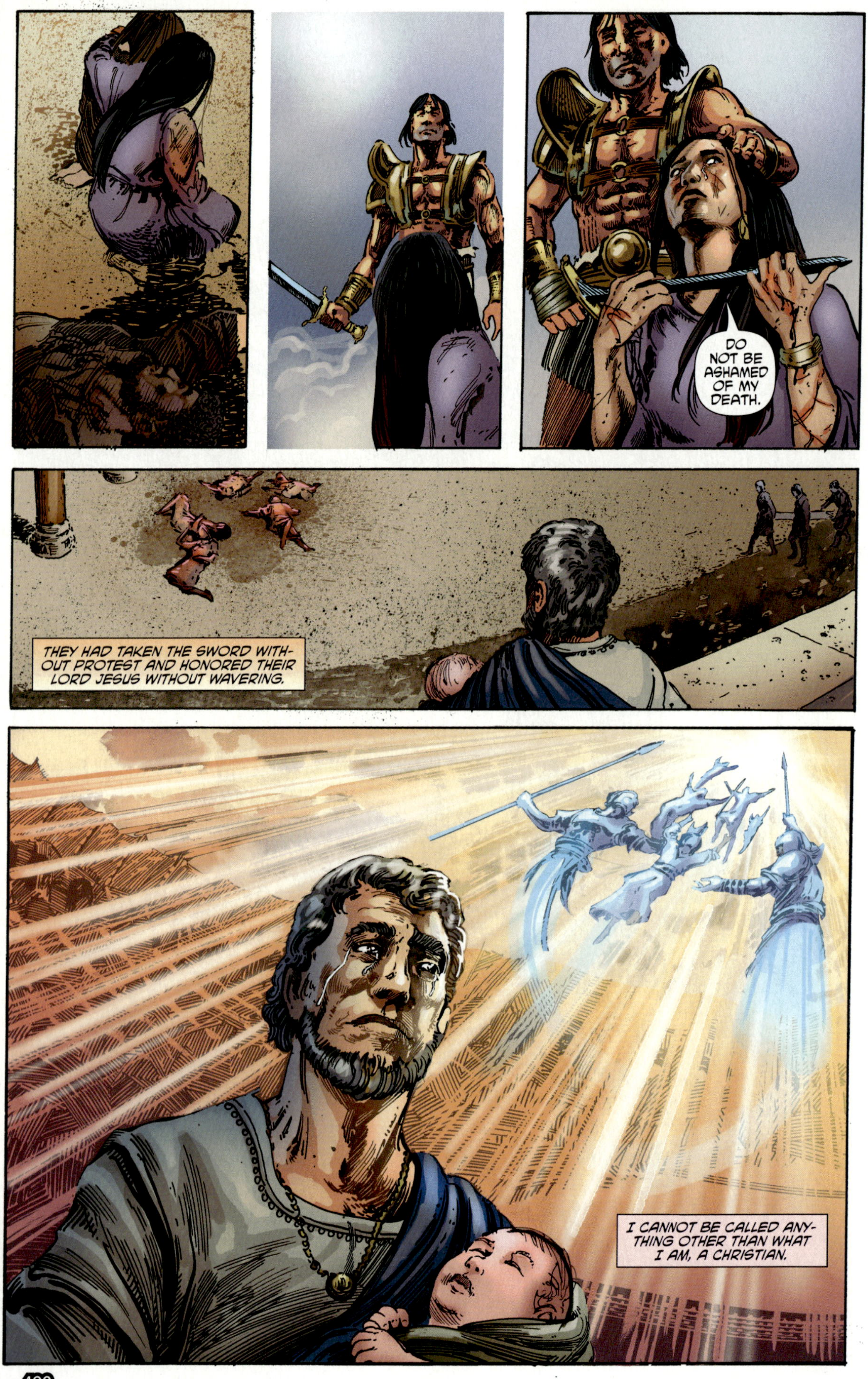
DO NOT BE ASHAMED OF MY DEATH.
THEY HAD TAKEN THE SWORD WITHOUT PROTEST AND HONORED THEIR LORD JESUS WITHOUT WAVERING.
I CANNOT BE CALLED ANYTHING OTHER THAN WHAT I AM, A CHRISTIAN.

KINGSTONE

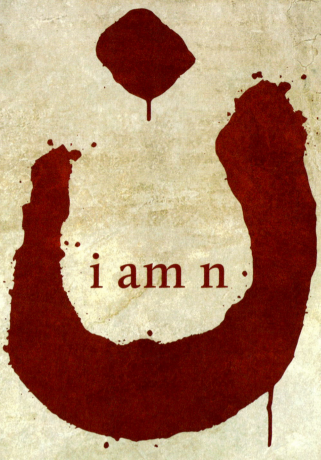

i am n

Inspiring Stories of Christians
Facing Islamic Extremists

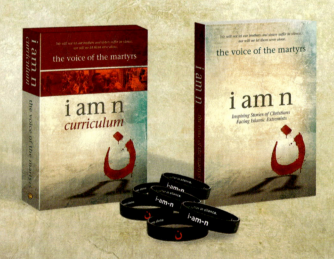

a new symbol for persecuted Christians

Within the first centuries following Jesus' death and resurrection, believers began to use several symbols to identify themselves as followers of Jesus Christ. One commonly used symbol was the "ichthus," from the Greek word meaning "fish."

The ichthus is thought to have been used by Christians in part as a secret symbol that wouldn't be recognized by persecutors. Today Christians are persecuted in more than 70 countries by governments and those who follow false religions and other ideologies that are hostile to Christ.

AINA (aina.org)

In Iraq, Islamic extremists used a symbol of their own to identify Christians. In Mosul, the Islamists used the Arabic "N" (pronounced nun) to label Christians' homes. The spray-painted "N" identified property as belonging to "Nazarenes," or followers of Jesus of Nazareth. By marking their property, the extremists were laying claim to it.

In addition, Iraqi believers were given an ultimatum: convert to Islam, pay an exorbitant tax, leave the area or be killed. Most Christians chose to flee, often with only the clothes on their backs.

We stand with our persecuted brothers and sisters, gladly identifying ourselves as "N" — followers of Jesus. We will not let them suffer alone.

Are You "N"?

If you would like to know more about what it means for our Christian brothers and sisters to live in the presence of Islamic extremists and to know how you can stand with them, please visit **i-am-n.com.**